Dictionary of Proper Names and Places in the Bible

Dictionary of Proper Names and Places in the Bible

By O. Odelain
and R. Séguineau

Preface by R. Tournay, O.P.

Translated and Adapted
by Matthew J. O'Connell

DOUBLEDAY & COMPANY, INC.
GARDEN CITY, NEW YORK
1981

This book was originally published in French under the title *Dictionnaire des Noms Propres de la Bible*

ISBN: 0-385-14924-7
Library of Congress Catalog Card Number: 79-8030

Printed in the United States of America

Library of Congress Cataloging in Publication Data

Odelain, O.
The dictionary of proper names and places in the Bible.

Rev. translation of Dictionnaire des noms propres de la Bible.
Includes indexes.
1. Bible—Names—Dictionaries. I. Séguineau, R., joint author. II. O'Connell, Matthew J. III. Title.
BS435.03313 220.3'21

Contents

Preface

There exists as yet no complete concordance for the Jerusalem Bible, but here at least is a dictionary *containing all the proper names to be found in the Old and New Testaments.* Such a complete inventory fills a real need, inasmuch as until now we have had at our disposal only the indexes or lists of names offered at the back of geographies or atlases of the Bible or histories of Israel. But O. Odelain and R. Séguineau have not been satisfied to give a complete list—almost four thousand entries—of the names of the persons and places mentioned in Scripture. Under each entry they also pull together, in brief form, the information that locates each name in its historical and geographical contexts and gives its meaning and various uses. As a result, they have painted an authentic sociological panorama of the people of Israel in terms of the persons and places in the biblical message.

As we read these scholarly notes, we shall be enabled to enter more fully into the very heart of the inspired message, for this message is not in any sense an ideology but takes concrete shape in a specific period of history and a specific human framework, in accordance with the logic inherent in the mystery of the Incarnation. Throughout the ancient East, the name was a substitute, as it were, for the person and shared in the very essence of beings and things. If a person or thing did not have a name, that person or thing did not exist. A change of name means a change of destiny; it means entering a new world (cf. Is 62:2; Rv 2:17; 3:12). *Nomen, omen!* In Israel, the divine name to some extent played the role that pagan peoples assigned to the images of their deities. The first Name mentioned in the Old Testament—and the one most often used—is YHWH, "I am" (Gn 2:4; Ex 3:14). The last Name that occurs, at the end of the Apocalypse (22:21), is that of Jesus, whose "name is above all other names."

Thanks, then, to this book of O. Odelain and R. Séguineau, the names of biblical persons and places take us into the theology of revelation and into the very mystery of the God who is transcendant and yet the friend of us human beings, the One who has sent us his Only Son, Jesus Christ, so that we might become his brothers and bear his Name in becoming Christians (Ac 11:26).

RAYMOND J. TOURNAY, O.P.
Director of the *École biblique et archéologique française* of Jerusalem

Introduction

I. GENERALITIES

1. From concordance to Dictionary

Unlike a *concordance* of the Bible, which follows the order of the books and, possibly with subdivisions, gives (all) the passages in which the same word is used, a *dictionary* supplies a note on each word. In this note, it does not follow the material succession of occurrences but handles these occurrences synthetically; that is, it reorders and organizes them as it takes into account both history and the various contributions made by the exegesis of the texts.

A concordance, especially if it is not purely verbal in character, provides a broader panorama and goes into far greater detail for words that occur with great frequency. A dictionary, on the other hand, offers information that is more accessible and more critical, especially in cases where a large mass of unorganized textual material would leave readers helpless and would force them either to attempt their own laborious synthesis or at least to single out for themselves the points that are essential. A dictionary entry, moreover, incorporates further important information, inasmuch as it will give references to passages where the name does not appear as such; thus "the man" of 1 K 20:42 is *Ben-hadad II,* who had been captured and then allowed to escape; the "great king of Israel" in Ezr 5:11 is *Solomon,* the builder of the temple; the eulogy of the high priest *Simon son of Onias,* who is mentioned only in Si 50:1, extends in fact to 50:21.

2. From common name to proper name

A common name corresponds to a species, a general idea, or a meaning. A proper name, on the other hand, *points to* individual persons or things: gods, *Apis, Baal, Yahweh;* human beings, *Abraham, Pilate;* places, *Jerusalem, Lebanon, Field of Blood;* rivers, *Jordan, Nile;* constellations, *Pleiades, Orion,* and so on, or to groups that possess their own historical reality and can therefore be "named": ethnic collectivities, *Hittites, Nabataeans;* groups sharing a philosophy, *Epicureans,* or a politics, *Zealots,* or a religious outlook, *Hasidaeans, Pharisees.*

The present dictionary embraces all the proper names in the Bible, from *Aaron* to *Zuzim,* from the book of Genesis, where *Yahweh* is the first name to appear in the Bible (Gn 2:4), to the Apocalypse, where the name of *Jesus* closes the New Testament (Rv 22:21). Some of the names given an entry are on the borderline between a dictionary of proper names and a dictionary of a given language (*Corner, Elohim, Pharaoh,* and others), whereas only after some hesitation has *Deep* (a personification to some extent) been included.

3. General statistics

The Dictionary lists 3,500 proper names (3,000 in the OT and 550 in the NT), of which 310 appear only in the NT; these names represent about 4,420 different persons, places, and so forth (3,800 in the OT, 600 in the NT), of which 380 are to be found only in the NT.

Some individuals and places have more than one name: *Gideon/Jerubbaal; John/Mark; Peter/Cephas/Simon; Sea of Chinnereth/Lake of Gennesaret/Sea of Galilee/Sea of Tiberias.* On the other hand, one and the same name is borne by different persons and places: thus, for persons, we find eight *Philips,* ten *Michaels,* thirteen *Josephs,* sixteen *Joshuas/Jesuses,* eighteen *Simeons/Simons,* twenty *Hananiahs/Ananiases,* twenty-five *Johns/Johanans,* thirty *Zechariahs.* Similarly, among towns there are two *Bethlehems,* two *Caesareas,* three *Bethanys,* four *Beth-shemeshes,* two *Gilgals,* five *Apheks/Aphekahs,* and eleven *Ramahs/Ramaths/Ramoths.*

The complete list of occurrences of proper names amounts to 37,540 (of which 5,040 are in the NT); in other words, roughly one eighth of all the words in the Bible.

Of the 4,420 persons and places mentioned in Scripture, 2,100, or about half, are named only once; 740 appear twice; 50, seven times, *Asherah, Goliath, Qoheleth, Jabbok* . . . ; 50 others, fifty times or more, *Bethlehem, Elisha, Noah;* 26, a hundred times or more, *Elijah, Canaan, Peter* . . . ; 5, two hundred times or more, *Joseph* the patriarch, *Joshua, Jordan, Pharaoh, Sabaoth;* 9, three hundred times or more, *Philistines, Solomon, Abraham, Babylon, Aaron, Levites, Jews, Jacob, King Saul;* 6, five hundred times or more, *Christ, Egypt, Moses, Judah, Jesus, Jerusalem;* 3, a thousand times or more, *David, Elohim, Israel.* The name *Yahweh* is used more than any other word in the Bible (not only more than other proper names, but even more than any common noun or verb; by comparison, the Hb. word *'amar,* "speak," occurs only 5,300 times): *Yahweh* is used 6,800 times.

4. Origin, development, deformation, transformation of proper names

The vast majority of biblical names are Hebrew in origin. But the Bible does show a certain number of names originating abroad. Sometimes these are simply transcribed; sometimes they are given a Hebrew or Greek form. In particular, there are Egyptian names, *Shishak, Tirhakah, Moses, Merari, Phinehas, Pithom, Shihor* . . . ; Accadian names, *Asshur, Calah, Shalmaneser, Sargon, Sennacherib* . . . ; Persian names, *Cyrus, Darius, Xerxes* . . . ; Greek names, *Alexander, Berenice, Demetrius, Heliodorus, Timothy, Nicopolis, Philadelphia* . . . ; Latin names, *Cornelius, Lucius, Memmius, Quintus, Forum of Appius, Puteoli.*

In the course of history, some names show different forms and undergo various kinds of change that can be explained as follows:

—By dialectal differences within the same language: thus there is a shift from *Yahweh* to *Yah, Yahu, Jeho, Jo.*

—By mistakes in reading and transmitting the text; for example, metathesis, by which *Ibleam* becomes *Bileam* or *Shalmai Shamlai;* confusion of letters, by which *Reuel* becomes *Deuel* or *Rhodanim Dodanim.*

—By the passage from one language to another: thus Egyptian *Hi-ku-pta* becomes Greek *Aiguptos,* Egypt; Accadian *Tukulti-Apil-Esharra* becomes Hebrew *Tiglat-Pil'eser* or *Tiglat-Pilneser,* Tiglath-pileser; Hebrew *Ashdod* becomes Greek *Azōtos; Zurishaddai* becomes *Sourisadai,* Sarasadai; *'Ekron* becomes *Akkarōn; 'Azza* becomes *Gaza; 'Amorah* becomes *Gomorrah; Jabneh* becomes *Iamnia, Jamnia; Re'u'el,* Reuel, becomes *Ragouēl,* Raguel; *Tahpanhes* becomes *Daphnē,* Daphne; *Hegai* becomes *Gai; Yamlek,* Jamlech, becomes *Iamlikou,* Iamleku.

—By an intention to insult or show contempt. The contempt may be directed to such pagan divinities as *Astarte, Marduk, Melech* or *Nebo;* for example, *Astarte* (Hb. *Ashtart*) becomes *Ashtaroth* and *Melech* becomes *Molech,* with the Hb. vocalization in both cases being borrowed from Hb. *boshet,* "shame"; *Marduk* is vocalized as *Merodach* on the basis of the Hb. *meborak,* "cursed"; *Abed Nabu* is deformed into *Abednego.* The contempt may also be directed to a person or place; thus *Tabeel,* "God is good" is vocalized as *Tabal,* "Good for nothing," in the Masoretic text; *Marratim,* "lagoon," becomes *Merathaim,* "Twofold rebellion" or "Twofold bitterness."

—By various historical circumstances: the destruction of a city or town, *Zephath* becoming *Hormah;* occupation by a new clan, as when *Laish* becomes *Dan;* influence of some individual, as when *Acco* becomes *Ptolemais;* a new political structure for a region, as when the old kingdom of Judah becomes *Ioudaia gē,* "land of the Jews," or *Judaea* (cf. the change from *Samaria* to *Samaritis, Edom* to *Idumaea*); a change of culture, as when the Egyptian city of *On* becomes the Greek *Heliopolis* or when the Hebrew name *Joshua* becomes *Jason* or *Jesus,* and Simeon (Hb. *Shim'ôn*) becomes Simon. Some names are translations: *Thomas,* "Twin," becomes *Didymus; Tabitha,* "Gazelle," becomes *Dorcas,* whereas *Numenius,* "[Born] at the new moon," probably translates the Hebrew *Hodesh.*

We may add that some proper names serve as a disguise for other proper names. This is the case with cryptograms that use a code language: *Leb-kamai* stands for *Kashdim,* that is, the Chaldaeans; *Sheshak* for *Babel;* whereas *Zimri,* which is perhaps to be read *Zimki,* may be a cryptogram for *Elam.*

5. Personal names and place names

a. A hundred or so proper names are borne both by human beings and by other entities: gods, *Amon, Baal, Gad, Hermes, Nebo;* places (in most instances), *Abel, Adam, Haran, Jephthah* (Iphthah), *Lydia, Tarshish, Jezreel;* columns of the temple, *Boaz, Jachin;* a well, *Sirah;* a hill, *Gareb.* A town and a constellation have the same name, *Chesil* (Orion).

b. The names of some cities or towns and of some features of the landscape refer to one or another person who enjoyed some degree of renown, for example, the threshing floor of *Araunah,* the oak of *Mamre,* the encampments of *Jair,* the garden of *Uzza,* the tower of *Hananel,* the portico of *Solomon,* the gate of *Joshua.* And it is easy to see the relationship between *Antioch* and *Antiochus, Seleucia* and *Seleucus, Ptolemais* and *Ptolemy, Philippi* and *Philip, Caesarea* and *Caesar, Tiberias* and *Tiberius, Antipatris* and *Antipater.*

c. In reading the Bible, we are struck by the relationship it very frequently establishes between human beings and places. To this end it uses—but in a way that we find surprising—the literary genre of the *genealogy;* it has even been said that "biblical history is first and foremost a genealogy." The sometimes monotonous succession of the terms *begot, father of,* and *son of* does not, however, necessarily mean we are dealing with strict genealogical trees that would enable us to trace backwards (cf. Lk 3) or forwards (cf. Mt 1) a succession of generations. This kind of "family handbook" may at times make a certain person the father of a town or a nation or may consider an ethnic group or a country as being the descendant of an eponymous ancestor, that is, of a famous individual who gave this group or country its name. The purpose of the author in thus describing the origin of the various peoples is to emphasize the fact that this origin does not depend solely on a certain stock of genes, but on immigrations, conquests, marriages, and alliances. Thus in Gn 34 the relations between "Shechem son of Hamor the Hivite" and "Dinah the daughter of Jacob" suggest the conquest of the town of Shechem, a "town of foreigners," by a group of Israelites. Similarly, in Nb 27, the names of the "daughters of Zelophehad" happen to be also the names of Manassite clans. In Ezr 2 repatriated Israelites who have lost any memory of their origins are registered under the names of their towns. This explains how the name of an individual can become that of a district and how a town can be incorporated as such into a genealogy.

The genealogies bring out, more than any books in a registry office could, "the cohesion of all the groups of Hebrews that were called to share a common destiny as part of Yahweh's people." The list of peoples in Gn 10 has a spiritual value: it points to the vocation all people have of becoming part of the posterity of Abraham, who was the descendant of Shem, the son of Noah, and the man by whom "all the tribes of the earth shall bless themselves."

6. Lists of proper names

a. In addition to the more or less full lists of the *tribes of Israel* that are indicated at the end of the dictionary (pp. 1041–1043), the Bible contains a large number of series of proper names: genealogies, lists of individuals, peoples, cities or towns, and so on. Sometimes the series of names are just that: simple lists, as, for example, the twelve Aramaean tribes descended from Nahor or the twelve sons of Ishmael or the twelve descendants of Esau. At other times there is greater expansion or development, as in the lists of the patriarchs before and after the flood or the stages of the Exodus or the twelve leaders who bring the offerings for the dedication of the altar in Nb 7:10–83. Sometimes the lists are quite short, like the list of the five kings of Midian, Nb 31:8, or of the seven deacons, Ac 6:5; sometimes they are quite lengthy, like the list of the peoples, Gn, or the list of those returning to Judah and Jerusalem from the exile, Ezr 2//Ne 7.

There would be no value in drawing up a list of all the lists of proper names (after all, a list begins when you have only two names!). In an appendix the reader will, however, find a listing of the more important and significant lists of proper names (pp. 1035–1040).

b. As is to be expected, the frequency with which proper names occur is greatest in the "historical" books. The most notable accumulation of such names occurs in chapters 1–9 of 1 Chronicles, which contains 1,680 mentions of proper names in only fourteen pages of text (Jerusalem Bible, 1966 ed., pp. 496–509). Second in the running for the record is Jos 15–21 (758 names). We may also mention Gn 10 (124), Ezr 2 (140), Ne 11 (140), and Ne 12 (176).

c. But the poetic, prophetic, and didactic books also contain some surprises. Thus there is a list of ten proper names in Ps 60:8–11, and a list of twenty in Ps 83:7–12. The Song of Songs contains forty-four proper names, and there are three in the short third Letter of John.

7. Meaning of proper names

a. The dictionary gives a translation for the greater number of proper names. In fact, some place names are even known and listed here under their English language equivalent, for example, the Valley of the *Acacias,* the *Water* Gate, *Fuller's* Field, the Valley of the *Hyenas,* the *Mortar,* the *Plain,* the Oak of *Tears,* the Sea of *Reeds,* the Wadi of the *Willows,* the Ascent of the *Scorpions,* the Rock of *Divisions.* Other names that are used in their original form could easily be used in translation: *Aijalon,* Stags; *Migdol,* Tower; *Bethel,* House of God; *Baskama,* Sycamores; *Kiriath-jearim,* Woodsville; *Neapolis,* New Town; *Mount Halak,* Bald Mountain. It is easy, moreover, to see, in certain Hebrew and Greek names, the equivalents of first names and surnames we now use in English: for example, *Baruch,* Benedict; *Barzillai;* Irons; *Beeri,* Wells; *Tikvah,* Hope; *Hakkatan,* Little; *Laban,* White; *Niger, Phinehas,* Black; *Edom, Rufus,* Rufus; *Tappuah,* Apple; *Sheresh,* Root; *Shual;* Fox.

b. The meaning of some names is clear by comparison with the corresponding common nouns or other parts of speech, for example, *Hieronymus* (English: Jerome) means "whose name is sacred"; *Philip* means "Friend of horses"; *Beerzeth* means "Well of the Olive Tree"; *Migdal-eder* means "Well of the Flock." A number of other proper names are "explained" by the biblical writers themselves. Sometimes the writers give a faithful translation, as in the case of the three wells mentioned in Gn 26:20–22: *Esek,* "Quarrel," *Sitnah,* "Accusation," and *Rehoboth,* "Large spaces." At other times, the writers offer a popular etymology, especially of the kind that plays on assonances, for example, *Penuel,* "Face of God," and that is often quite unrelated to the real meaning of the name. For example, *Abraham,* "The Father loves," is explained in Gn 17:5 by *'Ab-hamôn,* "father of a multitude," *Babel,* "Gate of God," in Gn 11:9 by *balal,* "confuse," *Samuel,* "Name of God," in 1 S 1:20 by *sha'al El,* "Asked of God." The names of the twelve sons of Jacob are explained in Gn 29:32–30:23 by means of verbal assonances connected with the circumstances of their respective births.

c. About 450 proper names in the Bible (400 personal names and 50 place names) are *theophoric* names, that is, they contain a reference to the godhead. The reference may be directly to the following:

—The common word for "God," namely, Hb. *El: Nathanael,* "God has given," or *Jezreel,* "God sows," or Gr. *Theos:* Theophilus, "He who loves God," or *Dositheus,* "Gift of God." There are more than 120 proper names of this kind.

—Substitutes for the name "God," for example, *Ab,* "the Father," as in *Absalom,* "The Father is peace"; or *Ah,* "the Brother," as in *Ahitub,* "My Brother is good"; or *Am,* "the Uncle, the Relative," as in *Amminadab,* "My Uncle is generous"; or *Adôn,* "the Lord," as in *Adoniram,* "My Lord is on high"; or *Melech,* "King," as in *Melchizedek,* "My King is justice"; or *Shaddai,* "Almighty," and *Zur,* "Rock," as in *Zurishaddai,* "My Rock is Shaddai." In all, there are about fifty proper names of this type.

—The proper name of the God of Israel, *Yahweh,* in its various forms, for example, *Nethaniah,* "Yah has given"; *Jehoiada,* "Yah knows"; *Jonadab,* "Yah is generous." In all, there are 130 proper names of this type.

—Various alien gods: *Baal* (*Ishbaal, Baal-peor . . . ,* about twenty names) and other gods: *Aton* (*Pithom*), *Apollo* (*Apollophanes*), *Arta, Artemis, Asshur, Bacchus, Bel, Bethel, Demeter, Gad, Hadad, Hermes, Horus, Lagamar, Marduk, Mot, Nebo, Neith, Nergal, Poseidon, Ra, Rimmon, Shulman, Sin, Zeus* (*Diotrephes*). These add up to about fifty proper names.

—An abbreviation or, most often, an elimination of one or other of these names, which results in hypocoristic forms: for example, *Micah* is a shortened form of *Michael,* "Who is like God?" or of *Micaiah,* "Who is like Yah?"; *Nathan* is a hypocoristic form of *Jonathan* or *Nethaniah,* "Yah has given," or else of *Elnathan* or *Nathanael,* "God has given." The dictionary lists about sixty such theophoric names.

d. The meaning of not a small number of names (including some more important ones) has been lost and remains a mystery to us: for example, *Aaron, Acco, Ammon, Ashkelon, Jericho, Jezebel, Shinar.* In other instances, the question mark that follows the meaning proposed shows that we are not quite sure of the origin of the word or that deformations and the awkward shifting of a name from one language to another render uncertain the translation being offered: for example, *Ahithophel, Balaam, Gideon, Sinai.*

II. THE PEOPLE OF THE BIBLE

A. PERSONAL NAMES

1. Meaning of personal names

In the Bible, just as throughout the ancient East, personal names almost always have a meaning, either secular or religious.

a. Names connected with the circumstances of the person's birth:

—Dates or contemporary events: *Haggai,* "Born on a day of festival"; *Geshem,* "Born in the season of the rains"; *Shabbethai,* "Born on a sabbath day"; *Ichabod,* "Where is the Glory?" or "Without Glory" (because of the defeat of Israel and the capture of the Ark);

—The father's situation: *Gershom,* "An alien there," the name given by Moses, when a refugee in Midian, to his eldest son;

—A child born after the loss of a previous child: *Shillem,* "[Yah] has replaced [the dead child]."

b. Names connected with a physical aspect or characteristic: *Edom* and *Rufus,* "Red, Red-headed"; *Esau,* "Shaggy, hairy"; *Gehazi,* "With protruding eyes"; *Zeresh,* "Hairy head"; *Naamah,* "Pretty"; *Dalphon,* "Sleepless"; *Nahor,* "Snorer"; *Peresh,* "Droppings," and *Galal,* "Dung," recall the Greek name "Copronymus."

c. Names connected with character, temperament, and so on: *Andrew,* "Virile"; *Jacob,* "Supplanter"; *Chislon,* "Dull, Stupid"; *Nabal,* "Brute"; *Naomi,* "My sweetness"; *Epaphroditus* and *Erastus,* "Lovable"; *Eumenes,* "Benevolent"; *Onesimus,* "Useful"; *Balaam,* "Glutton"; *Ikkesh,* "Depraved."

d. Names of animals: *Leah* and *Rebekah,* "Cow"; *Eglah,* "Heifer"; *Becher,* "Young camel"; *Hamor,* "Ass"; *Elon,* "Ram"; *Immer,* "Sheep"; *Rachel,* "Sheep"; *Caleb,* "Dog"; *Zeeb,* "Wolf"; *Hezir,* "Wild boar, Pig"; *Dishon, Epher,* and *Tabitha,* "Gazelle"; *Jael,* "Antelope"; *Arieh,* "Lion"; *Achbor,* "Mouse"; *Hagab,* "Grasshopper"; *Deborah,* "Bee"; *Gaal,* "Beetle"; *Nahash,* "Serpent"; *Shephupham,* "Viper"; *Tahash,* "Dolphin"; *Nimshi,* "Mangosteen"; *Zippor,* "Bird"; *Oreb,* "Raven"; *Jonah,* "Dove"; *Aiah,* "Vulture, Kite"; *Hoglah, Kore,* "Partridge"; *Nekoda,* "Moor-hen"; *Parosh,* "Flea."

e. Names of trees, plants, flowers, fruits: *Elon,* "Terebinth"; *Tamar,* "Palm tree"; *Zalaph,* "Caper-bush"; *Rimmon,* "Pomegranate"; *Koz,* "Thorn-bush"; *Habakkuk,* "Basil, Mint"; *Susanna,* "Lily"; *Rhoda,* "Rose"; *Azzur,* "Medlar"; *Diblaim,* "Figs."

f. Theophoric names. See above.

g. Symbolic names: *Emmanuel,* "God with us"; *Shear-jashub,* "A remnant will return"; *Maher-shalal-hash-baz,* "Speedy-spoil-quick-booty"; *Jezreel,* "God sows"; *Jesus:* "Savior."

h. Various other names: *Achsah,* "Ring"; *Anak,* "Necklace"; *Zeror,* "Pebble"; *Cephas,* "Rock"; *Kish,* "Gift"; *Barak, Lappidoth,* and *Regem,* "Lightning"; *Idbash,* "Honey"; *Berenice,* "Victory"; and so on.

2. Surnames, double names, titles

a. About thirty individuals have a surname:

—Some of the Seleucid and Lagide kings: *Epiphanes* (Alexander Balas and Antiochus IV), *Eupator* (Antiochus V), *Trypho* (Diodotus), *Philometor* (Ptolemy VI), *the Great* (Antiochus III);

—The five sons of Mattathias: *Gaddi* (John), *Thassi* (Simon), *Maccabaeus* (Judas), *Avaran* (Eleazar), *Apphus* (Jonathan);

—High-ranking officials: *the Ammonite* (Tobiah); *Macron* (Ptolemy);

—Important individuals in the NT: *Barnabus* (Joseph); *Barsabbas* (Joseph and Jude); *Boanerges* (James and John); *Iscariot* (Simon and Judas); *Justus* (Joseph and Jesus); *Nazarene* (Jesus); *Mark* (John); *Niger* (Simeon); *Paul* (Saul); *the Younger* (James); *Zealot* (Simon).

b. Some important persons receive a new name: *Tiglath-pileser,* king of the Assyrians, takes the name of *Pul* when he takes power at Babylon; *Eliakim,* king of Judah, has his name changed to *Jehoiakim* by Pharaoh Neco, and Nebuchadnezzar decides that *Mattaniah* is to be called *Zedekiah* (coronation names? names indicating vassal status?). We may also note the double names of *Shallum/Jehoahaz, Azariah/Uzziah, Jedidiah/Solomon.*

The change of name, in other cases, denotes a change of destiny: *Abram* becomes *Abraham, Sarai* becomes *Sarah, Jacob* becomes *Israel.*

c. Some names that sound like proper names are in fact titles indicating sovereignty: *Pharaoh, Jareb, Caesar, Augustus, Kandake.* Even a name designating a function is misinterpreted as a proper name: *rab shakek,* "chief cupbearer" becomes *Rabshakeh.*

3. Patronymics

In giving the name of an individual, the Bible, interested as it is in genealogies, often immediately follows it with the name of the individual's father. The mention of *son of* or *daughter of* corresponds to the use of a patronymic suffix in Slavic and North German languages: Andrei *Petrovich,* Anders *Petersson,* Andrew son of Peter.

a) Of the 1,700 personal names given in the Bible 300 names (borne by 400 persons) are patronymics pure and simple; by this is meant that the father plays no other role in the texts but that of giving his name to his son or daughter: Joshua *son of Nun,* Caleb *son of Jephunneh,* Balak *son of Zippor,* Jeroboam *son of Nabat,* Alexander *son of Philip,* Matthew *son of Alphaeus,* Levi *son of Alphaeus,* Simon *son of John,* or Simon *Bar-jonah.* The name of the father preceded by the word for *son of* (Hb. *ben;* Aram, *bar*) or *daughter of* (Hb. *bat*) suffices at times to name this son or daughter. This is the case, for example, with five of Solomon's administrators, *Son of Hur, Son of Deker, Son of Hesed, Son of Abinadab,* and *Son of Geber,* with a high-ranking official at Damascus, *Son of Tabeel,* and with one of Judah's wives, *Bath-shua.* Ptolemy, the military commissioner for Jericho, is on one occasion designated simply by his patronymic, *the son of Abubus.* Although the name of the father, in this type of proper name, is never found by itself, that of the son will often be used without mention of the father: *Joshua, Caleb, Balak, Jeroboam, Simon.*

b) In 1,200 other cases, the father, while providing a patronymic, also has an independent existence and more or less detailed personal "history" in the Bible. Thus *Jesse* is mentioned 48 times, but only on 19 occasions does he provide a patronymic for his son David. The same is true of the kings of Judah. In the NT we may mention *Zechariah,* who is mentioned nine times, but only once in the expression "John *son of Zechariah.*" A patronymic by itself can refer to one or more sons; for example, *the son of Jesse* means David; *the sons of Zebedee* means James and John.

c) In exceptional cases it is the mother who gives an identifying name to her children; for example, Jozacar *son of Shimeath;* Jehozabad *son of Shomer* or *Shimrith.* The most notable case is that of *Zeruiah,* daughter of Jesse and sister of David. Her name occurs 26 times, but of these it is on 23 occasions a matronymic for her sons Abishai, Asahel, and Joab, either individually: Abishai *son of Zeruiah;* Joab *son of Zeruiah,* or collectively: *the sons of Zeruiah.*

B. SOCIOLOGICAL PANORAMA

What kind of people do we find in the Bible?

The Bible names between 3,000 and 3,100 individuals, of whom 2,900 are men and only 170 are women. The vast majority are members of the Israelite people, and less than 500, or hardly one-sixth, are from other nations.

Many are people we might think of as insignificant because they are but names buried in a list or are mentioned only in passing. From their midst emerge the prominent personalities, those who "make history" because they play a determining role in the development of peoples and institutions: *Abraham, Moses, David, Ezra, Jesus, Paul.* In between, there are those who have a history, though it is sometimes quite short, or a precise role, though it is sometimes quite modest. In this intermediate group there is a whole gallery of figures: men of the people and persons of high rank; lowly servants and prestigious leaders; kings and shepherds, prophets, priests, generals and lawmakers, workers and artists, rich landowners, leaders of clans or tribes, authorities of every type, ambassadors, wise people and fools; incorruptible men like *Eleazar* and *Razis,* and traitors like *Doeg* and *Rhodocus;* executioners and martyrs; heroes and cowards; men of the Resistance, like *Judas Maccabaeus,* and collaborators, like *Simon,* the administrator of the temple; faithful friends, like *Jonathan* and *David, Jesus* and the family of *Martha, Mary,* and *Lazarus;* saints and sinners; believers and infidels. There are individuals who are solidly ensconced within history, others who in addition to having a historical existence have become literary types (*Nebuchadnezzar,* for example), and still others who are straight out of legend (King *Og*). There are individuals with a symbolic role, like *Judith,* and individuals that are literary fictions, like the poor man *Lazarus* or the good *Samaritan.* The Bible is thus a mirror of humanity: in it we find men and women as the chroniclers saw them and the poets imagined them.

1. Kings and emperors

The Bible mentions about 175 kings and emperors, about 50 of them belonging to Israel, the rest to other nations.

a) *In Israel*

Before the establishment of the monarchy, power was possessed in Israel by the great leaders of the people, such as *Moses* and *Joshua;* later on by the judges, both the "great" judges: *Othniel, Ehud, Deborah,* and *Barak, Gideon, Jephthah, Samson,* and the "lesser" judges: *Shamgar, Tola, Jair, Ibzan, Elon, Abdon.* An attempt at monarchy with *Abimelech,* "king of Shechem," is unsuccessful. *Samuel,* who is both judge and prophet, anoints the first king, *Saul,* who is succeeded by his son *Ishbaal.* But it is *David* and *Solomon* who set the monarchy on a firm footing. After Solomon, 19 kings and one queen (*Athaliah*), all of the Davidic dynasty, reign successively in Judah from 931 to 587 (see: JUDAH *d*); and 19 kings, belonging to 9 different dynasties or families, reign on the throne of Israel from 931 to 722 (see: ISRAEL *d*).

Kings reappear—but with very limited powers—under Roman domination, in the persons of *Herod the Great* and his successors.

b) *Other nations*

The Bible mentions as heads of the great powers (we are referring to kings who are named or are at least identifiable) seven or eight: PHARAOHS, and eight: LAGIDE kings in Egypt; six kings of: ASSYRIA; three kings of: BABYLON; two kings of the Medes, *Cyaxares* and *Astyages;* seven kings of: PERSIA; four kings of: MACEDONIA; fourteen: SELEUCID kings in Syria; and four Roman emperors: CAESAR.

Among the small kingdoms and city-states, we find a king of Sparta, *Areios;* two kings of Pergamum, *Attalus* and *Eumenes;* one king of Cappadocia, *Ariarathes;* six kings of Aram at: DAMASCUS; one king of Zobah, *Hadadezer;* one king of Geshur, *Talmai;* one king of Hamath, *Tou;* two kings of Tyre and Sidon, *Hiram* and *Ethbaal;* three kings of: AMMON; four kings of: MOAB; two kings of Nabataeans, *Aretas I* and *Aretas IV;* ten kings of: EDOM; seven kings of: MIDIAN; one king of Amalek, *Agag;* two kings of the Philistines, *Ahimelech* and *Achish;* eight kings of Canaan, *Horam, Jabin, Jobab,* and: ADONI-ZEDEK (with his allies); two Amorite kings, *Og* and *Sihon;* the nine kings of Gn 14, *Melchizedek* and: AMRAPHEL, BERA; one king of Massa, *Lemuel.*

See also: ARIOCH 2; ARPACHSHAD 2; BELSHAZZAR; DARIUS 4.

And see Chronological Table IV.

2. Leaders, officials, civil authorities

The Bible supplies us with a rather large number of names of men who exercise authority at quite varied levels, whether in Israel or abroad. In addition to tribal leaders and leaders of clans or families, who are listed in an appendix to the dictionary (page 408), and to elders (men like *Chabris* and *Charmis*), who are usually mentioned only collectively and form municipal councils as it were, we must single out high officials and the various administrative authorities.

a) *In Israel:*

—in the period of the monarchy: masters of the palace or prime ministers, *Arza, Obadiah, Jotham, Shebnah, Eliakim* and perhaps *Azrikam;* scribes or secretaries, *Elihoreph, Ahijah, Eliakim, Shebnah, Shaphan, Elishama, Jehonathan;* heralds, *Jehoshaphat* and two *Joahs;* one head of the prefects, *Azariah;* one man in charge of forced labor, *Adoram;* advisers to the king, *Ahithophel, Zechariah;* armor-bearers (aides-de-camp), *David, Bidkar, Pekah;* friends of the king, *Hushai, Zabud;* eunuchs,

Ebed-melech, Nathan-melech; chamberlains, *Seraiah, Blastus;* twelve district administrators (in the time of Solomon), 1 K 4:8–19; governors of capital cities: at Jerusalem, *Joshua, Maaseiah;* at Samaria, *Zebul, Amon;* police officials, *Joash, Maaseiah, Jerahmeel;*

—in the period of Babylonian, Persian, Greek and Roman occupation, governors or high commissioners are named: *Gedaliah, Sheshbazzar, Zerubbabel, Nehemiah, Jonathan;* an ethnarch, *Simon;* tetrarchs, *Herod, Philip;* district leaders, *Rephaiah,* two *Shallums, Malchijah, Nehemiah, Hashabiah;* administrators of cities, *Hanani, Hananiah.*

b) *In other countries we find:*

—in Babylon: a high official, *Nebushazban;* a head of the palace staff, *Ashpenaz;*

—in Persia: a grand vizier or prime minister, *Haman;* a chief cupbearer, *Nehemiah;* a secretary (of state) for Jewish affairs, *Ezra;* a royal treasurer, *Mithredath;* provincial governors, *Tattenai, Rehum, Sanballat, Tobiah, Geshem;* an inspector of the royal park, *Asaph;*

—in the Syria of the Seleucids: regents of the kingdom, *Lysias* and *Philip;* ministers, *Heliodorus, Lasthenes;* military commissioners (governors), *Apollonius, Gorgias, Cendebaeus, Ptolemy, Hegemonides;* representatives of the king, *Philip, Andronicus;*

—in the Roman Empire: consuls, *Lucius, Scipio;* proconsuls, *Gallio, Sergius Paulus;* legates, *Quintus Memmius, Titus Manius, Quirinius;* procurators or governors, *Pilate, Felix, Porcius Festus;* a chief magistrate of Malta, *Publius;* a member of the Areopagus at Athens, *Dionysius.*

3. Military men

The Bible names a certain number of army commanders, generals, and officers.

In Israel: *Barak,* in the time of the judges; *Abner,* under Saul; *Joab,* under David; *Eliab,* under Solomon; *Adnah, Jehohanan, Amasiah, Eliada, Jehozabad,* under Jehoshaphat; *Hananiah, Jeiel, Maaseiah,* under Uzziah; *Ishmael, Johanan, Jonathan, Seraiah, Jaazaniah,* under Gedaliah; *Judas Maccabaeus* and his officers *Zechariah, Dositheus, Sosipater, Azariah, Joseph; Jonathan Maccabaeus* and his officers *Mattathias, Judas; Simon Maccabaeus* and his officers *John* and *Judas,* who are his sons, and *Jonathan.*

In other countries: the Philistine *Phicol;* the Canaanite *Sisera;* the Aramaeans *Shobach* and *Naaman;* the Babylonians *Nergal-sharezer* and *Nebuzaradan;* the Syrians *Nicanor* and *Seron;* mercenary captains, *Apollonius, Crates;* Romans, *Lysias,* a tribune, and *Cornelius* and *Julius,* centurions.

In addition to these officers, we must mention champions and heroes like those of David (List, pages 412–13); *Zichri,* an Ephraimite hero; *Goliath* the Philistine; and so on.

The royal bodyguard consists of a corps of foreign mercenaries: the *Cherethites* and *Pelethites* under David; the *Carians* under Athaliah.

4. Prophets

The Bible applies the title of prophet—seer, man of God—to quite diverse individuals. Sometimes the role of such people goes far beyond the prophetic function in the strict sense; this is true of *Moses,* for example. In other cases the individuals are called prophets only in passing, as in the case of *Abraham, Eldad,* and *Medad.*

In the category of prophets, "men of the Word and men of the Spirit, mainstays of the covenant and witnesses to the future," we can put about forty persons who take part in a movement that lasts from the period of the monarchy to the end of the Persian period. Among them are professionals, prophets by trade, members of a body of prophets; *Zedekiah son of Chenaanah.* Others are prophets by calling: *Amos, Isaiah, Jeremiah, Ezekiel.* There are strong personalities like *Samuel, Nathan, Elijah,* and *Elisha,* and men whose role is more modest, like the two *Odeds, Azariah, Eliezer, Hanan,* and the two *Shemaiahs;* intransigent men like *Hosea* and *Jeremiah,* and self-satisfied men like *Hananiah, Ahab,* and *Zedekiah;* aristocrats like *Isaiah* and peasants like *Amos;* priests like *Jeremiah, Ezekiel,* and the two *Zechariahs.* Some are imprisoned because of their message: *Hanani, Micaiah son of Imlah, Jeremiah;* others are faithful to the Word at the cost of their lives: *Zechariah* and *Uriah.*

The writings of thirteen of these prophets have come down to us: the discourses, namely, of *Amos, Hosea, Micah of Moresheth, Isaiah, Zephaniah, Jeremiah, Nahum, Habakkuk, Ezekiel, Haggai, Zechariah, Obadiah* and *Joel;* the book of Jonah (4th cent.) is attributed to the prophet *Jonah son of Amittai,* a contemporary of Jeroboam II, and the book of *Malachi* belongs to an anonymous prophet of the 5th cent. The Bible also mentions writings (now lost) of *Gad, Nathan* (?), *Ahijah of Shiloh, Elijah, Jehu, Shemaiah, Iddo,* and *Hozai.*

The prophetic role was also exercised by women: *Miriam, Deborah, Huldah, Noadiah,* and *Anna.*

The NT mentions Christian prophets: *Agabus,* the prophets and teachers of Antioch, *Barnabas, Simeon Niger, Lucius of Cyrene, Manaen* and *Saul/Paul,* as well as *Jude* and *Silas. Jesus* himself is regarded as the prophet foretold in Dt 18:15.

Outside of Israel, only one soothsayer and seer is mentioned in the Bible: *Balaam.*

5. Priests, Levites and synagogue leaders

a) *Priests*

The Bible mentions about 210 Israelite priests. Most of these names come in the work of the chronicler (Chronicles, Ezra, Nehemiah); there are a few priests mentioned in Gn 46, Ex 6, Nb 3 and 26.

Before the time of Solomon the priests referred to as such are the administrators of local sanctuaries: *Eli* and his sons *Hophni* and *Phinehas* at Shiloh; *Ahimelech* at Nob; *Jonathan,* the grandson of Moses, at Dan; or else they are in the personal service of the king, as for example *Ahijah* with Saul, *Abiathar* and *Zadok* with David.

Once Solomon has established the central sanctuary at Jerusalem, we find a real organization of the priesthood taking place (but this does not reach into the schismatic kingdom of the north, in which only one priest is named: *Amaziah* at the sanctuary of Bethel). As members of this hierarchy the Bible presents, in first place, the leaders of the priesthood or the high priests: from Solomon to the fall of Jerusalem, *Zadok, Azariah, Amaziah, Jehoiada, Azariah, Uriah, Azariah, Hilkiah,* and *Seraiah;* from the return from exile to the period of the Maccabees, *Jeshua, Joiakim, Eliashib, Joiada, Johanan, Jaddua, Onias I, Simon, Onias II, Onias III, Jason, Menelaus, Alcimus, Jonathan* [*Maccabaeus*] and *Simon* [*Maccabaeus*]; at the beginning of the Christian era, *Annas, Caiaphas, Ananias.* Alongside the high priests there are the priests second in command who have charge of the temple police: *Pashhur,*

Jehoiada, Zephaniah, Jehoiakim; an overseer of the priests, *Zabdiel;* a provost or treasurer of the temple, *Simon;* a superintendent of the temple storehouses, *Shelemiah;* a priest in charge of the temple chambers, *Eliashib.*

Some priests are assigned to teaching: *Elishama, Jehoram;* others are prophets, *Jeremiah, Ezekiel,* and the two *Zechariahs,* or scribes (that is, secretary of state for Jewish affairs), *Ezra,* or ambassadors, *Eupolemus.* One priest, *Mattathias,* leads the armed rebellion against hellenization.

After the exile, the two priestly lines, that of Zadok and Abiathar, are linked to *Aaron* as an eponymous ancestor through his sons, *Eleazar* father of *Phinehas* for Zadok, and *Ithamar* for Abiathar. These two families provide twenty-four classes of priests; Zechariah, father of John the Baptist, belongs to the eighth class, that of *Abijah.*

Only five non-Israelite priests are named: *Melchizedek,* priest of God Most High (El Elyon) and king of Salem; *Potiphera,* Egyptian priest at On; *Jethro,* a Midianite priest; *Ethbaal,* priest of Astarte and king of Tyre and Sidon; and *Mattan,* priest of Baal at Jerusalem.

b) *Levites*

The Bible names about 300 Levites, the vast majority of these names being in the works of the chronicler. See: LEVI; List, page 416.

In the NT Barnabas is said to be a Levite from Cyprus.

c) *Synagogue leaders*

The leaders or presidents of the synagogues—laymen chosen from among the more important members of the community—appear only in the NT; there are three of them: *Jairus* at Capernaum, *Crispus* and *Sosthenes* at Corinth.

6. Other avocations and functions

Among the other trades or professions represented in the Bible we may mention shepherds, *Abel, Jacob;* stockbreeders, *Jabal, Nabal, Amos, Job;* farmers, *Cain, Boaz, Naboth;* fishermen, *Peter, James* (*Zebedee* is a fisherman who employs others); a smith, *Tubal-cain;* a foundryman, *Alexander;* artists with many skills (engravers, seamsters, sculptors . . .), *Bezalel, Oholiab;* a bronzeworker, *Hiram;* metalsmiths, *Malchijah, Uzziel, Demetrius;* a leather-tanner, *Simon;* tentmakers, *Aquila, Paul;* a perfumer, *Hananiah;* a prefect of liturgical vestments (a kind of sacristan), *Shallum;* a lawyer, *Zenas;* an advocate, *Tertullus;* a professor, *Tyrannus;* writers, *Jason of Cyrene, Jesus son of Sira;* a translator, *Lysimachus;* Scripture scholars, *Ezra, Gamaliel, Apollos;* secretaries, *Baruch, Tertius;* magicians, *Simon, Bar-jesus;* tax collectors, *Matthew, Zacchaeus;* an executioner, *Arioch;* a doctor, *Luke;* slaves, servants, domestics, *Jarha,* Sheshan's servant, who ends up by marrying his master's daughter; *Purah,* Gideon's servant; *Zeba,* servant of King Saul, then of his son Meribbaal; *Gehazi,* servant of the prophet Elisha; *Malchus,* servant of the high priest (Annas or Caiaphas); *Onesimus,* slave of Philemon.

7. Challengers, revolutionaries

Along with those who simply reject a particular authority, as *Dathan* and *Abiram* reject that of Moses, there are others who actively oppose an established regime and endeavor, sometimes unsuccessfully, to overthrow it: *Gaal* at Shechem, *Absalom* at Jerusalem, or to secede from it, *Sheba* the Benjaminite, *Jeroboam son of Nebat.*

Even more numerous are the violent men who by means of assassination succeed either in overthrowing the man in power: *Baanah* and *Rechab* kill King Ishbaal; *Jozacar* and *Jehozabad* kill King Jehoash; *Ishmael* kills Gedaliah the governor; *Adrammelech* and *Sharezer* kill their father, King Sennacherib; *Zabdiel* kills King Alexander Balas; or in transferring power to the man of their own choice: *Jehoiada,* head of the priesthood in Jerusalem, puts his nephew Jehoash on the throne as the result of a plot against Athaliah; or in taking power themselves: in the northern kingdom *Baasha, Zimri, Jehu, Shallum, Menahem, Pekah,* and *Hoshea* all reach the throne in this way.

When the country is occupied by foreign powers, nationalist, terrorist, and revolutionary movements spring up. It is the priest *Mattathias,* father of the "Maccabees," who forms the first guerrilla movement against the Seleucids in defense of religious and political freedom for the Jewish people. *Judith* is the very type of Jewish resistance. In the time of Jesus there are insurrectional groups bent on ridding Palestine of the Romans; the NT mentions as their leaders *Theudas* and *Judas the Galilean.* Among the *Zealots* are one of the Twelve, *Simon,* and perhaps *Barabbas;* it may be that *Judas* had had links with terrorist groups.

8. Women

We do not know the personal names of about forty of the women the Bible mentions. It describes them by the name of their father or husband: the wife and two daughters of Lot, the wife of Potiphar, the six daughters of Jethro, the daughter of Jephthah, the mother and the wife of Samson, the wife of Phinehas son of Eli, the wife of Jeroboam I, the wife of Naaman and her young serving-maid, the wife of the prophet Isaiah, the wife of the prophet Ezekiel, the wife and first daughters of Job, the wife of Pilate, the four daughters of Philip the evangelist. Or else it describes them by naming the town they live in: the woman of Thebez, the witch of En-dor, the woman of Abel-beth-maacah, the woman of Tekoa, the woman of Shunem, the wife of Zarephath, the widow of Nain, the young soothsayer at Philippi. Or it describes them by their country of origin: the queen of Sheba, the Canaanite woman, the Samaritan woman. Or, finally, it describes them by a title: the Kandake of Ethiopia, the Tahpenes (or Great Lady) of Egypt.

Without being directly named, four women can be identified: *Laodice* and *Berenice,* wives of Antiochus II; *Cleopatra,* the daughter of Antiochus the Great; and *Salome,* the daughter of Herodias.

Most of the women named are Israelite or Jewish: *Bathsheba, Esther, Hannah, Mary.* However, not a few are of foreign birth: Egyptian, *Asenath, Cleopatra;* Midianite, *Zipporah;* Moabite, *Ruth, Shomer;* Ammonite, *Naamah, Shimeath;* Canaanite, *Bath-shua, Tamar;* Hittite, *Basemath, Judith;* Phoenician, *Jezebel;* Aramaean, *Leah, Rachel;* Syrian, *Antiochis;* Greek, *Damaris, Phoebe;* Roman, *Claudia.*

Most of the women are wives—and mothers, in a number of instances—: *Hannah, Naomi, Susanna, Mary;* wives of kings, *Ahinoam, Jezebel, Cleopatra;* of a prime minister, *Zeresh;* of a royal steward, *Joanna;* of an administrator, *Basemath, Taphat;* of a priest, *Elizabeth, Jehosheba. . . .* Some of them are concubines: *Keturah, Rizpah, Antiochis;* others are prostitutes: *Rahab, Cozbi, Gomer;* one is an adulteress: *Bathsheba.*

Along with women who play but a modest role in society, there are those who have public functions or professions or trades. Thus we find one reigning queen, *Athaliah;* queens who are wives of kings, *Vashti, Esther;* queen mothers or "Great Ladies," of which there are sixteen in Judah, *Bathsheba, Naamah, Hamital,* and so forth, and two in Israel, *Zeruah* and *Jezebel.* There are heroines: *Deborah, Jael, Judith;* prophetesses: *Miriam, Deborah, Huldah, Noadiah, Anna;* a deaconess, *Phoebe;* a seamstress, *Tabitha;* a tentmaker, *Priscilla;* a trader, *Chloe;* a dealer in purple dye, *Lydia;* two midwives, *Shiphrah* and *Puah;* a nurse, *Deborah;* shepherdesses, *Rachel, Zipporah;* servants and domestics, *Hagar, Bilhah, Zilpah, Rhoda.* See the List on pages 418–20.

For the women in the company of Jesus, see no. 10, below, and the List on pages 421–23.

9. Children, youths

There is reference to or a description of the childhood of several biblical persons: *Isaac, Ishmael, Moses, Samuel, Jesus,* and so on. On the other hand, some individuals in the Bible are known to us only as children or youths.

We know the names (which describe a whole program) of the prophet Isaiah's two little boys, *Shear-jashub* and *Maher-shalal-hash-baz,* and of the three children of the prophet Hosea, two boys, *Jezreel* and *No-people-of-mine,* and a girl, *Unloved.* We also know the names of three children who died young: *Abijah,* son of King Jeroboam I, and *Abiram* and *Segub,* the sons of Hiel of Bethel. We know nothing about little *Ichabod* except the fact of his birth. Finally, we can mention two young men, *Jether,* the eldest son of Gideon, and *Eutychus* of Troas. Other children or young people are mentioned, but their names are not given; for example, the first child of David and Bathsheba, the son of the woman of Shunem, the daughter of Jairus, the son of the widow of Nain, the daughter of the Canaanite woman, the nephew of Paul.

10. Christians

The NT has preserved for us the names of about 150 disciples of Jesus or early Christians; of these 30 are women. Among those who met Jesus during his earthly life, sympathized with him, and even became his disciples, some do not appear again after Easter. This is true of *Joseph* and *Simon,* "brothers of the Lord," *Lazarus* and his sisters *Mary* and *Martha, Joseph of Arimathaea* and *Nicodemus, Mary of Magdala, Mary the mother of James, Joanna, Salome* and *Susanna, Zacchaeus* and *Zebedee.*

a) *Geographical distribution*

After Pentecost, Christian communities came into being in various places. Known members of such local communities are found in Palestine, at *Jerusalem* where the Church comes into existence around the *Twelve* and *Mary,* at *Jaffa* and *Caesarea;* in Syria, at *Damascus,* where Saul is converted; and above all at *Antioch,* which becomes a center for the spread of the Gospel. Then, owing, among other factors, to the missionary journeys of Paul, we find communities on the island of Cyprus at *Paphos;* in Asia Minor, at *Lystra, Colossae, Laodicea, Ephesus, Pergamum,* and *Troas;* in Macedonia, at *Philippi, Doberus, Thessalonika,* and *Beroea;* in Greece, at *Athens, Corinth,* and *Cenchreae;* in Italy, at *Rome.* (For the names of these local Christians see the List, pages 421–23.)

b) *Religious and professional circles*

Among these first Christians there are many Jews: Palestinian Jews ("Hebrews"), the *Twelve (Peter, James, John . . . Matthew), Mary* the mother of Jesus, *James the Younger, Joseph Barsabbas, Judas Barsabbas, Mary* and her son *Mark, Ananaias* and *Sapphira, Tabitha* . . . ; Jews from the Diaspora, ("Hellenists"), such as the *Seven (Stephen, Philip . . . Nicolaus),* the five prophets of Antioch *(Barnabas, Simeon . . . Saul), Aquila* and *Priscilla, Andronicus, Aristobulus, Timothy* whose father was Greek and whose mother was Jewish.

At a very early date we also find pagans (some of them, like *Cornelius,* already sympathetic to Judaism): pagans of Greek origin, *Dionysius, Damaris, Apelles, Tryphaena, Tryphosa,* and of Roman origin, *Claudia, Cornelius, Julia, Rufus, Urbanus.*

The circles they represent and the functions they exercise are varied. We find slaves and freedmen: *Onesimus, Rhoda, Ampliatus, Hermas, Herodion, Nereus, Patrobas, Persis;* fishermen: *Peter, Andrew, James,* and *John;* a foundryman; *Alexander;* tentmakers: *Aquila* and *Priscilla;* a seamstress: *Tabitha;* a trader: *Lydia;* a tax collector: *Matthew;* a treasurer: *Erastus;* a doctor: *Luke;* a lawyer: *Zenas;* a centurion: *Cornelius;* a council member: *Dionysius;* a proconsul: *Sergius Paulus.*

c) *Types of Christians*

Here again there is a great variety. There are Apostles of indefatigable zeal and strong character: *Paul, Barnabas, Silas, Aquila, Priscilla, Mark, Luke, Timothy, Titus;* martyrs: *Stephen, Antipas;* disinterested individuals: *Barnabas,* and others attached to their goods: *Ananias* and *Sapphira;* an ambitious leader of a community: *Diotrephes,* and missionaries who carry out their task faithfully: *Gaius, Demetrius;* gracious and devout Christians: *Phoebe* the deaconess, *Persis* and *Mary;* lukewarm or cowardly companions: *Demas, Hermogenes, Phygelus;* heretics: *Philetus, Hymenaeus,* and *Alexander;* members of dissident sects: the *Nicolaitans, Jezebel. . . .* In short, we see a Church in which the Church of every age can recognize its own features.

III. THE GEOGRAPHY OF THE BIBLE

1. The world of the Bible

Because God's revelation of himself takes place in history, it is also geographical and topographical in character, and "biblical history" is interwoven with "biblical journeys": the ebb and flow of peoples, military victories and routs, invasions, occupations, deportations, movements of nomads, commercial exchanges by land and sea, missions of every kind, pilgrimages, and so on. The people of the Bible are, in every respect, people on the move. On the roads of the Bible, the names of individuals and peoples are closely associated, in their destinies, with the *places,* countries, and towns through which they pass or where they settle for a while. It can be said that in a sense even places are in motion: political and religious capitals shift, towns disappear, sometimes to be reestablished a little later. And if the hills are more "stable" and the rivers relatively faithful to their course, the face of the "Bible lands" changes in the course of its history.

But what is the reality covered by the expression "Bible lands"? The geographical sweep of the Bible has for its center the *Navel of the Earth* (a name for Jerusalem as the center of the world). To the west it reaches the "islands of the nations" (symbolized by the name of *Tarshish*—in Spain?); to the east, *India;* to the north, the shores of the Black Sea and *Armenia;* to the south, *Arabia* and *Ethiopia.*

2. Meaning of place names

a. A number of place names share a common component that acts as a kind of prefix: *Abel, Beer, Beth, En, Gath, Hazar. Abel* means "meadow," for example, *Abel-meholah,* "Meadow of the dance"; *Beer* means "well," for example, *Beer-elim,* "Well of the gods *or* of the terebinths," *Beeroth,* "The wells"; *Beth* means "house, temple, castle-fortress" and finally "place," for example, *Beth-haggan,* "House of the garden," *Beth-marcaboth,* "House of the chariots," *Beth-pazzez,* "Place where they smash," *Beth-ha-jeshimoth,* "House of the devastations," *Beth-dagon, Beth-shemesh; En* means "fountain, spring," for example, *Enaim,* "The two springs," *En-dor,* "Spring of Dor," *En-gedi,* "Spring of the kid"; *Gath* means "press" and, more broadly, an agricultural or viticultural installation, whence the meaning "farm," for example, *Gath-hepher,* "Press of the well," *Gath-rimmon,* "Press of the pomegranate," *Gethsemane,* "Olive press"; *Hazar* means "park, square, village," for example, *Hazer-hatticon,* "Park of the middle," *Hazar-susah,* "Park of the cavalry."

b. Many names reflect a facet of the terrain: a height or hill, *Acropolis, Ophel, Bozkath, Dabbesheth, Gibeon, Ramah;* a lookout point, *Dok, Mizpah;* a break in the terrain, *Zela Haeleph,* "Rib of beef," or *The foothills;* a depression, *Coele-Syria,* "Hollow Syria"; a bowl, *Mortar.* They may reflect location by a river: *Mesopotamia,* "[Land] between the two rivers," *Amphipolis,* "City surrounded [by a river]." Or a particular appearance or form: *The Ladder of Tyre, Chinnereth,* "Lyre," *Joppa* and *Shaphir,* "The beautiful," *Gihon,* "The gushing," *Jordan,* "The descender." Or a color: *Lebanon,* "White [mountain]," *Libnah,* "White [town]," *Zalmon,* "Dark [mountain]," the *Red Sea, Adummim,* "The red [earth]." Or the vegetation: *Shittim,* acacias, *Elon* and *Elim,* oaks *or* terebinths, *Bethphage,* fig-trees, *Enrimmon,* pomegranates, *Beerzeth,* olive trees. Or the neighborhood of a source of water, *Nahalal;* or of a public dump, *Hinnom;* or of quarries, *Shebarim;* or of a hot spring, *Hammath.* Or a place where animals pass through or gather: goats, *En-gedi;* stags, *Aijalon;* horses, *Hazar-susim;* foxes, *Hazar-shual;* hyenas, *Zeboim.*

c. Other names recall historical events: *Pentapolis, Decapolis* (the act of confederating five, or ten, towns), *Tiberias,* "City of Tiberius," *Caesarea,* "City of Caesar." Or popular traditions: *Hill of Foreskins; Valley of Beracah* ("Blessing"); *Beth-pazzez,* "Place where they smash"; *Beth-ha-jeshimoth,* "House of the devastations"; *Massah, Meribah,* "Trial" and "Quarrel"; *Esek,* "Quarrel"; *Beersheba,* "Well of the Seven *or* of the Oath."

d. On *theophoric* place-names, see above.

3. Physical geography

a. *Mountains and hills*

We do not know the precise location of many of the mountains, hills, and heights mentioned in the Bible, for example, the Hill of *Ammah,* Mount *Ephron,* the Hill of *Gareb,* Mount *Misar,* and so on.

Here is the distribution of the more important or better known mountains:

In Cisjordania: in the south, *Mount Halak,* the *Highlands (of Judah), Mount Zion,* the *Mount of Olives;* in the center, the *Highlands of Ephraim, Mount Ebal* and

Mount Gerizim, Mount Gilboa, and *Mount Carmel;* in the north *Mount Tabor.* In Transjordania, the *Abarim* chain with the heights of *Nebo* and *Pisgah.* In the Sinai Peninsula, *Mount Sinai* or *Horeb.* In Syria the *Lebanon* and *Anti-Lebanon* ranges with *Mount Hermon* and *Mount Amana.* In the southern Caucasus, *Mount Ararat.*

b. *Plains and valleys*

To begin with, there are the major plains or valleys, such as the *Plain of Jezreel,* prolonged by the *Plain of Beth-shan* ("the Great Plain"), the *Plain of Sharon* and the *Plain of the Jordan* in Israel, the *Vale of Lebanon* in Lebanon, and the *Plain of Aram* or *Paddan-aram* in Mesopotamia. The Bible also mentions many other valleys, usually small, in Palestine. West of the Jordan there are the *Valley of Achor* and the *Valley of the Hyenas;* south of the Dead Sea there are the *Valley of Siddim* and the *Valley of Salt;* west of the Dead Sea there are the *Valley of Beracah* and the *Valley of Eshcol;* near Jerusalem there are the *Valley of the Weeper,* the *Valley of the Rephaim,* and the *Valley of the King,* and perhaps the *Wadi of Acacias;* on the Mediterranean slopes there are the *Valleys of Zephathah, of the Terebinth, of Sorek,* and *of Iphtahel.*

Finally, there are two valleys with a symbolic significance: the *Valley of Jehoshaphat* and the *Valley of Hamon-gog.*

c. *Rivers and wadis*

By far the most frequently mentioned river of Palestine is evidently the *Jordan.* Of its tributaries there are, to the east, the *Jabbok* (the *Yarmuk* is never mentioned) and streams or wadis such as the *Cherith,* and perhaps the *Nimrim* and the wadi of the *Willows.* To the west, there are the wadis *Mochmur* and *Perat.* Some streams empty into the Dead Sea: on the east, the *Arnon;* in the south, the *Zered;* to the west, the *Kidron.* Into the Mediterranean flow the *River of Egypt,* the *Besor,* the *Gaash,* the *Kanah,* the *Libnath,* and the *Kishon.*

Outside of Israel are the *Nile* in Egypt; the *Abana* and the *Pharpar* in Damascus; the *Eleutherus* in Phoenicia; the *Tigris* and *Euphrates* (with the *Habor,* a left-bank tributary of the Euphrates) and the canals named *Ahava, Chebar,* and *Sud* in Mesopotamia; and the *Ulai,* which provides water for Susa.

Unidentifiable are the *Abron* and two of the rivers of Paradise, the *Gihon* and the *Pishon.*

d. *Seas, lakes, islands*

Despite seventeen different names for them, the Bible speaks, in the last analysis, of only four seas or lakes: the Mediterranean (and three of its parts: the *Adriatic,* the *seas of Cilicia* and *Pamphylia,* and the *Syrtis* Gulf, or Gulf of Cyrene), the *Red Sea,* the *Dead Sea,* and the *Sea of Chinnereth* or *Lake of Gennesaret.*

The islands named or alluded to are thirteen in number, all located in the: MEDITERRANEAN.

e. *Wildernesses* or *deserts*

The wilderness or desert plays a fairly important role in the Bible. But, apart from the *wilderness of Damascus,* which is mentioned in 1 K 19:15, all the other wildernesses explicitly named are in southern Palestine and in its prolongation, the Sinai Peninsula. In southern Palestine there are the *wilderness of Judah* or *Judaea* (which includes the *wildernesses of Tekoa, Jeruel, En-gedi, Ziph,* and *Maon*) and the *Negeb,* which extends from the *wilderness of Beersheba* to the *wilderness of Kadesh,* with the *wilderness of Edom* to its left. In the Sinai Peninsula there are the *wildernesses of Sin, Shur, Zin, Paran,* and *Sinai.*

f. *Forests*

Apart from the well-known *forest of Lebanon,* the Bible mentions only three forests, with the site of all three being uncertain: the *forest of Hereth,* 1 S 22:5, the *forest of Ephraim,* 2 S 18:6, and the *forest of the Negeb,* Ez 21:2–3.

4. Human geography

a. *Countries, peoples, clans*

It is difficult to give a precise number for countries or peoples. Natural boundaries change very little, but national frontiers, populations, names of nations, and areas of influence change as history wills. The birth of a new empire not only means a regrouping of provinces but often involves exchanges, transfers, or interminglings of peoples. The world of Herodotus (5th cent.) is no longer the world of Homer (9th cent.) and not yet the world of Strabo (1st cent.). An atlas of the Bible shows the world of the Near East wearing a different face as it presents the age of the (Egyptian) New Kingdom with its capital at Thebes, or the Assyrian empire in its heyday, or the Persian empire, or Greek hegemony, or Roman power.

We must, therefore, be careful of words that are far from having the same content in different contexts. *Canaanite,* for example, does not have the same meaning when it applies to the pre-Israelite population of the Holy Land as when it is used of the Syrophoenician woman of Mt 15:22//Mk 7:26, to say nothing of *Kananaios* (lit. "Canaanite," but meaning "Zealot") as used of the Apostle Simon. The *Hittites,* who were occupying Canaan at the time of the Israelite conquest, are but very distantly connected with the great Anatolian empire that disappeared about 1200 B.C. *Israel* can mean the kingdom of David and Solomon or the northern kingdom or even, after 722, the kingdom of Judah. *Judah,* for its part, sometimes refers solely to the tribe of Judah, sometimes to the kingdom of Judah, including Benjamin, and sometimes to the more limited territory of *Judaea,* which is a kind of canton with Jerusalem as its center. *Idumaea* is another name for *Edom,* but the territories to which the two names refer overlap only in part, for the Edomites had gradually been displaced from the east to the west. In Maccabees *Asia* is the kingdom of the Seleucids, but in the NT it is the proconsular province of the Romans. The *Greeks* are for the most part the representatives of a culture rather than Greek nationals. The *Romans* in Ac 25:16 are those who embody the empire's judicial power, and in many passages of St. John, the *Jews* means the religious authorities and not the people as such.

The word "country" (or "land") can be used in the Bible of large areas: *Egypt, Ethiopia, Arabia, Mesopotamia, Assyria, Chaldaea, Elam, Persia, Media, India, Greece, Macedonia, Italy, Spain.* Between these lands, *Canaan* (which becomes the land of *Israel*) and its neighbors, *Phoenicia, Philistia, Syria, Moab, Edom,* and *Midian,* form a land bridge between Africa and Asia. "Country" or "land" is also used of provinces: *Samaria, Galilee, Galatia, Bithynia, Pontus;* of regions: *land of Gilead;* of territories allotted to tribes: *land of Judah, of Benjamin, of Naphtali, of Zebulun, land of the Jews* (= Judaea); of the limited area adjacent to or surrounding a city or town: *land of Hepher, of Shaalim, of Shalishah, of Shual, of Sinim, of Tob.*

The peoples named in the Bible are sometimes the populations of the "great nations": *Egyptians, Babylonians, Assyrians, Persians, Medes, Elamites, Syrians, Arabs,*

Greeks, Romans; sometimes of more or less important clans, some of which are difficult to identify. Of these clans, in turn, some have "gentilicial" names: *Ahashtarites, Ashurites, Dananites, Kenites, Kennizzites, Meunites, Nephisites, Shumathites;* others bear the name of a chieftain: *Amalek, Dumah, Ephah, Hazor, Ishi, Nadab, Pekod, Shoa;* still others are named after an eponymous ancestor whose "sons" the members of the tribe or clan are said to be: the *sons of Ammon, Anak, Baean, Bezai, Cheleoud, Jambri, Phasiron, Rassis, Sheth.* The English translation does not always show this "sonship": the *Israelites* are in fact the *Bene-Israel,* the *sons of Israel;* the same holds for the *Benjaminites, Ephraimites, Judaeans, Manassites,* and so on.

When the Israelites conquered Canaan, they did not get rid of the former populations, as Jg 1:21, 29–35, bears witness. The Bible even names a certain number of foreigners who in one or other manner became part of the Israelite people: *Canaanites* such as Bath-shua (wife of Judah) and the wife of Simeon; *Hittites* such as Ephron and Uriah; an *Edomite,* Doeg; *Moabites* like Ruth and Shimrith; *Ammonites* like Shobi and Zelek; *Philistines* like Ittai and Obed-edom, who were from Gath; *Egyptians* like Asenath, Jarha, and Bithiah; as *Ethiopian,* Ebed-melech; an *Ishmaelite,* Obil.

b. *Cities and towns*

1] Statistics

The term meaning "city" or "town" can be applied in the Bible to large cities like *Antioch in Syria* and *Corinth,* which numbered respectively 300,000 and over a half-million inhabitants at the beginning of the Christian era, and to little towns and even simple villages, such as *Anathoth, Bethlehem,* and *Nazareth.*

There are about 700 such cities and towns named in the Bible (300 of them only once): 550 in Palestine and Transjordania taken together, most of these being in Cisjordania (see the Lists of towns, page 409); 150 in other countries: Egypt, 16; Phoenicia, 8; Aram-Syria, 20; Mesopotamia (Assyria-Babylonia), 28; Persia-Elam-Media, 4; Asia Minor, 30; Greece-Macedonia, 13; Italy, 5; Mediterranean islands, 7.

2] Categories of cities and towns

In addition to the great national capitals, *Asshur, Nineveh, Babylon, Memphis, Jerusalem, Rabbah of the Ammonites, Damascus, Antioch, Athens,* there are provincial capitals like those of the Roman provinces: *Tarsus* (Cilicia), *Ephesus* (Asia), *Thessalonika* (Macedonia), *Corinth* (Achaia). There are cantonal or district centers, *Beth-hac-cherem, Mizpah, Beth-zur, Keilah* (without naming the various centers, Jos 15:21–62 presents the eleven cantons of the land of Judah). There are the main cities or towns of the somewhat larger districts or territories, *Aphairema, Lydda, Ramathaim,* in the Judaea of the Seleucids. There are fortified towns, *Lachish, Beth-zur, Gezer, Aijalon, Megiddo, Taanach;* cities of refuge, *Hebron, Shechem, Kedesh, Bezer, Ramoth-gilead,* and *Golan* in Israel, and *Daphne* in Syria; "holy" cities, *Beersheba, Mamre, Nob, Bethel, Gilgal, Shiloh, Shechem, Dan,* and, of course, *Jerusalem,* the holy city beyond all others, and, outside of Israel, *Daphne* in Syria, famous for its shrine of Apollo, and *Ephesus,* "holy city of great Diana"; Levitical cities, *Hebron, Libnah, Gibeon, Geba, Anathoth, Shechem, Gezer;* a city with the special status of a Roman colony, *Philippi.*

To these various classifications we may add the port cities (about forty of them) that are distributed as follows: on the Black Sea (which is not named explicitly) *Sampsames;* on the Red Sea, *Ezion-geber;* on the shores of the Mediterranean, *Alexandria* in Egypt, *Jamnia, Joppa, Caesarea, Acco/Ptolemais, Tyre, Sidon, Gebal/Byblos, Tripolis, Orthosia,* and *Seleucia* on the Syro-Palestinian coast; *Side, Attalia, Phaselis,*

Myra, Patara, Myndos, Miletus, Ephesus, Smyrna, Adramyttium, Assos, and *Troas* on the coasts of Asia Minor; *Neapolis* in Macedonia; *Cenchreae* in Greece; *Rhegium* and *Puteoli* in Italy; *Syracuse* in Sicily; *Lasea* and *Phoenix* in Crete; *Mitylene* on the island of Lesbos; *Rhodes* on the island of Rhodes; *Paphos* and *Salamis* on the island of Cyprus; and *Arvad* facing the Syrian coast.

Some cities or towns are linked together in federations, like the Gibeonite Tetrapolis of *Gibeon, Beeroth, Chephirah* and *Kiriath-jearim;* the Pentapolis on the Dead Sea plain, *Sodom, Gomorrah, Zeboiim, Admah,* and *Zoar;* the Philistine Pentapolis, *Ashdod, Ashkelon, Gaza, Gath,* and *Ekron;* the Decapolis, *Scythopolis, Philadelphia, Gerasa,* [*Pella*], *Gadara,* [*Abila, Hippos, Dion, Canatha*], and *Damascus.*

3] *Exploring the towns . . .*

In most cases the Bible gives no details regarding the topography, layout, or monuments of a town or city. But there are a few exceptions. The chief exception concerns Jerusalem. The Bible names many of the gates in the city wall: *Sheep Gate,* the *Gate of the Sons of the People, Fountain Gate, Dung Gate, Fish Gate, Gate of the Potsherds . . .* ; the towers, *Tower of the Furnaces, of Hananel;* the fortress [*Antonia*]; the *temple* and the royal palace, with the *Entry of the Horses, Water Gate, Watch Gate,* and the *Gate of the Felled Tree-trunk;* the sectors known as *Mortar* and *New Quarter* or *New Town;* the street of the *Bakers; Gihon Spring* and the *Well of the Dragon;* the pools of *Bethzatha* and *Shiloah.*

The Bible also refers to the following: at Shechem, the temple of *El-berith* and the *Migdal-shechem* or acropolis of the town; at Samaria, the *Ophel* and the *Pool;* at Rabbah of the Ammonites, *water town* or the lower city, and the *town* or acropolis; at Heshbon, the gate of *Bath-rabbim* and the pools; at Damascus, *Straight Street;* at Ephesus, the theater and the lecture hall of *Tyrannus.*

For a fairly large number of towns the existence of one or more synagogues is mentioned: *Capernaum, Nazareth, Jerusalem, Damascus, Salamis, Antioch in Pisidia, Iconium, Thessalonika, Beroea, Athens, Corinth,* and *Ephesus.*

4] *Yesterday and today*

The cities and towns mentioned in the Bible have had quite varied subsequent histories.

Many have simply disappeared. Of these, some are unknown to geographers: *Bealoth, Cyamon, Dalmanutha, Eglath Shelishiyah, Kiriath-huzoth,* or difficult to locate accurately, *Almon-diblathaim, Elkosh, Tarshish.* Others that were famous in their day have been identified by archaeological excavation: in Israel, *Lachish, Caesarea, Shechem, Tirzah, Megiddo* (with its twenty towns one atop the other), *Capernaum, Hazor;* in Egypt, *Memphis* (the ruins of which supplied material for building such nearby cities as Cairo); in Mesopotamia, *Ur, Babylon, Nineveh;* in Persia, *Susa* and *Persepolis;* in Turkey, *Perga, Ephesus, Miletus.*

Over the centuries some cities have been destroyed and rebuilt many times, sometimes on the very ruins of the old, sometimes close by (present-day *Jericho* is 2 km from *Tell es-Sultan,* site of the ancient town). Some have declined and become villages, like *Samaria* (the modern *Sebastiyeh*) or *Beth-shan* (the modern *Beit Shean*), whereas others, on the contrary, have developed into relatively important modern cities, *Beersheba, Ashdod, Hebron, Bethlehem, Nazareth, Acco, Tyre* (modern *Es Sur*), *Sidon* (modern *Saida*), *Antioch* in Syria (modern *Antakya*), *Attalia* (modern *Antalya*), *Syene* (modern *Aswan*), and even into large urban complexes, like *Gaza, Joppa* (modern *Tel Aviv–Yafo*), *Jerusalem, Rabbah of the Ammonites* (modern *Amman*), *Iconium* (modern *Konya*), *Smyrna* (modern *Izmir*), *Thessalonika, Corinth, Athens, Rome.*

c. *Special place-names*

Throughout the Bible, usually in relation to places outside the cities and towns, we find a number of traditional names reflecting some peculiarity of the topography or some historical incident. Not infrequently the biblical writer himself adverts to this phenomenon by saying, for example, "He gave this place the name . . . ," "They called this spot . . . ," or "At the place called. . . ." See Gn 28:19, *Bethel;* 32:31, *Penuel;* 33:17, *Succoth;* Ex 15:23, *Marah;* 17:7, *Massah* and *Meribah;* Nb 11:3, *Taberah;* Mt 27:33, *Golgotha;* Jn 19:13, *Pavement;* Rv 16:16, *Armageddon.* In many instances, the meaning given is the result of popular etymology.

This kind of place-name preserves the memory of a manifestation of God, a historical event, or a legend. The spots may be landmarks along a road, famous places of worship, tracks followed by animals, or a celebrated tree or grove. We may mention, for example, places where Yahweh has appeared, *Yahweh-nissi, Yahweh-Peace, Yahweh Provides;* threshing floors of *Araunah,* of the *Bramble* (Goren-ha-atad), of the *Javelin* (Nacon); stones, *Stone of Bohan, Sliding Stone;* rocks, *Rock of Etam, Rock of Rimmon, Rock of Divisions, Rock of Oreb, Rocks of the Wild Goats;* fields, *Field of Blood, Field of Sides, Fuller's Field, Field of Spies;* springs (*En-*), *Spring of Judgment, Spring of Harod* (or *Trembling*); trees, *Oak of Zanaan-nim, Oak of Mamre, Oak of Moreh* (or *Diviner's Oak*), *Oak of Tears, Oak of Tabor, Deborah's Palm;* ascents (or descents), of *Adummim,* of the *Armory,* of *Beth-horon,* of the *Flower* (Ziz), of *Gur,* of *Heres,* of *Luhith,* of *Scorpions.* Other places with this type of special name include the *Idols,* the *Huts, Uzza's Breach,* the *Well of Sirah,* the *Height of the Jawbone* (Ramath-lehi), *Winepress of the Wolf* (Zeeb), the *Valley of the Terebinth,* the *Valley of Jehoshaphat,* the *Tombs of Greed* (Kibroth-hattaavah).

IV. RELIGION AND MYTHOLOGY

a. *Mythical peoples*

The Bible has preserved for us the names of some legendary giants of prehistoric times: the *Nephilim,* the *Titans,* the *Rephaim* of Bashan and Gilead, the *Anakim* of Cisjordania, the *Zamzummim* of Ammon, the *Emim* of Moab. The *Horites* are also to be numbered among these legendary enemies who are defeated by the four kings of Gn 14; cf. Dt 2:10–12, 20–22.

b. *Dwelling place of the dead*

The only proper names alluding to the existence of man after death are *Sheol* and *Hades*—translated as Sheol, Hades, dwelling of the dead, hell, underworld—where the dead live on in a dreary half-life. It is a realm ruled by the figure to whom Job refers as the *King of Terrors.* On the lips of Christ the Greek word *Gehenna* ("hell") becomes the symbol of the place that is supremely accursed and of eternal punishment.

c. *Cosmic powers. Angels and demons*

Some texts present the mighty deeds of God, and especially the miracle at the Red Sea, as a victory of Yahweh over cosmic powers that are described in personal terms: the *Sea* (Hb. *Yam*), the *Dragon* (Hb. *Tannin*), *Leviathan, Rahab,* the *Deep* (Hb. *Tehom*). The descriptions remind us of the struggle of the Babylonian god

Marduk against *Tiamat* or of the Canaanite god *Baal* against his enemies, *Yam,* "Prince Sea," and *Mot,* "Death."

The Bible often speaks of angels, but for the most part these are nameless: "The angel of Yahweh *or* of the Lord," "an angel," "an angel of God *or* from heaven," or they are mentioned in a global manner: "some angels," "the angels." The only three angels named are *Raphael, Gabriel,* and *Michael.*

The Bible says nothing about the battles and struggles for ascendancy among the gods, as described in the ancient mythologies. It does, however, on a number of occasions refer to evil forces that are opposed to God and are described in personal terms: *Satan, Beliar, Beelzebul, Asmodeus, Azazel,* and *Lilith.*

d. *God and the gods*

Though the Bible is a book about humanity and a book about the world, it is also and above all a book about *God.* By a patient process of education God wishes to teach biblical people to "break with idolatry"—the "other gods" of Ex 23:13—about sixty of these are named or alluded to (see: GODS)—in order to "become servants of the real, living God," 1 Th 1:9, the one God in whom Jews, Christians, and Muslims believe (see: YAHWEH). God and the gods are present within biblical history by the power that they exercise or that is attributed to them, by the temples, steles, and trees dedicated to them, by the worship and prayers offered to them, by the persons and places that bear their names (cf. above, on theophoric names).

Sacred history, which has its origin in the first words spoken by God the creator, Gn 1:1–3, 26, will end at the moment when the Son, the Word of God made flesh, will, at his final coming, Rv 22:20, "hand over the kingdom to God the Father, having done away with every sovereignty, authority and power . . . so that God may be all in all," 1 Co 15:24, 28. The land of the Bible will be replaced by the ideal promised land, the real "land of the living." All the cities built since *Enoch,* the first city, and *Babel,* the place where the peoples were divided and scattered, will make way for the everlasting city, "the city founded by God," Heb 11:16, the *new Jerusalem,* Rv 21:2, to which the people of the Bible, these "strangers and nomads," are en route, and in which the race that sprang from the first *Adam* will recover its unity around the new *Adam.*

O. ODELAIN and R. SÉGUINEAU

Translator's Note

This English version of the *Dictionary of Proper Names and Places in the Bible* has been adapted for the use of readers of *The Jerusalem Bible*. (All references are to the original edition of 1966; the later *Reader's Edition* Americanizes the spelling used in the translation, and also slightly modifies the form of some proper names.) As a general rule, therefore, the alphabetical list of entries is limited to names that actually appear in the text of *The Jerusalem Bible*. There are, however, some bracketed entries. In addition to those which are bracketed because they are not found as such in the original texts of the Bible (see below: "Using the Dictionary"), I have included some others which, although found in the original texts and in the French edition of the *Dictionary*, are not in *The Jerusalem Bible* and yet seemed worth retaining, for example, [ELOAH] and [ELOHIM].

For the modern identification of biblical places I have followed Denis Baly and A. D. Tushingham, *Atlas of the Biblical World* (New York: World, 1971) and, secondarily, *Webster's Geographical Dictionary*.

Using the Dictionary

Depending on the importance of the name in question, an entry may contain the following items:

1. the proper name
2. its frequency in the Bible
3. its transcription in the original language or one of the other ancient languages
4. its meaning
5. its etymological kinships
6. the body of the article
7. references to other articles.

Some points of explanation regarding each of these items:

1. **The proper name:** in boldface capital letters.

a) The *spelling* is that of the *Jerusalem Bible* (Garden City, New York: Doubleday & Company, Inc., 1966). Entries that are bracketed, for example, **[ACHAEMENIDS],** are names that do not occur as such in the Bible.

b) The *name* may be simple, for example, **AARON; DAVID,** or composite, for example, **ADONI-ZEDEK; TIGLATH-PILESER.** It may be followed by other points of information derived from the biblical text and indicating either a kinship relation (son, daughter, wife, father, mother . . . of), for example, **son of Alphaeus** (JAMES 4); **mother of James** (MARY 6), or a place of origin, for example, **of Shunem** (ABISHAG); **the Tishbite** (ELIJAH 1), or a title or function, for example, **king of Salem** (MELCHIZEDEK); **governor of Judaea** (PILATE).

These secondary items are in upper- and lower-case boldface type.

c) When a name has several spellings in English, they are all included under the name that is the most representative or the best known in English, for example, **JOHN, Johanan, Jehohanan,** but each of these other spellings has its own entry in the alphabetical order.

2. **The frequency of the proper name:** number given in parentheses.

This number shows how many times the name is found throughout the Bible, for example, **ANDREW** (13); **JESUS** (923).

a) The number refers to the original text. In translations the proper name is often omitted for stylistic reasons (and replaced by a pronoun) or, on the contrary, is supplied for the sake of clarity. The same holds for indications of the place of origin; the Hebrew or Greek text may have *Gibeonite* or *Sidonian,* where English prefers "of (or from) Gibeon or Sidon."

b) No figure is given immediately after the entry when the name in question is borne by more than one person or place. In these cases the number is given after each subentry, for example, **ABEL:** 1. **Abel** (12) . . . ; 2. **Abel** (1) . . . ; 3. **Abel** (1).

c) The number thus given in parentheses is not necessarily matched by the number of references in the body of the article. These are several reasons for this: (1) to give references for the 923 occurrences of *Jesus,* the 1,150 of *David* or the 6,800 of *Yahweh* would have been impossible and useless; (2) some occurrences of a name may be found under another proper name to which reference is made, for example, *Jesse* occurs 48 times, but 19 of these are to be looked for under DAVID; (3) finally, the references given are meant to point to essentials: thus the same reference may be given more than once in order to provide evidence for different statements, for example, 1 K 11:1–3 tells both of the luxurious life of Solomon and his perilous religious tolerance.

d) When several names are grouped together, the frequency of each is indicated in connection with the occurrence of the name in the alphabetical order, e.g., **AQUILA** (6) and **Prisca** or **Priscilla; HANANIAH** 18. **Ananaias** (3) and his wife **Sapphira.** This rule is followed unless the several names are used an equal number of times, for example, **AHIMAN** 1. **Ahiman, Sheshai,** and **Talmai** (3); **DATHAN** and **Abiram** (11).

e) For names that occur with great frequency there is a breakdown for the different books, or groups of books, of the Bible; cf., for example, **AARON; ABRAHAM; ISRAEL; YAHWEH.**

f) A number denoting frequency is also given for each of the elements that goes with the proper name, for example, **JOHN** 22. **John** (91) **son of Zechariah** (1), called **the Baptist** (15).

It has been decided, however, not to give numbers for the frequency of the expressions "king of Israel" and "king of Judah," in order to avoid an excess of numbers and parentheses, for example, **JEHU** 2. **Jehu** (49) **son of Jehoshaphat** (2) **son of Nimshi** (5), tenth king of Israel (841–814).

3. **The transcription of the name in an ancient language:** in *italics.*

a) It is introduced by a suitable abbreviation: Hb., Aram., and so on. As we have decided not to use diacritical marks and unusual type fonts, these transcriptions make no pretence at being scholarly.

b) It is given when required in order to distinguish English homophones, for example, **ABEL,** or useful in order to discern the original behind an English name that is too unlike the original, for example, **AARON,** or to facilitate comparison with other words or other languages, for example, **NEBUCHADNEZZAR.**

4. **The meaning of the name:** in "quotation marks."

When no meaning is given, this is because the meaning is completely unknown or very uncertain.

When several names are grouped together, for example, **Gideon** = **Jerubbaal; Oreb** and **Zeeb,** the meaning of each name is given under the alphabetical listing of that name: **GIDEON; JERUBBAAL; OREB; ZEEB.**

Light is sometimes cast on the meaning of a name by a reference that is preceded by "see," for example, **AHAZ,** "[Yah] grasps [in order to guide]," see Ps 73:23.

Consultation of the *Index of English Equivalents* will allow the reader to compare various proper names having the same meaning.

5. **Etymological kinships between proper names:** in (parentheses).

After the meaning of a name or, if no meaning is given, immediately after the proper name or its transcription, certain references may be given:

a) with "cf.,"

either to a related word, for example, **BETH-PAZZEZ** (cf. Happizzez); **HAPPIZZEZ** (cf. Beth-pazzez),

or to a key word (or even several key words), under which all the words from the same root are listed, for example, **EBED-MELECH** refers to *Ebed* and *Melech.* Under *Ebed* there are references to eleven words from the same root, and under *Melech* to twenty-four words.

b) with "see,"

to a proper name with the same meaning but derived from a different root or belonging to a different language, for example, **IR HAHERES** Ac*f.* Heres . . . . See Amphipolis; Kiriath); **ZADOK** (cf. Adoni-zedek . . . . See Justus).

The Index of English Equivalents will enable the reader to extend the range of these relationships between names.

6. **The body of the article.** Except for those proper names where the reader is simply directed to another entry, for example, **JOHANAN.** See: JOHN; **OCHRAN** (5), (cf. Achar), father of: PAGIEL, the articles of the dictionary contain two types of material: a more or less lengthy text and more or less numerous references that are meant to support the statements of the text. The respective importance of the two types of material varies both according to the subject being treated and to the frequency of the name.

The importance of the personality of *Ezekiel,* as suggested in the 48 chapters of his book, is disproportionate to the three occurrences of his name. *Holofernes,* on the other hand, is named 24 times, yet he is given only a short article. Malta is named only once, but reference is being made to it throughout thirteen verses, Ac 27:43–28:11.

Articles may have two kinds of subdivision:

a) When a proper name covers a single homogeneous reality, it may be subdivided into simple paragraphs, or into sections preceded by *a, b, c* . . . and a subtitle, for example, **AARON,** *a. Aaron and the Exodus,* and so on.

b) When the same proper name belongs to more than one person or place, the article is subdivided into 1, 2, 3, and so on, for example, **ABEL** 1 . . . 2 . . . 3; **ZECHARIAH** 1 . . . 30.

Some of these subdivisions, of course, may in turn have several sections or paragraphs, for example, **JOHN** 22; **JUDAH** 1, 7, 12.

When a proper name has one or more equivalents, these are introduced by an = sign (possibly followed by a ?, if the identification is not certain) and are printed in boldface, for example, **HEBRON** 1. **Hebron** = **Kiriath-arba; CHINNERETH** b. **Sea of Chinnereth** = **Lake of Gennesaret** = **Sea of Galilee** = **Sea of Tiberias.**

N.B. The articles of this dictionary can be read in two different ways: in order to *obtain a quick overview* of a given subject, the reader will find it sufficient to read the article while ignoring the references; in order to *study in detail* a given person or place, the reader must consult the references given in support of the text.

7. **References to other articles:** preceded by "See:" or simply by a colon, and printed in CAPITALS AND SMALL CAPITALS.

Such references may be given in the *course of an article,* for example, in the text under **JUDAH** 1. *d,* which deals with the kingdom of Judah, reference is made to ISRAEL *d* (the northern kingdom) and, further on, to DAVID *b* (the reign and dynasty of David). Most often, however, these references are given at the *end of an article, section, or numbered subdivision.* In these instances the references complement the article in either or both of two ways:

a) They indicate the entry or entries where the reader will find those uses of a name which are not treated under the name itself, for example, **NEBAT** (26) refers to JEROBOAM 1, where the latter is said 26 times to be the **son of Nebat.**

b) They list articles that provide further information on the subject being treated, for example, **JUDAH** 1. *d,* which deals with the kingdom of Judah, refers the reader to the twenty kings of Judah: ABIJAH 2, and so on, and to the capital of Judah: JERUSALEM. The article **JERUSALEM** refers, at the end, to other names for the city: ARIEL 2; JEBUS, and so on, to its kings: ADONI-ZEDEK, and so on, to its hills, fountains, gates, and quarters.

The references to other articles are generally in alphabetical order.

Abbreviations and Various Sigla

abbrev.	abbreviation
acc.	according
Accad.	Accadian
Arab.	Arabic
Aram.	Aramaic
Babyl.	Babylonian
cf.	confer, compare
ch.	chapter
corr.	correction
DB	Deuterocanonical Books
E	East
e.g.	for example
Egypt.	Egyptian
fem.	feminine
ff.	following verses
Gr.	Greek
Hb.	Hebrew
JB	Jerusalem Bible
K	*Ketib,* that which is written
Kh.	*Khirbet* (= Ruin)
km	kilometer
Lat.	Latin
lit.	literally
LXX	Septuagint
m	meter
N	North
Nabat.	Nabataean
NT	New Testament
OT	Old Testament
p	parallel passage in the gospels
Pers.	Persian
Phoen.	Phoenician
prol.	prologue of Sirach
Q	*Qere,* that which is to be read
Rom.	Roman
S	South
Sumer.	Sumerian
Ugar.	Ugaritic
v., vv.	verse, verses
W	West
(358)	number of times a word occurs
/	equivalence or association of two proper names
//	parallel passage
×	times (5× = 5 times)
±	approximately
=	equivalent to
?	doubtful
[ ]	proper name not found as such in the Bible

References to the Bible

The names of the "books" of the Bible are abbreviated as in the Jerusalem Bible (cf. the following list of abbreviations). If an abbreviation occurs without any following number, the reference is to the book as a whole, for example, Gn; 1 Ch; Jn. The lack of any abbreviation before a number (chapter or chapter and verse) means that the reference is to the book most recently mentioned.

A simple number after an abbreviation refers the reader either to an entire chapter: 1 S 7, or to a verse in those books that have only one chapter: Ob 21; Phm 25; 2 Jn 13; 3 Jn 15; Jude 25.

A colon separates chapter and verse: Jg 4:6; a comma separates two verses: Jg 4:6, 12; 5:1, 12. An en dash shows that the reference is to several successive verses: 2 S 2:17–24, or to two or more successive chapters: 2 S 9–20, or parts of chapters: Ex 5:1–6:13.

The books of the Bible in alphabetical order of abbreviations

Ac	Acts	Ho	Hosea
Am	Amos	Is	Isaiah
Ba	Baruch	Jb	Job
1 Ch	1 Chronicles	Jdt	Judith
2 Ch	2 Chronicles	Jg	Judges
1 Co	1 Corinthians	Jl	Joel
2 Co	2 Corinthians	Jm	James
Col	Colossians	Jn	John
Dn	Daniel	1 Jn	1 John
Dt	Deuteronomy	2 Jn	2 John
Ep	Ephesians	3 Jn	3 John
Est	Esther	Jon	Jonah
Ex	Exodus	Jos	Joshua
Ezk	Ezekiel	Jr	Jeremiah
Ezr	Ezra	Jude	Jude
Ga	Galatians	1 K	1 Kings
Gn	Genesis	2 K	2 Kings
Hab	Habakkuk	Lk	Luke
Heb	Hebrews	Lm	Lamentations
Hg	Haggai	Lv	Leviticus

1 M	1 Maccabees
2 M	2 Maccabees
Mi	Micah
Mk	Mark
Ml	Malachi
Mt	Matthew
Na	Nahum
Nb	Numbers
Ne	Nehemiah
Ob	Obadiah
1 P	1 Peter
2 P	2 Peter
Ph	Philippians
Phm	Philemon
Pr	Proverbs
Ps	Psalms
Qo	Ecclesiastes
Rm	Romans
Rt	Ruth
Rv	Revelation
1 S	1 Samuel
2 S	2 Samuel
Sg	Song of Songs
Si	Ecclesiasticus
Tb	Tobit
1 Th	1 Thessalonians
2 Th	2 Thessalonians
1 Tm	1 Timothy
2 Tm	2 Timothy
Tt	Titus
Ws	Wisdom
Zc	Zechariah
Zp	Zephaniah

Dictionary of Proper Names and Places in the Bible

A

AARON (358), Hb. *'Aharon,* brother of Moses and Miriam, of the tribe of Levi, assistant to Moses and ancestor of the priestly class. Aaron appears 300× in the Pentateuch, then in Jos 21:4, 10, 13, 19; 24:5, 33; Jg 20–28; 1 S 12:6, 8; Ch-Ezr-Ne: 24×; Tb 1:7; 1 M 7:14; Ps: 9×; Si: 6×; Mi 6:1; NT: 5× (Lk 1:5; Ac 7:40; Heb 5:4; 7:11; 9:4).

a. Aaron and the Exodus

Aaron is given by God to Moses as his interpreter, Ex 4:14–30, or his prophet, Ex 7:1–2. With Moses he comes before Pharaoh to convince him to let the Hebrews depart, Ex 5:1–6:13; 7:1–7, and to overcome his stubbornness by afflicting him with the "plagues" of Egypt, Ex 7–12. He helps Moses during the Exodus and the long forty-year journey through the wilderness, cf. Nb 33:1; Jos 24:5; 1 S 12:6, 8; Ps 77:21; 105:26–27; Mi 6:4, in leading to the Promised Land a people ever ready to complain and rebel, Ex 16–19; Nb 14; 16; 20; Ps 106:16. He supports Moses' arms during the battle against Amalek, Ex 17:10–12, helps him take a census of the people, Nb 1–4, accompanies him on the mountain, Ex 19:24, where he is allowed to see the God of Israel, Ex 24:10. While Moses is meeting God alone on Sinai, Aaron, under pressure from the people, molds a golden calf and permits Israel to engage in idolatry, Ex 32; cf. Ac 7:40. Along with Miriam, Aaron shows himself jealous of Moses, Nb 12. Yahweh rebukes Moses and Aaron for their disbelief, Nb 20:12, which they will pay for by not entering the Promised Land. Aaron dies on Mount Hor, Nb 20:23–29; Dt 32:50, or at Moserah, Dt 10:6, at the age of 123, Nb 33:39.

b. Aaron and the Priesthood

Aaron a Levite, Ex 4:14, son of Amram and Jochebed, is a member of a rather unimportant clan (the Amramites) of the tribe of Levi, Ex 6:16–20; Nb 26:58–59; 1 Ch 5:27–29; 23:13; cf. Ex 2:1. The episode of Aaron's branch, Nb 17:16–26; cf. Heb 9:4, exhibits him as the one responsible for the tribe. He marries Elisheba, who bears him four sons: Nadab, Abihu, Eleazar, and Ithamar. In Ex 28–29 Moses consecrates Aaron and his sons so that they may exercise the priesthood of Yahweh, cf. Ex 29:44; Lv 8–9; Ps 133:2; Si 45:6–22, 25. Aaron is called a priest about 15×, and high priest, Ezr 7:5; cf. Heb 9:7 citing Lv 16:2–3. And in fact he appears as the first high priest, the leader of the priest sons of Aaron (about 20×), so that the expressions "Aaron and his sons," Ex 27:21, and so on, "the sons of Aaron," Ex 28:40, and so on, "you and your sons," Nb 18:1, 2, 7–9, the "house of Aaron," Ps 115:10, 12; 118:3; 135:19, "a descendant of Aaron," Lk 1:5; cf. Nb

18:11, 19, designate the priestly caste, those set apart to consecrate the most holy things, burn incense before Yahweh, serve him and bless in his name forever, 1 Ch 23:13, preside at worship, bless the people, make atonement for the people, enlighten Israel on his Law, Si 45:15–17. Because of his consecration Aaron is called holy, Si 45:6, Yahweh's holy one, Ps 106:16; his intercessory power is emphasized in Nb 17:6–15; cf. Ws 18:20–25; Ps 99:6. Except in ch. 1 and 11–12, Heb treats of the priesthood of Christ as contrasted with that of the old covenant as represented by Aaron. Himself called by God as Aaron had been, 5:4, Jesus ushers in a new priesthood, which breaks with that of Aaron and is in continuity with the mysterious priesthood of Melchizedek, 7:11.

Father of: ABIHU 1; ELEAZAR 1; ITHAMAR 1; NADAB 1.

Principal "descendants": EZRA 2; PHINEHAS 1; ZADOK 1. See List, pp. 000–000.

AB-, "Father," cf. Dt 32:6; 2 S 7:14; Ps 68:6; 89:27; Is 9:5 . . . , a divine title that is a component of many proper names.

ABADDON (6), "Perdition, Destruction" (cf. Asmodeus), a poetic name for the dwelling place of the dead, Jb 26:6; 28:22; 31:12; Ps 88:12; Pr 15:11, may be the name of a divinity of the lower world. Rv 9:11 calls the angel of the abyss *Abaddon* and tells us that his Greek name is **Apollyon,** "Destroyer," which reminds us of the Greek god *Apollo*. See: SHEOL.

ABAGTHA (1), a eunuch mentioned along with: MEHUMAN.

ABANA (1), (Q*Amana*), a river that runs down from the Anti-Lebanon and is one of the "rivers of Damascus" (the other is the Pharpar), 2 K 5:12.

ABANDONED (1). See: AZUBAH.

ABARIM (6), (cf. Iye-abarim), a mountain range east of the Jordan and the Dead Sea, one of the final stages of the Exodus, Nb 33:47–48. One of its summits is Nebo, from which Moses saw the Promised Land, Nb 27:12; Dt 32:49. A personified Jerusalem is urged to climb the heights of Lebanon, Bashan, and Abarim and cry out its distress there, Jr 22:20. The destruction of Moab is shouted from the Abarim (corr. of Hb. *Horonaim*), Jr 48:5. Gog and his army will be buried in the valley of the Abarim, Ezk 39:11. See: HAMON-GOG.

ABDA (1), "Servant" (cf. Ebed), father of: ADORAM.

ABDEEL (1), "Servant of God" (cf. Ebed), father of: SHELEMIAH 2.

ABDI, abbrev. of *Obadiah,* "Servant of Yah" (cf. Ebed).

1. **Abdi** (1), a Levite of the clan of Merari, father of Kishi, ancestor of Ethan the cantor, 1 Ch 6:29. Compare with the following.

2. **Abdi** (1), a Levite of the clan of Merari, father of: KISH 4.

3. **Abdi** (1), an Israelite of the sons of Elam, married to a foreign wife, whom he puts away, Ezr 10:26.

ABDIEL (1), "Servant of God" (cf. Ebed), father of: AHI 1.

ABDON, "Little servant" (cf. Ebed).

1. **Abdon son of Hillel, of Pirathon** (2), a "lesser" judge for eight years. "He had forty sons and thirty grandsons who rode on seventy donkeys' colts," Jg 12:13–15. In 1 S 12:11 some correct Hb. *Bedan to Abdon;* others, to *Barak,* with the Gr.

2. **Abdon** (1), a Benjaminite of the sons of Shashak, head of a family at Jerusalem, 1 Ch 8:23.

3. **Abdon** (2), a Benjaminite, first son of Jeiel, who is also called *Abi-gibeon,* "father of Gibeon," 1 Ch 8:30//9:36.

4. **Abdon son of Micah** (1). See: ACHBOR 2.

5. **Abdon** (3), a town in Asher, Jos 19:28 (var. of Hb. *Ebron*), east of

Achzib, assigned to the Levites of the clan of Gershon, Jos 21:30//1 Ch 6:59.

ABEDNEGO (15), a distortion of the Aram. *Abed-Nabu,* "Servant of Nabu," a name given to: AZARIAH 21.

ABEL, Hb. 1: *Hebel,* "Vapor, Smoke, *whence* Vanity," Accad. *aplu,* "Son"; 2–3: *'Abel,* "Brook *or* Meadow" (cf. composite names with Abel-).

1. **Abel** (12), son of Adam and Eve, a shepherd whose offering is pleasing to God, unlike that of his older brother Cain. The latter kills his brother out of jealousy, Gn 4:2–16, 25; Ws 10:3; Mt 23:35 p; Heb 11:4; 1 Jn 3:12. Acc. to Heb 12:24 the blood of Jesus "pleads more insistently" than that of Abel.

2. **Abel** (1). See: ABEL-BETH-MAACAH.

ABEL-BETH-MAACAH (4), "Meadow of the House of Maacah" (cf. Maacah), a fortified town near Dan, in the extreme north of Palestine, where Joab, commander of David's army, puts an end to the revolt of Sheba, son of Bichri, 2 S 20:14–22. It is captured at the same time as Ijon by Ben-hadad, king of Aram, 1 K 15:20, and later on by Tiglath-pileser, king of Assyria, 2 K 15:29.

= **Abel** (1), 2 S 20:18.

= **Abel-maim** (1), 2 Ch 16:4.

= ? **Beth-maacah** (1), 2 S 23:34 (corr. of Hb. *son of a Maacathite*) native place of: ELIPHELET 2. Today *Tell Abil el-Qamh.*

ABEL-HASH-SHITTIM (1), "Meadow of the acacias." See: SHITTIM 1.

ABEL-KERAMIN (1), "Meadow of the vines" (cf. Beth-hac-cherem), east of the Jordan. Jephthah pursues the Ammonites there, Jg 11:33.

ABEL-MAIM (1), "Meadow of the waters" (cf. Waters), Gr. *Abelmain.* See: ABEL-BETH-MAACAH.

ABEL-MEHOLAH (3), "Meadow of the dance," a town in the Jordan valley to which the Midianites flee when pursued by Gideon, Jg 7:22. In Solomon's fifth district, 1 K 4:12.

= **Meholah** (2), 1 S 18:19; 2 S 21:8. Native place of: ADRIEL; ELISHA.

ABEL-MIZRAIM (1), "Meadow of Egypt" or "Mourning of Egypt" (play on the words *'abel/'ebel,* "meadow/mourning"), identified with Goren-ha-atad across the Jordan, where the sons of Jacob made their lament for him, Gn 50:11–12. Site unknown.

ABIALBON (1), one of David's champions, 2 S 23:31.

= **Abiel from Beth-ha-arabah,** 1 Ch 11:32.

ABIASAPH (1), "My Father adds" (cf. Asaph), a Levite of the clan of Kohath, one of the three sons and clans of Korah, Ex 6:24.

= **Ebiasaph** (1), an ancestor of Samuel, 1 Ch 6:8, 22, of Heman the cantor, 1 Ch 6:22, and of: SHALLUM 6.

ABIATHAR (30), "The Father has in superabundance" (cf. Jether), **son of Ahimelech** (4), **son of Ahitub** (1), 1 S 22:20; 23:6; 30:7; 2 S 8:17, a descendant of Eli the priest, sole survivor of the massacre of the priests of Nob, joins David in his wanderings, 1 S 22:20–23, and carries the ephod containing the lots for consulting Yahweh, 23:6–9; 30:7.

Abiathar and Zadok, priests together under David, 2 S 8:17; 20:25; cf. 1 K 4:4; 1 Ch 15:11. When David flees from his son Absalom, they accompany him with the Ark of the Covenant into the valley of the Kidron; at the king's command they return to Jerusalem, 2 S 15:24–29, for the purpose of keeping him informed, through their two sons, of the developing situation, 2 S 15:35–36; 17:15–16. At the death of Absalom they urge the elders of Judah to be the first to call David back to his throne, 19:12–15. In the dispute over David's successor Abiathar sides with Adonijah whereas Zadok sides with Solomon, 1 K 1:7–45; cf. 2:22. After David's death Solomon sends Abiathar into exile at Anathoth, thus depriving him of the priesthood, to the benefit of Zadok, 1 K 2:26–27, 35; cf. 1 S 2:31–35.

Acc. to 1 Ch 27:34 Abiathar succeeded Ahitophel as David's counselor.

Related to Aaron, cf. 1 Ch 24:3. See List, p. 000.

= **Abiathar** (1), Mk 2:26 who refers to 1 S 21:2–7, where the reference is in fact to Ahimelech, father of Abiathar.

Father of: AHIMELECH 2; JONATHAN 3.

ABIDA (2), Hb. *'Abida',* "The Father knows" (cf. Jada), one of the five sons of Midian, called sons of Keturah, Abraham's concubine, Gn 25:4//1 Ch 1:33.

ABIDAN (5), "My Father is judge" (cf. Dan), **son of Gideoni** (5), in charge of the tribe of Benjamin, Nb 2:22; 7:60; 10:24, appointed to conduct the census of his tribe, Nb 1:11, brings the offering for the dedication of the altar on the ninth day, Nb 7:60–65.

ABIEL, "My Father is God."

1. **Abiel** (2), grandfather of King Saul and of Abner, 1 S 14:51. Father of: KISH 1.

2. **Abiel from Beth-ha-arabah** (1). See: ABIALBON.

ABI-ETAM (1), one of the sons of Hur, linked with Judah, 1 Ch 4:3. Some scholars interpret the name as meaning "the father of Etham." See: ETHAM 3.

ABIEZER, "My Father is help" (cf. Ezer).

1. **Abiezer** (4), second son (Machir, father of Gilead, being the eldest) and a clan of Manasseh, Jos 17:2, or son of Malchath the sister of Gilead, 1 Ch 7:18. Gideon is the most famous member of the clan of Abiezer.

= **Iezer** (1), eldest son of Gilead son of Machir, whose descendants form the **Iezerite** clan, Nb 26:30.

See: JOASH 1; OPHAR 1.

2. **Abiezer from Anathoth** (3), a Benjaminite, one of David's champions, 2 S 23:27//1 Ch 11:28, in charge of the (military) service for the ninth month, 1 Ch 27:12.

ABIGAIL, Hb. *'Abigayil* (or *'Abigal,* 1 S 25:32; 2 S 3:3; 17:25).

1. **Abigail** (14), **wife of Nabal of Carmel** (5), by her unselfish initiative prevents the murderous vengeance of David upon her husband. After Nabal's death David takes her as his second wife, 1 S 25. She follows David into exile at the home of Achish in Gath, 1 S 27:3, is a prisoner of the Amalekites, 1 S 30:5, accompanies David to Hebron, where he is anointed king, 2 S 2:2. David's second son, Chileab, 2 S 3:3 (//1 Ch 3:1: *Daniel*), is born to Abigail at Hebron.

2. **Abigail** (3), daughter of Jesse (acc. to Gr.; "daughter of Nahash" acc. to Hb.), sister of David, wife of Ithra or Jether the Ishmaelite, 2 S 17:25; 1 Ch 2:16–17. Mother of: AMASA 1.

ABI-GIBEON (2). See: JEIEL 2.

ABIHAIL, "My Father is mighty" (cf. Ben-hail).

1. **Abihail** (1), father of: ZURIEL.

2. **Abihail** (1), ancestor of the Gadites, who were sorted into various groups in the time of Jotham king of Judah, 1 Ch 5:14–17.

3. **Abihail** (2), Gr. *Aminadab,* Est 2:15; 9:29, father of: ESTHER.

4. **Abihail** (1), wife of Abishur, of the clan of Jerahmeel, 1 Ch 2:29.

5. **Abihail** (1), mother of: MAHALATH 2.

ABIHU, Gr. *Abioud,* "My Father is he."

1. **Abihu** (12), son of Aaron, whose history is linked to that of his older brother: NADAB 1.

2. **Abiud** (2), son of Zerubbabel and ancestor of Jesus, acc. to Mt 1:13.

ABIJAH, Gr. *Abia,* "My Father of Yah" (cf. Eliab; Joab).

1. **Abijah** (2), younger son of Sam-

uel, a venal judge at Beersheba like his elder brother Joel, 1 S 8:2–5; cf. 6:13.

2. **Abijah** (17) or **Abijam** (5), second king of Judah (913–911), son of Rehoboam, 1 Ch 3:10, and of Maacah daughter of Absalom, 1 K 15:1, 2; 2 Ch 11:20, 22, or of Micaiah daughter of Uriel, 2 Ch 13:2. Prepared for his future role by his father, 2 Ch 11:22, he succeeds him and rules three years at Jerusalem, 1 K 14:31–15:8//2 Ch 12:16–13:23. A war between him and Jeroboam I, king of Israel, mentioned in 1 K 15:7, is presented in 2 Ch 13:2–18, as a holy war that is preceded by a speech of justification by Abijah to Jeroboam and ends with the overwhelming victory of Judah. Abijah is an ancestor of Jesus, Mt 1:7.

His son and successor: ASA 1.

3. **Abijah** (1), son of Jeroboam, first king of Israel, dead at an early age, 1 K 14:1–18; "it is in him alone of the House of Jeroboam that anything pleasing to Yahweh, the God of Israel, is found," 14:13.

4. **Abijah daughter of Zechariah** (2), mother of King Hezekiah, 2 K 18:2 (Hb. *Abi*); 2 Ch 29:1.

5. **Abijah** (1), a Benjaminite, one of the nine sons of Becher, a fighting man and head of a family, 1 Ch 7:8–9.

6. **Abijah** (2), head of the eighth priestly class, 1 Ch 24:10, the one to which Zechariah, father of John the Baptist, belongs, Lk 1:5.

7. **Abijah** (3), a priest who returns from the exile with Zerubbabel, Ne 12:4, a cosigner of the pledge to observe the Law, Ne 8:10, gives his name to a priestly family, Ne 12:17.

ABIJAM (5), 1 K 14:31–15:8. See: ABIJAH 2.

ABILENE (1), a territory with its capital at *Abila* in the Anti-Lebanon, NW of Damascus. Tetrarchy of Lysanias, Lk 3:1.

ABIMELECH, "My Father is king" (cf. Melech).

1. **Abimelech** (24), **king of Gerar** (1), takes Sarah for himself after Abraham introduces her as his sister. Warned in time, Abimelech returns Sarah and escapes divine punishment, Gn 20. This Elohist narrative—a doublet of Gn 12:10–20 (Yahwist tradition) in which Pharaoh replaces Abimelech—has a parallel in Gn 26:1–11, a Yahwist narrative involving Abimelech, king of the Philistines (2), Isaac, and the latter's wife Rebekah. The covenant concluded at Beersheba between Abraham and Abimelech, Gn 21:22–32, likewise has its counterpart in Gn 26:15–33, where Isaac replaces Abraham.

2. **Abimelech** (41), **son of Jerubbaal** (40), that is, of Gideon, Jg 8:31. After murdering his seventy brothers, Abimelech has himself proclaimed king at Shechem. In a well-known fable Jotham, youngest son of Jerubbaal and sole survivor, compares Abimelech to a thorn bush that the trees call upon to be their king. Three years later, the Shechemites rebel against Abimelech but are put down. But during the siege of the town of Thebez Abimelech dies, his skull shattered by a millstone, which a woman throws down on him from the rampart, Jg 9; cf. 2 S 11:21 (Hb. *Abimelech son of Jerubbesheth*) and 22 (acc. to Gr.).

3. **Abimelech** (1), Ps 34:1. See: ACHISH.

4. **Abimelech** (1), 1 Ch 18:16, corr. to: AHIMELECH 2.

ABINADAB, "My Father is generous" (cf. Nadab).

1. **Abinadab** (4), third son of King Saul, 1 Ch 8:33//9:39, killed in the battle of Gilboa, 1 S 31:2//1 Ch 10:2.

2. **Abinadab** (3), second son of Jesse and brother of David, 1 Ch 2:13; 1 S 16:8, one of the "three eldest sons of Jesse [who] followed Saul to the war," 1 S 17:13–30.

3. **Abinadab** (5), a resident of Kiriath-jearim, whose house is built on a hill.

It is in his house that the Ark of the Covenant of Yahweh is placed on its arrival from Beth-shemesh, 1 S 7:1–2, and it is from his house that the Ark is transferred, much later, to Jerusalem, 2 S 6:3–8//1 Ch 13:7. Father of: AHIO 1; ELEAZAR 2; UZZAH 1.

4. **Son of Abinadab** (1), married to Taphath, Solomon's daughter, and administrator of Solomon's fourth district, 1 K 4:11.

ABINOAM (4), "My Father is gracious" (cf. Naomi), Jg 4:6, 12; 5:1, 12, father of: BARAK.

ABIRAM, Gr. *Abiron,* "My Father is on high" (cf. Ramah).

1. **Abiram** (11), son of Eliab the Reubenite. His story is closely connected with that of his brother: DATHAN.

2. **Abiram** (1), eldest son of Hiel of Bethel, dies (the victim of a foundation sacrifice?) during the rebuilding of Jericho, 1 K 16:34.

ABISHAG of Shunem (5), a beautiful young woman who looks after the elderly King David, 1 K 1:3–4, 15. After the death of David, Adonijah seeks her in marriage, but this claim to royalty seals his doom, 1 K 2:17–22.

ABISHAI (25), Hb. *'Abishai* or *'Abshai,* "Father of Ishai" or "My Father is an offering," see Is 18:7 (cf. Jesse), **son of Zeruiah** (9), **brother of Joab** (4) and of Asahel, a nephew of David, 1 Ch 2:13–16, leader of the Thirty, an elite corps, and one of the champions most devoted to David: to protect David he is ready to pin Saul to the ground, 1 S 26:6–9, to cut off Shimei's head, 2 S 16:5–11, to prevent the king from pardoning Shimei, 2 S 19:22–23, and he kills the Philistine champion, 2 S 21:16–17. According to 2 S 3:30, 39, Abishai joins Joab in the assassination of Abner, thus avenging the murder of their brother Asahel, 2 S 2:17–24. Abishai and Joab rout the Ammonites, 2 S 10:9–14, pursue Absalom, 2 S 18:2–14, and Sheba the rebellious Benjaminite, 2 S 20:6–10. Abishai conquers 18,000 Edomites in the Valley of Salt, 1 Ch 18:12, although 2 S 8:13 attributes this exploit to David, and Ps 60:2 to Joab. David complains on several occasions of the violence of these two sons of Zeruiah, 2 S 3:39; 19:23; cf. 1 S 26:9; 2 S 16:10; 19:23.

ABISHUA, "My Father is noble, magnanimous" (cf. Shua 1).

1. **Abishua** (4), son of Phinehas, descendant of Aaron and ancestor of Zadok the priest, 1 Ch 5:30, 31; 6:35; Ezr 7:5.

2. **Abishua** (1), son of Bela, who was Benjamin's first-born son, 1 Ch 8:4.

ABISHUR (2), son of Shammai, husband of Abihail, father of Ahban and Molid, of the clan of Jerahmeel, 1 Ch 2:28–29.

ABITAL (2), "My Father is dew" (cf. Hamital), one of David's wives, mother of: SHEPHATIAH 1.

ABITUB (1), "My Father is good" (cf. Tob), a Benjaminite, son of Gera (or of Shaharaim) and of Hushim, and brother of Elpaal, 1 Ch 8:11.

ABIUD. See: ABIHU 2.

ABNER (63), "The Father is the lamp," see Ps 18:28 (cf. Ner), **son of Ner** (12), a Benjaminite, cousin of Saul and leader of his army, 1 S 14:50–51; cf. 17:55–57; 20:25. When David is pursued by Saul's army, he derides Abner for the way the latter protects the king, 1 S 26:5–16. At the death of Saul, Abner makes Ishbaal, son of Saul, the king of Israel, 2 S 2:8–10. With Ishbaal's followers Abner attacks Joab and David's followers. In the battle of Gibeon Abner kills Asahel, Joab's brother, who has come in pursuit of him, 2 S 2:12–32. When Abner takes one of Saul's concubines for himself, he quarrels with Ishbaal, 2 S 3:6–8, and goes over to David's side, 2 S 3:9–21.

On leaving Hebron, where David has held a feast for him, Abner meets Joab, who treacherously slays him in revenge for the death of Asahel, 2 S 3:22–27; cf. 4:1. Abner is buried at Hebron, 2 S 4:12. Sorrow of David, who, on learning of the murder, declares himself innocent of it and makes a lament over Abner, 2 S 3:27–39. David will instruct Solomon to take revenge for Abner, 1 K 2:5, 32. 1 Ch 26:28 refers to offerings dedicated by Abner.

Father of: JAASIEL 2.

ABRAHAM (258), "The Father loves" (acc. to Accad.) or **Abram** (61), "The Father is on high" (cf. Ramah). *Abram* occurs in Gn 11:26–17:5; 1 Ch 1:27; Ne 9:7; *Abraham* in Gn 17:6–50:23 (133×); Ex to Dt (18×); Ch to Ne (9×); Ps (4×); Is to Mi (7×); deuterocanonical books (2×); NT (73×).

a. History of Abraham (ca. 1850 B.C.): Gn 11:26–25:11.

Born into a polytheistic Aramaean clan, Jos 24:2, 14–15, that had settled at Ur in Lower Mesopotamia and had for ancestor Terah, a descendant of Shem, Gn 11:10, 24–27, the son of Noah, Gn 5:32, Abram with his wife Sarai and his nephew Lot goes to Haran, 11:31. It is there that God calls him to go to an unknown land, Heb 11:8, and promises him countless descendants, Gn 12:1–3. At the age of 75, Abram leaves Haran for the land of Canaan, Gn 12:4–5, and settles at Hebron, 13:18.

Gn 14 tells the story of the campaign of the four kings from the east, the meeting of Abram with Melchizedek and with the king of Sodom, cf. Heb 7:1–10.

At the age of 86, Abram has a son, Ishmael, born to him of Hagar, Sarai's Egyptian servant, Gn 16. But this boy is not the "child of the promise," 17:19; cf. Ga 4:28; Rm 9:7–9. God makes a covenant with Abram, changes the latter's name to Abraham, "father of a multitude of nations," Gn 17:4–6, renews the promise of a posterity to which a land will be given as a permanent possession and imposes on Abraham and his descendants after him the sign of circumcision, 17:6 ff. Isaac, heir to the promises, Heb 11:9, is born to a man 100 years old and a wife of 90, 17:17; 18:11; Rm 4:19; Heb 11:11–12, in keeping with the renewal of the promise to Abraham and Sarah during the apparition at Mamre, Gn 18:9–15. The birth of Isaac leads to the dismissal of Hagar and Ishmael, so that the son of the serving woman may not inherit with the son of the promise, Gn 21:8–14. But God now requires Abraham to sacrifice his son, Gn 22. After having tested Abraham's faith, 1 M 2:52; Ws 10:5; Heb 11:17, God confirms his promise of a posterity. The same promise will be renewed to Isaac "in return for Abraham's obedience," Gn 26:3–5; cf. Si 44:22–23. At the death of Sarah, Abraham buys the property at Machpelah, near Hebron, Gn 23. Before dying, he sends one of his servants back to Mesopotamia to look for a wife for his son Isaac, Gn 24. The story of Abraham ends in Gn 25 with the linking to Abraham, via his concubine Keturah, of the peoples of Arabia, 25:1–4, and with the mention of the death of Abraham at the age of 175 and his burial at Machpelah, 25:7–11.

b. Person of Abraham

Friend of God, 2 Ch 20:7; Is 41:8; Dn 3:35; Jm 2:23; cf. Gn 17:1–2; 18:17; 19:29. Cf. *el-Khalil* ("The Friend"), the Arabic name for Hebron.

Servant of God, Ex 32:13; Dt 9:27; 2 M 1:2; Ps 105:6, 42.

A believer, acknowledged as just because of his faith, Gn 15:6; 26:5; 1 M 2:52; Si 44:20; Rm 4:3–9, 12–16; Ga 3:6–9; Heb 11:8–17; Jm 2:21–23.

Generous host, Gn 18:1–8; cf. Heb 13:2.

Intercessor in the well-known prayer in behalf of Sodom, Gn 18:22–23.

c. Abraham, Isaac, Jacob

The call of Abraham to faith is so important in the history of the revelation of God that God presents himself or is presented as the God of Abraham (8), Gn 24:27, 42, 48; 26:24; 31:53; Est 4:17[f,y]; Ps 47:10, the God of Abraham and Isaac (3), Gn 28:13; 31:42; 32:10, the God of Abraham, Isaac, and Jacob or Israel (12), Ex 3:6, 15–16; 4:5; 1 K 18:36; 1 Ch 29:18; 2 Ch 30:6; Mt 22:32 p; Ac 3:13; 7:32.

The explicit reference to the first three ancestors of the chosen people, namely, Abraham, Isaac, and Jacob (= Israel), occurs about thirty times in the Bible: it is to them that Yahweh promised and gave the land, Gn 35:12; 50:24; Ex 6:8; 33:1; Nb 32:11; Dt 1:8; 6:10; 9:5; 30:20; 34:4; Ba 2:34; it is with them that he entered into a covenant and to them that he gave his oath, Ex 2:24; Lv 26:42; Dt 29:12; 2 K 13:23; 1 Ch 16:16–17//Ps 105:6–10; 2 M 1:2; Si 44:22–23. It is to them, his servants, Ex 32:13; Dt 9:27, that he appeared, Ex 6:3, these men who were "our ancestors from the beginning," Tb 4:12; cf. Ex 3:6, 15–16; 4:5; Dt 1:8; 6:10; 9:5; 29:12; 30:20; 1 Ch 29:18; Ac 3:13, and who have the place of honor at the feast in the kingdom, Mt 8:11; Lk 13:28; cf. 16:22–23. The three names are also found together in Jdt 8:26; Jr 33:26; Dn 3:35, and, as ancestors of Jesus, in Mt 1:2; Lk 3:34.

d. Posterity of Abraham

The ties between the people to whom the land (the land of Abraham, Tb 14:7) is given, and "the rock you were hewn from," Is 51:1, is expressed in two types of formula:

Abraham our (or *your*) *father,* Jos 24:3; Si 44:19; Is 51:2; cf. 63:16; Lk 3:8; 16:24, 30; Jn 8:39, 53, 56; Ac 7:2; Rm 4:12, 16; Jm 2:21, our ancestor, Rm 4:1.

The descendants of Abraham, 2 Ch 20:7; 1 M 12:21; Is 41:8; Ac 13:26; Rm 11:1, the descendants or posterity of Abraham, Jr 33:26; Lk 1:55; Jn 8:33, 37; Rm 9:7; 2 Co 11:22; Ga 3:16, 29; Heb 2:16, the sons or children of Abraham, Mt 3:9 p; Lk 13:16; 19:9; Jn 8:39; cf. Gn 12:2, 7; 13:16; 15:13, and so on; Si 44:19; Is 63:16; Ez 33:24.

Authentic membership in the new Israel, the true people of Abraham, does not require blood descent; those who appeal to the faith of Abraham and "do as Abraham did," Jn 8:39, are the children of Abraham, Ga 3:7; the posterity that belongs to the faith of Abraham, who is the father of all of us, Rm 4:16, even pagans, Ga 3:14. Jesus himself, Mt 1:1; Lk 3:23, 34; Ga 3:16, and those who belong to him, Ga 3:29, are among the descendants of Abraham, but Jesus, the son of Abraham, Mt 1:1, the son of God, Mk 1:1, is greater than Abraham, Jn 8:53, and can say to the Jews: "Before Abraham ever was, I Am," Jn 8:58.

His wife: SARAH 1.

His concubines: HAGAR, KETURAH.

His sons: ISAAC; ISHMAEL 1; MIDIAN. . . .

ABRAM. See: ABRAHAM.

ABRON (2), Gr. *Abrōna,* an unknown river, Jdt 2:24.

ABRONAH (2), Hb. *'Abronah,* Gr. *Ebrōna,* a stage of the Exodus, before Ezion-geber, Nb 33:34–35.

ABSALOM, "My Father is peace" (cf. Salem).

1. **Absalom** (107), third son of David, born of Maacah at Hebron, 2 S 3:3//1 Ch 3:2, famous for his beauty and his hair, 2 S 14:25–26. He has three sons and a daughter, Tamar, 2 S 14:27.

To avenge the honor of his sister

Tamar, Absalom has his half-brother Amnon murdered, then flees to Talmai king of Geshur, 2 S 13. With the help of a quick-witted woman of Tekoa, Joab gets David to allow the return of Absalom, who wins the king's forgiveness, 2 S 14. Exploiting the latent enmity between the northern tribes and Judah, Absalom wins the hearts of the people of Israel, 15:1–6, then goes to Hebron, where with Ahithophel he foments a rebellion against David, 15:7–12. The latter, forced to flee, 15:13–29; cf. 1 K 2:7; Ps 3:1, wins the aid of Hushai and defeats the plans of Absalom, 2 K 15: 30–37; cf. 16:15–19. On the advice of Ahitophel, Absalom takes David's concubine, 2 S 16:20–23; then he consults Ahitophel and Hushai, in that order, and, to his undoing, accepts the advice of Hushai, 2 S 17. Absalom's army is defeated by David's troops, and Absalom himself, his hair caught in an oak, is killed by Joab, 2 S 18:5–17; cf. 19:11, and buried under the **Pillar of Absalom,** 18:18. Sorrow of David at the news of Absalom's death, 19:1–9.

2. **Absalom** (4), father of: MAACAH 9. Same as the preceding?

3. **Absalom** (3), one of the Jewish envoys to Lysias, 2 M 11:16–17. Father of: JONATHAN 17; MATTITHIAH 7.

ABUBUS (2), probably a name of Arabic origin, father of: PTOLEMY 11.

ACACIAS (Wadi of). See: SHITTIM 2.

ACCAD (1), Sumer. *Agade,* a city of Babylonia, Gn 10:10, whose name is used for the northern section of Lower Mesopotamia as distinguished from the land of Sumer, which is further south.

ACCO (2), a coastal town N of Mt. Carmel. The Canaanite town is assigned to Asher, Jos 19:30 (corr. of Hb. *'Ummah*), although the Israelites are unable to take it, Jg 1:31.

= **Ptolemais** (19), the name given to Acco in the Hellenistic period (after Ptolemy II Philadelphus, who enlarged the city). Jonathan meets Alexander Balas there on the occasion of the latter's marriage to Cleopatra, daughter of Ptolemy VI, 1 M 10:1, 56–60; later he meets Demetrius II there during the siege of the Citadel of Jerusalem, 11:20–24, and finally is taken prisoner there by Trypho, 12:39–50; 13:12. Ptolemais is also mentioned in the Maccabaean wars, in 1 M 5:15, 22, 55; 2 M 13:24–25.

On his return from his third missionary journey, Paul spends a day with the Christians of the city, Ac 21:7. During the Crusades the city was renamed *Saint-Jean-d'Acre.* Today *Akko.*

See: OCINA.

ACCOS (1), 1 M 8:17. See: KOZ 2.

[ACHAEMENIDS], "[Descendants] of Achaemenes," a Persian dynasty, some kings of which are named in the Bible: CYRUS; DARIUS; XERXES; ARTAXERXES 1.

ACHAIA (10), (cf. Achaicus), a Roman province that includes the Peloponnesus and Greece (except for Macedonia and Epirus). Paul stays there during his second missionary journey, 1 Th 1:7–8; cf. Ac 17:15–18:18; Apollos goes there later on, Ac 18:27–19:1. Before ending his third journey, Paul plans to pass through Achaia, Ac 19:21; he stays there for three months, Ac 20:2 (where *Greece* is equivalent to *Achaia*). A little earlier, he had written a new letter "to the church of God at Corinth and to all the saints in the whole of Achaia," 2 Co 1:1. Among the latter, "the Stephanas family . . . were the first-fruits of Achaia," 1 Co 16:15. Like the Christians of Macedonia, and even earlier than they, the Christians of Achaia take an active role in Paul's collection for the impoverished church of Jerusalem, Rm 15:26–27; 2 Co 9:2 (ch. 9 is probably a short letter on this subject addressed to the churches of Achaia), cf. 1 Co 16:1 ff. On the other hand, Paul boasts of never having accepted anything for himself from the Christians of Achaia, 2 Co 11:10.

Proconsul: GALLIO.

Capital of the province: CORINTH.

Cities: ATHENS; CENCHREAE.

ACHAICUS (1), "Man from Achaia," a Christian of Corinth who went to Ephesus with Stephanas and Fortunatus, probably to deliver to Paul the letter from the Christians of Corinth, 1 Co 16:17; cf. 7:1.

ACHAN (6), Hb. *'Akân* (cf. Jacan), **son of Carmi, son** (or of the family) **of Zabdi** (2), **son** (or of the clan) **of Zerah** (4), **of the tribe of Judah** (4). At the capture of Jericho he violates the law of the ban, Jos 7:1. Result: repulse of Joshua at Ai. Joshua discovers the culprit, who admits his guilt and is stoned to death with his entire family in the Vale of Achor, Jos 7:16–25; cf. 22:20.

= **Achar** (1), son of Carmi, 1 Ch 2:7.

ACHAR (1), "Bringer of ill-fortune" (cf. Achor; Ochran). See: ACHAN.

ACHBOR, "The mouse."

1. **Achbor** (3), father of the king of Edom: BAAL-HANAN 1.

2. **Achbor** (2), **son of Micaiah** (1), a member of the delegation led by the high priest Hilkiah and sent by King Josiah to consult Huldah the prophetess after the discovery of the Book of the Law, 2 K 22:12–30.

= **Abdon son of Micah** (1), 2 Ch 34: 20–28.

3. **Achbor** (2), same as the preceding? Father of: ELNATHAN 1.

ACHIM (2), an ancestor of Jesus acc. to Mt 1:14.

ACHIOR (13), Hb. *'Ahi'or,* "My Brother is a light" (cf. Ur 2). In the mouth of Achior, leader of the Ammonite troops—a personage seemingly inspired by the figure of Ahikar, a wise and good pagan, Tb 1:21—the author of Jdt places a recall of the history of Israel for the information of Holofernes, the Assyrian general, Jdt 5:5–21; cf. 11:9. When handed over to the Israelites, Achior tells them of Holofernes' threats, 5:22–6:20. After Judith's feat and Israel's victory, Achior converts to Judaism, 14:5–10.

ACHISH (21), **son of Maoch** (1) or **of Maacah** (1), **king of Gath** (4). It is with him that David takes refuge in order to escape Saul's hatred, after stopping at the sanctuary of Nob; but the words of Achish's servants put David on guard and he skillfully plays the madman, 1 S 21:11–16; cf. Ps 34:1, where Achish is called Abimelech. The theme of David's stay among the Philistines is developed more fully by another tradition in 1 S 27–29; David goes with 600 men into Philistine territory, 27:1–4, where Achish gives him the town of Ziklag, which David uses as a base for raids into the desert, 27:5–17. Achish wishes to involve David in a battle against Saul, but David gives an ambiguous answer to the Philistine, 28:1–2, who, under pressure from his own generals, who are hostile to David, asks the latter to leave Philistine territory, 29:1–11. It is with Achish that two slaves of Shimei take refuge; Shimei pays with his life for going to Gath after them, 1 K 2:39–42.

ACHOR (5), "Misfortune" (cf. Achar), a valley not far from Jericho, on the frontier between Judah and Benjamin, Jos 15:7; where Achan, who after the capture of Jericho had violated the ban, is stoned with his entire family, Jos 7:24–26. However, this "Vale of Misfortune" will in the future become a "gateway of hope," Hos 2:17; cf. Is 65:10.

ACHSAH (5), "Foot bangle" (cf. Is 3:16), daughter of Caleb, 1 Ch 2:49, given as wife to Othniel, son of Kenaz, after the latter has captured the town of Kiriath-sepher (= Hebron). Settled in an oasis of the Negeb, Jos 15:16–19//Jg 1:12–15.

ACHSHAPH (3), a Canaanite town, Jos 11:1, whose king is conquered by the

Israelites, Jos 12:20, and which is given to the tribe of Asher, Jos 19:25.

ACHZIB (cf. Cozbi).

1. **Achzib** (1), a town in the lowlands of Judah, Jos 15:44.

= **Beth-achzib** (1), Mi 1:14 (corr. of Hb. *the house of Achzib*).

= **Chezib** (1), Gn 38:5, a town of the Canaanite, Shua, whose daughter marries Judah.

= ? **Cozeba** (1), 1 Ch 4:22, connected with Judah through Shelah.

2. **Achzib** (2), a Canaanite town N of Acco, on the border of Asher, Jos 19:29, which this tribe is unable to occupy, Jg 1:31.

[ADAD]. See: ADRAMMELECH.

ADADAH (1), Jos 15:22. See: AROER 3.

ADAH, Hb. *'Adah,* "Ornament" (cf. Adaiah; Adiel; Adithaim; Eleadah; Iddo).

1. **Adah** (3), first wife of Lamech and mother of Jabal and Jubal, Gn 4:19–21, 23.

2. **Adah** (15), **daughter of Elon the Hittite** (1), wife of Esau, Gn 36:2, mother of Eliphaz, 36:4, 10, and called mother of the sons or chiefs of Eliphaz, 36:11–12, 15–16.

ADAIAH, Hb. *Adaya, Adayahu,* "Yahweh has adorned himself" (cf. Adah).

1. **Adaiah** (1), father of: JEDIDAH.

2. **Adaiah** (1), a Levite of the clan of Gershon, an ancestor of Asaph the cantor, 1 Ch 6:26.

3. **Adaiah** (1), a Benjaminite of the sons of Shimei, head of a family at Jerusalem, 1 Ch 8:21.

4. **Adaiah** (1), father of: MAASEIAH 2.

5. **Adaiah** (1), an ancestor of: MAASEIAH 15.

6. **Adaiah son of Jeroham—son of Pelaliah, son of Amzi, son of Zechariah** (1)—**son of Pashhur, son of Malchijah** (2), a priest living in Jerusalem after the return from exile, 1 Ch 9:12//Ne 11:12.

7. **Adaiah** (1). See: JEDAIAH 4.

8. **Adaiah** (1), an Israelite of the sons of Binnui, married to a foreign wife, whom he puts away, Ezr 10:39.

ADALIA (1), brother of: PARSHANDATHA.

ADAM, "Of red earth" (cf. Adamah).

1. **Adam** (19). The Hb. word *'adam* (540) is connected with *'adamah,* "soil, tillable red earth." It is habitually translated as *man* or *human beings,* but in 19 instances translation by a proper name is required. Except in Lk 3:38 the expression "son of Adam"—Hb. *ben 'adam* (108, of which 93 in Ezk) or, plural, *bene (ha) 'Adam* (47)—which is found especially in poetical texts, Nb 23:19; Ps 8:5; 80:18 . . . ; Si 40:1, can also be translated by *a man, a human being, men, human beings.*

From men to Adam. But the expression *sons of Adam* as meaning "human beings" emphasizes their relation to "the father of the world, the first being to be fashioned, created alone," Ws 10:1; cf. Jb 15:7; 20:4; cf. Dt 4:32, and their state of weakness: made from nothing, 2 M 7:28, human beings are taken from the earth, Gn 2:7; Ws 7:1; Si 33:10, which they are to till and take care of, Gn 2:15; cf. 3:17–19, and to which they will eventually return, Si 17:1; cf. 17:32, after having given back to God, Qo 12:7, the breath God has placed in them, Gn 2:7; Nb 16:22; Zc 12:2; Ml 2:15; Heb 12:9. However, this human being whom the creator of the world formed, 2 M 7:23; cf. Is 45:12, has been made by God in his own image, Gn 1:26–27; 5:2; 9:6; Ws 2:23, destined for incorruptibility, Ws 2:23; cf. 2 P 1:4, and given a share in God's power over the world, Gn 2:19; Ws 9:2; 10:2. Adam, son of God, Lk 3:38, is thus the single source from which God produces the human race, Ml 2:15; Ac 17:26, and the lead individual, as it were, of the human collectivity, Gn 5; 1 Ch 1:1; Ws 10:1; Si 49:16; Jude 14.

Adam dies at the age of 940, after having begotten Cain, Abel who is replaced by Seth, Gn 4:1–2, 25, and then sons and daughters, Gn 5:3–5.

Adam and the "helpmate" whom God gives him, Gn 2:18; Tb 8:6, and whom he calls "Eve" because she is the mother of all those who live, Gn 3:20, are presented as the first couple created by God, 1 Tm 2:13, "these two [from whom] the human race was born," Tb 8:6.

The new Adam. Adam, the first man, taken from the earth, 1 Co 15:45–47, the first sinner, whose sin brings death to all his descendants, Rm 5:12, is the figure of the one who was to come, Rm 5:14, that is, Christ, the second Adam, the last Adam, coming not from the earth but from heaven, 1 Co 15:47, the type of the new man who is created in God's way, in the goodness and holiness of the truth, cf. Ep 4:24, the source of grace, Rm 5:17–19, and a life-giving spirit, 1 Co 15:45.

2. **Adam** (2), a town on the Jordan at the mouth of the Jabbok, Jos 3:16, where Israel "violated the covenant," Ho 6:7 (corr. of Hb. *like Adam* or *like man*).

ADAMAH (1), "Red earth" (cf. Adam; Adummim; Edom), a town in Naphtali, Jos 19:36.

ADAMI-NEGEB (1), a town between the Sea of Chinnereth and Mount Tabor, Jos 19:33.

ADASA (2). See: HADASHAH.

ADBEEL (2), one of the twelve sons and clan chiefs of Ishmael, Gn 25:13//1 Ch 1:29.

ADDAN (1) or **Addon** (1), an otherwise unknown town in Babylonia to which Israelites were exiled, Ezr 2:59//Ne 7:61.

ADDAR

1. **Addar** (1). See: ARD.
2. **Addar** (1). See: HAZAR-ADDAR.

ADDI (1), an ancestor of Jesus acc. to Lk 3:28.

ADDON (1). See: ADDAN.

ADIDA (2) **in the Lowlands** (1). See: HADID.

ADIEL, "God has adorned himself" (cf. Adah).

1. **Adiel** (1), a Simeonite clan chief, 1 Ch 4:36–38.
2. **Adiel** (1), father of the priest Maasai. See: AMASAI 4.
3. **Adiel** (1), father of: AZMAVETH 4.

ADIN (4), "Voluptuous" (cf. Eden 2), an Israelite, a leader of the people whose sons return from the exile with Zerubbabel, Ezr 2:15//Ne 7:20, and with Ezra, Ezr 8:6. He signs the pledge to observe the Law, Ne 10:17.

ADINA (1), (cf. Eden 2), **son of Shiza the Reubenite** (1), one of David's champions, leader of the Reubenites and in charge of the Thirty, 1 Ch 11:42.

ADITHAIM (1), "The two ornaments" (cf. Adah). See: HADID.

ADLAI (1), father of: SHAPHAT 5.

ADMAH (5), Gr. *Adama,* a town in the Pentapolis, near Sodom and Gomorrah, Gn 10:19, and punished at the same time as these, Dt 29:22; Ho 11:8; cf. Ws 10:6.

King: SHINAB.

ADMATHA (1), name of a Persian official mentioned with: MEMUCAN.

ADMIN (1), a descendant of Perez and ancestor of David and Jesus, Lk 3:33; cf. Mt 1:4; Rt 4:19; 1 Ch 2:9–10.

ADNA, Hb. *'Adna'* (cf. Eden 2).

1. **Adna** (1), an Israelite of the sons of Pahath-moab, married to a foreign wife, whom he puts away, Ezr 10:30.
2. **Adna** (1), head of the priestly family of Harim in the time of the high priest Joiakim, Ne 12:15.

ADNAH, Hb. *'Adnah.*

1. **Adnah** (1), a Manassite leader who rallies to David before the latter becomes king, 1 Ch 12:21.

2. **Adnah** (1), an officer in the army of Judah under Jehoshaphat, 2 Ch 17:14.

ADONAI (± 450), Gr. *Kyrios.* See: YAHWEH *d.*

ADONIJAH, Hb. *'Adoniyyah, 'Adoniyyahu,* "Yah is my lord."

1. **Adonijah** (24), **son of Haggith** (5), fourth of the sons of David born at Hebron, 2 S 3:2–4//1 Ch 3:1–2, in David's old age make known his claim to the kingship and is supported by Joab, cf. 1 K 2:28, and Abiathar, 1 K 1:5–10. Nathan and Bathsheba intervene with David to make known Adonijah's plot, 1 K 1:11–27. David then has Solomon anointed king, vv. 28–40. At this news, vv. 41–48, Adonijah in terror clings to the horns of the altar, and Solomon pardons him, vv. 49–53. After David's death Adonijah seeks as wife Abishag of Shunem, who has cared for David in his illness, 1 K 1:1–4; because of this aspiration Solomon has him put to death, 1 K 2:13–25.

2. **Adonijah** (1), one of the eight Levites sent by King Jehoshaphat, along with two priests and five officers, to instruct the towns of Judah in the Law, 2 Ch 17:7–9.

3. **Adonijah** (1), a leader of the people and a cosigner of the pledge to observe the Law, Ne 10:17.

ADONIKAM (3), "My Lord is standing" (cf. Jakim), an Israelite and family head whose sons return from the exile with Zerubbabel, Ezr 2:13//Ne 7:18, and with Ezra, Ezr 8:13.

[ADONIS], "My lord." "Plants for Adonis" in Is 17:10 is lit. "plants of delight," but the allusion is doubtless to the "gardens of Adonis." See: TAMMUZ.

ADONI-ZEDEK (2), "My Lord is justice" (cf. Zadok), **king of Jerusalem** (5), forms a coalition with the neighboring Amorite kings **(Debir king of Eglon, Hoham king of Hebron, Piram king of Jarmuth, Japhia king of Lachish)** against Gibeon. Joshua intervenes and defeats the five kings, who take refuge in the cave of Makkedah. After being executed by hanging, their bodies thrown into the cave, Jos 10:1–26; cf. 12:10.

Acc. to Jg 1:5–7 Adoni-zedek (3×; corr. of Hb. *Adoni-bezek* to harmonize it with Jos 10:1–3) is defeated at Bezek by the sons of Judah who apply the law of the talion to him as he had applied it to his enemies; he dies at Jerusalem.

ADORA (1). See: ADORAIM.

ADORAIM (1), 8 km W of Hebron (today *Dura*), a fortified town restored by Rehoboam, 2 Ch 11:9.

= **Adora** (1), the road which Trypho takes in invading Judah, 1 M 13:20.

ADORAM (5), abbrev. of *Adoniram,* "My Lord is on high" (cf. Ramah), **son of Abda** (1), 1 K 4:6, in charge of forced labor under David, 2 S 20:24, then under Solomon, 1 K 4:6 and 5:28 (where Hb. has *Adoniram*). At the accession of Rehoboam he is stoned to death by the Israelites, to whom the young king has sent him as an envoy, 1 K 12:18//2 Ch 10:18 (Hb. *Hadoram*).

ADRAMMELECH, Accad. *Adadmilki,* "[The god] Adad is king" or "Adad is counsellor" (cf. Melech).

1. **Adrammelech** (1), an Assyrian god in whose honor the people of Sepharvaim sometimes burn their children, 2 K 17:31.

2. **Adrammelech** (2) and **Sharezer** (2), two of the sons of Sennacherib king of Assyria, who assassinate their father in the temple of Nisroch and then take refuge in the land of Ararat, 2 K 19:37//Is 37:38; cf. 2 Ch 32:21; Tb 1:21.

ADRAMYTTIUM (1), a port of Mysia, today *Edremit* in Turkey. At Caesarea, Paul embarks in a ship from Adramyttium, Ac 27:2.

ADRIATIC (1), in antiquity, the part of the Mediterranean located between Greece, Italy, and Africa. Paul is caught by a storm and shipwrecked on the Adriatic, Ac 27:27.

ADRIEL (2), parallel form of *Azriel* (cf. Eder), **son of Barzillai** (1), **of Meholah** (2), marries Merab, Saul's eldest daughter, who had been promised to David, 1 S 18:19; she gives him five sons, who will later be impaled by the Gibeonites, 2 S 21:8–9.

ADUEL (1), a Naphtalite, ancestor of Tobit and Tobias, Tb 1:1.

ADULLAM (12), Gr. *Odollam,* a Canaanite town whose king is defeated by Joshua, Jos 12:15, located in the lowlands of Judah, 15:35; cf. Mi 1:15, restored by Rehoboam, 2 Ch 11:7. Some people of Judah settle there on their return from the exile, Ne 11:30. Near the town is a *cave* in which David takes refuge during his flight from Saul, 1 S 22:1; 2 S 23:13//1 Ch 11:15. Judas Maccabaeus offers a sacrifice there for the dead, 2 M 12:38. About 25 km SW of Jerusalem. Native place of: HIRAH.

ADULLAMITE (3), Gn 38:1, 12, 20, of or from: ADULLAM.

ADUMMIM (Ascent of) (2), "The Red (pl.)" (cf. *Adamah*), on the border of Judah and Benjamin, Jos 15:7; 18:17. Halfway between Jerusalem and Jericho.

[AEGEAN], the part of the Mediterranean that is located between Greece, Crete, and Asia Minor. Many islands are located in it: CHIOS; COS; DELOS; LESBOS; PATMOS; RHODES; SAMOS; SAMOTHRACE.

AENEAS (1), a paralytic at Lydda, whom Peter cures, Ac 9:33–35.

AENON (1), "The springs" (cf. En-), near Salim. Location uncertain: some km S of Scythopolis? at Ain Farah? A place of abundant water, where John baptizes, Jn 3:23.

[AESHMA]. See: ASMODEUS.

AESORA (1), Gr. *Aisōra,* a town NW of Shechem, Jdt 4:4.

[AFRICA]. See: CYRENE; EGYPT; ETHIOPIA; LIBYA.

AGABUS (2), a Christian prophet of Jerusalem, comes to Antioch, where he predicts a famine, Ac 11:27–28. Later, at Caesarea, he predicts Paul's arrest, Ac 21:10–11.

AGAG, AGAGITE

1. **Agag** (8), **king of the Amalekites** (3), conquered (cf. Nb 24:7) and taken prisoner. Saul spares him in violation of the law of the ban, 1 S 15:8–9, 20. Samuel "butchered Agag before Yahweh at Gilgal," 1 S 15:32–33.

2. **Agagite** or **from the land of Agag** (6), that is, native of an unknown country or, more probably, a descendant of the preceding Agag. The term is applied to Haman, the persecutor of the Jews, Est 1:1r; 3:1, 10; 8:3, 5; 9:24. See: HAMAN 1.

AGAGITE. See: AGAG 2.

AGRIPPA, Gr. *Agrippos,* Lat. *Agrippa.*

1. **Herod [Agrippa I].** See: HEROD 3.
2. **[Herod] Agrippa II.** See: HEROD 4.

AGUR son of Jakeh (1), of the Arabian tribe of Massa, a wise man to whom Pr 30:1–14 is attributed.

AHAB, Hb. *'Ah'ab,* "Brother of the Father" (cf. Ab-; Ahi).

1. **Ahab** (91), **son of Omri** (3), seventh king of Israel (874–853), of the third dynasty. The Bible describes the reign of Ahab as that of a wicked king who was worse than his predecessors, 1 K 16:28–30, who was seduced into idolatry by his wife Jezebel, a Phoenician woman, 1 K 16:31–33; cf. 21:25–26; 2 K 10:18; 21:3, and whom the prophet Elijah regarded as the "scourge of Israel," 1 K 18:17–18. At the request of Elijah, Ahab gathers Israel for a sacrifice on Mount Carmel: massacre of the prophets of Baal, 18:19–40. Elijah tells Ahab that

the drought will end, 18:41–46. Two victorious campaigns of Ahab against the Aramaeans, 20. At the urging of his wife, Ahab has Naboth wrongly accused in order that he may steal the latter's vineyard, 21:1–16. Elijah pronounces God's condemnation, 21:17–24, against Ahab, who repents, so that Yahweh will postpone punishment until the time of Ahab's son Jehoram, 21:27–29. Campaign of Ahab and Jehoshaphat against the Aramaeans. Ahab dies in battle at Ramoth-gilead and is buried at Samaria, 22:1–38//2 Ch 18:2–34. The Bible preserves the memory of the building Ahab undertook, 1 K 22:39, but, above all, of the evil conduct of the house of Ahab, 2 K 8:18//2 Ch 21:6; 13; 2 K 8:27// 2 Ch 22:2–4; Mi 6:16, which Jehu will be commissioned to punish, 2 K 9:7–9; 10; 21:13; 2 Ch 22:7–8.

His sons: AHAZIAH 1 (his successor); JEHORAM.

His daughter: ATHALIAH 1.

2. **Ahab** (2), **son of Kolaiah** (1), a false prophet contemporary with Jeremiah; he is cursed and handed over, along with Zedekiah, to Nebuchadnezzar, who has them both burned alive, Jr 29:21–23.

AHARHEL son of Harum (1), of the clan of Ashhur, in Judah, 1 Ch 4:8.

AHASBAI (1), "My refuge is in Yahweh"? (cf. Mahseiah), father of the champion: ELIPHELET 2.

AHASHTARITES (1), a Judaean clan of the sons of Naarah, of Calebite origin, 1 Ch 4:6.

AHASUERUS. See: XERXES.

AHAVA (3), unidentified town and river or canal in Babylonia, Ezr 8:15, 21, 31.

AHAZ, Hb. *'Ahaz,* abbrev. of *'Ahazyah,* "[Yah] grasps [in order to guide]," see Ps 73:23 (cf. Ahaziah; Ahuzzam; Ahuzzath; Ahzai; Jehoahaz).

1. **Ahaz** (39), **son of Jotham** (2), **son of Uzziah** (1), second king of Judah (736–713). A contemporary of Pekah, 2 K 16:1, and Hoshea, 2 K 17:1, kings of Israel, and of the prophets Hosea, Ho 1:1, Isaiah, Is 1:1, and Micah, Mi 1:1. Instead of imitating the uprightness of his ancestor David, 2 K 16:2//2 Ch 28:1–2, he is unfaithful to Yahweh, 2 Ch 28:19, and imitates the conduct of the kings of Israel, 2 K 16:3, by heaping wrong on wrong, cf. Si 49:4. He is upbraided in particular for having sacrificed his son to Molech, 2 K 16:3, for having offered sacrifices on the high places, 2 K 16:4, and, cf. 2 K 23:12, for having replaced the altar in the Jerusalem temple with an altar fashioned after the model of the one in the temple at Damascus, 2 K 16:10–16, and having removed some of the furniture of the temple, 2 K 16: 17–18. When besieged by a coalition of Israelites and Syrians, 2 K 16:5; Is 7: 1–2, Ahaz buys the help of Tiglath-pileser, king of Assyria, 2 Ch 28:16, by handing over the treasures of the temple to him, 2 K 16:5–9, and this despite the intervention of Isaiah, who urges him to trust in God alone, Is 7:1–9, and to ask God for a sign. Ahaz refuses, but Isaiah nonetheless announces, Is 7:10–16, the birth of Immanuel, a sign of God's fidelity to the Davidic dynasty.

In 2 K 20:11//Is 38:8 the "steps of Ahaz" probably refer not to a sundial in the strict sense but to a monumental staircase Ahaz had built in order to reach his lofty chamber.

Ahaz is an ancestor of Jesus, Mt 1:9.

His son and successor: HEZEKIAH 2.

2. **Ahaz** (3), a Benjaminite, descendant of King Saul, son of Micah, and ancestor of the sons of Azel, 1 Ch 8:35–36// 9:42.

AHAZIAH, "Yah grasps [in order to guide]" (cf. Ahaz), Gr. *Ochozias.*

1. **Ahaziah** (7), **son of Ahab** (2) and his successor, eighth king of Israel (853–852), of the third dynasty, a contemporary of Jehoshaphat of Judah, 1 K 22: 40, 52. He attempts to band with the latter in order to build ships at Ezion-

geber, 1 K 22:50; 2 Ch 20:35–37. After a serious fall he consults the god Baalzebub at Ekron. The prophet Elijah condemns this action and predicts Ahaziah's death, which occurs a short time later. His brother Jehoram succeeds him, 2 K 1:2–18.

2. **Ahaziah** (35), **son of Jehoram** (4) and his successor, sixth king of Judah (841), 2 K 8:24–26; 1 Ch 3:11. He supports his relative, King Jehoram of Israel, in the latter's war against Hazael, king of Aram. It is during a visit to Jehoram, who is laid up at Jezreel by wounds received in war, that the conspiracy of Jehu breaks out. The two kings, Jehoram and Ahaziah, are assassinated along with many members of their families, 2 K 8:29; 9:16–23, 27, 29; 10:12–15; 2 Ch 22:1–9. Athaliah, mother of Ahaziah, 2 K 8:26; 11:1, succeeds her son, 2 K 11:3.

Brother of: JEHOSHEBA.
Father of: JOASH 5.
Grandfather of: AMAZIAH 1.

AHBAN (1), son of Abishur and Abihail, of the clan of Jerahmeel, 1 Ch 2:29.

AHER (1), 1 Ch 7:12, a descendant of Benjamin or perhaps of Dan (if v. 12 comes from a genealogy of Dan).

AHI, "My Brother" (cf. the composites with Ahi- that follow and Ahian; Ahio; Hiel), **son of Abdiel, son of Guni** (1), a Gadite, head of the family of the sons of Abihail, 1 Ch 5:15.

AHIAH (1), a leader of the people and cosigner of the pledge to observe the Law, Ne 10:27.

AHIAM (2), **son of Sharar, from** [Q]**Harar** ([K] **the Ararite)** (1), 2 S 23:33, or **son of Sachar, from Harar** (1), 1 Ch 11:35, one of David's champions.

AHIAN (1), "Little brother" (cf. Ahi), a Manassite, son of Shemida, 1 Ch 7:19.

AHIEZER, "My Brother is help" (cf. Ezer).

1. **Ahiezer son of Ammishaddai** (5), leader of the tribe of Dan, Nb 2:25; 7:66; 10:25, put in charge of the census of his tribe, Nb 1:12, brings the offering for the dedication of the altar on the tenth day, Nb 7:66–71.

2. **Ahiezer** (1), a Benjaminite leader, joins David's side before the latter becomes king, 1 Ch 12:3.

AHIHUD, "My Brother is majesty" (cf. Hod).

1. **Ahihud son of Shelomi** (1), leader, for the tribe of Asher, in the allocation of Canaan, Nb 34:27.

2. **Ahihud** (1), a Benjaminite, one of the sons of Ehud, 1 Ch 8:7.

AHIJAH, "Yah is my brother."

1. **Ahijah** (2), **son of Ahitub** (1), a priest, descendant of Eli, 1 S 14:3; he carries the divinatory ephod in a war of Saul against the Philistines, 1 S 14:18. He is probably to be distinguished from Ahimelech, 1 S 21:2–4, who is rather his brother.

2. **Ahijah** (1). See: ELIHOREPH.

3. **Ahijah** (12) **of Shiloh** (5), a prophet. By a symbolic action (cutting a cloak in twelve pieces), he tells Jeroboam son of Nebat of his future kingship over the ten tribes of the north, 1 K 11:29–39; cf. 12:15; 2 Ch 10:15. Later, when he is very old and blind, he receives a visit from the wife of Jeroboam: to her he predicts the proximate death of her sick young son and the future annihilation of the dynasty, 1 K 14:2–18; 15:29. The chronicler mentions among the sources he has consulted "the Prophecy of Ahijah of Shiloh," 2 Ch 9:29.

4. **Ahijah** (4), father of the king of Israel: BAASHA.

5. **Ahijah** (1), son of Jerahmeel, 1 Ch 2:25.

6. **Ahijah** (1), a Benjaminite, of the sons of Ehud, who are family heads of the people from Geba that migrated to Manahath, 1 Ch 8:7.

7. **Ahijah the Pelonite** (1), one of David's champions, 1 Ch 11:36.

AHIKAM (20), "My Brother is standing" (cf. Jakim), **son of Shaphan** (3), is a member of the delegation (made up of the high priest Hilkiah; Shaphan, the secretary of the king and father of Ahikam, and so on) sent by King Josiah to consult with Huldah the prophetess after the discovery of the Book of the Law, 2 K 22:12–20//2 Ch 34:20–28. In the reign of Jehoiakim he intervenes in behalf of Jeremiah, who is in danger of death after his discourse against the temple, Jr 26:24.

Father of: GEDALIAH 4.

AHIKAR (9), Gr. *Achi(a)charos,* "My Brother is precious," **son of Anael** (1). Minister of Sennacherib and Esarhaddon, kings of Assyria, and described as a relative—cousin or nephew—of Tobit, Tb 1:21–22, he intercedes to permit the return of Tobit to Nineveh after the latter has been delated as a secret burier of Jews, 1:22, and for two years he provides the upkeep of the blind Tobit, 2:10. When Tobit is cured, Ahikar shares his joy along with another cousin, Nadab, 11:18. Owing to the plotting of Nadab, whom he had adopted as his successor at the court, Ahikar is put to the torture, then rehabilitated because of his good works, 14:10 (the other Gr. text gives *Manasseh* for *Ahikar*). In Tb 14:15 perhaps read *Cyaxares* for Gr. *Ahikar*).

AHILUD

1. **Ahilud** (4), father of: JEHOSHAPHAT 3.

2. **Ahilud** (1), father of: BAANAH 3.

AHIMAAZ, "My Brother is angry" (cf. Maaz).

1. **Ahimaaz** (1), father of: AHINOAM 1.

2. **Ahimaaz** (13), **son of Zadok** (3), cf. 1 Ch 5:34; 6:28. This priest's son, together with Jonathan, son of the priest Abiathar, serves as liaison with David when the latter takes flight, 2 S 15:27, 36. Stationed at the Fuller's Spring, they are discovered by a spy of Absalom, and they hide at Bahurim, whence they go to warn David, 2 S 17:17–21. Ahimaaz comes on the scene again after the death of Absalom, when he pursues and gets ahead of the Cushite whom Joab sends to tell David of Absalom's death, 2 S 18:19–32.

3. **Ahimaaz** (1), married to Basemath, a daughter of Solomon; he is prefect in Naphtali, Solomon's eighth district, 1 K 4:14.

AHIMAN

1. **Ahiman, Sheshai,** and **Talmai** (3), the three sons of: ANAK.

2. **Ahiman** (1), a gatekeeper living in Jerusalem after the return from exile, 1 Ch 9:17.

AHIMELECH, "My Brother is king" (cf. Melech).

1. **Ahimelech** (12), **son of Ahitub** (4), a priest, a descendant of Eli, often identified with Ahijah (cf. 1 S 14:3), but is rather his brother and is attached to the sanctuary at Nob. Related to Saul by Doeg the Edomite, cf. Ps 52:2, for having given food (the loaves of offering) and the sword of Goliath to David when the latter is fleeing, he is put to death with his family and the eighty-five priests of Nob. Only Abiathar escapes the massacre, 1 S 21:2–10; 22:9–22; cf. Mt 12 3–4 p.

Father of: ABIATHAR.

2. **Ahimelech** (5), **son of Abiathar** (3), described as among the sons of Ithamar, 1 Ch 24:3, 6, 31, a priest under David at the same time as Zadok. In 2 S 8:17 some read *Abiathar son of Ahimelech* instead of *Ahimelech son of Abiathar;* in 1 Ch 18:16 *Ahimelech* is doubtless to be read for Hb. *Abimelech.*

3. **Ahimelech the Hittite** (1) accompanies David in his flight, 1 S 26:6.

AHIMOTH (1), "My Brother is Mot" (cf. Mot) or Accad. *Ahi-miti,* "My Brother is my support," brother of Amasai, a descendant of Levi through Kohath, and an ancestor of Samuel acc.

to 1 Ch 6:10. (Cf. Mahath son of Amasai, 1 Ch 6:20.)

AHINADAB (1), "My Brother is generous" (cf. Nadab), **son of Iddo** (1), administrator of Solomon's seventh district, at Mahanaim, 1 K 4:14.

AHINOAM, "My Brother is gracious" (cf. Naomi).

1. **Ahinoam daughter of Ahimaaz** (1), wife of King Saul, 1 S 14:50.

2. **Ahinoam of Jezreel** (6), first wife of David, 1 S 25:43, whom she accompanies into exile as guest of Achish of Gath, 1 S 27:3; she is a prisoner of the Amalekites, 1 S 30:5, and goes up to Hebron when David is anointed king, 2 S 2:2. She bears David's first son, Amnon, at Hebron, 2 S 3:2//1 Ch 3:1. She is always mentioned with—and before—Abigail, David's second wife.

AHIO, "Little brother" (cf. Ahi).

1. **Ahio** (3), **son of Abinadab** (1), from Kiriath-jearim; with his brother Uzzah he leads the cart that is carrying the Ark from his father's house to Jerusalem, 2 S 6:3–4//1 Ch 13:7.

2. **Ahio** (2), a Benjaminite of Gibeon, 1 Ch 8:31//9:37.

AHIRA son of Enan (5), leader of the tribe of Naphtali, Nb 2:29; 7:78; 10:27, put in charge of the census of his tribe, Nb 1:15, brings the offering for the dedication of the altar on the twelfth day, Nb 7:78–83.

AHIRAM (2), "My Brother is on high" (cf. Ramah), third son of Benjamin, Nb 26:38; 1 Ch 8:1 (corr. of Hb. *'Ahrah*), gives his name to the **Ahiramite** clan, Nb 26:38.

AHIRAMITE (1), of the clan of: AHIRAM.

AHISAMACH (3), "My Brother is my support" (cf. Semachiah), a Danite, father of: OHOLIAB.

AHISHARAR (1), a Benjaminite of the sons of Jediael, a champion and head of a family, 1 Ch 7:10–11.

AHITHOPHEL (2), "My Brother is drunk"?, **the Gilonite** (2), 2 S 15:12; 23:24, counselor of David, 1 Ch 27:33. He allows himself to be won over by Absalom, 2 S 15:12, to the despair of David, who, to thwart Ahithophel, secures the help of his friend Hushai the Archite and sends him to offer his services to Absalom so that he may spy on the latter and be able then to warn Zadok and Abiathar, 2 S 15:31–37. It is on the advice of Ahithophel that Absalom takes the concubines of David, his father, because "the advice Ahithophel gave was like an oracle from God," 2 S 16:20–23. But when Ahithophel proposes to set out immediately with 12,000 men in pursuit of David, Absalom approves instead the advice of Hushai. Foreseeing the consequences of his failure, Ahithophel goes home and hangs himself, 2 S 17:1–23. He will be replaced by Jehoiada and Abiathar, 1 Ch 27:34.

Father of: ELIAM 2.

AHITUB, Gr. *Achitob,* "My Brother is good" (cf. Tob).

1. **Ahitub** (5), grandson of the priest Eli, 1 S 14:3. Father of: AHIJAH 1; AHIMELECH 1; grandfather of: ABIATHAR.

2. **Ahitub** (10), father, 2 S 8:17; 1 Ch 5:33–34, 37–38 (repetition of vv. 33–34); 6:37; 18:16; Ezr 7:2, or grandfather, 1 Ch 9:11; Ne 11:11, of: ZADOK 1.

3. **Ahitub** (1), Jdt 8:1, a Simeonite, ancestor of: JUDITH.

AHLAB (1), a Canaanite town that retained its independence for a long time, Jg 1:31.

AHLAI, "Ah! Would to God that . . ." or "Brother of my God"?

1. **Ahlai** (1), son of Sheshan, a descendant of Jerahmeel, 1 Ch 2:31.

2. **Ahlai** (1), father of: ZABAD 3.

AHOAH (1), a Benjaminite, one of the sons of Bela, 1 Ch 8:4. To be compared with the following.

AHOH (from) or **AHOHITE** (5), of the clan of Ahoh in Benjamin. See: ELEAZAR 3; ZALMON 1.

AHUMAI (1), a descendant of Judah through Shobal; a Zorathite clan, 1 Ch 4:2.

AHUZZAM (1), (cf. Ahaz), a Judaean clan of the sons of Naarah, of Calebite origin, 1 Ch 4:6.

AHUZZATH (1), (cf. Ahaz), a friend of Abimelech, whom he accompanies on his visit to Isaac, Gn 26:26.

AHZAI (1), Ne 11:13.
= **Jahzerah** (1), 1 Ch 9:12. Ancestor of the priest: AMASAI 4.

AI (35), "Ruin," in Hb. always with the article, *ha-ʿAi.* A Canaanite town, 2 or 3 km SE of Bethel, with which it is named several times, especially in specifying the location of one of Abraham's first campsites in the Promised Land, Gn 12:8; 13:3, and in the list of returning exiles, Ezr 2:28//Ne 7:32. After a first repulse before Ai, Jos 7:2–5, owing to a violation of the ban in taking Jericho, Joshua punishes the guilty party and passes to the attack again. He sets up an ambush against Ai, takes the town, applies the ban to it, and hangs its king, 8:1–29; cf. 9:3; 10:1–2; 12:9.
= **Aiath** (1), the name of the rebuilt city, Is 10:28. Today *et-Tell.* Compare with: AVVIM; AYYAH.

AIAH, Hb. *ʾAyyah,* "Vulture, kite."
1. **Aiah** (2), elder son of Zibeon, himself the third son of Seir, Gn 36:24// 1 Ch 1:40.
2. **Aiah** (1), father of: RIZPAH.

AIATH (1). See: AI.

AIJALON (10), "Place of stags," 20 km W of Jerusalem. A Canaanite town that long retained its independence, despite the struggles against the Canaanites under Joshua, Jos 10:12; it is inhabited by Danites, Jos 19:42, and assigned to the Levite sons of Kohath, Jos 21:24 (taken from the tribe of Dan)//1 Ch 6:54 (from Ephraim). Aijalon, in Solomon's third district, 1 K 4:9 (Hb. *Elon*), is a fortified town rebuilt by Jeroboam, 2 Ch 11:10. Rivalry with the Benjaminite town of Gath, 1 Ch 8:13. Under Saul the Philistines are defeated at Aijalon, 1 S 14:31, but under Ahaz the latter occupy the town, 2 Ch 28:18. Today *Tell el-Qog* near *Yalu.*

AIN, Hb. *ʿAyîn,* "Spring" (cf. Aenon; En-; Enaim; Enam; Enan; Fountain. Cf. Dragon; Judgement; Tappuah).
1. **Ain** (1), W of Riblah, in the area of Damascus, Nb 34:11.
2. **Ain** (2), a town in the Negeb of Judah, allotted to the tribe of Simeon, Jos 19:7//1 Ch 4:31.

AKAN (1), third son of Ezer, Gn 36:27.
= **Jaakan** (1), 1 Ch 1:42.

AKKOS (1). See: Koz 2.

AKKUB
1. **Akkub** (1), one of the seven sons of Elioenai, a descendant of King Jehoiachin, 1 Ch 3:24.
2. **Akkub** (5), **Shallum** (5) or **Meshullam** (1), and **Talmon** (5), three gatekeepers always associated with one another, heads of families of gatekeepers who return from the exile with Zerubbabel, Ezr 2:42//Ne 7:45, remain at Jerusalem, 1 Ch 9:17//Ne 11:19, and guard the storehouses near the gates, Ne 12:25.
3. **Akkub** (1), one of the Levites who explain the Law to the people during its solemn reading by Ezra, Ne 8:7.
4. **Akkub** (1), head of a family of "oblates" who return from the exile with Zerubbabel, Ezr 2:45.

AKRABATTENE (1), district of Akrabatta, probably the modern *Aqrabah,* SE of Shechem. Judas Maccabaeus engages in battle there with the sons of Esau, 1 M 5:3.

ALCIMUS (15), "Valiant" (cf. Jakim), a Jew converted to Hellenism, a usurping high priest who succeeds a similar usurper, Menelaus, and has himself confirmed in office by Demetrius I, 1 M 7:5–9; 2 M 14:3, 13. He accompanies Bacchides, governor of the Trans-euphrates, to Judaea and makes hypocritical proposals to the scribes and Hasidaeans; Bacchides makes him responsible for the province of Judaea, where his wrongdoing draws the hostility of Judas and his followers, 1 M 7:8–25. Jealous of the friendship between Judas and Nicanor, Alcimus denounces the latter to Demetrius, 2 M 14:26–27. After the death of Nicanor, Demetrius again sends Bacchides and Alcimus to Judaea for a battle in which Judas Maccabaeus will be killed, 1 M 9:1–18. Paralysis strikes Alcimus at the moment when he has begun the demolition of the wall separating the two courts of the temple, and he dies ca. 157 B.C., 1 M 9:54–57.

ALEMA (2). See: HELAM.

ALEMETH

1. **Alemeth** (2), in Benjamin, among the sons of Becher, 1 Ch 7:8; a Levite town, 1 Ch 6:45.

= **Almon** (1), Jos 21:18. Always associated with Anathoth. The modern *Khirbet Almit,* 2 km NE of Anathoth.

2. **Alemeth** (2), a Benjaminite, one of the three sons of Jehoaddah, a descendant of King Saul, 1 Ch 8:36//9:42.

[ALEPPO]. See: BEROEA 1.

ALEXANDER, Gr. *Alexandros,* "He who protects men" (cf. Alexandrian; Andrew).

1. **Alexander [the Great]** (3), **son of Philip** (2), king of Macedonia (333–323): 1 M 1:1–8 summarizes his conquest of the Persian Empire and, after his death, the division of his realm among his generals; 1 M 6:2 mentions a temple at Elymais, which contains rich armor left there by Alexander. Dn alludes to the kingdom of Alexander in 2:40 (*iron*) and 7:7 (*the fourth beast with iron teeth*), and to Alexander himself, 8:5–8, 21–22 (*the he-goat*); 11:3–4.

2. **Alexander [Balas]** (24), son (?) of Antiochus Epiphanes and surnamed **Epiphanes** (1), 1 M 10:1, king of Syria (150–145). Rivalry between Alexander and Demetrius I to get an alliance with Jonathan: Alexander installs Jonathan as high priest, 1 M 10:1–45; the latter sides with Alexander, who wages war on Demetrius, vv. 46–50. Alliance of Alexander and Egypt (he marries Cleopatra), vv. 51–58, and with Jonathan, vv. 59–66. Alexander is disturbed by the return of Demetrius II, v. 68, then receives the good news of the defeat of Apollonius, governor of Coele-Syria, by Jonathan, to whom Alexander awards many honors, vv. 88–89. During a battle with Ptolemy, Alexander flees; Zabdiel the Arab cuts off his head, 1 M 11:1–20; Trypho had been a supporter of Alexander, 1 M 11:39.

Father of: ANTIOCHUS 5.

3. **Alexander** (1), brother of Rufus and son of Simon of Cyrene, Mk 15:21.

4. **Alexander** (1), from a family of high priests, present at the trial of Peter and John before the Sanhedrin, Ac 4:6.

5. **Alexander** (2), a Jew who seeks to intervene, unsuccessfully, in the riot of the silversmiths at Ephesus, Ac 19:33–34.

6. **Alexander** (2), a coppersmith, a Christian excluded from the community, 1 Tm 1:20, becomes a bitter opponent of the word, 2 Tm 4:14–15.

ALEXANDRIA. See: ALEXANDRIAN.

ALEXANDRIAN (4), belonging to Alexandria, a city founded by Alexander the Great at the NW end of the Nile delta, where there is a sizable Jewish community, of which Apollos is a member, Ac 18:24. Members of the community debate with Stephen at Jerusalem, Ac 6:9

ff. The city is the home port of many ships, Ac 27:6; 28:11.

ALIAH (1). See: ALVAH.

ALIAN (1). See: ALVAN.

ALLAMMELECH (1), (cf. Melech), a town in Asher, Jos 19:26.

ALMIGHTY (33), Gr. *Pantokratōr,* a title applied to God:

—in the OT, in Jdt 4:13; 8:13; 15:10; 16:5, 17; Est 4:17b; 2 M (12×); Ws 7:25; Si 42:17; 50:14, 17; Ba 3:1. It may also translate Hb. *Sebaoth*, "armies, powers," in the expression *Yahweh Sebaoth* (see: YAHWEH) or the Hb. *shaddai* (see: SHADDAI).

—in the NT (10×), 2 Co 6:18; Rv 1:8; 4:8; 11:17; 15:3; 16:7, 14; 19:6, 15; 21:22.

Cf. *the Mighty One of Israel,* Is 1:24; *the Mighty One of Jacob,* Gn 49:24; Ps 132:2, 5; Is 49:26; *Omnipotence* or *the Power,* Ws 1:3; Mt 26:64//Mk 14:62// Lk 22:69; Ac 8:10.

ALMODAD (2), first of the thirteen sons of Joktan, a tribe or territory in southern Arabia that is not identifiable, Gn 10:26//1 Ch 1:20.

ALMON (1). See: ALEMETH 1.

ALMON-DIBLATHAIM (2), (cf. Diblaim), a town in Moab between Dibon (-gad) and Nebo, a stage of the exodus, Nb 33:46–47.

= ? **Beth-diblathaim** (1), Jr 48:22, mentioned on the stele of Mesha. Site uncertain.

ALPHAEUS, Gr. *Halphaios* (cf. Chalphi).

1. **Alphaeus** (4), Mt 10:3//Mk 3:18// Lk 6:15//Ac 1:13, father of James the Apostle; see: JACOB 4. Alphaeus is identified by some with Clopas, Jn 19:25.

2. **Alphaeus** (1), Mk 2:14, father of the Apostle Levi or: MATTHEW.

ALUSH (2), a stage of the Exodus, in the wilderness of Sinai, before Rephidim, Nb 33:13–14.

ALVAH (1) or **Aliah** (1), "Height" (cf. Alvan; Elealeh; Eli; Jaalah; Jael; Wild Goats), one of the leaders (or clans) of Edom, Gn 36:40//1 Ch 1:51.

ALVAN (1) or **Alian** (1), (cf. Alvah), first of the five sons of Shobal, son of Seir, Gn 36:23//1 Ch 1:40.

AM- (or **-am**), "Paternal uncle, Relative, *whence* People," used as a divine title forming—by way of prefix or suffix—many composite proper names (cf. Ammiel; Ammihud; Amminadab; Ammishaddai; Ammizabad; Amram (?); Aniam; Ben-ammi; Eliam; Ithream; Jekameam; Jeroboam; Rehoboam).

AMAD (1), "People forever," a town in Asher, Jos 19:26.

AMAL (1), "Difficulty," an Asherite, son of Helem, a champion and head of family, 1 Ch 7:35.

AMALEK (39). See: AMALEKITES.

AMALEKITES (12), Hb. *'Amaleq* (39). Presented as descended from Esau, Gn 36:12, 16; 1 Ch 1:36, this very ancient nomad people, cf. Nb 24:20, lives in the Negeb and the mountainous district of Seir, Gn 14:7; Nb 13:29; 14:25. In the Sinai, Joshua defeats the Amalekites with whom God "is at war from age to age," Ex 17:8–16; Dt 25:17–18; cf. 1 Ch 4:43; Ps 83:8, and whose memory "you are to blot out," Dt 25:19; Nb 24:20. When Israel has almost reached the promised land, it is defeated by the Amalekites at Hormah, Nb 14:40–45. In the time of the judges the Amalekites enter into an alliance against Israel with the Moabites and Ammonites, Jg 3:13, then with Midian, Jg 6:3–6, 33; 7:12; 10:12. Saul leads a holy war against Amalek, 1 S 14:48; 15:1–7, but spares their king Agag, whom Samuel then butchers, 15: 8–24, 32–33. David leads a raid against the Amalekites, 1 S 27:8. They in turn raid the Negeb and Ziklag, 1 S 30:1–4; campaign of David against the Amalekites, 1 S 30:4–31; 2 S 1:1; cf. 2 S 8:12;

1 Ch 18:11. It is an Amalekite who comes to tell David that Saul has fallen on Gilboa; David has him put to death, 2 S 1:2–16.

King: AGAG.

AMAM (1), a town in the Negeb of Judah, Jos 15:26.

AMANA (1), (cf. Amon 1–3), one of the heights of the Anti-Lebanon, Sg 4:8.

AMARIAH, "Yah speaks" (cf. Omri).

1. **Amariah** (6), a descendant of Aaron and grandfather of Zadok the priest, 1 Ch 5:33, 37 (repetition of v. 33); 6:37; Ezr 7:3.

2. **Amariah** (1), second of the four sons of Hebron, a Levite of the clan of Kohath, 1 Ch 23:19//24:23.

3. **Amariah** (1), chief priest in the time of King Jehoshaphat, 2 Ch 19:11.

4. **Amariah** (1), one of the six Levites put under command of Kore, son of Imnah, for distribution of food in the time of King Hezekiah, 2 Ch 31:15.

5. **Amariah** (1), ancestor of the prophet: ZEPHANIAH 2.

6. **Amariah** (3), a priest who returns from the exile with Zerubbabel and Jeshua, Ne 12:2, cosigns the pledge to observe the Law, Ne 10:4, and whose family is headed by Jehohanan in the time of the high priest Joiakim, Ne 12:13.

7. **Amariah** (1), an Israelite of the sons of Zaccai, married to a foreign wife, whom he puts away, Ezr 10:42.

8. **Amariah** (1), a Judaean, a descendant of Perez and ancestor of: ATHAIAH.

AMASA, "[Yah] carries" (cf. Amos 2).

1. **Amasa** (15), **son of Jether** (3) or **Ithra** (1), **the Ishmaelite** (2), and of Abigail, the sister of David; a cousin of Joab and, like him, cousin of Absalom and nephew of David, 2 S 17:25; cf. 1 Ch 2:17. Absalom makes him the military leader of his rebellion, 2 S 17:25; to win him over, David makes him leader of the army of Judah in place of Joab, 2 S 19:12–14. Joab, without David's knowledge, treacherously strikes Amasa with the sword near the great stone of Gibeon, 2 S 20:4–13. When David is dying, he bids Solomon avenge this assassination, 1 K 2:5–6. Joab's complicity in the conspiracy of Adonijah gives Solomon the occasion to have Joab executed in revenge for Amasa and Abner, 1 K 2:32.

2. **Amasa son of Hadlai** (1), one of the four officers of the northern kingdom, 2 Ch 28:12, who at the appeal of the prophet Oded take pity on their Judaean brothers who are prisoners and give them relief and their freedom, vv. 5–15.

AMASAI, Amashai.

1. **Amasai** (3), a Levite of the clan of Kohath, brother of Ahimoth, 1 Ch 6:10. Father of: MAHATH 1.

2. **Amasai** (1), leader of the Thirty, pronounces a prophetic oracle about David, 1 Ch 12:19. In 1 Ch 11:20 the leader of the Thirty is said to be *Abishai,* brother of Joab.

3. **Amasai** (1), one of the priests who sound the trumpet before the Ark, 1 Ch 15:24.

4. **Amashai son of Azarel, son of Ahzai, son of Meshillemoth, son of Immer** (1), Ne 11:13.

= **Maasai son of Adiel, son of Jahzerah, son of Meshullam, son of Meshillemith, son of Immer** (1), 1 Ch 9:12, a priest at Jerusalem after the exile.

AMASHAI. See: AMASAI 4.

AMASIAH (1), "Yah carries" (cf. Amos 2), son of Zichri (1), "volunteered for Yahweh's service," an officer in the army of King Jehoshaphat, 2 Ch 17:16.

AMAW (Land of the sons of) (1), in northern Syria, Nb 22:5. Other possible readings: *land of the sons of his people* or *land of his kinsmen.*

AMAZIAH, "Yah is strong" (cf. Amos; Amzi).

1. **Amaziah** (35), **son of Jehoash** (6), **son of Ahaziah** (2), ninth king of Judah (796–781).

Successor to Jehoash, 2 K 12:22// 1 Ch 24:27; 1 Ch 3:12, Amaziah earns qualified praise, 2 K 14:1–4//2 Ch 25: 1–2; cf. 2 K 15:3//2 Ch 26:4. He executes his father's murderers but spares their sons, 2 K 14:5–6//2 Ch 25:3–4.

With a view to a war against the Edomites, he conducts a census of Judah, and enrolls Ephraimite mercenaries, but at the urging of a man of God he sends the mercenaries home and overcomes 10,000 Edomites in the Valley of Salt, 2 Ch 25:5–12; cf. 2 K 14:7. He then introduces the gods of Seir into Judah, but a prophet foretells his coming punishment, 2 Ch 25:14–16. Buoyed up by his victory over Edom, Amaziah, "the thistle of Lebanon," confronts Joash of Israel at Beth-shemesh, but he is captured and taken to Jerusalem, where Joash takes the treasures of the temple and the royal palace, 2 K 14:8–17//2 Ch 25:17–25. Threatened by a conspiracy, Amaziah flees to Lachish, where he is overtaken and killed, 2 K 14:18–20//2 Ch 25: 26–28.

His mother: JEHOADDIN.

His son and successor: UZZIAH.

2. **Amaziah** (3), a priest of the sanctuary of Bethel. To Jeroboam II he accuses the prophet Amos of a conspiracy and expels him from Bethel. Amos answers by referring to his own mission from Yahweh and predicting the punishment that awaits the priest and his family, Am 7:10–17.

3. **Amaziah** (1), a Simeonite, father of: JOSHAH.

4. **Amaziah** (1), a Levite of the clan of Merari, an ancestor of Ethan the cantor, 1 Ch 6:30.

AMI (1), a derivative of: AMON 3.

AMITTAI (2), (cf. Amon 1–3), 2 K 14:25; Jon 1:1, father of the prophet: JONAH 1.

AMMAH (Hill of), Hb. *Gib'at-'Ammah,* "to the east of the valley, on the road to Giah," 2 S 2:24. Site not identified.

[AMMANITIS] or **Ammonite territory** (2), the area around the ancient city of Rabbah of the Ammonites, 2 M 4:26; 5:7. Its inhabitants are called Ammonites (lit., sons of Ammon) in 1 M 5:6.

In Ammanitis: TOBIJAH 6.

Governors: HYRCANUS 1; TOBIJAH 4.

AMMIEL, "My Uncle is God" (cf. Am-).

1. **Ammiel son of Gemalli** (1), a clan leader of the tribe of Dan, sent by Moses as representative of his tribe in the reconnaissance of Canaan, Nb 13:12.

2. **Ammiel** (3), father of: MACHIR 2.

3. **Ammiel** (1). See: ELIAM 1.

4. **Ammiel** (1), a gatekeeper, sixth son of Obed-edom, 1 Ch 26:5.

AMMIHUD, "My Uncle is majesty" (cf. Am-; Hod).

1. **Ammihud** (6), an Ephraimite, ancestor of Joshua son of Nun, 1 Ch 7:26. Father of: ELISHAMA 1.

2. **Ammihud** (1), father of: SAMUEL 1.

3. **Ammihud** (1), father of: PEDAHEL.

4. **Ammihud** (1), ([K]*Ammihur*), father of: TALMAI 2.

5. **Ammihud** (1), father of: UTHAI.

AMMINADAB, Gr. *Aminadab,* "My Uncle is generous" (cf. Am-; Nadab).

1. **Amminadab** (10), a Judaean, descendant of Perez and ancestor of David, Rt 4:19–20; 1 Ch 2:10, and of Jesus, Mt 1:4; Lk 3:33. Father of: NAHSHON; ELIZABETH 1.

2. **Amminadab** (1), son of Kohath, father of Korah, and ancestor of Samuel acc. to 1 Ch 6:7.

3. **Amminadab** (2), a descendant of Kohath, head of a family in the clan of Uzziel, takes part in the transfer of the Ark of the Covenant, 1 Ch 15:10–11.

AMMISHADDAI (5), "My Uncle is Shaddai" (cf. Am-; Shaddai). Father of: AHIEZER 1.

AMMIZABAD (1), "My Uncle has made a gift" (cf Am-; Zabad), son of the champion Benaiah, son of Jehoiada, 1 Ch 27:6.

AMMON, AMMONITES, and **Sons of Ammon** (136), (cf. *Ben-ammi*), a land and a people E of the lower reaches of the Jordan.

a. Ammon and Moab, Ammonites and Moabites

The Ammonites are connected, in the popular account in Gn 19:36–39, with an ancestor *Ben-ammi,* "Son of my kinsman," who was born of incest between Lot, nephew of Abraham, and his younger daughter, just as Moab was of incest between Lot and his elder daughter.

Of Aramaean origin, Ammonites and Moabites, "the sons of Lot," Dt 2:9, 19; Ps 83:9, often appear together, frequently as enemies of Israel: at the Exodus from Egypt, Dt 2:19–21, 37; cf. Jg 11:15; Dt 23:5, in the time of the judges, Jg 3:12–13, under Saul, 1 S 14:47, under David, 2 S 8:12//1 Ch 18:11, under Jehoshaphat, 2 Ch 20:1–23, under Jehoiakim, 2 K 24:2. Cf. Ps 83:6–9; Jdt 5:2; 7:17–18. Israel and its leaders allow themselves to be corrupted by Ammonite and Moabite customs and divinities, Jg 10:6; 1 K 11:1–7, 33; 2 K 23:13; Ezr 9:1; Ne 13:23. Acc. to Dt 23:4, cited by Ne 13:1–2, "no Ammonite or Moabite is to be admitted to the assembly of Yahweh." Ammon and Moab are linked in prophetic oracles, Is 11:14; Jr 9:24–25; 25:21; 27:2–3; 49:1–6; Ezk 25:1–7; Dn 11:40–41; Am 1:13–14; Zp 2:8–11.

b. Ammon, Ammonite, Region of the Ammonites

When the Israelites conquer the land of Sihon, king of the Amorites, they stop at the Jabbok, "the Ammonite frontier," Nb 21:24; cf. Dt 2:37; 3:16; Jos 13:10. The sons of Gad receive as their portion "half the country of the Ammonites as far as Aroer facing Rabbah," Jos 13:25. Jephthah's entire mission is connected with oppression by the Ammonites, Jg 10:6–12:3. Saul conquers the Ammonites, whose king, Nahash, is threatening Jabesh-gilead, 1 S 11:1–11. The insulting behavior of Hanun, king of the Ammonites, to David's ambassadors, 2 S 10:1–5//1 Ch 19:1–5, leads to a first victorious campaign of the Israelites and their Aramaean allies, 2 S 10:6–19//1 Ch 19:6–19, then to a second campaign, during which Uriah the Hittite dies and which ends with the capture of Rabbah, the capital, 2 S 11; 12:26–31//1 Ch 20:1, 3. The Ammonites pay tribute to Uzziah, 2 Ch 26:8, then to Jotham, 2 Ch 27:5. After assassinating Gedaliah, Ishmael flees, with the prisoners he has taken, to the Ammonites, Jr 41:10, 15. Ezekiel announces the punishment of Ammon, Ezk 21:33–37. When the exiles return, the Ammonites try to oppose the rebuilding, Ne 4:1–2. In the time of the Maccabees, Judas "engaged them in many encounters," 1 M 5:6–7; and the high priest Jason, who favors the hellenization of the Jews, is forced on two occasions to take refuge in Ammonite territory, 2 M 4:26; 5:7.

Kings: Baalis; Hanun 1; Nahash 1.

Ammonites: Achior; Naamah 2; Shimeath; Tobijah 4; Zelek.

National god: Milcom.

Capital: Rabbah 1.

See: [Ammanitis]; Chephar-ammoni.

AMMONITES. See: Ammon.

AMNON, "Faithful" (cf. Amon 1–3).

1. **Amnon** (17), eldest son of David, born of Ahinoam of Jezreel at Hebron, 2 S 3:2//1 Ch 3:1. He falls in love with his half-sister Tamar, gets her to his house by trickery, and rapes her, 2 S 13:1–18. Absalom guesses the outrage done his sister by Amnon (Hb. *Aminon,* 13:20) and breaks with his brother, vv. 19–22. Two years later, during a ban-

quet he gives, Absalom has Amnon killed and goes into exile, vv. 23–33. Three years later, having "recovered from Amnon's death," David allows Absalom to return to Jerusalem, vv. 37–39.

2. **Amnon** (1), a Judaean, of the sons of Shimon, 1 Ch 4:20.

AMOK (2), (cf. Beth-emek; Emek-kezez), Accad. *Emqu,* "Capable," a priest who returns from exile with Zerubbabel and Jeshua, Ne 12:7, and gives his name to a priestly family, Ne 12:20.

AMON, Hb. 1–3: "Faithful" (cf. Amana; Amittai; Amnon; Heman?).

1. **Amon** (2), governor of the city of Samaria, to whom King Ahab sends the prophet Micaiah, son of Imlah, to be imprisoned, 1 K 22:26//2 Ch 18:25.

2. **Amon** (16), fifteenth king of Judah (642–640), son of Manasseh, 1 Ch 3:14, and of Meshullemeth, is, like his father, an idolater and unfaithful to Yahweh; he dies the victim of a conspiracy of his servants, 2 K 21:18–24//2 Ch 35:20–25. He is buried beside his father in the garden of Uzza, 2 K 21:26. Amon is named by Mt 1:10 (Gr. *Amōs*) among the ancestors of Jesus. His son and successor: JOSIAH 1.

3. **Amon** (1), head of a family of Solomon's slaves who return from the exile, Ne 7:59.

= **Ami** (1), Ezr 2:57.

4. **Amon** (2), Egypt. "Hidden," an Egyptian god represented in various human and animal forms (especially with the head of a ram); god of the city of Thebes (= No), to whom Jeremiah announces a "visit" from Yahweh, Jr 46:25. City of Amon: No.

AMORITES (87), Sumer. *Mar-tu* (to be connected with the city of *Mari*), a small pre-Israelite Semitic tribe that had come from Mesopotamia. Depicted as sons of Canaan, that is, as a Canaanite clan, Gn 10:15–16, the Amorites are in fact often synonymous with the Canaanites in the Bible: compare, for example, Nb 14:39–45 and Dt 1:41–44, and they are named 22× in the list of the "seven nations," Ac 13:19, who occupy the land of Canaan at the time of the Conquest and remain there for a long time after, cf. Jg 3:5; 1 S 7:14; 2 S 21:2; 1 K 9:20. The Amorites are mentioned even in the period of the patriarchs, when the four kings of the east invade the area south of the Dead Sea, Gn 14:1, 5, 7. The land of Canaan is also called the "land of the Amorites," Nb 21:13, 31; Jos 24:8; Jg 10:8, 11; 11:21–22; Jdt 5:15; cf. 1:44. In the Conquest, cf. Gn 48:22, Israel is to dispossess the inhabitants of this land and take over their towns, Nb 21:25, 31–32; 32:39; Dt 1:7; Jos 24:8, 18; Jg 11:21–23; cf. Nb 22:2. The Amorites, "men tall as cedars and strong as oaks," Am 2:9–10; cf. Dt 9:1–2, impress the Israelites, who are afraid of falling into their power, Dt 1:27; Jos 7:7. In fact, Israel is repulsed by the Amorites on several occasions, Dt 1:44; Jg 1:34–35, but Yahweh delivers it from this oppression, Jg 10:11. "The wickedness of the Amorites," Gn 15:16, and their idolatry are denounced a number of times, Jos 24:15; Jg 6:10; 1 K 21:21; 2 K 21:11; cf. Ex 23:24; 34:14–16. Ezekiel reminds Jerusalem that, though chosen by Yahweh and conquered by David, it has retained something of its pagan origins: "your father was an Amorite and your mother a Hittite," Ezk 16:3, 45, where "Amorite" and "Hittite" designate simply the people of Canaan.

The Amorites, named among the seven nations of: CANAAN *a.*

The five Amorite kings west of the Jordan: ADONI-ZEDEK.

The two Amorite kings east of the Jordan: OG; SIHON.

Amorite: MAMRE.

AMOS, Amoz

1. **Amoz** (13), Hb. *'Amoz,* Gr. *Amōs,* "Strong," abbrev. of *Amaziah,* 2 K 19:

2, 20; 20:1; 2 Ch 26:22; 32:20, 32; Is 1:1; 2:1; 13:1; 20:2; 37:2, 21; 38:1, father of the prophet: ISAIAH.

2. **Amos** (8), Hb. *'Amos,* Gr. *Amōs,* "Carrier" (cf. Amasiah).

The Book of Amos (9 chs.), one of the twelve "minor prophets," uses the name of the prophet 7×, Am 1:1; 7:8–14; 8:2. The name appears again in Tb 2:6, which cites Am 8:10. The NT refers 2× to the Book of Amos without naming the prophet: Ac 7:42 = Am 5:25–27 Gr., and Ac 15:16–17 = Am 9:11–12.

A native of Tekoa, Am 1:1, south of Jerusalem, where he had been a shepherd and looked after sycamores, Amos exercises his prophetic ministry, 1–9, around 750 B.C. under Jeroboam II of Israel and Uzziah of Judah, 1:1, in Israel and especially at Bethel, a royal sanctuary, where he comes in conflict with the priest Amaziah, 7:10–17. Compelled by the word of Yahweh, 3:3–8, even though he is not a professional prophet, 7:14, Amos is known above all for his attacks on the luxury of the rich who oppress the poor, 4:1; 6, and on purely formalistic worship, 4:4–5; 7:21–23, for his emphasis on seeking God, 5:4–6, and for his prediction of hunger for the word of God, 8:11–12.

3. **Amos** (1), Gr. *Amōs,* an ancestor of Jesus acc. to Lk 3:25.

4. **Amos** (1), Gr. *Amōs,* Mt 1:10 Gr., see: AMON 2.

AMOZ. See AMOS 1.

AMPHIPOLIS (1), "What is around the city" (cf. Decapolis; Heliopolis; Heracleopolis; Hierapolis; Neapolis; Nicopolis; Pentapolis; Persepolis; Scythopolis; Tripolis; see Ir Haheres), a city of Macedonia, almost completely *surrounded* by the river Strymon (whence the name of the city). During his second missionary journey Paul passes through the city on his way from Philippi to Thessalonika, Ac 17:1.

AMPLIATUS (1), a Roman Christian dear to Paul who greets him in his letter to the Romans, Rm 16:8.

AMRAM, "The Uncle is on high"? (cf. Ramah).

1. **Amram** (13), first of the four sons of Kohath son of Levi, Ex 6:18; Nb 26:58; 1 Ch 5:28; 23:12, marries Jochebed, his aunt, who bears him Aaron, Moses, Ex 6:20; 1 Ch 23:13, and Miriam, Nb 26:59; 1 Ch 5:29; cf. Ex 2:1–10. He dies at the age of 137, Ex 6:20.

Grouped under his name, his descendants form the first of the clans of Kohath, the clan of the **sons of Amram,** Nb 3:19; 1 Ch 6:3–4; 24:20, or **Amramite** clan, Nb 3:27, whose functions are specified in 1 Ch 26:23–28; cf. 23:25–32.

2. **Amram** (1), an Israelite of the sons of Bani, married to a foreign wife, whom he puts away, Ezr 10:34.

AMRAMITE (2), Nb 3:27; 1 Ch 26:23, belonging to the clan of: AMRAM 1.

AMRAPHEL (2), Accad. *Amur-pi-el,* "The mouth of God has spoken"?, **king of Shinar** (2), along with his allies **Arioch, king of Ellasar** (2), **Chedorlaomer, king of Elam** (2), and **Tidal, king of the Goiim** (2), crushes various small tribes and the five kings of the rebellious towns in the Valley of Siddim (Sodom, Gomorrah, and so on). Abraham, whose nephew Lot has been taken prisoner, goes after Amraphel and his allies and defeats them in turn north of Damascus, Gn 14:1–15, 17; cf. Heb 7:1; *Amraphel* is not to be confused with *Hammurabi.*

AMZI, abbrev. of *Amaziah.*

1. **Amzi** (1), a Levite of the clan of Merari and an ancestor of Ethan the cantor, 1 Ch 6:31.

2. **Amzi** (1), Ne 11:12, an ancestor of the priest: ADAIAH 6.

ANAB (2), "Grape," a town formerly belonging to the Anakim, Jos 11:21, in the highlands of Judah, Jos 15:50. About 20 km SW of Hebron. Today *Aneb.*

ANAEL (1), a Naphtalite, brother of Tobit and father of: AHIKAR.

ANAH

1. **Anah** (6), the fourth of the sons of Seir, Gn 36:20//1 Ch 1:38, and leaders (or clans) of the Horites, Gn 36:29. He has a son Dishon, Gn 36:25//1 Ch 1:41, and a daughter: OHOLIBAMAH 1. Compare with the following.

2. **Anah** (6), **younger son of Zibeon** (2), the latter being the third son of Seir, 1 Ch 1:40; a shepherd, he discovers the (hot) springs in the wilderness, Gn 36:24. His daughter: OHOLIBAMAH 2, becomes one of the wives of Esau. In Gn 36:2, 14, Hb. reads *Anah daughter of Zibeon.* Compare with the preceding.

ANAHARATH (1), a town in Issachar, Jos 19:19.

ANAIAH, "Yah answers."

1. **Anaiah** (1), a lay notable who stands on Ezra's right during the solemn reading of the Law, Ne 8:4.

2. **Anaiah** (1), a leader of the people, cosigner of the pledge to observe the Law, Ne 10:23.

ANAK (10) and his sons or descendants, **the Anakim** (9), "the [men with the] necklaces." The spies sent into Canaan by Moses reach Hebron, where **Ahiman, Sheshai** and **Talmai,** the three sons of Anak, live, Nb 13:22. Caleb takes Hebron from the three sons of Anak, Jos 15:14; cf. Jg 1:20, and the tribe of Judah marches against them and defeats them, Jg 1:10.

The pre-Israelite population of Palestine, which lived in "the highlands of the Amorites," Dt 1:28; cf. Jos 14:12, is presented as a race of giants, Nb 13:28–33; Dt 9:12, as are the Rephaim, Dt 2:10–11, 21. Wiped out in the highlands by Joshua, they continue to live at Gaza, Gath, and Ashdod, Jos 11:21–22. The ancient name of Hebron, Kiriath-arba, is connected, acc. to one tradition, with a certain **Arba,** "the greatest man of the Anakim," Jos 14:15, the "chief city of the Anakim," Jos 15:13; 21:11.

See: GOLIATH; NEPHILIM; REPHAIM 1; TITANS.

ANAKIM. See: ANAK.

ANAM (People of) (2), Hb. *'Anamim,* a people connected with Egypt, Gn 10:13//1 Ch 1:11; Anam is unidentified, but perhaps a town between Jerusalem and Gezer, which Solomon receives from Pharaoh as part of a dowry, cf. 1 K 9:16–17.

ANAMMELECH (1), (cf. Melech, which suggests Molech), one of the gods in whose honor the people of Sepharvaim offer their children in sacrifice, 2 K 17:31.

ANAN (1), "Storm-cloud" (cf. Anani; Ananiah), a leader of the people, cosigner of the pledge to observe the Law, Ne 10:27.

ANANI (1), a derivative of *Ananiah,* one of the seven sons of Elioenai, a descendant of King Jehoiachin, 1 Ch 3:24.

ANANIAH, "Yah has shown himself" (cf. Anan).

1. **Ananiah** (1), identical with: BETHANY 1.

2. **Ananiah** (1), ancestor of: AZARIAH 18.

ANANIAS. See: HANANIAH.

ANANIEL. See: HANANEL.

ANATH (2), Ugar. "Spring," name of a fiery goddess of the West Semites, sister of Baal (cf. Anathoth; Atargatis; Beth-anath; Beth-anoth). *Son of Anath* in Jg 3:31 perhaps means "a native of Beth-anath." See: SHAMGAR.

ANATHOTH (cf. Anath).

1. **Anathoth** (14) **in the territory of Benjamin** (2), 6 km NE of Jerusalem (near the modern *Anata*), a Levite town, Jos 21:18//1 Ch 6:45, of Benjamin, Jr 1:1; cf. Ne 11:32; 1 Ch 7:8, native place

especially of the priestly family of Abiathar, 1 K 2:26, of Jeremiah, Jr 1:1; 29:27, and of his cousin Hanamel, who owns a field there, Jr 32:7–9. Jeremiah will have to suffer at the hands of his fellow townsmen, Jr 11:21–23, of whom 128 will return from exile, Ezr 2:23// Ne 7:27. Anathoth is also mentioned as one of the stages for the invader from the north on his way to Jerusalem, Is 10:30. Native place of: ABIEZER 2; JEHU 3.

2. **Anathoth** (1), a leader of the people, cosigner of the pledge to observe the Law, Ne 10:20. To be connected with the preceding?

ANDREW (13), a Gr. name, "The virile one" (cf. Alexander; Andronicus; Nicanor), brother of Simon Peter, Mt 4:18; Mk 1:16; Jn 1:40; 6:8, a native of Bethsaida, Jn 1:44, lives in the same house as Peter at Capernaum, Mk 1:29. With Peter, James, and John, he makes a group of four privileged disciples: he is among the first four called (fishermen from the lake whom Jesus invites to become fishers of men), Mt 4:18–20// Mk 1:16–18; cf. Lk 5:1–11, where Andrew, who is not named, is nonetheless meant, as the plurals in vv. 5–7 show. In the lists of the Twelve, he is mentioned either second, Mt 10:2; Lk 6:14, or fourth, Mk 3:18; Ac 1:13. Acc. to Mk 13:3 the discourse of Jesus on the destruction of the temple is directed primarily to these four disciples. Acc. to Jn, Andrew was first a disciple of John the Baptist, then one of the first disciples of Jesus, Jn 1:35–42. Before the multiplication of the loaves, he tells Jesus that a boy is present who has five loaves and two fishes, Jn 6:8. Finally, with Philip, he mediates between the people of Greek background and Jesus, Jn 12:21–22.

See: TWELVE; List, page 417.

ANDRONICUS, "Conqueror of men" (cf. Andrew; Bernice; Eunice; Nicanor; Nicodemus; Nicolaus; Nicopolis; Thessalonika).

1. **Andronicus** (1), a deputy of Antiochus Epiphanes; at the instigation of Menelaus and in contempt for the rights of sanctuary, he murders the high priest Onias III; he is himself put to death by the king, 2 M 4:31–38.

2. **Andronicus** (1), a commissioner of King Antiochus Epiphanes, probably residing in Shechem, at the foot of Mount Gerizim, 2 M 5:23.

3. **Andronicus** (1), mentioned with Junias as a Roman Christian, a relative of Paul and his companion in captivity, who preceded him as a Christian, Rm 16:7.

ANEM (1). See: EN-GANNIM 2.

ANER

1. **Aner** (2), brother of the Amorite Mamre, Gn 14:13, accompanies Abraham in his successful pursuit of the four great kings, Gn 14:24.

2. **Aner** (1), 1 Ch 6:55. See: TAANACH.

ANGLE (5), Hb. *Miqzoa'*, at Jerusalem. King Uzziah builds a tower there, 2 Ch 26:9, at the intersection of the walls, Ne 3:19–20, 24–25. On the east side of the city.

ANIAM (1), a Manassite, son of Shemida, 1 Ch 7:19.

ANIM (1), a town in the highlands of Judah, 20 km S of Hebron, Jos 15:50.

ANNA. See: HANNAH.

ANNAS (4), Gr. *Hannas,* father-in-law of Caiaphas, high priest from 6–15 A.D., but whose influence remains dominant during the pontificate of Caiaphas, so that the text speaks of the "pontificate of Annas and Caiaphas" in relation to the first activity of John the Baptist (the fifteenth year of Tiberius = 27 A.D.), Lk 3:1. When arrested, Jesus is taken first to Annas, Jn 18:13, 24. Annas is still a member of the Sanhedrin when Peter and John appear before it, Ac 4:5–6.

ANTHOTHIJAH (1), a Benjaminite of the sons of Shashak, head of a family at Jerusalem, 1 Ch 8:24.

ANTICHRIST (5). The term appears only in the Letters of John, in the singular number as personification of a power hostile to Christ, 1 Jn 2:18, 22; 4:3–4 (*he is here, in the world*); 2 Jn 7, and in the plural, 1 Jn 2:18, as a designation for those who are moved by the spirit of the Antichrist, 1 Jn 4:3, who attack especially the true faith in Christ and whose activity is manifested especially in the "last times."

Elsewhere in the NT the equivalents of Antichrist are **the Rebel, the Lost One, the Enemy,** "who claims to be so much greater than all that men call 'god,' " 2 Th 2:3–4, 8, and also **the Beast** or rather the two beasts, Rv 13. In the OT the opposition to God is personified by **Satan,** 1 Ch 21:1; Jb 1:6; Zc 3:1–2, or **the devil,** Ws 2:24; cf. Gn 3.

ANTI-LEBANON (1), a chain of hills separated from Mount Lebanon by the Vale of Lebanon. Nebuchadnezzar addresses a message to its inhabitants, among others, Jdt 1:7.

ANTIOCH, "[The city of] Antiochus" (cf. Antiochus).

1. **Antioch** (28) in Syria, on the Orontes, founded around 300 B.C. by Seleucus I; capital of his kingdom, then of the Roman province of Syria. Today *Antakya.*

When Hellenism makes its way into Israel, some Jews who have become citizens of Antioch are called "Antiochists from Jerusalem," 2 M 4:19; cf. v.9. There is a sizable Jewish colony at Antioch, 2 M 4:36. After looting the temple of Jerusalem, Antiochus Epiphanes returns in haste to Antioch, 2 M 5:21; from there he departs on an expedition against Persia, 1 M 3:37. At Antioch, Lysias recruits foreigners before returning to Judaea, 1 M 4:35. Defeated by the Jews, Nicanor takes refuge at Antioch, 2 M 8:35. The Roman legates send word to the Jews of their arrival at Antioch, 2 M 11:36. On returning to Jerusalem, Antiochus V finds his capital in the hands of Philip and must recapture the city from him, 1 M 6:63; cf. 2 M 13:23–26. When Demetrius I becomes king, he goes to Antioch, "the crown lands of his ancestors," 1 M 7:1–2. He orders Nicanor to bring Judas Maccabaeus there in chains, 2 M 14:27. Learning of the arrival of Demetrius II in Syria, Alexander Balas returns to Antioch, 1 M 10:68. Ptolemy VI traitorously invades Syria and enters Antioch, 1 M 11:13. Demetrius II, who is aided by Jonathan at Antioch, 1 M 11:44–51, is attacked by Trypho, general of Alexander Balas, who seizes the city, 1 M 11:56.

After the martyrdom of Stephen, Antioch is evangelized by Christians whom persecution has forced from Jerusalem, Ac 11:19–21, then by Barnabas and Paul, who remain there for a year, Ac 11:22–26. Antioch becomes, after Jerusalem, the second center for the spread of the Christian faith. "It was at Antioch that the disciples were first called 'Christians,' " Ac 11:26. The Church of Antioch, where there were prophets and teachers, sends Barnabas and Paul on a mission, Ac 13:1–3. It is to Antioch that Paul returns after his first missionary journeys, either with Barnabas, Ac 14:26; 15:35, or alone, Ac 18:22. Between the Church at Jerusalem with its "Jewish" majority and the Church of Antioch, in which most are "pagans," there are frequent exchanges as is shown by the visit of Agabus, Ac 11:27, the discussion of problems raised by certain points in the Mosaic Law, Ac 15:22–35, and the visit of Peter to Antioch, where Paul "opposes him to his face," Ga 2:11–14.

Native place of: NICOLAUS.
Port of Antioch: SELEUCIA.
Near Antioch: DAPHNE.

2. **Antioch** (4) **in Pisidia** (2), principal city of the province of Pisidia in Asia Minor. Paul and Barnabas visit this city

during the first missionary journey, Ac 13:13–14, and preach there on several successive sabbaths, Ac 13:15–44. Faced with the hostility of the Jews who influence ladies of high society and leading men of the city, Paul and Barnabas shake the dust from their feet and leave for Iconium, Ac 13:45–51. They reach Lystra, where Jews from Antioch and Iconium pursue them in a hostile spirit, Ac 14:19, then Derbe, from which they return to Antioch, there to strengthen the spirits of the disciples, Ac 14:21–22. In 2 Tm 3:11, Paul mentions "the persecutions and hardships that came to me in places like Antioch."

See: GALATIA 1.

ANTIOCHIS (1), (cf. Antiochus), a concubine of Antiochus Epiphanes, to whom he gives the towns of Tarsus and Mallus in Cilicia as a present, 2 M 4:30.

ANTIOCHISTS in or **from Jerusalem** (2), 2 M 4:9, 19. See: ANTIOCH 1.

ANTIOCHUS, Gr. *Antiochos* (cf. Antioch; Antiochis). Antiochus I–Antiochus VI belong to the dynasty of the: SELEUCIDS.

1. **[Antiochus II Theos],** king of Syria (261–246).

= **King of the North** (1). Dn 11:6 alludes to his marriage to a second wife, Berenice, daughter of Ptolemy II, "the daughter of the king of the South," and to his death as well as to the death of Berenice and their child, all three poisoned by Laodice, first wife of Antiochus II. Father of: SELEUCUS 2.

2. **Antiochus III** (2), **the Great** (1), son of Seleucus II, called king of Asia, that is, king of Syria (223–187). He is conquered by the consul Lucius Cornelius Scipio at Magnesia on the Sipylus in 189 and is forced by the treaty of Apamea to pay an enormous tribute, 1 M 8:6–8.

= **King of the North** (3). Dn 11:10–19 refers to several incidents of his life: a first campaign against Egypt, in which he conquers Palestine, v. 10; his defeat by Ptolemy IV at Raphia (217), vv. 11–12; his counteroffensive and capture of Sidon after the battle of Paneion, v. 16; the marriage of his daughter Cleopatra, whom he gives to Ptolemy V in the hope of annexing Egypt, a hope that is disappointed because Cleopatra then defends the interests of Egypt, v. 17; his attacks on the cities of Asia Minor that are dependents of Egypt; and finally the Roman intervention and his crushing defeat at Magnesia on the Sipylus by Lucius Cornelius Scipio, "the magistrate," v. 18. Antiochus dies during the looting of a temple of Bel at Elymais, v. 19. See: List, page 466.

Father of: ANTIOCHUS 3; SELEUCUS 4.

3. **Antiochus IV** (25) **Epiphanes** (5), **son of Antiochus III** (1), king of Syria (175–164). A hostage at Rome before becoming king, this "sinful offshoot," 1 M 1:10; cf. 1 M 2:48, 62; 2 M 10:10, leads several campaigns against Egypt, 1 M 1:16–20; 2 M 5:11, loots the temple at Jerusalem, 1 M 1:21–24//2 M 5:15–21, imposes hellenization on Israel, 1 M 1:41–63//2 M 6:1–11, and before visiting Persia "in order to accumulate substantial funds," orders Lysias to "destroy the power of Israel and the remnant of Jerusalem," 1 M 3:27–37; cf. 2 M 2:20. He dies in Persia, acknowledging that the wrongs inflicted on Jerusalem were the cause of his wretched end, 1 M 6:1–17//2 M 1:13–16; 9:1–20; 10:9; cf. 11:23. In 2 M several further items of information are added: Antiochus is acclaimed at Jerusalem, 4:21–22; on his return from Cilicia, where he had gone to put down a rebellion, "he wept" on learning of the hateful crime committed against the high priest Onias, and punishes Andronicus, the murderer, 4:30–31, 36–38; yet he also tortures to death seven brothers and their mother, 2 M 7; finally, he is the author of one of four letters about the peace treaty with the Jews, 11:27–33.

In Dn numerous references are made to Antiochus and his history. The prophet symbolizes him as the "little horn," 7:8, with an arrogant mouth, cf. 7:25; 11:36; 1 M 1:24; 2 M 5:17. Chs. 5–17 describe his expansionist policy in regard to Egypt and Judaea, the profanation of the temple, the abolition of Jewish worship, and the dedication of the temple to Olympian Zeus, whereas 9:26–27 predicts the condemnation and death of Antiochus. In Dn 11, still in an allusory manner, the stages of Antiochus' life are given in greater detail, especially his persecution of the Jews, vv. 21–39, and his end, vv. 40–45.

His sons: ALEXANDER 2 ?; ANTIOCHUS 4.

His concubine: ANTIOCHIS.

4. **Antiochus V** (13) **Eupator** (5), **son of Antiochus [Epiphanes]** (1), king of Syria (164–161). As a child, he is put by his father in the care of Lysias, 1 M 3:13, then in that of Philip, 1 M 6:14–15, 55; cf. 2 M 9:25. At his father's death he succeeds to the throne and receives the name Eupator, 1 M 6:16–17; cf. 2 M 2:20; 10:10, 13. After a campaign against Judah, 1 M 6:28–54//2 M 13:1–2, 9–10, he grants the Jews religious freedom, 1 M 6:55–63//2 M 11:22–26; 13:20–26. He is the author of one of the four letters on the peace treaty with the Jews, 2 M 11:22–26. He orders the execution of the criminal high priest Menelaus, 2 M 13:3–4. He is slain at the same time as Lysias, and Demetrius I succeeds him, 1 M 7:2–4//2 M 13:2.

5. **Antiochus VI [Dionysos]** (5), **son of Alexander [Balas]** (1), king of Syria (145–142). While still a child he reigns under the protectorate of one of his generals [Diodotus] Trypho, 1 M 11:39–40, 54–55, confirms Jonathan as high priest, names him governor of Coele-Syria, and makes Simon military commander of the coastal zone, 11:57–59. He is treacherously killed by the ambitious Trypho, 12:39–40; 13:31–32.

6. **Antiochus VII [Sidetes]** (6), **son of Demetrius I** (1), king of Syria (138–129). He writes Simon Maccabaeus a letter in which he confirms the latter's titles, 1 M 15:1–9; he besieges Trypho in Dor, vv. 10–14; then, during the siege, he refuses military help from Simon, turns hostile to the latter, and threatens him, vv. 25–36.

7. **Antiochus** (1), father of: NUMENIUS.

ANTIPAS, abbrev. of *Antipatros* (cf. Antipater).

1. **[Antipas].** See: HEROD 2.

2. **Antipas** (1), a Christian martyr of Pergamum, a center of emperor worship; he must choose between the Lord Jesus and the Roman emperor, Rv 2:13.

ANTIPATER, Gr. *Antipatros,* "In the place of the father" (cf. Antipas; Antipatris; Cleopatra; Cleopas; Eupator; Patrobas; Patroclus).

1. **Antipater son of Jason** (2) is, with Numenius son of Antiochus, a Jewish ambassador to Sparta and Rome, 1 M 12:16–17; 14:22.

2. **[Antipater],** father of: HEROD 1.

ANTIPATRIS (1), from the name of Antipater 2, a city built by Herod the Great on the site of the ancient: APHEK 1.

[ANTONIA], a fortress built by Herod in 37 B.C. in honor of the triumvir Antony at the NW corner of the temple in Jerusalem, on the site of the ancient acropolis, 2 M 4:12, 28; 5:5; cf. Ne 2:8; 7:2. A Roman garrison is quartered there, cf. Ac 21:34–40; 22:24; 23:10, 16, 32.

ANUB (1), son of Koz, of the Calebite clan, 1 Ch 4:8. In Judah.

APELLES (1), Gr. *Apellēs,* a Roman Christian "who has gone through so much for Christ" and whom Paul greets, Rm 16:10.

APHAIREMA (1). See: EPHRAIM 4.

APHEK, Aphekah.

1. **Aphek** (3), a town in the coastal plain whose king is conquered by Joshua, Jos 12:18; an encampment of the Philistines, 1 S 4:1; 29:1.

= **Antipatris** (1), where Paul is taken by night when being transferred from Jerusalem to Caesarea, Ac 23:31.

2. **Aphek** (3), a town east of the Sea of Chinnereth. Ben-Hadad II, king of Aram, is defeated there by Ahab, king of Israel, 1 K 20:26–30. The prophet Elisha tells Joash, king of Israel, that he will defeat the Aramaeans there, 2 K 13:17. Today *Fiq*.

3. **Aphek** (1), a town in Asher, Jos 19:30.

= **Aphik** (1), a Phoenician town that remained independent, Jg 1:31. Probably *Tell Kurdane* near Akko.

4. **Aphekah** (1), a town in the highlands of Judah, Jos 15:53.

5. **Aphekah** (1), in Phoenicia, in the territory of Sidon, Jos 13:4. Perhaps *Afka,* NE of Beirut.

APHEKAH. See: APHEK 4–5.

APHIAH (1), 1 S 9:1, a Benjaminite, ancestor of: KISH 1.

APHIK (1). See: APHEK 3.

[APIRU]. See: HEBREW 1.

APIS (1), Gr. name of the Egypt. *Hapi,* the sacred bull, an incarnation of the god Ptah, tutelary deity of Memphis. In his lifetime he was raised near the temple of Ptah; at his death he was entombed in the Serapeum and became an *Osiris-Apis* or *Osar-Api,* Jr 46:15 (acc. to Gr.); in the same verse the Strong One (or *Bull* acc. to some translations) likewise designates Apis).

[APOLLO], (cf. Apollonia; Apollonius; Apollophanes; Apollos), a Greek god with many attributes. See: ABADDON (Rv 9:11); DAPHNE.

APOLLONIA (1), (cf. Apollo), a city in Macedonia, halfway between Amphipolis and Thessalonika, through which Paul passes on his second missionary journey, Ac 17:1.

APOLLONIUS, Gr. *Apollonios* (cf. Apollo).

1. **Apollonius** (4), **son of Menestheus** (2), **of Tarsus** (1), **military commissioner for Coele-Syria and Phoenicia** (2), 2 M 3:5; 4:4, from 175 to 164 B.C., Simon, administrator of the temple, tells him that the temple treasury is swollen with wealth. Apollonius tells King Seleucus IV, who sends Heliodorus to seize it, 2 M 3:6–8. The high priest Onias is disturbed at the evil influence of Apollonius over Simon and goes to the king, 2 M 4:4–6. Apollonius is the Syrian delegate at the wedding of Ptolemy VI Philometor, 2 M 4:21.

Father of: APOLLONIUS 4.

2. **Apollonius** (3), **the mysarch** [= commander of mercenaries from Mysia] (2), is sent on an expedition against Jerusalem, which "he deals a terrible blow," 1 M 1:29–32; 2 M 5:24–26. During a second expedition against Israel, he is defeated and killed by Judas, who takes his sword, 1 M 3:10–12.

3. **Apollonius son of Gennaeus** (1), one of the five military commissioners of Syria who "would not allow the Jews to live in peace and quiet," 2 M 12:2.

4. **Apollonius** (5), son of Apollonius 1, **governor of Coele-Syria** (1), a general of Demetrius II, provokes Jonathan to battle but is defeated, 1 M 10:69–85.

APOLLOPHANES (1), "Manifestation of Apollo" (cf. Apollo; Epiphanes), is slain along with Timotheus and Chaereas by the soldiers of Judas Maccabaeus when they take Gezer, 2 M 10:37.

APOLLOS (10), abbrev. of *Apollonios,* a Jew from Alexandria, "an eloquent man, with a sound knowledge of the scriptures . . . he had been given instruction in the Way of the Lord and . . . was accurate in all the details he taught about Jesus," Ac 18:24–25. At Ephesus, Priscilla and Aquila "gave him further instruction about the Way," 18:26, before his departure for Corinth, 18:27–28; 19:1. The influence of Apollos is such that it causes some to become infatuated with his views and gives rise in the Church of Corinth to cliques, against which Paul inveighs, 1 Co 1:11–12; 3:4–6, 22; 4:6; cf. 16:12. Along with Zenas the lawyer he is perhaps commissioned to bring Titus the letter that Paul addresses to him, Tt 3:13.

APOLLYON (1), "Destroyer," Rv 9:11. See: ABADDON.

APPHIA (1), a Christian woman in the community of Colossae, perhaps the wife of Philemon and mother of Archippus, Phm 2.

APPHUS (1), "The Favorite *or* The Crafty"?, 1 M 2:5, a surname of: JONATHAN 16.

APPIUS. See: FORUM OF APPIUS.

[APRIES]. See: HOPHRA.

AQUILA (6), a native of Pontus, and Prisca or Priscilla, a Jewish Christian couple. Paul meets them at Corinth when they arrive from Rome, whence they have been driven by an edict of Claudius against the Jews; Paul and they become friends and work together at making tents, Ac 18:2–3. A Christian community gathers in their home, Rm 16:5; 1 Co 16:19. Paul calls them his fellow workers; he owes them a great deal, as do the churches among the pagans, Rm 16:3–4. When he leaves Corinth at the end of his second journey, Priscilla and Aquila accompany him as far as Ephesus, Ac 18:18–29. There they complete the Christian formation of Apollos, Ac 18:26. At the end of his life Paul bids Timothy give his greetings to Prisca and Aquila, 2 Tm 4:19.

AR (4), Hb. *'Ar,* a fortified town in Moab, which controls the valleys of the Arnon, Nb 21:15. Ar even stands for the land of Moab, Dt 2:9, 18, 29.

= **Ar of Moab** (3), destroyed several times, Nb 21:28; Is 15:1. In Nb 22:36 *Ar of Moab* is a corr. for Hb. *city of Moab.*

ARA (1), an Asherite, one of the three sons of Ithran, a stout fighting man and head of a family, 1 Ch 7:38.

ARAB

1. **Arab** (2), a town in the highlands of Judah, Jos 15:52. 12 km SE of Hebron. Native place of: PAARAI.

2. **Arab.** See: ARAB(S), ARABIA.

ARABAH (25), Hb. *'Arabah,* "Steppe" (cf. Abraham; Beth-Arabah), a depression in which are located the Sea of Chinnereth, the Jordan, and the Dead Sea and which extends to the Gulf of Aqaba. Now *al-Ghor.*

a. **The Arabah** (19), (in one or other of its parts, to the exclusion of the Sea of the Arabah).

During the Exodus the Israelites travel "by the Arabah and Elath and Ezion-geber road," Dt 2:8. The Arabah, which Israel occupies, constitutes a part of the Promised Land, Dt 1:1, 7; 4:49; Jos 11:2, 16; 12:1, 8; cf. Jos 8:14. It had previously been the domain of the Canaanites, Dt 11:30, or of Sihon, Jos 12:3. The Arabah is the frontier between the tribes on either side of the Jordan, Dt 3:17, whereas the border of Benjamin reaches to the Arabah, Jos 18:18. When one crosses the Jordan, one is passing through the Arabah, 2 S 2:29 (Abner); 4:7 (Rechab and his brother); 2 K 25:4//Jr 39:4//52:7 (Zedekiah).

Part of the Arabah between the southern end of the Dead Sea and the Gulf of Aqaba: SALT 2.

b. **Sea of the Arabah** (5). See: DEAD SEA.

c. **The wadi of the Arabah** (1), Am 6:14, must empty into the Jordan, not far from the Dead Sea, and mark the southern border of the northern kingdom.

ARABIA. See: ARAB(S), ARABIA.

ARAB(S) (16), **ARABIA** (9), Hb. *'Arab,*

"Man of the Steppe" (cf. Arabah), a collection of nomad clans in the Syro-Arabian wilderness, later a kingdom SE of Israel and in particular the kingdom of the *Nabataeans.* The earliest mention of this people is perhaps in Jr 3:2, where the prophet compares Israel to a prostitute who "waited by the roadside for clients like an Arab in the desert."

The Arabs pay tribute of gold and silver to Solomon, 2 Ch 9:14//1 K 10:15 (corr. of Hb.), of rams and he-goats to Jehoshaphat, 2 Ch 17:11; they engage in trade with Tyre, Ezk 27:21. In the time of Jehoram they attack Judah, 2 Ch 21:16–17, and take part in the murder of the king's elder sons, 2 Ch 22:1. Uzziah resists them, 2 Ch 26:7. The prophets utter threatening oracles against them, Is 13:20; 21:13–17; Jr 25:23–24; 49:28–33. At the return from the exile the Arabs are among those most eager to prevent the Jews from rebuilding, Ne 4:1. In the time of the Maccabees Timotheus enlists Arabs as auxiliaries in his army, 1 M 5:39. Alexander Balas takes refuge in Arabia but has his head cut off by Zabdiel the Arab, 1 M 11:16–17. Jonathan defeats Arabs called *Zabadaeans,* 1 M 12:31–32. Arabia is mentioned as part of the route of Holofernes' army, Jdt 2:25–26.

Arabia: NABATAEANS.

Arabs: GESHEM; IAMLEKU; ZABDIEL.

See also: CROP-HEADS; CUSH 1; EAST 1; HAZOR 5; ISHMAEL 1; KEDAR; KETURAH.

ARAD, "Wild Ass."

1. **Arad** (4), a Canaanite town in the Negeb whose king is defeated by Israel, Nb 21:1; 33:40; Jos 12:14, becomes a town of Judah. The Kenites, who are related to Moses, dwell in the **Negeb of Judah at the Ascent of Arad,** Jg 1:16. Today *Tell Arad,* about 30 km S of Hebron.

2. **Arad** (1), a Benjaminite of the sons of Beriah, head of a family at Jerusalem, 1 Ch 8:15.

ARADUS (1). See: ARVAD.

ARAH

1. **Arah** (1), an Asherite, one of the three sons of Ulla, a fighting man and head of a family, 1 Ch 7:39.

2. **Arah** (2), an Israelite, head of a family whose sons return from the exile with Zerubbabel, Ezr 2:5//Ne 7:10. Father of: SHECANIAH 7.

3. **Arah** (conjecture for Hb. *Me'arah,* "cave"), **which the Sidonians hold,** Jos 13:4. Unknown.

ARAM

1. **Aram, Aramaean** (144), Hb. *'Aram,* Gr. *Syria, Syros,* designates peoples living in northern Palestine.

a. The *Aramaeans* are connected with Shem through an eponymous ancestor *Aram,* either directly, Gn 10:22/1 Ch 1:17, or through Kemuel, one of the twelve sons of Nahor, who is a descendant of Shem, Gn 22:20–24; cf. Gn 11:10–24. Aram has as sons Uz, Hul, Gether, and Mash (or Meshech), Gn 10:23//1 Ch 1:17. The Aramaeans are said to be originally from Kir, Am 9:7; cf. Am 1:5, which is perhaps identical with Ur in Lower Mesopotamia. Their language is called *Aramaic* in 2 K 18:26//Is 36:11; Ezk 4:7; Dn 2:4, *Syriac* in 2 M 15:36 (Gr.), and *Hebrew* in the NT. The Aramaeans appear in almost constant conflict with Israel: even back in the time of the Conquest, when Aram and Geshur take the Encampments of Jair, 1 Ch 2:23, from the sons of Machir, who had been born of an Aramaean concubine of Manasseh, 1 Ch 7:14; and later under David, 2 S 10:15–18//1 Ch 19:16–19; cf. 2 S 8:12, and at the time of the destruction of Jerusalem, 2 K 24:2; Jr 35:11.

The Israelites serve the gods of Aram, Jg 10:6, as does King Ahaz later on, 2 Ch 28:23. Corrections of *Aram* to *Edom* are sometimes proposed, Jg 3:8, 10; 2 S 8:13; 1 K 11:25; 2 Ch 20:2; Ez 16:57; 27:16.

Cities: ARPAD; HAMATH 1.

b. Small Aramaean kingdoms around Damascus: BETH-REHOB; GESHUR; MAACAH 1; TOB; ZOBAH.

c. Aramaean kingdom of: DAMASCUS.

d. **Aram Naharaiim, Paddan-aram,** and **Aram beyond the river.** See: MESOPOTAMIA.

e. **Syria** (15), **Syrian** (1), Gr. *Syria,* abbrev. of *Assyria,* Gr. name for *Aram,* refers in 1 M to the main part of the Greek Empire of the Seleucids, who are hostile to the Jews, 1 M 7:39; 10:67; 11:2, 60; Antioch is its capital. Acc. to Jdt 1:12, Nebuchadnezzar swears "to take revenge on all the territories of Cilicia, Damascene and Syria . . . and to ravage them with the sword."

In the NT the name refers to the Roman province of Syria. Churches were established very early at Damascus, Ac 9, and at Antioch, Ac 11:19–20. The Apostles send them a letter, Ac 15:23, and Paul visits them several times, Ac 15:41; 18:18; 20:13; 21:3; Ga 1:21. In Mt 4:24 *Syria* means for practical purposes Galilee and its environs, cf. Mk 1:28.

Another name: NORTH 1.

Kings: SELEUCIDS.

Governor: QUIRINIUS.

General: SERON.

Syrian or Aramaean: NAAMAN 3.

Capital: ANTIOCH 1.

f. **Coele-Syria** (1), originally the valley of the Bekaa, between Lebanon and the Anti-Lebanon, later Palestine and Phoenicia.

Military commander: APOLLONIUS 4.

Frontier: ELEUTHERUS.

Coele-Syria and Phoenicia (5), the region Heliodorus sets out to inspect, 2 M 3:8.

Military commanders: APOLLONIUS 1; LYSIAS 1; PTOLEMY 9.

g. **Syrophoenician** (1), from Syrophoenicia, a district belonging to the Roman province of Syria; native place of the woman whose daughter Jesus cures, Mk 7:26//Mt 15:22 (*Canaanite*).

2. **Aram** (1), an Asherite, third son of Shomer, a fighting man and head of a family, 1 Ch 7:34.

ARAMAEANS. See: ARAM 1.

ARAM NAHARAIIM (5), "Aram of the Two Rivers [Tigris and Euphrates]." See: MESOPOTAMIA.

ARAN (2), second son of Dishan, who was seventh son of Seir, Gn 36:28//1 Ch 1:42 (Hb. *son of Dishon*).

ARARAT (5), Accad. *Urartu,* is a name for Armenia, Jr 51:27, where the two sons of Sennacherib flee after murdering their father, 2 K 19:37//Is 37:38; cf. Tb 1:21. Ararat is also the mountain where Noah's ark lands, Gn 8:4.

ARAUNAH (9), in 2 S 24 = **Ornan** (12), in 1 and 2 Ch, **the Jebusite** (6), a person of Hittite or Hurrite origin, owns a threshing floor at Jerusalem, which David buys in order to build an altar on it. Araunah provides the oxen and wood for the sacrifice, but David pays for them, 2 S 24:16–25//1 Ch 21:15–26. David offers a sacrifice there, 1 Ch 21:28. Solomon later builds the temple on this spot, 2 Ch 3:1. Acc. to 1 Ch 21:20, Ornan has four sons. The Hb. text of 2 S 24:23 perhaps reflects a tradition in which Araunah is a Jebusite king.

ARBA. See: ANAK; KIRIATH-ARBA.

ARBATTA (1), probably the *Narbatene* of Josephus, between Galilee and Samaria. Simon Maccabaeus evacuates the Jewish women and children from it, 1 M 5:23.

ARBELA (1), today *Kh. Irbid,* NW of Tiberias; in its territory is Mesaloth, which is besieged and captured by Alcimus and Bacchides, 1 M 9:2.

ARCHELAUS (1), "Leader of the people" (cf. Archippus; Aristarchus), son of Herod the Great and Malthake, brother of Herod Antipas, ethnarch of Judaea, Samaria, and Idumaea (4 B.C.–6 A.D.). When JOSEPH "learnt that Archelaus had succeeded Herod as ruler of Judaea," he goes and settles at Nazareth, Mt 2:22. Archelaus was exiled to Vienne in Gaul.

ARCHIPPUS (2), "Leader of cavalry"? (cf. Archelaus; Philip), a Christian in the community of Colossae, Col 4:17, and perhaps the son of Philemon and Apphia, Phm 2.

ARCHITE (6), a clan, probably Canaanite, settled SW of Bethel, Jos 16:2. Archites: HUSHAI 1; ATAROTH-ADDER.

ARD (2), "Hunchback" (cf. Ardon), son of Benjamin, Gn 46:21, or son of Bela son of Benjamin, Nb 26:40. The descendants of Ard form the **Ardite** clan, Nb 26:40.

= ? **Addar** (1), 1 Ch 8:3.

ARDITE (1), belonging to the clan of: ARD.

ARDON (1), (cf. Ard), son of Caleb and his wife Azubah, 1 Ch 2:18.

AREIOS (1), (cf. Areopagus), king of the Spartans (1), (309–265), sends a letter to the high priest Onias in which he says that the Jews and Spartans are "brothers, and of the race of Abraham," 1 M 12:20; cf. 12:7 (corr. of Gr. *Dareios*).

ARELI (2), last of the seven sons of Gad, Gn 46:16, gives his name to the **Arelite** clan, Nb 26:17.

ARELITE (1), belonging to the clan of: ARELI.

AREOPAGITE (1), member of the Areopagus. See: DIONYSUS 2.

AREOPAGUS (2), Gr. *Areios pagos,* "Hill of Ares" (cf. Areios; Areopagite; Ares), west of the Acropolis at Athens. Originally, the city council met there, but in Paul's time it meets near the Agora. It is difficult to decide whether it is on the hill or before the council, Ac 17:19, 22, that Paul speaks of the unknown god and the resurrection, Ac 17:22–31.

[ARES], (cf. Areopagus), Greek god of war, identified with Mars by the Romans.

ARETAS, Arab. *Harita,* "Metal worker."

1. **Aretas I** (1), a Nabataean king, imprisons the usurping high priest Jason at Petra, but the latter manages to escape, 2 M 5:8 (where Aretas is called "the Arab despot").

2. **Aretas IV** (1), a Nabataean king whose ethnarch at Damascus cannot prevent Paul's escape, 2 Co 11:32. See: HEROD 2.

ARGOB (4), a region of Bashan, east of the Sea of Chinnereth. The confederation of Argob includes many towns of which the eastern half-tribe of Manasseh takes possession, Dt 3:4, 13. Later, Jair, son of Manasseh, seizes the confederation of Argob and gives it his own name, "The Encampments of Jair," Dt 3:14. Under Solomon the territory of Argob is part of the sixth district, 1 K 4:13.

ARIARATHES V (1), king of Cappadocia (162–131), a friend of the Romans, one of those to whom the letter promulgating the alliance between the Jews and Romans is sent, 1 M 15:22.

ARIDAI (1), a Pers. name, brother of: PARSHANDATHA.

ARIDATHA (1), a Pers. name, brother of: PARSHANDATHA.

ARIEL, Hb. *'Ari'el,* "Lion of God *or* Hearth of God."

1. **Ariel** (1), one of the messengers Ezra sends to Iddo, Ezr 8:16.

2. **Ariel** (6), a symbolic name given to Jerusalem, Is 29:1–2, 7; 33:7 (corr.). Perhaps to be connected with Ezk 43:15–16, Hb. *har'el* or *'ari'êl,* "hearth of the altar," on which the victims of sacrifice were burned; then Ariel would express the sacred character of Jerusalem.

ARIMATHAEA (2). See: RAMAH 2.

ARIOCH

1. **Arioch, king of Ellasar** (2), ally of: AMRAPHEL.

2. **Arioch, king of the Elymaeans** (1), fights alongside Nebuchadnezzar acc. to Jdt 1:6.

3. **Arioch** (5), head of King Nebuchadnezzar's executioners. When ordered to execute the Babylonian sages because of their inability to interpret the king's dreams, he brings Daniel to the king, and Daniel explains the dream, Dn 2:14–15, 24–25.

ARISAI (1), a brother of: PARSHANDATHA.

ARISTARCHUS (5), "Sovereign master" (cf. Archelaus; Aristobulus), **a Macedonian** (2) **from Thessalonika** (1), traveling companion of Paul, Ac 19:29 (at Ephesus during the riot of the silversmiths); 20:4 (from Greece to Syria); 27:2 (from Caesarea to Rome), and his companion in prison, Ac 27:2; Col 4:10; Phm 24, where Paul speaks of him as a colleague.

ARISTOBULUS, "Of excellent counsel" (cf. Aristarchus; Eubulus).

1. **Aristobulus** (1), a Jewish scholar of Alexandria, "tutor to King Ptolemy and one of the family of the anointed priests," 2 M 1:10.

2. **Aristobulus** (1), a Roman (Jew?) who had had slaves or freedmen who became Christians, Rm 16:10.

ARKITE (2), a tribe of the Phoenician coast, connected with Canaan, Gn 10: 17//1 Ch 1:15.

ARMAGEDDON (1), "Mountains of Megiddo" (cf. Megiddo), place where the kings of earth will gather for the Great Day, Rv 16:16. A symbol of disaster since the defeat of Josiah, cf. 2 K 23:29.

[ARMENIA]. See: ARARAT; TOGARMAH.

ARMONI (1), one of the two sons of Saul and Rizpah whom David hands over to the Gibeonites to be tortured, 2 S 21:8.

ARMOURY (Slope up to the) (1), Hb. *Nesheq,* "Weapons," probably [*House of*] *Weapons,* in Jerusalem, south of the royal palace, Ne 3:19.

ARNAN (1), a descendant of King Jehoiachin via Zerubbabel and Hananiah, 1 Ch 3:21.

ARNI (1), a descendant of Perez, an ancestor of David and Jesus, Lk 3:33. Cf. Mt 1:3; Rt 4:19; 1 Ch 2:9–10.

ARNON (25), "[The river] bordered by laurels *or* pines," see Is 44:14 (cf. Oren), a river on the eastern side of the Dead Sea, it is usually mentioned as being the (theoretical) eastern boundary of Moab, Nb 21:13–14; 22:36; Jg 11:18; cf. Is 16:2; Jr 48:19, and the southern boundary of the Transjordanian tribes of Israel, Nb 21:24; 26:28; Dt 2:24; 3:8; 16; Jos 12:1; Jg 11:22, 26. It is described as the southern boundary of Ammon in Jg 11:13. Today *Wadi Mujib.*

On the Arnon: AROER 1.

AR OF MOAB (3). See: AR.

AROD (1), Nb 26:17, or **Arodi** (1), Gn 46:16, sixth of the seven sons of Gad, gives his name to the **Arodite** clan, Nb 26:17.

ARODI (1). See: AROD.

ARODITE (1), belonging to the clan of: AROD.

AROER

1. **Aroer** (12), **on the edge of the wadi Arnon** (7), a town in Gad, Nb 32:34, or in Reuben, Jos 13:16; 1 Ch 5:8, and finally in Moab, Jr 48:20; cf. Is 16:2. Like the Arnon it is usually mentioned as marking the frontier of the realm of Sihon, king of the Amorites, Dt 2:36; 3:12; 4:48; Jos 12:2; 13:9, 16, which is conquered by Israel, Jg 11:26, or of the territory inspected by Joab during the census, 2 S 24:5, or of the land taken

from Israel by Hazael, king of Aram, 2 K 10:33. Today *Kh. ʿAraʿir.*

2. **Aroer** (3), a town in Gad, facing Rabbah of the Ammonites, Jos 13:25. Jephthah "harassed them [the Ammonites] from Aroer almost to Minnith," Jg 11:33.

Native place of: HOTHAM.

3. **Aroer** (2), a town in the Negeb of Judah, Jos 15:22 (Hb. *ʿAdʿadah*). David sends a share of the booty to the elders of Aroer, 1 S 30:28.

AROERITE (1), 1 Ch 11:44, a man from: AROER 2.

ARPACHSHAD, Arphaxad, Gr. *Arphaxad.*

1. **Arpachshad** (9), son of Shem and father of Shelah, Gn 10:22, 24//1 Ch 1:17, 18; Gn 11:10–13//1 Ch 1:24.

= **Arphaxad** (1), an ancestor of Jesus, Lk 3:36. Probably the Hurrites of *Arrapah,* east of the Tigris. In the region of Kirkuk.

2. **Arphaxad (5), king of the Medes at Ecbatana** (1), unknown to historians. His name suggests that of Phraortes (675–653), founder of the kingdom of Media. Jdt 1:1–5, 13–15, describe him as having been crushed by Nebuchadnezzar.

ARPAD (6), Accad. *Arpadda,* a city of Syria, 30 km N of Aleppo. It was destroyed at the same time as Hamath by Sennacherib, king of Assyria, 2 K 18:34//Is 36:19; 2 K 19:13//Is 37:13; cf. Is 10:9, and a century later it fell into a panic, as did Hamath, at the threat from Babylonia, Jr 49:23. Today *Tell Erfad.*

ARPHAXAD. See: ARPACHSHAD.

ARSACES (3), **king of Persia and Media** (2). This is Mithradates I, whose dynastic name was Arsaces VI (171–138), founder of the Parthian Empire. He captures Demetrius II, who had invaded his territory, 1 M 14:2–3. He is one of the addressees of the letter promulgating the Jewish-Roman alliance, 1 M 15:22.

[ARTA]. See: ARTAXERXES.

ARTAXERXES, Hb. *'Artahshast(a),* Gr. *Arthasastha* (Ezr; Ne) or *Artaxerxes* (Est), Iran. *Artahshasa,* "He who has a kingdom of justice *or* He who has *Arta* [the personified world order] for his kingdom."

1. **Artaxerxes** (15), **king of Persia** (4) or **of the Persians** (1) (465–423). This is Artaxerxes I Longimanus, successor of Xerxes, in whose reign the activity of Ezra and Nehemiah is generally situated.

In the time of Artaxerxes the Persian officials in Samaria write to the king to delate the Jews, who are rebuilding Jerusalem, Ezr 4:7–23. Acc. to Ezr 6:14 the elders of the Jews complete the rebuilding of the temple "in accordance with the order . . . of Cyrus and of Darius and [in the Hb. text] of Artaxerxes, king of Persia," but the mention of the last-named is an anachronism. Acc. to Ezr 7:1–29; 8:1, Ezra goes up to Jerusalem with a group of family heads in the seventh year of King Artaxerxes, with a document given him by "the king of kings," 7:12, authorizing him to inspect Judah and bring to Jerusalem the silver and gold offered by the Persian court. For his part, Nehemiah, cupbearer to the king, Ne 1:11, is authorized by the king to go the land of Judah, Ne 2:1–9, of which he has been appointed governor, from the twentieth to the thirty-second year of King Artaxerxes, 5:14, who is called king of Babylon, Ne 13:6. The apocryphal Memoirs of Nehemiah, 2 M 2:13, tell how Nehemiah, sent by the king of Persia, discovers the sacred fire from the ancient sanctuary, 2 M 1:18–26.

2. **Artaxerxes.** See: XERXES.

See: ACHAEMENIDS.

ARTEMAS (1), probably an abbrev. of *Artemidōros,* "Gift of Artemis" (cf. Dositheus), perhaps a delegate of Paul in Crete, Tt 3:12. Otherwise unknown.

[ARTEMIS]. See: DIANA.

ARUBBOTH (1), "Windows *or* Sluicegates"?, in the third district of Solomon, on the border between Samaria and Carmel, 1 K 4:10.

ARUMAH (1), a town SE of Shechem where Abimelech resides after the defeat of Gaal, Jg 9:41.

= **Rumah** (1), native town of Zebidah, mother of King Jehoiakim, 2 K 23:36. Today *Kh. el-'Ormah.*

ARVAD (2), Gr. *Aradios, Arados,* an island north of Tripolis, 3 km from the mainland. Today *Ruwad.* Its inhabitants, the Arvadites, are of Canaanite origin, Gn 10:18//1 Ch 1:16. Arvad furnishes Tyre with oarsmen and soldiers, Ezk 27:8, 11.

= **Aradus** (1), to which the letter of the consul Lucius promulgating the alliance of Jews and Romans is sent, 1 M 15:23.

ARVADITES (2), inhabitants of: ARVAD.

ARZA (1), master of the palace at Tirzah. It is in his house that King Elah of Israel is assassinated while drunk, 1 K 16:9.

ASA, Hb. *'Asa',* "Myrtle *or* Healer"?

1. **Asa** (59), third king of Judah (911–870). Succeeding his father Abijam, 1 K 15:8//2 Ch 13:23; cf. 1 Ch 3:10, in the twentieth year of Jeroboam I of Israel, 1 K 15:9, he has a long reign of forty-one years, 15:10, which makes him the contemporary of many kings of Israel: Nadab, 1 K 15:25; Baasha, 15:28, 23; Elah, 16:8; Zimri, 16:10, 15; Omri, 16:23; cf. Ahab, 16:29.

The first ten years of his reign are peaceful, 2 Ch 13:23, but cf. 2 Ch 15:19. Attacked by Baasha, Asa uses the treasures of the temple and palace to buy the help of Ben-hadad I, king of Damascus, 1 K 15:16–20//2 Ch 16:1–4; but the prophet Hanani reproaches him because he "relied on the king of Aram and not on Yahweh," and Asa puts him in prison, 2 Ch 16:7–10. Asa takes the stone and timber with which Baasha had been fortifying Ramah and uses it to fortify Geba and Mizpah, 1 K 15:17, 22//2 Ch 16:1–6, where he builds a cistern as a precaution against Baasha, Jr 41:9. He conquers some towns of Ephraim, 2 Ch 15:8; cf. 17:2. Asa has a sizable army, 2 Ch 14:7; he crushes Zerah the Cushite who has invaded Judah, 2 Ch 14:8–14. "Asa did what is right in the eyes of Yahweh," 1 K 15:11, 14//2 Ch 14:1; 15:17; cf. 1 K 22:43//2 Ch 30:32; 21:12. He drives the sacred prostitutes from the country, 1 K 15:12 (but not all of them, 1 K 22:47); he abolishes the high places, 2 Ch 14:2–4 (but 1 K 15:14//2 Ch 15:17 says that they "were not abolished") and the idols, even that of his grandmother, 1 K 15:13//2 Ch 15:16. Acc. to 2 Ch 15:1–15 it is at the urging of the prophet Azariah that Asa undertakes this religious reform that also entails a solemn sacrifice and renewal of the covenant. In old age he suffers from a disease of the feet, 1 K 15:23//2 Ch 16:12, which the chronicler perhaps regards as a punishment for his treatment of Hanani and for "treating part of the population harshly too," 2 Ch 16:10. The chronicler adds that "he turned in his sickness, not to Yahweh, but to doctors," 2 Ch 16:12. When he dies, 1 K 15:24, they light a huge fire for him, 2 Ch 16:13–14.

Asa (var.; Gr. *Asaph*) is listed among the ancestors of Jesus, Mt 1:7–8.

His grandmother: MAACAH 9.

His son and successor: JOSHAPHAT 6.

2. **Asa** (1), father of the Levite: BERECHIAH 6.

ASAHEL, Hb. *'Asah'el,* "God makes" (cf. Amasai; Asaiah; Asiel; Elasah; Jaasau; Jaasiel; Maaseiah).

1. **Asahel** (15), **brother of Joab** (3) and Abishai. The second of the three sons of Zeruiah, 2 S 2:18; 1 Ch 2:16. As a member of the elite corps of the Thirty, 2 S 23:24//1 Ch 11:26 he is linked especially to the battle of Gibeon. "As swift-footed as a wild gazelle," he goes in pursuit of Abner, Saul's commander-in-chief. Because Asahel refuses to break off the pursuit, Abner strikes him in the belly, 2 S

2:18–23, 30–32. Asahel will be avenged by his two brothers Joab and Abishai, who will assassinate Abner at Hebron, 2 S 3:27–30. The chronicler makes him commissioner for (military) service for the fourth month, 1 Ch 27:7.

2. **Asahel** (1), one of the eight Levites sent by King Jehoshaphat, along with two priests and five officers, to instruct the towns of Judah in the Law, 2 Ch 17:7–9.

3. **Asahel** (1), one of the ten Levites assisting Conaniah and Shimei in the time of King Hezekiah, 2 Ch 31:12–13.

4. **Asahel** (1), father of: JONATHAN 12.

ASAIAH, "Yah has made" (cf. Asahel).

1. **Asaiah** (3), a Levite of the clan of Merari, whose genealogy is given in 1 Ch 6:14–15, an official who takes part in the transfer of the Ark of the Covenant, 1 Ch 15:6, 11.

2. **Asaiah** (1), a Simeonite, leader of a clan, 1 Ch 4:36–40.

3. **Asaiah** (1), a Judaean, a Shilonite living at Jerusalem, 1 Ch 9:5.

4. **Asaiah** (3), a minister of the king and member of the delegation led by the high priest Hilkiah and sent by Josiah to consult the prophetess Huldah after the discovery of the Book of the Law, 2 K 22:12–20//2 Ch 34:20–28.

ASAPH, Hb. *'Asaph,* "[God] adds *or* [God] gathers" (cf. Abiasaph; Joseph).

1. **Asaph** (41), **son of Berechiah** (2), is, with Heman and Jeduthun (or Ethan), one of the three eponymous ancestors of the cantors. He appears only in 1 and 2 Ch; Ezr; Ne; Ps. Acc. to 1 Ch 6:24–28 he belongs among the descendants of Gershon son of Levi. But Ezr 2:41//Ne 7:44, in telling of the return from exile of 128 (or 148) cantors, sons of Asaph, distinguishes them from the Levites, whereas Ezr 3:10 identifies them with the latter.

Asaph takes part in the ceremony of the transfer of the Ark as a singer and cymbal-player, 1 Ch 15:17, 19; cf. 2 Ch 5:12; Ezr 3:10. David places him directly "before the ark of Yahweh, to commemorate, glorify and praise Yahweh," 1 Ch 16:4–5, 7, and "to maintain a permanent ministry before the ark as each day's ritual required," 1 Ch 16:37; cf. 2 Ch 35:15. The sons of Asaph are in charge of four classes of cantors, the first, third, fifth, and seventh, 1 Ch 25:2, 9–10, 12, 14, whereas charge of the other twenty is given to the sons of Heman and Jeduthun.

As a singer and musician Asaph, like Heman and Jeduthun, plays a prophetic role, 1 Ch 25:1–2; 2 Ch 29:30. Ne 12:46 claims that "from the days of David and Asaph, there had been guilds of cantors and canticles of praise and thanksgiving to God." In the time of Hezekiah praise is sung to Yahweh "in the words of David and of Asaph the seer," 2 Ch 29:30. There may have been a Psalter of Asaph comprising, among others, Ps 50 and 73–83.

Descendants: JAHAZIEL 4; MATTANIAH 3, 4, 5; UZZI 5; ZACCUR 4; ZECHARIAH 16, 17, 26.

2. **Asaph** (4), father of the herald: JOAH 1.

3. **Asaph** (1), keeper of the royal park of Artaxerxes, from whom Nehemiah will receive the timber needed for the rebuilding, Ne 2:8.

ASARAMEL (1), transcription of Hb. *Hazar 'am-el,* "Enclosure of the people of God" (cf. Hazar-). Probably the outer court of the temple at Jerusalem. 1 M 14:27.

ASAREL (1), fourth of the sons of Jehallelel, a clan connected with Caleb, 1 Ch 4:16.

ASENATH (3), Hb. from Egypt. *Ns-Nit,* "Belonging to [the goddess] Neith," **daughter of Potiphera priest of On** (3), wife given to Joseph by Pharaoh, Gn 41:45; she bears him two sons, Manasseh and Ephraim, Gn 41:50; 46:20.

ASHAN, "Smoke."

1. **Ashan** (1), a town in the lowlands of Judah, Jos 15:42.

= **Borashan** (1), 1 S 30:30.

2. **Ashan** (2), a town in Simeon, Jos 19:7//1 Ch 4:32. To be connected with the preceding?

3. **Ashan** (1), one of the preceding?, a Levite town, 1 Ch 6:44 (//Jos 21:16: *Ayin,* which some correct to *Ashan* with the Gr.).

ASHARELAH (1), a cantor among the sons of Asaph, 1 Ch 25:2.

= **Jesharelah** (1), leader of the seventh class of cantors, 1 Ch 25:14.

ASHBEL (3), a son of Benjamin: the second, Nb 26:38; 1 Ch 8:1, or the third, Gn 46:21 (missing from 1 Ch 7:6). His descendants form the **Ashbelite** clan, Nb 26:38.

ASHBELITE (1), belonging to the clan of: ASHBEL.

ASHDOD (17), Gr. *Azōtos.* Formerly a fief of the Anakim, Jos 11:22, then a town in the Philistine Pentapolis, located in the SW of Palestine, between Gaza and Joppa. It is part of those "regions of the Philistines" that the elderly Joshua has not yet conquered, Jos 13:2–3. It is assigned to Judah, Jos 15:46–47.

After capturing the Ark, the Philistines take it to Ashdod and place it in the temple of their god, Dagon, but the residents of the town are afflicted with tumors, 1 S 5; 6:17–18. King Uzziah razes the walls of Ashdod, 2 Ch 26:6. The town is captured by Sargon II in 711, Is 20:1. The prophets utter threats against Ashdod, Am 1:8; Jr 25:20; Zp 2:4; Zc 9:6. The **Ashdodites** show hostility to the repatriates as the latter seek to rebuild the walls of Jerusalem, Ne 4:12. However, some Jews marry women from Ashdod, Ne 13:23. Their children speak the language of Ashdod and eventually forget the language of their fathers, Ne 13:24.

= **Azotus** (13). In the time of the Maccabees it is attacked by Judas, 1 M 5:68; cf. 4:15, by Jonathan, who routs Apollonius there and burns the town and the temple of Dagon, 10:77–85; 11:4, by John Hyrcanus who sets fire to the town and the neighboring countryside, 16:10. Simon establishes a Jewish settlement there, 14:34. In Jdt 2:28 the invasion of Holofernes terrifies the population of Azotus. Philip the deacon evangelizes the town and the surrounding region, Ac 8:40.

Some correct *Ashdod* to *Assyria* in Am 3:9, and Gr. *Azotos* to *Azara* in 1 M 9:15.

See: PENTAPOLIS 2; PHILISTINES.

ASHDODITE (1), Ne 4:1, of or from: ASHDOD.

ASHER (44), Gr. *Aser,* popular etymology: "What happiness! *and* Women will call me happy," see Gn 30:13.

Asher is the son of Jacob and Zilpah, Leah's servingwoman, Gn 30:12–13; 36:26. He has four sons and a daughter, Gn 46:17; 1 Ch 7:30–31, and the clans of Asher number five, Nb 26:44–47. In the lists of the Israelite tribes, Asher, eponymous ancestor of the tribe of the same name, holds one of the last five places (except in Ezk 48:2 and Rv 7:6).

The territory occupied by Asher is described in Jos 19:24–31; it is bordered on the west by the Mediterranean, Jg 5:17. It is a rich land because of Carmel, cf. Gn 49:20; Dt 33:24–25. Asher is part of Solomon's ninth district, 1 K 4:16. Some towns of Asher are assigned to the Levite sons of Gershon, Jos 21:6, 30//1 Ch 6:47, 59. The numbers of the tribe vary between 41,500, Nb 1:41, 53,400, Nb 26:47, and 26,000 men, 1 Ch 7:30–40.

Asher supports Gideon in his campaign against Midian, Jg 6:35; 7:23. Acc. to the chronicler, 40,000 men come from Asher to take part in the coronation of King David at Hebron, 1 Ch 12:37, and some to take part in King Hezekiah's Passover assembly. Asher in the lists of the tribes: List, pp. 410–11.

Native place of: AHIHUD; HANNAH 3; PAGIEL; SETHUR.

Chief city: ACCO.

ASHERAH (7), identified with the Ugar. goddess *Athirat,* spouse of the supreme god El (some question this identification). In the Bible Asherah is a Canaanite divinity of fruitfulness, often confused with Astarte and associated with Baal, Jg 3:7; 1 K 18:19; 2 K 23:4–7. The grandmother of King Asa has an idol of Asherah made, 1 K 15:13//2 Ch 15:16, and King Manasseh places one in the temple, 2 K 21:7, but Josiah burns it, 2 K 23:4. Asherah is also the name for a *sacred pole,* an emblem of the divinity and a symbol of fruitfulness, which is set up near sanctuaries, Ex 34:13; Dt 16:21; and so forth.

ASHERITE (1), Jg 1:32, belonging to the tribe of: ASHER. Some correct Ashurites in 2 S 2:9 to *Asherites.*

ASHHUR, father of Tekoa (2), is, acc. to 1 Ch 2:24, a son of Caleb and therefore belongs to Judah; acc. to 1 Ch 4:5, he is the father of several groups, vv. 6–10, likewise belonging to Judah.

ASHIMA (1), Hb. *'Ashima'*, Syrian goddess imported into Samaria by the people of Hamath, 2 K 17:30. In Am 8:4 the "sin" (Hb. *'ashmah*) of Samaria is an ironical deformation of Ashima (JB corrects to *Ashimah*), unless it is intended as a scornful reference to a sanctuary in Samaria.

ASHKELON (12), Gr. *Askalōn,* a city of the Philistine Pentapolis, Jos 13:3, located on the coast between Ashdod and Gaza.

Judah fails to take Ashkelon and its territory, Jg 1:18. Samson kills thirty men there, Jg 14:19. When the Ark is sent back, the Philistines of Ashkelon pay a tumor of gold as reparation, 1 S 6:17–18. Ashkelon is named with Gath in David's elegy at the deaths of Saul and Jonathan, 2 S 1:20. It is the object of threats from the prophets, Am 1:8; Is 25:20; 47:5–7; Zp 2:4, 7; Zc 9:5.

= **Askalon** (4). To avoid the fate of Azotus, the residents of Askalon give Jonathan Maccabaeus an honorable welcome, 1 M 10:86; 11:60. When Simon reaches Askalon, he turns on Joppa, 1 M 12:33. In Jdt 2:28 the advance of Holofernes' troops throws the people of Askalon into a terror.

ASHKENAZ (3), first of the three sons of Gomer, Gn 10:3//1 Ch 1:6, refers in Jr 51:27 to the: SCYTHIANS, whom Jeremiah is calling, along with other peoples, to attack Babylon.

ASHNAH

1. **Ashnah** (1), a town in the lowlands of Judah, Jos 15:33. Unknown.

2. **Ashnah** (1), another town in the lowlands of Judah, Jos 15:43. Perhaps the modern *Idna,* 13 km W of Hebron.

ASHPENAZ (1), chief eunuch at the court of Nebuchadnezzar, Dn 1:3.

ASHTAROTH (7), "[Place of] Astarte" (cf. Astarte), a town about 35 km E of the Sea of Chinnereth. Ashtaroth and Edrei, royal city of Og, king of Bashan, Dt 1:4//Jos 12:4; Jos 9:10; 13:12, pass to the eastern half-tribe of Manasseh, Jos 13:21. Ashtaroth is assigned to the Levite sons of Gershon, 1 Ch 6:56//Jos 21:27 (corr. of Hb. *Be'eshterâh*).

= **Asteroth-karnaim** (1), where Chedor-laomer and his allies defeat the Rephaim, Gn 14:5.

Native place of: UZZIAH 1.

ASHURITES (1), Hb. *'Ashuri* (which some correct to *Asherites*), 2 S 2:9. Perhaps to be identified with: ASSYRIA 2.

ASHVATH (1), an Asherite, last of the three sons of Japhlet, a fighting man and head of a family, 1 Ch 7:33.

ASIA (28). In the Books of the Maccabees, the name designates the kingdom of the Seleucids (Asia Minor and western Asia), which passes to the Romans after the defeat of Antiochus III at Magnesia on the Sipylus. "Kings of Asia" or "wear the crown of Asia" are expressions applied to: ANTIOCHUS 2; PTOLEMY 6; SELEUCUS 4; TRYPHO.

The horses of Asia, raised by the Parthians on the plateaus of Iran are famous, 2 M 10:24.

In the NT Asia means the Roman proconsular province (= Mysia, Lydia, Caria, and sometimes Phrygia), Ac 2:9; 16:6; 20:4; 27:2. Jews and proselytes from Asia are in Jerusalem on the first Christian Pentecost, Ac 2:9. Some years later, they are found debating with Stephen, Ac 6:9. Later, some of them rouse the people of Jerusalem against Paul, Ac 21:27; cf. 24:19. A major part of Paul's ministry is carried on in Asia, Ac 20:8, first in Phrygia, Ac 16:6, then in the province of Asia in general, 19:10, 22, 26; cf. 27:2. There he effects many conversions, 19:26, after that of Epaenetus, Rm 16:6; finds companions in his apostolate, Ac 20:4 (some of whom will abandon him, 2 Tm 1:15); and experiences trials, 2 Co 1:8 (especially at Ephesus, 1 Co 15:32, which contains the temple of Diana, Ac 19:27). In writing to the Corinthians, Paul sends greetings to the churches of Asia, 1 Co 16:19. Peter, 1 P 1:1, and John, Rv 1:4–3:22, write to the churches of Asia.

Capital of the Roman province of Asia: EPHESUS.

Asia Minor (= present-day Turkey): BITHYNIA; CAPPADOCIA; CARIA; CILICIA; GALATIA 1; LYCAONIA; LYCIA; LYDIA 1; MYSIA; PAMPHYLIA; PHRYGIA; PISIDIA; PONTUS.

ASIEL (cf. Asahel).

1. **Asiel** (1), a Simeonite, ancestor of: JEHU 5.

2. **Asiel** (1), Tb 1:2, a Naphtalite, ancestor of Tobit and Tobias.

ASKALON. See: ASHKELON.

ASMODEUS (2), "He who destroys"? (see Abaddon), antithesis of the angel Raphael, "God heals." In the *Testament of Solomon,* he is an enemy of conjugal union, as he is in Tb 3:8, 17, where he is called "that worst of demons." Sometimes identified with *Aeshma,* one of the seven demons of Parsism.

ASNAH (1), an Egypt. name, head of a family of "oblates" who return from the exile, Ezr 2:50.

ASPATHA (1), a Pers. name, brother of: PARSHANDATHA.

ASPHAR (1), a cistern in the desert of Tekoa, SE of Bethlehem, where Simon and Jonathan Maccabaeus take refuge, 1 M 9:33. Perhaps the cisterns of *Kh. bîr ez-Zaʿfaran,* 6 km S of Tekoa.

ASRIEL (3), son of Manasseh and his Aramaean concubine, 1 Ch 7:14, or son of Gilead (and grandson of Manasseh), Nb 26:31. The sons of Asriel form the **Asrielite** clan, Nb 26:31; cf. Jos 17:2.

ASRIELITE (1), belonging to the clan of: ASRIEL.

ASSHUR. See: ASSYRIA.

ASSHURITES (1), Hb. *'Ashshurim,* descendants, through Dedan, of Jokshan, who was a son of Abraham and his concubine Keturah, Gn 25:1–4. Perhaps to be identified with: ASSYRIA 2.

ASSIR, "Prisoner" (cf. Moseroth).

1. **Assir** (2), a descendant of Levi through Kohath; a son and clan of Korah, Ex 6:24; given as an ancestor of Samuel, 1 Ch 6:7.

2. **Assir** (2), a descendant of the preceding, given as an ancestor of Samuel, 1 Ch 6:8, and of Heman the cantor, 6:23.

ASSOS (2), a port of Mysia, where Paul embarks on his return to Jerusalem at the end of his third missionary journey, Ac 20:13–14.

ASSURBANIPAL (1), Aram. *'Asnappar* (cf. Asshur), son of Esarhaddon and king of Assyria (669–630?), deports some peoples from Lower Mesopotamia to Samaria, Ezr 4:10. There is an allusion in Na 3:8–9 to the capture of Thebes by Assurbanipal.

ASSYRIA, Hb. *'Ashshur,* Gr. *Assour, Assyrios* (cf. Assurbanipal; Esarhaddon).

1. **Asshur, Assyria, Assyrian** (181), a city, country, and people on the Tigris "beyond the River" (= Euphrates), Is 7:20, a region corresponding to Upper Mesopotamia (northern part of modern Iraq).

The word. Asshur is the name of the oldest capital (replaced by Nineveh) and mentioned, it seems, in Gn 2:14 and Ezk 27:23. Asshur also designates the national god whose name is part of the names of Kings Assurbanipal and Esarhaddon. Everywhere else Asshur refers to Assyria.

Asshur is connected with an ancestor *Asshur* or *Ashur,* a descendant of Shem, Gn 10:22//1 Ch 1:17. Acc. to Gn 10:11 this Asshur came from the land of Shinar (= Babylonia) and was "builder of Nineveh," but some critics interpret the text as saying: "[Nimrod] came from [Shinar] for Asshur and built Nineveh," cf. Mi 5:6 (*land of Nimrod = land of Asshur*). More than half (94) of the uses of the word *Assyria* occur in the expression "king(s) of Assyria"; on twenty occasions there is question either of the kings of Assyria collectively or of a particular king who is difficult to identify. In Is 7:17, 20; 8:7; cf. 8:4, the mention of the "king of Assyria" seems to be a gloss.

The Assyrian empire. The apogee of Assyrian power in the eighth century (Tiglath-pileser III, 745–727) coincides with the period of the kings of Israel and of Judah. Under Pekah of Israel the first deportation of Israelites occurs, 2 K 15:29; cf. Am 5:27, which Tb 1:2–3, 10, wrongly attributes to Shalmaneser V; other deportations will follow, especially under Sargon II, 2 K 17:6, 23; cf. Jr 50:17. Assyria launches a campaign against Judah at the beginning of the seventh century. Sennacherib attacks the western coalition of which Hezekiah is a member, 2 K 18:13, 14; cf. 20:6//Is 38:6, but he fails, 2 K 19:35//Is 37:36//Si 48:21.

A number of texts refer to the cruelty that accompanies the Assyrian invasions, 2 K 19:11, 17–19//Is 37:11, 18–20; 2 Ch 30:6; Ne 9:32; cf. Ho 13:15 (*the wind from the East*), which explains the threats of the prophets against Assyria and against Nineveh in particular, Is 10:5–13; 14:25; 30:27–33; 31:4–9; Mi 5:4–5; Zp 2:13. The insolence of the king of Assyria will be punished, Is 10:12; Zc 10:11; his armies will go down, like those of other powers, into the underworld, Ezk 32:22. And the terrible oracle of Nahum, 1:14; 2–3, finds an echo in Tb 14:4, 15. The theme of Assyrian oppression provides the context for Jdt: Judith, "the Jewess," is set over against Holofernes, "general-in-chief of the Assyrian army," 5:1; 6:1; 13:13, and the army of the *sons of Asshur* (Hb.), an expression peculiar to Jdt, 6:17; 7:17–24; 12:13; 14:2–3, 12, an imposing and formidable army, 2:14–18; 9:7; 16:3–4, that is finally defeated before Bethulia, 8:9; 10:11; 14:19; 15:6.

Assyria and Egypt. Located between these two powerful neighbors, Israel is like a place of passage for invasions, 2 K 23:29; Is 20:4, and a small country threatened now by the one, now by the other, and therefore tempted to appeal to the one against the other. Whereas Egypt oppresses the Hebrew people at its beginnings, it is Assyria that puts an end to the history of the kingdom of Israel, Is 52:4; Ho 9:3; 10:6; 11:5. The people of God looks to illusory alliances, ineffective help, at one time from Egypt, at another from Assyria, Jr 2:18; Lm 5:6; Ezk 16:26–29; 23:3–27; Ho 5:13; 7:11–13; 8:9; 12:2. But God will bring the exiles back from Egypt and Assyria, Is 11:11–16; 27:12–13; Ho 11:11; Zc 10:10. And some day the oppressor states will be converted, the route followed by the invaders will become a road for peaceful communication, and a single divine blessing will bring the three peoples together: "Blessed be my people Egypt, Assyria my creation, and Israel my heritage," Is 19:22–25.

Kings: ASSURBANIPAL; ESARHADDON; SARGON; SENNACHERIB; SHALMANESAR; TIGLATH-PILESER; and, improperly, DARIUS 1; NEBUCHADNEZZAR.

Gods: ASSHUR (mentioned earlier); NISROCH.

Cities: CALAH; NINEVEH; REHOBOTH-IR; RESEN.

2. **Asshur** (4), an Arabian tribe in the south of Palestine, Nb 24:22–24; Ps 83:9. Probably Gn 25:18 and perhaps 2 S 2:9, if the Hb. is not emended.

See: ASHURITES; ASSHURITES.

ASSYRIAN. See: ASSYRIA 1.

ASTARTE (9), Hb. *'Ashtoret*—an insulting deformation of *Ashtart,* vocalized like the Hb. *bosheth,* "shame"; see Molech; Topheth; likewise Evil-merodach—(cf. Ashtaroth; Asteroth-karnaim), goddess of love and fruitfulness, corresponding to the Ugar. *Athtart,* the Babyl. *Ishtar,* and the Aram. *Atar.* She is venerated at Sidon and adopted by King Solomon, 1 K 11:5, 33; 2 K 23:13. She has a temple among the Philistines, 1 S 31:10. In the plural, *the Baals and the Astartes* signify the Canaanite divinities by which the Israelites so often let themselves be seduced, Jg 10:6; 1 S 7:3–4; 12:10. Finally, Astarte and Asherah are sometimes confused, cf. Jg 3:7; 2 K 23:4.

See: ATARGATIS; ISHTAR.

ASTEROTH-KARNAIM (1), "Astarte with the two horns" (cf. Astarte; Karnaim). See: ASHTAROTH.

ASTYAGES (1), last king of the Medes, conquered by Cyrus (ca. 550), who succeeds him, Dn 14:1.

ASYNCRITUS (1), "Incomparable," a Christian of Rome whom Paul greets, Rm 16:14.

ATARAH (1), "Crown, Diadem" (cf. Ataroth), one of the wives of Jerahmeel, mother of Onam, 1 Ch 2:26.

ATARGATEION (1), (cf. Atargatis), a temple of the goddess Atargatis, 2 M 12:26.

= ? **Carnaim** (2), temple of Asteroth-karnaim, "Astarte with the two horns," where Judas Maccabaeus slaughters 25,000 foes, 2 M 12:21, 26.

[ATARGATIS], Aram. *'Atar'atah* (made up of variants of the names of the two divinities *Athtar* and *Anath*), great Syrian goddess of the Hellenistic period, identified with Asteroth-karnaim. Astarte and Atargatis were both assimilated to the heavenly Aphrodite. See: ATARGATEION.

ATAROTH, "Crowns" (cf. Atarah; Ataroth-addar; Atroth-beth-joab; Atroth-shophan).

1. **Ataroth** (2), a town in Gad, Nb 32:3, 34. Today *Kh. 'Ataruz,* about 10 km E of the Dead Sea.

2. **Ataroth** (1), a town on the border of Ephraim and Manasseh, Jos 16:7. N of Jericho.

3. **Ataroth** (1), a town on the borders of the Archites, Jos 16:2.

= **Ataroth-addar** (2), on the border of Ephraim and Benjamin, Jos 16:5; 18:13.

ATAROTH-ADDAR (2), (cf. Ataroth). See: ATAROTH 3.

ATER, "Bent, Bowed."

1. **Ater** (3), an Israelite, head of a family whose sons return from the exile with Zerubbabel, Ezr 2:16//Ne 7:21, cosigner of the pledge to observe the Law, Ne 10:18.

= **Hezekiah** (2), Ezr 2:16//Ne 7:21. In Ne 10:18 **Hezekiah** (1) is distinct from Ater.

2. **Ater** (2), head of a family of gatekeepers who return from the exile with Zerubbabel, Ezr 2:42//Ne 7:45.

ATHACH (1), 1 S 30:30, a town of Judah. Some correct Hb. *Atak* to *Eter.*

ATHAIAH (1), "Yah is superior"?, **son of Uzziah, son of Zechariah, son of Amariah, son of Shephatiah, son of Mehalalel** (1), a Judaean, descendant of Perez, settled in Jerusalem after the exile, Ne 11:4.

ATHALIAH, Hb. *'Atalyah, 'Atalyahu,* "Yah is exalted" (cf. Athlai).

1. **Athaliah** (15), **daughter of Ahab** (2) and of Jezebel. Wife of Jehoram, king of Judah, 2 K 8:18//2 Ch 21:6, this **[grand]daughter of Omri** (2), is the mother of Ahaziah, king of Judah, 2 K 8:26// 2 Ch 22:2. After the assassination of the latter, Athaliah massacres all those of royal stock; only young Jehoash escapes the slaughter and lives in hiding during the six years of Athaliah's reign (841–835), 2 K 11:1–3//2 Ch 22:10–12. A coup d'état organized by the priest Jehoiada overthrows her; she is put to death, and Jehoash succeeds her, 2 K 11:13–16, 20//2 Ch 23:12–15, 21. She had shown a great deal of favor to the cult of Baal, 2 Ch 24:7; cf. 2 K 12:18.

2. **Athaliah** (1), a Benjaminite of the sons of Jeroham, head of a family at Jerusalem, 1 Ch 8:26.

3. **Athaliah** (1), of the sons of Elam, father of: ISAIAH 5.

ATHARIM (1), Nb 21:1. Unknown.

ATHENIAN (1), a citizen of Athens, Ac 17:21. See: ATHENS.

ATHENOBIUS (2), "friend of the king" Antiochus VII and his messenger to Simon Maccabaeus in order to obtain from the latter the restoration of towns he had captured outside of Judaea, 1 M 15:28–36.

ATHENS (4), a Greek city of Achaia, without a political role since the fourth century, but remaining at the center of Hellenistic culture. There is an allusion to its democratic institutions in 2 M 9:15.

Ac 17:15–18:1 shows Paul's first contact with Athens. During his second missionary journey he is forced to leave Macedonia; he comes to Athens with Timothy, whom he very soon sends to Thessalonika, 1 Th 3:1. While awaiting the return of Silas and Timothy, Paul walks around Athens and is revolted at the signs of this "city given over to idolatry." In the synagogue he debates with the Jews and in the marketplace with passersby and even with Epicurean and Stoic philosophers. Before the Council of the Areopagus he pronounces the most typical of his addresses in preaching to pagans, vv. 21–31, but the theme of resurrection, completely alien to Hellenism, provokes mockery from his hearers. Only a few individuals accept the Christian message, among them Dionysius the Areopagite and a woman named Damaris. His failure is almost complete. Paul leaves Athens for Corinth and in his preaching renounces henceforth the "show of oratory"; cf. 2 Co 2:1–5.

See: AREOPAGUS.

ATHLAI (1), (cf. Athaliah), an Israelite of the sons of Bebai, married to a foreign wife, whom he puts away, Ezr 10:28.

[ATHTAR]. See: ATARGATIS.

[ATON]. See: PITHOM.

ATROTH-BETH-JOAB (1), "Crown of the house of Joab" (cf. Ataroth), a town of Judah, linked with Judah through Hur and Salma, 1 Ch 2:54.

ATROTH-SHOPHAN (1), (cf. Ataroth), a town in Gad, Nb 32:35.

ATTAI

1. **Attai** (2), son of the daughter of Sheshan and of his Egyptian slave Jarha, of the clan of Jerahmeel, 1 Ch 2:35–36.

2. **Attai** (1), a Gadite who rallies to David before the latter becomes king, 1 Ch 12:12 (cf. vv. 9–16).

3. **Attai** (1), second son of Maacah and King Rehoboam, 2 Ch 11:20.

ATTALIA (1), Gr. *Attaleia* (cf. Attalus), a port of Pamphylia, built by King Attalus II. At the end of their first missionary journey Paul and Barnabas take ship there for their return to Antioch in Syria, Ac 14:25–26. Today *Antalya* (in Turkey).

ATTALUS II (1), (cf. Attalia), king of Pergamum (159–138), a friend of the Romans, an addressee of the letter of the consul Lucius promulgating the treaty between the Jews and the Romans, 1 M 15:20.

AUGUST. See: AUGUSTUS 2.

AUGUSTA (1), Gr. *Sebastē,* name of a cohort, probably assigned to the emperor's service; one of its centurions is Julius, Ac 27:1.

AUGUSTUS

1. **Augustus** (1), Gr. *Augoustos,* a Gr. transcription of the Lat. *Augustus,* Roman emperor (27 B.C.–14 A.D.). Lk 2:1 speaks of "Caesar Augustus" issuing "a decree for a census of the whole world to be taken."

2. **August** (2), Gr. *Sebastos,* a title, like Caesar, of the reigning Roman emperor, Ac 25:21, 25.

AURANUS (1), (cf. Avaran?), "a man advanced in years and no less in folly," leads 3,000 men of Lysimachus in an act of aggression against Jerusalem, 2 M 4:40.

AVARAN (1), "The Awakened *or* He who pierces"? (cf. Auranus?), surname of: ELEAZAR 9.

AVITH (12), capital of Hadad, king of Edom, Gn 36:35//1 Ch 1:46.

AVVA (1), a town in Syria, perhaps on the Orontes (today *Tell Kafr Aya*)?, taken by the Assyrians; its inhabitants, the **Avvites,** are deported to Samaria, where they introduce their gods, Nibhaz and Tartak, 2 K 17:24, 31.

= **Ivvah** (1), whose gods, 2 K 18:34, and kings are powerless to save their people from the hand of Sennacherib, 2 K 19:13//Is 37:13.

AVVIM (1), a town in Benjamin, Jos 18:23. Linked to Bethel. See: AI; AYYAH.

AVVITES

1. **Avvites** (3), seminomads settled near Gaza, Dt 2:23; Jos 13:3.

2. **Avvites** (1), 2 K 17:31, inhabitants of: AVVA.

AYYAH (2), Hb. *'Ayyah,* fem. of *'Ai,* a town inhabited by Ephraimites, 1 Ch 7:28, and Benjaminites, Ne 11:31. Associated with Bethel. See: AI 1; AVVIM.

AZALIAH (2), "Yahweh sets aside" (cf. Beth-ezel), father of: SHAPHAN 1.

AZANIAH (1), "Yah has heard" (cf. Jaazaniah; Ozni), father of the Levite: JOSHUA 7.

AZAREL, "God has helped" (cf. Ezer).

1. **Azarel** (1), a Korahite, rallies to David before the latter becomes king, 1 Ch 12:7.

2. **Azarel** (1). See: UZZIEL 3.

3. **Azarel son of Jeroham** (1), commissioner for the tribe of Dan, 1 Ch 27:22.

4. **Azarel** (1), an Israelite of the sons of Zaccai, married to a foreign wife, whom he puts away, Ezr 10:41.

5. **Azarel** (1), father of: AMASHAI.

6. **Azarel** (1), a Levite, a son of Asaph (?), an instrumentalist at the dedication of the wall of Jerusalem, Ne 12:36.

AZARIAH, Azariahu, Azarias, Hb. *'Azaryah, 'Azaryahu,* "Yah has helped," Gr. and Lat. *Azarias* (cf. Ezer).

1. **Azariah** (1), son of Ethan, descended from Judah through Zerah, 1 Ch 2:8.

2. **Azariah** (2), a descendant of Attai and ancestor of Elishama, of the clan of Jerahmeel, 1 Ch 2:38–39.

3. **Azariah son of Nathan** (1), head of Solomon's prefects, 1 K 4:5.

4. **Azariah son of Zadok** (1), a priest in the time of Solomon, 1 K 4:2.

= **Azariah** (2), 1 Ch 5:35 (the remark

in v. 36 about *Azariah* is better suited to the *Azariah* of v. 35).

5. **Azariah** (3), ancestor of Zadok and of the preceding, Ezr 7:3; 1 Ch 5:36–37 (which belongs with the series *Amariah-Ahitub-Zadok,* which is a repetition of vv. 33–34; cf. //Ezr 7:3–4).

6. **Azariah** (4), a descendant of Zadok and of the two preceding, 1 Ch 5:39, 40; 9:11; Ezr 7:1. To be identified with one of the two following?

7. **Azariah** (2), [descendant of Zadok], a high priest. Along with "eighty brave priests" he opposes King Uzziah, who wishes to offer incense in the temple, 2 Ch 26:17, 20.

8. **Azariah** (2), a high priest "of the family of Zadok" in the time of King Hezekiah, 2 Ch 31:10, 13.

9. **Azariah** (1), a cosigner of the pledge to observe the Law, Ne 10:3, a trumpeter at the dedication of the wall of Jerusalem, Ne 12:33: one or two priests.

To be compared with: EZRA 3.

10. **Azariah son of Oded** (1), a prophet, exhorts King Asa to undertake a religious reform, 2 Ch 15:1–8.

11. **Azariah** (1) and **Azariahu** (1), two of the six sons of King Jehoshaphat of Judah who are assassinated by their eldest brother, Jehoram, after his accession to the throne, 2 Ch 21:2–4, 13.

12. **Azariah** (9), in the Hb. text another name for king: UZZIAH 4.

13. **Azariah son of Jeroham** (1) and **Azariah son of Obed** (1), two of the five commanders of hundreds who are involved in the conspiracy against Athaliah, 2 Ch 23:1–14.

14. **Azariah son of Jehohanan** (1), one of the four officers of the northern kingdom, 2 Ch 28:12, who heed the plea of the prophet Oded, take pity on their brothers from Judah who are imprisoned, help them, and set them free, vv. 5–15.

15. **Azariah son of Hoshaiah** (1), a Judaean officer. See: JEZANIAH 2.

16. **Azariah** (2), a descendant of Levi; father of: JOEL 5.

17. **Azariah son of Jehallelel** (1), a Levite of the clan of Merari, takes part in the purification of the temple during the reform of Hezekiah, 2 Ch 29:12.

18. **Azariah son of Maaseiah, son of Ananiah** (1), a volunteer in the rebuilding of the wall of Jerusalem, Ne 3:23–24.

19. **Azariah** (1). See: SERAIAH 9.

20. **Azariah** (1), a Levite, explains the Law to the people during its solemn reading by Ezra, Ne 8:7.

21. **Azariah** (10), renamed **Abednego** (15), one of Daniel's three companions. See: HANANIAH 17.

22. **Azarias** (6) **son of the great Ananias** (1). See: RAPHAEL 1.

23. **Azariah** (3), a leader of the people, given responsibility, along with Joseph, son of Zechariah, and in the absence of Judas and Simon Maccabaeus, for keeping Judaea at peace, 1 M 5:18–19. Eager for glory, the two disobey their orders, march on Jamnia, and are routed, 1 M 5:56–62.

= **Esdrias** (2), 2 M 8:23 (corr. of Gr. *Eleazar*), ordered by Judas to read the sacred book aloud before battle; he takes part in the campaign against Gorgias on the borders of Idumaea, 2 M 12:36 (corr. of Gr. *Esdris*).

AZARIAHU. See: AZARIAH 11.

AZARIAS. See: AZARIAH 22.

AZAZ (1), abbrev. of *Azaziah,* a Reubenite, father of: BELA 3.

AZAZEL (4), wrongly interpreted by Gr. and Lat. as "scapegoat," is a demon, a satyr living in the desert. On the feast of Atonement he is sent a goat, which symbolically carries with it all the sins of Israel, Lv 16:8, 10, 26.

AZAZIAH, "Yah shows himself to be strong" (cf. Azaz; Aziza; Azzan; Maaziah; Uzzah; Uzzi; Uzziah; Uzziel).

1. **Azaziah** (1), a Levite, a lyre player before the Ark, 1 Ch 15:21.

2. **Azaziah** (1), an Ephraimite, father of: Hosea 4.

3. **Azaziah** (1), one of the ten Levites who assist Conaniah and Shimei in the time of King Hezekiah, 2 Ch 31:12–13.

AZBUK (1), father of: Nehemiah 3.

AZEKAH (7), about 30 km SW of Jerusalem. Joshua defeats the coalition of Canaanite kings there, Jos 10:10–11. A town in the lowlands of Judah, Jos 15:35, occupied by the Philistines, 1 S 17:1, fortified by Rehoboam, 2 Ch 11:9. Azekah resists for a time the siege laid to it by Nebuchadnezzar, Jr 34:7; it is reoccupied by the men of Judah on their return from exile, Ne 11:30. Today *Tell Zakaria.*

AZEL (6), "Noble," a Benjaminite, a descendant of Saul; he has six sons, 1 Ch 8:37–38//9:43–44.

AZGAD (1), Hb. "Gad is mighty" (cf. Gad), Pers. *Izgad,* "Messenger," a layman, head of a family whose sons return from the exile with Zerubbabel, Ezr 2:12//Ne 7:17, and Ezra, Ezr 8:12, a cosigner of the pledge to observe the Law, Ne 10:16.

AZIZA (1), (cf. Azaziah), an Israelite of the sons of Zattu, married to a foreign wife, whom he puts away, Ezr 10:27.

AZMAVETH

1. **Azmaveth from Bahurim** (2), 2 S 23:31, or **from Baharum,** 1 Ch 11:33, one of David's champions.

2. **Azmaveth** (2), a Benjaminite, one of the three sons of Jehoaddah, 1 Ch 8:36, or of Jarab, 1 Ch 9:42, a descendant of King Saul.

3. **Azmaveth** (1), 1 Ch 12:3, a Benjaminite, father of Pelet and: Jeziel. But "sons of Azmaveth" may mean "from the town of Azmaveth" (cf. the following no. 5).

4. **Azmaveth son of Adiel** (1), commissioner for the king's stores, 1 Ch 27:25.

5. **Azmaveth** (1), a town in Benjamin, near Anathoth, 7 km NNE of Jerusalem. Cantors come from Azmaveth to take part in the dedication of the wall of Jerusalem, Ne 12:29.

= **Beth-azmaveth** (1). "Men of Beth-azmaveth" return from the exile with Zerubbabel, Ezr 2:24//Ne 7:28. Today *Hizma.*

AZMON (3), a town on the southern frontier of Judah, near Kadesh-barnea and the wadi of Egypt, Nb 34:4–5; Jos 15:4.

AZNOTH-TABOR (1), (cf. Tabor), on the border of Naphtali, Jos 19:34. Perhaps the modern *Kh. Umm Jubeil,* north of Mount Tabor.

AZOR (2), a form derived from *Azariah;* an ancestor of Jesus acc. to Mt 1:13–14.

AZOTUS (13). See: Ashdod.

AZRIEL, "My help is God" (cf. Ezer).

1. **Azriel** (1), one of the family heads of the eastern half-tribe of Manasseh, 1 Ch 5:24.

2. **Azriel** (1), father of: Jeremoth 8.

3. **Azriel** (1), father of: Seraiah 2.

AZRIKAM, "My help arises," see Ps 44:27 (cf. Ezer; Jakim).

1. **Azrikam** (1), controller of the palace under King Ahaz, slain by Zichri the Ephraimite, 2 Ch 28:7.

2. **Azrikam** (2), a Benjaminite, firstborn son of Azel, a descendant of King Saul, 1 Ch 8:38//9:44.

3. **Azrikam** (2), ancestor of the Levite: Shemaiah 7.

4. **Azrikam** (1), last of the three sons of Neariah, a descendant of King Jehoiachin, 1 Ch 3:23.

AZUBAH, "Abandoned, Forsaken."

1. **Azubah** (2), wife of Caleb, 1 Ch 2:18–19 (usually v. 18 is corrected, which in Hb. reads literally: *Caleb . . . became father of Azubah*).

2. **Azubah daughter of Shilhi** (2),

mother of King Jehoshaphat of Judah, 1 K 22:42//2 Ch 20:31.

3. **Abandoned** (1), a symbolic name for Jerusalem, Is 62:4.

AZZAN (1), (cf. Azaziah), an Issacharite, father of: PALTIEL 1.

AZZUR, abbrev. of *Azariah;* or "Medlar."

1. **Azzur** (1), father of: HANANIAH 4.

2. **Azzur** (1), father of: JAAZANIAH 4.

3. **Azzur** (1), a leader of the people, cosigner of the pledge to observe the Law, Ne 10:18.

B

BAAL, Hb. *Ba'al,* "Master, Owner, *whence* Husband" (cf. Baalah; Baalath; Baara; Bealiah; Bealoth; Bel; Eshbaal; Ethbaal; Gur-baal; Ishbaal; Jerubbaal; Kiriath-baal; Meribbaal; and the composites of Baal- that follow this entry).

1. **Baal** (78), Canaanite god of the storm and the rain, owner of the soil whose fruitfulness he guarantees: his death was celebrated (cf. Dt 14:1) at the beginning of the summer, when the vegetation dried up. He is sometimes associated with *Astarte* (or *Asherah*), goddess of love and fertility, 2 K 21:3–7; 23:4–13. But Baal, the Baals, *the Baals and the Astartes,* Jg 2:11–13; 3:7; 10:6–10; 1 S 12:10, are most often a collective name for quite varied divinities, the "other gods," Dt 13:3; 2 K 5:17 . . . , the "foreign gods" that are paralleled specifically with the Astartes in 1 S 7:3–4. When associated with a place (cf. Baal-hermon; Baal-peor; and so on), Baal designates the god who owns and protects or is "patron" of the place; the cult of these various Baals corresponds with regionalist aspirations. In reaction against the cult of Baal, names with *Baal* as a component part have often been emended in Hebrew: *Baal* is replaced by *El, Yah,* or *bosheth,* "shame" (see: BAAL-BERITH; BEELIADA; MERIBBAAL; and so on). "Shame" even becomes a proper name for the idol of Baal, Ho 4:7; 9:10; Jr 11:13.

Israel is frequently tempted either to abandon Yahweh and serve the Baals, Jg 3:7; 10:6–10; 1 S 12:10; 1 K 18:18; 2 K 17:16; Jr 23:27; Ho 2:10–19, or to settle for a syncretist religion that offers a single worship to Yahweh and Baal together, cf. 2 K 23:4–5, or shifts from the one to the other, 1 K 18:21; Jr 7:9–10. In the period of the judges Gideon leads a strong but vain attack against the cult of Baal, Jg 6:25–32; at his death the Israelites "again began to prostitute themselves to the Baals," Jg 8:33.

In the northern kingdom, Ahab—and his son Ahaziah after him, 1 K 22:54—favors the cult of Baal, 1 K 16:31–32. This god comes on the scene as a rival of Yahweh: On Carmel Elijah forces Israel to choose between the living God, cf. 1 K 17:1, and this Baal, who is often absent or asleep, 1 K 18:18–40. Amid the general apostasy, 2 K 17:16; cf. Ho 4:7; 11:2; 13:1; Tb 1:5, "seven thousand in Israel: all the knees that have not bent before Baal," are spared by Yahweh, 1 K 19:18; cf. Rm 11:4. By treachery Jehu wipes out the followers and cult of Baal, 2 K 10:18–28. Under Jeroboam II Hosea sharply attacks the cult of Baal, Ho 2:10–19, and reminds the people of the apostasy at Beth-peor, 9:10.

In Judah, Zephaniah, 1:4, then and above all Jeremiah, denounce the prophets who speak in the name of Baal, Jr 2:8; 23:13, the Judaeans and Israelites who have built high places and altars for him, Jr 11:13; 19:5; 32:35, have offered him incense, 7:9; 11:17; 32:29, have sworn by him, 12:16, in short, have followed the Baals, Jr 2:3; 9:13. Athaliah, 2 Ch 24:7, Ahaz, 2 Ch 28:2, Manasseh, 2 K 21:3–7//2 Ch 33:3–7, are characterized by their devotion to Baal, whereas Jehoshaphat does not "have recourse to the Baals," 2 Ch 17:3, and at Athaliah's death the people of Judah demolish the temple of Baal and kill his priest, 2 K 11:18//2 Ch 23:17. Josiah's religious reform rids the temple of cult objects made for Baal, suppresses the priests and faithful of the god, and profanes his high places and altars, 2 K 23:4–14//2 Ch 34:3–7.

See: ASHERAH; ASTARTE; HADAD 1.

2. **Baal** (1), a Reubenite, a descendant of Joel and father of Beerah, 1 Ch 5:5.

3. **Baal** (2), a Benjaminite of Gibeon, 1 Ch 8:30//9:36.

4. **Baal** (1), 1 Ch 4:33 (Hb.). See: BAALATH 3.

BAALAH, Hb. *Ba'alah,* "Mistress, Lady" (cf. Baal; Bealoth).

1. **Baalah** (4) **of Judah** (1). See: KIRIATH-JEARIM; BAALATH 1–2.

2. **Baalah** (1), a town of the sons of Judah in the Negeb, Jos 15:29.

= **Balah** (1), Jos 19:3, formerly occupied by Simeonites.

= **Bilhah** (1), 1 Ch 4:29.

See: BAALATH 1–3; BAALATH-BEER.

3. **Baalah** (1), a hill on the NW frontier of Judah, Jos 15:11. See BAALATH 2.

BAALATH, "Lady" (cf. Baal).

1. **Baalath** (1), a town in Dan, Jos 19:44. Identical with: BAALAH 1 or 2.

2. **Baalath** (2), a town fortified by King Solomon, 1 K 9:18//2 Ch 8:6. Identical with: BAALAH 1, 2, or 3.

3. **Baalath** (1), (corr. of Hb. *Baal*), a town assigned to Simeon, 1 Ch 4:33.

= **Baalath-beer** (1), Jos 19:8. Probably identical with BAALAH 2.

BAALATH-BEER (1), "Lady of the well" (cf. Baal). See: BAALATH 3.

BAAL-BERITH (2), "Baal of the covenant," a god Baal worshipped under this name by the Canaanites of Shechem and adopted by the Israelites, Jg 8:33; 9:4.

= **El-berith** (1), Jg 9:46, in whose temple the leading men of Migdal-shechem take refuge.

BAAL-GAD (3), "Baal of [the god] Gad" (cf. Gad), located "in the Vale of Lebanon below Mount Hermon," Jos 11:17; 13:5. The expression "from Baal-gad . . . to Mount Halak" (and the reverse) is probably a more specific way of indicating the northern and southern limits of the territory of the twelve tribes, Jos 11:17; 12:7. Cf. the more popular expression "from Dan to Beersheba." To be connected (?) with: BAAL-HERMON.

BAAL-HAMON (1), "Master of a multitude *or* of wealth" (cf. Hamonah), an unknown town, Sg 8:11.

BAAL-HANAN, "Baal has been gracious," to be compared with the Phoen. *Hannibal,* "Thanks to Baal" (cf. Hanan).

1. **Baal-hanan** (4), **son of Achbor** (3), king of Edom, Gn 36:38–39//1 Ch 1:49–50.

2. **Baal-hanan of Geder** (1), commissioner for the olives and sycamores in the lowlands, 1 Ch 27:28.

BAAL-HAZOR (1), "Baal of Hazor" (cf. Hazor), a town 25 km N of Jerusalem, "near Ephraim." It is there that Absalom has his half-brother Ammon assassinated in revenge for the rape of his sister Tamar, 2 S 13:23.

= **Hazor** (1), a town occupied by Benjaminites after the return from the exile, Ne 11:33.

BAAL-HERMON (2), (cf. Hermon), a sanctuary dedicated to Baal or a town on the slopes of Mount Hermon, southern boundary of the Hittite area, Jg 3:3, and northern boundary of the eastern half-tribe of Manasseh, 1 Ch 5:23.

To be connected (?) with: BAAL-GAD.

BAALIS (1), "Son of delights"?, **king of**

the Ammonites (1), sends Ishmael son of Nethaniah to murder Gedaliah, the governor, Jr 40:14.

BAAL-MEON (3), "Master of Meon," a town of Reuben, Nb 32:38; 1 Ch 5:8, then of Moab. Ezk 25:9 announces its destruction.

= **Beth-baal-meon** (1), Jos 13:17, a town in Reuben.

= **Beth-meon** (1), Jr 48:25, a town in Moab.

= **Beon** (1), Nb 32:3, a town claimed by the Transjordanian tribes. Today *Ma'in,* 7 km SW of Madaba.

BAAL-PEOR, "Master of Peor," Gr. *Beelphegōr* (cf. Peor).

1. **Baal of Peor, Baal-peor** (4), a local god of Mount Peor, to whom Israel "commits itself" by debauching with Moabite women and by offering him sacrifices before they enter the Promised Land, Nb 25:3, 5; Dt 4:3; Ps 106:28. In Ho 9:10 the name Baal is replaced by the contemptuous Hb. word *bosheth,* "shame."

= **Peor** (1), a local form of Baal. In the priestly tradition "the Peor affair," Nb 25:8; 31:16, or "the sin at Peor," Jos 22:17, calls to mind the double infidelity of Israel to Yahweh: through contact with the Moabite woman (see earlier) and through contact with the Midianite Cozbi, cf. Nb 25:6–18.

2. **Baal-peor** (1), a high place of the god Baal of Peor. The Israelites worship the idol there and are punished for it, Dt 4:3; Ho 9:10.

Near to: BETH-PEOR. Cf. also PEOR 1.

BAAL-PERAZIM (4), "Master of the breaches" (cf. Perez), a place S of Jerusalem?, where David defeats the Philistines and says: "Yahweh has made a breach in my enemies for me like a breach the waters make," 2 S 5:20// 1 Ch 14:11.

= **Perazim** (Mount) (1), Is 28:21.

BAAL-SHALISHAH (1), "Baal of Shalishah." See: SHALISHAH.

[BAAL-SHAMEM], "Master of heaven," a Phoenician god assimilated to Olympian Zeus. See: ZEUS.

BAAL-TAMAR (1), "Baal of the palm tree," in Benjamin, NW of Gibeah, Jg 20:33.

BAALZEBUB, "Baal of the flies," Gr. *Baal muia, Bee(l)zebul,* Lat. *Beelzebub,* a scornful distortion of *Baal-Zebul,* "Baal the Prince," a Canaanite god venerated especially at Ekron. The gospels use the original name to designate the prince of demons.

1. **Baalzebub, the god of Ekron** (1). King Ahaziah of Israel consults him on the question of an illness. The prophet Elijah, an enemy of Baal-worship, objects: "Is there no God in Israel?" and tells the king of his impending death, 2 K 1:2–6, 16.

2. **Beelzebul** (7), **the prince of devils** (4). Jesus is regarded by his enemies as Beelzebul, Mt 10:25, or as possessed by Beelzebul, Mk 3:22; they also claim that he casts out demons by Beelzebul's power, Mt 12:24, 27//Lk 11:15–19; cf. Mt. 9:34; Mk 3:22.

BAAL-ZEPHON (3), "Baal of the North" (cf. Zaphon). In the sixth century the god Baal-zephon is listed at the head of the divinities of Tahpanhes. A town associated with Pi-hahiroth, a stage in the Exodus before the crossing of the Red Sea, Ex 14:2, 9; Nb 33:7.

BAANA. See: BAANAH 3–4.

BAANAH, Baana, Hb. 1–2, 6–7: *Ba'anah;* 3–5: *Ba'ana'.*

1. **Baanah** and **Rechab** (4), **sons of Rimmon of Beeroth** (3), a Benjaminite, leader of freebooters in the service of Ishbaal, son of Saul, 2 S 4:2. During the siesta hour they slip into their master's house, kill him, behead him, and bring his head to David. The latter has these "bandits" executed for having "killed an honest man." Their bodies, with hands and feet cut off, are hung beside the Pool of Hebron, 4:5–12.

2. **Baanah** (2), father of: HELED.

3. **Baana son of Ahilud** (1), administrator of Solomon's fifth district, 1 K 4:12.

4. **Baana son of Hushai** (1), administrator of Solomon's ninth district, 1 K 4:16.

5. **Baanah** (2), one of the twelve leaders on the return from the exile, Ezr 2:2//Ne 7:7.

6. **Baanah** (1), a leader of the people, cosigner of the pledge to observe the Law, Ne 10:28.

BAARA (1), abbrev. of *Ba'alram,* "Baal is on high" (cf. Baal; Ramah), one of the two wives repudiated by the Benjaminite Gera, 1 Ch 8:8.

BAASEIAH (1), an ancestor of Asaph the cantor, 1 Ch 6:25.

BAASHA (28), Hb. *Ba'sha',* Gr. *Baasa,* **son of Ahijah** (4), **of the House of Issachar** (1), third king of Israel, founder of the second dynasty. This usurper murders his king, Nadab, during the siege of Gibbethon, has himself proclaimed king, and exterminates the royal family of Jeroboam, 1 K 15:27–29, 33; cf. 14: 14. There are frequent skirmishes between him and his neighbor, Asa, king of Judah, 1 K 15:16, 32. But when Baasha fortifies Ramah in order to blockade Asa, the latter reacts, cf. Jr 41:9, and buys the support of Ben-hadad, king of Aram; Baasha withdraws, 1 K 16:5–6. A stern judgment is passed on Baasha: he followed the example of Jeroboam and therefore his dynasty will suffer the same fate as that of Jeroboam, 1 K 15: 34; 16:1–4, 7; 21:22; 2 K 9:9. In fact, Zimri will destroy it entirely, 1 K 16: 11–13.

His son and successor: ELAH 3.

BABEL. See: BABYLON.

BABYLON, BABYLONIA, BABYLONIAN (327), Hb. *Babel,* Accad. *Bab-ilu,* "Gate of God" (cf. Zerubbabel), Gr. *Babylōn,* a city, country, and people of Lower Mesopotamia (the southern part of modern Iraq).

a. Babylon and biblical history

The earliest biblical texts on Babylon are Gn 10:10, where Babel is listed among the capitals of the empire of the Mesopotamian hero Nimrod, and Gn 11:2–9, which alludes to the famous ziggurats (stepped pyramidal temple towers), especially that of the city's great temple, and artificially connects *Babel* with the Hb. *balal,* "mix up, confuse," the confusion of languages being regarded as the punishment for idolatry and for man's presumption in claiming that he can "guarantee the unity of the human race by a politico-religious imperialism of which Babylon is an example," cf. Is 13:19; 14:4; Jr 51:41, 53; Dn 4:27.

After the fall of the kingdom of Israel in 721, the kings of Assyria several times deport Babylonians to Samaria, 2 K 17: 24–41; cf. Ezr 4:2, 9–10. When Hezekiah, after his miraculous recovery, rejoices at the visit of the messengers from the Babylonian king Merodach-baladan, cf. 2 Ch 32:31, Isaiah announces that some day the wealth in Hezekiah's palace will be carted off to Babylon and that some of his descendants will be "eunuchs in the palace of the king of Babylon," 2 K 20:14–18//Is 39:3–7. And, in fact, Babylon appears in the Bible chiefly as the power that puts an end to the kingdom of Judah and as the land of exile. Babylon will see the arrival of several waves of deportees, 2 K 24:16; 25:28; 1 Ch 9:1; 2 Ch 36:20; Ezr 2:1; 5:12; Jr 20:4–6; 39:9; 40:1; Mi 4:10; Ac 7:43; cf. Am 5:27 ("far beyond Damascus"), and among them will be kings of Judah: Manasseh,2 Ch 33:11, later Jehoiakim, 2 Ch 36:6, Jehoiachin, 2 K 24: 15–16; 25:28; cf. 2 Ch 36:10; Jr 24: 1; 27:20; 28:4; Ba 1:9; Mt 1:11–12, 17, and Zedekiah, 2 K 25:7//Jr 39:

7//52:11; Jr 32:5; 34:2. Cf. Ezk 12: 13; 17:12–20. The treasures of the temple as well as the riches of the royal palace will likewise be carried off to Babylon, 2 K 20:17//Is 39:6; 2 K 25: 13//Jr 52:17; 2 Ch 36:7, 10, 18; Ezr 5:14; 6:5; Jr 20:5; 27:16–22; 28:3. Jeremiah urges the exiles, now far from their country and the temple, Ps 137, not to heed the false prophets among them, Jr 29:8–9, 15, 21–23; for in fact the time of trial will be long, Ba 6:1–2: let the exiles therefore settle down and even pray for the city to which Yahweh has deported them, Jr 29:4–7, 28, and in which some Jews will play an important role, as sages, Dn 2:12–27, 48; 4:3–5; 5:7–29, or as officials, Dn 2:48–49; 3:12, 30. But they must not worship the gods of Babylon, Is 21:9; 46:1–2; Ba 6:3–4; cf. Dn 3:1; 14:3, 23. The exile in Babylon lasts about 50 years (587–538). The figure 70, Jr 25:11–12; 29:10; Dn 9:2; cf. Zc 1:12, is a round number but may also designate the approximate length of time during which the worship in the temple has been interrupted (587–515), 2 Ch 36:21–22.

The fall of the "virgin, daughter of Babylon," Ps 137:8; Is 47:1; Jr 50:42; 51:33; Zc 2:11—or **daughter of the Chaldaeans,** Is 47:1, 5, "the jewel and boast of the Chaldaeans," Is 13:19, also called **Sheshak,** Jr 25:26; 51:41—is often predicted by the prophets, Is 13:1–22; 14:4–23; 21:1–9; 43:14; 46:1–13; 48: 14; Jr 50; 51, as a punishment by Yahweh, who avenges his oppressed people, Ps 137:8; Is 21:10; 47:3; 48:14; Jr 51:6, 24, 35. It takes place in 539, when Cyrus of Persia invests the city and promulgates the edict putting an end to the captivity, Ezr 1:11; 2:1; 7:6; 8:1; Zc 6:10, and the furnishings of the temple are brought back, Ezr 1:7–11; 5:14; 6:5, together with the silver and gold collected in the province, Ezr 7:15–16. The joyous return to the homeland is depicted as a new Exodus, a repetition of the deliverance from slavery in Egypt, Is 11:15–16; 35:6–10; 40:1–5; 41:18; 43:19–20; 51: 11; Ps 126; and so on. But Babylon, like the other pagan neighbors of Israel, is called to receive the knowledge some day of the true God, Ps 87:4. The city and country also mentioned in Tb 14:4; 1 M 6:4; 2 M 8:20.

b. Babylon as a symbol

Just as, at the beginning of history, Babylon is the great city that seeks to dethrone God, Gn 11:2–9, so, too, from the time of the exile, Babylon—which destroyed Jerusalem, slaughtered its inhabitants, burned the temple, deported its elites, 2 Ch 36:17–21, thus attacking the very structures of the holy nation in order to make it lose its identity—becomes the symbol of all the empires that oppose God and his people; its king, Nebuchadnezzar, becomes the very type of the proud and sacrilegious ruler, Is 14; Dn 2; 3; 4:26–27. Over against the new Jerusalem, religious center of the holy land, in which there will be only "a humble and lowly people . . . who . . . will seek refuge in the name of Yahweh," Zp 3:12–13, there stands "Great Babylon," Dn 4:27; Rv 12:8; 17:5, 18; 18:2, 10, 16, 19, 21, in her "arrogance against Yahweh," Jr 50:29–32, "sovereign lady of the kingdoms" who claims to be "eternal (Hb.) sovereign lady" and proclaims "I, and none besides me," Is 47:5–7, 8–10. Over against the fiancée and bride, Ho 2; Is 62:4–5; Rv 21:2, stands the "famous prostitute," Rv 17; 19:2; cf. Hab 2:15–16; Jr 51:7, who leads nations astray by her sorceries, Is 47:9, 12; Rv 18:23.

In the Apocalypse, Babylon stands for Rome, "the great city which has authority over all the rulers on earth," 17:18, and which sits on "seven hills," 17:9; this city's authorities are responsible for persecution of the young Church, 18:24. After acting as the cup with which God intoxicates the nations, Jr 51:7, and the hammer with which he pounds the entire world, Jr 50:23; 51:20–23; cf. Is 14:6, and especially the chosen people, Is 21:20, Babylon, in which the members of the Church are in exile, 1 P 5:13; cf. 1:1, which is allied with Satan (the Dragon), Rv 12:9, and with Antichrist (the Beast), Rv 13; 17, will in its turn "drink the full winecup of his [God's] anger," Rv 16:19, and will be annihilated by being hurled into the sea, as it were, Rv 18:21, or burned in an everlasting furnace, Rv 18:9–10, 18; 19:3. Its punishment will evoke the Alleluia of the citizens of God's city, Rv 19.

See: CHALDAEA; MERATHAIM; SHESHAK; SHINAR.

Kings: EVIL-MERODACH; MERODACH-BALADAN; NEBUCHADNEZZAR. See also: ARTAXERXES 1; BELSHAZZAR; CYRUS; PUL.

Gods: BEL; ISHTAR; MARDUK; NEBO 4; NERGAL.

Canals: AHAVA; CHEBAR; SUD.

BACCHIDES (2), "Son *or* Descendant of Bacchus," **governor of the country beyond the river** [Euphrates] (1), M 7:8.

Demetrius I sends him twice to Judaea in company with the high priest Alcimus. The first time, he makes hypocritical offers of peace to the Jews and executes those who go over to him but have been compromised in the rebellion, 7:9–20. The second time, he defeats the Jews at the battle of Beerzeth, in which Judas Maccabaeus dies, 9:25–26; he pursues but does not capture Jonathan, the successor of Judas, 9:32–34, 43–49. He then fortifies his positions in Judaea, 9:50–57; cf. 10:12; at the death of Alcimus he returns to the king. He comes to Judaea a third time to besiege Jonathan and Simon in Bethbasi. He fails and makes peace with Jonathan, 9:58–72. In 2 M 8:30 a battle is mentioned of Judas against Timotheus and Bacchides, in which the latter are defeated.

[BACCHUS], (cf. Bacchides). See: DIONYSUS 1.

BAEAN (Sons of) (1), a seminomadic tribe, probably Arabian, which holds travelers for ransom; Judas burns them in their towers, where they have taken refuge, 1 M 5:4–5.

BAGOAS (6), a common name among the Persian eunuchs; "the eunuch in charge of his [Holofernes'] personal affairs," Jdt 12:11, 13, 15; 13:1, 3. He discovers the decapitated body of Holofernes, 14:13–18.

BAHARUM (1), 1 Ch 11:33. See: AZMAVETH 1.

BAHURIM (7), a town in Benjamin, east of the Mount of Olives on the road from Jerusalem to the Jordan valley. It is here that Michal, on her return to David, leaves her husband Paltiel, 2 S 3:16. David, on his flight from Absalom, passes by Bahurim, where Shimei curses him, 2 S 16:5. Jonathan and Ahimaaz, carrying a message to David, escape the search of Absalom's servants by hiding in a cistern of the town, 2 S 17:18.

Native place of: SHIMEI 6.

BAKBAKKAR (1). See: BAKBUKIAH.

BAKBUK (2), "Pitcher" (cf. Bakbukiah), head of a family of "oblates" who return from the exile, Ezr 2:51//Ne 7:53.

BAKBUKIAH (3), (cf. Bakbuk), a Levite, a cantor in the time of the high priest Jeshua, Ne 12:9, 25; lives in Jerusalem, Ne 11:17.

= **Bakbakkar** (1), 1 Ch 9:15, residing in Jerusalem.

BAKERS (Street of the) (1), Hb. *'Ophim,* in Jerusalem, the street where the bakeries are located, Jr 37:21.

BALAAM, Gr. and Lat. transcription of Hb. *Bil'am,* "Glutton"? (cf. Bela?).

1. **Balaam** (63), **son of Beor** (9), a

soothsayer, Jos 13:22. His story has for its context the conquest of Transjordania by Israel. After Israel's defeat of the Amorites, Balak, king of Moab, summons Balaam so that he may curse Israel, but Balaam utters a series of blessings instead, cf. Mi 6:5. In Nb 22–24 are found two traditions (Elohist and Yahwist) intermingled: in one, Balaam is an Aramaean soothsayer from the banks of the Euphrates, 22:5; 23:7, a worshipper of Yahweh, 22:18, whom God authorizes to answer the summons of the king of Moab, 22:20. In the other tradition, it is against God's will that Balaam attempts to go to the king of Moab; he is prevented by an angel (episode of the donkey, which can see the angel; 22:22–35).

The oracles of Balaam consist of four blessings upon Israel: 23:7–10, "See, a people dwelling apart . . ."; 23:18–24, "Yahweh his God is with him . . ."; 24: 3–9, "His king is greater than Agag . . ."; 24:15–19, "a star from Jacob takes the leadership. . . . It crushes the brows of Moab. . . . Edom becomes a conquered land." These oracles are followed by three curses, which foretell the end of the Amalekites, the Kenites, and the Sea-people.

Elsewhere the Bible makes Balaam an enemy of Israel: he blesses Israel, but against his will, Dt 23:5–6; Jos 24:9–10; cf. Ne 13:2; at Peor he is the one who incites Israel to idolatry, Nb 31:16; finally, he is linked to the Midianites, with whom he dies at the hands of the Israelites, Nb 31:8; Jos 13:22. The NT follows this same line of thought: Balaam becomes the very type of the false teacher, 2 P 2:15; Jude 11; Rv 2:14.

2. **Bileam** (1), 1 Ch 6:55. See: IBLEAM.

BALADAN (2), Accad. *Apal-iddina*, "[The god] has given a son," father of: MERODACH-BALADAN.

BALAH (1). See: BAALAH 2.

BALAK (44), **son of Zippor** (7), **king of Moab** (6). When Israel crushes the Amorites, Balak summons Balaam the soothsayer to curse Israel; the uttering of a curse will infallibly guarantee victory. Instead of the expected curse, Balaam utters blessings on Israel, Nb 22: 21–8, 35–41; 23; 24:10–14, 25; cf. Jos 24:9; Jg 11:25; Mi 6:5; Rv 2:14.

BALAMON (1), Jdt 8:3 = ? **Balbaim** (1), Jdt 7:3, both associated with Dothan.

= ? **Belmain** (1), Jdt 4:4. Site unknown (var. *Abelmain*).

BALBAIM (1). See: BALAMON.

BAMOTH (2), "High places" (cf. Oholibamah), in Moab, NE of the Dead Sea. One of the final stages of the Exodus, Nb 21:19–20.

= **Bamoth-baal** (2), from which Balaam can see part of the Israelite camp, Nb 22:41; assigned to Reuben, Jos 13: 17.

BAMOTH-BAAL (2), "High places of Baal." See: BAMOTH.

BANI (cf. Benaiah).

1. **Bani the Gadite** (1), one of David's champions, 2 S 23:36.

2. **Bani** (1), a Levite of the clan of Merari, an ancestor of Ethan the cantor, 1 Ch 6:31.

3. **Bani** (1), a Judaean, ancestor of: UTHAI 1.

4. **Bani** (4), an Israelite, head of a family whose sons return from the exile with Zerubbabel, Ezr 2:10//Ne 7:15 (*Binnui*), and with Ezra, Ezr 8:10; among them are a number of men married to foreign wives, whom they put away, Ezr 10:34. Bani, a leader of the people, is one of the cosigners of the pledge to observe the Law, Ne 10:15.

5. **Bani** (1), same as the preceding?, father of: REHUM 3.

6. **Bani** (4), one of the Levites who explain the Law during its solemn reading by Ezra, Ne 8:7, take part in the cere-

mony of the confession of sins and urge the people to bless God, Ne 9:4–5, and sign the pledge to observe the Law, Ne 10:14.

7. **Bani** (1), a descendant of Asaph, father of: Uzzi 5.

BAPTIST (15), Gr. *Baptistēs, Baptizōn,* "He who immerses," Mt 3:1//Mk 1:4; Mt 11:11–12; 14:2//Mk 6:14; Mt 14: 8//Mk 6:24–25; Mt 16:14//Mk 8: 28//Lk 9:19; Mt 17:13; Lk 7:20, 33. See: John 22.

BARABBAS (11), Aram. *Bar-'abba,* "Son of the Father," whose first name (acc. to variants) is **Jesus,** "a notorious prisoner," Mt 27:16, "a murderer," Ac 3:14, "a brigand" (a term often applied to the Zealots because of their violence-ridden political and religious activity), Jn 18:40, doubtless the leader of the rebellion against the Roman occupation, cf. Mk 15:7; Lk 23:19, 25. Manipulated by the chief priests, the Jewish crowd wins from Pilate the liberation of Barabbas and the infliction on Jesus of the punishment Barabbas deserved, Mt 27:15–26//Mk 15:6–15//Lk 23:13–25.

BARACHEL (2), Hb. *Barak'el,* "God blesses" (cf. Beracah), father of: Elihu 5.

BARACHIAH. See: Berechiah 4.

BARAK (15), "Lightning flash," **son of Abinoam** (4), **from Kedesh in Naphtali** (1). At the urging of Deborah the prophetess, Barak gathers fighters from Naphtali and Zebulun; from Mount Tabor he attacks the Canaanite army of Sisera, which he crushes at Taanach. It is not Barak, however, but a woman, Jael, who wins the glory of killing Sisera, Jg 4:6–22. This episode is also recounted in a poem, the "Song of Deborah," one of the oldest texts of the Bible, Jg 5. Barak is thus among the "greater" judges, the liberators of Israel, cf. 1 S 12:11; Heb 11:32.

BARECHIAH (1). See: Berechiah 4.

BARIAH (1), one of the six sons of Shecaniah, a descendant of King Jehoiachin of Judah, 1 Ch 3:22.

BAR-JESUS (1), Aram. "Son of Jesus *or* of Joshua," Ac 13:6.

= **Elymas** (1), at Paphos (in Cyprus), a Jewish magician in the entourage of the proconsul Sergius Paulus, whom he seeks to turn away from the Christian faith. Paul intervenes forcefully, and the magician is struck blind, Ac 13:6–12.

BARKOS (2), a head of a family of "oblates" who return from the exile, Ezr 2:53//Ne 7:55.

BARNABAS (28), acc. to Ac 4:36, "son of encouragement," probably in the sense of "He who is able to encourage" (cf. Ac 11:23), a surname given by the Apostles to **Joseph, a Levite of Cypriot origin** (1), Ac 4:36, a cousin of Mark, Col 1:10, a generous man, Ac 4:36–37, "a good man, filled with the Holy Spirit and with faith," Ac 11:24, called an Apostle in Ac 14:4, 14.

At Jerusalem, where he first comes on the scene, he does not hesitate to be in the company of the new convert, Saul, of whom the majority remain suspicious, and to introduce him to the apostles, Ac 9:26–27. Sent by the Church of Jerusalem to Antioch in Syria, he urges the young community on and introduces to it Saul, whom he has sought out at Tarsus; he and Saul work together at Antioch for a year, 11:22–26. Together they go up to Jerusalem with the funds collected at Antioch for the impoverished brethren in the holy city, 11:29–30, and return together with Mark, 12:25. A list of the "prophets and teachers" of the Church at Antioch has Barnabas at the head of the list and Saul at the end, 13:1. Sent as missionaries by the Church of Antioch, Ac 13:2–3, Barnabas and Saul bring the Gospel both to Jews and to pagans. Stages of the journey: Cyprus, 13:5–12; Perga in Pamphylia, where Mark leaves them, 13:13; Antioch in Pisidia; 13:14–

52; Iconium, 14:1–6; Lystra, where Barnabas is mistaken for Zeus and Paul for Hermes, 14:7–19; Derbe, and return to Antioch in Syria, 14:20–28. At Antioch a serious crisis arises: "Are pagans who embrace the Christian faith to be forced to undergo circumcision?" As men with personal missionary experience, Barnabas and Paul are commissioned to bring the problem to those in charge of the Church at Jerusalem, Ac 15:1–4, 12; cf. Ga 2:1–12, and it is to these same two, as men "who have dedicated their lives to the name of our Lord Jesus Christ," that the Council's resolutions are entrusted for communication to the Church of Antioch, where the two will be staying for a while longer, Ac 15:22–25. As they are about to set out on their mission once again, the two disagree completely and part company: Paul, refusing the companionship of Mark, who had left them once before, sets out with Silas for Asia Minor, whereas Barnabas and Mark embark for Cyprus, 15:36–40. Paul and Barnabas may have worked together later on, 1 Co 9:6.

BARSABBAS, Aram. *Bar-saba,* "Son of the noble one," or *Bar-shabba,* "Son of the sabbath."

1. **Barsabbas** (1), another name of: JOSEPH 12.

2. **Barsabbas** (1), surname of: JUDAH 16.

BARTHOLOMEW (4), Aram. Bartolmai, "Son of Tolmai" (cf. Talmai), appears only in the lists of the Twelve, where his name occurs in the second group (with Philip, Thomas, and Matthew, either in the second place, Mt 10:3; Mk 3:18; Lk 6:14, or the third, Ac 1:13). It is probably because both are associated with Philip that Bartholomew has been identified with Nathanael, cf. Jn 1:45–46.

See: TWELVE; List, page 000.

BARTIMAEUS (1), Aram. "Son of Timaeus," **son of Timaeus** (1), a blind beggar; at his petition he is healed by Jesus as the latter is leaving Jericho, Mk 10:46–52.

BARUCH, Hb. *Baruk,* "Blessed" (cf. Beracah).

1. **Baruch** (25), **son of Neriah** (9) or **Neraiah** (1), **son of Mahseiah** (2) (cf. Ba 1:1 for a fuller genealogy), secretary of Jeremiah. It is to him that Jeremiah entrusts the deed of purchase for the field belonging to Hanamel of Anathoth, Jr 32:12–16. In the fourth year of Jehoiakim (605) Jeremiah, who is forbidden entry into the temple, dictates to Baruch the oracles pronounced since the beginning of his ministry, Jr 36:4–8, 18. In December 604, Baruch reads these to the people in the temple, 36:9–1, then to the officials, 36:11–17. On the advice of the latter, Baruch and Jeremiah go into hiding. The king burns the scroll and orders the arrest of the parties responsible for it, 36:19, 26. Baruch rewrites a scroll identical with the first, 36:27, 32. As a reward, Jeremiah predicts for him, not success in great projects, but the saving of his life, 45:1–5. After the fall of Jerusalem, the rebellious men of Judah blame Jeremiah for letting Baruch influence him; the prophet and his secretary are led off to Egypt, 43:3, 6. Acc. to Ba 1:1–18 Baruch himself writes at Babylon the book that bears his name. He supposedly reads it to the deportees, then sends it to Jerusalem to be read there. He also recovers the furnishings belonging to the temple.

Probably brother of: SERAIAH 3.

2. **Baruch son of Zabbai (QZaccai)** (1), restores the wall of Jerusalem "from the Angle as far as the door of Eliashib, the high priest," Ne 3:20.

3. **Baruch** (1), a priest, cosigner of the pledge to observe the Law, Ne 10:7.

4. **Baruch** (1), a man of Judah, father of: MAASEIAH 15.

BARZILLAI, "Of iron."

1. **Barzillai** (7), **the Gileadite** (5) **from Rogelim** (2), a very rich old man who devotes his life and property to David

during the latter's exile at Mahanaim. Because of his great age he declines David's offer to have him spend the rest of his life in the royal palace, 2 S 17:27–28; 19:32–40. When dying, David urges Solomon to treat the sons of Barzillai with kindness, 1 K 2:7. See the following entry.

His son: CHIMHAM.

2. **Barzillai** (4), a priest, son-in-law of the preceding, whose name he adopts. His descendants, after the return from exile, cannot prove their authentic Israelite origin, Ezr 2:61–62//Ne 7:63–64.

3. **Barzillai** (1), father of: ADRIEL.

BASEMATH, "Perfumed."

1. **Basemath** (6), **daughter of Elon the Hittite** (1), Gn 26:34, or **daughter of Ishmael and sister of Nebaioth** (1), Gn 36:3; she is one of the wives of Esau, to whom she bears a son, Reuel, Gn 36:4, 10; the sons of the latter are called sons of Basemath, Gn 36:13, 17.

2. **Basemath daughter of Solomon** (1), wife of Ahimaaz, prefect of Solomon's eighth district, 1 K 4:15.

BASHAN (6), "Smooth land, *therefore* without rocks and fertile," a plateau east of the Sea of Chinnereth, between Hermon and the Yarmuk, a region famous for its wooded hills, Ps 68:15, 22; Is 33:9; Jr 22:20; Na 1:4, its oaks, Is 2:13; Ezk 27:6; Zc 11:2, its pastures and cattle, Dt 32:14; Ps 22:13; Jr 50:19; Ezk 39:18; Am 4:1; Mi 7:14, and its savage beasts, Dt 33:22. Realm of the Amorite king Og, Jos 12:5, conquered by Israel, Dt 3:1// Nb 21:33, including in particular the confederation of Argob, Dt 3:4–14, or Encampments of Jair, Dt 3:14; Jos 13:30–31, it falls to the lot of the eastern half-tribe of Manasseh, Jos 13:11–12; 17:1, 5; 21:6//1 Ch 6:47; Jos 22:7; 2 K 10:33; 1 Ch 5:23, and to the tribe of Gad, 1 Ch 5:11–16. It is part of Solomon's twelfth district, 1 K 4:13. The name Bashan survives in the Greco-Roman *Batanea.*

Towns: ASHTAROTH; EDREI 1; GOLAN; SALECAH.

King: OG 1.

See: GILEAD 1*d*.

BASKAMA (1), Peshitta *Beth-sekma,* "House of the sycamore," at the eastern end of the promontory of Carmel. Trypho kills Jonathan there, 1 M 13:23.

[BAST]. See: PI-BESETH.

BATH-GALLIM (1), "Daughter of Gallim." See: GALLIM 2.

BATH-RABBIM (1), "Daughter of many, *whence* Populous, Large" (cf. Rabbah), name of a much-used gate, perhaps in Heshbon, a town of the Transjordan, Sg 7:5.

BATHSHEBA (11), Hb. *Bat-Sheba',* "Daughter of opulence" (cf. Sheba), **daughter of Eliam (1), wife of Uriah** (5) **the Hittite** (2), a "very beautiful" woman, whom David seduces while her husband is at war. Bathsheba conceives, and David arranges to have Uriah die on the battlefield, 2 S 11:2–17. After the period of mourning, Bathsheba becomes David's wife, 2 S 11:26–27. The prophet Nathan reproaches David for his twofold sin, 12:9–10; cf. Ps 51:1. "The child that Uriah's wife had borne to David" dies, 2 S 12:15. Bathsheba bears a second son, Solomon, 12:24.

Nathan and Bathsheba plot for the succession to the elderly king David: the latter chooses Solomon and sets aside his eldest son, Adonijah, 1 K 1:11–21, 28–31. Finally Bathsheba meets with a total refusal from the young king when she asks him to give Abishag of Shunem to Adonijah for a wife, 1 K 2:13–24.

= **Bath-shua daughter of Ammiel** (1), 1 Ch 3:5, who has four sons by David: Shimea, Shobab, Nathan, and Solomon.

There is an allusion to Bathsheba as "Uriah's wife" in the genealogy of Jesus, Mt 1:6.

BATH-SHUA, "Daughter of Shua" (cf. Shua 1).

1. **Bath-shua the Canaanite woman** (1), 1 Ch 2:3.

= **The daughter of Shua** (2) **the Canaanite** (1), Gn 38:2–5, 12, wife of Judah (son of Jacob), to whom she gives three sons: Er, Onan, and Shelah.

2. **Bath-shua daughter of Ammiel** (1). See: BATHSHEBA.

BAZLITH (1). See: BAZLUTH.

BAZLUTH (1), Ezr 2:52, head of a family of "oblates" who return from the Exile.

= **Bazlith** (1), Ne 7:54.

BEALIAH (1), "Yah is master" (cf. Baal), a Benjaminite who rallies to David before the latter becomes king, 1 Ch 12:6.

BEALOTH (1), "Ladies" (cf. Baaloth), a town in the Negeb of Judah, Jos 15:24. Unknown.

BEAR (2), Hb. *'Ash, 'Ayish,* Jb 9:9; 38:32, a constellation.

See: MANSIONS OF THE SOUTH.

BEAST, Aram. *hevah* (10), Gr. *thērion* (37), symbol of totalitarian political power that is hostile to the people of God. Dn 7 has four beasts, one each for the Babylonian Empire and the kingdoms of the Medes, the Persians, and Alexander. Rv 13 and 17 speak of *the beast from the sea,* namely, the Roman Empire; *the beast from the ground,* which is also called "the false prophet," that is, the power of communication that is completely at the service of the first beast; the defeat of these two is certain. Cf. also Rv 11:7; 14:9, 11; 15:2; 16:2, 13; 19:19–20; 20:4, 10.

See: BEHEMOTH; DEEP; LEVIATHAN.

BEAUTIFUL GATE (2), a gate of the Jerusalem temple, also called the "Corinthian" gate and leading from the outer court (or Court of the Gentiles) to the first inner court (or Court of the Women), Ac 3:2, 10. Peter cures a paralytic there.

BEBAI, Accad. *Bibi,* "Infant," Gr. *Babi, Bebai.*

1. **Bebai** (6), head of a family whose sons return from the exile with Zerubbabel, Ezr 2:11//Ne 7:16, or with Ezra, Ezr 8:11, and among whom are some men who have married foreign wives; these they put away, Ezr 10:28. Bebai is a cosigner of the pledge to observe the Law, Ne 10:16.

Father of: ZECHARIAH 24.

2. **Bebai** (1), Gr. *Bebai,* Jdt 15:4, an unknown town in Israel.

BECHER, "Young camel" (cf. Becorath).

1. **Becher** (4), second son of Benjamin acc. to Gn 46:21 and 1 Ch 7:6, whose descendants form the clan of the sons of Becher, 1 Ch 7:8–9.

2. **Becher** (1), second son of Ephraim, whose descendants form the **Becherite** clan, Nb 26:35.

= ? **Bered** (1), son of Shuthelah, son of Ephraim, 1 Ch 7:20.

BECHERITE (1), (cf. Becorath), belonging to the clan of: BECHER 2.

BECORATH (1), "First-born" (cf. Becher; Becherite; Bichri; Bichrite), a Benjaminite, ancestor of Saul and of: KISH 1.

BECTILETH (2), an unknown town. Acc. to Jdt 2:21 it is a three days' march (northward) from Nineveh.

BEDAD (2), father of the Edomite king: HADAD 2.

BEDAN (1), a Manassite, descendant of Machir through Sheresh and Ulam; he is listed among the sons of Gilead, 1 Ch 7:17.

BEDIAH (1), perhaps an abbrev. of Hb. *'Abedyah,* "Servant of Yahweh," or of Hb. *beyad yah,* "By the hand, that is, by the mediation of Yah" (cf. Ebed), an Israelite of the sons of Bani, married to a foreign wife, whom he puts away, Ezr 10:35.

BEELIADA (2), Hb. *Be'elyada',* "Baal knows" (cf. Jada), 1 Ch 14:7.

= **Eliada** (2), 2 S 5:16 (which some correct to *Beeliada*); 1 Ch 3:8, one of the sons of David that are born at Jerusalem.

BEELZEBUL (7). See: BAALZEBUB.

BEER, "Well" (cf. Baalath-beer; Beerah; Beer-elim; Beeri; Beeroth; Beersheba; Beerzeth).

1. **Beer** (1), a stage of the Exodus, north of the Arnon, in Moab, Nb 21:16. = ? **Beer-elim** (1), Is 15:8.

2. **Beer** (1), a town located perhaps west of Beth-shan, where Jotham takes refuge to escape Abimelech, Jg 9:21.

BEERAH (cf. Beer).

1. **Beerah** (1), a descendant of Joel, a prince of the Reubenites who is deported by Tiglath-pileser, 1 Ch 5:4–6.

2. **Beerah** (1), an Asherite, one of the eleven sons of Zophah, 1 Ch 7:37.

BEER-ELIM (1), "Well of the gods *or* of the terebinths" (cf. Beer; El; Elim). See: BEER 1.

BEERI, "Of the well" (cf. Beer).

1. **Beeri the Hittite** (1), father of: JUDITH 1.

2. **Beeri** (1), father of the prophet: HOSHEA 3.

BEEROTH (11), "The wells" (cf. Beer), one of the four Gibeonite towns, Jos 9:17, assigned to Benjamin, Jos 18:25; 2 S 4:2. The people of Beeroth emigrate to Gittaim, 2 S 4:3. Some men from Beeroth return from the exile with Zerubbabel, Ezr 2:25//Ne 7:29.

= **Beerzeth** (1), site of the battle of the Jews against Bacchides during which Judas Maccabaeus is slain, 1 M 9:4. Variant of Gr. *Berea.*

Native place of: NAHARAI; RIMMON 4.

BEERSHEBA (34), Gr. transcription of Hb. *Be'er-Sheba',* "Well of the seven [lambs] *or* Well of the oath" (cf. Beer; Sheba).

Beersheba is the scene of a covenant between Abraham and Abimelech regarding a well, for ownership of which Abraham gives Abimelech *seven* lambs, Gn 21:25–32. A parallel account, 26:23–33, has Abimelech and Isaac on the stage: there is a covenant and exchange of *oaths;* the well is given the name "Sheba, and hence the town is named Beersheba to this day," v. 33. Earlier, Hagar, when driven out by Sarah, takes refuge in the wilderness of Beersheba, 21:14. Abraham, too, dwells there; there he calls upon El Olam, "the everlasting God," 21:33; Isaac calls upon the God of his father Abraham, 26:23–25, and Jacob upon the God of his father Isaac, 46:1. Beersheba is the place from which Jacob sets out for Mesopotamia, 28:10, and a stopping place where he receives divine promises on his way down into Egypt, 46:1–6. This patriarchal sanctuary is still a place of pilgrimage in the period of the monarchy, Am 5:5; 8:14.

Beersheba is a town in the Negeb of Judah, Jos 15:28. The sons of Samuel are judges in Beersheba, 1 S 8:2. The prophet Elijah passes through it, 1 K 19:3, on his way to Horeb. At the southern end of Judah, 2 K 23:8; 2 Ch 19:4, Beersheba thus marks the southern frontier of Israelite territory, the northern frontier being Dan; cf. the expression *from Dan to Beersheba* (7), Jg 20:1; 1 S 3:20; 2 S 3:10; 17:11; 24:2, 15; 1 K 5:5, or *from Beersheba to Dan* (2), 1 Ch 21:2; 2 Ch 30:5; cf. 2 S 24:6–7; Am 8:14. Beersheba is reoccupied by the sons of Judah after the return from exile, Ne 11:27, 30. Today *Be'er Sheva'.*

Native place of: ZIBIAH.

BEERZETH (1), "Well of the olive tree" (cf. Beer), 1 M 9:4. See: BEEROTH.

= ? **Birzaith** (1), 1 Ch 7:31, whose father, Malchiel, is an Asherite.

Today *Birzeit,* 25 km N of Jerusalem.

BEHEMOTH (1), plural of Hb. *Behemah,* "Beast, Cattle." This is the Beast, the brute beast par excellence, at once of the land and of the sea, regarded as an animal both sacred and demonic. In Jb 40:

15–24, Behemoth refers to the hippopotamus, a symbol of brute power, of which God is master but which man cannot domesticate.

See: LEVIATHAN.

BEL (18), like Baal means "Master" (cf. Belshazzar); usually it refers to Marduk (Merodach), Jr 50:2, the supreme god of Babylon, cf. Dn 14:3–22, 28. With the fall of Babylon, Bel too collapses, Is 46:1; Jr 51:44; he is a deaf and powerless god, Ba 6:40.

Father of: NEBO 4.

BELA, "Swallowed up"? (cf. Balaam).

1. **Bela** (4), **son of Beor** (2), king of Edom at Dinhabah, Gn 36:32–33//1 Ch 1:43–44.

2. **Bela** (7), first-born son of Benjamin, Gn 46:21; Nb 26:38; 1 Ch 7:6; 8:1. The three lists of Bela's sons do not agree; Nb 26:40 lists two sons; 1 Ch 7:7, five; and 1 Ch 8:3–5, eight. His descendants form the **Belaite** clan, Nb 26:38, which is divided into two subclans, the Ardite and the Naamite, Nb 26:40.

3. **Bela son of Azaz, son of Shema, son of Joel** (1), a Reubenite, 1 Ch 5:8.

4. **Bela** (2), Gn 14:2, 8, a town identified with: ZOAR. Its king is allied with: BERA.

BELAITE (1), Nb 26:38, belonging to the Benjaminite clan of: BELA 2.

BELIAL (5), Hb. *beli-ya'al,* "Useless, good-for-nothing, *or* Whence one does not return," (25× in all in the OT) is usually translated by a generic name, such as "scoundrel," when applied to persons, Dt 13:4; Jg 19:22; 20:13; and so on, or "evil, mean," when applied to things, Dt 15:9; and so on. In some instances the word Belial appears in the translation and refers to death or the lower world, 2 S 22:5//Ps 18:4; cf. Ps 41:8, or Satan (perhaps in Ps 101:3; Pr 16:27) or his representatives, Na 1:11; 2:1.

See: BELIAR.

BELIAR (1), another form of *Belial,* refers in 2 Co 6:15 to Satan, the adversary of Christ.

BELMAIN (1). See: BALAMON.

BELOVED, Hb. *Ruhamah.* See: UNLOVED.

BELSHAZZAR (10), Hb. and Aram. *Belsha'zzar,* Accad. *Bel-shar-uzur,* "Bel, protect the king," Gr. *Baltasar,* Lat. *Baltassar* (cf. Bel; Sharezer), **king of Babylon** (1), Dn 7:1, **the Chaldaean king** (1), Dn 5:30, and son of Nebuchadnezzar, Ba 1:11–12; cf. Dn 5:18, 22. In fact, the historical Belshazzar was son of Nabonidus and never had the title of king. In Ba 1:11–12 prayers are asked for a long life for Nebuchadnezzar and Belshazzar. In Dn 5 the banquet given by Belshazzar is described. During it a mysterious hand writes mysterious words on the wall. During the ensuing night Belshazzar is assassinated. Two dreams of Daniel are dated from the reign of Belshazzar, Dn 7:1; 8:1.

BELTESHAZZAR (10), Hb. and Aram. *Beltsha'zzar,* Accad. *Belit-shar-uzur,* "Protect the life of the king," Gr. *Baltasar* (cf. Sanballat; Sharezer), Dn 1:7; 2:26; 4:5–6, 15–16; 5:12; 10:1, a name given to: DANIEL 4.

BENAIAH, "Yah builds," Gr. *Banaias* (cf. Bani; Binnui; Bunni; Ibneiah; Ibnijah; Jabneh; Jabneel).

1. **Benaiah** (24), **son of Jehoiada** (20), **from Kabzeel** (2), one of David's champions, the most illustrious of the Thirty; he kills two Moabite champions, an Egyptian of great stature, and a lion in a cistern, 2 S 23:20–23//1 Ch 11:22–25. Commander of David's personal bodyguard, 2 S 8:18//20:23//1 Ch 18:17, he supports Solomon's candidacy for the succession against Adonijah, 1 K 1:8–44. At the new king's order he executes Adonijah, 1 K 2:25, Joab, 2:29–34, and Shimei, 2:46. Solomon makes him com-

mander of the army, 1 K 2:35; 4:4. The chronicler makes him responsible for the (military) service of the third month, 1 Ch 27:5–6.

Father of: AMMIZABAD.

2. **Benaiah from Pirathon** (3), one of David's champions, 2 S 23:30//1 Ch 11:31. The chronicler makes him an Ephraimite, responsible for the (military) service of the eleventh month, 1 Ch 27:14.

3. **Benaiah** (1), a Simeonite, head of a clan, 1 Ch 4:36.

4. **Benaiah** (3), a Levite, a gatekeeper assigned to the service of the Ark, 1 Ch 15:18, a lyre player, 15:20; 16:5.

5. **Benaiah** (2), a priest, a trumpeter before the Ark, 1 Ch 15:24; 16:6.

6. **Benaiah** (1), to be compared with 1 above, father of: JEHOIADA 2.

7. **Benaiah** (1), a descendant of Asaph and ancestor of: JAHAZIEL 4.

8. **Benaiah** (1), one of the ten Levites assisting Conaniah and Shimei in the time of King Hezekiah, 2 Ch 31:13.

9. **Benaiah** (2), father of: PELATIAH 2.

10. **Benaiah** (4), four Israelites, all married to foreign wives, whom they put away: the first, of the sons of Parosh, Ezr 10:25; the second, of the sons of Pahath-moab, 10:30; the third, of the sons of Bani, 10:35; and the fourth, of the sons of Nebo, 10:43.

BEN-ALLON (1), "Son of Allon," a Simeonite and clan leader, 1 Ch 4:37.

BEN-AMMI (1), "Son of my relative" (cf. Am-; Ammon), a name given to the ancestor of the Ammonites, Gn 19:38.

BEN-BUZ (1), "Son of Buz." See: BUZ 2.

BENE-AMMON, "Sons of Ammon" (cf. Ammon), a biblical name for the Ammonites, for example, Gn 19:38.

BENE-BERAK (1), Accad. *Banai Barqa,* a town in Dan, Jos 19:45, 8 km SE of Joppa.

BENE-HASHEM (1), "Sons of Hashem," from Gizon (1). See: JASHEN.

BENE-JAAKAN (3), "Sons of Jaakan" (cf. Jaakan), a stage of the Exodus, in the Wilderness of Sin, Nb 33:31–32; Dt 10:6.

BEN-GILEAD (1), "Son of Gilead." See: GILEAD 3.

BEN-HADAD, "Son of Hadad" (cf. Hadad 1–4).

1. **Ben-hadad I** (4), **son of Tabrimmon, son of Hezion** (1), **the king of Aram** (4), **who lived in Damascus** (2), about 900 B.C. Allied with Baasha of Israel, he accepts the gold and silver Asa of Judah offers him and invades the kingdom of Baasha; the latter withdraws his army from the borders of Judah, 1 K 15:18–20//2 Ch 16:2–4. Acc. to 2 Ch 16:7 Hanani the seer blames Asa for having sought help from the king of Aram.

2. **Ben-hadad II** (16), **king of Aram** (10), probably the son and successor of the preceding, around 875 B.C. Because Ahab refuses to meet his demands, Ben-hadad besieges Samaria, 1 K 20:1–12, but Ahab inflicts a serious defeat on him, 20:13–21. In a second campaign, at Aphek, the king of Aram surrenders to Ahab, who concludes a treaty with him and gives him his freedom, 20:22–34, 42. Three years later Ahab attacks Ben-hadad for taking Ramoth-gilead from him, but loses his life there, 1 K 22:1–35//2 Ch 18:1–34. Ben-hadad besieges Samaria again, but unsuccessfully, 2 K 6:24–7:16. He falls ill and sends Hazael to consult Elisha; when Hazael returns, he murders Ben-hadad and reigns in his place, 2 K 8:7–15.

It is perhaps Ben-hadad II, the "king of Aram," whose commander-in-chief is: NAAMAN 3.

3. **Ben-hadad III** (5), **son of Hazael** (2), king of Aram ca. 797–773, oppresses the Israelites in the time of Kings

Jehoahaz, 2 K 13:3–4, and Joash; the latter strikes him "three times," 2 K 13:16–25. This is undoubtedly the Ben-hadad to whom Am 1:4 and Jr 49:27 are referring.

BEN-HAIL (1), "Son of Hail *or* The courageous" (cf. Abihail), one of the five officers sent by King Jehoshaphat, along with two priests and eight Levites, to instruct the towns of Judah in the Law, 2 Ch 17:7–9.

BEN-HANAN (1), "Son of Hanan." See: HANAN 9.

BEN-HINNOM (Valley of) (9). See: HINNOM.

BEN-HURI (1), "Son of Huri" (cf. Hur), a Gadite, of the sons of Abihail, 1 Ch 5:14 ff.

BEN-JAHDO (1), "Son of Jahdo," a Gadite of the sons of Abihail, 1 Ch 5:14.

BENJAMIN, Hb. *Binyamin,* "Son of the right hand, that is, of the South" (cf. Jamin).

1. **Benjamin** (165), last of the sons of Jacob, and a tribe of Israel, second son of Rachel (after Joseph). Before dying, Rachel calls him **Ben-oni,** "Son of my sorrow," but Jacob changes this name of ill-omen to *Benjamin,* Gn 35:18. Benjamin is the only son of Jacob born in the Promised Land, between Bethel and Ephrath, Gn 35:16. He is mentioned 12× in the story of Joseph, his elder brother, to whom he is linked by the special affection his father has for them, Gn 42–45. Three lists of the sons and descendants of Benjamin are given: Gn 40:21; 1 Ch 7:6–12; 8, and a list of clans, Nb 26:38–41. The military strength of the tribe varies acc. to the censuses: 35,400, Nb 1:37; 45,600, Nb 26:41; 54,434, 1 Ch 7:6–11.

The tribe's territory is located west of the Jordan between the territories of Judah, Dan, and Ephraim: it is described in Jos 18:11–28, which names five of its hillsides, or flanks, to which Dt 33:12 alludes. Jerusalem, on the frontier of Judah, is mentioned among the towns of Benjamin, Jos 18:28, but before the conquest of Jerusalem by David, neither Judah, Jos 15:63, nor Benjamin, Jg 1:21, is able to expel the Jebusites from it. Under Solomon, Benjamin belongs to the eleventh district, 1 K 4:18. Some towns of the tribe are assigned to the Levites, Jos 21:4–17, 18//1 Ch 6:45, 50. Rocky and not very fertile, the country, 1 S 9:4; Jr 37:12, is a place of passage; brigandage is perhaps one of the resources of the Benjaminites, Gn 49:27.

Benjamin is a tribe with a combative spirit; its warriors are able, Jg 20:16, and cruel, Gn 49:27; cf. Jg 3:15–16, as is attested especially by the implacable war between Israelites and Benjaminites after the crime at Gibeah, Jg 19–21; this war almost deprived Israel of one of its tribes. Saul, first king of Israel, is a Benjaminite, 1 S 9–10; cf. 2 S 21:14; 1 Ch 12:2; Ac 13:21. The enmity between Benjamin and Judah, 2 S 2, continues after the country has rallied to David, 2 S 3:19; cf. 1 Ch 12:7, as is shown, for example, by the cursing of Shimei, 2 S 16:5–6, or the rebellion of Sheba, 2 S 20. At the time of the schism, Rehoboam tries to mobilize Judah and Benjamin in order to reconquer Israel, 1 K 12:21–23//2 Ch 11:5–12, 23; he fortifies towns in Judah and in Benjamin, 2 Ch 11:20–23. Henceforth the life of Benjamin is inseparable from that of Judah in the area of military organization (under Asa, 2 Ch 14:7, Jehoshaphat, 2 Ch 17:14, 17, Amaziah, 2 Ch 25:5; and so on) and in the area of religious reform (under Asa, 2 Ch 15:1–9; Hezekiah, 2 Ch 31:1; and Josiah, 2 Ch 34:9, 32). At the return from the exile, Benjaminites and Judaeans reoccupy the land, Ezr 1:5; 4:1; 10:9, either at Jerusalem, Ne 11:4–8//1 Ch 9:3–9, or in the province, Ne 11:31–32, as Jr 32:8, 44; 33:13, had foretold.

In Dt 33:13, where Benjamin is called "beloved of Yahweh" with whom "he rests in safety," Benjamin's location near the temple of Jerusalem (or of Shiloh) is alluded to. For Benjamin in the lists of the tribes, see List, pages 410–11.

Famous Benjaminites: JONATHAN 2; PAUL 1; SAUL 4. See also: ABIDAN; ABIEZER 2; CUSH 2; EHUD; ELIDAD; KISH 1; MORDECAI 2; PALTI 1; SHEBA 2; SHIMEI 5–6.

Principal towns: ANATHOTH; GEBA; GIBEAH 1.

2. **Benjamin Gate** (5), a gate on the north side of the temple and of Jerusalem, Jr 37:13; 38:7; Ezk 48:32; Zc 14:10. Some distinguish it from "the Gate of Benjamin, the upper gate leading into the Temple," where Jeremiah is put in the stocks, Jr 20:2, and which is perhaps the: UPPER GATE 1.

3. **Benjamin** (1), a Benjaminite of the sons of Jediael, a fighting man and head of a family, 1 Ch 7:10.

4. **Benjamin** (1), an Israelite of the sons of Harim, married to a foreign wife, whom he puts away, Ezr 10:32.

5. **Benjamin** (1), a volunteer in the rebuilding of the wall, Ne 3:23.

BENJAMINITE (13), Hb. *Ben-Yemini* or *Ish-Yemini,* Jg 3:15; 19:16; 1 S 9:1, 4, 21; 22:7; 2 S 16:11; 19:17; 20:1; 1 K 2:8; 1 Ch 27:12; Est 2:5; Ps 7:1. See: BENJAMIN 1.

BEN-JAROAH (1), "Son of Jaroah," a Gadite of the sons of Abihail, 1 Ch 5:14.

BEN-JEDAIAH (1), "Son of Jedaiah." See: JEDAIAH 6.

BEN-JESHISHAI (1), "Son of Jeshishai," a Gadite of the sons of Abihail, 1 Ch 5:14.

BEN-JOHANAN (1), "Son of John" (corr. of Hb. *Hanan*), **son of Igdaliah** (1). See: JOHN 10.

BEN-MICHAEL (1), "Son of Michael." See: MICHAEL 8.

BEN-ONI (1), "Son of my sorrow" (cf. Beth-aven; Bikath-aven), Gn 35:18, name given by the dying Rachel to her son: BENJAMIN 1.

BEN-SHEMAIAH (1), "Son of Shemaiah." See: SHEMAIAH 5.

BEN-SHIMRI (1), "Son of Shimri." See: SHIMRI 1.

BEN-SHIPHI (1), "Son of Shiphi," a Simeonite, head of a clan, 1 Ch 4:37.

BEN-SIRA (2), "Son of Sira." See: JOSHUA 10.

BEN-ZOHETH (1), "Son of Zoheth." See: ZOHETH 2.

BEON (1). See: BAAL-MEON.

BEOR

1. **Beor** (1), father of the Edomite king: BELA 1.

2. **Beor** (9), father of the soothsayer: BALAAM 1.

BERA (1), "Out of spitefulness," **king of Sodom** (6), together with **Birsha** (1) **king of Gomorrah** (3), **Shinab** (1) **king of Admah** (2), **Shemeber** (1), **king of Zeboiim** (2), and **the king of Bela** (2), form a coalition against their common oppressor, Chedor-laomer. The confrontation in the Valley of Siddim ends in the defeat of the king of Sodom and his allies. Abraham pursues Chedor-laomer successfully and restores all the recovered booty to the king of Sodom so that the latter may not be able to say, "I enriched Abram," Gn 14.

BERACAH, "Blessing" (cf. Barachel; Baruch; Berechiah; Jeberechiah).

1. **Beracah** (1), a Benjaminite, rallies to David before the latter becomes king, 1 Ch 12:3.

2. **Valley of Beracah** (2), perhaps between Tekoa and Engedi, where Jehoshaphat and his army "bless Yahweh"

after their victory over Ammon, Moab, and Edom, 2 Ch 20:25–26.

BERAIAH (1), "Yah has created," a Benjaminite of the sons of Shimei, head of a family at Jerusalem, 1 Ch 8:21.

BERECHIAH, Barachiah, Jeberechiah, "Yahweh blesses," Gr. *Barachia* (cf. Beracah).

1. **Berechiah** (2), 1 Ch 6:24; 15:17, father of: ASAPH 1.

2. **Berechiah** (1), a Levite, a gatekeeper for the Ark, 1 Ch 15:23.

3. **Berechiah son of Meshillemoth** (1), one of the four officers of the northern kingdom, 2 Ch 28:12, who heed the plea of the prophet Oded, take pity on their brothers from Judah who are imprisoned, help them, and set them free, cf. vv. 5–15.

4. **Barachiah** (1), father of: ZECHARIAH 6.

5. **Jeberechiah** (1), father of: ZECHARIAH 8.

6. **Berechiah** (2), father of: ZECHARIAH 22.

7. **Berechiah** (1), one of the five sons of Meshullam, a descendant of King Jehoiachin, 1 Ch 3:20.

8. **Berechiah son of Asa, son of Elkanah** (1), a Levite who after the return from the exile lives "in the villages of the Netophathites," 1 Ch 9:16.

9. **Berechiah** (3), father of: MESHULLAM 14.

BERED

1. **Bered** (1). See: BECHER 2.

2. **Bered** (1), a town near Kadesh; between Kadesh and Bered is the well of Lahai Roi, Gn 16:14.

[BERENICE], Bernice, Gr. "Bringer of victory" (cf. Andronicus).

1. **[Berenice],** daughter of Ptolemy II Philadelphus, wife of: ANTIOCHUS 1.

2. **Bernice** (3), daughter of Herod Agrippa I, sister of Agrippa II and of Drusilla, lives with her brother. During a stay at Caesarea she is present when Paul appears before her brother Agrippa and Festus, the governor, Ac 25:13, 23; 26:30.

BERI (1), an Asherite, one of the eleven sons of Zophah, 1 Ch 7:36.

BERIAH, Hb. *Beri'ah.*

1. **Beriah** (6), last (fourth or third) of the sons of Asher, has two sons, Heber and Malchiah, Gn 46:17//1 Ch 7:30–31. His descendants form the **Beriite** clan, Nb 26:44–45.

2. **Beriah** (1), a son born to Ephraim after the death of his other sons, 1 Ch 7:23, where the name Beriah is connected with Hb. *bera'ah,* "in misfortune." Beriah, an Ephraimite clan, perhaps settled in Benjamin. Cf. the following entry.

3. **Beriah** (2), a Benjaminite, one of the heads of families at Aijalon who conquered the people of Gath, 1 Ch 8:13. His brothers and sons are listed in vv. 14–16. Cf. the preceding entry.

4. **Beriah** (2), a Levite of the clan of Gershon, last of the four sons of Shimei, 1 Ch 23:10, 11.

BERIITE (1), belonging to the clan of: BERIAH 1.

BERNICE (3). See: [BERENICE] 2.

BEROEA, Gr. *Beroia.*

1. **Beroea** (1), name given by Seleucus I to the city today known as Aleppo (100 km E of Antioch in Syria). It is here that, in keeping with the local manner of execution, Menelaus dies by the punishment of ashes, 2 M 13:4–6.

2. **Beroea** (3), a city in Macedonia west of Thessalonika. Paul, Silas, and Timothy visit it during their second missionary journey, after having had to leave Thessalonika abruptly. The Jews of Beroea prove more receptive than those of Thessalonika. But the arrival of the latter forces Paul to leave for Athens, whereas Silas and Timothy stay at Beroea a while longer, Ac 17:10–14. Today, *Werria.*

Native city of: SOPATER.

BEROTHAH (1), a town on the theoretical northern frontier of the Promised Land, between Hamath and Damascus, Ezk 47:16.

= ? **Berothai** (1), a town in the kingdom of Zobah, N of Damascus, where "David took a great quantity of bronze," 2 S 8:8(//1 Ch 18:8 *Cun*).

BEROTHAI (1). See: BEROTHAH.

BESAI (2), head of a family of "oblates" who return from the exile, Ezr 2:49//Ne 7:52.

BESODEIAH (1), "In the secret of Yah"?, father of: MESHULLAM 13.

BESOR (Wadi) (3), where David leaves two hundred of his men to rest, 1 S 30:9–10, 21. Today a tributary or the main channel of the *Nahal Besor*.

BETAH (1), a town in the kingdom of Zobah, captured and looted by David, 2 S 8:8.

BETEN (1), "Pistachio"? (cf. Betonim?), a town in Asher, Jos 19:25. Today *Kh. Ibtin,* about 20 km SE of Akko.

BETH-ACHZIB (1). See: ACHZIB 1.

BETH-ANATH (2), "House of [the goddess] Anath" (cf. Anath), linked with Beth-shemesh. A town in Upper Galilee that long retained its independence, Jg 1:31; a fortified town of Naphtali, Jos 19:38. Location not definitively established.

BETH-ANOTH (1), "House of [the goddess] Anath"? (cf. Anath), a town in the highlands of Judah, Jos 15:59.

= ? **Bethany** (1), Jdt 1:9. Today *Kh. Beit Anum,* a few km N of Hebron.

BETHANY, Gr. *Bethania,* Hb. *Beth-'ani,* "House of the poor man *or* House of Ananiah."

1. **Bethany** (1). See: BETH-ANOTH.

2. **Bethany** (11), a town on the eastern slopes of the Mount of Olives, 3 km E of Jerusalem, Jn 11:18. A village, Lk 11:38, frequented by Jesus, especially during the last days of his life, Mk 11:1–12//Mt 21:1, 17; Lk 19:29, where Martha, Mary, and Lazarus live, Jn 11:1; 12:1, who welcome him into their home, Lk 10:38–42, as does Simon the leper, Mt 26:6–13; Mk 14:3–9, in whose house the "anointing at Bethany" takes place, cf. Jn 12:1–11. It is at Bethany that Jesus raises Lazarus from the dead, Jn 11, and it is here that the Ascension takes place acc. to Lk 24:50–51.

= **Ananiah** (1), occupied by Benjaminites after the return from exile, Ne 11:32. Today *el-'Azariyeh.*

3. **Bethany** (1), a town "on the far side of the Jordan, where John was baptizing," Jn 1:28 (var. *Bethabara*). Site uncertain.

BETH-ARABAH (4), "House of the steppe" (cf. Arabah), a border town between Judah and Benjamin, Jos 15:6; 18:18 (acc. to Gr.); listed among the towns of the Judaean wilderness, Jos 15:61, or among the towns of Benjamin, Jos 18:22. SE of Jericho, *'Ain Gharbeh.*

Native place of: ABIEL 2.

BETH-ARBEL (1), a town laid waste by Shalman, king of Moab, Ho 10:14. Probably the modern *Irbid* in northern Transjordania.

BETH-ASHBEA (1), "House of abundance" (cf. Sheba), a town in Judah where a clan of linenworkers lived, 1 Ch 4:21.

BETH-AVEN (7), "House of iniquity *or* nothingness" (cf. Ben-oni; Bikath-aven), is a name derisively applied to Bethel, "House of God," which had become a place of idolatrous worship, Ho 4:15; 5:8; 10:5; cf. Am 5:5. But in Jos 7:2 Beth-aven is distinct from Bethel. The same in Jos 18:12–13: the territory of Benjamin "ended at the wilderness of Beth-aven. Thence it continued towards Luz . . . which is now Bethel." 1 S 13:5 says only that Michmash is "to the east of Beth-aven." Some follow the Gr. and correct *Beth-aven* to *Beth-horon* in 1 S 14:23.

BETH-AZMAVETH (2). See: AZMAVETH 5.

BETH-BAAL-MEON (1), "House of Baal of Meon." See: BAAL-MEON.

BETH-BARAH (2), probably S of Beth-shan. The people of Ephraim occupy the water points there before the Midianites, Jg 7:24.

BETHBASI (2), a town between Bethlehem and Tekoa, doubtless founded by the "sons of Bezai" after the return from exile, cf. Ezr 2:17. Restored by Jonathan and Simon, this town is besieged by Bacchides, but he is defeated by Simon, 1 M 9:62–68. Today *Beit Bassa.*

BETH-BIRI (1), a town occupied by the sons of Simeon, 1 Ch 4:31 (// Jos 19:6, *Beth-lebaoth*).

BETH-CAR (1), "House of the ram *or* of the grass land," mentioned with Mizpah in Benjamin, 1 S 7:11. Site unknown.

BETH-DAGON, "House of Dagon" (cf. Dagon).

1. **Beth-dagon** (1), a town in the lowlands of Judah, Jos 15:41. Probably between Lod and Joppa.

2. **Beth-dagon** (1), on the frontier of Asher, Jos 19:27.

3. **Beth-dagon** (1), a temple of Dagon at Azotus, burned by Jonathan, 1 M 10:83–84; 11:4. See: DAGON.

BETH-DIBLATHAIM (1), (cf. Diblaim). See: ALMON-DIBLATHAIM.

BETH-EDEN (1), "House of pleasure"? (cf. Eden 4?), Am 1:5, difficult to identify; perhaps a symbolic name for Damascus.

BETH-EKED (2) **OF THE SHEPHERDS** (1), 2 K 10:12, 14, where, near a cistern, the brothers of King Ahaziah of Judah are slaughtered. Probably *Beit Qad,* 5 km E of *Jenin.*

BETHEL, "House of God," see Gn 28: 16–17, 22.

1. **Bethel** (75), a town 17 km N of Jerusalem on the road to Shechem, Jg 20:31; 21:19.

= **Luz** (7), a Canaanite town near which there was a sacred tree, Gn 35:8; cf. Jg 4:5, and a sanctuary where the god Bethel was venerated. Subsequently, the Israelites changed the name of *Luz* to *Bethel,* Gn 28:19; 35:6; 48:3; Jos 16:2; 18:13; Jg 1:23.

Bethel is one of the camping places of Abraham, Gn 12:8; 13:3, and Jacob, Gn 28:10–22. From there Abraham sees the land God is giving him, Gn 13:14; it is there that the dream of "Jacob's ladder" occurs, Gn 28:10–22, and that God appears to Jacob, Gn 35:1–15; 48: 31 cf. Ho 12:5. Thus Bethel becomes a sanctuary of the patriarchs. Along with Ai, it is one of the first towns conquered by Joshua, Jos 7:2; 8:9–17; cf. 12:9, 16. Listed among the towns of Benjamin, Jos 18:22, it is in fact on the borders of Benjamin, Jos 18:13, and occupied by Ephraim, Jos 16:1–2; 1 Ch 7:28. Acc. to Jg 1:22–26 the house of Joseph took Bethel thanks to the treachery of one of its inhabitants who was let go free and established another town named Luz elsewhere. The Israelites go to Bethel to consult God, Jg 20:18, 26; 21:2; 1 S 10:7, or to meet the judges, 1 S 7:16; cf. Jg 4:5. In the ninth century the town is the residence of a brotherhood of prophets centered around Elijah and Elisha, 2 K 2:1–3; cf. 1 K 13. After the schism, Bethel becomes for the northern kingdom the national center of worship, with its golden calf, "the sin of Jeroboam," 1 K 12:26–33; 13; cf. 2 K 10:29; 23:4, 15–20. Amos launches a violent attack on this cult, Am 3:14; 4:4; 5:5–6; cf. Tb 2:6, and is expelled from Bethel by the priest Amaziah. Hosea waxes ironical about Bethel, the "house of God" that has become *Beth-aven,* "the house of nothingness," 5:8; 10:5, 15. After the fall of Samaria one of the deported priests is brought to Bethel to teach the Law to the people transferred there from Babylon, 2 K 17:28. Josiah's religious reform affects Bethel, where the altars and high places are destroyed, 2 K 23: 14, 15–20. After the edict of Cyrus, some residents of Bethel return from exile, Ezr 2:28//Ne 7:32, and some Benjaminites occupy the town, Ne 11:31. In the time of the Maccabees, Bethel is one of the towns of Judah that Bacchides fortifies, 1 M 9:50.

Native place of: HIEL.

See: TEARS.

2. **Bethel** (1), a Canaanite divinity venerated at Bethel, mentioned in Jr 48:13, and whose name is a component of various proper names mentioned in Aramaean inscriptions.

BETH-EMEK (1), "House of the plain" (cf. Amok), a town in Asher, Jos 19:27. Today *Tell Mimas,* NE of Akko.

BETHER (1), acc. to the Gr., a town in the highlands of Judah, Jos 15:59.

BETH-EZEL (1), "House aside" (cf. Azaliah), probably a town in the lowlands of Judah, whose destruction Mi 1:11 announces.

BETH-GADER (1), "House of the enclosure" (cf. Geder), a town of Calebite origin in Judah, 1 Ch 2:51. Probably identical with: GEDOR 1.

BETH-GAMUL (1), "House of retribution" (cf. Gamaliel), a town of Moab whose "judgement" Jr 48:23 announces. A few km NE of Aroer, at *Kh. el-Jumeil.*

BETH-GILGAL (1), (cf. Gilgal), in the neighborhood of Jerusalem, Ne 12:29.

BETH-HAC-CHEREM (2), "House of the vineyard" (cf. Abel-keramim; Carmel; Carmi?), a town in Judah, probably near Bethlehem, Jr 6:1; a district center after the exile, Ne 3:16.

= **Carem** (1), in the highlands of Judah, Jos 15:59 (acc. to Gr.).

BETH-HAGGAN (1), "House of the garden" (cf. En-gannim), a town on the road by which Ahaziah, king of Judah, flees after seeing the murder of King Jehoram of Israel, 2 K 9:27. The modern *Jenin,* S of Jezreel.

BETH-HA-JESHIMOTH (1), "House of the devastations," a few km E of where the Jordan empties into the Dead Sea. Final stage of the Exodus, Nb 33:49, on the borders of the kingdom of Sihon, Jos 12:3, a town of Reuben, Jos 13:20, then of Moab, Ezk 25:9. Today probably *Tell el-ʿAzeimah.*

BETH-HANAN (1), a town between Aijalon and Gibeon, in Solomon's second district, 1 K 4:9. Today *Beit Anan.*

BETH-HARAM (1), Jos 13:27, a town of Gad.

= **Beth-haran** (1), Nb 32:36. Today *Tell Iktanu?*, a few km E of the Jordan.

BETH-HARAN (1). See: BETH-HARAM.

BETH-HOGLAH (3), "House of the partridge" (cf. Hoglah), 5 km SE of Jericho, Jos 15:6; 18:19, listed among the towns of Benjamin, 18:21. Today *Deir Hajlah.*

BETH-HORON (19), "House of [the god] Horon," two neighboring towns in Ephraim, 1 Ch 7:24; Jos 16:3, 5, on the border of Benjamin, Jos 18:13, 14.

Upper Beth-horon (2), Jos 16:5; 2 Ch 8:5. Today *Beit ʿUr el-Fauqa,* 16 km NW of Jerusalem.

Lower Beth-horon (4), Jos 16:3; 18: 13; 1 K 9:17; 2 Ch 8:5. Today *Beit ʿUr et-Tahta,* 18 km NW of Jerusalem.

On the usual invasion route *(ascent, descent of Beth-horon)* Jos 10:10–11; cf. Si 46:6; 1 S 13:18; 14:23 (corr. acc. to Gr. of Hb. *Beth-aven*); 1 M 3:16, 24; cf. 7:39. Beth-horon is fortified by Solomon, 1 K 9:17; 2 Ch 8:5, and later on by Bacchides, 1 M 9:50. It is sacked by mercenaries of King Amaziah, 2 Ch 25: 13. The town is assigned to Levites of the clan of Kohath, Jos 21:22//1 Ch 6:53. The Book of Judith locates it in Samaria, Jdt 4:4.

See: HORONITE.

BETH-LEAPHRAH (1), a play on words with *'aphar,* "dust," Mi 1:10; a town in the lowlands of Judah. Site unknown.

BETH-LEBAOTH (1), "House of the lionesses," a town of the Negeb, occupied by the sons of Simeon, Jos 19:6.

= **Lebaoth** (1), which becomes a town of Judah, Jos 15:32.

BETHLEHEM, "House of bread *or* House of [the divinity] Lahmu" (cf. Lahmi).

1. **Bethlehem** (47) **of Judah** (10) or **of Judaea** (2), 8 km S of Jerusalem.

= **Ephrathah** (4), residence of the Calebite clan of Ephrathah, which gives its name to the town, 1 Ch 4:4; Jos 15:59 (acc. to Gr.); Rt 1:2; 4:11; 1 S 17:12; Mi 5:1. The mention of Bethlehem in connection with Ephrathah in Gn 35:19 and 48:7 is a gloss and refers to another Ephrathah north of Jerusalem.

Bethlehem is listed among the towns in the highlands of Judah, Jos 15:59 (acc. to Gr.). It is briefly occupied by the Philistines, 2 S 23:14–16//1 Ch 11:16–18. It is restored by Rehoboam, 2 Ch 11:6. Bethlehemites are mentioned in the convoys of repatriates, Ezr 2:21//Ne 7:26. Native place of the Levite who stays with Micah the Ephraimite and becomes priest for the sanctuary of Dan, Jg 17:7–13; native place of the unfortunate concubine of a Levite of Ephraim, Jg 19, but, above all, native place of the ancestors of the royal house of Judah: Elimelech, husband of Naomi and father-in-law of Ruth, Rt 1:1–2, 19–22; Boaz, 2:4; 4. It is to Bethlehem and the sons of Jesse that Samuel comes to choose a king, 1 S 16:1, 4 ff. Bethlehem is "David's own town," 1 S 20:6; cf. 20:28; Lk 2:4, 11; Jn 7:42. It is also the native place of David's cousins, Joab, Abishai, and Asahel, cf. 2 S 2:32. Jesus, "a descendant of David," is, in accordance with the messianic prophecy of Micah, Mi 5:1; cf. Mt 2:5–6, born in Bethlehem, Mt 2:1; Lk 2:11; Jn 7:42.

See: EPHRATHAH 1.

Native place of: BOAZ; ELHANAN 1–2; ELIMELECH; JESSE.

Near Bethlehem: KHAN KIMHAM.

2. **Bethlehem** (3), listed among the towns of Zebulun, Jos 19:15, native place of Ibzan the judge, Jg 12:8–10 (though in this case there may be question of Bethlehem 1). Today *Beit Lahm,* 11 km W of Nazareth.

BETHLEHEMITE (4), 1 S 16:1, 18; 17:58; 2 S 21:19, of or from: BETHLELEM 1.

BETH-MAACAH (1), "House of Maacah" (cf. Maacah), 2 S 23:34 (corr. of Hb. *son of a Maacathite*). See: ABEL-BETH-MAACAH.

BETH-MARCABOTH (2), "House of the chariots" (cf. Rechab), a town in the Negeb, occupied by the sons of Simeon, Jos 19:5; 1 Ch 4:31 (//Jos 15:31: *Madmannah*).

BETH-MEON (1), "House of Meon" (cf. Meon). See: BAAL-MEON.

BETH-MILLO, "House of the embankment" (cf. Imlah).

1. **Beth-millo** (1). See: MILLO.

2. **Beth-millo** (3). See: MIGDAL-SHECHEM.

BETH-NIMRAH (2), cf. Accad. *Namru,* "Limpid" (cf. Nimrim), a town in Gad east of the Jordan, Nb 32:36; Jos 13:27.

= **Nimrah** (1), Nb 32:3. Perhaps on the shore of the "waters of Nimrim," Is 15:6; Jr 48:34.

BETH-PAZZEZ (1), "Place where they smash" (cf. Happizzez), listed among the towns of Issachar, Jos 19:21.

BETH-PELET (3), "House of the survivor" (cf. Pelet 1–2), a town in the Negeb of Judah, Jos 15:27, occupied by Judaeans at the return from the exile, Ne 11:26.
Native place of: HELEZ 1.
To be connected (?) with: PELET 1–2; PELETHITES; PELONITE.

BETH-PEOR (4), "House of Peor" (cf. Peor), a town in the steppes of Moab, Dt 3:29; 4:46, opposite which Moses is buried, Dt 34:6, assigned to Reuben, Jos 13:20. NW of Mount Nebo.
Near: BAAL-PEOR 2.

BETHPHAGE (3), "House of figs," a town near Bethany, on the slopes of the Mount of Olives. Jesus sends his disciples there for the ass's colt he is to ride into Jerusalem, Mk 11:1–2//Mt 21:1//Lk 19:29.

BETHRAPHA (1), "House of Rapha" (cf. Raphael), a town of Calebite origin in Judah, 1 Ch 4:12. Site unknown.

BETH-REHOB (2), "House of the [market] place" (cf. Rehob), Jg 18:28; 1 S 14:47.
= **Rehob** (2), a territory (or town) in the Vale of Lebanon, N of Laish in Dan, Jg 18:28; the scouts sent out by Moses reach it, Nb 13:21. An Aramaean people, 2 S 10:6, at war with Saul, 1 S 14:47 (acc. to Gr.), allied with the Ammonites against David, who defeats them, 2 S 10:6–14.

BETHSAIDA (7), "House of the fishery" (cf. Sidon), **in Galilee** (1), Jn 12:21, on the north shore of the Sea of Chinnereth, east of the Jordan. Hometown of the Apostles Peter, Andrew, and Philip, Jn 1:44; 12:21, not far from which a "multiplication of loaves" occurs, Lk 9:10; cf. Mk 6:45. Jesus heals a blind man there, Mk 8:22–26. He utters a lament over Bethsaida and the nearby towns, Mt 11:21//Lk 10:13.

BETH-SHAN (3) or **BETH-SHEAN** (6), Gr. *Baithsan,* Lat. *Bethsan,* "House of rest *or* House of [the serpent-goddess] Sha'an," a strategic point between Jezreel/Esdraelon (20 km to the W) and the Jordan (5 km to the E). A town of Manasseh, Jos 17:11; 1 Ch 7:29, where the Canaanites continued to dwell for a long time, Jos 17:16; Jg 1:27; occupied by the Philistines who hang the corpses of Saul and his sons from its walls, 1 S 31:10–12; 2 S 21:12; in Solomon's fifth district, 1 K 4:12. Judas comes to Beth-shan after destroying Ephron, 1 M 5:52, and Trypho and Jonathan meet there, 1 M 12:40–41.
= **Scythopolis** (3), whose friendliness to the Jews averts from it the cruel fate of Ephron, 2 M 12:29–30. Holofernes camps there, Jdt 3:10. Today *Beit Shean.*
See: DECAPOLIS; PLAIN 2.

BETH-SHEMESH, "House *or* Temple of the sun" (cf. Samson).
1. **Beth-shemesh** (17), a town in the lowlands on the border between Judah and Dan, Jos 15:10, assigned to the Levites of the clan of Kohath, Jos 21:16//1 Ch 6:44, in the second district of Solomon, 1 K 4:9. The Ark of Yahweh stops there on its return from Philistine territory, 1 S 6:9–20. Amaziah of Judah provokes Joash of Israel, who takes him prisoner there, 2 K 14:8–13//2 Ch 25:20–23. It is captured by the Philistines in the time of Ahaz, 2 Ch 28:18. Today *Tell el-Rumeileh.*
= **Har-heres** (1), an Amorite town that long retained its independence, Jg 1:35.
= **Irshemesh** (1), occupied by Dan, Jos 19:41. Native place of: JOSHUA 2.
2. **Beth-shemesh** (1), a town on the border between Issachar and Naphtali, Jos 19:22.
3. **Beth-shemesh** (3), a town in Naphtali in Upper Galilee, Jos 19:38, that long retained its independence, Jg 1:33.
4. **Beth-shemesh** (1) is the equivalent of *Heliopolis,* an Egypt. name for which was *On,* Jr 43:13. See: ON 1.

BETH-SHITTAH (1), "House of the acacias" (cf. Shittim), a town between

Jezreel and Beth-shan, to which the Midianites flee after being defeated by Gideon, Jg 7:22. Today *Shattah*.

BETH-TAPPUAH (1), "House of the apple tree" (cf. Tappuah), a town in the highlands of Judah, Jos 15:53. 8 km W of Hebron.

BETH-TOGARMAH (2). See: TOGARMAH.

BETHUEL

1. **Bethuel** (9) **the Aramaean** (2), one of the twelve sons born to Nahor of his wife Milcah, Gn 22:22–23, a nephew of Abraham, cf. 22:20, father of Laban, 28:5, and Rebekah, 22:23; 28:2, maternal grandfather of Jacob, 28:2. In the marriage of Rebekah to Isaac, Bethuel plays a secondary role, 24:50–51, as compared with that of Rebekah's brother (Laban), 24:29, 33, and mother (not named), cf. 24:28, 53, 55–60.

Father of: LABAN 1; REBEKAH.

2. **Bethuel** (1), a town of Simeon in the Negeb, 1 Ch 4:30.

= **Bethul** (1), Jos 19:4 (//15:30: *Chesil*).

BETHUL (1). See: BETHUEL 2.

BETHULIA (2), a town not otherwise known (its name reminds us of Bethuel, Bethul, Bethel), native place of Judith, Jdt 8:2–4; 16:21–23, described as occupying a key position that commands the approach to Judah through Samaria, 4:6–7; cf. 8:21. Holofernes besieges it, 7, after having handed over Achior the Ammonite to its inhabitants, 6:10–14; 11:9. Judith exhorts the elders of the town to resistance, 8:9–10, and saves Bethulia by killing Holofernes, 10:6; 11:9; 12:7; 13:10; 15:3; 16:21, 23.

BETHZAITH (1), "Olive-oil factory": Bacchides slaughters Jews there and throws them "into the great cistern," 1 M 7:19. Probably *Beit Z'ita,* 6 km N of Beth-zur, where there is a cistern with spiral steps.

BETHZATHA (1), "Ditch" (var. *Bethesda,* "House of mercy," *Bethsaida,* or *Belsetha*), Jn 5:2, at Jerusalem, near the Sheep Gate, a pool (Sheep Pool) with five porticoes, under which "were crowds of sick people—blind, lame, paralysed." Jesus cures a sick man there on the sabbath, Jn 5:2–9.

BETHZECHARIAH (2), a town 10 km N of Beth-zur and 20 km SW of Jerusalem. Judas Maccabaeus is defeated there by King Antiochus V, who uses elephants in the battle, 1 M 6:32–47; cf. 2 M 13:1–2, 15–16. Today *Kh. Beit Zakariyeh.*

BETH-ZUR (19), "House of the rock," Gr. *Baithsour* (cf. Zur), about 8 km NW of Hebron. A town in the highlands of Judah, Jos 15:58, of Calebite origin, 1 Ch 2:45, rebuilt by Rehoboam, 2 Ch 11:7, it becomes a district center in Judaea under Nehemiah, Ne 3:16.

It occupies a strategic position in southern Judaea, facing Idumaea, 1 M 4:29; 2 M 11:5, and is fortified by Judas Maccabaeus, 1 M 4:61; 6:7, 26, besieged and captured by Antiochus V, 1 M 6:31–50; 2 M 13:19–22, fortified by Bacchides, 1 M 9:52; 10:14, and finally recaptured by Simon Maccabaeus, 1 M 11:65–66; 14:7, 33.

BETOMESTHAIM (2), associated with Bethulia, "two towns facing Esdraelon, toward the plain of Dothan," Jdt 4:6; 15:4. Not otherwise known.

BETONIM (1), (cf. Beten?), beyond the Jordan, a town of Gad, Jos 13:26. Today *Kh. Batneh.*

BETWEEN THE TWO WALLS (4), Hb. *Bên ha-Homotayim,* at Jerusalem:

—name of a *gate* near the royal garden, on the SE side of the city, by which King Zedekiah escapes during the siege of the city by Nebuchadnezzar, 2 K 25:4//Jr 39:4//52:7.

—name of a *reservoir* near this gate, Is 22:11.

BEZAI (3), a derivative of *Bezalel;* head of a family whose sons return from the exile with Zerubbabel, Ezr 2:17//Ne 7:23, a leader of the people and cosigner of the pledge to observe the Law, Ne 10:19. See: BETHBASI.

BEZALEL, Hb. *Bezal'el,* "In the shadow of God" (cf. Bezai; Zillah).

1. **Bezalel** (8), **son of Uri** (4), **son of Hur** (3), **of the tribe of Judah** (3), an artist who, together with Oholiab, son of Ahisamach, of the tribe of Dan, constructs the sanctuary and produces the various cult furnishings, Ex 31:2–11; 35:30–35; 36:1–2; 37:1–29; 38:22–23; cf. 1 Ch 2:20; 2 Ch 1:5.

2. **Bezalel** (1), an Israelite of the sons of Pahath-moab, married to a foreign wife, whom he puts away, Ezr 10:30.

BEZEK

1. **Bezek** (1), a town between Shechem and Beth-shan. Saul reviews the Israelite army there, 1 S 11:8. Today *Kh. Ibziq.*

2. **Bezek** (1), perhaps W of Beth-horon or, less probably, identical with the preceding. Judah and Simeon defeat Adonizedek there, Jg 1:4–5.

BEZER, "Fortress," Gr. *Bosor* (cf. Bosor; Bozrah; Mibzar).

1. **Bezer** (4), a town of refuge in Reuben, Dt 4:43//Jos 20:8, assigned to Levites of the clan of Merari, 1 Ch 6:63//Jos 21:36 (acc. to Gr.).

Probably the same as: BOZRAH 2.

2. **Bezer** (1), an Asherite, one of the eleven sons of Zophah, 1 Ch 7:37.

BICHRI (8), (cf. Becorath), a Benjaminite, father of: SHEBA 2.

BICHRITE (1), 2 S 20:14 (corr. of Hb. *Berites*), a partisan of Sheba, son of Bichri.

BIDKAR (1), "Son of Deker"? equerry of Jehu, throws the corpse of King Jehoram into the field of Naboth of Jezreel, 2 K 9:25–26.

BIGTHA (1), a Persian name; a eunuch listed with: MEHUMAN.

BIGTHAN and **Teresh** (3), Persian names, two eunuchs who are palace guards; their plot against Ahasuerus is uncovered and reported by Mordecai, Est 1:1m–r (corr. of Gr. *Gabatha* and *Tharra*); 2:21–23; 6:2 (Hb. *Bigtana'*).

BIGVAI (7), one of the twelve leaders in the return from exile, Ezr 2:2//Ne 7:7, head of a family whose sons return from exile, Ezr 2:14//Ne 7:19; cf. Ezr 8:14; some of the latter have married foreign wives, whom they put away, Ezr 10:29 (corr. of Hb. *Bani*). Bigvai is one of the leaders of the people who sign the pledge to observe the Law, Ne 10:17.

BIKATH-AVEN (1), "Valley of wickedness *or* nothingness" (cf. Ben-oni; Beth-aven; Vale of Lebanon), Am 1:5, difficult to identify; perhaps a symbolic name for Damascus.

BILDAD (5), (cf. Eldad?), **of Shuah** (5), Eliphaz of Teman and Zophar of Naamath are "three of his friends" who come to visit Job in his trials and to "offer him sympathy and consolation," Jb 2:11; 8:1; 18:1; 25:1; cf. 32:1. In the end God is angry with them "for not speaking truthfully about me as my servant Job has done," 42:7–10.

BILEAM. See: BALAAM 2.

BILGAH (4), a priest, leader of the fifteenth class of priests, 1 Ch 24:14; cf. Ne 12:18, returns from the exile with Jeshua, Ne 12:5.

= **Bilgai** (1), a cosigner of the pledge to observe the Law, Ne 10:9. In the priestly class of Bilgah: SIMEON 6.

BILGAI. See: BILGAH.

BILHAH

1. **Bilhah** (10), a slave girl of Laban, then of his daughter Rachel, Gn 29:29, then concubine of Jacob, raped by Reuben, Gn 35:22. From the union of Jacob and Bilhah come Dan and Naphtali, Gn 30:3–8; 35:25 (and their clans, Gn 46:

23–25//1 Ch 7:12–13), half-brothers of Joseph, Gn 37:2.

2. **Bilhah** (1). See: BAALAH 2.

BILHAN

1. **Bilhan** (2), first of the four sons of Ezer, himself the sixth son of Seir, Gn 36:27//1 Ch 1:42.

2. **Bilhan** (2), a Benjaminite of the clan of Jediael, 1 Ch 7:10–11.

BILSHAN (2), Accad. *Be-el-shu-nu,* "Their Lord," one of the twelve leaders in the return from the exile, Ezr 2:2// Ne 7:7.

BIMHAL (1), an Asherite, second of the three sons of Japhlet, a fighting man and head of a family, 1 Ch 7:33.

BINEA (2), a Benjaminite, son of Moza, a descendant of King Saul and ancestor of the sons of Azel, 1 Ch 8:37//9:42.

BINNUI (cf. Benaiah).

1. **Binnui** (2), an Israelite, head of a family whose sons return from the exile with Zerubbabel, Ne 7:15 (//Ezr 2:10: *Bani*). Some of them have married foreign wives, whom they now put away, Ezr 10:38 (where *of the sons of Binnui* is probably to be read for *Bani and Binnui*).

2. **Binnui** (1), an Israelite of the sons of Pahath-moab, married to a foreign wife, whom he puts away, Ezr 10:30.

3. **Binnui** (7), **son of Henadad** (3), a Levite, Ne 12:8, probably among the heads of the Levites, 12:24 (corr. of Hb. *ben,* "son of"), ruler of half the district of Keilah, 3:18 (read *Binnui* instead of Hb. *Bavvai*), a volunteer in rebuilding the wall of Jerusalem, 3:24; present at the ceremony of atonement, 9:4; cosigner of the pledge to observe the Law, 10:10.

Father (?) of: NOADIAH.

BIRSHA (1), "Out of wickedness"? (cf. Cushan-rishathaim), **king of Gomorrah** (3), Gn 14:2, 8, 10, ally of: BERA.

BIRZAITH (1), "Well of the olive tree." See: BEERZETH.

BITHIAH (1), Egypt. "Queen," daughter of Pharaoh, wife of Mered, mother of several sons, in the genealogy of Caleb, 1 Ch 4:17–18.

BITHYNIA (2), a region in NW Asia Minor that, together with Pontus, forms a Roman province. Despite Paul's desire to go there, he does not visit it on his second missionary journey, Ac 16:7, but in the time of 1 P 1:1 there are Christians there.

BIZIOTHIAH (1), an otherwise unknown town in the Negeb of Judah, Jos 15:28. Some correct to *benôtêah,* "her [that is, Beersheba's] dependencies."

BIZTHA (1), a eunuch mentioned with: MEHUMAN.

BLASTUS (1), chamberlain of Herod Agrippa I, mediator between the Tyrians and the king, Ac 12:20.

BOANERGES (1), "Sons of thunder," a name Jesus gives to James and John, the sons of Zebedee, Mk 3:17; cf. Lk 9:54.

BOAZ, "In him is strength."

1. **Boaz** (25), a rich Judaean landowner at Bethlehem, a close relative by marriage of Ruth the Moabitess. The latter's husband having died, Boaz has a right of "redemption" over her, Rt 2–3. After the withdrawal of a closer *goel* or "redeemer," Boaz marries her and she gives him a son, Obed. The latter will be the father of Jesse and grandfather of David, Rt 4; cf. 1 Ch 2:11–15. Mt 1:5 makes Boaz the son of Rahab and, like Lk 3:2, an ancestor of Jesus.

2. **Boaz** (2). See: JACHIN 3.

BOCHERU (1), (cf. Becorath), a Benjaminite, second of the six sons of Azel, a descendant of King Saul, whom some insert for "his first-born" (Gr.) in order to reach the total of six sons in 1 Ch 8:38//9:44.

BOCHIM (1), "The weepers"? (cf. Tears), an etymology explained in Jg 2:5 by the tears the Israelites shed there. Site unknown. Jg 2:1 has *Bochim* in Hb., but some correct it to *Bethel,* following the Gr.

BOHAN (2), "Thumb"? See: STONE 1.

BORASHAN (1), "Cistern of smoke." See: ASHAN 1.

BOSOR (2), (cf. Bezer), a town in Gilead, where Jews are blockaded; Judas Maccabaeus liberates them, 1 M 5:26, 36. 65 km E of the Sea of Chinnereth. Today *Busr el-Hariri.*

BOZEZ (1) and **Seneh,** two rocky spurs dominating a pass, "the first . . . to the north facing Michmash, the other to the south facing Geba," 1 S 14:4–5.

BOZKATH (2), "Height," a town near Lachish, in the lowlands of Judah, Jos 15:39, native place of Jedidah, mother of King Josiah, 2 K 22:1.

BOZRAH, "Fortress," Gr. *Bosor, Bosorra* (cf. Bezer).

1. **Bozrah** (7), the modern *Buseireh,* about 40 km S of the Dead Sea. Many prophetic threats are leveled at this ancient capital of Edom, Is 34:6; Jr 49:13, 22; Am 1:12 and Is 63:1; cf. Rv 19:13. The "fortified city" of Ps 108:10 is probably Bozrah. In Mi 2:12 "in the fold" is doubtless to be read for Hb. *at Bozrah.*

Native place of king: JOBAB 2.

2. **Bozrah** (1), a town in Moab on which Jr 48:24 pronounces "judgement." Probably the same as: BEZER 1.

3. **Bozrah** (2), a town in Gilead, where Jews are blockaded; Judas Maccabaeus captures and destroys it, 1 M 5:26, 28. 40 km SE of Bosor. The *Bostra* of the Greeks and Romans. Today *Bosra eski-Sham.*

BRANCH (2), Hb. *zemah,* Gr. *anatolē,* "Rising (sun)," see Lk 1:78. A messianic name, Zc 3:8; cf. Jr 23:5, applied to Zerubbabel, Zc 6:13 (see JB note).

BUKKI (cf. Bukkiah).

1. **Bukki son of Jogli** (1), represents the tribe of Dan in the allocation of Canaan, Nb 34:22.

2. **Bukki** (4), a descendant of Aaron and ancestor of Zadok, 1 Ch 5:31; 6:36; Ezr 7:4.

BUKKIAH (2), (cf. Bukki), of the sons of Heman, leader of the sixth class of cantors, 1 Ch 25:4, 13.

BUNAH (1), one of the sons of Jerahmeel, a descendant of Judah, 1 Ch 2:25.

BUNNI (cf. Benaiah).

1. **Bunni** (1), ancestor of the Levite: SHEMAIAH 7.

2. **Bunni** (1), a Levite taking part in the prayer of confession of sins, Ne 9:4.

3. **Bunni** (1), a leader of the people and cosigner of the pledge to observe the Law, Ne 10:16.

BUZ

1. **Buz** (2), one of the twelve sons of Nahor, Abraham's brother, that were born of his wife Milcah, Gn 22:21. An Arabian tribe of NW Arabia, Jr 25:23. See: BUZITE.

2. **Ben-buz** (1), a Gadite, among the sons of Abihail, or, acc. to another reading, *Buz,* ancestor of Abihail, 1 Ch 5:14.

BUZI (1), a priest, father of the prophet: EZEKIEL 1.

BUZITE (2), Hb. *Buzi,* belonging to the Arabian tribe of Buz. See: ELIHU 5.

[BYBLOS]. See: GEBAL 1.

C

CABBON (1), a town in the lowlands of Judah, Jos 15:40.

CABUL (2), "As nothing *or* Swamp"?, a town in Asher, SE of Acco, Jos 19:27. The towns Solomon gives to Hiram of Tyre are called *the land of Cabul,* 1 K 9:13.

CAESAR (29), Gr. *Kaisar,* Lat. *Caesar,* initially a surname of the *gens Julia,* made famous by *Julius Caesar* (100–44 B.C.), and later a title of the reigning Roman emperor.

The NT uses the term only in the second sense, Mt 22:17–21//Mk 12:14–17//Lk 20:22–25; 23:2; Jn 19:12, 15; Ac 17:7. In Ac 25:8, 10, 12, 21; 26:32; 27:24; 28:19, the reigning Caesar is *Nero* (54–68 A.D.).

Caesar: AUGUSTUS 1; TIBERIUS.

Another Roman emperor: CLAUDIUS 1.

CAESAREA, the name of cities built in honor of Caesar [Augustus].

1. **Caesarea** (15), a Mediterranean port 50 km N of Joppa, built by Herod the Great between 12 and 9 B.C.

Paul takes ship there for Tarsus, Ac 9:30, and probably again when being brought to Rome as a prisoner, cf. 27:1–2; he lands there on returning from his second and third missionary journeys, 18:22; 21:8. Herod Agrippa I dies there, Ac 12:19–23; Agrippa II stays there for a time with Bernice, 25:13; the Roman procurators reside there, 25:1, 6; there is a Roman garrison there. After his arrest Paul is transferred there, 23:23, 33, and spends two years in prison there, 25:4, 13. There are Christians at Caesarea at a very early date: Peter baptizes the centurion Cornelius there, Ac 10:1, 24; cf. 11:11. Philip the evangelist lives there, 8:40, with his family; Paul stays with him for a while at the end of his third missionary journey, 21:8–16.

2. **Caesarea Philippi** (2), a city located near the sources of the Jordan, rebuilt about 3 or 2 B.C. by Herod Philip. It is in this neighborhood that Peter acknowledges Jesus as the Christ, the Son of God, Mt 16:13//Mk 8:27. Today *Banias.*

CAIAPHAS (9), son-in-law of Annas, Jn 18:13, high priest (18–36 A.D.), and therefore president of the Sanhedrin, the tribunal that passes judgment on Jesus, Mt 26:3, 57–58; Jn 18:13–14, 24, 28, and on the Apostles Peter and John, Ac 4:6. Acc. to Jn 11:49; 18:14, he advises getting rid of Jesus in order to maintain public peace and order. It is in his reign that John the Baptist begins to preach, Lk 3:2.

CAIN, Gr. and Lat. form of *Qayîn,* "(black)smith"; popular etymology in Gn 4:1, "I have acquired" (cf. Kenan; Kenites; Tubal-cain).

1. **Cain** (19).

a. The eponymous ancestor of the Kenites. Acc. to the Yahwist account in

Gn 4, first-born son of Adam and Eve and brother of Abel. A farmer, he becomes jealous of his brother, a shepherd, and kills him, 4:1–16; cf. Heb 11:4. He is the prototype of the wicked or unjust man, Ws 10:3, the murderer of the innocent, Mt 23:35; 1 Jn 3:12; Jude 11.

Descendants of Cain, Gn 4:17–24 (Yahwist genealogy).

= **Kenan** (6), son of Enosh and father of Mahalalel, Gn 5:9–14; 1 Ch 1:2 (priestly genealogy).

= **Cainan** (1), ancestor of Jesus, Lk 3:38.

b. The tribe of Cain or the Kenites. Nomads—brothers of the Rechabites, 1 Ch 2:55—connected with the Midianites, cf. Jg 1:16 and Nb 10:29, allied with the Amalekites, 1 S 15:6, then with Israel, 1 S 30:29, they become dispersed, Nb 24:21–22: they are found in the plain of Jezreel, Jg 4:11, but live chiefly in the Judaean Negeb, Gn 15:19; 1 S 27:10 (*Negeb of the Kenites*).

Kenites: HEBER 2; HOBAB.

To be connected (?) with the: KENIZZITES.

2. **Kain** (1), a town in the highlands of Judah, Jos 15:57.

CAINAN

1. **Cainan** (1). See: CAIN 1*a*.

2. **Cainan** (1), acc. to Lk 3:36, a descendant of Shem and the preceding, and an ancestor of Jesus.

CALAH (2), Accad. *Kalhu,* called "the great city," Gn 10:11–12. Ancient capital of Assyria. Today *Nimrud,* 30 km SE of Nineveh.

CALCOL (2), is listed with Heman and Darda and with Ethan the Ezrahite as the best-known sages of Canaan, 1 K 5:11. He is likewise listed among the five sons of Zerah, son of Judah in 1 Ch 2:6.

CALEB (39), "Dog" (cf. Chelub), **son of Jephunneh** (16), also called **the Kenizzite** (3), Nb 32:12; Jos 14:6, 14; brother of Kenaz, Jos 15:17//Jg 1:13; 3:9; cf. 1 Ch 4:15, that is, a non-Israelite.

Caleb is nonetheless described as one of the twelve scouts whom Moses sends from Kadesh to reconnoiter the Promised Land: he even represents the tribe of Judah on this occasion, Nb 13:6, as he does in the allocation of the land, Nb 34:19. With Joshua he reacts against the general defeatism induced by the difficulties of the conquest, Nb 13:30; 14:6; therefore, he will enter Canaan with Joshua, Nb 14:24, 30, 38; 26:65; Dt 1:36, and will occupy the region of Hebron, Jos 14:6–14; 15:13–19//Jg 1:10–15, 20; Jos 21:12; 1 Ch 6:41; 1 M 2:56, south of which lies *the Negeb of Caleb,* 1 S 30:14. There is a eulogy of Caleb in Si 46:7–9.

The genealogies of 1 Ch show the assimilation of the clan of Caleb to the tribe of Judah: Caleb is there called the son of Hezron, the grandson of Judah, 1 Ch 2:18; cf. 2:24. His posterity is listed in 1 Ch 2:18–24, 42–50.

= **Chelubai** (1), 1 Ch 2:9, son of Hezron.

= **Chelub** (1), 1 Ch 4:11; cf. vv. 11–20.

His brother: JERAHMEEL 1.

His wives and concubines: AZUBAH 1; EPHAH 1; EPHRATH 1; MAACAH 2.

His daughter: ACHSAH.

CALEBITE (1), 1 S 25:3, belonging to the clan of: CALEB. See: NABAL.

CALLISTHENES (1), probably a hellenizing Jew, burned alive by Judas Maccabaeus, 2 M 8:33.

CALNEH (1), a prosperous city in Syria, Am 6:2.

= **Calno** (1), taken, like Carchemish and Hamath, by Tiglath-pileser III, king of Assyria, Is 10:9.

Ca. 25 km NE of Aleppo.

CALNO (1). See: CALNEH.

CALVARY. See: GOLGOTHA.

CAMP OF DAN. See: DAN 3.

CANA in Galilee. See: KANAH 3.

CANAAN (105), Hb. *Kena'ân,* "[Country of the] purple" (cf. Chenaanah), an area of the Palestino-Phoenician coast, former name of the Promised Land, which becomes the land of: ISRAEL *c.* The Yahwist account, Gn 9:22–27, connects Canaan with Ham, who is said to be the father both of Canaan and Egypt (Misraim), which dominates this area, Gn 10:6. The territory of Canaan extends from southern Phoenicia (a name that also means "purple"), that is, from the region of Tyre and Sidon, Is 23:1, 11–12; cf. Mt 15:21–22//Mk 7:26, to the Negeb, cf. Gn 10:19; 2 S 24:7.

a. "The ancient inhabitants of your holy land" (cf. Ws 12:3). The Canaanite clans are listed in Gn 10:15–18//1 Ch 1:13–16. In this list of eleven proper names there are six—Canaan, Heth (the Hittites), the Jebusites, the Amorites, the Girgashites, and the Hivites—that will, along with the Perizzites, often be associated, in variable order, to designate the pre-Israelite populations of Palestine, the "seven nations in Canaan," Ac 13:19.

As a matter of fact, we find:

—three lists of seven: Amorites, Canaanites, Girgashites, Hittites, Hivites, Jebusites, Perizzites, Dt 7:1; Jos 3:10, 24:11;

—twelve lists of six, two of which omit the Hivites, Gn 15:20–21; Ne 9:8, and ten of which omit the Girgashites, Ex 3:8, 17; 23:23; 32:2; 34:11; Dt 20:17; Jos 9:1; 11:3; 12:8; Jg 3:5;

—five lists of five, Ezk 13:5; 1 K 9:20//2 Ch 8:7; Ezr 9:1; Jdt 5:15–16 (the names omitted vary from list to list);

—one list of four: Amorites, Canaanites, Hittites, Jebusites, Nb 23:29;

—three lists of three: Canaanites, Hivites (or: Amorites), Hittites, Ex 23:28; 2 S 24:6–7; Ezk 16:3;

—six lists of two: Amorites and Canaanites, Dt 1:7; Jos 7:7–9; Canaanites and Perizzites, Gn 13:7; 34:30; Canaanites and Hittites (Hb. *Hivites*), Jg 3:3; Amorites and Hittites, Ezk 16:45.

b. The land of Canaan and the Canaanites. The land of Canaan, for which Abraham sets out, Gn 11:31; 12:1, 5–6; cf. Jdt 5:9, where he settles with his family, Gn 13:12; 16:3; cf. 23:2, 19; Jos 24:3, where Isaac also lives, Gn 31:18; 37:1, and Jacob, Gn 33:18; 35:6; 42:5 (cf. Jdt 5:10; Ac 7:11); Gn 42:13, 29–32; 44:8; 45:17, 25; 46:6, 31; 47:1–4, 13–15; 48:7; 50:11, is the land "promised," Ac 7:5; Heb 11:9; cf. Gn 12:7; 13:15; 15:18; 17:8; 26:2–3; 35:12; Ex 6:4; 13:11; Dt 1:8, and given, Lv 25:38; Dt 32:49; 1 Ch 16:18//Ps 105:11, a good and excellent land, Nb 14:7; Dt 8:7; 11:10–17, a land "where milk and honey flow" (22×), Ex 3:8 . . . Si 46:8 . . . Ezk 20:6, 15, but which must be reconnoitered, Nb 13:1–14:9, then conquered by force of arms, Ex 23:23–33; Jos 7:7–9; 9:1–2; 17:16; 24:11; Jg 3:1–2; 5:19; Ne 9:24. This conquest fulfills the curse of Noah in which the subjection of Canaan, son of Ham, to Shem, ancestor of Israel, is announced, Gn 9:24–26. Although in some instances Israel applies the ban to Canaanites and their towns, Nb 21:3; cf. Dt 7:2; 20:17, most often the Canaanites live on beside the Israelites, Jos 16:10; 17:12–13; Jg 1:1–35; 3:1, 5; 1 K 9:20–21, and enter into mixed marriages with them, Gn 24:3, 37; 28:1, 6–7; 34:9; 36:2; 38:2//1 Ch 2:3; Gn 46:10//Ex 6:15; 34:16; Dt 7:3; Jos 23:12; Jg 3:6, which lead, despite warnings, Ex 34:15–16; Lv 18:3; Dt 7:4–6; 20:18, to the adoption of idolatrous practices, Jg 3:5–6; Ezr 9:1–2; Ps 106:38; Ws 12:3–11.

The prophets at times remind Israel of its "Canaanite origin," Ezk 16:3, 45. Hosea even gives Ephraim/Israel the name of the people whose land it took, a name it deserves to bear, Ho 12:8, because it has inherited the defects, cf. Dn 13:56, of the people of Canaan, Zp 1:11; Israel is a merchant, a trafficker: the Hb. *Kena'ân* has this meaning in Jb 40:30; Pr 31:24; Is 23:8; Zc 14:21. In Zp 2:5 the parallel between Canaan and the land of the Philistines (Hb. *Pelishtim*) shows how "Canaan" became "Palestine." Is 19:18 foretells that in an Egypt that has been converted to the true God, "there will be five towns speaking the language of Canaan."

King: JABIN.

Principal divinities: ANATH; ASTARTE; BAAL 1; MOT.

Canaanites: BATH-SHUA 1; SAUL 2.

"In the land of Canaan": SHILOH.

CANAANITE

1. **Canaanite** (67), Hb. *Kena'ani,* of or from: CANAAN.

N.B. The *Canaanite* woman of Mt. 15:22 is a *Syrophoenician,* Mk 7:26.

2. **Canaanite** (2), Aram. *Qanana,* Gr. *Kananaios.* See: ZEALOT.

CANNEH (1), Accad. *Kannu,* associated with Haran and Eden, a trade depot on the middle Euphrates, Ezk 27:23.

CAPERNAUM (16), Hb. *Kephar Nahum,* "Town of Nahum" (cf. Chephar-ammoni; Nahum), **a town in Galilee** (1), Lk 4:31, on the NW shore of the Lake of Genneseret (Sea of Chinnereth), 4 km from the mouth of the Jordan.

On leaving Nazareth, Jesus takes up residence there, Mt 4:13; cf. Jn 2:12. It is "his own town," Mt 9:1; we find him in "the house," Mk 2:1; 9:33—probably Peter's house, Mk 1:29–33—and in the synagogue where he speaks, Mk 1:21//Lk 4:31; Jn 6:59 (on the bread of life). It is the center for his early activity, Lk 4:23, where he works numerous cures, Mt 8:5//Lk 7:1; Jn 4:46; Mk 1:30–34; 2:1 ff.; and so on. It is here that he returns after journeying through the area, Mt 17:24; Jn 6:17, 24. But Capernaum has not understood the message of Jesus and faces a lamentable fate, Mt 11:23–24//Lk 10:15. Today *Tell Hum.*

CAPHARSALAMA (1), "Valley of Peace" (cf. Chephar-ammoni), near Gibeon. Victory of Judas Maccabaeus over Nicanor, 1 M 7:31. Today *Kh. Salameh.*

CAPHTOR (3), an island, Jr 47:4, from which the Philistines originally come, Gn 10:14//1 Ch 1:12; Am 9:7, to settle on the Palestinian coast, Dt 2:23.

Probably the island of: CRETE, or the islands of the Aegean Sea.

CAPHTORIM (1), Dt 2:23, people of: CAPHTOR.

CAPPADOCIA (2), a region in the center of Asia Minor, a Roman province after 17 B.C., where some Jews live, Ac 2:9, and, later, Christians, 1 P 1:1.

King: ARIARATHES.

CARCHEMISH (3) **on the Euphrates** (5), an Aramaean city taken and destroyed by Sargon, king of Assyria in 717, Is 10:9. In 609 Pharaoh Neco comes to the aid of the Assyrians on the Euphrates, at Carchemish, 2 K 23:29//2 Ch 35:20; he is defeated there in 605 by Nebuchadnezzar, Jr 46:2–12. Today *Jerablus* on the Turko-Syrian border, 100 km NE of Aleppo.

CAREM (1). See: BETH-HAC-CHEREM.

CARIA (1), a region of SW Asia Minor, an addressee of the letter of the consul Lucius promulgating the Jewish-Roman alliance, 1 M 15:23. See: CARIANS.

Cities: CNIDUS; HALICARNASSUS; MILETUS; MYNDOS; TROGYLLIUM.

CARIANS (2), mercenaries hailing from Caria and forming the royal guard in Judah in the time of Athaliah, 2 K 11:4, 19.

CARKAS (1), a eunuch mentioned with: MEHUMAN.

CARMEL, Hb. *Karmel,* "Orchard" (cf. Beth-hac-cherem).

1. **Carmel** (16), a mountain overlooking the plain of Jezreel and the Mediterranean (height: 552 m), in the southern part of the territory of Asher, Jos 19:26. Elijah summons Israel there to choose

between Yahweh and Baal: sacrifices of the prophets of Baal and sacrifice of Elijah, 1 K 18:19–43. Place of retreat for Elijah, 1 K 18:42, and Elisha, 2 K 2:25; 4:25–29. Carmel is often paralleled with Lebanon, Bashan, the plain of Sharon, or Tabor, because it is a beautiful mountain, Sg 7:6; Jr 46:18; Am 9:3, rich in vegetation, Is 33:9; 35:2; Jr 50:19; Am 1:2; Na 1:4.

Acc. to Jdt 1:8, Nebuchadnezzar calls on the people of Carmel to rally to him.

On Carmel: JOKNEAM.

2. **Carmel** (16), a town in the highlands of Judah, Jos 15:55. Saul goes there "to raise himself a monument," 1 S 15:12. David sends a share of booty to the elders of Carmel, 30:29 (corr. of Hb. *Rakal*). King Uzziah has vineyards there, 2 Ch 26:10 (but some translate *Karmel* here as "orchards"). 12 km S of Hebron. Today *Kh. el-Karmil.*

Native place of: HEZRO; NABAL.

3. **[Carmel],** name of a storm- and rain-god similar to Baal.

CARMI, "My vine"? (cf. Beth-haccherem).

1. **Carmi** (4), fourth and last son of Reuben, Gn 46:9; Ex 6:14; 1 Ch 5:3, whose descendants form the **Carmite** clan, Nb 26:6.

2. **Carmi** (4), a descendant of Judah, 1 Ch 4:1, father of: ACHAN.

CARMITE (1), belonging to the clan of: CARMI 1.

CARNAIM (5), Gr. transcription of Hb. *Karnayim,* "the two horns" (cf. Asterothkarnaim; Mascara), a town 40 km E of the Sea of Chinnereth. In the time of the Maccabees, Jews are imprisoned there; Judas launches an expedition and frees his coreligionists, destroying the city and its sanctuary, the *Karnion,* 1 M 5:26, 43–44//2 M 12:21–26.

= **Karnaim** (1), reconquered by Jeroboam II, king of Israel, Am 6:13.

CARPUS (1), Gr. *Karpos,* "Fruit," a Christian of Troas in whose house Paul has left a cloak that Timothy is to bring back, 2 Tm 4:13.

CARSHENA (1), an officer mentioned with: MEMUCAN.

CASIPHIA (2), a town in Babylonia where there is a Jewish community headed by Iddo, Ezr 8:17. Location unknown.

CASLUH (1). See: CUSLUH.

CASPIN (1). See: CHASPHO.

CASSIA (1), Hb. *Kezi'ah,* second of the three daughters born to Job after his testing; he gives her inheritance rights, Jb 42:14.

[CASTOR and Pollux]. See: TWINS.

CAUDA (1), Gr. *Kauda,* var. of *Klauda,* a small island S of Crete, Ac 27:16. Today *Gavdos.*

CENCHREAE (2), the eastern port of Corinth, on the Aegean Sea. In fulfillment of a vow Paul has his hair cut off there, Ac 18:18, before departing for Syria at the end of his second missionary journey. The church at Cenchreae has a deaconess, Phoebe, Rm 16:1.

CENDEBAEUS (5), governor of the coastal region of Palestine under Antiochus VII, fortifies Kedron and harasses Judaea. John Hyrcanus meets and routs him, 1 M 15:38–41; 16:1, 4–10.

CEPHAS (9), Aram. *Kepha,* "Rock" (compare with Hb. *Zur*). See: PETER.

CHABRIS (3), **son of Gothoniel** (1), and **Charmis son of Melchiel,** two elders of Bethulia, associated with Uzziah son of Micah, Jdt 6:15; 8:10; 10:6.

CHAEREAS (2), military commander at Gezer, slain with Timotheus, his brother, and Apollophanes by Judas Maccabaeus, 2 M 10:32, 37.

CHALDAEA, CHALDAEANS (87), Hb. *Kasdim* (cf. Chesed), a land and people giving their name to Lower Mesopotamia and later to Babylonia.

If we prescind from some texts recalling that the Israelites are the descendants of the Chaldaeans, Jdt 5:5–6 (see: UR 1) and from the allegory of Ezekiel, Ezk 16:29; 23:14–23, which alludes to the alliances of Israel with its Egyptian, Assyrian, and Chaldaean (or Babylonian) neighbors (alliances that represented so many infidelities), the term is used almost entirely with reference to the period in which the Neo-Babylonians impose their yoke on the Near East at the end of the seventh century. Hab 1–2 describes the invasion of the Chaldaeans, a "fierce and fiery people," 1:6, a scourge of God. When Jehoiakim rebels, ca. 600, Nebuchadnezzar sends armed bands, especially of Chaldaeans, to destroy Judah, 2 K 24:2. But the Chaldaeans are mentioned chiefly in connection with the events that bring the downfall of Judah: the siege of Jerusalem, the destruction of the city and the temple, the deportation of King Zedekiah and the population, the installation of Gedaliah at Mizpah as governor of the country, 2 K 25//Jr 39:4–10; 40: 9–10; 41:1–3, 17–18; 52:7–8, 14–17; cf. Ba 1:1–2; Ezk 12:13. Jeremiah finds himself involved in these events, which he predicts as inevitable, Jr 22:25; 32:4–29; 37, with such vigor that he is accused of being a collaborator: "You are deserting to the Chaldaeans!" (Jr 37:13–14). But the exiles, who are now settled in the land of the Chaldaeans, cf. Ezk 1:3; 11:24, are exhorted to hope, Jr 24:5; 32:25, 43. The day will come when the blood of Jerusalem will be avenged on the inhabitants of Chaldaea, Jr 51:35; cf. Ps 137:8; when Yahweh will punish them, Is 43:14; Jr 50–51; when the deportees will leave Babylon and the land of the Chaldaeans, Is 48:20. Dn 9:1 alludes to the conquest of the kingdom of Chaldaea.

In Jb 1:17 *Chaldaeans* designates plundering nomads, and in Dn 2:2, 4, 5, 10; 3:8; 4:4; 5:7–11, it refers to soothsayers who practice astrology because the latter was at that time regarded as having originated in Chaldaea.

In Dn 1:4, "the language and literature of the *Chaldaeans*" refers to the cuneiform writing in which the educated were trained.

Eponymous ancestor: CHESED.

"Kings of the Chaldaeans": BELSHAZZAR; NEBUCHADNEZZAR.

Chaldaeans = ? sons of: CHELEOUD.

Cities: BABYLON; UR 1.

Anagram of Chaldaeans: LEB-KAMAI.

CHALPHI (1), Aram. *Halphaï,* abbrev. of Nabat. *Halaph-ilâhaï,* "God has replaced [a dead child]," Gr. *Halphaios* (cf. Alphaeus. See Shillem), father of: JUDAH 8.

CHANANIAH (1). See: CHENANIAH 2.

CHAPHENATH (1), phonetic var. of Aram. *Kaphelta,* "The Double," perhaps a translation of Hb. *ha-mishneh,* "The new [city]" of 2 K 22:14; Zp 1:10; a new quarter of Jerusalem, NW of the temple, 1 M 12:37.

See: NEW TOWN.

CHARAX (1), probably a fortified town in Transjordania where the governor of the Ammonite territory resides, 2 M 12:17.

CHARMIS (3), **son of Melchiel** (1). See: CHABRIS.

CHASPHO (2), a town in Gilead, 15 km E of the Sea of Chinnereth; some Jews are rescued there by Judas Maccabaeus, 1 M 5:26, 36.

= **Caspin** (1), "a certain fortified town, enclosed by ramparts," 2 M 12: 13–16.

CHEBAR (8), called a river but probably the canal running beside the Euphrates between Babylon and Warka. Among the people of Judah who are deported there is the prophet Ezekiel, Ezk 1:1, 3; 3:15, 23; 10:15, 20, 22; 43:3.

CHEDOR-LAOMER (5), "Servant of [the goddess] Lagamar," Lat. *Chodorlahomer,* **king of Elam** (2), an ally of: AMRAPHEL.

CHELAL (1), an Israelite of the sons of Pahath-moab, married to a foreign wife, whom he puts away, Ezr 10:30.

CHELEON (1), Jdt 2:23. Unknown.

CHELEOUD (The sons of) (1), Jdt 1:6, probably the: CHALDAEANS.

CHELOUS (1), an unknown town that Jdt 1:9 seems to locate near Beersheba.

CHELUB, "Cage, Basket"? (cf. Caleb?; Chelubai).

1. **Chelub** (1). See: CALEB.
2. **Chelub** (1), father of: EZRI.

CHELUBAI (1), derived from *Chelub* or *Caleb,* 1 Ch 2:9. See: CALEB.

CHELUHI (1), an Israelite of the sons of Bani, married to a foreign wife, whom he puts away, Ezr 10:35.

CHEMOSH (8), Gr. *Chamōs,* national god of Moab, Nb 21:29; Jr 48:7, 13, 46 (and not of the Ammonites, despite Jr 11:24), for whom Solomon builds a sanctuary east of Jerusalem, 1 K 11:7, 33; 2 K 23:13.

CHENAANAH, Hb. *Kena'anah* (cf. Canaan?).

1. **Chenaanah** (4), father of the prophet: ZEDEKIAH 1.

2. **Chenaanah** (1), a Benjaminite of the sons of Jediael, head of a family and a stout fighting man, 1 Ch 7:10–11.

CHENANI (2), abbrev. of *Chenaniah,* a Levite associated with Bani, takes part in the penitential liturgy, Ne 9:4, and cosigns the pledge to observe the Law, Ne 10:14 (corr. of Hb. *Beninu*).

CHENANIAH, "Yah is steadfast" (cf. Chenani; Jehoiachin).

1. **Chenaniah** (2), a chief of the Levites, in charge of transferring the Ark under David, 1 Ch 15:22, 27.

2. **Chananiah** (1), a Levite descended from Izhar, of the clan of Kohath. He and his sons are "assigned to outside duties for Israel as scribes and judges," 1 Ch 26:29.

CHEPHAR-AMMONI (1), "Village of the Ammonite" (cf. Capernaum; Capharsalama; Chephirah; Hac-chepirim), Q*Kephar-ha-'Ammonah,* a town in Benjamin, Jos 18:24.

CHEPHIRAH (4), "Young lioness *or* Little town" (cf. Chephar-ammoni), one of the four towns in the Gibeonite confederacy, Jos 9:17, in Benjamin, Jos 18:26. The people of Chephirah return from the exile with Zerubbabel, Ezr 2:25//Ne 7:29.

CHERAN (2), last of the four sons of Dishon, 1 Ch 1:41//Gn 36:26 (Hb. *Dishan*), son of Seir.

CHERETHITES (10), a people kin to the Philistines, 1 S 30:14, practically identified with the latter in Ezk 25:16 and Zp 2:5 (here some translate *Cherethites* as *Cretans;* cf. Gn 10:14, where the Philistines are said to be originally from *Caphtor,* that is, Crete).

Associated with the **Pelethites**—a word that is perhaps a variant of *Philistines*—the Cherethites form the personal bodyguard of David, 2 S 15:18; 20:7; 1 K 1:38, 44. Their leader is Benaiah, son of Jehoiada, 2 S 8:18//20:23; 1 Ch 18:17.

CHERITH (2), a wadi on the left bank of the Jordan, beside which the prophet Elijah hides, 1 K 17:3–6.

CHERUB (2), a town in Babylonia to which Israelites are exiled, Ezr 2:59//Ne 7:61. Site unknown.

CHESALON (1), (cf. Chislon), on the border of Dan and Judah, NE of Beth-shemesh, Jos 15:10. About 20 km W of Jerusalem. See: JEARIM.

CHESED (1), (cf. Chaldaea), one of the twelve sons of Nahor, brother of

Abraham, born of his wife Milcah; eponymous ancestor of the Chaldaeans, Gn 22:22.

CHESIL, "Insolent, Bold" (cf. Chislon).

1. **Chesil** (1), a town in the Negeb of Judah, Jos 15:30 (//Jos 19:4, *Bethul* //1 Ch 4:30, *Bethuel,* a town of Simeon in the Negeb).

2. **Orion** (3), Hb. *Kesil,* Jb 9:9; 38: 31; Am 5:8, a constellation. See: MANSIONS OF THE SOUTH.

CHESULLOTH (1), (cf. Chislon), "Loins, Sides," Jos 19:18.

= **Chisloth-tabor** (1), Jos 19:12, a town of Issachar on the border of Zebulun. Perhaps *Iksal,* 8 km SE of Nazareth.

CHETEPH (1), "Shoulder, Side," a town on the border of Judah and Benjamin, near Beth-arabah, Jos 18:18.

CHEZIB (1), (cf. Cozbi). See: ACHZIB 1.

CHILEAB (1), second son of David, born at Hebron of Abigail, former wife of Nabal of Carmel, 2 S 3:3.

= **Daniel** (1), 1 Ch 3:1.

CHILION (3), "Weakness, Fragility," an Ephrathite from Bethlehem of Judah, one of the two sons of Elimelech and Naomi, husband of Orpah the Moabite and brother-in-law of Ruth, Rt 1:2–5; 4:9–10.

CHILMAD (1), a trading town in Babylonia? Ezk 27:23. Some correct to Hb. *kol Madaï,* "all of Media."

CHIMHAM

1. **Chimham** (3), son of Barzillai. When David returns from his exile at Mahanaim, where Barzillai had generously provided for the king's needs, Chimham accompanies him to Jerusalem in place of his elderly father, 2 S 19:38–39, 41.

2. **Khan Kimham** (1), name of an encampment or caravanserai near Bethlehem where Johanan and the Judaeans with him stop on their flight into Egypt, Jr 41:17.

CHINNERETH (4), "Lyre"?

a. **Chinnereth** (2), a town of Naphtali, Jos 19:35, on the NW shore of the sea of the same name, cf. Dt 3:17.

= **Chinneroth** (2), Jos 11:2 (corr. of Hb. *Kinaroth*), conquered by Ben-hadad, king of Aram, 1 K 15:20.

= **Gennesaret** (2), where Jesus lands after crossing the lake, Mk 6:53//Mt 14:34.

b. **Sea of Chinnereth** (2) or **of Chinneroth** (2), Jos 12:3. It is 209 m below sea level; length, 21 km; breadth, 12 km. It marks the NE frontier of the Promised Land, Nb 34:11, and the NW frontier of the kingdom of Sihon, Jos 12:3, which became the territory of the tribe of Gad, Jos 13:27.

= **Lake of Gennesaret** (2), near which Judas Maccabaeus and his army camp, 1 M 11:67, and where Jesus calls his first disciples, Peter, Andrew, James, and John, Lk 5:1–11.

= **Sea of Galilee** (5), Mt 4:18//Mk 1:16, call of the first disciples; Mt 15: 29//Mk 7:31; Jn 6:1, presence of Jesus.

= **Sea of Tiberias** (2), Jn 6:1; cf. 6:22–25. In Jn 21:1 the risen Jesus shows himself to the disciples there.

Other uses of *sea* (Mt, Mk, Jn) or *lake* (Lk) to refer to the Sea of Chinnereth: Mt 8:24–27//Mk 4:36–41//Lk 8:23–25, the calming of the sea; Mt 8: 32//Mk 5:13; Lk 8:33, the herd of pigs driven into the lake; Mt 13:1//Mk 4:1, Jesus teaches there; Mt 14:25–26//Mk 6:48–50//Jn 6:16–20, Jesus walks on the lake. See also Mt 4:13; 17:27; Mk 2:13; 3:7; 5:1, 21.

Towns by the lake: BETHSAIDA 1; CAPERNAUM; CHORAZIN; MAGDALA; TIBERIAS.

CHINNEROTH (4). See: CHINNERETH.

CHIOS (1), an island in the Aegean Sea, west of Smyrna, Paul perhaps stops there, Ac 20:15.

CHISLON (1), "Dull, Stupid" (cf. Chesalon; Chesil; Chesulloth; Chisloth-tabor), a Benjaminite, father of: ELIDAD.

CHISLOTH-TABOR (1), "Sides of Tabor" (cf. Chislon; Tabor). See: CHESULLOTH.

CHITLISH (1), a town in the lowlands of Judah, Jos 15:40.

CHLOE (1), a trader? manufacturer? whose employees travel about on business, in particular to Ephesus, where Paul meets them, 1 Co 1:11.

CHOBA (3), Jdt 4:4; 15:4, 5, an otherwise unknown town in Palestine.

CHORAZIN (2), Lat. *Corozain,* a town in Galilee, 3 km N of Capernaum. Jesus laments its fate, Mt 11:21//Lk 10:13.

CHOUS (1), on the wadi Mochmur, Jdt 7:18. NE of Shechem?

CHRIST (540). See: JESUS *b.*

CHRISTIAN (3), Ac 11:26; 26:28; 1 P 4:16, a follower of: CHRIST.

CHUZA, steward of Herod [Antipas] (1), Lk 8:3, husband of: JOANNA.

CILICIA (18), a region of SE Asia Minor, which became a Roman province in 57 B.C.

Cilicia, a coastal country, Ac 27:5, with a mountainous hinterland, "Upper Cilicia," Jdt 2:21, is invaded by the troops of Holofernes, Jdt 1:7–12; 2:25. Two uprisings in this area against the Seleucids are recorded, 1 M 11:24; 2 M 4:30–31, 36. In Jerusalem, Jews from Cilicia debate with Stephen, Ac 6:9. Paul, who hails from Cilicia (Tarsus), stays there for several years after his conversion, Ga 1:21; cf. Ac 9:30; 11:25. A little later, he visits and strengthens the churches of this province, Ac 15:23, 41. Cilicia (Hb. *Keve,* 4×) is one of the places that furnishes Solomon with horses, 1 K 10:28//2 Ch 1:16.

Towns: MALLUS; TARSUS.

[CISJORDAN]. See: JORDAN 4.

CITADEL (28), Gr. *Akra.* See: JERUSALEM *a.*

CITY OF DAVID (49), Hb. *'Ir David.* See: JERUSALEM *a.*

CITY OF PALM TREES. See: PALM TREES.

CITY OF SALT (1). See: SALT 3.

CLAUDIA (1), (cf. Claudius), a Christian woman of Rome, 2 Tm 4:21.

CLAUDIUS, Gr. *Klaudios,* Lat. *Claudius,* "Lame" (cf. Claudia. See Paseah).

1. **Claudius** (2), full name *Tiberius Claudius Nero,* Roman emperor (41–54). From his reign dates an edict expelling the Jews from Rome, Ac 18:2, and a famine, Ac 11:28.

2. **Claudius** (1). See: LYSIAS 3.

CLEMENT (1), a Christian of Philippi, Ph 4:3.

CLEOPAS, abbrev. of Gr. *Kleopatros,* pronounced in Semitic, *Qlôpha',* Gr. *Klōpas* (cf. Cleopatra).

1. **Cleopas** (1), Lk 24:18, one of the two "disciples at Emmaus," vv. 13–35.

2. **Clopas** (1), Jn 19:25, husband (rather than father) of (?): MARY 6. Identified by some with: ALPHAEUS 1.

CLEOPATRA, Gr. *Kleopatra* (cf. Cleopas; Patroclus; Antipater).

1. **[Cleopatra],** daughter of Antiochus the Great and wife of Ptolemy V Epiphanes. See: ANTIOCHUS 2.

2. **Cleopatra** (2), daughter of Ptolemy VI Philometor, wife of Alexander Balas, 1 M 10:57–58, then of Demetrius II, 11:9–12.

3. **Cleopatra** (1), Est 10:3[1], wife of: PTOLEMY 8.

CLOPAS. See: CLEOPAS 2.

CNIDUS (2), a city of Caria on the SW coast of Asia Minor. It receives the letter of the consul Lucius promulgating the alliance between Jews and Romans, 1 M 15:23. Mentioned in connection with Paul's journey by sea to Rome, Ac 27:7. Today *Cape Krio.*

COASTAL REGION (1), Gr. *Paralia,* "Shore, Littoral," 1 M 15:38, probably the official name for the administrative area elsewhere described in terms of its boundaries: "from the Ladder of Tyre to the frontiers of Egypt," 1 M 11:59, or "from Ptolemais to the territory of the Gerrenians," 2 M 13:24.

District center: JAMNIA.

See: JABNEEL 1.

Commander-in-chief: CENDEBAEUS; GORGIAS; HEGEMONIDES; SIMEON 5.

COELE-SYRIA (1), "Hollow Syria." See: ARAM 1*f*.

COL-HOZEH (cf. Hazael).

1. **Col-hozeh** (1), father of: SHALLUM 15.

2. **Col-hozeh** (1), ancestor of: MAASEIAH 15.

COLOSSAE (1), a city in Phrygia near Laodicea and Hierapolis, 200 km E of Ephesus. Epaphras, a native of Colossae, establishes the churches of these three cities; Paul addresses a letter to these communities, which he has not visited, Col 1:1; cf. 2:1; 4:13–17.

Member of the Church at Colossae: PHILEMON.

CONANIAH (cf. Jehoiachin).

1. **Conaniah** (2) and **Shimei** his brother and assistant; both are Levites, and under King Hezekiah are in charge of the offerings brought to the temple. They are aided by ten overseers, 2 Ch 31:12–13.

2. **Conaniah** (1), one of the six heads of the Levites under Josiah, 2 Ch 35:9.

CONIAH (3), Hb. *Konyahu,* abbrev. of *Jekonyahu.* See: JEHOIACHIN.

CORINTH (6), a Greek city, capital of the Roman province of Achaia, populous (more than 500,000 inhabitants, of which two-thirds were slaves), cosmopolitan (two ports), dissolute in its morals.

First stay of Paul (winter, 50–summer, 52): during his second missionary journey, after his failure at Athens, Paul evangelizes Corinth, where his message reaches the poor above all, cf. 1 Co 1:26–28. He becomes a friend of Aquila and Priscilla, Ac 18:1–11. He writes to the Christians of Thessalonika, *1 and 2 Th.* The hostility of the Jews causes him to appear before the proconsul Gallio, who declares he has no competency in this area. Paul goes to Syria, Ac 18:12–18. Apollos, coming from Ephesus, eloquently preaches the Gospel to the Jews of the city, 18:27–19:1. During the third missionary journey and while staying at Ephesus (54–57), Paul receives bad news from Corinth and writes a *first letter,* 1 Co 5:9–13 (a lost letter, unless 2 Co 6:14–7:1 is a part of it). After receiving further news, 1 Co 1:11, and questions sent to him in writing, 1 Co 7:1, Paul sends a *second letter* (= 1 Co 1–16). But Titus, coming to Corinth to prepare for the collection announced in 1 Co 16:1–4, informs Paul that his letter has had meager results.

Second stay. A quick visit of Paul to Corinth, 2 Co 12:14; 13:1–2, is the occasion for a brief and violent confrontation. Returning to Ephesus, he writes a *third letter,* a stern one, 2 Co 2:3–4; 7:8–12 (a lost letter, unless it = 2 Co 10–13). A little later, in Macedonia, Paul receives good news from Titus, cf. 2 Co 7:13; he then writes a *fourth letter* (= 2 Co 1–9; but ch. 9 is perhaps an independent note in the collection).

Third stay (winter 57–58), cf. Ac 20:3, during which he composes the *letter to the Romans.*

Port: CENCHREAE.

Province: ACHAIA.

Synagogue leaders: CRISPUS; SOSTHENES 1.

Christians: CHLOE; GAIUS 3; STEPHANAS.

See: ZEUS.

CORINTHIANS (2), Ac 18:8; 2 Co 6:11, of or from: CORINTH.

CORNELIUS (8), "one of the centurions of the Italica cohort stationed in Caesarea. . . . He and the whole of his household were devout and God-fearing, and he gave generously to Jewish causes and prayed constantly to God," Ac 10:1–2. The whole of ch. 10 tells of the vision of this Roman officer garrisoned at Caesarea and of Peter's ecstasy at Jaffa, both intended to promote the access of the "pagans" to the faith. Cornelius and his household receive the Holy Spirit and are baptized. In Ac 11:1–18 Peter justifies his attitude toward Cornelius and his household to the Church at Jerusalem.

CORNER (Gate of the) (5), Hb. *Pinnah,* on the NW side of Jerusalem. Jehoash, king of Israel, demolishes the wall between this gate and the Gate of Ephraim, 2 K 14:13//2 Ch 25:23. King Uzziah repairs the damage and fortifies the Gate of the Corner, 2 Ch 26:9. Other destructions will be followed by other repairs, Jr 31:38; Zc 14:10.

See: FURNACES.

COS (2), a small island in the Aegean, west of Caria; a copy of the consul Lucius' letter promulgating the Jewish-Roman alliance is sent here, 1 M 15:23. Paul stops here on his return from his third missionary journey, Ac 21:1.

COSAM (1), an ancestor of Jesus acc. to Lk 3:28.

COZBI (2), "Luxuriant" (cf. Achzib; Chezib; Cozeba), **daughter of Zur** (1), **a Midianite woman** (3), whom Phinehas pierces with a lance, as he does the Simeonite Zimri, son of Salu, with whom she had probably engaged in sacral prostitution, Nb 25:6–18; cf. 1 M 2:26.

COZEBA (1), (cf. Cozbi). See: ACHZIB 1.

CRAFTSMEN (Valley of the) (1), Hb. *Geharashim,* a place occupied by Benjaminites after the return from exile, Ne 11:35. Formerly Kenizzite, 1 Ch 4:14. Location uncertain.

CRATES (1), "Mighty," **commander of the Cypriots** (i.e., mercenaries) (1), replaces Sostratus in charge of the acropolis at Jerusalem, 2 M 4:29.

CRESCENS (1), co-worker of Paul, journeys to Galatia, that is, to Gaul rather than to Galatia in Asia Minor, 2 Tm 4:10.

CRETANS (2), Ac 2:11; Tt 1:12, inhabitants of: CRETE.

CRETE (6), an island in the southern Aegean Sea, the largest in the eastern Mediterranean. Demetrius II recruits mercenaries there, cf. 1 M 11:38, before returning to Antioch, 1 M 10:67. Some Cretan Jews are in Jerusalem for the first Christian Pentecost, Ac 2:11. During his journey to Rome Paul, a prisoner, stops at Fair Havens, Ac 27:7–15. Later, he leaves Titus in Crete to complete the organization of the local church, Tt 1:5. Using a Cretan proverb, Tt 1:12, he warns his follower against false teachers.

Another name for the island: CAPHTOR.

Towns: FAIR HAVENS; GORTYNA; LASEA; PHOENIX.

Cape: SALMONE.

CRISPUS (2), president of the synagogue in Corinth, Ac 18:8, baptized by Paul, 1 Co 1:14.

CROP-HEADS (3), Hb. *Kezuze Pe'ah* (cf. Emek-keziz), Arabian tribes that, acc. to Herodotus, wear their hair cut into a round pad and shave their temples, Jr 9:25; 25:23; 49:32, a practice forbidden in Israel, cf. Lv 19:27.

CUB (1), an unknown country, Ezk 30:5. Perhaps read (with Gr.) *Lub,* that is, Libya.

CUN (1), a town in the kingdom of Zobah, north of Damascus; 1 Ch 18:8 (//2 S 8:8, *Berothai*).

CUSH

1. **Cush** (29), (cf. Cushi), Gr. *Aithiopia,* **Ethiopia** (3), a country south of the second cataract of the Nile, the Nubia or Ethiopia of the ancients; south of Egypt, Ezk 29:10; 30:4–5, 9; Jdt 1:10, on the frontiers of the known world, Am 9:7, at the western end of the Persian Empire of Ahasuerus, Est 1:1; 3:13[a]; 8:9, 12[b]. A people of black skin, cf. Is 18:2; Jr 13:23.

The XXVth dynasty (715–663) ruling Egypt is Cushite, and its kings suffer heavy defeats at the hands of Assyria, Is 18:1–7; 20:3–5; Zp 2:12; Na 3:8. See: TIRHAKAH.

Ethiopians are naturally to be found in the Egyptian armies, 2 Ch 12:3; Jr 46:9. They are also to be found in Judah, 2 S 18:21–23, 31–32. See: EBED-MELECH.

Cush is sometimes allied with the enemies of God's people, at the side of Gog, Ezk 38:5, or of the persecutor Antiochus Epiphanes, Dn 11:43. But some day Ethiopia will be converted and be joined to the people of God, Ps 68:31; 87:4; Zp 3:10. An Ethiopian (cf. Is 11: 11), a high-ranking official of the kandake or queen of Ethiopia, accepts the Gospel on the occasion of a pilgrimage to Jerusalem, Ac 8:27–39. Cush seems rather to mean SW Arabia in Gn 2:13; 10:7–8//1 Ch 1:9–10; 2 Ch 21:16; Jb 28:19; Is 43:3; 45:14.

Cushites: ZIPPORAH; ZERAH 6.

2. **Cush the Benjaminite** (1), Ps 7:1, perhaps an enemy of David. The translations have seen in him the Cushite who brings news of Absalom's death, cf. 2 S 18:21–32.

CUSHAN (1), Hab 3:7, perhaps an archaic name for: MIDIAN. The translations have taken the word to be a derivative of Cush (Ethiopia).

CUSHAN-RISHATHAIM (4), "Cushan of twofold wickedness" (cf. Birsha?), king of Aram Naharaim (but some correct to *king of Edom*). He enslaves the Israelites for eight years, at the end of which he is overcome by the judge Othniel son of Kenaz, Jg 3:8–10.

CUSHI (cf. Cush 1).

1. **Cushi** (1), father of the prophet: ZEPHANIAH 2.

2. **Cushi** (1), father of: SHELEMAIAH 1.

CUSHITE or **Ethiopian** (27), Hb. *Kushi,* inhabitant of: CUSH OR ETHIOPIA.

CUSLUH or **Casluh (People of)** (2), Hb. *Kasluhim,* an unidentified people connected with Egypt; the Philistines are originally not from Cusluh but from Caphtor, Gn 10:14//1 Ch 1:12 (*Casluh*).

CUTHAH (2), 2 K 17:24 (Hb. *Cuth*), 30 (Hb. *Cuthah*), Accad. *Kutu,* a town 30 km NE of Babylon, taken by the Assyrians, who deport its inhabitants to Samaria, where they introduce the worship of their god Nergal.

CYAMON (1), facing Esdraelon, Jdt 7:3. Site unknown.

CYAXARES, king of Media (1), (633–584), destroyer of the Assyrian empire. Tb 14:15 refers to the fall of Nineveh and the deportation of its inhabitants by Cyaxares (the name is a conjecture based on the Gr. *Ahikar;* var. are *Nebuchadnezzar* and *Ahasuerus*).

CYPRIOT (4), 2 M 4:29; Ac 4:36; 11: 20; 21:16, of or from: CYPRUS.

CYPRUS (7), an island in the eastern Mediterranean, under the domination of the Ptolemies—Ptolemy Macron was governor of it, 2 M 10:12–13—and later of the Seleucids. A copy of the consul Lucius' letter promulgating the alliance between the Jews and the Romans is sent there, 1 M 15:23. The island becomes a Roman province in 22 B.C.

The Gospel reaches Cyprus at a very early date: first, in Jewish circles, thanks to the Jewish Christians who leave Palestine after the martyrdom of Stephen, Ac 11:19, then in pagan circles, thanks to Paul, Barnabas, and Mark, 13:4–13 (conversion of Sergius Paulus the proconsul); 15:39. Cypriots are among the first Jewish Christians to preach the Gospel to the pagans of Antioch, Ac 11:20. During his journeys by sea Paul sights Cyprus several times, Ac 21:3; 27:4.

"The islands across the sea," Jr 25:22, perhaps include Cyprus.

Native place of: BARNABAS; MNASON.

Leaders of Cypriot mercenaries: CRATES; NICANOR 2.

Other possible names for the island: ELISHAH; KITTIM.

Towns: PAPHOS; SALAMIS.

CYRENE (2), Gr. *Kyrēnē,* 1 M 15:23; 2 M 2:23, a city in North Africa, in present-day Libya, about 800 km W of Alexandria, a Greek colony, then a Roman province from 75 B.C. A large Jewish population; a copy of the consul Lucius' letter on the alliance of Jews and Romans is sent to Cyrene, 1 M 15:23; on the first Christian Pentecost Jews from this area are in Jerusalem, Ac 2:10, where they have a synagogue, 6:9. Jewish Christians from Cyrene are among the founders of the Church of Antioch in Syria, 11:20.

Native place of: JASON 4; LUCIUS 2; SIMEON 15.

Gulf of Cyrene: SYRTIS.

CYRUS [the Great] (24), Hb. *Kôresh,* Pers. *Kurush,* "Shepherd" (cf. Is 44:28), **king of Persia** (11), **the Persian** (2), **king of Babylon** (1) (550–529).

The Book of Consolation gives the exiles from Judah the hope of proximate liberation by announcing, at first in veiled terms, Is 41:2–5, 25–27; 42:1–9, then by name, Is 44:28; 45:1–4, the victorious progress of Cyrus, who is given the title of "Shepherd," Is 44:28, "Anointed," Is 45:1, "Servant" and "Chosen One" of Yahweh, Is 42:1. In October 539, Cyrus enters Babylon. In 538 he issues the edict ending the captivity of the Jews and ordering the rebuilding of the temple in Jerusalem and the return of the sacred vessels to the sanctuary, 2 Ch 36:22–23// Ezr 1:1–5; cf. Ezr 1:7–8; 3:7; 4:3–4; 5:13–17; 6:2–3, 14.

The history of Daniel is presented as lasting into the reign of Cyrus the Persian, Dn 1:21; 6:29; 10:1; 14:1–2.

See: ACHAEMENIDS.

D

DABBESHETH (1), "Hump," on the border of Zebulun, beside the Kishon, Jos 19:11. 10 km N of Megiddo.

DAGON (16), Ugar. *Dgn,* Accad. *Dagan* (cf. Beth-dagon), a divinity in the Amorite pantheon of Mari in Mesopotamia; later adopted at Ugarit (Syria) and in Palestine. In the OT Dagon is the principal god of the Philistines; his most famous temple is at Ashdod (= Azotus), Jg 16:23–24; 1 S 5:2–7; 1 Ch 10:10. The temple of Dagon at Azotus will be burned by Jonathan, 1 M 10:83–84; 11:4.

DALMANUTHA (1), Mk 8:10 (//Mt 15:39, *Magadan*). Location unknown.

DALMATIA (1). See: ILLYRICUM.

DALPHON (1), Accad. *Dullupu,* "Sleepless" (cf. Jidlaph), brother of: PARSHANDATHA.

DAMARIS (1), an Athenian woman converted to the Christian faith at the same time as Dionysius the Areopagite, Ac 17:34.

DAMASCENE (1), Jdt 1:12, another name for the territory of: DAMASCUS.

DAMASCUS (67), a city at the foot of Mount Hermon (cf. Sg 7:5) at the edge of the Syrian desert. An important commercial center, Ezk 27:18; cf. Am 3:12. On the northern frontier of the Promised Land, cf. Ezk 47:16–18; 48:1; Zc 9:1.

As *capital of the powerful Aramaean kingdom,* Damascus, often victorious and cruel, Am 1:3–5, is a permanent threat to Israel: under David, 2 S 8:5–6//1 Ch 18:5–6; under Solomon with Rezon, 1 K 11:23–25; under Ahab and Jehoram with Ben-hadad II and Hazael, 1 K 20:24; 2 K 8:7–9; under Jeroboam II, who "recovered Damascus and Hamath for Israel," 2 K 14:28 (JB note); under Ahaz with Rezin, but Damascus is captured by Tiglath-pileser, the Assyrian (ca. 732), 2 K 16:9; Is 7:8; 8:4; 10:9; 17:1–3, and the Israelites of the north are deported "far beyond Damascus," Am 5:27. Following his meeting with Tiglath-pileser at Damascus, Ahaz erects at Jerusalem an altar like the one in Damascus, 2 K 16:10–12; cf. 2 Ch 28:23. In 605, after the downfall of Assyria and the defeat of Egypt at Carchemish, Jr 49:23–27 announces the proximate destruction of Damascus by Babylon.

Kings of Aram at Damascus: BEN-HADAD 1–2; HAZAEL; REZIN; REZON.

Native city of: ELIEZER 1; NAAMAN 3.

Symbolic names (?) for Damascus: BETH-EDEN; BIKATH-AVEN.

In the *Syria of the Seleucids* (or Lagides), the place of Damascus is taken by Antioch. In 1 M 11:62 and 12:32, the presence of Jonathan at Damascus is mentioned. Acc. to Jdt 1:7, 12; 2:27 the Damascus area is invaded by Nebuchadnezzar, but his troops are finally defeated near Damascus itself, 15:5.

From 63 B.C. on, *Damascus is part of the Decapolis.* There is a sizable Jewish community there, cf. Ac 9:2. It is on the road to Damascus, ca. 34 or 36, that Saul, on his way to arrest Christians, is called by Christ, Ac 9:1–9//22:5–11; 26:12–16, and sent by him to the house of Judas in "Straight Street," where he meets Ananias, Ac 9:10–18//22:12–16; it is at Damascus that the new convert begins to preach Christ, Ac 9:19–22, 27; cf. 26:20. Around 36 or 38 Paul returns to Damascus, 2 Co 11:32; Ga 1:17, where he escapes arrest by King Aretas' ethnarch, 2 Co 11:33.

Rivers of Damascus: ABANA; PHARPAR.

North of Damascus: HOBAH.

See: ARAM 1; DECAPOLIS.

DAN, from Hb. root *din,* "to judge," see Gn 30:6; 49:16 (cf. Abidan; Daniel; Dinah).

1. **Dan** (51), son of Jacob and of Bilhah, Rachel's servant, Gn 30:6; 35:25, eponymous ancestor of one of the twelve tribes of Israel. A small tribe (despite the census figures in the priestly account, Nb 1:39; 2:25; 26:42), Dan contains only one clan, Nb 26:42; cf. Gn 46:23, six hundred men acc. to Jg 18:11.

The territory of Dan is located west of Benjamin between Ephraim, Judah, and the Mediterranean, Jos 19:40–46. But pressure from the Amorites, Jg 1:34–35, then from the Philistines, Jg 13–16, leads to the migrations of the Danites to northern Palestine around the town of Laish, Jg 18; Jos 19:47. Dan is also described in poems in Gn 49:16–17 (judge/Dan); Dt 33:32 (lion/Laish); Jg 5:17 (sailors).

Levitical towns of Dan; Jos 21:5, 23.

Dan in the lists of the tribes: see List, pages 410–11.

Danites: AHIEZER 1; AMMIEL 1; AZAREL 3; BUKKI; HIRAM 2; MANOAH; OHOLIAB; SAMSON; SHELOMITH 1.

2. **Dan** (23), a town near one of the sources of the Jordan, 5 km W of Banias. Before its conquest by the Danites it is called:

= **Laish** (4), Jg 18:7, 14 (Hb.), 27–29.

= **Leshem** (2), Jos 19:47.

= ? **Lesha** (1), Gn 10:19 (northern boundary of Canaan).

Dan is in the extreme north of the Promised Land, Dt 34:1; cf. Jr 4:18; 8:16; Gn 14:14. The expression *from Dan to Beersheba* thus indicates the northern and southern boundaries of Israel, Jg 20:1; 1 S 3:20; 2 S 3:10; 17:11; 24:2, 15; 1 K 5:5; in 1 Ch 21:2; 2 Ch 30:5, the formula is reversed: *from Beersheba to Dan,* cf. 2 S 24:6–7; Am 8:14.

King Jeroboam sets up the golden calf, 1 K 12:29–30; cf. 2 K 10:29; Am 8:14; Tb 1:5, in a sanctuary that is already old, cf. Jg 17–18; 2 S 28:10. The city is taken by Ben-hadad, king of Aram, 1 K 15:20//2 Ch 16:4.

3. **Camp of Dan** (2), Hb. *Mahane-Dan,* a temporary property of the Danites, near Zorah, Jg 13:25; 18:12.

4. **Dan** (1), an Arabian tribe like Uzal?, Ezk 27:19 (Hb. *Vedan*).

DANANITES (2), among the peoples of the islands and coasts of the Mediterranean, connected with Javan, Gn 10:4 (corr. of Hb. *Dodanim*)//1 Ch 1:7 (corr. of Hb. *Rodanim*).

DANEL. See: DANIEL.

DANIEL, Danel, Hb. *Daniyy'el* or *Dani'el,* "God is judge" (cf. Dan).

1. **Danel** (3), a popular hero of antiquity, known in the Ugaritic texts for his wisdom and justice, cf. Ezk 28:3, but whose presence along with Noah and Job in a sinful land is not enough to avert chastisement from it, Ezk 14:14–20.

2. **Daniel** (1). See: CHILEAB.

3. **Daniel** (2), a priest among the sons of Ithamar; he returns from the exile with Ezra, Ezr 8:2, and is a cosigner of the pledge to observe the Law, Ne 10:7.

4. **Daniel** (126), a young man of Judah, deported with Hananiah, Mishael, and Azariah to the court of Nebuchadnezzar, Dn 1:3–21, where he is given the name **Belteshazzar,** Dn 1:7. When the Babylo-

nian sages prove helpless, Daniel intervenes to explain the meaning of the king's dream about the composite statue and is given a high rank at the court, 2. Belteshazzar, "a man in whom lives the spirit of God Most Holy," cf. 5:11, 14; 13:45, and whom "no mystery puts . . . at a loss," 4:5–6, explains to the king the dream about the tree that forecasts the king's madness, 4. During "Belshazzar's feast" Daniel explains to the king the meaning of the mysterious writing on the wall, 5. Envied by the satraps, Daniel "for his singleness of heart was rescued from the lion's jaw," 6; cf. 1 M 2:60.

Daniel's dream: the four beasts and the Ancient of Days, Dn 7. His vision of the ram and the he-goat is explained by Gabriel, 8. Gabriel also explains to Daniel, "son of man," 8:17, "a man specially chosen," 9:23; 10:11, 19, the prophecy of the seventy weeks and the "disastrous abomination," 9:1–27; cf. Mt 24:15. A vision of a man dressed in linen: the time of wrath and of the end, Dn 10–12. The figure of Daniel appears again in *Susanna and the Judgement of Daniel,* Dn 13, *Daniel and the Priests of Baal,* 14:1–22, and *Daniel and the Dragon*, 14:23–42.

DANITE (5), Jg 13:2; 18:1, 11, 30; 1 Ch 12:36, belonging to the tribe of: DAN 1.

DANNAH (1), Accad. *Dannatu,* "Fortress" (cf. Medan), a town in the highlands of Judah, Jos 15:49.

DAPHNE, "Laurel," a nymph changed into a laurel at the moment when Apollo catches her.

1. **Daphne, near Antioch** (1), famous for its sanctuary of Apollo, enjoying the right of asylum. Menelaus has the high priest Onias murdered there when the latter has taken sanctuary, 2 M 4:33–34. It is 8 km S of Antioch in Syria.

2. **[Daphne],** classical name for: TAHPANHES.

DARA (1), one of the sons of Zerah, 1 Ch 2:6.

DARDA (1), associated with Heman and Cacol as a celebrated sage, 1 K 5:11.

DARIUS, Gr. *Dareios,* Hb. *Daryavesh,* Old Pers. *Darayavahus,* "The one who upholds the good."

1. **Darius I [Hystaspis]** (16), **king of Persia** (2) (522–486), Ezr 4:5, 24, authorizes the Jews, in the second year of his reign (520), to carry on the reconstruction of the temple, Ezr 5:5–7; 6:1–14, which is finished in his sixth year (515), Ezr 6:15. The activity of the prophet Haggai is dated from the second year of Darius' reign, Hg 1:1, 15; 2:10; that of the prophet Zechariah from the second, Zc 1:1, 7, and fourth years, Zc 7:1. In Ezr 6:22, the "king of Assyria" is Darius, Assyria here standing for all of Mesopotamia (and not the kingdom of Assyria, which has long since disappeared).

2. **Darius II (Nothos) the Persian** (1), king of Persia (423–405), Ne 12:22, although some think the reference here is to Darius III.

3. **Darius III [Codomannus], king of the Persians and Medes** (1) (336–330), conquered by Alexander the Great, 1 M 1:1.

4. **Darius** (8) **son of Artaxerxes** (Hb. *of Ahasuerus = Xerxes*), **of Median stock** (1), Dn 9:1, the Mede, Dn 6:1; 11:1, appoints Daniel a grand vizier, is forced to throw him into the lions' pit, and then rescues him from it, Dn 6:2–29. This King Darius is unknown to historians.

See: ACHAEMENIDS.

DARK MOUNTAIN (1). See: ZALMON 3.

DARKON (2), head of a family of Solomon's slaves who return from the exile, Ezr 2:56//Ne 7:58.

DATHAN and **Abiram** (11), **sons of Eliab** (4), Reubenites, Nb 16:1, 12; 26:9; Dt 11:6. The Yahwist-Elohist story of their rebellion, Nb 16:1–2, 12–15, 25,

26, 27–34 (an account woven into the priestly story of the rebellion of Korah against Aaron), tells of how during the Exodus the two men reject the authority of Moses as leader of Israel and refuse to follow him on the journey to Canaan. The blasphemy of Dathan and Abiram consists in saying that the "land where milk and honey flow" is not the Promised Land but Egypt, where Israel had been enslaved, 16:12–15. A collective punishment strikes the rebels and their families, 16:25–34. Cf. Dt 11:6; Ps 106:7; Si 45:18.

DATHEMA (1), a fortress in Transjordania where the persecuted Israelites of Gilead take refuge, 1 M 5:9. Site not identified.

DAVID (1,150), "Beloved," see 1 S 16: 21–22; 18:1, 5, 16, 22, 28; 20:17 (cf. Dodai; Dodavahu; Dodo; Eldad; Elidad; Jedidah; Jedidiah; Medad; Bildad?; Iddo?), but *david* is perhaps only a common noun meaning "commander, military leader" that has become a proper name; cf. the *davidum* of the Mari tablets.

= **son of Jesse** (19): 1 S 16:18; 20:27, 30–31; 22:7–13; 25:10; 2 S 20:1; 23:1; 1 K 12:16; 1 Ch 10:14; 12:19; 29:26; 2 Ch 10:16; Si 45:25; Ac 13:22.

King of Judah and Israel (1010–970).

a. History of David: 1 S 16–31; 2 S; 1 K 1–2; 1 Ch 11–29. Apart from the closely knit account in 2 S 9–20, to which is to be added 1 K 1–2, the story has the composite character of a text in which traditions are intermingled and doublets are to be found. Even before being named as the eighth son of Jesse the Bethlehemite and the man whom Samuel privately "anoints where he stood with his brothers," 1 S 16:1–13, David is presented as the one whom God has singled out as recipient of the kingship belonging to Saul, the one chosen but now rejected, 1 S 13:14; 15:28; cf. 28:17; 2 S 3:10; 1 Ch 10:14.

Young David, harpist acc. to 1 S 16: 14–23, a shepherd acc. to 1 S 17:12, 15, 20, 28, enters the court of Saul whose armor-bearer he becomes. His victory over the giant Goliath, a type of the Philistine foe whom David will be confronting throughout his life, 1 S 17:1–53; cf. 19:8; 23:1, 28; 28:1; 2 S 5:17–25; Si 47:7—but among whom he also finds refuge, 1 S 21:11–16; 27–28—awakens a morbid jealousy in Saul, who several times attempts, 1 S 18:10–16; 19:9–17; 23:14–28, to kill the man he knows to be his rival. After becoming the son-in-law of the king, who gives him his younger daughter Michal, 1 S 18:17–30, and although protected by the friendship of Saul's son Jonathan, 1 S 18:2–3; 19:1–7; 20:17, 23; 23:16–18, David is forced to flee the court, 1 S 20; he becomes the leader of a raiding band, a man sometimes artful, 1 S 27:10–11, and cruel, 1 S 30:16–17, pursued by Saul, whom he escapes and whom he on the other hand spares, 1 S 22–26:25. Cf. Ps 63:1.

After Saul's death, cf. 2 S 1, David is anointed at Hebron, first as king of Judah, 2 S 2:1–4, 11, then, thanks to the allegiance of Abner, Saul's general, as king of Israel, 2 S 5:1–3//1 Ch 11:1–3. He captures Jerusalem and makes it his capital, 2 S 5:6–10//1 Ch 11:4–9, and has the Ark of God transferred to it, 2 S 6:1–23//1 Ch 13; cf. Ps 132:6–10, 13–14. At the moment when he is resolving to build a temple for Yahweh, the prophet Nathan solemnly tells him that instead Yahweh will build David a "house" by assuring the permanence of his dynasty, 2 S 7//1 Ch 17.

Victorious wars against the Philistines, Moabites, Aramaeans, Edomites, 2 S 8, and Ammonites, 2 S 11//1 Ch 20:1, which lead to the formation of a transitory empire. Twofold crime of David: adultery with Bathsheba and murder of Uriah, 2 S 11. The end of his reign is darkened by the rebellions of Absalom his son, 2 S 15–18, and Sheba the Benjaminite, 2 S 20, as well as by the intrigues for the succession, 1 K 1. David gives Solomon sovereignty over Israel, 1 K 1:28–33; cf. 1 Ch 23:1. David dies and is buried in the Citadel of David, 1 K 2:10.

b. Reign and dynasty of David. "David was thirty years old when he became king, and he reigned for forty years. He reigned in Hebron over Judah for seven years and six months; then he reigned in Jerusalem over all Israel and Judah for thirty-three years," 2 S 5:4–5//2:11// 1 Ch 3:4; cf. 29:26–27.

David, second king of Israel, leaves a lasting mark on the kingship, so that the throne of Israel, 1 K 2:4; 8:25; 9:5; Si 47:11; Jr 33:17, becomes the *throne of David* (25×), 2 S 7:16; 1 K 2:45; 1 M 2:57; Ps 132:11–12; Is 9:6. The fundamental text is 2 S 7:11–16//1 Ch 17: 11–14: "Yahweh Sabaoth says this . . . Yahweh will make you *a House* (33×). . . . Your House and your sovereignty will always stand secure before me and your throne be established for ever." For David and his sons who "sit on the sovereign throne of Yahweh over Israel" this "royal succession from father to one son exclusively," Si 45:25, is an unbreakable covenant, 1 Ch 28:5; 29:23; 2 Ch 13:5, 8; cf. 21:7; 23:3. The royal house of Judah is indistinguishable from the *house of David,* Jr 21:11–12; cf. Is 7:2, 13, and into Jerusalem, where "the royal tribunals of David" are, Ps 122:5, "kings occupying the throne of David will continue to make their entry," Jr 17:25; 22: 2–4. With the fall of the kingdom of Judah, the mention of David's name becomes an invitation to look to the future: "The days are coming . . . when I will raise up a virtuous Branch for David," Jr 23:5//33:15; Israel and Judah "will serve Yahweh their God and David their king whom I will raise up for them," Jr 30:9; cf. Ho 3:5. The expression "my servant David," Ezk 34:23–24; 37:24–25; Jr 33:21; Ps 144:10, becomes a messianic title. The davidic dynasty will culminate in Jesus *Son of David* (14×), Mt 1:1; 9:27; 12:23; 15: 22; 20:30–31; 21:9, 15; 22:42–45; Mk 10:47–48; 12:35–37; Lk 18:38–39; 20: 41–44; cf. Lk 1:32; 3:31, of the line of David, Rm 1:3; cf. Lk 2:4, root of Jesse, Rm 15:12, and of David, Rv 5:5, the one who has the key of David, Rv 3:7; cf. Is 22:22.

c. Person of David. Handsome, 1 S 16:12, 18, a valiant warrior, 1 S 16:18; 2 S 17:8; 1 Ch 22:8; 28:3; Ps 89:20, loved by men, 1 S 18:5, 16, 22, 28, faithful to his king, 1 S 22:14, whom he respects because Yahweh has anointed him, 1 S 24:7; 26:9, and to his friends, 2 S 9:7; cf. 1:26, kind like God, 2 S 9:3; cf. 1 S 20:14, like to an angel of God, 1 S 29:9; 2 S 14:17; 19:28, full of humility, 1 S 18:23; 2 S 7:18; 12:13; 24:17, of mercy, 1 S 24:10–12, 17–20; cf. 26, David is first and foremost the man of God, 2 Ch 8:14; Ne 12:24, 36, who is with him, 1 S 16:18; 17:37; 18:12, 14, 28; 20:13; 2 S 5:10, and who is the God of David, 2 K 20:5//Is 38:5; 2 Ch 21: 12. He is the servant of God, Ps 36:1; Ac 4:25; 13:36; cf. 2 S 3:18; 1 K 3:6; Ps 89:4, 21; Jr 33:21; and so on, a man after God's heart, 1 S 13:14; Ac 13:22, who has chosen him, 1 S 16:1–12; 1 K 8:16//2 Ch 6:6; Si 47:22, walking before God in fidelity, justice, and uprightness of heart, I K 3:6, in generosity of heart, 1 M 2:57, and love of God, Si 47:8, 22. He is an ideal and model king, cf. Ps 101, whose behavior serves as a rule for judging—and especially for condemning—his successors, 1 K 3:3, 14; 9:4; 11:4, 6, 33, 38; 14:8; 15:3–5, 11; 2 K 14:3; 16:2; 18:3; 22:2; 2 Ch 7:17; 11:17; 17:3; Si 49:4. The promises made to David and his dynasty, 2 S 7:5–16, bind Yahweh forever, 2 S 3:9; 1 K 6:12; 8:15, 24–26; 9:5; 2 K 8:19; 21:7; 2 Ch 1:9; 21:7; Ps 89:4, 29, 36, 50; 132:11; Si 47:22; Is 55:3 (cf. 2 Ch 6:42), so that Yahweh feels himself obliged "for the sake of my servant David," 1 K 11:13, 32, 34; 15:4; 2 K 8:19//2 Ch 21:7; 2 K 19:34//Is 37:35; 2 K 20:6; Ps 132:10; Si 47:12 (*thanks to him*), despite the shadows over his reign and the weaknesses of the man himself.

He who "pastured Israel with unselfish care and led them with a sensitive hand," Ps 78:72, is also "the singer of the songs of Israel," 2 S 23:1; cf. 22:1//Ps 18:1, the harpist, 1 S 16:16–23; 18:10; 19:9, who, later on, during the transferral of the Ark, dances before it, 2 S 6:5, 14–16, 21. Acc. to the chronicler it is he who draws up the plan for the temple, 1 Ch 22; 28, and prepares for the building of it, 29, organizes the chanting, music, and worship of the temple, 1 Ch 6:16; 15:16; 16:4–8, 37; 25:1; 2 Ch 7:6; 23:18; 29: 25–30; Ne 12:2–4. The musical instruments of David are mentioned in Am 6:5. The Psalter attributes 74 psalms to David: 3–9; 11–32; 34–41; 51–65; 68–70; 86; 101; 103; 108–110; 122; 124; 131; 133; 138–145; cf. 2 M 2:13; Si 47:8–10; Mt 22:42–45; Ac 1:16, 20; 2:25, 34; 4:25; Rm 4:6; 11:9; Heb 4:7.

d. David as figure of Christ. David, *king* of Israel, 2 S 6:20; 2 Ch 8:11; 29: 27; 35:4; Ezr 3:10, *shepherd* of Israel, 2 S 5:2; 7:8; Ps 78:70–72, *prophet* inspired by God's Spirit, 1 S 16:13; 2 S 23:2; Mt 22:43; Ac 1:16; cf. Is 11:2; 2 S 14:17, and *priest,* 2 S 6:13–14, 17–18, is one of the most important figures of Christ. As new David, born like David at Bethlehem, Lk 2:11; Jn 7:42, root of Jesse, Rm 15:12; cf. Is 11:1, to whom God will give the throne of David his father, Lk 1:32, Jesus is the true king of Israel, Mt 27:42//Mk 15:32; Jn 1:49; 12:13; cf. Ac 1:6, the true shepherd of Israel, Mt 2:6; cf. Mi 5:3; Ezk 34:23–24. He is a prophet, Mt 21:11; Lk 7:16, endowed with the Spirit of God, Mt 3:16; Lk 4:18; cf. Is 11:2. He is appointed priest by a divine oath as unbreakable, Ps 110:4; Heb 5:6, as the one that protects the dynasty of David and the high place of Zion, Ps 132:11–14. A shared love for the house of God unites them, 1 Ch 29:3; Ps 26:8; 69:10; Jn 2:17; cf. Lk 2:49. The sight of David climbing the Mount of Olives in tears, 2 S 15:30, and accepting the insults of Shimei as he goes, 2 S 16:5–14, reminds us of the agony in the garden of Gethsemane, Lk 22:39–44, and the insults hurled at Jesus on the way of the cross. David is only the lamp of Israel, 2 S 21:17; Jesus is the light of the world, Jn 8:12.

His wives: ABIGAIL 1; AHINOAM 2; BATHSHEBA; MICHAL.

His sons: ABSALOM 1; ADONIJAH 1; AMNON 1; JEREMOTH 7; SOLOMON 1.

Other sons: List, page 414.

His champions: List, pages 412–13.

Citadel and City of David: JERUSALEM *a.*

Town of David: BETHLEHEM 1.

Tower of David (unknown): Sg 4:4.

[DEAD] (Sea). 392 m below sea level; length, 76 km; width, 16 km; salinity, 25%.

= **Sea of the Arabah** (5), Hb. *yam ha-ʿarabah,* into which the waters of the Jordan flow, Jos 3:16. It serves as SW border for the territory of the Transjordanian tribes of Israel, Dt 3:17; 4:49; Jos 12:3, and southern limit of the kingdom of Jeroboam II, 2 K 14:25.

= **Salt Sea** (9), Hb. *yam ha-mèlah,* identified with the Sea of the Arabah, Dt 3:17; Jos 3:16; 12:3, marks the SE frontier of the Promised Land, Nb 34:3, 12, which is at the same time the eastern frontier of Judah, Jos 12:2, 5 (in these four passages the Salt Sea is paralleled with the Great Sea, that is, the Mediterranean) and of Benjamin, Jos 18:19. In Gn 14:3 the Salt Sea is identified with the Valley of Siddim.

= **Eastern Sea** (3), Hb. *yam ha-qadmoni,* marks the eastern boundary of Israel, just as the Great Sea or Western Sea sets the western boundary, Ezk 47: 18–19; Jl 2:20; Zc 14:8.

The Dead Sea is also paralleled with the Mediterranean in the expression "from sea to sea," Ps 72:8//Zc 9:10; Mi 7:12; Am 8:12, which indicates the ideal limits of the Promised Land. Other uses of "sea" as meaning the Dead Sea,

2 Ch 20:2; Is 16:8//Jr 48:32; Ezk 39:11.

See: ARABAH; PLAIN 1; SODOM.

DEBIR, "He who is behind" (cf. Dobrath?).

1. **Debir** (1), **king of Eglon** (4), an Amorite, allied with: ADONI-ZEDEK.

2. **Debir** (1), a former Canaanite town taken by the clan of Caleb, Jg 1:11–13//Jos 15:15–17 (by Joshua acc. to Jos 10:38–39; cf. 11:21; 12:13), listed among the towns in the highlands of Judah, Jos 15:49, assigned to the Levites of the clan of Kohath, Jos 21:15//1 Ch 6:43.

= **Kiriath-sepher** (4), former name of Debir, Jg 1:11–12//Jos 15:15–16. 13 km S of Hebron.

= **Kiriath-sannah** (1), former name of Debir, acc. to Jos 15:49.

3. **Debir** (1), on the border of Judah, Jos 15:7, NW of the Dead Sea. Location unknown.

DEBORAH, Gr. *Debbōra,* "Bee."

1. **Deborah, nurse of Rebekah** (1), buried below Bethel, under the Oak of Tears, Gn 35:8.

2. **Deborah** (8), **wife of Lappidoth** (1), both prophetess and judge, exercises her functions beneath "Deborah's Palm," between Ramah and Bethel, Jg 4:4–5. At Deborah's call, urged on by her and in her shadow as it were, Barak attacks and crushes Sisera's army at Taanach, 4:6–22.

The "Song of Deborah," Jg 5, one of the oldest texts of the Bible, retells the story in poetic form, and calls Deborah "a mother in Israel," 5:7. Other prophetesses: MARY 1.

3. **Deborah, mother of Ananiel** (1), ancestress of Tobit and Tobias, Tb 1:8.

DECAPOLIS (3), "The Ten Cities" (cf. Amphipolis). Between 63 B.C. and 100 A.D., a confederation of ten cities belonging to the Roman province of Syria; comprising Scythopolis (= Beth-shan) west of the Jordan and, east of the Jordan (running from S to N), Philadelphia (today *Amman*), Gerasa, [Pella], Gadara, Abila, [Hippo, Dion, Canathan] (these last four being east of the Sea of Chinnereth), and Damascus.

Jesus encounters a possessed man at Gerasa or Gadara, Lk 8:26–39//Mt 8:28–34//Mk 5:1–20. Other contacts with Jesus, Mt 4:25; Mk 7:31.

DECISION (Valley of) (2), Hb. *Haruz.* See: JOSHAPHAT 7.

DEDAN (11), a tribe in northern Arabia, on the borders of Edom, Jr 49:8; Ezk 25:13. (Should we follow some interpreters and see an Edomite town in Jr 49:8 and Ezk 25:13?)

Two genealogies for Dedan (associated with Sheba): one connects him with Ham through Cush, Gn 10:7//1 Ch 1:9; the other makes him a grandson of Abraham and his concubine Keturah, Gn 25:3//1 Ch 1:32.

A people of caravaneers, Is 21:13; Jr 25:23//*Tema*); Ezk 38:13 (//*Sheba*), trading with Tyre among others, Ezk 27:15, 20.

DEDANITES (1), Is 21:13, inhabitants of: DEDAN.

DEEP, Hb. *Tehôm,* "Primordial abyss," Gr. *Abyssos,* the formless mass of original waters, calls to mind the Babylonian *Tiamat,* the dragon of primordial chaos whom Marduk conquers when he organizes the cosmos. So, too, the Hb. *Yam,* "Sea, Ocean," Gr. *Thalassa,* calls to mind *Yam,* the god of the sea at Ugarit, the unfortunate adversary of Baal. In its poetry the Bible at times makes use of the imagery of the Babylonian and Ugaritic myths: Yahweh conquers the sea and the monsters who dwell in it. *Tehom:* Gn 1:2; 49:25; Jb 28:14; Is 51:10; Ha 3:10 . . . ; cf. Lk 8:31; Rv 11:7; 17:8; 20:3. *Yam:* Jb 7:12; 26:12; 28:14; 38:8–11; Ps 74:13–14; 89:10–11; Is 27:1; Dn 7:3 . . . ; cf. Mk 4:39–41; Rv 21:1.

See: BEAST; LEVIATHAN; RAHAB 1.

DEKER (Son of) (1), (cf. Bidkar), prefect of Solomon's second district, 1 K 4:9.

DELAIAH, "Yah has extricated [from danger]."

1. **Delaiah** (2), **son of Shemaiah** (1), one of the officials of King Jehoiakim who are overwhelmed by the reading of Jeremiah's oracles and unsuccessfully urge the king not to burn the book, Jr 36:12, 25.

2. **Delaiah** (1), head of a family whose sons, returning from the exile, cannot prove their authentic Israelite origin, Ezr 2:60//Ne 7:62.

3. **Delaiah** (1), father of: SHEMAIAH 22.

4. **Delaiah** (1), one of the seven sons of Elioenai, a descendant of King Jehoiachin, 1 Ch 3:24.

5. **Delaiah** (1), head of the twenty-third class of priests, 1 Ch 24:18.

DELILAH (6), "Coquette" in old Arabic, a woman of the Vale of Sorek with whom Samson falls in love; through trickery she learns the secret of his strength and betrays him to the Philistines, Jg 16:4–20.

DELOS (1), an island in the Aegean Sea; it receives a copy of the consul Lucius' letter promulgating the alliance of the Romans and the Jews, 1 M 15:23. Excavations have uncovered a synagogue there.

DEMAS (3), abbrev. of *Demetrius*?, associated with Luke, a fellow worker of Paul, Col 4:14; Phm 24, whom he deserts "for love of this life," 2 Tm 4:10.

DEMETRIUS, Gr. *Dēmētrios,* "of Demeter [Greek goddess of the cultivated soil]." For 1–2, see: SELEUCIDS.

1. **Demetrius I [Soter]** (2), **son of Seleucus IV** (2), 1 M 7:1; 2 M 14:1, king of Syria (161–150).

After escaping from Rome, where he had been held as a hostage, he succeeds young Antiochus V, whose murder he arranges. To repress the Jewish rebellion, he twice sends Bacchides and Alcimus, as well as Nicanor, to Judaea, 1 M 7:1–26//2 M 14:1–13; 1 M 9:1 ff.; cf. 2 M 14:26–27. But Demetrius is warned by the Romans, who are allied with the Jews, 1 M 8:31–32.

In the competition between Demetrius and Alexander Balas for the throne, despite significant offers from the former, Jonathan Maccabaeus sides with Alexander, 1 M 10:1–47. The two kings meet in battle and Demetrius dies, 10:48–50, 52.

Father of: ANTIOCHUS 6; DEMETRIUS 2.

2. **Demetrius II [Nicator]** (26), **son of Demetrius** (1), king of Syria (145–138 and 129–125).

On arrival from Crete he appoints Apollonius his general: the latter is defeated by Jonathan, 1 M 10:67–89. The candidacy of Demetrius for the kingship is supported by Ptolemy VI, who takes back his daughter, the wife of Alexander Balas, and gives her to Demetrius. Alexander, defeated, is assassinated, and Demetrius becomes king, 1 M 11:9–19. Demetrius grants the Jews a charter; the Jews support him at Antioch, 1 M 11:20–52, but the king quarrels with Jonathan, who enters into an alliance with young Antiochus VI and opposes Demetrius, 11:53–74; 12:24–34. After Jonathan's death, Demetrius bestows his favors on Simon Maccabaeus, 13:34–42; 14:38 ff. Consul Lucius' letter promulgating the Jewish-Roman alliance is sent to him, 15:22. In the reign of Demetrius, the Jews of Jerusalem write to the Jews of Egypt, 2 M 1:7. Demetrius is a prisoner of Mithradates I Arsaces, king of the Parthians, 1 M 14:1–3.

3. **Demetrius** (2), a silversmith at Ephesus, makes miniature shrines of Diana. The spread of Christianity cuts into his trade, and he organizes a protest at the theater in Ephesus. Because of the increasing agitation the town clerk of the city points out to Demetrius that there

are more lawful ways of getting a hearing, Ac 19:24–38.

4. **Demetrius** (1), an important member of the local church where Diotrephes is causing trouble or else a missionary who is being recommended to Gaius, 3 Jn 12.

DEMOPHON (1), (cf. Nicodemus), one of the five Syrian military commissioners who "would not allow the Jews to live in peace and quiet," 2 M 12:2.

DERBE (4), a town in Lycaonia in Asia Minor, between Iconium and Tarsus. Paul visits it during his first missionary journey with Barnabas, Ac 14:6, 20, and during his second missionary journey in the company of Silas, Ac 16:1.

Native place of: GAIUS 2.

DESSAU (1). See: HADASHAH.

DESTRUCTION. See: ABADDON; IR HA-HERES; OLIVES (MOUNT OF) (2 K 23:13).

DIANA (5), Gr. *Artemis* (cf. Artemas. See Phoebe), mother goddess of Ephesus. Acc. to Ac 19:23–40 there is a riot by the silversmiths of the city of Ephesus, which is "the guardian of the temple of great Diana and of her statue that fell from heaven," v. 35. Paul's preaching against false gods, v. 26, may take work from the craftsmen who make silver shrines of Diana, vv. 24–25, and take away "all the prestige of a goddess venerated all over Asia, yes, and everywhere in the civilised world," v. 27. Only the town clerk manages to calm the crowd, which shouts for more than two hours, "Great is Diana of the Ephesians!" vv. 28, 34.

See: NANAEA.

[DIASPORA]. See: DISPERSION.

DIBLAIM (1), "Two fig-cakes" (cf. Diblathaim), Ho 1:3, father of: GOMER.

DIBLATHAIM (cf. Diblaim). See: ALMON-DIBLATHAIM; BETH-DIBLATHAIM.

DIBON

1. **Dibon** (8), a Moabite town destroyed by the Amorites, Nb 21:30, rebuilt by the Gadites, Nb 32:34, assigned to the Reubenites, Nb 32:3; Jos 13:9, 17, belongs later to the Moabites, Is 15:2, 9 (Hb. *Dimon*); Jr 48:18, 22.

= **Dibon-gad** (2), a stage of the Exodus, Nb 33:45–46. 20 km E of the Dead Sea and 5 km N of the Arnon. Today *Tell Dhiban,* where the discovery was made in 1868 of the stele of the Moabite king: MESHA 4.

2. **Dibon** (1), a town inherited by sons of Judah after the return from the exile, Ne 11:25.

= **Dimon** (1), a town in the Negeb of Judah, Jos 15:22 (corr. of Hb. *Dimonah*).

DIBON-GAD (2). See: DIBON 1.

DIBRI (1), a Danite, father of: SHELOMITH 1.

DIKLAH (2), cf. Aram. "Date-palm," one of the thirteen sons of Joktan, a tribe or territory in southern Arabia, not identified, Gn 10:27//1 Ch 1:21.

DILEAN (1), Hb. root *dl*ʿ, "to protrude," a town in the lowlands of Judah, Jos 15:38.

DIMON (1). See: DIBON 2.

DINAH (8), "Lawsuit" (cf. Dan), daughter of Jacob (3), Gn 34:3, 7, 19, and of Leah, Gn 30:21; 34:1; 46:15; raped by Shechem and then asked by him in marriage; blood vengeance is exacted in a treacherous manner by Simeon and Levi, her brothers, Gn 34; cf. 49:5–7; Jdt 9:2–4.

DINHABAH (2), a town of Bela, king of Edom, Gn 36:42//1 Ch 1:43.

[DIODOTUS]. See: TRYPHO.

DIONYSIUS (1). See: DIONYSUS 2.

[DIONYSOS]. See: DIONYSUS 3.

DIONYSUS, Gr. *Dionysos* (cf. Zeus).

1. **Dionysus** (2), Greek god of wine

and ecstasy, also called *Bacchus,* celebrated especially at the *Dionysiaca* or *festival of Dionysus.* Under Antiochus Epiphanes the Jews "were forced to wear ivy wreaths and walk in the Dionysiac procession [lit.: a procession in honor of Dionysus]," 2 M 6:7. Nicanor threatens to erect a shrine to Dionysus in place of the temple at Jerusalem, 14:33.

2. **Dionysius the Areopagite** (1), converted to the Christian faith as a result of Paul's discourse at Athens, Ac 17:34.

3. **[Dionysos],** surname of: ANTIOCHUS 5.

DIOTREPHES (1), "Nurseling of Zeus" (cf. Zeus), leader of a Christian community, an ambitious man and a fierce opponent of the work of evangelization directed by "the Elder," 3 Jn 9–10.

DIPHATH (1), 1 Ch 1:6. See: RIPHATH.

DISHAN (5), (cf. Dishon), last of the seven sons of Seir the Horite, Gn 36:21//1 Ch 1:38, and of the chiefs of the Horites, Gn 36:30. He has two sons: Uz and Aran, Gn 36:28//1 Ch 1:42 (Hb. *Dishon*). In Gn 36:26 read *Dishon* for Hb. *Dishan.*

DISHON, "Gazelle, Wild goat"? (cf. Dishan).

1. **Dishon** (5), fifth of the sons of Seir the Horite, Gn 36:21//1 Ch 1:28, and of the chiefs of the Horites, Gn 36:20. He has four sons, Gn 36:26 (corr. of Hb. *Dishan*)//1 Ch 1:41.

2. **Dishon** (2), son of Anah, himself the fourth son of Seir, Gn 36:25//1 Ch 1:41.

DISPERSION (2), Gr. *diaspora,* Jm 1:1; 1 P 1:1. The Dispersion or Diaspora includes all Israelites and, later, all Jews living outside of Palestine. Causes: the Assyrian (after the fall of Samaria, 722/721) and Babylonian (after the fall of Jerusalem, 587) deportations, at the end of which many Jews stayed where they were; but there were also commercial, professional, and other reasons. Principal centers: Alexandria (Egypt), Antioch (Syria), Babylon (Mesopotamia), and Rome. Jewish population of the Dispersion at the beginning of the Christian era: perhaps 7,000,000, in comparison to less than 1,000,000 in Palestine.

On the geographical extent of the Dispersion, cf. Is 11:11; 1 M 15:22–23; Ac 2:9–11; Jn 7:35.

DIVINERS' OAK (1), Hb. *Me'ônenîm,* Jg 9:37, probably the same as the Oak of: MOREH 2.

DIVISIONS (Rock of) (1), Hb. *Sela'-ha-Mahleqot,* a place in the wilderness of Maon, where Saul breaks off his pursuit of David, 1 S 23:25–28.

DIZAHAB (1), "Who has gold" (cf. Mezahab), in Transjordania, Dt 1:1. Site unknown.

DOBERUS (1), Ac 20:4, var. of Gr. *Derbē.* A town in Macedonia between Philippi and Amphipolis. Native place of: GAIUS 2.

DOBRATH (3), (cf. Debir?), on the frontier of Zebulun, Jos 19:12, a town of Issachar, 19:20 (acc. to the Gr.; Hb. *ha-Rabbit*), assigned to Levites of the clan of Gershon, 21:28//1 Ch 6:57. South of Mount Tabor.

DODAI (1), (cf. David), **the Ahohite** (1). See: ELEAZAR 3.

DODAVAHU (1), "Beloved of Yahweh" (cf. David), father of: ELIEZER 5.

DODO, "His beloved" (cf. David).

1. **Dodo** (1), an Issacharite, ancestor of: TOLA 2.

2. **Dodo son of Joash** (1), a descendant of Rapha, armed with a spear weighing three hundred shekels of bronze, slain by Abishai, 2 S 21:15–16.

3. **Dodo** (2), father of: ELHANAN 2.

4. **Dodo** (2), father of: ELEAZAR 3.

DOEG (6) **the Edomite** (5), the chief of Saul's guardsmen, 1 S 21:8 (or the best of his runners, cf. 1 S 22:17). He tells Saul that he saw Ahimelech the priest of Nob consult Yahweh for David and give the latter provisions and the sword of Goliath, 22:9–10; cf. Ps 52:2. At Saul's orders he puts to death eighty-five priests of Nob together with the population of the place. Only Abiathar escapes, 22:18–22.

DOK (1), "Observation point"?, a small fortress where Ptolemy, son of Abubus, assassinates Simon Maccabaeus in 134, 1 M 16:15. Probably located atop the *Jebel Qaruntul,* west of Jericho.

DOPHKAH (2), Hb. *Dophqah* from the root *dphq,* "to strike," a stage of the Exodus after the wilderness of Sin, Nb 33:12–13.

DOR (10), (cf. En-dor), a town on the Mediterranean coast, south of Carmel, occupied by Canaanites, Jos 11:2, the king of Dor is defeated by the Israelites, Jos 12:23, the town and its dependencies are assigned to Manasseh and Asher, Jos 17:11; 1 Ch 7:29, but in fact Dor remains in Canaanite hands for a long time, Jg 1:27. Under Solomon, the fourth district, the "region of Dor," has the king's son-in-law for its administrator, 1 K 4:11. Antiochus VII besieges Trypho at Dor, 1 M 15:11–14, 25.

DORCAS (2). See: TABITHA.

DORYMENES (2), father of: PTOLEMY 9.

DOSITHEUS, "Gift of God" (cf. Artemas; Heliodorus; Theodotus; Zenas. See Nathan).

1. **Dositheus** (1), "who affirmed that he was a priest and Levite," in company with his son Ptolemy brings the Book of Esther to the community in Egypt, Est 10:3[1].

2. **Dositheus** (3), a Tubian, 2 M 12:35, general of the army of Judas Maccabaeus, 12:19, captures Timotheus during a campaign in the country of the Tubians, 12:24, but is wounded in Idumaea while trying to take Gorgias alive, 12:35.

DOTHAN (8), a town 25 km N of Shechem. It is here that Gn 37:17–28 locates the selling of Joseph by his brothers and here that acc. to 2 K 6:13–19 Elisha captures an Aramaean detachment sent out to arrest him. Holofernes pitches camp here (Gr. *Dōtaia*). It is not far from Bethulia, Jdt 4:6; 7:3, 18; 8:3 (in all these passages, Gr. *Dōthaim*).

DRAGON, Hb. *Tannin, Tannim.*

1. **Dragon** or **Serpent** or **Monster** or **Beast** (7), associated with Leviathan, Is 27:1, or Rahab, Is 51:9, a fabled animal found in Babylonian mythology: it dwells in the sea and is the symbol of the primeval chaos and disorder that God masters at the creation, Is 27:1; 51:9; Jr 51:34; Ps 74:13; Jb 7:12; cf. Ezk 29:3; 32:2 (*crocodile*).

See: DEEP; LEVIATHAN; RAHAB 1; SATAN.

2. **Well of the Dragon** (1), (cf. Ain), at Jerusalem, a well or fountain that Ne 2:13 locates between the Valley Gate and the Dung Gate.

DRUSILLA (1), a Jewish woman, youngest daughter of Herod Agrippa I, sister of Agrippa II and Bernice. She leaves her first husband, Aziz, king of Emesa, to marry Felix, Roman procurator of Judaea. Before her and her second husband, Paul speaks of faith in Christ Jesus, righteousness, and self-control, Ac 24:24–25.

DUMAH, "Silence"?

1. **Dumah** (3), one of the twelve sons of Ishmael, Gn 25:14//1 Ch 1:30, a tribe in northern Arabia, probably in the neighborhood of Edom, Is 21:11 (read Gr. *Idumaea* for Hb. *Dumah*). Today an oasis in Saudi Arabia, 450 km E of Aqaba.

2. **Dumah** (1), a town in the high-

lands of Judah, Jos 15:52. 15 km SW of Hebron. Today *ed-Domeh.*

DUNG GATE (4), Hb. *'Ashpôt,* south of Jerusalem, near the rubbish heap of the city. On the route Nehemiah follows in his nocturnal inspection of the wall, Ne 2:13; restored under Nehemiah, 3:13 ([Q]*Dung Gate;* [K]*Gate of the Cheeses*), 14; on the route of the procession for the dedication of the wall, 12:31. Later called the "Gate of the Essenes."

Identical (?) with the Gate of the: POTSHERDS.

DURA (1), Accad. *Duru,* "Wall, Strong castle," a plain in Babylonia, Dn 3:1. Site not identifiable.

E

EAST

1. **East** (13), Hb. *Kèdèm,* "Front, East" (cf. Eastern; Kadmiel; Kadmonites; Kedemah; Kedemoth).

The **sons of the East,** whose eponymous ancestor is *Kedemah,* one of the twelve sons of Ishmael, Gn 25:15, are a nomadic tribe in the wilderness of northern Transjordania and the wilderness of Syria. Job belongs to them, Jb 1:3. They are famous for their wisdom, 1 K 5:10. In the time of the Judges, they, like Midian and Amalek, conduct raids on Israel, Jg 6:3, 33; 7:12; 8:10. They dominate Ammon and Moab for a while, Ezk 25:4, 10, but they in their turn will be pillaged, Is 11:14, and crushed, Jr 49:28.

The **East Country,** Gn 25:6, or the **Land of the sons of the East,** Gn 29:1, is probably to be located to the NE of Israel, S of Damascus.

The **hills of Kedem,** Nb 23:7, form the hilly border of the Syrian wilderness, unless it refers to the region between Phoenicia and Syria.

2. **East** (1), Hb. *Mizrah,* "Rising" (cf. Ezrahite; Izrahiah; Zerah; Zerahiah; Zerahite). The **East Gate** is located in the eastern wall of the temple; in the time of Nehemiah, Shemaiah son of Shecaniah is its keeper, Ne 3:29.

EASTERN (Sea) (3), Hb. *Qadmoni* (cf. East 1). See: DEAD (SEA).

EBAL, Hb. *'Ebal.*

1. **Ebal** (5). See: GERIZIM.

2. **Ebal** (2), third of the five sons of Shobal, son of Seir, Gn 36:23//1 Ch 1:40.

EBED, "Servant" (cf. Abda; Abdeel; Abdi; Abdiel; Abdon; Abednego; Bediah?; Ebed-melech; Obadiah; Obed; Obed-edom).

1. **Ebed** (5) (Hb. corrected by some to *Obed*), Jg 9:26, 28, 31, 35, father of: GAAL.

2. **Ebed son of Jonathan** (1), head of a family of the sons of Adin who return from the exile with Ezra, Ezr 8:6.

EBED-MELECH (6), "Servant of the king *or* Servant of [the god] Melech" (cf. Ebed; Melech), **the Cushite** (4), a eunuch at the court of King Zedekiah. After speaking to the king, Ebed-melech pulls Jeremiah from the cistern into which he has been thrown, Jr 38:7–13. In return, the prophet predicts that in the coming destruction of Jerusalem, Ebed-melech's life will be saved, 39:16–18.

EBENEZER (3), "Stone of help" (cf. Ezer; Stone), a place of several confrontations between Israelites and Philistines in the time of Samuel: defeats of Israel, 1 S 4:1; 5:1 (capture of the Ark); defeat of the Philistines, 7:11–12 (the "Stone of Help" or *Ebenezer* is the memorial of Israel's victory, erected by Samuel). The site in 1 S 7 (*//Mizpah*) seems different from that in chs. 4 and 5 (*//Aphek*).

EBER (cf. Hebrew).

1. **Eber** (12), grandson of Arpachshad and father of Peleg and Joktan, Gn 10: 24–25 (Yahwist account)//1 Ch 1:18–19; great-grandson of Shem and father of Peleg, Gn 11:14–17 (priestly account)//1 Ch 1:25//Lk 3:35. The two genealogies are finally harmonized in Gn 10:21 (Yahwist), where Shem is called the ancestor of all *the sons of Eber,* who are to be connected with the *Hebrews,* the group to which Israel belongs, cf. Nb 24:24.

2. **Eber** (1), a Gadite, head of a family, 1 Ch 5:13.

3. **Eber** (1), a Benjaminite of the sons of Elpaal, settled in the area of Lud, 1 Ch 8:12.

4. **Eber** (1), a Benjaminite of the sons of Shashak, head of a family at Jerusalem, 1 Ch 8:22.

5. **Eber** (1), head of the priestly family of Amok in the time of the high priest Joiakim, Ne 12:20.

EBEZ (1), (cf. Ibzan), a town in Issachar, Jos 19:20.

EBIASAPH (4), "The Father adds" (cf. Joseph), 1 Ch 6:8, 22; 9:19; 26:1 (corr. of Hb. *Asaph*). See: ABIASAPH.

ECBATANA (14), Aram. *'Ahmeta',* Gr. *Ekbatana,* **in Media** (3), Tb 3:7; 14:13, 14, **in the province of Media** (1), Ezr 6:2, capital of Media, summer residence of the Persian kings, cf. Jdt 1:1–2, 14. Under Darius a document is discovered in the archives of the city concerning the rebuilding of the temple at Jerusalem, Ezr 6:2. Antiochus Epiphanes stops there on his return from Persia, 2 M 9:3. Native city of Raguel, father-in-law of Tobias, Tb 3:7; cf. 5:6; 6:6–10; 7:1, then of Tobias himself, 14:12–14. Today *Hamadan,* 700 km NE of Persepolis.

ECCLESIASTES (cf. Ecclesiasticus). See: QOHELETH.

[ECCLESIASTICUS], a very ancient name for the book of Ben Sira (see: JOSHUA 10), given because of the importance the Church assigned to this book in the instruction of neophytes (cf. Ecclesiastes).

EDEN

1. **Eden** (15), Hb. *'Eden,* Accad. *Edinu,* Sumer. *Edin,* "Steppe, Desert," but interpreted by Israel as "Delight, Pleasure." A topographical name that cannot be localized, Gn 2:8; 4:16. Used in several ways:

—*Eden* as distinct from the *garden* (Hb. *gan;* Gr. *paradeisos*): a river arising in Eden waters a garden planted with magnificent trees, among them "the tree of life" and "the tree of the knowledge of good and evil," Gn 2:8, 10; cf. Rv 2:7.

—*Garden of Eden:* man is its cultivator and guardian, Gn 2:15, but loses it by his sin, 3:23–24; contrasted with the wasteland or desert, Ezk 36:35; Jl 2:3; cf. Si 24:30.

—*Eden* identified with the *garden of Yahweh* and contrasted here again with the desert and steppe as a place of joy, thanksgiving, and music, Is 51:3; identified with the *garden of God,* famous for its trees, Ezk 31:9, 16, 18, enclosed by a wall of precious stones, Ezk 28:13; cf. Rv 21:18–20.

In Si 40:17, 27 charity and fear of the Lord are compared to a *paradise* (Hb. *Eden*) of blessing. Jesus promises the "good thief" that he will be with him in Paradise, Lk 23:43. Finally, the image of the garden of Eden is the inspiration for Rv 22:1–2; cf. Ezk 47:1–12.

2. **Eden** (1), "Delight" (cf. Adin; Adina; Adna), **son of Joah** (1), a Levite of the clan of Gershon, takes part in the purification of the temple during the reform of Hezekiah, 2 Ch 29:12.

= **Iddo** (1), son of Joah, 1 Ch 6:6.

3. **Eden** (1), one of the six Levites assigned to Kore, son of Imnah, for distributing rations, 2 Ch 31:15.

4. **Eden** (3), Accad. *Bit Adini* (cf. Beth-eden), a town on the middle Euphrates, taken by the Assyrians, cf. 2 K 19:12//Is 37:12, trades with Tyre, Ezk 27:23.

EDENITES (2), lit. "sons of Eden," 2 K 19:12//Is 37:12, inhabitants of: EDEN 4.

EDER, Hb. *'Eder;* 1–3: a form parallel to *Ezer* (cf. Adriel); 4: "Flock."

1. **Eder** (1), a Benjaminite of the sons of Beriah, head of a family at Jerusalem, 1 Ch 8:15.

2. **Eder** (1), a Levite of the clan of Merari, second of the three sons of Mushi, 1 Ch 23:23; 24:30.

3. **Eder** (1), a town of Judah "toward the boundary of Edom in the Negeb," Jos 15:21.

EDNA (7), (cf. Adna; Adnah), wife of Raguel, mother of Sarah, and mother-in-law of Tobias, Tb 7:2–3, 8, 13–16; 8:4, 11–12, 18; 21; 10:12–13; 14:13.

EDOM (100), Hb. *'Edom,* Gr. *Edōm, Idumaea,* "Red" (cf. Adamah; Obed-edom; see Rufus).

A people living between the Dead Sea and the Gulf of Aqaba, first to the east, then to the west of the Valley of Salt, cf. Jos. 15:1, 21; Jg 1:36.

Acc. to Gn 25:30; 36:1, 8–9, 43, the eponymous ancestor of Edom is Esau, twin brother of Jacob, the latter being ancestor of Israel. Consequently, the land of Edom is sometimes called **Esau,** Jr 49:8, 10; Ob 6, **the Mount of Esau,** Ob 8–9, 19, 21, **the House of Esau,** Ob 18, and the Edomites are called **the sons of Esau,** Dt 2:4, 8, 12, 22, 29; Jdt 7:8, 18; 1 M 5:3, 65.

Edom/Esau settles in the land of Seir, Gn 32:4; 33:14, 16; 36:6–9; Dt 2:4–5, 8, 29; Jos 24:4, after the sons of Esau have expelled the Horites, Dt 2:12, 22. This explains why Edom may be called **Seir,** Is 21:11; Ezk 25:8; cf. Nb 24:18; Jg 5:4, or the **mountain of Seir,** Ezk 35:2–3, 7, 15, and the Edomites **the sons of Seir,** 2 Ch 25:11, 14, or **the mountain folk of Seir,** 2 Ch 20:10, 22–23; cf. Si 50:26.

Two lists of the chiefs or clans of Edom, Gn 36:15–19 and 36:40–43// 1 Ch 1:51–54, as well as a list of the kings of Edom, probably prior to the occupation of the country by Israel, Gn 36:31–39//1 Ch 1:43–50.

During the Exodus Israel skirts Edom, Nb 20:14–21, 23; 21:4; 33:37; Jg 11:17–18; 2 Ch 20:10, but cf. Dt 2:1–8, 29. In the time of the judges, an attempt is made by Edom to settle in the southern part of Judah, Jg 3:8–10 (if *Aram* is corrected to *Edom*). War between Saul and Edom, 1 S 14:47. Conquest of Edom by David and administrative organization of it, 2 S 8:13–14; 1 K 11:15–16; Ps 60:2; cf. 1 Ch 18:11. Solomon marries Edomite women, 1 K 11:1; he develops the port of Ezion-geber on the Red Sea in Edom, 1 K 9:26. Then Edom perhaps regains a certain independence, 1 K 11:14, 17–25, but loses it again, 22:48. Jehoshaphat of Judah crushes a coalition of Moabites, Ammonites, and Edomites, 2 Ch 20:2, 10, 22–23. The king of Judah and his vassal the king of Edom support Jehoram of Israel in his campaign against Mesha of Moab, 2 K 3:8–9, 12. Edom throws off the domination of Judah under Jehoram, 2 K 8:20–22, but is defeated by Amaziah, 2 K 14:7, 10. Taking advantage of the Syro-Ephraimite war against Ahaz, Edom recovers Elath from Judah, 2 K 16:6; cf. 2 Ch 28:17. When Jerusalem falls (587), Edom, under the pressure perhaps of the Nabataeans, who have occupied part of the country, invades Judah and plunders it, Ps 137:7; Lm 4: 21–22; Ezk 25:12; 35:5, 12, 15; 36:5; Ob 10–16. From this time on, Edom, although a people of the same blood stock as Israel, Dt 2:4, 8; 23:8; Am 1:11; Ob 10, 12; Ml 1:2, becomes the archetypal enemy of Jerusalem, cf. Ps 83:7; Dn 11:41, upon whom the prophets call down the avenging judgment of God, Is 34; 63:1–6; Jr 49:7–22; Ezk 25:12–14; 35; Jl 4:19; Ob; Ml 1:3–5. When Israel is once again restored, it will dominate Edom anew, Nb 24:18; Ps 60:10–11; Is 11:14; Ob 19; Am 9:12.

N.B. In Hb. *'Edom* and *'Aram* are easily confused; corr. therefore are to be made in Jg 3:8, 10; 2 S 8:13; 1 K 11:25; 2 K 3:26; 16:6; 2 Ch 20:2; Ezk 27:16.

See: ESAU; SEIR 1; TEMAN; ÜZ 4.

Kings: BAAL-HANAN 1; BELA 1; CUSHAN-RISHATHAIM; HADAD 2–4; HUSHAM; JOBAB; SAMLAH; SAUL 1.

Edomite: DOEG.

Principal towns: BOZRAH; ROCK 1.

= **Idumaea** (7), Gr. name for Edom, which, since the fall of Jerusalem (587) occupies southern Palestine as far as Hebron. On the borders of Idumaea and Judaea, confrontations between Judas Maccabaeus and the Seleucid armies, 1 M 4:15, 29. To protect himself from attacks originating in Idumaea, like the one launched later on by Antiochus V, 1 M 6:31, Judas fortifies Beth-zur, 1 M 4:61. Military expeditions of Judas against Idumaea, 1 M 5:3, 65; 2 M 10:15–23; 12:32–37.

In the crowds that press around Jesus there are Idumaeans, Mk 3:8.

Military commissioner of Idumaea: GORGIAS.

Idumaeans: HEROD 1–5.

EDOMITE (12), Dt 23:8; 1 S 21:8; 22:9, 18, 22; 1 K 11:1, 14, 17; 2 K 16:6; 2 Ch 25:14; 28:17; Ps 52, belonging to: EDOM.

EDREI

1. **Edrei** (7), in Bashan, a royal town of Og, conquered by Israel and occupied by the sons of Machir, son of Manasseh, Nb 21:33//Dt 3:1; Dt 1:4; 3:10; Jos 12:4; 13:12, 31. Today *Der'a,* 106 km S of Damascus.

2. **Edrei** (1), a fortified town of Naphtali, Jos 19:37. Site unknown.

EGLAH (2), "Heifer" (cf. Eglath; Shelishiyah; Eglon; En-eglaim), mother of Ithream, sixth of the sons of David who are born at Hebron, 2 S 3:5//1 Ch 3:3.

EGLAIM (1), Hb. *'Eglayim,* a town in Moab, Is 15:8. SW of present-day *Kerak.*

EGLATH SHELISHIYAH (2), "The third [town] of the heifer *or* The three-[year-old] heifer"? (cf. Eglah), a town in Moab associated with Horonaim, Is 15:5; Jr 48:34. Site unknown.

EGLON (cf. Eglah).

1. **Eglon king of Moab** (5), thanks to a coalition with the Ammonites and Amalekites, takes possession of the City of Palms (Jericho), which he enslaves for eighteen years. The Benjaminite judge Ehud puts an end to his reign by treacherously stabbing him, Jg 3:12–25; cf. 1 S 12:9.

2. **Eglon** (8), a royal Canaanite city taken by Joshua, Jos 10:34–37; in the lowlands of Judah, Jos 15:39, W of Hebron.

King: DEBIR 1.

EGREBEL (1), a town "near Chous on the wadi Mochmur," Jdt 7:18. NE of Shechem?

EGYPT (753), Gr. *Aigyptos* (58), Egypt. *Hi-ku-ptah,* "House of the being of Ptah," Hb.: MISRAIM. A land along the lower course of the Nile, at the SW end of the Fertile Crescent, divided into "nomes" or provinces, Is 19:13, and comprising Upper Egypt, Tb 8:3 (from Elephantine to Memphis) and Lower Egypt (from Memphis to the Mediterranean); adjacent to Palestine, which extends "as far as the approaches of Egypt," 2 Ch 26:8, to the Egyptian border, 1 K 5:1//2 Ch 9:26; 1 M 3:32; 11:59, or as far as the: WADI OF EGYPT.

Egypt enters into biblical history in the patriarchal period in the form of a *land of refuge.* Abram goes there because of a famine in Canaan, Gn 12:10–13:1. For the same reason Jacob sends his sons to Egypt, Gn 42:1, where they discover their brother Joseph, whom they had sold into slavery and who has become "lord of the land," Gn 42–45. At Pharaoh's invitation, Jacob, too, comes to this land of plenty, Gn 45:16–20; 46–49, and settles there with his family, Gn 46:8–27; Ex 1:1–5; Jdt 5:10, which multiplies there, Ex 1:6–7. It is there that Jacob dies, as does Joseph, Gn 50. In later times Egypt again acts as land of refuge for outlaws, like Jeroboam, 1 K 11:40; 12:2, Uriah, Jr 26:21–22, the Edomite Hadad, 1 K 11:17–18, Joseph and Mary, Mt 2:13–19, and for those who fear invasion or occupation, Jr 41:16–18; but flight into Egypt is sometimes a bad risk, Jr 42:13–22.

Egypt appears above all (more than 400×), however, as a *land of oppression,* Ex 1:8–14; 2:23–24; 3:7–9, 16–17; 5:4–23; 6:5–9; 18:9–10; Nb 20:15; Jg 10:11–12; 1 S 12:8; Ws 10:15; 19:16; Heb 11:25–26, a place of slavery and a house of servitude, Ex 13:3, 14; 20:2; Dt 5:15; 6:12, 21; 7:8; 8:14; 13:6, 11; 15:15; 16:12; 24:18, 22; 26:6–8; Jos 24:17; Jg 6:8–9; 1 S 2:27; Ne 9:17; Jdt 5:11; Jr 34:13; Mi 6:4, a "furnace of iron," Dt 4:20; 1 K 8:51; Jr 11:4, from which God enables his people to "go out" or "go up," Ex 3:17; 7:4; Lv 11:45; 19:36; 26:13; Nb 15:41; Dt 8:14; 20:1; Jg 2:12, by the agency of Moses and Aaron, Ex 3:10–12; 6:13, 26; 14:11; 17:3; 32:1, 7, 23; Nb 20:16; Dt 9:12, by multiplying signs and wonders in Egypt, Ex 3:20; 4:21; 7:3; Nb 14:22; Dt 6:22; Jos 9:9; Ps 78:12, 43; 106:7, 13, 21–22; 135:9; Ws 10:16; Jr 32:20–21; Ac 7:36, which are in fact judgments and punishments: the "plagues of Egypt," Ex 3:20; 7–12; 15:26; 18:8; 19:4; Nb 3:13; 8:17; Dt 4:34; 7:15–19; 28:27–60; 1 S 4:8; Jdt 5:12; Ps 78:51; 81:6; 105:27–38; Am 4:10. The "coming out of Egypt," Ex 19:1; Nb 1:1; 9:1; 33:38; Dt 9:7; 16:3; Jg 19:30; 2 K 21:15; Is 11:16; Jr 7:25; Mi 7:15, was a deliverance, Ex 3:8; 6:6; 18:9–10; Dt 7:8; 9:26; Jg 6:9; 1 S 10:18; Ac 7:34, a redemption, Dt 13:6; 15:15; 24:18; 2 S 7:23; 1 Ch 17:21; Est 4:17[g]; Mi 6:4; Ac 7:35, a salvation, Jg 10:12; Jude 5. The theme of the Exodus (150×) is taken up in Ws 10:12–12:27 and 16:1–19:22, but without the name of Egypt being mentioned.

Yet this land of exile, Ws 19:10; Ac 13:17, in which the Israelites lived as aliens, Gn 15:13; Ex 2:22; 22:20; 23:9; Lv 19:34; Dt 10:19; 23:8; Ac 7:6, for 430 years, Ex 12:40; cf. Gn 15:13; Ga 3:17; Nb 20:15, and to which God threatens to send them back, Dt 28:68; Ho 8:13; 9:3, is remembered by them as a *seductive land men dream of,* a land "where milk and honey flow," Nb 16:13, a land "where we were able to sit down to pans of meat and could eat bread to our heart's content," Ex 16:3; Nb 11:4–6; cf. Gn 41:29–31, and whither they were tempted to return, Ex 13:17; 14:11–12; Nb 14:2–4; Ac 7:39. An important trading center, Gn 37:25–26; Is 45:14, famous especially for its fabrics, Pr 7:16; Is 19:9–10; Ezk 27:7, its horses, Dt 17:16; 1 K 10:28–29//2 Ch 1:16–17; 9:28; Is 31:3. A seat of culture and wisdom, Gn 41:8; 1 K 5:10; Is 19:11–12; Ws 17:7; Si prol. 29; Ac 7:22. Many Jewish colonies have come into existence in Egypt, cf. 2 M 1:1, 10; Si prol. 27–34; cf. Ac 2:5–10, especially at Elephantine. Egypt is consequently a military power to which Israel, when the threat from the east—Assyria, Babylon—causes unease, is tempted to have recourse, either by asking help from it, 2 K 18:21–24//Is 36:6–9, or by seeking refuge in it (cf. earlier). The prophets remind their people that "the Egyptian is a man, not a god," Is 31:3, that Egypt's aid is "futile and empty," Is 30:2–7, because Egypt is a "broken reed," 2 K 18:21//Is 36:6. In addition to the lack of faith that such recourse to Egypt betrays, the action puts the Israelites in danger of falling into idolatry, Lv 18:3; Ezr 9:1; Ezk 20:7–8, because of Egypt's false gods and its magicians, Is 19:1, 3. Egypt, the dwelling place of demons, Tb 8:3, is the type of those powers that are idolatrous and hostile to the people of God, Rv 11:8; cf. Ws 11:15–16; 12:23–27; 15:14–19.

Instrument of God's plan in the past but punished even at that time, *Egypt in its turn trembles* before those it once terrorized, and it will experience the day when Yahweh will rise up against it, Is 19; Jr 46; Ezk 29–32, to annihilate its pride and turn the land into a desolation, Ezk 32:12–15; cf. Jl 4:19; Dn 11:42. But Egypt will be converted, and whereas the Pharaoh of the Exodus arrogantly said: "Who is Yahweh? . . . I know nothing of Yahweh," Ex 5:2, some day "there will be an altar to Yahweh in the center of the land of Egypt," Is 19:19, and the race of Egypt, along with all the races of the world, will be forced, under pain of punishment, to go up to Jerusalem "to worship the King, Yahweh Sabaoth, and to keep the feast of Tabernacles," Zc 14:16–19.

Egypt and Assyria: ASSYRIA 1.

See: CUSH 1; GOSHEN 1; HAM; PATHROS; RAHAB 1; SOUTH 1.

Kings: LAGIDES; PHARAOH.

Egyptians: HAGAR; JARHA; POTIPHAR.

Cities: ALEXANDRIA; HANES; IR HAHERES; MEMPHIS; MIGDOL; NO; ON 1; PI-BESETH; PITHOM; RAMESES 2; SAIS; SIN 3; SYENE; TAHPANHES; ZOAN.

Another place: ABEL-MIZRAIM.

Sea: RED (SEA).

Rivers: NILE; WADI OF EGYPT.

Gods: AMON 4; APIS; HORUS; PTAH; RA.

EGYPTIAN (36), Gn 12:12, 14; 16:1, 3; 21:9; 25:12; 39:1–2, 5; 43:32; Ex 1:19; 2:11–12, 14, 19; Lv 24:10; Dt 23:8; 26:6; Jos 24:7; 1 S 30:11, 13; 2 S 23:21; 1 Ch 2:34; 11:23; Ezr 9:1; Jdt 5:12; Ac 7:22, 24, 28; 21:38; Heb 11:29, of or from: EGYPT.

EGYPT (Sea of). See: RED (SEA).

EHI (1), acc. to Gn 46:21 one of the ten sons of Benjamin.

EHUD (cf. Ohad).

1. **Ehud** (10), **son of Gera** (1), **a Benjaminite** (1). He "judges" or, rather, "delivers," cf. Jg 3:15, his tribe from the Moabite yoke. At the presentation of the tribute, he stabs Eglon, king of Moab, who had occupied Jericho for eighteen years, 3:15–26; 4:1. In 1 Ch 8:3, read *Gera father of Ehud* for Hb. *Gera and Abihud.* His descendants are family heads at Geba, 1 Ch 8:6–7.

2. **Ehud** (1), a Benjaminite of the sons of Jediael, a fighting man and head of a family, 1 Ch 7:10. To be connected. (?) with the preceding?

EKER (1), "Descendant," last of the three sons of Ram, of the clan of Jerahmeel, 1 Ch 2:27.

EKRON (23), Gr. *Akkarōn,* "The City" (cf. Kiriath). A city of the Philistine Pentapolis, Jos 13:3; 1 S 6:16–18, where the Ark of the Covenant remains after its capture by the Philistines and before its return to the Israelites, 1 S 5:10–12; 6:1–12, 16–18. There are numerous prophetic oracles against the Philistine cities and Ekron in particular, Jr 25:20; Am 1:8; Zp 2:4, and Zc 9:5, 7, who foretells the incorporation of the city into the Promised Land.

Ekron is counted among the towns of the Judaean lowlands in Jos 15:45–46; cf. Jg 1:18 (but see 19b); 1 S 7:14; 17:52, and among the towns of Dan in Jos 19:43. Acc. to Jos 15:11, it is on the border of Judah and Dan.

Ekron is given to Jonathan Maccabaeus by Alexander Balas, 1 M 10:89. 35 km W of Jerusalem. Today *Tell el-Muqanna'.*

God of Ekron: BAALZEBUB 1.

EKRONITE or **of Ekron** (2), Jos 13:3; 1 S 5:10, inhabitant of: EKRON.

EL, "Power"?, Accad. *ilu,* Arab. *allah,* as a proper name signifies the supreme god of the Phoenician pantheon (see: ASHERAH). El is adored under different names in the Canaanite sanctuaries of Bethel, Beersheba, Mamre, and so on. In the period when the patriarchs become sedentary, the God of Abraham, Isaac, or Jacob, the God of Israel, is identified with the high god El, cf. Gn 33:20; he is called *El Elyon,* God Most High, Gn 14:18–22 (at Jerusalem), *El-berith,* God of covenant, Jg 9:46; cf. 8:33 (at Shechem), *El Bethel* (Hb.), God Bethel or God of Bethel, Gn 35:7 (at Bethel), *El Olam,* God of eternity, Gn 21:33 (at Beersheba), *El Roi,* God of vision, Gn 16:13 (at Lahai Roi in the Negeb), *El Shaddai* (see: SHADDAI) at Mamre. See also perhaps *El Qannah,* the jealous God, Ex 20:5; 34:14; Dt 4:24; 5:9; 6:15; cf. Jos 24:19; Na 1:2.

El is a component part of many names such as *El-ijah, Eli-melech,* or *Isra-el, Jo-el,* and so on.

See: ELOAH; ELOHIM; LORD; SHADDAI; YAHWEH.

ELA. See: ELAH 6.

ELAH, Ela, Hb. 1–5: *'Elah,* "Oak" (cf. Elim; Terebinth); 6–7: *'Ela'*.

1. **Elah** (2), one of the chiefs (or clans) of Edom, Gn 35:41//1 Ch 1:52.

2. **Elah** (2), acc. to 1 Ch 4:15, son of Caleb and father of Kenaz. To be connected (?) with the preceding.

3. **Elah** (4), **son of Baasha** (1), fourth king of Israel (886–885), of the second dynasty, succeeds his father. His capital is Tirzah. A contemporary of Asa of Judah. He and all his family are murdered by Zimri, who takes his place, 1 K 16:6, 8–14.

4. **Elah** (4), father of the king of Israel: HOSHEA 2.

5. **Elah son of Uzzi, son of Michri** (1), a Benjaminite, head of a family living in Jerusalem after the exile, 1 Ch 9:8.

6. **Ela** (1), father of: SHIMEI 8.

7. **Elah** (1), father of: SHAMMAH 3.

ELAM, Hb. *'Elam.*

1. **Elam** (17), linked to Shem in the priestly tradition, Gn 10:22//1 Ch 1:17, a country in the eastern part of Lower Mesopotamia, in present-day Iran, around Susa. Elamites are among the populations shifted to Samaria by Assurbanipal, Ezr 4:9, and Elamite mercenaries, expert bowmen, are in the Assyrian armies, Is 22:6. Elam is one of the countries of the Jewish diaspora, Is 11:11; Ac 2:9; cf. Tb 2:10. Babylon will one day be occupied by Elam and the Medes, Is 21:2, but Elam, in turn, will experience the terror of invasions, Jr 25:25; 49:34–39; cf. Ezk 32:24. Elam is a province of the Seleucid Empire, Dn 8:2.

= **Elymais** (1), Tb 2:10, the Hellenistic name for the country of Elam.

King: CHEDOR-LAOMER.

Capital: SUSA.

See: ELYMAIS 2; ELYMAEANS.

2. **Elam** (2), a town in Judah, reoccupied after the return from the exile, Ezr 2:31//Ne 7:24. W of Beth-zur.

3. **Elam** (1), a Benjaminite of the sons of Shashak, head of a family at Jerusalem, 1 Ch 8:24.

4. **Elam** (1), a Korahite, a gatekeeper, fifth of the seven sons of Meshelemaiah, 1 Ch 26:3.

5. **Elam** (6), head of a family whose sons return from the exile with Zerubbabel, Ezr 2:7//Ne 7:12, and with Ezra, Ezr 8:7. Some of them had married foreign wives, whom they now put away, Ezr 10:26. Elam signs the pledge to observe the Law, Ne 10:15.

Among his sons: SHECANIAH 5.

6. **Elam** (1), a priest, takes part in the dedication of the wall at Jerusalem, Ne 12:42.

ELAMITES (2), Ezr 4:9; Ac 2:9, inhabitants of: ELAM 1.

ELASA (1), a town where Judas Maccabaeus pitches camp, 1 M 9:5. Perhaps *Kh. Ilasa* near Beth-horon.

ELASAH. See: ELEASAH 3–4.

ELATH (8), Hb. *'Elat, 'Elot* (cf. Elim), a stage of the Exodus, Dt 2:8, on the shore of the Red Sea, at the head of the

Gulf of Aqaba, near the town of Ezion-geber (with which Elath may have been confused at one time), 1 K 9:26//2 Ch 8:17. The town is rebuilt by Uzziah of Judah, 2 K 14:22//2 Ch 26:2, and definitively reoccupied by Edomites under Ahaz, 2 K 16:6.

A possible name in antiquity: EL-PARAN.

EL-BERITH (1), "God of covenant." See: BAAL-BERITH.

ELDAAH (2), "God desires," one of the five sons of Midian, who are said to be the sons of Keturah, Abraham's concubine, Gn 25:4//1 Ch 1:33.

ELDAD (2), "God has loved" (cf. David), associated with Medad, both of them inspired Israelites, Nb 11:26–27.

ELEAD (1), Hb. *'El'ad,* "God has witnessed" (cf. Joed). See: ERAN.

ELEADAH (1), Hb. *'El'adah,* "God has adorned" (cf. Adah). See: ERAN.

ELEALEH (5), Hb. *'El'aleh,* "God ascends"? (cf. Alvah), a town in Transjordania, always linked with Heshbon, occupied by Reuben, Nb 32:37; cf. 32:3, then by Moab, Is 15:4; 16:9; Jr 48:34. Today *El-Al,* 4 km N of Heshbon.

ELEASAH, Elasah, Hb. *'El'asah,* "God has made" (inverted form of *Asahel*).

1. **Eleasah** (2), a descendant of the daughter of Sheshan, of the clan of Jerahmeel, 1 Ch 2:39–40.

2. **Eleasah** (1), a Benjaminite, a descendant of King Saul and an ancestor of the sons of Azel, 1 Ch 8:37//9:43.

3. **Elasah son of Shaphan** (1) and **Gemariah son of Hilkiah,** messengers from King Zedekiah to King Nebuchadnezzar and bearers of Jeremiah's letter to the first people deported to Babylon, Jr 29:3.

4. **Elasah** (1), a priest of the sons of Pashhur, married to a foreign wife, whom he puts away, Ezr 10:22.

ELEAZAR, Gr. transcription of Hb. *'El'azar,* "God has called" (cf. Ezer).

1. **Eleazar** (64), **son of Aaron** (12). Known from the priestly tradition. Third of Aaron's four sons and a priest like the others, Ex 6:23; 28:1; Nb 26:60; 1 Ch 5:29. After the death of Nadab and Abihu, he exercises the priesthood with his brother Ithamar, Lv 10:6, 12, 16; Nb 3:2–4; 1 Ch 24:1–2. Chief of the Levite leaders, Nb 3:32, he succeeds Aaron, Nb 20:25–28; Dt 10:6, takes part in the census of Israel, Nb 26:1, 3, 63, in the division of the booty, Nb 31:12–54, and in the allocation of the Promised Land, Nb 34:17; Jos 14:1; 19:51; cf. Nb 32:2, 28; Jos 21:1. He is buried at Gibeah, Jos 24:33.

Acc. to 1 Ch 24:3–6 the *sons of Eleazar* comprise sixteen classes of priests as compared to the eight of the sons of Ithamar.

Father of: PHINEHAS 1.

Ancestor of: ZADOK 1.

2. **Eleazar** (1), son of Abinadab, guardian of the Ark of the Covenant at Kiriath-jearim, 1 S 7:1.

3. **Eleazar son of Dodo the Ahohite** (2), one of David's three champions, 2 S 23:9–10//1 Ch 11:12–14.

= **Dodai the Ahohite** (1), in charge of the (military) service for the seventh month, 1 Ch 27:4.

4. **Eleazar** (1), a Levite of the clan of Merari, son of Mahli, has only daughters, 1 Ch 23:21–22; 24:28.

5. **Eleazar son of Phinehas** (1), assistant to the priest Meremoth in the temple at Jerusalem, Ezr 8:33.

6. **Eleazar** (1), an Israelite of the sons of Parosh, married to a foreign wife, whom he puts away, Ezr 10:25.

7. **Eleazar** (1), a priest who takes part with Nehemiah in the dedication of the Jerusalem wall, Ne 12:42.

8. **Eleazar** (1). See: JOSHUA 10.

9. **Eleazar** (2), called **Avaran** (2), one of the four brothers of Judas Mac-

cabaeus, 1 M 2:5, dies a hero in the battle of Bethzechariah, 6:43–44.

10. **Eleazar** (1), father of: JASON 1.

11. **Eleazar** (1), an elderly Jew, a teacher of the Law, and a martyr under Antiochus Epiphanes, 2 M 6:18–31.

12. **Eleazar** (2), an ancestor of Jesus acc. to Mt 1:15.

[ELEPHANTINE]. See: SYENE.

ELEUTHERUS (1), Gr. *Eleutheros,* "Free," a river that is the NW boundary of Coele-Syria, 1 M 11:7; 12:30. North of Tripolis. Today *Nahr el-Kebir.*

ELEVEN (4), designation of the group of Apostles chosen by Jesus, during the period between the death of Judas Iscariot and his replacement by Matthias, Mk 16:14; Lk 24:9, 33; cf. Mt 28:16; Ac 1:26 (Gr.).

See: TWELVE.

ELHANAN, "God shows favor" (cf. Hanan).

1. **Elhanan son of Jair** (2), **from Bethlehem** (1), kills Goliath of Gath at Gob in a battle against the Philistines, 2 S 21:19 (*son of Jair,* corr. of Hb. *son of Jaarah Orgim*) //1 Ch 20:5, where Elhanan kills Lahmi, brother of Goliath.

2. **Elhanan son of Dodo, from Bethlehem** (2), one of David's champions, 2 S 23:24//1 Ch 11:26.

ELI, Heli, Hb. *'Eli,* Gr. *Heli,* "[Yah] is raised up"? (cf. Alvah).

1. **Eli** (33), **the priest of Yahweh at [the sanctuary of] Shiloh** (1), 1 S 14:3, witness of the distress of Hannah, who is barren, then of her joy when she brings her son Samuel to him, 1 S 1:9–18, 25–28; 2:11, 20, witness also of the calling of young Samuel, 3:1–18, and the misconduct of his own two sons, 2:12–17, 22–27. He dies at the age of 98 on learning of the brutal death of his sons and the capture of the Ark by the Philistines, 4:1, 12–18. Eli is regarded as a judge in 1 S 4:18. He is the ancestor of the priest Abiathar, who will be replaced by Zadok under Solomon, 1 K 2:27; cf. 1 S 2:25–36.

Father of: HOPHNI; PHINEHAS 2.

Ancestor of: AHITUB 1; ICHABOD.

2. **Heli** (1), ancestor of Jesus, acc. to Lk 3:23.

ELIAB, "My God is Father" (cf. Joab).

1. **Eliab son of Helon** (5), leader of the tribe of Zebulun, Nb 2:7; 7:24; 10:16, in charge of the census for his tribe, Nb 1:9; brings the offering for the dedication of the altar on the third day, Nb 7:24–29.

2. **Eliab** (5), son of Pallu, a Reubenite, Nb 16:1; 26:8–9; Dt 11:6. Father of Abiram and: DATHAN.

3. **Eliab** (6), eldest son of Jesse and brother of David, 1 Ch 2:13; 1 S 16:6, one of the "three eldest sons of Jesse" who "followed Saul to the war," 1 S 17:13–30.

= ? **Elihu** (1), leader of the tribe of Judah, 1 Ch 27:18.

Father of: MAHALATH 2.

4. **Eliab** (1). See: ELIHU 1.

5. **Eliab son of Joab** (1), leader of the army of Solomon, 1 K 4:6 (acc. to Gr.).

6. **Eliab** (1), a Gadite who rallies to David before the latter becomes king, 1 Ch 12:10 (cf. vv. 9–16).

7. **Eliab** (3), a Levite, a gatekeeper attached to the service of the Ark, 1 Ch 15:18, and a harpist, 15:20; 16:5.

8. **Eliab** (1), a Simeonite, an ancestor of Judith, Jdt 8:1.

ELIADA, "God knows" (cf. Jada).

1. **Eliada** (1). See: BEELIADA.

2. **Eliada** (1), father of the king of Damascus: REZON.

3. **Eliada** (1), a Benjaminite, a "valiant champion with two hundred thousand, armed with bow and shield," in the service of King Jehoshaphat, 2 Ch 17:17.

ELIAHBA (2), "God hides," **from Shaalbon** (2), one of David's champions, 2 S 23:32//1 Ch 11:33.

ELIAKIM, "God sets upright" (cf. Jakim).

1. **Eliakim** (9), **son of Hilkiah** (6),

master of the palace for King Hezekiah. He had succeeded Shebna in the office when the latter was deposed. Is 22:15–25 announces this removal and proclaims that Eliakim "shall be a father to the inhabitants of Jerusalem and to the House of Judah," but that his house in turn will fall.

In 701, at the siege of Jerusalem by Sennacherib, he heads the Judaean delegation sent to negotiate with the commander-in-chief of the Assyrian armies, 2 K 18:18–19:2//Is 36:3–37:3.

2. **Eliakim** (2), the name, before his elevation, of: JEHOIAKIM 1.

3. **Eliakim** (1), a priest, a trumpeter at the dedication of the wall of Jerusalem, Ne 12:41.

4. **Eliakim** (2), two ancestors of Jesus, Mt 1:13; Lk 3:30.

ELIAM, "My God is Uncle" (cf. Am-).

1. **Eliam** (1), 2 S 11:3 = **Ammiel** (1), 1 Ch 3:5 (the components of the name *'Eli'am* are inverted in *'Ammi'el*), father of: BATHSHEBA.

2. **Eliam son of Ahithophel, from Gilo** (1), one of David's champions, 2 S 23:34.

ELIASAPH, "God has added" (cf. Joseph).

1. **Eliasaph son of Reuel** (5), leader of the tribe of Gad, Nb 2:14; 7:42; 10:20, in charge of the census of his tribe, Nb 1:14, brings the offering for the dedication of the altar on the sixth day, Nb 7:42–47. In all these texts, except 2:14, *Reuel* is a corr. of *Deuel.*

2. **Eliasaph son of Lael** (1), leader of the house of the Levites of Gershon, Nb 3:24.

ELIASHIB, "God causes to return *or* reestablishes" (cf. Jashub).

1. **Eliashib** (1), a priest, leader of the eleventh class of priests, 1 Ch 24:12.

2. **Eliashib** (9), a high priest, son of Joiakim and grandson of Jeshua, Ne 12:10, takes part in the rebuilding of the wall of Jerusalem, Ne 3:1; 20–21. In his time a record is made in the temple archives of the heads of the priestly families, Ne 12:22.

His son and grandson: JEHOIADA 6; JOHN 12.

3. **Eliashib** (2), a priest, in charge of the temple chambers. A near relative of Tobiah, he furnishes a chamber for him, thus rousing the anger of Nehemiah, Ne 13:4–7.

4. **Eliashib** (1), one of the seven sons of Elioenai, a descendant of King Jehoiachin, 1 Ch 3:24.

5. **Eliashib** (3), a singer, Ezr 10:24, an Israelite of the sons of Zattu, 10:27, and an Israelite of the sons of Bani, 10:36; all three are married to foreign wives, whom they put away.

ELIATHAH (2), "You are my God," of the sons of Heman, 1 Ch 25:4, leader of the twentieth class of cantors, 1 Ch 25:27.

ELIDAD (1), "My God has loved" (cf. David), **son of Chislon** (1), representative of the tribe of Benjamin in the allocation of Canaan, Nb 34:21.

ELIEHOENAI, Elioenai, Elioenei, "Toward Yah my eyes," cf. Ps 25:15.

1. **Eliehoenai** (1), a gatekeeper, a Korahite, seventh son of Meshelemiah, 1 Ch 26:3.

2. **Eliehoenai son of Zerahiah** (1), head of the family of the sons of Pahath-moab, who returns from the exile with Ezra, Ezr 8:4.

3. **Elioenai** (2), first of the three sons of Neariah, a descendant of King Jehoiachin and father of seven sons, 1 Ch 3:23–24.

4. **Elioenei** (1), a Simeonite, leader of a clan, 1 Ch 4:36–37.

5. **Elioenai** (1), a Benjaminite of the sons of Becher, 1 Ch 7:8.

6. **Elioenai** (1), corr. acc. to Gr. (Hb. *Elienai*); a Benjaminite of the sons of Shimei, head of a family at Jerusalem, 1 Ch 8:20.

7. **Elioenai** (1), an Israelite of the

sons of Zattu, married to a foreign wife, whom he puts away, Ezr 10:27.

8. **Elioenai** (2), a priest of the sons of Pashhur, married to a foreign wife, whom he puts away, Ezr 10:22; a priest and trumpeter at the dedication of the wall of Jerusalem, Ne 12:41. These are one person or two different persons.

ELIEL, "My God is El" (cf. El).

1. **Eliel** (1), head of a family in the eastern half tribe of Manasseh, 1 Ch 5:24.

2. **Eliel** (1). See: ELIHU 1.

3. **Eliel** (1), a Benjaminite of the sons of Shimei, head of a family in Jerusalem, 1 Ch 8:20.

4. **Eliel** (1), a Benjaminite of the sons of Shashak, head of a family in Jerusalem, 1 Ch 8:22.

5. **Eliel the Mahavite** (1), one of David's champions, 1 Ch 11:46.

6. **Eliel** (1), another of David's champions, 1 Ch 11:47.

7. **Eliel** (1), a Gadite who rallies to David before the latter becomes king, 1 Ch 12:12 (cf. vv. 9–16).

8. **Eliel** (2), a Levite of the sons of Hebron, of the clan of Kohath, takes part in the transferral of the Ark, 1 Ch 15:9, 11.

9. **Eliel** (1), one of the ten Levites assisting Conaniah and Shimei in the time of King Hezekiah, 2 Ch 31:13.

ELIEZER, "My God is help" (cf. Ezer).

1. **Eliezer** (1), son of Moses and brother of: GERSHOM 1.

2. **Eliezer** (1), a Benjaminite, one of the nine sons of Becher, a fighting man and head of a family, 1 Ch 7:8.

3. **Eliezer** (1), a priest, a trumpeter during the transferral of the Ark, 1 Ch 15:24.

4. **Eliezer son of Zichri** (1), chief officer for the Reubenites, 1 Ch 27:16.

5. **Eliezer son of Dodavahu of Mareshah** (1), a prophet, condemns the alliance of Jehoshaphat of Judah with Ahaziah of Israel for the common use of the port of Ezion-geber, 2 Ch 20:37.

6. **Eliezer** (1), one of Ezra's messengers to Iddo, Ezr 8:16.

7. **Eliezer** (3), a priest of the sons of Jeshua, Ezr 10:18; a Levite, 10:23; and an Israelite of the sons of Harim, 10:31—all married to foreign wives, whom they put away.

8. **Eliezer** (1), an ancestor of Jesus acc. to Lk 3:29.

ELIHOREPH (1) and **Ahijah, sons of Shisha** (1), two brothers, secretaries of King Solomon, 1 K 4:3.

ELIHU, "He is my God."

1. **Elihu** (1), an ancestor of Samuel, an Ephraimite, 1 S 1:1.

= **Eliab** (1), 1 Ch 6:12, an ancestor of Samuel and a descendant of Levi.

= **Eliel** (1), 1 Ch 6:19.

2. **Elihu** (1), a Manassite chief who rallies to David before the latter becomes king, 1 Ch 12:21.

3. **Elihu** (1), a gatekeeper, one of the sons of Shemaiah, son of Obed-edom, 1 Ch 26:7.

4. **Elihu, brother of David** (1), 1 Ch 27:18. See: ELIAB 3.

5. **Elihu** (7), **son of Barachel the Buzite** (2), Jb 32:2, 16, fourth interlocutor of Job, after the "three friends." Four discourses: Jb 32:6–37:24; he decides against both Job and his friends, attempts to justify God's behavior, defends the pedagogical value of suffering, and praises the omnipotent wisdom of God.

ELIJAH, Hb. *'Eliyyah, 'Eliyyahu,* Gr. *Elias,* "My God is Yah" (cf. Eliel; Joel).

1. **Elijah** (101), **the Tishbite** (6) or **of Tishbe in Gilead** (1), a prophet, a "man of God," 2 K 1:9–12, in the time of Ahab.

During the great drought, Elijah at the wadi Cherith, 1 K 17:2–6, then at Zarephath in the widow's house (miracle of the meal and the oil; raising of a child from the dead), 17:7–24; cf. Lk 4:25–26. Meeting with Obadiah, master of the palace, a believer in Yahweh, 18:1–5, and with Ahab, the king, a follower of Baal, 18:16–19. Elijah on Carmel: "How long . . . do you mean to hobble first on one leg then on the other? If Yahweh is God, follow him; if Baal, follow him," (v. 21); the prophets of Baal, the sacrifices, 18:20–40. End of the drought, 18: 41–46; cf. Jm 5:17–18. Flight of Elijah to Horeb, 1 K 19:1–8; his meeting with God and his threefold mission, 19:9–18; cf. Si 48:7–8; Rm 11:2. He calls Elisha to follow him, 19:19–21; 2 K 3:11. Elijah predicts the punishment of Ahab and his house for the murder of Naboth of Jezreel, 1 K 21:17–29; cf. 2 K 9:36; 10:10, 17, and the death of Ahaziah, successor of Ahab, 2 K 1:3–17. Ascension of Elijah, 2 K 2:1–15; 1 M 2:58.

Beginning in Ml 3:23–24 Elijah is regarded by one whole tradition as precursor of the Messiah. Jesus says that John the Baptist fills this role, Mt 11:14; 17:10–13//Mk 9:11–13; cf. Lk 1:17; Jn 1:21, 25, whereas others see the prophet Elijah in Jesus himself, Mt 16: 14//Mk 8:28//Lk 9:19; Mk 6:15//Lk 9:8; cf. Mt 27:47–49//Mk 15:35–36. Elijah is with Moses on the mountain of transfiguration, Mt 17:3–8//Mk 9:4–8//Lk 9:30–36.

Si 48:1–11 is an encomium of Elijah, and 2 Ch 21:12 speaks of something written by Elijah that has come into the hands of Jehoram, king of Judah.

2. **Elijah** (1), a Benjaminite of the sons of Jeroham, head of a family in Jerusalem, 1 Ch 8:27.

3. **Elijah** (1), a priest of the sons of Harim, married to a foreign wife, whom he puts away, Ezr 10:21.

4. **Elijah** (1), an Israelite of the sons of Elam, married to a foreign wife, whom he puts away, Ezr 10:26.

5. **Elijah** (1), a Simeonite, an ancestor of Judith, Jdt 8:1.

ELIKA from Harod (1), one of David's champions, 2 S 23:25.

ELIM (6), Hb. *'Elim,* "Terebinths, Green oaks" (cf. Beer-elim; Elah 1–5; Elon 3–5; El-paran; Elath?), a stage of the Exodus "where twelve water springs were, and seventy palm trees," Ex 15:27; 16:1; Nb 33:9–10. On the coast of the Gulf of Suez.

ELIMELECH (6), "My God is King" (cf. Melech), an Ephrathite from Bethlehem in Judah. A famine causes him to become an exile in Moab with his wife Naomi and his two sons, Rt 1:1–3. After his death and that of his sons his patrimony is "redeemed" by a relative, Boaz, who also marries the widow of one of his sons, Ruth the Moabitess, 2:1, 3; 4:3, 9.

ELIOENAI (8), a derivative of: ELIEHOENAI.

ELIOENEI (1). See: ELIEHOENAI 4.

ELIPHAZ, "My God is fine gold"? or, acc. to Old Arabic, "God is conqueror."

1. **Eliphaz** (9), **first-born son of Esau** (2), and Adah, Gn 36:4, 15; 1 Ch 1:35, eponymous ancestor of five Edomite chiefs or clans: Gatam, Kenaz, Omar, Teman and Zepho; Amalek is connected with these clans, Gn 36:10–12, 15–16; 1 Ch 1:36.

2. **Eliphaz of Teman** (6), Bildad of Shuah, and Zophar of Naamath, "three of his friends" who come to visit Job in his trials and to bemoan and console him, Jb 2:11; 4:1; 15:1; 22:1; cf. 32:1. In the end God blames them "for not speaking truthfully about me as my servant Job has done," 42:7–10.

ELIPHELEHU (2), "May my God distinguish him" (cf. Pelaiah 1), a Levite, a gatekeeper in the service of the Ark, 1 Ch 15:18, a player of the octave lyre, 15:21.

ELIPHELET, "My God rescues" (cf. Pelet 1–2).

1. **Eliphelet** (4), one of the sons of David born in Jerusalem, 2 S 5:16// 1 Ch 3:8//14:7. In 1 Ch 14:5 the parallel *Elpelet* seems to be an addition.

2. **Eliphelet son of Ahasbai, from Beth-maacah** (1), 2 S 23:34, one of David's champions.

= **Eliphelet of Ur** (1), 1 Ch 11:35 (Hb. *Eliphel*).

3. **Eliphelet** (1), a Benjaminite, third son of Eshek, a descendant of King Saul, 1 Ch 8:39.

4. **Eliphelet** (1), an Israelite of the sons of Adonikam who returns from the exile with Ezra, Ezr 8:13; cf. 2:13.

5. **Eliphelet** (1), an Israelite of the sons of Hashum, married to a foreign wife, whom he puts away, Ezr 10:33.

ELISHA (60), "God has helped" (cf. Isaiah?), **son of Shaphat** (4), **of Abel Meholah** (1), 1 K 19:16, a prophet, a "man of God" (29), 2 K 4:9, 21; and so on; "prophet of Samaria," 5:3; cf. 2:25. Called by the prophet Elijah, 1 K 19:16–21, he becomes the latter's servant and disciple, and after the master's ascension he inherits his spirit, 1 K 19:21; 2 K 2:1–18; cf. 3:11.

Many miracles are attributed to him: water purified, 2 K 2:19–22, punishment of insolent children, 2:23–25, increase of oil, 4:1–7, raising to life of the Shunammitess' son, 4:8–37; cf. 8:1–6, soup purified of poison, 4:38–41, multiplication of loaves, 4:42–44, healing of Naaman the leper, 5:1–27; cf. Lk 4:27, axe found, 6:1–7, capture of an Aramaean detachment, 6:8–23. Elisha is consulted by the kings of Judah, Israel, and Edom, who are at war with Moab, 2 K 3:11–19. He intervenes in the siege of Samaria by the Aramaeans, 6:31–7:2, 16–20, tells Hazael that he will rule over Aram, 8:7–15, and sends one of his disciples to anoint Jehu king, 9:1–13. Elisha falls ill and dies, 2 K 13:14–19. Contact with his corpse brings a dead man back to life, 2 K 13:20–21; cf. Si 48:12–14.

ELISHAH (3), presented in the list of peoples as "son of Javan" (Ionia), along with Tarshish, the Kittim, and the Dananites, Gn 10:4//1 Ch 1:7. Producer of purple cloth, Ezk 27:7. Probably signifies: CYPRUS.

ELISHAMA, "God has heard" (cf. Shemaiah).

1. **Elishama son of Ammihud** (6), leader of the tribe of Ephraim, Nb 2:18; 7:48; 10:22, in charge of the census of his tribe, Nb 1:10, brings the offering for the dedication of the altar on the seventh day, 7:48–53. Ancestor of Joshua, son of Nun, 1 Ch 7:26.

2. **Elishama** (1), 1 Ch 3:6, a son of David. See: ELISHUA.

3. **Elishama** (3), one of the sons of David born in Jerusalem, 2 S 5:16; 1 Ch 3:8; 14:7.

4. **Elishama** (3), a scribe, one of the ministers of King Jehoiakim, who read the book of Jeremiah's oracles, Jr 36:12, 20–21.

5. **Elishama** (2), grandfather of: ISHMAEL 5.

6. **Elishama** (1), a descendant of the daughter of Sheshan, of the clan of Jerahmeel, 1 Ch 2:41.

7. **Elishama** (1), one of the two priests whom King Jehoshaphat sends, along with five officers and eight Levites, to instruct the towns of Judah in the Law, 2 Ch 17:8.

ELISHAPHAT (1), "God has judged" (cf. Shephathiah), **son of Zichri** (1), one of the five commanders of hundreds who take part in the plot against Athaliah, 2 Ch 23:1–15.

ELISHEBA (1). See: ELIZABETH 1.

ELISHUA (2), "My God is noble, magnanimous" (cf. Shua 1), one of the sons of David born in Jerusalem, 2 S 5:15; 1 Ch 14:5.

= **Elishama** (1), 1 Ch 3:6.

ELIUD (2), "My God is Majesty" (cf. Hod), an ancestor of Jesus acc. to Mt 1:14–15.

ELIZABETH, Gr. form of Hb. *'Elisheba'*, "My God is plenitude"? (cf. Sheba).

1. **Elisheba daughter of Amminadab** (1), sister of Nahshon, wife of Aaron, and mother of Nadab, Abihu, Eleazar, and Ithamar, Ex 6:23.

2. **Elizabeth** (9), a descendant of Aaron, wife of the priest Zechariah, Lk 1:5, relative of Mary, 1:36, barren and elderly, 1:7, 18, then mother of John the Baptist, 1:24, 36, 57, 60. The latter's birth is foretold to Zechariah, 1:13, and preceded by a visit from Mary, whose faith Elizabeth praises, 1:40–42.

ELIZAPHAN, Elzaphan, "My God has protected" (cf. Zephaniah).

1. **Elizaphan** (3) or **Elzaphan** (2), **son of Uzziel** (2), Ex 6:22, leader of the house of the clan of Kohath, Nb 3:30, in charge of removing the corpses of Nadab and Abihu from the sanctuary, Lv 10:4. Acc. to the chronicler, sons of Elizaphan take part in the transferral of the Ark under David, 1 Ch 15:8, and in the purification of the temple under Hezekiah, 2 Ch 29:13.

2. **Elizaphan son of Parnach** (1), representative of the tribe of Zebulun in the allocation of Canaan, Nb 34:25.

ELIZUR (5), "My God is a rock" (cf. Zur), **son of Shedeur** (5), in charge of the tribe of Reuben, Nb 2:10; 7:30; 10:18, responsible for the census of his tribe, Nb 1:5, brings the offering for the dedication of the altar on the fourth day, Nb 7:30–35.

ELKANAH, "God has created *or* God has taken possession" (cf. Mikneiah).

1. **Elkanah** (11), an Ephraimite from Ramathaim, husband of Hannah, who is barren but his preferred wife, and of Peninnah. After a pilgrimage to the sanctuary at Shiloh, he receives from Hannah a son, Samuel, 1 S 1:1–8, 19–25; 2:11, 19–21; 1 Ch 6:13, 19. 1 Ch 6:12//6:19 makes Elkanah a Levite of the clan of Kohath.

2. **Elkanah** (5), several Levites who are descendants of Kohath and, acc. to 1 Ch 6, ancestors of Samuel and the preceding Elkanah, Ex 6:24//1 Ch 6:8; 6:10//6:21; 6:11//6:20.

3. **Elkanah** (1), 1 Ch 9:16, ancestor of the Levite: BERECHIAH 8. To be connected (?) with the preceding.

4. **Elkanah** (1), with Berechiah, a Levite gatekeeper in the service of the Ark, 1 Ch 15:23.

5. **Elkanah** (1), a Korahite who rallies to David before the latter becomes king, 1 Ch 12:7.

6. **Elkanah** (1), second-in-command of King Ahaz, slain by Zichri during the Syro-Ephraimite war, 2 Ch 28:7.

ELKIAH (1). See: HILKIAH 11.

ELKOSH (1), native place of the prophet Nahum, Na 1:1. Impossible to locate with certainty: In Judah (Epiphanius)? In Galilee (St. Jerome)? North of Nineveh (a sixteenth-century tradition)? Capernaum, "town of Nahum"?

ELLASAR (2), a city in Mesopotamia, Gn 14:1, 9. Formerly identified, mistakenly, with Larsa.

King: ARIOCH 1.

ELMADAM (1), an ancestor of Jesus acc. to Lk 3:28.

ELNAAM (1), "God is gracious, agreeable" (cf. Naomi), father of Jeribai and: JOSHAVIAH.

ELNATHAN, "God has given" (cf. Nathan).

1. **Elnathan** (3), **son of Achbor** (2), at the order of King Jehoiakim brings the prophet Uriah back from Egypt, whither he had fled, Jr 26:22–23. Four years later he is among the ministers of the same Jehoiakim who are overwhelmed as they listen to the book of Jeremiah's oracles and who urge the king, unsuccessfully, not to burn the book, Jr 36:12, 25.

2. **Elnathan** (1), same as the preceding? Father of: NEHUSHTA.

3. **Elnathan** (3), three of Ezra's messengers to Iddo, Ezr 8:16 (the third is omitted by some).

[ELOAH] (58), singular of *Elohim,* used 58× in the Hb. text, almost exclusively in poetic passages where it almost always refers to the only true God, Hab 3:3; Jb 3:4–40:2 (42×); Dt 32:15, 17; Ps 18:32; 50:22; 114:7; 139:19; Pr 30:5; Ne 9:17.

[ELOHIM] (2,550 in Hb. text), plural of *Eloah,* sometimes refers to several gods, but usually to one (Elohim is then used with a verb or attribute in the singular), who is either the true God (the majority of instances) or an idol (Chemosh in Jg 11:24; Baalzebub in 2 K 1:2; and so on).
See: EL; LORD; YAHWEH.

ELON, Hb. *'Elôn,* 1–2: "Ram"; 3–5: "Terebinth, Oak" (cf. Elim).
1. **Elon the Hittite** (2), father of: ADAH 2; BASEMATH 1.
2. **Elon of Zebulun** (2), a "lesser" judge, Jg 12:11–12.
3. **Elon** (2), second of the three sons of Zebulun, Gn 46:14; his descendants form the **Elonite** clan, Nb 26:26.
4. **Elon** (2), a town in Dan, Jos 19:43. In 1 K 4:9 *Aijalon* is probably to be read for Hb. *Elon.*
5. **Elon** (1), a town of Zebulun where the judge Elon is buried, Jg 12:12.

ELONITE (1), belonging to the clan of: ELON 3.

ELPAAL (3), "God has acted" (cf. Peullethai), a Benjaminite, a son (or brother) of Shaharaim, 1 Ch 8:11, whose sons live in Ono and Lud, 8:12, or at Jerusalem, 8:17.

EL-PARAN (1), "Oak of Paran" (cf. Elim; Paran), Gn 14:6, perhaps an ancient name for: ELATH.

ELPELET (1), (cf. Pelet 1–2), 1 Ch 14:5. See ELIPHELET 1.

ELTEKE (1). See: ELTEKEH.

ELTEKEH or **Elteke** (2), a town in Dan, Jos 19:44, assigned to the Levites of the clan of Kohath, 21:23. Location uncertain.

ELTEKON (1), a town in the highlands of Judah, Jos 15:59.

ELTOLAD (2), a town in the Negeb of Judah, Jos 15:30, that had belonged to the Simeonites, Jos 19:4.
= **Tolad** (1), 1 Ch 4:29. Location unknown.

ELUZAI (1), a Benjaminite who rallies to David before the latter becomes king, 1 Ch 12:6.

ELYMAEANS (1), probably the inhabitants of Elymais (the Hellenistic name for Elam), Jdt 1:6.
King: ARIOCH 2.

ELYMAIS
1. **Elymais** (1), the Greek name for: ELAM 1.
2. **Elymais** (1), an otherwise unknown city in Persia, 1 M 6:1.

ELYMAS (1), "The wise man"? See: BAR-JESUS.

ELZABAD, "God gives a gift" (cf. Zabad).
1. **Elzabad** (1), a Gadite, a fighting man who rallies to David before the latter becomes king, 1 Ch 12:13 (cf. vv. 9–16).
2. **Elzabad** (1), a gatekeeper, one of the sons of Shemaiah, son of Obed-edom, 1 Ch 26:7.

ELZAPHAN. See: ELIZAPHAN 1.

EMEK-KEZIZ (1), "Plain of separation"? (cf. Amok; Crop-heads), a town in Benjamin, Jos 18:21.

EMIM (3), "Frightening beings," Gn 14:5; Dt 2:10–11. See: REPHAIM 1.

EMMANUEL (1). See: IMMANUEL.

EMMAUS
1. **Emmaus** (4) **in the Lowlands** (1), site of a battle between the Syrian army under Gorgias and Nicanor and the

troops of Judas Maccabaeus, 1 M 3:40, 57; 4; one of the fortresses built by Bacchides in Judaea, 9:50–51. 30 km W of Jerusalem. Today *Imwas*.

2. **Emmaus** (1), a town sixty stadia (12 km) from Jerusalem where the risen Jesus appears to two disciples, one of whom is Cleopas, Lk 24:13–32. Difficult to identify: same as the preceding, with sixty stadia being corrected to one hundred and sixty? Or Mozah, which is sixty stadia round trip?

EN-, construct state of Hb. *'Ayîn,* "Spring, Fountain," forms part of a number of place-names listed in the following pages (cf. also Ain).

ENAIM (2), "The two springs" (cf. En-). See: ENAM.

ENAM (1), "The two springs" (cf. En-), a town in the lowlands of Judah, Jos 15:34.

= **Enaim** (2), near "the road to Timnah," where Judah meets Tamar, his daughter-in-law, and mistakes her for a prostitute, Gn 38:14, 21.

ENAN (5), (cf. En-), father of: AHIRA.

ENCAMPMENTS OF JAIR (6), Hb. *Havvôt Ya'ir*. See: JAIR 1.

EN-DOR (3), "Spring of Dor" (cf. En-; Dor), the place where Gideon defeats Midian, Ps 83:10 (*En-harod* acc. to Jg 7:1), a town of Manasseh in Issachar, Jos 17:11 (but some regard this as a repetition of *Dor*), native place of the necromancer whom Saul consults before his death, 1 S 28:7. Not far from the modern *Indur,* south of Tabor.

EN-EGLAIM (1), "Spring of the heifers" (cf. En-; Eglah), a town on the shore of the Dead Sea, associated with En-gedi, Ezk 47:10. Site unknown.

EN-GANNIM, "Spring of the gardens" (cf. En-; Beth-haggan).

1. **En-gannim** (1), a town in the lowlands of Judah, Jos 15:34.

2. **En-gannim** (2), a town of Issachar, Jos 19:21, assigned to the Levites of the clan of Gershon, Jos 21:29.

= **Anem** (1), 1 Ch 6:58.

EN-GEDI, or **Engedi** (7), Gr. *Engaddi,* "Spring of the kid" (En-; Hazar-gaddah), a town in the wilderness of Judah, Jos 15:62, near which David hides, 1 S 24: 1–2; on the shore of the Dead Sea, Ezk 47:10, identified in 2 Ch 20:2 with Hazazon-tamar, an oasis where vine, palm, and cypress are found, Sg 1:14; Si 24:14. At about the middle of the west bank of the Dead Sea.

EN-HADDAH (1), a town in Issachar, Jos 19:21. 10 km SW of the Sea of Chinnereth.

EN-HAKKORE (1), "Spring of the invoker," cf. Jg 15:18, or "Spring of the partridge" (cf. Kore), name of a spring at Lehi, Jg 15:19.

EN-HAROD (1), "Spring of trembling"? (cf. En-; Harod), an encampment of Gideon near that of Midian, Jg 7:1–3. 3 km SE of Jezreel, at the foot of Mount Gilboa.

EN-HAZOR (1), "Spring of Hazor" (cf. En-; Hazor), a fortified town in Naphtali, Jos 19:37.

ENOCH, Hanoch, Hb. *Hanok,* Gr. *Henōch,* "Inauguration, Dedication."

1. **Enoch** (14), son of Cain and father of Irad (Yahwist genealogy), Gn 4:17–18; son of Jared and father of Methuselah (priestly genealogy), Gn 5:18–23; 1 Ch 1:3. An antediluvian patriarch. "Enoch lived for three hundred and sixty-five years. Enoch walked with God. Then he vanished because God took him," Gn 5:22–24; Si 44:16; 49:14; Heb 11:5. An ancestor of Jesus acc. to Lk 3:37. A prophecy is attributed to him, Jude 14, which is in fact a citation from the *Book of Enoch.*

2. **Hanoch** (2), one of the five sons of Midian, a grandson of Abraham and his concubine Keturah, Gn 25:4//1 Ch

1:13. Cf. the town of *el-Hanakiya* in western Saudi Arabia.

3. **Hanoch** (4), first of the four sons of Reuben, Gn 46:9; Ex 6:14; 1 Ch 5:3; his descendants form the **Hanochite** clan, Nb 26:5.

4. **Enoch** (1), acc. to Gn 4:17 the first town built by Cain.

ENOS (1). See: ENOSH.

ENOSH (7), Gr. *Enōs*, "Man," son of Seth, "the first to invoke the name of Yahweh," Gn 4:26 (Yahwist tradition), father of Kenan, Gn 5:6–11 (priestly tradition)//1 Ch 1:1.

= **Enos** (1), an ancestor of Jesus, Lk 3:38. An antediluvian patriarch.

ENRIMMON (1), "Spring of the pomegranate" (cf. En-; Rimmon 1–4). See: RIMMON 1.

EN-ROGEL (2), a place, "Fuller's Spring," on the border of Judah and Benjamin, Jos 15:7; 18:16. See: FULLER 1.

EN-SHEMESH (2), "Spring of the sun" (cf. En-; Samson), on the border of Judah and Benjamin, Jos 15:7; 18:17. East of the Mount of Olives.

EPAENETUS (1), "Praiseworthy," a Christian living at Rome, one of the first converts from Asia, Rm 16:6.

EPAPHRAS (3), abbrev. of Gr. *Epaphroditos*. A Christian of Colossae, Col 4:12, a founder of the Church at Colossae and perhaps also of those at Laodicea and Hierapolis, Col 1:7–8; 4:12–13, a fellow prisoner with Paul at Rome, Phm 22.

EPAPHRODITUS (2), "Lovable, Charming" (cf. Epaphras), a Christian of Philippi, sent by this Church to bring the collection to Paul in prison; a co-worker of Paul, he falls ill and wants to return to Philippi, Ph 2:25–30; 4:18.

EPHAH

1. **Ephah** (3), an Arabian tribe, Is 60:6, related to the Midianites, Gn 25:4//1 Ch 1:33 (son of Midian, son of Keturah, Abraham's concubine).

2. **Ephah, concubine of Caleb** (1), 1 Ch 2:46.

3. **Ephah** (1), a Calebite of the sons of Jahdai, 1 Ch 2:47.

EPHAI (1), (Q*Ephai;* K*Ophai*), **the Netophathite** (1), Jr 40:8 (//2 K 25:23, *the Netophathite*). His sons are among the Judaean officers in the entourage of Johanan, son of Kareah, after the capture of Jerusalem by Nebuchadnezzar, cf. Jr 40:13; 41:11, 13, 16; 42:8; 43:4–5.

EPHER, "Gazelle" (cf. Ephron).

1. **Epher** (2), a Midianite clan, Gn 25:4//1 Ch 1:33 (son of Midian, son of Keturah, Abraham's concubine).

2. **Epher** (1), one of the sons of Ezrah, attached to Caleb, 1 Ch 4:17.

3. **Epher** (1), one of the family heads in the eastern half tribe of Manasseh, 1 Ch 5:24.

EPHES-DAMMIM (1), between Socoh and Azekah, an encampment of the Philistines, 1 S 17:1.

= **Pas-dammim** (1), where Eleazar, son of Dodo, one of David's champions, confronts the Philistines, 1 Ch 11:13 (omitted in //2 S 23:9). Precise location uncertain.

EPHESIAN (5), Ac 19:28, 34–35; 21:29, inhabitant of: EPHESUS.

EPHESUS (16), an important port on the eastern shore of the Aegean Sea, capital of the Roman province of Asia, "guardian of the temple of great Diana," Ac 19:35, and religious center of Asia Minor, cf. Rv 1:11; 2:1–7.

Leaving Corinth for Syria, at the end of his second journey, summer 52, Paul stops at Ephesus, Ac 18:19–21, where he leaves Priscilla and Aquila, who meet Apollos there, 18:24–26. During his third journey Paul stays there "two years" and "three months," Ac 19:8, 10—three years acc. to Ac 20:31—or from 54 to

57. There he completes the Christian formation of the disciples of John the Baptist, Ac 19:1–8, founds the Church of Ephesus, preaching in the synagogue, then in the lecture hall of Tyrannus, Ac 19:8–10, performing miracles that some Jewish exorcists try in vain to duplicate, Ac 19:11–20. Paul's preaching, which threatens the prestige of Diana and the local trade in miniature shrines, leads to a riot of the silversmiths and the gathering of the populace in the theater of the town, Ac 19:23–40. Ephesus is a favorable place for Paul's apostolic activity, 1 Co 16:8–9; some individuals, like Onesiphorus, help him, 2 Tm 1:18, but enemies such as Alexander the coppersmith, 2 Tm 4:14–15, are also numerous, 1 Co 16:8; cf. 1 Co 15:32; 1 Tm 1:3. Timothy, 1 Tm 1:3, and Tychicus, 2 Tm 4:12, are mentioned among the authorities in the Church of Ephesus.

It is from Ephesus that Paul writes the *first letter to the Corinthians,* the *letter to the Galatians,* and perhaps the *letter to the Philippians.* On his return from Macedonia, Paul summons the elders of Ephesus to Miletus and leaves them his pastoral testament in one of the great discourses in Acts, Ac 20:16–38. The fact that in Ep 1:1 the mention of "[the saints] who are at Ephesus" is missing in a number of manuscripts suggests perhaps that Ephesians was a circular letter addressed to all the communities Paul had founded.

Native town of: TROPHIMUS.

EPHLAL (2), (cf. Pelaliah), a descendant of the daughter of Sheshan, of the clan of Jerahmeel, 1 Ch 2:37.

EPHOD (1), a Manassite, father of: HANNIEL 1.

EPHRAIM, "Fertile [land]"; a popular etymology, Gn 41:52 (cf. Ephrathah).

1. **Ephraim** (184), son of Joseph and Asenath, younger brother of Manasseh, born like the latter in Egypt, Gn 41:52, and, like him, adopted by Jacob, who gives him priority over his older brother, Gn 48:1–20. Eponymous ancestor of the tribe of the same name.

Descendants and clans of Ephraim, Nb 26:35–37; 1 Ch 7:20–28. Several censuses of the tribe, Nb 1:32; 2:18; 26:37. Mixed population of Canaanites and Ephraimites, Jos 16:10; Jg 1:29. Possible emigration of clans, for example, the clan of Beriah (see: BERIAH 2–3).

Ephraim and Manasseh form two tribes, Jos 14:4, sometimes called **Joseph,** Gn 49:22; Dt 27:12, or the **sons of Joseph,** Nb 26:28–37; Jos 16:1–4; 17:14–18; 1 Ch 7:29, often associated, Dt 34:2; Ps 60:9//108:9; Is 9:20; 2 Ch 30:1; 34:6, 9. In Rv 7:8 "Joseph" refers to the tribe of Ephraim.

The territory of Ephraim is defined in Jos 16:5–10. It includes the **highlands of Ephraim** (32) or "highlands of Israel," between Benjamin and Manasseh, Jos 11:16–21, colonized by Ephraim and Manasseh, Jos 17:15–18, but with Ephraim in a preponderant position and intending to maintain its hegemony, Gn 48:19–20; Jg 8:1–3; 12:1–6, by spreading extensively into Manasseh as far as Shechem, Jos 20:7, and Samaria, Is 7:9. Native place or scene of the activity of the lesser judges Ehud, Jg 3:27, Deborah, 4:5, Tola, 10:1, and Abdon, 12:15; of Micah, whose priest is taken from him, 17:1, 8; 18:2, 13; of the Levite whose concubine is brutalized, 19:1, 18; of Sheba, who rebels against David, 2 S 20:21. Ephraim becomes the most important of the northern tribes, cf. 2 S 2:9, and the nucleus of the future kingdom of Israel, to the point where "Ephraim" (64×, of which 37 are in Hosea and 12 in Isaiah, Is 7; 9; 11; 17; 28) is a name, often in poetic texts, for the northern kingdom. Thus Ephraim is called the "first-born son" of God, Jr 31:9, just as Israel is, Ex 4:2, 22. Solomon makes the highlands of Ephraim the first district of the united kingdom,

1 K 4:8, but at his death the Ephraimite Jeroboam leads a rebellion, which ends in the separation of Judah and Ephraim, Is 7:17; cf. Ps 78:67. Asa of Judah occupies towns of Ephraim, 2 Ch 15:8–9, over which his son Jehoshaphat appoints governors, 2 Ch 17:2; 19:4. On the eve of the war against Edom, Amaziah dismisses his Ephraimite mercenaries, 2 Ch 25:7, 10. After the Syro-Ephraimite attack on Ahaz, cf. Is 7:2, 5, some officers from Ephraim liberate their fellow Judaean prisoners, 2 Ch 28:12. Ephraim's power is shattered, cf. Is 7:8–9; 17:3; 28:1, 3. The religious reforms of Hezekiah, 2 Ch 30:1, 10, 18; 31:1, and Josiah, 2 Ch 34:6, 9, find an echo in some Ephraimites. Like Ephraim, Judah will be cast off, Jr 7:15. Ephraim, however, will be restored some day, Jr 31:9, 18–20, and be reconciled to Judah, Ps 60:9; Is 11:13; Ezk 37:16, 19; Zc 9:10.

Ephraim in the lists of tribes: List, pages 410–11.

Other Ephraimites: BENAIAH 2; ELISHAMA 1; ELKANAH 1–2; HELEZ 1; JEROBOAM 1; JOSHUA 1; SAMUEL 2; ZICHRI 10.

Towns in (the highlands of) Ephraim: GIBEAH 3; PIRATHON; RAMAH 2; SHAMIR 3; SHECHEM; TIMNATH-SERAH.

See: ZEMARAIM.

2. **Gate of Ephraim** (4), in the north wall of Jerusalem, 2 K 14:13//2 Ch 25:23; in front of it is a square where the people make shelters out of branches, Ne 8:16. On the route of the procession for the dedication of the wall, Ne 12:39.

3. **Forest of Ephraim** (1), where Absalom is slain, 2 S 18:6. In Transjordania near Mahanaim.

4. **Ephraim** (2), a town near Baal-hazor, 2 S 13:23. It is near the desert, and Jesus withdraws there, Jn 11:54.

= **Ephrath** (4) or **Ephrathah** (1), near Bethel; Rachel dies there and is buried there, Gn 35:16, 19; 48:7. The identification with Bethlehem is a late gloss, cf. 1 S 10:2; Jr 31:15. The Ark of the Covenant stops there, Ps 132:6.

= **Ophrah** (2), attacked by the Philistines, 1 S 13:17, listed among the towns of Benjamin.

= **Ephron** (1), conquered by Abijah of Judah, 2 Ch 13:19.

= **Aphairema** (1), capital of one of three nomes or districts, probably conquered by Judas Maccabaeus, 1 M 11:34.

Today *et-Taiyebeh,* 20 km NE of Jerusalem.

5. **Ephraim** (2), (corr. of Hb. *Appaim*), a descendant of Onam, of the clan of Jerahmeel, 1 Ch 2:30–31.

EPHRAIMITE (3), Hb. *'Ephrati,* Jg 12:5; 1 S 1:1 (or: *Ephrathite*); 1 K 11:26, belonging to the tribe of: EPHRAIM 1.

EPHRATH

1. **Ephrath** (1), wife of Caleb, 1 Ch 2:19.

= ? **Ephrathah** 1.

2. **Ephrath** (1), Gn 48:7. See: EPHRAIM 4.

EPHRATHAH, "Fruitful" (cf. Ephraim).

1. **Ephrathah** (8), wife of Hezron, then of Caleb, 1 Ch 2:24, mother of Hur, 2:50, himself father of Bethlehem, 4:4 (cf. 2:51, 54), whence the identification of Ephrath or Ephrathah with: BETHLEHEM 1; consequently, the designation **Ephrathites from Bethlehem** that is given to Elimelech and his sons, Rt 1:2, and to Jesse, father of David, 1 S 17:12.

2. **Ephrathah** (1). See: EPHRAIM 4.

EPHRATHITE (3), Hb. *'Ephrati,* Rt 1:2; 1 S 1:1 (or: *Ephraimite*); 17:12, belonging to: EPHRATHAH 1.

EPHRON (cf. Epher).

1. **Ephron** (12), **son of Zohar** (2) **the Hittite** (5), from whom Abraham buys the field and cave of Machpelah, Gn 23:8–18; cf. 25:9; 49:29–30; 50:13. See: MACHPELAH.

2. **Ephron** (1), a mountain on the border of Judah and Benjamin, Jos 15:9. Not identified.

3. **Ephron** (1). See: EPHRAIM 4.

4. **Ephron** (2), a fortified town across

the Jordan, destroyed by Judas Maccabaeus, 1 M 5:46–51//2 M 12:27–28. Opposite Beth-shan. Today *et-Taiyebeh.*

EPICUREANS (1), philosophers and disciples of Epicurus. Paul meets some of them in Athens, Ac 17:18.

EPIPHANES, Gr. *Epiphanēs,* "[God] manifests" (cf. Apollophanes).

1. **Epiphanes** (5), surname of: ANTIOCHUS 3.

2. **Epiphanes** (1), surname of: ALEXANDER 2.

3. **[Epiphanes],** surname of: PTOLEMY 5.

ER, "Vigilant" (cf. Jair 4).

1. **Er** (9), first-born of the three sons of Judah and Bath-shua the Canaanite woman and first husband of Tamar; he dies in Canaan, Gn 38:3, 6–7; 46:12//Nb 26:19//1 Ch 2:3.

2. **Er** (1), son of Shelah, son of Judah, and father of Lecah, 1 Ch 4:21.

3. **Er** (1), an ancestor of Jesus acc. to Lk 3:28.

ERAN (1), son of Shuthelah, son of Ephraim, whose descendants form the **Eranite** clan, Nb 26:36.

= ? **Elead** (1), 1 Ch 7:21.

= ? **Eleadah** (1), 1 Ch 7:20.

= ? **Ladan** (1), 1 Ch 7:26, an ancestor of Joshua, son of Nun.

ERANITE (1), of the Ephraimite clan of: ERAN.

ERASTUS, Gr. *Erastos,* "Lovable, Loving."

1. **Erastus** (1), a co-worker of Paul at Ephesus; Paul sends him to Macedonia with Timothy, Ac 19:22.

2. **Erastus** (2), a Christian, city treasurer of Corinth, Rm 16:23; 2 Tm 4:20. To be identified (?) with the preceding.

ERECH, Hb. *'Erek,* one of the capitals of the kingdom of Nimrod, Gn 10:10.

= **Uruk** (1), whose inhabitants Assurbanipal deports to Samaria and elsewhere in the western Transeuphrates region, Ezr 4:9. A town in Lower Mesopotamia on the left bank of the Euphrates. Today *Warka.*

ERI (2), the fifth of the seven sons of Gad, Gn 46:16, whose descendants form the **Erite** clan, Nb 26:16.

ERITE (1), belonging to the clan of: ERI.

ESARHADDON (6), Accad. *Assur-aha-iddîn,* "[The god] Asshur has given a brother," **king of Assyria** (2) (680–669). After the assassination of his father, Sennacherib, who was slain by two of his sons, he becomes king, 2 K 19:37//Tb 1:21//Is 37:38. His generals capture Manasseh, king of Judah, 2 Ch 33:11. The deportation mentioned in Ezr 4:2 is perhaps connected with the Egyptian campaign of Esarhaddon and the capture of Tyre. In his reign Ahikar is restored to his office as chancellor of the exchequer, Tb 1:22, and Tobit is authorized to return home. In the three passages of Tb, Esarhaddon is a corr. for Gr. *Sacherdonos.*

Father of: ASSURBANIPAL.

ESAU (105), Hb. *'Esav,* "Shaggy, hairy," see Gn 25:25; 27:11, elder son of Isaac and Rebekah, twin brother of Jacob, Gn 25:25–26; 28:5; 35:29; Jos 24:4; 1 Ch 1:34; Ml 1:2, a skillful hunter, Gn 25:27–28. He loses his right as first-born to Jacob, Gn 25:29–34; cf. Heb 11:20; 12:16–17, and the paternal blessing connected with it, Gn 27:1–40; cf. 28:6; Rm 9:13. Esau's hatred of Jacob, Gn 27:41–45; cf. 35:1; Ws 10:10, then the reconciliation of the two brothers, Gn 32:4–21; 33:1–17.

Esau is identified with: EDOM.

His wives: ADAH 2; BASEMATH 1; JUDITH 1; MAHALATH 1; OHOLIBAMAH 2.

His sons: ELIPHAZ 1; JALAM; JEUSH 1; KORAH 1; REUEL 1.

ESDRAELON (4), Hellenistic name of: JEZREEL 2.

ESDRIAS (2). See: AZARIAH 23.

ESEK (1), "Quarrel," name of a well over which the shepherds of Gerar and those of Isaac quarrel, Gn 26:20. Linked with the wells of *Sitnah* and *Rehoboth.* Between Gerar and Beersheba.

ESHAN (1), a town in the highlands of Judah, Jos 15:52. 16 km SW of Hebron.

ESHBAAL (2), "Man of Baal." See: ISHBAAL 1.

ESHBAN (2), second of the four sons of Dishon, 1 Ch 1:41//Gn 36:36 (Hb. *Dishan*), son of Seir.

ESHCOL (6), "Cluster (of grapes)," brother of Mamre and Aner, Gn 14:13, 24. **The Valley of Eshcol** (4) is near Hebron: the scouts Moses sends to reconnoiter Canaan report "a cluster of grapes which two of them carried away on a pole," Nb 13:23–24//Dt 1:23–25; Nb 32:9.

ESHEK (1), a Benjaminite, father of three sons, 1 Ch 8:39.

ESHTAOL (8), "Place where they consult [the oracle]" (cf. Saul). A town always associated with: ZORAH.

ESHTEMOA (6), "Place where they hear [the oracle]" (cf. Shemaiah), attached to the Calebite clan, 1 Ch 4:17 (by Ezra), 19 (Eshtemoa is called **Maacathite**). A town in the highlands of Judah, Jos 15: 50; cf. 1 S 30:28, assigned to the Levites of the clan of Kohath, Jos 21:24//1 Ch 6:42. 15 km S of Hebron.

ESHTON (2), of Calebite origin. With it are connected in particular Bethrapha and Irnahash, 1 Ch 4:11–12.

ESLI (1), Gr. *Hesli,* an ancestor of Jesus acc. to Lk 3:25.

ESTHER (59), Accad. *Ishtar,* Pers. *Stareh,* "Star"; acc. to the rabbinic tradition, "The Hidden One," cf. Dt 31:17; **daughter of Abihail** (2), Est 2:15; 9:29.

A Jewish orphan, young and beautiful, deported to Persia, raised by her cousin and tutor, Mordecai, and married to King Ahasuerus, to whom she "did not reveal her race or kindred," 2. Urged by Mordecai, she goes to the king and reveals the plan of Haman, the chancellor, to liquidate the Jews, 3–5. Esther obtains the punishment of Haman, whose house is given to her, and the rehabilitation of the Jews, who are authorized to slaughter their enemies; she establishes by ordinance the feast of Purim, 7–9. The Greek additions to the book put on Esther's lips an impassioned prayer in which the queen links her destiny with that of her people (I/we) and invokes the justice of God, 4:17[k–z].

= **Hadassah** (1), Est 2:7.

ETAM. See: ETHAM 2–4.

ETHAM, Etam, Hb. 1: *'Etam*; 2–4: *'Etam,* "Bird of prey"?

1. **Etham** (4), on the edge of the desert of the same name, Nb 33:8, a stage of the Exodus between Succoth and Migdol, Ex 13:20//Nb 33:6–7. On the eastern frontier of Egypt. Site uncertain.

2. **Rock of Etam** (2), a steep precipice in Judah. Samson withdraws to a cave there, Jg 15:8, 11, 13.

3. **Etam** (2), a town in the highlands of Judah, Jos 15:59 (acc. to Gr.), restored by Rehoboam, 2 Ch 11:6.

See: ABI-ETAM.

4. **Etam** (1). See: ETHER 2.

ETHAN, Hb. *'Etân,* "Constant, permanent" (cf. Jathniel).

1. **Ethan (7) the Ezrahite** (2) is mentioned in 1 K 5:11 with Heman, Calcol, and Darda as among the wise men probably best known in Canaan. Doubtless because of a confusion between Hb. *'Ezrahi,* "native," and *Zerah,* 1 Ch 2:6 makes Ethan one of the five sons of Zerah, a descendant of Judah. Finally, the chronicler associates Ethan with Heman and Asaph. He is thus one of David's three great cantors, who are connected with the three great Levitic lines of Merari, Kohath, and Gershom, 1 Ch 6:29. In this context Ethan is **son of**

Kishi, 6:29, or **Kushaiah,** 15:17. He plays the cymbals when the Ark is being transferred, 15:19. Ps 89 is attributed to Ethan the Ezrahite, v. 1.

In other parallels with Asaph and Heman, Ethan is replaced by JEDUTHUN.

Father of: AZARIAH 1.

2. **Ethan** (1), a Levite of the clan of Gershom, ancestor of Asaph, 1 Ch 6:27.

ETHBAAL (1), Hb. *'Etba'al,* "Baal with him" (cf. Ithiel), **king of the Sidonians** (1), 1 K 16:31. A priest of Astarte who becomes king of Tyre and Sidon. Father of: JEZEBEL 1.

ETHER

1. **Ether** (1), a town in the lowlands of Judah, Jos 15:42. 25 km W of Hebron.

2. **Ether** (1), a town of Simeon, Jos 19:7 (*//Tochen,* 1 Ch 4:32).

= ? **Etam** (1), 1 Ch 4:32, in the list of towns of Simeon. 8 km W of Beersheba.

ETHIOPIA, Gr. name, "[Lands of the] burnt *or* black faces." See: CUSH 1.

ETHIOPIAN. See: CUSH 1.

ETHNAN (1), "Gift, present" (cf. Nathan), son of Helah and Ashhur, a descendant of Caleb, in Judah, 1 Ch 4:7.

ETHNI (1), a descendant of Gershom, son of Levi, and an ancestor of Asaph the cantor, 1 Ch 6:26.

[ETRUSCANS]. See: TIRAS.

EUBULUS (1), "Of good counsel" (cf. Aristobulus; Euergetes; Eumenes; Eunice; Eupator; Eupolemus; Eutychus; Evodia), a Christian of Rome, 2 Tm 4:21.

EUERGETES, a Gr. name, "Benefactor" (cf. Eubulus).

1. **Euergetes** (1), surname of: PTOLEMY 7.

2. **[Euergetes],** surname of: PTOLEMY 3.

EUMENES (1), "Benevolent" (cf. Eubulus), king of Pergamum (197–160). After the defeat of Antiochus the Great at Magnesia on the Sipylus, Eumenes II, whose cavalry had helped the Romans to victory, receives from them "the Indian territory, with Media, Lydia, and some of their best provinces," 1 M 8:8.

EUNICE (1), a name of Gr. origin, "Fine victory" (cf. Eubulus; Andronicus), a Jewish woman of Lystra who becomes a Christian, marries a Greek, and is mother of Timothy, Ac 16:1. Paul praises her faith, 2 Tm 1:5. See: LOIS.

EUPATOR (5), "Born of a noble father" (cf. Eubulus; Antipater), 1 M 6:17; 2 M 2:20; 10:10, 13; 13:1, surname of: ANTIOCHUS 4.

EUPHRATES (25), Hb. *Perat'*, Old Pers. *Ufratu,* called **the River** (17), **the great river** (5): the longest river of western Asia (2,270 km), on the banks of which Babylon is situated, cf. Jr 51:63, and which with the Tigris gives Mesopotamia its name.

Described as one of the four rivers of Paradise, Gn 2:14; cf. Si 24:26, the Euphrates is mentioned chiefly as the NE frontier of the Promised Land, Gn 15:18; Ex 23:31; Dt 1:7; 11:24; Jos 1:4; cf. 1 Ch 5:9, the boundary of Solomon's kingdom, 1 K 5:1//2 Ch 9:26; cf. 1 K 5:4, and as a border of the ideal Palestine, Ps 72:8; 80:12; Si 44:21; Is 27:12; Zc 9:10; conquered by Nebuchadnezzar, 2 K 24:7, and occupied by the Seleucids, 1 M 3:32; the frontier crossed by the repatriates, Is 11:15; 27:12. The troops of Antiochus IV will cross it eastwards, 1 M 3:37, the soldiers of Holofernes westwards, Jdt 2:24; cf. 1:6, and the Parthian warriors who threaten the Roman Empire, also moving westwards, Rv 9:14; 16:12. The River stands for Assyrian power in Is 8:7 and Jr 2:18.

Some regard the *Euphrates* of Jr 13:4–7 as being the *Wadi Farah* N of Anathoth.

Tributary: HABOR.

Cities and towns on the Euphrates:

BABYLON; CARCHEMISH; PETHOR; REHOBOTH-HAN-NAHAR?; TIPHSAH.

EUPOLEMUS (2), "Skilled *or* Fortunate in war" (cf. Eubulus), **son of John [of the family] of Accos** (1), is commissioned by Judas Maccabaeus to go to Rome with Jason, son of Eleazar, to make a treaty of friendship with the Romans, 1 M 8:17 ff.; 2 M 4:11.

Son of: JOHN 20.

EUTYCHUS (1), "Of good fortune, Lucky" (cf. Eubulus; Syntyche; Tychicus. See: FORTUNATUS; GAD), a young man of Troas. Overcome by sleep during a sermon of Paul, he falls from the third story and is killed. Paul restores him to life, Ac 20:7–12, with gestures that recall those of Elijah, 1 K 17:21, and Elisha, 2 K 4:34.

EVE (5), Hb. *Havvah,* "Living"? (cf. Jehiel), "taken from man" and "built" by God, Gn 2:22; cf. 1 Tm 2:13, "a helpmate suitable" for man, "bone from his bones, and flesh from his flesh," Gn 2:19–20, 23; cf. Tb 8:6, "mother of all those who live," Gn 3:20, seduced by the serpent, 2 Co 11:3; 1 Tm 2:14; Gn 3:1–6; cf. Si 25:24, mother of Cain and Abel, Gn 4:1.

With Adam, Eve is the eponymous ancestor of the human race, cf. Gn 1:26–27; 1 Co 11:8–12.

See: ADAM 1.

EVI (2), one of the five Midianite kings, vassals of King Sihon of the Amorites, Jos 13:21, who are conquered and put to death by the Israelites during the Exodus, Nb 31:8.

EVIL-MERODACH (2), a deliberate deformation, "Accursed madman" (cf. Astarte), of the Babyl. *Avil Marduk,* "Man of Marduk" (cf. Merodach), **king of Babylon** (3) (561–560), son and successor of Nebuchadnezzar. He frees Jehoiachin, king of Judah, after a captivity of thirty-seven years, 2 K 25:27–30//Jr 52:31–34.

EVODIA (1), "Good journey" (cf. Eubulus), a Christian woman of Philippi whom Paul exhorts "to come to agreement" with Syntyche. Both women "were a help to me when I was fighting to defend the Good News," Ph 4:2.

EZBAI (1), 1 Ch 11:37, father of: NAARAI. See: PAARAI.

EZBON

1. **Ezbon** (1). See: OZNI.

2. **Ezbon** (1), a Benjaminite, first of the five sons of Bela, head of a family and a fighting man, 1 Ch 7:7.

EZEKIEL, Jehezkel, Hb. *Yehezq'el,* "May God make strong *or* obstinate," see Ezk 3:8–9 (cf. Hizki).

1. **Ezekiel** (3) **son of Buzi** (1), Ezk 1:3, a priest of Jerusalem, taken to Babylonia probably during the first deportation under Jehoiachin of Judah in 598. In 593, Ezk 1:2 the breakthrough of the glory of Yahweh into his life turns this simple priest into a prophet, 2:5; 3:10–11, a "sentry to the House of Israel," 3:17; 33:2, 7, commissioned to "warn the [wicked man] to renounce his evil ways," 3:18, and to "confront Jerusalem with her filthy crimes," 16:2. The fall of the city, of which Ezekiel learns from a fugitive, 33:21, transforms the preacher of condemnation into a preacher of salvation.

Ezekiel is named only in Si 49:8–9 and twice in the book that bears his name (1:3; 24:24), but the book is nonetheless a very "personal" one. Starting in 1:4, the prophet constantly speaks in the first person and reports the words that Yahweh speaks to him, a "son of man." This last expression (92×), 2:1, 8; 3:1, 4, 10, 17; etc., emphasizes the distance separating man's weakness from the "glory of Yahweh," 1:28; 3:23; 8:4; 10:4; 43:2. Ezekiel several times calls attention to the grip of the hand or the Spirit of God: "the hand of the Lord came (fell) on me," 1:3 (Gr.); 3:22; 8:1; 33:22; 37:1; 40:1, "the spirit came into me," 2:2;

3:24, "fell on me," 11:5, "lifted me up," 3:12, 14; 8:3; 11:1, 24; 43:5. The prophet turns the spotlight on himself as he tells of the trials God sends him (for example, his muteness, 3:24–27; the death of his wife, 24:16–17) and of the symbolic actions he is bidden to perform in mime (for example, the siege of Jerusalem, 4:1–5:17; the departure of the deportees, 12:1–16; the distress of the exile, 12:17–20; the reunion of the two kingdoms, 37:15–28). He describes his astonishing visions in detail: the chariot of Yahweh, 1:4–28; cf. 10; the book he eats, 2; the sins and punishment of Jerusalem, 8–10; the dry and then revitalized bones, 37:1–14; the new Jerusalem with its temple and ideal worship and well as a renewed Palestine, 40–48.

These final chapters, "the Torah of Ezekiel," make this prophet a first-rate witness to the influence that the priestly class and tradition will have from the time of the exile on. Ezekiel also introduces a new literary genre, the apocalyptic, cf. the colossal struggle of Gog, king of Magog, with the people of God, 38–39. Ezekiel's message effects above all a spiritualization of religious life: emphasis on personal responsibility, 14:12–23; 18, ritual as valuable because of the sentiments that inspire it, interior renewal of heart and spirit, 11:9; 18:31; 36:26–27, an emphasis, this, that will lead to worship in spirit, Jn 4:24.

2. **Jehezkel** (1), a priest, leader of the twentieth class of priests, 1 Ch 24:16.

EZEM (3), "Bone"?, a town in the Negeb of Judah, Jos 15:29, having belonged to the sons of Simeon, Jos 19:3//1 Ch 4:29. Perhaps 25 km SE of Beersheba.

EZER, Hb. *'Ezer,* "Succor, help" (cf. Abiezer; Ahiezer; Azarel; Azariah; Azor; Azriel; Azrikam; Ebenezer; Eleazar; Eliezer; Ezra; Ezri; Hadadezer; Iezer; Jazer; Joezer; Lazarus; Romamti-ezer). Compare with *Eder*.

1. **Ezer** (5), sixth of the sons of Seir the Horite, Gn 36:21//1 Ch 1:28, and of the chiefs of the Horites, Gn 36:30. He has three sons, Gn 36:27//1 Ch 1:42.

2. **Ezer** (1), one of the sons of Hur, the first-born of Ephrathah and Caleb, 1 Ch 4:4.

3. **Ezer** (1), a son of Ephraim, 1 Ch 7:21.

4. **Ezer** (1), a Gadite who rallies to David before the latter becomes king, 1 Ch 12:10 (cf. vv. 9–16).

5. **Ezer son of Jeshua** (1), ruler of Mizpah, a volunteer in rebuilding the wall of Jerusalem, Ne 3:19.

6. **Ezer** (1), a priest, takes part in the ceremony of the dedication of the Jerusalem wall, Ne 12:42.

EZION-GEBER (7), (cf. Geber), "which is near Elath on the shores of the Red Sea," 1 K 9:26, at the head of the Gulf of Aqaba. A stage of the Exodus, Nb 33:35–36; Dt 2:8. A naval dockyard and commercial port under Solomon, 1 K 9:26//2 Ch 8:17, which Jehoshaphat attempts unsuccessfully to revitalize, 1 K 22:49//2 Ch 20:36. At one period the town was confused with: ELATH.

EZRA, Ezrah, Hb. *'Ezrah* and Aram. *'Ezra'*, "[God is] helper" (cf. Ezer).

1. **Ezrah** (1), an ancestor of groups connected with Caleb, 1 Ch 4:17–18.

2. **Ezra** (25), **priest** (8), **scribe** (10), a descendant of Aaron through Zadok, Ezr 7:1–5, "a scribe versed in the Law of Moses," 7:6, a man who "had devoted himself to the study of the Law of Yahweh, to practising it and to teaching Israel its laws and customs," 7:10–11, secretary for Jewish affairs, 7:12, 22, at the court of the Persian king Artaxerxes (I or II, for the chronology of Ezra and Nehemiah raises difficult problems). As bearer of a letter from Artaxerxes he travels from Babylon to Jerusalem with a company of about 1,500 fellow Jews, 8:1–14, who are joined on the way by 258 Levites and "oblates," 8:15–20. He restores the worship of Yahweh, 8:31–

35, dissolves the marriages of Jews with foreign women, 9:1–10, 44; cf. Ne 9:1–2, proceeds to a solemn reading of the Law and the celebration of the feast of Tabernacles, Ne 8:1–18. The chronicler makes Ezra a contemporary of the priest Joiakim, son of Jeshua, Ne 12:26 (cf. 3 following), and has Ezra taking part in the procession for the dedication of the Jerusalem wall, Ne 12:36 (cf. 4 following).

3. **Ezra** (2), a priest who returns from the exile with Zerubbabel, Ne 12:1, head of a priestly family in the time of the high priest Joiakim, Ne 12:13. To be compared with: AZARIAH 9.

4. **Ezra** (1), a priest, a trumpeter at the dedication of the wall of Jerusalem, Ne 12:33.

EZRAH. See: EZRA 1.

EZRAHITE (3), "Native *or* [Son] of Zerah" (cf. Zerah), 1 K 5:11; Ps 89:1, see: ETHAN 1; Ps 88:1, see: HEMAN.

EZRI (1), "My help" (cf. Ezer), **son of Chelub** (1), commissioner for the agricultural workers, 1 Ch 27:26.

F

FAIR HAVENS (1), Gr. *Kaloi Limenes,* near the town of Lasea, a bay on the southern coast of the island of Crete. Paul stops there on his voyage to Rome, Ac 27:8.

FEAR OF ISAAC. See: KINSMAN OF ISAAC.

FELIX (9), "Happy," a freedman, brother of Pallas, Agrippina's favorite, procurator of Judaea (52 to 59 or 60), husband of: DRUSILLA. It is to him, at Caesarea, that Lysias sends Paul, who has just been arrested in Jerusalem, Ac 23:24–35. Paul appears before the tribunal of Felix, 24:1–22. A little later Felix and his wife Drusilla hear Paul speaking "on the subject of faith in Christ Jesus," 24:24–25. He leaves Paul in prison, in the hope of receiving a bribe from him and in order to please the Jews. He is succeeded by Porcius Festus, 24:26–27; 25:14.

FELLED TREE-TRUNK (Gate of the) (1), Hb. *Shalleket,* a gate of the temple in Jerusalem, 1 Ch 26:16. Unidentified.

[FERTILE CRESCENT], an area in the shape of a crescent, starting from Egypt, covering Palestine and Syria, and curving back SE between the Tigris and the Euphrates, and ending at the Persian Gulf.

FESTUS (13), "Festive, merry" (cf. Haggi). **Porcius** (1) **Festus,** procurator of Judaea (60–62), succeeds Felix, Ac 24:27. He rejects the request of the Jewish authorities that Paul be transferred from Caesarea to Jerusalem but yields to Paul's demand that as a Roman citizen he be tried by an imperial court in Rome, 25:1–12. He informs King Agrippa II of Paul's case and presents the prisoner to the king, 25:13–24; 26:24–25, 32.

FIELD OF BLOOD. See: HAKELDAMA.

FIELD OF SIDES. See: ZIDDIM 2.

FIELDS-OF-THE-FOREST (1), Hb. *Sede Ya'ar* (cf. Jaar), Ps 132:6, a poetic reference to: KIRIATH-JEARIM.

FISH (Gate) (4), Hb. *Dagim,* on the northern side of Jerusalem, west of the Tower of Hananel. There was doubtless a fish market, supplied perhaps by Tyrians, near this gate. The Fish Gate, Zp 1:10, is restored under King Manasseh, 2 Ch 33:14, and rebuilt under Nehemiah, Ne 3:3; 12:39.

FIVE CITIES. See: PENTAPOLIS 1.

FLEEING SERPENT (1), Hb. *Bariah,* Jb 26:13. See: LEVIATHAN.

FOOTHILLS (1), Hb. *'shdt,* last stage of the Exodus before the entry into Canaan, Dt 33:2; cf. 3:17.

FORESKINS (Hill of) (1), Hb. *Gib'at ha-'Aralôt,* acc. to Jos 5:3, the place at Gilgal where the Israelites were circumcised as they entered the Promised Land. Perhaps a place where there was a bed of flints.

FOREST OF LEBANON (Hall of the) (6), Hb. *Ya'ar ha-Lebanôn* (cf. Jaar; Lebanon), beside the temple in Jerusalem, a building erected by Solomon that is named after the great pillared hall with its forty-five columns made of cedar from Lebanon; it may have served as an arsenal, 1 K 7:2; 10:17, 21//2 Ch 9:16, 20; Is 22:8.

FORTUNATUS (1), "Fortunate" (see Eutychus), a Christian of Corinth who, with Stephanas and Achaicus, goes to Ephesus, probably in order to bring Paul the letter from the Christians of Corinth, 1 Co 16:17; cf. 7:1.

FORUM OF APPIUS (1), a town 65 km S of Rome. Christians from Rome meet Paul there, Ac 28:15.

FOUNDATION (Gate of) (1), Hb. *Yesod,* a gate of the temple, 2 Ch 23:5.

FOUNTAIN (Gate) (3), Hb. *'Ayîn* (cf. Ain), on the southeastern side of Jerusalem, on the route Nehemiah follows during his nocturnal inspection of the wall, Ne 2:14; repaired by Shallum, son of Col-hozeh, 3:15; on the route of the procession for the dedication of the wall, 12:37.

FREEDMEN (1), Gr. *Libertinoi,* Jews freed from slavery or their descendants (in 63 B.C. some Jews had been sold into slavery at Rome). They have a synagogue in Jerusalem. Members of this synagogue debate with Stephen, Ac 6:9.

FULLER

1. **Fuller's Spring** (2), Hb. *'En Rogel* (cf. Rogelim), on the border of Judah and Benjamin, outside Jerusalem, 2 S 17:17, distinct from the spring of Gihon, 1 K 1:9 (cf. vv. 33–45). At the junction of the valleys of the Kidron and of Hinnom, 300 m S of Siloam. Today *Bir Ayyub* (Well of Job).

2. **Fuller's Field** (3), Hb. *Sedeh Kobes,* near Fuller's Spring, 2 K 18:17//Is 36:2; 7:3.

FURNACES (Tower of the) (1), Hb. *Tannûrim,* at the NW corner of Jerusalem, repaired under Nehemiah, Ne 3:11; on the route of the procession for the dedication of the wall, 12:38. Probably identical with the tower, cf. 2 Ch 26:9, built by King Uzziah at the Gate of the: CORNER.

G

GAAL (9), "Beetle," **son of Ebed** (5), a Canaanite adventurer, perhaps a Shechemite; he leads a movement of rebellion by the Shechemites against Abimelech, whose representative at Shechem is Zebul. A battle between Gaal and Abimelech ends in the defeat of Gaal, Jg 9:26–41.

GAASH
1. **Mount Gaash** (2), a mountain in the SW of the highlands of Ephraim; burial place of Joshua, Jos 24:30//Jg 2:9.
2. **Wadis of Gaash** (2), native place of: HIDDAI.

GABAEL, "God is raised up" (cf. Geba), Lat. *Gabelus.*
1. **Gabael** (1), a Naphtalite, an ancestor of Tobit and Tobias, Tb 1:1.
2. **Gabael** (7), **brother of Gabrias** (1), Tb 1:14, or **son of Gabrias** (1), 4:20, cousin of Tobit, 9:6. Tobit had left once a deposit of silver with Gabael in Media. Tobias' journey to recover this silver is one of the themes of the Book of Tobit, Tb 4:1–3, 20; 5:1–6; 9:1–6; 10:2.

[GABELENE]. See: GEBAL 2.

GABBATHA (1), Aram. "Height" (cf. Jogbehah). See: PAVEMENT.

GABRIAS (2), (cf. Geber), father or brother of: GABAEL 2.

GABRIEL (4), "Man of God *or* God is strong" (cf. Geber), the angel sent to explain Daniel's visions to him, Dn 8:16–26; 9:21–23, and to tell Zechariah of the birth of John the Baptist, Lk 1:11–20, and Mary of the birth of Jesus, Lk 1:26–38.

GAD, "Fortune, Luck" (cf. Azgad; Baal-gad; Gaddi; Gaddiel; Gadi; Gadites; Migdal-gad. See Eutychus).
1. **Gad** (1), an Aramaean god of fortune, Is 65:11.
2. **Gad** (59), son of Jacob and of Zilpah, servant of Leah, who says at his birth: "What good fortune!", Gn 30:10–11, eponymous ancestor of a tribe of Israel. Note the parallel between his name and that of his uterine brother, Asher: "Happiness." The sons and clans of Gad are listed in Gn 46:16; Nb 26:15–18, and in a list peculiar to the chronicler and that may derive from a census under Jeroboam II, 1 Ch 5:11–17. The number of men able to bear arms is given in Nb 1:25 and 26:15.

The territory of Gad is described in Jos 13:24–29; cf. 1 Ch 5:16; it extends east of the Jordan between the Arnon to the south and the Jabbok to the north, and its towns are listed in Nb 32:34–36. In Jg 5:17 the tribe of Gad is designated by its territory, Gilead. The establishment of the three Transjordanian tribes, Gad between Reuben to the south and Manasseh to the north, is narrated in Nb 32 and Jos 22; cf. Dt 3:12–16; 4:43//Jos 20:8; Dt 29:7; Jos 1:12; 4:12; 12:6; 13:8;

18:7. Gad increases its territory at the expense of Reuben, Dt 33:20–21; cf. 33:6. Occupying fertile land suited for flocks but near the desert, it retains the nomadic way of life, obliged as it is to defend itself against raids by nomads, Gn 49:19; cf. 1 Ch 5:11, 22; Jr 49:1. Conquered by Hazael of Damascus in the time of Jehu, 2 K 10:32, the three tribes are deported a century later by the Assyrians, 1 Ch 5:26. Some Gadites are among the first to rally to David, 1 Ch 12: 9–15.

Gad in the lists of the tribes: List, pages 410–11.

Native land of: BANI 1.

3. **Gad** (13), a prophet and the king's seer. Adviser to David at the beginning of his life as a wanderer, 1 S 22:5, he intervenes especially in the matter of the census, 2 S 24:11–17//1 Ch 21:7–17, and in the building of the altar on the threshing floor of Araunah, 2 S 24:18–19//1 Ch 21:18–19. The chronicler also refers to an "Annals of Gad the seer," 1 Ch 29:29, and to his zeal for the cultus, 2 Ch 29:25.

[GADARA]. See: GADARENES.

GADARENES (Country of the) (1). The center of it is at Gadara, a town of the Decapolis, 10 km SE of the Sea of Chinnereth. Jesus meets two demoniacs there, Mt 8:28.

GADDI, "My fortune" (cf. Gad).

1. **Gaddi son of Susi** (1), leader of a clan of Manasseh, sent by Moses as representative of his tribe in the reconnaissance of Canaan, Nb 13:11.

2. **Gaddi** (1), 1 M 2:2, a surname of John Maccabaeus. See: JOHN 19.

GADDIEL (1), "My fortune is God" (cf. Gad), **son of Sodi** (1), leader of a clan of Zebulun, sent by Moses as representative of his tribe in the reconnaissance of Canaan, Nb 13:10.

GADI (2), "Of Gad" (cf. Gad), father of king: MENAHEM 1.

GADITES (16), Nb 34:14; Dt 3:12, 16; 4:43; 29:7; Jos 1:12; 12:6; 13:8; 22:1; 2 S 23:36; 2 K 10:33; 1 Ch 5:18, 26; 12:9, 38; 26:32, belonging to the tribe of: GAD 2.

GAHAM (1), "Flame"?, one of the twelve sons of Nahor, brother of Abraham, and of his concubine Reumah, Gn 22:24.

GAHAR (2), "[Born in a year] poor in rain," head of a family of "oblates" who return from the exile, Ezr 2:47//Ne 7: 49.

GAIUS, Gr. form of Lat. *Caius*.

1. **Gaius, a Macedonian** (1), a traveling companion of Paul and a prisoner of the rioters at Ephesus, Ac 19:29. See the next entry.

2. **Gaius from Doberus** (Gr.: *from Derbe*) (1), a traveling companion of Paul. If *Doberus* is retained, this Gaius is perhaps identical with the preceding. Acc. to the Gr. text, he would be from Lycaonia, Ac 20:4.

3. **Gaius** (2), of Corinth, baptized by Paul, 1 Co 1:14, receives Paul into his home, Rm 16:23.

4. **Gaius** (1), a Christian believer to whom the third letter of John is addressed, 3 Jn 1.

GALAL, "Dung heap, Dung" (cf. Gilgal).

1. **Galal** (1), a Levite living in Jerusalem after the exile, 1 Ch 9:15.

2. **Galal** (1), a Levite, son of Jeduthun and ancestor of: OBADIAH 11.

GALATIA, Gr. *Galatia*. The same word is used for *Gaul*.

1. **Galatia** (3) in Asia Minor: either the Roman province created in 25 B.C. and extending from Pamphylia to Pontus and from the Roman province of Asia to Cappadocia, 1 P 1:1; or rather the region in the northern part of the province of Galatia around Ancyra (the present-day Ankara), occupied since 300 B.C. by a people of Celtic origin, the Galatians.

Paul passes through the **Galatian country** (2) on his second missionary journey, Ac 16:6. An illness that lengthens his stay there gives him an opportunity to preach the Gospel, cf. Ga 4:13–15. He travels there again on his third missionary journey, Ac 18:23. It is probably at the end of his stay in Ephesus that he writes the letter to the Galatians, Ga 1:2; 3:1, a strong letter: against the Judaizers who are perverting the Gospel, Paul states that salvation is not won by carrying out the terms of the Law but is received through faith in Jesus Christ. The churches of Galatia contribute to the great collection for the impoverished Church of Jerusalem, 1 Co 16:1.

Regions of the Roman province: LYCAONIA; PISIDIA.

Towns: ANTIOCH 2; DERBE; ICONIUM; LYSTRA.

2. **Galatia** (1), either the preceding or, rather, **Gaul,** 2 Tm 4:10. In 1 M 8:12 the reference is doubtless to the Cisalpine Gauls and in 2 M 8:20 perhaps to Gallic mercenaries.

GALATIAN (4), Gr. *Galatēs,* 2 M 8:20; Ga 3:1; Gr. *Galatikos,* Ac 16:6; 18:23. See: GALATIA 1 and 2.

GALEED (2), Hb. *Galʿed,* popular etymology "Heap [of stones for a] witness" (cf. Gilgal; Joed), Aram. *Yegar-sahaduta,* boundary between Laban and Jacob, Aram and Israel, Gn 31:47–48, cf. v. 52.

= **Jegar-sahadutha** (1), Gn 31:47.

See: GILEAD 1.

GALILEAN (11), Mt 26:69; Mk 14:70; Lk 13:1–2; 22:59; 23:6; Jn 4:45; Ac 1:11; 2:7; 5:37, of or from: GALILEE.

GALILEE (81), Hb. *Galil,* "District" (cf. Gilgal), a region west of the Sea of Chinnereth and north of the plain of Jezreel, corresponding to the territory of the tribes of Zebulun and Naphtali, called *Galilee* [or: *province*] *of the nations,* or *heathen Galilee,* Is 8:23//Mt 4:15; 1 M 5:15, a designation explained by the presence of foreigners who are there owing to invasions and deportations, 2 K 15:29. Galilee is already mentioned in 1 K 9:11 where Solomon "gave Hiram twenty towns in the land of Galilee," and in Jos 12:23 (Gr.). The northern part is called **Upper Galilee,** Tb 1:2; cf. 1:5; Jdt 1:8. In the time of the Maccabees, Simon conducts a campaign there to free the Jews of Galilee and bring them back to Judaea, 1 M 5:14–23; cf. 1 M 12:47–49.

Galilee is connected especially with the Gospel. Though born in Judaea, Jesus spends his entire hidden life at Nazareth in Galilee, Mt 2:22–23; 3:13. It is in the area that is under Herod's jurisdiction, Mk 6:21; Lk 23:6–7, and ready for revolt against the occupier, cf. Ac 5:37; Lk 13:1, that he begins his ministry, Mt 4:12–13; Lk 23:5; Ac 10:37, and exercises it most of the time, traveling through the region in every direction, Mt 4:23; Jn 7:1, rousing the crowds, Mk 1:28; Lk 5:17. Consequently, he is called **the Galilean,** Mt 26:69; Lk 23:6, with overtones of scorn for the ignorance of the people in that area, Jn 7:41–42, 52. It is in Galilee that Jesus chooses his Apostles, Mk 14:70; Mt 26:69–73; Lk 22:59; Jn 1:43; Ac 1:11; 2:7; 13:31, and meets the women who aid him until his death, Lk 23:49, 53. It is there that he meets his Apostles after his resurrection, Mt 26:32 //Mk 14:28; Mt 28:7//Mk 16:7 (cf. Lk 24:6); Mt 28:10, 16.

Sea of Galilee: CHINNERETH *b.*

Towns: BETHSAIDA 1; CANA 2; CAPERNAUM; KEDESH 2; NAZARETH; TIBERIAS.

Tetrarch: HEROD 2.

Galilean: JUDAS 11.

GALLIM, "Pile of rocks" (cf. Gilgal).

1. **Gallim** (1), acc. to the Gr. a town in the highlands of Judah, Jos 15:59. Today *Beit Jala.*

2. **Gallim** (1), a town in Benjamin, 1 S 25:44.

= **Bath-gallim** (1), Is 10:30. Perhaps *Kh. Kaʿkul,* 4 km N of Jerusalem.

Native place of: PALTIEL 2.

GALLIO (3), brother of Seneca the philosopher. Proconsul of Achaia (51–52 or 52–53), he refuses to get involved in the religious conflict between the Jews of

Corinth and Paul and has Sosthenes, the synagogue leader, beaten, Ac 18:12–17.

GAMALIEL, "My reward is God" (cf. Beth-gamul; Gamul; Gemalli).

1. **Gamaliel son of Pedahzur** (5), leader of the tribe of Manasseh, Nb 2:20; 7:54; 10:23; in charge of the census of his tribe, Nb 11:10; brings the offering for the dedication of the altar on the eighth day, Nb 7:54–59.

2. **Gamaliel** (2) the Elder, a Pharisee, "a doctor of the Law and respected by the whole people"; his intervention in the Sanhedrin leads to the release of the Apostles, Ac 5:34. Teacher of Saul of Tarsus, Ac 22:3.

GAMUL (1), "Satiated" (cf. Gamaliel), leader of the twenty-second class of priests, 1 Ch 24:17.

GAREB

1. **Gareb from Jattir** (corr. of Hb. *the Ithrite*) (2), one of David's champions, 2 S 23:38//1 Ch 11:40.

2. **Hill of Gareb** (1), a height that Jeremiah locates at or near Jerusalem, Jr 31:39. Otherwise unknown.

GARMITE (1), 1 Ch 4:19. See: KEILAH.

GASHMU (1), another form of: GESHEM.

GASIN (1), a town on the border of Judah and Benjamin, Jos 18:15 (acc. to Gr.; Hb. *west*). Some km W of Jerusalem.

GATAM (3), Hb. *Ga'tam,* one of the sons of Eliphaz, called sons of Adah, Esau's wife, Gn 36:11–12//1 Ch 1:36; one of the chiefs (or clans) of Edom, Gn 36:16.

GATE BETWEEN THE TWO WALLS (3). See: BETWEEN THE TWO WALLS.

GATH, Gr. *Geth,* "Press" (cf. Gath-hepher; Gath-rimmon; Gethsemane; Gittaim; Moresheth-gath).

1. **Gath** (30) **in Philistia** (1), an ancient fief of the Anakim, Jos 11:22 (see: GOLIATH), a town in the Philistine Pentapolis, Jos 13:1; 1 S 7:14, whose inhabitants are afflicted with tumors after capturing the Ark, 1 S 5:8–9; 6:17–18, where David finds refuge, 1 S 21:11–16; 27:1–12; cf. Ps 56:1, whither the slaves of Shimei flee, 1 K 2:39–41. The inhabitants, ready to rejoice at the death of Saul, 2 S 1:20; cf. Mi 1:10, become vassals of David, 2 S 6:10–11//1 Ch 13:13; 2 S 15:18–22; 1 Ch 18:1. The town is rebuilt by Rehoboam, 2 Ch 11:8, taken by Hazael of Damascus, 2 K 12:18. "Gath in Philistia" falls under the onslaught of Sargon in 77, Am 6:2. 25 km E of Ashkelon.

King: ACHISH.

Native place of: GOLIATH; ITTAI 1; OBED-EDOM.

2. **Gath** (3), a town associated with Ephraim, 1 Ch 7:21, and with Benjamin, 8:13, razed by Uzziah, 2 Ch 26:6.

= **Gittaim** (2), inhabited by Benjaminites from Beeroth, 2 S 4:3, reoccupied by Benjaminites after the exile, Ne 11:33.

GATH-HEPHER (2), "Press of the well" (cf. Gath; Hepher 1), a town on the border of Zebulun, Jos 19:13. 5 km NE of Nazareth.

Native place of the prophet: JONAH 1.

GATH-RIMMON (4), "Press of the pomegranate" (cf. Gath; Rimmon 1–4), a town of Dan, Jos 19:45, assigned to Levites of the clan of Kohath, Jos 21:24 (in Dan)//1 Ch 6:54 (in Ephraim).

Hb. *Gath-rimmon* in Jos 21:25 is probably to be corrected to *Jibleam.*

[GAUL]. See: GALATIA 2.

[GAULANITIS], Gr. name for the region of: GOLAN.

GAZA (22), Hb. *'Azzah,* "The strong one [fem.]"?, an ancient fief of the Anakim, Jos 11:22. Most important town in the Philistine Pentapolis, Jos 13:3; Jr 25:20, located in the extreme SW of Palestine, Gn 10:19; Dt 2:23; 2 K 18:8, and of the lands from the Euphrates westward, 1 K 5:4. Assigned to Judah, Jos 15:47, but only in theory, cf. Jg 1:18–19; Jos 10:41;

threatened by Midianite invasions, Jg 6:4. Samson escapes from the people of Gaza by carrying off the gates of the town, Jg 16:1–3; later on, a prisoner at Gaza, Jg 16:21, he dies there while taking revenge on the Philistines. When the Ark is released, the people of Gaza pay a golden tumor in reparation, 1 S 6:17–18. Gaza is the object of threats from the prophets, Am 1:6–7; Zp 2:4; Jr 47:1, 5; Zc 9:5. The "fortified city" of Dn 11:15 perhaps refers to it. Jonathan Maccabaeus besieges the city but spares it, 1 M 11:61–62.

On the road from Jerusalem to Gaza, Philip the deacon baptizes the Ethiopian eunuch, Ac 8:26.

In 1 M 13:43 read Gr. *Gazara* (that is, Gezer) for Gr. *Gaza.*

GAZEZ (2), "[Born at the time of the] shearing"?, son or grandson of Ephah, concubine of Caleb, 1 Ch 2:46.

GAZZAM (2), head of a family of "oblates" who return from the exile, Ezr 2:48 //Ne 7:51.

GEBA (20), Hb. *Geba'* or *Gaba',* "Hill" (cf. Gabael; Gibeah; Gibeon; Gilboa), **of Benjamin** (3). A town in Benjamin, Jos 18:24, assigned to the Levites of the clan of Kohath, Jos 21:19//1 Ch 6:45. Near Gibeah (to the SW), Jg 20:33–34, Michmash (to the NE), 1 S 13:16; 14:5, and Ramah (to the NW), Is 10:29. A border town, 1 K 15:22//2 Ch 16:6 (kingdom of Asa), 2 K 23:8 (kingdom of Josiah); Zc 14:10. Some people of Geba are among those returning from exile, Ezr 2:26//Ne 7:30, and the town of Geba is then reoccupied by Benjaminites, Ne 11:31. Some Levite cantors from the countryside around Geba take part in the dedication of the Jerusalem wall, Ne 12:29. The notice in 1 Ch 8:6 may be a transformed version of the story in Jg 20. Holofernes camps between Geba and Scythopolis, Jdt 3:10.

Many corrections are proposed of *Geba* to *Gibeah* 1, in Jg 20:10; 1 S 13:3, to *Gibeon* in 2 S 5:25, and of Hb. *Gibeah* to *Geba* in 1 S 13:2, 15; 14:2, 16. Today *Jeba',* 10 km N of Jerusalem.

GEBAL

1. **Gebal** (1), "Hill," a Phoenician town, more or less dependent economically on Tyre, Ezk 27:9. Its inhabitants, the **Giblites,** take part in the building of Solomon's temple, 1 K 5:32. The **country of the Gebalites** is part of the ideal Promised Land, Jos 13:5. Gebal is the later *Byblos* of the Greeks. On the Lebanese coast, 30 km N of Beirut. Today *Jubail.*

2. **Gebal** (1), that is, *Gabalene,* a district of Idumaea to the north of Petra, Ps 83:7.

GEBALITES (1). See: GEBAL 1.

GEBER, "The virile one, The man" (cf. Ezion-geber; Gabrias; Gabriel; Gibbar).

1. **Geber son of Uri** (1), prefect of Solomon's twelfth district, 1 K 4:19.

2. **Son of Geber** (1), administrator of Solomon's sixth district, 1 K 4:13.

GEBIM (1), "Cisterns," an unidentified town N of Jerusalem, whose inhabitants flee before the invader from the north, Is 10:31.

GEDALIAH, "Yah has magnified" (cf. Giddalti; Giddel; Haggadol; Igdaliah; Magdala; Migdal-eder; Migdalel; Migdal-gad; Migdal-shechem; Migdol).

1. **Gedaliah** (2), of the sons of Jeduthun, leader of the second class of cantors, 1 Ch 25:3, 9.

2. **Gedaliah** (1), ancestor of the prophet: ZEPHANIAH 2.

3. **Gedaliah son of Pashhur** (1), one of the four ministers of King Zedekiah, who, during the siege of Jerusalem by the Chaldaeans, have Jeremiah thrown into a cistern, accusing him of demoralizing with his prophecies the last defenders of the city, Jr 38:1–6.

4. **Gedaliah** (27), **son of Ahikam** (16),

son of Shaphan (7), appointed governor of Judah by the king of Babylon in 587; he is for loyal collaboration with the occupier, 2 K 25:22–24//Jr 40:7–12, a protector and friend of Jeremiah, Jr 39:14; 40:5–6; 43:6. Baalis, king of the Ammonites, foments a plot against him, but Gedaliah refuses to credit this, Jr 40:13–16; he is assassinated by Ishmael, 2 K 25:25//Jr 41:1–3; cf. 41:4–18.

5. **Gedaliah** (1), a priest, married to a foreign wife, whom he puts away, Ezr 10:18.

GEDER (1), "Enclosure of stones" (cf. Beth-geder; Gederah; Gederoth; Gederothaim; Gedor 1–2), an unidentified Canaanite town, Jos 12:13. Identical (?) with: GEDERAH, GEDEROTH, GEDEROTHAIM, or GEDOR.

Native place of: BAAL-HANAN 2.

GEDERAH (2), "Enclosure" (cf. Geder), a town in the lowlands of Judah, Jos 15:36, in which potters, the descendants of Shelah, reside, 1 Ch 4:23.

GEDEROTH (3), "The enclosures" (cf. Geder), a town in the lowlands of Judah, Jos 15:41; taken by the Philistines in the time of Ahaz, 2 Ch 28:18.

Native place, 1 Ch 12:7, of: JOZABAD 2.

GEDEROTHAIM (1), "The two enclosures" (cf. Geder), a town in the lowlands of Judah, Jos 15:36 (perhaps a dittography for *Gederah*).

GEDOR, Hb. 1–2: "Enclosure" (cf. Geder); 3: "Pock-marked."

1. **Gedor** (4), a town in the highlands of Judah, Jos 15:58, formerly Calebite, 1 Ch 4:4, 18. *Gerar* is probably to be read with the Gr. instead of Hb. *Gedor* in 1 Ch 4:39. 13 km SW of Bethlehem.

See: BETH-GADER.

2. **Gedor** (1), a town in Benjamin, 1 Ch 12:8. Native place of: ZEBADIAH 3.

3. **Gedor** (2), a Benjaminite of Gibeon, 1 Ch 8:31//9:37.

GEHARASHIM (1). See: CRAFTSMEN (VALLEY OF THE).

GEHAZI (12), "With protruding eyes"?, Gr. *Giezi,* servant of the prophet Elisha. The latter sends him to the woman of Shunem, then to the bed of her son, 2 K 4:12–36; cf. 8:45. He is struck with leprosy because of his duplicity and greed in connection with the healing of Naaman, 2 K 5:20–27.

GEMALLI (1), (cf. Gamaliel), father of: AMMIEL 1.

GEMARIAH, "Yah has brought to term" (cf. Gomer).

1. **Gemariah son of Hilkiah** (1). See: ELASAH 3.

2. **Gemariah** (4), **son of Shaphan** (3), one of the ministers of King Jehoiakim who are overwhelmed when they hear the book of Jeremiah's oracles, and who endeavor, unsuccessfully, to keep the king from burning it, Jr 36:10–12, 25.

Father of: MICAIAH 13.

GENNAEUS (1), Gr. *Gennaios*, "Noble, chivalrous," father of: APOLLONIUS 3.

GENNESARET (4), 1 M 11:67; Mt 14:34//Mk 6:53; Lk 5:1. See: CHINNERETH.

GENUBATH (2), "Stolen"?, son of the Edomite prince Hadad and of the sister of Tahpenes, raised at the court of the Pharaoh, 1 K 11:20.

GERA, "Who has taken refuge [with the deity]" (cf. Gershom; Gur-baal).

1. **Gera** (4), a son of Benjamin, Gn 46:21, or son of Bela, son of Benjamin, 1 Ch 8:3, 5. Father of: EHUD 1.

2. **Gera** (1), a Benjaminite, one of the sons of Ehud who are heads of families among the inhabitants of Geba who migrate to Manahath, 1 Ch 8:7.

3. **Gera** (1), a Benjaminite, father of: SHIMEI 6.

GERAR (10), a border town between Palestine and Egypt, Gn 10:19, where Abraham stays, 20:1–18, as does Isaac, who digs some wells in the neighborhood, 26. The town seems to have been a Philistine possession, 26:1, 8. Acc. to

1 Ch 4:39 (Gr.; Hb. *Gedor*), the Simeonites look for pastures in the area. Asa of Judah pursues the Cushites as far as Gerar, 2 Ch 14:11–12. Halfway between Gaza and Beersheba.

King: ABIMELECH 1.

[GERASA]. See: GERASENES.

GERASENES (Country of the) (1), Mk 5:1//Lk 8:26, 37, the center of which is Gerasa, a town of the Decapolis. 55 km SE of the Sea of Chinnereth. Today *Jerash*.

GERIZIM (6) and **Ebal,** two mountains overlooking the city of Shechem, the first to the south (868 m), the second to the north (938 m). After crossing the Jordan, Joshua builds an altar on Mount Ebal, offers a sacrifice, and reads the Law to the people who are standing "half of them in front of Mount Gerizim and half in front of Mount Ebal," Jos 8:30–33; cf. Dt 11:29–30; 27:4 (Hb. *Ebal;* var. *Gerizim*), 12–13. From Mount Gerizim Jotham ridicules the kingship of Abimelech, Jg 9:7. From these mountains Abimelech launches his army against rebellious Shechem, Jg 9:36. In the time of the Maccabees, Antiochus Epiphanes installs Andronicus as his representative "on Mount Gerizim" (that is, probably at Shechem), 2 M 5:23, and desecrates the Samaritan temple on Gerizim by dedicating it to Zeus, Patron of Strangers, 2 M 6:2.

The Samaritan woman reminds Jesus of the worship traditionally offered on this mountain by her people, Jn 4:20–21.

See: NAVEL OF THE LAND; ZALMON 2.

[GERRA]. See: GERRENIANS.

GERRENIANS (1), inhabitants of *Gerra,* a town near Pelusium, on the borders of Egypt. Acc. to 2 M 13:24 the territory of the Gerrenians is the southern limit of the military commissioner for the coastal region.

GERSHOM, popular etymology "An alien there," see Ex 2:22; 18:3 (cf. Gera).

1. **Gershom** (6) and **Eliezer,** sons of Moses and Zipporah, both born in a foreign land, that is, Midian, Ex 2:22; 4:20; 18:2–6; cf. Ac 7:29, Levites of the clan of Kohath, 1 Ch 23:15–17; 26:24–25.

Father of: JONATHAN 1.

2. **Gershom** (7), in 1 Ch 6:1, 2, 5, 28, 47, 56; 15:7, the name given to: GERSHON.

3. **Gershom** (1), a descendant of the priest Phinehas, who returns from the exile with Ezra, Ezr 8:2.

GERSHON (17), (see: GERSHOM 2), first of the three sons of Levi, Gn 46:11//Ex 6:16; Nb 3:17; 1 Ch 5:27; 6:1. Eponymous ancestor of the Gershonites, he and his brothers, Kohath and Merari, with whom he is always associated, originate the three great classes of Levites, Nb 26:57; 1 Ch 23:6–7. A census gives 2,630 sons of Gershon, Nb 4:38–41. These are subdivided into two clans, the *Libnite* and the *Shimeite,* Nb 3:21–23; cf. 26:58. Their function in the service of the tabernacle is described in Nb 3:25–26; 4:24–28; 7:7; 10:17; cf. 1 Ch 15:7. Thirty towns are assigned to them in Issachar, Asher, Naphtali, and eastern Manasseh, Jos 21:6, 27–33//1 Ch 6:47, 56–66. Asaph, one of the three great cantors, is given as a descendant of Gershom, 1 Ch 6:24–28.

See: List, page 416.

Among his sons: LIBNI 1; SHIMEI 3.

GERSHONITE (13), Nb 3:21, 23–24; 4:24, 27–28; 26:57; Jos 21:33; 1 Ch 23:7; 26:21; 2 Ch 29:8, 12, belonging to the clan of: GERSHON.

GESHAN (1), a Calebite of the sons of Jahdai, 1 Ch 2:47.

GESHEM (3), "[Born in the season of the] rains," **the Arab** (2), governor of the Arab federation of Kedar, whose territory extends to the southern end of Transjordania and Palestine. With Sanballat, governor of Samaria, and Tobiah, governor of the Ammonite territory, he tries to prevent the rebuilding of the wall of Jerusalem that is being undertaken by Nehemiah, Ne 2:19; 6:1, 2.

= **Gashmu** (1), Ne 6:6.

GESHUR (9) **in Aram** (1), 2 S 15:8, or **Geshurites** (4), a kingdom to the east of the Sea of Chinnereth, on the border of eastern Manasseh, Dt 3:14; cf. Jos 12:5; 1 Ch 2:23, assigned to the Transjordanian tribes but never occupied by them, Jos 13:11, 13. After the assassination of Amnon, Absalom takes refuge there at the court of the king of Geshur, where he remains for three years, 2 S 13:38; 14:23, 32; 15:8.

King: TALMAI 2.

GESHURITES

1. **Geshurites** (4). See: GESHUR.
2. **Geshurites** (2), one of the tribes of the Negeb, Jos 13:2, against which David leads raids, 1 S 27:8.

GETHER (2), one of the four sons of Aram, Gn 10:23//1 Ch 1:17. An Aramaean tribe.

GETHSEMANE (2), "Olive press" (cf. Gath; Mishmannah), an estate in the Kidron Valley, at the foot of the Mount of Olives, where Jesus endures his agony and where his arrest takes place, Mt 26:36//Mk 14:32; cf. Lk 22:40; Jn 18:1–2, who speaks of a "garden" where "Jesus had often met his disciples."

GEUEL (1), "Majesty of God"?, **son of Machi** (1), a clan leader of the tribe of Gad, sent by Moses as representative of his tribe in the reconnaissance of Canaan, Nb 13:15.

GEZER (28), Gr. *Gazara,* "Enclosure"?, a Canaanite town of strategic importance on the northern border of the Philistine territory, 2 S 5:25//1 Ch 14:16; 20:4, claimed by Ephraim, Jos 16:3, 10; Jg 1:29; 1 Ch 7:28, assigned to the Levites of the clan of Kohath, Jos 21:21//1 Ch 6:52. Pharaoh takes the town, burns it, and gives it as a wedding gift to his daughter, the wife of Solomon; the latter rebuilds it, 1 K 9:15, 17.

A citadel and center of a Seleucid administrative district, 2 M 10:32, scene of a battle between Syrians and Jews, 1 M 4:15; 7:45; besieged and destroyed by Judas Maccabaeus, 2 M 10:33–38, rebuilt by Bacchides, 1 M 9:52, conquered by Simon Maccabaeus, who installs his son John there, 13:43–48, 53; 14:7, 34; 16:1, 19–21. Antiochus VII demands it back from Simon, but in vain, 15:28–36. 30 km W of Jerusalem on the road from Jerusalem to Joppa.

King: HORAM.

GHOSTS. See: REPHAIM 3.

GIAH (1), "Bubbling, gushing" (cf. Gihon), near Gibeon, 2 S 2:24. Site not identified.

GIANTS. See: NEPHILIM.

GIBBAR (1), (cf. Geber), Ezr 2:20. See: GIBEON.

GIBBETHON, "Hillock; Vault"?, a town in Dan, Jos 19:44, assigned to the Levites of the clan of Kohath, 21:23, then **a Philistine town** (2), besieged by the Israelites under Kings Nadab, 1 K 15:27, and Elah, 16:15, 17. Site not identified.

GIBEA (1). See: GIBEAH 2.

GIBEAH, Hb. *Gib'ah* (*Gib'a'* in no. 2, below, 1 Ch 2:49).

1. **Gibeah** (44) **in Benjamin** (8), Jg 19:14; 20:4, 10 (corr.); 1 S 13:2, 15; 14:16; 2 S 23:29; 1 Ch 11:31, **of Saul** (3), 1 S 11:4; 15:34; Is 10:29, **of God** (1), 1 S 10:5.

The inhabitants of Gibeah commit an abominable crime against a Levite of Ephraim when they refuse him hospitality and brutalize his concubine so that she dies, Jg 19:12–30; cf. Ho 9:9; 10:9. Israel then launches a punitive war against Gibeah and against Benjamin, which sides with Gibeah, Jg 20:1–44. Gibeah is occupied by the Philistines for a time, 1 S 10:5; 13:3 (corr.). It is the native place of Saul, 1 S 10:26, where, after being anointed king, he experiences ecstasy when he meets a group of prophets, 1 S 10:5, 10, 13 (Gr.); it is also his capital, 1 S 11:4; 15:34; 22:6; 23:19; 26:1; Is 10:29. Gibeah is listed among the towns of Benjamin, Jos 18:28 (corr. of Hb. *Gib'at*, "Gibeat"; some link *Gibeat* to the next word and read *Gibeat-kiriath*). Today *Tell el-Ful,* 6 km N of Jerusalem.

Native place of: HASSHEMAR; ITTAI 2; MAACAH 9.

Corr. of Hb. *Gibeah* to *Geba* in 1 S 13:2, 15; 14:2, 16, and to *Gibeon* in 2 S 21:6.

2. **Gibeah** (1) or **Gibea** (1), a town in the highlands of Judah, Jos 15:57, formerly Calebite, 1 Ch 2:49.

3. **Gibeah** (1), the town of Phinehas, where his father, the priest Eleazar, is buried. In the highlands of Ephraim, Jos 24:33. Some translate *Gibeah* here as "hill."

GIBEON (41), Hb. *Gib'ôn,* "Height" (cf. Geba). The Gibeonites, a federation of four towns (Gibeon, Chephirah, Beeroth and Kiriath-jearim, Jos 9:17), form a Hivite enclave in Canaanite territory, Jos 9:7; 11:19. They enter into an alliance with Israel, but because of the trick used to obtain this agreement, they receive an inferior status in Israel as "woodcutters and water carriers," Jos 9:3–27. A coalition of five Amorite kings against Gibeon is crushed by Joshua, Jos 10:1–13, 41. But Saul violates the ancient treaty by putting Gibeonites to death; to expiate this crime, David hands over to the Gibeonites seven descendants of the oath-violating king for torture, 2 S 21:1–9. Scene of a confrontation between partisans of Saul and partisans of David, 2 S 2:12–16, 24; 3:30, and of a victory of David over the Philistines, 2 S 5:25 (corr. of Hb. *Geba*) //1 Ch 14:16; cf. Is 28:21. Famous high place or sanctuary (where Solomon offers sacrifices), 1 K 3:4–5//2 Ch 1:3, 6–7; 1 K 9:2; 1 Ch 16:39; 21:29; 2 Ch 1:13.

Gibeon is listed among the towns of Benjamin, Jos 18:25, and assigned to the Levites of the clan of Kohath, 21:17. The chronicler gives a list of individuals living at Gibeon, 1 Ch 8:29–30//9:35–36. Among the Israelites returning from the exile are some Gibeonites, Ne 7:25 (// Ezr 2:20, *Gibbar*).

Pool of Gibeon, 2 S 2:13–14; Jr 41:12. 9 km NW of Jerusalem. Today *el-Jib.*

Native place of: HANANIAH 4; ISHMAIAH; MELATIAH.

GIBEONITES or **of (from) Gibeon** (8), 2 S 21:1–4, 9; 1 Ch 12:4; Ne 3:7, inhabitants of: GIBEON.

GIBLITES (2), of or from: GEBAL 1.

GIDDALTI (2), "I have magnified [God]" (cf. Gedaliah), of the sons of Heman, 1 Ch 25:4, head of the twenty-second class of cantors, 25:29.

GIDDEL, "Very great" (cf. Gedaliah).

1. **Giddel** (2), head of a family of "oblates" who return from the exile, Ezr 2:47//Ne 7:49.

2. **Giddel** (2), head of a family of Solomon's slaves who return from the exile, Ezr 2:56//Ne 7:58.

GIDEON, Hb. *Gid'ôn,* "Swordfish; Cutter; With his hand cut off"? (cf. Gideoni).

1. **Gideon** (39) = **Jerubbaal** (14), **son of Joash** (5), one of the "greater" judges, a native of Ophrah of Abiezer, Jg 6:11, in the tribe of Manasseh, Jos 17:2, is called by God to "rescue" Israel from oppression by the Midianites, Jg 6:12–24; cf. 1 S 12:11; Heb 11:32. He destroys the altar of Baal, which wins him the surname Jerubbaal, Jg 6:25–32. Reassured of the authenticity of his mission by the sign of the fleece, 6:36–40, Gideon reduces the number of his fighters at En-harod and carries on a campaign west of the Jordan against Midian, whose two leaders Oreb and Zeeb he kills, 7:1–8:3; cf. Ps 83:12; Is 10:26. Gideon pursues the enemy across the Jordan and takes revenge on the people of Succoth and Penuel and on the two kings of Midian,

Zebah and Zalmunna, Jg 8:4–21. He refuses kingship but he makes an ephod, thus causing idolatry, 8:22, 27. He has seventy sons, 8:30, whom Abimelech, son of his concubine, 8:31, will massacre, 9:2–5, 18, 24–56. He dies old and forgotten, 8:29–35.

Sons of Jerubbaal: ABIMELECH 2; JOTHAM 1.

2. **Gideon** (1), a Simeonite, ancestor of Judith, Jdt 8:1.

GIDEONI (5), (cf. Gideon), a Benjaminite, father of: ABIDAN.

GIHON, "The Gushing"? (cf. Giah).

1. **Gihon** (2), one of the rivers of the earthly paradise, Gn 2:13; Si 24:27.

2. **Gihon** (5), originally the only spring providing Jerusalem with water, located in the Kidron Valley, SE of and outside the walls (cf. 2 Ch 33:14), on the side of the hill on which the city is built. Solomon is anointed king there, 1 K 1:33, 38, 45. A first tunnel, the work of the Canaanites, links the city with the spring: Joah must have used it in capturing Jerusalem, 2 S 5:8. It is replaced by a conduit that is partly open to the sky, cf. Is 7:3; 8:6; 22:9–22. Later on, Hezekiah has a conduit dug in the rock to bring Gihon's water to the Pool of Siloam within the walls, 2 Ch 32:30; cf. 2 K 20:20; Si 48:17. Today *'Ain Sittna Maryam* or *'Ain Umm ed-Daraj.*

GILALAI (1), a priest or Levite, an instrumentalist at the dedication of the wall of Jerusalem, Ne 12:36.

GILBOA (8), "Country of hills" (cf. Geba), a highland (altitude 500 m) located between the plain of Jezreel and the Jordan, W of Beth-shan. The Israelites are defeated there by the Philistines; Saul and his sons die there, 1 S 28:4; 31:1, 8// 1 Ch 10:1, 8; 2 S 1:6, 21; 21:12.

GILEAD, Hb. *Gil'ad,* "Hard, uneven [ground]," a biblical etymology. See: GALEED.

1. **Gilead** (130), a country in Transjordania; the territory indicated by the name can differ:

a. Primitive Gilead: highlands, Gn 31:21, 23, 25, between the Jabbok and the country of Jazer, Nb 31:1, near Mizpah, Jg 10:17; 11:11, bordering on the Ammonites, cf. 2 S 17:24–26. The country of Jephthah, Jg 11:1, who became its chief and military leader against the neighboring Ammonites, Jg 10:17–18; 11:1–12, 29, and Ephraimites, 12:4–7. Distinct from Machir, it designates the territory of Gad, Jg 5:14, 17.

b. Land of Machir and eastern Manasseh, between the Jabbok and the Yarmuk, Nb 32:39–40; Dt 3:15; Jos 13:11; 17:5–6; 1 Ch 27:21. Consequently, Gilead is called "son of Machir son of Manasseh," 1 Ch 7:17; cf. Nb 26:29; Jos 17:1; 1 Ch 2:21, 23; 7:14, and from it come the clans of Gilead, which are called "clans of Manasseh," Nb 26:30–34.

c. All of Transjordania, comprising one half of Gilead which is south of the Jabbok and is occupied by Reuben and Gad, and the other half, which is north of the Jabbok and is occupied by eastern Manasseh, Dt 3:12–13; Jos 12:2–6; 13:31; 22:9, 13, 15, 32; 2 K 10:33.

d. In Hellenistic times Gilead names a land that reaches to the north of the Yarmuk (see: BASHAN). Judas Maccabaeus conducts a campaign there to free Jewish prisoners and takes reprisal on the towns of the area, 1 M 5:9–11, 17–20, 25–45, 55. Trypho also goes there, 1 M 13:32. While Ezk 48:17 excludes Gilead from the Promised Land, a widespread view favors the return of the region to Israel, Ps 60:9//108:9; Jr 50:19; Ob 19; Mi 7:14; Zc 10:10.

Gilead is famous for its medicinal plants, Gn 37:25; Jr 8:22; 46:11, its pastures, Nb 32:1; Sg 4:1//6:5; Jr 50:19; Mi 7:14, its forests, Jr 22:6.

Gileadites: BARZILLAI 1; JAIR 2; JEPHTHAH 1.

Towns in Gilead: JABESH 1; MIZPAH 2; PAMAH 10; TISHBE 1.

Towns in Hellenistic Gilead: BOSOR; BOZRAH 1; CARNAIM; CHASPHO; DATHEMA; EPHRON 4; HELAM; MAKED; RAPHON.

See Transjordania, under: JORDAN 3.

2. **Gilead** (2), a town in Transjordania, Ho 6:8; 12:12. Not identified.

3. **Ben-gilead** (1), a Gadite of the sons of Abihail, 1 Ch 5:14–17, or, acc. to another reading, *Gilead,* ancestor of Abihail.

GILEADITE (11), inhabitant of: GILEAD 1.

GILGAL. Gr. *Galgala,* "Circle of stones" (cf. Beth-gilgal; Galal; Galeed; Galilee; Gallim).

1. **Gilgal** (36), between the Jordan and Jericho, probably NE of the latter, cf. Jos 4:19. Precise location uncertain.

First encampment of the Israelites on entering Canaan after crossing the Jordan, Jos 4:19–20; cf. Mi 6:5; circumcision of the people and celebration of the Passover, Jos 5:9–10 (theophany, 5:13–15), conclusion of treaty with the Gibeonites, 9:6, point of departure for the conquest of Canaan, 10:6–9, 15, 43; 14:6; cf. Jg 2:1. Chief sanctuary of Benjamin: Samuel and Saul offer sacrifice there, 1 S 10:8; 13:7–9, 12–15; 15:12–13, 21; cf. 1 S 7:16. Saul is proclaimed king there, 1 S 11:14–15, then rejected by Samuel, cf. 15:26. Samuel there slays Agag, king of the Amalekites, 15:33. After the death of Absalom, David stops at Gilgal on his return from exile, 2 S 19:16, 41. The worship at Gilgal will be condemned by the prophets, Ho 4:15; 9:15; 12:12; Am 4:4; 5:5.

Near Gilgal: IDOLS.

2. **Gilgal** (3), in the highlands of Ephraim between Shiloh and Bethel, or perhaps at the foot of Mount Gerizim, cf. Dt 11:30. The prophets Elijah and Elisha go there, 2 K 2:1; 4:38.

GILO. See: GILOH.

GILOH, Gilo (2), a town in the highlands of Judah, Jos 15:51; cf. 2 S 15:12. Today *Kh. Jala,* 10 km NW of Jerusalem. Native place of: AHITHOPHEL.

GILONITE (2), 2 S 15:12, of or from: GILOH.

GIMZO (1), a town in the lowlands, captured by the Philistines in the time of Ahaz, 2 Ch 28:18. Native place of: JASHEN.

GINATH (2), father of: TIBNI.

GINNETHOI (1), a priest who returns from exile with Zerubbabel, Ne 12:4.

GINNETHON (2), a priest, cosigner of the pledge to observe the Law, Ne 10:7, gives his name to a priestly family, 12:16.

GIRGASHITES (8), one of the peoples of Canaan, perhaps originally from Asia Minor, Gn 10:16; 15:21; Dt 7:1; Jos 3:10; 24:11; 1 Ch 1:14; Ne 9:8; Jdt 5:16.

See: CANAAN *a.*

GIRZITES (1), one of the Negeb tribes against which David conducts raids, 1 S 27:8.

GISHPA (1), head of the "oblates," Ne 11:21.

GITTAIM (2), "The two presses" (cf. Gath). See: GATH 2.

GITTITE (13), 2 S 15:18–19; 18:2, of or from: GATH 1.

GIZON (1), 1 Ch 11:34, native place of: BENE-HASHEM. Probably identical with: GIMZO.

GOAH (1), Jr 31:39; Zc 14:5 (text corrected), at Jerusalem, perhaps at juncture of the valleys of Hinnom and the Kidron.

GOB (2), an otherwise unknown Philistine town, 2 S 21:18 (//1 Ch 20:4, *Gezer*), 19, where two of David's champions win renown; one of them, Elhanan of Bethlehem, kills Goliath.

GOD. See: EL; ELOAH; ELOHIM; LORD; SHADDAI; YAHWEH.

GODS, listed acc. to the countries where they are worshipped; but the lines of demarcation are not always clear.

Ammon: MILCOM.

Aram, Assyria, Babylonia, Canaan, Phoenicia:

Aram: ASHIMA; GAD 1; MENI.

Assyria: [ADAD]; ADRAMMELECH; ANAMMELECH; [ASSHUR] (see: ASSYRIA 1); NIBHAZ; NISROCH; [SHULMAN]; TARTAK.

Babylonia: BEL; [ISHTAR]; KAIWAN; MARDUK; NANAEA; NEBO 4; NERGAL; [NINURTA]; SAKKUTH (cf. SUCCOTH-BENOTH); [SIN 1]; TAMMUZ.

Canaan: ASHERAH; ASTARTE; BAAL 1; BAAL-BERITH; BETHEL 2; [HORON]; MELECH 2; MOLECH; MOT.

Phoenicia: ANATH; [BAAL-SHAMEM]; [HADAD 1]; HADAD-RIMMON; [MELKART].

Egypt: AMON 4; APIS; [ATON]; [BAST] (see: PI-BESETH); [HORUS]; [NEITH]; [PTAH]; [RA].

Elam: [LAGAMAR].

Greek and Hellenistic world: [ADONIS]; [APOLLO]; [ARTEMIS]; [ATARGATIS]; [DAPHNE] (see: DAPHNE); [DEMETER] (see: DEMETRIUS); DIONYSUS 1; HERCULES; HERMES 1; [POSEIDON]; TWINS; ZEUS.

Moab: CHEMOSH.

Philistia: BAAL-ZEBUB; DAGON.

GOG (cf. Hamon-gog).

1. **Gog** (1), a Reubenite, a descendant of Joel and an ancestor of Beerah, 1 Ch 5:4.

2. **Gog** (10), **prince of Rosh, Meshech and Tubal** (3), **in the land of Magog** (1). The name can be compared with *Gyges,* king of Lydia (= Magog); some regard Gog as a revival of the name of *Agag,* king of Amalek and traditional enemy of Israel, cf. Nb 24:7 (Hb. *Agag;* Gr. *Gog*).

In Ezk 38–39 Gog personifies the powers hostile to the people of God: he comes from the north, Ezk 38:6, 15, which is the direction from which the great invasions come, cf. Jr 4:6–7; this barbarian conqueror, like Babylon, is the instrument of God's wrath, which subjects Israel to a final test, 38:7–9, 14, before itself being crushed and buried with its multitudes in the valley of Hamon-gog, 39:11–16.

In Rv 20:7–10, *Gog and Magog* are both symbols of the world's hostility to the Church.

GOIIM (3), "Nations" (cf. Harosheth-ha-goiim; Galilee of the nations).

1. **Goiim** (2), Gn 14:1, 9, whose king is: TIDAL.

2. **Goiim** (1), near Gilgal or, acc. to the Gr., in Galilee. Joshua defeats its Amorite king, Jos 12:23. (Some translate: "the king of the nations.")

GOLAN in Bashan (4), a city of refuge for the eastern half-tribe of Manasseh, Dt 4:43//Jos 20:8, assigned to the Levites of the clan of Gershon, Jos 21:27//1 Ch 6:56. 30 km E of the Sea of Chinnereth. Golan gave its name to *Gaulanitis,* the Gr. name for the region, today the *Golan Heights.*

GOLGOTHA (3), Aram. *Gulgolta,* "Place of the skull," Gr. *Kranion* (4), "Skull," Lat. *Calvaria,* whence *Calvary,* probably the name of a rock that was shaped like a skull. Outside the wall of Jerusalem, cf. Mt 27:32; Heb 13:12, where Jesus is crucified, Mt 27:33//Mk 15:22//Lk 23:33 (who omits *Golgotha*)//Jn 19:17. Tradition locates Golgotha on the site of the present Basilica of the Holy Sepulcher.

GOLIATH (7), **the Philistine** (32), **from Gath** (4), a "giant" and "mighty warrior," Si 47:4–5; cf. 1 S 17:4, perhaps a descendant of the Anakim, cf. Jos 11:22, whom David faces and conquers in single combat with unequal weapons, 1 S 17; 18:6; 19:5; 21:10; 22:10; Si 47:4; cf. 1 M 4:30. Acc. to 2 S 21:19 it is Elhanan, son of Jair, who kills Goliath the Gittite. It seems that the original account in 1 S 17 related a victory of David over an anonymous adversary, "the Philistine" (29× in this chapter); subsequently there was added in 17:4 and 23 the explanation: "his name was Goliath, from Gath." In attributing to Elhanan the death of Lahmi, brother of Goliath, 1 Ch 20:5, 11 is attempting to harmonize the traditions.

GOMER

1. **Gomer** (5), one of the seven sons of Japheth and father of three peoples, one of which, Togarmah, Gn 10:2–3//1 Ch 1:5–6, figures with Beth-togarmah among the allies of Gog, Ezk 38:6. Probably the *Cimmerians* of eastern Asia Minor.

See: ZIMRI 5.

2. **Gomer** (1), "Fulfillment"? (cf. Gemariah), or "Burning coal"?, **daughter of Diblaim** (1), wife of the prophet: HOSHEA 3.

GOMORRAH (23), Hb. *'Amorah,* a town of the Pentapolis, always linked with: SODOM.

GOREN-HA-ATAD (2), "Threshing floor of the bramble," across the Jordan, identified with *Abel-mizraim*, where Jacob was supposedly buried, Gn 50:10–11. Site uncertain.

See: MACHPELAH.

GORGIAS (11), "friend" of Antiochus IV Epiphanes, 1 M 3:38, "a professional general of wide military experience," 2 M 8:9, routed by Judas Maccabaeus at Emmaus, 1 M 4:1–25; conqueror of Joseph and Azariah at Jamnia (capital of the coastal region of which Gorgias was probably the military commissioner), 1 M 5:55–62; military commissioner of Idumaea, 2 M 10:14; 12:32, where his troops are again defeated by Judas, while he himself manages to escape to Marisa, 2 M 12:32–37.

GORTYNA (1), a town in Crete to which the letter of the consul Lucius on the Roman-Jewish alliance is sent, 1 M 15:23.

GOSHEN

1. **Land of Goshen** (11) or **Goshen** (2), Gn 46:28–29, Gr. *Gesem,* a fertile region of Egypt that the Bible locates in the eastern part of the Nile delta. Joseph, "lord of all Egypt," settles his father and brothers there, Gn 45:9–10; 46:28–34, and Pharaoh authorizes them to stay there because of their flocks, Gn 47:1–6, 27; 50:8. During the "plagues" in Egypt the land of Goshen is spared, Ex 8:18; 9:26. Nebuchadnezzar sends his summons to Goshen among others, Jdt 1:9; Goshen is unknown to Egyptologists.

2. **Goshen** (1), Gr. *Gosom,* a town in the highlands of Judah, Jos 15:51. The **region of Goshen** or **land of Goshen** (2) is the area around this town, Jos 10:41; 11:16. Site unknown.

GOTHONIEL (1). See: OTHNIEL 2.

GOZAN (3), Accad. *Guzana,* a town in Upper Mesopotamia, on the upper reaches of the Habor, not far from Haran, conquered by Sennacherib, 2 K 19:12//Is 37:12.

River: HABOR.

GREAT PLAIN (2). See: PLAIN 2.

GREAT SEA (12). See: MEDITERRANEAN.

GREECE, Gr. *Hellas.*

a. **Javan** (2), Gr. *Hellas, Hellēnos,* refers first of all to *Ionia* and the *Greeks of Ionia* in Asia Minor. The list of peoples in Gn 10 makes Javan a son of Japheth; the sons of Javan are the peoples of the Mediterranean islands, Gn 10:2–4//1 Ch 1:5, 7. Javan trades in slaves, bronze, and so forth, with Tyre, Ezk 27:13, 19; Jl 4:6; cf. Is 66:19. Javan is also the *continental Greece* of Alexander the Great, king of Macedonia and the Greeks, Dn 8:21; 10:20; 11:2; cf. Zc 9:13.

b. **Greece** (3), Gr. *Hellas. Hellas,* 1 M 1:1, refers either to continental Greece, Ionia, and the islands of the Aegean, or simply to Ionia, where Alexander undertakes the conquest of the Persian Empire, or to the Hellenistic Empire, cf. 1 M 6:2.

The Greeks, 1 M 8:9, probably refers to the *Achaian League,* which Rome crushed in 146 B.C.

Finally, *Greece* in Ac 20:2 refers to the Roman province of *Achaia.*

See: ACHAIA; KITTIM; MACEDONIA; SICYON; SPARTA.

See: GREEK.

GREEK (32), Gr. *Hellēn,* a person belonging to the Hellenistic civilization that was born of the exchange between Greek and Oriental cultures that came about through the conquests of Alexander the Great, cf. 1 M 1:10; 8:18 (where *Greeks* refers to the *Seleucids*).

The opposition of **Greek and Barbarian,** which is of the cultural order and prescinds from ethnic origin, divides mankind into civilized peoples (of Greek language and culture) and uncivilized (barbarian), Rm 1:14.

The opposition of **Jew and Greek,** which is religious and has no reference to culture, divides mankind into those who belong to the chosen people (the Jews) and the rest of the world (Greeks and pagans), 2 M 4:36; 11:2; and so on. Owing to the Diaspora, people sympathetic to the Jewish religion are found among the Greeks, cf. Jn 12:20.

The Gospel is preached to Jews and Greeks alike, Ac 11:20; 14:1; 17:4; 18:4; 19:10; 20:21. Paul states: "While the Jews demand miracles and the Greeks look for wisdom, here are we preaching a crucified Christ; to the Jews an obstacle that they cannot get over, to the pagans madness, but to those who have been called, whether they are Jews or Greeks, a Christ who is the power and wisdom of God," 1 Co 1:22–24; cf. Rm 1:16; 2:9–10; 3:9; 10:12; 1 Co 10:32; 12:13; Col 3:11.

See: GREECE; HELLENISTS.

GUARDS (Gate of the) (1), Hb. *Razim,* at Jerusalem, the gate connecting the temple with the royal palace, 2 K 11:19 (//2 Ch 23:20: *Upper Gate*).

GUDGODAH (2). See: HOR-HAGGIDGAD.

GUNI

1. **Guni** (3), second of the four sons of Naphtali, Gn 46:24//1 Ch 7:13, whose descendants form the **Gunite** clan, Nb 26:48.

2. **Guni** (1), a Gadite, ancestor of: AHI 1.

GUNITE (1), belonging to the clan of: GUNI 1.

GUR (Slope of) (1), near Ibleam. Ahaziah, king of Judah, is mortally wounded there, 2 K 9:27.

GUR-BAAL (1), "Residence of Baal" (cf. Baal; Gera), occupied by an Arab population, 2 Ch 26:7. Location unknown.

[GYGES]. See: GOG 2.

H

HABAIAH (1) or **Hobaiah** (1), "Yah hides himself," head of a family whose sons on returning from the exile cannot prove their authentic Israelite origin, Ezr 2:61//Ne 7:63.

HABAKKUK (9), "Basil, Mint"?, a prophet at the end of the seventh century, author of an oracle against the Chaldaeans, Hab 1:1–2:20, and of a "A Prayer . . . tone as for dirges," 3:1–19. One of the twelve "minor prophets." Later tradition gives him a role in re-editing the story of "Daniel in the lions' den," Dn 14:33–39. In 14:1 the LXX has the title: "From the prophecy of Habakkuk son of Joshua of the tribe of Levi."

HABAZZINIAH (1), a Rechabite, ancestor of: JAAZANIAH 1.

HABER. See: HEBER 4.

HABOR, a river of Gozan (3), a left-bank tributary of the Euphrates, 2 K 17:6//18:11; 1 Ch 5:26. Today the *Khabur*.

HACALIAH (2), "Hope in Yah," see Ps 33:20; Is 8:17 (cf. Hachilah), father of: NEHEMIAH 2.

HAC-CHEPHRIM (1), "The villages" (cf. Chephar-ammoni), **in the Vale of Ono** (1), where Sanballat and Geshem invite Nehemiah to meet them, Ne 6:2. Near Lod.

HACHILAH (Hill of) (3), (cf. Hacaliah), a hill between En-gedi and Ziph, where David hides and where Saul pursues him, 1 S 23:19; 26:1, 3.

HACHMONI (1), 1 Ch 27:32, father of: JEHIEL 3.

HACHMONITE (2), 2 S 23:8; 1 Ch 11:11. Son of Hachmoni? See: ISHBAAL 2; JASHOBEAM 1.

HADAD, Hb. with *he,* 1–4 (cf. Ben-hadad; Hadadezer; Hadad-rimmon; Hadoram 2–3; Henadad); with *heth,* 5: "Sharp."

1. **[Hadad],** a Phoenician god of the storm (see: Baal), not mentioned as such in the Bible, but used as a personal name (cf. 2–4) or as a component in proper names (cf. the following).

2. **Hadad** (4), **son of Bedad** (2), king of Edom, conqueror of the Midianites in Moab, Gn 36:35–36//1 Ch 1:46–47.

3. **Hadad** (3), another king of Edom, whose wife is Mehetabel, daughter of Matred, from Me-zahab, Gn 36:39 (*Hadad* is a corr. of Hb. *Hadar*); 1 Ch 1:50–51.

4. **Hadad** (7), a young Edomite prince, flees to Egypt after the defeat of his country by David. He marries Pharoah's sister-in-law, who gives him a son, Genubath. At the death of David he returns to his own country, where he resists Solomon, 1 K 11:14–25.

5. **Hadad** (2), one of the twelve sons

of Ishmael, or Arabian clans, Gn 25: 15//1 Ch 1:30.

HADADEZER (21), "Hadad is help" (cf. Ezer; Hadad 1–4), **son of Rehob** (2), **king of Zobah** (7). Despite help from the Aramaeans of Damascus, he is conquered by David, 2 S 8:3–6//1 Ch 18: 3–7; cf. Ps 60:2, who takes extensive booty, 2 S 8:7–12//1 Ch 18:7–11. Another version of this war is given in 2 S 10:15–19//1 Ch 19:16–19.

See: REZON.

HADAD-RIMMON (1), (cf. Hadad 1–4; Rimmon 5), a Phoenician divinity of vegetation, thought to die each year after the harvests. This death was celebrated annually; the celebration must have had a special character in the fertile plain of Megiddo, Zc 12:11.

HADASHAH (1), "New [town]" (cf. New (Gate). See Hazor-hadattah; Neapolis; New Quarter), Gr. *Adasa,* a town in the lowlands of Judah, Jos 15:37.

= **Adasa** (2), victory of Judas Maccabaeus over Nicanor, who dies in the battle, 1 M 7:40, 45.

= ? **Dessau** (1), battle between the Jews and Nicanor, 2 M 14:16.

Between Jerusalem and Beth-horon.

HADASSAH (1), "Myrtle," the Hebrew name of: ESTHER.

HADES. See: SHEOL.

HADID (3), (cf. Hadad 5), a town near Lod and Ono, from which some exiled Jews had come, Ezr 2:33//Ne 7: 37, inhabited by Benjaminites after the exile, Ne 11:34.

= **Adida** (2) **in the Lowlands** (1), fortified by Simon, 1 M 12:38, and occupied by him, 13:13.

= **Adithaim** (1), a town in the lowlands of Judah, Jos 15:36. 6 km NE of Lod.

HADLAI (1), father of: AMASA 2.

HADORAM, "Hadad is raised up" (cf. Hadad; Ramah).

1. **Hadoram** (2), one of the thirteen sons of Joktan, Gn 10:27//1 Ch 1:21. A tribe in southern Arabia.

2. **Hadoram** (2), son of Tou, king of Hamath, comes in his father's name to congratulate David on his victory over Hadadezer, 1 Ch 18:9–11//2 S 8:9–10 (corr. of Hb. *Joram* to *Hadoram*).

HADRACH (1), Accad. *Hatarikka,* a town in northern Syria, Zc 9:1.

HAELEPH (1), Jos 18:28. See: ZELA.

HAGAB (1), "Grasshopper" (cf. Hagabah), head of a family of "oblates" who return from the exile, Ezr 2:46.

HAGABAH (2), fem. of *Hagab,* head of a family of "oblates" who return from the exile, Ezr 2:45//Ne 7:48.

HAGAR (15), **the Egyptian** (4), servant of Sarah, gives Abraham a son, Ishmael, Gn 16:1–16. But at the request of Sarah, Abraham expels Hagar and her son, 21: 9–20, who is the future father of the twelve Arabian tribes, 25:12, which Ba 3:23 calls the sons of Hagar. For Paul, Hagar represents the covenant of Sinai and the state of servitude that characterizes it, whereas Sarah symbolizes the freedom of the true children of Abraham, Ga 4:24–26. Her descendants are the: HAGRITES.

HAGGADOL (1), "The Great" (cf. Gedaliah), father of: ZABDIEL 2.

HAGGAI (11), "[Born on a day of] festival" (cf. Haggi), a prophet contemporary with Zechariah, Ezr 5:1; 6:14, and with the rebuilding of the temple, 520 B.C. The two chapters of the book of Haggai (one of the twelve "minor prophets") contains the prophet's exhortation to the governor, Zerubbabel, and the high priest, Joshua, urging them to rebuild the temple, Hg 1:1–15; the prediction of the future glory of the temple, 2:1–19, and of a period of agricultural prosperity, 2:15–19; a consultation with the priests regarding clean and unclean, 2:10–14; and a promise to Zerubbabel, 2:20–23.

HAGGI (2), "[Born on a day of] festival" (cf. Haggai; Haggiah; Haggith. See Festus), the second of the seven sons of Gad, Gn 46:16, whose descendants form the **Haggite** clan, Nb 26:15.

HAGGIAH (1), "Yah is my festival," see Ex 10:9 (cf. Haggi), a Levite, a descendant of Merari and father of Asaiah, 1 Ch 6:15.

HAGGITE (1), belonging to the clan of: HAGGI.

HAGGITH (5), "[Born on a day of] festival" (cf. Haggi), 2 S 3:4//1 Ch 3:2; 1 K 1:5, 11; 2:13, one of David's wives, mother of: ADONIJAH.

HAGRI (1), father of: MIBHAR.

HAGRITES (5), Hb. *Hagri,* descendants of: HAGAR, the mother of Ishmael; an Arabian tribe in Transjordania. In the time of Saul they enslave the Reubenites, 1 Ch 5:10 (but the Hb. text permits a reading that reverses the situation). Finally, the Hagrites are subjected to the Transjordanian tribes of Israel until the Assyrian deportation, 1 Ch 5:18–22. In Ps 83:7, the Hagrites are listed among the many enemies of Israel.

Hagrite: JAZIZ.

HAKELDAMA (1), Aram. "Bloody Acre" (cf. Hilkiah), Gr. *chōrion haimatos,* bought with the price of Judas' betrayal, and place of the traitor's death, Ac 1:19.

= **Field of Blood** (1), Gr. *agros haimatos,* so named in an allusion to the blood of Jesus and identified with the "potter's field" of Mt 27:8–10; cf. Zc 11:12–13; Jr 18:2–3; 19:1–2; 32:6–15. Acc. to ancient tradition it was located in the Valley of Hinnom.

HAKKATAN (1), "The little one," father of: JOHN 11.

HAKKOZ (5), "The thorn." See: Koz 2.

HAKUPHA (2), head of a family of "oblates" who return from the exile, Ezr 2:51//Ne 7:53.

HALAH (3), a town in Upper Mesopotamia where the Assyrian kings deport the Israelites of the Transjordanian tribes, 1 Ch 5:26, and those of the kingdom of Samaria, 2 K 17:6//18:11.

HALAK (Mount) (2), "Smooth, Bald," **which rises toward Seir** (2), southern limit of the conquests of Joshua, Jos 11:17; 12:7. Today *Jebel Halaq,* south of Beersheba.

HALHUL (1), a town in the highlands of Judah, Jos 15:58. 6 km N of Hebron.

HALI (1), a town in Asher, Jos 19:25. About 10 km SE of Aphek.

HALICARNASSUS (1), a city of Caria in Asia Minor, to which, among others, the letter of the consul Lucius promulgating the alliance of Romans and Jews is sent, 1 M 15:23.

HALLOHESH (2), "The spellbinder *or* The soothsayer," a leader of the people, cosigner of the pledge to observe the Law, Ne 10:25. Father of: SHALLUM 14.

HAM

1. **Ham** (16), Gr. and Lat. *Cham.* Etymology? Second of the three sons of Noah (priestly tradition), Gn 5:32; 6:10; 10:1; 1 Ch 1:4; the youngest (Yahwist tradition), Gn 9:24. With his brothers he is saved from the flood, Gn 7:13; 9:18. He is said to be the father of Cush (Ethiopia and Nubia), Misraim (Egypt), Put (Arabia? Libya?), and Canaan, Gn 10:6//1 Ch 1:8. This last-named is subject to Israel, son of Shem, because, unlike his brothers, Ham did not "cover his father's nakedness," Gn 9:22–27. Under Hezekiah, some descendants of Ham are wiped out by Simeonites, 1 Ch 4:40.

In Ps 78:51; 105:23, 27; 106:22 the "tents" or "land" of Ham refer to Egypt.

2. **Ham** (1), a town in Transjordania. The Zuzim are defeated there by Chedorlaomer, Gn 14:5. 30 km E of Beth-shan.

HAMAN (63), a Pers. name, "The Great," Hb. *Hamân,* **son of Hammedatha** (8), **the Agagite** or **from Agag** (6), first minister of the Persian court under Ahasuerus, Est 3:1; because of the Jew Mordecai's refusal to do obeissance to him, 3:2–5, he determines to wipe out the entire Jewish people, 3:6. For a gift of 10,000 talents, 3:9; 4:7, he obtains a decree of extermination, which he sends by letter to all the provinces, 3:7–13; 8:5, 12[r]. Invited by Esther to a first, then a second banquet, Haman, at the urging of his wife Zeresh and his friends, meanwhile has a gallows prepared for Mordecai, 5:9–14. When the king learns that Mordecai has saved his, the king's, life by denouncing a plot of two of his eunuchs, he compels Haman to honor Mordecai, 6:1–13. During the banquet Esther asks Ahasuerus to punish Haman, the enemy of the Jews. Haman is hanged on the gallows he had prepared for Mordecai, 6:14–7:10; 8:7, 12[r]; 9:25. The royal favor then passes to the Jews: the home of Haman is given to Esther, 8:1–2; Haman's letters are revoked, and the Jews are given permission to exterminate their enemies, 8:3–12. The ten sons of Haman are among the victims of Jewish vengeance, 9:7–14, 25.

"In the Aramaic text of Esther, the struggle between Haman and Mordecai corresponds to the struggles between Agag and Saul, between Amalek and Israel, and even between Esau and Jacob" ([French] *Ecumenical Translation of the Bible*).

HAMATH

1. **Hamath** (24), a city of Syria on the Orontes, halfway between Aleppo and Damascus, today known as *Hama.*

Connected with Canaan in the list of peoples, Gn 10:18//1 Ch 1:16. An important center, Am 6:2 (*Hamath the great*), its name extends to an entire territory, 2 Ch 8:4; cf. Ezk 47:12 (see: RIBLAH), which under David and Solomon has the status of a vassal or allied kingdom, 2 K 14:27; cf. 2 S 8:9–10. Destroyed by Sennacherib, king of Assyria, at the same time as Arpad, 2 K 18:34//Is 36:19; 2 K 19:13//Is 37:13; cf. Is 10:9, its inhabitants are deported to Samaria to replace the Israelites; there they fashion a god for themselves, 2 K 17:24–32. After the defeat of Egypt at Carchemish, Hamath and Arpad are "in confusion" at the threat from Babylonia, Jr 49:23. After the fall of Jerusalem, a part of the people of Judah will be deported to Hamath, Is 11:11.

Jonathan Maccabaeus goes to the region of Hamath (Gr. *Amathitis*) in order to halt the troops of Demetrius there, 1 M 12:25.

In the region of Hamath: RIBLAH.
King: TOU.

2. **The Pass of Hamath** (12), Hb. *Lebo-Hamat,* first outpost in the kingdom of Hamath, on the theoretical northern boundary of the Promised Land, Nb 13:21; 34:8; Jos 13:5//Jg 3:3; Ezk 47:15, 20; 48:1; cf. Zc 9:2, and the northern limit of the kingdom of David and Solomon, 1 K 8:65//2 Ch 7:8; 2 K 14:25; Am 6:14; 1 Ch 13:5. Modern *Lebweh,* in the northern part of the Bekaa.

HAMATHITE (2), Gn 10:18//1 Ch 1:16, of or from: HAMATH.

HAMATH OF ZOBAH (1) ? Apart from 2 Ch 8:3 the Bible always treats *Hamath* and *Zobah* as distinct geographical entities.

HAMITAL (2) or **Hamutal** (1), "My father-in-law is dew" (cf. Abital), daughter of Jeremiah (3), from Libnah, mother of two kings of Judah: Jehoahaz, 2 K 23:31 (*Hamutal*) and Zedekiah, 2 K 24:18//Jr 52:1.

HAMMATH (2), "Warm spring" (cf. Hammon), a fortified town in Naphtali,

Jos 19:35. Occupied at one time by Kenites and Rechabites, 1 Ch 2:55.

= **Hammoth-dor** (1), a town of Naphtali, assigned to Levites of the clan of Gershon, Jos 21:32. 3 km from Tiberias.

= To be distinguished (?) from: HAMMON 2.

HAMMEDATHA (8), Hb. *Hammedata'*, Gr. *Hamadathos,* Est 1:1[r]; 3:1, 10; 8:5, 12[k,r]; 9:10, 24, father of: HAMAN.

HAMMON, "Warm spring" (cf. Hammath).

1. **Hammon** (1), a town in Asher, Jos 19:28.

2. **Hammon** (1), a town in Naphtali, assigned to Levites of the clan of Gershon, 1 Ch 6:61. To be distinguished (?) from: HAMMOTH-DOR.

HAMMOTH-DOR (1). See: HAMMATH.

HAMMUEL (1), a Simeonite, descendant of Shaul and ancestor of Shimei, 1 Ch 4:26.

HAMONAH (1), "Multitude" (cf. Baal-hamon; Hamon-gog), an unidentified town, linked with Hamon-gog, Ezk 39:16.

HAMON-GOG (Valley of) (2), "Multitude of Gog" (cf. Hamonah), Ezk 39:11, 15.

= **Valley of the Abarim** (1), (cf. the Abarim hills in Moab), "on the east of the Sea—the valley that turns back the traveler," Ezk 39:11, and reminds one of the deep and precipitous valley of the Arnon. There Gog and his entire army will be buried.

HAMOR (13), "Ass," **the Hivite** (1), a prince of the country, Gn 34:2, asks for Dinah, the daughter of Jacob, as wife for his son Shechem, who has violated her, and proposes a general matrimonial alliance with the sons of Jacob. The latter accept on condition that the men of Shechem submit to circumcision. This is only a trick; Simeon and Levi kill Hamor and Shechem, Gn 34:4, 6, 8, 13, 18, 20, 24, 26.

The sons of Hamor, the father of Shechem (2), a clan settled at Shechem, Jg 9:28, from which Jacob buys a field where he sets up his tent, Gn 33:19 and where Joseph will be buried, Jos 24:32. Ac 7:16 represents a nonbiblical tradition.

HAMRAN (1). See: HEMDAN.

HAMUL (3), "Spared," second son of Perez, son of Judah, Gn 46:12//1 Ch 2:5, whose descendants form the **Hamulite** clan, Nb 26:21.

HAMULITE (1), belonging to the clan of: HAMUL.

HAMUTAL (1). See: HAMITAL.

HANAMEL (4), a derived form of *Hananel,* "God has shown favor" (cf. Hanan), **son of Shallum** (1), cousin-german of Jeremiah. During the siege of Jerusalem, Jeremiah uses his right of priority in purchasing and buys a field from Hanamel at Anathoth. The purchase is symbolic of better days to come, Jr 32:7–9, 12.

HANAN, abbrev. of *Hananiah,* "Yah has shown favor" (cf. Baal-hanan; Elhanan; Hanamel; Hananel; Hanani; Hananiah; Hannah; Hanniel; Hanun; Henadad; John; Tahan; Tehinnah).

1. **Hanan** (1), a Benjaminite of the sons of Shashak, head of a family at Jerusalem, 1 Ch 8:23.

2. **Hanan** (2), a Benjaminite, one of the six sons of Azel, 1 Ch 8:38//9:44.

3. **Hanan son of Maacah** (1), one of David's champions, 1 Ch 11:43.

4. **Hanan** (2), head of a family of "oblates" who return from the exile, Ezr 2:46//Ne 7:49.

5. **Hanan** (2), one of the Levites who explains the Law to the people during its solemn reading by Ezra, Ne 8:7; a co-signer of the pledge to observe the Law, Ne 10:11.

6. **Hanan son of Zaccur, son of Mattaniah** (1), a man of integrity, one of the supervisors of the temple storehouses in the time of Nehemiah, Ne 13:13.

7. **Hanan** (2), two leaders of the people, cosigners of the pledge to observe the Law, Ne 10:23, 27.

8. **Ben-hanan** (1), one of the sons of Shimei, 1 Ch 4:20, in Judah.

HANANEL, Gr. *Ananeel, Ananiel,* "God has shown favor" (cf. Hanan).

1. **Tower of Hananel** (4), at Jerusalem, in the northern sector of the city, between Fish Gate and Sheep Gate, Ne 3:1; 12:39; Jr 31:38; Zc 4:10.

2. **Ananiel** (2), a Naphtalite, son of Deborah, Tb 1:8, ancestor of Tobit and Tobias, Tb 1:1.

HANANI, probably an abbrev. of *Hananiah* (cf. Hanan).

1. **Hanani** (5), a seer, is thrown into prison by King Asa because he blames the king for having sought support from the king of Aram instead of from God, 2 Ch 16:7 ff. Father of the prophet: JEHU 1.

2. **Hanani** (2), of the sons of Heman, leader of the eighteenth class of cantors, 1 Ch 25:4, 25.

3. **Hanani** (1), a priest, of the sons of Immer, married to a foreign wife, whom he puts away, Ezr 10:20.

4. **Hanani** (2) informs his kinsman, Nehemiah, then at Susa, of the critical situation of the Jews who have returned to Jerusalem, Ne 1:2. With Hananiah he shares the responsibility for administering Jerusalem, Ne 7:2.

5. **Hanani** (1), a priest and instrumentalist at the dedication of the wall of Jerusalem, Ne 12:36.

HANANIAH, Ananias, Hb. *Hananyah, Hananyahu,* "Yah has shown favor" (cf. Hanan), Gr. *Ananias.*

1. **Hananiah** (1), a Benjaminite of the sons of Shashak, head of a family in Jerusalem, 1 Ch 8:24.

2. **Hananiah** (2), of the sons of Heman, leader of the sixteenth class of cantors, 1 Ch 25:4, 23.

3. **Hananiah** (1), commander-in-chief of the armies of King Uzziah, 2 Ch 26:11.

4. **Hananiah** (9), **son of Azzur, a Gibeonite** (1), a prophet. By a symbolic action (breaking the yoke Jeremiah is wearing), he announces the proximate return of the exiles from Babylon. Jeremiah expresses reservations but hopes that Hananiah's words will come true. But shortly thereafter, under God's inspiration, Jeremiah returns and proclaims that "an iron yoke is what I [Yahweh] now lay on the necks of all those nations," that Hananiah has not received a prophetic mission from God, and that he will die that very year. In fact, Hananiah dies two months later, Jr 28:1–17.

5. **Hananiah** (1), father of: ZEDEKIAH 3.

6. **Hananiah** (1), ancestor of: IRIJAH.

7. **Hananiah** (2), second son of Zerubbabel, a descendant of King Jehoiachin, 1 Ch 3:19 (compare with Mt 1:13); his posterity is given in 1 Ch 3:21.

8. **Hananiah** (1), an Israelite of the sons of Bebai, married to a foreign wife, whom he puts away, Ezr 10:28.

9. **Hananiah** (1), a perfumer, a volunteer in rebuilding the wall of Jerusalem, Ne 3:8.

10. **Hananiah son of Shelemiah** (1), another volunteer in the rebuilding of the Jerusalem wall, Ne 3:30.

11. **Hananiah** (1), commander of the citadel of Jerusalem, "a trustworthy man and God-fearing above the ordinary," Ne 7:2.

12. **Hananiah** (1), a leader of the people and cosigner of the pledge to observe the Law, Ne 10:24.

13. **Hananiah** (1), head of the priestly family of Jeremiah in the days of the high priest Joiakim, Ne 12:12.

14. **Hananiah** (1), a priest, a trum-

peter at the dedication of the wall of Jerusalem, Ne 12:41.

15. **Ananias** (2) **the Great** (1) and his brother **Jathan** (Hb. *Nathan* or *Nathaniah*), the two sons of the great Shemaiah, accompany Tobias on his pilgrimage to Jerusalem, Tb 5:14. The great Ananias is father of Azarias, the name under which the angel Raphael presents himself to Tobias, Tb 5:13.

16. **Ananias** (1), a Simeonite, an ancestor of Judith, Jdt 8:1.

17. **Hananiah** (8) is always associated with **Mishael** (8) and **Azariah** (10); all three are the companions of Daniel. These young Jews, "without any physical defect, of good appearance, trained in every kind of wisdom, well-informed, quick at learning," are chosen from among the Judaean deportees to become counselors of King Nebuchadnezzar. Each of them receives a new name: Hananiah is called **Shadrach** (15), Mishael **Meshach** (15), and Azariah **Abednego** (15). They are given a special education. They win out in a first test of ten days by refusing to violate the dietary prescriptions of the Law: the king "found them ten times better than all the magicians and enchanters in his kingdom," Dn 1:3–20. Threatened with death along with all the sages of Babylon, the three assist Daniel with their prayers; he alone is able to interpret the king's dream, Dn 2:12–18, and his three companions are then put in charge of the affairs of the province of Babylon, Dn 2:12–18, 49. On refusing to adore the golden statue erected on the plain of Dura, the three officials are thrown into a furnace, Dn 3:1–23. In the midst of the flames they walk about listening to the canticle of Azariah, Dn 3:45–50 (Gr.); cf. 1 M 2:59, and they sing the "canticle of creatures," Dn 3:51–88 (Gr.). Seeing this miracle, Nebuchadnezzar praises the God of Shadrach, Meshach, and Abednego and gives them a position of eminence at Babylon, Dn 3:24–30.

18. **Ananias** (3) and his wife **Sapphira,** Jewish Christians of Jerusalem. After selling a piece of property, love of money makes them attempt to deceive the Apostles and, through them, the Holy Spirit. Both are struck dead, Ac 5:1–10.

19. **Ananias** (6), a Jewish Christian of Damascus, is sent to "Straight Street," to the house of Judas, in order to lay hands on Saul of Tarsus that he may recover his sight and be filled with the Holy Spirit, Ac 9:10–17; cf. 22:12–16.

20. **Ananias** (2), son of Nebedaios, appointed high priest ca. 47 A.D., deposed in 51 or 52, or later on in 59, dies at the hands of Zealots in 66, at the beginning of the Jewish uprising against Rome. When Paul appears before the Sanhedrin at Jerusalem, Ananias "breaks the Law" by ordering his attendants to strike Paul on the mouth. Paul replies: "God will surely strike you, you whitewashed wall" (a prophecy of Ananias' violent death?), Ac 23:2–5. Ananias then goes to Caesarea to lodge a complaint against Paul with Felix, the governor, Ac 24:1.

HANES (1), a city in the Nile delta, probably *Heracleopolis,* about 100 km south of Cairo. An embassy sent by Hezekiah to ask for Egyptian help will reach Hanes, but the results will be disappointing, Is 30:4.

HANNAH, Anna, Gr. *Anna,* "Favor" (cf. Hanan).

1. **Hannah** (13), mother of Samuel. Hannah, favorite wife of Elkanah, is barren and must suffer the sarcasms of her rival Peninnah, 1 S 1:1–8. During a pilgrimage to Shiloh she asks Yahweh for a son whom she will dedicate to him, 1 S 1:9–11. Comforted by Eli the priest, she returns with her husband to Ramah, where she bears a son whom she names Samuel, 1 S 1:12–23. Once the child has been weaned, she presents him in the temple at Shiloh in order to "make him over" to Yahweh, 1 S 1:24–28, and she

praises God in a song that is an anticipation of the Magnificat, 1 S 2:1–10. She returns each year to see Samuel, 1 S 2:19–20. She has three other sons and two daughters, 1 S 2:21.

2. **Anna** (9), wife of Tobit and mother of Tobias, Tb 1:9, taken from Tobit for a time and then restored to him, Tb 1:20; 2:1. When her husband is blinded, Anna becomes a weaver, but she reproaches Tobit for the uselessness of his good works, 2:11–14. She is disturbed by the departure of her son, 5:18–6:1, and his prolonged absence, 10:1–4; cf. 6:15, watches the road by which he is to return, and welcomes him back, 11:5–9. Tobias carries out his father's recommendations in his dealings with his mother, 4:3–4; 14:9–12.

3. **Anna daughter of Phanuel** (1), of the tribe of Asher, a widow and prophetess; at the age of 84 and together with Simeon, she welcomes the child Jesus to the temple, Lk 2:36–38.

Other prophetesses: MARY 1.

HANNATHON (1), a town on the border of Zebulun, Jos 19:14.

HANNIEL, "Favor of God" (cf. Hanan).

1. **Hanniel son of Ephod** (1), representative of Manasseh in the allocation of Canaan, Nb 34:23.

2. **Hanniel** (1), an Asherite, one of the three sons of Ulla, head of a family, 1 Ch 7:39.

HANOCH. See: ENOCH.

HANOCHITE (1), belonging to the clan of: ENOCH 3.

HANUN, "Favored" (cf. Hanan).

1. **Hanun** (9), **son of Nahash** (2), king of the Ammonites, who shames the embassy David sends him with condolences on the death of his father, 2 S 10:1–4//1 Ch 19:2–4. This serious insult leads to David's first campaign against the Ammonites, 2 S 10:6–7//1 Ch 19:6–7.

2. **Hanun** (1), with the help of the inhabitants of Zanoah, repairs the Valley Gate and part of the Jerusalem wall, Ne 3:13.

3. **Hanun son of Zalaph** (1), another volunteer in the rebuilding of the Jerusalem wall, Ne 3:30.

HAPHARAIM (1), "The two wells" (cf. Hepher 1), a town in Issachar, Jos 19:19.

HAPPIZZEZ (1), "The smasher" (cf. Beth-pazzes), a priest, leader of the eighteenth priestly class, 1 Ch 24:15.

HARADAH (2), "Fright"? (cf. Harod), a stage of the Exodus, Nb 33:24–25.

HARAN, Hb. with *he:* 1–2, Gr. *Arran* (cf. Beth-haran); with *heth:* 3–4, Gr. *Charran.*

1. **Haran** (6), brother of Abram and Nahor, dies at Ur of the Chaldaeans, Gn 11:26–28. Father of: ISCAH; LOT; MILCAH 1.

2. **Haran** (1), one of the three sons of Shimei, a Levite of the clan of Gershon, 1 Ch 23:9.

3. **Haran** (2), one of the sons of Ephah, concubine of Caleb, and father of Gazez, 1 Ch 2:46.

4. **Haran** (12), Accad. *Harranu,* "Street," city of the patriarchs Abraham, Gn 11:31–32; 12:4–5; Ac 7:2, 4, and Jacob, Gn 27:43; 28:10; 29:4, captured by the Assyrians, 2 K 19:12//Is 37:12. Trade with Tyre, Ezk 27:23. In Upper Mesopotamia. Today *Harran* in Turkey.

HARAR (from), or **Hararite** (5), from an unknown town or clan. See: AHIAM; JONATHAN 5; SHAMMAH 3.

HARBONA (2), "Bold"? (cf. Horeb). Pers. "Donkey-driver," one of the seven eunuchs in the personal service of King Ahasuerus and charged with bringing Queen Vashti before the king, Est 1:10–15. It is he who suggests hanging Haman

on the gallows prepared for Mordecai, Est 7:8–9. The Gr. in 7:9 has *Bougathan*.
See: MEHUMAN.

HAREPH (1), (cf. Hariph), a Judaean, son of Hur and father of Beth-gader, 1 Ch 2:51.

HARHAS (1) = **Hasrah** (1), ancestor of: SHALLUM 7.

HAR-HERES (1), "Mountain of the sun" (cf. Heres). See: BETH-SHEMESH 1.

HARHUR (2), "Subject to fever"?, head of a family of "oblates" who return from the exile, Ezr 2:51//Ne 7:53.

HARIM, "[With a] cleft [nose]" (cf. Harumaph)? or "Consecrated"?

1. **Harim** (6), a priest leader of the third priestly class, 1 Ch 24:8. He, Ne 12:3 (corr. of Hb. *Rehum*), and his sons return from the exile, Ezr 2:39//Ne 7:42; some of them have married foreign wives, whom they put away, Ezr 10:21. He is a cosigner of the pledge to observe the Law, Ne 10:6. Under Joiakim the head of this family is Adna, Ne 10:28.

2. **Harim** (4), head of a family whose sons return from the exile, Ezr 2:32//Ne 7:25; some of these have married foreign wives, whom they put away, Ezr 10:31. A cosigner of the pledge to observe the Law, Ne 10:28.

Father of: MALCHIJAH 8.

HARIPH, "Autumn" (cf. Hareph).

1. **Hariph** (1) of Benjamin. A town or clan leader? Several men from Hariph rally to David, 1 Ch 12:6.

2. **Hariph** (2), to be identified with the preceding? His sons return from the exile, Ne 7:24 (//Ezr 2:18, *Jorah*). A cosigner of the pledge to observe the Law, Ne 10:20.

HARNEPHER (1), Egypt. *Hr nfr*, "Horus is merciful" (cf. Horus), an Asherite, one of the eleven sons of Zophah, head of a family, 1 Ch 7:36.

HAROD (from) (2), "Trembling"? (cf. En-harod; Haradah), perhaps a native of En-harod, 2 S 23:25.

See: ELIKA; SHAMMAH 4.

HAROEH (1), "The seer" (cf. Irijah; Lahai Roi; Reaiah; Yahweh Provides), son of Shobal, son of Hur, in Judah, 1 Ch 2:52.

HAROSHETH-HA-GOIIM (2), "The wooded region of the nations" (cf. Goiim; Horesh), native place of Sisera, Jg 4:2, and scene of his defeat by Barak, the judge, Jg 4:13, 16. In Galilee, precise location uncertain. Perhaps near the modern Haifa.

HARSHA (2), (cf. Tel-harsha), head of a family of "oblates" who return from the exile, Ezr 2:52//Ne 7:54.

HARUM (1), (cf. Horam), father of: AHARHEL.

HARUMAPH (1), "With the cleft nose" (cf. Harim. See: ZILPAH), father of: JEDAIAH 5.

HARUZ (1), father of the queen-mother: MESHULLEMETH.

HASADIAH, "Yah is faithful" (cf. Hesed).

1. **Hasadiah** (1), one of the five sons of Meshullam, a descendant of King Jehoiachin, 1 Ch 3:20.

2. **Hasadiah** (1), var. *Sedei,* ancestor of Baruch, Ba 1:1.

HASHABIAH, "Yah has taken into account" (cf. Hashbaddanah; Hashubah; Hasshub; Heshbon?).

1. **Hashabiah** (1), a descendant of Merari, ancestor of Ethan the cantor, 1 Ch 6:30.

2. **Hashabiah** (2), of the sons of Jeduthun, leader of the twelfth class of cantors, 1 Ch 25:3, 19.

3. **Hashabiah** (1), a Levite of the clan of Hebron, assigned "to guard Israel west of Jordan," 1 Ch 26:30.

4. **Hashabiah son of Kemuel** (1), commissioner for the Levites, 1 Ch 27:17.

5. **Hashabiah** (1), one of the six heads of the Levites under Josiah, 2 Ch 35:9.

6. **Hashabiah** (6), a Levite of the sons of Merari, always linked with Sherebiah; among those charged with bringing the temple utensils back from the exile, Ezr 8:19, 24; a cosigner of the pledge to observe the Law, Ne 10:12; one of the heads of the Levites under Joiakim, Ne 12:24. An ancestor of: SHEMAIAH 7.

One or more individuals.

7. **Hashabiah** (1), a Levite, ruler of half the district of Keilah, a volunteer in rebuilding the wall of Jerusalem, Ne 3:17.

8. **Hashabiah** (1), a descendant of Asaph, ancestor of: UZZI 5.

9. **Hashabiah** (1), head of the priestly family of Hilkiah in the time of the high priest Joiakim, Ne 12:21.

HASHABNAH (1), a leader of the people and cosigner of the pledge to observe the Law, Ne 10:26.

HASHABNEIAH

1. **Hashabneiah** (1), father of: HATTUSH 2.

2. **Hashabneiah** (1), a Levite who takes part in the penitential liturgy, Ne 9:5.

HASHBADDANAH (1), (cf. Hashabiah), an important layman who stands at Ezra's left during the solemn reading of the Law, Ne 8:4.

HASHEM. See: BENE-HASHEM.

HASHUBAH (1), "Respect" (cf. Hashabiah), one of the five sons of Meshullam, a descendant of King Jehoiachin, 1 Ch 3:20.

HASHUM (5), (cf. Hashmonah; Heshmon; Husham?; Hushim), an Israelite, head of a family. His sons return from the exile with Zerubbabel, Ezr 2:19//Ne 7:22; some of them have married foreign wives, whom they put away, Ezr 10:33. He stands on Ezra's left during the solemn reading of the Law, Ne 8:4, and signs the pledge to observe the Law, 10:19.

HASIDAEANS (3), Gr. *Asidaioi,* Hb. *Hasidim,* "Pious" (cf. Hesed), "a community of . . . stout fighting men of Israel, each one a volunteer on the side of the Law," 1 M 2:42, a community born under Antiochus Epiphanes out of hostility to hellenization, forming the shock troops of Judas Maccabaeus, 2 M 14:6, yet not binding themselves to follow Hasmonaean policy, 1 M 7:13–16. From 150 B.C. on, the Hasidaeans split into Pharisees and Essenes.

[HASMONAEANS], the family and dynasty of the Maccabees, from the name of their ancestor *(Ha)shmonai* (= ? *Simeon*), cf. 1 M 2:1.

Among the Hasmonaeans: MATTATHIAH 6; JUDAH 7; JONATHAN 19; JOHN 21; HEROD 1–5. See: Chronological Table 3.

HASMONAH (2), (cf. Hashum), a stage of the Exodus, Nb 33:29–30.

To be connected (?) with: HESHMON.

HASRAH (1). See: HARHAS.

HASSENAAH (1). See: SENAAH.

HASSENUAH (cf. Senaah).

1. **Hassenuah** (1), a Benjaminite, ancestor of: SALLU 1.

2. **Hassenuah** (1), a Benjaminite, father of: JUDAH 4.

HASSHEMAR (1), (cf. Shemaiah), **from Gibeah** (1), father of: JOASH 3.

HASSHUB, "Respected" (cf. Hashabiah).

1. **Hasshub** (1), father of the Levite: SHEMAIAH 7.

2. **Hasshub son of Pahath-moab** (1), a volunteer in the rebuilding of the wall of Jerusalem, Ne 3:11.

3. **Hasshub** (1), another volunteer in the rebuilding of the wall of Jerusalem, Ne 3:23.

4. **Hasshub** (1), a leader of the people and a cosigner of the pledge to observe the Law, Ne 10:24.

HASSOPHERETH (1), "Secretariat; Chancellery" (cf. Kiriath-sepher; Mispar;

Sophrites), head of a family of Solomon's slaves, Ezr 2:55.

= **Sophereth** (1), Ne 7:57.

HASUPHA (2), head of a family of "oblates" who return from the exile, Ezr 2:43//Ne 7:46.

HATHACH (4), a eunuch in the service of Esther, acts as go-between for her and Mordecai, Est 4:5–12. In the Gr. version *Hachrathaios* corresponds to *Hathach,* 4:5, 9–10, 12–13.

HATHATH (1), "Fright"?, a Kenizzite, son of Othniel, 1 Ch 4:13.

HATIPHA (2), head of a family of "oblates" who return from the exile, Ezr 2:54//Ne 7:56.

HATITA (2), head of a family of gatekeepers who return from the exile, Ezr 2:42//Ne 7:45.

HATTIL (2), head of a family of Solomon's slaves who return from the exile, Ezr 2:57//Ne 7:59.

HATTUSH

1. **Hattush** (2), a descendant of David who returns from the exile with Ezra; a son or grandson of Shecaniah, Ezr 8:2–3; 1 Ch 3:22.

2. **Hattush son of Hashabneiah** (1), a volunteer in the rebuilding of the Jerusalem wall, Ne 3:10.

3. **Hattush** (2), a priest who returns from the exile with Zerubbabel, Ne 12:2, a cosigner of the pledge to observe the Law, Ne 10:5.

HAURAN (2), known to the Assyrians, a territory with unclear limits, located east of the Sea of Chinnereth and doubtless including the Jebel Druze. On the NE border of the Promised Land, Ezr 47:16, 18.

HAVILAH (7), a country encircled by the river Pishon, rich in gold and precious stones, Gn 2:11; described, along with Seba, as "sons of Cush," Gn 10:7//1 Ch 1:9, or, with Sheba and Ophir, as "sons of Joktan," Gn 10:29//1 Ch 1:23. The expression "from Havilah to Shur," indicates the limits of the territory of the Ishmaelite, Gn 25:18, or Amalekite, 1 S 15:7, nomads. In southern Arabia.

HAZAEL (23), "God has seen" (cf. Colhozeh; Hazaiah; Haziel; Hozai; Jahaziel; Jahzeiah; Mahazioth), **king of Aram** (14), **king of Damascus** (1), around 844 B.C. Anointed king of Aram by Elijah, 1 K 19:15–17, he hears Elijah proclaim God's plan for him: he will be great both in power and in cruelty, 2 K 8:7–14; cf. Am 1:3–4. An officer of Ben-hadad II, he assassinates his master and rules in his place, 2 K 8:15. He repulses the attacks of Ahaziah and Jehoram at Ramoth-gilead, 2 K 8:28–29//2 Ch 22:5–6; cf. 2 K 9:14–15; he defeats Israel under Jehu, 2 K 10:32, and under Jehoahaz, from whom he takes some towns, 2 K 13:3–7, 22–25; he attacks Jerusalem, but the tribute paid by Joash of Judah to the king of Damascus, 2 Ch 24:23, causes him to renounce his plan of capturing the city, 2 K 12:18–19// 2 Ch 24:23–24.

Father of: BEN-HADAD 3.

HAZAIAH (1), "Yah has seen" (cf. Hazael), ancestor of: MAASEIAH 15.

HAZAR-, "Enclosure, Square, Park, Village," a component of many proper names (cf. the following composite names, as well as Asaramel; Hazeroth; Hazor, and names based on this last).

HAZAR-ADDAR (1), (cf. Hazar-), on the southern border of the Promised Land, Nb 34:4.

= ? **Hezron** (1) and **Addar** (1), on the southern border of Judah, Jos 15:3. Location unknown.

HAZAR-ENAN (4), (cf. Hazar-), a town on the theoretical NE frontier of the Promised Land or of Israel, Nb 34:9–10; Ezk 47:17; 48:1.

= **Hazer-hat-ticon** (1), Ezk 47:16.

HAZAR-GADDAH (1), (cf. Hazar-; Engedi), a town in the Negeb of Judah, Jos 15:27.

HAZARMAVETH (2), "Park of Mot *or* of Death" (cf. Hazar-; Mot), one of the thirteen sons of Joktan, Gn 10:26//1 Ch 1:20. A country in southern Arabia. Today *el-Hadhramaut*.

HAZAR-SHUAL (4), "Park of the Fox" (cf. Hazar-; Shual), in the Negeb, a town of the sons of Simeon, Jos 19:3//1 Ch 4:28, absorbed by Judah, Jos 15:28, and inhabited by Judaeans after the exile, Ne 11:27.

HAZAR-SUSAH (1), "Park of the Cavalry" (cf. Hazar-; Horses), a town of the sons of Simeon, in the Negeb, Jos 19:5.

= **Hazar-susim** (1), 1 Ch 4:31.

HAZAR-SUSIM (1), "Park of the Horses" (cf. Hazar-; Horses). See: HAZAR-SUSAH.

HAZAZON-TAMAR (2). See: TAMAR 4.

HAZER-HAT-TICON (1), "Park of the Middle" (cf. Hazar-; Middle Gate). See: HAZAR-ENAN.

HAZEROTH (6), "Parks" (cf. Hazar-), a stage of the Exodus, in the wilderness, Nb 11:35 (where Miriam and Aaron rebel against Moses, cf. 12:1–15), 12:16; 33:17–18; Dt 1:1.

HAZIEL (1), "Vision of God" (cf. Hazael), a Levite of the clan of Gershon, one of the three sons of Shimei, listed among the heads of families of Ladan, 1 Ch 23:9.

HAZO (1), one of the twelve sons of Nahor, brother of Abraham, born to him of his wife Milcah, Gn 22:22.

HAZOR, Gr. *Asōr,* "Enclosure" (cf. Baal-hazor; En-hazor; Hazar-).

1. **Hazor** (13), ancient Canaanite principal city, taken and burned by Joshua, Jos 11:10–13, listed among the fortified towns of Naphtali, Jos 19:36, fortified by Solomon, 1 K 9:15. Tiglath-pileser captures it from King Pekah of Israel and deports its populace to Assyria, 2 K 15:29. Tobit is from Thisbe near Hazor (corr.; Gr. *Asser*). It is at Hazor that Judas Maccabaeus after an initial defeat wins out over the generals of Demetrius II, 1 M 11:67.

Well known from Egyptian texts. About 15 km N of the Sea of Chinnereth. Today *Tell el-Qedah.*

King: JABIN.

Commander of the army: SISERA 1.

2. **Hazor** (1), a town in the Negeb of Judah, Jos 15:23.

3. **Hazor** (1). See: KERIOTH-HEZRON.

4. **Hazor** (1). See: BAAL-HAZOR.

5. **Hazor** (3), collective name for some seminomadic Arabs as distinct from the Beduin of the desert; conquered by Nebuchadnezzar, Jr 49:28, 30, 33.

HAZOR-HADATTAH (1), "Hazor the New" (cf. Hazor; Hadashah), a town in the Negeb of Judah, Jos 15:25.

HAZZELELPONI (1), "Give me shade, you who turn to me!" (cf. Zillah; Penuel), sister of the sons of Hur, 1 Ch 4:3. In Judah.

HAZZOBEBAH (1), one of the sons of Koz, 1 Ch 4:8. In Judah.

HEBER, Haber, "Companion" (cf. Hebron).

1. **Heber** (4), son of Beriah, son of Asher, Gn 46:17//1 Ch 7:30–31. He has three sons and one daughter, 1 Ch 7:32. His descendants form the **Heberite** clan, Nb 26:45, one of the clans of Asher.

2. **Heber** (5), **the Kenite** (4), leader of a group of seminomadic Kenites camping in Galilee, Jg 4:11, and living in peace with Jabin, king of Hazor, 4:17.

Husband of: JAEL.

3. **Heber** (1), father of Soco, among the sons of Bitiah, in Judah, 1 Ch 4:18.

4. **Haber** (1), a Benjaminite, of the sons of Elpaal, head of a family in Jerusalem, 1 Ch 8:17.

HEBERITE (1), belonging to the clan of: HEBER 1.

HEBREW, Hb. *'Ibri,* "The man from beyond [the Euphrates]" (cf. Eber).

1. **Hebrew(s)** (42), an ethnic group linked to Shem through: EBER 1; cf. Gn 10:21; corresponds to the *Habiru/Apiru* of Egyptian and Mesopotamian texts from the second millennium B.C.

The word designates the Israelites as opposed to the Egyptians, Gn 39:14, 17; 40:15; 41:12; 43:32; Ex 1:15–19; 2:6–13, or the Philistines, 1 S 4:6–9; 13:3, 19; 14:11, 21; 29:3, or, in legal texts, any foreigners, Ex 21:2; Dt 15:12; Jr 34:9, 14. Applied to Abraham at a later date, Gn 14:13. Yahweh is called the God of the Hebrews, Ex 3:18; 5:3; 7:16; 9:1. After Jeremiah the word, which has become archaic and is applied to the Jews, takes on a solemn tone, Jon 1:9; Jdt 10:12; 12:11; 14:18; 2 M 7:31; 11:13; 15:37; 2 Co 11:22; Ph 3:5.

In Ac 6:1 "Hebrews" means Jews born in Palestine, speaking Aramaic, and converted to Christianity, as distinct from "Hellenists" or Jews born outside Palestine, speaking Greek, and likewise converted to Christianity.

Hebrew refers to the Hebrew language in Si prol. 22; Rv 9:11; 16:16 (cf. the "language of [his, their] ancestors," 2 M 7:8, 21, 27; 12:37; 15:29) and to the Aramaic language or writing in Jn 5:2; 19:13; 17:20; 20:16; Ac 21:40; 22:2; 26:14.

2. **Ibri** (1), a Levite of the clan of Merari, one of the leaders of the sons of Jaaziah, 1 Ch 24:27.

HEBRON, "[Place of the] covenant" (cf. Heber).

1. **Hebron** (68), a patriarchal sanctuary where Abraham, Gn 13:18, Isaac, 35:27, and Jacob, 37:13–14, spend some time; and where Sarah is buried, Gn 23:2, 10–19. A town in the highlands of Judah, Jos 15:54; a city of refuge, Jos 20:7, assigned to the Levites of the clan of Kohath, Jos 21:11–13//1 Ch 6:40–42.

This ancient principal town of the Anakim, "founded seven years before Tanis in Egypt," is captured by the Calebites, Nb 13:22–25; Jos 10:36–37, 39; 11:21; 14:13–15; 15:13–14, 54; 21:12–13//1 Ch 6:41–42; Jg 1:10, 20; cf. 1 Ch 2:42–43.

David is proclaimed king there, 2 S 5:1–3//1 Ch 11:1–3; cf. 1 Ch 12:24–39, and makes it his first capital, 2 S 2:1–3, 11; 3:19–20; 5:5; 1 K 2:11; 1 Ch 3:4; 29:27. His first sons are born there, 2 S 3:2–5//1 Ch 3:1–4. Abner is assassinated and buried there, 2 S 3:19–32; 4:1, 12. When Absalom rebels, he has himself proclaimed king at Hebron, 2 S 15:7–10. The town is rebuilt by Rehoboam, 2 Ch 11:10. Taken from the Idumaeans by Judas Maccabaeus, 1 M 5:65.

= **Kiriath-arba** (9), identified with Hebron in Gn 23:2; 35:27; Jos 14:15; 15:13, 54; 20:7; 21:11; Jg 1:10, inhabited by Judaeans after the exile, Ne 11:25.

Today *Hebron,* in Arabic *el-Khalil* ("The Friend," which is the name given to Abraham in Is 41:8; Jm 2:23). 40 km S of Jerusalem.

See: MACHPELAH; MAMRE.

2. **Hebron** (8), the third of the four sons of Kohath, son of Levi, Ex 6:18; Nb 3:19; 1 Ch 5:28; 6:3; 23:12. He has four sons, 1 Ch 23:19//24:23. The descendants of Hebron form the **Hebronite** clan, Nb 3:27, which is listed among the clans of Levi in Nb 26:58 (acc. to the ancient list of the Levitic tribes—which differs from the canonical division into Gershonite, Kohathite, and Merarite clans—the Hebronites originally lived in the town of: HEBRON 1). They are initially associated with the transfer of the Ark, 1 Ch 15:9. Later on, other functions are assigned to them, 1 Ch 26:30–32; cf. 23:25–32.

HEBRONITE (6), Nb 3:27; 26:58; 1 Ch 26:23, 30–31, belonging to the clan of: HEBRON 2.

HEGAI (4), Gr. *Gai,* a eunuch who is responsible for the harem of Ahasuerus and to whose care Esther the Jewess is entrusted, Est 2:3, 8–9, 15.

HEGEMONIDES (1), "Governor," a military commissioner, under Antiochus V, for the Palestinian coastal region, "from Ptolemais to the territory of the Gerrenians," 2 M 13:24.

HELAH (2), "Rust," one of the wives of Ashhur, mother of several clans connected with Judah, 1 Ch 4:5, 7.

HELAM (2), a town in Transjordania, about 60 km E of the Sea of Chinnereth. David does battle there with the Aramaean army of Hadadezer, 2 S 10:16–17.

= **Alema** (2), which Judas Maccabaeus burns after having liberated its Jewish prisoners, 1 M 5:26, 35.

HELBON (1), an area N of Damascus, famous for its wine, Ezk 27:18.

HELDAI (cf. Heled).

1. **Heldai from Netophah, of Othniel** (1). See: HELED.

2. **Heldai** (2), one of the deported who return from Babylon to Jerusalem and show themselves especially generous, Zc 6:10, 14 (corr. of Hb. *Helem*).

HELED (2), "Duration," **son of Baanah, from Netophah** (2), one of David's champions, 2 S 23:29 (var. of Hb. *Heleb*); 1 Ch 11:30.

= **Heldai from Netophah, of Othniel** (1), in charge of the (military) service for the twelfth month, 1 Ch 27:15.

HELEK (2), abbrev. of *Hilkiah?* Second of the second group of the sons of Manasseh, Jos 17:2, or second of the sons of Gilead (who is grandson of Manasseh), whose descendants form the **Helekite** clan, Nb 26:30.

= ? **Likhi** (1), son of Shemida (son of Manasseh), 1 Ch 7:19.

HELEKITE (1), belonging to the clan of: HELEK.

HELEM (1), a descendant of Asher and father of four sons, 1 Ch 7:35.

HELEPH (1), a town on the border of Naphtali, Jos 19:33. Perhaps NE of Tabor.

HELEZ, an abbrev. "[Yah] has extricated, rescued."

1. **Helez** (3), **from Beth-pelet** (1), 2 S 23:26, or **the Pelonite** (2), 1 Ch 11:27, one of David's champions, **an Ephraimite** (1), in charge of the (military) service for the seventh month, 1 Ch 27:10.

2. **Helez** (2), a descendant of Jerahmeel through Sheshan, 1 Ch 2:37.

HELI (1). See: ELI 2.

HELIODORUS (12), "Gift of the sun" (cf. Heliopolis; Dositheus. See Samson), chancellor of Seleucus IV, king of Syria. Commissioned to take the treasures of the temple, he is saved by the prayers of the Jews and is converted, 2 M 3:7–40; cf. 4:1; 5:18.

HELIOPOLIS, "City of the sun" (cf. Amphipolis; Heliodorus. See Samson). See: ON 1.

To be identified (?) with: IR HAHERES.

HELKAI (1), a derivative of *Hilkiah?* Head of the priestly family of Meremoth in the time of the high priest Joiakim, Ne 12:15.

HELKATH, "Parcel, Field" (cf. Hilkiah).

1. **Helkath** (2), a town of the tribe of Asher, Jos 19:25, assigned to the Levites of the clan of Gershon, Jos 21:31.

= **Hukok** (1), 1 Ch 6:60.

2. **Field of Sides** (1). See: ZIDDIM 2.

HELL (12). See: HINNOM.

HELLAS. See: GREECE *b.*

[HELLENISM], the civilization that began with the conquests of Alexander the Great and arose from the interaction between Greek culture and eastern culture, 2 M 4:13. See: GREEK.

HELLENISTS (2), (cf. Greek), Jews born outside of Palestine and speaking Greek (as their maternal or usual tongue), as contrasted with the "Hebrews," that is, Jews born in Palestine and speaking Aramaic, Ac 6:1. Generally speaking, the former are more open to the Gospel message, cf. Ac 11:20–21; yet it is among them that the newly converted Saul meets with opposition, Ac 9:29.

HELON (5), a Zebulunite, father of: ELIAB 1.

HEMAM (1), Gn 36:22, second son of Lotan, who is himself the first son of Seir.

= **Homam** (1), 1 Ch 1:39.

HEMAN (17), "Faithful"? (cf. Amon), is mentioned in 1 K 5:11 with Ethan the Ezrahite, Calcol, and Darda as among the wise men probably best known in Canaan. With them he is also listed among the five sons of Zerah, son of Judah in 1 Ch 2:6; there may be a confusion here between Hb. *'Ezrahi,* "Ezrahite or native," Ps 88:1, and *Zerah.*

Elsewhere, in 1 and 2 Ch, Heman is always associated with Asaph and Ethan (or Jeduthun). He is thus one of David's great cantors, eponymous ancestors of the cantors and instrumentalists, cf. 2 Ch 35:15. Belonging to the clan of Kohath, son of Levi, Heman is the **son of Joel** (2) and grandson of Samuel, 1 Ch 6:18; 15:17; at his right hand stands Asaph and at his left Ethan, 1 Ch 6:24, 29. He takes part in the ceremony for the transfer of the Ark, 1 Ch 15:17, 19; cf. 2 Ch 5:12, and in the sacrifices offered on the high place of Gibeon, 1 Ch 16:41–42.

The **sons of Heman,** "the king's seer," 1 Ch 25:1, 4–6, are in charge of fourteen classes of cantors, 25:13, 16, 18, 20, 22–31. Note that the last nine names of the sons of Heman form a fragment of a psalm: "Be gracious to me, Yahweh, be gracious to me, you are my God! I have increased, I have raised myself up, you are the help I have sought! Grant me many visions!"

Among his sons: SHIMEI 11.

HEMDAN (1), Gn 36:26, first of the four sons of Dishon (Hb. *Dishan*), himself the fifth son of Seir.

= **Hamran** (1), 1 Ch 1:41.

HENA (3), listed with Hamath, Arpad, Sepharvaim, and Ivvah as among the towns conquered by the Assyrians, 2 K 18:34; 19:13//Is 37:13. Probably in Upper Mesopotamia.

HENADAD (3), "Hadad is gracious" (cf. Hadad 1–4; Hanan), a Levite, father of: BINNUI 3.

HEPHER, Hb. 1: "Well" (cf. Gath-hepher; Hapharaim).

1. **Hepher** (2), a Canaanite town whose king is defeated by Joshua, Jos 12:17. In Solomon's third district, 1 K 4:10. In the northern part of the coastal plain.

2. **Hepher** (5), sixth son of Manasseh, Jos 17:2, or sixth son of Gilead, whose descendants form the **Hepherite** clan, Nb 26:32. To be connected with the preceding?

Father of: ZELOPHEHAD.

3. **Hepher** (1), a Judaean clan of the sons of Naarah, of Calebite origin, 1 Ch 4:6.

4. **Hepher from Mecherah** (1), 1 Ch 11:36, one of David's champions.

HEPHERITE (1), belonging to the clan of: HEPHER 2.

HEPHZIBAH, "My delight is in her."

1. **Hephzibah** (1), mother of King Manasseh of Judah, 2 K 21:1.

2. **My Delight** (1), a name of the new Jerusalem, Is 62:4.

[HERACLEOPOLIS], (cf. Amphipolis; Hercules). See: HANES.

HERCULES (1), Lat. name of the Gr. god Heracles (cf. Heracleopolis); a Gr. hero venerated at Tyre, where he is identified with the god Melkart. On the occasion of the quinquennial games at Tyre, the high priest Jason sends 300 silver drachmas for a sacrifice to Hercules, 2 M 4:19–20.

HERES (Ascent of) (1), "Sun"? (cf. Har-heres; Ir Haheres; Timnath-heres. See Heliopolis; Samson), taken by Gideon after the defeat of the Midianite kings, Jg 8:13. In Transjordania, in the area of Succoth.

HERESH (1), a Levite living in Jerusalem after the exile, 1 Ch 9:15.

HERETH (1), probably in the neighborhood of Adullam and Keilah. David takes refuge in the forest there, 1 S 22:5.

HERMAS (1), (cf. Hermes), a Christian of Rome, Rm 16:14.

HERMES, Gr. name of the Roman god *Mercury,* messenger of the gods (cf. Hermas; Hermogenes).

1. **Hermes** (1), the god for whom Paul is mistaken at Lystra, "since Paul was the principal speaker," Ac 14:12.

2. **Hermes** (1), a Christian of Rome, Rm 16:14.

HERMOGENES (1), (cf. Hermes), one of the Christians of Asia who "refuse to have anything to do with" Paul, 2 Tm 1:15.

HERMON (16), "Forbidden, sacred place" (cf. Baal-hermon; Hormah), the highest peak (2814 m) of the Anti-Lebanon, overlooking the Bekaa.

Northern boundary of the kingdom of Og of Bashan, Jos 12:15; 13:11, conquered by the Israelites, Dt 3:8; 4:48; Jos 12:1; cf. Am 4:3 (corr. of Hb. *Harmôn*) and occupied by sons of Manasseh, 1 Ch 5:23.

The word occurs in poetic texts, Ps 42:4 (Hb. *the Hermons*); 89:13; 133:3; Si 24:13.

= **Senir** (4), Amorite name for Hermon. Dt 3:9; 1 Ch 5:23; Sg 4:8; Ezk 27:5.

= **Sirion** (3), Sidonian name for Hermon, Dt 3:9; 4:48; Ps 29:6.

See: BAAL-HERMON.

At the foot of Hermon: BAAL-GAD; MIZPAH 3.

HEROD, from the Gr. *herōs,* "Noble, Demigod" (cf. Herodians; Herodias; Herodion). See: Chronological Table 3, page 467.

1. **Herod [the Great]** (11), son of an Idumaean, Antipater, and an Arabian princess, **king of Judaea** (1), Lk 1:5, and of Samaria (37–4 B.C.). A bloodthirsty dictator. A great builder, he founds, among other cities, the city of: CAESAREA 1, cf. Ac 23:35.

It is in his reign that Lk 1:5 places the birth of John the Baptist, and Mt 2:1–22 the birth of Jesus at Bethlehem, the visit of the Magi, the slaughter of the children at Bethlehem (for which Herod is responsible), and the flight of Joseph, Mary, and Jesus to Egypt.

Father of: ARCHELAUS; HEROD 2, 5–6; PHILIP 6.

Grandfather of: HEROD 3–4; HERODIAS.

2. **Herod [Antipas]** (27), son of Herod the Great and Malthake, **tetrarch of Galilee** (1), Lk 3:1, and of Peraea (4 B.C.–39 A.D.), called a king, Mk 6:14. He puts away his wife, the daughter of Aretas IV, and marries Herodias, wife of his brother Philip. John the Baptist condemns this violation of Jewish law; Herod has him imprisoned and later decapitated, Mk 6:17–28//Mt 14:3–11; Lk 3:19–20. Herod hears tell of Jesus, Mk 6:14–16//Mt 14:1–2//Lk 9:7–9; cf. 23:8, and, acc. to the Pharisees, wants to kill him, Lk 13:31. As a Galilean, Jesus is under Herod's jurisdiction and therefore, during his passion, appears before the tetrarch of Galilee, who treats him with contempt and makes fun of him, Lk 23:7–11, 15; cf. Ac 4:27.

Herod is tricky; Jesus speaks of him as "that fox," Lk 13:32; cf. Mk 8:15.

He is first the enemy, then the friend, of Pilate, Lk 23:12.

See: HERODIANS; HERODIAS.

Childhood friend: MENAHEM 2.

Steward: CHUZA.

3. **Herod [Agrippa I]** (5), grandson of Herod the Great, king of Judaea and Samaria (41–44 A.D.), persecutes the leaders of the early Church: he has James beheaded and Peter imprisoned, Ac 12: 1–11, 19a. He dies a terrible death at Caesarea, 12:19b–23.

Father of: BERNICE; DRUSILLA; HEROD 4.

4. **[Herod] Agrippa II** (11), son of the preceding, king of Chalcis (48–53), then of the tetrarchies of Philip and Lysanias (53–95). In company with his sister Bernice, with whom he lives in an incestuous union, he visits Festus, the procurator at Caesarea. On this occasion Paul appears as a prisoner before him and declares his conviction that Agrippa knows the events that have taken place (the death and resurrection of Jesus) and believes in the prophets. Agrippa would have been in favor of Paul's being set free, Ac 25:13–26:32.

5. **[Herod] Philip** (2), son of Herod the Great and Mariamne II, first husband of Herodias, Mt 14:3//Mk 6:17.

See: HEROD 2.

Father of: SALOME 2.

6. **[Herod] Philip** (3), son of Herod the Great and Cleopatra, tetrarch of Ituraea and Trachonitis (1) (4 B.C.–34 A.D.), Lk 3:1. He rebuilds the city of: CAESAREA 1.

HERODIANS (3), (cf. Herod), Jews who are partisans of the Herodian dynasty, especially of Herod Antipas, and hostile to Jesus, Mt 22:16//Mk 12:12; Mk 3:6; cf. Mk 8:15.

HERODIAS (6), (cf. Herod), granddaughter of Herod the Great, abandons her first husband (who is also her uncle), Herod Philip, and marries another uncle, Herod Antipas. She incites the latter to put John the Baptist to death for denouncing this illegitimate union, Mt 14:3//Mk 6:17, 19//Lk 3:19.

Mother of: SALOME 2.

HERODION (1), (cf. Herod), a Jewish Christian of Rome, a fellow countryman of Paul, Rm 16:11.

HESED (Son of) (1), "Fidelity, Solidarity" (cf. Hasidaeans; Hasadiah; Jushab-hesed), administrator of Solomon's third district, 1 K 4:10.

HESHBON (39), "Plan, scheme," see Jr 48:2 (cf. Hashabiah?), **city of Sihon** (2) in Transjordania.

Occupied by Israelites, Nb 21:25–30; Jg 11:26; Jdt 5:15, assigned to Reuben, Nb 32:37; Jos 13:17, on the border of Gad, Jos 13:26, assigned to Levites of the clan of Merari, Jos 21:39//1 Ch 6:66, but finally Moabite, Is 15:4; Jr 48:34, or conquered by the Ammonites, Jr 48:2; 49:3. Heshbon, with the nearby towns of Elealeh and Sebam, is a region of pastures, Nb 32:1–4; Jos 21:39; of vineyards, Is 16:8–9; Jr 48:32, of water pools, Sg 7:5.

Today *Hisban,* 35 km E of Jericho.

Residence of king: SIHON.

HESHMON (1), (cf. Hashum), a town in the Negeb of Judah, Jos 15:27. To be connected (?) with: HASHMONAH.

HETH (14). See: HITTITES.

HETHLON (2), on the ideal northern border of the Holy Land, Ezk 47:15; 48:1.

HEZEKIAH, Jehizkiah, Hizkiah, Hb. *Hizqiyyah,* "My strength is Yah," see 2 K 18:6–7, *Yehizqiyyah, Yehizqiyyahu,* "May Yah strengthen" (cf. Hizki).

1. **Jehizkiah son of Shallum** (1), one of the four officers of the northern kingdom, 2 Ch 28:12, who in response to the appeal of the prophet Oded, take pity on their Judaean brothers in prison, supply their needs, and set them free, vv. 5–12.

2. **Hezekiah** (131), **son of Ahaz** (1) and Abijah, thirteenth king of Judah

(716–687). Associated with his father since 728, cf. 2 K 18:9–10, he becomes really the successor to Ahaz, 2 K 18:1// 2 Ch 29:1, only in 716, five years after the fall of the northern kingdom. A contemporary of the prophets Hosea, Ho 1:1, Isaiah, Is 1:1, Micah, Mi 1:1; Jr 26:18–19, "he did what is pleasing to Yahweh. . . . [and] put his trust in the God of Israel. . . . He was devoted to Yahweh," 2 K 18:3–7; cf. 2 Ch 31:20–21, meriting, along with David and Josiah, the unreserved praise of Ben Sira, Si 48:22; 49:4. Regarding the reign of Hezekiah, the Bible recalls:

—the public works he undertakes in Jerusalem "to bring water into the city," 2 K 20:20//2 Ch 32:30; cf. Si 48:17, and to fortify it, 2 Ch 32:5;

—the literary activity he fosters at the court where a collection of proverbs is made, Pr 25:1;

—the religious reform he undertakes: purification of the temple, the renewal of the clergy and the cultus, celebration of a solemn Passover, organization of the offering of the first-fruits and the tithes, 2 Ch 29:3–31:21;

—his illness, his prayer, his cure, 2 K 20:1–11//Is 38:1–6, 21–22, 7–8, his canticle of thanksgiving, Is 38:9–20;

—his contacts with Merodach-baladan, king of Babylon, who sends an embassy to him in about 703, both to congratulate him on his cure and to try to make an ally of him against Assyria, 2 K 20:12–19//Is 39:1–8; cf. 2 Ch 32:23, 25, 31. The self-centered reply that Hezekiah gives Isaiah, 2 K 20:19, who predicts the later Babylonian invasion, has been deleted by the chronicler, who emphasizes the glory, wealth, and piety of the king of Judah, 2 Ch 32:26–29;

—his unpleasant dealings with Sennacherib, king of Assyria, against whom he rebels in about 705, 2 K 18:7; it is difficult to determine whether there were two campaigns against Sennacherib in Palestine, in 701 and 690, or only one, in 701. Acc. to 2 K 18:13–16//Is 36:1, Hezekiah eliminates the Assyrian threat by paying a tribute. The chronicler adds an account of the military preparations made by Hezekiah, whom he exalts, 2 Ch 32:2–8. Another account, 2 K 18:17–19, 37//Is 36:21–37:38; cf. 2 Ch 32:9–26, gives a great many more details: parleys between Sennacherib and Hezekiah, intervention of Isaiah, unexpected liberation of Jerusalem, cf. 2 M 15:22.

Hezekiah is listed among the ancestors of Jesus, Mt 1:9–10.

His son and successor: MANASSEH 2.

3. **Hezekiah** (1), ancestor of: ZEPHANIAH 2.

4. **Hizkiah** (1), second of the three sons of Neariah, a descendant of King Jehoiachin, 1 Ch 3:23.

5. **Hezekiah** (3). See: ATER 1.

HEZION (1), "Vision" (cf. Hazael), an ancestor of: BEN-HADAD 1.

HEZIR, "Wild boar, Pig."

1. **Hezir** (1), head of the seventeenth priestly class, 1 Ch 24:15.

2. **Hezir** (1), a leader of the people and cosigner of the pledge to observe the Law, Ne 10:21.

HEZRO from Carmel (2), 2 S 23:35// 1 Ch 11:37, one of David's champions.

HEZRON

1. **Hezron** (4), third of the four sons of Reuben, Gn 46:9; Ex 6:14; 1 Ch 3:5, whose sons form the **Hezronite** clan, Nb 26:6.

2. **Hezron** (15), son of Perez, son of Judah, and brother of Hamul, Gn 46:12//1 Ch 2:5; cf. 4:1, whose descendants form the **Hezronite** clan, Nb 26:21. Father of Ram and ancestor of David, Rt 4:18–19; 1 Ch 2:5. Acc. to 1 Ch 2:9, 18, 24–25, he is also father of Caleb and Jerahmeel. Acc. to 1 Ch 2:21 he "married the daughter of Machir, father of Gilead." He is an ancestor of Jesus, Mt 1:3; Lk 3:33.

3. **Hezron** (1), a town of Judah, Jos 15:3. See: HAZAR-ADDAR.

HEZRONITE (2), belonging to the clan of: HEZRON 1 or 2.

HIDDAI (1), 2 S 23:30 = **Hurai** (1), 1 Ch 11:32, **from the wadis of Gaash** (2), one of David's champions.

HIEL (1), abbrev. of *Ahiel,* gr. *Achiel,* "My Brother is God" (cf. Ahi), **of Bethel** (1), rebuilds Jericho in the time of Ahab. At this time his two sons die (victims of a foundation sacrifice?), 1 K 16:34; cf. Jos 6:26.

HIERAPOLIS (1), "Sacred city" (cf. Amphipolis), a city of Phrygia in Asia Minor, notable especially for its hot springs, near Laodicea, Col 4:13. See: COLOSSAE.

HIERONYMUS (1), "Sacred name" (cf. Hierapolis), one of the five military commissioners for Syria who "would not allow the Jews to live in peace and quiet," 2 M 12:2.

HIGHLANDS, Hb. *Har* (cf. Hor).

1. **The Highlands** (12), refers in whole or in part to the chain of hills that runs north-south through Galilee, Samaria, and Judaea. The word is often used in parallel with Negeb and: LOWLANDS.

2. **The Highlands of Ephraim** (32). See: EPHRAIM 1.

HILEN (1). See: HOLON 1.

HILKIAH, Hb. *Hilqiyya, Hilqiyyahu,* Gr. *Chelkias, Elkia,* Lat. *Helcias,* "My share is Yah" (cf. Hakeldama; Helek?; Helkai?; Helkath).

1. **Hilkiah** (6), father of: ELIAKIM 1.

2. **Hilkiah** (22), a high priest, a descendant of Zadok, son of Shallum or Meshullam, 1 Ch 5:38–39; 9:11; Ne 11:11, ancestor of Ezra, Ezr 7:1. During the work on the temple he discovers the Book of the Law (in all probability the legislative part of our present Book of Deuteronomy), 2 K 22:3–10//2 Ch 34:8–9. As a result of this discovery and at the request of King Josiah, he leads a delegation to the prophetess Huldah, 2 K 22:11–20//2 Ch 34:19–28, takes part in the religious reform of Josiah, 2 K 23:4, 24; 2 Ch 35:8.

Father of: JOIAKIM 2.

3. **Hilkiah** (1), a descendant of Merari and an ancestor of Ethan the cantor, 1 Ch 6:30.

4. **Hilkiah** (1), a gatekeeper, second of the sons of Hosah, a descendant of Merari, 1 Ch 26:11.

5. **Hilkiah** (1), Jr 1:1, father of the prophet: JEREMIAH.

6. **Hilkiah** (1), father of: GEMARIAH 1.

7. **Hilkiah** (1), an ancestor of Baruch, the secretary of Jeremiah, Ba 1:1.

8. **Hilkiah** (1), an important layman, stands at Ezra's right during the solemn reading of the Law, Ne 8:4.

9. **Hilkiah** (2), a priest who returns from the exile with Zerubbabel, Ne 12:7. In the time of the high priest Joiakim, Hashabiah is the head of his family, Ne 12:21.

10. **Hilkiah** (3), Dn 13:2, 29, 63, father of: SUSANNA 1.

11. **Hilkiah** (1) and **Elkiah** (1), two Simeonites, ancestors of Judith, Jdt 8:1.

HILLEL (2), "He has praised" (cf. Jehallelel; Mahalalel), father of the judge: ABDON 1.

HILL OF GAREB (1). See: GAREB 2.

HINNOM (3), Jos 15:8; 18:16; Ne 11:30, or **Ben-hinnom** (9), or **The Sons of Hinnom** (1) **(Valley of).** A valley west and south of Jerusalem, on the border of Judah and Benjamin, Jos 15:8; 18:16; Ne 11:30. Called simply **The Valley** in Jr 2:23, it is famous chiefly for the abominable religious practices of the Israelites who there "built the high place of Topheth . . . to burn their sons and daughters," Jr 7:31–32; 19:2, 6; 32:35, in honor of Molech, cf. Lv 18:21, the example being given by Kings Ahaz, 2 Ch 28:3, and Manasseh, 33:6. Josiah desecrates this high place, 2 K 23:10. Read

Valley of Hinnom for *Valley of vision* (Hb.) or *Valley of Zion* (Gr.), in Is 22:1, 5.

From the city one went out to this valley by the Gate of the: VALLEY.

= HELL (12), Gr. *geenna.* Changed into a public refuse-dump and permanent place for burning, this valley, the "hell of fire," Mt 5:22; 18:9, "where their worm does not die nor their fire go out," Mk 9:47–48; cf. Is 66:24, becomes the symbol of the accursed spot par excellence and of eternal punishment, Mt 5:22–30//Mk 9:43–48; Mt 18:8–9, where God can destroy both the body and the soul, Mt 10:28//Lk 12:5, of those he condemns, Lt 25:15, 33; cf. 25:41, 46. In Jm 3:6 the fire of hell is used to describe the power of evil that is at work in sins of the tongue that can set fire to the whole world.

See: SHEOL.

HIRAH (2), **the Adullamite** (3), friend of Judah and his go-between with Tamar, Gn 38:1, 12, 20.

HIRAM, abbrev. of *Ahiram,* "My Brother is on high" (cf. Ramah).

1. **Hiram** (19) or **Huram** (7), 2 Ch 2:2, 10–11; 8:2, 18; 9:10, 21, **king of Tyre** (6), a contemporary and friend of David and Solomon. He provides David with material and craftsmen for building the royal palace, 2 S 5:11//1 Ch 14:1, and Solomon with the same for building the temple, 1 K 5:15–26//2 Ch 2:2–11; 1 K 5:32. He helps Solomon arm a fleet, 1 K 9:26–28//2 Ch 8:17–18, and has trade agreements with him, 1 K 10:11, 22//2 Ch 9:10, 21. Acc. to 1 K 9:10–14 Solomon gives Hiram "twenty-two towns in the land of Galilee," which do not please him; but cf.//2 Ch 8:1–2.

2. **Hiram** (4) or **Huram** (2), 2 Ch 4:11, or **Huram-abi** (2), 2 Ch 2:12; 4:16, **from Tyre** (1), a bronze worker, son of a Tyrian father and a Naphtalite, 1 K 7:13, or Danite, 2 Ch 2:12, mother, he does all the bronze work for the temple of Solomon, 1 K 7:13–47//2 Ch 2:12–13; 4:11–16.

HITTITES (48), in the Bible, does not refer to the great Anatolian empire that disappeared around 1200 B.C., but to one of the non-Israelite peoples of Syro-Palestine. The Hittites are one of the "seven peoples" of: CANAAN *a.* Among the foreign wives of Solomon are some Hittite women, 1 K 11:1. The land of the Hittites is northern Syria, 1 K 10:29//2 Ch 1:17; 2 K 7:6, or Syro-Palestine, Jos 1:4; Jg 1:26; cf. 3:3 (corr. of Hb. *Hivites*).

= **Sons of Heth** or **daughters of Heth** (21), whose eponymous ancestor, **Heth** (2), is called son of Canaan in the Yahwist tradition, Gn 10:15//1 Ch 1:13 (perhaps an allusion to the ancient Hittite empire). Abraham buys Machpelah from the sons of Heth as a burial place for Sarah, Gn 23:3–20; 25:10; 49:32. At Beersheba, Esau chooses wives from among the daughters of Heth, Gn 27:46.

Hittites: AHIMELECH 3; BEERI 1; ELON 1; EPHRON 1; URIAH 1.

In the land of the Hittites: KADESH 2.

HIVITES (2), a pre-Israelite people of Cisjordania: CANAAN *a.* The presence of Hivites at Gibeon, Jos 9:7; 11:19, and Shechem, Gn 34:2, is noted. Some correct *Hivite* to *Hittite* in Jg 3:3, or to *Horite* in Gn 36:2.

Hivite: HAMOR.

HIZKI (1), "My strength is [Yah or El]" (cf. Ezekiel; Hezekiah), a Benjaminite of the sons of Elpaal, head of a family in Jerusalem, 1 Ch 8:17.

HIZKIAH (1). See: HEZEKIAH 4.

HOBAB (2), **the Kenite** (1), Jg 1:16, **father-in-law of Moses** (3), Jg 4:11. In Nb 10:29 ff. Hobab is called *son of Reuel the Midianite.*

See: JETHRO.

HOBAH, north of Damascus (1), the place where Abraham defeats the four kings, Gn 14:15.

HOBAIAH (1). See: HABAIAH.

HOD (1), "Majesty" (cf. Ahihud; Ammihud; Eliud; Hodiah; Ishbod), an Asherite, one of the eleven sons of Zophah, head of a family, 1 Ch 7:37.

HODAVIAH, "Celebate Yah," see Ps 118:1.

1. **Hodaviah** (1), head of a family of Levites who return from the exile with Zerubbabel. Ezr 2:40. He superintends the workmen at the temple, Ezr 3:9 (corr. of Hb. *Jehudah*) and signs the pledge to observe the Law, Ne 10:11 (corr. of Hb. *Hodiah*).

= **Hodiah** (1), Ne 7:43.

2. **Hodaviah** (1), of the eastern half-tribe of Manasseh, a fighting man and head of a family, 1 Ch 5:24.

3. **Hodaviah** (1), a Benjaminite, ancestor of: SALLU 1.

4. **Hodaviah** (1), one of the seven sons of Elioenai, a descendant of King Jehoiachin, 1 Ch 3:24.

HODIAH, "Yah is Majesty" (cf. Hod).

1. **Hodiah** (1), whose wife is sister of Naham, connected with Caleb, 1 Ch 4:19.

2. **Hodiah** (1). See: HODAVIAH 1.

3. **Hodiah** (3), among the Levites who explain the Law to the people during its solemn reading by Ezra Ne 8:7, urge the people to bless God during the penitential liturgy, Ne 9:5, and sign the pledge to observe the Law, Ne 10:14.

4. **Hodiah** (1), a leader of the people, a cosigner of the pledge to observe the Law, Ne 10:19.

HOGLAH (4), "Partridge" (cf. Beth-hoglah), Nb 26:33; 27:1; 36:11; Jos 17:3, in Manasseh, one of the five daughters of: ZELOPHEHAD.

HOHAM (1), **king of Hebron** (4), an Amorite, allied with: ADONI-ZEDEK.

HOLOFERNES (44), a Pers. name, commander-in-chief of the armies of Nebuchadnezzar, king of the Assyrians, Jdt 2:4; 4:1. After a lightning campaign he threatens Judaea, 4–7. During the siege of Bethulia, Judith, thanks to her faith, her resourcefulness, and her beauty, succeeds in decapitating him, 10–13; 16:5–9; cf. also 15:11; 16:19.

HOLON

1. **Holon** (2), a town in the highlands of Judah, Jos 15:51, assigned to the Levites of the clan of Kohath, Jos 21:15.

= **Hilen** (1), 1 Ch 6:43. 16 km NNW of Hebron.

2. **Holon** (1), a town in Moab, Jr 48:21. Otherwise unknown.

HOLY LAND (4), Hb. *'admat (ha-) qôdèsh,* Gr. *hagia gē.* The reference is first of all to the ground, the piece of earth, where God manifests himself, for example, Mount Sinai, where God reveals his most holy name to Moses: "Come no nearer. Take off your shoes, for the place on which you stand is *holy ground,*" Ex 3:5–6; cf. 19:12. Similarly the spot near Jericho where the captain of Yahweh's army appears to Joshua is declared "holy," Jos 5:15. The presence of God gives a place a sacred character, as Jacob realizes at Bethel: "Yahweh is in this place and I never knew it! . . . How awe-inspiring this place is! This is nothing less than a house of God; this is the gate of heaven!" Gn 28:16–17.

It is in Zc 2:16 that the land of Israel is called for the first time the *Holy Land.* The expression reappears in 2 M 1:7 and Ws 12:3 ("your holy land"). It is also said to be a "holy place," 2 M 1:29, a "sanctuary," Ex 15:17; Ps 114:2. This land is holy because it is "the land of Yahweh," Is 14:2; Hos 9:3; cf. 2 Ch 7:20; Ws 12:3; Jr 16:18, "the heritage of Yahweh," 1 S 26:19; 2 S 14:16. To this land which he has given to his people and whose capital, Jerusalem, "Zion of the Holy One of Israel," Is 60:14, is Yahweh's "city founded on the holy mountain," Ps 87:1–3, Yahweh, the Holy One of Israel, is bound in a special way, to the point where David does not think he can honor him in a foreign land, 1 S 26:19, and that Naaman brings some Israelite earth to Damascus in order that he may worship God there, 2 K 5:17.

Profaned and defiled by the Israelites, Is 24:5; Jr 16:18; Ezk 36:17, the ideal Holy Land will, in the perspective of the postexilic prophets, someday be wholely purified and made sacred, Ezk 47:13–48:35; Zc 14. The entire earth, however, belongs to God, Ex 19:5; Lv 25:23; Dt 10:14; Ps 24:1, and the human beings to whom God has given it, Ps 115:16; Gn 1:28, are simply "God's tenants," cf. Lv 25:23. It is already holy inasmuch as it is God's footstool, Is 66:1//Mt 5:35//Ac 7:49. Above all, as Origen said, since the Son of God came upon this earth where his Gospel is to be spread to the ends of the world, Mt 26:13; Ac 1:8; 13:47; Rm 10:18, "all the earth is holy."

HOMAM (1). See: HEMAM.

HOPHNI (5), Egypt. *Hfn(r),* "Tadpole," Gr. *Ophni,* brother of: PHINEHAS 2.

HOPHRA (1), Hb. of Egypt. *Ouahibri* or *Hâibria,* Gr. *Apries,* **Pharaoh** (5), **king of Egypt** (2) (589–569). He comes to Palestine to resist Nebuchadnezzar, who is besieging Jerusalem, but is forced to return to his own country, Jr 37:5–7, 11. Jeremiah calls him "Much-noise-but-he-lets-the-chance-slip-by," 46:17. The proximate death of Hophra—he will be assassinated by the followers of Amasis—is predicted in Jr 44:30. It is perhaps to him that the military action against Gaza is to be attributed, Jr 47:1.

HOR (Mount), Hb. *Hor ha-Har* (cf. Highlands).

1. **Mount Hor** (10), on the border of Edom, a stage of the Exodus, where Aaron dies, Nb 20:22–28; 21:4; 33:37–41; Dt 32:50. Identical (?) with: MOSEROTH.

2. **Mount Hor** (2), a town on the northern border of the Promised Land, Nb 34:7–8. Site unknown.

HORAM (1), (cf. Harum) **king of Gezer** (2), comes to the aid of Lachish and is defeated by Joshua, Jos 10:33; 12:12.

HOREB (18), "Dry, Desertlike"? (cf. Harbona). See: SINAI.

HOREM (1), a town in Naphtali, Jos 19:38.

HORESH (4), "Forest" (cf. Harosheth-ha-goiim), in the wilderness of Ziph. David flees there to escape Saul's wrath and is visited by Jonathan, 1 S 23:15–16, 18–19. At least 10 km S of Hebron.

HOR-HAGGIDGAD (2), Nb 33:32, 33, a stage of the Exodus.

= **Gudgodah** (2), Dt 10:7.

HORI

1. **Hori** (2), eldest of the sons of Lotan, son of Seir, Gn 36:22//1 Ch 1:39.

2. **Hori** (1), a Simeonite, father of: SHAPHAT 1.

HORITES (8), Accad. *Hurru,* an ancient people occupying the highlands of Seir, Gn 14:6, dispossessed by the Edomites, Dt 2:12, 22. They are probably descendants of the Hurrites, whose presence in Palestine is attested in the fifteenth and fourteenth centuries B.C., a period in which Egypt. documents call Palestine *Huru.*

HORMAH (9), meaning connected by Nb 21:3 and Jg 1:17 with the Hb. *herem,* "anathema, ban" (cf. Hermon). An old Canaanite town: scene of the defeat of the Israelites by the Amalekites and Canaanites, Nb 14:45//Dt 1:44, then of the Israelite victory over the Canaanites, Nb 21:3; cf. Jos 12:14. A town in the Negeb of Judah, Jos 15:30; 1 S 30:30, formerly a town of Simeon, Jos 19:4//1 Ch 4:30.

= **Zephath** (1), ancient name of this town, Jg 1:17.

[HORON], (cf. Beth-horon; Horonaim?), a god known at Ugarit, capable of attacking but also of healing serpent bites. Later identified with *Asclepius.*

HORONAIM (4), "Two holes *or* Double Horon"? (cf. Horon), a town in Moab, Is 15:5; Jr 48:3 (corr. to *Abarim*), 5, 34. Its name is found on the stele of Mesha. Not identified with certainty.
See: HORONITE.

HORONITE (3), Ne 2:10, 19; 13:28, coming either from Beth-horon or from Horonaim. See: SANBALLAT.

HORSES (Entry of the) (4), Hb. *Susim* (cf. Hazar-susah. See Archippus), gate at Jerusalem, 2 K 11:16//2 Ch 23:15, in the eastern wall toward the Kidron, Jr 31:40, or perhaps between the royal palace and the temple precincts, Ne 3:28. It probably gave access to the king's stables.

[HORUS], Egypt. *Hor* (cf. Harnepher; Hur; Shihor), an Egyptian god represented by a falcon or a man with a falcon's head. See: NILE (Jr 2:18; Is 23:3).

HOSAH
1. **Hosah** (4) of the clan of Merari, a gatekeeper, 1 Ch 16:38, whose four sons are named, 26:10–11, 16.
2. **Hosah** (1), a town in Asher, Jos 19:29. Some km S of Tyre.

HOSEA (3). See: HOSHEA 3.

HOSHAIAH, "Yah has saved" (cf. Isaiah).
1. **Hoshaiah** (2), father of: AZARIAH 15.
2. **Hoshaiah** (1), one of the leaders of Judah who take part in the dedication of the wall of Jerusalem, Ne 12:32.

HOSHAMA (1), "Yah hears" (cf. Shemaiah), one of the sons born to King Jehoiachin when a prisoner at Babylon, 1 Ch 3:17.

HOSHEA, Hb. *Hoshéa',* Gr. *Osēe,* "[Yah] saves" (cf. Isaiah).
1. **Hoshea son of Nun** (3). See: JOSHUA 1.
2. **Hoshea** (8), **son of Elah** (4), nineteenth and last king of Israel (732–724). He reaches the throne after assassinating his predecessor, 2 K 15:30. A contemporary of Ahaz, 2 K 17:1, and Hezekiah, 2 K 18:1, kings of Judah. He pays tribute to the king of Assyria, but when he ceases payment and looks for help from Egypt, he is taken prisoner by the king of Assyria, 2 K 17:1–6//18:9–11.
3. **Hosea** (3) **son of Beeri** (1), the "first" of the twelve "Minor Prophets," a contemporary of Amos. His ministry is exercised in the northern kingdom under Jeroboam II, Hos 1:1, and probably under the following kings, at a period marked by a series of palace revolutions and by Assyrian conquests that will end in the fall of the kingdom. For Hosea it is a time of dramatic marital experience in his own life: he marries **Gomer daughter of Diblaim,** whom he loves passionately, but this woman is unfaithful to him and goes in for (sacral?) prostitution. He has three children—two boys and a girl—to whom he gives symbolic names: **Jezreel** (which calls to mind the massacre of the dynasty of Omri), *Lo-Ammi,* **"No-People-of-Mine,"** and *Lo-Ruhamah,* **"Unloved,"** Hos 1:2–9; cf. 2:24–25; 3:1–3. . . . "In loving Gomer as she was, Hosea grasped and was able to express the love of the Lord for his people as it was" ([French] *Ecumenical Translation of the Bible*).
4. **Hoshea son of Azaziah** (1), commissioner for the tribe of Ephraim, 1 Ch 27:20.
5. **Hoshea** (1), a leader of the people, a cosigner of the pledge to observe the Law, Ne 10:24.

HOTHAM, "Seal."
1. **Hotham** (1), an Asherite, one of the three sons of Heber, son of Beriah, 1 Ch 7:32.
2. **Hotham the Aroerite** (1), father of Jeiel and: SHAMA.

HOTHIR (2), "Abundance" (cf. Jether), one of the sons of Heman, leader of the twenty-first class of cantors, 1 Ch 25:4, 28.

HOZAI (1), "Seer" (cf. Hazael), an otherwise unknown prophet whose annals are mentioned in 2 Ch 33:19 as giving the details of the conversion of King Manasseh.

HUBBAH (1), an Asherite, one of the sons of Shomer, head of a family, 1 Ch 7:34.

HUKKOK
1. **Hukkok** (1), a town on the border of Zebulun and Naphtali, Jos 19:34.
2. **Hukok** (1). See: HELKATH 1.

HUKOK (1). See: HUKKOK 2.

HUL (2), one of the four sons of Aram, Gn 10:23//1 Ch 1:17.

HULDAH, wife of Shallum (2), a prophetess whom Josiah consults after the discovery of the Book of the Law in the temple, 2 K 22:14–20//2 Ch 34:22–28. Other prophetesses: MARY 1.

HUMTAH (1), a town in the highlands of Judah, Jos 15:54.

HUPHAM (1). See: HUPPIM 1.

HUPHAMITE (1), belonging to the clan of: HUPPIM 1.

HUPPAH (1), "Canopy," head of the thirteenth priestly class, 1 Ch 24:13.

HUPPIM
1. **Huppim** (1), a son of Benjamin, Gn 46:21.
= **Hupham** (1), whose descendants form the **Huphamite** clan, Nb 26:39.
= ? **Huram** (1), 1 Ch 8:5, son of Bela, son of Benjamin.
2. **Huppim** (2), associated with Shuppim and connected with Benjamin in 1 Ch 7:12 (but v. 12 may have belonged to a genealogy of *Dan*) and with Manasseh in 1 Ch 7:15.

HUR, Egypt. *Hor,* "[God] Horus" (cf. Horus), Accad. *Huru,* "Child" (cf. Huri).
1. **Hur** (3), companion of Moses and Aaron, Ex 17:10, 12; 24:14.
2. **Hur** (9), son of Caleb by Ephrath or Ephrathah, whose first-born he is called, 1 Ch 2:19; 4:4. His posterity is given in 1 Ch 2:50–51; 4:3–4. He is listed among the sons of Judah. Ancestor of: BEZALEL 1.
3. **Hur** (2), one of the five Midianite kings who are vassals of Sihon, king of the Amorites, Jos 13:21, and are conquered and put to death by the Israelites during the Exodus, Nb 31:8.
4. **Son of Hur** (1), administrator of Solomon's first district, 1 K 4:8.
5. **Hur** (1), father of: REPHAIAH 5.

HURAI (1). See: HIDDAI.

HURAM
1. **Huram** (1). See: HUPPIM 1.
2. **Huram** (7). See: HIRAM 1.
3. **Huram** (2). See: HIRAM 2.

HURAM-ABI (2), "Huram is my father." See: HIRAM 2.

HURI (1), (cf. Hur). See: BEN-HURI.

HUSHAH (1), 1 Ch 4:4, a town in Judah. West of Bethlehem. Native place of: SIBBECAI.

HUSHAI
1. **Hushai** (13) **the Archite** (5), companion and friend of David, 2 S 15:32, 37; 1 Ch 27:33, whose fidelity and resourcefulness during the rebellion of Absalom succeed in frustrating the plans of Ahithophel, the king's former adviser, who has gone over to the service of the rebellious son, 2 S 16:16–18; 17:5–15.
2. **Hushai** (1), father of: BAANAH 4. To be identified (?) with the preceding?

HUSHAM (4), (cf. Hashum?) **of the land of the Temanites** (2), king of Edom, Gn 36:34–35//1 Ch 1:45–46.

HUSHATITE (5), from: HUSHAH.

HUSHIM (cf. Hashum).

1. **Hushim** (2). See: SHUHAM.

2. **Hushim** (2), a wife dismissed by the Benjaminite Gera, 1 Ch 8:8. Mother of Ahitub and Elpaal, 8:11.

HUTS (6), Hb. *Naioth,* dwellings of the prophets, cf. 2 K 6:1–2, at Ramah, or else a spot thus called at Ramah, 1 S 19:18–19, 22–23; 20:1.

HYDASPES (1), a river, Jdt 1:6. Probably the river at Susa (and therefore the: ULAI) rather than a tributary of the Indus.

HYENAS (Valley of the) (1), between Ramah and Jericho, 1 S 13:18.

HYMENAEUS (2), Gr. *Hymenaios,* "[God of] marriage," a heretical Christian who is excluded from the community, 1 Tm 1:20; 2 Tm 2:17–18.

HYRCANUS, Gr. *Hyrkanos,* "[Conqueror] of the Hyrcaneans *or* Native of Hyrcania."

1. **Hyrcanus son of Tobias** (1). Acc. to 2 M 3:11 he had deposited a sum of silver in the temple treasury.

2. **[Hyrcanus I].** See: JOHN 21; Chronological Table 3.

I

IAMLEKU (1), "[God] reigns" (cf. Jamlech; Melech), **the Arab** (1). This prince, perhaps the son of Zabdiel, cf. 1 M 11:7, probably lives at Chalcis, south of Aleppo. He is in charge of the education of the young son of Alexander Balas, the future king Antiochus VI, 1 M 11:39 (corr. of Gr. *Eimalkouai*).

IBHAR (3), "Choice" (cf. Mibhar), one of David's sons born at Jerusalem, 2 S 5:15//1 Ch 3:6//14:5.

IBLEAM, Jibleam (5), Hb. *Yibl'am,* a former Canaanite town that long retained its independence, Jg 1:27, between Manasseh and Issachar, Jos 17:11. Near Ibleam, on the Slope of Gur, King Ahaziah of Judah is mortally wounded, 2 K 9:27. Acc. to the Gr. recension of Lucian, Zechariah, king of Israel is assassinated at Ibleam, 2 K 15:10. The town of Jibleam is assigned to Levites of the clan of Kohath, Jos 21:25 (corr. of Hb. *Gath-rimmon*).

= **Bileam** (1), 1 Ch 6:55.

IBNEIAH (1), "Yah builds" (cf. Benaiah), **son of Jeroham** (1), head of a Benjaminite family settled in Jerusalem, 1 Ch 9:8.

IBNIJAH (1), "Yah builds" (cf. Benaiah), a Benjaminite, ancestor of: MESHULLAM 6.

IBRI (1). See: HEBREW 2.

IBSAM (1), an Issacharite, one of the heads of the families of Tola, 1 Ch 7:2.

IBZAN (2), (cf. Ebez), **of Bethlehem** (1), in Zebulun? One of the "lesser" judges of Israel, Jg 12:8–10.

ICHABOD (2), "Where is the Glory?" or an abbrev. of *Abikabod,* "My Father is Glory" or of *Ahikabod,* "My Brother is Glory"; popular etymology: "Without glory," 1 S 4:21 (cf. Jochebed?), **son of Phinehas son of Eli** (1), born on the day the Ark is captured by the Philistines and the day when his father, his uncle Hophni, his mother, and his grandfather, the priest Eli, all die, 1 S 4:21. Brother of Ahitub, 1 S 14:3.

ICONIUM (6), a city of Lycaonia in Asia Minor. During their first missionary journey Barnabas and Paul preach the Gospel there. Jews and pagans oppose his activity, Ac 13:51; 14:1–7, 19, 21; 16:2; 2 Tm 3:11. Today *Konya* in Turkey.

IDBASH (1), "Honey," among the sons of Hur, connected with Judah, 1 Ch 4:3.

IDDO, Hb. 1: *Yiddo* (cf. David); 2: *'Iddo;* 3–7: *'Iddo'* or *'Iddo* (= ? Oded).

1. **Iddo son of Zechariah** (1), commissioner for the half tribe of Manasseh in Gad, 1 Ch 27:21.

2. **Iddo** (2), **the leading man in the region of Casiphia** (1) in Babylonia. Be-

fore journeying to Jerusalem, Ezra sends to Iddo to get servants for the temple, Ezr 8:17.

3. **Iddo** (1), father of the administrator: AHINADAB.

4. **Iddo** (3), a seer or prophet to whom 2 Ch 12:15 attributes Annals recording the history of King Rehoboam, and 2 Ch 13:22 a Midrash on the history of King Abijah. Acc. to 2 Ch 9:29 he has a vision regarding Jeroboam.

5. **Iddo** (4), father of the prophet: ZECHARIAH 22.

6. **Iddo** (1), 1 Ch 6:6. See: EDEN 2.

7. **Iddo** (2), head of a priestly family who returns from the exile with Zerubbabel, Ne 12:4. In the time of the high priest Joiakim this family has Zechariah for its head, Ne 12:16.

IDOLS (2), Hb. *Pesilim,* posts or hewn stones used as a topographical reference point, Jg 3:19, 26. Near: GILGAL 1.

IDUMAEA (7). See: EDOM.

IDUMAEAN (2), 2 M 10:15–16, an inhabitant of: IDUMAEA.

IEZER (1), abbrev. of *Abiezer,* Nb 26:30. See: ABIEZER 1.

IEZERITE (1), Nb 26:30, of the Manassite clan of Iezer or: ABIEZER 1.

IGAL, Hb. *Yig'al,* "He ransoms."

1. **Igal son of Joseph** (1), chief of an Issacharite clan, sent by Moses to represent his tribe in the reconnaissance of Canaan, Nb 13:7.

2. **Igal son of Nathan, from Zobah** (1), 2 S 23:36.

= **Joel the brother of Nathan** (1), 1 Ch 11:38, one of David's champions.

3. **Igal** (1), one of the six sons of Shecaniah, a descendant of King Jehoiachin, 1 Ch 3:22.

IGDALIAH (1), "Yah is great" (cf. Gedaliah), father of: BEN-JOHANAN.

IIM, Iyim, "Ruins" (cf. Iye-abarim).

1. **Iim** (1), a town in the Negeb of Judah, Jos 15:29.

2. **Iyim** (1). See: IYE-ABARIM.

IJON (3), a town captured at the same time as Abel-beth-maacah by Ben-hadad, king of Aram, 1 K 15:20//2 Ch 16:4, and later by Tiglath-pileser, king of Assyria, 2 K 15:29. In the extreme north of Palestine, about 10 km N of Abel-beth-maacah.

IKKESH (3), "Crooked *or* Depraved," father of: IRA 2.

ILAI from Ahoh (1). See: ZALMON 1.

ILLYRICUM (1), a region of NW Macedonia; a Roman province from 27 B.C. on. Paul preaches the Gospel there, Rm 15:19.

= **Dalmatia** (1), visited by Titus, 2 Tm 4:10. Today part of Yugoslavia.

IMLAH (4), Hb. *Imlah, Imla'* (cf. Millo), father of the prophet: MICAH 7.

IMMANUEL (2), **Emmanuel** (1), Hb. *'Immanu'el,* "With us [is] God," see Ex 17:7; Ps 46; etc. (cf. Ithiel?), a symbolic name of a descendant of the house of David, foretold to Ahaz, Is 7:14; 8:8–10; the name designates not only Hezekiah but, beyond him, the Messiah, Jesus, son of Joseph, acc. to Mt 1:23 (*Emmanuel*).

In Rv 21:3 *God-with-them* is an equivalent of *Immanuel.*

IMMER, "Sheep."

1. **Immer** (7), head of the sixteenth priestly class, 1 Ch 24:14. The **sons of Immer** return from the exile with Zerubbabel, Ezr 2:37//Ne 7:40. Some of them put away their foreign wives, Ezr 10:20.

Father of: PASHHUR 1.

Ancestor of: AMASHAI.

2. **Immer** (1), father of: ZADOK 3.

3. **Immer** (2), a town in Babylonia where some deported Jews live, Ezr 2:59//Ne 7:61.

IMNA (1). See: IMNAH 3.

IMNAH, Hb. 1–2: *Yimnah* (cf. Meni); 3: *Yimna'*.

1. **Imnah** (3), first of the sons of Asher, Gn 46:17; 1 Ch 7:30, whose descendants form the **Imnite** clan, Nb 26:44.

2. **Imnah** (1), father of: KORE 2.

3. **Imna** (1), an Asherite, one of the sons of Helem, 1 Ch 7:35.

IMNITE (1), belonging to the clan of: IMNAH 1.

IMRAH (1), an Asherite, one of the eleven sons of Zophah, 1 Ch 7:36.

IMRI, abbrev. of *Amariah,* "Yah speaks."

1. **Imri** (1), a Judaean, ancestor of: UTHAI 1.

2. **Imri** (1), father of: ZACCUR 5.

INDIA (4). The word is found only in Est 1:1; 3:13[a]; 8:9, 12[b], in the phrase *from India to Ethiopia,* which expresses the eastern and western boundaries of the Persian Empire of Ahasuerus. Acc. to 1 M 8:8 Antiochus the Great, after his defeat at Magnesia on the Sipylus in 189, cedes to the Romans *the Indian territory,* among others, but in fact India never belonged, even partially, to the Seleucids; but *Indian* here is perhaps a corruption of *Ionian*.

In 1 M 6:37 the elephant driver is called in Gr. *indos,* "hindu," because the animal comes from India.

INDIAN (1), 1 M 8:8. See: INDIA.

[IONIA], ancient name for the Asiatic coastal region of the Aegean Sea between Phocaea and Miletus, peopled by Greeks from Greece and including in particular the cities of Miletus and Ephesus. See: GREECE *a;* INDIA.

IPHDEIAH (1), (cf. Pedaiah), a Benjaminite, one of the eleven sons of Shashak, head of a family at Jerusalem, 1 Ch 8:25.

IPHTAH (1). See: JEPHTHAH 2.

IPHTAHEL (Vale or **Plain of)** (2), "God opens, rescues" (cf. Jephthah), between the territory of Zebulun and the territory of Asher, Jos 19:14, 27.

IR, Hb. *'Ir,* 1: "Ass" (cf. Ira; Iram; Iri); 2: "Town, city."

1. **Ir** (1), 1 Ch 7:12, a Benjaminite (compare with: Iri) or Danite (if v. 12 really belongs to a genealogy of Dan).

2. **Ir.** See: CITY OF DAVID; CITY OF SALT; IR HAHERES; IRNAHASH; IRSHEMESH; PALM TREES (CITY OF); REHOBOTH-IR.

IRA (cf. Ir).

1. **Ira the Jairite** (1), a priest of David, 2 S 20:26. Perhaps a doublet of no. 3, following.

2. **Ira son of Ikkesh, from Tekoa** (2), one of David's champions, 2 S 23:26// 1 Ch 11:28, in charge of the (military) service for the sixth month, 1 Ch 27:9.

3. **Ira from Jattir** (corr. of Hb. *the Ithrite*) (2), one of David's champions, 2 S 23:38//1 Ch 11:40.

IRAD (2), son of Enoch and father of Mehujael, Gn 4:18 (Yahwist genealogy).

= **Jared** (7), son of Mahalael and father of Enoch, Gn 5:15–16, 18–19 (priestly genealogy); cf. 1 Ch 1:2. An ancestor of Jesus, Lk 3:37. One of the antediluvian patriarchs.

IRALAH (1), a town in Zebulun, Jos 19:15 (var. of Hb. *Yideala*).

IRAM (2), (cf. Ir), one of the chiefs (or clans) of Edom, Gn 36:43//1 Ch 1:54.

[IRAN]. See: ELAM 1; MEDIA; PARTHIANS; PERSIA.

The "upper provinces," 1 M 3:37; 6:1, or "upland satrapies," 2 M 9:25, refer to the Iranian plateau.

IR HAHERES (1), "City of the sun" (cf. Heres; Irnahash; Irshemesh; Rehoboth-ir. See Amphipolis; Kiriath) or "City of destruction," acc. as *heres* is read with *he* or *heth.* One of the five cities of Egypt that will speak "the language of Canaan" (that is, Hebrew) when Egypt is reconciled with Assyria and Israel, Is 19:18. Perhaps identical with: HELIOPOLIS.

IRI (1), (cf. Ir), a Benjaminite, head of a family, one of the five sons of Bela, 1 Ch 7:7. Compare with: IR 1.

IRIJAH (2), "Yah sees" (cf. Haroeh), **son of Shelemaiah son of Hananiah** (1), sentry at the Benjamin Gate in Jerusalem. He arrests Jeremiah, accusing him of going over to the enemy (the Chaldaeans) and hands him over to the authorities of the city, Jr 37:13–14.

IRNAHASH (1), "City rich in copper *or* City of Nahash" (cf. Nahash), a town in Judah, of Calebite origin, 1 Ch 4:12.

IRPEEL (1), (cf. Raphael), a town in Benjamin, Jos 18:27.

IRSHEMESH (1), "City of the sun" (cf. Samson). See: BETH-SHEMESH 1.

IRU (1), one of the sons of Caleb, 1 Ch 4:15.

ISAAC (140), Hb. *Yizhak,* "May [God] laugh, smile, be kind," **son of Abraham** (1). Born of a hundred-year-old father and a nonagenarian mother, Gn 17:17, circumcised on the eighth day, Gn 21:4; Ac 7:8, Isaac grows up with his half-brother Ishmael until the day when Sarah forces Abraham to send Hagar and her son away, Gn 21:8, 14. Offered in sacrifice by his father, Isaac is saved at the last moment, Gn 22; Heb 11:17–18; Jm 2:21. At the age of forty he marries Rebekah, Gn 25:20, whose hand has been sought for him in Mesopotamia, Gn 24:4, 14, 62–67. At the age of sixty he begets Esau and Jacob, Gn 25:26; cf. Jos 24:24; Rm 9:10–11. A famine sends him to Gerar and the area of Beersheba, where he grows rich and digs wells, Gn 26. As an old man he "gave his blessing to Jacob and Esau for the still distant future," Gn 27; Heb 11:20. He dies at the age of 180, Gn 35:27–29, and is buried at Machpelah, 49:31.

Isaac, child of laughter, Gn 17:17; 18:12; cf. 21:9, is above all the child of the promise, Rm 9:7–9; Ga 4:28, by a twofold title: he is solemnly promised to Abraham and Sarah, Gn 15:4; 17:15–22; 18:9–15; 21:1, and he is entrusted with the promises of the covenant, Gn 17:19; 21:12; 22:17. In becoming a child of sacrifice, Isaac becomes the means of testing Abraham's faith in God's fidelity, Heb 11:17–18. The personality of Isaac, son of Abraham and father of Jacob, Gn 48:15; Jos 24:3–4; 1 Ch 1:34; Mt 1:2; Lk 3:34, does not emerge strongly from the patriarchal stories, but he is a key figure in sacred history, so that Genesis can speak of the *God of Isaac,* 46:1, a God who is also called the *Kinsman* [or: *Fear*] *of Isaac,* 31:42, 53, and Paul can speak of Isaac as "our ancestor Isaac," Rm 9:10.

Isaac and *the house of Isaac,* in Am 7:9, 16, refer to the northern kingdom (Israel).

Abraham, Isaac, and Jacob: ABRAHAM *c*.

ISAIAH, Jeshaiah, Gr. *Esaias,* Hb. *Yesha'yah, Yesha'yahu,* "Yah is salvation" (cf. Elisha?; Hosea; Hoshaiah; Ishi; Mesha 3–4. See Joshua).

1. **Isaiah** (46) **son of Amoz** (13), a prophet in Judah.

The prophet Isaiah

His vocation dates from the year of the death of King Uzziah (740 B.C.), Is 6, and his ministry is exercised during the reigns of Jotham, Ahaz, and Hezekiah in Judah, Is 1:1. Acc. to Jewish tradition he was executed by King Manasseh.

Isaiah attacks first of all the moral corruption attendant upon the prosperity of Judah, Is 1–5. At the time of the Syro-Ephraimite coalition, ca. 734, he attempts in vain to prevent King Ahaz from turning to Assyria for help, Is 7–11; he intervenes again in 705, when Hezekiah rebels against Assyria, 2 K 18:7. Sennacherib invades Palestine, but Isaiah supports Hezekiah in his resistance and assures him that Jerusalem will be saved, 2 K 19:1–7//Is 37:1–7; cf. Si 48:20–22. Acc. to 2 Ch 32:20 the prophet joins Hezekiah in his prayer, cf. 2 K 19:15// Is 37:15. Oracle of Isaiah against Sennacherib, 2 K 19:20–34//Is 37:21–35. Hezekiah falls ill, turns to Isaiah, and is cured, 2 K 20:1–11//Is 38:1–8, 21–22. Isaiah reproaches Hezekiah after the embassy from Merodach-baladan, king of Babylon, 2 K 20:12–19//Is 39:1–8. Isaiah's own family takes part in his ministry: his wife, who is described as a prophetess, Is 8:1, and his two sons, Shear-jashub and Maher-shalal-hash-baz, whose names are symbolic and who, like their father, Is 20:2–3, are signs and portents in Israel, Is 7:3; 8:1–4, 18; cf. 10: 21–22. He also doubtless has disciples who continue his work.

The book of Isaiah

Half of the occurrences of the name "Isaiah" refer not to the prophet himself but to the "book of Isaiah": 2× in 2 Ch (26:22; 32:32) and 21× in the NT (Mt 3:3//Mk 1:2//Lk 3:4//Jn 1:23; Mt 4: 14; 8:17; 12:17; 13:14; 15:7//Mk 7:6; Lk 4:17, 20; Jn 12:38–41; Ac 8:28, 30; 28:25; Rm 9:27, 29; 10:16, 20; 15:12). The NT has, in addition, about forty citations of Isaiah that are not expressly attributed to the prophet.

More than half of the oracles transmitted under the name of Isaiah are generally regarded as later than the period of the prophet himself, and the collection of 66 chapters is a library of prophecy, a summa of Israelite prophecy. The critics like to distinguish three major collections: First Isaiah (1–39); Second Isaiah (40–55); Third Isaiah (56–66). The whole collection, however, is attributed to the greatest of the prophets, the witness to the holiness of a God who is at once utterly transcendent and yet present to the world and its history.

2. **Jeshaiah** (1), son or grandson of Hananiah, a descendant of King Jehoiachin, 1 Ch 3:21.

3. **Jeshaiah** (2), of the sons of Jeduthun, leader of the eighth class of cantors, 1 Ch 25:3, 15.

4. **Jeshaiah** (1), a Levite of the clan of Kohath, a descendant of Moses through Eliezer, among those in charge of the treasury of consecrated offerings, 1 Ch 26:25.

5. **Jeshaiah son of Athaliah** (1), head of a family of the sons of Elam, who returns from the exile with Ezra, Ezr 8:7.

6. **Jeshaiah** (1), a Levite of the sons of Merari, part of the convoy that brings the temple furnishings back from Babylon, Ezr 8:19.

7. **Jeshaiah** (1), a Benjaminite, acc. to Ne 11:7 an ancestor of: SALLU 1.

ISCAH (1), a daughter of Haran, brother of Abraham, and sister of Lot and Milcah, Gn 11:29 (Yahwist tradition).

ISCARIOT (12), Gr. *Iskariōtēs* (9×), Mt 10:4; 26:14; Mk 14:43; Lk 22:3; Jn 6:71; 12:4; 13:2, 26; 14:22, or *Iscariōth* (3×), Mk 3:19; 14:10; Lk 6:16, a name difficult to interpret: in Hb. *Ish Qeriyyot,* "a man from Kerioth" (cf. Jos 15:25); in Aram. *Ishqarya,* "False, lying, hypocritical," or *Iaskar iothe,* "He who handed him over," Mk 3:19; Mt 10:4 . . . ; Gr. *Sikarios,* "Hired killer," equivalent to *Zealot* (note that in the lists of the Twelve in Mt 10:4 and Mk 3:19, Judas Iscariot immediately follows Simon the Zealot).

Surname of the Apostle who betrays Jesus: JUDAH 12, and of his father: SIMEON 12.

ISHBAAL, "Man of Baal" (cf. Baal).

1. **Ishbaal** (12), (corr. of Hb. *Ishbosheth,* "man of shame") **son of Saul** (8). At Saul's death Abner makes Ishbaal, then forty years old, the king of Israel at Mahanaim; he will reign for two years, 2 S 2:8–10. At Gibeon a battle is fought between the young soldiers of David and those of Ishbaal, 2:12–15. Ishbaal sus-

pects Abner, his commander-in-chief, of a desire to become king, 3:7–11. He yields to David's demands when the latter claims his wife Michal (sister of Ishbaal), 3:14–15. The murder of Abner causes Ishbaal to lose heart, 4:1. A little later he himself is assassinated by two of his chieftains, Rechab and Baanah, who go over to David, but the latter has them executed and buries Ishbaal at Hebron beside Abner, 4:2–12.

= **Eshbaal** (2), brother of Jonathan, Malchi-shua, and Abinadab, 1 Ch 8:33/ 9:39.

= **Ishvi** (1), 1 S 14:49.

2. **Ishbaal the Hachmonite** (1), acc. to Gr. (corr. of Hb. *living in the Tahkmonite dwelling*), one of David's champions, leader of the Three, 2 S 23:8.

= **Jashobeam the Hachmonite** (1), 1 Ch 11:11.

= **Jashobeam son of Zabdiel** (1), of the Judaean clan of Perez, in charge of the (military) service for the first month, 1 Ch 27:2.

3. **Ishbaal** (1), acc. to Gr. (corr. of Hb. *Yeshebab*), in charge of the fourteenth priestly class, 1 Ch 24:13.

ISHBAH (1), one of the sons of Bithiah (daughter of Pharaoh) and father of Eshtemoa. Connected with Caleb, 1 Ch 4:17, 18.

ISHBAK (2), (cf. Shobek), one of the six sons of Abraham and his concubine Keturah; a people or region of Arabia, Gn 25:2//1 Ch 1:32.

ISHHOD (1), "Man of Majesty" (cf. Hod), a Manassite, son of Malchath, 1 Ch 7:18.

ISHI, "My salvation" (cf. Isaiah).

1. **Ishi** (2), a descendant of Jerahmeel through Onam and Shammai, father of Sheshan, 1 Ch 2:31.

2. **Ishi** (1), father of Zoheth and Ben-zoheth. Connected with the Calebite group, 1 Ch 4:20. To be connected with the preceding?

3. **The sons of Ishi** (1), Simeonite chiefs settled in the highlands of Seir, 1 Ch 4:42–43.

4. **Ishi** (1), a Manassite, head of a clan, 1 Ch 5:24.

ISHMA (1), Hb. *Yishma'*, abbrev. of *Yishma''el,* "God hears" (cf. Shemaiah), among the sons of Hur, connected with Judah, 1 Ch 4:3.

ISHMAEL, Hb. *Yishma''el,* "God hears," see Gn 16:11 (cf. Shemaiah).

1. **Ishmael** (20), **son of Abraham** (2) and the Egyptian woman Hagar, who is Sarah's servant, Gn 16:3–16; cf. 1 Ch 1:28. He is foretold to his mother as being "a wild ass of a man," Gn 16:12. Circumcised at thirteen, 17:23–26, Ishmael is later sent away by Sarah, who does not want to see him inherit with her son Isaac, 21:8–21; cf. Ga 4:22–30. He buries his father Abraham at Machpelah, Gn 25:9, and dies at the age of 137, 25:17. Although not the child of the promise, he is blessed by God, and the twelve princes whom he begets (the eponymous ancestors of the twelve Arabian tribes, who are peoples as independent and footloose as the wild ass) will be "a great nation," Gn 17:20; 21:18; 25:12–16//1 Ch 1:29–31.

Joseph is sold to Ishmaelite traders who carry him off to Egypt, Gn 37:25–28; 39:1. Victory of Gideon over the Ishmaelites, cf. Jg 8:24. A campaign of Holofernes against "sons of Ishmael," Jdt 2:23. In Ps 83:6 the Ishmaelites are among the traditional enemies of Israel.

Daughters of Ishmael and Ishmaelites: Basemath 1; Jether; Mahalath 1; Obil.

2. **Ishmael** (2), a Benjaminite, one of the six sons of Azel, a descendant of Saul, 1 Ch 8:38//9:44.

3. **Ishmael** (1), father of: Zebadiah 7.

4. **Ishmael son of Jehohanan** (1), one of the five commanders of hundreds who are in the plot against Athaliah, 2 Ch 23:1–15.

5. **Ishmael** (23), **son of Nethaniah**

(16), **son of Elishama** (2), a Judaean officer of Davidic descent who resists the Babylonian occupiers after the fall of Jerusalem. At the instigation of Baalis, king of the Ammonites, he assassinates Gedaliah, the governor appointed by Nebuchadnezzar, at Mizpah, Jr 40:7–9// 2 K 25:23–25; Jr 40:14–16; 41:1–3. At Mizpah he also assassinates eighty men of Shiloh and Samaria and throws their corpses into a large cistern, and he also imprisons the survivors there. Judaean officers free the latter, and Ishmael takes refuge among the Ammonites, Jr 41: 6–18.

6. **Ishmael** (1), a priest, of the sons of Pashhur, married to a foreign wife, whom he puts away, Ezr 10:22.

ISHMAELITES (7), Gn 37:25, 27–28; 39:1; Jg 8:24; Ps 83:7, descendants of: ISHMAEL 1.

ISHMAIAH, "Yah hears" (cf. Shemaiah).

1. **Ishmaiah from Gibeon** (1), "a champion among the Thirty, and over the Thirty," who rallies to David before the latter becomes king, 1 Ch 12:4.

2. **Ishmaiah son of Obadiah** (1), leader of the tribe of Zebulun, 1 Ch 27: 19.

ISHMERAI (1), abbrev. of *Shemariah?* A Benjaminite of the sons of Elpaal, head of a family in Jerusalem, 1 Ch 8:18.

ISHPAH (1), a Benjaminite of the sons of Beriah, head of a family in Jerusalem, 1 Ch 8:16.

ISHPAN (1), a Benjaminite of the sons of Shashak, head of a family in Jerusalem, 1 Ch 8:22.

[ISHTAR], (cf. Esther), Assyro-Babylonian goddess of love and war, daughter of Sin (moon god) and sister of Shemesh (sun god), often called "Beauty" in Assyrian writings; identified with the planet Venus and venerated under the name Astarte in Canaan. In Na 2:8 "Lady" (JB) or "Statue" is probably the statue of Ishtar, goddess of Nineveh. In Jr 7:18; 44:17, 19, 25, the *Queen of Heaven* refers to Ishtar, whom some Judaeans are worshipping (offering incense, cakes representing the naked goddess, and so on).

ISHVAH (2), (cf. Shaveh), second of the sons of Asher, acc. to Gn 46:17// 1 Ch 7:30.

ISHVI (cf. Shaveh).

1. **Ishvi** (3), third son of Asher, acc. to Gn 46:17//1 Ch 7:30, whose descendants form the **Ishvite** clan, Nb 26: 44.

2. **Ishvi** (1), 1 S 14:49. See: ISHBAAL 1.

ISHVITE (1), belonging to the clan of: ISHVI 1.

ISMACHIAH (1), "Yah sustains" (cf. Semachiah), one of the ten Levites assisting Conaniah and Shimei in the time of King Hezekiah, 2 Ch 31:13.

ISRAEL (2,760), "May God struggle, show his strength," see Gn 32:29; Ho 12:5, *or* "May God reign, be Lord" (cf. Sarah; Seraiah). The word occurs: In the Hb. OT (2,500×): Pentateuch, 584; Jos to Kings, 1,334; 1–2 Ch-Ezr-Ne, 357; Ps, 62; Is, 92; Jr, 124; Ezk, 184; Dn, 4; minor prophets, 104; Pr, 1; Qo, 1; Sg, 1. Not in Est, Tb, Jos, Hab, or Hg.

In the deuterocanonical writings (190×): Tb, 17; Jdt, 53; Est, 7; 1 M, 65; 2 M, 5; Si, 18; Ba, 19; Dh, 7. Not in Ws.

In the NT (70×): Mt, 12; Mk, 2; Lk, 12; Jn, 4; Ac, 15; Rm, 12; 1 Co, 1; 2 Co, 2; Ga, 1; Ep, 1; Ph, 2; Heb, 3; Rv, 3. Not in the other books.

a. Israel = the patriarch Jacob (± 50×)

The name Israel is given to Jacob at the time of his wrestling with God, Gn 33:29, and the divine manifestation at Bethel, 35:10; cf. 1 K 18:31; 2 K 17:34. In this usage it is found 34× in Gn

33:20–35:21–22; 37:3, 13; 42–50, and 15× in the remainder of the Bible, 1 Ch 29:10 (Israel our ancestor//Jn 4:12; cf. Is 63:16); Jdt 8:1; Dn 3:35; Ho 12:13 . . .

See: JACOB 1 *a*.

b. The tribes of Israel

After renewing with Isaac, Gn 26:3–5, the covenant made with Abraham, Gn 17:19, God makes the covenant "rest on the head" of Jacob/Israel and his descendants, who are the eponymous ancestors of the twelve tribes of Israel, Si 44:22–23. These tribes give the people of God its basic structure. The texts speak of: *the tribes of Israel* (50×), Gn 49:16, 28; Nb 31:4 . . . Zc 9:1, or *of the sons of Israel* (9×), Nb 30:2; 32:28; 36:8–9; Jos 4:5–8; 14:1; 19:51; 21:1, *the twelve tribes of Israel* (4×), Ex 24:4; Ezk 47:13; Mt 19:28; Lk 22:30, or *of the sons of Israel* (2×), Rv 7:4; 21:12. In Gn 49:28 the twelve tribes are described as connected with the twelve sons of Jacob/Israel; their birth is told in Gn 29:32–30:25; 35:17 ff., where the first list occurs; *Reuben, Simeon, Levi, Judah, Dan, Naphtali, Gad, Asher, Issachar, Zebulun, Joseph, Benjamin*. In the thirty lists of the tribes that the Bible contains, we may note three points:

Levi is often missing, for it is a tribe apart, which "has no share or inheritance with his brothers; Yahweh is his inheritance," Dt 10:9.

Joseph is sometimes represented by his two sons *Ephraim* and *Manasseh* or is mentioned with one of these. Manasseh is often divided into eastern Manasseh (M^e) and western Manasseh (M^w).

The tribes are listed in varying order, yet there are some constants. See: List, pages 410–11.

c. The land of Israel

The *country* or *land* (Hb. *'erez*) *of Israel,* which is the modern name, is mentioned only 11× in the Bible: 1 S 13:19; 1 Ch 22:2; 2 Ch 2:16; 30:35; 34:7; Ezk 27:17; 40:2; 47:17, to which we must add the Gr. passages in Tb 1:4; 14:4–5; Mt 2:20–21. In addition, we find in Hebrew: *the soil* (Hb. *'adamah*) *of Israel,* in Ezk (17×), 7:2–38:19; *the territory* (Hb. *gebul*) *of Israel,* Jg 19:29; 1 S 7:13; 11:3, 7; 27:1; 2 S 21:5; 1 K 1:3; 1 Ch 21:12; Ezk 11:10–11; Ml 1:5; cf. Jdt 14:4; 15:4; 1 M 2:46; 9:23; *the mountains of Israel* (18×), Ez 6:2–39:4; *the* [*twelve*] *tribes of Israel,* Jg 18:1; 2 S 20:14; 24:2; 1 K 8:16; 11:32; 14:21; 2 K 21:7; 2 Ch 6:5; 12:13; 33:7; Tb 1:4; Ezk 47:22, or simply *Israel,* Gn 49:7; Lv 20:2; Jos 13:13; Jg 5:2; 1 S 9:9; 18:6; 2 S 20:19; 24:15; 1 M 9:27, or *all Israel,* Dt 18:6; 1 S 3:20; 2 S 14:25; 17:11; 1 K 5:27. Note that in the period of the divided kingdom (931–721) the expressions *land of Israel,* 2 K 5:2, 4; 6:23, *territory of Israel,* 2 K 10:32; 14:25, or *Israel,* 2 K 5:12, can refer to the northern kingdom.

The ideal borders of the land of Israel, those of the kingdom of David and Solomon, are described in detail in Nb 34:1–15 and Ezk 47:13–21. They are also indicated in stereotyped formulas such as: *from Dan to Beersheba* (see: DAN 2); *from the Pass of Hamath to the Arabah* or *to the wadi of Egypt* (see: HAMATH 2); *from the wadi of Egypt to the Euphrates* (see: EUPHRATES); *from sea to sea* (see: DEAD SEA).

The expression "land of Israel" replaces the older name, land of: CANAAN b, and the land of the Philistines, Gn 21:32, 34; Zp 2:5.

See: HOLY LAND; PROMISED LAND.

d. Israel = Northern kingdom

In many texts *Israel* designates not the entire people of the twelve tribes or the territory shared by all the tribes, but a more political entity, namely, the "ten tribes" of the north, 1 K 11:31, 35, often identified with the most important of them, Ephraim, Ho 11:8, as opposed to the tribe of Judah, 1 K 11:36; 12:20; 2 K 17:18; Is 11:13, which had absorbed Simeon. As early as Jg 1 and 5, Judah and Simeon seem to lead an existence that is independent of the other tribes. Later on, David is first anointed as king of Judah, 2 S 2:4, whereas Abner makes Ishbaal "king over all Israel," 2 S 2:9, which shows that the expression *all Israel* (158×), referring to either the people or the land, is far from always having the same extension. The battle of Gibeon involves Israel and Judah, 2 S 2:12–28. After seven years David is anointed king "over all Israel and Judah," 2 S 5:5. At the death of Solomon in 931, "the sovereignty was split in two, from Ephraim arose a rebel kingdom," Si 47:21, whose rallying cry was "To your tents, Israel!" 1 K 12:16; 2 S 20:1. Henceforward, for two centuries, that is, until the capture of Samaria in 721, the two kingdoms live as brothers, and often as enemies, and the history of "the two Houses of Israel," Is 8:14, is linked to that of their respective kings.

Other titles: EPHRAIM 1; SAMARIA.

Kings: AHAB 1; AHAZIAH 1; BAASHA; ELAH 3; HOSHEA 2; JEHOAHAZ 1; JEHORAM 4; JEHU 2; JEROBOAM 1; JOASH 6; MENAHEM 1; NADAB 4; OMRI 4; PEKAH; PEKAHIAH; SHALLUM 4; ZECHARIAH 9; ZIMRI 4.

Capitals: SAMARIA *a;* TIRZAH 2; SHECHEM and PENUEL, 1 K 12:25.

e. Israel = Judah

The expression in Is 8:14, "the two Houses of Israel," shows that the prophets do not like to admit the fact of the schism, cf. Is 5:7. After the fall of Samaria the term *Israel* recovers its religious meaning. It is applied to "all that is left of Israel," that is, the kingdom of Judah, Ezk 9:8; 11:13, which becomes the center to which all of Israel relates. For the chronicler, Judah is the true Israel: Jehoshaphat, king of Judah, is called king of Israel, 2 Ch 21:2; so too is Ahaz, 28:19. After the fall of Jerusalem in 587 and the exile to Babylon, the term "Judaean" or "Jew(ish)" has a racial and national meaning and is used chiefly by foreigners, Ezr 4:12, Ne 3:33–34; 2 M 9:4; however, the term "Israel" continues to refer to the twelve tribes and to the people of the covenant. The Jewish nation, cf. 2 M 10:8; 11:48–52; 18:35; Ac 10:32, remains the people of Israel, Ezr 2:2; 6:17; 10:5; Mt 10:6; 27:9; Lk 1:16; Ac 13:17, and Palestine, though occupied, remains the land of Israel, Mt 2:20–21; 8:10; 10:23; Jn 3:10.

f. Israel, people of God

In addition to the expression "the tribes of Israel" the following are also used, in the Hebrew, to refer to the people of the covenant:

—*the people of Israel* (17×), Jos 8:33; 2 S 8:7; Ezr 2:2; 7:13; 9:1; Jdt 4:8; 7:10; 1 M 5:60; Ac 4:10, 27 (the peoples); 13:17, 24. Note that "people of Israel" may refer at times to the northern tribes as opposed to Judah, 2 S 19:41; 1 K 16:21.

—*Israel my (your, his) people* (90×), Ex 7:4; 18:1; Dt 21:8; 26:15; 1 K 6:13; 8:16–66, and so on; Mt 2:6; Lk 2:32.

—*the community of Israel* (11×), Ex 12:3, 6, 19, 47; Lv 4:13; Nb 16:9; 32:4; Jos 22:18, 20; 1 K 8:5; 2 Ch 5:6, or *of the sons of Israel* (31×), Ex 16:1–10; 17:1; 35:1–20; and so on.

—*the assembly of Israel* (15×), Lv 16:17; Dt 31:30; Jos 8:35; 1 K 8:14; 1 M 4:59; Si 50:13, or *of the sons of Israel,* Si 50:20.

—*the house of Israel* (138×), Ex 16:31; Jos 21:45; Ps 98:3; 115:9, 12; 118:2; 135:19; Is 5:7; Jr 2:4; Ezk (82×); Mt 10:6; 15:24; Ac 2:36; 7:42; Heb 8:8, 10.

—the *people* or *men of Israel* (56×), Nb 25:8, 14; Dt 27:14; 29:9; Jos 9:6–7; 10:24; Jg–2 S (43×); 1 K 8:2; 1 Ch 10:1, 7; 16:3; 2 Ch 5:3.

—*Israel* (± 650×), Gn 48:20; Ex 4:22; 5:2; 9:4; and so on; Dt 4:1; 5:1; 6:3–4, 9:1; 20:3; Ba 3:24; 4:4, etc.; Rm 11:7, 25–26.

—*the Virgin of Israel* (4×), Jr 18:13; 31:4, 21; Am 5:2.

g. The God of Israel (200×)

God is linked to Israel in a special way, in accordance with the classical formulation of the covenant: "I will be your God and you shall be my people," Lv 26:12; cf. Gn 17:8; Jr 31:33; Rv 21:3. This special bond appears in the formulas:

—*Yahweh God of Israel* (120×), Ex 5:1; 32:27; Jos 7:13, and so on.

—*Lord God of Israel* (5×), Jdt 12:8; 13:7; Est 4:17[k]; Ba 2:11; Lk 1:68.

—*Lord Yahweh God of Israel,* Ex 34:23.

—*Almighty Lord, God of Israel,* Ba 3:1, 4.

—*God of Israel* (50×), Gn 33:20 (El, God of Israel); Ex 24:10; Nb 16:9; Jos 22:16; 1 S 1:17 . . . Ps 68:9; Ezk 43:2; Mt 15:31; Ac 13:17.

—*God of the armies of Israel,* 1 S 17:45.

—*God of all the clans of Israel,* Jr 31:1.

—*God of the heritage of Israel,* Jdt 9:12.

—*God in Israel,* 1 S 17:46; 1 K 18:36; 2 K 1:3, 6, 16; 5:15; *over Israel,* 2 S 7:26; *for Israel,* 1 Ch 17:24.

—*Holy One of Israel* (35×), 2 K 19:22; Ps 71:22; 78:41; 89:19; Is (27×); Jr 50:29; 51:5; Ezk 37:28; 39:7.

—*the Stone of Israel,* Gn 49:24.

—*the Rock of Israel,* 2 S 23:3; Is 30:29.

—*the Glory of Israel,* 1 S 15:29.

—*the Mighty One of Israel,* Is 1:24.

—*The King of Israel,* Is 44:6; Zp 3:15; cf. 1 S 8:7; 1 Ch 28:5; Is 43:15.

h. The new Israel

The prophets foretell the reunification of the two kingdoms and gathering of the scattered Israelites into the true kingdom of David, Ezk 36:24; 37:15–25; Jr 3:18; Is 27:12, all twelve tribes included, Ezk 48:1–7, under the authority and protection of the "God of all the clans of Israel," Jr 31:1. But this will be a new people, the remnant of Israel, Is 4:3; 10:20–22; cf. Rm 9:27; Is 11:11; Jr 31:7; Mi 2:12; it will be purified, animated by a new spirit, Ezk 11:19; 18:31, ruled by a new covenant, Jr 31:31–34. It will be the new Israel that is no longer "the Israel according to the flesh," 1 Co 10:18 (literal translation), that is, the Israel of history, with its roots in its land, for "not all those who descend from Israel [= Jacob] are Israel," Rm 9:6. This new Israel will be "the Israel of God," Ga 6:16.

While Israel retains its privilege as the people "called first," as the first-born son, Ex 4:22; Si 36:11; cf. Rm 9:4–5, yet the pagans must someday become part of the new Israel, cf. Ps 47:9–10. Christ established his Church on the model of the old Israel and gave his twelve Apostles the power to "judge the twelve tribes of Israel," Mt 19:18. The Israelites from whom Christ was descended acc. to the flesh, Rm 9:5, are urged to follow the example of Nathanael, a true Israelite, Jn 1:47, and see in Christ the Glory of Israel, Lk 2:32, the king of Israel, Mt 27:42; Jn 1:49, the savior of Israel, Ac 13:23, in short, the hope of Israel, Ac 28:20.

ISRAELITE (14), in the original text is applied to individuals, Lv 24:10–11; 2 S 17:25; Jn 1:47; Rm 11:1, and to the people of Israel, Ac 2:22; 3:12; 5:25; 13:16. . . . In translations it also renders such Hb. expressions as *sons of Israel* (± 680×), *people* or *men of Israel,* and so on.

ISSACHAR, Gr. transcription of Hb. *Yissaskar,* a defective spelling of *Yissakar,* from the Hb. root *sakar,* "to give wages," see Gn 30:18 (cf. Sachar).

1. **Issachar** (43), fifth son of Jacob and Leah, Gn 30:17–18, eponymous ancestor of one of the twelve tribes of Israel. Four clans are linked to Issachar: those of Tola (further details in 1 Ch 7:2–5), Puvah, Jashub and Shimron, Nb 26:23–25; Gn 46:13//1 Ch 7:1. Various censuses of the tribe in Nb 1:28–29; 2:5–6; 26:23–25; 1 Ch 12:33; cf. Rv 7:7. The territory of Issachar, described in Jos 19:17–23; cf. 17:10–11, is bounded on the S by Manasseh, on the NW by Zebulun, on the NE by Naphtali, and on the E by the Jordan. Issachar, therefore, occupies the rich plain of Jezreel but is subject to the Canaanite yoke, Gn 49:14–15; cf. Jg 5:15. Later on, like Zebulun, it takes up trading and frequents the sanctuary on Mount Tabor, Dt 33:18–19. In the time of Solomon, Issachar constitutes the tenth district of the united kingdom, 1 K 4:17. Some towns of Issachar are assigned to Levites of the clan of Gershon, Jos 21:6, 28–29//1 Ch 6:47, 57–58. The chronicler mentions the presence of Issacharites at the Passover of Hezekiah, 2 Ch 30:18.

Issachar in the lists of the tribes: List, pages 410–11.

Issacharites: BAASHA; IGAL 1; NATHANAEL 1; OMRI 3; PALTIEL 1; TOLA 1–2; UZZIAH 2.

2. **Issachar** (1), a Levite gatekeeper, second son of Obed-edom, 1 Ch 26:5.

ISSHIAH, Isshijah, Hb. *Yishshiyya, Yishshiyyahu.*

1. **Isshiah** (1), an Issacharite, one of the five military chiefs of the sons of Uzzi, 1 Ch 7:3–5.

2. **Isshiah** (2), a Levite of the clan of Kohath, second of the sons of Uzziel 1 Ch 23:20. The sons of Isshiah have Zechariah as their leader, 1 Ch 24:25.

3. **Isshiah** (1), a Levite of the clan of Kohath, a descendant of Amram, leader of the sons of Rehabiah, 1 Ch 24:21.

4. **Isshijah** (1), an Israelite of the sons of Harim, married to a foreign wife whom he puts away, Ezr 10:31.

5. **Isshiah** (1), a Korahite, who rallies to David before the latter becomes king 1 Ch 12:7.

ISSHIJAH (1). See: ISSHIAH 4.

ITALICA (1), (cf. Italy), Ac 10:1, the name of a cohort made up in principle of Italian soldiers; one of its centurions is: CORNELIUS.

ITALY (4), present-day Italy, since the time of Caesar. There are Jewish, cf. Ac 18:2, and Christian communities there: in Heb 13:24 "the saints of Italy" refers to Christians who reside in Italy or are Italians settled outside of Italy. For his appearance before the imperial tribunal, Paul embarks at Caesarea for Italy; at Myra in Lycia he boards an Alexandrian ship bound for Italy, Ac 27:1, 6.

See: ITALICA.

Cities and towns: FORUM OF APPIUS; PUTEOLI; RHEGIUM; ROME; THREE TAVERNS.

ITHAI (1). See: ITTAI 2.

ITHAMAR (21), abbrev. of *Abitamar,* **son of Aaron** (10), known from the priestly tradition. A priest, last of the four sons of Aaron, Ex 6:23; 28:1; Nb 3:2; 26:60; 1 Ch 5:29; 24:1, he exercises the priesthood with his brother Eleazar after the death of his older brothers Nadab and Abihu, Nb 3:4; Lv 10:6, 12, 16; 1 Ch 24:2. The Levites of the clans of Gershon and Merari are under his direction, Ex 38:21; Nb 4:28, 33; 7:8.

The sons of Ithamar comprise eight classes of priests as compared with the sixteen of the sons of Eleazar, 1 Ch 24:3–6. Some sons of Ithamar are among the priests who return from the exile, Ezr 8:2.

With the line of Ithamar is connected: AHIMELECH 2.

ITHIEL, "God is with me"? (cf. Ethbaal; Ittai? See Immanuel).

1. **Ithiel** (1), Ne 11:7, a Benjaminite, an ancestor of: SALLU 1.

2. **Ithiel** (2), son or protégé of Agur? Pr 30:1. Some correct Hb. *le'iti'el* to *la'iti'el,* "I am weary, O God."

ITHLAH (1), Jos 19:42 (Gr. *Silata*), a town of the tribe of Dan. Associated with Aijalon.

ITHMAH the Moabite (1), one of David's champions, 1 Ch 11:46.

ITHNAN (1), (cf. Jathniel), a town in the Negeb of Judah, Jos 15:23.

ITHRA (1), (cf. Jether). See: JETHER 2.

ITHRAN (cf. Jether).

1. **Ithran** (2), third of the four sons of Dishon, 1 Ch 1:41//Gn 36:26 (Hb. *son of Dishan*), son of Seir.

2. **Ithran** (2), an Asherite of the sons of Zophah, father of Jephunneh, Pispa, and Ara, 1 Ch 7:37, 38 (corr. of Hb. *Jether*).

ITHREAM (2), Hb. *Yitr'am,* sixth son of David, born of Eglah at Hebron, 2 S 3:5//1 Ch 3:3.

ITHRITE (5), Hb. *Yitri.* "The Ithrites" are one of the clans of Judah that are descended from Shobal, 1 Ch 2:53.

ITTAH-KAZIN (1), locative of the Hb. *'Et-qazin,* "Time of the magistrate"? On the border of Zebulun, not far from Gath-hepher, Jos 19:13.

ITTAI, abbrev. of *Ithiel?*

1. **Ittai** (7) **the Gittite** (3), a leader of foreign troops who enters David's service, perhaps at the head of 600 men from Gath, 2 S 15:18–22. He is one of the three officers (along with Joab and Abishai) to whom David gives charge of the troops who accompany him on his flight from Absalom, 2 S 18:2, 5, 12.

2. **Ittai** (1) **son of Ribai, from Gibeah of Benjamin** (1), one of David's champions, 2 S 23:29.

= **Ithai** (1), 1 Ch 11:31.

ITURAEA (1). See: JETUR.

IVVAH (3). See: AVVA.

IYE-ABARIM (2), "Ruins of Abarim" (cf. Iim), a stage of the Exodus "in the wilderness that borders Moab, towards the sunrise," Nb 21:11–12, in Moab, 33:44.

= **Iyim** (1), Nb 33:45.

IYIM (1). See: IIM.

IZHAR (9), "Brilliance, Clarity," second of the four sons of Kohath, son of Levi, Ex 6:18; Nb 3:19; 1 Ch 5:28; 6:3; 23:12. His sons, Ex 6:21; 1 Ch 23:18; 24:22, form the **Izharite** clan, Nb 3:27. Like the other sons of Kohath, these are at first responsible for the Ark and later on helpers of the priests in the temple, cf. 1 Ch 23:25, 32. In addition, the Izharites are assigned duties of a secular kind, those of scribe and judge, 1 Ch 26:23, 29.

Father of: KORAH 3.

IZHARITE (4), Nb 3:27; 1 Ch 24:22; 26:23, 29, belonging to the clan of: IZHAR.

IZLIAH (1), a Benjaminite of the sons of Elpaal, head of a family at Jerusalem, 1 Ch 8:18.

IZRAHIAH, Jezrahiah, "Yah will arise *or* will shine" (cf. East 2).

1. **Izrahiah** (2), an Issacharite, one of the five military leaders of the sons of Uzzi, 1 Ch 7:3–5.

2. **Jezrahiah** (1), leader of the can-

tors at the dedication of the Jerusalem wall, Ne 12:42.

IZRAHITE (1), 1 Ch 27:8. See: SHAMMAH 4.

IZRI (1). See: ZERI.

IZZIAH (1), (cf. Jaziz), an Israelite of the sons of Parosh, married to a foreign wife, whom he puts away, Ezr 10:25.

J

JAAKAN (1), (cf. Bene-jaakan). See: AKAN.

JAAKOBAH (1), (cf. Jacob), a Simeonite, head of a clan, 1 Ch 4:36–40.

JAALAH (2), "Gazelle" (cf. Alvah), head of a family of Solomon's slaves who return from the exile, Ezr 2:56//Ne 7:58.

JAAR (1), Hb. *Ya'ar,* "Woods, forest," appears as a component of several names (cf. Fields-of-the-Forest; Jearim; Kiriath-jearim). See: KIRIATH-JEARIM.

JAARESHAIAH (1), a Benjaminite of the sons of Jeroham, head of a family at Jerusalem, 1 Ch 8:27.

JAASAU (1), (cf. Asahel), an Israelite of the sons of Bani, married to a foreign wife, whom he puts away, Ezr 10:37.

JAASIEL, Hb. *Ya'asi'el,* "God has done" (cf. Asahel).

1. **Jaasiel from Zoba** (1), one of David's champions, 1 Ch 11:47 (Hb. *he from Zoba*).

2. **Jaasiel son of Abner** (1), commissioner for the tribe of Benjamin, 1 Ch 27:21.

JAAZANIAH, "Yah hears" (cf. Azaniah).

1. **Jaazaniah son of Jeremiah son of Habazziniah** (1), clan leader of the Rechabites, whom the prophet Jeremiah brings to the temple, Jr 35:3.

2. **Jaazaniah the Maacathite** (1) or **Jezaniah son of the Maacathite** (1), an officer of the Judaean army who rallies to Gedaliah after the fall of Jerusalem, 2 K 25:23//Jr 40:8.

= ? **Azariah son of Hoshaiah** (2). After the murder of Gedaliah he, along with Johanan, son of Kareah, is one of the officers who refuse to listen to Jeremiah's advice not to flee to Egypt but to remain in Judah, Jr 42:1 (where *Azariah* is a corr. of Hb. *Jezaniah*); 43:2.

3. **Jaazaniah son of Shaphan** (1), one of the elders of Israel who in the time of the prophet Ezekiel give themselves up to idolatry in the temple, Ezk 8:11.

4. **Jaazaniah son of Azzur** (1), one of the leaders of the people whom Ezekiel blames for giving bad advice to the people after the first siege of the city and whom he threatens with punishment, Ezk 11:1 ff.

JAAZIAH (1), a Levite of the clan of Merari, father of three sons, 1 Ch 24:26–27.

JAAZIEL (2), Hb. *Ya'azi'el,* a Levite gatekeeper in the service of the Ark, 1 Ch 15:18, a player of the keyed harp, 15:20 (Hb. *Aziel*).

JABAL (1), suggests Hb. *ybl,* "lead, guide" (cf. Obil), son of Lamech and Adah, ancestor of livestock breeders, Gn 4:20.

JABBOK (7), left-bank tributary of the Jordan. It is at the ford of the Jabbok that Jacob "wrestles with an angel," Gn 32.23. The Jabbok marks the northern boundary of the Ammonites, Dt 3:16; Jos 12:2; Jg 11:13, 22; cf. Nb 21:24; Dt 2:37. Today *Nahr ez-Zerka,* "Blue River," which rises near Amman.

JABESH, "Dry."

1. **Jabesh** (21) **in Gilead** (12), a town in Transjordania. It does not take part in the war against Benjamin, but its maidens are given to the Benjaminites so that the numbers of the tribe may be restored, Jg 21:8–14. Saul the Benjaminite goes to the aid of Jabesh and defeats the Ammonites, who are besieging the town, 1 S 11:1–5, 9. On learning that the corpses of Saul and his sons are hanging from the wall of Beth-shan, the warriors of Jabesh cross the Jordan and remove the bodies, which will be cremated at Jabesh and buried "under the tamarisk of Jabesh," 1 S 31: 11–13//1 Ch 10:11–12; cf. 2 S 21:12. David expresses his gratitude to the people of Jabesh for this gesture and urges them to rally to him as king, 2 S 2:4–7. About 15 km SE of Beth-shan.

2. **Jabesh** (3), father of: SHALLUM 4.

JABESH-GILEAD. See: JABESH 1.

JABEZ, Hb. *Ya'bez.*

1. **Jabez** (1), in Judah, dwelling place of the Sophrite clans, 1 Ch 2:55.

2. **Jabez** (3), connected with *'ozeb,* "distress," 1 Ch 4:9. In the Ashhur group in Judah, Jabez "won himself more honour than his brothers" and addresses a prayer to the God of Israel, 1 Ch 4: 9–10.

JABIN (8), **king of Hazor** (4), **king of Canaan** (4), leader of the coalition of kings of northern Canaan that is conquered under Joshua, Jos 11:1, 10; 12: 19; Sisera is commander of his army acc. to Jg 4:2, 7, 17, 23–24; cf. Ps 83:10.

JABNEEL, "God causes to be built" (cf. Benaiah).

1. **Jabneel** (1), a town halfway between Joppa and Ashdod. On the NW border of Judah, Jos 15:11.

= **Jabneh** (1), taken from the Philistines by King Uzziah, 2 Ch 26:6.

= **Jamnia** (6), chief town of the coastal region, cf. 1 M 15:38, 40. Judas Maccabaeus pursues the army of Gorgias, which has been routed at Emmaus, as far as the plain of Jamnia, 1 M 4:15; he burns the harbor of Jamnia and its fleet, 2 M 12: 8–9. Gorgias soon takes revenge by routing Joseph and Azariah, the commanders of the Jewish army, who were marching on Jamnia, 1 M 5:58–61. Later on, Apollonius, governor of Coele-Syria, assembles an army there, 1 M 10:69, that will be defeated by Jonathan near Azotus. Cendebaeus, appointed commander-in-chief of the coastal region, arrives at Jamnia, 1 M 15:40, and invades Judaea. Jamnia is also mentioned in Jdt 2:28.

2. **Jabneel** (1), a town in Naphtali, Jos 19:33, SW of the Sea of Chinnereth.

JABNEH (1), (cf. Benaiah). See: JABNEEL 1.

JACAN (1), Hb. *Ya'kan* (cf. Achan), a Gadite, head of a family, 1 Ch 5:13.

JACHIN, "[God] makes firm" (cf. Jehoiachin).

1. **Jachin** (3), one of the sons of Simeon, son of Jacob, Gn 46:10//Ex 6: 15, whose descendants form the **Jachinite** clan, Nb 26:12.

= **Jarib** (1), one of the (five) sons of Simeon, 1 Ch 4:24.

2. **Jachin** (3), a priest living at Jerusalem, 1 Ch 9:10//Ne 11:10 (acc. to Hb.), head of the twenty-first priestly class, 1 Ch 24:17.

3. **Jachin** (2) and **Boaz,** names of the two bronze pillars in the vestibule of the temple at Jerusalem, the former standing at the right, the latter at the left, 1 K 7: 15–22//2 Ch 3:15–17.

JACHINITE (1), belonging to the clan of: JACHIN 1.

JACOB, James, Hb. *Ya'aqob,* abbrev. of south Arabic *Ya'aqob'el,* "Let God protect," connected with Hb. *'aqéb,* "heel" in Gn 25:26, and with Hb. *'aqab,* supplant, deceive," in Gn 27:36; Ho 12:4; Jr 9:3; Gr. *Iakōbos, Iakōb* (cf. Jaakobah).

1. **Jacob** (394), son of Isaac and Rebekah.

a. The patriarch

Twin brother of Esau, but born after him, Gn 25:21–26; cf. Jos 24:4; 1 Ch 1:34, Jacob supplants his brother by buying his birthright from him for a dish of lentil soup, Gn 25:29–34, then by getting from the aged Isaac, with Rebekah's help, the blessing reserved for the first-born, Gn 27:1–40; He 11:20. To escape the wrath of Esau and to choose a wife from the stock of his ancestors, Jacob leaves for Mesopotamia, Gn 27:41–28:5; cf. Ho 12:13; Jdt 8:26. On the way, at Bethel, the dream of "Jacob's ladder," Gn 28:10–20. Having come to Paddan-aram, he marries Leah and Rachel, the daughters of Laban. Deceived by his father-in-law, he cheats him in turn and grows rich at his expense, 29–30. Birth in Mesopotamia of the first eleven sons of Jacob, as well as of his daughter Dinah, 29:31–30:24. Jacob flees from Laban's house, 31–32. On the return journey to Canaan: "Jacob wrestles" with God and his name is changed to Israel, 32:23–33; cf. 35:10; 1 K 18:31; 2 K 17:34 ("Israel" is the name used for the patriarch Jacob 50×); he meets Esau, 33. At Shechem Jacob learns of the rape of Dinah and the vengeance taken by Simeon and Levi, 34. Jacob goes up to Bethel, where God appears to him, 35:1–15, Birth of Benjamin, the twelfth son of Jacob, in Canaan, 35:16–20. Story of Jacob and his son Joseph, 37; 42–48. Jacob settles in Egypt, 47; cf. Dt 26:5; Jos 24:4; 1 S 12:8; Ac 7:12–15: he adopts the two sons of Joseph, Gn 48:1–20; Heb 11:21, and gives Joseph the district of Shechem, Gn 48:21–22; cf. 33:18–20; Jos 24:32 (where Jn 4:5–6 locates the "well of Jacob"). Before dying he blesses his sons, Gn 49:1–23; Heb 11:20, who "make up the tribes of Israel, twelve in number," Gn 49:28; cf. 1 K 18:31. After spending seventeen years in Egypt, he dies at the age of 147, Gn 47:8, 28; 49:33, is embalmed, then transferred to Canaan, 50:1–14. "A quiet man, staying at home among the tents," Gn 25:27, the favorite of Rebekah, 25:28; 27:46, chosen by God, Ps 105:6, who prefers him to his older brother, Ml 1:2; Rm 9:13, Jacob is given a kindly judgment in Ws 10:10, which speaks him as a "virtuous man," but a harsh judgment in Is 43:27 and Ho 12:3–5, 13. His cleverness, his trickery, his recourse to lies in dealing with his brother, Gn 25:29–30; 32:4–5; 33:1–2, his father, 27:18–24, and his father-in-law, 30:32–33, are made to serve the plan of God, who "caused the covenant to rest on the head of Jacob," Si 44:23, so that Jacob, too, can be called "our father," Jn 4:12; cf. 1 Ch 29:10; Is 58:14. His name is connected with several sanctuaries and towns: Beersheba, Gn 28:10; 46:1–2, Bethel, 28:11–22; 31:13; 35:1–15; 48:3–4, Galeed, 31:43–54, Mahanaim, 32:1–3, Peniel, 32:31, Succoth, 33:17, Shechem, 33:18–20.

b. The house of Jacob

More than 180× *Jacob* is a collective name for the people of Israel,

—either used by itself, 1 S 12:8; 1 M 3:45; Ps 44:5; 79:7; 85:2; 99:4; Si 46:14; 47:22; 49:10; Is 17:4; 27:9; 59:20; Jr 10:25; 30:7; 46:27; Ob 10,

—or in various expressions: House of Jacob (24), Ex 19:3; 1 M 1:28; Ps 114:1; Is 2:5–6; 58:1; Jr 5:20; Ob 17–18, the sons of Jacob, 2 K 17:34; 1 Ch 16:13; Ps 77:16; 105:6; cf. Gn 49:1, the tribes of Jacob, Si 36:10; 48:10; Is 49:6; cf. 1 K 18:31, the race of Jacob, Ps 22:23; Is 45:19; Ex 20:5; cf. Is 65:9, the posterity of Jacob, 1 M 5:2, the remnant of Jacob, Is 10:21; Mi 5:6–7, the well of Jacob, Dt 33:28; cf. Is 65:9, the vineyard (corr. of Hb.) of Jacob, Na 2:3, the assembly or assemblies of Jacob, Dt 33:4; Si 24:23,

—or in parallel with Israel (90), Gn 49:7; Nb 23:7, 10, 21, 23; 24:5, 17–19; Dt 33:10; Ps 78:5, 21, 71; Si 45:5, and so on, or with Jeshurun (= Israel), Dt

32:15; 33:4–5; Is 44:2. Jacob, as the people, is called a servant, Is 44:1–2; 45:4; 48:20; Jr 46:27–28, God's chosen one, Ps 105:6; 135:41; Is 41:8, a poor worm, Is 41:14; cf. Am 7:2–5, magnificence of Jacob, Na 2:3 (Hb.).

The Holy Land is called the inheritance of Jacob, Si 23:12; 24:8; 44:22; cf. Gn 28:13; 35:12; Is 58:14; Ezk 28:25; 37: 25, the pride of Jacob, Ps 47:4; Am 8:7, the dwelling, the tents of Jacob, Ps 87:2; Jr 30:18; Lm 2:2; Ml 2:12; cf. Nb 24:5.

c. The God of Jacob (17)

2 S 23:1, 3; Ps 20:2; 24:6; 46:4, 8, 12; 59:14; 75:10; 76:7; 81:2, 5; 84:9; 94:7; 114:7; 146:5; Is 2:3//Mi 4:2; cf. Gn 50: 17. This is the God who appeared to Jacob at Bethel, Gn 28:11–22; 31:13; 48:3–4.

Other expressions: *The God of the house of Jacob,* Is 29:22, *God, ruler in Jacob,* Ps 59:13, *the Holy One of Jacob,* Is 29:23, *Jacob's king,* Is 41:21; cf. Lk 1:35, *the Mighty One of Jacob,* Gn 49: 24; Ps 132:2, 5; Is 49:26; 60:16, *the portion of Jacob,* Jr 10:16; 51:19, *the pride of Jacob,* Am 8:7; cf. 6:8 (Hb.).

God of Abraham, Isaac and Jacob. See: ABRAHAM *c.*

Daughter of Jacob: DINAH.

See: ISRAEL.

2. **Jacob** (2), acc. to Mt 1:15–16, the father of Joseph, the husband of Mary, mother of Jesus.

3. **James** (21) **son of Zebedee** (10), (the Elder), one of the Twelve, always associated with his brother John. Together the two ask Jesus for the first two places (of honor and authority) in his new kingdom, Mk 10:35–41; cf. Mt 20:20–24, and call down fire from heaven on a Samaritan village that refuses to receive them, Lk 9:54. Jesus surnames them *Bôanērges,* "Sons of Thunder," Mk 3:17. Sometimes the two brothers are called simply by their patronymic, *the sons of Zebedee,* Mt 20:20; 26:37; 27:56; Jn 21:2; cf. Mt 10:2; Mk 1:19; 3:17; 10:35; Lk 5:10.

Always in association with his brother John, James is among the privileged disciples:

—either among *the four* (Peter, Andrew, James, and John): the first ones called, while they are still fishermen on the Sea of Galilee, Mk 1:19//Mt 4:21; Lk 5:10 (here James and John are called Simon's partners), they make up the first group of Apostles in the lists of the Twelve, Mt 10:2; Mk 3:16–18; Lk 6:14; Ac 1:13, are with Jesus in Peter's house at Capernaum, Mk 1:29, and are given the advantage of private instruction on the fall of Jerusalem, Mk 13:3.

—or among *the three* (Peter, James, and John): they are witnesses of the raising of Jairus' daughter, Mk 5:37–40// Lk 8:51, of the transfiguration of Jesus, Mk 9:2//Mt 17:1//Lk 9:28, and of his agony in Gethsemane, Mk 14:33//Mt 26:37. We find them on the lakeshore during an appearance of the risen Jesus, Jn 21:2.

Herod Agrippa I has James beheaded, and Peter is thrown into prison, Ac 12:2 (Easter 44).

See: TWELVE; List, page 417.

4. **James the son of Alphaeus** (4), leading man in the third group of Apostles in the lists of the Twelve, Mt 10:3; Mk 3:18; Lk 6:15; Ac 1:13. Some identify him with the following.

See: TWELVE; List, page 417.

5. **James** (15) **the Younger** (1), Mk 15:40, "the brother of the Lord," Ga 1: 19, or, with Joset (= Joseph), Jude, and Simon, a "brother" of Jesus, Mt 13:55// Mk 6:3. He is not one of the Twelve, but he sees the risen Jesus, 1 Co 15:7. An important person in the Church of Jerusalem, Ac 12:17; Ga 2:12, whom Paul meets on several occasions, Ac 15:13–21; 21:18; Ga 1:19; 2:9. Tradition assigns him the authorship of a canonical letter, Jm 1:1. Sometimes identified with the preceding.

Son of: MARY 6.

Brother of: JUDAH 13.

6. **James** (2), father (rather than

brother) of Judas, one of the Twelve. See: JUDAH 14.

JADA (2), Hb. *Yada'*, "He knows" (cf. Abida; Beeliada; Eliada; Jaddua; Jediael; Jehoiada; Shemida), grandson of Jerahmeel through Onam, 1 Ch 2:28. His descendants are listed in 1 Ch 2.32–33.

JADDAI (1), Ezr 10:43 (acc. to Q), an Israelite of the sons of Nebo, married to a foreign wife, whom he puts away.

JADDUA (cf. Jada).

1. **Jaddua** (1), a leader of the people and cosigner of the pledge to observe the Law, Ne 10:22.

2. **Jaddua** (2), son of Johanan, a Jewish high priest in about 400 B.C., Ne 12:11, 22.

JADON of Meronoth (1), a volunteer in the rebuilding of the Jerusalem wall, Ne 3:7.

JAEL (6), "Antelope" (cf. Alvah; Wild Goats), **wife of Heber** (3), **the Kenite** (2), offers hospitality in her tent to Sisera, who has been defeated by Barak; while he sleeps, she kills him by driving a peg into his temple, Jg 4:17–22; cf. 5:6, 24.

JAFFA. See: JOPPA.

JAGUR (1), a town in the Negeb of Judah, Jos 15:21. Today *Tell Ghurr,* 20 km E of Beersheba.

JAHATH

1. **Jahath** (2), a descendant of Judah through Shobal, father of the Zorathite clans, 1 Ch. 4:2.

2. **Jahath** (4), a Levite of the clan of Gershon, the son of Libni acc. to 1 Ch. 6:5; the son of Gershon, father of Shimei and ancestor of Asaph the cantor acc. to 1 Ch 6:27–28; the eldest son of Shimei acc. to 1 Ch 23:10–11.

3. **Jahath** (1), a Levite of the clan of Kohath, of the family of Izhar, of the sons of Shelomoth, 1 Ch 24:22.

4. **Jahath** (1), a Levite of the clan of Merari, one of the supervisors of the work of restoring the temple under Josiah, 2 Ch 34:12.

JAHAZ (7), a town in Moab, Is 15: 4//Jr 48:34. It is here that Sihon, king of the Amorites, is defeated by Israel, Nb 21:23//Dt 2:32; Jg 11:20. A town belonging to Reuben, Jos 13:18, assigned to the Levites of the clan of Merari, Jos 21: 36 (//1 Ch 6:63, *Jahzah*).

= **Jahzah** (2), 1 Ch 6:63; Jr 48:21, a town in Moab.

JAHAZIEL, "God sees" (cf. Hazael).

1. **Jahaziel** (1), a Benjaminite who rallies to David before the latter becomes king, 1 Ch 12:5.

2. **Jahaziel** (1), a priest, a trumpeter before the Ark, 1 Ch 16.6.

3. **Jahaziel** (2), a Levite of the clan of Kohath, third of the four sons of Hebron, 1 Ch 23:19//24:23.

4. **Jahaziel son of Zechariah son of Benaiah son of Jeiel son of Mattaniah** (1), a Levite of the sons of Asaph. This cantor, who lives in the time of King Jehoshaphat, has the prophetic spirit, 2 Ch 20:14–17.

5. **Jahaziel** (1), father of: SHECANIAH 4.

JAHDAI (1), connected with Caleb, father of six sons, 1 Ch 2:47.

JAHDIEL (1), Hb. *Yahdi'el,* "God rejoices" (cf. Jehdeiah), a Manassite, head of a clan, 1 Ch 5:24.

JAHDO. See: BEN-JAHDO.

JAHLEEL (2), Hb. *Yahle'el,* "Wait for God!", last of the three sons of Zebulun, Gn 46:14, whose descendants form the **Jahleelite** clan, Nb 26:26.

JAHLEELITE (1), belonging to the clan of: JAHLEEL.

JAHMAI (1), an Issacharite, one of the heads of the families of Tola, 1 Ch 7:2.

JAHZAH (2). See: JAHAZ.

JAHZEEL (2), "Yah divides, apportions," first of the four sons of Naphtali,

Gn 46:24, whose descendants form the **Jahzeelite** clan, Nb 26:48.
= **Jahziel** (1), 1 Ch 7:13.

JAHZEELITE (1), belonging to the clan of: JAHZEEL.

JAHZEIAH (1), "Yah sees" (cf. Hazael), **son of Tikvah** (1), one of the opponents of the procedure for dissolving marriages with foreign women, Ezr 10:15.

JAHZERAH (1), 1 Ch 9:12.
= ? **Ahzai** (1), Ne 11:13.
An ancestor of the priest: AMASAI 4.

JAHZIEL (1). See: JAHZEEL.

JAIR, Hb. 1–3: *Ya'ir,* Gr. *Iaïr, Iaïros* (cf. Ur 2); 4: *Ya'ir,* Gr. *Iaïr* (cf. Er).

1. **Jair son of Manasseh** (3), Nb 32:41; Dt 3:14; 1 K 4:13, occupies the **Encampments of Jair** (6), which comprise sixty, Jos 13:30; 1 K 4:13, thirty, Jg 10:4, or twenty-three towns, 1 Ch 2:22. The Encampments of Jair are identified, Dt 3:14, with "the whole confederation of Argob" and located by Jg 10:4 and 1 K 4:13 (sixth district of Solomon) in Gilead and by Jos 13:30 in Bashan. Acc. to 1 Ch 2:22–23 Jair is the son of Segub and grandson of Hezron of Judah and of the daughter of Machir; and the Encampments were conquered by Geshur and Aram.

Jairite: IRA 1.

2. **Jair** (2) **of Gilead** (1), a "lesser" judge. "He had thirty sons who rode on thirty donkeys' colts; and they possessed thirty towns," Jg 10:3–5.

3. **Jair** (2), a Benjaminite, father of: MORDECAI 2.

4. **Jair** (2), father of: ELHANAN 1.

5. **Jairus** (2), **a synagogue official** (5), at Capernaum, father of a little girl who dies at the age of twelve. At the plea of Jairus, Jesus raises the child to life, Mk 5:22–24, 35–42//Mk 8:41–42, 49–56; cf. Mt 9:18–19, 23–26.

JAIRITE (1) 2 S 20:26, of or from: JAIR 1.

JAIRUS (2), Gr. *Iaïros.* See: JAIR 5.

JAKEH (1), "Foresightful," father of: AGUR.

JAKIM, "He makes to stand, sets erect" (cf. Adonikam; Ahikam; Alcimus; Azrikam; Eliakim; Jekameam; Jekamiah; Joiakim; Jokim?; Kemuel).

1. **Jakim** (1), a Benjaminite of the sons of Shimei, head of a family at Jerusalem, 1 Ch 8:19.

2. **Jakim** (1), a priest, leader of the twelfth priestly class, 1 Ch 24:12.

JALAM (4), Hb. *Ya'lam,* "Young man," a chief (or clan) of Edom, second of the three sons of Esau and Oholibamah, Gn 36:5, 14, 18; cf. 1 Ch 1:35.

JALON (1), one of the sons of Ezrah, connected with the Calebites, 1 Ch 4:17.

JAMBRES (1). See: JANNES.

JAMBRI (Sons of) (2), a probably Arabian tribe, distinct from the Nabataeans; one of its clans was settled at Medeba. The sons of Jambri seize John, brother of Judas Maccabaeus, and execute him. His brothers Jonathan and Simon avenge him by massacring a wedding procession of the sons of Jambri, 1 M 9:36–40.

JAMES. See: JACOB 3–6.

JAMIN, ["Right] hand = Good side, *whence* Opportunity; = South" (cf. Benjamin; Mijamin?; Miniamin?; Teman).

1. **Jamin** (4), second of the six, Gn 46:10; Ex 6:15, or five, 1 Ch 4:24, sons of Simeon, son of Jacob, whose descendants form the **Jaminite** clan, Nb 26:12.

2. **Jamin** (1), second of the three sons of Ram, of the clan of Jerahmeel, 1 Ch 2:27.

3. **Jamin** (1), one of the Levites who explain the law to the people during its solemn reading by Ezra, Ne 8:7.

JAMINITE (1), belonging to the clan of: JAMIN 1.

JAMLECH (1), (cf. Iamleku; Melech), a Simeonite, head of a clan, 1 Ch 4:34 ff.

JAMNIA (6). See: JABNEEL 1.

JANAI (1), Hb. *Ya'nai,* a Gadite living in Bashan, 1 Ch 5:12.

JANNAI (1), an ancestor of Jesus acc. to Lk 3:24.

JANNES (1) and **Jambres,** 2 Tm 3:8. Acc. to Jewish tradition, the names of the magicians who vie with Moses in Ex 7:11, 22; 8:3, and so on.

JANOAH (cf. Nahath).

1. **Janoah** (2), a town on the NE border of Ephraim, Jos 16:6–7 (Hb. *Yanohah*). About 10 km SE of Shechem.

2. **Janoah** (1), a town in Galilee captured by Tiglath-pileser, king of Assyria, in the time of Pekah, king of Israel, 2 K 15:29.

JANUM (1), "He sleeps"? —a town in the highlands of Judah, Jos 15:53.

JAPHETH, Hb. *Yephet,* "May he extend," see Gn 9:27.

1. **Japheth** (12), one of the three sons of Noah, Gn 5:32, 6:10; 1 Ch 1:4, who are saved from the flood along with their father, Gn 7:13; 9:18; 10:1. Japheth is one of the ancestors of postdiluvian mankind; the geographical area occupied by his posterity covers Asia Minor, the islands of the Mediterranean, Gn 10:2–5; cf. 1 Ch 1:5–6, and the Palestinian coast, cf. Gn 9:27.

2. **Japheth** (1), Jdt 2:25. To be identified with the preceding?

JAPHIA, Hb. *Yaphia'* (cf. Mephaath).

1. **Japhia** (1), **king of Lachish** (4), an Amorite, allied with: ADONI-ZEDEK.

2. **Japhia** (3), one of David's sons born at Jerusalem, 2 S 5:15//1 Ch 3:7// 14:6.

3. **Japhia** (1), a town on the border of Zebulun, Jos 19:12. About 10 km W of Mount Tabor.

JAPHLET (3), (cf. Pelet 1–2), an Asherite of the clan of Beriah, son of Heber and father of three sons, acc. to 1 Ch 7:32–33. The portion of the **Japhletites** is located between Bethel and Beth-horon acc. to Jos 16:3.

JAPHLETITES (1), (cf. Pelet 1–2), related to: JAPHLET.

JARAH (2), Hb. *Ya'rah.* See: JEHOADDAH.

JARED, Accad. *(w)ardu,* "Servant."

1. **Jared** (7). See: IRAD.

2. **Jered** (1), father of Gedor, among the sons of Bithiah, 1 Ch 4:18.

JARHA (2), Hb. *Yarha',* an Egyptian slave of Sheshan of the clan of Jerahmeel. Having no sons (but cf. 1 Ch 2:31), Sheshan gives his daughter in marriage to Jarha, who assures him of a posterity through many generations, 1 Ch 2:34–41.

JARIB, "He renders justice" (cf. Joiarib; Meribah).

1. **Jarib** (1). See: JACHIN 1.

2. **Jarib** (1), one of Ezra's messengers to Iddo, Ezr 8:16.

3. **Jarib** (1), a priest, married to a foreign wife, whom he puts away, Ezr 10:18.

JARMUTH

1. **Jarmuth** (6), a former Canaanite town in the lowlands of Judah, Jos 15:35, reoccupied by Judaeans after the return from the exile, Ne 11:29. 18 km W of Bethlehem.

King: PIRAM.

2. **Jarmuth** (1). See: RAMAH 11.

JAROAH (1), (cf. Jerah). See: BEN-JAROAH.

JASHEN (1), "Sleeper," **from Gimzo** (1), one of David's champions, 2 S 23:32. (Hb. *the sons of* [= *Bene-*] *Jashen.* JB adds *from Gimzo* by referring to 1 Ch 11:34 and correcting Hb. *from Gizon*).

= **Bene-hashem from Gizon** (1), 1 Ch 11:34.

JASHIB (1), "[Yah] causes to return" (cf. Jashub), Jos 17:7, acc. to the Gr. (Hb. *yoshebe,* "the inhabitants"), a town on the border of Manasseh and Ephraim. Near Tappuah.

JASHOBEAM, Hb. *Yashob'am.*

1. **Jashobeam** (1), **the Hachmonite** (1) or the **son of Zabdiel** (1). See: ISHBAAL 2.

2. **Jashobeam** (1), a Korahite who rallies to David before the latter becomes king, 1 Ch 12:7.

JASHUB, "[Yah] will return" (cf. Eliashib; Jashib; Meshobab; Shear-jashub; Shobab).

1. **Jashub** (3), third of the four sons of Issachar, Gn 46:13 (corr. of Hb. *Yob*)//1 Ch 7:1, whose descendants form the **Jashubite** clan, Nb 26:24.

2. **Jashub** (1), an Israelite of the sons of Bigvai, married to a foreign wife, whom he puts away, Ezr 10:29.

JASHUBITE (1), belonging to the clan of: JASHUB 1.

JASOL (1), probably a town SE of Jerusalem (to be connected with the *wadi Jasol,* a tributary of the Kidron), Zc 14:5 (acc. to Gr.; Hb. *Azal*).

JASON, Gr. form of *Jesus* or *Joshua.*

1. **Jason son of Eleazar** (1), sent by Judas Maccabaeus to Rome, together with Eupolemus, to conclude a treaty of friendship with the Romans, 1 M 8:17 ff.

2. **Jason** (2), father of the ambassador: ANTIPATER 1.

3. **Jason** (10), brother of the high priest Onias III, 2 M 4:7, whom he supplants. Having become high priest, (175–172) this "godless wretch," 4:13, a "vile" man, 4:19, actively promotes the hellenization of the Jews but he is supplanted in turn by Menelaus, 2 M 1:7; 4:7–26. He fails in his attempt to regain power and dies at Sparta, 2 M 5:5–10.

4. **Jason of Cyrene** (1), author of a work of which 2 M is said to be a digest, 2 M 2:23.

5. **Jason** (4), a Jew of Thessalonika, who welcomes Paul and Silas to his home. For this reason some Jews hale him before the city council. He is released after giving security, Ac 17:5–9. Same as the following?

6. **Jason** (1), a Jewish Christian of Corinth, a compatriot of Paul, Rm 16:21. Identical with the preceding?

JATHAN (1), Tb 5:14, brother of Ananias. See: HANANIAH 15.

JATHNIEL (1), "God is constant" (cf. Ethan; Ithnan), a gatekeeper, a Korahite, fourth son of Meshelemiah, 1 Ch 26:2.

JATTIR (4), (cf. Jether), a town in the highlands of Judah, Jos 15:48; cf. 1 S 30:27, assigned to the Levites of the clan of Kohath, Jos 21:14//1 Ch 6:43.

Native place of: GAREB 1; IRA 3.

JAVAN (12). See: GREECE *a.*

JAVELIN (1), Hb. *Kidon.* See: NACON.

JAZER (15), Hb. *Ya'zer,* Gr. *Iazēr* (cf. Ezri), a town in Transjordania on the Ammonite border, Nb 21:24 (acc. to Gr.), reconnoitered and captured by Israel, Nb 21:32. The **land of Jazer,** "an ideal region for raising stock," is claimed by Gad and Reuben, Nb 32:1–3. Gad occupies Jazer, Nb 32:35; Jos 13:25, which is also a Levite town of the clan of Merari, Jos 21:39//1 Ch 6:66. Jazer is included in the census under David, 2 S 24:5; cf. 1 Ch 26:31. Later on, the town is in Moabite hands, Is 16:8–9//Jr 48:32. Jazer is captured by Judas Maccabaeus, 1 M 5:8. 29 km W of Amman.

JAZIZ (1), (cf. Izziah; Jeziel), **the Hagrite** (1), in charge of the king's flocks, 1 Ch 27:31.

JEARIM (1), Hb. *Ye'arim,* "Forests," a

mountain near Kiriath-jearim and Chesalon, Jos 15:10.

JEATHERAI (1), Hb. *Ye'atrai,* a Levite descended from Gershom, 1 Ch 6:6.

JEBERECHIAH (1). See: BERECHIAH 5.

JEBUS (4), a biblical name for ancient Jerusalem, Jg 19:10–11; 1 Ch 11:4–5, derived from the name of its inhabitants, the Jebusites, cf. Jos 15:8, 63; 18:16, 28; 2 S 5:6, 8; Zc 9:7. As a matter of fact, Jerusalem was never called Jebus.
See: JEBUSITES.

JEBUSITES (41), a pre-Israelite population of: CANAAN *a,* known in the Bible as inhabiting Jerusalem. See: JEBUS.
Jebusite: ARAUNAH.

JECHONIAH. See: JEHOIACHIN.

JECOLIAH (2), "Yah can," of Jerusalem, mother of King Uzziah of Judah, 2 K 15:2//2 Ch 26:3.

JEDAIAH, Hb. 1–4: *Jeda'yah,* "Yah knows" (cf. Jada); 5–6: *Jedayah.*

1. **Jedaiah** (7) **son of Joiakim son of Seraiah son of Hilkiah son of Meshullam son of Zadok son of Meraioth son of Ahitub** (1), (corr. of Hb. *son of Joiarib, Jachin, Seraiah son of Hilkiah . . . son of Ahitub*), Ne 11:10, head of the second priestly class, 1 Ch 24:7. The family of Jedaiah, which is that of the high priest Jeshua, returns from the exile with Zerubbabel, Ezr 2:36//Ne 7:39; cf. Ne 12:6, and lives in Jerusalem, 1 Ch 9:10//Ne 11:10. In the time of the high priest Joiakim its head is Uzzi, Ne 12:19.

2. **Jedaiah** (2), a priest who returns from the exile with Zerubbabel, Ne 12:7. In the time of the high priest Joiakim, Nethanel is the head of the family of Jedaiah, Ne 12:21.

3. **Jedaiah** (2), one of the deportees who return from Babylon to Jerusalem and prove especially generous, Zc 6:10, 14.

4. **Jedaiah** (1), (corr. of Hb. *and Adaiah*), an Israelite of the sons of Bigvai, married to a foreign wife, whom he puts away, Ezr 10:29.

5. **Jedaiah son of Harumaph** (1), a volunteer in the rebuilding of the wall of Jerusalem, Ne 3:10.

6. *Ben-jedaiah* (1), a Simeonite, chief of a clan, 1 Ch 4:37.

JEDIAEL, "God knows" (cf. Jada).

1. **Jediael** (3), the last of the three sons of Benjamin, 1 Ch 7:6, whose descendants form the clan of the **sons of Jediael,** 1 Ch 7:10–11.

2. **Jediael son of Shimri** (1), brother of Joha the Tizite, one of David's champions, 1 Ch 11:45.

3. **Jediael** (1), a Manassite commander who rallies to David before the latter becomes king, 1 Ch 12:21.

4. **Jediael** (1), a Korahite gatekeeper, second son of Meshelemiah, 1 Ch 26:2.

JEDIDAH (1), "Beloved" (cf. David), **daughter of Adaiah** (1), a native of Bozkath, mother of King Josiah, 2 K 22:1.

JEDIDIAH (1), "Loved by Yah," see Dt 33:12 (cf. David). See: SOLOMON 1.

JEDUTHUN (17), or: ETHAN 1, is, with Asaph and Heman, one of the three great cantors of David who are the eponymous ancestors of the cantors and instrumentalists. Under David, Jeduthun takes part in the offering of sacrifices on the high place of Gibeon, 1 Ch 16:41–42, and, under Solomon, in the ceremony of moving the Ark into the temple, 2 Ch 5:12. He is described as prophesying to the sound of the lyre, 1 Ch 25:3, and as "the king's seer," 2 Ch 35:15.

The **sons of Jeduthun** are in charge of six classes of cantors, the second, fourth, eighth, tenth, twelfth, and fourteenth, 1 Ch 25:1, 3, 6, 9, 11, 15, 17, 19, 21. They take part in the religious reforms of Hezekiah, 2 Ch 29:14, and Josiah, 2 Ch 35:15. Acc. to 1 Ch 16:42, some sons of Jeduthun are gatekeepers; see: OBED-EDOM.

Three psalms are attributed to Jeduthun (Hb. *Jeditûn*), Ps 39; 62; 77.

Among his sons: OBADIAH 11.

JEGAR-SAHADUTHA (1), Aram. "Heap [of stones for a] witness." See: GALEED.

JEHALLELEL, "He will praise God" (cf. Hillel).

1. **Jehallelel** (1), father of several sons, 1 Ch 4:16.

2. **Jehallelel** (1), father of: AZARIAH 17.

JEHDEIAH, "May Yah rejoice" (cf. Jahdiel).

1. **Jehdeiah** (1), a Levite of the clan of Kohath, of the sons of Shubael, 1 Ch 24:20.

2. **Jehdeiah of Meranoth** (1), commissioner for the king's donkeys, 1 Ch 27:30.

JEHEZKEL (1). See: EZEKIEL 2.

JEHIAH (1), "May Yah live!" (cf. Jehiel), with Obed-edom a gatekeeper in the service of the Ark, 1 Ch 15:24.

JEHIEL, Hb. *Yehi'el,* "May God live!" (cf. Eve; Jehiah; Mehujael).

1. **Jehiel** (2), a Levite gatekeeper in the service of the Ark, 1 Ch 15:18, a player of the keyed harp, 1 Ch 15:20; 16:5.

2. **Jehiel** (2), a Levite of the clan of Gershon, the first of the three sons of Ladan, 1 Ch 23:8, administrator of the temple treasuries, 1 Ch 29:8, as will be his descendants, the **Jehielites,** 1 Ch 26: 21–22.

3. **Jehiel son of Hachmoni** (1), in charge of David's children, 1 Ch 27:32.

4. **Jehiel** (1), one of the six sons of King Jehoshaphat of Judah who are assassinated by their eldest brother, Jehoram, after his accession to the throne, 2 Ch 21:2–4, 13.

5. **Jehiel,** a Levite, of the sons of Heman, takes part in the purification of the temple during the reform of Hezekiah, 2 Ch 29:14.

6. **Jehiel** (1), one of the ten Levites who assist Conaniah and Shimei in the time of King Hezekiah, 2 Ch 31:13.

7. **Jehiel** (1), a priest, one of the chiefs of the temple under Josiah, 2 Ch 35:8.

8. **Jehiel** (1), father of: OBADIAH 9.

9. **Jehiel** (1), a priest, of the sons of Harim, married to a foreign wife, whom he puts away, Ezr 10:21.

10. **Jehiel** (2), an Israelite of the sons of Elam, married to a foreign wife, whom he puts away, Ezr 10:2, 26. Father of: SHECANIAH 5.

JEHIELITES (2), descendants of: JEHIEL 2.

JEHIZKIAH (1). See: HEZEKIAH 1.

JEHO. See: YAHWEH *a.*

JEHOADDAH (2), Hb. *Yeho'addah,* a Benjaminite, a descendant of Saul, father of three sons and ancestor of the sons of Azel, 1 Ch 8:36.

= **Jarah** (2), 1 Ch 9:42.

JEHOADDAN. See: JEHOADDIN.

JEHOADDIN or **Jehoaddan** (2) of Jerusalem, mother of King Amaziah of Judah, 2 K 14:2//2 Ch 25:1.

JEHOAHAZ, Joahaz, Hb. *Yeho'ahaz, Yo'ahaz,* "Yah lays hold of [in order to lead]" (cf. Ahaz).

1. **Jehoahaz** (15) **son of Jehu** (2), eleventh king of Israel (814–798) of the fourth dynasty. A difficult reign because Israel is being oppressed by the kings of Aram: Hazael, then Ben-hahad III. His army is finally reduced to "fifty horsemen, ten chariots and ten thousand foot soldiers." Jehoahaz is buried in Samaria, 2 K 10:35; 13:1–9, 22, 25.

His son and successor: Joash 6.

2. **Jehoahaz** (6) **son of Josiah** (2) and of Hamutal, seventeenth king of Judah (609). He is proclaimed king after his father's tragic death at Megiddo. Pharaoh

Neco deposes him three months later and exiles him to Egypt, where he dies, 2 K 23:30–34//2 Ch 36:1–4; cf. Jr 22:10–12 (*the man who has gone away*); Ezk 9:3–4.

= **Shallum** (2) **son of Josiah** (1), Jr 22:10–11; 1 Ch 3:15.

His son and successor: JEHOIAKIM 1.

3. **Joahaz** (1), father of: JOAH 2.

JEHOASH. See: JOASH 5.

JEHOHANAN. See: JOHN.

JEHOIACHIN (11), Hb. *Yehoyakin, Yoyakin,* "Yah has established, strengthened" (cf. Chenaniah; Chenani; Jachin; Meconah; Nacon) nineteenth king of Judah (598–597), son of Jehoiakim and Nehushta, reigns three months, 2 K 24:6, 8//2 Ch 36:8–9. Nebuchadnezzar besieges Jerusalem; Jehoiachin surrenders and is deported to Babylon with the queen mother and other personages, 2 K 24:12, 15; cf. Ezk 1:2. Thirty-seven years later, he is pardoned by the son and successor of Nebuchadnezzar, 2 K 25:27–30//Jr 52:31–34.

= **Coniah** (3), Hb. *Konyahu,* **son of Jehoiakim** (1) or **of Josiah** (1). Jeremiah predicts his captivity, Jr 22:24, 28. Zedekiah succeeds him, Jr 37:1.

= **Jeconiah** (12), Hb. *Yekonyah(u),* Gr. *Iechonias,* **son of Jehoiakim** (4), the exile, Jr 24:1; 27:20; 28:4; 29:2; Est 1:1[c]; 2:6; Ba 1:3, 9. His posterity is listed in 1 Ch 3:16–24; cf. Jr 22:30. An ancestor of Jesus, Mt 1:11–12.

JEHOIADA, Joiada, "Yah knows" (cf. Jada).

1. **Jehoiada** (21), father of: BENAIAH 1. The chronicler has Jehoiada in command of the Aaronites, 1 Ch 12:28, and gives him the title of chief priest, 1 Ch 27:5.

2. **Jehoiada son of Benaiah** (1), acc. to 1 Ch 27:34, is, with Abiathar, the successor of Ahithophel as counselor of David. To the identified (?) with the preceding.

3. **Jehoiada** (29), head of the priests in Jerusalem under Athaliah and Joash. His marriage to Jehosheba, 2 Ch 22:11, connects him with the royal family; he becomes the son-in-law of Jehoram, the brother-in-law of Ahaziah, and the uncle of Joash. He organizes the plot that leads to the fall of Athaliah and the accession of young King Joash, 2 K 11:4–16//2 Ch 23:1–15. A fervent Yahwist, he effects a religious reform that rids Jerusalem of the cult of Baal, 2 K 11:17–19//2 Ch 23:16–20. He exercises a lengthy tutelage over Joash, whom he has instructed in the Law, 2 K 12:3, 7–10//2 Ch 24:2–14, but the king turns to other advisers at the death of Jehoiada, 2 Ch 24:17, 22. Jehoiada dies at the age of 130 and is buried with the kings, 2 Ch 24:15.

Father of: ZECHARIAH 6.

4. **Jehoiada** (1), a priest, a contemporary of Jeremiah, is in charge of order in the temple and is replaced by Zephaniah, Jr 29:26.

5. **Joiada son of Paseah** (1), takes part in the rebuilding of the gate of the New Quarter, Ne 3:6.

6. **Joiada** (3) or **Jehoiada** (1), **son of Eliashib** (2), Ne 12:10–11, a high priest. In his time, the heads of the priestly families are recorded in the temple archives, Ne 12:22. One of his sons marries a foreign woman, the daughter of Sanballat the Horonite; Nehemiah expels him from Jerusalem, Ne 13:28.

JEHOIAKIM, Joiakim, Joakim, Gr. *Iōakim,* Hb. *Yehoyaqim, Yoyaquim,* "Yah causes to stand upright" (cf. Jakim).

1. **Jehoiakim** (38) [second] **son of Josiah** (11), 1 Ch 3:15, and of Zebidah, 2 K 23:36//2 Ch 36:5, eighteenth king of Judah (609–598).

= **Eliakim** (2), the young man's name before his enthronement; the name *Jehoiakim* is given him by Pharaoh Neco when the latter makes him king in place of his brother Jehoahaz, 2 K 23:34//2 Ch 36:4. From the time of his accession Jehoiakim is forced to levy a tax to pay for the heavy tribute demanded by the Egyptian overlord, 2 K 23:33, 35. In 605–604 he becomes a vassal of Nebuchadnezzar, but three years later he revolts. Armed bands of Chaldaeans, Aramaeans, Moabites, and Ammonites ravage the country, 2 K 24:1–4; cf. Dn 1:1. In 598 Jehoiakim dies, 2 K 24:5–6. The activity of the prophet Jeremiah goes on throughout his reign, Jr 1:3. Several oracles are dated from this period, Jr 26:1; 35:1, and especially from the fourth year, Jr 25:1; 36:1; 45:1; 46:2. As each section of the first edition of Jeremiah's oracles is read to the king, he burns the scroll, Jr 36:9, 16–32. The prophet will have harsh words to say of the king, Jr 22:13–19; cf. 2 K 23:37; 24:19; 2 Ch 36:8. Another prophet, Uriah, son of Shemaiah, pays with his life for a message that displeases the monarch, Jr 26:21–23.

His son and successor: JEHOIACHIN.

2. **Jehoiakim son of Hilkiah son of Shallum** (1), Ba 1:7, a priest, probably second in command, who remains in the half-ruined temple of Jerusalem. It is to be noted that his genealogy is that of the high priests descended from Zadok.

3. **Joiakim** (4) **son of Jeshua son of Jozadak** (1), Ne 12:10, 12, 26, a high priest who exercises his office before the exile.

Father of: JEDAIAH 1.

4. **Joakim** (4), name of the high priest in Jdt 4:6, 8, 14; 15:8.

5. **Joakim** (6), a rich Jew of Babylon. His fellow religionists frequent his house in great numbers. His wife Susanna remains faithful to him despite the threat of death, Dn 13:1, 4, 6, 28–29, 63.

JEHOIARIB (2). See: JOIARIB 1.

JEHONADAB. See: JONADAB.

JEHONATHAN. See: JONATHAN 8, 15.

JEHORAM, Joram, Hb. *Yehoram, Yoram,* "Yah is high" (cf. Ramah).

1. **Joram** (1), a Levite of the clan of Kohath, a descendant of Moses via Eliezer; among those in charge of the treasuries of votive offerings, 1 Ch 26:25.

2. **Jehoram** (1), one of the two priests sent by King Jehoshaphat, along with five officers and eight Levites, to instruct the towns of Judah in the Law, 2 Ch 17:7–9.

3. **Jehoram** (26) **son of Ahab** (8), ninth king of Israel (852–841), of the third dynasty, succeeds his brother Ahaziah, 2 K 1:17. A contemporary of the kings of Judah—Jehoshaphat, 2 K 3:1, Jehoram, 8:16, and Ahaziah, 8:25; 9:29.

With the aid of Jehoshaphat—or rather Jehoram—of Judah, and of the latter's vassal, the king of Edom, he launches an expedition against Mesha, king of Moab, not without having consulted the prophet Elijah. He crushes the Moabites but, seeing the king of Moab sacrificing his own son on the wall of Kir-hareseth, where he is besieged, Jehoram panics and returns to his own country, 2 K 3:6–27. Later on, with the help of Ahaziah of Judah, he wages war on Hazael, king of Aram, at Ramoth-gilead. Wounded, he returns to Jezreel to recover, 2 K 8:28–29//2 Ch 22:5–6. During his absence Jehu at Ramoth-gilead prepares to usurp power and then goes to Jezreel, where he assassinates Jehoram and Ahaziah, 2 K 9:14–26//2 Ch 22:6–8; cf. 1 K 21:29.

In 2 K 3:2 a much less severe judgment is passed on Jehoram than on his father, Ahab.

4. **Jehoram** (22) **son of Jehoshaphat** (2), fifth king of Judah (848–841), succeeds his father, 1 K 22:51//2 Ch 21:1; cf. 1 Ch 3:11. A contemporary of Jehoram, king of Israel, 2 K 1:17; 8:16. Husband of Athaliah, 2 K 8:18//2 Ch 21:6.

It is doubtless he, and not his father Jehoshaphat, who, with his vassal the king of Edom, supports Jehoram of Israel in an expedition against Mesha, king of

Moab, 2 K 3:7–27. Some years later Edom throws off the domination of Jehoram and regains its independence, 2 K 8:21–22//2 Ch 21:9–10.

According to 2 Ch 21, Jehoram, eldest son of Jehoshaphat, massacred his six brothers once he was in secure possession of the kingship, vv. 2–4, 13; a document of the prophet Elijah issued a severe condemnation of him, vv. 11–15; he also suffered a stinging defeat at the hands of the Philistines and Arabs and was buried without the honors usually given to kings, vv. 16–20.

An ancestor (Joram) of Jesus, according to Mt 1:8.

His son and successor: AHAZIAH 2.

His daughter: JEHOSHEBA.

JEHOSHAPHAT. See: JOSHAPHAT.

JEHOSHEBA (3), Gr. *Iōsabeth* (cf. Sheba), **daughter of King Jehoram, sister of Ahaziah** (2) and, acc. to 2 Ch, wife of the priest Jehoiada. She saves her nephew Jehoash from the slaughter of the royal family by Athaliah and keeps him hidden for six years in an outbuilding of the temple, 2 K 11:2–3//2 Ch 22:11–12.

[JEHOVAH]. See: YAHWEH *d.*

JEHOZABAD. See: JOZABAD 10–12.

JEHOZADAK. See: JOZADAK.

JEHU, Lat. transcription of Hb. *Yehu'*, abbrev. of *Yôhu'*, "It is he, Yah."

1. **Jehu** (5), **son of Hanani** (4), a prophet. He predicts the extermination of the house of Baasha, king of Israel, 1 K 16:1, 7, 12. Acc. to 2 Ch 19:2 he condemns the military support given by Jehoshaphat, king of Judah, to Ahab, king of Israel. He is supposed to have written a history of King Jehoshaphat, 2 Ch 20:34.

2. **Jehu** (49) **son of Jehoshaphat** (2) **son of Nimshi** (5), tenth king of Israel (841–814), founder of the fourth dynasty. At Ramoth-gilead, which he defends against the Aramaeans, and while King Jehoram is nursing his wounds at Jezreel, Jehu is anointed king by a disciple of Elisha, 2 K 9:1–10, who thus carries out the mission entrusted to the prophet Elijah, 1 K 19:16–17. He is then proclaimed king of Israel by his staff, 2 K 9:11–13. He goes to Jezreel and assassinates Jehoram of Israel; Ahaziah, king of Judah, who is visiting the wounded man; and Jezebel, the queen mother, 9:14–37. At Samaria he also wipes out the royal families of Israel and Judah, 10:1–17; cf. 2 Ch 22:7–9. Then, with the help of Jonadab the Rechabite, he slaughters the followers of Baal and destroys the temple of the god, 10:18–28. In contrast to 2 K 10:30// 15:12, Hosea condemns all this bloodshed, Ho 1:4. But the long reign of Jehu does not escape criticism in 2 K 10:29, 31, 34–36.

His son and successor: JEHOAHAZ 1.

His grandson: JOASH 6.

3. **Jehu from Anathoth** (1), a Benjaminite who goes over to David before the latter becomes king, 1 Ch 12:3.

4. **Jehu** (2), a descendant of the daughter of Sheshan, of the clan of Jerahmeel, 1 Ch 2:38.

5. **Jehu son of Joshibiah son of Seraiah son of Asiel** (1), a Simeonite, leader of a clan, 1 Ch 4:35–36.

JEHUCAL (1). See: JUCAL.

JEHUD (1), a town in Dan, Jos 19:45.

JEHUDI (4), "Judaean, Jewish" (cf. Judah), **son of Nethaniah** (1) and (Hb. *son of*) **Shelemiah son of Cushi** (1), two (or one) messenger(s) from the officials of King Jehoiakim to Baruch. Jehudi reads the scroll of Jeremiah's oracles to the king, and the king cuts off each section with a scribe's knife and throws it into the fire, Jr 36:14, 21, 23.

JEIEL, Hb. *Je'i'el.* In 2 and 5: [Q]*Je'i'el,* [K]*Je'u'el.*

1. **Jeiel** (1), a Reubenite, of the sons of Joel, 1 Ch 5:7.

2. **Jeiel** (1), a Benjaminite, also called *Abi-gibeon,* "father of Gibeon." His wife is Maacah. He is an ancestor of King Saul, 1 Ch 9:35–39.

3. **Jeiel** (1), brother of: SHAMA.

4. **Jeiel** (4), a Levite gatekeeper associated with Obed-edom, in the service of the Ark, 1 Ch 15:18, a player of the octave lyre, 1 Ch 15:21; 16:5 (at the beginning of this verse, Hb. mentions another *Jeiel,* which some correct to *Uzziel* and others to *Aziel*).

5. **Jeiel** (1), a descendant of Asaph and ancestor of: JAHAZIEL 4.

6. **Jeiel** (1), a scribe in the army of King Uzziah, 2 Ch 26:11.

7. **Jeiel** (1), one of the six heads of the Levites under Josiah, 2 Ch 35:9.

8. **Jeiel** (1), an Israelite of the sons of Adonikam, returns from the exile with Ezra, Ezr 8:13.

9. **Jeiel** (1), an Israelite of the sons of Nebo, married to a foreign wife, whom he puts away, Ezr 10:43.

JEKABZEEL (1), "May God gather together." See: KABZEEL.

JEKAMEAM (2), Hb. *Yeqam'eam,* "May the Uncle establish!" (cf. Jakim), a Levite of the clan of Kohath, last of the four sons of Hebron, 1 Ch 23:19//24:23.

JEKAMIAH, "May Yah establish!" (cf. Jakim).

1. **Jekamiah** (2), a descendant of the daughter of Sheshan, of the clan of Jerahmeel, 1 Ch 2:41.

2. **Jekamiah** (1), one of the sons born to King Jehoiachin while a prisoner at Babylon, 1 Ch 3:18.

JEKUTHIEL (1), father of Zanoah, among the sons of Bithiah, in Judah, 1 Ch 4:18.

JEMUEL (2). See: NEMUEL 1.

JEPHTHAH, Gr. and Lat. transcription of Hb. *Yiphtah,* "[God] opens, rescues" (cf. Iphtahel; Pethahiah).

1. **Jephthah** (30), **the Gileadite** (3), Jg 11:1, 40; 12:7, one of the "greater" judges and saviors of Israel, 1 S 12:11; Heb 11:32.

Son of a prostitute and rejected by his brothers, he becomes leader of a raiding band in the land of Tob, Jg 11:1–3. Faced with the Ammonite threat, the elders of Gilead ask Jephthah to be their leader; he lays down his conditions, 11:4–11. Fruitless parlays between Jephthah and the Ammonites (who are here confused with the Moabites), 11:12–28. Vow of Jephthah, who, after his victory over the Ammonites, 11:29–33, offers his daughter in sacrifice, 11:34–40. Jephthah's victory is a source of uneasiness to Ephraim, which has no intention of giving up its supremacy over the other tribes: war between Gilead, led by Jephthah, and Ephraim, 12:1–6. He dies after being judge in Israel for six years, 12:7.

2. **Ephtah** (1), a town in the lowlands of Judah, Jos 15:43.

JEPHUNNEH (cf. Penuel).

1. **Jephunneh** (16), father of: CALEB.

2. **Jephunneh** (1), an Asherite, one of the sons of Ithran, 1 Ch 7:38.

JERAH (2), "Month" (cf. Jaroah), the fourth of the thirteen sons of Joktan, a tribe or territory in southern Arabia, Gn 10:26//1 Ch 1:20.

JERAHMEEL, "May God have pity!" (cf. Jeroham).

1. **Jerahmeel** (6), brother of Caleb, 1 Ch 2:42, or his eldest brother, cf. 1 Ch 2:9. The list of his descendants is given in 1 Ch 2:25–33. His home is to be looked for in southern Palestine: 1 S 27:10 speaks of the **Negeb of Jerahmeel** along with the Negeb of Judah and the Negeb of the Kenites, and 1 S 30:29 mentions towns of Jerahmeel alongside towns of the Kenite. Connected with Judah, Jerahmeel becomes in 1 Ch 2:25 the eldest son of Hezron (who was a grandson of Judah).

2. **Jerahmeel** (1), a Levite, a son of Kish, of the clan of Merari, 1 Ch 24:29.

3. **Jerahmeel** (1), a "son of the king," that is, a prince of the blood or perhaps a police officer. With Seraiah, son of Azriel, and Shelemiah, son of Abdeel, he is ordered by King Jehoiakim to arrest Jeremiah the prophet and Baruch his secretary, Jr 36:26.

JERED (1). See: JARED 2.

JEREMAI (1), abbrev. of *Yirmeya,* "Jeremiah"?, an Israelite of the sons of Hashum, married to a foreign wife, whom he puts away, Ezr 10:33.

JEREMIAH, Gr. *Ieremias,* Hb. *Yirmeyah, Yirmeyahu,* "Yah raises up" (cf. Ramah) or "Yah opens [the womb]"?

1. **Jeremiah** (145) **son of Hilkiah** (1), one of the great prophets of Israel, from Anathoth, 6 km NE of Jerusalem, of a priestly family, Jr 1:1, perhaps a descendant of the priest Abiathar.

The prophetic activity of Jeremiah takes place between the thirteenth year of Josiah (626), Jr 1:2–3; 25:3 (some date his calling as late as 609–608, 1:4–19), and the period that follows upon the fall of Jerusalem (587). During these forty years, which are those of the last kings of Judah, Jeremiah shares the darkest days of his people's history: the tragic death of King Josiah at Megiddo (609), cf. 2 Ch 35:25, and the resultant complete failure of the religious reform Josiah had undertaken; progressive expansion of the Babylonian empire in Palestine from 605 on, cf. Jr 46:2, and, as a result of an attempted revolt, the crushing of the kingdom of Judah in 587.

Some biographical accounts enable us to determine some dates in the prophet's activity: ca. 608, discourse against the fetishized temple, Jr 26; cf. 7:1–8:3; 605–604, first two editions of his oracles, 36; cf. 45:1; 597 or 594, call for submission to the king of Babylon in order to avoid disaster, and altercation with the prophet Hananiah, 27–28; a little later, a letter to the deportees in Babylon (a letter that is decisive for the future of the Diaspora), 29; 588–587, unpleasant dealings with King Zedekiah and his officials during the second siege of Jerusalem, 32–34; 37–39; 587, destruction of Jerusalem: Jeremiah, treated with consideration by the conqueror, chosen to remain with those not deported. After the murder of Gedaliah, he is carried off to Egypt by a group of Judaeans who fear reprisals from the conqueror, 40–44.

Jeremiah's task is to warn especially the authorities, priests, prophets, and kings of the misfortune, cf. Jr 1:10; 20:8; Si 49:8, that threatens the country, 16:10–13, unless there is a conversion, cf. 3–5. In order to underscore his words and bring out their irrevocability, Jeremiah does many symbolic actions: purchase of a loincloth, which he hides and later recovers, 13:1–11; purchase of a jug, which he breaks, 19:1–15; visit to the potter, 18:1–12; wearing of a yoke, 27–28; purchase of a field at Anathoth, 32; laying of a foundation for a throne, 43:8–13. He makes a sign of his very life: he has neither wife nor children; he takes part in neither feasting nor mourning, 16:1–9. But no one listens to him, Jr 25:3; 37:2; 2 Ch 36:12. He receives little sympathy except from the son and grandson of Shaphan, namely Ahikam, Jr 26:24, and Gedaliah, 39:14; 40:5–6; 43:6, from Ebed-melek the Cushite, 38:7–13, and from his faithful friend and secretary: BARUCH 1. On the other hand, he is subjected to much persecution because of the word he proclaims: threats of death from his own people at Anathoth, perhaps because of the part he plays in the reform of Josiah, 11:18–22; placement in the stocks by Pashhur, captain of the temple police, 20:1–3; new threats of death from the priests and other prophets after the discourse against the temple, 26; strong opposition from the prophet Hananiah, 28; prohibition against entering the temple, cf. 36:5; destruction by King Jehoiakim of the first edition of his oracles, 36. Accused of planning to go over to the enemy, he is arrested, beaten, imprisoned, threatened with death, 37:11–16, cast into a cistern, 38:1–13, and finally locked up in the Court of the Guard of the royal palace, 37:21; 38:13, 28; cf. 32:2.

And what an interior drama goes on in this sensitive and generous heart! Jeremiah has left us witness of it in his "confessions," which are an intimate dialogue with God, 11:18–12:6; 15:10–21; 17:14–18; 18:18–23; 20:7–18. He is a tormented man who complains to God of his loneliness, of the hatred that surrounds him, of the success of the wicked; who has doubts about a mission from which he cannot disengage himself; who curses the day he was born and yet asserts that the word of God fills him with joy. The religion of the heart that he experienced so intensely doubtless prepared him for defining the religion of the new covenant, 31:31–34; cf. Heb 8:10–12.

During the troubled age of the Maccabees, Jeremiah is regarded as the friend of his people and a powerful intercessor, 2 M 15:13–16; cf. 2:1–8.

In the time of Jesus some Jews await the return of Jeremiah, Mt 16:14.

Mt 2:17 cites Jr 31:15 (Rachel weeping for her exiled children), and Mt 27:9 attributes an oracle of Zechariah (11:12–13) to Jeremiah.

2. **Jeremiah** (1), father of the Rechabite: JAAZANIAH 1.

3. **Jeremiah** (3), father of the queen mother: HAMITAL.

4. **Jeremiah** (1), a Manassite, leader of a clan, 1 Ch 5:24.

5. **Jeremiah** (2), a Benjaminite, 1 Ch 12:5, and a Gadite, 1 Ch 12:11, both of whom rally to David before the latter becomes king.

6. **Jeremiah** (1), another Gadite who rallies to David before the latter becomes king, 1 Ch 12:14.

7. **Jeremiah** (3), head of a priestly family who returns from the exile with Zerubbabel, Ne 12:1, a cosigner of the pledge to observe the Law, Ne 10:3. In the time of the high priest Joiakim the family of Jeremiah has Hananiah for its head, Ne 12:12.

8. **Jeremiah** (1), a priest and trumpeter who takes part in the dedication of the wall of Jerusalem, Ne 12:34.

JEREMOTH, Jerimoth

1. **Jeremoth** (1), a Benjaminite, one of the nine sons of Becher, a fighting man and head of a family, 1 Ch 7:8–9.

2. **Jeremoth** (1), a Benjaminite of the sons of Beriah, head of a family at Jerusalem, 1 Ch 8:14.

3. **Jerimoth** (1), a Benjaminite, one of the five sons of Bela, a fighting man and head of a family, 1 Ch 7:7.

4. **Jeremoth** (1), 1 Ch 23:23, the last of the three sons of Mushi, of the Levitic clan of Merari.

= **Jerimoth** (1), 1 Ch 24:30.

5. **Jerimoth** (1), of the sons of Heman, 1 Ch 25:4.

= **Jeremoth** (1), head of the fifteenth class of cantors, 1 Ch 25:22.

6. **Jerimoth** (1), a Benjaminite who rallies to David before the latter becomes king, 1 Ch 12:6.

7. **Jerimoth** (1), a son of David, 2 Ch 11:18, father of: MAHALATH 2.

8. **Jeremoth son of Azriel** (1), commissioner for the tribe of Naphtali, 1 Ch 27:19.

9. **Jerimoth** (1), one of the ten Levites who assist Conaniah and Shimei in the time of King Hezekiah, 2 Ch 31:13.

10. **Jeremoth** (1), three Israelites, married to foreign wives, whom they put away: the first, of the sons of Elam, Ezr 10:26; the second, of the sons of Zattu, 10:27; the third, of the sons of Bigvai, 10:29 *(QJeramoth)*.

JERIAH (2) or **Jerijah** (1), "Foundation of Yah" (cf. Jeruel), a Levite of the clan of Kohath, first of the four sons of Hebron, 1 Ch 23:19//24:23, and their leader, 26:31.

JERIBAI (1), brother of: JOSHAVIAH.

JERICHO (69), Hb. *Yeriho.*

a. The city

Lowest-lying in the world (± 300 m below sea level), situated in the depression created by the Jordan valley, north of the Dead Sea, 35 km NE of Jerusalem. In the course of history the city has been located on different sites.

= **City of Palm Trees** (3), Dt 34:3; 2 Ch 28:15, occupied by Eglon, king of Moab, who will be assassinated there by Ehud the judge, Jg 3:13.

On the wall of Jericho stands the house of Rahab the prostitute, who welcomes the emissaries of Joshua, Jos 2:1–3; cf. 6:22–25. The Canaanite city conquered by Joshua is put under the ban, Jos 5:13; 6:1–7.2; cf. 8:2; 9:3; 10:1, 28, 30; 12:9; 24:11; 2 M 12:15; Heb 11:30.

A town of Benjamin, Jos 18:21, Jericho is near the border of Ephraim, Jos 16:1, 7; 18:12. On their return from Rabbah, David's humiliated envoys stay there until their beards grow back, 2 S 10:5//1 Ch 19:5. The town is rebuilt in the time of Ahab by Hiel of Bethel, 1 K 16:34; cf. Jos 6:26. A group of prophets resides there; Elijah and Elisha are mentioned among them, 2 K 2:4, 5, 15, 18 (ascension of Elijah; purification of the town's water, 2:19–22). After the exile Jews reoccupy the town, Ezr 2:34// Ne 7:36, and the people of Jericho take part in rebuilding the wall of Jerusalem, Ne 3:2. In the period of the Maccabees Bacchides fortifies the town, 1 M 9:50, and Simon Maccabaeus and two of his sons inspect it, 1 M 16:14; these three are murdered not far from there in the small fortress of Dok. Jdt 4:4 connects Jericho with Samaria. Si 24:14 praises the roses (oleanders?) of Jericho.

Outside the town Jesus cures two blind men, Mt 20:29//Lk 18:35 (one blind man)//Mk 10:46 (one blind man, Bartimaeus). Zacchaeus welcomes Jesus into his home at Jericho, Lk 19:1–9. It is on the road from Jerusalem to Jericho, which passes through the wilderness of Judah, that Jesus locates the story of the Good Samaritan, Lk 10:30.

b. The Plain of Jericho

The Chaldaeans capture King Zedekiah there, 2 K 25:5//Jr 39:5; 52:8. The town of Gilgal is located there, Jos 5:10; cf. 4:19. Ptolemy will be "military commissioner for the plain of Jericho," 1 M 16:11.

c. Opposite Jericho

Israel crosses the Jordan there at the end of the Exodus, Jos 3:16; cf. 4:13. There too, beyond the Jordan, are the steppes of: MOAB, Mount Nebo, Dt 32:49; 34:1, and the territory of the Transjordanian tribes of Israel, Nb 34:15; Jos 20:8; 1 Ch 6:63.

"The Jordan opposite Jericho": JORDAN 1.

JERIEL (1), (cf. Jeruel), an Issacharite, one of the family heads of Tola, 1 Ch 7:2.

JERIJAH (1). See: JERIAH.

JERIMOTH. See: JEREMOTH.

JERIOTH (1), Hb. *Yeri'ot,* son of Caleb and his wife Azubah, 1 Ch 2:18.

JEROBOAM, Gr. *Ieroboam,* Hb. *Yarob'am,* "May the people increase" (cf. Rabbah).

1. **Jeroboam** (91) **son of Nebat** (26) and **of Zeruah** (1), an Ephraimite from Zeredah, 1 K 11:26, first king of Israel (931–910), 1 K 14:20, founder of the first dynasty. Appointed by Solomon, 1 K 11:11, 26; 2 Ch 13:6, as overseer of the Ephraimites and Manassites engaged in forced labor on the Millo in Jerusalem, he receives support from prophetic circles, cf. 2 Ch 9:29, and leads

a revolt against the authoritarianism of King Solomon; he is forced to flee into Egypt, where he remains until the death of Solomon, 1 K 11:26–40. At the assembly in Shechem the northern tribes, led by Jeroboam, reject the authority of the new king Rehoboam, 1 K 12:1–15// 2 Ch 10:1–15. Jeroboam becomes king of the northern tribes (political schism), 1 K 12:20–25. At Bethel and Dan he builds two sanctuaries as rivals of the Jerusalem temple (religious schism), 1 K 12:26–33; cf. 2 Ch 11:14–15; Tb 1:5. A contemporary of Rehoboam, Jeroboam is also a contemporary of Abijah, 1 K 15:1, and Asa, 15:9. Wars with Rehoboam, 1 K 14:30//15:6; 2 Ch 12:15; cf. 2 Ch 11:4, and with Abijah, 1 K 15:7//2 Ch 13:2–20 (defeat of Jeroboam). Capitals: Shechem, then Penuel, 1 K 12:25, finally Tirzah, 14:17.

The prophets pass a harsh judgment on the behavior of Jeroboam, cf. 1 K 13:1–9; 14:1–16; 2 K 23:5. "The sin of Jeroboam": building of high places, recruitment as clergy of any who wanted to be, 1 K 13:33, making of false gods, or in short, the rejection of Yahweh, 1 K 14:9, led Israel into sin, 1 K 15:30; 2 K 13:6; 17:21–22; Si 47:24; it also led to Israel's punishment, 1 K 14:15–16, the sins of the dynasty of Jeroboam, 1 K 13:34, the fall of this dynasty, 1 K 14:10–14; 15:29; cf. 16:3, 7; 21:22; 2 K 9:9, and finally the sins of all the kings of Israel: Nadab, 1 K 15:26, Baasha, 15:34, Zimri, 16:19, Omri, 16:26, Ahab, 16:31, Ahaziah, 22:53, Jehoram, 2 K 3:3, Jehu, 10:29, 31, Jehoahaz, 13:2, Joash, 13:11, Jeroboam II, 14:24, Zechariah, 15:9, Menahem, 15:18, Pekahiah, 15:24, and Pekah, 15:28.

Father of: Abijah 3; Nadab 4 (his successor).

2. **Jeroboam** (14) **son of Joash** (4) and his successor, thirteenth king of Israel (783–743), fourth in the dynasty of Jehu, 2 K 13:13//14:16. A contemporary of the kings of Judah, Amaziah, 2 K 14:23, and especially Uzziah, 15:1, and of the prophets Jonah, 2 K 14:25, Amos, Am 1:1, and Hosea, Ho 1:1. Profiting from the weakened state of Aram and Assyria, he "recovered the territory of Israel from the Pass of Hamath as far as the Sea of the Arabah [its ancient boundaries; the Sea of the Arabah is the Dead Sea]," 2 K 14:25–29; cf. 13:5; Am 6:13–14; 1 Ch 5:17. The prosperity of his long reign leads to social injustices, which are denounced by the prophets Amos—who is accused of plotting against the king by Amaziah, priest of Bethel—and Hosea.

His son and successor: Zechariah 9.

JEROHAM, "May he be seized with pity!" (cf. Jerahmeel; Rehum; Unloved).

1. **Jeroham** (2), an Ephraimite, grandfather of Samuel, 1 S 1:1; 1 Ch 6:12, 19.

2. **Jeroham** (1), a Benjaminite, father of six sons who are heads of families at Jerusalem, 1 Ch 8:26.

3. **Jeroham** (1), same as the preceding? Father of: Ibneiah.

4. **Jeroham from Gedor** (1), a Benjaminite, father of Zebadiah and Joelah.

5. **Jeroham** (2), father of the priest: Adaiah 6.

6. **Jeroham** (1), a Danite, father of: Azarel 3.

7. **Jeroham** (1), father of: Azariah 13.

JERUBBAAL (13), "May Baal show himself great!" (cf. Baal; Rabbah), or "May Baal defend [the bearer of the name]!". Popular etymology in Jg 6:32: "May Baal plead against him"; Jg 7:1; 8:29, 35; 9:1, 2, 5, 16, 19, 24, 28, 57; 1 S 12:11. Identified with: Gideon 1.

JERUEL (1), Hb. *Yeru'el,* "Foundation of God" (cf. Jeriah; Jeriel; Jerusalem), a wilderness where, under Jehoshaphat, a coalition of Moab, Ammon, and Edom against Israel is defeated, 2 Ch 20:16. SE of Tekoa.

JERUSALEM, (950), Hb. *Yerushalaim* (670), "Foundation of [the god] Shalem" (cf. Jeruel; Salem), Accad. *Urushalimu,* Gr. *Hierousalem* (180) or *Hierosolyma* (100); Arab. *El Quds,* "The Holy," see Is 52:1.

OT, 670 (not in the Pentateuch); DB, 136; NT, 140 (Gospels, 67; Ac 59).

a. The Citadel of David (49)

Citadel of David is not a synonym for Jerusalem: the expression, which originates with David himself, refers to the old *fortress of Zion,* 2 S 5:6–9//1 Ch 11:4–8; 1 K 8:1//2 Ch 5:2, a kind of acropolis located SE of Jerusalem and reached by stairs cut into the rock, Ne 3:15; 12:37. David captures it from the: JEBUSITES, settles in it, surrounds it with a wall that will be often destroyed, rebuilt—and relocated, 1 K 11:27; 2 Ch 32:5; 33:14; Is 22:9. He puts up buildings there, 1 Ch 15:1, moves the Ark of the covenant into it, 2 S 6:10–16//1 Ch 13:13–14; 15:25–29; 2 Ch 8:11. Hezekiah directs the waters of Gihon into the Citadel, 2 Ch 32:30; cf. 2 K 20:20; Si 48:17.

The Citadel of David serves as a *royal cemetery:* David is buried there, 1 K 2:10, as are Solomon, 1 K 11:43, ten of the kings of Judah, 1 K 14:31; 15:8, 24; 22:51; 2 K 8:24; 9:28; 12:22; 14:20; 15:7, 38; 16:20; cf. 2 Ch 32:33; Ne 3:16, and the priest Jehoiada, 2 Ch 24:16.

In the time of the Maccabees the name "City of David," 1 M 2:31; 7:32; 14:36, is also given to the great western hill. This quarter, now known as the *Citadel* (28), Gr. *Akra,* 1 M 1:33; 9:52; 12:36, or Citadel of Jerusalem, 1 M 6:26; 9:53; 10:32; 15:28, houses the Syro-Macedonian garrison, 1 M 3:43; 11:41, and the hellenized Jews, 1 M 4:2. Besieged by Judas Maccabaeus, 1 M 6:18–32; cf. 2 M 15:31, 35, it is taken and purified by his brother Simon, 1 M 13:49–52; 14:7, who settles Jewish soldiers in it, 14:36–37.

b. Zion (176)

OT, 154: 2 S–2 Ch, 6; Ps, 38; Sg, 1; Is, 47; Jr, 15; Lm, 15; Minor Prophets, 30.—DB, 15: 1 M, 8; Si, 4; Ba, 3.—NT, 7: Mt 21:5; Jn 12:15; Rm 9:33; 11:26; Heb 12:22; 1 P 2:6; Rv 14:1.

The name *Zion* refers first of all to the mountain, Mount Zion (30), 2 K 19:31//Is 37:32; 1 M 4:37; 6:62; Ps 2:6; 48:3, 12; 125:1; Is 4:5; 29:8, the heights of Zion, Jr 31:11, the hill of Jerusalem, Is 10:32; cf. 31:4, on which the fortress of Zion was built. The texts also speak of the mountain of Yahweh, Is 2:3//Mi 4:2; cf. Ps 2:6, the holy mountain, Is 27:13; Jl 4:17; Ps 48:2, the temple hill, 1 M 16:20; Jr 26:18//Mi 3:12; cf. Is 2:2. The use of the plural, "the heights of Zion," Ps 133:2, the "holy mountains," Ps 87:1 (Hb.), situates Mount Zion in the group of hills of which it is a part and thus leads to a broader use of the term. In fact, it is subsequently extended to the entire city, which is called *daughter of Zion* (24), Ps 9:14; Is 1:8; 10:32; 16:1; 62:11; Jr 4:31; 6:2, 23; Lm 2:1–18, *virgin daughter of Zion* (3), 2 K 19:21//Is 37:22; Lm 2:13. Jerusalem is called dweller in Zion, Is 12:6; Jr 51:35; Is 10:24 (cf. the inverse idea in Is 30:19), so that "Zion" occurs either in strict parallelism with Jerusalem, Ps 51:20; 102–22; 147:12; Si 24:10–11; Is 4:3; 33:20; 40:9; 52:1; 62:1; 64:9, and is even called *daughter of Jerusalem,* Lm 2:13, 15; Zp 3:14; Mi 4:8; Zc 9:9, or as equivalent to and a substitute for Jerusalem, Ps 65:2, 69:36; 87:2, 5; 102:14; 126:1; Si 48:18; Is 33:5; 49:14. The dwellers in Jerusalem are called Zion's children, Ps 149:2 and sons of Zion, Jl 2:23. The women of the city are called daughters of Jerusalem, Sg 1:5; 2:7; 3:5, 10 (Hb.); 5:8, 16; 8:4; Lk 23:28; cf. Lm 3:51, or daughters of Zion, Sg 3:11; Is 3:16–17; 4:4.

c. The city of God

Mount Zion and Jerusalem are the site and the city that Yahweh has *chosen* (18), 1 K 8:44, 48; 11:13, 32; 2 K 23:27; 2 Ch 5:6; 6:34, 38; Tb 1:4; Ps 78:68; 132:12; Si 49:6; Zc 1:17; 2:16; 3:2, in order to give his name a home, 1 K 8:16; 11:36; 14:21; 2 K 21:4; cf. 2 K 20:6//Is 38:6; Jr 25:29; Dn 9:18, and which He has given to Israel, Jr 23:39. Jerusalem is *holy* (20): "Jerusalem, the holy city," Ne 11:1; Tb 13:9–10; Si 36:12; Is 52:1; Dn 3:28; Ap 21:2, 10, "the holy city," Ne 11:18; 1 M 2:7; 2 M 1:12; 3:1; 9:14; 15:14; Si 49:6; Is 48:2; Dn 9:24. It is a holy place, Jl 4:17; Ob 17; cf. 1 M 10:31; Ps 46:5 (Hb.); Jr 31:40; Zc 14:21. Jerusalem is the *city of Yahweh,* Ps 48:8; 10:8, the "Zion of the Holy One of Israel," Is 60:14; Jr 31:38, the "city of God," Ps 87:3; cf. Is 45:13; Dn 9:16, 19, 24, the "city of our God," Ps 48:1, 8, the "city of my God," Rv 3:12, the "city of the Great King," Ps 48:2//Mt 5:35; cf. Is 24:23, the "Throne of Yahweh," Jr 3:17. It is the *dwelling place of Yahweh,* who resides on Zion, Ps 9:12; 74:2; 76:3; 132:13–14; Jl 4:17, 21; Is 8:18; 18:7; cf. Jr 31:6, who dwells in the midst of Jerusalem, Ps 135:21; Ws 9:8; Si 36:12; Zp 3:16–17; Zc 8:3; cf. Ezk 48:35, in the temple or sanctuary of Jerusalem, 2 Ch 36:23; Ezr 1:2, 4–5; 2:68; 3:8; 4:24; 5:14–17; 6:3, 5; 7:16, 17, 27; Dn 5:3; cf. 2 K 21:4; 2 Ch 3:1; 36:14; Ps 116:19, so that God is said to be "the God of Jerusalem," 2 Ch 32:19; cf. Ezr 7:19, of Zion, Ps 146:10, the God who is in Jerusalem, Ezr 1:3, the God of Israel who dwells in Jerusalem, Ezr 7:15.

d. The capital of Israel

By reason of its location between the tribes of the South and those of the North, Jerusalem, a Canaanite town, Jos 10:1–2; Jg 1:7; cf. Gn 14:18, captured by David, becomes the political center of the twelve tribe federation; cf. the expression "the gate of my people," Ob 13; Mi 1:9. It is the capital of the kingdom of David, 2 S 5:5//1 Ch 3:4, and of Soloman, 1 K 11:42//2 Ch 9:30; cf. Qo 1:1, 12, 16; 2:7, 9. By bringing the Ark of the Covenant there, David also makes Jerusalem the national sanctuary that replaces Shiloh, Ps 78:60, 68; cf. 1 S 1:3–4, and to which the Israelite, must go up at fixed times, cf. Ex 23:17; 34:23–24; Dt 16:16; 31:11, in order to seek and see the face of Yahweh, Ps 42:3; cf. Dt 12:5; Am 5:4. Jerusalem, where Yahweh dwells and speaks, is the new Sinai: "the Lord has left Sinai for his sanctuary," Ps 68:17–18, and henceforth "the Law will go out from Zion, and the oracle of Yahweh from Jerusalem," Is 2:3//Mi 4:2.

What Jerusalem means to the Israelites is expressed with enthusiastic fervor in one of the fifteen "songs of ascents," Ps 122: "Jerusalem restored! The city, one united whole! Here the tribes come up, the tribes of Yahweh, they come to praise Yahweh's name . . . here where the tribunals of justice are, the royal tribunals of David." What a joy it is to go there, Ps 84:2–3; 122:1–2; 1 M 5:54; Is 35:10; 51:11; Jr 31:12, and to abide, Ps 27:4–5; 84, in this "city of our feasts," Is 33:20. "The beloved city," Si 24:11; cf. Ps 78:68; 87:2, the all-beautiful, Ps 50:2; Sg 6:4; Jr 6:2, joy of all the earth, Lm 2:15; whose walls are so admirable, Ps 48:13, is the focus of the thoughts of the children of Zion who must never forget her, Ps 137:1, 5–6; Jr 51:50.

e. Jerusalem—Judah

Conquered by David the Judaean, 2 S 5:6–9 (despite Jos 15:8, 63; Jg 1:8), it is the primary city of Judah, as is shown by the expression "daughter (or virgin daughter) of Judah" (3), Lm 1:15; 2:2, 5, and cf. Ezr 1:2, 3. When Israel breaks off from the House of David in 931, 1 K 12:19 and only the tribe of Judah rallies to the House of David, 1 K 12:20; 2 K 17:18. Jerusalem becomes the residence of the kings of Judah, 1 K 12:18; cf. the formula, so-and-so "became king of Judah and reigned . . . in Jerusalem" (38), 1 K 14:21; 15:1–2, 9–10; 22:41–42, and so on. See: JUDAH 1 *d*.

The southern kingdom and its capital are often mentioned together: Judah and Jerusalem, 2 K 23:1, 5, 24; 24:20; 1 Ch 5:41; Is 1:1; 2:1; Jr 4:5, and so on, the people of Judah (or Judaea) and the inhabitants of Jerusalem, 2 K 23:2; 2 M 1:1, 10; Is 22:21; Jr 25:2; 35:13; 36:31; Lk 6:17, Jerusalem (or Zion) and the towns (or daughters) of Judah, Ne 11:3; Ps 48:12; 69:36; Is 40:9; Jr 7:17, 34; 9:10; 25:18; 36:9. Also to be noted is the expression *the daughter of my people* (15), a personification of Judah or Jerusalem, Is 22:4; Jr 4:11; 6:26; 8:11, 19–23; 9:6; 14:17; Lm 2:11; 3:48; 4:3; 6:10. After the fall of Samaria, its rival in the northern kingdom, Jerusalem becomes more than ever the city to which the eyes of faithful Israelites are turned, Jr 50:5. After the return from the Exile Jerusalem ceases to be politically important in the land of the Jews. The role it plays is exclusively religious, and the power of the priesthood is dominant.

f. Jerusalem and the beginnings of Christianity

When Jesus is born, Jerusalem is the capital of Judaea, which in turn is part of the Roman province of Syria. As the residence of the Jewish authorities, the Sanhedrin and the high priest (the religious and the political spheres are fused), it is also the focus of the hopes of a spiritual elite who are waiting for "Israel's comforting," Lk 2:25, and "the deliverance of Jerusalem," Lk 2:38. The child Jesus is carried to Jerusalem so that he may be presented in the temple; Lk 2:22–23; at the age of twelve, the boy Jesus makes his first pilgrimage as a son of Israel and encounters the teachers of the Law in the temple that he calls his Father's house, Lk 2:41–50. During his public life he goes up to the holy city on several occasions for the feasts, Mt 20:17–18; Mk 10:32–33; 15:41; Lk 18:31; 19:28; Jn 5:1; 7:8–10; Ac 13:31. At the feast of Passover he cleanses the temple, Jn 2:13–23. It is at Jerusalem that he will establish the new covenant, Mt 26:18, take his departure, Lk 9:51, and die as a prophet, 13:33. The mission of Jesus is brought to completion at Jerusalem: Passion, Resurrection, appearances, Ascension, Lk 24:50. There too the Apostles receive the Spirit of Pentecost, Ac 1:4–5, 12. It is from Jerusalem, where the first Christian community is founded, that the preachers of the Gospel set out, Ac 1:8; 5:28; 6:7. A violent persecution arises against the Church of this city, Ac 8:1; Paul, who was brought up at Jerusalem, Ac 22:3; 26:4, persecutes the Christians there, Ac 9:2, 13, 21; 26:10; once converted, he preaches Christ there, Ac 9:26–28; cf. Rm 15:19. Subsequently he returns several times to Jerusalem, Ac 13:13; 15:2; 18:22; 20:16–22; 21:4–31; 24:11–22; Rm 15:25–28; 1 Co 16:3–4. Jerusalem is the mother Church: at the "council of Jerusalem," Ac 15, this Church settles the problems caused by the accession of pagans to the faith, cf. Ac 16:4; Ga 1:18, and sends an envoy to Antioch to verify the foundation of its Church, Ac 11:22. But Jerusalem sees its influence wane as the Churches of Corinth, Ephesus, and Rome are established.

g. Sins and punishments of Jerusalem

"What a harlot she has become, the faithful city," Is 1:21: her kings have given themselves to idolatry, 2 K 16:3–4; 21:3–9. "You have built as many incense altars to Baal as Jerusalem has streets," Jr 11:13; cf. Ezk 16; 23. Jerusalem has abandoned the covenant of Yahweh, Jr 22:8–9. She is a rebellious and wicked city, Ezk 9:9; Ezr 4:12, 15, a city of oppression, Jr 6:6, a city of bloodshed, Ezk 22:2–9; 7:23; 11:6; Is 4:4, unclean, Jr 13:27, and tyrannical, Zp 3:1, like Sodom or Egypt, Rv 11:8. Just as Saul had been a chosen king but was rejected, so Jerusalem, "the chosen City" that has rejected Yahweh, Jr 15:6, is rejected by him, 2 K 25:27; Jr 23:39, and made an "outcast," Jr 30:17. Yahweh turns against this city to its sorrow, Jr 21:10; 39:16, sends destruction upon it, Ezk 9:1–2; 14:21, abandons his temple, Ezk 10:18–19, which will suffer the same fate as the temple of Shiloh, Jr 7:14. The capture of the city by the Babylonians in 587 will be the climax of its punishment, for it represents the great judgment of God, "the day of Jerusalem," Ps 137:7.

At the dawning of the messianic age, Jerusalem, its leaders and its priests, reject the messenger of God, whom they crucify outside the gates of the city, Mt 27:32 p; Heb 13:12; cf. Ac 7:58, and Jesus repeats the prophetic curses on the city, Mt 23:37–39//Lk 13:34–35; 19:41–44; 21:20–24 p; 23:28–31; cf. Ezk 15:6. The destruction of Jerusalem in 70 A.D. will fulfill the predictions of Jesus.

h. The new Jerusalem, the city to come

God is faithful: the guilty city has been punished, being handed over to the Chaldaeans, Jr 32:24, but it will be ransomed, Is 52:9, and consoled, Is 40:1–2; cf. Ezk 14:22, it will be rebuilt by Yahweh, Jr 31:38, who will "again make Jerusalem his very own," Zc 1:14–17; 2:16. Purified of her dross, she will become once again a City of Integrity, a Faithful City, Is 1:25–27. But the texts that describe this new Jerusalem—"placed in the middle of the nations," Ezk 5:5; cf. Jr 33:9, which will stream toward her and toward the name of Yahweh in Jerusalem, Jr 3:17; Is 2:2–3//Mi 4:1–2, Is 66:18–20, the navel of the earth, Ezk 38:12, the gate of the nations, Ezk 26:2, the mother of the peoples, Ps 87:5—allow theology to shape geography. The city and its inhabitants are gradually transfigured, Is 60; 62. Jerusalem becomes an ideal city standing outside of reality, Tb 13:8–17; cf. Rv 21. The "present Jerusalem" gives way to the "Jerusalem above," Ga 4:25–26, to the new and heavenly Jerusalem, Rv 3:12; 21:2, 10; Heb 12:22, the city prepared by God, Heb 11:16, who is its architect and builder, Heb 11:10. It is this Jerusalem, the city that is "to come," that the Christian is seeking, Heb 13:14, for he knows that it is no longer at Jerusalem or in any other place that true worshipers are to worship the Father, cf. Jn 4:21: it is in the body of the risen Christ, the new temple of the new covenant, in which "lives the fulness of divinity," Col 2:9, that the presence of God is henceforth to be found, Heb 10:20; Ph 3:20–21.

Other names for Jerusalem: ARIEL 3; HEPHZIBAH 2; JEBUS; MIGDAL-EDER 2; NAVEL OF THE LAND 2; OHOLIBAH; ROCK 8; SALEM 2.

Kings: ADONI-ZEDEK and kings of: JUDAH 1 *d*.

Hills: GOLGOTHA; MORIAH; OLIVES (MOUNT OF).

Fountains, pools, springs: BETHZATHA; DRAGON 2; FULLER 1; GIHON 2; SHILOAH 1.

Gates in the wall: BENJAMIN 2; BETWEEN THE TWO WALLS; CORNER; DUNG; EPHRAIM 2; FISH; FOUNTAIN; JOSHUA 3; MIDDLE; NEW TOWN; POTSHERDS; SHEEP; SONS OF THE PEOPLE; VALLEY; WATCH 1.

Gates of the temple or royal palace: BEAUTIFUL; BENJAMIN 2; EAST 2; FELLED TREE-TRUNK; FOUNDATION; HORSES; NEW; UPPER; WATCH 2; WATER.

Quarters: CHAPHENATHA; MORTAR; NEW TOWN.

Street: BAKERS.

Towers, fortress: ANTONIA; FURNACES; HANANEL 1; SHILOAH 2.

Valleys: HINNOM; KIDRON.

Various: ASARAMEL; GETHSEMANE; HAKELDAMA; MILLO; OPHEL 1.

JERUSHA daughter of Zadok (2), mother of Jotham, king of Judah, 2 K 15:33//2 Ch 27:1.

JESHAIAH. See: ISAIAH 2–7.

JESHANAH (2), "Old [town]," a town taken by Abijah of Judah from Jeroboam, 2 Ch 13:19. Samuel erects an *Ebenezer* or "Stone of Help" between Mizpah and Jeshanah.

JESHARELAH (1). See: ASHARELAH.

JESHER (1), son of Caleb and his wife Azubah, 1 Ch 2:18.

JESHISHAI (1), "Decrepit." See: BEN-JESHISHAI.

JESHOHAIAH (1), a Simeonite, head of a clan, 1 Ch 4:36.

JESHUA. See: JOSHUA.

JESHURUN (4), perhaps a diminutive of Hb. *yashar,* "upright," a name given to Jacob or Israel, Dt 32:15; 33:5, 26; Is 44:2.

JESIMIEL (1), "God establishes," a Simeonite, head of a clan, 1 Ch 4:36.

JESSE (48), Hb. *Ishai,* "Man of Yah"? (cf. Abishai), **the Bethlehemite** (3), 1 S 16:1, 18; 17:58, **an Ephrathite from Bethlehem of Judah** (1), 1 S 17:12. Jesse, a descendant of Judah through Perez, is son of Obed and grandson of Boaz, Rt 4:17, 22; 1 Ch 2:12; Mt 1:5. It is from among his eight sons—but 1 Ch 2:13–15 names only seven—that Samuel in the course of a sacrifice chooses David, the youngest, and anoints him king, 1 S 16:3–19; 17:12–20. Later on, where David is forced to flee the wrath of Saul, he sends his father and mother to safety in Moab, 1 S 22:3–4, the country from which his ancestress Ruth had come, Rt 1:22; 4:10. Jesse is, above all, the "stock" or "root," Is 11:1, 10, of the royal family of Judah and the ancestor of Jesus the Messiah, Mt 1:5–16//Lk 3:23–32, in whom Paul sees the "root of Jesse," Rm 15:12.

His sons: DAVID; ELIAB 3.

His daughters: ABIGAIL 2; ZERUIAH.

His great-granddaughter: MAHALATH 2.

JESUS (923), (cf. Joshua).

a. "Life of Jesus"

Born—in about the sixth year before our era—at Bethlehem in Judaea, Mt 2:1; Lk 2:1, of the Virgin Mary, Mk 6:3; Mt 1:18–25; 13:55; Lk 1:26–38; 2:1–20; Jn 2:1; 6:42; Ac 1:14; Ga 4:4, regarded as the son of Joseph the carpenter, Mt 13:55; Lk 3:23; Jn 1:45; 6:42, a descendant of David, Lk 1:37, 62, of the tribe of Judah, Heb 7:14, circumcised on the eighth day, he receives the name Jesus, Lk 2:21; cf. Mt 1:21, 25; Lk 1:31. After being presented in the temple by his parents, Lk 2:22–38, he returns with them "to Galilee, to their own town of Nazareth. Meanwhile, the child grew to maturity, and he was filled with wisdom; and God's favour was with him," Lk 2:39–40; cf. 4:16. At twelve years, the age of religious adulthood in Judaism, he accompanies his parents to Jerusalem, Lk 2:41–50. The "hidden life" of Jesus at Nazareth, where he plies the trade of a carpenter, Mk 6:3, explains various appellations (in Greek) of Jesus: *from Nazareth* (3), Mt 21:11; Jn 1:45–46; Ac 10:37; *the Nazarene* (6), Mk 1:24//Lk 4:34; Mk 10:47; 14:67; 16:6; Lk 24:19; *the Nazarean* (12), Mt 2:23; 26:71; Lk 18:37; Jn 18:5, 7; 19:19; Ac 2:22; 3:6; 4:10; 6:14; 22:8; 26:9; *the Galilean,* Mt 26:69; cf. Lk 23:6.

When "about thirty years old," Lk 3:23, in the fifteenth year of the emperor Tiberius (28 or 29 A.D.), Lk 3:1, after being proclaimed by his cousin John the Baptist, Ac 13:24, Jesus comes forward to be baptized in the Jordan, Mt 3:13–19 p; then he withdraws into the desert,

Mt 4:1–11. Then the ministry of Jesus begins. He chooses some disciples, "the Twelve," Mk 3:13–19 p, then others, Lk 10:1–2. He travels about the towns and villages, Mt 9:35, without having any fixed residence acc. to Mt 8:20//Lk 9:58, but with Capernaum as a base, Mt 4:13; cf. Jn 1:38–39. He proclaims the good news of the kingdom, Mt 4:23, reveals the Father, Jn 1:18; 8:38, cures the sick and infirm, Mt 4:24; 8:1–17, goes about doing good, Ac 10:38, provides many "signs" in order to rouse faith in his word, Jn 7:31; 20:30–31. He establishes his Church, Mt 16:13–20. He speaks simply and yet mysteriously, in parables, Mt 13:3–4; Mk 4:10–11; Lk 8:10, with the authority of a prophet, Mt 7:29; 21:23; Mk 1:27; Mt 8:27—"there is something greater than Jonah here," Lk 11:32—to such an extent that men can say: "There has never been anybody who has spoken like him," Jn 7:46. On several occasions, Mt 16:21–23 p; 17:22–23 p; 20:17–19 p, he foretells the apparent failure of his ministry, his violent death, but also his resurrection and the fruit to be borne by the seed that falls on the ground and dies, Jn 12:24. And in fact Jesus is "rejected by the elders and chief priests and scribes," Lk 9:22, by his generation, Lk 17:25; Mt 21:42 p. After having instituted the New Covenant, Lk 22:19–20, he is arrested by the Jewish authorities, brought before the judgment seat of the Roman procurator Pilate, who has him scourged and crucified, most likely on Friday, April 7, in the year 30, Mt 26:36–27:57 p. Placed in the tomb that same evening, he rises "on the third day," Mt 27:56–28:6 p. "For forty days" he shows himself alive to his disciples and then, on the Mount of Olives, he is taken up to heaven, Lk 24; cf. Ac 1:1–11.

b. Principal names of Jesus

Jesus (923) occurs 572× in the Gospels (270× as the subject of the verbs *speak, say* or *answer*): Mt, 155; Mk, 80; Lk, 87; Jn, 250.

The relationship between the meaning of the name Jesus: "The Lord saves," cf. Mt 1:25; Lk 1:31; 2:21, and the fundamental mission of Jesus is brought out in Mt 1:21 and underscored about 30×; Jesus is called *savior* (16), Lk 2:11; Jn 4:42; Ac 5:31; 13:23; Ep 5:23; Ph 3:20; 2 Tm 1:10; Tt 1:4; 2:13; 3:6; 2 P 1:1, 11; 2:20; 3:2, 18; 1 Jn 4:14; he has come to "save," to bring "salvation" (14), Lk 1:69–71; 2:30; 19:10; Jn 3:17; 10:9; 12:47; Ac 4:12; 15:11; 1 Tm 1:15; 2 Tm 2:10; Heb 2:10; 5:9; 7:25; 9:28. Among the texts that highlight the name of Jesus are to be noted: "this Jesus," Ac 1:11; 2:32, 36; 5:30; 6:14; "Jesus, the King of the Jews," Mt 27:37; Jn 19:19; cf. Ac 17:7; "I am Jesus," Ac 9:5; 22:8; 26:15; "a man called Jesus," Ac 25:19; "a new Jesus," 2 Co 11:4; "Jesus who was crucified," Mt 28:5; "your holy servant Jesus," Ac 4:27, 30; "the Good News of Jesus," Ac 8:35; cf. Mk 1:1; "the life and death of Jesus," 2 Co 4:10–11; "the marks of Jesus," Ga 6:17; "Jesus, the Son of God," Heb 4:14; "Jesus, who leads us in our faith," Heb 12:2; to "acknowledge Jesus," 1 Jn 4:2; "I, Jesus," Rv 22:15.

Christ (540), Gr. *Christos,* "Anointed," a translation of the Hb. *Meshiah,* which is transcribed 2× by Gr. *Messias,* "Messiah," Jn 1:41; 4:25.

Jesus presents himself or is presented as: the one whom God has anointed, Lk 4:18; Ac 4:27; 10:38; Heb 1:9, as the one whom God "has made . . . both Lord and Christ," Ac 2:36, whence the title *Christ,* which is given to him: in Greek "the Christ" (145), Mt 1:17; Ac 26:23; Rm 7:4 . . . Rv 20:4, 6; and "Christ" (158), Mk 9:41; Rm 5:6; 6:4 . . . 1 P 5:14. In most instances "Christ" has become another proper name of Jesus: *Jesus* and *Christ* are then interchangeable, cf. "Philip proclaimed the Christ to them," Ac 8:5, and Saul "began preaching . . . Jesus," Ac 9:20; "the blood of Jesus," Heb 10:19, and "the blood of Christ," Heb 9:14.

The name "Christ" is used about 40× in a solemn manner: "Jesus who is called Christ," Mt 1:16; 27:17, 22; "Christ the Lord," Lk 2:11; "the Christ of the Lord," Lk 2:26; "the Christ of God," Lk 9:20; 23:35; cf. Ac 3:18; 4:26; Rv 11:15; 12:10; "Christ, a king," Lk 23:2; cf. Mk 15:32; "the Christ, the Son of God," Mt 26:63; Jn 11:27; cf. Mk 1:1. The Christ is he who was "predestined" for men, Ac 3:20, and whose coming the Jews were awaiting, Mt 2:4; 11:2–3; Jn 1:41; 4:25, 29; 7:26–27, 31, 41–42. The activity of John the Baptist, Lk 3:15; Jn 1:20, 25–26; 3:28, then, and above all, of Jesus, Mt 11:2–3, intrigues men and raises the question: Is Jesus the Christ? Mt 26:63 p; Jn 4:29; 10:24. The Good News is that Jesus is the Christ, Ac 5:42; Rm 15:19; 2 Co 2:12; cf. Ac 9:22; 17:3; 18:5, 28, and true faith is to acknowledge him as such, Mt 16:16; Jn 1:45; 9:22; 11:27; 20:31; 1 Jn 2:22; 5:1. Christ is the son of: DAVID *b,* but also a Messiah whose glory comes by way of the cross, Lk 24:26, 46; Jn 12:34; Ac 3:18; 17:3; 26:23.

See: ANTICHRIST.

Jesus and *Christ* are linked 236× to form a two-part name. The most frequent form of it, *Jesus Christ* (140) occurs 6× in the Gospels: Mt 1:1, 18; 16:21; Mk 1:1; Jn 1:17; 17:3, and 134× from Ac 2:38 to Rv 1:5. *Christ Jesus* occurs 90×, Ac 24:24; Rm 1:1 to Phm 23, and (in Greek) *the Christ Jesus* 6×: Ac 5:42; Ga 5:24; 6:12; Ep 3:1, 11; Col 2:6.

Lord, Gr. *Kyrios* (which in the LXX translates the Hb. *Yahweh*), is applied 450× to Jesus (145× to God in the NT); to this name we must add 50 texts in which it is not clear whether the title is being given to God or to Jesus: Ac 8:22; 1 Co 3:5; and so on, and 55 others in which it can apply either to God or to Jesus or to a human authority: Mt 10: 24–25; 24:45; and so on. We find: *the Lord* (200): 33× in the Gospels, Mt 3:3; 21:3; Mk 16:20; Lk 7:13; 10:1, 39; 17:5; Jn 11:2; 20:2, 18, 20, 25; 21:7, 12 . . . ; 23× in Ac: 2:20, 47; 5:14; 9:1 . . . ; 18× in Rm; 48× in 1 and 2 Co; 34× in Ep–Ph–Col; 22× in 1–2 Th. *Lord!* (87), addressed to Jesus, of which 76 are in the Gospels, Mt 7:21–22; 8:2 . . . Jn 21:21; 10× in Ac: 1:6; 7:60 . . . ; and Heb 1:10. *My Lord,* Mt 22:44; Lk 1:43; Jn 20:13, 28; Ac 2:34; Ph 3:8. *Our Lord,* 1 Tm 1:14; 2 Tm 1:8; Heb 7:14; 2 P 1:2; 3:15. *Their Lord:* Rv 11:8. (*The*) *Lord Jesus* (31), Lk 24:3; Ac (13), 1:21; 4:33 . . . Rv 22:20, 21. *Our Lord Jesus* (9), Ac 20:21; 1 Co 5:4; 2 Co 1:14; 1 Th 2:19; 3:11, 13; 2 Th 1:8, 12; Heb 13:20. *Jesus our Lord,* Rm 4:24; 1 Co 9:1. *The Lord Christ,* Col 3:13, 24; 1 P 3:15; *our Lord Christ,* Rm 16:18. *The Lord Jesus Christ* (22), Ac 11:17; Rm 1:7; 13:14; Ep 1:2; 6:23; Jm 1:1. *Our Lord Jesus Christ* (40), Ac 15:26; Rm 5:1, 11 . . . Jude 4, 17, 21. *Jesus Christ our Lord* (6), Rm 1:4; 5:21; 7:25; 1 Co 1:2, 9; Jude 25. *Christ Jesus our Lord* (7), Rm 6:23; 8:39; 1 Co 15:31; 2 Co 4:5; 1 Tm 1:2, 12; 2 Tm 1:2; *the Christ Jesus our Lord,* Ep 3:11; *Christ Jesus, Lord,* 2 Co 4:5; *the Christ Jesus the Lord,* Col 2:6; *Christ Jesus my Lord,* Ph 3:8.

In about 20 texts, the "lordship" or authority, 2 P 2:10, of Christ is solemnly affirmed: in the explanation Jesus gives of Ps 110:1 in Mt 22:42–45 p and in the following texts: "a saviour . . . Christ the Lord," Lk 2:11; "You call me Master and Lord," Jn 13:13; "God has made this Jesus . . . both Lord and Christ," Ac 2:36; "Jesus Christ is Lord of all men," Ac 10:36; "Jesus is Lord," Rm 10:9; 1 Co 12:31; Ph 2:11; "Lord both of the dead and of the living," Rm 14:9; "all belong to the same Lord," Rm 10:12; "there is one Lord, Jesus Christ," 1 Co 8:6; Ep 4:5; "the Lord of Glory," 1 Co 2:8; cf. Jm 2:1; "the Lord of Peace," 2 Th 3:16; "our Lord and saviour Jesus Christ," 2 P 1:11; 3:18; cf. 2:20; "our only Master and Lord, Jesus Christ," Jude 4; cf. Jn 13:13; "the Lord of lords," Rv 17:14; 19:16.

In the Christ, in Christ, in the Lord. Whereas the term "Christian" appears only 3× in the NT, Ac 11:26; 26:28; 1 P 4:16, the relation of the Christian to Christ and the behavior proper to a Christian find expression in various formulas: [in union] with the Christ, Col 2:20; 3:1; and so on; belonging to Christ, to the Lord, Mk 9:41; Rm 14:8; 1 Co 1:12; 3:23; 2 Co 10:7; Ga 3:29; 5:34; to have the Spirit of Christ, Rm 8:9; to become sharers of Christ, Heb 3:14; [to live] according to Christ, Col 2:8; according to the Lord, 2 Co 11:17; in a manner worthy of the Lord, Col 1:10.

But the most frequent expressions (not always reflected in the English translation) are: *In Christ* (30), Rm 12:5; 16:7, 9, 10; 1 Co 3:1; 4:10, 15; 15:18, 19; 2 Co 2:17; 3:14; 5:17, 19; 12:2, 19; Ga 1:22; 2:17; Ep 1:3; 4:32; Ph 1:13; 2:1; Col 1:2, 28; 2:5; 1 Th 4:16; Phm 8, 20; 1 P 3:16; 5:10, 14. *In the Christ* (5), 1 Co 15:22; 2 Co 2:14; Ep 1:10, 12, 20. *In Jesus Christ,* Ga 3:14. *In Christ Jesus* (48), Rm 3:24; 6:11, 23; 8:1, 2, 39; 15:17; 16:3; 1 Co 1:2, 4, 30; 4:15, 17; 15:31; 16:24; Ga 2:4; 3:26, 28; 5:6; Ep 1:1; 2:6, 7, 10, 13; 3:6, 11, 21; Ph 1:1, 26; 2:5; 3:3, 14; 4:7, 19, 21; Col 1:4; 1 Th 2:14; 5:18; 1 Tm 1:14; 3:13; 2 Tm 1:1, 9, 13; 2:1, 10; 3:12, 15; Phm 23. *In the Lord* (42), Ac 11:23; Rm 16:2, 8, 11–13, 22; 1 Co 4:17; 7:22, 39; 9:1–2; 11:11; 15:58; 16:19; 2 Co 2:12; Ga 5:10; Ep 2:21; 4:1, 17; 5:8; 6:1, 10, 21; Ph 1:14; 2:24, 29; 3:1; 4:1–2, 4, 10; Col 3:18, 20; 4:7, 17; 1 Th 3:8; 5:12; 2 Th 3:4; Phm 16, 20; Rv 14:13. *In the Lord Jesus* (4), Rm 14:14; Ep 1:15; Ph 2:19; 1 Th 4:1. *In the Lord Jesus Christ* (3), 1 Th 1:1; 2 Th 1:1; 3:12. *In him:* 1 Co 1:20; Ep 1:11, 13; Ph 3:9; Col 11:16–17; and so on. In most instances these formulas are the equivalent of "Christian, in a Christian manner": 2 Tm 3:12, to live in Christ Jesus = to live as a Christian, and so on.

Son of Man (88), a title applied to Jesus 84× in the Gospels (Mt, 31; Mk, 14; Lk, 26; Jn, 14) and in Ac 7:56; Heb 2:6; Rv 1:13; 14:14.

In the plural (sons of men or sons of Adam), the expression, frequent in the OT, rare in the NT, Mk 3:28 and Ep 3:5, means simply "men, human beings" with, at times, an emphasis on the weakness of man, who is God's creature. In the singular it has most often the same meaning. It is addressed 93× to Ezekiel and 1× to Daniel, Dn 8:17, in a context of prophetic vision in which God is bringing home to man the distance between God and himself, cf. Nb 23:19; 1 S 15:29; Jb 9:32, and so on. But in two passages, Dn 7:13: "I saw, coming on the clouds of heaven, one like a son of man," and 10:16: "someone looking like a son of man came and touched my lips," it "signifies a man who is mysteriously more than human" (JB).

When Jesus uses the expression, most often (but not always, cf. Mt 16:27; 24:30) in reference to himself, it is at times equivalent simply to "I, me"; compare Mt 16:13: "Who do people say the Son of Man is?" and Mk 8:27: "Who do people say I am?" Elsewhere the meaning is: "the man that I am": cf. Mt 8:20; 12:40; Mk 9:9. But in most cases Jesus by using it puts himself forward as the promised Messiah whose glory is veiled by his humanity, Mt 11:19//Lk 7:34, and by his suffering, Mt 17:12, 22; 20:18 p; Jn 3:14. When Caiaphas asks Jesus "to tell us if you are the Christ, the Son of God," Jesus answers: "The words are your own. Moreover, I tell you that from this time onward you will see the Son of Man seated at the right hand of the Power and coming on the clouds of heaven," Mt 26:64 p. The Son of Man claims the divine power to forgive sins, Mt 12:8 p; he is the sovereign judge of the human race, Jn 5:27; cf. Mt 19:28;

25:31. And the Son of Man—Jesus—solemnly attributes to himself the name that God applies to himself in the OT: "When you have lifted up the Son of Man, then you will know that I am He," Jn 8:28.

Son of God (122). The relationship between God and Jesus is expressed in the phrase "Son of God" (46)—with its variants, "son of the living God," Mt 16:16; "son of the Most High God," Mk 5:7//Lk 8:28; "Son of the Most High," Lk 1:32; "Son of the Blessed One," Mk 14:61—or its equivalent, the possessive "my, your, his Son" (38), or else by the unqualified term "the Son" (36), Jn 3:35; 5:19–20; 6:40; 8:36; 14:13, which implies the correlative "the Father" (207), especially in Jn (120), Jn 1:18; 3:35; 4:21–23; 5:17–45, and so on.

In most instances, the expression "Son of God," especially when linked to the term "Christ," has a messianic meaning and expresses the divine sonship of Jesus, Mt 16:16; Mt 26:63//Mk 14:61; Rm 1:4; 2 Co 1:19; Ga 2:20; Ep 4:13; Heb 4:14; 6:6; 1 Jn 3:8; 5:5, the begotten of God, 1 Jn 5:18; cf. Jn 1:13; Ac 13:33; Heb 1:5; 5:5. But at times the intention may be to refer only to a being of extraordinary power who enjoys the favor of God by an exceptional title, Mt 4:3, 6; 14:33; 27:40, 54; Mk 15:39.

The Name is applied 105× to Jesus, with "the Name" being used without further qualification 2×, Ac 5:41; 3 Jn 7. Because the Jews reserved the phrase to God himself in order to avoid pronouncing the name "Yahweh," its application to Jesus designates him as the Lord. It is the name above every name, Ph 2:9; Ep 1:20–21; Heb 1:4, a new name that he alone knows, Rv 3:12; 19:12–13, 16, and by which the hostile Jews point to Jesus, "this name," Ac 4:17; 5:28; 9:21. This name is freighted with the authority and power of Jesus, Ac 4:7–12. It is "the honourable name" that is invoked, Jm 2:7, over those who are baptized in the name of Jesus, Mt 28:19; Ac 2:38; 8:16; 10:48; 19:5; 22:16.

c. Other titles and various epithets applied to Jesus

—Adam (second *or* last), 1 Co 15:45–49.

—Advocate, Paraclete, Jn 14:16; 1 Jn 2:1.

—Alpha and Omega, Beginning and End, First and Last, Rv 22:13; cf. 3:14; Col 1:18.

—Amen, Rv 3:14; cf. 2 Co 1:19.

—Apostle and high priest of our religion, Heb 3:1.

—Beloved, Ep 1:6; cf. Col 1:13 and Mt 3:17; 12:18; and so on.

—Bread of life, Jn 6:35, 41, 48, 51.

—Brother of men, Rm 8:29; cf. Mk 3:33 p; Heb 2:11–12, 17.

—Copy *or* imprint of the substance of God, Heb 1:3.

—Emmanuel, Mt 1:23.

—End of the Law, Rm 10:4.

—Faithful, Rv 19:11; cf. 2 Th 3:3; Heb 2:17; 3:2; Rv 1:5; 3:14.

—First-born, Heb 1:6; of every creature, Col 1:15, from among the dead, Col 1:18; Rv 1:5.

—Gate, Jn 10:7, 9.

—Gentle and humble in heart, Mt 11:28.

—God, Mt 1:23; Jn 1:1; 5:18; 20:28; Rm 9:5; Col 2:9; Tt 2:13; 2 P 1:1–5; 1 Jn 5:20.

—He (7), pronoun used emphatically to designate the glorious Christ, Jn 19:35; 1 Jn 2:6; 3:3, 5, 7, 16; 4:17.

—He who was, who is to come, Mt 11:3; Lk 7:19; Jn 6:14; 11:27; Rm 5:14.

—Head, Ep 1:22; 4:15; Col 1:18; 2:10, 19; cf. Ep 1:10; Heb 2:10.

—Holy, Lk 1:35; Ac 3:14; 4:27, 30; 1 Jn 2:20; Rv 3:7, Holy One of God, Mk 1:24; Lk 4:34; Jn 6:69.

—"I am," Jn 8:24, 28, 58; 13:19; cf. Ex 3:14; Heb 13:8.

—Image of God, 2 Co 4:4; Col 1:15.

—Judge, Ac 10:42; 2 Tm 4:1, 8; Jm 5:9; cf. 2 Co 5:10.

—Keystone, Mt 21:42 p; Ac 4:11; 1 P 2:4–7.

—King, Mt 25:34–40; Lk 19:38; 23:2; Jn 18:37; Ac 17:7; Rv 17:14; 19:16, of Israel (3), Mt 27:42; Jn 1:49; 12:13, of the Jews (18), Mt 2:2; 27:11, 29, 37; Mk 15:2, 9, 12, 18, 26; Lk 23:3, 37–38; Jn 18:33–39; 19:3, 19, 21.

—Lamb of God, Jn 1:29, 36; cf. Ac 8:32; 1 P 1:19, *or* Lamb (27), Rv 5:6–22:3.

—Leader, Mt 2:6; Ac 5:31, of life, Ac 3:15, of faith, Heb 12:2, of salvation, Heb 2:10.

—Light, Jn 1:9; 8:12.

—Lion of Judah, Rv 5:5.

—Man, Jn 10:33; 1 Co 15:21, 47; 1 Tm 2:5; cf. Jn 1:14; Rm 9:5; Ep 2:14; Col 1:22; Heb 5:7; 10:20; 1 P 4:1; 1 Jn 4:2.

—Master, Gr. *Kyrios*. See: JESUS *b*, Lord.

—Master (who teaches), Gr. *didaskalos* (46), Mt 5:19; . . . Jn 20:16. See: Rabbi (below).

—Mediator, 1 Tm 2:5; Heb 8:6; 9:15; 12:24.

—Messiah. See: JESUS *b*, Christ.

—Morning Star, 2 P 1:19; Rv 2:28; 22:16.

—Passover, 1 Co 5:7. See: Lamb (above).

—Peace, Ep 2:14; 2 Th 3:16.

—Priest, high priest, Heb 2:17–10:21.

—Prophet, Mt 21:11; Lk 7:16; 13:33; 24:19; Jn 4:19; 9:17; cf. Ac 3:22–23; 7:37.

—Rabbi (12), "Master," Gr. *didaskalos*, Mt 26:25, 49; Mk 9:5; 11:21; 14:45; Jn 1:38, 49; 3:2; 4:31; 6:25; 9:2; 11:8, *and* Rabbuni, Mk 10:51; Jn 20:16.

—Root of Jesse, Rm 15:12, of David, Rv 5:5; 22:16; cf. Son of David.

—Resurrection, Jn 11:25.

—Rising Sun, Lk 1:78.

—Rock, 1 Co 10:4.

—Servant, Mt 12:18; Ac 3:13, 26; 4:27, 30.

—Shepherd, Jn 10:11–12; Mt 2:6; 26:31; Heb 13:20; 1 P 2:25; 5:4; Rv 2:27; 7:17; 12:5; 19:15.

—Sign to be contradicted, Lk 2:34.

—Son of Abraham, Mt 1:1.

—Son of David. See: DAVID *b*.

—Spouse, Mt 9:15 p; Jn 3:29; Rv 21:2.

—Stumbling-stone, Rm 9:32–33; 1 P 2:8.

—Teacher, Guide, Mt 23:10.

—Temple, Mt 26:61 p; Jn 2:19–21; Rv 21:22.

—Vine, Jn 15:1, 5.

—Way, truth, and life, Jn 14:4–6.

—Wisdom of God, 1 Co 1:24, 30.

—Word (6), Jn 1:1, 14; 1 Jn 1:1; Rv 19:13.

[For others named *Jesus*, see: JOSHUA.]

JETHER, "Remnant, Superabundance" (cf. Abiathar; Hothir; Ithra; Ithran; Jattir; Jethro).

1. **Jether** (1), eldest son of Gideon. His father orders him to kill the Midianite kings Zebah and Zalmunna, "but the boy did not draw his sword; he dared not; he was still only a lad," Jg 8:20.

2. **Jether** (3) **the Ishmaelite** (1), 1 K 2:5, 32; 1 Ch 2:17.

= **Ithra the Ishmaelite** (corr. of Hb. *Israelite*) (1), 2 S 17:25, father of: AMASA 1.

3. **Jether** (2), a descendant of Jerahmeel through Onam and Jada, dies leaving no sons, 1 Ch 2:32.

4. **Jether** (1), one of the sons of Ezrah, connected with Caleb, 1 Ch 4:17.

5. **Jether** (1), 1 Ch 7:38. See: ITHRAN 2.

JETHETH (2), one of the chiefs (or clans) of Edom, Gn 36:40//1 Ch 1:51.

JETHRO (10), Hb. *Yitrô* (cf. Jether), **father-in-law of Moses** (7), **priest of Midian** (2), acc. to the Elohist tradition. Jethro gives his daughter Zipporah in marriage to Moses after the latter has fled from Egypt, Ex 2:16, 18 (the reference to *Reuel* here must be secondary), 21. Moses, a shepherd of Jethro's flocks, 3:1, leaves Midian to return to Egypt, 4:18. During the Exodus Jethro, accompanied by Zipporah, meets Moses, blesses Yahweh, who has rescued Israel, offers sacrifices, gives useful advice to Moses regarding the appointment of judges, and then returns to his own country, 18:1–27.

Acc. to the Yahwist tradition, Moses' father-in-law is: HOBAB.

JETUR (3), one of the twelve sons of Ishmael, Gn 25:15//1 Ch 1:21, an Arabian tribe in Transjordania that is allied with the Hagrites against the Transjordanian tribes of Israel, 1 Ch 5:19.

= **Ituraea** (1), a country whose capital is Chalcis; east of the upper waters of the Jordan and belonging to the tetrarchy of Philip, Lk 3:1.

JEUEL, Hb. *Ye'u'el.*

1. **Jeuel** (1), a Judaean of the clan of Zerah, lives in Jerusalem after the exile, 1 Ch 9:6.

2. **Jeuel** (1), a Levite, of the sons of Elizaphan (clan of Kohath), takes part in the purification of the temple during the reform of Hezekiah, 2 Ch 29:13.

JEUSH, Hb. *Ye'ush* (cf. Joash 7–8).

1. **Jeush** (4), a chief (or clan) of Edom, first of the three sons of Esau and Oholibamah, Gn 36:5, 14, 18; cf. 1 Ch 1:35.

2. **Jeush** (1), a Benjaminite of the sons of Jediael, head of a family and a valiant fighting man, 1 Ch 7:10.

3. **Jeush** (1), a Benjaminite, second of the three sons of Eshek, 1 Ch 8:39.

4. **Jeush** (1), first of the three sons of Mahalath and King Rehoboam, 2 Ch 11:19.

5. **Jeush** (2), a Levite of the clan of Gershon, third of the four sons of Shimei, 1 Ch 23:10–11.

JEUZ (1), Hb. *Ye'uz,* a Benjaminite, head of a family, in Moab, 1 Ch 8:10.

JEW, JEWISH (375). See: JUDAH 1 *e.*

JEZANIAH (1). See: JAAZANIAH 2.

JEZATHA (1), Hb. *Vayezata',* brother of: PARSHANDATHA.

JEZEBEL, Hb. *'Izebel* (cf. Zebul).

1. **Jezebel** (22), **daughter of Ethbaal king of the Sidonians** (1), wife of King Ahab of Israel, 1 K 16:31. She is a bad influence on her husband, 1 K 21:25, and on her son, King Jehoram, 2 K 9:22. She persecutes the prophets of Yahweh, 1 K 18:4, 13; 19:1–2, while promoting the idolatrous worship of Baal, 1 K 18:19. In order to gain for her husband a vineyard he covets, she does not hesitate to flout the law by having its owner, Naboth of Jezreel, stoned, 1 K 21:4–16. Elijah predicts Jezebel's ignominious death, 1 K 21:23; cf. 2 K 9:7, 10. During the triumphal entry of Jehu into Jezreel, she is thrown from the window of her palace and dies wretchedly, 2 K 9:30–37.

Mother of: ATHALIAH 1.

2. **Jezebel** (1), a probably symbolic name (with reference to the preceding) of a pseudoprophetess of the Nicolaitan sect, Rv 2:20.

JEZER (2), "Work," third of the four sons of Naphtali, Gn 46:24; 1 Ch 7:13, whose descendants form the **Jezerite** clan, Nb 26:49.

JEZERITE, Hb. *Yizri,* belonging to the clan of: JEZER.

JEZIEL (1), (cf. Jaziz) and **Pelet, sons of Azmaveth** (1), two Benjaminite brothers who rally to David before the latter becomes king, 1 Ch 12:3 ([K]*Jezuel*).

JEZRAHIAH (1). See: IZRAHIAH 2.

JEZREEL, *Hb. Jezre' 'el,* "God sows," Gr. *Iezrael* (cf. Zerubbabel).

1. **Jezreel** (8), a town in the highlands

of Judah, Jos 15:56, of Calebite origin, cf. 1 Ch 4:3. Native place of: AHINOAM 2.

2. **Jezreel** (39) in Issachar.

a. Town

In the south of Issachar, Jos 19:18, in Solomon's fifth district, 1 K 4:12. Ahab builds a palace there, 21:1, which becomes his secondary residence, 18:45–46, and that of his successors. Jehoram comes there to recover after the battle of Ramoth-gilead and is visited by King Ahaziah of Judah, 2 K 8:29//2 Ch 22:6; 2 K 9:13. After killing Jehoram in the plain of Jezreel, 2 K 9:22–25, and mortally wounding Ahaziah, 9:27, Jehu makes his entry into Jezreel: on his orders Jezebel is put to death, 9:30–37; cf. 1 K 21:23//2 K 9:10, the heads of the "seventy sons of Ahab" are brought to him from Samaria, and the survivors of the House of Ahab are annihilated, 2 K 10:1–11; cf. Ho 1:4–5; 2:2, 24–25.

= **Esdraelon** (3), Jdt 3:9; 4:6; 7:3.

15 km E of Megiddo.

Native place of: NABOTH.

b. Plain or **valley** (Hb. *'Emek*) **of Jezreel**

A triangular-shaped valley stretching between Beth-shan and Mount Carmel, watered by the river: KISHON and its tributaries. Passageway between Assyria and Egypt, defended by the fortress of: MEGIDDO to the west and by the fortified towns of: TAANACH, IBLEAM and BETH-SHAN. Classic battlefield of the Holy Land, good for chariot warfare, Jos 17:16. In the time of Gideon "all Midian and Amalek and the sons of the East" assemble there, Jg 6:33; 7:12. Israelites and Philistines meet there in a battle in which King Saul dies, 1 S 29:1, 11; cf. 2 S 4:4. The royal rule of Ishbaal, son of Saul, extends to Jezreel, 2 S 2:9.

Hosea—whose eldest son receives the prophetic name of *Jezreel* (cf. no. 3, below)—announces to the dynasty of Jehu the punishment for the crimes committed at Jezreel, Ho 1:4–5. But the fertility of the plain of Jezreel, indicated in its very name "God sows," serves the prophet as a symbol for predicting the birth of a new people whose sons, "sown in the country," Ho 2:24–25, "will spread far beyond their country; so great will be the day of Jezreel," Ho 2:2.

= **Plain of Esdraelon** (1), Jdt 1:8.

3. **Jezreel** (1), eldest son—whose name is symbolic—of the prophet Hosea, Ho 1:4. See above, 2 *b*.

JIBLEAM (1), Jos 21:25. See: IBLEAM.

JIDLAPH (1), (cf. Dalphon), one of the twelve sons of Nahor, brother of Abraham, born to him of his wife Milcah, Gn 22:22.

JO. See: YAHWEH *a*.

JOAB, Hb. *Yo'ab,* "Yah is Father" (cf. Abijah).

1. **Joab** (142) **son of Zeruiah** (12), brother of Abishai and Asahel, nephew of David.

As David's general. 2 S 8:16//20:23; 1 Ch 18:15; 27:34, he wins renown in many battles: against Israel, whose king at the time is Ishbaal, 2 S 2:12–32; in the assault for the capture of Jerusalem, 1 Ch 11:6–8; against Edom, 1 K 11:15–16; Ps 60:2; and in two campaigns against the Ammonites, 2 S 10:6–14//1 Ch 19:6–15 and 2 S 11:1–25; 12:26–29//1 Ch 20:1. After the murder of David's son Amnon, Joab negotiates the return of Absalom from exile at Geshur, 2 S 14. During Absalom's rebellion he commands one of the bodies of soldiers that remain loyal to David, captures Absalom, and kills him with his own hands, 18:1–29. On this occasion he reproaches the king for an excessive display of grief, 19:1–8. Joab falls into disgrace, and his cousin Amasa is appointed commander-in-chief by David in his place, 19:14; cf. 17:25. Taking advantage of the rebellion of Sheba, son of Bichri, Joab kills Amasa—as treacherously as he had formerly killed Abner, the murderer of his brother Asahel, 2 S 3:32–39—rallies the army to himself, and triumphs over Sheba, 20:4–22. Joab does not seem to have approved of the census of the people ordered by David, 2 S 24:8–9//1 Ch 21:2–6; cf. 27:23–24. In the matter of David's successor, he sides with Adonijah, 1 K 1:7, 19, 41. When Solomon takes the throne, he has Joab killed near the altar where he has taken refuge. 1 K 2:5, 22, 27–35; cf. 11:21. In 1 Ch 26:28 offerings of Joab among the temple treasures are mentioned.

His son: ELIAB 5.

His armor-bearer: NAHARAI.

2. **Joab** (1), a Kenizzite, father of Geharashim, 1 Ch 4:14.

3. **Joab** (3), Ezr 2:6//Ne 7:11; Ezr 8:9, one or two heads of families who return from the exile.

JOAH, "Yah is brother" (cf. Ahi).

1. **Joah** (6) **son of Asaph** (4), herald of King Hezekiah. In 701, during the siege of Jerusalem by the Assyrian armies, he takes part with Eliakim, master of the palace, and Shebnah, the secretary, in the legation commissioned to negotiate with the cupbearer-in-chief of Sennacherib, king of Assyria, 2 K 18:26, 37//Is 36:3, 11, 22.

2. **Joah son of Joahaz** (1), herald of King Josiah. He accompanies Shaphan, the secretary, and Maaseiah, governor of the city, to the high priest Hilkiah in order to bring payment for the workers who are restoring the temple, 2 Ch 34:8–9.

3. **Joah** (3) **son of Zimnah** (1), a Levite of the clan of Gershon, 1 Ch 6:5–6, takes part in the purification of the temple during the reform of Hezekiah, 2 Ch 29:12. Father of: EDEN 2.

4. **Joah** (1), a gatekeeper, third of the eight sons of Obed-edom, 1 Ch 26:4.

JOAHAZ (1). See: JEHOAHAZ 3.

JOAKIM. See: JEHOIAKIM.

JOANAN. See: JOHN 17.

JOANNA (2), Gr. *Iōanna* (cf. John), **wife of Herod's steward Chuza** (1), is one of the women who accompany Jesus and the Twelve and help them out of their own resources, Lk 8:3. She is also among the women who tell the Apostles of the resurrection of Jesus, Lk 24:10.

JOARIB. See: JOIARIB 1.

JOASH, Jehoash, Hb. 1–6: *Yo'ash, Yeho'ash,* "Yah has given"; 7–8: *Yo'ash,* "Yah helps" (cf. Jeush).

1. **Joash** (9) [of the Manassite clan] **of Abiezer** (1), father of Gideon, lives at Ophrah, Jg 6:11; 8:32. When the townspeople demand the head of his son because the latter has destroyed the altar of Baal, Joash replies: "If he [Baal] is a god, let him plead for himself," 6:30–31.

See: GIDEON 1.

2. **Joash** (1), one of the sons of Shelah, son of Judah, 1 Ch 4:22.

3. **Joash son of Hasshemar from Gibeah** (1), a Benjaminite who rallies to David before the latter becomes king, 1 Ch 12:3.

4. **Joash** (2), a "prince," receives from Ahab, king of Israel, the order to imprison the prophet Micaiah, son of Imlah, 1 K 22:26–27//2 Ch 18:25–26.

5. **Jehoash** or **Joash** (26) **son of Ahaziah** (3), 2 K 11:2; 13:1; 2 Ch 22:11; cf. 1 Ch 3:11, and of Zibiah, 2 K 12:2, eighth king of Judah (835–796). A contemporary of the kings of Israel Jehu, 2 K 12:1, Jehoahaz, 13:1, and Joash, 13:10. Sole survivor of the massacre of the royal family by Athaliah, he is hidden in the temple and raised there by his Aunt Jehosheba, 2 K 11:1–3//2 Ch 22:10–12. As the result of a plot laid by the priest Jehoiada, Athaliah is assassinated and Jehoash is proclaimed king; he is seven years old, 2 K 11:4–20//2 Ch 23. He will restore the temple, 2 K 12:5–17//2 Ch 24:4–6.

In 2 K 12:3 a flattering judgment is passed on him: "Jehoash did what is pleasing to Yahweh all his life, having been instructed by Jehoiada the priest." The viewpoint adopted in 2 Ch 24:17–22 is different: at the death of Jehoiada, Jehoash rejects further clerical tutelage; the prophet Zechariah, Jehoiada's son, reproaches the king for having "deserted Yahweh"; Jehoash has him stoned. Hazael, king of Aram, threatens Jerusalem, and Jehoash turns him away by paying very heavy tribute, 2 K 12:18–19//2 Ch 24:23–24. A plot is hatched against him, and he is killed by two of his officers at Beth-millo, 2 K 12:21–22//2 Ch 24:25–26.

His son and successor: AMAZIAH 1.

6. **Joash** or **Jehoash** (25) **son of Jehoahaz** (7) **son of Jehu** (2), 2 K 14:8//2 Ch 25:17, twelfth king of Israel (798–783), of the fourth dynasty. A contemporary of the kings of Judah Jehoash, 2 K 13:10, and Amaziah, 14:1; cf. 14:17//2 Ch 25:25. Two wars, two victories. First, against the Aramaeans: Joash recovers from Ben-hadad III the towns of Israel that had been occupied since the reign of Hazael, 2 K 13:14–19 (oracle of Elisha predicting the victory), 22–25. Later, against Amaziah, king of Judah: Joash captures him at Beth-shemesh, destroys part of the wall of Jerusalem, and pillages the treasures of the temple and the royal palace, 2 K 13:12; 14:8–15//2 Ch 25:17–24. He is buried in Samaria, 2 K 13:12; 14:16.

His son and successor: JEROBOAM 2.

7. **Joash** (1), a Benjaminite, one of the nine sons of Becher, a fighting man and head of a clan, 1 Ch 7:8.

8. **Joash** (1), commissioner for the stores of oil under David, 1 Ch 27:28.

JOB (59), Hb. *'Iyyob,* "He whom they treat as an enemy *or* He who turns to God *or* Where is the father"?, like Noah and Daniel, a popular hero well known in Israelite tradition, Ezk 14:14, 20. Principal figure in the book bearing his name.

According to the prose prologue, Job, who is of the land of Uz in Edom, is both the most fortunate of the sons of the East and a great servant of God. In a series of savage blows he loses his possessions, his children, and his health. But he refuses to curse God as his wife bids him to do. Three of his friends, Eliphaz of Teman, Bildad of Shuah, and Zophar of Naamath, come to "offer him sympathy and consolation," 1–2. A series of verse dialogues: of Job with the three friends, 3–31; with a fourth friend, Elihu, 32–37; and with Yahweh, 38:1–42:6, describes the relationship between the suffering man and God. In the prose epilogue the three friends are blamed "for not speaking truthfully about me as my servant Job has done." Job intercedes for them. He also recovers health, wealth, and family and patriarchal longevity, 42:7–17.

In the NT only Jm 5:11 mentions Job, emphasizing his exemplary patience.

JOBAB

1. **Jobab** (2), the last of the thirteen sons of Joktan, a tribe or territory of SE Arabia, Gn 10:29//1 Ch 1:23.

2. **Jobab** (4) **son of Zerah, from Bozrah** (2), a king of Edom whose reign falls between those of Bela and Husham, Gn 36:33–34//1 Ch 1:44–45.

3. **Jobab king of Madon** (1), one of the kings of North Canaan who form a coalition with Jabin, king of Hazor, against the Israelites, Jos 11:1.

4. **Jobab** (1), a Benjaminite, head of a family in Moab, 1 Ch 8:9.

5. **Jobab** (1), a Benjaminite of the sons of Elpaal, head of a family in Jerusalem, 1 Ch 8:18.

JOCHEBED (2), "Yah is glory"? (cf. Ichabod), **daughter of Levi** (2), born in Egypt, wife of her nephew Amram and mother of Moses, Aaron, and Miriam, Ex 6:20; Nb 26:59; cf. Ex 2:1–9.

JODA (1), Gr. *Iōda,* an ancestor of Jesus acc. to Lk 3:26.

JOED (1), Hb. *Yo'ed,* "Yah is witness" (cf. Oded; Elead; Galeed), Ne 11:7, a Benjaminite, ancestor of: SALLU 1.

JOEL, Hb. *Yo'el,* "Yah is God" (cf. Eli).

1. **Joel** (1), an Ephraimite, elder son of Samuel, a venal judge, like his brother Abijah, at Beersheba, 1 S 8:2–5. To be compared with 6.

2. **Joel** (1), a Simeonite, head of a clan, 1 Ch 4:35–40.

3. **Joel** (2), connected with Reuben, father of several clans, 1 Ch 5:4–8.

4. **Joel** (1), a Gadite living in Bashan, 1 Ch 5:12.

5. **Joel son of Azariah** (2), a Levite of the clan of Kohath, associated with: MAHATH 1.

6. **Joel** (2), a Levite of the clan of Kohath, a son of Samuel acc. to the chronicler and father of the cantor: HEMAN. To be compared with 1.

7. **Joel** (1), an Isaacharite, one of the five military chiefs of the sons of Uzzi, 1 Ch 7:3–5.

8. **Joel, the brother of Nathan** (1). See: IGAL 2.

9. **Joel** (4), a Levite of the clan of Gershon, takes part in the transferral of the Ark under David, 1 Ch 15:7, 11; one of the three family heads of Ladan, 23:8, in charge of the treasuries of the temple, 26:22.

10. **Joel son of Pedaiah** (1), commissioner for the western half-tribe of Manasseh, 1 Ch 27:20.

11. **Joel** (1), an Israelite of the sons of Nebo, married to a foreign wife, whom he puts away, Ezr 10:43.

12. **Joel son of Zichri** (1), a Benjaminite leader at Jerusalem, Ne 11:9.

13. **Joel** (2) **son of Pethuel** (1), Jl 1:1, one of the twelve "minor prophets." Nothing is known of his life. Perhaps a prophet at the end of the prophetic line? Or a "cultic" prophet who had liturgical functions in the temple? In any event, in his message he is above all the prophet of the outpouring of the Spirit, of Pentecost, cf. Ac 2:16, and the prophet of repentance.

JOELAH (1), Hb. *Yo'e'lah,* and **Zebadiah, sons of Jeroham from Gedor** (1), two Benjaminite brothers who rally to David before the latter becomes king, 1 Ch 12:8.

JOEZER (1), "Yah is help" (cf. Ezer), a Korahite who rallies to David before the latter becomes king, 1 Ch 12:7.

JOGBEHAH (2), "Height" (cf. Gabbatha), a town built by the Gadites, Nb 32:35. Not far away, the victory of Gideon over the Midianites Zebah and Zalmunna, Jg 8:11 (var. *Jogbohah*). Today *Jubeihat,* 13 km NW of Amman.

JOGLI (1), a Danite, father of: BUKKI 1.

JOHA

1. **Joha** (1), a Benjaminite of the sons of Beriah, head of a family at Jerusalem, 1 Ch 8:16.

2. **Joha the Tizite** (1), brother of Jediael, son of Shimri, one of David's champions, 1 Ch 11:45.

JOHANAN. See: JOHN.

JOHN, Johanan, Jehohanan, Gr. *Iōannēs,* Hb. *Yohanan, Yehohanan,* "Yah has shown favor" (cf. Hanan, Joanna; Onias).

1. **Johanan** (2), a priest of the line of Zadok, 1 Ch 5:35–36.

2. **Johanan** (1), a Benjaminite who rallies to David before the latter becomes king, 1 Ch 12:5.

3. **Johanan** (1), a Gadite who rallies to David before the latter becomes king, 1 Ch 12:13.

4. **Jehohanan** (1), a gatekeeper, a Korahite, sixth son of Meshelemiah, 1 Ch 26:3.

5. **Jehohanan** (1), a Judaean, an army officer under Jehoshaphat, 2 Ch 17:15.

6. **Jehohanan** (1), father of: ISHMAEL 4.

7. **Jehohanan** (1), father of: AZARIAH 14.

8. **Johanan** (1), eldest son of Josiah, 1 Ch 3:15.

9. **Johanan** (15) **son of Kareah** (14), leader of the Jewish officers who after

the fall of Jerusalem rally to Gedaliah, the governor appointed by the Chaldaean conquerors, Jr 40:7–8//2 K 25:23–24. He warns Gedaliah of the plot being hatched against him and even proposes to have Ishmael the assassin done away with, but Gedaliah does not believe him, Jr 40:13–16. On hearing of Gedaliah's murder and the other crimes of Ishmael, Johanan sets out in pursuit of him, but Ishmael escapes, 41:11–18. Then, against the advice of Jeremiah, Johanan leads to Egypt the other officers, the people who support them, and the prophet himself, in order to find refuge there from possible reprisal by the Chaldaeans, Jr 42:1, 8; 43:1–7.

10. **Ben-johanan son of Igdaliah** (1), a "man of God." In the time of Jeremiah a room in the temple is assigned to his sons; the prophet meets the Rechabites there, Jr 35:4.

11. **Johanan son of Hakkatan** (1), head of the family of the sons of Azgad, who returns from exile with Ezra, Ezr 8:12.

12. **Jehohanan son of Eliashib** (1) has a room in the temple where Ezra spends a night in fasting, Ezr 10:6.

= ? **Johanan** (1) **grandson** (Hb. *son*) **of Eliashib** (1), high priest, Ne 12:11 (probably read *Yohanan* for Hb. *Yonatân*), 22, 23.

13. **Jehohanan** (1), an Israelite of the sons of Bebai, married to a foreign wife, whom he dismisses, Ezr 10:28.

14. **Jehohanan** (1), son of Tobiah the Ammonite, husband of the daughter of Meshullam, son of Berechiah, Ne 6:18.

15. **Jehohanan** (1), head of the priestly family of Amariah in the time of the high priest Joiakim, Ne 12:13.

16. **Jehohanan** (1), a priest, takes part with Nehemiah in the ceremony for the dedication of the Jerusalem wall, Ne 12:42.

17. **Johanan** (1), fifth of the seven sons of Elioenai, a descendant of Zerubbabel and King Jehoiachin, 1 Ch 3:24.

= ? **Joanan** (1), likewise a descendant of Zerubbabel and an ancestor of Jesus, Lk 3:27.

18. **John** (1), 1 M 2:1, father of: MATTATHIAS 6.

19. **John** (4), known as **Gaddi** (1), the oldest of the five sons of Mattathias, 1 M 2:2, in charge of the baggage convoy of the Maccabaean army, assassinated by the Arabian tribe of the sons of Jambri and avenged by his brothers Jonathan and Simon, 1 M 9:35–42. To be identified (?) with John, one of the two Jewish envoys to Lysias, 2 M 11:17.

20. **John** (2), of the priestly family of Accos, 1 M 8:17. Thanks to his efforts, the Jews win certain freedoms from the reigning Seleucids, 2 M 4:11.

Father of: EUPOLEMUS.

21. **John [Hyrcanus I]** (8), son of Simon Maccabaeus and brother of Judas and Mattathias, 1 M 16:2, 14. His father puts him in command of the troops at Gezer, 1 M 13:53. Victory of John over Cendebaeus, 1 M 16:1–10. His father and his two brothers are assassinated by Ptolemy, son of Abubus, and John himself barely escapes a plot instigated by the same Ptolemy, 16:13–22. John succeeds his father (134–104), exercises the high priesthood, and rebuilds the walls of Jerusalem, 16:23–34.

22. **John** (91) **son of Zechariah** (1), Lk 3:2, and of Elizabeth, called **the Baptist** (15).

His activity is located in the Judaean wilderness, Mt 3:1, near the Jordan, Mt 3:13; Mk 1:4; Lk 3:3, and at Bethany, Jn 1:28; cf. 10:40, or at Aenon, Jn 3:23. It begins "in the fifteenth year of Tiberius Caesar's reign" (perhaps in 27), Lk 3:1, and ends (around 29?) with his imprisonment, Mt 4:12//Mk 1:14; cf. Mt 11:2; Jn 3:24, and his decapitation by order of Herod Antipas, Mt 14:3–12//Mk 6:17–29; Lk 3:19–20; 9:9, whose illegitimate marriage with his niece and sister-in-law Herodias John has denounced.

John's activity is characterized by a summons to conversion, that is, an unconditional return to the God of the covenant, and by a baptism that is a sign of this conversion and is given to Jews once and for all, Mt 3:1–10//Mk 1:2–6//Lk 3:1–14; Jn 4:1; cf. Ac 19: 3–4. The Gospels establish *a very close link between John the Baptist and Jesus,* while at the same time emphasizing the radical differences between them: Lk parallels the infancy of John, 1:13–25, 57–66, 76, 80, and that of Jesus, while making the former subordinate to the latter. John precedes and announces the Messiah. John's baptism is a baptism of water, that of the Messiah will be a baptism of fire (the difference between this prediction and the activity of Jesus will lead in the future to John's question: Are you he who is to come? Mt 11: 2–4//Lk 7:18–23) and of Spirit, Mt 3:11–12//Mk 1:7–8//Lk 3:15–18//Jn 1:26–27. John baptizes Jesus, Mt 3:13–17//Mk 1:9–11//Lk 3:21–22, but Mt notes that John wants to reverse their roles. John and his disciples fast; Jesus and his disciples do not fast, Mt 11:18–19; cf. Mt 3:4; 9:14. Jesus will be regarded at times as a reincarnation of John, Mt 14:2//Mk 6:14//Lk 9:7; cf. Mt 16:14//Mk 8:28//Lk 9:19.

The fourth Gospel regards John primarily as a witness, Jn 1:6–8; 5:33–36; 10:41, a man who bears witness before the Jewish authorities, 1:19, and before Israel, 1:31, that he is not himself the Messiah but only the Messiah's forerunner, 1:20; 3:28, that he has seen the Spirit descend from heaven and remain upon Jesus, 1:33, that Jesus is the Lamb of God, 1:29, 36, and the Son of God, 1:34. Once his testimony has been given, John gradually stands aside and lets Jesus take the stage—some disciples, 1:35–40, then the crowd, 3:26; cf. 10:40–41, leave John to join Jesus—"he must grow greater, I must grow smaller," 3:30; cf. 4:1.

Jesus will say of John that he is more than a prophet, the greatest man of the old covenant, the new Elijah, Mt 11:7–14//Lk 7:24–30; 16:16; Mt 17:11–13//Mk 9:11–13.

A community of believers has been established around John: these **disciples of John** practice fasting, Mt 9:14//Mk 2:18; Lk 5:33; John has taught them to pray, Lk 11:1; they ask themselves whether their master is not the Messiah, Lk 3:15; Jn 1:19–20; 3:25–28; Ac 13: 25; it is from among them that Jesus recruits his first disciples, Jn 1:35–40; they bury the body of John, Mt 14:12. This community will remain in existence long after the death of John, Ac 18:25; 19:1–4.

23. **John** (34) **brother of James** (2), **son of Zebedee** (2), one of the Twelve.

Often associated with his brother James. See: Jacob 3.

Likewise associated with Peter, the Apostle. Together they make the preparations for the last Passover of Jesus, Lk 22:8. After Pentecost they heal a cripple in the temple whither they have gone to pray, Ac 3:1, 3, 4, 11. When the Sanhedrin forbid them to speak of Jesus, they answer that they cannot remain silent about what they have seen and heard, Ac 4:1, 13, 19–21. Later on, they go to Samaria to put the seal of approval on the mission of Philip, one of the seven deacons, Ac 8:14–25.

Tradition had identified **the disciple whom Jesus loved** (5) with John, the Apostle, Jn 19:26 (at the foot of the cross); this disciple is likewise associated with Peter in Jn 13:23 (at the Last Supper) and 21:7, 20 (on the shore of the Sea of Tiberias during an appearance of the risen Jesus). He is also identified with **the other disciple** (6) in Jn 20:2, and, as such, again associated with Peter, Jn 18: 15–16 (in the courtyard of the high priest's palace); Jn 20:2–10 (at the empty tomb). John, who is also mentioned in Mk 9:38//Lk 9:49, is associated in Ga 2:9 with Cephas and James, the brother of the Lord, in a meeting with Paul and Barnabas.

Tradition is not unanimous on the

identity of the author of the Apocalypse, whose name is John, an exile on the island of Patmos for his faith and his preaching, Rv 1:1, 4–9; 22:8.

See: TWELVE; List, page 417.

24. **John** (4), Jn 1:42; 21:15–17.

= **Jonah** (1), Mt 16:17, father of Simon: PETER 1.

25. **John** (5), Ac 12:12, 25; 13:5, 13; 15:37. See: MARK.

JOIADA. See: JEHOIADA.

JOIAKIM. See: JEHOIAKIM.

JOIARIB, Jehoiarib, "Yah renders justice," Gr. *Iōarib* (cf. Jarib).

1. **Joiarib** (3), a priest who returns from the exile with Zerubbabel, Ne 12:6. In the time of the high priest Joiakim, Mattenai is head of the priestly family of Joiarib, Ne 12:19. In Ne 11:10, *Joiakim* is perhaps to be read for Hb. *Joiarib.* See: JEDAIAH 1.

= **Jehoiarib** (2), head of the first priestly class, 1 Ch 24:7, lives at Jerusalem, 1 Ch 9:10.

= **Joarib** (2), 1 M 2:1; 14:29, to whose line the Maccabees belong. See: MATTITHIAH 6; SIMEON 5.

2. **Joiarib** (1), a Judaean, an ancestor of: MAASEIAH 15.

3. **Joiarib** (1), one of Ezra's messengers to Iddo, Ezr 8:16 (omitted by some).

JOKDEAM (1), a town in the highlands of Judah, Jos 15:56.

JOKIM (1), derived from *Joiakim?* A descendant of Judah through Shelah, 1 Ch 4:22.

JOKMEAM (2), Hb. *Yoqmeʿam.* See: JOKNEAM.

JOKNEAM (3), Hb. *Yoqneʿam,* **in Carmel** (1), an ancient Canaanite town known to the Egyptians. Its king figures in the list of kings conquered by Joshua, Jos 12:22. A town of Zebulun, Jos 19:11, assigned to the Levites of the clan of Merari.

= **Jokmeam** (2), a town in Solomon's fifth district, 1 K 4:12. By a mistake it replaces *Kibzaim* in 1 Ch 6:53 (cf.//Jos 21:22). Today *Tell Qeimun,* 12 km NW of Megiddo.

JOKSHAN (4), one of the sons of Abraham and his concubine Keturah, father of Sheba and Dedan, peoples of Arabia, Gn 10:25–30//1 Ch 1:19–23.

JOKTAN (6), son of Eber, brother of Peleg, father of the tribes of south Arabia, among them Havilah, Ophir, and Sheba, Gn 10:25–30//1 Ch 1:19–23.

JOKTHEEL, Hb. *Yoqteʾel.*

1. **Joktheel** (1), a town in the lowlands of Judah, Jos 15:38.

2. **Joktheel** (1). See: ROCK 1.

JONADAB, Jehonadab, "Yah is generous (cf. Nadab).

1. **Jonadab** (5), **son of Shimeah** (2), nephew of David, cousin and friend of Amnon, "a very shrewd man." He advises Amnon, who is infatuated with his half-sister Tamar, to feign illness so that the king, his father, will send the young girl to wait on him in his room, 2 S 13:3–5. After the murder of Amnon, he tells David that the rumor is false that has all of the king's sons assassinated, 13:32–35.

2. **Jonadab** (3), Jr 35:6, 10, 19, or **Jehonadab** (7), 2 K 10:15, 23; Jr 35:8, 14, 16, 18. See: RECHAB 2.

JONAH, Gr. *Iōnas,* Hb. *Yonah,* "Dove."

1. **Jonah** (30) **son of Amittai** (2), **from Gath-hepher** (1), a prophet, predicts that Jeroboam II, king of Israel, will extend the country to its ancient frontiers, 2 K 14:25.

His name has been attached to the marvel-filled and ironical story told in the Book of Jonah, one of the twelve "minor" prophets. God's call to life is addressed to all beings: to the Jewish prophet who has fallen into the depths of the abyss; to the pagans of Nineveh, sworn enemies of Israel; and to the countless animals, Jon 1; 2:1, 11; 3–4; Tb 14:4 (var.).

Jesus refers his unbelieving hearers, who ask him for miracles, to "the sign of the prophet Jonah" (probably to Jonah's preaching and restoration to life), Mt 12:39–41//Lk 11:29–32.

2. **Jonah** (1). See: JOHN 24.

JONAM (1), Gr. *Iōnam,* an ancestor of Jesus, Lk 3:30.

JONATHAN, Hb. *Yehonatân, Yonatân,* "Yah has given" (cf. Nathan), Gr. *Iōnathan, Iōnathas, Iōnathēs.*

1. **Jonathan son of Gershom son of Moses** (1), Jg 18:30, a Levite of Bethlehem in Judah. Initially a priest for an individual man, Micah, in the highlands of Ephraim, Jg 17:7–13, he accompanies the Danites in their migration to the North of Palestine and becomes their priest, as do his sons after him, in the sanctuary of Dan, 18:3–6, 15–30.

2. **Jonathan** (96) **son of Saul** (5), 1 S 14:1; 19:1; 23:16; 2 S 21:7; 1 M 4:30; cf. 1 S 14:49; 31:2. When the country is occupied by the Philistines, Jonathan takes the initiative in a war of liberation: he kills the Philistine governor, 1 S 13: 2–3; with his armor-bearer he attacks an enemy post, where he causes a panic and wins the victory of Michmash, 13:16, 22; 14:1–23; cf. 1 M 4:30. But Jonathan has broken the fast imposed before the battle, and his father, Saul, demands punishment; the intervention of the people saves Jonathan from death, 1 S 14: 24–30, 36–45. Deep friendship binds Jonathan and David together: the son of Saul gives David his cloak and weapons, enters into an agreement with him, 18: 1–4, intervenes with his father in David's behalf, 19:1–7, or, according to another tradition, facilitates David's flight, 20; 21:1, and visits him when he is in hiding at Horesh, 23:16–18.

On learning of the death of Jonathan, who has been slain by the Philistines in the battle of Gilboa, 31:2//1 Ch 10:2; cf. 2 S 4:4, David weeps for him whose "love to me [was] more wonderful than the love of a woman," 2 S 1:4–5, 12, 17–27. Out of loyalty to this friendship, David welcomes into his house Jonathan's son Meribbaal, 2 S 9:1, 7; cf. 4:4; 21:7, and transfers his friend's bones to his family tomb, 2 S 21:12–14.

Father of: MERIBBAAL 2.

3. **Jonathan** (6) **son of Abiathar** (2). This priest's son serves, with Ahimaaz, son of the priest Zadok, as liaison for David when the latter flees from Absalom, 2 S 15:27, 36. Stationed at the Fuller's Spring, Jonathan and Ahimaaz are discovered by one of Absalom's spies and hide at Bahurim, whence they go to warn David, 2 S 17:17–21. It is Jonathan who brings news to Adonijah that David has chosen Solomon as his successor, 1 K 1:42–43.

4. **Jonathan son of Shimeah** (2), a nephew of David, at Gath kills a Philistine giant who is descended from Rapha, 2 S 21:20–21//1 Ch 20:6–7.

5. **Jonathan son of Shammah, from Harar** (1), 2 S 23:32–33 (corr. of Hb. [*the sons of Jashen:*] *Jonathan, Shammah the Hararite*), one of David's champions.

= **Jonathan son of Shagee, from Harar** (1), 1 Ch 11:34.

6. **Jonathan son of Uzziah** (1), commissioner for the king's stores in provincial towns, villages, and castles, 1 Ch 27:25.

7. **Jonathan, David's uncle** (1), counselor and scribe, in charge of the royal children, along with Jehiel, son of Hachmoni, 1 Ch 27:32.

8. **Jehonathan** (1), one of the eight Levites sent by Jehoshaphat, along with two priests and five officers, to instruct the towns of Judah in the Law, 2 Ch 17: 7–9.

9. **Jonathan** (3), a scribe. It is in an underground cell of his house, which has been turned into a prison, that Jeremiah undergoes a painful imprisonment, Jr 37: 15, 20; 38:26.

10. **Jonathan** (2), a descendant of Jerahmeel, 1 Ch 2:32–33.

11. **Jonathan** (1), father of: EBED 2.

12. **Jonathan son of Asahel** (1), one of

those opposed to the procedure for dealing with marriages to foreign women, Ezr 10:15.

13. **Jonathan** (1), a high priest who, according to 2 M 1:23, exercised his ministry in the time of Nehemiah.

14. **Jonathan** (1) and **Jehonathan** (1), two heads of priestly families in the time of the high priest Joiakim, one of the family of Malluchi, Ne 12:14, of the other of the family of Shemaiah, Ne 12:18.

15. **Jonathan** (1), a descendant of Asaph, father of: ZECHARIAH 26.

16. **Jonathan** (85), surnamed **Apphus** (1), 1 M 2:5, leader of the Jews (in 160) and high priest (153–143). He fights first at the side of his brother Judas Maccabaeus, cf. 2 M 8:22, especially during the expedition aimed at liberating the Jewish prisoners in the land of Gilead, 1 M 5:17, 24–55. At the death of Judas, 1 M 9:19, Jonathan takes over the leadership of the resistance, 9:28–31. Threatened by Bacchides, he goes to hide in the desert of Tekoa, 9:32–49, but at Bethbasi he defeats Bacchides, 9:58–72. He then resides at Michmash, where he begins "to judge the people," 9:73. From 152 on, the kings of Syria vie for the favor of Jonathan: Alexander Balas appoints him high priest, and Demetrius I offers the Jews a charter, which Jonathan rejects, 10:1–47. Jonathan meets two kings, Alexander and Ptolemy Philometor, at Ptolemais: he is appointed military commissioner and governor general, 10:59–66. Near Azotus he routs the army of Demetrius II under the command of Apollonius, 10:67–89; cf. 11:4–6.

After the death of Alexander and Philometor, Demetrius II becomes king and confirms Jonathan in his functions and prerogatives by a new charter, 11:20–37. When an insurrection takes place at Antioch in Syria, Jonathan comes to Demetrius' aid, but a little while later the king falls out with him, 11:38–53. Antiochus VI, with the help of Trypho, expels Demetrius II and once again grants Jonathan the favors formerly bestowed on him by Antiochus' father, Alexander Balas; he even appoints him military commissioner of Coele-Syria, 11:57–62, where Jonathan routs the generals of Demetrius II, 11:63–74; 12:24–32. Jonathan sends envoys to Rome and Sparta, 12:1–23; cf. 14:16–18. In 143, Trypho imprisons Jonathan at Ptolemais and executes him later on, 12:39–53; 13:12–25; 14:16. His brother Simon succeeds him, 13:8, 14.

17. **Jonathan son of Absalom** (1), one of Simon Maccabaeus' generals. He occupies Joppa after having expelled its pagan population, 1 M 13:11.

18. **Jonathan** (1), a member of a priestly family, takes part in the hearing of Peter and John by the Sanhedrin, Ac 4:6.

JOPPA, Jaffa (25), Gr. *Ioppē,* Hb. *Yapho* or *Yapho',* whence *Jaffa,* "The Beautiful"?, on the border of the territory of Dan, Jos 19:46, serves as seaport for Jerusalem, 2 Ch 2:15; Ezr 3:7; Jon 1:3; 1 M 14:5.

In the time of the Maccabees, Antiochus Epiphanes spends some time there, 2 M 4:21. Judas burns the harbor in reprisal for the drowning of the city's Jews, 2 M 12:3, 7. Joppa capitulates to Jonathan, 1 M 10:75–76, who meets King Ptolemy Philometor there, 11:6. Simon Maccabaeus occupies the city, 1 M 12:33; 13:11; 14:5, 34, for which he agrees to pay a fine to Antiochus VII, 15:18–35.

The Apostle Peter comes from Lydda to Jaffa in order to restore Tabitha to life, Ac 9:36, 38, 42. He stays for a while in the house of Simon, a leather tanner who lives beside the sea, 9:43; 11:5. It is from Jaffa that Peter is called to the house of Cornelius, the centurion at Caesarea, 10:5, 8, 32; 11:13, whither he goes in company with some Christians of Jaffa, 10:23.

Today *Yafa,* in the southern part of Tel Aviv.

JORAH (1), head of a family of Israelites who return from the exile with Zerubbabel, Ezr 2:18 (//Ne 7:24, *Hariph*).

JORAI (1), a Gadite, head of a family, 1 Ch 5:13.

JORAM. See: JEHORAM.

JORDAN, Gr. *Iordanēs,* Hb. *Yardên,* "The Descender"?

1. **Jordan** (147), the largest river in Palestine. Rising from various springs at the foot of Mount Hermon, it descends in a torrent, cf. Jb 40:23, to the Sea of Chinnereth (210 m below sea level), then runs 140 km further as the crow flies, and, after very many meanderings, reaches the Dead Sea (392 m below sea level). Between these two seas and along the river banks tropical vegetation, Jr 12:5, where lions dwell, Jr 49:19; 50:44; Zc 11:3.

The expression *Jordan opposite* (or *near* or *facing*) *Jericho* occurs 13×, Nb 22:1; 26:3, 63; 31:12; 33:48, 50; 34:15; 35:1; 36:15; Jos 13:32; 16:1; 20:8; 1 Ch 6:63.

The Jordan forms the eastern boundary of Canaan or the Promised Land, Nb 34:12; Ezk 47:18; cf. Jos 23:4, of the tribes of Judah, Jos 15:5, Benjamin, 18:12, 19–20, Ephraim and western Manasseh, 16:7, Issachar, 19:22, and Naphtali, 19:33–34, and it forms the western boundary of the territories of Reuben, Gad, and eastern Manasseh, Nb 32:5, 21, 29; Dt 3:17; Jos 13:23, 27; 22:25; cf. Jg 11:13, 22; 2 S 24:5.

The Jordan has a number of fords used throughout biblical history by Jacob, Gn 32:11, the Moabites, Jg 3:28, Gideon and the Midianites, 7:24; 8:4, the Ammonites, 10:9; Ephraim and Gilead, 12:5, the Philistines and the Israelites, 1 S 13:7, David attacking the Aramaeans, 2 S 10:17, then fleeing from his son Absalom, 2 S 17:22, 24; 19:16–19, 32–42; 20:2; 1 K 2:8 . . . , Judas Maccabaeus and his brothers, 1 M 5:24, 52; 9:42–48. The most famous crossing, however, is that of Israel under the leadership of Joshua, Jos 1:2—and not of Moses, Dt 3:27; 4:21–22; 31:2—for the conquest of the Promised Land, Nb 35:10; Dt 2:29; 4:26; 9:1; 11:31; 12:10; 27:2, 4, 12; 30:18; 31:13; 32:47; Jos 1:11; 3–4 (parallel with the crossing of the Red Sea, Jos 4:23; cf. Ps 66:6; 114:3, 5); Jos 5:1; 7:7; 24:11; Jdt 5:15. Elijah and especially Elisha stay for a more or less lengthy period on the banks of the Jordan, 2 K 2:6–7, 13; 6:2, 4; Elisha will send Naaman the Aramaean to cleanse himself of his leprosy in the waters of the river, 2 K 5:10–14.

It is in the Jordan that John baptizes the crowds who come to him, Mt 3:5–6//Mk 1:5//Lk 3:3, and Jesus in particular, Mt 3:13//Mk 1:9; cf. Lk 4:1.

Tributaries: CHERITH; JABBOK. The Yarmuq is not named in the Bible.

2. **Plain** (11) of the Jordan. See: PLAIN 1; ARABAH *a*.

3. **Beyond the Jordan** [= *Transjordania*] (4), Hb. *'Eber ha-Yardên,* Gr. *Peran tou Iordanou* (whence the name *Peraea*). Here, east of the Jordan, are located the ancient kingdoms of Sihon and Og, Dt 1:5; 3:8; 4:46–47, 49; Jos 2:10; 9:10; 12:1; 24:8, which become the territories of Reuben, Gad, and eastern Manasseh, Nb 32:19, 32; 34:15; Jos 1:14–15; 13:8, 27, 32; 14:3; 18:7; 22:4; Jg 5:17; 10:8; 1 S 31:7; 1 Ch 12:38; cf. Is 8:23; Mt 4:15.

Among the hearers of Jesus are people from Transjordania (or Peraea), Mt 4:25//Mk 3:8. Jesus himself goes to this region, Mt 19:1//Mk 10:1; Jn 3:26; 10:40.

Beyond the Jordan: ABEL-MIZRAIM; BETHANY 2; the Plains of MOAB.

4. **Beyond the Jordan** [= *Cisjordania*] (11). The country west of the Jordan, occupied by the Amorite kings, Jos 5:1; 9:1; 12:7, which becomes the land of Israel, Dt 3:25, that of the other ten tribes, Nb 32:19; Dt 3:20; Jos 22:7; Jg 7:25. See also 1 Ch 26:30; Jdt 1:9.

JORIM (1), Gr. *Iōrim,* an ancestor of Jesus acc. to Lk 3:29.

JORKEAM (1), a descendant of Caleb, 1 Ch 2:44.

JOSECH (1), Gr. *Iōsech,* an ancestor of Jesus acc. to Lk 3:26.

JOSEPH, Hb. *Yoseph,* "May [God] add [other children to the one just born]," see Gn 30:24. (Cf. Ebiasaph; Eliasaph; Josiphiah; Asaph.)

1. **Joseph** (220) **son of Israel** (2), 1 Ch 5:1; 7:29.

a. The patriarch

First son of Jacob and Rachel, born in Upper Mesopotamia, Gn 30:23–25; 33:2, 7; 48:7. Darling of his father, favored with dreams that promise him a brilliant future, Joseph is on both accounts envied by his brothers, who sell him, 37. In Egypt, he first experiences humiliation as a slave and a prisoner, Gn 39. But in this country of wise men and soothsayers Joseph soon proves the clear superiority of the wisdom with which he is endowed by interpreting the dreams of Egyptian officials, 40, then those of Pharaoh himself (the seven cows and the seven ears of corn), 41:1–32, as he will prove it in his agrarian policy of war against the scourge of famine, 41:46–57; 46:13–26. The lowly shepherd then attains to the highest dignities: he is appointed prime minister—on this occasion he receives the Egyptian name of *Zaphenath-paneah*—and enters the ranks of the highest nobility of Egypt by marrying Asenath, daughter of Potiphera, priest of On, who gives him two sons, Manasseh and Ephraim, 41:37–45, 50–52, later adopted by Jacob, 48:1–23.

The story of Joseph is inseparable from that of "his brothers." The latter, forced by famine—like the Egyptians, 41:55—"go to Joseph," who tests them, 42–44, before revealing himself to them, 45:1–15. Joseph settles his brothers and his father Jacob in the land of Goshen, 45:9–47:12. After his father's death, in an action that prefigures the future Exodus, cf. 48:21; 50:24–25, Joseph transfers the body of Jacob to Canaan, 50:1–14; cf. 47:29; he forgives his brothers for their earlier crime against him and explains the key to the entire sequence of events: "The evil you planned to do me has by God's design been turned to good, that he might bring about, as indeed he has, the deliverance of a numerous people," 50:12–21; cf. 45:5–8. Joseph dies at the age of 110, the ideal age according to Egyptian wisdom, 50:22–26. Cf. also Ex 1:6, 8; 13:19; Jos 24:32; 1 M 2:53; Ps 105:17; Ws 10:13–14: Ac 7:9–18; Heb 11:22.

b. Joseph, the sons of Joseph, the tribe of Joseph, the house of Joseph

These also refer to:

—a group of tribes, comprising especially Ephraim and Manasseh, Nb 36:1–5; Jos 24:32; 1 K 11:28, but also Benjamin, 2 S 19:21;

—the northern kingdom, Ps 78:67; Ezk 37:16, 19; Am 5:6, 15; 6:6; Zc 10:6; Ob 18;

—all of Israel, Ps 77:16; 80:2; 81:6.

Joseph in the list of tribes: List, pages 410–11. See: EPHRAIM 1; MANASSEH 1.

2. **Joseph** (1), an Issacharite, father of: IGAL 1.

3. **Joseph** (2), of the sons of Asaph, head of the first class of cantors, 1 Ch 25:2, 9.

4. **Joseph** (1), an Israelite of the sons of Zaccai, married to a foreign woman, whom he dismisses, Ezr 10:42.

5. **Joseph** (1), head of the priestly family of Shebaniah in the time of the high priest Joiakim, Ne 12:14.

6. **Joseph** (1), a Simeonite, an ancestor of Judith, Jdt 8:1.

7. **Joseph** (5) **son of Zechariah** (2), a general who, along with Azariah, has the

task of keeping the peace in Judaea during the absence of Simon Maccabaeus, 1 M 5:18–19. Eager to win renown, the two march on Jamnia and are routed, 1 M 5:56–62. He had earlier taken part with Judas Maccabaeus in the campaign against Nicanor, 2 M 8:22, and with Zacchaeus (his father?) and Simon Maccabaeus in the siege of the Idumaean fortresses, 2 M 10:19.

8. **Joseph** (2), two ancestors of Jesus and of the following Joseph, acc. to Lk 3:24, 30.

9. **Joseph** (14), son of Jacob acc. to Mt 1:16 or son of Heli acc. to Lk 3:23, a descendant of David, Mt 1:20; Lk 1:27; 2:4, husband of Mary, Mt 1:16, 18–20, 24–25; Lk 1:27; 2:4; cf. 2:16, regarded as the father of Jesus, Lk 3:23; 4:22//Mt 13:55; Jn 1:45; 6:42, a carpenter by trade, Mt 13:55; cf. Mk 6:3, lives in Nazareth, Mt 2:23; Lk 2:4, 39, 51. Unlike Mary, Joseph makes no appearance during the public life of Jesus.

10. **Joseph** (2), Mt 13:55; 27:56.

= **Joset** (3), Mk 6:3; 15:40, 47, son of MARY 6, brother of James the Younger, Simon, and Jude, "brother" of Jesus.

11. **Joseph** (6) **of Arimathaea** (4), a wealthy man, member of the Sanhedrin, disciple of Jesus, obtains permission from Pilate to take the body of Jesus and buries it in his own tomb, Mt 27:57–60//Mk 15:43–46//Lk 23:50–53//Jn 19:38–42.

12. **Joseph,** known as **Barsabbas,** surnamed **Justus** (1), a candidate to take the place of Judas Iscariot; Matthias, the other candidate, is chosen, Ac 1:23.

13. **Joseph** (1), Ac 4:36. See: BARNABAS.

JOSET (3), Gr. *Iōsēs.* See: JOSEPH 10.

JOSHAH son of Amaziah (1), a Simeonite, leader of a clan, 1 Ch 4:34.

JOSHAPHAT, Jehoshaphat, Gr. *Iōsaphat,* Hb. *Yehoshaphat, Yoshaphat,* "Yah judges" (cf. Shephathiah. See Daniel).

1. **Joshaphat the Mithnite** (1), one of David's champions, 1 Ch 11:43.

2. **Joshaphat** (1), a priest, a trumpeter before the Ark, 1 Ch 15:24.

3. **Jehoshaphat son of Ahilud** (4), recorder under David and Solomon, 2 S 8:16; 20:24; 1 K 4:3; 1 Ch 18:15.

4. **Johoshaphat son of Paruah** (1), administrator of Solomon's tenth district, which is Issachar, 1 K 4:17.

5. **Jehoshaphat** (2), 2 K 9:2, 14, father of: JEHU 2.

6. **Jehoshaphat** (77) **son of Asa** (1) and of Azubah, daughter of Shilhi, 1 K 22:42//2 Ch 20:31–32, fourth king of Judah (870–848), succeeds his brother, 1 K 15:24; cf. 1 Ch 3:10. Contemporary of the kings of Judah: Ahab, 1 K 22:41, Ahaziah, 22:52; and Jehoram, 2 K 3:1; 8:16.

His reign is marked by peace with Israel, 1 K 22:45. Jehoshaphat even supports Ahab in his campaign against the Aramaeans of Ramoth-gilead, a campaign in connection with which the prophets are consulted, especially Micaiah, son of Imlah, 1 K 22:1–33//2 Ch 18:1–31. (On the return, meeting of Jehoshaphat and the prophet Jehu, 2 Ch 19:1–3.) The support given to Jehoram, king of Israel, in his expedition against Mesha, king of Moab, probably comes from Jehoram, king of Judah, rather than from his father, Jehoshaphat, 2 K 3:7–27. 2 Ch 20:1–30 reports a war of Jehoshaphat against the Moabites and their allies, the Ammonites and the Meunites. Jehoshaphat undertakes to build trading ships at Ezion-geber, but the venture finally fails, 1 K 22:49–50//2 Ch 20:36–37.

The chronicler emphasizes Jehoshaphat's consolidation of power, his concern for the Law, his well-organized army, 2 Ch 17, his reforms in the area of justice, 19:4–11. Jehoshaphat "sought Yahweh with all his heart," 2 Ch 22:9; cf. 1 K 22:43–44, 47//2 Ch 20:32; 21:12. This eulogy ranks Jehoshaphat among the three great kings of Judah, alongside Hezekiah and Josiah.

An ancestor of Jesus acc. to Mt 1:8. His son and successor: JEHORAM 5.

7. **Valley of Jehoshaphat** (2), Jl 4:2, 12, a valley with the symbolic name "God judges," an imaginary place where Yahweh passes judgment on the nations, called in 4:14 the "Valley of Decision" (or "Valley of Threshing *or* of the Drag"). A late tradition identifies it with the Kidron Valley, SE of the Temple of Jerusalem.

JOSHAVIAH and **Jeribai, sons of Elnaam** (1), two brothers who are among David's champions, 1 Ch 11:46.

JOSHBEKASHAH (2), of the sons of Heman, 1 Ch 25:4, head of the seventeenth class of cantors, 25:24.

JOSHIBIAH (1), father of: JEHU 5.

JOSHUA, Lat. transcription of Hb. *Yehoshuaʿ* or *Yéshuaʿ*, Gr. *Iēsous,* Jesus, or *Iasōn,* Jason, "Yah is generous" (cf. Shua) or "Yah saves" (cf. Isaiah).

1. **Joshua** (210) **son of Nun** (27), an Ephraimite.

= **Hoshea son of Nun** (3), Nb 13:8, 16; Dt 32:44.

Joshua, *servant of Moses,* Ex 24:13; 33:11; Nb 11:28; Dt 1:38, in the wilderness during the Exodus is victorious over Amalek, whom he engages in battle, Ex 17:9–14, accompanies Moses on Mount Sinai, Ex 24:13 (Elohist tradition), takes part as the representative of his tribe in the reconnaissance of the Promised Land, Nb 13:8, and, seconded only by Caleb, is in favor of occupying Canaan, Nb 14:6; cf. 14:30–31, 38; 26:65; 32:12; Dt 1:38. He *succeeds Moses* as leader of the community, Nb 27:15–33, which he must bring into Canaan, Dt 1:38; 3:21, 28; 31:3, 7, 14, 23; 34:9.

Acc. to the Book of Joshua (see the different point of view of Jg 1 regarding the conquest) Joshua crosses the Jordan, 1–3, erects a memorial at Gilgal, 4, circumcises the Israelites, 5:2–9, captures Jericho, 5:13–6:27; cf. 2 M 12:15; 1 K 16:34, then Ai, Jos 7–8, offers a sacrifice on Mount Ebal, 8:30–35, makes a treaty with the Gibeonites, 9, goes to their aid, crushes the five Amorite kings, then conquers the southern, 10, and northern towns, 11, of Canaan, cf. 12:7. He then portions out the land among the tribes, 14:1, 6, 13; 15:13; 17:4, 14–18; 18:3, 8, 10; 19:51, and himself receives as his share the town of Timnath-serah in the highlands of Ephraim, 19:49–50; cf. 24: 30//Jg 2:9. His career is climaxed by the great assembly at Shechem, where he gathers all the tribes, which together choose Yahweh, Jos 24. He dies at the age of 110, Jos 24:29//Jg 2:8; cf. Jg 1:1; 2:21. A genealogy of Joshua is given in 1 Ch 7:25–27. There is a eulogy of Joshua in Si 46:1–6; cf. 1 M 2:55.

The NT thinks of Joshua primarily as the man who leads the Israelites into the Promised Land, Ac 7:45; Heb 4:8.

2. **Joshua of Beth-shemesh** (2), owner of the field where the Ark of the Lord halts on its return from the land of the Philistines, 1 S 6:14, 18.

3. **Joshua** (1), governor of Jerusalem, otherwise unknown. His name is given to a gate of the city near which there is a high place in the time of King Josiah, 2 K 23:8.

4. **Jeshua** (1), leader of the ninth class of priests, 1 Ch 24:11.

5. **Jeshua** (1), one of the six Levites under the command of Kore, son of Imnah, for the distribution of food in the time of King Hezekiah, 2 Ch 31:15.

6. **Jeshua** (26) **son of Jozadak** (5) or **Jehozadak** (6), a descendant of: ZADOK 1.

After the return from the exile, Ezr 2:36//Ne 7:39; 12:7, first high priest, associated with David's descendant: ZERUBBABEL.

Among his descendants are some priests married to foreign women, whom they put away, Ezr 10:18.

Father of: JEHOIAKIM 3.

7. **Jeshua** (10) **son of Azaniah** (1), and

Kadmiel, Levites associated with one another, contemporaries of the high priest Jeshua, Ne 12:8, 24, return from the exile with Zerubbabel, Ezr 2:40//Ne 7:43, are among the Levites directing the work of rebuilding the temple, Ezr 3:9, in charge of the penitential ceremony of Ne 9:4–5, and cosigners of the pledge to observe the Law, Ne 10:10. Ne 8:7 lists Jeshua among the Levites who explain the Law to the people during its solemn reading by Ezra.

Father (?) of: JOZABAD 6.

8. **Jeshua** (2), an Israelite, head of a family, related to Pahath-moab, whose sons return from the exile with Zerubbabel, Ezr 2:6//Ne 7:11.

9. **Jeshua** (1), father of: EZER 5.

10. **Jesus** (4) **son of Sira** (3), Si prol., title, and 7; 50:27; 51, title, and subscription.

= **Eleazar of Jerusalem** (1), Si 50:27, author of the book of: ECCLESIASTICUS.

11. **Joshua** (1), father of: HABAKKUK.

12. **Joshua** (1), an ancestor of Jesus of Nazareth acc. to Lk 3:29.

13. **Jesus** (932) **of Nazareth.** See: JESUS.

14. **Jesus** surnamed **Justus** (1), a Jewish Christian, coworker with Paul, Col 4:11.

15. **Jesus** (1), Mt 27:16. See: BARABBAS.

16. **Jeshua** (1), a town of the Negeb occupied by Judaeans, Ne 11:26.

17. See: JASON.

JOSIAH, Hb. *Yo'shiyyah, Yo'shiyyahu,* "Yah supports"?

1. **Josiah** (56) **son of Amon** (3) and of Jedidah, 2 K 22:1, sixteenth king of Judah (640–609), succeeds his father, 2 K 21:24, 26//2 Ch 33:25. A contemporary of the prophets Zephaniah, Zp 1:1, Jeremiah, 1:2; 3:6; 25:3; 36:2, and probably Nahum.

After the wicked reigns of his predecessors, that of Josiah is notable chiefly for an important religious reform. Acc. to 2 Ch 34:3–7 the king is engaged in it from 628 on. In 622 on the occasion of the restoration and purification of the temple the discovery is made of the Book of the Law (probably the legislative section of our Deuteronomy): it is read to the king, who sends a delegation to consult the prophetess Huldah about it, 2 K 22:3–20//2 Ch 34:8–28. The reform movement is then strengthened and is extended not only to Jerusalem and Judah but to the part of the northern kingdom that has been reconquered as a result of the decline of Assyria: the sanctuaries of the idols are destroyed, their priests slaughtered, the covenant is renewed, and a solemn Passover is celebrated at Jerusalem, 2 K 23:1–24//2 Ch 34:29–33; 35:1–18. Josiah is killed at Megiddo as he tries to prevent the passage of Pharaoh Neco, who is going to the help of Assyria, 2 K 23:29–30//2 Ch 35:20–24; cf. Jr 22:10 (*the man who is dead*). Josiah is the last king of Judah, after David, Jehoshaphat, and Hezekiah, to be praised by the Deuteronomist, 2 K 22:2//2 Ch 34:2; 2 K 23:25; cf. Si 49:1–4.

His sons and successors: JEHOAHAZ 2; JEHOIAKIM 1; ZEDEKIAH 4.

2. **Josiah** (1) **son of Zephaniah** (2), one of the deportees who return from Babylon to Jerusalem and show themselves especially generous, Zc 6:10, 14.

JOSIPHIAH (1), "May Yah add [other children]" (cf. Joseph), father of: SHELOMITH 4.

JOTBAH (1), "Attractiveness, charm" (cf. Mehetabel), native place of Meshullemeth, mother of King Amon of Judah, 2 K 21:19. About 20 km N of Nazareth.

JOTBATHAH (3), "Attractiveness, charm" (cf. Mehetabel), a stage of the Exodus, north of the Gulf of Aqaba, Nb 33:33–34, "a land of water-streams," Dt 10:7.

JOTHAM, "Yah is whole, perfect," Gr. *Iōatham.*

1. **Jotham** (4), the youngest **son of**

Jerubbaal/Gideon (2), escapes the massacre of his brothers at the hands of their half-brother Abimelech, Jg 9:5, 21, who becomes king of Shechem. The famous "Jotham's fable" is violently hostile to the institution of kingship, which it regards as useless, Jg 9:7–15; cf. 9:57.

2. **Jotham** (20) **son of Uzziah** (2), 2 K 15:30, 32; cf. 1 Ch 3:12, and of Jerusha, 2 K 15:33//2 Ch 27:1, eleventh king of Judah (740–736). A contemporary of Pekah, king of Israel, 2 K 15: 32 (but not of King Hoshea, despite 2 K 15:30, which is contradicted by 17:1) and of the prophets Hosea, Ho 1:1, Isaiah, Is 1:1, and Micah, Mi 1:1.

Coregent with his father, who is afflicted with leprosy, he succeeds him at his death, 2 K 15:5–7//2 Ch 26:21, 23. Acc. to 2 K 15:34–38, he builds the Upper Gate of the temple and, at the end of his reign, sees the beginning of the Syro-Ephraimite war against Judah. The chronicler also mentions work on the wall of the Ophel, the building of towns, and a war against the Ammonites; finally, he agrees with 2 K in saying that Jotham "did what is pleasing to Yahweh," 2 Ch 27:2–9. A census of the Gadites was supposedly taken in the period of Jotham, 1 Ch 5:17. Jotham is listed as an ancestor of Jesus, Mt 1:9.

His son and successor: AHAZ 1.

3. **Jotham** (1), a Calebite of the sons of Jahdai, 1 Ch 2:47.

JOZABAD, Jehozabad, "Yah has bestowed" (cf. Zabad).

1. **Jozabad** (1). See: JOZACAR.

2. **Jozabad from Gederoth** (1), a Benjaminite who rallies to David before the latter becomes king, 1 Ch 12:5.

3. **Jozabad** (2), two Manassite chiefs who rally to David before he becomes king, 1 Ch 12:21.

4. **Jozabad** (1), one of the ten Levites assisting Conaniah and Shimei in the time of King Hezekiah, 2 Ch 31:13.

5. **Jozabad** (1), one of the six heads of the Levites under Josiah, 2 Ch 35:9.

6. **Jozabad son of Jeshua** (1), one of the Levites who assist the priest Meremoth in the Jerusalem temple, Ezr 8:33.

7. **Jozabad** (1), a priest, of the sons of Pashhur, married to a foreign wife, whom he puts away, Ezr 10:22.

8. **Jozabad** (1), a Levite, married to a foreign wife, whom he puts away, Ezr 10:23.

9. **Jozabad** (2), a Levite, explains the Law to the people during its solemn reading by Ezra, Ne 8:7; responsible for the outside work of the temple, Ne 11:16. One or two individuals.

10. **Jehozabad** (2) **son of Shomer** (1), 2 K 12:22, or **son of Shimrith the Moabitess,** 2 Ch 24:26, one of the assassins of King Joash of Judah.

See: JOZACAR.

11. **Jehozabad** (1), a gatekeeper, second of the eight sons of Obed-edom, 1 Ch 26:4.

12. **Jehozabad** (1), a Benjaminite, an officer in the army of King Jehoshaphat of Judah, 2 Ch 17:18.

JOZACAR (1), "Yah has remembered" (cf. Zechariah), **son of Shimeath** (1), 2 K 12:22 (*Jozacar* is a var. of Hb. *Jozabad*).

= **Zabad son of Shimeath the Ammonite woman** (1), 2 Ch 24:26, one of the assassins of King Joash of Judah.

See: JOZABAD 10.

JOZADAK (6), Gr. *Iōsedek,* "Yah is just" (cf. Zadok), a priest, Ezr 3:2, 8; 5:2; 10:18; Ne 12:26; Si 49:12.

= **Jehozadak** (8), Hg 1:1, 12, 14; 2:2, 4; Zc 6:11, son of Seraiah, a descendant of Aaron through Zadok, exiled to Babylon.

Father of: JOSHUA 6.

Grandfather of: JEHOIAKIM 3.

JUBAL (1), suggests Hb. *yôbel,* "Horn, trumpet," son of Lamech and Adah, "ancestor of all who play the lyre and the flute," Gn 4:21.

JUCAL son of Shelemiah (1), one of the four officials of King Zedekiah who, during the Chaldaean siege of Jerusalem, have Jeremiah thrown into a cistern on the grounds that his words are demoralizing the remaining defenders of the city, Jr 38:1–6.

= **Jehucal son of Shelemiah** (1), a messenger sent at an earlier date from King Zedekiah to Jeremiah, Jr 37:3.

JUDAEA (96). See: JUDAH 1 *e*.

JUDAEAN (13), of Judaea or of: JUDAH 1 *b, e*.

JUDAH, Judas, Jude, Hb. *Yehudah,* Gr. *Iouda, Ioudas,* connected in Gn 29:35; cf. 49:8, with *Yadah,* "praise," perhaps an abbrev. of *Yehud'el,* "God be praised" (cf. Jew; Jehudi; Judith).

1. **Judah** (877), son of Jacob and Leah, eponymous ancestor of the tribe of the same name.

a. The son of Jacob and his descendants

Presented as the fourth son of Jacob and Leah, Gn 29:35; cf. 35:22–23; 46: 8–12; Ex 1:1–2, Judah plays, in the Yahwist story of Joseph, the role of restrainer, which is assigned to Reuben in the Elohist story: when his brothers want to kill Joseph, he advises them to sell him instead to an Ishmaelite caravan that is on its way to Egypt, Gn 37:25–27. Later on, in Egypt, he pleads with Joseph in behalf of Benjamin, 44:18–34. And it is Judah whom his father, Israel, "sent . . . ahead to Joseph, so that the latter [Joseph] might present himself to him in Goshen," 46:28. The story of Judah and Tamar, Gn 38, is a Yahwist tradition having to do with the origins of the tribe. "Judah left his brothers," marries a Canaanite woman named Bath-shua, by whom he has three sons, Er, Onan, and Shelah, Gn 38:1–5. By trickery Tamar, a widow, becomes pregnant by her father-in-law, Judah, himself a widower, and gives him twins, Perez and Zerah, Gn 38: 6–30. "Judah had five sons in all," 1 Ch 2:3–4; cf. Gn 46:12. The clans of Judah are mentioned in Nb 26:20–22; cf. Nb 1:26; Jos 7:17; Jg 17:7; 1 S 23:23; Mi 5:1; Mt 2:6.

b. The tribe of Judah

"The sons of Judah" (50), Nb 10:14; Jos 18:11, 14; Jg 1:8; and so on, "the House of Judah" (40), 2 S 2:4, 7, 10–11; . . . Zc 12:4, "The men *or* people of Judah" (37), Jg 15:10; 1 S 11:8; 15:4; 2 S 19:41; 2 K 14:21; . . . "the men of Judah" (13), 2 K 16:6; 25: 25; Jr 32:12–52:30, or simply "Judah," Jos 18:5; 2 K 24:20; 2 Ch 28:19, form the largest of the tribes, cf. Nb 1:27; 2:9; 26:22. This is doubtless due to the fact that it has absorbed not only some Simeonites, cf. 1 Ch 4:27, but foreign elements as well: Canaanites, Gn 38, Kenizzites, Calebites, and Jerahmeelites, 1 Ch 2; cf. Jos 14:6, 14; Jg 1:9–15, and as a result is the most complex and least "Israelite" of the tribes. It is also the most important tribe in Israel's history. In the thirty lists of the tribes (see: List, pages 410–11) Judah appears 11× in fourth place, which is in accordance with the order of its "birth," 3× in third place, 2× in second place, and 11× in first place. A primary role is attributed to it in the conquest of the Promised Land: "Judah is to attack first," Jg 1:2; and the text adds that "Yahweh was with Judah," Jg 1:19a. The "blessing of Jacob" proclaims the preeminence of Judah among his brothers and the perdurance of the royal house of Judah: "Judah . . . your father's sons shall do you homage. . . . The sceptre shall not pass from Judah," Gn 49:8, 10. Thus it is the only tribe mentioned in the genealogy of Jesus: "Jacob the father of Judah and his brothers," Mt 1:2. "But it seems that it is under David and through David that the tribe of Judah discovered its true identity" (R. de Vaux). And, in fact, it is David, a Judaean from Bethlehem, 1 S 16:1; 20:6, who unites the elements of the tribe, 1 S 30:26–31, as he takes up residence at Hebron, 2 S 2:1–3, the Calebite town, Jos 14:13. Judah in the south corresponds to the principal tribe in the north, Ephraim or the house of Joseph. The choice of Yahweh falls on Judah; on Zion, its capital; and on David, the most illustrious of the "sons of Judah," Ps 78:67–70. Jesus, son of David, "came from Judah," Heb 7:14, and is the Lion of the tribe of Judah, Rv 5:5; cf. Gn 49:9.

Judah in the lists of the tribes: List, pages 410–11.

Members of the tribe: AKAN; BEZALEL; NAHSHON.

c. The land of Judah

Some scholars think that Judah was first a geographical name, the name of a region, like Ephraim or Naphtali, which then gave its name to the tribe that settled in the area; this tribe then found an eponymous ancestor for itself in the person of Judah, son of Jacob.

The tribe of Judah and the tribe of Simeon, whose inheritance "was taken out of the portion of the sons of Judah," Jos 19:9, occupy the whole of southern Palestine, below the non-Israelite barrier of Gezer, the Gibeonite towns, and Jerusalem; consequently, it is to a certain degree isolated from the tribes of the north, which explains Judah's spirit of independence, Gn 38:1; Dt 33:7, and fosters the development in the north of the causes of the future schism. This northern boundary, described in detail in Jos 15:5–11, is that of Judah in the reign of David. The other boundaries of Judah, to the south (the wadi of Egypt), east (the Dead Sea, 15:5) and west (the Great Sea, 15:12), coincide with the ideal borders of the Promised Land.

The "land of Judah" (47), Dt 34:2; Rt 1:7; 1 S 22:5; 30:16; 1 M 3:39; Mt 2:6, or simply "Judah," Jg 15:9; 1 S 23:3, contains four regions:

—the *highlands,* Jos 11:21; 15:48; 20:7; 21:11; 2 Ch 21:11; 27:4; Lk 1:39, 65, which extends from north of Bethlehem (altitude of Jerusalem, 790 m) to south of Hebron (1010 m);

—the *hilly area* located between the highlands to the east and the coastal plain to the west, and called the: LOWLANDS;

—*the wilderness* of Judah, Jg 1:16; Ps 63:1 (cf. 1 S 22–24); Mt 3:1, a barren area east of the Jerusalem-Hebron line;

—the *Negeb* of Judah. See: NEGEB 1.

Jos 15:21–63 apportions out the towns of Judah according to these four regions. We also find 56× the global designation *the towns of Judah,* 2 K 23:8; 2 Ch 10:17 . . . 39:14; Ps 69:36; Jr 1:15, several times in Jr with Jerusalem, Jr 11:6, 12; 17:26; 44:6; cf. Zc 1:12, and 2× the "daughters of Judah," Ps 48:11; 97:8. The "town in the hill country of Judah" in Lk 1:39 is usually identified as Ain Karim.

Principal towns: BEERSHEBA; BETHLEHEM 1; BETH-SHEMESH 1; HEBRON 1; JERUSALEM.

d. The kingdom of Judah

The two anointings at Hebron of David, whom "all Israel and Judah loved," 1 S 18:16, make him king of Judah, 2 S 2:4, *and* king of Israel, 2 S 5:1–5: the two groups, Judaeans and Israelites, acknowledge David as king, but they remain distinct, partly because of the independent spirit of the southern tribes and of the great families at Hebron. David exercises a double monarchy: for thirty-three years David "reigned in Jerusalem over all Israel and Judah," 2 S 5:5, and national unity, maintained under David and Solomon, though in an incomplete manner, has its basis only in the personality of the king. When the intransigence of Rehoboam, 1 K 12, after the death of Solomon in 931, leads to the schism of the ten northern tribes; the disintegration of the "united kingdom" is simply a return to the situation that had prevailed since the conquest. Only the tribe of Judah remains faithful of the House of David, 1 K 12:20; cf. 2 K 17:21, and at the same time to a more authentic form of the national religion, 1 K 12:27; 13:1–2; 2 K 23:4–20, even if "Judah did not keep the commandments of Yahweh their God either," 2 K 17:19. After an often hostile coexistence for more than two hundred years, 1 K 12–2 K 17 (see: ISRAEL *d*), the kingdom of Judah, over which Hezekiah is reigning (716–687) at the time of the fall of Samaria in 721, outlasts its brother in the north for 134 years, 2 K 17:18; 18–25. The most outstanding reign is that of Josiah (640–609), promoter of a religious reform, 2 K 23:4–14, which extends even into the former kingdom of the north, 2 K 23:15–20. In the reign of Zedekiah, Jerusalem falls into the hands of Nebuchadnezzar, in 587, and the people of Judah are deported to Babylon, 2 K 25:1–21. Over those left behind in the land of Judah, Nebuchadnezzar places Gedaliah, who is soon assassinated by Ishmael, 2 K 25:22–26//Jr 40:5–41:18. The kingdom of Judah then becomes a province of the Babylonian empire.

The "kings of Judah" are mentioned globally 21×: 1 S 27:6; 2 K 18:5; Si 49:4; Jr 8:1; 17:19; cf. Jr 22:30; there is mention also of the "royal house of Judah," 2 Ch 22:10; Jr 21:11, and (6×) of the "palace of the king of Judah," Jr 22:1, 6; 27:18–21; 32:2; 38:22; cf. 33:4. Twenty kings, all of the Davidic dynasty (see: DAVID *b*), sit successively on the throne of Judah, from the beginning of the schism to the end of the kingdom in 587; see: ABIJAH 2; AHAZ 1; AHAZIAH 2; AMAZIAH 1; AMON 2; ASA 1; ATHALIAH 1; HEZEKIAH 2; JEHOAHAZ 2; JEHOIACHIN; JEHOIAKIM 1; JEHORAM 5; JOASH 5; JOSHAPHAT 6; JOSIAH 1; JOTHAM 2; MANASSEH 2; REHOBOAM; UZZIAH 4; ZEDEKIAH 4.

Capital: JERUSALEM.

e. Judaea and the Jews

After the return from exile, the land of Judah, where the repatriates, the "remnant of Judah," Jr 40:15; 42:15, 19; 43:5; 44:12, 14, 28; Zp 2:7, settle, is now simply the "district" or "province" of Judah, Ezr 5:8; cf. Ne 1:3, whose towns are listed in Ne 3:1–32. Round about are settled groups from neighboring nations, Edomites, Ammonites, Arabs. In Greek this province is called *Ioudaia* (with the word *chōra* or *gē* understood, cf. Jn 3:22), that is, the "Judaean *or* Jewish land," whence *Judaea* (96: DB, 52, with 40 in 1 and 2 M; NT, 44); we also find "the countryside of Judaea," Ac 10:39. But the relatively small territory of Judaea, cf. 1 M 3:35, is gradually enlarged through the annexations effected by the Maccabees, cf. 1 M 5:3, 8, 50, and so on. "The sons *or* people of Judah" are henceforth preferably called *the Jews* (375×), Hb. *yehudi* (75) (Ezr–Ne, 16; Est, 53), Gr. *Ioudaioi* (300: DB, 106; NT, 194): the two words can be translated "Judaean *or* Jewish." We also find: "the Jewish people" (7), 1 M 8:20, 29; 12:6; 14:20; 15:17; 2 M 11:16, 34; Ac 12:11; "the Jewish nation" (10), 1 M 8:23, 25, 27; 10:25; 11:30, 33; 12:3; 13:36; 15:2; 2 M 10:8; Ac 10:22, "the nation of the Jews," 2 M 15:12. With the term "Jewish" (*ioudaios*) are connected "Judaism" (Gr. *ioudaismos*) (6), 2 M 2:21; 8:1; 14:38; Ga 1:13–14; "Judaic *or* Jewish" (Gr. *ioudaikos*) (3), 2 M 13:21; Ga 2:14; Tt 1:14; "Judaize" (Gr. *ioudaizein*), Ga 2:14; cf. Est 8:17; Dn 14:28; 1 Co 9:20.

At the beginning of the Christian era the vast majority of Jews live outside of

Judaea and even outside of Palestine, in the Diaspora. The word "Jew" has a primarily racial and national meaning, Est 10:3; 1 M 2:23; Ac 16:1, 20; 21:39. The Jews speak *Judaean* or *Jewish*, 2 K 18:26; 2 Ch 32:18; Is 36:11, 13; Ne 13:24, which is actually *Aramaic*. But the Jews of the Diaspora speak Greek, whence the name "Greeks," Jn 7:35, that is applied to these Jews, cf. Ac 6:1. In the Gospel of John "the Jews" often designates the Jewish authorities hostile to Jesus, Jn 1:19; 2:18; 5:10; 7:13; 9:22; 18:12; 19:38; 20:19.

Judah and Israel: ISRAEL *e*.

Governors: NEHEMIAH 2; ZERUBBABEL; FELIX; FESTUS; PILATE.

"Prince of Judah": SHESHBAZZAR.

Kings of Judaea: ARCHELAUS; HEROD 1, 3.

"King of the Jews": JESUS *c*.

Jews: GREEK; MORDECAI 2.

2. **Judah** (1), a variant in Ezr 3:9. See: HODAVIAH 1.

3. **Judah** (1), a Levite, married to a foreign woman, whom he puts away, Ezr 10:23.

4. **Judah son of Hassenuah** (1), a Benjaminite, second in command of the city of Jerusalem, Ne 11:9.

5. **Judah** (1), a Levite who returns from exile with Zerubbabel and Jeshua, Ne 12:8.

6. **Judah** (2), a priest, Ne 12:34, and a son of Asaph, Ne 12:36: both men take part in the dedication of the wall of Jerusalem.

7. **Judas** (123) called **Maccabaeus** (31), leader of the Jews (166–160).

Third son of the priest Mattathias, 1 M 2:4, he withdraws with his father and brothers into the wilderness and highlands, 1 M 2:28; 2 M 5:27, where he "assembled about six thousand" villagers, 2 M 8:1–8, 16. At the death of his father he is the first of the five brothers to take charge of the Jewish resistance to Hellenism, 1 M 3:1–2; cf. 2:66.

After a series of successes against Apollonius, 1 M 3:10–12, and Seron, 3:13–24, against Gorgias at Emmaus, 1 M 3:38–4:27, against Lysias at Beth-zur, 4:26–35//2 M 11:1–12, after reprisal raids against Joppa and Jamnia, 2 M 12:1–9, Judas proceeds to the purification of the temple and the dedication of the altar, 1 M 4:36–61//2 M 10:1–8. Expedition against the Idumaeans and the Ammonites, 1 M 5:1–18//2 M 10:14–25, into Galilee and Gilead, then into Idumaea and Philistia, 1 M 5:9–68//2 M 12:10–45. Siege of the Citadel of Jerusalem by Judas Maccabaeus, 1 M 6:18–27, who wins the day at Modein, 2 M 13:9–17, but is repulsed at Beth-zur and Bethzechariah, 1 M 6:28–47. Friendship of Judas and the Syrian military leader Nicanor, 2 M 14:18–26. Then Judas defeats Nicanor when the latter turns hostile again, at Capharsalama, 1 M 7:25–32, and at Adasa, where he kills him, 1 M 7:39–50//2 M 15:25–36. After having made a treaty with the Romans, 1 M 8:1, 17–20, Judas is conquered and slain by Bacchides at Beerzeth, 1 M 9:1–18.

The two "Books of the Maccabees"—which owe their title to the surname of the most famous of Mattathias' sons—eulogize, 1 M 3:3–9, 25–26; 2 M 15:30, the "hero Judas" or "valiant Judas," 1 M 5:63; 2 M 12:42; 14:18, "strong and brave from his youth," 1 M 2:66, "the man who saved Israel single-handed," 1 M 9:21, and whose "other deeds . . . and all his titles to greatness have not been recorded; but they were very many," 1 M 9:22 (cf. Jn 20:30; 21:25), "the man who had devoted himself entirely, body and soul, to the service of his countrymen, and had always preserved the love he had felt even in youth for those of his own race," 2 M 15:30, the leaders of the Hasidaeans, 2 M 14:6, protected by the Lord, 2 M 13:17, to whom he often prays before battle, 1 M 4:30–33; 7:41–42; cf. 2 M 10:4, 16, 25, 38; 11:6; 12:15, 36, 38–45; 13:10, 12. His trust in God is summed up in his two battle cries: "Help from God," 2 M 8:23, and

"Victory from God," 13:15, and shines through in the impassioned exhortations he addresses to his troops, 1 M 3:18–22, 58–60; 4:8–11, 17–18; 5:32; 9:8–10; 2 M 8:16–21; 11:7; 13:14. The two feasts of the Dedication (*Hanukkah*), 1 M 4:59, and the Day of Nicanor, 1 M 7:49, were instituted to commemorate his exploits.

8. **Judas son of Chalphi** (1), one of the generals in the army of Jonathan Maccabaeus, 1 M 11:70.

9. **Judas** (3), one of the sons of Simon [Maccabaeus]. With his brother John Hyrcanus, he shares the command in a victorious military action against Cendebaeus, during which he is wounded, 1 M 16:2, 9. With his father and his brother Mattathias he is assassinated by Ptolemy, son of Abubus, during a journey of inspection in the area of Jericho, 1 M 16:13–21.

10. **Judah** (1), one of the ancestors of Jesus, Lk 3:30.

11. **Judas the Galilean** (1), a leader of Jewish rebels against the Romans, a precursor of the Zealots, contemporary with the birth of Jesus, Ac 5:37.

12. **Judas** (22) **Iscariot** (9), **son of Simon Iscariot** (3). Named last in the lists of the Apostles (see: TWELVE; List, page 417), Judas is described by two phrases:

—*one of the Twelve,* Mt 26:14, 47; Mk 14:10, 20, 43; Lk 22:47, Jn 6:71; cf. "numbered among the Twelve," Lk 22:3; "one of his disciples," Jn 12:4; "which of them," Lk 22:23; "having been one of our number," Ac 1:17;

—*he who handed Jesus over; the traitor,* Mt 26:15–16//Mk 14:10–11//Lk 22:4–6. The formula accompanies the name of Judas (9×), Mt 10:4//Mk 3:19//Lk 6:16; Mt 26:25; 27:3; Jn 6:71; 12:4; 18:2, 5, or it serves as a more or less veiled reference to him, Mt 26:21–24//Mk 14:18–21//Lk 22:21–23; Mt 26:45–46//Mk 14:41–42//Jn 6:64, 71. The action of Judas—who, in order to effect the betrayal and to indicate "where he was," Jn 11:57, makes use of the very sign of friendship, the kiss, Mt 26:48–49//Mk 14:44–45//Lk 22:47–48—is explained by his love of money, Mt 26:14–16; Jn 12:6; 13:29, and by the influence of Satan, Lk 22:3; Jn 6:70; 13:2, 27. The death of Judas is related in Mt 27:5 and Ac 1:15–18.

13. **Jude** (3), brother of Jesus, Mt 13:55//Mk 6:3, probably identical with the "brother of James" in Jude 1.

14. **Judas** or **Jude** (3) **son** (or **brother**) **of James** (2), one of the Twelve, Lk 6:16//Ac 1:13, corresponding to the *Thaddaeus* (var. *Lebbaeus*) of Mt 10:3//Mk 3:18. Judas is mentioned also in Jn 14:21.

See: TWELVE; List, page 417.

15. **Judas** (1), a Jewish Christian?, living in Damascus in Straight Street. It is at his house that Ananias meets Saul of Tarsus after the latter's conversion, Ac 9:11.

16. **Judas** (3), surnamed **Barsabbas** (1), a Jewish Christian, a prophet, sent with Silas as a delegate from the Church of Jerusalem to the Church of Antioch in Syria, Ac 15:22, 27, 32.

JUDAISM (6). See: JUDAH 1 *e*.

JUDAS. See: JUDAH 7–9, 11–12, 14–16.

JUDE. See: JUDAH 13–14.

JUDGEMENT (Spring of) (1), Hb. *'En-mishpat* (cf. Ain; Shephathiah).

See: KADESH 1.

JUDITH, Hb. *Yehudit,* "Judaean woman, Jewess" (cf. Judah).

1. **Judith, daughter of Beeri the Hittite** (1), one of the Hittite wives of Esau, Gn 26:34.

2. **Judith** (32), **daughter of Merari** (2), a descendant of Simeon, Jdt 8:1; cf. 9:2, 12, a young widow, beautiful, prudent, devout, and determined, whose intervention, 9–16, saves the small Jewish nation from the threat that Nebuchadnezzar, symbol of the powers of evil,

represents for the entire world. After encouraging the people of besieged Bethulia, she uses trickery to meet Holofernes, the Persian general, whom she kills, thereby causing the rout of his army and meriting the blessing of ancient Israel: "You are the glory of Jerusalem! You are the great pride of Israel! You are the highest honour of our race!" 15:9.

JULIA (1), (cf. Julius), a Christian woman of Rome, Rm 16:15.

JULIUS (2), (cf. Julia), **centurion of the Augustan cohort** (1), in charge of bringing Paul as prisoner from Caesarea to Rome, Ac 27:1. Full of good will toward Paul during the stopover at Sidon, 27:3, he does not heed Paul's warnings about the crossing, 27:11, yet, bent on saving Paul, he resists the soldiers who wish to kill the prisoners when the ship founders, 27:43.

JUNIAS (1), a man or woman (*Junia?*) mentioned with Andronicus as a Christian of Rome; both are compatriots of Paul and his companions in captivity and have even preceded him in the apostolate, Rm 16:7.

JUSHAB-HESED (1), (cf. Hesed), one of the five sons of Meshullam, a descendant of King Jehoiachin, 1 Ch 3:20.

JUSTUS, "The just one" (cf. Zedekiah).

1. **Justus** (1), surname of: JOSEPH 12.

2. **Justus** (1), a Jewish sympathizer. It is in his house—next door to the synagogue—that he welcomes Paul when the latter breaks with the synagogue of Corinth, Ac 18:7.

3. **Justus** (1), surname of: JOSHUA 14.

JUTTAH (2), a town in the highlands of Judah, Jos 15:55, assigned to the Levites of the clan of Kohath, Jos 21:16. 9 km S of Hebron.

K

KABZEEL (3), "God gathers together" (cf. Kibzaim), a town in the Negeb of Judah, Jos 15:21.

= **Jekabzeel** (1), occupied by the sons of Judah after the exile, Ne 11:25. Location unknown.

Native place of: BENAIAH 1.

KADESH, "Holy" (cf. Kedesh).

1. **Kadesh** (15) or **Kadesh-barnea** (11), principal oasis in the northern part of the Sinai, 75 km S of Beersheba, in the wilderness of Paran, Nb 13:26, or of Zin, Nb 33:36, or of Kadesh, Ps 29:8, and north of the River of Egypt, cf. Jdt 1:9, on the southern border of the Promised Land, Nb 34:4; cf. Jos 10:41, and of Judah, Jos 15:3. A residence of the patriarchs, Gn 16:14; 20:1. Above all, an important stage of the Exodus, Dt 1:2, 19, 46; 2:14; 9:23; Jg 11:16–17; Jdt 5:14: burial place of Miriam, Nb 20:1; exploration of Canaan, Nb 13:26; 32:8; cf. Jos 14:6–7; attempt to enter the Promised Land, followed by a repulse, Nb 14:39–45; dispatch of messengers to the king of Edom, Nb 20:14–21. Some think that Nb 33:36–37 is referring to a different Kadesh, which is doubtless to be located east of the Gulf of Aqaba.

= **Spring of Judgement** (1), occupied by the four kings, Gn 14:7.

= ? **Kedesh** (1), among the towns of the Judaean Negeb, Jos 15:23.

Today *Ein Qudei* or *Ein Qudeirat*.

See: MERIBAH.

2. **Kadesh in the land of the Hittites** (1), acc. to the Gr. of 2 S 24:6 (Hb.? *of Tahtim Hodshi*; or ? *in the lowlands at Hodshi*), on the upper reaches of the Orontes. Included in David's census. Known to the Egyptians.

KADESH-BARNEA (11), (*Barnea*, unknown, is perhaps a personal name), Nb 32:8; 34:4; Dt 1:2, 19; 2:14; 9:23; Jos 10:41, 14:6, 7; 15:3; Jdt 5:14). See: KADESH 1.

KADMIEL (8), "God is before me" (cf. East 1), a Levite associated with: JOSHUA 7.

KADMONITES (1), "The Easterners" (cf. East 1), one of the peoples of pre-Israelite Palestine, perhaps living east of the Jordan, Gn 15:19.

KAIN (1). See: CAIN 2.

KAIWAN (1), (corr. of Hb. *Kiyyûn*), linked with *Sakkuth* (corr. of Hb. *Sikkut*), Am 5:26, probably Babylonian divinities whose cult was introduced into Samaria after the fall of the northern kingdom (721).

= **Rephan** (1), var. of Gr. *Rompha*, Ac 7:43.

KALLAI (1), a priest, head of the priestly family of Sallai in the time of the high priest Joiakim, Ne 12:20.

KAMON (1), in Gilead, the place where the judge Jair is buried, Jg 10:5. Halfway between the Sea of Chinnereth and Ramoth-gilead.

KANAH, "Reed."

1. **Kanah** (2), a river between Ephraim and Manasseh, Jos 16:8; 17:9.
2. **Kanah** (1), a town in Asher, Jos 19:28. SE of Tyre.
3. **Cana in Galilee** (4), a town 14 km NE of Nazareth; today *Kh. Qana* (not *Kafr Kanna*).

Invited to a wedding there, Jesus changes water into wine, Jn 2:1–11; later, he meets there a court official, whose son he cures, Jn 4:46–54.

Native place of: NATHANAEL 12.

KANDAKE (1), a title designating the queen of Ethiopia, just as Pharaoh is a title meaning king of Egypt. One of her important officials is converted to the Christian faith, Ac 8:27–39.

KAREAH (14), "Bald" (cf. Korah), father of: JOHN 9; JONATHAN 10.

KARKA (1), Hb. *Qarqa'*, "Ground" (cf. Karkor), a town on the southern border of Judah, Jos 15:3.

KARKOR (1), "Ground" (cf. Karka), in Transjordania, a town where the troops of Zebah and Zalmunna are stationed, Jg 8:10. Unknown.

KARNAIM (1), "The two horns." See: CARNAIM.

KARTAH (1), "The town" (cf. Kiriath), a town of Zebulun, assigned to the Levites of the clan of Merari, Jos 21:34. Today *Atlit,* SW of Carmel.

KASERIN (1), acc. to Tb 11:1 a town opposite Nineveh.

KATTATH (1), a town in Zebulun, Jos 19:15.

= ? **Kitron** (1), a Canaanite town that long remains independent, Jg 1:30.

KEDAR (12), "Swarthy" (cf. Kidron), one of the twelve sons of Ishmael, Gn 25:13//1 Ch 1:29, a nomadic Arabian tribe in Transjordania, Ps 120:5; Sg 1:5; Is 42:11, famous for its courageous bowmen, Is 21:17, and its flocks, Is 60:7; Ezk 27:21. Several prophetic oracles predict the destruction of Kedar, Is 21:16–17; Jr 49:28.

KEDEM. See: EAST 1.

KEDEMAH (2), (cf. East 1), one of the twelve sons of Ishmael, Gn 25:15//1 Ch 1:31, eponymous ancestor of the sons of the: EAST 1.

KEDEMOTH (4), (cf. East 1), one of the final stages of the Exodus, Dt 2:26 (*wilderness of Kedemoth*), a town of Reuben, Jos 13:18, assigned to the Levites of the clan of Merari, Jos 21:37//1 Ch 6:64. Probably N of the Arnon.

KEDESH, "Holy," Gr. *Kedes, Kadēs,* Lat. *Cedes, Cades* (cf. Kadesh).

1. **Kedesh** (1). See: KADESH 1.
2. **Kedesh** (9), **of Naphtali** (2), **in Galilee** (4), an ancient Canaanite town, Jos 12:22; a fortified town occupied by Naphtali, Jos 19:37, a town of refuge, Jos 20:7, assigned to the Levites of the clan of Gershon, Jos 21:32//1 Ch 6:61, captured by Tiglath-pileser III, king of Assyria, 2 K 15:29. Scene of a victory of Judas Maccabaeus over the generals of Demetrius II, 1 M 11:63, 73.

= **Kadesh** (corr. of Gr. *Kydios*)-**Naphtali in Upper Galilee** (1), Tb 1:2.

Native place of: BARAK.

3. **Kedesh** (3), at the foot of Mount Tabor; Barak assembles Zebulun and Naphtali there before launching his attack on Sisera, Jg 4:9–11. A town of Issachar assigned to the Levites of the clan of Gershon, 1 Ch 6:57.

= **Kishion** (2), a town of Issachar, Jos 19:20, assigned to the Levites, 21:28.

KEDRON (3). See: KIDRON 2.

KEHELATHAH (2), "Assembly" (cf. Makheloth; Qoheleth), a stage of the Exodus in the wilderness, Nb 33:22–23.

KEILAH (18), Hb. *Qeʿilah,* a town in the lowlands of Judah, Jos 15:44. David rescues Keilah when it is besieged by the Philistines; suspecting the inhabitants of wanting to hand him over to Saul, who is pursuing him, David leaves it, 1 S 23: 1–13. In the time of Nehemiah, Keilah is a district center, Ne 3:17–18. Today *Tell Qila,* 15 km NW of Hebron. On the origins of *Keilah the Garmite* cf. 1 Ch 4:19.

KELAIAH (1), Ezr 10:23. See: KELITA.

KELITA (3) = **Kelaiah** (1), among the Levites who explain the Law to the people during its solemn reading by Ezra, Ne 8:7, sign the pledge to observe the Law, Ne 10:11, and put away the foreign wives they have married, Ezr 10:23.

KEMUEL (cf. Jakim).

1. **Kemuel** (1), one of the twelve sons of Nahor, brother of Abraham, born of his wife Milcah; father of Aram, Gn 22:21.

2. **Kemuel son of Shiphtan** (1), represents the tribe of Ephraim in the allocation of Canaan, Nb 34:24.

3. **Kemuel** (1), father of: HASHABIAH 4.

KENAN (6), Gr. *Kainan.* See: CAIN 1 *a.*

KENATH (2), a town in eastern Manasseh, conquered by Nobah, a Manassite, who gives it his own name, Nb 32:42; later captured by Aram and Geshur, 1 Ch 2:23.

KENAZ (11), (cf. Kenizzite), last of the five sons of Eliphaz who are called sons of Adah, wife of Esau, Gn 36:11//1 Ch 1:36, one of the chiefs (or clans) of Edom, Gn 36:15, 42//1 Ch 1:53.

Brother of Caleb and father of: OTHNIEL 1.

Grandson of Caleb, 1 Ch 4:15.

KENITES. See CAIN 1 *b.*

KENIZZITE (4), a descendant of Kenaz, one of the peoples of pre-Israelite Palestine, living in the south of Palestine, Gn 15:19.

Kenizzite: CALEB.

To be connected (?) with the Kenites: CAIN 1 *b.*

KERIOTH (2), Gr. *Kariōth,* "The towns" (cf. Kiriath), principal town of Moab acc. to Am 2:2, listed among the other towns of Moab, Jr 48:24.

KERIOTH-HEZRON (1), (cf. Kerioth; Hezron), a town in the Negeb of Judah, Jos 15:25.

= **Hazor** (1), Jos 15:25.

20 km S of Hebron. Some exegetes distinguish *Kerioth* and *Hezron* as two different towns.

KEROS (2), head of a family of "oblates" who return from the exile, Ezr 2:44//Ne 7:47.

KETURAH (4), from the same root as Hb. *qetoret,* "incense" (cf. Kitron), concubine of Abraham, mother of the peoples of Arabia, among which we may single out Midian, Sheba, and Dedan, Gn 25:1–6//1 Ch 1:32–33.

KHAN KIMHAM (1). See: CHIMHAM 2.

KIBROTH-HATTAAVAH (5), "Tombs [of the tribe?] of Taavah," or, acc. to the tradition, "Tombs of Greed," a stage of the Exodus in the Sinai wilderness, Nb 33:16–17, where Israel rebels against its God, Dt 9:22; "it was there that they buried the people who had indulged their greed," Nb 11:33–34.

KIBZAIM (1), (cf. Kabzeel), a town of Ephraim assigned to the Levites of the clan of Kohath, Jos 21:22 (//1 Ch 6:53, where *Jokmeam* is wrongly listed).

KIDRON, Hb. *Qidrôn,* "Dark, murky" (cf. Kedar), Gr. *Kedrōn.*

1. *Kidron* (12), a river and valley be-

tween Jerusalem and the Mount of Olives, which David crosses, 2 S 15:23, 30, as do Shimei on his way to Gath to look for his runaway slaves, 1 K 2:37, and, later on, Jesus, Jn 18:1, on his way to the Mount of Olives. During his inspection of the wall of Jerusalem, Nehemiah returns by way of the Valley [of Kidron] Gate, Ne 2:15. The valley or "fields" of Kidron, where the Gihon spring is, 2 Ch 33:14, serves as a place for refuse: there are thrown the altars, posts, and statues of idols that polluted the temple and the holy city, 1 K 15:13//2 Ch 15:16; 2 K 23:4–12; 2 Ch 29:16; 30:14. But some day "the whole valley, with its dead and its ashes, and all the fields beside the wadi Kidron . . . will be consecrated to Yahweh," Jr 31:40.

2. **Kedron** (3), a town south of Jamnia, rebuilt and fortified by Cendebaeus, 1 M 15:39–41; 16:9.

KINAH (1), a town in the Negeb of Judah, Jos 15:22. 35 km E of Beersheba.

KING, Hb. *Melek* (cf. Melech).

1. **King's Pool** (1), Ne 2:14, perhaps the pool constructed by Hezekiah. See: BETWEEN THE TWO WALLS.

2. **Valley of the King** (2), Gn 14:17, probably near Jerusalem, where Absalom has a pillar erected to himself, 2 S 18:18. The latter is not to be identified with the tomb to be seen in the Kidron Valley; this dates from the Hellenistic period.

= **Valley of Shaveh** (1), where Abraham, the king of Sodom, and Melchizedek meet after the defeat of Chedorlaomer and his allies, Gn 14:17.

KINSMAN OF ISAAC (2), Hb. *Pahad Yizhaq* (cf. Zelophehad), a divine name (formerly translated as "Fear of Isaac"), Gn 31:42, 53.

KIR

1. **Kir** (4), a country in Mesopotamia, probably alongside Elam, Is 22:6. Native land of the Aramaeans, Am 9:7. In 732 Tiglath-pileser deports the Aramaeans of Damascus to Kir, 2 K 16:9; cf. Am. 1:5.

2. **Kir** (1), Is 15:1, Moabite "Wall" and, by extension, "Town" (cf. Kiriath), called *Keriho* on the Mesha stele. See: KIR-HERES.

KIR-HARESETH. See: KIR-HERES.

KIR-HERES (2), "Town of Potsherds" (cf. Potsherds); acc. to Gr., *Kir-hadash*, "New Town," capital of Moab, whose fate the prophets lament, Jr 48:31, 36.

= **Kir-hareseth** (2), Is 16:7, 11, seriously threatened by the coalition of Jehoram of Israel and Jehoram of Judah in the time of Mesha, king of Moab, 2 K 3:25.

= **Kir** (1), devastated at the same time as the land of Moab, Is 15:1; cf. 24:10.

Today *el-Kerak,* east of the Dead Sea, on a precipitous hill.

KIRIATH (1), "The Town" (cf. Ekron; Kartah; Kartan; Kerioth; Kerioth-hezron; Kir 2; Kiriathaim; and the composites with Kiriath that follow. See: Ir Haheres; Amphipolis), Jos 18:28. See: KIRIATH-JEARIM.

KIRIATHAIM, "The Two Towns" (cf. Kiriath).

1. **Kiriathaim** (6), a town to the east of the Dead Sea. In the plain of Kiriathaim (Hb. *Shave-Qiryatayim*); defeat of the Emim by the four kings of the east, Gn 14:5. Kiriathaim is in the territory of Reuben, Nb 32:37; Jos 13:19, and later in that of Moab, Jr 48:1, 23; Ezk 25:9 (Hb. *Qiryatamah*).

2. **Kiriathaim** (1), perhaps identical with: RAKKATH.

KIRIATH-ARBA (9), "Town of the Four [Clans or Quarters?]" or "Town of Arba" (cf. Kiriath). See: HEBRON 1.

KIRIATH-BAAL (2), "Town of Baal" (cf. Kiriath; Baal), Jos 15:60; 18:14. See: KIRIATH-JEARIM.

KIRIATH-HUZOTH (1), "Town of Streets" (cf. Kiriath), in Transjordania, an unidentified town where Balaam and Balak meet, Nb 22:39.

KIRIATH-JEARIM (19), "Town of the Woodlands" (cf. Kiriath; Jaar) **in Judah** (2), Jg 18:12; 1 Ch 13:6, or **a city of the sons of Judah** (1), Jos 18:14.

One of the four towns in the Gibeonite federation, Jos 9:17, on the border between Judah and Benjamin, Jos 15:9–10; 18:14–15. A town in the highlands of Judah, Jos 15:60. The chronicler connects Kiriath-jearim with Judah through Shobal and Hur, 1 Ch 2:50, 52–53. The Danites camp there on their migration to the north, Jg 18:12. After being given back by the Philistines, the Ark stays there, 1 S 6:21; 7:1–2, until David brings it back to Jerusalem, 1 Ch 13:5–6//2 S 6:2; 2 Ch 1:4; cf. Ps 132:6. Among the Israelites returning from the exile are men of Kiriath-jearim, Ezr 2:25 (Hb. *Kiriath-'arim*) //Ne 7:29.

= **Kiriath** (1), Jos 18:28, listed among the towns of Benjamin (some connect *Kiriath* with the preceding word and read *Gibeah-kiriath*).

= **Kiriath-baal** (2), Jos 15:60; 18:14.

= **Baalah** (4) **of Judah** (1), Jos 15:9–10; 2 S 6:2 (Hb. *Ba'ale-Yehudah*)//1 Ch 13:6.

= **Fields of the Forest** (or: *Fields of Jaar*) (1), Ps 132:6.

Native place of: URIAH 3.

KIRIATH-SANNAH (1), (cf. Kiriath), Jos 15:49. See: DEBIR 2.

KIRIATH-SEPHER (5), "Town of the Book" (cf. Kiriath; Hassophereth). See: DEBIR 2.

KISH, Gr. *Kis,* Lat. *Cis,* Accad. *Qashu,* "Gift" (cf. Kishi; Kushaiah).

1. **Kish** (16) **son of Abiel son of Zeror son of Becorath son of Aphiah** (1), 1 S 9:1; cf. 14:51, a Benjaminite, a man of quality, father of Saul, 1 S 9:3; 14:51; 2 S 21:14; 1 Ch 8:33//9:39.

Father of: SAUL.

Ancestor of: MORDECAI 2.

2. **Kish** (2), a Benjaminite, uncle of the preceding, 1 Ch 8:30//9:36.

3. **Kish** (4), younger brother of Eleazar, a Levite of the clan of Merari, whose sons marry their cousins, the daughters of Eleazar, 1 Ch 23:21–22; 24:29.

4. **Kish son of Abdi** (1), a Levite of the clan of Merari; during the reform of Hezekiah he takes part in the purification of the temple, 2 Ch 29:12–15.

KISHI (1), (cf. Kish), son of Abdi, a Levite of the clan of Merari, father of Ethan the cantor, 1 Ch 6:29.

= **Kushaiah** (1), father of Ethan, 1 Ch 15:17.

KISHION (2). See: KEDESH 3.

KISHON (6), a river that flows from the foot of Carmel and empties into the Mediterranean north of Haifa. The meeting of Barak and Sisera and the latter's defeat take place at the wadi Kishon, Jg 4:7, 13; 5:21; Ps 83:10. Near the wadi Kishon the prophet Elijah slaughters the prophets of Baal, 1 K 18:40.

See: LIBNATH.

KITRON (1), (cf. Keturah). See: KATTATH.

KITTIM (11), Gr. *Kitioi, Kitieis, Chettiim.*

Originally the Kittim are the inhabitants of the town of Kition on the island of Cyprus and, by extension, the Cypriots generally, Is 23:1, 12.

In the list of peoples the Kittim are linked to Elishah, Tarshish, and the Dananites as "Javan's sons," Gn 10:4//1 Ch 1:7. Then the word acquires a broader meaning and refers not only to Cyprus but to the islands and shores of the Mediterranean, that is, to all the seafaring peoples, Nb 24:24; Jr 2:10; Ezk 27:6.

In 1 M 1:1 and 8:5 "Kittim" refers to Macedonia, from whence Alexander the Great had come and of which Perseus, son of Philip V, was king. In Dn

11:30 the Kittim are probably the Romans.

KOA (1), Ezk 23:23, a Chaldaean tribe living to the east of Babylonia; sometimes identified with the *Qutu* of the cuneiform inscriptions.

KOHATH (32), Gr. *Kaath,* second of the three sons of Levi, Gn 46:11//Ex 6:16; Nb 3:17; 1 Ch 5:27; 6:1, dies at the age of 133 years, Ex 6:18. Eponymous ancestor of the **Kohathites,** he and his brothers Gershon and Merari, with whom he is always associated, form the three great classes of Levites, Nb 26:57; 1 Ch 23:6, 12–13. A census shows 2,750 sons of Kohath, Nb 4:34–37. These are subdivided into four clans: the Amramite, the Izharite, the Hebronite, and the Uzzielite, Nb 3:27; 1 Ch 23:12.

The function of the sons of Kohath in the service of the Tabernacle is described in Nb 3:31; 4:4–15; 7:9; 10:21; cf. 1 Ch 9:32; 15:5; 2 Ch 20:19; 29:12; 34:12. Twenty-three towns are assigned to them: thirteen for the sons of Aaron in Judah, Simeon, and Benjamin, and then for the other sons of Kohath in Ephraim, Dan, and western Manasseh, Jos 21:4–5, 10–26//1 Ch 6:39–46, 51–55.

Among the descendants of Kohath, the chronicler puts Samuel, 1 Ch 6:7 ff.; and Heman, one of the three great cantors, 1 Ch 6:18, 23. See: List, page 000. Among his sons: AMRAM 1; KORAH 3.

KOHATHITE or **of Kohath** (15), Nb 3:27, 30; 4:18, 34, 37; 10:21; 26:57; Jos 21:4, 10; 1 Ch 6:18, 39; 9:32; 2 Ch 20:19; 29:12; 34:12, a descendant of: KOHATH.

KOLA (1). See: KONA.

KOLAIAH, "Yah has spoken" (see Amariah).

1. **Kolaiah** (1), Ne 11:7, a Benjaminite, an ancestor of: SALLU 1.

2. **Kolaiah** (1), father of: AHAB 2.

KONA (1), Jdt 4:4 = ? **Kola** (1), Jdt 15:4, both described as located in Samaria. Not identifiable.

KORAH, "Baldness"? (cf. Kareah), Gr. *Kore,* Lat. *Core.*

1. **Korah** (4), an Edomite chief (or clan), last of the three sons of Esau and Oholibamah, Gn 36:5, 14, 18; cf. 1 Ch 1:35.

2. **Korah** (1), a Calebite, of the sons of Hebron, 1 Ch 2:43.

3. **Korah** (33) **son of Izhar son of Kohath son of Levi** (2), Ex 6:21; Nb 16:1; 1 Ch 6:22–23; cf. 1 Ch 6:7. List, page 416.

The priestly account in Nb 16:1–11, 16–24, 27, 32, 35 (woven into the Yahwist-Elohist account of the political rebellion of the Reubenites Dathan and Abiram) describes the rebellion of Korah against Aaron as a claim to the exercise of priesthood. This higher status is refused them, and the priesthood remains the privilege of the descendants of Aaron. Cf. Nb 17:5, 14; 26:9–11; 27:3; Ps 106:16; Si 45:18; Jude 11.

The Korahites: the sons of Korah did not perish when their father was punished, Nb 26:11. They form a clan of Levi, that is, the **Korahite** clan, Nb 26:58 (this ancient list of the Levitic clans—different from the canonical distribution into Gershonite, Kohathite and Merarite clans—seems to see the Korahites as originating in the region of Hebron; see, earlier: KORAH 2); cf. Ex 6:24. They are gatekeepers, 1 Ch 9:19, or cantors, 2 Ch 20:19—Heman, one of the three great cantors, is a descendant of Korah, 1 Ch 6:22—and to the sons of Korah are attributed Ps 42; 44–49; 84; 85; 87; 88. Acc. to 1 Ch 12:7 Korahites are among the first to rally to David.

Son of Korah *or* the Korahite: SHALLUM 11.

KORAHITES (8), Ex 6:24; Nb 26:58; 1 Ch 9:19, 31; 12:7; 26:1, 19; 2 Ch 20:19, belonging to the clan of: KORAH 3.

KORE, Hb. *Qore‘,* "Partridge," Gr. *Kōre,* Lat. *Core* (cf. En-hakkore).

1. **Kore** (2), a Korahite, father of: SHALLUM 11.

2. **Kore son of Imnah** (1), a Levite and gatekeeper, 2 Ch 31:14.

KOZ, Hakkoz, Gr. *Akkos,* "Thornbush."

1. **Koz** (1), father of several clans connected with Judah through Ashhur, 1 Ch 4:8.

2. **Hakkoz** (4) or **Accos** (1), leader of the seventh priestly class, 1 Ch 24:10. Among the priests who return from the exile **the sons of Hakkoz** cannot prove their authentic Israelite origin, Ezr 2:61//Ne 7:63. Among his descendants: EUPOLEMUS; MEREMOTH.

KULON (1), acc. to the Gr., a town in the highlands of Judah, Jos 15:59.

KUSHAIAH (1), "Gift of Yah" (cf. Kish). See: KISHI.

L

LAADAH (1), Hb. *La'dah* (cf. Ladan), father of Mareshah and son of Shelah, son of Judah, 1 Ch 4:21. See: LIBNI 1.

LABAN, "The White" (cf. Lebanah; Lebanon; Lebonah; Libnah, Libnath).

1. **Laban** (54) **son of Bethuel** (1), Gn 28:5, **son of Nahor** (1), 29:5, **the Aramaean** (4), 25:20; 28:5; 31:20, 24, brother of Rebekah, 24:29–30; 27:43, uncle of Jacob, 29:10; Jdt 8:26.

When Jacob comes to him, Laban, using trickery, gives him as wives first Leah, then Rachel, Gn 29; cf. 46:18, 25. But Laban has met someone more cunning than he, for Jacob enriches himself at Laban's expense, 30:25–43, and, despite Laban's watchfulness, flees with the family and great wealth he has acquired in his father-in-law's house, 31:1–21. Laban overtakes him and concludes a treaty with him, 31:22–54; 32:1.

2. **Laban** (1), Dt 1:1, a town in Moab. Unknown.

[LACEDAEMONIANS]. See: SPARTA.

LACHISH (24), a very old Canaanite town conquered by Joshua acc. to Jos 10:31–35, whose king at the time is Japhia, an ally of: ADONI-ZEDEK.

A town in the lowlands of Judah, Jos 15:39, fortified by King Rehoboam, 2 Ch 11:9. As a result of a conspiracy, King Amaziah of Judah is pursued there and assassinated, 2 K 14:19//2 Ch 25:27. Sennacherib, king of Assyria, occupies it and, it seems, sets up his headquarters there for his attack on Jerusalem, 2 K 18:14, 17; 19:8//Is 36:2; 37:8; 2 Ch 32:9; cf. Mi 1:13. A century later, Nebuchadnezzar besieges Lachish simultaneously with Jerusalem, Jr 34:7, and captures both. The town is reoccupied by Judaeans after the exile, Ne 11:30. Today *Tell ad-Duweir,* halfway between Jerusalem and Gaza.

LADAN, Hb. *La'dân* (cf. Laadah).

1. **Ladan** (1), an Ephraimite. See: ERAN.

2. **Ladan** (6), a Levite, 1 Ch 23:7–9; 26:21. See: LIBNI 1.

LADDER OF TYRE (1), Gr. *Klimax Tyrou,* between Tyre and Ptolemais, at Cap Blanc or, lower down, at *Ras en-Naqurah*: a stepped coastal road between the sea and the cliffs. Northern boundary of Simon Maccabaeus' military responsibility, 1 M 11:59.

LAEL (1), "Who belongs to God" (cf. Lemuel), father of: ELIASAPH 2.

[LAGAMAR]. See: CHEDOR-LAOMER.

[LAGIDES], a Hellenistic dynasty ruling Egypt after the death of Alexander the Great, founded by the Macedonian, Ptolemy, son of Lagos, one of Alexander's generals.

See: PTOLEMY 1–8; SELEUCIDS.

LAHAD (1), a Zorathite clan, connected with Judah through Shobal, 1 Ch 4:2.

LAHAI ROI (3), "Of the Living One who sees me" (cf. Haroeh), name of a well—and perhaps earlier of a local divinity—to which are linked traditions about Hagar, the servant of Sarah, Gn 16:14, and about Isaac, 24:62, 25:11. "Between Kadesh and Bered," Gn 16:14. Site unknown.

LAHMAS (1), a town in the lowlands of Judah, Jos 15:40. Today *Kh. el-Lahm.*

LAHMI, brother of Goliath of Gath (1), a Philistine slain by Elhanan, 1 Ch 20:5. In the parallel passage, 2 S 21:19, Goliath of Gath is slain by Elhanan of Bethlehem. *Lahmi* may be a deformation of *Beth-ha-Lahmi* that is due to the chronicler, who is attempting to harmonize 2 S 21:19 and 1 S 17 (where it is David who slays Goliath).

[LAHMU]. See: BETHLEHEM.

LAISH, Hb. *Layish,* "Lion," Gr. *Lais* (cf. Laishah).

1. **Laish** (4), ancient name of the city of: DAN 2.

2. **Laish** (2), father of: PALTIEL 2.

LAISHAH (1), Hb. *Layeshah*, "Lioness" (cf. Laish. See Lebaoth), a town of Benjamin near Anathoth, some km NE of Jerusalem, threatened by an invasion of enemies from the north, Is 10:30.

LAKKUM (1), a frontier town of Naphtali, some km S of the Sea of Chinnereth, Jos 19:33.

LAMB. See: JESUS *c.*

LAMECH (11), Hb. *Lemek,* Gr. *Lamech;* acc. to the Yahwist genealogy, he is the son of Methushael, Gn 4:18, and has two wives: Adah, who bears him Jabal and Jubal, and Zillah, who bears him Tubal-cain and Naamah, 4:19–23. In his clan blood vengeance takes horrible forms.

Acc. to the Elohist genealogy, Lamech is the son of Methuselah, Gn 5:25–26, and father of Noah, 5:28–31; cf. 1 Ch 1:3. He dies at the age of 777 years.

Acc. to Lk 3:36 he is an ancestor of Jesus.

[LAODICE], first wife of: ANTIOCHUS 1.

LAODICEA (6), a city of Phrygia in Asia Minor, near Colossae and Hierapolis. It has a Christian community founded not by Paul but probably by Epaphras, Col 2:1; 4:12–13. To this church are addressed a lost letter of Paul, Col 4:15–16, and one of the letters to the seven churches, Rv 1:11; 3:14–22.

LAODICEANS (1), Col 4:16, Christians of: LAODICEA.

LAPPIDOTH (1), "Torches, Lightnings"?, husband of the prophetess: DEBORAH 2.

LASEA (1), Ac 27:8, a town on the southern coast of the island of Crete, near Fair Havens.

LASTHENES (2), a Cretan, a minister of Demetrius II, king of Syria. It is in a letter addressed to Lasthenes that Demetrius promulgates the new charter in favor of the Jews, 1 M 11:31–32.

LAZARUS, Gr. *Lazaros,* from Hb. *'El'azar*, "Eleazar," "God has given help" (cf. Ezer).

1. **Lazarus** (11) of Bethany, brother of Martha and Mary, a friend of Jesus. He falls ill and dies; Jesus restores him to life, Jn 11:1–5, 11, 14, 17, 43–44; cf. 12:17. Before his own death Jesus dines in the house of Lazarus, Jn 12:1–2, 9–11.

2. **Lazarus** (4), Lk 16:19–31. The only example of a figure in parable—here the poor man—receiving a name; the reason is perhaps to be found in the meaning of the name itself.

LEAH (34), Hb. *Le'ah,* "Cow" (see Rebekah), daughter of Laban and elder sister of Rachel, Gn 29:16–17, given to Jacob as his first wife by trickery, 29: 23–25, mother of Reuben, Simeon, Levi, and Judah, 29:30–35; cf. 30:14–15, then of Issachar, Zebulun, and a daughter Dinah, 30:16–21; cf. 34:1; 35:23; 46:15. Through her servant Zilpah she is also mother of Gad and Asher, 30:9–13; cf. 35:26; 46:18. She is also associated with Rachel in Gn 31:4, 14, 33; 33:1–2, 7; Rt 4:11. Acc. to Gn 49:31, she is buried at Machpelah near Hebron.

LEBANAH (2), "Whiteness; Full Moon" (cf. Laban), head of a family of "oblates" who return from the exile, Ezr 2:45//Ne 7:48.

LEBANON (73), "White" (cf. Laban), a chain of mountains 170 km long, parallel to the northern coast of Palestine, cf. Jos 9:1; some of its summits are more than 3,000 m high. Occupied by the Hittites (Hb. *Hivites*), Jg 3:3, Lebanon is regarded as being within the theoretical boundaries of the Promised Land, Dt 1:7; 3:25; 11:24; Jos 1:4; 13:5–6; 1 K 9:19; Zc 10:10.

The area is renowned for its forests, especially of cedar and cypress, Jg 9:15; 1 K 5:13, 20–23, 28; 2 K 19:23; Ezr 3:7; Ps 29:5; 92:13; 104:16; Sg 3:9; 5:15; Si 24:13; 50:12; Is 2:13; 14:8; 29:17; 33:9; 35:2; 37:24; 60:13; Jr 23:6, 23; Ezk 17:3; 27:5; 31:3, 16; Ho 14:6–8; Hab 2:17; Zc 11:1, for its flora, 2 K 14:9; Ps 72:16; Sg 4:11; Na 1:4, and its fauna, Sg 4:8; Is 40:16, its snows, Jr 18:24, and its waters, Sg 4:15.

See: ANTI-LEBANON; FOREST OF LEBANON; HERMON; VALE OF LEBANON.

LEBAOTH (1), "Lionesses" (cf. Laishah). See: BETH-LEBAOTH.

LEB-KAMAI (1), "Heart of those who rise against me," a cryptogram for Hb. *Kashdim,* "Chaldaeans, Chaldaea," Jr 51:1. See: SHESHAK.

LEBONAH (1), derived from *Lebanah* (cf. Laban), a town halfway between Bethel and Shechem, NW of Shiloh, Jg 21:19.

LECAH (1), a town of Judah, connected with Shelah through Er, 1 Ch 4:21.

LEHAB (People of) (2), Hb. *Lehabim,* a people connected with Egypt, Gn 10:13//1 Ch 1:11; refers perhaps to the *Libyans.* But it may refer instead to a town between Jerusalem and Gezer that Solomon receives as a dowry from Pharaoh, cf. 1 K 9:16–17.

LEHI (5), "Jawbone," a town of Judah—not identifiable—near Philistia, with which is connected an episode in the struggle of Samson against the Philistines, Jg 15:9, 14, 17, 19. Acc. to some translations it is at Lehi that Shamma the Hararite, a fighting man, singlehandedly defeats an army of Philistines, 2 S 23:11.

See: EN-HAKKORE; RAMATH-LEHI.

LEMUEL (2), "Who belongs to God" (cf. Lael), king of the Arabian tribe of Massa, Pr 31:1, 4, a wise man to whom Pr 31:1–9 is attributed.

[LESBOS], an island in the NE Aegean Sea, the principal port of which is: MITYLENE.

LESHA (1). See: DAN 2.

LESHEM (2). See: DAN 2.

LETUSHIM (1), an Arabian tribe connected through Dedan with Jokshan, one of Abraham's sons by his concubine Keturah, Gn 25:3.

LEUMMIM (1), "Hordes," an Arabian tribe connected through Dedan with Jokshan, one of Abraham's sons by his concubine Keturah, Gn 25:3.

LEVI, "United to, Joined to," see Gn 29:34; Nb 18:2–4.

1. **Levi, sons of Levi, Levites** (370). The word occurs 4× in Lv (25:32–33) and 182× in the work of the chronicler (1–2 Ch, Ezr, Ne).

Acc. to Gn 29:34, Levi is the third son of Jacob and Leah, born after Simeon and before Judah. Gn 34:25–31 tells of the cruel and treacherous vengeance of Simeon and Levi on Shechem, who had raped their sister Dinah, and of the bitter reproaches Jacob addresses to them. The blessing in Gn 49:5–7 still links Simeon and Levi in blame for their "malicious plans" and ruthless rage (against Shechem) and announces the dispersion of these two tribes. We may think that Levi followed Simeon to the south, where the latter will gradually be absorbed by Judah. For it is to be observed that Levi, Simeon, and Judah are all three the sons of Leah; that in the lists of the tribes (see: List, pages 410–11) Levi, whose name occurs 13×, comes 10× immediately before or after Judah or Simeon; that the ancient division of the Levitical clans in Nb 26:58 points to the Levites as living in the south, at Hebron and Libnah; that the Levite in Micah's service comes from Judah, Jg 17:7; 18:30, and the Levite of Jg 19:1, who lives in Ephraim, comes to Judah to look for a concubine.

The priestly tribe. The secular tribe of Levi disappeared, therefore. Its surviving members seem to have then specialized in cultic functions. Originally, of course, we find priests from other tribes beside Levi: Ephraimites, like the son of Micah, Jg 17:5 (note that on the first possible occasion Micah prefers a Levite to him, Jg 17:12), or Samuel, 1 S 2:18; 7:9; Judaeans, 2 S 8:18; Manassites, 2 S 20:26.

The descendants of Levi thus appear as set apart to exercise sacral functions, Nb 1:50; 3:6–7; they are offered to God in place of the firstborn sons of Israel, Nb 3:12; 8:16. In the affair of the golden calf they show themselves especially zealous for Yahweh, Ex 32:26–29; cf. Dt. 33:8–11. Their numbers are not counted as are those of the other tribes, Nb 1:47–49, and they have no territory, as do the other tribes, because "Yahweh the God of Israel is their inheritance," Jos 13:33; 14:3–4; 18:7; cf. Nb 18:20; Dt 10:9 . . . They live dispersed in villages belonging to the other tribes, cf. Nb 35:2–8; Jos 21//1 Ch 6:39–66, as resident aliens, Dt 12:12, 18; 14:27, 29 . . . , having as their income the tithes paid to them, Nb 18:20–24; cf. Heb 7:5–11.

For the Deuteronomist (7th cent.), the tribe of Levi has been set apart to carry the Ark of the Covenant, serve Yahweh, and bless the people, Dt 10:8; 31:9, 25. Every Levite can exercise the priesthood, Dt 18:6–7, but this rule will not always be respected, cf. 2 K 23:9. The distinction between priests and Levites comes into existence once the small sanctuaries are abandoned to the advantage of the great ones, such as Jerusalem or Bethel; the distinction is explicit in Ezk 44:10–31; 45:4–5; 48:10–13. In the view of the priestly writer (5th cent.), Aaron is the first high priest of Israel, his sons alone are legitimate priests, cf. Ex 28–29; 39; Nb 16–18, and the other descendants of Levi are "given" or joined to the priests in order to serve them and serve the tabernacle, Nb 3:6–12; 8:6–26; 18:1–7.

The number of Levites returning from the exile is very small compared to the number of priests, Ezr 2:36–40//Ne 7:39–43; Ezr 8:18–19, but in the time of Ezra and Nehemiah we find other Levites, Ne 3:17–18; 10:10–14; 11:18, who are distinct from the cantors, the gatekeepers, the "oblates," and the slaves of Solomon, cf. Ezr 2:40–58.

Around 300, the chronicler, though maintaining the distinction between priests and Levites, gives considerable importance to the Levites who play a preponderant part in connection with the Ark of the Covenant, 1 Ch 15–16, in the temple, 23–26, and in carrying out the religious reforms of Hezekiah, 2 Ch 29–31, and Josiah, 34–35. Some Levites, who no longer have the Ark to carry, 1 Ch 23:26, are assigned to the choral office, 1 Ch 16:4. By this action the other cantors are assimilated to the Levites. This is how the three leading cantors, Hemen, Asaph, and Ethan/Jeduthun are attached respectively to Kohath, Gershom, and Merari, sons of Levi and ancestors of the three groups of Levites, 1 Ch 6:18–32. Similarly, the gatekeepers receive as ancestors Kore and Obed-edom, 1 Ch 26:1–19, two descendants of Levi, the former via Kohath, the second via Merari, according to the chronicler.

In addition to the offices of cantor, musician, and gatekeeper, the sons of Levi assume other responsibilities, such as the administration of the temple, 1 Ch 9:26, 26:20–21; 2 Ch 24:6, 11; 31:11–15, the slaughtering and dismembering of the sacrificial victims, 2 Ch 29:34; 35:11, the offices of scribe and judge, 1 Ch 23:4, and of teaching, cf. 2 Ch 17:8–9; 35:3; Ne 8:7, 9.

Levi in the lists of the tribes; List, pages 410–11.

Posterity of Levi: List, page 416.

Levites: BARNABAS; JONATHAN 1.

Daughter of Levi: JOCHEBED.

2. **Levi** (2), two ancestors of Jesus, Lk 3:24, 29.

3. **Levi** (3). See: MATTHEW.

LEVIATHAN (6), Hb. *Livyatân,* Ugar. *Lotân,* in Phoenician mythology a seven-headed monster of the primeval chaos, Jb 3:8; cf. 7:12, described as a fleeing serpent and a twisting serpent, Is 27:1 (where it is paralleled with the sea dragon). A symbol of disorder and an embodiment of the power of evil, it is overcome by Yahweh at the creation and at the crossing of the Red Sea, Ps 74:14. In Jb 40:25–41:26 it refers to the crocodile, cf. Ps 104:26, and may be an allusion to Egypt, the enemy of Israel.

The Dragon of Rv 12:3 presents some traits of this serpent of chaos.

See: BEAST; DEEP; RAHAB 1.

LEVITES (242), Hb. *Leviim* (239), Gr. *Leuitēs* (3), Lk 10:32; Jn 1:19; Ac 4:36. See: LEVI 1.

LIBNAH, "White" (cf. Laban).

1. **Libnah** (2), a stage of the Israelites in the desert between Sinai and Kadesh, Nb 33:20–21. Otherwise unknown.

2. **Libnah** (16), an ancient Canaanite royal town captured by Joshua acc. to Jos 10:29–32, 39; 12:15. A town in the lowlands of Judah, Jos 15:42, assigned to the Levites of the clan of Kohath, Jos 21:13//1 Ch 6:42. See: LIBNI 1. Under Jehoram, Libnah is occupied by the Philistines, cf. 2 K 8:22//2 Ch 21:10. In the time of Hezekiah it is besieged by Sennacherib, 2 K 19:8//Is 37:8. Native place of Hamital, mother of Jehoahaz and Zedekiah, kings of Judah, 2 K 23:31//24:18; Jr 52:1. Probably 10 km S of Ekron.

LIBNATH (The streams of the) (1), "Whiteness" (cf. Laban), on the southern border of Asher, Jos 19:26. Perhaps the modern *Nahr ez-Zerqa* or the *Kishon.*

LIBNI (cf. Libnah).

1. **Libni** (4) is, like Shimei, a son of Gershon, son of Levi, Ex 6:17//Nb 3:18//1 Ch 6:2, 5. His descendants form the **Libnite** clan, Nb 3:21; acc. to the ancient list of Levitical clans in Nb 26:58 (which differs from the canonical division into Gershonite, Kohathite, and Merarite clans), the Libnites originally resided in the town of: LIBNAH 2.

= **Ladan** (6) who is likewise presented with Shimei as a son and Levitical clan of Gershon, 1 Ch 23:7–9; 26:21.

Father of: JEHIEL 2.

2. **Libni** (1), a Levite of the clan of Merari, son of Mahli and father of Shimei, 1 Ch 6:14.

LIBNITE (2), Nb 3:21; 26:58, belonging to the clan of: LIBNI 1.

LIBYA (1), a country west of Egypt, near Cyrene. Some Jews from this area are in Jerusalem for the first Christian Pentecost, Ac 2:10. See: CUB; LIBYANS.

LIBYANS (4), Hb. *Lubim,* natives of Libya, mentioned with the Cushites as auxiliaries of the Egyptian armies, 2 Ch 12:3; 16.8; Dn 11:43; Na 3:9. See: LEHAB; LIBYA; PUT.

LIKHI (1), a metathesis (?) for Hb. *Helqi,* "Helekite," 1 Ch 7:19. See: HELEK.

LILITH (1), Accad. *Lilitu,* a female demon, probably of the storm, which in Palestine becomes a nocturnal ghost ("night" in Hb. is *layelah*), Is 34:14.

LINUS (1), a Christian of Rome, 2 Tm 4:21.

LOD (3) or **Lud** (1), Gr. *Lydda,* a town linked with Ono, occupied after the exile by Jews, Ezr 2:33//Ne 7:37, of Benjamin, Ne 11:35; cf. 1 Ch 8:12 (*Lud*).

= **Lydda** (4), capital of one of the three districts annexed by Jonathan Maccabaeus, 1 M 11:34; cf. 10:30, 38; 11:28, 57. The Apostle Peter heals Aeneas, a paralytic, there, Ac 9:32, 35, 38. About 15 km SW of Joppa.

LO-DEBAR (5), "Nothing," a town in Transjordania, in the territory of Gad, Jos 13:26 (Hb. *Lidebir*), probably reconquered by Joash or Jeroboam II, kings of Israel, Am 6:13 (Hb. *Lo-Dabar*).

Native place of: MACHIR 2.

LOIS (1), grandmother of Timothy, 2 Tm 1:5. See: EUNICE.

LORD, Gr. *Kyrios,* translation of Hb. *'Adôn* or Aram. *Mara'* or Hb. *YHWH,* "Yahweh." See: JESUS *b*; YAHWEH *d*.

LOT (38), (cf. Lotan), acc. to the priestly tradition is **son of Haran** (1) and nephew of Abraham, with whom he emigrates from Ur, then from Haran to Canaan, Gn 11:27, 31; 12:5. Acc. to the Yahwist tradition, Lot settles in the Jordan valley at Sodom, 13:1–14. The only just man in a city of sinners, he escapes the destruction that strikes Sodom and the surrounding area, whereas "the wife of Lot looked back, and was turned into a pillar of salt," 19:1–29; cf. Ws 10:6–7; 19:17; Si 16:8; 2 P 2:7–8, and Lk 17:28–32 for whom this chastisement prefigures the judgment at the end of time. Gn 19:30–38 describes the Moabites and Ammonites as the fruits of Lot's incest with his daughters. Cf. Dt 2:9, 19; Ps 83:8, where Moab and Ammon are called the "sons of Lot." Acc. to the (independent) tradition in Gn 14, Lot is made a prisoner of the four allied kings and then rescued by Abraham in a surprise attack.

LOTAN (7), (cf. Lot), first of the sons of Seir the Horite, Gn 36:20//1 Ch 1:38, and of the chiefs (or clans) of the Horites, Gn 36:29. He has two sons, Hori and Hemam or Homam, and a sister Timna.

[LOWER EGYPT, LOWER MESOPOTAMIA]. See: EGYPT; MESOPOTAMIA.

LOWLANDS, Hb. *Shephelah,* Gr. *Sephela* or *Pedinē,* "Plain."

1. **The Lowlands** (20), usually means the region between the highlands of Judah and the Mediterranean coastal plain (occupied by the Philistines); it is the area of the hills of Judah, Jos 10:40; 11:16; 12:8; Jg 1:9; 2 Ch 28:18; Jr 17:26; 32:44; 33:13; Ob 19; Zc 7:7. In Dt 1:7; Jos 9:1, the lowlands are clearly distinguished from the coastal plain, vv. 45–47; Ob 19. In most of the passages cited the lowlands are associated with the highlands (of Judah) and the Negeb (of Judah). In the lowlands stock farming is carried on, 2 Ch 26:10, as is the growing of sycamores, 1 K 10:27//2 Ch 1:15; 9:27, and olive trees, 1 Ch 27:28.

Towns: ADIDA; EMMAUS 1. See also the list in Jos 15:33–47.

2. **The Lowlands** (2), in Jos 11:16 is the region west of the highlands of Ephraim, and in Jos 11:2 perhaps the plain N of Carmel.

LUCIUS, Gr. *Leukios* or *Loukios* (cf. Luke), a name of Roman origin.

1. **Lucius** (1), whose full name is *Lucius Caecilius Metellus Calvus,* Roman consul in 142 B.C., 1 M 15:16–24 gives

the text of his letter promulgating the treaty between the Romans and the Jews, as well as the names of the kings, cities, islands and territories to which it is addressed.

2. **Lucius of Cyrene** (1), one of the five "prophets and teachers" of the Church of Antioch, Ac 13:1–2.

3. **Lucius** (1), a compatriot of Paul, a Jewish Christian of Corinth, Rm 16:21 (Gr. text).

LUD

1. **Lud** (6), a people connected with Egypt (Misraim) in the Yahwist genealogy, Gn 10:13//1 Ch 1:11, and with Shem in the priestly genealogy, Gn 10: 22//1 Ch 1:17. Other passages always parallel it with Put, Is 66:19; Jr 46:9; Ezk 27:10; 30:5; Jdt 2:23, so that Lud may refer to an African people on the coast of the Red Sea. Some interpreters identify the Lud of Gn 10:22//1 Ch 1:17 and Is 66:19 with Lydia. Others see in the Lud of Gn 10:13 a town between Jerusalem and Gezer, which Solomon supposedly received as a dowry from Pharaoh.

2. **Lud** (1), 1 Ch 8:12. See: LOD.

LUHITH (Slopes of) (2), in Moab, Is 15:5; Jr 48:5. Difficult to locate. Perhaps in the western part of the country.

LUKE (3), Gr. *Loukas* (cf. Lucius), a physician and, with Demas, a co-worker of Paul, Col 4:14; Phm 24; 2 Tm 4:11. "The brother" in 2 Co 8:18 may be Luke. Perhaps, too, he is included with Paul in the passages of Acts that are written in the first person plural, Ac 16:10–17; 20: 5–15; 21:1–18; 27:1–28:16. Tradition makes him the author of the third gospel and of the Acts of the Apostles.

LUZ, "Almond."

1. **Luz** (7), ancient name of: BETHEL 1.

2. **Luz** (1), a town in the country of the Hittites. Acc. to Jg 1:26, it was founded by an inhabitant of Bethel after he had betrayed Bethel to the house of Joseph.

LYCAONIA (1), a region of high plateaus in the NW of Cilicia, in present-day Turkey; joined in 25 B.C. to the Roman province of Galatia. The language of the country was still *Lycaonian* in some areas, Ac 14:11. Paul preaches the Gospel there during his first two missionary journeys, Ac 14:6; cf. 16:1.

Cities: DERBE; ICONIUM; LYSTRA.

LYCIA (2), a region of Asia Minor on the southern coast, in modern Turkey. The letter of the consul Lucius promulgating the alliance between Romans and Jews is addressed to it among others, 1 M 15:23. From 43 A.D. on, Lycia and Pamphylia form a Roman province.

Cities: MYRA; PATARA; PHASELIS.

LYDDA (4). See: LOD.

LYDIA

1. **Lydia** (1), a region in Asia Minor on the Aegean Sea, between Mysia and Caria. After his defeat at Magnesia on the Sipylus in 189, Antiochus the Great is forced to cede Lydia to Eumenes, king of Pergamum, 1 M 8:8. In 133 B.C. Lydia is incorporated into the Roman province of Asia.

See: LUD; MAGOG.

Cities: PHILADELPHIA 1; SARDIS; SMYRNA; THYATIRA.

2. **Lydia** (2), a dealer in purple dye, from Thyatira in Lydia, now residing at Philippi. Sympathetic to Judaism, she is converted to the Christian faith and receives baptism together with her household, during Paul's second missionary journey. She offers hospitality to Paul, who, on emerging from prison, returns to her house to say farewell to the Christian community of the city, Ac 16:14–15, 40.

LYSANIAS (1), "Who dispels sadness" (cf. Lysimachus), **tetrarch of Abilene** (1), at the time when John the Baptist begins his ministry, Lk 3:1.

LYSIAS

1. **Lysias** (23), **high commissioner for Coele-Syria and Phoenicia** (1), 2 M 10:11, "a nobleman belonging to the royal family," regent of Syria in the absence of King Antiochus Epiphanes, 1 M 3:32–36. In order to put down the Jewish revolt, Lysias sends an army into Judaea, but it is defeated at Emmaus, 1 M 3:38–40; 4:1–27. The next year he campaigns in person against the Jews, but is defeated near Beth-zur, 1 M 4:28–35//2 M 11:1–12; cf. 1 M 6:6. Peace talks and letters from Lysias to the Jews, 2 M 11:13–21; cf. 11:35–36; 12:1. At the accession of the very youthful Antiochus V Eupator, 1 M 6:17, Lysias conducts a new campaign against the Jews, who suffer defeats at Beth-zur and Bethzechariah and a siege at Jerusalem, 1 M 6:28–54; cf. 2 M 13:1–4. Lysias then persuades Antiochus to deal with the Jews, 1 M 6:55–60; 2 M 13:23–26: a letter of Antiochus V to Lysias, 2 M 11:22–26. In 161, Lysias is handed over by his army to Demetrius I and assassinated at the same time as Antiochus V, 1 M 7:2–4//2 M 14:2.

2. **Lysias** (1), probably leader of the town of Ephron, which is captured by Judas Maccabaeus, 2 M 12:27. Corr. to *Lysanias?*

3. **Lysias** (3), full name **Claudius Lysias** (1), Ac 23:26; 24:7 (var.), 22, a Roman tribune at the fortress Antonia in Jerusalem. He had had to pay a large sum to acquire Roman citizenship, Ac 22:24–29. It is he who rescues Paul from the Jews as they prepare to lynch him in the temple, Ac 21:31–39, has him appear before the Sanhedrin, 22:30 and, learning of a Jewish plot against Paul, has him transferred to Caesarea, 23:12–33.

LYSIMACHUS, "Who causes combat to cease" (cf. Lysanias).

1. **Lysimachus** (6), brother of the high priest Menelaus, and himself interim high priest, dies in the temple at the hands of the mob for numerous sacrilegious thefts, 2 M 4:29, 39–42.

2. **Lysimachus son of Ptolemy** (1), of the Jewish community in Jerusalem, translator of the Book of Esther, acc. to Est 10:3[1].

LYSTRA (6), a city in Lycaonia about 30 km south of Iconium. Paul, accompanied by Barnabas, preaches the Gospel there during his first missionary journey and heals a cripple there. He is taken to be Hermes, and Barnabas is taken to be Zeus. The arrival of Jews from Iconium turns the people against the Apostles, and Paul is stoned. The next day he goes to Derbe, Ac 14:6–20; cf. 2 Tm 3:11. On his return from his first journey he again passes through Lystra, Ac 14:21–22. During his second journey Paul, in company with Silas, stops there again. When he leaves, he takes with him Timothy, who is a native of Lystra and will become his favorite disciple, Ac 16:1–3.

M

MAACAH, Hb. *Ma'akah* (cf. Abel-beth-maacah; Beth-maacah).

1. **Maacah** (6), one of the twelve sons of Nahor, brother of Abraham, and of his concubine Reumah, Gn 22:24. An Aramaean people—the **Maacathites**—to the east of the Upper Jordan, on the borders of Israel, Dt 3:14; Jos 12:5; 13:11, 13, allied with the Ammonites against David, 2 S 10:6, 8//1 Ch 19:6–7.

2. **Maacah** (1), a concubine of Caleb, from whom several clans descend, 1 Ch 2:48–49. To her are probably attached: ESHTEMOA and JAAZANIAH 2.

3. **Maacah** (2), sister and wife of Machir, 1 Ch 7:15–16.

4. **Maacah** (2), wife of Abi-gibeon, 1 Ch 8:29, or of Jeiel, 1 Ch 9:35.

5. **Maacah** (1), father of: HANAN 3.

6. **Maacah** (1), father of: SHEPHATIAH 3.

7. **Maacah** (1), 1 K 2:39.

= **Maoch** (1), 1 S 27:2, father of: ACHISH.

8. **Maacah** (7) **daughter of Talmai king of Geshur** (2), wife of David and mother of Absalom, 2 S 3:3//1 Ch 3:2.

Mother of: TAMAR 2.

9. **Maacah** (7) **daughter of Absalom** (4), favorite wife of Rehoboam, king of Judah, 2 Ch 11:21, mother of Abijah, among others, 1 K 15:2; 2 Ch 11:20, 22, and grandmother of Asa, 1 K 15:10; the latter deprives her of her dignity as queen mother, 1 K 15:13.

= **Micaiah daughter of Uriel from Gibeah** (1), mother of Abijah, 2 Ch 13:2.

MAACATHITE, Hb. *Ma'akati.*

1. **Maacathite** (5), Dt 3:14; Jos 12:5; 13:11, 13; 2 S 23:34 (some correct to *Beth-maacah*), from the land of: MAACAH 1.

2. **Maacathite** (3), 2 K 25:23//Jr 40:8; 1 Ch 4:19, belonging to the Calebite clan of: MAACAH 2.

MAADAI (1), abbrev. of *Maadiah,* an Israelite of the sons of Bani, married to a foreign wife, whom he puts away, Ezr 10:34.

MAADIAH (1), Hb. *Ma'adyah* (cf. Maadai), a priest who returns from the exile with Zerubbabel, Ne 12:5.

= **Moadiah** (1), gives his name to a priestly family, the head of which, in the time of the high priest Joiakim, is Piltai, Ne 12:17.

MAAI (1), a Levite, a son of Asaph (?), an instrumentalist at the dedication of the wall of Jerusalem, Ne 12:36.

MAARATH (1), a town in the highlands of Judah, Jos 15:59.

MAASAI (1), acc. to Gr.; Hb. *Ma'sai,* abbrev. of *Maaseyahu.* See: AMASAI 4.

MAASEIAH, "Work of Yah" (cf. Asahel).

1. **Maaseiah** (2), a Levite gatekeeper attached to the service of the Ark, 1 Ch 15:18, player of the keyed harp, 15:20.

2. **Maaseiah son of Adaiah** (1), an officer involved in the plot against Athaliah, 2 Ch 23:1–14.

3. **Maaseiah** (1), an official (in charge of enrollment? a leader?) in the army of King Uzziah, 2 Ch 26:11.

4. **Maaseiah** (1), a Judaean, "son of the king" (= a police officer?), killed by Zichri during the Syrophoenician war, 2 Ch 28:7.

5. **Maaseiah** (1), governor of Jerusalem under Josiah. He accompanies Shaphan, the secretary, and Joah, the herald of the king, to the high priest Hilkiah in order to take care of the payment of the workers who are restoring the temple, 2 Ch 34:8–13.

6. **Maaseiah** (3), a priest, father of: ZEPHANIAH 3.

7. **Maaseiah** (1), father of the prophet: ZEDEKIAH 2.

8. **Maaseiah son of Shallum** (1), guardian of the threshold, for whom an apartment is reserved in the temple, Jr 35:4.

9. **Maaseiah** (1), three priests married to foreign women, whom they put away: the first, of the sons of Jeshua, Ezr 10:18; the second, of the sons of Harim, 10:21; the third, of the sons of Pashhur, 10:22.

10. **Maaseiah** (1), an Israelite of the sons of Pahath-moab, married to a foreign woman, whom he puts away, Ezr 10:30.

11. **Maaseiah** (1), father of: AZARIAH 18.

12. **Maaseiah** (1), a lay notable who stands on Ezra's right during the solemn reading of the Law, Ne 8:4.

13. **Maaseiah** (1), a Levite, explains the Law to the people during the same solemn reading, Ne 8:7.

14. **Maaseiah** (1), a leader of the people, a cosigner of the pledge to observe the Law, Ne 10:26.

15. **Maaseiah son of Baruch son of Col-hozeh son of Adaiah son of Joiarib son of Zechariah** (1), a Judaean of the clan of Shelah, settled in Jerusalem after the exile, Ne 11:5.

16. **Maaseiah** (1), a Benjaminite, an ancestor of: SALLU 1.

17. **Maaseiah** (2), two priests who take part with Nehemiah in the dedication of the Jerusalem wall, Ne 12:41–42.

MAATH (1). See: MAHATH 3.

MAAZ (1), "Anger" (cf. Ahimaaz), first of the three sons of Ram, of the clan of Jerahmeel, 1 Ch 2:27.

MAAZIAH, "Yah is a fortress" (cf. Azaziah).

1. **Maaziah** (1), leader of the twenty-fourth priestly class, 1 Ch 24:18.

2. **Maaziah** (1), a priest, cosigner of the pledge to observe the Law, Ne 10:9.

MACCABAEUS (31), Gr. *Makkabaios,* Hb. *Maqqaba,* "Hammer"? (see Mark), or *Maqqebai,* "Appointed by Yahweh"?, a surname of the most celebrated of the sons of Mattathias, being coupled with the name of **Judas** (9), 1 M 2:4, 66; 3:1; 5:24; 8:20; 2 M 2:10; 5:27; 8:1; 14:6, or used by itself (22), 1 M 5:34; 2 M 8:5, 16; 10:1, 16; 19:21, 25, 30, 33–35; 11:6–7, 15; 12:19–20; 13:24; 14:27–30; 15:7–21. See: JUDAH 7.

MACEDON. See: MACEDONIA.

MACEDONIA or **Macedon** (22), a region in northern Greece.

Native land of Alexander the Great, 1 M 1:1, of Haman, Est 8:12[k, o]. Four thousand Macedonians take part in a battle in Babylonia, 2 M 8:20.

A Roman province (capital: Thessalonika), where Paul during his second missionary journey founds some especially dynamic churches, Ac 16:9–14; 18:5; cf. Ph 4:15, which he visits during his third journey, Ac 19:21–22; 20:1–6; cf. 1 Co 16:5; 2 Co 1:16; 2:13; 7:5–6, and on a fourth journey, 1 Tm 1:3. Generous participation of the Macedonian Christians in the great collection for the impoverished church of Jerusalem, Rm 15:26–27; 2 Co 8:1–15; 9:1–4, and generosity to Paul in his personal needs, 2 Co 11:9.

Another name: KITTIM.

Cities and towns: AMPHIPOLIS; APOLLONIA; BEROEA 2; DOBERUS; NEAPOLIS; PHILIPPI; THESSALONIKA.

Kings: ALEXANDER 1; PERSEUS; PHILIP 1–2.

Macedonian companions of Paul: ARISTARCHUS; GAIUS 1.

MACEDONIAN or **of Macedon** (11), Est 8:12[k, o]; 1 M 1:1; 6:2; 2 M 8:20; Ac 16:9; 19:29; 27:2; 2 Co 9:2, 4, from or of: MACEDONIA.

MACHBANNAI (1), a Gadite who rallies to David before the latter becomes king, 1 Ch 12:14 (cf. vv. 9–16).

MACHBENAH (1), a descendant of Maacah, Caleb's concubine, 1 Ch 2:49.

MACHI (1), a Gadite, father of: GEUEL.

MACHIR, "The one sold; He who hires himself out; The mercenary."

1. **Machir** (19), **son of Manasseh** (7), Gn 50:23; Nb 32:39–40; 36:1; Jos 13:31; 17:3; 1 Ch 7:17, or "Manasseh's eldest son," Jos 17:1, named—with his clan, the **Machirite** clan—at the head of the clans of Manasseh, Nb 26:29–34; Jos 17:1 ff., **father of Gilead** (4), Jos 17:1; 1 Ch 2:21, 23; 7:14. Acc. to Gn 50:23, the sons of Machir are born in Egypt "on Joseph's lap," that is, are adopted by Joseph. Acc. to 1 Ch 2:21, there are links between Machir and Judah.

Machir, "a fighting man," Jos 17:1, conquers Gilead, Nb 32:39–40, where he settles, Dt 3:15; Jos 13:31. The ancient passage in Jg 5:14 speaks of Machir as a tribe on a par with Ephraim, Benjamin, Zebulun, Issachar, and Naphtali, whereas Manasseh is not mentioned. It is probable that Machir was supplanted and absorbed by Manasseh, as Simeon was by Judah and Reuben by Gad.

See: GILEAD 1; ZELOPHEHAD.

2. **Machir son of Ammiel at Lo-debar** (3) remains loyal to the house of Saul and in particular to Meribbaal, son of Jonathan, 2 S 9:4–5; he aids David when the latter is a fugitive, 2 S 17:27–29.

MACHIRITE (1), Nb 26:29, belonging to the clan of: MACHIR 1.

MACHPELAH (6), "Double," a property and cave **opposite Mamre** (5), which Abraham buys in order to bury Sarah there, Gn 23:7–20. In time, it will serve as burial place for Abraham, Gn 25:8–10, Isaac and Rebekah, Leah and Jacob, Gn 49:30–31; 50:13 (but cf. Gn 50:10–11 and Ac 7:16). Traditionally identified with the *Haram al-Khalil* at Hebron.

MACRON (1), "Long-head," a surname of: PTOLEMY 10.

MADMANNAH (2), "Dung heap" (cf. Madmenah), a town in the Negeb of Judah, Jos 15:31, of Calebite origin, 1 Ch 2:49.

MADMEN (1), (cf. Madmenah), a town of Moab, perhaps S of the Arnon, Jr 48:2.

MADMENAH (1), "Dung heap" (cf. Madmannah; Madmen), an unidentified town, NE of Jerusalem, Is 10:31.

MADON (2), Jos 11:1; 12:19. See: MEROM.

MAGADAN (1), an unidentified place, Mt 15:39 (//Mk 8:10, *Dalmanutha*).

MAGBISH (1), a town of Judah (or a Judaean town), whose sons return from the exile with Zerubbabel, Ezr 2:30.

MAGDALA (14), from the Hb. *Migdal*, "Tower" (cf. Gedaliah), a town on the west shore of the Sea of Chinnereth, N of Tiberias. Native place of: MARY 4.

MAGDALENE, of or from: MAGDALA.

MAGDIEL (2), "God is my best gift *or*

God is my honor" (cf. Megiddo), one of the chiefs (or clans) of Edom, Gn 36:43//1 Ch 1:54.

[MAGNESIA ON THE SIPYLUS], a city in Asia Minor where in 189 B.C. Lucius Cornelius Scipio, a Roman consul, crushes Antiochus the Great. Today *Manisa* in Turkey, 40 km NE of Izmir (Smyrna).

MAGOG (5), "Land of Gog" (cf. Gog), one of the seven sons of Japheth, Gn 10:2//1 Ch 1:5 (= *Lydia* in Asia Minor). Described as the country where Gog reigns, in Ezk 38:2 and 39:6, and as a symbol, along with Gog, of the pagan nations united against the people of God, Rv 20:8–9.

MAGPIASH (1), a leader of the people, a cosigner of the pledge to observe the Law, Ne 10:21.

MAHALAB (2), a Phoenician town on the border of Asher, Jos 19:29 (corr. of Hb. *Mehebel*). NE of Tyre.

MAHALALEL, Gr. *Maleleēl*, "Praise of God" (cf. Hillel).

1. **Mahalalel** (7), son of Kenan and father of Jared, Gn 5:12–17 (priestly genealogy); cf. 1 Ch 1:1. Acc. to Lk 3:37, an ancestor of Jesus. An antediluvian patriarch.

= **Mehujael** (2), son of Irad and father of Methushael, Gn 4:18 (Yahwist genealogy).

2. **Mehalalel** (1), an ancestor of: ATHAIAH.

MAHALATH

1. **Mahalath daughter of Abraham's son Ishmael and sister of Nebaioth** (1), a wife of Esau, Gn 28:9.

2. **Mahalath daughter of Jerimoth son of David** (1) and **of Abihail daughter of Eliab son of Jesse** (1), one of the wives of King Rehoboam, to whom she gives three sons, 2 Ch 11:18–19.

MAHANAIM (13), "The Two Camps," see Gn 32:3, 8, 11 (cf. Camp of Dan). Place of a confrontation between Jacob and some angels of God, Gn 32:3. A town in Transjordania, S of the Jabbok, on the border of Gad and Manasseh, Jos 13:26, 30, assigned to the Levites of the clan of Merari, Jos 21:38//1 Ch 6:65. In the seventh district of Solomon, 1 K 4:14. Refuge of Saul's son Ishbaal after he has become king, 2 S 2:8, 12, 29, and of David when fleeing from his son Absalom, 2 S 17:24, 27; cf. 19:33; 1 K 2:8.

MAHARAI from Netophah (3), one of David's champions, 2 S 23:28//1 Ch 11:30. Acc. to 1 Ch 27:13, which calls him a Zerahite, he is in charge of the (military) service for the tenth month.

MAHATH, Gr. *Maath*.

1. **Mahath son of Amasai** (2), a Levite of the clan of Kohath, associated with Joel, son of Azariah, in the genealogy of the cantor Heman, 1 Ch 6:20–21, and in the account of the purification of the temple during the reform of Hezekiah, 2 Ch 29:12. Cf. Ahimoth, brother of Amasai, 1 Ch 6:10.

2. **Mahath** (1), one of the ten Levites who assist Conaniah and Shimei in the time of Hezekiah, 2 Ch 31:13.

3. **Maath** (1), an ancestor of Jesus acc. to Lk 3:26.

MAHAVITE (1), 1 Ch 11:46 (corr. of Hb. *Mahavim*, "the Mahavites". See: ELIEL 5.

MAHAZIOTH (2), "Visions" (cf. Hazael), of the sons of Heman, head of the twenty-third class of cantors, 1 Ch 25:4, 30.

MAHER - SHALAL - HASH - BAZ (2), "Speedy-spoil-quick-booty," a prophetic name given to the second son of Isaiah, Is 8:1–4.

MAHLAH

1. **Mahlah** (4), Nb 26:33; 27:1; 36:11; Jos 17:3, a Manassite, first of the five daughters of: ZELOPHEHAD.

2. **Mahlah** (1), a Manassite, one of the

three children of Malcath, 1 Ch 7:18. To be connected with the preceding.

MAHLI (cf. Mahlon).

1. **Mahli** (19) is, with Mushi, a son of Merari, son of Levi, Ex 6:19; Nb 3:20; 1 Ch 6:4, 14; 23:21; 24:26. His descendants form the Mahlite clan, Nb 3:33; 26:58.

Descendants: ASAIAH 1; ELEAZAR 4; KISH 3; SHEREBAIAH.

2. **Mahli** (3), a Levite of the clan of Merari, one of the three sons of Mushi, 1 Ch 23:23//24:30, an ancestor of Ethan the cantor, 1 Ch 6:32.

MAHLITE (2), belonging to the Levitic clan of: MAHLI 1.

MAHLON (4), "Listlessness"? (cf. Mahli ?), an Ephrathite from Bethlehem in Judah, one of the two sons of Elimelech and Naomi, first husband of Ruth the Moabitess; he dies childless, Rt 1:2–5; 4:9–10.

MAHSEIAH, Gr. *Maasaias,* Lat. *Maasias,* "Yah is a refuge" (cf. Ahasbai).

1. **Mahseiah** (2), Jr 32:12; Ba 1:1, father of Neriah and grandfather of: BARUCH 1.

2. **Mahseiah** (1), Jr 51:59, probably the same as the preceding; acc. to the Hb. text, father of Neriah and grandfather of: SERAIAH 3.

MAKAZ (1), in the second district of Solomon, 1 K 4:9. Location unknown.

MAKED (2), a town in the NE of Hellenistic Gilead, where Jews live who are freed by Judas Maccabaeus, 1 M 5:26, 36.

MAKHELOTH (2), "Gatherings" (cf. Kehelathah), a stage of the Exodus between Sinai and Kadesh, Nb 33:25–26.

MAKKEDAH (9), an ancient Canaanite royal town conquered by Joshua, Jos 10:28–29; 12:16. Five Canaanite kings hide in a cave near the town; after executing them, Joshua buries them in the cave, Jos 10:10, 16–27. A town in the lowlands of Judah, Jos 15:11. Site unknown.

MALACHI (1), "My messenger," a name drawn from Ml 3:1, and designating an anonymous prophet active ca. 450, Ml 1:1. The "last" of the twelve "minor" prophets.

MALCAM (1), (cf. Melech), a Benjaminite, head of a family in Moab, 1 Ch 8:9 (Gr. *Malkom*).

MALCHATH (1), "Royalty"? (cf. Melech), a Manassite, sister of Gilead (?) and mother of Abiezer, Ishhod, and Mahlah, 1 Ch 7:18.

MALCHIAH (1). See: MALCHIJAH 1.

MALCHIEL, Melchiel, Gr. *Melchiel,* "My king is God" (cf. Melech).

1. **Malchiel** (3), son of Beriah son of Asher, Gn 46:17//1 Ch 7:31, whose descendants form the **Malchielite** clan, Nb 26:45.

2. **Melchiel** (1), Jdt 6:15, father of: CHARMIS.

MALCHIELITE (1), belonging to the clan of: MALCHIEL 1.

MALCHIJAH, Malchiah, "My King is Yah" (cf. Melech).

1. **Malchiah** (1), a prince of the blood, into whose cistern Jeremiah is thrown, Jr 38:6.

2. **Malchiah** (2), father of: PASHHUR 3.

3. **Malchijah** (1), an ancestor of Asaph the cantor, 1 Ch 6:25.

4. **Malchijah** (2), ancestor of the priest: ADAIAH 6.

5. **Malchijah** (1), leader of the fifth priestly class, 1 Ch 24:9.

6. **Malchijah** (2), two Israelites of the sons of Parosh, married to foreign women, whom they put away, Ezr 10:25.

7. **Malchijah** (1), an Israelite of the sons of Harim, married to a foreign woman, whom he puts away, Ezr 10:31.

8. **Malchijah son of Harim** (1), a volunteer in the rebuilding of the Jerusalem wall, Ne 3:11. Same as the preceding?

9. **Malchijah son of Rechab** (1), ruler of the district of Beth-hac-cherem, a volunteer in the rebuilding of the Jerusalem wall, Ne 3:14.

10. **Malchijah** (1), of the goldsmiths' guild, another volunteer in the rebuilding, Ne 3:31.

11. **Malchijah** (1), a lay notable who stands at Ezra's left during the solemn reading of the Law, Ne 8:4.

12. **Malchijah** (1), a priest, a cosigner of the pledge to observe the Law, Ne 10:4.

13. **Malchijah** (1), a priest, present at the dedication of the Jerusalem wall, Ne 12:42.

MALCHIRAM (1), "My King is on high" (cf. Melech; Ramah), one of the sons of King Jehoiachin, born to him while a captive at Babylon, 1 Ch 3:18.

MALCHISHUA (5), (cf. Melech; Shua 1), one of the three sons of King Saul, 1 S 14:49; 1 Ch 8:33//9:39, who die in the battle of Gilboa, 1 S 31:2//1 Ch 10:2.

MALCHUS (1), Gr. and Lat. form of Nabat. *Maliku,* "king" (cf. Melech), a servant of the high priest; Peter cuts off his ear, Jn 18:10; cf. Mt 26:51.

MALLOTHI (2), of the sons of Heman, head of the nineteenth class of cantors, 1 Ch 25:4, 26.

MALLUCH, a recent form of Hb. *Melek,* "king" (cf. Melech).

1. **Malluch** (1), a Levite of the clan of Merari, an ancestor of Ethan the cantor, 1 Ch 6:29.

2. **Malluch** (1), an Israelite of the sons of Bigvai, married to a foreign wife, whom he puts away, Ezr 10:29.

3. **Malluch** (1), an Israelite of the sons of Harim, married to a foreign wife, whom he puts away, Ezr 10:32.

4. **Malluch** (2) or **Malluchi** (1), a priest who returns from the exile, Ne 12:2, a cosigner of the pledge to observe the Law, Ne 10:5, gives his name to a priestly family, Ne 12:14 (corr. of Hb. *Meliku*).

5. **Malluch** (1), a leader of the people and a cosigner of the pledge to observe the Law, Ne 10:28.

MALLUCHI (1). See: MALLUCH 4.

MALLUS (1), Gr. *Mallōtai,* a city of Cilicia, on the coast, whose inhabitants rebel against Antiochus Epiphanes, 2 M 4:30.

MALTA, Gr. *Melitē,* an island in the Mediterranean, S of Sicily, where Paul receives a welcome after his shipwreck and where he heals the sick, Ac 28:1–10.

Prefect of the island: PUBLIUS.

MAMRE (10), Hb. *Mamre',* Gr. *Membre,* an Amorite, brother of Eshcol and Aner, host and ally of Abraham, Gn 14:13, 24, gives his name to an **oak grove** (Hb. *oaks;* Gr. *oak*), which becomes the residence and sanctuary of the patriarchs, Gn 13:18; 14:13; 35:27, and scene of the well-known appearance of the "three men" to Abraham, Gn 18:1–6.

Traditionally located 3 km N of Hebron, at *Ramat el-Khalil.*

Opposite Mamre: MACHPELAH.

MANACH (1). See: MANAHATH 2.

MANAEN (1). See: MENAHEM 2.

MANAHATH (cf. Nahath).

1. **Manahath** (2), second son of Shobal, himself the second son of Seir, Gn 36:23//1 Ch 1:40.

2. **Manahath** (1), a town to which the inhabitants of Geba are exiled, 1 Ch 8:6.

= **Manach** (1), a town in the highlands of Judah, Jos 15:59 (acc. to Gr.). Its inhabitants, the **Manahathites,** are regarded as descendants of "Hur, the first-born of Ephrathah" through Shobal, 1 Ch 2:52 (corr. of Hb. *Menuhot*) and through Salma, 2:54.

MANAHATHITES (2), Hb. *Manahti,* of or from: MANAHATH 2.

MANASSEH, Gr. *Manassē(s)*, Hb. *Menashshè,* connected in Gn 41:51 with Hb. *nashah,* "to forget."

1. **Mannaseh** (125) **son of Joseph** (4), Nb 27:1; 32:33; 36:12; Jos 17:1–2, and a tribe of Israel.

Elder son of Joseph and Asenath, daughter of Potiphera, born in Egypt, Gn 41:50–51; 46:20, 27. Together with his brother Ephraim blessed by Jacob, who adopts them as his own sons but transfers preeminence to Ephraim, Gn 48:1–20.

Posterity and clans of Manasseh, Nb 26:29–34; cf. Jos 17:1–6; 1 Ch 7:14–19. The "weakest" clan of Manasseh is that of Abiezer, to which Gideon belongs, Jg 6:15. Censuses of the tribe, Nb 1:34–35; 2:20–21; 26:29–34. Population mingled with the Canaanites, Jg 1:27. (See: SHECHEM).

Manasseh and **Ephraim** form two tribes, Jos 14:4, still designated by the name of **Joseph,** Gn 49:22; Dt 27:12, or **the sons of Joseph,** Nb 26:28–37; Jos 16:1–4; 17:14–18; 1 Ch 7:49, often associated with each other, Dt 34:2; 2 Ch 30:1; 34:6, 9; Ps 60:9//108:9; Ps 80:3; Is 9:20. The two tribes together possess the most extensive and richest sector of the Holy Land and the national sanctuary of Shechem and later that of Shiloh.

Manasseh is made up of *two half tribes,* Jos 13:7–8; 21:5–6, 25, 27; 1 Ch 27:20–21: one whose territory is located *west* of the Jordan (western Manasseh), Jos 17:7–13; cf. Jg 1:27–28; 1 Ch 7:29, the other whose territory is *east* of the Jordan (eastern Manasseh), Jos 13:29–31; cf. 1 Ch 5:23–26; the latter half-tribe, by reason of its geographical position, is often associated with Reuben and Gad, Nb 32:33–41; 34:14–15; Dt 3:12–16; 4:43; 29:7; Jos 1:12–13; 4:12; 12:16; 13:8; 18:7; 22 (the affair of the altar erected on the banks of the Jordan); 2 K 10:33; 1 Ch 5:18, 26 (deportation to Assyria); 26:32.

His "sons": GILEAD 1; JAIR 1; MACHIR 1; ZELOPHEHAD.

Manasseh in the lists of the tribes: List, pages 410–11.

Sister tribe: EPHRAIM.

2. **Manasseh** (26), fourteenth king of Judah (687–642). **Son of Hezekiah** (1), Jr 15:4; 1 Ch 3:13, and of Hephzibah, 2 K 21:1, he succeeds to his father, 2 K 20:21//2 Ch 32:33, at the age of twelve and rules for fifty-five years, 2 K 21:1// 2 Ch 33:1. He takes the opposite course from the religious reform of his father: high places rebuilt, worship of Baal, Astarte, and the whole heavenly host, altars rebuilt in the temple (Josiah will demolish them, 2 K 23:12), necromancers and soothsayers reintroduced, sacrifice of his own son, killing of innocent people (Jewish tradition attributes the death of the prophet Isaiah to him), 2 K 21:2–16//2 Ch 33:1–10. The sins of Manasseh will remain infamous, 2 K 21:20; 23:26; 24:3; Jr 15:4; cf. Si 49:4. Acc. to 2 Ch 33:11 Manasseh was led a prisoner to Babylon by the Assyrians. As a result of this misfortune he was converted, 2 Ch 33:12–16, 18–19 (cf. *the prayer of Manasseh*), 23. He is buried in the garden of Uzza, 2 K 21:18//2 Ch 33:20.

Manasseh is one of the ancestors of Jesus, Mt 1:10.

His son and successor: AMON 2.

3. **Manasseh** (1), an Israelite of the sons of Pahath-moab, married to a foreign woman, whom he puts away, Ezr 10:30.

4. **Manasseh** (1), an Israelite of the sons of Hashum, married to a foreign woman, whom he puts away, Ezr 10:33.

5. **Manasseh** (6), a Simeonite, husband of Judith, Jdt 8:2, 7; 10:3; 16:22–24.

MANASSITES or **of Manasseh** (4), Dt 4:43; 29:7; 2 K 10:33; 1 Ch 26:32, belonging to the tribe of: MANASSEH 1.

MANIUS (1), full name **Titus Manius** (1), one of the Roman ambassadors sent to Antioch and authors of a letter to the Jews regarding the peace treaty with the Romans, 2 M 11:34.

MANOAH (18), "Place of rest" (cf. Nahath), a Danite of Zorah, father of Samson, Jg 13; 14:1–11; 16:31.

MANSIONS OF THE SOUTH (1), Hb. *Hadre Temân,* a constellation, Jb 9:9. Other constellations: BEAR; ORION; PLEIADES.

MAOCH (1). See: MAACAH 7.

MAON (8), Hb. *Ma'on,* "Hiding place, refuge; Dwelling" (cf. Beth-meon), a town in the highlands of Judah, Jos 15:55, of Calebite origin, 1 Ch 2:45. Saul pursues David into the wilderness of Maon, 1 S 23:24–28; 25:1 (corr. of Hb. *Paran*). Native place of Nabal of Carmel, 1 S 25:2–3. 15 km S of Hebron. Today *Tell Ma'in.*

MARA (1). See: MARAH 2.

MARAALAH, Hb. *Mar'alah,* a town on the border of Zebulun, Jos 19:11. Perhaps *Tell Ghalta* in the valley of the Kishon.

MARAH, "Bitter" (cf. Maroth; Merathaim).

1. **Marah** (5), first stage of the Exodus after the crossing of the Red Sea, Nb 33:8–9; complaints of the people at the bitter water that Moses renders sweet, Ex 15:22–25.

See: MASSAH 2.

2. **Mara** (1), a surname ("Bitter") that Naomi ("My sweetness"), mother-in-law of Ruth, gives herself on her return from Moab, Rt 1:20–21.

[MARDUK]. See: MERODACH.

MARESHAH (8), Hb. *Mare'shah* and *Mareshah,* Gr. *Marisa,* "Summit," a town in the lowlands of Judah, Jos 15:44; cf. Mi 1:15, formerly Calebite, 1 Ch 2:42; 4:21, fortified by Rehoboam, 2 Ch 11:8, scene of a confrontation between King Asa and Zerah the Cushite.

= **Marisa** (2), through which Judas Maccabaeus passes, 1 M 5:66 (corr. of Gr. *Samaria*); place of refuge for Gorgias, the military commissioner, 2 M 12:35.

Native place of: ELIEZER 6.

[MARI]. See: AMORITES.

MARISA (2). See: MARESHAH.

MARK (8), a name of Roman origin, "Hammer" (see Maccabaeus), surname of **John** (5), son of Mary, Ac 12:12, 25; 15:37, cousin of Barnabas, Col 4:10. He leaves Jerusalem to accompany Barnabas and Saul to Antioch, Ac 12:25, helps them during the first part of the first missionary journey, then leaves them, Ac 13:5, 13; later on, he goes to Cyprus with Barnabas, Ac 15:37–39. He is with Paul during the latter's first imprisonment in Rome, Col 4:10; Phm 24, and at the end of his life Paul asks for his "useful" help, 2 Tm 4:11. He is also found in the company of Peter, 1 P 5:13.

MAROTH (1), "Bitterness" (cf. Marah), a town in the lowlands of Judah, Mi 1:12.

[MARRATIM]. See: MERATHAIM.

MARSENA (1), a Persian name, an officer mentioned with: MEMUCAN.

MARTHA (13), after the Aram. "Mistress," sister of Mary and Lazarus, of Bethany. Mistress of a hospitable, active, even busy house, Lk 10:38–41; Jn 12:2. Martha is also the person who, at the death of her brother, acknowledges Jesus as Messiah and Son of God and the source of all resurrection, Jn 11:1–5, 19–39.

MARY, Hb. *Miryam,* Gr. *Maria*(*m*), "Seeress *or* Lady"?

1. **Miriam** (14), sister of Moses and Aaron, daughter of Amram and Jochebed, of the tribe of Levi, Nb 26:59// 1 Ch 5:29; cf. Ex 2:1–8, a prophetess, Ex 15:20–21, joins Aaron in rebelling against Moses, who had married a Cushite woman, is struck with leprosy, then healed at Moses' prayer, Nb 12:1–15; cf. Dt 24:9, dies at Kadesh, Nb 20:1. She

is mentioned with Moses and Aaron in Mi 6:4 as leader of Israel in the Exodus from Egypt. Other prophetesses: DEBORAH 2; HANNAH 3; HULDAH; NOADIAH 2.

2. **Miriam** (1), a Calebite, son (or daughter) of Bithiah, daughter of Pharaoh, 1 Ch 4:17.

3. **Mary** (19), mother of Jesus.

a. In the "Infancy Gospels"

Mt and Lk: Mary, wife of Joseph, Mt 1:16, is pregnant by the action of the Holy Spirit, Mt 1:18; Lk 1:27, 35, at Bethlehem bears a son, Jesus, Mt 1:25; 2:1; Lk 2:4–7, then lives at Nazareth, Mt 2:23; Lk 2:39.

Mt: Joseph refuses to repudiate Mary, who is pregnant, 1:19–24. After the birth of Jesus, the wise men visit Mary, 2:11, who takes refuge for a while in Egypt with Joseph and Jesus, 2:13–15, then goes back to Nazareth, 2:19–23.

Lk: The angel Gabriel tells Mary, "so highly favoured," 1:28, of the birth of Jesus, 1:26–37; she agrees, calling herself "the handmaid of the Lord," 1:38. She goes to visit her cousin Elizabeth, 1:39–56, and in her presence proclaims her gratitude in the *Magnificat*. After giving birth to Jesus, she receives the visit of the shepherds, 2:16. In the temple, hearing with amazement what they say of the child, she learns from Simeon that she herself will suffer in the drama centered around her son, 2:22–34. If she does not understand the answer Jesus gives her when he stays behind in the temple at the age of twelve, without his parents' knowing it, yet "she treasured all these things and pondered them in her heart," 2:19, 41–51.

b. In the rest of the NT

Mary comes on the scene several times during the public life of Jesus: she accompanies him to the marriage at Cana, Jn 2:1–5, then to Capernaum, Jn 2:12; one day when she wants to talk to him, Jesus says that "anyone who does the will of my Father in heaven, he is . . . my mother," Mt 12:46–50//Mk 3:31–35//Lk 8:19–21; on another occasion, to a woman in the audience who extols Mary's happiness at having such a son, Lk 11:27; cf. 1:48, Jesus replies that true happiness comes from hearing and observing the word of God. Surprised at finding Jesus so wise and performing such miracles, the people of Nazareth exclaim: "Is not his mother the woman called Mary?" Mt 13:55//Mk 6:7; cf. Jn 6:42. Mary stands near the cross, from which the dying Jesus entrusts her to the beloved disciple and the beloved disciple to her, Jn 19:25–27. After the Ascension "the mother of Jesus" joins "in continuous prayer" with the Apostles and some women, Ac 1:14.

In Galatians, Paul reminds his readers that "God sent his Son, born of a woman," Ga 4:4; cf. Is 7:14; Mi 5:2. Finally some see in the woman of Rv 12 an evocation of Mary either as mother of the Messiah or as a figure of the Church.

4. **Mary** (14) **of Magdala** or **the Magdalene** (12). Delivered by Jesus from "seven demons," Lk 8:2; Mk 16:9 (note that Luke does not identify her with the sinful woman of 7:36–50, whose name he tactfully suppresses), Mary is one of the group of women who accompany Jesus since the days in Galilee, Lk 8:2, stand by the cross, Mt 27:55–56//Mk 15:40–41//Jn 19:25; cf. Lk 23:49, attend to the burial, Mt 27:61//Mk 15:4; cf. Lk 23:56, buy spices for anointing the corpse, Mk 16:1, and are at the empty tomb, Mt 28:1 ff.//Mk 16:2 ff.//Jn 20:1–2; cf. Lk 24:1 ff.

Mary Magdalene is the first to see the risen Jesus, Jn 20:11–18; Mk 16:9, and is one of the women who bring the Apostles the news of the resurrection, Lk 24:9–10; Jn 20:18; cf. Mt 28:8; Mk 16:8.

5. **Mary** (11), of Bethany, sister of Martha and Lazarus, Jn 11:1–5. Shown several times at the feet of Jesus, Lk

10:39; Jn 11:32; 12:3, Mary proves more attentive in listening to the words of Jesus than in helping in the tasks of the house. Jesus comments: "It is Mary who has chosen the better part; it is not to be taken from her," Lk 10:38–42. When Lazarus has died, we find her in the house surrounded by Jews who have come to comfort her, Jn 11:19–20, 45. At her sister's summons she immediately goes to Jesus, who is moved by her tears and himself weeps, Jn 11:18–35. A few days before the death of Jesus, during a meal at Bethany, Mary pours perfume over his feet, Jn 12:1–7; cf. 11:2. This "anointing at Bethany" is regarded by most exegetes as a different incident from the one narrated in Lk 7:36–50, and the anonymous sinful woman of Luke is not to be identified with Mary of Bethany or with Mary Magdalene. Yet the view that sees the three women as one and same person, Mary of Magdala, lacks neither defenders nor arguments.

6. **Mary** (7) **mother of James** (4), Mt 27:56; Mk 15:40; 16:1; Lk 24:10, **and of Joseph** (1), Mt 27:56, or **Joset** (2), Mk 15:40, 47.

= ? **Mary the [wife] of Clopas** (1), sister of Mary, mother of Jesus, Jn 19:25. Except in Mk 16:9; Lk 8:2, and Jn 20, she is associated with: MARY 4.

7. **Mary** (1), mother of Mark. It is in her house at Jerusalem that the first disciples of Jesus gather and that Peter seeks refuge when he emerges from prison, Ac 12:12–17.

Her servant: RHODA.

8. **Mary** (1), a Christian woman active at Rome, Rm 16:6.

MASCARA (1), Hb. *Keren ha-Pûk* (cf. Carnaim), the last of the three daughters born to Job after his testing and to whom he gives inheritance rights, Jb 42:14.

MASH (1), one of the four sons of Aram, son of Shem, Gn 10:23. An Aramaean tribe.

= **Meshech** (1), 1 Ch 1:17.

MASHAL (1). See: MISHAL.

MASREKAH (2), in Edom, a royal city of Samlah, Gn 36:36//1 Ch 1:47.

MASSA (4). See: MASSAH 1.

MASSAH, Massa.

1. **Massa** (4), Hb. *Massa'*, "Oracle," one of the twelve sons of Ishmael, Gn 25:14//1 Ch 1:30; an Ishmaelite tribe of northern Arabia, Pr 30:1; 31:1.

2. **Massah** (1), Hb. *Massah,* "Trial, temptation," symbolic name of a spring on the route of the Exodus, at which Israel puts God to the test by its complaining, Ex 17:7; Dt 6:16; 9:22; 33:8; Ps 95:8–9; cf. Heb 3:8–9, 15, 17.

See: MARAH 1; MERIBAH; REPHIDIM.

MATRED (2), "Who pursues," father (or mother) of: MEHEBABEL.

MATRI (2), the Benjaminite clan of King Saul, 1 S 10:21.

MATTAN, "Gift," abbrev. of *Mattaniah,* Gr. *Matthan* (cf. Nathan).

1. **Mattan** (2), a priest of Baal who is killed at the same time as Athaliah, 2 K 11:18//2 Ch 23:17.

2. **Mattan** (1), father of: SHEPHATIAH 5.

3. **Matthan** (2), an ancestor of Jesus acc. to Mt 1:15.

MATTANAH (2), "Donation" (cf. Nathan), a stage of the Exodus before Transjordania, Nb 21:18.

MATTANIAH, "Gift of God" (cf. Nathan. See Dositheus).

1. **Mattaniah** (1), name, before his accession to the throne, of: ZEDEKIAH 4.

2. **Mattaniah** (2), of the sons of Heman, leader of the ninth class of cantors, 1 Ch 25:4, 16.

3. **Mattaniah** (1), of the sons of Asaph, ancestor of: JAHAZIEL 4.

4. **Mattaniah** (1), a Levite of the sons of Asaph, takes part in the purification

of the temple during the reform of King Hezekiah, 2 Ch 29:13.

5. **Mattaniah** (6) **son of Micah** (3) or **Micaiah** (1), **son of Zaccur** (1)—or **of Zichri** (1) or **of Zabdi** (1)—**son of Asaph** (3), a cantor, Ne 12:8, 25, lives in Jerusalem after returning from the exile, 1 Ch 9:15//Ne 11:17.

Ancestor of: UZZI 5; ZECHARIAH 26.

6. **Mattaniah** (1), ancestor of: HANAN 6.

7. **Mattaniah** (4), four Israelites married to foreign wives, whom they put away: the first, of the sons of Elam, Ezr 10:26; the second, of the sons of Zattu, 10:27; the third, of the sons of Pahath-moab, 10:30; the fourth, of the sons of Bani, 10:37.

MATTATHA (1), an ancestor of Jesus acc. to Lk 3:31.

MATTATHIAS. See: MATTITHIAH.

MATTATTAH (1), (cf. Nathan), an Israelite of the sons of Hashum, married to a foreign wife, whom he puts away, Ezr 10:33.

MATTENAI, abbrev. of *Mattaniah* (cf. Nathan).

1. **Mattenai** (2), two Israelites married to foreign wives, whom they put away: the first, of the sons of Hashum, Ezr 10:33; the second of the sons of Bani, 10:37.

2. **Mattenai** (1), head of the priestly family of Joiarib in the time of the high priest Joiakim, Ne 12:19.

MATTHAN (1). See: MATTAN 3.

MATTHAT (1), an ancestor of Jesus acc. to Lk 3:29.

MATTHEW (5), Gr. *Matthaios,* derived from Hb. *Mattai* or *Matya,* abbrev. of *Mattenai* or *Mattithiah* (cf. Nathan). See: TWELVE; List, page 000. A tax collector at Capernaum who becomes one of the twelve Apostles, Mt 9:9, among whom he is listed in seventh, Mk 3:18; Lk 6:15, or eighth place, Ac 1:13.

= **Levi** (2), Lk 5:27, 29, or **Levi son of Alphaeus** (1), Mk 2:14.

MATTHIAS (2), abbrev. of *Mattathias* (cf. Nathan), a disciple chosen instead of Joseph Barsabbas to take the place of Judas Iscariot and thus complete the group of twelve Apostles, Ac 1:22–26.

See: TWELVE; List, page 417.

MATTITHIAH, Mattathias, Gr. *Mattathias,* "Gift of Yah" (cf. Nathan).

1. **Mattithiah, the first-born of Shallum the Korahite** (1), a Levite, 1 Ch 9:31.

2. **Mattithiah** (3), a Levite gatekeeper in the service of the Ark, 1 Ch 15:18, a player of the octave lyre, 15:21; 16:5.

3. **Mattithiah** (2), of the sons of Jeduthun, head of the fourteenth class of cantors, 1 Ch 25:3, 21.

4. **Mattithiah** (1), an Israelite of the sons of Nebo, married to a foreign woman, whom he puts away, Ezr 10:43.

5. **Mattithiah** (1), a lay notable who stands at Ezra's right during the solemn reading of the Law, Ne 8:4.

6. **Mattathias** (11) **son of John, son of Simeon, a priest of the line of Joarib** (1), settled at Modein, father of five sons, Judas Maccabaeus among them, 1 M 2:1–5. Refusing to abandon "the Law and its observances," he takes the lead in the resistance to hellenism, takes to the hills, and launches a holy war, 1 M 2:6–28, 39–48. Dies a few months later, in 166 B.C., 1 M 2:69–70.

Father of: ELEAZAR 9; JOHN 19; JONATHAN 17; JUDAH 7; SIMEON 5.

7. **Mattathias son of Absalom** (1), a general in the army of Judas Maccabaeus, 1 M 11:70.

8. **Mattathias** (1), son of Simon Maccabaeus, grandson of: MATTATHIAS 6, brother of John Hyrcanus, assassinated with his father and his brother Judas by Ptolemy, son of Abubus, 1 M 16:14.

9. **Mattathias** (1), one of the three

messengers sent by Nicanor to the Jews, 2 M 14:19.

10. **Mattathias** (2), two ancestors of Jesus acc. to Lk 3:25–26.

MECHERAH (from) (1), location unknown. Native place of: HEPHER 4.

MECONAH (1), "Residence" (cf. Jehoiachin), a town of Judah, Ne 11:28. Not identified.

MEDAD (2), associated with Eldad, both of them Israelites who have the gift of prophecy, Nb 11:26–27.

MEDAN (2), from an Accad. root *dananu,* "be strong" (cf. Dannah), one of the six sons of Abraham by his concubine Keturah, Gn 25:2//1 Ch 1:32.

MEDEBA (6), Hb. *Medba',* Gr. *Mēdaba,* a former town of Moab, destroyed, Nb 21:30, assigned to Reuben, Jos 13:9, 16, mentioned in the first campaign of David against the Ammonites, 1 Ch 19:7, and passing again into Moabite hands, Is 15:2. Occupied at the beginning of the Maccabaean period by the Arabian tribe of the sons of Jambri, 1 M 9:36. Today *Madaba,* 32 km S of Amman.

MEDES, MEDIA (56), Hb. *Madai,* an Iranian tribe in NE Babylonia. In the list of peoples the Medes are one of the seven sons of Japheth, Gn 10:2//1 Ch 1:5. The Assyrians deport as far as Media some Israelites from the fallen kingdom of Samaria, 2 K 17:6//18:11; cf. Tb 1:14–15; 5:2–10; 6:6, 10; 11:15; 14:4, 12, 15. It is under attack from Media that Babylon will fall, acc. to the prophets, Is 13:17; 21:2; Jr 51:11, 28. But the kings of the Medes will be punished in their turn, Jr 25:25. Antiochus the Great loses Media (corruption of *Mysia?*), 1 M 8:8. King Demetrius II invades it but is captured there, 1 M 14:1–3. Medes and Persians are associated in Jdt 16:10; Est 1:3–19; 10:2; Dn 5:28; 6:9–16; 8:20; cf. 7:5–6; 1 M 6:56.

Jews from Media are among those present in Jerusalem on the first Christian Pentecost, Ac 2:9.

Kings: ARPHAXAD; ARSACES; ASTYAGES; CYAXARES; DARIUS 3.

Mede: DARIUS 4.

Cities: ECBATANA; RHAGES.

MEDIA. See: MEDES.

[MEDITERRANEAN] (Sea), often paralleled with the: DEAD SEA, is designated by various expressions that indicate in a broad manner the western frontier of Canaan, the Promised Land, or of one of the coastal tribes.

= **Great Sea** (12), Hb. *ha-yam ha-gadôl,* Nb 34:6–7; Jos 1:4; 9:1; 15:12, 47; 23:4; Ezk 47:15, 19–20; 48:28. In Ezk 47:10 *Great Sea* refers to the Mediterranean as such; cf. *the sea,* 1 K 5:23; and so forth.

= **Western Sea** (4), Hb. *ha-yam ha-'aharôn,* Dt 11:24; 34:2; Jl 2:20; Zc 14:8.

= **The Philistine Sea** (1), Hb. *yam Pelishtim,* Ex 23:31.

Parts of the Mediterranean: ADRIATIC; seas of Cilicia and Pamphylia, Ac 27:5.

Islands: ARVAD; CAUDA; CHIOS; COS; CRETE; CYPRUS; LESBOS; MALTA; PATMOS; RHODES; SAMOS; SAMOTHRACE; SICILY.

Ports: ASSOS; ATHENS; ATTALIA; CENCHREAE; CAESAREA 1; DELOS; EPHESUS; JOPPA; MILETUS; NEAPOLIS; PUTEOLI; SELEUCIA; SIDON; TROAS; TYRE.

MEGIDDO (12), (cf. Magdiel), an important Canaanite royal city, SE of Carmel, dominating the plain of Jezreel, on the route from Egypt to Syria and Mesopotamia, frequently associated with Taanach, Jos 12:21; Jg 5:19, and so on, assigned to Manasseh, Issachar, and Asher, but independent for a long time, Jos 17:11–12; Jg 1:27; 1 Ch 7:29. Rebuilt by Solomon, 1 K 9:15; in the fifth district of his kingdom, 1 K 4:12. King Ahaziah of Judah takes refuge there when wounded and dies there, 2 K 9:27.

Josiah is killed there by Pharaoh Neco when he attempts to intercept him, 2 K 23:29–30//2 Ch 35:22. On its fertile plain the cult of the Phoenician god Hadad-rimmon is celebrated, Zc 12:11. Today *Tell el-Mutasellim.*

See: ARMAGEDDON.

MEHALALEL (1). See: MAHALALEL 2.

MEHETABEL, Hb. *Mehetab'el,* "God does good" (cf. Jotbah; Jotbathah).

1. **Mehetabel daughter of Matred from** (Hb. *daughter of*) **Me-zahab** (2), wife of the king of Edom: HADAD 3.

2. **Mehetabel** (1), an ancestor of: SHEMAIAH 22.

MEHIDA (2), head of a family of "oblates" who return from the exile, Ezr 2:52//Ne 7:54.

MEHIR (1), "Wages, Price," son of Chelub (= Caleb) and father of Eshton, 1 Ch 4:11.

MEHOLAH (2), "Dance." See: ABEL-MEHOLAH.

MEHUJAEL (2), "God causes to live" (cf. Jeiel). See: MAHALALEL 1.

MEHUMAN (1) and **Biztha, Harbona, Bigtha, Abagtha, Zethar** and **Carkas** (1× each except for Harbona, who is mentioned again in Est 7:9): the seven eunuchs in the personal service of King Ahasuerus, Est 1:10–15. Est Gr. gives the following list: *Hamān, Bazān, Tharra, Borazē, Zatholta, Abataza, Tharabē.*

ME-JARKON (1), "Waters of the Jarkon," a town on the NW border of Dan, Jos 19:46. Some correct the passage acc. to the Gr.

MELATIAH (1), "Yah has rescued" (cf. Pelet), **of Gibeon** (1), a volunteer in the rebuilding the wall of Jerusalem, Ne 3:7.

MELCHI (2), "My King" (cf. Melech), two ancestors of Jesus acc. to Lk 3:24, 28.

MELCHIEL (1). See: MALCHIEL 2.

MELCHIZEDEK (11), "My King is justice" (cf. Melech; Zadok), **king of Salem** (3). In Gn 14:17–20, a brief and mysterious appearance, in the account of Lot's rescue, of this priest-king of Salem (probably Jerusalem), a worshipper of the Most High God, who brings bread and wine and pronounces a blessing on Abraham, who then gives him a tithe of the booty he has taken. In Ps 110:4 Melchizedek is a figure of David, who is, in turn, a figure of the priest-king Messiah.

In Heb, Melchizedek is a prophetic figure of Christ. Having "no father, mother or ancestry," Melchizedek is outside of time, becomes like the Son of God, and exercises an eternal priesthood, 7:1–3. By this fact the priesthood of Melchizedek is superior to that of the Jewish priests: not only are the latter mortal, but in the person of their ancestor Abraham they gave tithes to Melchizedek and received his blessing, 7:4–10. Jesus who, like Melchizedek, is not of priestly descent, is a "priest of the order of Melchizedek," 7:11–19; cf. 5:6, 10; 6:20.

MELEA (1), an ancestor of Jesus acc. to Lk 3:31.

MELECH (2), Hb. *Melek,* "King" (cf. Abimelech; Adrammelech; Ahimelech; Allammelech; Anammelech; Ebed-melech; Elimelech; Iamleku; Jamlech; King; Malcam; Malcath; Malchiah; Malchiel; Malchiram; Malchishua; Malchus; Malluch; Melchi; Melchizedek; Milcah; Milcom; Molech; Nathan-melech), one of the sons of Micah, grandson of King Saul, 1 Ch 8:35//9:41.

[MELKART], a god of the underworld, venerated at Tyre and Carthage. In his honor games were celebrated every four years. Assimilated to: HERCULES.

MEMMIUS (1), full name **Quintus Memmius,** one of the Roman ambassadors to Antioch and authors of a letter to the Jews regarding the peace treaty with the Romans, 2 M 11:34.

MEMPHIS (1), Gr. name for the Hb. *Noph* (7) or *Moph* (1); Egypt. *Mn-nfr,* Accad. *Mempi, Mimpi,* Jdt 1:10; Ho 9:6.

= **Noph** (7), where there is a colony of Judaean refugees, Jr 44:1, is witness to the humiliation of Israel, Jr 2:16, but will be destroyed in its turn, Is 19:13; Jr 46:14, 19; Ezk 30:13, 16 (Hb.).

MEMUCAN (3) and **Carshena, Shethar, Admatha, Tarshish, Meres, Marsena,** the seven administrators of Persia and Media who have access to the presence of King Ahaseurus, Est 1:14–21. Est Gr. mentions along with *Mouchaios* (= *Memucan*) (2), only three officials: *Arkessios, Sarsathaios* and *Malesear.*

MENAHEM, Gr. *Manaen,* "Consoler" (cf. Nahum).

1. **Menahem** (8), **son of Gadi** (2), sixteenth king of Israel (743–738), founder of the fifth dynasty. He succeeds Shallum after assassinating him, inflicts harsh punishment on the town of Tappuah for resisting him, is supported by Tiglath-pileser, king of Assyria, to whom he pays a heavy tribute; at his death his son Pekahiah succeeds to the throne, 2 K 15:14–22.

Father of: PEKAHIAH.

2. **Manaen** (1), "who had been brought up with Herod the tetrarch," one of the "prophets and teachers" of the Church of Antioch, Ac 13:1.

MENELAUS (17), Gr. *Menelaos,* **brother of Simon** (1), of the priestly class of Bilgah. High priest from 172 to 163 B.C., traitor to his country and his office, he has the high priest Onias assassinated, 2 M 4:23–50, and guides Antiochus Epiphanes in the looting of the temple, 2 M 5:5–23. Peacemaking delegate of Antiochus Epiphanes to the Jewish senate, 2 M 11:27–32, but condemned by Antiochus Eupator to the punishment of ashes and executed at Beroea, 2 M 13:1–8.

MENESTHEUS (2), father of: APOLLONIUS 1.

MENI (1), "Apportionment, Destiny" (cf. Imnah 1–2), an otherwise unknown god, perhaps a god of destiny, Is 65:11.

MENNA (1), an ancestor of Jesus acc. to Lk 3:31.

[MEON]. See: BAAL-MEON; MEUNITES.

MEONOTHAI (2), one of the sons of Othniel, son of Kenaz, a descendant of Caleb, 1 Ch 4:13–14.

MEPHAATH (4), Hb. *Mepha'at* (cf. Japhia), a town of the tribe of Reuben, Jos 13:18, assigned to the Levites of the clan of Merari, Jos 21:37//1 Ch 6:64, then a town of Moab, Jr 48:21. Location uncertain.

MERAB (4), (cf. Rabbah), **daughter of Saul** (2), 1 S 18:19; 2 S 21:8 (var. *Merab;* Hb. *Mikal*), older sister of Michal, 1 S 14:49, promised to David but given to Adriel of Meholah, 1 S 18:17–19, to whom she bears five sons, 2 S 21:8–9.

MERAIAH (1), Hb. *Merayah,* derived from *Meriyyah,* "Loved by Yah," head of the priestly family of Seraiah in the time of the high priest Joiakim, Ne 12:12.

MERAIOTH (1), acc. to the genealogies either the father of the high priest Zadok, 1 Ch 9:11; Ne 11:11, or an ancestor of the same, 1 Ch 5:32–33; 6:37; Ezr 7:3.

MERANOTH (1). See: MERONOTH.

MERARI, an Egypt. name, "Beloved."

1. **Merari** (34), habitually presented as the last of the three sons of Levi, Gn 46:11//Ex 6:16; Nb 3:17; 1 Ch 5:27; 6:1. Eponymous ancestor of the **Merarites,** he constitutes one of the three great classes of Levites, along with his brothers Gershon and Kohath, with

whom he is always paralleled, Nb 26:57; 1 Ch 23:6. The Merarites are subdivided into two clans, the Mahlite and the Mushite, Nb 3:33; cf. 26:58. Acc. to one census they numbered 3,200, Nb 4:42–45. Their function in the service of the temple is specified in Nb 3:36–37; 4:31–33; 7:8; 10:17; cf. 1 Ch 15:6, 17; 26:10, 19. Twelve towns chosen from the tribes of Reuben, Gad, and Zebulun are reserved for them, Jos 21:7, 34–40//1 Ch 6:48, 62–66.

Ethan, one of the three great cantors, is given as a descendant of Merari, 1 Ch 6:29–32. See: List, page 416.

Father of: MAHLI and MUSHI.

2. **Merari** (2), a Simeonite, father of: JUDITH 2.

MERARITE (3), Nb 3:33, 35; 26:57, belonging to the clan of: MERARI 1.

MERATHAIM (1), "Twofold rebellion *or* Twofold bitterness" (cf. Marah), a Jewish deformation of the Babyl. *Marratim,* "Lagoon," the region around the mouth of the Tigris and Euphrates, Jr 50:21.

MERCURY. See: HERMES 1.

MERED (2), "Rebellion"?, son of Ezrah and husband of Bithiah, the daughter of Pharaoh; attached to Caleb, 1 Ch 4:17–18.

MEREMOTH, acc. to Ugar. "Moth has blessed" (cf. Meribbaal; Mot).

1. **Meremoth** (5) **son of Uriah** (3) **son of Hakkoz** (2), a priest who returns from the exile with Zerubbabel and Jeshua, Ne 12:3, receives the temple vessels brought by the exiles, Ezr 8:33, takes part in the rebuilding of the Jerusalem wall, Ne 3:4, 21, signs the pledge to observe the Law, Ne 10:6, and gives his name to a priestly family, Ne 12:15.

2. **Meremoth** (1), an Israelite of the sons of Bani, married to a foreign wife, whom he puts away, Ezr 10:36.

MERES (1), a Persian name?, an officer mentioned with: MEMUCAN.

MERIBAH (7), "Contention, Quarrel" (cf. Jarib).

Symbolic name of a spring that leaps from the rock at the touch of Moses' rod and at which the Israelites slake their thirst during the Exodus. Ex 17:1–7 locates the event at Rephidim (in the southern part of the Sinai wilderness), where Nb 20:1–13 locates the same episode at Kadesh, and Dt 32:51 at Meribah of Kadesh; cf. Nb 27:14. At this place of *grumbling,* Ex 17:2, 7, Moses and Aaron find themselves forbidden entry into the Promised Land, Nb 20:12, 24; 27:14. The episode at Meribah is also mentioned in Dt 33:8; Ps 81:8; 95:8; 106:32.

= **Meribah of Kadesh** (4), one of the places marking the southern frontier of the Promised Land, Ezk 47:19; 48:28.

Another name of this spring: MASSAH 2.

MERIBAH OF KADESH or **in Kadesh** or **Meribath-kadesh** (4), (cf. Meribah; Kadesh), Nb 27:14; Dt 32:51; Ezk 47:19; 48:28. See: MERIBAH.

MERIBATH-KADESH (1). See: MERIBAH OF KADESH.

MERIBBAAL, "Baal is champion *or* Baal is advocate"; acc. to Ugar., "Baal has blessed" (cf. Baal; Meremoth). Except in 1 Ch 8:34; 9:40, *Meribbaal* is a var. of Hb. *Mephibosheth*).

1. **Meribbaal** (1), one of the two sons of Saul and Rizpah, whom David hands over to the Gibeonites to be tortured, 2 S 21:8.

2. **Meribbaal** (18), **son of Jonathan** (6) **son of Saul** (4), 2 S 4:4; 21:7; 1 Ch 8:34//9:40. Crippled in both feet from the age of five, 2 S 4:4; 9:3, 13, received into the household of Machir, son of Ammiel, at Lo-debar, he is welcomed at court by David, who, in memory of Jonathan, restores to him all the estates of his grandfather Saul, 2 S 9. During the rebellion of Absalom, instead of accompanying David, who is forced to flee, he remains at Jerusalem. His servant Ziba

accuses him to David of cherishing secret hopes of regaining his grandfather's throne, 2 S 16:1–4. After Absalom's death Meribbaal succeeds in justifying himself, but David forces him to give half of his estates to Ziba, 2 S 19:25–31.

Father of: MICAH 1.

MERODACH (1), (cf. Mordecai; Evil-merodach; Merodach-baladan), biblical vocalization (acc. to Hb. *meborak,* "cursed") of *Marduk,* principal god of Babylon, habitually referred to by the name Bel, Jr 50:2.

MERODACH-BALADAN (2), Accad. *Marduk-apal-iddina,* "Marduk has given a son" (cf. Merodach; Baladan), **son of Baladan** (2), king of Babylon (721–710, 703). He sends an embassy to King Hezekiah of Judah to deliver letters and a gift, 2 K 20:12//Is 39:1–8.

MEROM (2), an old Canaanite town. It is at the **waters of Merom** that acc. to Jos 11:5–9 Joshua crushes the coalition of northern Canaanite kings against Israel. In Jos 11:1 and 12:19 the Gr. has *king of Merom* for Hb. *king of Madon.* A few km NW of Safed; cf. the modern *Meirun.*

MERONOTH (1) or **Meranoth** (1) **(of),** a town near Gibeon; native place of: JADON; JEHDEIAH 2.

MEROZ (1), Jg 5:23, a town cursed in the canticle of Deborah. S of Kedesh in Naphtali; today *Kh. Marus.*

MESALOTH (1), Gr. *Maisalōth,* from Hb. *Mesillôt,* "Paths," in the territory of Arbela; a town taken by the army of Bacchides, 1 M 9:2. W of the Sea of Chinnereth.

MESHA, Hb. 1: *Mesha'*; 2: *Mêsha'*; 3–4: *Mêsha'*, "[God] saves" (cf. Isaiah).

1. **Mesha** (1), habitat of the sons of Joktan, Arabian tribes, Gn 10:30. To be identified (?) with: MASSAH 1.

2. **Mesha** (1), a Benjaminite, head of a family in Moab, 1 Ch 8:9.

3. **Mesha** (1), firstborn of Caleb and father of Ziph, 1 Ch 2:42 (Gr. *Marisa*).

4. **Mesha** (1), **king of Moab** (4), pays the king of Israel a tribute of "a hundred thousand lambs and the wool of a hundred thousand rams." At the death of Ahab he rebels, but he is defeated by Jehoram, king of Israel, who is supported by the king of Judah (Jehoshaphat or, rather, his son Jehoram) and the king of Edom: besieged in his capital, Kir-hareseth, he sacrifices his son on the wall; panic lays hold of the conquerors, who depart, 2 K 3:4–27.

The stele of Mesha in the Louvre tells us that Moab was subject to Israel under Omri and that, under the son of Omri, King Mesha rebelled.

MESHACH (15), Gr. *Misach,* name given to: MISHAEL 3.

MESHECH

1. **Meshech** (9) and **Tubal,** two of the seven sons of Japheth, Gn 10:2 (var. *Moshek*)//1 Ch 1:5, trading with Tyre, Ezk 27:13. Peoples of Asia Minor: probably Phrygia and Cilicia or peoples on the coast of the Black Sea. Gog is said to be "prince of Rosh, Meshech and Tubal," Ezk 38:2–3; 39:1. Meshech and Tubal are also associated in Is 66:19 (Gr.) and Ezk 32:26. In Ps 120:5 Meshech (land of the Moschoi) is paralleled with Kedar.

2. **Meshech** (1). See: MASH.

MESHELEMIAH (4), "Yah has replaced" (cf. Salem). See: SHALLUM 11.

MESHEZABEL, Hb. *Meshezab'el,* "God saves" (cf. Nebushazban).

1. **Meshezabel** (1), ancestor of: MESHULLAM 14.

2. **Meshezabel** (1), a leader of the people and cosigner of the pledge to observe the Law, Ne 10:22.

3. **Meshezabel** (1), father of: PETHAHIAH 3.

MESHILLEMITH, Meshillemoth, "Replacement" (cf. Salem).

1. **Meshillemoth** (1), father of: BERECHIAH 3.

2. **Meshillemoth** (1) or **Meshillemith** (1), ancestor of the priest: AMASAI 4.

MESHOBAB (1), (cf. Jashub), a Simeonite, leader of a clan, 1 Ch 4:34; 38–41.

MESHULLAM, "Replaced" (cf. Salem).

1. **Meshullam** (1), ancestor of: SHAPHAN 1.

2. **Meshullam** (1), son of Zerubbabel, a descendant of King Jehoiachin, 1 Ch 3:19.

3. **Meshullam** (1), a Gadite, head of a family, 1 Ch 5:13.

4. **Meshullam** (1), a Benjaminite of the sons of Elpaal, head of a family at Jerusalem, 1 Ch 8:17.

5. **Meshullam** (2), a Benjaminite father of: SALLU 1.

6. **Meshullam son of Shephatiah son of Reuel son of Ibnijah** (1), a Benjaminite, head of a family at Jerusalem after the exile, 1 Ch 9:8.

7. **Meshullam** (2), a priest. See: SHALLUM 6.

8. **Meshullam** (1), 1 Ch 9:12, an ancestor of the priest: AMASAI 4.

9. **Meshullam** (1), a Levite of the clan of Kohath, one of the overseers in the restoration of the temple under Josiah, 2 Ch 34:12.

10. **Meshullam** (2), one of Ezra's messengers to Iddo, Ezr 8:16, one of his attendants during the solemn reading of the Law, Ne 8:4: one or two individuals.

11. **Meshullam** (1), one of those who oppose the procedure for the breaking of marriages with foreign women, Ezr 10:15.

12. **Meshullam** (1), an Israelite of the sons of Bigvai, married to a foreign woman, whom he puts away, Ezr 10:29.

13. **Meshullam son of Besodeiah** (1), takes part in the restoration of the gate of the New Quarter, Ne 3:6.

14. **Meshullam son of Berechiah** (3), **son of Meshezabel** (1), another volunteer in the reconstruction, Ne 3:4, 30; his daughter is married to Jehohanan, son of Tobiah the Ammonite, Ne 6:18.

15. **Meshullam** (1), a leader of the people, a cosigner of the pledge to observe the Law, Ne 10:21.

16. **Meshullam** (1), a priest, a cosigner of the pledge to observe the Law, Ne 10:8, a trumpeter at the dedication of the wall of Jerusalem, Ne 12:33: one or two individuals.

17. **Meshullam** (1), head of the priestly family of Ezra in the time of Joiakim, Ne 12:13.

18. **Meshullam** (1), head of the priestly family of Ginnethon in the time of Joiakim, Ne 12:16.

19. **Meshullam** (1). See: SHALLUM 11.

MESHULLEMETH (1), "Replaced" (cf. Salem), **daughter of Haruz** (1), from Jotbah, mother of King Amon of Judah, 2 K 21:19.

MESOPOTAMIA (6), Gr. *Mesopotamia,* "[Land] between the Rivers [Euphrates and Tigris]," designates:

a. either, in a broad sense, the area on both sides of the Tigris and Euphrates (*Lower* and *Upper Mesopotamia*), where there is a Jewish colony that is represented in Jerusalem at the first Christian Pentecost, Ac 2:9.

= **Beyond the River** (5), (eastern Transeuphratean area), the country from which God sends Abraham forth, Jos 24:2–3, 14–15; cf. Gn 12:1, and to which Israel will one day be exiled, 1 K 14:15;

b. or the lower part of this region (*Lower Mesopotamia*), the ancient land of the Chaldaeans, where Abraham lives before moving to Haran, Ac 7:2;

c. or, more usually, the region surrounded on three sides by the great bend in the upper Euphrates (*Upper Mesopotamia*), cf. Jdt 2:24, having Haran as its capital, the region that the patriarchs inhabit, Jdt 5:6–9.

= **Syrian Mesopotamia** (1), Jdt 8:26.

= **Aram Naharaiim** (5), "Aram of the Two Rivers," Gr. *Mesopotamia, Mesopotamia Syrias* or *Syria potamōn,* country of Abraham before his settlement in Canaan and to which he sends his servant to seek a wife for his son Isaac, Gn 24: 2–10. Native land of Balaam, Dt 23:5; cf. Nb 23:7. Kingdom of Cushan-rishathaim (acc. to Hb.). David several times defeats the army of Aram Naharaiim, 1 Ch 19:6; Ps 60:2.

= **Paddan-aram** (10), "Plain of Aram," Gr. *Mesopotamia* or *Mesopotamia Syrias,* a word perhaps explained by "the plains of Aram" in Ho 12:13. Native land of Bethuel, Isaac's father-in-law, Gn 25:20, to which Jacob goes in quest of a wife, Gn 28:2–7, where he becomes wealthy, Gn 31:18, where eleven of his sons are born, Gn 35:26; 46:15, a country that he leaves in order to return to Canaan, Gn 33:18; 35:9. In Dt 26:5 Jacob is called "a wandering Aramaean."

= **Paddan** (1), Gn 48:7.

Aramaeans [of Paddan-aram]: BETHUEL 1; LABAN 1.

= **Aram beyond the River [Euphrates]** (1), 2 S 10:16//1 Ch 19:6.

See: EUPHRATES; TIGRIS.

See: ASSYRIA; BABYLON; CHALDAEA.

MESSIAH. See: JESUS *b.*

METHUSELAH (6), Gr. *Mathousala,* Hb. *Metushelah,* "Man of [the god] Shelah *or* of the Javelin"? (cf. Shelah), son of Enoch and father of Lamech, the longest-lived of the antediluvian patriarchs (969 years), Gn 5:21–27 (priestly genealogy); cf. 1 Ch 1:3. An ancestor of Jesus acc. to Lk 3:37.

= **Methushael** (2), son of Mehujael and father of Lamech, Gn 4:18 (Yahwist genealogy).

METHUSHAEL (2), "Man of God," Gr. *Mathousala.* See: METHUSELAH.

MEUNITES (4), Hb. *Me'unim,* a tribe whose name suggests *Meon,* a town located SE of Petra, 2 Ch 20:1 (corrected by some acc. to Gr. *Minaioi* and transcribed as *Maonites* by others); 26:7. Among the "oblates" who return from the exile are some of the Meunites, Ezr 2:50//Ne 7:52.

ME-ZAHAB (2), "Waters of gold" (cf. Water Gate), place of origin (or ancestor) of: MEHETABEL 1.

MIBHAR (1), "Choice" (cf. Ibhar), **son of Hagri** (1), one of David's champions, 1 Ch 11:38.

MIBSAM

1. **Mibsam** (2), one of the twelve sons and clan leaders of Ishmael, Gn 25:13// 1 Ch 1:29.

2. **Mibsam** (1), a Simeonite, a descendant of Shaul and ancestor of Shimei, 1 Ch 4:25.

MIBZAR (2), "Fortress" (cf. Bezer), one of the leaders (or clans) of Edom, Gn 36:42//1 Ch 1:53.

MICA. See: MICAH 1–2.

MICAH, Mica, Micaiah, Micayehu, Hb. *Mika'* or *Mikah,* "Who is like . . . ?" (cf. Ex 15:11; Is 44:7), abbrev. of *Mikaya, Mikayahu, Mikayehu,* "Who is like Yah?" Gr. *Micha, Michaias,* or of *Mikael,* "Who is like God?" (cf. Michael). The name *Mica* or *Micah* in the following list takes various forms in Hb.: 1–2: *Mika';* 4–6 and 9: *Mikah;* 3: *Mika'* and *Mikah;* 7: *Mikah* and *Mikayehu;* 8: [K]*Mikayah,* [Q]*Mikah.*

1. **Mica** (1) or **Micah** (4), a Benjaminite, son of Meribbaal, a descendant of King Saul, 2 S 9:12; 1 Ch 8:34//9:40, father of several sons, 1 Ch 8:35//9:41.

2. **Mica** (1), a Levite, cosigner of the pledge to observe the Law, Ne 10:12.

3. **Micah** (3) or **Micaiah** (1), a descendant of Asaph, father of: MATTANIAH 5, and ancestor of: UZZI 5; ZECHARIAH 26.

4. **Micah** (1), a Reubenite, a descendant of Joel and ancestor of Beerah, 1 Ch 5:5.

5. **Micah** (4), a Levite of the clan of Kohath, first son of Uzziel. The leader of the *sons of Micah* is Shamir, 1 Ch 23:20; 24:24–25.

6. **Micah** (19) or **Micayehu** (2), an Ephraimite who has a private sanctuary with an idol and a priest, Jg 17. Some scouts preparing for the migration of the Danites stop at Micah's house and consult his priest about the outcome of their activity, Jg 18:1–6. During their migration the Danites seize the idol and priest of Micah, who protests in vain, Jg 18:13–31.

7. **Micaiah** (18) **son of Imlah** (4), a prophet in the time of Ahab. Ahab, king of Israel, consults him before an expedition against Ramoth-gilead. Micaiah first gives an ironical answer. Then he describes the vision he has had of Yahweh and, alone against four hundred prophets of the court, predicts the failure of the expedition. This frankness earns him a blow from the prophet Zedekiah and imprisonment by the governor of the city, while Ahab leaves for the war where he will die, 1 K 22:5–28//2 Ch 18:7–27.

8. **Micah of Moresheth** (2), a prophet in the reigns of Jotham, Ahaz, and Hezekiah, Mi 1:1, a contemporary of Isaiah. One of the twelve "Minor Prophets." He is cited by name in Jr 26:18–19 for an oracle against Jerusalem, a prophecy of misfortune that nonetheless brought no vengeance upon him.

9. **Micah** (1) or **Micaiah** (1), father of: ACHBOR 2.

10. **Micaiah** (1), a priest, a trumpeter at the dedication of the wall of Jerusalem, Ne 12:41.

11. **Micaiah daughter of Uriel** (1). See: MAACAH 9.

12. **Micaiah** (1), one of the five officers whom King Jehoshaphat sends with two priests and eight Levites to instruct the towns of Judah in the Law, 2 Ch 17:7–9.

13. **Micaiah** (2) **son of Gemariah, son of Shaphan** (1), reports to the officials of King Jehoiakim, among them his own father, what he has just heard during the reading of Jeremiah's oracles, Jr 36:11–13.

14. **Micah** (1), father of: UZZIAH 7.

MICAIAH. See: MICAH 3, 7, 9–13.

MICAYEHU. See: MICAH 6.

MICHAEL, "Who is like God?" (cf. Micah; Michal; Mishael).

1. **Michael** (1), father of: SETHUR.

2. **Michael** (1), an ancestor of Asaph the cantor, 1 Ch 6:25.

3. **Michael** (2), an Issacharite, one of the five military leaders of the sons of Uzzi, 1 Ch 7:3–5. Father of: OMRI 3.

4. **Michael** (1), a Benjaminite of the sons of Beriah, head of a family in Jerusalem, 1 Ch 8:16.

5. **Michael** (1), a Manassite, a fighting man who rallies to David, an officer in the army, 1 Ch 12:21.

6. **Michael** (1), one of the six sons of King Jehoshaphat of Judah who are assassinated by their eldest brother, Jehoram, after his accession to the throne, 2 Ch 21:2–4, 13.

7. **Michael** (1), a Gadite, head of a family, 1 Ch 5:13.

8. **Ben-michael** (1), a Gadite of the sons of Abihail, 1 Ch 5:14.

9. **Michael** (1), father of: ZEBADIAH 8.

10. **Michael** (5), guardian angel of the people of God, called "prince," Dn 10:13, 21; 12:1, "archangel," adversary of Satan, Jude 9 (cf. Zc 3:1–2); Rv 12:7.

MICHAL (18), abbrev. of *Michael,* **daughter of Saul** (8), younger sister of Merab, 1 S 14:49, falls in love with David, 18:20–28, who wins her for his wife after killing 200 Philistines, 18:27. She saves David's life when he is threatened with death by Saul, 19:11–17. Saul then gives her as wife to Palti, son of Laish, 25:44. After Saul's death David claims her from Ishbaal, son of Saul, 2 S 3:13–16, but henceforth stays aloof from this woman, who scorns his behavior, 2 S 6:16–23; cf. 1 Ch 15:29. In 2 S 21:8, Hb. *Mikal;* var. *Merab.*

MICHMASH (12), Gr. *Machmas,* "Hidden place," a town north of Jerusalem, cf. Is 10:28, where Jonathan, son of Saul, distinguishes himself in a victorious battle against the Philistines, 1 S 13:2–23; 14:5, 31. One hundred and twenty-two men of Michmash return from the exile with Zerubbabel, Ezr 2:27//Ne 7:31. Some Benjaminites reside in this town, Ne 11:31. Jonathan, brother of Judas Maccabaeus, settles here and begins to "judge the people," 1 M 9:73. 12 km N of Jerusalem. Facing Michmash is: BOZEZ.

MICHMETATH (2), **opposite Shechem** (1), a peculiarity of the terrain or a town on the border of Ephraim and Manasseh, Jos 16:6; 17:7.

MICHRI (1), a Benjaminite, an ancestor of: ELAH 5.

MIDDIN (1), a town in the wilderness of Judah, Jos 15:61.

MIDDLE GATE (1), Hb. *Tavek* (cf. Hazer-hat-ticon), at Jerusalem, probably in the interior of the city. Nebuchadnezzar's officers establish their quarters there, Jr 39:3.

MIDIAN (63), Hb. *Midyân,* one of the six sons of Abraham and his concubine Keturah, Gn 25:2//1 Ch 1:32. Midian's sons are listed in Gn 25:4//1 Ch 1:33. Nomadic tribes usually located east of the Gulf of Aqaba, more probably in the Sinai peninsula, cf. 1 K 11:18; Ha 3:6–7. Defeat of Midian by Edom in Moab, Gn 36:35//1 Ch 1:46.

Moses goes into exile in Midian, Ex 2:15//Ac 7:29, where he marries the daughter of a priest of Midian, Ex 2:16–18; from there God sends him back to Egypt to free his people, Ex 4:19 ff. As Israel approaches, the elders of Moab and Midian consult Balaam, Nb 22:4, 7 ff. — Affair of the Midianite woman Cozbi and the Israelite Zimri, Nb 25:6–18; cf. 1 M 2:26. — Holy war against Midian: massacre of the five kings of Midian, Nb 31:1–12; cf. Jos 13:21. To end Midianite oppression of Israel, Jg 6:1–16, two victorious campaigns of Gideon: west of the Jordan, with the execution of the two Midianite chieftains, Oreb and Zeeb, Jg 6:33; 7:1–8:3; east of the Jordan, with the execution of the two kings of Midian, Zebah and Zalmunna, Jg 8:4–28; cf. 9:17; 10:12; Ps 83:10–12; Is 9:3 ("day of Midian"); 10:26. Midian is crushed by Holofernes, Jdt 2:26.

A trading people, Gn 37:28, 36; Ba 3:23; cf. Is 60:6.

A possible archaic name of Midian: CUSHAN.

Native land of: JETHRO; REUEL 2.

MIDIANITE (8), Gn 37:28, 36; Nb 10:29; 25:6, 14–15, 17; 31:2, of or from: MIDIAN.

MIGDAL-EDER, "Tower of the Flock" (cf. Gedaliah).

1. **Migdal-eder** (1), S of Bethel. It is in this area that Reuben commits incest with Bilhah, Jacob's concubine, Gn 35:21.

2. **Tower of the Flock** (1), symbolic name for Jerusalem, Mi 4:8.

MIGDALEL (1), "Tower of God" (cf. Gedaliah), a fortified town in Naphtali, Jos 19:38.

MIGDAL-GAD (1), "Tower of Gad" (cf. Gad; Gedaliah), a town in the lowlands of Judah, Jos 15:37.

MIGDAL-SHECHEM (3), "Tower of Shechem" (cf. Gedaliah; Shechem), doubtless the acropolis of Shechem, Jg 9:46, 47, 49.

= probably **Beth-millo** (3), Jg 9:6, 20.

MIGDOL (6), "Tower" (cf. Gedaliah), a frontier town in the extreme NE of Egypt. The Israelites camp near it during the Exodus, Ex 14:2; Nb 33:7. Judaeans live there in the time of Jeremiah, Jr 44:1. The ruin of the city is foretold, Jr 46:14. The expression *from Migdol to Syene* indicates the northern and southern frontiers of Egypt, Ezk 29:10; 30:6.

MIGHTY. See: ALMIGHTY.

MIGRON (2), a place near Michmash, in Benjamin, Is 10:28. In 1 S 14:2 some correct Hb. *at Migron* to *near the threshing floor.*

MIJAMIN (cf. Jamin?).

1. **Mijamin** (1), head of the fifth priestly class, 1 Ch 24:9.

2. **Mijamin** (2), a priest who returns from the exile with Zerubbabel, Ne 12:5, and is a cosigner of the pledge to observe the Law, Ne 10:8.

= **Miniamin** (1), name of a priestly family in the time of Joiakim, Ne 12:17.

3. **Mijamin** (1), an Israelite of the sons of Parosh, married to a foreign wife, whom he puts away, Ezr 10:25.

4. **Mijamin** (1), a priest, a trumpeter at the dedication of the Jerusalem wall, Ne 12:34.

MIKLOTH (4), a Benjaminite, father of Shimeah, granduncle of Saul, 1 Ch 8:31 (restored acc. to 9:37), 32//9:37–38.

MIKNEIAH (2), "Possession of Yah" (cf. Elkanah), a Levite gatekeeper in the service of the Ark, 1 Ch 15:18, a player of the octave lyre, 15:21.

MILALAI (1), a Levite, a son of Asaph (?), an instrumentalist at the dedication of the wall of Jerusalem, Ne 12:36.

MILCAH, "Queen" (cf. Melech).

1. **Milcah** (7), **daughter of Haran** (1), Gn 11:28, gives eight sons to Nahor, a brother of Abraham, Gn 22:20–23; one of these is Bethuel, father of Rebekah, Gn 24:15, 24, 47.

2. **Milcah** (4), Nb 26:33; 27:1; 36:11; Jos 17:3, in Manasseh, one of the five daughters of: ZELOPHEHAD.

MILCOM (5), "King" (cf. Melech), national god of the Ammonites, **the Ammonite abomination** (3). After the capture of Rabbah, David takes the precious stone that adorned the head of the god's statue, 2 S 12:30//1 Ch 20:2 (acc. to Gr.). Later, Solomon venerates Milcom, 1 K 11:5, 33, builds a sanctuary for him, 1 K 11:7 (acc. to Gr.; Hb. *Molek*); King Josiah profanes it, 2 K 23:13, while at the same time Zephaniah denounces the cult of Milcom, Zp 1:5 (corr. of Hb. *Melek*).

MILETUS (3), a port in Caria, on the west coast of Asia Minor, 50 km S of Ephesus. On his return from his third missionary journey Paul summons the elders of the church of Ephesus there and makes an important address that is his pastoral testament, Ac 20:15–38. At the end of his life, Paul passes through Miletus again and leaves Trophimus ill there, 2 Tm 4:20.

MILLO (6), "Terrace *or* Embankment" (cf. Imlah). Mentioned by an anachronism in 2 S 5:9 and 1 Ch 11:8, it was in fact built under Solomon, 1 K 9:15, 24; 11:27, and restored under Hezekiah, 2 Ch 32:5. It was probably a fortified earthen platform or embankment, N of the city of David, at Jerusalem.

= probably **Beth-millo** (1), where King Jehoash is assassinated, 2 K 12:21.

MINIAMIN (cf. Jamin?).

1. **Miniamin** (1), one of the six Levites assigned to assist Kore, son of Imnah, in the distribution of food in the time of King Hezekiah, 2 Ch 31:15.

2. **Miniamin** (1), a priest, a trumpeter at the dedication of the wall of Jerusalem, Ne 12:41.

3. **Miniamin** (1). See: MIJAMIN 2.

MINNI (1), Jr 51:27. A region of Armenia, around Lake Van.

MINNITH (2), a town in the country of Ammon, Jg 11:33, which gives its name to a variety of grain, Ezk 27:17. 15 km SW of Rabbah.

MIRIAM. See: MARY 1–2.

MIRMAH (1), "Deceit," a Benjaminite, head of a family in Moab, 1 Ch 8:9.

MISHAEL, "Who belongs to God? *or* Who is what God is?" (cf. Michael).

1. **Mishael** (2), a Levite of the clan of Kohath, one of the three sons of Uzziel, Ex 6:22, appointed by Moses to remove the bodies of Nadab and Abihu from the sanctuary, Lv 10:4.

2. **Mishael** (1), a lay notable who stands on Ezra's left during the solemn reading of the Law, Ne 8:4.

3. **Mishael** (8), whose name is changed to **Meshach** (15), one of Daniel's three companions. See: HANANIAH 17.

MISHAL (2), a town in Asher, Jos 19:26, assigned to the Levites of the clan of Gershon, Jos 21:30.

= **Mashal** (1), 1 Ch 6:59.

MISHAM (1), a Benjaminite of the sons of Elpaal, settled in the area of Lud (= Lod), 1 Ch 8:12.

MISHMA, "Hearsay, Rumor" (cf. Shemaiah).

1. **Mishma** (2), one of the twelve sons or clan leaders of Ishmael, Gn 25:14//1 Ch 1:30.

2. **Mishma** (2), a Simeonite, a descendant of Shaul and ancestor of Shimei, 1 Ch 4:25.

MISHMANNAH (1), "Fat morsel, Good morsel" (cf. Gethsemane), a Gadite who rallies to David before the latter becomes king, 1 Ch 12:11.

MISHRAITES (1), Hb. *Mishra'i,* a clan of Judah, descended from Shobal, 1 Ch 2:53.

MISPAR (1), "Number *or* Narrative" (cf. Hassophereth), one of the twelve leaders on the return from the exile, Ezr 2:2.

= **Mispereth** (1), Ne 7:7.

MISPERETH (1). See: MISPAR.

MISRAIM, Hb. name for Egypt; the dual form of the word includes *Upper* and *Lower Egypt.* Misraim is regarded as one of Ham's sons, Gn 10:6//1 Ch 1:8, and his posterity is given in Gn 10:13–14//1 Ch 1:11–12. See: EGYPT.

MISREPHOTH-MAIM (2), "Burnings of waters, *that is,* Saltpans," a town on the NW frontier of the Promised Land, Jos 11:8; 13:6. Between Tyre and Acco.

MITHKAH (2), "Sweetness," a stage of the Exodus between Sinai and Kadesh, Nb 33:28–29.

MITHNITE (1), indicating the (unknown) place of origin of: JOSHAPHAT 1.

[MITHRIDATES]. See: MITHREDATH 2.

MITHREDATH, a Persian name, "Gift of Minhras."

1. **Mithredath** (2), treasurer of Cyrus, king of Persia, commissioned with restoring to Sheshbazzar the furnishings of the temple, Ezr 1:8; an official of the king of Persia in Samaria, and one of the authors of the letter complaining to Artaxerxes about the rebuilding that is going on at Jerusalem, Ezr 4:7. One or two individuals.

2. **[Mithridates I],** king of the Parthians. See: ARSACES.

MITYLENE (1), a port on the island of Lesbos, in the Aegean Sea, where Paul spends a night on his return from his third missionary journey, Ac 20:14–15.

MIZPAH, Mizpeh, Gr. *Massēpha* or *Maspha,* "(The) Lookout, (The) Watchpost" (cf. Zaphon; Spies).

1. **Mizpah** (36) or **Mizpeh** (1), a town of Benjamin, Jos 18:26 (Hb. *Hamizpeh*).

A traditional place of assembly for Israel:—in the time of the Judges when Israel binds itself by oath to take vengeance for the crime of the people of Gibeah, Jg 20:1, 3; 21:1, 5, 8;—in the time of Samuel, when the people offer a libation and fast while Samuel offers sacrifice and "judges" Israel, 1 S 7:5–12; cf. 7:16, and when Saul is appointed king by lot, 1 S 10:17–27. King Asa fortifies the town and has a large cistern built there, 1 K 15:22//2 Ch 16:6; Jr 41:9. Gedaliah is appointed to govern the country there and dies there at the assassin's hand, Jr 40–41//2 K 25:23–25. In the time of Nehemiah the people of Mizpah, center for the district, take part in the rebuilding of the Jerusalem wall, Ne 3:7, 15, 19. It is at Mizpah (Gr. *Maspha*) that the Jews assemble to fast and hear the Law read before the battle of Emmaus, 1 M 3:46–57. 13 km N of Jerusalem, probably the modern *Tell en-Nasbeh.*

2. **Mizpah** (4), beyond the Jordan, south of the Jabbok, border between Laban and Jacob, Gn 31:48–49, native place of Jephthah, cf. Jg 10:17; 11:14; site of a sanctuary, Jg 11:11.

= **Mizpah in Gilead** (2), Jg 11:29.

= **Ramath-mizpeh** (1), a town of the Gadites, Jos 13:26.

3. **Mizpah** (2), "under Hermon," Jos 11:3, 8. Place not identified.

4. **Mizpah in Moab** (1), a town of Moab where David puts his parents to protect them from Saul's vengence, 1 S 22:3.

5. **Mizpah** (1), Ho 5:1, one of the preceding towns, but it is not possible to determine which one of them.

6. **Mizpeh** (1), a town in the lowlands of Judah, Jos 15:38.

MIZPEH. See: MIZPAH.

MIZZAH (3), last of the four sons and chiefs of Reuel in Edom, called sons of Basemath, wife of Esau, Gn 36:13, 17; 1 Ch 1:37.

MNASON, a Cypriot (1), "one of the earliest disciples," probably living halfway between Caesarea and Jerusalem, welcomes Paul to his home on the latter's return from his third missionary journey, Ac 21:16.

MOAB (193), Hb. *Mo'ab,* popular etymology acc. to Gn 19:37: "Sprung from the father *or* Water of the father" (cf. Pahath-moab).

Country and people of Transjordania, east of the Dead Sea. A fertile plateau sometimes called the **Plains of Moab,** Nb 22:1; 26:3; 31:12; 33:48–50; 36:13; Dt 34:1; Jos 13:32, sometimes the **Country of Moab,** Gn 36:35//1 Ch 1:46; Nb 21:20; Rt 1:1–6, 22; 2:6; 4:3; 1 Ch 8:8. It is in Moab that Yahweh orders Moses to allocate Canaan, Nb 33:50–36:12; that Moses expounds the Law, Dt 1:5, makes the covenant, Dt 28:69, and receives the Law and commandments, Nb 36:13. It is from there, on Mount Nebo, that Moses sees the Promised Land before he dies, Dt 34:1–6.

Moabites and Ammonites, "sons of Lot," Dt 2:9, 19; Ps 83:9, are often mentioned together: in the story of Lot, Gn 19:36–38, these two peoples are presented as relatives of the Israelites, with whom they are frequently at odds, Ps 83:6–9; cf. Jdt 5:2. Balak, the king of Moab, opposes Israel during the conquest of Canaan, Nb 22–24. In the time of the Judges, another Moabite king, Eglon, oppresses Israel, Jg 3:12–30. Saul makes war on Moab, 1 S 14:47; David makes the Moabites subject to him, 2 S 8:2, 12//1 Ch 18:2, 11. Moabites and Ammonites attack Jehoshaphat of Judah, 2 Ch 20:1–23. Under Jehoram, king of Israel, a victorious expedition of Israel and Judah against Mesha of Moab, 2 K 3:4–27. Under Jehoiakim, attacks of the Moabites and Ammonites against Judah, 2 K 24:2.

Israel and its leaders allow themselves to be seduced by the customs and divinities of Moab, Nb 25:1–2; Jg 10:6; 1 K 11:1–7, 33; 2 K 23:13; Ezr 9:1; Ne 13:23. Israel's hostility to Moab is clear in Dt 23:4–5, which forbids the "Moabite or Ammonite . . . to be admitted to the assembly of Yahweh," and in the many prophetic oracles against Moab, Is 11:14; 15; 16; 25:10; Jr 9:24–25; 25:21; 27:2–3; 48 (Moab is mentioned 34× in this ch.); Ezk 25:8–11; Am 2:1–2; Zp

2:8–11. Nonetheless, David will entrust his parents to the king of Moab in time of danger, 1 S 22:3–4, and at the siege of Jerusalem some Judaeans will take refuge in Moab, Jr 40:11. Above all, a Moabite woman, Ruth, Rt 1:22, etc., will become an ancestress of David and thus of the Messiah, Rt 4:13, 17–22; Mt 1:15–16.

Kings: BALAK; EGLON 1; MESHA 4; SHALMAN.

Moabites: ITHMAH; ORPAH; RUTH; SHIMRITH.

National god: CHEMOSH.

Mountains: ABARIM; NEBO.

River: ARNON.

Towns: AR; AROER 1; BAAL-MEON; BETH-DIBLATHAIM; BETH-GAMUL; BETH-HA-JESHIMOTH; BETH-PEOR; DIBON 1; ELEALEH; HESHBON; HORONAIM; JAZER; KIR-HERES; KIRIATHAIM; MEDEBA; MIZPAH 4; NEBO 2.

MOABITE (16), Dt 2:11, 29; 23:4; Rt 1:4, 22; 2:2, 6; 4:5, 10; 1 K 11:1; 1 Ch 11:46; 2 Ch 24:26; Ezr 9:1; Ne 13:1, of or from: MOAB.

MOADIAH (1). See: MAADIAH.

MOCHMUR (Wadi) (1), Jdt 7:18. Perhaps E of Shechem.

MODEIN (8), a town where Mattathias, father of the Maccabees, has settled, 1 M 2:1. Having refused to sacrifice to idols on the altar of Modein, 1 M 2:23, Mattathias and his sons leave the town for the hills. Judas wins a victory near Modein, 2 M 13:14 ff., and Simon, marching against Cendebaeus, spends a night there with his army, 1 M 16:4. Mattathias, 1 M 2:70, Judas, 9:19, and Jonathan, 13:25, are buried at Modein. Simon, their brother, erects a monument over their tomb, 13:27–30.

30 km NW of Jerusalem.

MOLADAH (4), a town in the Negeb of Judah, Jos 15:26; cf. Ne 11:26, formerly a town of Simeon, Jos 19:2// 1 Ch 4:28.

MOLECH (8), Gr. and Lat. *Moloch* (cf. Melech), a contemptuous deformation of *Melek,* "king," vocalized like the Hb. *boshet,* "shame" (the King of Shame) (see Astarte), a word of Phoenician origin designating a type of sacrifice, understood in Israel as the name of a god, Lv 18:21; 20:2–5; 2 K 23:10; Is 30:33; 57:9; Jr 32:35. In 1 K 11:7 some read *Milcom* for Hb. *Molek.*

= **Moloch** (1), Ac 7:43.

MOLID (1), "Who begets," son of Abishur and Abihail, of the clan of Jerahmeel, 2 Ch 2:29.

MOLOCH (1). See: MOLECH; TERRORS.

MONEY (5), Aram. *Mamôn,* "wealth," a personification ("Mammon") of money, a power that enslaves the world, Mt 6:24//Lk 16:13; Lk 16:9, 11; cf. Si 31:8.

MONSTER. See: DRAGON.

MOPH (1). See: MEMPHIS.

MORDECAI, Hb. *Mordocai* or *Mordecai,* "Of Marduk" (cf. Merodach).

1. **Mordecai** (2), one of the twelve leaders on the return from the exile, Ezr 2:2//Ne 7:7.

2. **Mordecai** (68) **son of Jair, son of Shimei, son of Kish** (2), a Benjaminite, Est 1:1[a]; 2:5, called **a Jew** (7), cousin and guardian of Esther, 2:7, 15, deported to Susa, 2:5.

His story, in the Gr. text, opens with a dream, 1:1[a-l] and closes with the explanation of this dream, 10:3[a-k]. Attached to the Chancellery, he uncovers a plot against King Ahasuerus, 2:21–22, but refuses to bend the knee before the prime minister, Haman, 3:2–6, who persuades the king to sign a decree of extermination against the Jews. Mordecai persuades Esther to intervene with the king, 4:1–17, while, for his part, he prays to the Lord, 4:17[a-h]. Haman erects a gallows for Mordecai, 5:9–14, but the king, after hearing the Record Book read to him, orders Haman to honor Mordecai, 6:1–13; then, after Esther's banquet, the king has Haman hung on the gallows prepared for Mordecai, 7:9–10. Mordecai is then advanced to the rank previously held by Haman, 8:1–2, 15; 9:4; 10:3, and obtains a decree rehabilitating the Jews, 8:12[a-x]. The Day of Mordecai will be identified with the feast of Purim, 9:20–32; 2 M 15:36.

MOREH, Hb. *Môreh,* "The Teacher, The Soothsayer."

1. **Hill of Moreh** (1), at the foot of which the Moabites camp in the time of Gideon, Jg 7:1. About 10 km S of Mount Tabor, the modern *Jebel ed-Dahi.*

2. **Oak of Moreh** (2), a sacred tree near Shechem, Gn 12:6; Dt 11:30; cf. Gn 35:4; Jos 24:26; Jg 9:6.

= probably **Diviners' Oak** (1), Jg 9:37.

MORESHETH (Of) (2), native of: MORESHETH-GATH, Mi 1:1; Jr 26:18.

MORESHETH-GATH (1), (cf. Gath), a town in the lowlands of Judah, near Gath, Mi 1:14. Native place of the prophet: MICAH 8.

MORIAH (Mount) (2), place of Isaac's sacrifice, Gn 22:2, identified with the hill on which the temple of Jerusalem is built, 2 Ch 3:1.

MORTAR (1), Hb. *Maktesh,* "Trough, Bowl," a quarter of Jerusalem located at a lower level, Zp 1:11.

[MOSCHOI]. See: MESHECH 1.

MOSERAH (1). See: MOSEROTH.

MOSEROTH (2), "Bonds" (cf. Assir), a stage of the Exodus, Nb 33:30–31.

= **Moserah** (1), where Aaron dies, Dt 10:6.

Identical (?) with: HOR 1.

MOSES (867), Hb. *Moshèh* (cf. Mushi), Gr. *Moysēs, Mosēs,* derived from the Egypt. *mos,* "son," as in Ahmosis, Tutmosis (cf. Rameses), interpreted by Ex 2:10 as connected with the Hb. verb *mashah* "to draw out" and meaning therefore "drawn [from the water]." The name of Moses appears 706× from Ex 2:10 to Jos 24:5; 16× from Jg to 2 K; 22× in Dn-Ezr-Ne-Ch; 8× in the DB, and 80× in the NT. Moses' career unfolds ca. 1250, the date generally accepted for the Exodus.

a. Moses and the Exodus

A member of the oppressed Hebrew people in Egypt, Ex 1; Ws 10:15, born on the banks of the Nile of a Levitical family, Ex 2:1; 6:16; 18:20; Nb 26:59; 1 Ch 5:27–29; 23:12–13, saved from drowning by the daughter of Pharaoh, Ex 2:1–10; Ws 18:5; Ac 7:20–21, Moses is instructed in all the wisdom of the Egyptians, Ac 7:22. At the age of forty, Ac 7:23, he becomes aware of the situation of his people, Ex 2:11, defends one of his mistreated brothers and kills an Egyptian; spurned by a fellow Jew, Ex 2:14; Ws 11:14; Ac 7:35, and fearing the anger of Pharaoh, he flees to Midian, where he marries Zipporah, daughter of Jethro, who gives him two sons, Ex 2:12–22. His travels through the wilderness bring him to Sinai/Horeb: meeting with God in the burning bush, mission given to Moses of freeing the Hebrews and leading them to the land promised to their fathers, revelation of the name of Yahweh, power to perform signs given to Moses, who also receives his brother Aaron as helper and interpreter, Ex 3:1–4:18. Moses then returns to Egypt, Ex 4:18–31. After many appeals to the king of Egypt, backed up by signs and wonders—the "plagues" of Egypt, Ex 5–13; cf. Dt 34:12; Ps 105:26; Ws 10:16; Si 45:2; Is 63:12—Moses, aided by Aaron, opens the way to freedom for his people by bringing them through the Red Sea, Ex 14–15, and then guiding them for forty years, Nb 32:13; Am 5:25, through the wilderness, Ex 15:22–18:27; Nb 11–14; 20–21.

On Mount Sinai the covenant is made and the Law given, Ex 19–24. After the incident of the golden calf, which provokes both the prayer and the anger of Moses, the covenant is renewed and the Law given once again, and Moses comes back down the mountain with radiant face, Ex 32–34, for he had seen the glory of God, Ex 33:18–23; cf. Ex 16:10; 24:16; 40:34–38; 2 M 2:8; Ps 99:7; Si 45:3, 5; 2 Co 3:7, 13. Having reached Moab opposite Jericho, Moses dies at the age of 120 on Mount Nebo, though he is still a vigorous man, Dt 34; cf. 2 M 2:4, leaving to Joshua the task of leading the people into Canaan.

The role of Moses (and Aaron) in the Exodus is recalled in Jos 24:5; 1 S 12:6, 8; 1 K 8:53; Ps 77:21; 105:26; Ws 10:15–11:16; Is 63:11–13; Ho 12:14; Mi 6:4; Ac 7:36; 1 Co 10:2; He 3:16; 11:29.

Principal traits of Moses' personality

Humblest man on earth, Nb 12:3; cf. Ex 3:11; 4:10; 6:12, 30; Si 45:4; a man of God, Dt 33:1; Jos 14:6; 1 Ch 23: 14; 2 Ch 30:16; Ezr 3:2; Ps 90:1; servant of God, of Yahweh, of the Lord (38), Nb 12:7; Dt 34:5; Jos (17); Is 63:11; Ba 1:20; 2:28; Ml 3:22; He 3:5; chosen by God, Ps 106:23; friend of God, Ex 33:11; beloved of God and men, Si 45:1; holy, Ws 11:1; Si 45:2, 4, 6, who speaks to God and to whom God speaks, Ex 6:28; 33:9–11; 34:29, 34–35; Nb 3:1, 14; 7:89; 12:2, 8; Ps 103:7; Si 45:5 (the formula, "Yahweh speaks *or* says to Moses," occurs over 200× from Ex to Dt); a prophet, that is, one who speaks in the name of God, Ex 19:6–7; Nb 11:24; Dt 18:15–20; 34:10; Ws 11:1; cf. Si 46:1; Ho 12:14; Ac 7:38, and who acts as mediator between God and men, Ex 20:18–21; 24:2; 34:2–3; Dt 5:1–5, Ga 3:19; cf. He 8:6; 9:15–16; whence his role as intercessor: in behalf of Pharoah, of his sister Miriam, and above all of his people, Ex 5:22–23; 8:4–8; 9:27–33; 10:16–18; 17:9–13; 32: 11–14, 30–32; Nb 11:2; 12:13; 14:13–19; 16:22; 21:7; Dt 9:25–29; 2 M 2:10 (cf. Lv 9:23–24); Ps 90:1; 99:6; 106:23; Si 45:3; Jr 15:1; alone with God, Ex 24:2; 34:2–5; cf. 19:12, 20–21; whom Yahweh knows face to face and who sees the form of Yahweh, Nb 12:8; cf. Ex 24:10; with whom God is, Jos 1:5, 17; 3:7; in whom wisdom dwells, Ws 10:16–17, and the spirit that he transmits, Nb 11:25; Dt 34:9; cf. Is 63:11. He is called a priest, Ps 99:6 (but see the punctuation in the JB); in fact, he is of the tribe of Levi, Ex 2:1, he consecrates Aaron and his sons as priests, Ex 28:1; 29; Lv 8–9; Si 45:6; he transmits to Eleazar the priesthood of Aaron, his father, Nb 20:23–28; he offers the sacrifice that sanctifies the people, Ex 19:24. With Aaron he blesses the people, Lv 9:23.

b. Moses and the Law

The most sacred part of the Jewish Bible—the five books of Gn, Ex, Lv, Nb, Dt (whence the Greek name "Pentateuch")—is called the Law, Si prol. 1; Mt 5:17; 12:5; and so on, the Law of Moses, Lk 24:44, and so on, the Book of the Law of Moses, Ne 8:1, or very simply "Moses," Lk 16:29, 31; 24:27; Ac 21:21; 26:22; 2 Co 3:15. In addition to numerous legislative provisions or laws in the narrow sense, *the Law* includes lengthy narrative sections and a whole body of teaching, the whole meant as a rule for the moral and religious life of the covenanted people of which Moses was leader and liberator. The authority of Moses has, for this reason, been extended to the book of origins (Gn), even though the name of Moses does not appear in it.

The statement of Jn 1:17, "the Law was given through Moses," is spelled out in a great variety of formulas, with the prototype possibly being the one in Ex 31:12–13: "Yahweh said this to Moses, 'Speak to the sons of Israel and say, "You must keep my sabbaths carefully."'" About 100×, especially in Lv, the words, "Yahweh spoke to Moses; he said . . . ," introduce a law. Among the most evocative formulas must be mentioned: "Moses went and told the people all the commands of Yahweh and all the ordinances," Ex 24:3; "the laws . . . which Yahweh laid down . . . through the mediation of Moses," Lv 26:46; "These are the commandments that Yahweh laid down for Moses on Mount Sinai, for the sons of Israel," Lv 27:34; "these commands that Yahweh has given to Moses (every single precept that Yahweh has laid on you through Moses)," Nb 15:22–23; "the decrees and laws and customs that Moses proclaimed to the sons of Israel," Dt 4:45; "the commandments and the Law which Moses the servant of Yahweh gave you," Jos 22:5; "the orders that Yahweh had given their fathers through Moses," Jg 3:4; "the statutes and the ordinances that Yahweh has prescribed to Moses for Israel," 1 Ch 22:13; "the book of the Law given through Moses," 2 Ch 34:14; "the Law of my servant Moses to whom at Horeb I prescribed laws and customs for the whole of Israel," Ml 3:22. The NT refers more than 40× to Moses as lawgiver or author of the book of the Law, to "the traditions that Moses handed down to us," Ac 6:14; cf. 15:1. Moses is presented not only as having said, ordained, and prescribed but also as having written the Law or one of its parts, Ex 24:4; 34:27–28; Nb 33:2; Dt 1:5; 31:9, 22, 24; Jos 8:32; Ba 2:28; Mk 12:19//Lk 20:28; Jn 1:45; 5:47; Rm 10:5. References could be added to "what is written" in the Law of Moses, Jos 8:31, 34–35; 23:6; 1 K 2:3; 2 K 14:6; 2 Ch 13:18; 35:12; Ezr 3:2; 6:18; Ne 13:1; Tb 7:12; Ba 2:2; Dn 9:11, 13; Lk 24:44; 1 Co 9:9, the reference being at times to some specific law, Mk 12:19, at other times to a nonlegislative passage of the Pentateuch, Jn 1:45.

c. Jesus, the new Moses

Moses, sent to Israel "as both leader and redeemer," Ac 7:35, is one of the great prefigurations of Christ, who is "the prophet like Moses" that is predicted for the last times, Dt 18:15; Ac 3:22; 7:37, the prophet par excellence, Jn 1:21, concerning whom Moses had written, Jn 5:46. Moses is present at the transfiguration of Christ, Mt 17:1–6 p, to emphasize the transition from the old covenant to the new and the coming of the only true mediator, Ga 3:19; 1 Tm 2:5; He 8:6; 9:15; 12:24, and redeemer, Ga 3:13; He 9:12. Like a guardian, Ga 3:24, the Law of Moses was to lead men to Christ who is the end, Rm 10:4, and who has come not to abolish it but to complete it, Mt 5:17, by bringing it to its perfection through the gift of grace and truth, Jn 1:17. And on a lowlying hill in Galilee, Mt 5:1, Jesus will proclaim the new Law, Mt 5:3–7:29, superior to the old, Mt 5:20, whose precepts had often become an intolerable burden, Mt 23:4. In bringing men the truth that sets them free, Jn 8:32, Jesus will offer them a yoke that is easy and a burden that is light, Mt 11:28–30.

Son of: AMRAM 1 and JOCHEBED.
Brother of: AARON; MARY 1.
Husband of: ZIPPORAH.
Son-in-law of: HOBAB; JETHRO.
Father of: GERSHOM 1.

MOST HIGH (27), Hb. *Elyon,* Gr. *Hypsistos,* an ancient divine name used in Phoenicia.

Most High (*Elyon*) is used as a proper name of the true God and thus designates him as the one who dwells in heaven, Is 14:14; cf. Nb 24:16; Dt 32:8; 2 S 22:14; Ps 7:18; 9:3; 18:14; 21:8; 46:5; 47:3; 50:14; 57:3; 73:11; 77:11; 78:17, 35, 56; 82:6; 83:19; 87:5; 91:1, 9; 92:2; 97:9; 107:11; Lm 3:35, 38; Tb

1:13; 4:11; Jdt 13:18; Ws 5:15; 6:3; Si (45×); Mt 5:7//Lk 8:28; Lk 1:32, 35, 76; 6:35; Ac 7:48; 16:17; Heb 7:11.

The "Most High God" (*El Elyon*) was probably the object of a cult at Jerusalem before the conquest of the city by David, cf. Gn 14:18–20; he is identified with the God of Abraham, Gn 14:22.

MOT (cf. Ahimoth; Hazarmaveth; Meremoth), a Ugar. name, a Canaanite god of drought or even a personification of death, Is 28:15, 18 (Hb. *maveth,* "death"), where the reference may be to death as such or to *Mot.* Cf. Dt 14:1.

MOZA, Mozah, Hb. 1–2: *Moza',* "Issue, Source"; 3: *Mozah.*

1. **Moza** (1), son of Ephah, Caleb's concubine, 1 Ch 2:46.

2. **Moza** (4), a Benjaminite, a descendant of King Saul and an ancestor of the sons of Azel, 1 Ch 8:36–37//9:42–43.

3. **Mozah** (1), a town of Benjamin, Jos 18:26.

MOZAH (1). See: MOZA 3.

MUPPIM (1), one of the sons of Benjamin, Gn 46:21.

MUSHI (8), (cf. Moses), is, with Mahli, a son of Merari, son of Levi, Ex 6:19; Nb 3:20; 1 Ch 6:4; 23:21; 24:26. His descendants, 1 Ch 23:23; 24:30, form the **Mushite** clan, Nb 3:33; 26:58 (this last listing of the Levitical clans is ancient and differs from the classical division into Gershonite, Kohathite, and Merarite clans; it seems to locate the home of the Levites in the area of Hebron). Among the descendants of Mushi is Ethan, one of the three great cantors, 1 Ch 6:32.

MUSHITE (2), belonging to the clan of: MUSHI.

MY-DELIGHT (1), Hb. *Hephzibah,* a symbolic name for Jerusalem, Is 62:4.

MYNDOS (1), a port of Caria, near Halicarnassus, to which the letter of the consul Lucius promulgating the alliance between the Romans and the Jews is sent, 1 M 15:23.

MYRA (2), a city in Lycia, Ac 27:5, in Asia Minor, on the Myros river; its port is called *Andriakē.* A center for the grain trade. Paul stops there on his third missionary journey, Ac 21:1 (var.) and during his transfer from Caesarea to Rome, Ac 27:5–6. Today *Demre* in Turkey.

MYSIA (2), a region in the NW part of modern Turkey, incorporated into the Roman province of Asia. Paul crosses it on his second, Ac 16:7–8, and third, cf. Ac 20:5–13, missionary journeys. The *mysarch* of 2 M 5:24 is the captain of the mercenaries from Mysia.

Towns: ADRAMYTTIUM; ASSOS; PERGAMUM; TROAS.

N

NAAM (1), "Gracious" (cf. Naomi), one of the sons of Caleb, son of Jephunneh, 1 Ch 4:15.

NAAMAH, "Gracious, Loved, Pretty" (cf. Naomi).

1. **Naamah** (1), daughter of Lamech, sister of Tubal-cain, perhaps the eponymous ancestress of the daughters of joy, Gn 4:22.

2. **Naamah the Ammonitess** (3), mother of King Rehoboam of Judah, 1 K 14:21, 31//2 Ch 12:13.

3. **Naamah** (1), a town in the lowlands of Judah, Jos 15:41.

NAAMAN (cf. Naomi).

1. **Naaman** (4), son of Benjamin, Gn 46:21, or son of Bela, son of Benjamin, Nb 26:40; 1 Ch 8:4, whose descendants form the **Naamite** clan, Nb 26:40.

2. **Naaman** (1), a Benjaminite of the sons of Ehud, who are heads of the families of Geba that migrate to Manahath, 1 Ch 8:7. Same as the preceding?

3. **Naaman** (12) **the Aramaean** (1), 2 K 5:20, or **the Syrian** (1), Lk 4:27, skilled army commander of the king of Aram, cured of leprosy by the prophet Elisha, who sends him to bathe in the Jordan, 2 K 5.

NAAMATH (Of) (4), Hb. *Na'amati,* probably an Idumaean or Arabian town, Jb 2:11; 11:1; 20:1; 42:9. Native place of: ZOPHAR.

NAAMITE (1), Nb 26:40, belonging to the Benjaminite clan of: NAAMAN 1.

NAARAH, Hb. *Na'arah,* "Young girl" (cf. Naarai?; Neariah?).

1. **Naarah** (3), one of the wives of Ashhur and mother of several clans attached to Judah, 1 Ch 4:5–6.

2. **Naarah** (1), a town on the border of Ephraim and Manasseh, Jos 16:7.

= **Naaran** (1), in Ephraim, 1 Ch 7:28. Probably 8 km NW of Jericho.

NAARAI (1), (cf. Naarah 1 ?), **son of Ezbai** (1). See: PAARAI.

NAARAN (1). See: NAARAH 2.

NABAL (21), "Brute, Fool, Wicked," see 1 S 25:25, a **Calebite** (1), a wealthy stock breeder at Carmel in the highlands of Judah. He refuses to pay David for the protection that the latter is providing for his flocks. Learning from his wife the next day that David is determined on revenge, he has an apoplectic fit and dies, 1 S 25:2–39.

Husband of: ABIGAIL 1.

NABATAEANS (2), a nomadic tribe of southern Arabian origin, settled later on in the former realm of the Edomites, with Petra as their capital. The Nabataeans will also control part of Transjordania. In the time of the Maccabees, the Nabataeans, hostile to the Jews at first, become their allies, 1 M 5:25//

2 M 12:10–12; 1 M 9:35. Some Nabataeans are among the Jews present in Jerusalem for the first Christian Pentecost, Ac 2:11 (*Arabs*). The Arabia of Ga 1:17 probably refers to the kingdom of the Nabataeans; cf. 4:25.

Kings: ARETAS 1, 2.

See: ARABIA.

Petra: ROCK 1.

NABOTH (22) **of Jezreel** (9), refuses to hand over his vineyard to King Ahab of Israel. With the help of false witnesses, Jezebel has Naboth stoned and gives the vineyard to her husband. Elijah straightway utters the sentence on the king: "In the place where the dogs licked the blood of Naboth, the dogs will lick your blood too," 1 K 21:1–19; cf. 2 K 9:21, 24–26.

[NABU]. See: NEBO 4.

NACON (Threshing floor of) (1), (cf. Jehoiachin), 2 S 6:6 = **Threshing floor of the Javelin,** 1 Ch 13:9.

While the Ark of God is being transferred from Kiriath-jearim to Jerusalem, Uzzah dies there after touching the Ark. The spot where he is struck down is given the name Perez-uzzah (2), 2 S 6:8//1 Ch 13:11. Site unknown.

NADAB, "[Yah] is generous" (cf. Abinadab; Ahinadab; Amminadab; Jonadab; Nedabiah).

1. **Nadab and Abihu** (12), **sons of Aaron** (7), older brothers of Eleazar and Ithamar, priests who die childless in punishment for a ritual sin: they "presented unlawful fire before Yahweh," Lv 10:1–5; cf. Ex 6:23; 24:1, 9; 28:1; Lv 16:1; Nb 3:2–4; 26:60–61; 1 Ch 5:29; 24:1–2. Note that the story in Lv 10:1–5 is meant as an introduction to the law on the mourning of priests, Lv 10:6–7.

2. **Nadab** (2), son of Shammai and father of Seled and Ephraim (Hb. *Appaim*), of the clan of Jerahmeel in Judah, 1 Ch 2:28, 30.

3. **Nadab** (2), a Benjaminite of Gibea, 1 Ch 8:30//9:36.

4. **Nadab** (4), **son of Jeroboam** (1) and his successor, second king of Israel (910–909), a contemporary of King Asa. While he is besieging the Philistine town of Gibbethon, he is assassinated by Baasha, one of his generals, who takes his place, 1 K 14:20; 15:25–31.

5. **Nadab** (5), acc. to Tb 11:18 (Gr *Nabad;* var. *Nasbas;* corr. *Nadan,* acc. to the *Wisdom of Ahikar*), a cousin of Tobit; with Ahikar he shares Tobit's joy at his cure. Acc. to Tb 14:10, Nadab (var. *Aman;* corr. *Nadan*) is punished for a crime against Ahikar, his adoptive father.

NADABATH (1). See: NEBO 2.

NAGGAI (1), an ancestor of Jesus acc. to Lk 3:25.

NAHALAL (2), "Watering place," a town of Zebulun, Jos 19:15, assigned to the Levites of the clan of Merari, Jos 21:35.

= **Nahalol** (1), a Canaanite town that long remains independent, Jg 1:30.

NAHALIEL (2), "River of God *or* God is my River" (cf. Wadi), or "God is my inheritance," one of the final stages of the Exodus, in Moab, Nb 21:19.

NAHALOL (1). See: NAHALAL.

NAHAM (1), "Consolation" (cf. Nahum), brother of Hodiah, in Judah, 1 Ch 4:19.

NAHAMANI (1), "Compassionate" (cf. Nahum), one of the twelve leaders on the return from exile, Ne 7:7. His name does not occur in the Hb. text of the parallel passage, Ezr 2:2.

NAHARAI from Beeroth (2), armor-bearer to Joab, son of Zeruiah, one of David's champions, 2 S 23:37//1 Ch 11:39.

NAHASH, "Serpent" (cf. Irnahash?; Nahshon; Nehushtan).

1. **Nahash** (7) **the Ammonite** (2), **king of the Ammonites** (2), 1 Ch 19:1// 2 S 10:1, lays siege to Jabesh-gilead.

Saul goes to the aid of the town and defeats Nahash, 1 S 11:1–11. Acc. to 1 S 12:12, it is this Ammonite threat that induces the Israelites to ask for a king.

Father of: HANUN 1.

2. **Nahash** (2), an Ammonite, father of: ABIGAIL 2; SHOBI.

NAHATH, "Rest" (cf. Janoah; Manahath; Manoah).

1. **Nahath** (3), first of the sons and chiefs of Reuel in Edom, called sons of Basemath, wife of Esau, Gn 36:13, 17; 1 Ch 1:37.

2. **Nahath** (1), a Levite of the clan of Kohath, an ancestor of Samuel acc. to 1 Ch 6:11 (*//Toah,* 1 Ch 6:19*//Tohu,* 1 S 1:1).

3. **Nahath** (1), one of the ten Levitical assistants of Conaniah and Shimei in the time of King Hezekiah, 2 Ch 31:13.

NAHBI son of Vophsi (1), a clan leader of the tribe of Naphtali, sent by Moses as representative of his tribe in the reconnaissance of Canaan, Nb 13:14.

NAHOR, Gr. *Nachor,* "Snorer."

1. **Nahor** (6), a postdiluvian patriarch, son of Serug, father of Terah and ancestor of Abraham, Gn 11:22–25; 1 Ch 1:26. Acc. to Lk 3:34 he is an ancestor of Jesus.

2. **Nahor** (12), **Abraham's brother** (1), Gn 22:23, son of Terah, Gn 11:26–27, lives in Mesopotamia, cf. Jdt 24:2. Acc. to the Yahwist tradition in Gn 22:20–24 (cf. the priestly tradition in Gn 10:23), Nahor is the ancestor of the Aramaean tribes: thus he is the father of twelve sons (cf. the twelve sons of Jacob and the twelve sons of Ishmael), eight by his wife Milcah (one of these is Bethuel, father of Laban and Rebekah, Gn 24:15, 24, 47) and four by his concubine Reumah. Gn 31:53 speaks of "the god of Nahor."

Ancestor of: LABAN 1.

3. **Nahor** (1), a town in the region of Haran in Upper Mesopotamia, which acquires a certain importance in the second millennium B.C. Abraham sends his servant there to look for a wife for his son Isaac, Gn 24:10.

NAHSHON (13), (cf. Nahash), Gr. *Naassōn,* **son of Amminadab** (5), leader of the tribe of Judah, Nb 2:3; 7:12; 10:14, in charge of the census of his tribe, Nb 1:7, brings the offering for the dedication of the altar on the first day, Nb 7:12–17. Acc. to Ex 6:23 he is the brother of Elisheba, the wife of Aaron. From the Judaean clan of Perez; he is an ancestor of David acc. to Rt 4:20; 1 Ch 2:10. Acc. to Mt 1:4; Lk 3:32, he is an ancestor of David and Jesus.

NAHUM, Gr. *Naoum,* "Consoled" (cf. Capernaum; Menahem; Naham; Nahamani; Nehemiah; Nehum; Noah?; Tanhumeth).

1. **Nahum** (2) **of Elkosh** (1), Na 1:1, one of the twelve "minor" prophets, predicts and describes—shortly before 612—the destruction of Nineveh. Tb 14:4 explicitly refers to Nahum's message.

2. **Nahum** (1), an ancestor of Jesus acc. to Lk 3:25.

NAIN (1), Lat. *Naim,* a town in Galilee where Jesus restores life to the only son of a widow, Lk 7:11–17. About 10 km SE of Nazareth.

NAIOTH (6). See: HUTS.

NANAEA (2), a Babylonian goddess, wife of the god: NEBO 4, venerated in Elam since 2000 B.C. and still venerated in the Roman period, identified with Artemis by the Greeks. It is in a temple of Nanaea, the *Nanaeon,* in Persia, that Antiochus IV is stoned and killed by priests of the goddess, 2 M 1:13–16.

NAOMI (21), Hb. *Na'omi,* "My gracious one, My sweetness" (cf. Abinoam; Ahinoam; Elnaam; Naam; Naamah; Naaman), leaves Bethlehem of Judah for Moab with her husband, Elimelech, and her sons, Mahlon and Chilion. There her husband soon dies, as do her sons who have married Moabite women, Ruth and Orpah. Naomi then returns to Bethlehem in company with Ruth, Rt 1. She advises her daughter-in-law to marry Boaz, who has a right of redemption over her, Rt 2:1, 18–23; 3:1–5, 16–18; 4:1–8. From this marriage is born a son, whom Naomi adopts: Obed, future grandfather of David, 4:14–17.

See: MARAH 2.

NAPHISH (3), "Great wealth," one of the twelve sons or clan chiefs of Ishmael, Gn 25:15//1 Ch 1:31. An Arabian tribe in Transjordania, in conflict with the Israelite tribes beyond the Jordan, 1 Ch 5:19.

NAPHTALI (57), "I have fought," popular etymology acc. to Gn 30:8.

Naphtali is the son of Jacob and of Bilhah, Rachel's servant—as is Dan—Gn 30:7, and eponymous ancestor of the tribe of the same name.

The territory of Naphtali is located west of the Sea of Chinnereth and the upper course of the Jordan, north of Zebulun and east of Asher, Jos 19:32–39: a hilly and wooded region, cf. Gn 49:21, an extensive land, cf. Dt 33:23.

Posterity and clans of Naphtali, Gn 46:24//1 Ch 7:13; Nb 26:48–50. Censuses, Nb 1:42–43; 2:30; 26:50. People of Naphtali are mingled with the Canaanites, Jg 1:33. Levitical towns, Jos 21:6, 32//1 Ch 6:47, 61. According to some scholars, Jg 5:18 is an old saying that recalls the active participation of Naphtali and Zebulun in the battle at the waters of Merom against the Canaanites, cf. Jos 11:5–8. In any case, a little later, "at Taanach, by Megiddo's waters," Naphtali and Zebulun triumph over Sisera in a battle in which the Israelites are led by Barak, a Naphtalite, Jg 4–5. The same two tribes also take part in the campaign of Gideon against Midian, Jg 6:35; cf. 7:23. Under Solomon, Naphtali is the eighth district of the kingdom, 1 K 4:15. Some ten years before the fall of Samaria, Tiglath-pileser conquers Naphtali and deports its people to Assyria, 2 K 15:29; cf. Is 8:23; Mt 4:15; Tb 1:4–5; 7:3. Acc. to 2 Ch 34:6 the reform of Josiah reached Naphtali, as that of Hezekiah had perhaps already done, Ps 68:28. Naphtali in the list of the tribes: Table, pages 410–11.

Naphtalites: HIRAM 2; TOBIJAH 7; TOBIT.

Town: KEDESH 2.

NAPHTUH (People of) (2), Hb. *Naphtuhim,* acc. to Egypt. "People of the Delta," linked with Egypt in Gn 10:13//1 Ch 1:11. Some interpreters take Naphtuh (or *Naphtuah*) to be a town between Jerusalem and Gezer that would have been part of the dowry Solomon received from Pharaoh.

NARCISSUS (1), a Roman, some of whose slaves or freedmen are Christians, Rm 16:11.

NATHAN, abbrev. of *Nethaniah,* "Yah has given" or of *Elnathan,* "God has given" (cf. Elnathan; Ethnan; Jonathan; Mattan; Mattanah; Mattaniah; Mattatha; Mattenai; Matthew; Matthias; Mattithiah; Nathanael; Nathan-melech; Nethaniah. See Dositheus; Zabad).

1. **Nathan** (5), one of the sons of David born at Jerusalem, 2 S 5:14//1 Ch 3:5//14:4. His clan is mentioned in Zc 12:12. Acc. to Lk 3:31, Nathan (Gr. *Natham*) is an ancestor of Jesus.

2. **Nathan** (2), 2 S 23:36//1 Ch 11:38. See: IGAL 2.

3. **Nathan** (33), a prophet. He comes on the scene at three important moments in David's life, Si 47:1. He tells the king that it is not he, David, who will build a house or temple for Yahweh, but that it is Yahweh who will make a house or dynasty for him, David, 2 S 7:2–4, 17//1 Ch 17:1–3, 15. He rebukes David for his two crimes against Uriah the Hittite, whom he has had killed after taking his

wife Bathsheba from him, 2 S 12:1, 5, 7, 13, 15, 25; cf. Ps 51:2. Finally, he plays an important role in the Davidic succession by lending all his authority to the candidacy of Solomon against that of Adonijah, 1 K 1:8–11, 22–24, 32–34, 38, 44–45. "The Annals of Nathan the prophet," 1 Ch 29:29; 2 Ch 9:29, probably refers not to an original document but to the texts of 2 S regarding Nathan. Acc. to 2 Ch 29:25, Nathan was the author of some ordinances regarding worship.

His sons (?): AZARIAH 3; ZABUD 1.

4. **Nathan** (2), grandson of the daughter of Sheshan and of Jarha the Egyptian, of the clan of Jerahmeel, in Judah, 1 Ch 2:36.

5. **Nathan** (1), an Israelite of the sons of Binnui, married to a foreign woman, whom he puts away, Ezr 10:39.

6. **Nathan** (1), one of Ezra's messengers to Iddo, Ezr 8:16.

NATHANAEL, Gr. and Lat. transcription of Hb. *Netan'el,* "God has given" (cf. Nathan).

1. **Nethanel son of Zuar** (5), leader of the tribe of Issachar, Nb 2:5; 7:18; 10: 15, in charge of the census of his tribe, Nb 1:8, brings the offering for the dedication of the altar on the second day, Nb 7:18–23.

2. **Nethanel** (1), fourth son of Jesse and brother of David, 1 Ch 2:14.

3. **Nethanel** (1), a priest, a trumpeter before the Ark, 1 Ch 15:24.

4. **Nethanel** (1), father of the Levite: SHEMAIAH 10.

5. **Nethanel** (1), a gatekeeper, fifth son of Obed-edom, 1 Ch 26:4.

6. **Nethanel** (1), one of the five officers sent by King Jehoshaphat, along with two priests and eight Levites, to instruct the towns of Judah in the Law, 2 Ch 17:7–9.

7. **Nethanel** (1), of the six heads of the Levites under King Josiah, 2 Ch 35:9.

8. **Nethanel** (1), a priest, of the sons of Pashhur, married to a foreign woman, whom he puts away, Ezr 10:22.

9. **Nethanel** (1), head of the priestly family of Jedaiah in the time of the high priest Joiakim, Ne 12:21.

10. **Nethanel** (1), a priest, an instrumentalist at the dedication of the wall of Jerusalem, Ne 12:36.

11. **Nathanael** (1), a Simeonite, an ancestor of Judith, Jdt 8:1.

12. **Nathanael** (6) **from Cana in Galilee** (1), Jn 21:2, devoted, it seems, to the study of Scripture (cf. the phrase "under the fig tree," Jn 1:48), one of the first disciples of Jesus, Jn 1:45–49. He is among those to whom the risen Jesus appears on the shore of the Sea of Tiberias, Jn 21:2. Nathanael has since the ninth century been identified with the Apostle Bartholomew, probably because both are associated with Philip, cf. Jn 1:45; Mt 10:3.

NATHAN-MELECH (1), "The King has given" (cf. Melech; Nathan), a eunuch with an apartment in the precincts of the temple, 2 K 23:11.

NAVEL OF THE LAND (or **Earth**), Hb. *Tabbur ha-'erez.*

1. **Navel of the Land** (1), a rounded hillock on the slopes of Mount Ebal or Mount Gerizim, Jg 9:37.

2. **Navel of the Earth** (1), a designation of Jerusalem as center of the world, Ezk 38:12; cf. 5:5.

NAZARENE or **of Nazareth.** In JB *Nazarene* translates Gr. *Nazoraios* (13) whereas *of Nazareth* translates Gr. *Nazarēnos* (6); cf. note on Mt 2:23.

The origin and meaning of *Nazoraios* are obscure (some derive it from Hb. *nazir;* see: NAZIRITES). *Nazarene* is applied 12× to Jesus, whose origin—*from Nazareth*—is thus indicated, Mt 2:23; 26:71; Lk 18:37; Jn 18:5, 7; 19:19; Ac 2:22; 3:6; 4:10; 6:14; 22:8; 26:9, and once to the disciples of Jesus, Ac 24:5.

Nazarēnos, "of Nazareth," is used only of Jesus.

NAZARETH (12), Gr. *Nazaret* (10), *Nazara* (2), **in Galilee** (5), a town about

30 km W of the southern end of the Sea of Chinnereth. The town where Joseph, Mary, and Jesus live, "their own town," Lk 2:39, 51. Acc. to Mt 2:23 Joseph settles there with his family after the birth of Jesus, but acc. to Lk 1:26–27 and 2:4 Mary and Joseph are already living there. Jesus leaves Nazareth to go and preach the good news, Mt 4:13 (Gr. *Nazara*); Mk 1:9. He returns to the town during his public life, Lk 4:16 (Gr. *Nazara*). Nazareth is "his home town," Mt 13:54//Lk 4:23//Mk 6:1. Cf. the expressions "Jesus the Nazarene," Lk 18:37, and so on, and "Jesus of Nazareth," Mk 1:24; 10:47; 14:67; 16:6; Lk 4:34; 24:19.

NAZIRITES (3), Gr. *naziraioi,* transcription of Hb. *nazir,* Jg 13:5, 7, 16–17, Jews who consecrate themselves to God in a special way and take a vow, for a limited period or for life, not to cut their hair, not to drink any fermented liquor, and not to go near a corpse, all this in accordance with regulations formulated in Nb 6. A ceremony marks the expiration of the vow, 1 M 3:49; cf. Ac 18:18; 21:23–26.

See: NAZARENE.

NEAH (1), a town of Zebulun, Jos 19:13.

NEAPOLIS (1), "New City" (cf. Numenius; Amphipolis. See Hadashah), port of Philippi in eastern Macedonia. Paul stops there on his second missionary journey, Ac 16:11.

NEARIAH (cf. Naarah 1).

1. **Neariah** (2), a descendant of King Jehoiachin, one of the sons of Shecaniah and father of three sons, 1 Ch 3:22–23.

2. **Neariah** (1), one of the Simeonite leaders settled in the highlands of Seir, 1 Ch 4:42–43.

NEBAI (1), a leader of the people and a cosigner of the pledge to observe the Law, Ne 10:20.

NEBAIOTH (5), first-born of the twelve sons or clan chiefs of Ishmael, Gn 25:13//1 Ch 1:29. An Arabian tribe famous for its rams, Is 60:7.

NEBALLAT (1), a town occupied by Benjaminites, Ne 11:34. 7 km NE of Lydda.

NEBAT (26), "God has regarded," an Ephraimite, father of: JEROBOAM 1.

NEBO

1. **Nebo** (2), a mountain 19 km E of the Jordan, opposite Jericho (alt., 838 m). Place of Moses' death, Dt 32:49–50; 34:1; cf. 2 M 2:4.

2. **Nebo** (7), a town on the slope of Mount Nebo, one of the final stages of the Exodus, Nb 33:47; a town of Reuben, Nb 32:3, 38; 1 Ch 5:8, then of Moab, Is 15:2; Jr 48:1, 22.

= ? **Nadabath** (1), 1 M 9:37.

3. **Nebo** (3), a town of Judah—same as Nob?—reoccupied by Israelites after the exile, Ezr 2:29//Ne 7:33; some of these put away the foreign wives they have married, Ezr 10:43.

4. **Nebo** (1), Accad. *Nabu* (cf. Abednego; Nebuchadnezzar; Nebushazban; Nebuzaradan), in Assyro-Babylonia, a god of writing and wisdom, interpreter and son of: BEL. Is 46:1 sees him collapse at the fall of Babylon.

Husband of: NANAEA.

NEBUCHADNEZZAR (117), Hb. *Nebukadre'zzar* and *Nebukadne'zzar,* Accad. *Nabu-kudurri-uzar,* "Nabu, protect the son!" Gr. *Nebuchodonosor* (cf. Nebo 4), **king of Babylon** (124) or **of the Babylonians** (2) (605–592).

The historical person

In 605, Nebuchadnezzar defeats the army of Pharaoh Neco at Carchemish, Jr 46:2; cf. 2 K 24:7. In 604 he invades Palestine for the first time, cf. Jr 36:29, obtains the submission of Jehoiakim, king of Judah, but three years later the latter rebels against the king of Babylon, 2 K 24:1–2. In 597, Nebuchadnezzar besieges Jerusalem, Jr 35:11; three months later King Jehoiachin surrenders and the first deportation of Jews takes place, 2 K 24:10–16//Jr 24:1; 27:19–20; 29:1–2; Ezk 17:12; 19:9; Est 1:1[c]; 2:6; Ba 1:9; Dn 1:1; cf. Jr 22:25; 29:1–23. Nebuchadnezzar appoints Zedekiah king over Judah, 2 K 24:17; Jr 37:1; Ezk 17:13. At the end of 589, Zedekiah rebels, Jr 52:3; Ezk 17:15. Nebuchadnezzar besieges Jerusalem and the other fortified places of Judah, cf. Jr 34:7; Ezk 24:2. Around the middle of 587 Jerusalem falls into the hands of the king of Babylon: capture of Zedekiah, destruction of the temple and Jerusalem, new deportation to Babylon, 2 K 25:1–21//Jr 39:1–10//52:4–27; 44:30; cf. Jr 50:17; 51:34; 52:29; 1 Ch 5:41; Ezr 1:7; 2:1; 5:12. Nebuchadnezzar appoints Gedaliah governor of Judah, 2 K 25:22–24//Jr 40:5–12; 41:2. During the difficult years that preceded the fall of Jerusalem, Jeremiah had advised submission to Nebuchadnezzar, Jr 27–28; 38:17–23; then, when the authorities refused to listen to him, he had predicted the tragic outcome of this rebellion, Jr 21:2–10; 32:1–5, 28, 36; 34:1–3; 37:17, 19; 38:3. At almost the same period Nebuchadnezzar attacks, among other, the Arabian tribes, cf. Jr 49:28, 30, and the fortified city of Tyre, Ezk 26:7 ff.; 29:18. In about 568/567 he marches on Egypt, Jr 46:13; cf. Jr 43:10–13; Ezk 29:19–20; 30:10–11; 24–25; 32:11.

His officers: NEBUSHAZBAN; NEBUZARADAN; NERGAL-SHAREZER.

The fictitious personage of literature

This is Nebuchadnezzar's role in Dn 1–4 (1: Daniel and his companions at the court of N.; 2: N.'s dream; 3: the golden statue erected by N.; 4: premonitory dream and madness of N.) and in Jdt, where he is called **king of the Assyrians** (6), Jdt 1:1, 7, 11; 2:1, 4; 4:1 (giving his general Holofernes the mission of punishing the west, 2:1–19, and forcing it "to worship Nebuchadnezzar alone," 3:8) and is covered with shame by a woman, Judith, 14:18. See also Ba 1:11–12.

Father of: BELSHAZZAR.

NEBUSHAZBAN (1), Accad. *Nabu-shezibanni,* "Nabu, save me!" (cf. Nebo 4; Meshezabel), a high-ranking official of Nebuchadnezzar, Jr 39:3 (corr. of Hb. *Sar-sekim*), 13.

NEBUZARADAN (15), Accad. *Nabu-zer-iddin,* "Nabu gives a posterity" (cf. Nebo 4), commander of Nebuchadnezzar's guard. At the end of July 587, Jerusalem surrenders; Nebuzaradan enters it, loots and burns the temple, destroys the city and deports its population, but leaves the humbler people behind in Judaea, putting them under the authority of Gedaliah, 2 K 25:8, 11, 20//Jr 39:9–10//52:12–26; Jr 41:10. He gives Jeremiah his freedom, Jr 39:11–13; 40:1–5. In 582 he proceeds to a new deportation of Judaeans, Jr 52:30.

NECO (8), Hb. form, Gr. *Nechao,* **king of Egypt** (5), is the Pharaoh Necas (609–594), son and successor of Psammetichus I. In 609 Necas goes to the aid of Assyria, which has reached its final hour; Josiah tries to stop him but Neco kills him, 2 K 23:29//2 Ch 35:20–22. In the same year he takes Jehoahaz, the successor of Josiah, as a captive to Egypt, replaces him with his brother Jehoiakim, and imposes a heavy tribute on Judah, 2 K 23:33–35//2 Ch 36:3–4. In 605 Necas is defeated at Carchemish by Nebuchadnezzar, Jr 46:2. Necas is perhaps the one who attacks Gaza, Jr 47:1.

NEDABIAH (1), "He whom Yah fills to overflowing" (cf. Nadab), one of the sons of King Jehoiachin, 1 Ch 3:18.

NEGEB, "Dry, *therefore* South, Southern section" (cf. Ramah of the Negeb).

1. **Negeb** (44), an area almost entirely desert in the south of Palestine. It is often associated with other regions of

Palestine that are formed by nature, especially the highlands and lowlands, Dt 1:7; Jos 10:40; 11:16; 12:8; 15:21–60; Jg 1:9; 2 Ch 28:18; Jr 17:26; 32:44; 33:13; Ob 19–20; Zc 7:7.

According to the clans that dwell in it, the Bible distinguishes between the **Negeb of Judah,** 1 S 27:10; 30:14; 2 S 24:7; 2 Ch 28:18, the **Negeb of Arad,** Jg 1:16, the **Negeb of Caleb,** 1 S 30:14; cf. Jos 15:19//Jg 1:15, the **Negeb of the Kenites,** the **Negeb of Jerahmeel,** 1 S 27:10, and the **Negeb of the Cherethites,** 1 S 30:14.

The patriarchs, Abraham, Gn 12:9; 13:1, 3; 20:1, and Isaac, Gn 24:62, and the scouts sent by Moses, Nb 13:17, 22, cross it. The tribe of Simeon has some towns in it, Jos 19:2–7//1 Ch 4:28–32, which will be absorbed by Judah, Jos 15:21–32; cf. Ne 11:26–29. A land of whirlwinds, Is 21:1, of torrents, Ps 126:4, and of various beasts, Is 30:6. Ezk 21:2–3, mentions a forest there.

2. **South.** See: SOUTH.

NEHELAM (Of) (3), a town or clan of: SHEMAIAH 3.

NEHEMIAH, Hb. *Nehemyah,* "Yah consoles" (cf. Nahum).

1. **Nehemiah** (2), one of the twelve who lead the exiles back to Palestine, Ezr 2:2//Ne 7:7.

2. **Nehemiah** (14) **son of Hacaliah** (2), Ne 1:1; 10:2, a Jewish layman, cupbearer at the court of Artaxerxes, king of Persia, one of the principal agents in the Jewish restoration after the exile, carries out two missions to Jerusalem and himself tells us of these.

First mission (445–433). Informed of the desperate situation at Jerusalem, Nehemiah secures official authorization to go to Jerusalem, Ne 2:1–10. He is later appointed governor of Judah, Ne 5:14; 12:26. In fifty-two days Nehemiah restores the wall of Jerusalem, and this despite the hostility of Sanballat, governor of Samaria, and his allies, 2:11–4:7; 6:1–19. He fights against the social injustice to which the ordinary Jews are subjected, 5:1–13, organizes the guards for the city, 7:1–3, as well as the repopulating of Jerusalem, 7:4–72. He always acts without selfish interest, 5:14–19. Second mission (before 424). To remedy certain disorders in the community, he takes the following steps: sanctions against Tobiah, payment to the Levites of their portions, respect for the sabbath, prohibition of mixed marriages, regulations for worship, 13:4–31.

Nehemiah is also mentioned in 2 M 1:18–23, 31, 33, 36; Si 49:13.

3. **Nehemiah son of Azbuk** (1), ruler of half the district of Beth-zur, a volunteer in the rebuilding of the Jerusalem wall, Ne 3:16.

NEHUM (1), (cf. Nahum). See: REHUM 1.

NEHUSHTA, daughter of Elnathan (1), mother of Jehoiachin, king of Judah, a native of Jerusalem, 2 K 24:8, deported to Babylon with her son, 2 K 24:12, 15; Jr 22:26–27; 29:2.

NEHUSHTAN (1), a word formed from Hb. *nahash,* "serpent," and *nehoshet,* "bronze" (cf. Nahash). Acc. to 2 K 18:4 it is "the bronze serpent that Moses had made": the Israelites worshipped it, and Hezekiah destroys it during his religious reform. Cf. Nb 21:4–9; Ws 16:6–7; Jn 3:14.

NEIEL (1), a town of Asher, Jos 19:27. About 10 km E of Acco.

[NEITH], a goddess honored at Sais in the Nile Delta. See: ASENATH.

NEKODA, Accad. *Niquddu,* "Moor hen."

1. **Nekoda** (2), head of a family of "oblates" who return from the exile, Ezr 2:48//Ne 7:50.

2. **Nekoda** (2), head of a family whose sons, on returning from the exile, cannot prove their authentic Israelite origin, Ezr 2:60//Ne 7:62.

NEMUEL

1. **Nemuel** (2), one of the sons of Simeon, son of Jacob, 1 Ch 4:24, whose descendants form the **Nemuelite** clan, Nb 26:12.

= **Jemuel** (2), Gn 46:10//Ex 6:15.

2. **Nemuel** (1), acc. to Nb 26:9 a Reubenite, brother of Dathan and Abiram.

NEMUELITE (1), belonging to the clan of: NEMUEL 1.

NEPHEG

1. **Nepheg** (1), son of Izhar, a Levite of the clan of Kohath, Ex 6:21.

2. **Nepheg** (3), one of the sons of David born at Jerusalem, 2 S 5:15//1 Ch 3:7//14:6.

NEPHILIM (1), a Hb. name meaning "Fallen [from heaven]," often translated as "Giants" (Nb 13:33): heroes born of the union between heavenly beings, "the sons of God," and mortals, "the daughters of men." Their disappearance is due to their condemnation by God because of their errors, Gn 6:4. Acc. to Nb 13:33 the sons of: ANAK are descended from them. Cf. also Si 16:7; Ba 3:26.

NEPHISITES or **Nephusites (Sons of the)** (2), a family of "oblates" who return from the exile, Ezr 2:50 (Hb. *Nephusim*)//Ne 7:52 (Hb. *Nephishsim*).

NEPHTOAH (Source of the Waters of) (2), a spring on the border of Judah and Benjamin, Jos 15:9; 18:15. 4 km NW of Jerusalem.

NEPHUSITES. See: NEPHISITES.

NER, "Lamp" (cf. Abner; Neri; Neriah).

1. **Ner** (15), a Benjaminite, son of Abiel, brother of Kish, father of Abner, 1 S 14:51, uncle of Saul, cf. 1 S 10:14–16, from Gibeon, 1 Ch 8:30//9:36.

Father of: ABNER.

2. **Ner** (2), a Benjaminite, father of Kish and grandfather of Saul, acc. to 1 Ch 8:33//9:39.

NERAIAH (1). See: NERIAH 1.

NEREUS (1), a Christian of Rome. He and his sister are greeted by Paul, Rm 16:15.

NERGAL (1), (cf. Nergal-sharezer), a Babylonian god of the underworld whose cult is brought to Samaria by people deported from Cuthah, 2 K 17:30.

See: TERRORS.

NERGAL-SHAREZER (3), Accad. *Nergal-sharri-uzur,* "Nergal, protect the king" (cf. Nergal; Sharezer), military leader of the king of Babylon. He enters Jerusalem after its fall in 587, Jr 39:3, 13.

NERI (1), (cf. Ner), an ancestor of Jesus acc. to Lk 3:27.

NERIAH (9) or **Neraiah** (1), Hb. *Neriyya, Neriyyahu,* Gr. *Nērias,* **son of Mahseiah** (2), Jr 32:2, 16; 36:4, 8, 14, 32; 43:3, 6; 45:1; Ba 1:1, father of: BARUCH 1.

[NERO]. See: CAESAR.

NETAIM (1), "Plantations," a town of Judah, perhaps in the lowlands, 1 Ch 4:23.

NETHANEL. See: NATHANAEL 1–10.

NETHANIAH, Hb. *Netanya, Netanyahu,* Gr. *Nathanias,* "Yah has given" (cf. Nathan).

1. **Nethaniah** (16), father of: ISHMAEL 5.

2. **Nethaniah** (2), of the sons of Asaph, head of the fifth class of cantors, 1 Ch 25:2, 12.

3. **Nethaniah** (1), one of the eight Levites sent by King Jehoshaphat, along with two priests and five officers, to instruct the towns of Judah in the Law, 2 Ch 17:7–9.

4. **Nethaniah** (1), father of: JEHUDI 2.

NETOPHAH (2), Ezr 2:22//Ne 7:26, a town 5 km SE of Bethlehem, whose population, the **Netophathites,** are Judaean in origin, 1 Ch 2:54. After the exile, Levites occupy the "villages of the Netophathites," 1 Ch 9:16; Ne 12:28.

Netophathites: EPHAI; HELED; MAHARAI; SERAIAH 6.

NETOPHATHITES. See: NETOPHAH.

NEW (Gate) (2), Hb. *Hadash* (cf. Hadashah), one of the gates of the temple in Jerusalem; the people gather there on one occasion for a trial of Jeremiah, Jr 26:10, and, on another, to hear a reading of his oracles, Jr 36:10.

NEW QUARTER. See: NEW TOWN.

NEW TOWN or **New Quarter** (4), Hb. *ha-Mishneh* (see Hadashah), in Jerusalem, NW of the temple, a new quarter due to the growth of the city, 2 K 22:14//2 Ch 34:22; Zp 1:10. The **Gate** of the same name, located in the wall, allows communication between the old city and the new quarter, Ne 3:6 (acc. to Syr.; Hb. *ha-Yeshanah,* "[Gate of] the Old"). Perhaps to be identified with the "Gate of Ephraim," cf. Ne 12:39.

See: CHAPHENATHA.

NEZIAH (1), head of a family of "oblates" who return from the exile, Ezr 2:54//Ne 7:56.

NEZIB (1), a town in the lowlands of Judah, Jos 15:43. About 10 km NW of Hebron.

NIBHAZ (1), an unknown divinity introduced into Samaria by the Avvites, 2 K 17:31.

NIBSHAN (1), a town in the wilderness of Judah, Jos 15:62.

NICANOR, Gr. *Nikanōr* (cf. Andronicus).

1. **Nicanor** (41) **son of Patroclus** (1), one of the king's "First Friends," 2 M 8:9, military commander in Syria. In 165, under Lysias, he is at Gorgias' side in the campaign against Judas Maccabaeus, a campaign that ends in a defeat at the hands of the Jews at Emmaus, 1 M 3:38–4:25//2 M 8:8–29, 34–36. Under Demetrius I in 161, he is again defeated by Judas—with whom he had for a short while, become friendly—at Capharsalama; at this time he utters threats against the temple, 1 M 7:36–38//2 M 14:12–36. Finally, in March 160, Nicanor is killed in a battle with Judas at Adasa, and his army is defeated. This Jewish victory will be celebrated each year on the thirteenth of Adar, which is called "Day of Nicanor," 1 M 7:39–49//2 M 15:1–36; cf. 1 M 9:1.

2. **Nicanor the Cypriarch** [leader of the mercenaries from Cyprus] (1), one of the five Syrian military commissioners who "would not allow the Jews to live in peace and quiet," 2 M 12:2.

3. **Nicanor** (1), one of the: SEVEN.

NICODEMUS (5), Gr. *Nikodēmos,* "Victorious people" (cf. Andronicus), a Pharisee and important Jew, "a teacher in Israel," comes to Jesus at night, Jn 3:1–10, cautiously defends Jesus before the Sanhedrin, Jn 7:50–51, and takes part in his burial, Jn 19:39.

NICOLAITANS (2), Christians with Gnostic tendencies who do not hesitate to take part in pagan ceremonies, Rv 2:6, 15. See: JEZEBEL 2.

NICOLAUS (1), "Victorious people" (cf. Andronicus), a proselyte from Antioch, one of the: SEVEN.

NICOPOLIS (1), "City of Victory" (cf. Amphipolis; Andronicus), a city in Epirus, on the eastern coast of Greece. Paul decides to spend the winter (of 65–66?) there and urges Titus to join him, Tt 3:12.

NIGER (1), a name of Lat. origin, "The Black" (see Phinehas). See: SIMEON 18.

NILE or **River** (46), Hb. *Ye'or* (derived from the Egyptian), **of Egypt** (2), the longest river in the world (6,671 km), the treasure of Egypt because of its muddy water, which, in its annual flooding, fertilizes the soil, Is 19:5–8; 23:3, 10; Jr 46:7–8; Am 8:8; 9:5; Zc 10:11.

See also Gn 41:1–3, 17–18 (seven fat cows and seven lean cows); Ex 1:22; 2:3, 5 (the infant Moses committed to the river); 4:9; 7:15–25, 28; 8:1–7; cf. Ps 78:44; Ws 11:6; 19:10 (the "plagues" of Egypt).

The Niles or **The Rivers** (16) (plural of Hb. *Ye'or*) **of Egypt** (4) are the arms of the Delta, 2 K 19:24; Is 7:18; Ezk 29:3–5, 10; 30:12; Na 3:8.

In Jr 2:18 Nile translates Hb. *Shihor,* derived from Egypt. *Shihor,* "Pool of Horus," a name for the eastern branch of the Nile that ends in Lake Manzala, near Daphne.

NIMRAH (1), (cf. Nimrim). See: BETH-NIMRAH.

NIMRIM (Waters of) (2), (cf. Beth-nimrah; Nimrah), an oasis in Moab, Is 15:6//Jr 48:34. Near the Dead Sea: either SE (cf. the *Wadi en-Numeirah*) or NE (cf. the *Wadi Nimrim*) of it.

NIMROD (4), a name to be connected with the Babyl. god *Ninurta,* god of the hunt or of war. Gn 10:8–10//1 Ch 1:10 connects Nimrod with Cush and describes him as a mighty hunter and the first potentate, with Babel, Erech, and Accad as his principal cities. In Mi 5:5 the land of Nimrod is Assyria.

NIMSHI (5), acc. to Ugar., "Mangosteen," ancestor of: JEHU 2.

NINEVEH (37), Hb. *Ninveh,* Gr. *Nineue,* Accad. *Ninua,* on the left bank of the Tigris, cf. Na 2:7, opposite the modern Mosul.

As a result of Tiglath-pileser's raids on Galilee, cf. 2 K 15:29, some Israelites are deported to Nineveh, Tb 1:3, 10, 17; 19, 22; 2:2; 7:3; 11:1, 15–17; 14:1, 9. Sennacherib makes it the capital of Assyria, 2 K 19:36//Is 37:37; Gn 10:11–12. The destruction of Nineveh (612) is predicted by Zp 2:13–15 and especially by Na 1–3; cf. Tb 14:4, 15. The conversion of Nineveh, "the great city" whose "wickedness has become known" to God—a conversion effected by the exhortations of Jonah—illustrates the saving love God has for all human beings, Jon 1:2 ff.; 3:2–10; 4:11; cf. Lk 11:30, 32//Mt 12:41. Jdt 1:1 makes Nineveh, "the great city," the capital of a Nebuchadnezzar, king of the Assyrians; cf. 2:21.

NINEVITES (4), Lk 11:30, inhabitants of: NINEVEH.

[NINURTA], (cf. Nimrod), Assyro-Babylonian god of war and fertility. See: NISROCH.

NISROCH (2), an unknown god of the Assyro-Babylonian pantheon; perhaps the reference is to *Ninurta, Nusku,* or *Marduk.* Acc. to 2 K 19:37//Is 37:38 he had a temple at Nineveh.

NO (4), "City," the *Thebes* of the Greeks, in Upper Egypt, capital of Egypt in the New Empire. City of the ram-god Amon, Jr 46:25. Ezk 30:14–16 foretells the destruction of No along with that of all Egypt.

= **No-Amon** (1), Na 3:8–9, sacked by the Assyrians under Assurbanipal in 663.

NOADIAH, Hb. *No'adyah,* "Encounter with Yah."

1. **Noadiah son of Binnui** (1), one of the Levites who attend the priest Meremoth in the temple of Jerusalem, Ezr 8:33.

2. **Noadiah** (1), a prophetess hostile to Nehemiah, Ne 6:14.

Other prophetesses: MARY 1.

NOAH

1. **Noah** (56), "Rest"; Gn 5:29 connects the name with the root *nhm,* "console" (cf. Nahum).

Acc. to the Yahwist tradition (J), Noah, a descendant of Cain (ancestor of the crafts) via Lamech, Gn 5:29, is the inventor of viticulture, Gn 9:20–27. The priestly tradition (P) connects Noah with Seth via Lamech, Gn 5:28. The two traditions agree in giving Noah three sons, Shem, Ham, and Japheth: J, Gn 9:18–19; P, Gn 5:32//6:10; 10:1,

32; cf. 1 Ch 1:4. They also make Noah the hero of the flood: he alone, with his family, escapes the punishment that strikes corrupt mankind, Gn 6:5–8:22. When the waters have subsided, God makes a covenant with Noah and the entire human race, a covenant that has the rainbow for its sign, Gn 9:1–17 (P); cf. Is 54:9. Noah is the just man, Ws 10:4; Ezk 14:14, 20, who is both saved, Heb 11:7; 1 P 3:20; 2 P 2:5; cf. Mt 24: 37–38//Lk 17:26–27, and savior insofar as he represents "the hope of the world," Ws 14:6; cf. Si 44:17–18. Noah is listed among the ancestors of Jesus in Lk 3:36.

2. **Noah** (4), Nb 26:33; 27:1; 36:11; Jos 17:3, in Manasseh, one of the five daughters of: ZELOPHEHAD.

NO-AMON (1), "City of Amon." See: No.

NOB (6), a town of priests, 1 S 22:19, and a sanctuary in which the priests of Shiloh take refuge after the disaster described in 1 S 4. David, fleeing the wrath of Saul, visits the priest Ahimelech there, who gives him the consecrated bread as food, as well as the sword of Goliath, 1 S 21:2–10; cf. Mt 12:4 p. Doeg the Edomite, a witness to the scene, betrays Ahimelech to Saul, who puts the town of Nob to the sword. Abiathar, who alone escapes, joins David, 1 S 22:9–20.

Acc. to Is 10:32, Nob is close to Jerusalem. After the exile the town is occupied once again by Benjaminites, Ne 11:32.

NOBAH

1. **Nobah** (1), a Manassite, seizes the town of Kenath and renames it after himself, Nb 32:42.

2. **Nobah** (1), Nb 32:42, a town in Gilead. See: KENATH.

3. **Nobah** (1), Jg 8:11, a town near Jogbehah, south of the Jabbok. Probably different from the preceding.

NOD (1), to be connected with Hb. *nad,* "vagabond, wanderer," see Gn 4:14, an (unidentifiable) country east of Eden, where Cain lives after the murder of his brother Abel, Gn 4:16.

NODAB (1), an Arabian tribe in conflict with the Israelite tribes in Transjordania, 1 Ch 5:19.

NOGAH (2), "Brilliance, Clarity," one of David's sons born at Jerusalem, acc. to 1 Ch 3:7//14:6.

NOHAH (1), fourth son of Benjamin, acc. to 1 Ch 8:2.

NO-PEOPLE-OF-MINE (1), Hb. *Lo-ammi,* a symbolic name, which the prophet Hosea gives to the second of his sons born of Gomer, Ho 1:9. Subsequently the name will be changed to "You-are-my-people" (*Ammi*), Ho 2:3, 25.

NOPH (7), Is 19:13; Jr 2:16; 44:1; 46:14, 19; Ezk 30:13, 16 (Hb.). See: MEMPHIS.

NOPHAH (1), Nb 21:30, a town of Moab. The Hb. text of this passage is unintelligible.

NORTH

1. **North** (6), Hb. *Zaphôn,* a term used in Dn 11:6–8, 13, 15, for: SYRIA.

"Kings of the North": ANTIOCHUS 1–2; SELEUCUS 2.

2. **[Northern Kingdom].** See: ISRAEL *d.*

NUMENIUS (4), "[Born] at the new moon" (cf. Neapolis), **son of Antiochus** (2), Jewish ambassador to Sparta and Rome, 1 M 12:16–17; 14:22, 24; 15:15.

NUN (30), an Ephraimite, father of: JOSHUA 1.

NYMPHA (1), a Christian woman of Laodicea in whose home the Christian community meets, Col 4:15.

O

OBADIAH, Gr. *Abdia(s)*, "Servant of Yah" (cf. Ebed).

1. **Obadiah** (1), an Issacharite, one of the five military commanders of the sons of Uzzi, 1 Ch 7:3–5.

2. **Obadiah** (2), a Benjaminite, one of the six sons of Azel, a descendant of King Saul, 1 Ch 8:38//9:44.

3. **Obadiah** (1), a Gadite chief who rallies to David before the latter becomes king, 1 Ch 12:10 (cf. vv. 9–16).

4. **Obadiah** (1), a Zebulunite, father of: ISHMAIAH 2.

5. **Obadiah** (7), master of the palace of King Ahab of Israel. A faithful believer in Yahweh, he saves the lives of a number of prophets of Yahweh during the persecution of Jezebel. Elijah bids him go and tell Ahab of his, Elijah's, presence, 1 K 18:3–16.

6. **Obadiah** (1), one of the five officers whom King Jehoshaphat sends, with two priests and eight Levites, to instruct the towns of Judah in the Law, 2 Ch 17:7–9.

7. **Obadiah** (1), a Levite of the clan of Merari, one of the supervisors of the work of restoring the temple under Josiah, 2 Ch 34:12.

8. **Obadiah** (1), a descendant of King Jehoiachin via Zerubbabel and Hananiah, 1 Ch 3:21.

9. **Obadiah son of Jehiel** (1), of the sons of Joab, a head of a family who returns from the exile with Ezra, Ezr 8:9.

10. **Obadiah** (1), a priest who cosigns the pledge to observe the Law, Ne 10:6.

11. **Obadiah (3) son of Shemaiah** (or **of Shammua**) **son of Galal son of Jeduthun** (2), a Levite cantor of Jerusalem, always associated with Bakbakkar and Mattaniah, 1 Ch 9:16//Ne 11:17 (Hb. *Abda*); Ne 12:25.

12. **Obadiah** (1), Ob 1, one of the twelve "minor prophets." We know nothing about him. The book bearing his name is the shortest in the OT: it announces the punishment of Edom for taking advantage of the fall of Jerusalem in 587 to invade southern Judaea.

OBAL (2), Hb. *'Obal,* one of the thirteen sons of Joktan, Gn 10:28//1 Ch 1:22. An unidentifiable tribe or area in southern Arabia.

OBED, Hb. *'Obed,* Gr. *Iōbed*, "Servant" (cf. Ebed).

1. **Obed** (5), father of: GAAL. See: EBED.

2. **Obed** (8), son of Boaz and Ruth the Moabitess, Rt 4:13–16, father of Jesse and grandfather of David, Rt 4:17, 21–22; 1 Ch 2:12. An ancestor of Jesus, Mt 1:5; Lk 3:32.

3. **Obed** (2), a descendant of the daughter of Sheshan and Jarha the Egyptian, of the clan of Jerahmeel, in Judah, 1 Ch 2:37–38.

4. **Obed** (1), one of David's champions, 1 Ch 11:47.

5. **Obed** (1), a gatekeeper, one of the sons of Shemaiah, son of Obed-edom, 1 Ch 26:7.

6. **Obed** (1), father of: AZARIAH 13.

OBED-EDOM (20), "Servant of Edom" (cf. Ebed; Edom), **of Gath** (3), a Philistine whose house is on the road from Kiriath-jearim to Jerusalem. During the transfer of the Ark, Uzzah dies suddenly; David, in consternation, leaves the Ark with Obed-edom. Three months later, learning that "Yahweh blessed Obed-edom and his whole family," David has the Ark brought to Jerusalem, 2 S 6:10–12//1 Ch 13:13–14; 15:25.

Acc. to the chronicler David makes Obed-edom a gatekeeper—and on occasion a player of the octave lyre—near the Ark, 1 Ch 15:18, 21, 24; 16:5. Obed-edom thereby becomes a son of Jeduthun—clan of Merari—and a Levite, 1 Ch 16:38 (see List, page 416). A group of gatekeepers is connected with him, 1 Ch 26:4–8, 15. Cf. 2 Ch 25:24.

OBIL (1), Hb. *'Obil* (cf. Jabal), **the Ishmaelite** (1), in charge of the king's camels, 1 Ch 27:30.

OBLATES, Hb. *Nethinim,* descendants of foreigners who exercise subordinate tasks in the temple at Jerusalem, cf. Jos 9:23–27; Ezk 44:7–9; Ezr 8:20; many of them return from the exile, Ezr 2:43–54, 58//Ne 7:46–56, 60; Ezr 8:20.

OBOTH (4), a stage of the Exodus, Nb 21:10–11; 33:43–44. S of the Dead Sea.

OCHRAN (5), (cf. Achar), father of: PAGIEL.

OCINA (1), a town on the Phoenician coast acc. to Jdt 2:28. Unknown. To be identified (?) with: Acco.

ODED, Hb. *'Oded,* = ? **Iddo** (cf. Joed).

1. **Oded** (2), a prophet in the time of Asa of Judah, acc. to 2 Ch 15:8 (Hb.). Father of the prophet: AZARIAH 10.

2. **Oded** (1), a prophet in Samaria, contemporary with King Ahaz of Judah, 2 Ch 28:9–11.

ODOMERA (1), probably chief of an Arabian tribe that is collaborating with Bacchides. He is defeated by Jonathan Maccabaeus, 1 M 9:66.

OG (22), Hb. *'Og,* name of a divinity?, **King of Bashan** (15), a probably legendary personage: last survivor of the Rephaim (his famous bed is probably a dolmen in the area of Ammon), Dt 3:11; Jos 12:4. The account of the conquest of his country—Bashan, cf. Jos 12:5—by Israel, Dt 3:1–6; cf. Nb 21:33–35, is modeled on that of the conquest of the kingdom of Sihon by Israel. Og is always paralleled with Sihon, Dt 1:4; 29:6; 1 K 4:19; Ne 9:22; Ps 135:11; 136:19–20; cf. the expression *the two Amorite kings,* Dt 3:8; 4:47; 31:4; Jos 2:10; 9:10; 24:12. His "kingdom" is assigned to eastern Manasseh, Dt 3:13; Jos 13:30–31.

His towns: ASHTAROTH; EDREI 1; SALECAH.

OHAD (2), (cf. Ehud), the third of the six sons of Simeon, Gn 46:10//Ex 6:15. His name does not occur in Hb 26:12–13 or in 1 Ch 4:24.

OHEL (1), Hb. *'Ohel,* "Tent" (cf. Oholah; Oholiab; Oholibah; Oholibamah), the second of the five sons of Meshullam, a descendant of King Jehoiachin, 1 Ch 3:20.

OHOLAH (5), "His tent" (cf. Ohel), Ezk 23:4, 5, 36, 44, a symbolic name for *Samaria.* Elder sister of Oholibah, *Jerusalem.* The two sisters, spouses of Yahweh, "prostituted themselves" with Egypt, Assyria, and Babylon. They will suffer the consequences of their wickedness.

OHOLIAB (5), "My tent is the Father" (cf. Ohel), **son of Ahisamach, of the tribe of Dan** (3), an artist associated with Bezalel of Judah in the building of the sanctuary and the fabrication of the various furnishings for worship, Ex 31:6; 35:34; 36:1–2; 38:23.

OHOLIBAH (6), "My tent [is] in Her" (cf. Ohel), Ezk 23:4, 11, 22, 36, 44, a symbolic name for Jerusalem. See: OHOLAH.

OHOLIBAMAH, "My tent is in the high place" (cf. Ohel; Bamoth).

1. **Oholibamah daughter of Anah** (1), Gn 36:25, granddaughter of Seir. To be compared with the following.

2. **Oholibamah** (5), **daughter of Anah** (3), **son** (Hb. *daughter*) **of Zibeon** (2), great-granddaughter of Seir, wife of Esau, Gn 36:2, and mother of the Edomite chiefs Jeush, Jalam, and Korah, Gn 36:5, 14, 18. To be compared with the preceding and the following.

3. **Oholibamah** (2), one of the chiefs (or clans) of Edom, Gn 36:41//1 Ch 1:52. To be compared with the two preceding.

OLIVES (Mount of) (16), Hb. *Har ha-Zetim* (cf. Beerzeth; Birzaith; Zetham?; Zethan), covered with many olive trees, cf. Ne 8:15, located east of Jerusalem, across the Kidron valley, cf. Jn 18:1.

David, fleeing from his son Absalom, climbs this hill in tears, 2 S 15:30, 32. Solomon builds high places there, especially for the gods Chemosh and Milcom, 1 K 11:7; consequently the Hb. text of 2 K 23:13 calls the Mount of Olives the *mount of Perdition* or *of the Destroyer* (cf. Ex 12:23; 2 S 24:16; Is 54:16; Pr 18:9). Leaving the temple, the Glory of God pauses on the Mount of Olives before joining the exiles at Babylon, Ezk 11:23, whereas on the day of the eschatological battle Yahweh's "feet will rest on the Mount of Olives," Zc 14:4–5.

Jesus goes there several times, especially during the days before his passion, Mt 21:1//Mk 11:1//Lk 19:29; Mt 24:3//Mk 13:3; Mt 26:30//Mk 14:26//Lk 22:39; Lk 19:37; 21:37; Jn 8:1. Luke locates the Ascension of Jesus on the Mount of Olives, cf. Ac 1:12.

See: BETHANY 1; BETHPHAGE; GETHSEMANE.

OLYMPAS (1), (cf. Olympian), a Christian of Rome, Rm 16:15.

OLYMPIAN (1), (cf. Olympas), of Olympus, the sacred mountain of the Greek gods. See: ZEUS.

OMAR (3), "Eloquent" (cf. Amariah), second of the sons of Eliphaz, who are called the sons of Adah, wife of Esau, Gn 36:11//1 Ch 1:36; one of the chiefs (or clans) of Edom, Gn 36:15.

OMRI, Hb. *'Omri.*

1. **Omri** (1), one of the sons of Becher, son of Benjamin, 1 Ch 7:8.

2. **Omri** (1), a Judaean, an ancestor of: UTHAI 1.

3. **Omri son of Michael** (1), commissioner for the tribe of Issachar, 1 Ch 27:18.

4. **Omri** (15), perhaps not of Israelite origin, sixth king of Israel (888–874), founder of the third dynasty. His accession to the throne is not an easy one. He crushes in its early stage the conspiracy of Zimri against his predecessor, King Elah, but he seems to have greater difficulty in eliminating the opposition of Tibni, son of Ginath, around whom a part of Israel rallies for a time, 1 K 16:16–22. At first he resides at Tirzah, like his predecessors; then on an empty hill he builds a town named Samaria, 1 K 16:24, which will continue as the capital of Israel until the fall of the kingdom in 721. He is at odds with Damascus, to which he is forced to yield some towns, cf. 1 K 20:34. "Omri did what is displeasing to Yahweh, and was worse than all his predecessors." This judgment of 1 K 16:25–26 condemns the king's religious outlook, cf. Mi 6:16; scholars agree that in other respects he was a great king.

Father of: AHAB 1.

Grandfather of: ATHALIAH 1.

ON, Hb. *'On.*

1. **On** (5), a town in Egypt, not far from Cairo, which had a temple of the sun god, Ra. On the Day of Yahweh against Egypt, the young people of On will be slaughtered, Ezk 30:17.

= **Heliopolis** (1), Gr. name for *On.* Jr 43:13 announces the coming of Nebuchadnezzar and the destruction in particular of "the obelisks of the *temple* of the sun (Hb. *Beth-shemesh*)" (thus the Hb. text; Gr. text has: "the obelisks of *Heliopolis* which are at *On*").

Native place of the priest Potiphera, father of: ASENATH.

2. **On** (1), "Power" (cf. Onam; Onan), **son of Peleth** (1), a Reubenite like Dathan and Abiram and associated with their rebellion against Moses, Nb 16:1.

ONAM (cf. On 2).

1. **Onam** (2), last of the five sons of Shobal, son of Seir, Gn 36:23//1 Ch 1:40.

2. **Onam** (2), son of Jerahmeel and Atarah, 1 Ch 2:26; his posterity is given in 2:28–41. In Judah.

ONAN (8), "The Strong"? (cf. On 2), second son of Judah and Bath-shua the Canaanite woman. His brother Er having died without an heir, Onan unwillingly marries his sister-in-law Tamar, Er's widow (cf. the levirate law, Dt 25:5–10), but refuses to beget (therefore, the term "onanism") a posterity that will not bear his name. His premature death is interpreted as a punishment for his action, Gn 38:4, 8–11; 46:12//Nb 26:19; 1 Ch 2:3.

ONESIMUS (2), Gr. *Onēsimos,* "Useful, Profitable," see Phm 11 (cf. Onesiphorus), a slave of Philemon at Colossae. He runs away from his master and meets Paul, who is then a prisoner. He is converted, and Paul makes a much-appreciated co-worker of him, Col 4:9. After a while, Paul sends him back to Philemon with a letter asking the latter to receive Onesimus "not as a slave any more, but . . . a dear brother," Phm 1, 10–18.

ONESIPHORUS (2), "Who brings a profit; Useful" (cf. Onesimus), a Christian, probably of Ephesus, helps and comforts Paul both at Ephesus and at Rome, 2 Tm 1:16–17; 4:19. It may be that at the time Paul writes to Timothy Onesiphorus is already dead.

ONIAS, shortened form of *Yohanân* (cf. John).

1. **Onias I** (4), a Jewish high priest contemporary with Alexander the Great. He is supposed to have received from Areios, king of the Spartans, a letter dealing with "friendship and alliance," 1 M 12:7–8, 19–20.

2. **Onias II** (1), a high priest, father of: SIMEON 4.

3. **Onias III** (15), son of Simon, grandson of the preceding. High priest (185–175), champion of orthodoxy, he defends the temple treasury against Heliodorus, 2 M 3:1–35. Slandered by Simon, the administrator of the temple, he goes to Antioch to justify himself, 2 M 4:1–6. The high priesthood is usurped by Onias' brother Jason, 2 M 4:7. Having taken refuge in the inviolable sanctuary of Daphne near Antioch, Onias denounces the thefts committed in the Jerusalem temple by the new usurping high priest, Menelaus. Menelaus has Onias assassinated in a treacherous manner (170), 2 M 4:32–38; cf. Dn 9:26; 11:22. Onias is also presented as an intercessor with God for his people, 2 M 15:12, 14; cf. 3:31–33; 4:5.

ONO (5), a town known to the Egyptians. Rebuilt by Benjaminites, 1 Ch 8:12. Occupied before the exile by Israelites, Ezr 2:33//Ne 7:37, and reinhabited after the exile by Benjaminites, Ne 11:35. 9 km NW of Lod.

In the valley of Ono: HAC-CHEPHERIM.

OPHEL, "Excrescence, *therefore* Hill, Height," a kind of acropolis.

1. **Ophel** (7), at Jerusalem, on the ancient Zion, cf. Mi 4:8, the southern part of the hill supporting the royal palace, Is 32:14. Ophel is restored by Kings Jotham, 2 Ch 27:3, and Manasseh, 2 Ch 33:14, and by Nehemiah, Ne 3:27. The "oblates" who serve in the temple live there, Ne 3:26 (Hb.); 11:21.

2. **Ophel** (1), at Samaria, a height on which the royal palace was probably built, 2 K 5:24.

OPHIR (16), one of the thirteen sons of Joktan, Gn 10:29//1 Ch 1:23. In southern Arabia, famous for its gold, 1 Ch 29:4; Jb 22:24; 28:16; Ps 45:10; Si 7:18; Is 13:12; Jr 10:9 (corr. of Hb. *Ouphaz*), and its precious stones, 1 K 10:11//2 Ch 9:10; Tb 13:17. People travel to Ophir by sea, 1 K 9:28//2 Ch 8:18, the Red Sea, 1 K 22:49.

OPHNI (1), a town in Benjamin, Jos 18:24. 5 km NW of Bethel. Today *Jifni.*

OPHRAH, "Gazelle"? (see Tabitha).

1. **Ophrah** (5) **of Abiezer** (2), in Manasseh, native place of Gideon. The latter is buried there in the tomb of his father, Joash, Jg 6:11, 24; 8:27, 32; 9:5.

2. **Ophrah** (2). See: EPHRAIM 4.

3. **Ophrah** (1), a descendant of Othniel, son of Kenaz, 1 Ch 4:14.

OREB (5), "Raven," and **Zeeb,** Midianite chiefs conquered by Gideon, Jg 7:25; 8:3; Ps 83:12. Their story is connected with places called **Oreb's Rock,** Jg 7:25; Is 10:26, and **Zeeb's Winepress,** Jg 7:25, the locations of which are unknown.

OREN (1), "Laurel" (cf. Arnon), one of the sons of Jerahmeel, in Judah, 1 Ch 2:25.

ORION (3). See: CHESIL 2.

ORNAN (12) **the Jebusite** (4). See: ARAUNAH.

ORPAH (2), "She who turns her back," a Moabite woman. At the death of her husband, Chilion, son of Elimelech, she "went back to her people," whereas Ruth followed Naomi, her mother-in-law, to Bethlehem, Rt 1:4, 14.

ORTHOSIA (1), a port on the Phoenician coast between Tripolis and the river Eleutherus. Trypho takes refuge there, 1 M 15:37.

OTHNI (1), abbrev. of *Othniel,* a gatekeeper, one of the sons of Shemaiah, son of Obed-edom, 1 Ch 26:7.

OTHNIEL, Hb. *'Otni'el,* Gr. *Gothoniel.*

1. **Othniel** (7) **son of Kenaz** (4) **Caleb's younger brother** (3). This nephew of Caleb conquers the town of Kiriath-sepher; for this exploit Caleb gives him his daughter Achsah to wife, as well as "the upper springs and the lower springs," Jos 15:16–19//Jg 1:12–15.

Acc. to Jg 3:8–11, this same Othniel, one of the "lesser" judges of Israel, rescues his people from oppression by Cushan-rishathaim, king of Edom (Hb. *king of Aram*).

Othniel is father of Hathath and Meonothai, 1 Ch 4:13.

See: HELDAI 1.

2. **Gothoniel** (1), father of: CHABRIS.

OX (1), a Simeonite, grandfather of Judith, Jdt 8:1.

OZEM

1. **Ozem** (1), sixth son of Jesse and brother of David, 1 Ch 2:15.

2. **Ozem** (1), one of the sons of Jerahmeel, in Judah, 1 Ch 2:25.

OZIEL (1). See: UZZIEL 6.

OZNI (1), (cf. Azaniah), fourth of the seven sons of Gad; his descendants form the **Oznite** clan, Nb 26:16.

= **Ezbon** (1), Gn 46:16.

OZNITE (1), belonging to the clan of: OZNI.

P

PAARAI from Arab (1), 2 S 23:35, one of David's champions.

= **Naarai son of Ezbai** (1), 1 Ch 11:37.

PADDAN (1), "Plain." See: MESOPOTAMIA *c*.

PADDAN-ARAM (10), "Plain of Aram." See: MESOPOTAMIA *c*.

PADON (2), (cf. Pedaiah), head of a family of "oblates" who return from the exile, Ezr 2:44//Ne 7:47.

PAGIEL son of Ochran (5), leader of the tribe of Asher, Nb 2:27; 7:72; 10:26, in charge of the census of his tribe, Nb 1:13, brings the offering for the dedication of the altar on the eleventh day, Nb 7:72–77.

PAHATH-MOAB (6), "Governor of Moab"? (cf. Moab), head of an Israelite family whose sons return from the exile, some with Zerubbabel and Jeshua, Ezr 2:6//Ne 7:11, others with Ezra, Ezr 8:4. Some of them put away the foreign wives they have married, Ezr 10:30–32. Pahath-moab is among the leaders of the people who sign the pledge to observe the Law, Ne 10:15.

Among his sons: HASSHUB 2.

PAI (1), Hb. *Pa'i.* See: PAU.

PALAL (1), "[Yah] has arbitrated" (cf. Pelaliah), **son of Uzai** (1), a volunteer in the rebuilding of the Jerusalem wall, Ne 3:25.

[PALESTINE], "Land of the Philistines." Originally the word referred to the coastal area S of Joppa and occupied by the Philistines; subsequently, it designates the country between Mount Lebanon and the Red Sea, the "Bible land" par excellence.

PALLU (5), (cf. Pelaiah 2), second of the four sons of Reuben, Gn 46:9//Ex 6:15//1 Ch 5:3. His descendants form the **Palluite** clan, Nb 26:5, to which Dathan and Abiram, sons of Eliab, belong, Nb 26:8.

Same (?) as: PELET 3.

PALLUITE (1), belonging to the clan of: PALLU.

PALM (Deborah's) (1), Hb. *Tomer* (cf. Tamar), Jg 4:5. See: DEBORAH 2.

PALM TREES (City of), Hb. *'Ir ha-Temarim.*

1. **City of Palm Trees** (3). See: JERICHO *a*.

2. **City of Palms** (1). See: TAMAR 4.

PALTI, abbrev. of *Paltiel* or *Pelatiah* (cf. Pelet 1–2).

1. **Palti son of Raphu** (1), a clan chief of the tribe of Benjamin, sent by Moses to represent his tribe in the reconnaissance of Canaan, Nb 13:9.

2. **Palti son of Laish, from Gallim** (1). See: PALTIEL 2.

PALTIEL, "God is my deliverance" (cf. Pelet 1–2).

1. **Paltiel son of Azzan** (1), leader representing the tribe of Issachar in the allocation of Canaan, Nb 34:26.

2. **Paltiel** (1) or **Palti** (1) **son of Laish** (1), second husband of Michal, daughter of Saul (the first husband having been David), 1 S 25:44; 2 S 3:15.

PAMPHYLIA (6), "[Land] of all the tribes," an area of Asia Minor on the southern coast between Lycia to the west and Cilicia to the east. From 43 B.C. on, Pamphylia and Lycia form a Roman province. Many Jews live there. The letter of the consul Lucius promulgating the alliance between the Romans and the Jews is addressed to Pamphylia among others, 1 M 15:23.

Some Jews from Pamphylia are in Jerusalem on the first Christian Pentecost, Ac 2:10. Paul and Barnabas preach the Gospel there, Ac 14:24; it is there that Mark leaves them, Ac 15:38. During his journey to Rome, Paul, a prisoner, sails by Pamphylia, Ac 27:5.

Towns: ATTALIA; PERGA; SIDE.

PAPHOS (2), a port on the southern coast of Cyprus. During their first missionary journey, Paul, Barnabas, and Mark, coming from Salamis, meet the Roman proconsul Sergius Paulus there. The latter, despite the hostility of the Jewish magician Bar-jesus, is converted. From Paphos the Apostles travel on to Pamphylia, Ac 13:6–13.

PARADISE. See: EDEN 1.

PARAH (1), a town of Benjamin, Jos 18:23. In the *Wadi Farah*, 6 km N of Anathoth.

PARAN, Hb. *Pa'rân.*

1. **Wilderness of Paran** (6). Ishmael stays there, Gn 21:21, as do the Israelites in the course of the Exodus, Nb 10:12; 12:16; 13:3, 26. David, pursued by Saul, takes refuge there, 1 S 25:1 (the Gr. *Maon* is probably to be read instead of Hb. *Paran*). Acc. to Nb 13:26, the wilderness of Paran is near Kadesh.

2. **Paran** (2), between Egypt and Midian, Dt 1:1; 1 K 11:18. Probably identical with the preceding.

3. **Mount Paran** (2), in Edom or Seir, Dt 33:2; Hab 3:3.

4. **El-paran** or "Oak of Paran." See: EL-PARAN.

PARBAR (2), a Persian word? Perhaps refers to a gallery or colonnade of the temple in Jerusalem, 1 Ch 26:18.

PARMASHTA (1), a Persian name, Accad. *Parushta,* brother of: PARSHANDATHA.

PARMENAS (1), one of the: SEVEN.

PARNACH (1), a Zebulunite, father of: ELIZAPHAN 2.

PAROSH (6), Hb. *Par'osh,* "Flea," head of an Israelite family whose sons return from the exile, some with Zerubbabel and Jeshua, Ezr 2:3//Ne 7:8, others with Ezra, Ezr 8:3. Some of them put away the foreign wives they have married, Ezr 10:25. Parosh is among the leaders of the people who sign the pledge to observe the Law, Ne 10:15.

Among his sons: PEDAIAH 3.

PARSHANDATHA (1), a Persian name, and **Dalphon, Aspatha, Poratha, Adalia, Aridatha, Parmashta, Arisai, Aridai,** and **Jezatha,** the ten sons of Haman, persecutor of the Jews, all hung with their father, Est 9:7–14; cf. 9:25. Est Gr. gives the following list: *Pharsanestain, Delphōn, Phasga, Phardatha, Barea, Sarbacha, Marmasin, Arouphaios, Arsaios, Zabouthaios.*

PARTHIANS (1), an Iranian tribe occupying the area SE of the Caspian Sea. The Parthians present in Jerusalem on the first Christian Pentecost are Jews of the Diaspora from Parthia, Ac 2:9. Allusion to the Parthians, Rv 6:2; 9:14 ff.; 16:12.

King: ARSACES.

PARUAH (1), an Issacharite, father of: JOSHAPHAT 4.

PARVAIM (1), an unidentifiable region, perhaps in southern Arabia? 2 Ch 3:6 speaks of it as a country where gold is found.

PASACH (1), an Asherite, first of the three sons of Japhlet, a fighting man and head of a family, 1 Ch 7:33–34.

PAS-DAMMIM (1). See: EPHES-DAMMIM.

PASEAH, "Lame" (cf. Tiphsah. See Claudius).

1. **Paseah** (1), one of the sons of Eshton, a descendant of Chelub (= Caleb), 1 Ch 4:12.

2. **Paseah** (2), head of a family of "oblates" who return from the exile, Ezr 2:49//Ne 7:51.

3. **Paseah** (1), father of: JEHOIADA 5.

PASHHUR

1. **Pashhur** (5) **son of Immer** (1), a priest, head of the temple police. He has the prophet Jeremiah beaten and put in the stocks for predicting the fall of Jerusalem. The next day, when Pashhur frees Jeremiah, the latter says to him: "Not Pashhur but Terror is Yahweh's name for you," and predicts that Pashhur will be deported to Babylon and will die and be buried there, for "you have prophesied lies," Jr 20:1–6.

2. **Pashhur** (1), same as the preceding?, father of the minister: GEDALIAH 3.

3. **Pashhur son of Malchiah** (2). Two appearances during the siege of Jerusalem: with the priest Zephaniah, son of Maaseiah, he consults the prophet Jeremiah on behalf of King Zedekiah, Jr 21:1 ff.; later, he is among the four ministers of Zedekiah who have Jeremiah thrown into a cistern on the grounds that his words are demoralizing the last defenders of the city, Jr 38:1–6.

4. **Pashhur** (2), son of Malchijah, an ancestor of the priest: ADAIAH 6.

5. **Pashhur** (4), head of a priestly family whose sons return from the exile, Ezr 2:38//Ne 7:41. Some of these put away the foreign wives they have married, Ezr 10:22. Pashhur is a cosigner of the pledge to observe the Law, Ne 10:4.

PASS OF HAMATH (12). See: HAMATH 2.

PATARA (1), a port of Lycia in Asia Minor. Paul stops there on his return from his third missionary journey, Ac 21:1.

PATHROS (5), Egypt. *Po-to-resi,* "Country of the South," is a name for Upper Egypt. The genealogies in Gn 10:14//1 Ch 1:12 connect Pathros with Egypt. "Pathros" is also associated with "Egypt" in the major prophets, Is 11:1; Jr 44:1, 5 (Israelites exiled to Pathros); Ezk 29:14 (Egyptians exiled far from Pathros); 30:14 (devastation of Pathros).

PATMOS (1), a small island in the Sporades in the Aegean Sea, west of Miletus. John, the author of the Apocalypse, is probably in exile there for preaching the faith, Rv 1:9.

PATROBAS (1), (cf. Antipater), a Roman Christian, Rm 16:15.

PATROCLUS (1), (cf. Antipater; Cleopatra), 2 M 8:9, father of: NICANOR 1.

PAU (1), Gn 36:39 = **Pai** (1), 1 Ch 1:50, a town in Edom, capital of the Edomite king Hadad. Location unknown.

PAUL, PAULUS, Gr. *Paulos.*

1. **Paul** (157), Roman surname of **Saul** (15) or, in Greek, *Saoul* (8) **of Tarsus** (2), an Apostle.

Paul: 127× in Ac 13:9–28:25; 29× in Rm to Phm (missing from Heb); 1× in 2 P 3:15.

Saul: Ac 7:58; 8:1, 3; 9:1, 8, 11, 22, 24; 11:25, 30; 12:25; 13:1–2, 7, 9.

Saoul (in Greek text): Ac 9:4, 17; 22:7, 13; 26:14.

a. The activity of Paul

A *Jew* (cf. Rm 9:3–4; 11:14) of the tribe of Benjamin, Rm 11:1, of a Palestinian family, "a Hebrew born of Hebrew parents," Ph 3:5, born at Tarsus in Cilicia, Ac 9:11; 21:39; cf. 9:30; 11:25; 22:3; 23:34, between 5 and 10 A.D., a Roman citizen from birth, Ac 16:37–38; 22:25–29; 23:27, Saul, circumsized on the eighth day, Ph 3:5, is raised as a Pharisee and strict observer of the Law, Ac 26:5; Ph 3:5, in the school of Gamaliel, Ac 22:3; cf. 5:34, and as a man "enthusiastic . . . for the traditions of my ancestors," Ga 1:14; Ac 22:3. While still a "young man" he is present, an approving witness, at the stoning of Stephen in about 34 or 36 A.D., Ac 7:58–8:1. "Breathing threats to slaughter the Lord's disciples," Ac 9:1–2, Saul comes on the scene initially as "a blasphemer" who "did all I could to injure and discredit the faith," 1 Tm 1:13, in Jesus, Ac 9:4–5// 22:7–8//26:14–15, of those who follow the new way (religion), Ac 9:2, 21; 22:4; 26:9–12, proper to the Church of God, Ac 8:3–4; 1 Co 15:9; Ga 1:13–14; Ph 3:6.

But, having been "captured" by Christ Jesus, Ph 3:12, who appeared to him on the road to Damascus, Ac 9:3–6//22: 6–10//26:12–18; Ac 9:27, and revealed himself to him, Ga 1:12, 15–16; 2:2; 1 Co 9:1; 15:8, thus drawing aside the veil that as yet remained for this reader of the OT, Saul *is converted* to the Lord, cf. 2 Co 3:14–16, in about the year 34 or 36. He who has until now "been acting in ignorance," 1 Tm 1:13, comes to the faith suddenly and in an abnormal and violent way, like someone "born when no one expected it," 1 Co 15:8, and dedicates himself with all his zeal, Ac 22:3; cf. 21:20, hitherto "misguided," cf. Rm 10:2, to Christ Jesus, who has "judged me faithful enough to call me to his service," 1 Tm 1:12. "For him I have accepted the loss of everything . . . if only I can have Christ and . . . know the power of his resurrection and . . . share his sufferings," Ph 3:8–10. Like the "scribe who becomes a disciple of the kingdom of heaven" and "brings out of his storeroom things both new and old," Mt 13:52; cf. 13:12, Paul "worship[s] the God of my ancestors according to the [new] Way" of Christ, "retaining my belief in all points of the Law and in what is written in the prophets," Ac 24:14. Having been a persecutor, he in turn endures "persecutions . . . for Christ's sake," 2 Co 12:10; cf. Ac 9:16; 13:50; Rm 8:35; 1 Co 4:12, Ga 5:11; 2 Co 4:9; 11:23–24; 1 Th 2: 15; 2 Tm 3:11.

After receiving baptism in the house of Judas at Damascus, Ac 9:11–18, Saul begins to preach to the Jews of the city, 9:20, that Jesus is the Christ, 9:22. Threatened by a Jewish plot, Saul flees the city, Ac 9:25; cf. 2 Co 11:33. Reaching Jerusalem, he is introduced to the Apostles by Barnabas, Ac 9:26–28. To escape the Jews, he flees from there "to Arabia," Ga 1:17, there returns to Tarsus, where he remains for some years, Ac 9:29–30. It is there that Barnabas will seek him out after the foundation of the Church at Antioch, Ac 11:22–25, in order to bring him to this city that will become the center of Hellenistic Christianity and, as such, the point of departure and return for Paul's missions to pagan countries, cf. Ac 14:26. Paul is one of the five "prophets and teachers" (that is, men entrusted with the responsibility of teaching) of the new community, Ac 13:1–2. Paul and Barnabas then spend a year in Antioch, "instructing a large number of people," those who will henceforth be called "Christians," Ac 11:26.

Saul/Paul, Ac 13:9, is then "sent" by Christ, Ac 22:21; 26:17; 1 Co 1:17; as the Twelve had been, Mt 10:5, 16 p; Jn 17:18; the title *Apostle* is used of him 20×: Ac 14:4, 14; Rm 1:1; 11:13; 1 Co 1:1; 4:9; 9:1–2; 15:9; 2 Co 1:1; Ga

1:1; Ep 1:1; Col 1:1; 1 Th 2:7; 1 Tm 1:1; 2:7; 2 Tm 1:1, 11; Tt 1:1. Paul's field of apostolate is the "pagan nations" (the "Gentiles") as contrasted with the Jewish "people," cf. Ac 15:23; Rm 16:4; "This man is my chosen instrument to bring my name before pagans," Ac 9:15; cf. 14:27; 15:7; 26:20; 28:28; Rm 1:15; 15:16; Ga 1:16; 2:2, 8–9; Ep 3:1, 8; 1 Th 2:16. And Paul calls himself "the apostle of the pagans," cf. Rm 11:13, and "a teacher of the faith and the truth to the pagans," 1 Tm 2:7. A tireless preacher, a man of great learning, Ac 26:24, who speaks Aramaic, Ac 21:40; cf. Ph 3:5, and Greek, Ac 21:37, and knows Hellenistic culture, Paul also works with his hands as a tentmaker, Ac 18:3; cf. 20:34; 1 Co 4:12; 1 Th 2:9; 2 Th 3:8.

The missionary vocation of Paul finds expression in three great *missionary journeys:*

First journey (46–48) in the company of Barnabas and John Mark: Antioch in Syria, Cyprus, Antioch in Pisidia, Iconium, Lystra, Derbe; Antioch in Syria, Ac 13:1–14:26.

Second journey (49–52), with Silas: Antioch in Syria, Cilicia, Lycaonia (where Paul makes Timothy his companion, at Lystra), Phrygia, Galatia, Mysia (Troas, where Luke joins Paul), Macedonia (Philippi, Amphipolis, Apollonia, Thessalonika, Beroea), Greece (Athens, Corinth), Ephesus, Antioch in Syria, Ac 15:36–18:22.

Third journey (53–58): Galatia, Phrygia, Ephesus (from 53 to 56), Corinth, Ephesus, Macedonia, Corinth, Macedonia, Mysia (Troas), Miletus, Ptolemais, Caesarea, Jerusalem, Ac 18:23–21:16.

In 58, Paul is arrested at Jerusalem, Ac 21:27–28, then transferred to Caesarea, Ac 23:23–24, where he remains a *prisoner* from 58 to 60. Having appealed to Caesar, he is brought to Rome, Ac 27, where he arrives only after being forced to winter in Malta owing to a shipwreck, Ac 28. Paul is set free in 63. Perhaps he then makes a journey to Spain, Rm 15:24–25, then others, to Asia Minor, 1 Tm 1:3; 2 Tm 4:20; Phm 22, to Macedonia, 1 Tm 1:3; 2 Tm 4:13, to Greece, Tt 3:12, to Crete, Tt 3:5. Paul sums up his life as a missionary for Christ in 2 Co 11:23–28, where he speaks of himself as "constantly travelling." It is thought that at the end of a *second imprisonment* at Rome, to which 2 Tm 1:8, 12; 2:9, allude, Paul was beheaded during the persecution of Nero, in 67.

b. The discourses and letters of Paul

The "Acts of the Apostles" are the Acts chiefly of Paul: 7:58–8:3; 9:1–30; 11:25–26; 12:25; 13–28. The book reports not only the journeys of Paul but *six major discourses* as well: in the synagogue of Antioch in Pisidia, 13:16–42, 46–47, before the Areopagus in Athens, 17:22–31, at Miletus to the elders of Ephesus, 20:18–35, on the steps of Fortress Antonia to the Jews of Jerusalem, 22:1–21, at Caesarea before the governor Felix, 24:10–21, and before King Agrippa, 26:2–30. To these must be added his preaching at Lystra, 14:15–17, and his declaration to the Jews of Rome, 28:25–28.

Paul's "theology," which is primarily a Christology, centered on the dead and risen Christ, is also developed in the *thirteen letters* that have been attributed to him since the beginning of the third century. The letter to the Hebrews, even though Paul's influence is detectable in it, is generally regarded as from another author; this view is confirmed by the order followed in the NT canon, which lists the letters of Paul according to decreasing length and puts Heb with its 13 chapters after the short note (22 verses) to Philemon.

These thirteen letters are occasional writings, called forth by particular circumstances; but, except for the letter to Philemon, they look beyond the immediate recipients to all the faithful of Christ.

Paul himself wants them read in public, 1 Th 5:27, and passed from one church to another, Col 4:16.

The most probable dates and places of composition for the lettters of Paul:

51, at Corinth: 1 and 2 Th (the first writings of the NT).

56, at Ephesus: Ph (?).

57, at Ephesus: 1 Co; Ga (?); in Macedonia: 2 Co.

57–58, at Corinth: Rm; Ga (?).

61–63, at Rome: letters during the (first) imprisonment: Ph (?); Col; Ep; Phm.

65, in Macedonia: 1 Tm; Tt.

67, at Rome, 2 Tm.

The discourses and letters of Paul are characterized by his love for Christ and his passionate zeal for the spread of the Gospel. They reveal a man of wisdom and learning, Ac 26:24, but there are "some points in his letter hard to understand," 2 P 3:16.

Chief figures connected with the ministry of Paul: APOLLOS; AQUILA; ARISTARCHUS; BARNABAS; MARK; SILAS; TIMOTHY 2; TITUS 2; TYCHICUS.

Places connected with the journeys of Paul: ASIA; GALATIA; MACEDONIA.

Also: ANTIOCH 1–2; ATHENS; CORINTH; DAMASCUS; EPHESUS; PHILIPPI; ROME.

2. **Sergius Paulus** (1), proconsul of Cyprus (46–47 or 49–50). At Paphos he "summoned Barnabas and Paul and asked to hear the word of God." Despite the opposition of the Jewish magician Barjesus, Sergius Paulus is converted to the Christian faith, Ac 13:7–12.

PAULUS. See: PAUL 2.

PAVEMENT (1), Gr. *Lithostratos,* in Aram. *Gabbatha,* "Height," the place where Pilate passes sentence on Jesus, Jn 19:13.

PEDAHEL (1), "God ransoms, delivers" (cf. Pedaiah), **son of Ammihud** (1), representative of the tribe of Naphtali in the allocation of Canaan, Nb 34:28.

PEDAHZUR (5). "The [God] Rock ransoms *or* delivers" (cf. Pedaiah; Zur), a Manassite, father of: GAMALIEL 1.

PEDAIAH, Hb. *Pedaya, Pedayahu,* "Yah ransoms, delivers" (cf. Iphdeiah; Padon; Pedahzur; Pedahel).

1. **Pedaiah** (1), father of the queen mother: ZEBIDAH.

2. **Pedaiah** (2), son of the imprisoned King Jehoiachin, and brother, with others, of Shealtiel, 1 Ch 3:17–18. Acc. to 1 Ch 3:19 he is father of Zerubbabel and Shimei; elsewhere, however, Shealtiel is 9× called the father of: ZERUBBABEL.

3. **Pedaiah son of Parosh** (1), a volunteer in the rebuilding of the Jerusalem wall, Ne 3:25.

4. **Pedaiah** (1) stands on Ezra's left during the solemn reading of the Law, Ne 8:4.

5. **Pedaiah** (1), Ne 11:7, a Benjaminite, an ancestor of: SALLU 1.

6. **Pedaiah** (1), a Levite of great honesty, one of the supervisors of the temple storehouse in the time of Nehemiah, Ne 13:13.

7. **Pedaiah** (1), a Manassite, father of: JOEL 10.

PEKAH (11), abbrev. of *Pekahiah,* **son of Remaliah** (13), eighteenth king of Israel (737–732), perhaps a native of Gilead. Equerry of King Menahem, he succeeds the latter after assassinating him, 2 K 15:25, 27. A contemporary of the kings of Judah, Jotham, and Ahaz, 2 K 15:32; 16:1.

With Rezin, king of Damascus, he forms a coalition against Assyria. When Ahaz, king of Judah, refuses to become part of it, Pekah and Rezin threaten Jerusalem, 2 K 15:37; 16:5, and the Davidic dynasty because they have in mind to replace Ahaz with the son of Tabeel, a man to their liking, Is 7:1, 4–9; cf. 8:6. Ahaz suffers heavy losses, 2 Ch 28:5–8. He then calls upon the king of Assyria, Tiglath-pileser III, who crushes the coalition, 2 K 16:7–9. Pekah loses Galilee and Gilead, 2 K 15:29 (he had already lost Naphtali the year before). He is assassinated by Hoshea, son of Elah, who succeeds him, 2 K 15:30.

PEKAHIAH (3), "Yah has opened [the eyes]" (cf. Pekah), **son of Menahem** (1), whom he succeeds. Seventeenth king of Israel (738–737), of the fifth dynasty. He dies at Samaria in the dungeon of the royal palace, assassinated by his equerry, Pekah, son of Ramaliah, 2 K 15:22–26.

PEKOD (2), a tribe of (nomadic) Aramaeans, in eastern Babylonia, Jr 50:21 (neighbors of Merathaim); Ezk 23:23. Pekod is known from cuneiform inscriptions.

PELAIAH, Hb. 1: *Pelayah* (cf. Eliphelehu; Pelonite); 2: *Pela'yah* (cf. Pallu).

1. **Pelaiah** (1), one of the sons of Elioenai, a descendant of King Jehoiachin, 1 Ch 3:24.

2. **Pelaiah** (2), among the Levites who explain the Law to the people during its solemn reading by Ezra, Ne 8:7, and who sign the pledge to observe the Law, Ne 10:11.

PELALIAH (1), "Yah has arbitrated" (cf. Palal; Ephlal), Ne 11:12, ancestor of the priest: ADAIAH 6.

PELATIAH, Hb. *Pelatya, Pelatyahu,* "Survivor of Yah" (cf. Pelet 1–2).

1. **Pelatiah** (1), one of the Simeonite chiefs settled in the highlands of Seir, 1 Ch 4:42.

2. **Pelatiah son of Benaiah** (2), one of the leaders of the people in Jerusalem whom the prophet Ezekiel accuses of giving bad advice to the people after the first siege of the city by the Babylonians. His death perhaps presages that of the survivors of Israel, Ezk 11:1, 13.

3. **Pelatiah** (1), son of Hananiah, a descendant of King Jehoiachin, 1 Ch 3:21.

4. **Pelatiah** (1), a leader of the people and cosigner of the pledge to observe the Law, Ne 10:23.

PELEG (8), Gr. *Phaleg* or *Phalek,* a descendant of Shem. Acc. to the Yahwist tradition, Peleg is the elder son of Eber and the brother of Joktan; his name supposedly means "Division," a possible allusion to an allocation of the countries, Gn 10:25//1 Ch 1:9. In the priestly tradition he is the son of Eber and father of Reu, Gn 11:16–19//1 Ch 1:25, an ancestor of Abraham. Acc. to Lk 3:35 (Gr. *Phalek*), he is an ancestor of Jesus.

PELET, Peleth, Hb. 1–2 (final *teth*): "Survivor" (cf. Beth-pelet; Eliphelet; Elpelet; Japhlet; Melatiah; Palti; Paltiel; Pelatiah; Piltai); 3–4 (final *tau*).

1. **Pelet** (1), a Calebite of the sons of Jahdai, 1 Ch 2:47.

2. **Pelet** (1), a Benjaminite, brother of: JEZIEL.

3. **Peleth** (1), son of Reuben, father of: ON 2. Same (?) as: PALLU.

4. **Peleth** (1), son of Jonathan, of the clan of Jerahmeel, 1 Ch 2:33.

PELETH. See: PELET 3–4.

PELETHITES (7), personal bodyguard of David, along with the: CHERETHITES.

PELONITE (3), (cf. Pelaiah 1), same (?) as **from Beth-pelet.** See: AHIJAH 7; HELEZ 1.

PENIEL (1), "Face of God," Gn 32:31, same as: PENUEL 1.

PENINNAH (3), "Pearl"?, second wife of Elkanah. Because she has given her husband sons and daughters "she would taunt" the first wife, Hannah, the future mother of Samuel, who at that time was barren, 1 S 1:2, 4–7.

[PENTAPOLIS], "The Five Cities" (cf. Amphipolis).

1. **Five Cities** (1), name given by Ws 10:6 to the *five* neighboring *cities* of Sodom, Gomorrah, Admah, Zeboiim, and Zoar, also called "the cities of the plain," Gn 13:12; 19:29. Cf. Ez 16:46, 55. In a coalition against the four great kings, Gn 14, they are destroyed, except for Zoar, in the same catastrophe, Gn 19. South of the Dead Sea.

See: ADMAH; SODOM; ZEBOIIM; ZOAR.

2. **[Pentapolis of the Philistines]**, cf. the "five" princes, Jos 13:3; 1 S 6:18; includes the Philistine cities of: ASHDOD; ASHKELON; EKRON; GATH 1; GAZA.

PENUEL, Gr. *Phanouēl,* "Face of God" (cf. Corner; Hazzelelponi; Jephunneh).

1. **Penuel** (7), place where Jacob meets God in a wrestling match, wins God's blessing by force, and receives the name Israel, Gn 32:31 (Hb. *Peniel*), 32. Gideon destroys the tower of Penuel and punishes the inhabitants of the town who have refused him bread, Jg 8:8–9, 17. Jeroboam I, king of Israel, fortifies it, 1 K 12:25. In Transjordania, on the Jabbok. Perhaps *Tulul edh-Dhahab.*

2. **Penuel** (1), father of Gedor, listed among the sons of Hur, 1 Ch 4:4. In Judah.

3. **Penuel** (1), a Benjaminite of the sons of Shashak, head of a family in Jerusalem, 1 Ch 8:25.

4. **Phanuel** (1), an Asherite, father of the prophetess: HANNAH 3.

PEOR, Gr. *Phogōr, Phagōr* (cf. Baal-peor; Beth-peor).

1. **Peor** (1), acc. to Nb 23:28, a mountain in Transjordania where Balaam and Balak offer a holocaust. From here they see Israel.

2. **Peor** (1), another name for Baal-peor, the god worshipped on this mountain. See: BAAL-PEOR 1–2.

3. **Peor** (1), Jos 15:59 (Gr.), a town in the highlands of Judah. 7 km SW of Bethlehem. Today *Kh. Faghur.*

[PERAEA]. See: JORDAN 3.

PERAZIM (Mount) (1), "Breaches" (cf. Perez). See: BAAL-PERAZIM.

PERESH (1), "Droppings," son of Machir and Maacah, in Manasseh, 1 Ch 7:16.

PEREZ (19), Gr. *Phares,* "Breach," see Gn 38:29 (cf. Baal-perazim; Perazim; Perezzite; Perez-uzzah; Rimmon-perez), **son of Judah** (1), 1 Ch 9:4.

Perez is born of the incestuous union of Judah with his daughter-in-law Tamar, who is probably a Canaanite woman. Twin brother of Zerah, Gn 38:27–30; Rt 4:12, he is the fourth of Judah's five sons, Gn 46:12; 1 Ch 2:3–4; cf. 4:1. Perez has two sons, Hezron and Hamul, Gn 46:12; Nb 26:21; 1 Ch 2:5. His descendants, 1 Ch 9:4; 27:3; Ne 11:4, 6, form the **Perezzite** clan, Nb 26:20. A genealogy of Perez down to David is given in Rt 4:18–22; cf. 1 Ch 2:5, 10–15; Mt 1:306; Lk 3:31–33. Perez is an ancestor of Jesus, Mt 1:3; Lk 3:33.

PEREZ-UZZAH (2), "Uzzah's Breach" (cf. Perez). See: NACON.

PEREZZITE (1), belonging to the clan of: PEREZ

PERGA (3) **in Pamphylia** (1), a religious center. Paul, accompanied by Barnabas, passes through it twice during his first missionary journey: outward bound (after the journey across Cyprus, when Mark leaves them, Ac 13:13–14, and homeward bound (from Antioch in Pisidia), when they preach the Gospel there, 14:25.

PERGAMUM (2), ancient capital of Mysia (which is incorporated in 129 into the Roman province of Asia). 130 km N of Ephesus. In this center of emperor worship there is a Christian community to which one of the letters to the seven churches is addressed. In this community are to be found such faithful witnesses as the martyr Antipas, but also heretics like the Nicolaitans, Rv 1:11; 2:12. Today *Bergama* in Turkey.

PERIDA (1). See: PERUDA.

PERIZZITES (24), Hb. *Perizzi,* "[Dwellers] in an open country," one of the pre-Israelite peoples of Canaan, Gn 13:7; Jg 1:4–5, living in the highlands of Ephraim, Jos 17:15, in the area of Shechem, Gn 34:20.

See: CANAAN *a.*

PERSEPOLIS (1), (cf. Amphipolis; Persia), one of the ancient capitals of the Achaemenid Persian Empire, destroyed by Alexander the Great. The temple of which 2 M 9:2 speaks is not in Persepolis but rather NW of it at Elymais, cf. 1 M 6:1.

PERSEUS king of the Kittim (1), son of Philip V of Macedonia, and last king of Macedonia, defeated by the Romans, 1 M 8:5, at Pydna in 168.

PERSIA, PERSIANS (57), Hb. *Paras, Parsi,* ancient Pers. *Persa,* Gr. *Persis, Persikē, Persēs* (cf. Persepolis; Persis), an Iranian tribe related to the: MEDES. Having gained preeminence over the latter, the Persians will dominate the Near East from the time of Cyrus the Great (555), from India to Egypt. In 331 the Persian Empire will collapse before Alexander the Great.

First mention of Persia in Ezk 27:10, where Persians serve in the army of Tyre, and in 38:5, where Persia fights beside Gog, king of Magog. When Cyrus captures Babylon in 539, the exile is brought to an end, 2 Ch 36:20; cf. 2 M 1:19; the kings of Persia show themselves especially cordial to the Jews, Ezr 9:9. Judaea becomes a province of the Persian Empire, cf. Ezr 4:9; 5:6; 6:6. The story told in the book of Esther takes place in Persia, Est 1:3, 19; 8:12[k, o, u], where a young Jewess who has been deported there becomes queen of Persia and saves her coreligionists from extermination.

High-ranking officers: MEMUCAN.

The Book of Daniel alludes to the conquest of Babylon by the Persians, 5:28, and the growth, then the fall of Persian power, 7:6 (*the third beast*); 8:3–4, 7, 20 (*the horn that rose the higher*); cf. 10:13, 20; 11:2. Antiochus Epiphanes, the persecutor of the Jews, travels through Persia; it is there that he dies, 1 M 3:31, 37; 6:1, 5, 56; 2 M 1:13; 9:1, 21.

Kings: CYPRUS; DARIUS 1–3; XERXES; ARTAXERXES 1; ARSACES.

Cities: ECBATANA; PERSEPOLIS; SUSA.

PERSIANS. See: PERSIA.

PERSIS (1), (cf. Persia), Greek name of a slave or freedwoman who was doubtless of Persian origin. A Christian woman very active in Rome and known to Paul, Rm 16:12.

PERUDA (1), Ezr 2:55, head of a family of Solomon's slaves who return from the exile.

= **Perida** (1), Ne 7:57.

PETER (154), Aram. *Képha,* Gr. *Petros,* "Rock" (cf. Rock), Gr. name corresponding to **Cephas** (9), the surname given to **Simon** (50) or **Simeon** (2) **son of John** (4) or **of Jonah** (1), the leading member of the Twelve. We find:

Cephas (9), Jn 1:42; 1 Co 1:12; 3:22; 9:5; 15:5; Ga 1:18; 2:9, 11, 14.

Peter: Gospels, 95; Ac, 56; and Ga 2:7; 1 P 1:1; 2 P 1:1; (the name Peter is used by itself 126×).

Simon (17), Mt 17:25; Mk 1:16, 29–30, 36; 14:37; Lk 4:38; 5:3–5, 10; 22:31; 24:34; Jn 1:41.

Simon called Peter (8), Mt 4:18; 10:2; Mk 3:16; Lk 6:14; Ac 10:5, 18, 32; 11:13.

Simon Peter (19), Mt 16:16; Lk 5:8; Jn 1:40; 6:8, 68; 13:6, 9, 24, 36; 18:10, 15, 25; 20:2, 6; 21:2–3, 7, 11, 15.

Simon son of John (4), Jn 1:42; 21: 15–17.
Simon son of Jonah, Mt 16:17.
Simeon, Ac 15:14.
Simeon Peter, 2 P 1:1.

a. Peter and Jesus

A native of Bethsaida, Jn 1:44, Peter, with his brother Andrew, Mt 4:18; Mk 1:16, 29; Jn 1:40, 44; 6:8, belongs to a group of fishermen "by the Sea of Galilee," Mt 4:18//Mk 1:16; Lk 5:2–10; Jn 21:2–11. Married, cf. 1 Co 9:5, he lives with Andrew at Capernaum, Mt 8:5, 14//Mk 1:21, 29–30//Lk 4:31, 38. The first one called, Mt 4:18 p, by Jesus (but cf. Jn 1:35–41), he is "first" of the Twelve, Mt 10:2. The "primacy" of Peter is solemnly affirmed at Caesarea Philippi when Simon, son of Jonah, in the name of the Twelve, acknowledges Jesus as "the Christ, the Son of the living God" and receives the new name *Peter* as foundation of the Church, Mt 16:13–19. Jesus also prays especially for Peter "that your faith may not fail, and once you have recovered, you in your turn must strengthen your brothers," Lk 22:32. Finally, after the resurrection, Jesus bestows on Peter the pastoral care of his flock, Jn 21:15–19. Peter's primacy is underscored by the first place he has in the lists of the: TWELVE; List, page 417. He is also mentioned at the head of the three Apostles closest to Jesus—Peter, James, and John—who are with him at the raising of the daughter of Jairus, Mk 5:37//Lk 8:51, at the Transfiguration, Mt 17:1–8//Mk 9:2–8//Lk 9:28–36, who hear him predict the end of Jerusalem and the end of the world, Mk 15:3, and who should have watched with him in the garden of Gethsemane, Mt 26:37// Mk 14:33. When he is mentioned with John, his name comes first, Lk 22:8; Jn 18:15; 20:2–3 (cf. 21:20–23); cf. below, *b.* He acts as the representative of the Twelve, Mt 17:24; Jn 13:24, and is named specifically along with a group of "disciples," Mk 16:7; he is the spokesman who addresses Jesus, Mt 14:28; 15: 15; 16:16, 22; 17:4 p; 18:21; 19:27 p; 26:33; Mk 11:21; Jn 6:68, and whom Jesus addresses, Mt 17:25; Mk 8:33; Lk 22:31; Jn 13:6–9; 18:11. Peter is the first —of the disciples—who is informed of the resurrection, Jn 20:2; Mk 16:7, and to whom the risen Jesus appears, 1 Co 15:5.

Called to the highest responsibility and endowed with great powers in the Church of Christ, Mt 16:18–19, Peter remains the "human being" whom the Gospels depict for us: full of fervor in commitment to Jesus, Mt 19:27//Mk 10:28//Lk 18: 28; Mt 26:33 p; Jn 6:68; 13:9, 37; 18:10, full of reverence for the Lord, Jn 21:7, but also presumptuous, Mt 26:33–35, rash, 14:28, lacking in courage, 26:40, even cowardly, 26:58, 69 p, ready to receive the revelation of the Father, 16:17, but ready, too, to oppose the plan of God, to the point where Jesus treats him as "Satan," 16:22–23//Mk 8:32–33; when all is said and done, recognizing himself to be a sinner, Lk 5:8, weeping bitterly for his sin, Mt 26:75 p, and redeeming his triple denial, Mt 26:69–75// Mk 14:66–72//Lk 22:56–61//Jn 18:17, 25–27, by a triple avowal of love, Jn 21:15–17.

b. The "Acts of Peter"

In their first section, the Acts of the Apostles are chiefly, 1:15–5:42; 8:14–25; 9:26–12:19; 15, the "Acts of Peter." From the beginning Peter is to the fore. At the head, as always, of the list of the Eleven who are gathered in Jerusalem after the Ascension, Ac 1:12–14, he immediately acts as head of the apostolic group by proceeding to a replacement for Judas, Ac 1:15–26. After the coming of the Spirit, even when he is accompanied by John, who is hardly more than his understudy, Ac 3:1, 3–4, 11; 4:1–13, 19;

8:14, it is he who addresses the people of Jerusalem, Ac 2:14–41; 3:12–26, the Sanhedrin, Ac 4:7–12, 19–20, the "Council of Jerusalem," Ac 15:7–11. Even if Paul, whom Peter welcomes at Jerusalem, Ga 1:18–19; cf. Ac 9:27, is the "apostle to the pagans," Rm 11:13, as contrasted with Peter, "the apostle of the circumcised," Ga 2:7–9, it is Peter who confers the Holy Spirit on the Samaritans evangelized by Philip, Ac 8:14–17; it is also he who, after the twofold vision at Jaffa, Ac 10:1–16, goes to Caesarea to Cornelius the centurion, 10:17–33, proclaims there that "Jesus Christ is Lord of all men," 10:34–43, and baptizes the first pagans, 10:44–48, thus opening "the door of faith to the pagans," 14:27; cf. 11:18; 15:14. Peter and Paul are thus seen as the two pillars of the Church. Paul "opposed Peter to his face," Ga 2:11, but this was not due to jealousy or desire to resist his authority, cf. 1 Co 1:12; 3:21–22; he criticized Peter for behaving badly by acting out of fear and duplicitously, Ga 2:12–14, but he did so out of concern to "strengthen" the unity of the Church in the truth, as Peter should have been doing by the Lord's command, Lk 22:31–32. Peter has also received the mission, Mt 16:19, of exercising discipline in the Church. He does this, for example, in dealing with Simon the magician, Ac 8:18–26, and the cheating couple, Ananias and Sapphira, Ac 5:1–11. In virtue of the power Jesus has given to the Twelve, Mt 10:8, he cures the lame man at the Beautiful Gate of the temple, Ac 3:1–11; Aeneas, the paralytic at Lydda, Ac 9:32–35; and many sick people who are placed along his route, so that "at least the shadow of Peter might fall across some of them as he went past," Ac 5:15–16, and he restores to life Tabitha, the seamstress at Jaffa, Ac 9:36–42.

Persecuted, yet "glad to have had the honour of suffering humiliation for the sake of the name," Ac 5:41, arrested, imprisoned, but twice miraculously freed, Ac 4:3, 21, 23; 5:18–19, 22–23; 12:1–19, Peter was to die by crucifixion at Rome—in about 64 or 67—thus fulfilling the prophecy of Jesus, who, in Jn 21:18–19, had predicted "the kind of death by which Peter would give glory to God."

Two letters are attributed to "Peter, apostle of Jesus Christ," 1 P 1:1; 2 P 1:1.

PETHAHIAH, "Yah opens [the womb?]" (cf. Jephthah).

1. **Pethahiah** (1), a priest, head of the nineteenth class of priests, 1 Ch 24:16.

2. **Pethahiah** (2), a Levite married to a foreign wife, whom he puts away, Ezr 10:23, takes part in the penitential liturgy of Ne 9:5.

3. **Pethahiah son of Meshezabel** (1), a Judaean of the clan of Zerah, the king of Persia's commissioner for Jewish affairs, Ne 11:24.

PETHOR (2), Accad. *Pitru,* **on the river** (1), Nb 22:5, **in Aram of the Two Rivers** (1), Dt 23:5, native place of Balaam. A city on the Euphrates, south of Carchemish.

PETHUEL (1), "Youthfulness of God," father of the prophet: JOEL 13.

[PETRA]. See: ROCK 1.

PEULLETHAI (1), (cf. Elpaal), a Levite gatekeeper, eighth son of Obed-edom, 1 Ch 26:5.

PHANUEL (1). See: PENUEL 4.

PHARAOH (277), Hb. *Par'oh,* Egypt. *Per-âa,* "Great House," a title for the king of Egypt (as Kandake is a title for the queen of Ethiopia).

Four Pharaohs are named: SHISHAK I (945–925); TIRHAKAH (685–664); NECO (609–594); HOPHRA (589–566). Other Pharaohs are not named, but we may think that:

—the *Pharaoh* (128) who oppresses the Hebrews and is involved in the events of the Exodus is: RAMESES II (1290–1224);

—the *Pharaoh* (5) who is Solomon's father-in-law is: PSUSENNIS II (955–950);

—the *Pharaoh* (4), to whom Hezekiah sends ambassadors, is: SHABATOKA (710–696).

Unidentifiable are:

—the *Pharaoh* (6), who is a contemporary of Abraham, Gn 12:10–20;

—the *Pharaoh* (90), who is a contemporary of Joseph, son of Jacob, Gn 40; 41; 45; 47; 50:4–9; cf. Ac 7:10, 13;

—the *Pharaohs* of 1 Ch 4:8; Jr 25:19; 46:25; Ezk 17:17; 29:2–3; 30:21–25; 31:2, 18; 32:2, 31–32.

PHARATHON (1). See: PIRATHON.

PHARISEE (98), Gr. *Pharisaios,* Hb. *Parush,* Aram. *Perishayya,* "Separated."

Members of a Jewish sect, Ac 23:6, 9; 26:5, that originated, as did the Essenes, in the movement of the: HASIDAEANS, the Pharisees are motivated by a concern to "separate themselves" from men in power, from unclean pagans, from sinners, Mt 9:11 p; Lk 15:2, from less fervent Jews, from the "people in the country" (cf. 2 K 24:14), "this rabble" that "knows nothing about the Law," Jn 7:49.

A scrupulous observance of all the commandments of the Law of Moses, Rm 2:17–20, and of the least details of "the tradition of the elders," Mt 15:2; Mk 7:3, 5; cf. Ga 1:14, constitutes the "justice," that is, virtue of the Pharisees, Mt 5:20; cf. Lk 18:9–14, which Paul boasts of having possessed, Ph 3:5–6. The Pharisaic tradition, "your tradition," Mt 15:3, 6; Mk 7:9, the "tradition which you have handed down," Mk 7:13, established by the rabbis, the majority of whom belonged to this party, cf. Mt 23:2, 7, finds in the Law (*Torah*) 613 precepts (248 commandments and 365 prohibitions) which must be "kept," Mt 19:20; 23:3; Mk 7:9; Ga 4:10. The Pharisees are often mentioned together with the scribes (61× in the NT), Mt 5:20; 12:38; 15:1; 23:2–29; Mk 2:16; 7:1, 5; Lk 5:21, 30; 6:7; 11:53; 15:2; Jn 8:3, the doctors of the Law, Lk 5:17; cf. Ac 5:34; 1 Tm 1:7, the lawyers, Mt 22:34–35; Lk 7:30; 10:25; 11:45–46, 52; 14:3.

The Pharisees reproach Jesus for breaking the sabbath, Mt 12:2 p; Lk 6:7; 14:1–31 Jn 9:13–14, the regulations for ritual cleanness, Mt 15:1–3; Mk 7:3–4; Lk 11:37–39, the law of fasting, Mt 9:14, for claiming to forgive sins, Lk 5:21, and for being more effective than they in expelling demons, Mt 9:34; 12:24. They try to trap him, Mt 19:3; 22:15, 35; Lk 11:54; 14:1; Jn 8:3, but instead they are themselves caught, Mt 19:8; 22:22, 46; Lk 5:22; 14:4–6. They "were furious," Lk 6:11, and "began a furious attack on him," 11:53.

Jesus, in turn, is very hard on the Pharisees, especially in Mt 23:1–36; Lk 11:37–53, and in the three parables of the barren fig tree, Mt 21:18–22, the two sons, Mt 21:28–32, and the murderous vinedressers, Mt 21:33–34, in which, the Pharisees realize, Jesus is "speaking about them," Mt 21:45. He who has come "not to abolish but to complete" the Law and the prophets, Mt 5:17, blames the Pharisees not for their teaching, Mt 23:2–3, but for their outlook: that precisely which we call "Phariseeism." Their knowledge of the Law fills them with arrogance, Lk 18:11–12; cf. Rm 2:17–20, and their practice of the Law makes them sure of their salvation. Their legalistic spirit leads them into pettiness and hypocrisy, Mt 12:1–2; 23:3–5, 27; Lk 12:1; "you . . . pay your tithe of mint and dill and cummin and have neglected the weightier matters of the Law—justice, mercy, good faith!" Mt 23:23//Lk 11:42. The Pharisaic tradition, under pretext of completing the Law of Moses, in fact makes it null and void, Mt 15:6, and thwarts the plan of God, Lk 7:30; it is simply a "human tradition," Mk 7:7–8. The Pharisees are blind guides, Mt 23:16–26; Rm 2:19, and avaricious as well, Lk 16:14.

While Phariseeism is an excess, there are good Pharisees, such men as Nicodemus and Gamaliel, more open than the Sadducees, with whom they are 7× linked, Mt 3:7; 16:1, 11–12; 22:34; Ac 23:6–9, the Pharisees believe in the resurrection, in angels and spirits, Ac 23:8, and sincerely look for the coming of the Messiah and the establishment of the Kingdom, as does the scribe who wins this response from Jesus: "You are not far from the kingdom of God," Mk 12:34.

See: GAMALIEL 2; NICODEMUS; SIMEON 13.

PHARPAR (1), a river that runs down from the Anti-Lebanon and, with the Abana, is one of the "rivers of Damascus," 2 K 5:12.

PHASELIS (1), a port of Lycia in Asia Minor, to which the letter of the consul Lucius promulgating the alliance of Romans and Jews is addressed, 1 M 15:23.

PHASIRON (The sons of) (1), probably an Arabian tribe collaborating with Bacchides and defeated by Jonathan Maccabaeus, 1 M 9:66.

PHICOL (3), Gn 21:22, 32; 26:26, commander of the army of: ABIMELECH 1.

PHILADELPHIA, Gr. *Philadelpheia,* from *Philadelphos,* "One who loves the brethren" (cf. Philetus).

1. **Philadelphia** (2), a city in Lydia in Asia Minor, founded by Attalus II Philadelphus (159–138 B.C.). The Christian community of the city, to which one of the letters to the seven churches is addressed, has remained constant in its faith despite persecution, Rv 1:11; 3:7–13. 130 km E of Smyrna (in Turkey).

2. **[Philadelphia],** name given to *Rabbah of the Ammonites* by Ptolemy II Philadephus (285–246). A city of the: DECAPOLIS. Today *Amman.*

PHILEMON (1), (cf. Philetus), a well-to-do Christian of Colossae, in whose house the Christian community of the city gathers. The letter called after him is addressed to him. Onesimus is doubtless his slave, Apphia is perhaps his wife, and Archippus is perhaps his son, Phm 1.

PHILETUS (1), Gr. *Philētos,* "Beloved" (cf. Philadelphia; Philemon; Philip; Philippi; Philologus; Philometor; Theophilus), a Christian heretic, 2 Tm 2:17.

PHILIP, Gr. *Philippos,* "Friend of horses" (cf. Philetus; Archippus. See Horses).

1. **Philip II** (2), king of Macedonia, father of: ALEXANDER 1.

2. **Philip V** (1), 1 M 8:5, king of Macedonia, defeated by the Romans at Cynoscephalae in 197.

3. **Philip** (5), friend of Antiochus Epiphanes, "his comrade," appointed by the latter as tutor of his son, the future king Antiochus V, and regent of the kingdom in place of Lysias, 1 M 6:14–16; cf. 3:32. At the death of Epiphanes, Philip takes refuge in Egypt with Ptolemy Philometor, 2 M 9:29. In due time he returns to Antioch to oust Lysias, 2 M 13:23, but is conquered by the latter, 1 M 6:55–56, 63.

4. **Philip** (3), **a Phrygian** (1), commissioner (*epistatēs*) of King Antiochus Epiphanes at Jerusalem, "by nature more barbarous than the man who appointed him," 2 M 5:22; 6:11; 8:8.

5. **[Herod] Philip** (2). See: HEROD 5.

6. **[Herod] Philip** (3). See: HEROD 6.

7. **Philip** (16), **from Bethsaida** (2) **in Galilee** (1), one of the Twelve. In the lists of the Twelve, he is the first-named in the second group of four Apostles, Mt 10:3//Mk 3:18//Lk 6:14//Ac 1:13. Acc. to Jn, Philip is a fellow townsman of Peter and Andrew; as soon as he himself has responded to the call of Jesus, he brings Nathanael to Jesus, 1:43–48. We find him with Andrew at the multiplication of the loaves; again with Andrew, he acts as intermediary between some people

of Greek background and Jesus, 12:20–22. Finally, it is he who asks Jesus for an evident manifestation of the Father, 14:8–9.

See: TWELVE; List, page 417.

8. **Philip** (16), one of the: SEVEN, the evangelist, Ac 21:8, proclaims the Good News in Samaria, 8:4–13, baptizes a high-ranking official of the queen of Ethiopia, 8, 26–40. When Paul is returning from his third missionary journey, Philip gives him hospitality in his home at Caesarea, in which his four daughters, all prophetesses, are living, 21:8–9.

Some modern exegetes agree with Polycrates of Ephesus and Eusebius of Caesarea in identifying this Philip with Philip the Apostle.

PHILIPPI (4), Gr. *Philippoi* (cf. Philip), owes its name to Philip II, father of Alexander the Great. A city in the first of the four districts that make up the Roman province of Macedonia, Philippi has been a Roman "colony" since 31 B.C. and, therefore, enjoys the same rights as the cities of Italy, Ac 16:12. Its population is Latin for the most part. The Jewish minority, which has no synagogue, meets outside the city on the banks of a river, 16:13.

Paul, accompanied by Silas and Timothy (and perhaps Luke) founds a Christian community there, one of the first in Europe, during his second missionary journey (ca. 49–50). Accused of stirring up trouble in the city, he is thrown into prison. Once set free, he goes to Thessalonika, Ac 16:11–40; cf. 1 Th 2:2. He passes through the city again at the end of his third missionary journey (Easter 58), Ac 20:6. In the letter that he writes to the Christians of Philippi, Ph 1:1, Paul shows a great affection for them, cf. 1:3–8; 4:1. The brotherly attitude of the Christians of Philippi had touched him so deeply that out of all the churches he had founded he will accept material help only from the community of Philippi, Ph 2:25; 4:10–19; cf. Ac 16:15, 40; 2 Co 11:8.

Christians of Philippi: CLEMENT, EVODIA, LYDIA 2; SYNTYCHE; SYZYGUS.

Port of Philippi: NEAPOLIS.

PHILISTIA (8), Hb. *Peleshet,* Assyr. *Palastu,* Gr. *Palaistinē,* an ancient name —appearing only in poetic texts, Ex 15:14; Ps 60:10; 83:8; 87:4; 108:10; Is 14:29, 31; Jl 4:4—for the country of the: PHILISTINES.

PHILISTINES (300), Hb. *Pelishti(m)*; Gr. *Phylistiim,* 11× (Gn 10:14–Jos 13:3; 1 M 3:24; Si 46:18; 47:7; 50:26), but everywhere else *allophyloi,* "foreigners," in the Greek text, as a translation of the Hb., as in 1 M 3:41; 4:22, 30; 5:66, 68. One of the "peoples of the sea," originally from Caphtor, Gn 10:14; 1 Ch 1:12; Am 9:7; cf. Dt 2:23; Jr 47:4, that is, from Crete or the Aegean islands, they settle on the coast of Canaan south of Carmel in about the 12th century B.C.

The **land of the Philistines** (19), Gn 21:32, 34; Ex 13:17; 1 S 27:1; 29:11; 30:16; 31:9; 1 K 5:1; 2 K 8:2–3; 1 Ch 10:9; 2 Ch 9:26; 1 M 3:24, 41; 4:22; 5:66, also called "Philistine territory," 1 S 6:1; 27:7, 11, or "the regions of the Philistines," Jos 13:2 (cf. 1 M 5:68) or "of Philistia," Jl 4:4, comprises the lowlands west of the Judaean hills, and the coastal plain.

Several times called "uncircumcised" (therefore non-Semitic), Jg 14:3; 15:18; 1 S 14:6; 17:26, 36; 31:4; 2 S 1:20; 1 Ch 10:4, the Philistines are politically a confederation of **five towns** (Pentapolis) governed by a prince. The "five chiefs of the Philistines" are listed in Jos 13:3 and 1 S 6:17–18. They are mentioned collectively 22×: Jg 3:3; 16:5–30; 1 S 5:8–11; 6:4–18; 7:7; 18:30; 29:2–9; 1 Ch 12:20; Si 46:18; cf. Jr 25:20, where they are called "kings." See: ASHDOD; ASHKELON; EKRON; GATH 1; GAZA.

Well-equipped with chariots, 1 S 13:5, and iron weapons, of which they seek to retain a monopoly over against Israel, 1 S 13:19–22, they endeavor to extend their domain inland to the highlands: their political unity and military strength long remain dangerous to Israel. In the time of the Judges, Yahweh "gave them [the Israelites] over into the power of the Philistines," Jg 10:7; 13:1; cf. 3:1–3, and Samson's activity is one long battle with the Philistine enemy, Jg 14–16. But Samson will only "begin to rescue Israel from the power of the Philistines," Jg 13:5, and the conquest of the Philistines is the later accomplishment of Saul, 1 S 13–14; 1 M 4:30 (although Saul dies on Mount Gilboa, defeated by the Philistines, 1 S 31; 2 S 1:20; 21:12), and of David, who is famous for his victorious combat with Goliath, 1 S 17, and for his many successes in dealing with the Philistines, 1 S 18: 17–27, 30; 19:8; 23:1–5; 2 S 5:17–25//1 Ch 14:8–16; 2 S 8:1, 12; 19:10; Si 47:7. The Philistine enemy, cf. Ps 83:8; Si 50:26; Is 9:11, is mentioned again in the reigns of Jehoshaphat of Judah, 2 Ch 17:11, Jehoram, 21:16–17, Uzziah, 26: 6–7, Ahaz, 28:18, and Hezekiah, 2 K 18:8, and in the oracles of the prophets, Is 2:6; 14:29–31; Jr 25:20; 47:1–7; Ezk 16:27, 57; 25:15–17; Am 1:8; Zp 2:5; Zc 9:6–7.

King: ABIMELECH 1.

"The Philistine": GOLIATH.

God: DAGON.

Another town: GIBBETHON.

The "Philistine sea": MEDITERRANEAN.

PHILOLOGUS (1), "One who loves to talk" (cf. Philetus), a Christian of Rome, Rm 16:15.

PHILOMETOR (3), "He who loves his mother" (cf. Philetus), 2 M 4:21; 9:29; 10:13. See: PTOLEMY 6.

PHINEHAS, Hb. form of Egypt. "The Black" (cf. Tahpanhes. See Niger), Gr. *Phinees.*

1. **Phinehas** (20), **son of Eleazar** (9) **son of Aaron** (3) and of a daughter of Putiel, Ex 6:25, distinguishes himself at Peor "in the affair of Cozbi" the Midianite woman whom he slays as he does the Israelite Zimri, whom she had seduced. This zeal of Phinehas in behalf of his God wins him the promise of a perpetual priesthood, Nb 25:7–8, 10–13; cf. 1 M 2:26, 54; Ps 106:30–31; Si 45:23–24. Because of this episode Phinehas takes part in the holy war against Midian, Nb 31:6, and, after an altar has been built on the banks of the Jordan, intervenes with the tribes of Transjordania to prevent a repetition of the "sin at Peor," Jos 22:17.

The reference to Phinehas, Jg 20:28, as being in the service of the Ark is probably a gloss. Acc. to the chronicler, Phinehas was at one time in charge of the guardians of the temple, 1 Ch 9:20. Acc. to 1 Ch 5:30//6:35//Ezr 7:5, Phinehas, grandson of Aaron, is an ancestor of Zadok. Among the priests who return from the exile are some sons of Phinehas, Ezr 8:2.

Town of Phinehas: GIBEAH 3.

2. **Phinehas** (7) and **Hophni** (5), **sons of Eli** (4), priests at the sanctuary of Shiloh, 1 S 1:3. These "scoundrels . . . treated the offering made to Yahweh with contempt," 2:12–17, and do not heed the reproaches of their father, 2:22–25. During a war between Israel and the Philistines the two sons of Eli, who are accompanying the Ark, are slain, 4:4, 11, 17; cf. 2:29, 34. On learning of her husband's death, the wife of Phinehas also dies as she bears a son, Ichabod, 4:19–22.

Father of: ICHABOD.

3. **Phinehas** (1), a priest, father of: ELEAZAR 5.

PHLEGON (1), "Burning," a Christian of Rome, Rm 16:14.

PHOEBE (1), Gr. *Phoibē,* "Shining" (surname of Artemis as assimilated to the Moon), "a deaconess of the church at Cenchreae . . . she has looked after a good many people, myself included," says

Paul, Rm 16:1–2. Perhaps she is the one who brings the Letter to the Romans from Corinth to Rome.

PHOENICIA (9), Gr. *Phoinikē,* "Date-palm or Purple"? (cf. Phoenix), a narrow strip of coast between Mount Lebanon and the Mediterranean, extending from Mount Carmel to the mouth of the Orontes. In 2 M 4:22, "Phoenicia" also includes the Palestinian coast. In the Maccabaean period it forms, together with Coele-Syria, a province whose successive governors are: APOLLONIUS 1; PTOLEMY 9; LYSIAS 1.

During his public life Jesus meets a Syrophoenican woman, Mk 7:24 (= Canaanite woman, Mt 15:22). The persecution to which Stephen falls victim drives the Christians of Jerusalem to bring the Gospel to the Jews living in Phoenicia, Ac 11:19. On their way to the "council" of Jerusalem, Paul and Barnabas visit the churches of Phoenicia, Ac 15:3. Paul passes through Phoenicia on his return from this third missionary journey, Ac 21:2.

Towns: ARVAD; GEBAL 1; SIDON; TRIPOLIS; TYRE.

Gods: ANATH; ASTARTE; BAAL 1; BAAL-SHAMEM; EL; HADAD 1; HADAD-RIMMON; [HORON]; [MELKART].

PHOENIX (1), Gr. *Phoinix* (cf. Phoenicia), a harbor on the southern coast of Crete, which the ship carrying Paul the prisoner and his companions tries to reach en route to Rome, Ac 27:12.

PHRYGIA (3), in Asia Minor, a region west of the Anatolian plateau, between Lydia and Cappadocia, attached to the Roman province of Asia in 103 B.C. From among the many Jews living in Phrygia, some are in Jerusalem on the first Christian Pentecost, Ac 2:10. Paul passes through Phrygia on his second and third missionary journeys, Ac 16:6; 18:23. The Christian communities already there were not founded by him.

Churches: COLOSSAE; HIERAPOLIS; LAODICEA.

PHRYGIAN (1), 2 M 5:22, a native of Phrygia. See: PHILIP 4.

PHYGELUS (1), a Christian of Asia Minor who for reasons unknown to us refuses to have anything more to do with Paul, 2 Tm 1:15.

PI-BESETH (1), from Egypt. *Pi-Bastit,* "House of Bast [cat-headed Egyptian goddess]" (cf. Pi-hahiroth; Pithom; Rameses 2), Gr. *Boubastos,* Bubastis, a town in the NE of the Nile Delta. On the day of the Lord against Egypt the young men of Pi-beseth will be massacred, Ezk 30:17.

PI-HAHIROTH (4), popular etymology, "Mouth of the canals"; Egypt. *Pi-Hrt,* "House of [the Syrian goddess] Hrt" (cf. Pi-beseth), **facing Baal-zephon** (3), a stage of the Exodus before the crossing of the Red Sea, Ex 14:2, 9; Nb 33:7, 8 (read *Pi-hahiroth* instead of Hb. *before Hahiroth*). East of the Nile Delta.

PILATE (55), surname of **Pontius** (3), **governor** (3) **of Judaea** (1), Lk 3:1, resides at Caesarea and goes up to Jerusalem for the major feasts. Hated by the Jews because of his stupid blunders and also because of bloody interventions such as the one reported in Lk 13:1. An enemy of Herod Antipas, he is later reconciled with him, Lk 23:12. He is already procurator of Judaea (26–36) when John the Baptist begins his ministry, Lk 3:1.

But Pilate is famous above all as the judge in the trial of Jesus, Mt 27:2, 11–26//Mk 15:1–15//Lk 23:1–24//Jn 18:28–19:16, 19–22, 31; cf. 1 Tm 6:13. Although acknowledging the innocence of Jesus, Lk 23:14–15, 22; Jn 19:4, 6, he hands him over to the shameful torment of the cross after giving in to the blackmail used by the Jews, Jn 19:12; cf. Ac 3:13; 4:27; 13:28, and having "washed his hands" of the affair, Mt 27:24. He allows Joseph of Arimathea to take the body of Jesus, Mt 27:58//Mk 15:43–44//Lk 23:52//Jn 19:38, but refuses the Jewish request that he change the inscription on the cross, Jn 19:21–22, and provide guards for the tomb, Mt 27:62–65.

PILDASH (1), one of the twelve sons of Nahor, brother of Abraham, born of his wife Milcah, Gn 22:22.

PILHA (1), a leader of the people and cosigner of the pledge to observe the Law, Ne 10:25.

PILTAI (1), (cf. Pelet 1–2), a priest, head of the priestly family of Moadiah in the time of the high priest Joiakim, Ne 12:17.

PINON (2), (cf. Punon), one of the chiefs (or clans) of Edom, Gn 36:41// 1 Ch 1:52.

PIRAM (1), **king of Jarmuth** (4), an Amorite, allied with: ADONI-ZEDEK.

PIRATHON (1), Hb. *Pir'atôn,* Gr. *Pharathōn,* a town of Ephraim where the "lesser" judge Abdon is buried, Jg 12:15.
= **Pharathon** (1), fortified by Bacchides, 1 M 9:50. 9 km SW of Shechem.

PISGAH (8), a mountain in Transjordania located near the Dead Sea, Dt 3:17; 4:49, opposite Jericho, Dt 34:1. Last stage of the Exodus before the Jordan, Nb 21:20. From Pisgah, Balaam prophecies regarding Israel, Nb 23:14, and Moses sees the Promised Land, Dt 3:27; 34:1. In the territory of Reuben, Jos 13:20; cf. 12:3.

PISHON (1), Gr. *Phisōn,* one of the four rivers of the earthly paradise. The Law is compared to it in Si 24:25.

PISIDIA (2), a region in Asia Minor between Phrygia to the north and Pamphylia to the south, in the Roman province of Galatia. Paul passes through it going and coming on his first missionary journey, Ac 14:24.
City: ANTIOCH 2.

PISPA (1), an Asherite, one of the three sons of Ithran, a stout fighting man and head of a family, 1 Ch 7:38.

PITHOM (1), Egypt. *Pr-itm,* "House of [the god] Aton," a store city in the eastern part of the Nile Delta, in the building of which the Hebrews take part, Ex 1:11. Perhaps *Tell Retabeh.*

PITHON (2), a Benjaminite, a descendant of King Saul and a son of Micah, 1 Ch 8:35//9:41.

PLAIN

1. **The Plain** or **area** or **stretch** (11), Hb. *Kikkar,* of the Jordan, the lowlying Jordan valley, Dt 34:3; 2 S 18:23; 1 K 7:46//2 Ch 4:17. In Gn 13:10–12; 19:17, 25, 28–29. The term designates this valley as prolonged to the south of the Dead Sea.

2. **The Great Plain** (2), Gr. *to pedion to mega,* between Beth-shan and the Jordan. Judas Maccabaeus and his brother Jonathan cross it, 1 M 5:52; 12:49.

3. **Plain of Aram,** Hb. *Paddan-aram.* See: MESOPOTAMIA *c.*

4. **Plain of:** JEZREEL 2 *b.*

PLEIADES (3), Hb. *Kimah,* Jb 9:9; 38:31; Am 5:8, a constellation. See: MANSIONS OF THE SOUTH.

POCHERETH - HAZ - ZEBAIM (2), "Trap for gazelles"? (cf. Zibia 2), head of a family of Solomon's slaves who return from the exile, Ezr 2:57//Ne 7:59.

[POLLUX and Castor]. See: TWINS.

PONTIUS (3), Lk 3:1; Ac 4:27; 1 Tm 6:13. See: PILATE.

PONTUS (2), Gr. *Pontos,* "High seas," an area in the northern part of Asia Minor, on the shores of the Black Sea, a Roman province since 65 B.C.

A sizable Jewish colony, represented in

Jerusalem on the first Christian Pentecost, Ac 2:9. Christian communities develop there later on, 1 P 1:1.

City: SAMPSAMES.

PORATHA (1), a Persian name, brother of: PARSHANDATHA.

PORCIUS (1), Ac 24:27. See: FESTUS.

[POSEIDON] (cf. Posidonius), Greek god of the sea, the *Neptune* of the Romans.

POSIDONIUS (1), "Of Poseidon" (cf. Poseidon), one of the three messengers of Nicanor to the Jews, 2 M 14:19.

POTIPHAR, abbrev. of **POTIPHERA,** Egypt. "He whom [the god] Ra has given," Lat. *Putiphar* (cf. Putiel).

1. **Potiphar** (2) **the Egyptian** (3), a eunuch of Pharaoh and commander of the guards, to whom Joseph, son of Jacob, is sold, Gn 37:36; 39:1, 2, 5; cf. 40:3–4; 41:10.

2. **Potiphera** (3), the Egyptian priest of On, father of: ASENATH.

POTIPHERA (3). See: POTIPHAR 2.

POTSHERDS (Gate of the) (1), Hb. *Harsit* (cf. Kir-heres), at Jerusalem, a gate leading, it seems, to the Valley of Ben-hinnom. Perhaps identical with: DUNG GATE. Jeremiah there performs the symbolic action of breaking a jug, Jr 19:2.

PRISCA (3) or **Priscilla** (3), wife of: AQUILA.

PROCHORUS (1), one of the: SEVEN.

PROMISED LAND, lit. "Land of the promise," Gr. *gē tēs epaggelias,* Heb 11:9; cf. Ac 7:5. The OT has no word corresponding to the verb "to promise"; the same idea is frequently expressed, however, in two basic formulas:

—"the land that Yahweh is giving you, as he promised [lit.: paid]" Ex 12:25; cf. Gn 12:7; 13:15; 15:7, 18; 17:8; 26:2–3; 35:12; Ex 6:4; Lv 14:34; 20:24; 25:2; Nb 14:8; Jos 1:2, and so on.

—"the land he swore to your fathers he would give you," Dt 7:13; cf. Gn 24:7; 50:23; Ex 6:8; 13:5, 11; 32:13; 33:1; Nb 11:12; 14:16, 23, 30; Dt (16×) 1:8; 6:10, 18, 23; 7:13; 8:1; 10:11; 11:21; 19:8; 26:3, 15; 27:3; 28:11; 30:20; 34:4; Jos 1:6; 21:43; Jg 2:1; Jr 11:5; 32:22; Ba 2:34; Ezk 20:6, 28, 42.

This promise of the gift of a country is not unconditional. Some of the Israelites who are en route to the Promised Land, the land of "rest," will not enter it because they have complained against Yahweh, Nb 14:30; 32:10–11; Dt 1:34–35; 2:14; 4:21; Ps 95:11; Ezk 20:15; Heb 4:3. And once settled in the land that Yahweh gives them, they will be torn from it if they prove unfaithful to the covenant, Dt 28:63; 29:27; 1 K 14:15; 2 Ch 7:20. Above and beyond the land of Israel, God promises to the just and the gentle a "new earth," 2 P 3:13; cf. Mt 5:4; Ps 37:9; Is 57:13; 60:21; 65:17; 66:22; Rv 21:1.

[PSUSENNIS II], Pharaoh (6), **king of Egypt** (2) (955–950), the last king of the twenty-first dynasty. He is probably the father of the "Pharaoh's daughter" whom Solomon marries, 1 K 3:1; 7:8; 9:16, 24; 11:1. He is also perhaps the Pharaoh of 1 K 11:7–22.

[PTAH], (cf. Egypt), an Egyptian god. See: APIS.

PTOLEMAIS (19), from the name *Ptolemy* [*Philadelphus*]. See: ACCO.

PTOLEMY (cf. Ptolemais).

1. **[Ptolemy I Soter],** son of Lagos, a general of Alexander the Great, cf. 1 M 1:6–9, first king of the Hellenistic dynasty in Egypt (306–285).

= **King of the South** (1), Dn 11:5; the prince who "will grow more powerful still" is: SELEUCUS I.

2. **[Ptolemy II Philadelphus],** king of Egypt (285–246).

= **King of the South** (1), Dn 11:6, father of: BERENICE 1.

3. **[Ptolemy III Euergetes I],** king of Egypt (246–221).

= **King of the South** (1), Dn 11:9. He seizes the Seleucid capital, Antioch, and carries off considerable booty, Dn 11:7–8.

4. **[Ptolemy IV Philopator],** king of Egypt (221–205).

= **King of the South** (1), Dn 11:11, a probable allusion to his victory over Antiochus the Great in the battle of Raphia, a victory not pressed home, v. 12.

5. **[Ptolemy V Epiphanes],** king of Egypt (205–180).

= **King of the South** (1), Dn 11:14. Conquered by Antiochus the Great, he must yield Palestine to him; he marries Cleopatra, daughter of Antiochus the Great; instead of seconding her father's plans for annexation, she takes the side of her new country, Egypt, cf. Dn 11:15–17.

6. **Ptolemy VI** (14), **Philometor** (3), **king of Egypt** (4) (180–145). In about 174 he marries, 2 M 4:21. In 169, during the first Egyptian campaign of Antiochus Epiphanes, he suffers a serious defeat, 1 M 1:18–20. In the following year, at the beginning of Antiochus' second Egyptian campaign, he is betrayed by Ptolemy Macron, high commissioner for Cyprus, who goes over to Antiochus, 2 M 10:13. (When Antiochus dies, his friend Philip joins Philometor, 2 M 9:29.) In 150 Ptolemy gives his daughter Cleopatra to Alexander Balas: meeting of the two kings at Ptolemais, where Jonathan Maccabaeus joins them, 1 M 10:51–60. But in the summer of 145 Ptolemy travels along the coast to Antioch, where he unites in his person the two crowns of Egypt and Asia. He takes his daughter back from Alexander and gives her to Demetrius II. Ptolemy does battle with Alexander, who is defeated and dies. Ptolemy dies shortly after, 1 M 11:1–18.

= **King of the South** (3), Dn 11:25–27: allusions to the defeat of Ptolemy (during the first Egyptian campaign of Antiochus), to the evil advisers around him, to the humiliating peace treaty he is forced to sign while a prisoner at Antioch. Cf. Dn 11:40.

7. **Ptolemy VII** (1), king of Egypt (145–117), to whom, among others, is addressed the letter of the consul Lucius promulgating the alliance between Jews and Romans.

= **Euergetes** (1), Si prol. 27.

8. **Ptolemy** (1), king of Egypt, married to Cleopatra, Est 10:3[1]. The reference is to Ptolemy VIII in 114–113 or to Ptolemy XII in 48–47.

9. **Ptolemy** (5) **son of Dorymenes** (2), **military commissioner for Coele-Syria and Phoenicia** (1), 2 M 8:8, associated with Nicanor and Gorgias in conducting the war on the Jews, 1 M 3:38 ff. A few years earlier Ptolemy had pleaded the cause of Menelaus, the criminal high priest, with Antiochus Epiphanes, 2 M 4:45–46.

In 2 M 6:8 *people of Ptolemais* is probably to be read in place of the Gr. *Ptolemy.*

10. **Ptolemy Macron** (1), military commissioner of Cyprus, "the first governor to treat the Jews with any justice." "Called traitor at every turn for having abandoned Cyprus, which had been entrusted to him by [Ptolemy] Philometor and for going over to Antiochus Epiphanes," he commits suicide, 2 M 10:12–13.

11. **Ptolemy** (3) **son of Abubus** (2), military commissioner for the plain of Jericho, son-in-law of the high priest Simon (Maccabaeus) whom he treacherously assassinates along with his two sons Mattathias and Judas in the small fortress of Dok above Jericho, 1 M 16:11–21.

12. **Ptolemy** (1), son of: DOSITHEUS 1.

13. **Ptolemy** (1), father of: LYSIMACHUS 2.

PUAH, Hb. 1–2: *Pu'ah,* "Madder"; 3: *Pu'ah,* Ugar. *Pgt,* "Young girl."

1. **Puah** (1), son of Dodo, father of: TOLA 2.

2. **Puah** (1). See: PUVAH.

3. **Puah** (1), one of the Hebrew midwives in Egypt, Ex 1:15–21.

PUBLIUS (2), chief magistrate of the island of Malta. He gives a friendly welcome to Paul and his companions after their escape from shipwreck in the Mediterranean. Paul cures Publius' father, who suffers from attacks of fever and dysentery, Ac 28:7–8.

PUDENS (1), a Christian of Rome known to Timothy, 2 Tm 4:21.

PUL (3), Accad. *Pûlu,* Babylonian name of: TIGLATH-PILESER.

PUNON (2), (cf. Pinon), a stage of the Exodus, Nb 33:42–43. Identified with *Feinan,* 40 km S of the Dead Sea.

PURAH (2), servant of Gideon, accompanies his master to the Midianite outposts, Jg 7:10–11.

PUT (9), Gr. *Phoud* or *Libyes,* occurs in the list of peoples alongside Cush, Egypt, and Canaan, Gn 10:6//1 Ch 1:8. In the prophets Put, which always refers to warriors, Na 3:9, is paralleled with Lud, Is 66:19 (Gr.; Hb. *Pul*); Ezk 27:10; Jdt 2:23, or with Cush, Ezk 38:5, or with both together, Jr 46:9; Ez 30:5.

Put doubtless refers to a people of the African coast, probably at the southern end of the Red Sea. Some interpreters take it as referring to Libya.

PUTEOLI (1), a port on the bay of Naples. The Christian community of the city welcomes Paul for a week on his way to Rome as a prisoner, Ac 28:13–14. The modern *Pozzuoli.*

PUTHITES (1), a clan of Judah, connected with Shobal and Hur, 1 Ch 2:53.

PUTIEL (1), a hybrid Egypto-Hebraic form, "He whom [the god] El has given" (cf. Potiphar). One of the daughters of Putiel marries the priest Eleazar, son of Aaron, and becomes mother of Phinehas, Ex 6:25.

PUVAH (2), second of the four sons of Issachar, Gn 46:13, whose descendants form the **Puvite** clan, Nb 26:23 (corr. of Hb. *Punite*).

= **Puah** (1), 1 Ch 7:1.

PUVITE (1), belonging to the clan of: PUVAH.

PYRRHUS (1), Lat. transcription of Gr. *Pyrros,* "Red fire," father of: SOPATER.

Q

QOHELETH (7), "The Assembly [personified]" (cf. Kehelathah), Gr. *Ekklēsiastēs,* whence *Ecclesiastes,* "President *or* Speaker of an Assembly" (cf. Ecclesiasticus), Qo 1:1–2, 12; 7:27; 12:8–10.

A wise man, Qo 1:3; 12:9–11, presented as "son of David, king in Jerusalem," and thus identified with Solomon, Qo 1:1, 12, whose "songs . . . proverbs . . . sayings and . . . retorts made [him] the wonder of the world," Si 47:14–17; cf. Qo 1:16; 2:9, and 1 K 3:12; 5:9–14; 10:1–13; Mt 12:42. Qoheleth states the case against the human happiness whose three components—wealth, love, and glory—seem to reach their climactic form in the life of Solomon, 1 K 10:4–5; 11:1–3; Mt 6:29; cf. Qo 1:12–2:12. The first and last words of the book, Qo 1:2 and 12:8 (apart from title and epilogue), are: "Vanity of vanities. All is vanity." The word *vanity* (literally *vapor, smoke*) occurs 38× in the book. By insisting that "the rich man's wealth will not let him sleep at all," Qo 5:11, Qoheleth prepares men to understand the later words: "Happy are the poor in spirit," Mt 5:3.

QUARTUS (1), "Fourth," a Christian of Corinth, Rm 16:23.

QUEEN OF HEAVEN (5). See: ISHTAR.

QUINTUS (1), "Fifth," **Memmius** (1). See: MEMMIUS.

QUIRINIUS (1), Gr. *Kyrēnios,* full name *Publius Sulpicius Quirinius,* **governor of Syria** (1), organizes the census of Palestine in 6 A.D. Did the first stages of the census of which Lk 2:2 speaks begin earlier? In any case, from the year 12 B.C. Quirinius was in charge of Roman policy in the Near East.

R

[RA], (cf. Potiphar; Rameses), Egypt. god of the sun, the center of whose worship is at: ON 1.

RAAMAH (5). See: RAMAH 7.

RAAMIAH (1). See: REELAIAH.

RABBAH, "The Great [City]" (cf. Bath-rabbim; Jeroboam; Jerubbaal; Merab).

1. **Rabbah** (9) or **Rabbah of the Ammonites** (5), Dt 3:11; 2 S 12:26; 17:27; Jr 49:2, capital of Ammon, located opposite Aroer (in Gad), Jos 13:25. To be seen there is the "bed of iron" of Og, king of Bashan, Dt 3:11. Besieged by Joab, the city will be taken by David, 2 S 11:1; 12:26–31 (distinction between the *water town,* or lower city, and the *town,* or acropolis)//1 Ch 20:1–3; cf. 2 S 10:3. In their oracles against the nations, the prophets predict the punishment of Ammon and of Rabbah in particular, Jr 49:2–3; Ezk 21:25; 25:5; Am 1:14.

In the Hellenistic period the city is called: PHILADELPHIA 2. Today *Amman,* capital of Jordan.

Native place of: SHOBI.

2. **Rabbah** (1), a town in the highlands of Judah, Jos 15:60.

RABSHAKEH (1), Gr. *Rapsakēs,* Hb. *rab shaqeh,* "Cupbearer-in-chief." What is simply the name for the function of Sennacherib's aide-de-camp, cf. 2 K 18: 17, 19, 26–28, is interpreted as a proper name by the Greek translator of Ecclesiasticus, Si 48:18.

RACHEL (48), Gr. and Lat. transcription of Hb. *Rahél,* "Sheep" (see Sheep Gate), younger daughter of Laban the Aramaean, a "shepherdess," "shapely and beautiful," whom Jacob prefers but cannot make his wife until he has first married her older sister Leah, Gn 29: 6–31; cf. Ho 12:13. Through her servant Bilhah she gives Jacob two sons, Dan and Naphtali, Gn 30:1–8; 35:25; 46:25, then herself bears Joseph, Gn 30:22–23, 25, and then, after reaching Canaan, cf. 31: 4–19, 31–35; 33:1–7, Benjamin, but dies in childbirth, 35:16–19 (cf. 48:7); 35: 24; 44:27; 46:19, 22. "Rachel and Leah . . . together built up the House of Israel," Rt 4:11.

The **tomb of Rachel,** Gn 35:20, is located on the border between Benjamin and Ephraim, 1 S 10:2, at Ramah (8 km N of Jerusalem), Jr 31:15; Mt 2:18.

See: EPHRAIM 4.

RADDAI (1), "Yah rules," fifth son of Jesse and brother of David, 1 Ch 2:14.

RAGAE. See: RHAGES.

RAGUEL. See: REUEL 5.

RAHAB, Hb. 1: *Rahab,* with *hé,* "Impetuous, Tempestuous"; 2: *Rahab,* with *heth.*

1. **Rahab** (6), one of the monsters of the primeval chaos, a mythical personification of the primordial waters, overcome by God in the course of creating, Jb 9:13; 26:12; Ps 89:11; it is also a

symbolic name for Egypt, Ps 87:4; Is 30:7. In Is 51:9 Rahab means the monster of primeval chaos but also evokes the idea of Egypt.

See: DEEP; LEVIATHAN.

2. **Rahab** (8) **the harlot** (5), of Jericho, saves the spies sent by Joshua by hiding them in her house. This action merits her and her family being spared when the Israelites capture Jericho, Jos 2:1–21; 6:17, 22–25.

Rahab is praised for her faith in Heb 11:31 and for her hospitality in Jm 2:25. According to Mt 1:5 she is the mother of Boaz (echo of a rabbinical legend) and an ancestress of Jesus.

RAHAM (1), "Vulture," a Calebite, son of Shema and father of Jorkeam, 1 Ch 2:44.

RAKEM (1). See: REKEM 4.

RAKKATH (1), "Bank, shore" (cf. Rakkon), a fortified town of Naphtali, Jos 19:35, assigned to the Levites of the clan of Gershon, 21:32 (Hb. *Qartan*).

= ? **Kiriathaim** (1), 1 Ch 6:61.

RAKKON (1), "Bank, shore" (cf. Rakkath), a town in Dan, Jos 19:46. Near the Mediterranean. Some correct the passage acc. to Gr.: *Jerakon*.

RAM (cf. Ramah).

1. **Ram** (6), son of Hezron, grandson of Perez, Rt 4:19; 1 Ch 2:9–10, a descendant of Judah. Acc. to Mt 1:4 (Gr. *Aram*), an ancestor of Jesus. Compare with the two following entries.

2. **Ram** (2), firstborn of Jerahmeel, 1 Ch 25:27. Compare with the preceding and the following.

3. **Ram** (1), clan to which Elihu, son of Barachel the Buzite, belongs, Jb 32:2. Compare with the two preceding.

RAMAH, Hb. 1–6, 8–11: *Ramah*, "Height," pl. *Ra(')mot;* construct state, *Ramat;* dual, *Ramatayim* (cf. Abiram; Abram; Ahiram; Amram; Baara; Hadoram 2–3; Hiram; Jehoram; Jeremai?; Jeremiah?; Jeremoth; Malchiram?; Ram; Raamiah?; Romamti-ezer; Rumah).

1. **Ramah** (16), a town near Bethel, Jg 4:5, and Gibeah, Jg 19:13, is in Benjamin, Jos 18:25. In the territory of Asa, king of Judah, it is occupied for a time by Baasha, king of Israel, 1 K 15:17, 21–22//2 Ch 16:1, 5–6. On the road taken by invaders of the kingdom of Judah, Is 10:29; Ho 5:8. After the fall of Judah the columns of the deported are gathered there, Jr 31:15; 40:1, and the people of Ramah themselves set out for exile, cf. Ezr 2:26//Ne 7:30. Ramah is reoccupied at the return from exile by sons of Benjamin, Ne 11:33. Place of Rachel's burial, Jr 31:15; cf. Mt 2:18. 8 km N of Jerusalem. Today *er-Ram*.

2. **Ramah** (15), a town in Ephraim, native place of Samuel: there he has his home, there he "judged Israel," 1 S 7:17; 8:4; 15:34; 16:13; it is there, too, that David in flight from Saul meets Samuel and together they dwell in the HUTS, the dwelling places of the prophets (or at NAIOTH, a district in Ramah), 1 S 19:18–23; 20:1. Samuel is buried there, 1 S 25:1//28:3. The parents of Samuel, Elkanah and Hannah, were already living at Ramah, 1 S 1:19; 2:11.

= **Ramathaim** (2), 1 S 1:1 (Hb. *Ramathyim-zophim*); center of a district recognized as belonging to the Jews, 1 M 11:34 (Gr. *Rathamin*); cf. 10:30.

= **Arimathaea** (4), native place of: JOSEPH 11. 14 km NE of Lod. Today *Rentis*.

3. **Ramah** (1), a town on the border of Asher, Jos 19:28. Identical with the following?

4. **Ramah** (1), a fortified town in Naphtali, Jos 19:36.

5. **Ramah of the Negeb** (2), a town of the sons of Benjamin, Jos 19:8, absorbed by Judah, 1 S 30:27 (Hb. *Ramoth of the Negeb*).

6. **Ramah** (1), one of the preceding towns, native place of: SHIMEI 10.

7. **Raamah** (5), acc. to the priestly tradition, one of the five sons of Cush and

father of Sheba and Dedan, Gn 10:7// 1 Ch 1:9. A tribe of southern Arabia engaged in trade with Tyre, Ezk 27:22.

8. **Ramath-lehi** (1), "Height of the Jawbone," a place-name explained by the weapon—the jawbone of an ass—that Samson uses in fighting the Philistines, Jg 15:17. See: LEHI.

9. **Ramath-mizpeh** (1), "Height of the Lookout." See: MIZPAH 2.

10. **Ramoth** (26) **in Gilead** (24), or **Ramoth-gilead,** a town of refuge for Gad, Dt 4:43//Jos 20:8, assigned to the Levites of the clan of Merari, Jos 21:38// 1 Ch 6:65, center of Solomon's sixth district, 1 K 4:13. Ramoth in Gilead is occupied by the Aramaeans; Ahab, king of Israel, supported by Jehoshaphat of Judah, tries to recapture it, but he is killed in front of the town, 1 K 22:3–6, 12, 15, 20, 29//2 Ch 18:2–5, 11, 14, 19, 28. His son Jehoram, supported by Ahaziah of Judah, takes the town back from the Aramaeans, but suffers wounds, which he goes to Jezreel to take care of. During this time, at Ramoth in Gilead, Jehu, who has received anointing as king from a disciple of Elisha, concocts a plot against his master, the king of Israel, 2 K 8:28, 29 (Hb. *Ramah*)//2 Ch 22:5, 6 (Hb. *Ramah*); 2 K 9:1–2, 4 ff., 14–15. 35 km E of Beth-shan. Today *Tell Ramith.*

11. **Ramoth** (1), 1 Ch 6:58, a town of Issachar, assigned to the Levites of the clan of Gershon.

= **Remeth** (1), Jos 19:21.

= **Jarmuth** (1), Jos 21:29.

RAMATHAIM (2), "The Two Heights." See: RAMAH 2.

RAMATH-LEHI (1). See: RAMAH 8.

RAMATH-MIZPEH (1). See: RAMAH 9.

RAMESES, Hb. *Ra'amsés* or *Ra'msés*, Egypt. "Ra has begotten him *or* Son of Ra" (cf. Ra; Moses).

1. **[Rameses II],** an Egyptian Pharaoh (1290–1224). He is probably the **Pharaoh** who oppresses the Hebrews, and it is doubtless in his reign that the Exodus takes place, cf. Ex 1:8–18:10. Repeated in Dt 6:21–22; 7:8–18; 11:3; 29:1; 34: 11; 1 S 2:27; 6:6; 2 K 17:7; Ne 9:9–10; Jdt 5:11; Ps 105:30; 135:8–9; 136:10–15; Ws 10:15; Ac 7:17–21; Rm 9:17; Heb 11:24–29.

2. **Rameses** (5), in Egypt. *Pi-ramses,* "House of Rameses" (cf. Pi-beseth), residence of Pharaoh Rameses II, in the eastern part of the Nile Delta, identified either with Tanis or with Qantir. Joseph settles his father and brothers in **the land of Rameses,** Gn 47:11. Pharaoh forces the Israelites to work at building the depot city of Rameses, Ex 1:11. This city is the point of departure for the Exodus of Israel to the Promised Land, Ex 12: 37; Nb 33:3, 5. Rameses is also mentioned in Jdt 1:9.

RAMIAH (1), (cf. Ramah?), an Israelite of the sons of Parosh, married to a foreign wife, whom he puts away, Ezr 10:25.

RAMOTH (1). See: RAMAH 11.

RAMOTH-GILEAD. See: RAMAH 10.

RAMOTH (26) **in Gilead** (24). See: RAMAH 10.

RAPHA, abbrev. of *Raphael?* (cf. Raphael).

1. **Rapha** (6), 2 S 21:16, 18, 20, 22; 1 Ch 20:6, 8, eponymous ancestor of: REPHAIM 1.

2. **Rapha** (1), fifth son of Benjamin acc. to 1 Ch 8:2.

3. **Raphah** (1), a Benjaminite, a descendant of King Saul and an ancestor of the sons of Azel, 1 Ch 8:37.

= **Rephaiah** (1), 1 Ch 9:43.

RAPHAH (1). See: RAPHA 3.

RAPHAEL, Gr. transcription of Hb. *Repha'el,* "God has healed" (cf. Beth-rapha; Irpeel; Rapha; Raphu; Rephaiah; Rephaim).

1. **Raphael** (14), an angel "sent to bring remedy" to Tobit and Sarah, Tb 3:17.

= **Azarias** (6) **son of the great Ananias** (1), the name under which the angel introduces himself to Tobit, Tb 5:13, and by which he is called by Tobias, 6:7, 14; 7:1, 9; 9:1.

Engaged as a guide, he accompanies Tobias to Media, where the latter is to recover a sum of money, 5:4. Thanks to the angel's intervention, Tobias escapes the attack of an enormous fish, from which he extracts valuable remedies, 6:7. Sarah is saved by becoming the wife of Tobias, her kinsman, 6:11, 14, 18; 7:1, 9; 8:2, 3, the money is recovered from Gabael, 9:1, 2, 5, and the aged Tobit regains his sight, 11:2, 7. Only at the end of his earthly mission does the angel reveal his true name, "Raphael, one of the seven angels who stand ever ready to enter the presence of the glory of the Lord," 12:15.

2. **Rephael** (1), a gatekeeper, one of the sons of Shemaiah, son of Obed-edom, 1 Ch 26:7.

RAPHAIM, Gr. *Raphain,* a Simeonite, an ancestor of Judith, Jdt 8:1.

RAPHON (1), a town in Hellenistic Gilead near which the armies of Judas Maccabaeus and Timotheus meet, 1 M 5:37. 50 km E of the Sea of Chinnereth. Identified with *er-Rafeh.*

RAPHU (1), (cf. Raphael), father of: PALTI 1.

RASSIS (Sons of) (1), looted by Holofernes, Jdt 2:23. An unidentified nomadic tribe.

RAZIS (1), "one of the elders of Jerusalem . . . a man who loved his countrymen and stood high in their esteem, and he was known as the father of the Jews because of his kindness." Charged with Judaism, he refuses to surrender to Nicanor and commits suicide in hope of the resurrection, 2 M 14:37–46.

RAZON. See: REZIN 1.

REAIAH, "Yah has seen" (cf. Haroeh).

1. **Reaiah son of Shobal** (1), father of the Zorathite clans, in Judah, 1 Ch 4:2.

2. **Reaiah** (1), a Reubenite, a descendant of Joel and an ancester of Beerah, 1 Ch 5:5.

3. **Reaiah** (2), head of a family of "oblates" who return from the exile, Ezr 2:47//Ne 7:50.

REBA (2), "Quarter," one of the five Midianite kings, vassals of Sihon, king of the Amorites, Jos 13:21, who are conquered and put to death by the Israelites during the Exodus, Nb 31:8.

REBEKAH (31), Hb. *Ribqah,* a metathesis of *Biqrah,* "Cow," (see Leah), Gr. *Rebekka,* **daughter of Bethuel** (3) the Aramaean of Paddan-aram, Gn 24: 15, 24; 25:20; cf. 22:23, sister of Laban the Aramaean, 24:29–30; 28:5; cf. 29: 12, wife of Isaac, 24:45–67; 25:20; 26: 7–8, and, after long barrenness, mother of Esau and Jacob, twin brothers, Gn 25:21–26; cf. 26:35; 27:42, 46. Rebekah prefers Jacob, 25:28, and helps him gain for himself the blessing reserved for the elder brother, Esau, 25:5–17; cf. Rm 9:10. She is buried in the cave of Machpelah, Gn 49:31.

Her nurse: DEBORAH 1.

RECAH (1), 1 Ch 4:12. See: RECHAB 2.

RECHAB (cf. Beth-marcaboth).

1. **Rechab** (4), brother of: BAANAH 1.

2. **Rechab** (9) gives his name to the **Rechabite** clan.

Their ancestor, Jr 35:6, **Jonadab** (3) or **Jehonadab** (7) **son of Rechab** (7), a fervent Yahwist who supports Jehu in his struggle against baalism, 2 K 10:15, 23, sets for his clan the ideal of the religion of the wilderness as experienced of old by the Israelite tribes: rejection of urban and agricultural civilization, Jr 35: 6–10. When the Babylonian troops advance on Jerusalem in 598, the Rechabites take refuge in the city, and Jeremiah holds them up to the people of Judah and Jerusalem as an example of fidelity, Jr 35:2–19.

Acc. to 1 Ch 2:55 the Rechabites are related to the Kenites, and acc. to 1 Ch 4:12 the men of Recah (= Rechab?) are descended from Caleb.

3. **Rechab** (1), father of: MALCHIJAH 9.

RECHABITE or **son of Rechab** (4), Jr 35:2, 3, 5, 18, belonging to the clan of: RECHAB 2.

RED (Sea) (3), Gr. *Erythra Thalassa,* a translation of the Hb. *Yam Suph,* "Sea of Reeds, or of Suph," dried up by God for the Exodus of Israel, Jdt 5:13; Heb 11:29; cf. 1 Co 10:1–2, scenes of miracles and signs, Ac 7:36.

= **Sea of Reeds** or **of Suph** (24), difficult to locate, because the expression covers several things:

—the place of the miraculous crossing of the sea by the Israelites on their way out of Egypt under the leadership of Moses, Ex 15:4, 22; Dt 11:4; Jos 2:10; 4:23; 24:6–7; Ne 9:9 ff.; Ps 106:7, 9, 22; 136:13, 15; cf. the passages in which only the word *sea* is used, Ex 14–15; Nb 33:8; Ps 66:6; 74:13; 77:17, 20; 78:13, 53; 114:1, 3, 5; Is 43:16; 50:2; 51:10; 63:11.

—the Gulf of Suez, Ex 10:19; 13:18; Nb 33:10–11.

—the Gulf of Aqaba, Nb 14:25; 21:4; Dt 1:40; 2:1; 1 K 9:26; Jr 49:21; Ex 23:31?; Jg 11:26?

= **Sea of Egypt** (2), which Yahweh will again dry up for a new Exodus, Is 11:15; Zc 10:10–11 (corr. of Hb.); cf. Is 10:26.

REEDS (Sea of). See: RED SEA.

REELAIAH (1), Ezr 2:2, one of the twelve leaders on the return from the exile.

= **Raamiah** (1), Ne 7:7.

REGEM (1), Accad. *Ragimu,* "Lightning [= epithet of the god Hadad]," a Calebite, one of the sons of Jahdai, 1 Ch 2:47.

REHABIAH (5), Hb. *Rehabya, Rehabyahu,* "Yah has given me room" (cf. Rehob), a Levite of the clan of Kohath, a grandson of Moses, first of the sons of Eliezer and father of a numerous posterity, 1 Ch 23:17; 24:21, among the officers responsible for the treasuries, 26:25.

REHOB, "[Market] Square" (cf. Rahab 2?; Rehabiah; Rehoboam; Rehoboth and its compounds).

1. **Rehob** (5), two towns of the tribe of Asher, Jos 19:28, 30, one of which remains Canaanite, Jg 1:31, whereas the other is assigned to the Levites of the clan of Gershon, Jos 21:31//1 Ch 6:60.

2. **Rehob** (2). See: BETH-REHOB.

3. **Rehob** (2), 2 S 8:3, 12, father of: HADADEZER. To be connected with the preceding.

4. **Rehob** (1), a Levite, a cosigner of the pledge to observe the Law, Ne 10:12.

REHOBOAM (53), Hb. *Rehab'am,* "The Uncle has given me room," see Ps 4:1, or "The people has increased" (cf. Rehob), **son of Solomon** (6) and of Naamah the Ammonitess, 1 K 14:21//2 Ch 12:13, first king of Judah after the schism (931–913).

Rehoboam succeeds to Solomon without difficulty, 1 K 11:43//1 Ch 9:31, as king of Judah, 1 K 12:27; 14:21//2 Ch 12:13, but when he goes to Shechem, place of assembly for the northern tribes, to be acknowledged by them as king of Israel, his intransigence (refusal to ease taxes) and his harshness (mission of Adoram, who is in charge of forced labor) provoke the political schism: Jeroboam cuts himself off from Judah, 1 K 12:1–19//2 Ch 10:1–18. When Abijah describes his father Rehoboam as "a young man and timid, unable to resist" the scoundrels of the north, 2 Ch 13:7, he is giving a tendentious version of the facts. Compare his statement with the stern judgment of Ben Sira: "the stupidest member of the nation [a play on the name Rehoboam], brainless Rehoboam, whose policy drove the nation to rebel," Si 47:23. The prophet Shemaiah dissuades Rehoboam from putting down this rebellion by force, 1 K 12:21–23//2 Ch 11:1–4, but "Rehoboam and Jeroboam were at war with each other throughout their reigns," 1 K 14:30// 2 Ch 12:15. Rehoboam fortifies some towns of Judah and Benjamin and puts commanders in them, 2 Ch 11:5, 12, 23. Supported by the priests and Levites who came from the north, Rehoboam "for three years . . . followed the example of David and Solomon," 2 Ch 11:17, but "no sooner was his royal authority securely consolidated than he, and all Israel with him, abandoned the Law of Yahweh," 2 Ch 12:1, 14; cf. 1 K 14: 22–24. The chronicler sees the invasion of Judah by King Sheshonk (Shishak) of Egypt as a punishment for this infidelity, 2 Ch 12:2–11//1 K 14:25–28, but it is one that makes the king humble himself, 2 Ch 12:6, 12.

Husband of: MAACAH 9; MAHALATH 1.
His son and successor: ABIJAH 2.

REHOBOTH (1), "Large spaces, Squares" (cf. Rehob), a well, associated with those of Esek and Sitnah, but concerning which there is no dispute, Gn 26:22. Between Gerar and Beersheba.

REHOBOTH-HAN-NAHAR (2), "The Squares of the River" (cf. Rehob), a town in Edom, south of the Dead Sea. Some read *Rehoboth-on-the-Euphrates*. In any case, a town belonging to the king of Edom: SAUL 1.

REHOBOTH-IR (1), "The Squares of the City" *or* "The City with the Large Squares" (cf. Rehob; Ir Haheres), a city listed with Nineveh and Calah, Gn 10: 11. Not identified.

REHUM (cf. Jeroham).

1. **Rehum** (1), Ezr 2:2, one of the twelve leaders of the exiles back to Jerusalem and Judah.

= **Nehum** (1), Ne 7:7.

2. **Rehum** (4), governor of Samaria (capital of the province that includes the region of Judah). He obtains from King Artaxerxes I a rescript ordering the suspension of the rebuilding of the Jerusalem temple and immediately enforces it, Ezr 4:8, 9, 17, 23.

His secretary: SHIMSHAI.

3. **Rehum son of Bani** (1), a Levite, a volunteer in rebuilding the wall of Jerusalem, Ne 3:17.

4. **Rehum** (1), a leader of the people, a cosigner of the pledge to observe the Law, Ne 10:26.

REKEM

1. **Rekem** (2), one of the five Amorite kings, vassals of Sihon, king of the Amorites, Jos 13:21, who are defeated and executed by the Israelites during the Exodus, Nb 31:8.

2. **Rekem** (1), a town of Benjamin, Jos 18:27.

3. **Rekem** (2), a Calebite, of the sons of Hebron, an ancestor of Maon through Shammai, 1 Ch 2:43–44.

4. **Rakem** (1), a Manassite, a descendant of Machir and Maacah, 1 Ch 7:16.

REMALIAH (13), father of king: PEKAH.

REMETH (1). See: RAMAH 11.

REPHAEL (1). See: RAPHAEL 3.

REPHAIAH, "Yah has healed" (cf. Raphael).

1. **Rephaiah** (1), a descendant of King Jehoiachin through Hananiah, 1 Ch 3:21.

2. **Rephaiah** (1), one of the Simeonite chiefs settled in the highlands of Seir, 1 Ch 4:42–43.

3. **Rephaiah** (1), an Issacharite, one of the family heads of Tola, 1 Ch 7:2.

4. **Rephaiah** (1). See: RAPHA 3.

5. **Rephaiah son of Hur** (1), in charge of a section of Jerusalem, a volunteer in the rebuilding of the city wall, Ne 3:9.

REPHAIM, Hb. *Repha'im,* "Healers" (cf. Raphael).

1. **Rephaim** (10) or **descendants of Rapha** (6). Fabled giants, "a great and numerous people, tall as the Anakim," Dt 2:21, who, before the coming of the

Israelites, lived in Transjordania, Gn 15:18–20; Jos 17:15, Bashan, Dt 3:13; Gn 14:5, Ammon (where they are called **Zamzummim,** Dt 2:20, or **Zuzim,** Gn 14:5) and Moab (where they are called **Emim,** Dt 2:10–11; Gn 14:5). To be compared with the Amorites, "men tall as cedars and strong as oaks," Am 2:9.

Four "descendants of Rapha" are mentioned in 2 S 21:16–22//1 Ch 20:4–8 as falling "at the hands of David and his guards."

See: ANAK; GOLIATH; NEPHILIM; OG; SAMSON.

2. **Valley** or **Plain of the Rephaim** (8), a valley or plain that kept the memory of its legendary population by the Rephaim. Near Jerusalem, on the boundary of Judah and Benjamin, Jos 15:8; 18:16; site of confrontation between the Israelites and the Philistines, 2 S 5:18, 22//1 Ch 14:9, 13; 2 S 23:13//1 Ch 11:15. A cultivated valley, Is 17:5. Precise location disputed.

3. **The Shades** or **the Ghosts** (8), a poetic name for the deceased, Jb 26:5; Ps 88:11; Pr 2:18; 9:18; 21:16; Is 14:9; 26:14, 19. In Hb. *Rephaim* from *raphah,* "to be weak."

REPHAN (1). See: KAIWAN.

REPHIDIM (5), "Place of rest," last stage of the Exodus before Mount Sinai, Ex 19:2; Nb 33:14–15, site of the miracle of the water from the rock, Ex 17:1 ff. Acc. to Ex 17:7–8 Rephidim is to be identified with Massah and Meribah, and there was a battle there between Israel and Amalek.

RESEN (1), a city located "between Nineveh and Calah," Gn 10:12. Not identified.

RESERVOIR BETWEEN THE TWO WALLS (1), at Jerusalem, near the: GATE BETWEEN THE TWO WALLS, Is 22:11.

REU (6), Gr. *Ragau* (cf. Reuel), acc. to the priestly tradition a postdiluvian patriarch, son of Peleg, father of Serug and ancestor of Abraham, Gn 11:18–21; 1 Ch 1:25. Acc. to Lk 3:35 an ancestor of Christ.

REUBEN (70), Hb. *Re'ubên,* popular etymology *Ra'ah be'onyi,* "He has seen my misery," **first-born of Jacob** (2), Gn 35:23; 46:8; cf. 49:3, or **first-born of Israel** (5), Ex 6:14; Nb 1:20; 26:5; 1 Ch 5:1, 3.

Eldest of the sons of Jacob, first child of Leah, Gn 29:32, Reuben is the eponymous ancestor of the tribe that bears his name. Fifteen times out of 30 he is named at the head of the lists of the tribes of Israel. As eldest, he undertakes (acc. to the Elohist tradition) to defend Joseph against his brothers when they wish to kill him, Gn 37:21–22, 29; 42:22, and offers his own sons as hostages in place of Benjamin, Gn 42:37. He loses his right of primogeniture because of his incest with Bilhah, his father Jacob's concubine, Gn 35:22; 1 Ch 5:1–2; cf. Gn 49:3–4.

The sons or clans of Reuben are four in number, Gn 46:9; Ex 6:14; Nb 26:5–7; 1 Ch 5:3–10. Censuses of the tribe are given in Nb 1:21 and 26:7. Reuben, Gad, and eastern Manasseh form the Transjordanian tribes; thus we frequently find the associations Reuben/Gad, Nb 32:1–2, 6, 25, 29, 31; Jos 22:25, 32–34, or Reuben/Gad/[eastern] half tribe of Manasseh, Nb 32:33–39; 34:14–15; Dt 3:12–16; 4:43; 29:7; Jos 1:12; 4:12; 12:6; 13:8; 18:7; 32:1–21; 2 K 10:33; 1 Ch 5:18, 26; 26:32. Acc. to Nb 32:1–4, Reuben and Gad settle in the land of Jazer and the original land of Gilead; the allocation of towns to each tribe suggests that Reuben occupies a territory in the midst of Gad. But acc. to Jos 13:15–28, Reuben is to the south, between the Arnon and the town of Heshbon, and Gad to the north.

Despite Nb 32:6–32; Jos 1:12–18; 22:1–9, Reuben and Gad doubtless did not take part in the conquest of Canaan; Jg 1 and Jos 1–11, which tell the story of the conquest, assign them no real role in it. If Reuben was originally an important group (cf., above, the expression "first-born"), it had lost its preeminence: cf. Gn 49:3–4; Dt 33:6 ("his small band of warriors"); after the period of the Judges, Reuben is no longer on the scene. It is doubtless due to this decline—which probably resulted from conflicts with Moab, Gad, and the nomads, cf. 1 Ch 5:10—that some Reubenites crossed over into Cisjordania: cf. the Stone of Bohan son of Reuben on the boundary between Judah and Benjamin, Jos 15:6; 18:18; the clans of Carmi and Hezron, which are both Reubenite and Judaean; the clan of Bela, which is Reubenite and Benjaminite; the incest of Reuben, which occurred at Migdal-eder south of Bethel, Gn 35: 21–22.

Reuben in the lists of the tribes: List, pages 410–11.

Reubenites: ADINA; BEERAH 1; DATHAN; ELIZUR; ELIEZER 5; SHAMMUA 1.

REUBENITE or **of Reuben** or **sons of Reuben** (19), Nb 26:7; 34:14; Dt 3:12, 16; 4:43; 29:7; Jos 1:12; 12:6; 13:8; 22:1; 2 K 10:33; 1 Ch 5:6, 26; 11:42; 12:38; 26:32; 27:16, belonging to the tribe of: REUBEN.

REUEL, Hb. *Re'u'el,* Gr. *Ragouēl,* "Friend of God" (cf. Reu).

1. **Reuel** (7) **son of Esau** (1), Gn 36:17, and of Basemath, Gn 36:4, 10; 1 Ch 1:35; father of four sons: Nahath, Zerah, Shammah, Mizzah, called sons of Basemath, Gn 36:13, and chiefs or clans of Reuel in Edom, Gn 36:17.

2. **Reuel** (2), Ex 2:18, **the Midianite** (1), Nb 10:29, father-in-law of Moses. See: JETHRO.

3. **Reuel** (5), a Gadite, father of: ELIASAPH 1.

4. **Reuel** (1), a Benjaminite, an ancestor of: MESHULLAM 6.

5. **Raguel** (22), a Jew living in Ecbatana, husband of Edna, father of Sarah and father-in-law of Tobias, Tb 6:11, 13; 7:1–15; 8:8, 11, 15; 9:5–6; 10:7–13; 14:12–13.

Father of: SARAH 2.

REUMAH (1), a concubine of Nahor, brother of Abraham, and mother of four sons: Tebah, Gaham, Tahash, and Maacah, Gn 22:24.

REZEPH (2), a town conquered by Sennacherib, 2 K 19:12//Is 37:12. Between Palmyra and the Euphrates.

REZIN, Accad. *Razunnu,* Gr. *Raassōn, Rasōn.*

1. **Rezin** or **Razon** (9), **king of Aram** (5) or **of the Aramaeans** (1), forms a Syro-Ephraimite coalition with Pekah, son of Remaliah, king of Israel, against the Assyrians. When Ahaz, king of Judah, refuses to become part of the coalition, they invade Judah and threaten Jerusalem, 2 K 15:37; 16:5; cf. Is 9:10?, as well as the Davidic dynasty because they propose to replace the reigning king with the son of Tabeel, a man to their liking, Is 7:1, 4–9; cf. 8:6. The king of the Aramaeans and Pekah inflict heavy losses on Ahaz, 2 Ch 28:5–8, who then appeals to Tiglath-pileser III, king of Assyria. The latter crushes the coalition; Rezin dies, 2 K 16:7–9. The Hb. text of 2 K 16:6 indicates that Rezin takes Elath from Ahaz and installs the Edomites there, who then join the Syro-Ephraimite coalition.

2. **Rezin** (2), head of a family of "oblates" who return from the exile, Ezr 2:48//Ne 7:50.

REZON son of Eliada (1), former servant of Hadadezer, king of Zobah, who becomes leader of a marauding band and then king of Damascus and enemy of Solomon, 1 K 11:23.

RHAGES (11) **in Media** (6), a city in the highlands, about 150 km NE of Ecbatana, not far from the modern Teheran. Native place of Gabael, with whom Tobit leaves a sum of money on deposit, Tb 1:14 (var.); 4:1, 20; 5:5 (var.), 6; 6:10 (var.), 13; 9:2, 5.

= **Ragae** (2), Jdt 1:5, 15, scene of the defeat of Arphaxad.

RHEGIUM (1), a port in southern Italy, the modern *Reggio di Calabria.* A port of call for Paul during his voyage from Malta to Rome, Ac 28:13.

RHESA (1), son of Zerubbabel and an ancestor of Jesus acc. to Lk 3:27.

RHODA (1), "Rose" (cf. Rhodes), a young servant girl of Mary, the mother of Mark. When Peter knocks at the door after being freed from prison, Rhoda recognizes his voice but in her joy forgets to open the door to him, Ac 12:13.

RHODES (2), "Rose," an island in the southeastern part of the Aegean Sea. There is a Jewish colony there; consequently, the letter of the consul Lucius promulgating the alliance of Romans and Jews is sent there, 1 M 15:23. Paul stops there briefly on his return from his second missionary journey, Ac 21:1.

RHODOCUS (1), a Jewish soldier who betrays his country, is arrested and executed, 2 M 13:21.

RIBAI (2), a Benjaminite, father of: ITTAI 2.

RIBLAH (12), **in the territory of Hamath** (5), a town on the Orontes, between Hamath and Damascus. Today *Ribleh.* Riblah is the most northerly point in Palestine, Ezk 6:14 (Hb. *Diblah*). It is at Riblah that Pharaoh Neco, in 609, puts Jehoahaz, king of Judah, in chains, 2 K 23:33. It is there, too, that Nebuchadnezzar, king of Babylon, sets up his headquarters and there that, after the fall of Jerusalem (587) he slaughters the sons of Zedekiah, puts out the latter's eyes, 2 K 25:6–7//Jr 39:5–7, and puts to death the most important men of Jerusalem, 2 K 25:20–21//Jr 52:26–27.

RIMMON, 1–4: Hb. "Pomegranate" (cf. Enrimmon; Gath-rimmon; Rimmon-perez); 5: Accad. *Ramanu* (cf. Hadad-rimmon; Tabrimmon).

1. **Rimmon** (4) **in the Negeb** (1), Zc 14:10, listed among the towns in the Negeb of Judah, Jos 15:32, formerly a town of Simeon, Jos 19:7//1 Ch 4:32.

= **Enrimmon** (1), reinhabited by the sons of Judah after the exile, Ne 11:29.

2. **Rimmon** (3), a border town of Zebulun, Jos 19:13, assigned to the Levites of the clan of Merari, Jos 21:35 (corr. of Hb. *Dimna*).

= **Rimmono** (1), 1 Ch 6:62.

3. **Rock of Rimmon** (14), a place of refuge for the Benjaminites who survive the war of extermination waged on them by Israel as a result of the crime at Gibeah, Jg 20:45–47; 21:13. 6 km E of Bethel. Today *Rammun.*

4. **Rimmon of Beeroth** (3), a Benjaminite, father of Rechab and of: BAANAH 1.

5. **Rimmon** (3), one of the names of *Hadad,* Aramaean storm god. Naaman, army commander of the king of Aram, frequents his temple at Damascus, in company with his master, 2 K 5:18.

RIMMONO (1). See: RIMMON 2.

RIMMON-PEREZ (2), "Pomegranate of the Breach" (cf. Rimmon 1–4; Perez), a stage of the Exodus, between Sinai and Kadesh, Nb 33:19–20.

RINNAH (1), "Clamor," a Judaean, one of the sons of Shimon, 1 Ch 4:20.

RIPHATH (1), one of the three sons of Gomer, son of Japheth, Gn 10:3.

= **Diphath** (1), 1 Ch 1:6.

An unidentified people.

RISSAH (2), a stage of the Exodus between Sinai and Kadesh, Nb 33:21–22.

RITHMAH (2), "Jennet," a stage of the Exodus between Sinai and Kadesh, Nb 33:18–19.

RIVER. See: EUPHRATES; JORDAN 1; NILE; WADI.

RIZIA (1), (cf. Tirzah?), an Asherite, one of the three sons of Ulla, head of a family and a stout fighting man, 1 Ch 7:39–40.

RIZPAH (4), "Burning stone," **daughter of Aiah** (4), a concubine of Saul, then of Abner, 2 S 3:7–8. By Saul she has two sons, Armoni and Meribbaal. When these have been tortured to death by the Gibeonites, Rizpah watches over their bodies for a whole season, until they are buried, 2 S 21:8–11.

ROCK, Hb. 1–4: *Sèla';* 5–8: *Zur* (cf. Zur. See Peter; Stone).

1. **The Rock** (7), Gr. *Petra,* a fortified town in the wilderness of Edom, Jg 1:36, conquered by Amaziah, king of Judah, 2 K 14:7//2 Ch 25:12, who gives it the name **Joktheel** (1), 2 K 14:7. The "city" of 2 M 5:8 is *Petra,* capital of the Nabataeans. Elsewhere, *The Rock,* often identified with the modern *Petra,* is probably to be located further north, in the region of Bozrah. It is possible that there is question of several cities with the same name. Cf. Is 16:1; 42:11; Jr 49:16; Ob 3.

2. **Rock of Etam** (2). See: ETHAM 2.

3. **Rock of Rimmon** (4). See: RIMMON 3.

4. **Rock of Divisions** (1). See: DIVISIONS.

5. **Rock of Oreb** (2), "Rock of the Raven." See: OREB.

6. **Field of Rocks** (1). See: ZIDDIM 2.

7. **Rocks of the Wild Goats** (1), 1 S 24:3, a spot near En-gedi, to which Saul pursues David.

8. **Rock-in-the-Plain** (1), Jr 21:13, name given to Jerusalem and to the Ophel, on which the royal palace is built.

ROGELIM (2), "The Fullers" (cf. Fuller 1), a town in Gad, native place of: BARZILLAI 1.

ROHGAH (1), an Asherite, one of the sons of Shomer, a stout fighting man and head of a family, 1 Ch 7:34.

ROMAMTI-EZER (2), "I have raised myself up, [you are my] help" (cf. Ramah; Ezer), of the sons of Heman, 1 Ch 25:4, leader of the twenty-fourth class of cantors, 25:31.

ROMAN (24), of or from: ROME.

ROME (20), capital of the Roman Empire. In the OT, the first allusion to Rome is found in Dn 11:30 where **Kittim** probably means the Romans. Shortly before the end of the second century B.C. the author of 1 M writes an enthusiastic encomium of the **Romans,** 1 M 8:1–16. Under Antiochus IV Epiphanes—a hostage at Rome before becoming king, 1 M 1:10, just as Demetrius I was to be later on, 1 M 7:1—two Roman ambassadors establish contact with the Jews, 2 M 11:34–38. Under Demetrius I, Judas Maccabaeus sends Eupolemus and Jason to conclude with the Romans, 1 M 8:17–32; cf. 2 M 4:11, an alliance that will be renewed by Jonathan, 1 M 12:1–4, 16, then by Simon, 1 M 14:16–19, 40; 15:15–24. Nicanor hopes by selling Jewish prisoners, to pay the tribute the king owes to the Romans, 2 M 8:10, 36.

The NT reminds us that Judaea is under Roman domination (since 63 B.C.), Jn 11:48, that there is a Jewish colony at Rome, Ac 2:10; cf. Ac 18:2, and that Philippi is a Roman colony, Ac 16:12, 21. The capital of the empire is connected especially with the ministry of Paul. Born a Roman citizen, Ac 22:28; cf. 16:37–38; 22:25–29; 23:27, Paul several times makes plans to go there, Rm 15:22; cf. Ac 19:21. From Corinth, during the winter of 57–58, he writes his "Letter to the Romans," Rm 1:7, 19.

Arrested at Jerusalem on Pentecost 58, Paul feels called by the Lord to bear witness for him in Rome, Ac 23:11. When transferred to Caesarea, he appeals to Caesar and to a trial at Rome, Ac 25:10, 12; cf. 28:17, the fairness of which he values, Ac 25:16; cf. 18:15; 28:16. An eventful journey brings him to Rome, Ac 27:1–28:14. He remains a prisoner there for two years (61–63), "in lodgings of his own," Ac 28:15–16, and "proclaiming the kingdom of God," 28:30–31. 2 Tm allows for a second imprisonment of Paul at Rome, 1:8; 2:9, where "Onesiphorus . . . has often been a comfort to me," 1:16–17. The Church of Rome, founded perhaps by Jewish colonials and proselytes who had returned there after the first Christian Pentecost, Ac 2:10, seems to have been made up chiefly of Christians converted from paganism, cf. Rm 1:5–6, 13; 11:13, with Jewish Christians in the minority; the distrustful reception that the Jews of Rome, Ac 28:21–28, give to Paul's message, suggest this. Paul greets twenty-eight members of this church in Rm 16:1–15.

Symbolic name: BABYLON *b*.
See: ITALY.
Emperors: CAESAR.
Consul: SCIPIO.
Proconsuls: GALLIO; PAUL 2.
Ambassadors: MANIUS; MEMMIUS.
Governors/Procurators: FELIX; FESTUS; PILATE; QUIRINIUS.
Tribune: LYSIAS 3.
Centurions: CORNELIUS; JULIUS.
Various: PUBLIUS; TERTULLUS.

ROSH (1), "Head," a son of Benjamin, Gn 46:21.

RUFUS, Gr. *Rouphos,* Lat. *Rufus,* "Russet, Red" (cf. Edom).

1. **Rufus** (1), brother of Alexander and son of Simon of Cyrene, Mk 15:21.

2. **Rufus** (1), a Christian of Rome. Paul regards Rufus' mother as his own, Rm 16:13. Same as the preceding?

RUMAH (1), (cf. Ramah). See: ARUMAH.

RUTH (13), "Friend, Companion," **the Moabitess** (7).

Central figure in the little book that bears her name and emphasizes both her foreignness to the people of the covenant, 2:10—she is a "Moabite woman," 1:4, 22; 2:2, 6, 21; 4:5, 10; cf. 1:1, 2, 6, 22; 4:3—and her familial piety, 3:10: after entering by her first marriage into an Ephrathite clan of Bethlehem in Judah, 1:1–5, she remains attached to Naomi, her mother-in-law, 1:14, 18, and returns with her to Bethlehem, 1:22, where she marries Boaz, a relative who has the right of redemption over her, 2:20; 4:9–10. Obed, the son born of this union, 4:13–17, is "father of David's father, Jesse," 4:17, 22, and wins for Ruth a place in the genealogy of Jesus, Mt 1:5.

S

SABAEANS (2), Jl 4:8 (Hb. *Sheba'im*); Jb 1:15 (Hb. *Sheba'*). See: SHEBA 1.

SABAOTH (282), Hb. *Zeba'ot,* Gr. *Sabaōth* (NT, 2×) or *tōn dynameōn,* "of armies" (= armies of Israel, 1 S 17:45; heavenly armies—angels, stars—Ps 103:21; Gn 2:1; Canaanite gods). See: YAHWEH *e*.

SABTAH (2), one of the five sons of Cush, Gn 10:7//1 Ch 1:9, acc. to the priestly tradition. In southern Arabia?

SABTECA (2), one of the five sons of Cush, Gn 10:7//1 Ch 1:9, acc. to the priestly tradition. In southern Arabia?

SACAR (1). See: SACHAR 2.

SACHAR, Sacar, "Wages" (cf. Issachar).

1. **Sachar** (1), = **Sharar** (1), father of: AHIAM.

2. **Sacar** (1), a gatekeeper, fourth son of Obed-edom, 1 Ch 26:4.

SACHIA (1), a Benjaminite, head of a family, in Moab, 1 Ch 8:10.

SADDUCEES (14), Hb. *Zadduq,* Aram. *Zadduqaya* (cf. Zadok), a party, Ac 5:17; 23:6, linked by its name with: ZADOK 1, whose members are drawn from the upper classes of the priesthood and the wealthy laity and who form the majority in the Sanhedrin. They differ from the Pharisees (with whom they are named 7×, Ac 23:7–8, and severely judged, Mt 3:7; 16:1, 6, 11–12) on three essential points:

—They stick exclusively to the written Law (cf. "Moses said," Mt 22:23–24; "We have it from Moses in writing," Mk 12:18–19//Lk 20:27–28) and regard priests as alone qualified to interpret it.

—"The Sadducees say there is neither resurrection nor angel nor spirit, while the Pharisees accept all three," Ac 23:8. Concerning the resurrection, they present Jesus with a tricky and ridiculous "case of conscience," and he answers them not with the text of Dn 12:2–3, which they reject, but with Ex 3:6, which is part of the Law of Moses, Mt 22:23–24//Mk 12:18–27//Lk 20:27–38.

—They are more involved politically and accept Roman domination. Being very influential with the authorities and especially hostile to Jesus, they seem to be responsible for his condemnation to death, cf. the part played by the chief priests in the passion stories, in which the Pharisees appear only in Jn 18:3. This hostility carries over to the disciples of Jesus, Ac 4:1; 5:17.

SAKKUTH (1). See: KAIWAN.

SALA

1. **Sala** (1). See: SHELAH 2.
2. **Sala** (1). See: SALMON.

[SALAMANU]. See: SHALMAN.

SALAMIEL (1). See: SHELUMIEL.

SALAMIS (1), a harbor on the eastern coast of Cyprus. Paul and Barnabas, accompanied by Mark, preach the Gospel in the synagogues there, Ac 13:5.

SALECAH (4), one of "the capital cities of Og in Bashan," Dt 3:10; cf. Jos 12:5, assigned to the Transjordanian tribes, Jos 13:11, inhabited by Gadites, 1 Ch 5:11. 120 km E of Beth-shan.

SALEM, Gr. transcription of Hb. *Shalem,* "safe and sound"; *Shalem* is also the name of a god known at Ugarit; the Hb. root of this word suggests *integrity, plenitude,* therefore *peace* (cf. Capharsalama; Jerusalem; Meshelemiah; Meshillemith; Meshullam; Meshullemeth; Salim; Salome; Shallum; Shalman; Shelemiah; Shelomi; Shelomith; Shelomoth; Shelumiel; Shillem; Solomon).

1. **Salem** (3), Gn 14:18; Heb 7:1–2, a town whose king is: MELCHIZEDEK. Identified by Jewish tradition with *Jerusalem,* by the Byzantines with *Salim.*

2. **Salem** (1), identified by Ps 76:2 with *Jerusalem.*

3. **The Salem valley** (1), Jdt 4:4. Today *Salim,* 5 km E of Shechem.

SALIM (1), (cf. Salem), Jn 3:23: "John was baptising at Aenon near Salim, where there was plenty of water." Site uncertain: near Scythopolis? at Ain Farah?

SALLAI

1. **Sallai** (1), a Benjaminite, settled in Jerusalem after the exile, Ne 11:8.

2. **Sallai** (1). See: SALLU 2.

SALLU, Hb. 1: *Sallu';* 2: *Sallu.*

1. **Sallu son of Meshullam** (2), a Benjaminite settled in Jerusalem after the exile; his genealogy as given in 1 Ch 9:7: *son of Hodaviah son of Hassenuah* differs from that in Ne 11:7: *son of Joed son of Pedaiah son of Kolaiah son of Maaseiah son of Ithiel son of Jeshaiah.*

2. **Sallu** (1) = **Sallai** (1), a priest who returns from the exile with Zerubbabel, Ne 12:7, gives his name to a priestly family whose head in the time of the high priest Joiakim is Kallai, Ne 12:20.

SALMA, Salmah

1. **Salma** (2). See: SALMON.

2. **Salma** (2), one of the sons of Hur, son of Judah, 1 Ch 2:51. Father of several Judaean clans, among them Bethlehem, Zorah, Netophah, 1 Ch 2:54.

3. **Salmah** (1), a nomadic Arabian tribe, Sg 1:5 (corr. of Hb. *Salomon*).

SALMAH (1). See: SALMA 3.

SALMON (4), Hb. and Gr. *Salmōn,* a descendant of Judah through Perez, is a son of Nahshon and father of Boaz, Rt 4:20 (Hb. *Salma;* var. *Salmon*), 21 (Hb. *Salmon;* var. *Salma*), and ancestor of David. Acc. to Mt 1:5, "Salmon was the father of Boaz, Rahab [the prostitute] being his mother."

= **Salma** (2), son of Nahshon and father of Boaz, 1 Ch 2:11.

= **Sala** (1), an ancestor of Jesus, Lk 3:32 (var. *Salmon*).

SALMONE (1), a cape on the eastern or southeastern coast of Crete, Ac 27:7.

SALOME, Gr. *Salōmē* (cf. Salem).

1. **Salome** (2), one of the women who follow and serve Jesus, beginning in Galilee, and stand near the cross, Mk 15:40. They buy the spices for anointing the corpse of Jesus and discover the empty tomb, Mk 16:1.

= ? **the mother of Zebedee's sons** (2), Mt 20:20; 27:55.

2. **[Salome] the daughter of Herodias** (2) and of Herod Philip. During the celebration of Herod's birthday and at her mother's request, she has the head of John the Baptist brought to her on a dish, Mk 6:21–28//Mt 14:6–11.

SALT, Hb. *Melah* (cf. Tel-melah).

1. **Salt Sea** (9). See: DEAD SEA.

2. **Valley of Salt** (5), a part of the Arabah, between the Dead Sea and the Gulf of Aqaba. The Edomites are de-

feated there by David, 2 S 8:13//1 Ch 18:12 (by Abishai)//Ps 60:2 (by Joab), and two centuries later by King Amaziah of Judah, 2 K 14:7//2 Ch 25:11.

3. **City of Salt** (1), Hb. *Ir-melah* or *Ir-ha-melah,* a town in the wilderness of Judah, Jos 15:62.

SALU (2), a Simeonite, father of: ZIMRI 1.

SAMARIA (130), Hb. *Shomrôn,* Aram. *Shamrayin,* "Guard tower"?, Gr. *Samar(e)ia* (cf. Shemariah).

a. Samaria, capital, kingdom, province

Samaria is initially the name of a hill in Canaan, 1 K 16:24; cf. Si 50:26 (Gr.); Am 3:9; 4:1; 6:1, which Omri, king of Israel, buys from a man named Shemer: on it Omri "built a town which he named Samaria after Shemer who had owned the hill," and which replaces Tirzah as capital of the northern kingdom, 1 K 16:23–24, 28; cf. Is 7:9; 8:4; 9:8; Ezk 16:53, 55. Henceforth the kings of Israel reside at Samaria, 1 K 16:29; 20:43; 21:1, 18; 22:52; 2 K 1:2; 3:1, 6; 10:36; 13:1, 10; 14:23; 15:8, 13, 17, 23, 27; 17:1; 2 Ch 18:2; 22:9, and it is the burial place of Kings Omri, 1 K 16:28, Ahab, 1 K 22:37; Jehu, 2 K 10:35, Jehoahaz, 2 K 13:9, and Joash, 2 K 13:13; 14:16. The court of Samaria is several times the scene of crimes and plots, with Jehu, who has the seventy sons of Ahab massacred at Jezreel and Samaria, 2 K 10:1–17; with Menahem, who assassinates Shallum, 2 K 15:14; Pekah, who assassinates Pekahiah, 2 K 15:25 (cf. Ho 8:4). Samaria is also the residence of prophets such as Elisha, 2 K 5:3 (cf. 2:25), and Oded, 2 Ch 28:9; cf. 2 K 23:18; Jr 23:13. Under Ahab the "governor of the city" is Amon, 1 K 22:26//2 Ch 18:25. As capital of Israel, Samaria is frequently paralleled with Jerusalem, the capital of Judah, 2 K 18:34–35//Is 36:19–20; 2 K 21:13; Tb 14:4; Is 10:11; Jr 23:13–14; Ezk 16:2, 46–47; 23; Am 6:1; Mi 1:1, 5. The city has an acropolis (*Ophel*), 2 K 5:24, and a pool, 1 K 22:38.

The name of the city is extended to the surrounding territory, which is called "the land of Samaria," 2 K 18:34–35//Is 36:19–20; cf. 2 K 17:26; Ob 19; "the mountains of Samaria," Jr 31:5; "Samaria," 2 K 17:24, 26. Samaria is coextensive with the northern kingdom or the kingdom of Israel: thus, Ahab and Ahaziah are called "kings of Samaria," 1 K 21:1; 2 K 1:3.

Threatened several times in the past by the Aramaeans, 1 K 20; 2 K 6:24–7:20; cf. 2 K 6:19–20, the city, besieged by Shalmaneser V, king of Assyria, in 724, falls in 721 under the assault of Sargon II, who deports the inhabitants to Assyria, 2 K 17:5–6//18:9–10, and establishes the province of *Samerina,* where he settles colonists from other lands, 2 K 17:24–25. After the fall of the kingdom, its territory becomes a province of the various empires that occupy Palestine, the Assyrian, cf. 2 K 17:24; Ezr 4:10, the Persian, cf. Ezr 4:17; Ne 3:34, the Hellenistic (Samaria, 1 M 3:10; 10:38; 2 M 15:1, is also called, in Greek, Samaritis, 1 M 10:30; 11:28, 34), and the Roman: at the beginning of the Christian era, Samaria is the central area of western Palestine between Galilee to the north and Judaea to the south, Jn 4:3–4; Ac 1:8; 9:31.

b. Sin and punishment of Samaria

In becoming the capital of the northern kingdom, Samaria inherits "the sin of Jeroboam" (see: JEROBOAM 1), 2 K 13:6; 17:21–22: "the altar that was at Bethel, the high place built by Jeroboam, son of Nebat, who had led Israel into sin," 2 K 23:15. "The sin [Hb.] of Samaria," Am 8:14, refers perhaps to the importation of the goddess Ashima(h) into Samaria, but it includes more broadly the schismatic cult established at Bethel, "the calf of Samaria," Ho 8:5–6; 10:5, that is, the golden calf set up by Jeroboam,

1 K 12:28–29, 32, "that sin of Israel," Ho 10:8. In a more general way, the prophets condemn not only the altar at Bethel but the temple of Baal and the sacred poles erected by Ahab, 1 K 16: 32–33; 2 K 10:26; 13:6, and "all the shrines of the high places in the towns of Samaria," 1 K 13:32; 2 K 18:34//Is 36:19; Is 10:10–11; cf. Ho 7:1. And they foretell punishment, Am 3:9–12; Ho 14:1; Is 8:4. After the fall of the northern kingdom and of its capital, the prophets point to these dramatic events as a sign that foretells the punishment of Judah and Jerusalem, which are guilty of sins like those of Samaria, 2 K 21:13; Is 10:11; Jr 23:13–14; cf. the symbolic story of Oholah (Samaria) and Oholibah (Jerusalem), Ezk 23; cf. 16:46–47.

Kingdom: ISRAEL *d*.
Governor: AMON 1.
Towns: BETHEL 1; SHECHEM; SYCHAR.
Mountains: GERIZIM.

c. The Samaritans

The word appears for the first time in 2 K 17:29, after the fall of the kingdom of Israel. It does not designate simply the inhabitants of the city or province of Samaria, but has both ethnic and religious overtones. The Samaritans are, to begin with, a mixed population, made up partly of Israelites descended from the northern tribes, especially Ephraim and Manasseh, and partly of colonists brought from other countries into this Assyrian province, 2 K 17:24; Ezr 4:4, 9–10. In addition, these foreigners brought their gods and customs with them, 2 K 17: 29–31, but they also begin to worship "the god of the country," thanks to a priest who was deported but then sent back to Samaria, 2 K 17:26–28; the result is the religious syncretism summed up in 2 K 17:41: "These nations, then, worshipped Yahweh and served their carved images as well, their children, too, and their children's children still behave today as their fathers behaved in the past." These are "the surrounding peoples," Ezr 3:3, who try to frustrate the efforts of the repatriated Jews to rebuild, Ezr 4:1–5, 6–24; Ne 3:34. The result is division and hostility between Jews and Samaritans; in the fourth century the latter build a schismatic altar on Mount Gerizim, 2 M 6:2; cf. Jn 4:20–21, and retain only the Pentateuch from the Jewish Bible. Acc. to Si 50:25–26, the Jews "detest" the Samaritans, "the stupid people living at Shechem." This feeling is still alive in the time of Christ, cf. Mt 10:5; Lk 9:52–53; Jn 4:9, and the name "Samaritan" is even thrown at Jesus as an insult, Jn 8:48. Yet Jesus does not hesitate to pass through Samaria, Lk 9: 52; 17:11; Jn 4:4. It is to a Samaritan woman that he speaks of the living water and of spiritual worship, Jn 4; it is Samaritans to whom he points as models of love of neighbor, Lk 10:29–37 (cf. the incident in 2 Ch 28:8–15) and of gratitude, Lk 17:11–18. His disciples are to be his "witnesses" throughout Judaea and Samaria, Ac 1:8: Samaria will be evangelized by Philip the deacon, Ac 8:1–9, Peter and John, 8:14–25 (meeting with Simon the magician), and Barnabas and Saul, 15:3.

SAMARITAN (12), 2 K 17:29; Mt 10:5; Lk 9:52; 10:33; 17:16; Jn 4:9, 39–40; 8:48; Ac 8:25. See: SAMARIA *c*.

SAMLAH (4) **of Masrekah** (2), a king of Edom. His predecessor is Hadad and his successor Shaul, Gn 36:36–37//1 Ch 1:47–48.

SAMOS (2), (cf. Samothrace), an island in the Aegean Sea, SW of Ephesus. There is a Jewish colony there, and the letter of the consul Lucius promulgating the alliance of Romans and Jews is, therefore, sent to Samos among other places, 1 M 15:23. Paul stops there as he returns from his third missionary journey, Ac 20:15.

SAMOTHRACE (1), Gr. *Samothrakē,* "Samos of Thrace" (cf. Samos; Thracian);

in the eighth century B.C. this island is colonized by people from the island of Samos. An island in the northern part of the Aegean Sea, near the Thracian coast. Paul stops there on his second missionary journey with Silas, Timothy, and probably Luke, Ac 16:11.

SAMPSAMES (1), a town in Pontus on the Black Sea, between Sinope and Trebizond. It has a Jewish colony, and the letter of the consul Lucius promulgating the alliance of Jews and Romans is addressed to it among others, 1 M 15:23. Today *Eski-samsun* in Turkey.

SAMSON (39), Hb. *Shimshôn,* diminutive of *Shèmèsh,* "Sun" (cf. Beth-shemesh; En-shemesh; Irshemesh; Shimshai; Shavsha? See Heliopolis; Heres; Ra).

Samson is presented in the Book of Judges as the last of the "greater" judges of Israel: consecrated to God from his mother's womb, "it is he who will begin to rescue Israel from the power of the Philistines," Jg 13:5. But he is neither a judge nor a liberator in the strict sense of the terms. He is rather a popular hero whose physical prowess against the Philistines is equaled only by his weakness for women; a man who always acts on his own and whose feats are aimed more at ridiculing the foe than at freeing the country from the yoke of the conqueror.

Birth into a Danite family at Zorah, Jg 13. Marriage to a Philistine woman; the riddle of "the strong and the sweet," 14. Burning of the Philistine crops and slaughter of a thousand Philistines with the jawbone of an ass, 15. At Gaza, a Philistine town, meeting with a prostitute and transferral of the town gates to a hill top, 16:1–3. Betrayal by Delilah and revenge of Samson, who dies but takes with him the Philistines who have gathered in the temple of their god Dagon, 16:4–31.

Heb 11:32 mentions Samson and three other judges: Gideon, Barak, and Jephthah.

SAMUEL, Hb. *Shemu'el,* "Name of God *or* His name is El" (cf. Shem). The popular etymology given in 1 S 1:20, "Requested," is better suited to Saul than to Samuel.

1. **Shemuel son of Ammihud** (1), represents the tribe of Simeon in the allocation of Canaan, Nb 34:20.

2. **Samuel** (144), an Ephraimite from Ramah, son of Elkanah and Hannah the barren, dedicated by his mother to the service of the sanctuary at Shiloh, where he passes his childhood with the priest Eli, 1 S 1:20–28; 2:11, 18–21, 26, and where in a "vision" he hears the word of God who consecrates him a *prophet,* 3.

A tradition originating in the sanctuary of Mizpah regards Samuel as a new Moses (cf. Ex 18:13–14 and 32:11), being at once a *judge,* that is, a liberator from Philistine oppression, and an *intercessor* with Yahweh for this victory, 1 S 7:2–14. Acc. to 7:15–8:3, Samuel is throughout his life an itinerant judge, and his sons after him are the last of the "lesser" judges, 8:1–5; 12:2. But it is in the establishment of the monarchy that Samuel plays an essential and decisive role. We have two parallel traditions on this subject. One points to a current of popular opinion that wants "a king to rule over us, like the other nations." Without favoring this outlook, Samuel reminds the people of the "rights of the king" and the abuses that accompany these, 8:4–22. He calls the people together at Mizpah, and there Saul is chosen king by lot, 10:17–25. Then Samuel withdraws into the background in favor of Saul, while also urging Israel to respect the rights of God, 12. Acc. to the other tradition, Samuel, a man of God, 9:6, a prophet or seer, 9:9, while at Ramah meets young Saul, who is looking for his father's she-donkeys, and anoints him king, 9:1–10:16. After the victory over the Ammonites, the people proclaim Saul king at the sanctuary of Gilgal, 11:15. The two traditions are harmonized in 11:12–14. Then comes the break between Saul and Samuel, 13:8–15; 15. "Samuel did not see Saul again to the day of his death," 15:35, but cf. 19:18–24, where David and Saul come to Samuel at Ramah, and 28:4–20, where at Saul's request the witch of En-dor summons up the ghost of Samuel. Once Saul has been rejected, Samuel goes to Bethlehem, where he gives anointing as king not to the older sons of Jesse, but to the youngest, David, 16:1–13; cf. 1 Ch 11:3. Samuel dies and is buried at Ramah, 25:1//28:3.

Tradition has looked upon Samuel primarily as a seer, 1 Ch 9:22; 26:28; 29:29, or a prophet, 2 Ch 35:18; Ac 3:24; 13:20; cf. Heb 11:32, and an intercessor equal to Moses, Ps 99:6; Jr 15:1. There is a encomium of Samuel in Si 46:13–20. The chronicler speaks of "the Annals of Samuel the seer," 1 Ch 29:29, and makes this Ephraimite priest, cf. 1 S 2:18; 7:9–10, a descendant of Levi through Kohath, 1 Ch 6:7–13, and an ancestor of Heman the cantor, 1 Ch 6:18–23.

3. **Shemuel** (1), an Issacharite, one of the family heads of Tola, 1 Ch 7:2.

SANBALLAT (10), Accad. *Sin-uballit,* "[The god] Sin gives life" (cf. Belteshazzar; Sin), **the Horonite** (3), Persian governor of Samaria. With Tobiah, governor of the Ammonite territory, and Geshem, governor of the Arab federation of Kedar, he attempts to block the rebuilding of the Jerusalem wall by Nehemiah, Ne 2:10, 19–20; 3:33–35. The vigilance of Nehemiah thwarts his plans and threats: an attack on the city, 4:1–3, intrigues against Nehemiah, calumnies, 6:1–14. Sanballat's son-in-law is a grandson of the high priest Eliashib, and Nehemiah is forced to expel him, 13:28.

SANSANNAH (1), a town in the Negeb of Judah, Jos 15:31. 15 km NE of Beersheba.

SAPH, a descendant of Rapha (1), 2 S 21:18 = **Sippai, a descendant of the Rephaim** (1), 1 Ch 20:4, slain by Sibbecai of Hushah in a war against the Philistines, at Gob or Gezer.

SAPPHIRA (1), Gr. *Sappheirē,* "Sapphire," wife of: HANANIAH 18.

SARAH, Gr. *Sarra,* "Princess, Sovereign" (cf. Israel; Seraiah).

1. **Sarah** (42) = **Sarai** (17), Gn 11:26–17:5, **wife of Abraham** (6), Gn 11:29, 31; 12:17; 16:1, 3; 20:18, and his half-sister, Gn 20:12. On two occasions Abraham will have his wife Sarah pass as his sister, in dealing with Pharaoh in Egypt, Gn 12:10–20 (Yahwist tradition), and with Abimelech, king of Gerar, Gn 20:1–17 (Elohist tradition).

Sarah accompanies Abraham from Ur to Haran, Gn 11:31, and thence to Canaan, Gn 12:5. Being barren, Sarah gives her Egyptian servant Hagar to Abraham so that she may have children by means of this servant, Gn 16:1–8; cf. 25:12. At the age of 90, Sarai receives the name Sarah and the promise of child and numerous descendants, Gn 17:15–22 (priestly tradition); cf. Rm 4:19. At Mamre, Yahweh announces that Sarah will soon bear a son; Sarah laughs, Gn 18:6–15 (Yahwist tradition); cf. Rm 9:9. Sarah gives birth to Isaac, Gn 21:1–7; cf. 24:36. Jealous now of Ishmael, she forces Abraham to send Hagar and her son away, Gn 21:8–12. She dies at the age of 127 at Hebron; Abraham buries her in the cave of Machpelah, Gn 23:1–20; cf. 25:10; 49:31.

Acc. to Is 51:1–2, Sarah is the ancestor of Israel. In Ga 4:22–31 Sarah, in virtue of her status as a free woman, prefigures the Jerusalem above, which gives birth to free men. Heb 11:11 praises the faith of Sarah, and 1 P 3:6 proposes her as a model wife.

2. **Sarah** (16) **the daughter of Raguel** (4), Tb 3:7, 17; 11:15, and of Edna. An unhappy bride who sees seven husbands die one after another on the wedding night, all slain by the demon Asmodeus,

she prays God to remove her from this life, Tb 3; cf. 12:12–14. On the advice of the angel Raphael, who overcomes the demon Asmodeus, Sarah marries young Tobias, 6:11–18; 7–8. With her husband she leaves Ecbatana and her family, 10: 7–12, to go to her parents-in-law, Tobit and his wife, at Nineveh, 11:15–17. At their death, Tobias, Sarah, and their children return to live in Ecbatana, 14:12.

SARAI (17), another form of: SARAH 1.

SARAPH (1), "Burning serpent" (cf. Misrephoth-maim), a descendant of Judah through Shelah, a clan that has emigrated to Moab and then resettles at Bethlehem, 1 Ch 4:22.

SARASADAI (1), Jdt 8:1. See: ZURISHADDAI.

SARDIS (3), ancient capital of Lydia in Asia Minor. One of the letters of the Apocalypse is addressed to the Christian community of the city: "You are reputed to be alive and yet are dead," Rv 1:11; 3:1–6. 80 km E of Smyrna.

Perhaps to be identified with: SEPHARAD.

SARGON II (1), Accad. *Sharru-ukîn,* **king of Assyria** (6), (721–705), successor of Shalmaneser V. At the beginning of his reign he captures the city of Samaria that his father had besieged for three years, deports its population to Assyria, and transfers people from Mesopotamia to Samaria, 2 K 17:6//18:11; 17:24–27. Ten years later he captures the Philistine town of Ashdod, Is 20:1.

His son and successor: SENNACHERIB.

SARID (2), "Survivor," a town in Zebulun, Jos 19:10, 12. Some read *Sadud* with some Gr. mss.

SATAN (54), Hb. *Satân,* "Accuser, Adversary," Gr. *diabolos* (OT), *Satanas* (NT) (cf. Sitnah).

In 18 instances the word *Satan* (from a root *satân/satam,* "to be opposed to") designates a personal being who is enemy both of God and of his faithful, cf. Si 21:27. In Jb 1:6–12; 2:1–7 (14×) and in Zc 3:1–2 (3×), where it is used in Hebrew with the article, "the Satan" is depicted as a member of the heavenly court along with "the Sons of God," Jb 1:6; 2:1, or with "the angel of Yahweh," Zc 3:1–2, and plays the part of "accuser" of Job and of the high priest Joshua. Acc. to 1 Ch 21:1 it is Satan (which has become a proper name) and no longer Yahweh himself (2 S 24:1) who incites David to take a census of Israel.

By always translating (*the*) *Satan* as *ho diabolos* (from *dia-ballō,* "to speak evil of, to calumniate"), the LXX, with the text of Ws 2:24: "the devil's envy," paves the way for the vocabulary of the NT in which the words *satanas* (usually with the article) and *diabolos* are used 35× each to refer to Satan. Jesus is tempted by Satan acc. to Mk 1:13, by the devil acc. to Mt 4:1; Lk 4:2. Peter and Judas, who oppose the plan of God, are treated, one as Satan, Mt 16:23// Mk 8:33, the other as a devil, Jn 6:70; cf. Lk 22:3; Jn 13:27. The equivalence of the two terms is also indicated in Rv 12:9; 20:2.

In contrast to God, who alone is good, Mt 19:17 p, Satan is **the evil one** (12), Mt 5:37 . . . 1 Jn 5:19, the enemy, Mt 13:39; Lk 10:19, the liar, Jn 8:44, the seducer, Rv 12:9; 20:7–8; cf. 1 Co 7:5; 2 Co 2:11; 2 Th 2:9; 1 Tm 5:15, identified with the serpent of Gn 3 in Rv 12:9; 20:2; 2 Co 11:3, possessor of a false knowledge, Rv 2:24; cf. Gn 3:5–6. As prince of this world, Jn 12:31; 14:30; 16:11; cf. Jm 3:15; Rv 2:13–15, god of this world, 2 Co 4:4; cf. Ep 2:2, he reigns over a kingdom of darkness, Ac 26:18; cf. Lk 22:53; Col 1:13, even if he disguises himself as an angel of light, 2 Co 11:14, and he has power over men, Lk 4:6; Jn 13:27; Ac 5:3; cf. Lk 13:16; 1 Co 5:5; 1 Tm 1:20. He opposes Jesus (temptation) and the Apostles, Lk 22:

31; 1 Th 2:18. By rejecting Christ, the Jews show that they are the sons of the devil, Jn 8:44, "the synagogue of Satan," Rv 2:9; 3:9. Satan is finally overcome by Christ, Lk 10:18; Jn 12:31; 14:30; 16: 11, 33; cf. Rv 12:7–8.

See: ABADDON; ANTICHRIST; BAALZEBUB 2; BELIAL; LEVIATHAN.

SAUL, Hb. *Sha'ûl,* Gr. *Saoul* (OT and NT), *Saulos* (NT), "Asked for [from God]" (cf. Eshtaol; Jishal; Shealtiel; Shelah; see Silas).

1. **Shaul** (4) **of Rehoboth-han-nahar** (2), king of Edom. His predecessor is Samlah and his successor Baal-hanan, Gn 36:37–38//1 Ch 1:48–49.

2. **Shaul** (4), **the son of the Canaanite woman** (2), the last of the sons of Simeon, son of Jacob, Gn 46:10//Ex 6:15; 1 Ch 4:24, whose descendants form the **Shaulite** clan, Nb 26:13.

3. **Shaul** (1), a Levite of the clan of Kohath, an ancestor of Samuel acc. to 1 Ch 6:9.

4. **Saul** (395) **son of Kish** (5), **a Benjaminite** (3), first king of Israel (1030–1010).

Reign of Saul

Born into a modest clan of Benjamin, 1 S 10:21, which itself is "the smallest of Israel's tribes," 1 S 9:21; cf. 9:1, 16; 1 Ch 12:1–2; Ac 13:21, living at Gibeah, 1 S 10:26; cf. 11:4; 15:34, Saul, while searching for his father's she-donkeys, happens to meet Samuel at Ramah, 1 S 9, and the latter privately anoints him king, 1 S 10:1; cf. Si 46:13. Acc. to other traditions connected with various sanctuaries, Saul, a young man, tall and handsome, 1 S 9:2; 10:23–24, is chosen by lot at Mizpah, 10:17–25, or else, after a lightning-swift victory over the Ammonites, 11:1–12, is proclaimed king at Gilgal, 11:12–15. Samuel, the last of the judges, yields place, in principle, to Saul, the first of the kings, 1 S 12; cf. Si 46:19.

From the beginning of his reign Saul assumes the role of the judges as liberators by fighting the Philistines, whose leader his son Jonathan kills at Gibeah, 1 S 13:3–4: battle of Michmash; a ritual fault of the people, provoked by an arbitrary decision on Saul's part, keeps the victory from being definitive, 13–14. He also does battle with the Amalekites; but, in sparing King Agag and setting aside the best of the sheep and cattle "to sacrifice them to Yahweh," he sins gravely against the law of the ban, 15:11–15. Samuel reproaches Saul for this sin, 15: 16–23, just as he repudiates the sacrifice Saul offers at Gilgal, without making very clear the reason for his doing so, 13:7–11; cf. 10:8. Samuel tells the king that Yahweh rejects him, 15:23, 26. And "Samuel did not see Saul again to the day of his death," 15:35.

From this time on "the spirit of Yahweh had left Saul and an evil spirit from Yahweh filled him with terror," 1 S 16:14. This text explains the entire subsequent story of Saul as narrated in 16–31. Inclined to rapturous emotion and prophetic delirium, cf. 10:9–12; 19:20–24, afflicted with neurotic anxiety until the end of his life, 28:5; 31:3 (Hb.), Saul directs his jealousy and hatred, 18:9–15, 28–29, at young David, whose valor he recognizes, 18:5, but in whom he sees a rival, 16:2; 18:6–8; 22:17. He gives David his daughter Michal in marriage in the hope that she will prove a snare for him, 18:17–30. The friendship of his son Jonathan with David, 18:1–4; 19:1–7; 20, rouses the king's wrath once more: Saul tries several times to kill David, 19:8–24; cf. 18:10–11. Learning that the priests of Nob have helped David, Saul has them massacred, 20:1–10; 22:6–22. The king of Israel sets out to take David's life, 23:15; 24:15; 26:20, and pursues him to Keilah, then into the wilderness, 23–24; 26. After sparing his enemy, 24:20; 26: 21, David takes refuge among the Philistines, and Saul "stopped searching for him," 27:1–4. Fearful of the Philistines at Mount Gilboa, Saul consults a witch at En-dor; she calls up the ghost of Samuel for him, and the king learns that defeat and death are at hand, 28:3–25; cf. Si 46:20. Saul and his sons die in the battle of Gilboa, 1 S 31:1–13//1 Ch 10:1–14; cf. 2 S 1:1–16; 2:4–7; 4:4, 10.

After Saul's death the struggle for power goes on between David and the **House of Saul** (16), 2 S 3:1, 6. Abner, commander of Saul's army, at first makes Ishbaal, son of Saul, the king of Israel, 2 S 2:8–10, whereas David is anointed king of Judah, 2 S 2:4. Soon, however, Abner agrees "to win all Israel over to" David, 2 S 3:12–21. Acc. to 1 Ch 12:30 "three thousand kinsmen of Saul" rally to David. The new king treats Saul's family with kindness, 2 S 9:1–2, but hands seven descendants of Saul over to the Gibeonites to be dismembered, as expiation for the king's breaking the treaty made with the Gibeonites by Joshua (cf. Jos 9:3–27), 2 S 21:1–9.

Person of Saul

Between Samuel, who withdraws into the background, 1 S 16:13 (cf. 12) and David, whose star is in the ascendant, 13:14; 15:28, Saul is, as it were, eclipsed first by the former, then by the latter and seems like a transitional figure between the age of the judges, 1 S 8:1–2, and the monarchy, 8:4–21, as he exercises a function that is an especially difficult test for the first man to hold the office. In fact, the story of Saul is chiefly a chain of incidents and comprises his relations first with Samuel, then with David; he is named all by himself only 33×: 13:16–14:52.

Saul is almost more a "judge" than a king, and more a military chieftain than an administrator, the only measure he takes being that of expelling "the necromancers and wizards from the country," 1 S 28:3. The summary of his reign emphasizes especially his battles, his deeds of valor, and his victories, 14:47–48. And it is of this valor and this success that David sings after the disaster at Gilboa, 2 S 1:19, 21–24, 27. The fact that Saul, despite his humility, 1 S 9:21; 10:22; 15:17, 24; 24:18; 26:21, and his upright intentions, 13:11–12; 14:41; 15:15, 20; is rejected by Yahweh, 15:23, 26; cf. 13:13–14; 15:11, 35; 18:12; 2 S 7:15; Ac 13:33, underscores both God's freedom of choice, 1 S 10:24; cf. 10:1; 15:17, and the requirement of fidelity to the word of God that is laid upon the one chosen, 15:22–23; cf. 1 Ch 10:13. The reign of Saul illustrates, in a tragic way, the difficulty involved in "sitting on the sovereign throne of Yahweh over Israel," cf. 1 Ch 28:5. Saul, "the anointed of Yahweh," 1 S 10:1; 12:3, 5; 24:7, 11; 26:9, 11, 16, 23; 2 S 1:14–16; Si 46:10, tries to find a compromise between the demands of Yahweh, who has chosen him, and the desires of the people who have acclaimed him. Samuel "the prophet" comes, even from beyond death, 1 S 28:16–18, to remind him of the unavoidable duty of obedience to God. Throughout the history of the monarchy the prophet will stand at the king's side to remind him that he is "the servant of Yahweh," cf. Nathan and David; Elijah and Ahab; and so on.

His sons: ISHBAAL 1; JONATHAN 2; MERIBBAAL 1, 2.

His daughters: MERAB; MICHAL.

His wife: AHINOAM 1.

His concubine: RIZPAH.

Of his clan: SHIMEI 6.

His native town: GIBEAH.

5. **Saul** (15) or, in Greek text, *Saoul* (8) **of Tarsus** (2). See: PAUL 1.

SCEVA (1), Gr. *Skeuas,* a Jewish high priest. His seven sons, itinerant exorcists from Ephesus, invoke the name of Jesus in their rites. "The man with the evil spirit . . . handled them so violently that they fled from that house naked and badly mauled," Ac 19:14–16.

[SCIPIO, Lucius Cornelius], a Roman consul, conqueror of Antiochus the Great at Magnesia on the Sipylus (Lydia) in

189. Scipio is doubtless the *magistrate* of Dn 11:18.

SCORPIONS (Ascent of the) (3), Hb. *'Aqrabim,* between the northern end of the Dead Sea and the wilderness of Zin, on the southern frontier of the Promised Land, Nb 34:4, and of Judah, Jos 15:3, between Judah and Edom, Jg 1:36.

SCYTHIANS (2), Gr. *Skythai* (cf. Scythopolis), a people on the northern shore of the Black Sea, considered barbarian, 2 M 4:47; Col 3:11. See: ASHKENAZ.

SCYTHOPOLIS (2), "City of the Scythians" (cf. Amphipolis; Scythians), Hellenistic name of: BETH-SHAN.

SEBA, Hb. *Seba',* Gr. *Saba,* son of Cush acc. to the priestly traditions, Gn 10:7// 1 Ch 1:9. Associated with Sheba, Ps 72:10, with Egypt and Cush, Is 43:3; cf. 45:14 (*men of Seba*). A region and people to the south of Egypt.

SEBAM (1). See: SIBMAH.

SECACAH (1), (cf. Succoth), a town in the wilderness of Judah, Jos 15:61.

SECUNDUS (1), "Second," **from Thessalonika** (1), a companion of Paul on his return from his third missionary journey (between Greece and Syria), Ac 20:4.

SEGUB

1. **Segub** (1), youngest son of Hiel of Bethel, dies (victim of a foundation sacrifice?) during the rebuilding of Jericho, 1 K 16:34.

2. **Segub** (2), son of Hezron the Judaean and of the daughter of Machir, and father of Jair, 1 Ch 2:21–22.

SEIR, Hb. *Se'ir,* "Hairy"? (cf. Seirah; Seorim?).

1. **Seir** (39), an area described as the **mountainous district** or **highlands of Seir** (16), Gn 14:6; 36:8–9; Dt 1:2; 2:1, 5; Jos 24:4; 1 Ch 4:42; 2 Ch 20:10, 22–23; Si 50:26 (Hb. *Seïr;* Gr. *Samaria*); Ezk 35:2–3, 7, 15. An area located between the Dead Sea and the Gulf of Aqaba, cf. Gn 14:6, in the region of Kadesh, Dt 1:2; 2:1, not far from Hormah, Dt 1:44, and Mount Halak, Jos 11:17//12:7. Formerly occupied by the: HORITES, of whom Seir the Horite is regarded as the eponymous ancestor, Gn 36:20–21, then taken from the Horites by: EDOM (which was originally located east of the Arabah). Acc. to 1 Ch 4:42, some Simeonites take up residence in the highlands of Seir and expel the Amalekites.

2. **Seir** (1), a mountainous area, distinct from the preceding, located west of Kiriath-jearim, between Judah and Benjamin, Jos 15:10.

To be identified (?) with: SEIRAH.

SEIRAH (1), (cf. Seir), place where Ehud hides after the murder of Eglon, Jg 3:26. Perhaps the region north of Jericho?

To be identified (?) with: SEIR 2.

SELED (2), son of Nadab, dies without sons; of the clan of Jerahmeel, 1 Ch 2:30.

SELEUCIA (2), (cf. Seleucus), port of Antioch in Syria, established by Seleucus I. Ptolemy VI occupies it, 1 M 11:8. Barnabas and Paul embark there for Cyprus at the beginning of their first missionary journey, Ac 13:4.

[SELEUCIDS], a Hellenistic dynasty founded by the Macedonian Seleucus I; it reigns over Asia (Syria and Babylonia) from 305 to 64 B.C. Cf. Dn 2:41–43 (*the kingdom*); 7:7–10 (*the ten horns*).

See: SELEUCUS 1–4; ANTIOCHUS 1–6.

SELEUCUS (cf. Seleucia).

1. **[Seleucus I Nicator],** king of Syria (305–281), the *prince* of Dn 11:5. A general of Alexander the Great, then, after the latter's death, a lieutenant of Ptolemy I, he carves out a vast empire in Asia and founds the Seleucid dynasty.

2. **[Seleucus II Callinicus],** son of Antiochus II, king of Syria (246–226).

= **king of the North** (2), suffers a serious defeat at the hands of Ptolemy III Euergetes, who strips him of a vast booty. Seleucus then launches a counteroffensive, Dn 11:7–9. Father of: ANTIOCHUS 2.

3. **[Seleucus III Ceraunus],** son of Seleucus II, king of Assyria (226–23), sets out on a campaign against Egypt with his brother Antiochus the Great, cf. Dn 11:10 (*his sons*). He dies at an assassin's hand.

4. **Seleucus IV [Philopator]** (3), son and successor of Antiochus the Great, called **king of Asia** (1), that is, of Syria (187–175). In 2 M 3:3 gifts he makes to the temple at Jerusalem are mentioned. But he also sends his minister Heliodorus to plunder the temple treasury, 2 M 5:18. At his death—assassinated by Heliodorus—his brother Antiochus Epiphanes succeeds him, 2 M 4:7. Cf. Dn 11:20 (*there will rise a man*). Father of: DEMETRIUS 1.

SEMACHIAH (1), "Yah has sustained" (cf. Ahisamach; Ismachiah), a gatekeeper, one of the sons of Shemaiah, son of Obed-edom, 1 Ch 26:7.

SEMEIN (1), an ancestor of Jesus acc. to Lk 3:26.

[SEMIRAMIS]. See: SHEMIRAMOTH.

SENAAH (2), (cf. Hassenuah), a town in Judah whose sons return from the exile with Zerubbabel, Ezr 2:35//Ne 7:38.

= **Hassenaah** (1), whose sons rebuild the Fish Gate at Jerusalem, Ne 3:3.

About 10 km NW of Jericho.

SENEH (1). See: BOZEZ.

SENIR, Gr. *Sanir*. See: HERMON.

SENNACHERIB (20), Hb. *Sanhérib,* Accad. *Sin-ahhe-eriba,* "Sin has replaced the brothers" (cf. Sin), **king of Assyria** (36), **the great king** (4), 2 K 18:19, 28//Is 36:4, 13 (704–681), son and successor of Sargon II (despite Tb 1:15).

When Hezekiah, king of Judah, rebels against Assyria, 2 K 18:7, Sennacherib invades Judah in 701 and captures the fortified towns of the country, 2 K 18:13//Is 31:1//2 Ch 32:1–8 (which describes the military preparations made by Hezekiah). Sennacherib does not take Jerusalem but imposes the payment of a tribute on the king of Judah, 2 K 18:14–16. The Assyrian Annals of Sennacherib confirm what is said in 2 K 18:13–16. In addition, two parallel accounts give the threats made by the king of Assyria against Jerusalem, the reaction of the prophet Isaiah to these threats, and the failure of Sennacherib with regard to Jerusalem. The first account, 2 K 18:17–19:19a//Is 36:2–37:9a: embassy of the cupbearer-in-chief of the king of Assyria to Jerusalem, //2 Ch 32:9–19; exhortation of Isaiah and retreat of Sennacherib, who must face an attack from Pharaoh Tirhakah, cf. Si 48:18; Na 1:11. Second account, 2 K 19:9b–36//Is 37:9b–37//2 Ch 32:17, 20–22: letter of Sennacherib to Hezekiah; intervention of Isaiah; departure of the Assyrian army that has been perhaps decimated by plague, cf. Tb 1:18; 1 M 7:41; 2 M 8:19; 15:22; Si 48:21. Are these two accounts dealing with one and the same campaign of Sennacherib, that of 701 (cf. above) or with two different campaigns: that of 701 and another in about 690? Sennacherib dies by assassination at the hands of two of his sons, Adrammelech and Sharezer, 2 K 19:37//Is 37:38//2 Ch 32:21–22; cf. Tb 1:21.

SENT. See: SILOAM.

SEORIM (1), (cf. Seir), leader of the fourth class of priests, 1 Ch 24:8.

SEPHAR (1), southern boundary of the area of the sons of Joktan, in Arabia, Gn 10:30.

SEPHARAD (1), Lat. *Bosphorus,* perhaps Sardis in Lydia. Some Jews from Jerusalem are exiled there, Ob 20.

SEPHARVAIM (6), a town captured, like Hamath and Arpad, by Sennacherib, king of Assyria, 2 K 19:13//Is 37:13.

In the face of the Assyrian onslaught, the gods of Sepharvaim—Adrammelech and Anammelech, in whose honor the people of the town burn their children, 2 K 17:31—prove completely powerless, 2 K 18:34//Is 36:19. The people of Sepharvaim are transferred to Samaria to replace the deported Israelites, 2 K 17:24. An unidentified town in Syria.

SEPHARVITES (1), 2 K 17:31, the people of: SEPHARVAIM.

SERAH (2), "Abundance," daughter of Asher, son of Jacob, Gn 46:17//1 Ch 7:30, Nb 26:46 (Hb. *Sarah*).

SERAIAH, "Yah struggles, shows himself strong *or* Yah reigns, is master" (cf. Israel; Sarah).

1. **Seraiah** (1), 2 S 8:17, secretary to David.

= **Sheva** (1), 2 S 20:25 (corr. of Hb. K*Sheya;* Q*Sheva*).

= *Shisha* (1), 1 K 4:3, father of Ahijah and: ELIHOREPH.

= **Shavsha** (1), 1 Ch 18:16.

2. **Seraiah son of Azriel** (1). See: JERAHMEEL 3.

3. **Seraiah** (3) **son of Mahseiah** (1), grand chamberlain, goes to Babylon in about 593 (with Zedekiah, king of Judah?). Jeremiah gives him an oracle on the future fall of Babylon. Seraiah is to read the oracle, then throw it into the Euphrates, saying: "So shall Babylon sink . . . ," Jr 51:59–64.

Probably brother of: BARUCH 1.

4. **Seraiah** (2), chief priest at the time when Jerusalem is taken, is led to Nebuchadnezzar at Riblah, where he is put to death, 2 K 25:18//Jr 52:24. Compare with the following.

5. **Seraiah** (4), a descendant of the high priest Zadok, 1 Ch 5:40; cf. Ne 11:11, father of Ezra, Ezr 7:1. Compare with the preceding.

6. **Seraiah son of Tanhumeth** (2), **the Netophathite** (1), an officer in the Judaean army who rallies to Gedaliah after the fall of Jerusalem, 2 K 25:23//Jr 40:8.

7. **Seraiah** (2), son of Kenaz, brother of Othniel and ancestor of Geharashim, 1 Ch 4:13.

8. **Seraiah** (1), a Simeonite, ancestor of: JEHU 5.

9. **Seraiah** (1), Ezr 2:2, one of the twelve leaders of the Jews on their return to Jerusalem.

= **Azariah** (1), Ne 7:7.

10. **Seraiah** (3), head of a priestly family who returns from the exile with Zerubbabel, Ne 12:1, signs the pledge to observe the Law, Ne 10:3. In the time of the high priest Joiakim, the head of the family of Seraiah is Meraiah, Ne 12:12.

SERED (2), first of the three sons of Zebulun, Gn 46:14, whose descendants form the **Seredite** clan, Nb 26:26.

SEREDITE (1), belonging to the Zebulunite clan of: SERED.

SERGIUS Paulus (1). See: PAUL 2.

SERON (2), **commander of the Syrian troops** (1), routed by Judas and his men at the descent of Beth-horon, 1 M 3:14, 23.

SERPENT. See: LEVIATHAN; SATAN.

SERUG (6), Gr. *Serouch,* acc. to the priestly tradition a postdiluvian patriarch, son of Ram, father of Nahor, and ancestor of Abraham, Gn 11:20–23; 1 Ch 1:26. An ancestor of Jesus acc. to Lk 3:35. Compare with Accad. *Sarugi,* a town near Haran.

SETH, Hb. *Shĕt,* popular etymology from the Hb. *shat,* "[God] has raised up, granted," see Gn 4:25.

1. **Seth** (10), acc. to the Yahwist tradition, is born of Adam and Eve after the murder of Abel by Cain. The son of Seth, Enosh, is "the first to invoke the name of Yahweh," Gn 4:25–26. Acc. to the priestly tradition, Seth, son of Adam and father of Enosh, dies at the age of

912, Gn 5:3–7; 1 Ch 1:1; cf. Si 49:16. Among the ancestors of Jesus, Lk 3:38. To be connected with the following?

2. **The sons of Sheth** (1), Nb 24:17, a Bedouin tribe or even the Moabites themselves. To be connected with the *Shutu,* a tribe of southeastern Palestine mentioned in Egyptian and Assyrian texts? See the preceding.

SETHUR (1), (cf. Sithri), **son of Michael** (1), a clan leader of the tribe of Asher, sent by Moses as representative of his tribe in the reconnaissance of Canaan, Nb 13:13.

SEVEN (The). Used without a further noun (1) in Ac 21:8. The number seven, which is, among other things, the number of the pagan peoples of: CANAAN (just as the number twelve is the number of the tribes of Israel) designates the assistants of the Apostles, "seven men of good reputation, filled with the Spirit and with wisdom," who are put in charge of the service (*diakonia,* whence the word *deacon*) at table, that is, probably to be administrators or stewards in the Christian community. The Seven all have Greek names and are, most of them at least, Hellenists. The Seven are: **Stephen, Philip, Prochorus, Nicanor, Timon, Parmenas,** and **Nicolaus,** Ac 6:1–6. Stephen and Philip will move from service at table to the service of the word.

SHA-ALABBIN (1), Jos 19:42. See: SHAALBIM.

SHAALBIM (2), a town occupied by the Amorites, Jg 1:35; in the second district of Solomon, 1 K 4:9. NW of Aijalon.

= **Sha-alabbin** (1), Jos 19:42, in the territory of Dan.

= **Shaalbon** (2), native place of: ELIAHBA.

SHAALBON (2). See: SHAALBIM.

SHAALIM (Land of) (1), in the highlands of Ephraim. Saul passes through it in search of his father's she-donkeys, 1 S 9:4.

SHAAPH (2), among the sons of Jahdai, 1 Ch 2:47, called son of Caleb and his concubine Maacah; father of Madmannah, 1 Ch 2:49.

SHAARAIM (3), "The Two Gates," a town in the lowlands of Judah, Jos 15:36, formerly occupied by Simeon, 1 Ch 4:31. Israel wins a victory over the Philistines there, 1 S 17:52.

SHAASHGAZ (1), Gr. *Gai,* a eunuch of King Ahasuerus, "custodian of the concubines," Est 2:14.

[SHABATOKA] is probably the Pharaoh to whom King Hezekiah of Judah sends ambassadors in about 703–702 to ask for military assistance against the threat from Assyria, 2 K 18:21//Is 36:6; 30:2–3; cf. 19:4 (*a cruel king*), 11.

SHABBETHAI (3), "[Born on a] sabbath [day]," a Levite, one of those who oppose the dissolution of mixed marriages, Ezr 10:15; he explains the Law to the people during its solemn reading by Ezra, Ne 8:7, and is one of those responsible for the outside work of the temple, Ne 11:16. One or several individuals.

SHADDAI (48), (cf. Ammishaddai; Shedeur ?; Zurishaddai), Gr. *Pantokratōr* (15), "The Almighty."

Shaddai could take its meaning from Accad. *shadû,* "The Mountain-dweller" or from Hb. *saday, sadêh* and another meaning of Accad. *shadû,* "He of the Fields, of the Steppe."

Two forms: used alone, **Shaddai** (40), Nb 24:4, 16; Rt 1:20–21, Jb (31); Ps 68:15; 91:1; Is 13:6; Ezk 1:24; Jl 1:15, or combined with El, **El Shaddai** (8), Gn 17:1; 28:3; 35:11; 43:14; 48:3; 49:25; Ex 6:3; Ezk 10:5.

Shaddai is an ancient divine name, perhaps originating in Upper Mesopotamia and brought with them by the ancestors of Israel. It would have been regarded as another name for El, whence the combination El Shaddai. Acc. to Ex 6:3, it is under the name of El Shaddai that God manifested himself to Abraham, Isaac, and Jacob, cf. Gn 17:1; 28:3; 35:11; 43:14; 48:3; 49:25.

SHADES. See: REPHAIM 3.

SHADRACH (15), name given to: HANANIAH 17.

SHAGEE (1), father of: JONATHAN 5.

SHAHARAIM (1), "[Born] at dawn *or* The Two Dawns" (cf. Shehariah), a Benjaminite living in the plains of Moab, 1 Ch 8:8. The Hb. text is poorly preserved. Some read: *He became father of Shaharaim;* others, *Shaharaim became father. . . .*

SHAHAZIMAH (1), from Hb. *shahaz,* "elevated place," a town in Issachar, between Mount Tabor and the Jordan, Jos 19:22.

[SHALEM], a god of Ugarit. See: SALEM.

SHALISHAH (1), in the highlands of Ephraim, 25 km NNE of Lod. Saul passes through the **land of Shalishah** when searching for his father's she-donkeys, 1 S 9:4.

= **Baal-shalishah** (1). With the twenty barley loaves brought by a man from Baal-shalishah, the prophet Elisha feeds a hundred people, 2 K 4:42.

SHALLUM, abbrev. of *Shelemiah* (cf. Salem).

1. **Shallum** (2), a descendant of the daughter of Sheshan, of the clan of Jerahmeel, 1 Ch 2:40–41.

2. **Shallum** (1), a Simeonite, a son of Shaul and ancestor of Shimei, 1 Ch 4:25.

3. **Shallum** (1), a Naphtalite. See: SHILLEM.

4. **Shallum** (4) **son of Jabesh** (3), the fifteenth king of Israel (743), a contemporary of Uzziah of Judah. He plots against Zechariah, king of Israel, assassinates him at Ibleam and assumes power. A month later he in turn is assassinated at Samaria by Menahem, who succeeds him, 2 K 15:10, 13–15.

5. **Shallum** (1), father of: HEZEKIAH 1.

6. **Shallum** (4), son of the high priest Zadok, a descendant of Aaron, 1 Ch 5:38–39//Ezr 7:2 (an ancestor of Ezra), and an ancestor (Gr. *Salōm*) of: JEHOIAKIM 2.

= **Meshullam** (2), 1 Ch 9:11//Ne 11:11.

7. **Shallum son of Tikvah, son of Harhas** (1), 2 K 22:14, or **son of Tokhath, son of Hasrah** (1), 2 Ch 34:22, husband of Huldah the prophetess, "the keeper of the wardrobe," that is, probably in charge of the vestments for the temple liturgy.

8. **Shallum** (2), another name for king: JEHOAHAZ 2.

9. **Shallum** (1), uncle of Jeremiah, father of: HANAMEL.

10. **Shallum** (1), father of: MAASEIAH 8.

11. **Shallum** (5), associated with Akkub and Talmon, all three gatekeepers living in Jerusalem, 1 Ch 9:17; cf. Ne 11:19, whose sons return from the exile with Zerubbabel, Ezr 2:42//Ne 7:45.

= ? **Meshullam** (1), also associated with Akkub and Talmon, Ne 12:25.

= **Shallum son of Kore, son of Ebiasaph, son of Korah** (1), 1 Ch 9:19, a keeper of the threshold for the Tent.

= **Shallum the Korahite** (1), 1 Ch 9:31, father of: MATTITHIAH 1.

= **Meshelemiah** (3) **son of Kore, one of the sons of Ebiasaph** (1), 1 Ch 26:1 (corr. of Hb. *Asaph*), father of seven sons, 1 Ch 26:2, 9.

= **Meshelemiah** (1), father of: ZECHARIAH 11.

= **Shelemiah** (1), 1 Ch 26:14.

12. **Shallum** (1), a gatekeeper, married to a foreign wife, whom he puts away, Ezr 10:24.

13. **Shallum** (1), an Israelite of the sons of Zaccai, married to a foreign wife, whom he puts away, Ezr 10:42.

14. **Shallum son of Hallohesh** (1), ruler of half the district of Jerusalem, takes part with his sons (corr. of Hb. *his daughters*) in rebuilding the wall of Jerusalem, Ne 3:12.

15. **Shallum son of Col-hozeh** (1), ruler of the district of Mizpah, a volunteer in the rebuilding the Jerusalem wall, Ne 3:15 (var. *Shallum*; Hb. *Shallun*).

SHALMAI (1), Ne 7:48, head of a family of "oblates" who return from the exile.

= **Shamlai** (1), Ezr 2:46 ([Q]*Shalmai*).

SHALMAN (1), (cf. Salem), probably *Salamann,* king of Moab, vassal of the Assyrian king Tiglath-pileser III. Shalman lays waste the town of Beth-arbel during a raid into Gilead, Ho 10:14.

SHALMANESER V (6), Hb. *Shalman'eser,* Accad. *Shulman-ashared,* "[The god] Shulman is superior," **king of Assyria** (6) (727–722), son and successor of Tiglath-pileser III.

Two campaigns against Hoshea, last king of Israel. In the first, Hoshea yields and must pay an annual tribute to the king of Assyria. Later on, when Hoshea stops sending the tribute and, in addition, seeks an alliance with Egypt, Shalmaneser imprisons him and besieges Samaria. The city falls three years later, at the beginning of the reign of Shalmaneser's successor, Sargon II, 2 K 17:3–5; 19:9–10. Cf. Tb 1:2, 13, 15, 16 (corr. of Gr. *Enemesser*).

SHAMA (1), abbrev. of *Shemaiah,* "Yah has heard," and **Jeiel, sons of Hotham the Aroerite** (1), two brothers, champions of David, 1 Ch 11:44.

SHAMGAR (2), a Hurrite name, **son of Anath** (2), acc. to Jg 3:31 one of the "lesser" judges of Israel; he routs 600 Philistines with an oxgoad, cf. 2 S 23:11–12. In Jg 5:6 Shamgar seems to be characterized in a different way from the judge.

SHAMHUTH (1), "[Born at the moment of a] catastrophe." See: SHAMMAH 4.

SHAMIR

1. **Shamir** (1), a Levite of the sons of Micah, of the Uzzielite clan, 1 Ch 24:24 ([K]*Shamur*).

2. **Shamir** (1), a town in the highlands of Judah, Jos 15:48. 20 km SW of Hebron.

3. **Shamir** (2), a town in the highlands of Ephraim, native place of the "lesser" judge Tola, Jg 10:1–2.

SHAMLAI (1). See: SHALMAI.

SHAMMA. See: SHAMMAH 3, 5.

SHAMMAH, Hb. 1–4: *Shammah;* 5: *Shamma'.*

1. **Shammah** (3), third of the four sons and chiefs of Reuel in Edom, called sons of Basemath, wife of Esau, Gn 36:13, 17; 1 Ch 1:37.

2. **Shammah** (2), third of the sons of Jesse and a brother of David, 1 S 16:9; 17:13; cf. 17:14–22.

= **Shimea** (5), 1 Ch 2:13, father of: JONADAB 1; JONATHAN 4.

3. **Shamma** (2) **son of Elah** (corr. of Hb. *Age*) (1), **the Hararite** (2), one of David's champions, victorious at Lehi in single combat against the Philistines, 2 S 23:11. Father of: JONATHAN 5.

4. **Shammah from Harod** (1), 2 S 23:25, another of David's champions.

= **Shammoth from Harod** (1), 1 Ch 11:27.

= **Shamhuth the Izrahite** (1), 1 Ch 27:8, in charge of the (military) service for the fifth month.

5. **Shamma** (1), an Asherite, one of the eleven sons of Zophah, 1 Ch 7:37.

SHAMMAI

1. **Shammai** (3), son of Onam and brother of Jada, of the clan of Jerah-

meel, 1 Ch 2:28, 32. His posterity is given, vv. 28–31.

2. **Shammai** (2), a Calebite, son of Rekem and father of Maon, 1 Ch 2:44–45.

3. **Shammai** (1), one of the sons of Bithiah, daughter of Pharaoh, and of Mered, 1 Ch 4:17. Connected with the Calebite group.

SHAMMOTH from Harod (1). See: SHAMMAH 4.

SHAMMUA, abbrev. of *Shemaiah.*

1. **Shammua son of Zaccur** (1), a clan leader of the tribe of Reuben, sent by Moses as representative of his tribe in the reconnaissance of Canaan, Nb 13:4.

2. **Shammua** (2), one of the sons of David born in Jerusalem, 2 S 5:14; 1 Ch 14:4.

= **Shimea** (1), 1 Ch 3:5.

3. **Shammua** (1) = **Shemaiah** (1), father of the Levite: OBADIAH 11.

4. **Shammua** (1), head of the priestly family of Bilgah in the time of the high priest Joiakim, Ne 12:18.

SHAMSHERAI (1), a composite of *Shimshai* and *Shamrai* (not used in the Bible), a Benjaminite of the sons of Jeroham, head of a family at Jerusalem, 1 Ch 8:26.

SHAPHAM (1), a Gadite living in Bashan, 1 Ch 5:12.

SHAPHAN, "Hyrax."

1. **Shaphan** (29), **son of Azaliah** (2) **son of Meshullam** (1), secretary of King Josiah. On an errand to the high priest Hilkiah for the purpose of arranging the salary of the workers who are rebuilding the temple, Shaphan learns that Hilkiah has just discovered, in the temple, the book of the Law (= legislative section of Deuteronomy). Hilkiah gives the book to Shaphan, who, after seeing its contents, takes it to the king and reads it to him, 2 K 22:3–10//2 Ch 34:8–9. Shaphan is a member of the delegation Josiah sends to consult Huldah the prophetess about the book, 2 K 22:12–15, 20//2 Ch 34:20–23, 28.

His sons and grandsons: AHIKAM; ELASAH 3; GEDALIAH 4; GEMARIAH 2; MICAH 13.

2. **Shaphan** (1), father of: JAAZANIAH 3.

SHAPHAT, abbrev. of *Shephathiah.*

1. **Shaphat son of Hori** (1), a clan leader in the tribe of Simeon, sent as representative of his tribe in the reconnaissance of Canaan, Nb 13:5.

2. **Shaphat** (4), 1 K 19:16, 19; 2 K 3:11; 6:31, father of the prophet: ELISHA.

3. **Shaphat** (1), one of the sons of Shecaniah, a descendant of King Jehoiachin, 1 Ch 3:22.

4. **Shaphat** (1), a Gadite living in Bashan, 1 Ch 5:12.

5. **Shaphat son of Adlai** (1), commissioner for cattle in the valleys under David, acc. to 1 Ch 27:29.

SHAPHIR (1), "Beauty" (cf. Shiphrah), a play on words with the Hb. *shophar,* "horn," a town in the lowlands of Judah, Mi 1:11.

SHARAI (1), an Israelite of the sons of Zaccai, married to a foreign wife, whom he puts away, Ezr 10:40.

SHARAR (1) = **Sachar** (1), father of: AHIAM.

SHAREZER, Hb. *Sar'ezer,* Accad. *Shar-uzur,* "Protect the king" (cf. Belshazzar; Belteshazzar; Nergal-sharezer; Shenazzar).

1. **Sharezer** (2), brother of: ADRAMMELECH 2.

2. **Sharezer** (1), a person sent by Bethel [the town?] for a consultation at Jerusalem regarding a commemorative fast, Zc 7:2.

SHARON, Gr. *Sarōn,* "Flat country."

1. **Sharon** (7), a coastal plain between Carmel and Joppa, rich in pastures, 1 Ch 27:29; Sg 2:1; Is 33:9; 35:2; 65:10. In

the list of Canaanite kings conquered by Joshua is *the king of Sharon,* Jos 12:18 (Hb. *Lasharon*). The plain of Sharon is evangelized by Peter the Apostle, Ac 9:35.

Native place of: SHITRAI.

2. **Sharon** (1), a region of pastures in Transjordania, occupied by Gadites, 1 Ch 5:16.

SHARUHEN (1). See: SHILHIM.

SHASHAI (1), an Israelite of the sons of Zaccai, married to a foreign wife, whom he puts away, Ezr 10:40.

SHASHAK (2), a Benjaminite whose eleven sons live at Jerusalem, 1 Ch 8:14, 22–25.

SHAUL. See: SAUL 1–3.

SHAULITE (1), belonging to the clan of: SAUL 2.

SHAVEH (1), "Plain" (cf. Isvah; Ishvi), a valley. See: KING 2.

SHAVSHA (1), (cf. Samson?). See: SERAIAH 1.

SHEAL (1), an Israelite of the sons of Bigvai, married to a foreign wife, whom he puts away, Ezr 10:29 ([K]*Jishal;* [Q]*Sheal*).

SHEALTIEL (10), Hb. *She'alti'el,* Gr. *Salathiel,* "I have asked God [for him]" (cf. Saul), 1 Ch 3:17; Ezr 3:2, 8; 5:2; Ne 12:1; Hg 1:1; 2:23, or Hb. *Shalti'el,* Hg 1:12, 14; 2:2, son of Jeconiah, the imprisoned king [= Jehoiachin], 1 Ch 3:17; Mt 1:12, and uncle of Zerubbabel, 1 Ch 3:17, or father of Zerubbabel, Mt 1:12; acc. to Lk 3:27, son of Neri and father of Zerubbabel. An ancesor of Jesus.

Father of: ZERUBBABEL.

SHEARIAH (2), a Benjaminite, one of the six sons of Azel, a descendant of King Saul, 1 Ch 8:38//9:44.

SHEAR-JASHUB (1), "A remnant will return *or* will be converted" (cf. Jashub), a prophetic name given to the first son of the prophet Isaiah, Is 7:3; cf. 10:21–22.

SHEBA, Hb. 1: *Sheba',* Gr. *Saba;* 2–3: *Shèba',* Gr. *Sabee,* "Seven, Fullness, *or* Oath" (cf. Beth-ashbea; Bathsheba; Beersheba; Elizabeth; Jehosheba).

1. **Sheba** (24). The priestly tradition connects Sheba with Ham via Cush, Gn 10:7//1 Ch 1:9, the Yahwist tradition connects it with Shem via Joktan, Gn 10:28//1 Ch 1:22, or with Abraham via Jokshan. Gn 25:3//1 Ch 1:32. The region occupied by this trading people, the **Sabaeans,** Jl 4:8; cf. Jb 6:19; Ezk 27:22–23; 38:13, is southern Arabia, renowned for its gold and precious stones, Ps 72:10, 15, its perfumes and incenses, Is 60:6; Jr 6:20; Ezk 27:22–24.

The queen of Sheba (8), learning of Solomon's reputation for wisdom, comes to Jerusalem to consult him, to bring him the wealth of her country, and undoubtedly also to enter into trade agreements with him, 1 K 10:1–13//2 Ch 9:1–12.

= **The Queen of the South** (1), a pagan queen more anxious to hear Solomon than the contemporaries of Jesus will be to listen to the wisdom of Christ, Mt 12:42//Lk 11:31.

In Jn 1:15 *Sabaeans* refers to plundering nomads.

2. **Sheba son of Bichri** (8), **a Benjaminite** (1), leads the men of Israel in a rebellion against David. Pursued by Abishai, Joab, and the champions of David, he is overtaken and besieged at Abel of Beth-maacah, where a woman delivers him up to Joab by throwing his head over the wall, 2 S 20:1–22.

3. **Sheba** (1), a Gadite, head of a family, 1 Ch 5:13.

SHEBANIAH (cf. Shebnah?).

1. **Shebaniah** (1), a priest, a trumpeter at the transferral of the Ark, 1 Ch 15:24.

2. **Shebaniah** (2), a priest, a cosigner of the pledge to observe the Law, Ne 10:5, gives his name to a priestly family

whose head, in the time of the high priest Joiakim, is Joseph, Ne 12:14.

= **Shecaniah** (1), a priest who returns from the exile with Zerubbabel, Ne 12:3.

3. **Shebaniah** (3), one of the Levites who takes part in the penitential ceremony of Ne 9:4–5 and signs the pledge to observe the Law, Ne 10:13.

SHEBARIM (1), "Stone pits, Quarries" (cf. Sheber), in the neighborhood of Ai, Jos 7:5.

SHEBER (1), "Break, crack" (cf. Shebarim) or "Wheat"?, one of the sons of Maacah, the concubine of Caleb, 1 Ch 2:48.

SHEBNA. See: SHEBNAH.

SHEBNAH, Shebna (9), abbrev. of *Shebaniah?,* master of the palace, more concerned about his own affairs than about those he administers. An oracle of Isaiah, Is 22:15–20, announces his removal and replacement by Eliakim, son of Hilkiah. In 701, during the siege of Jerusalem by Sennacherib, Shebnah, now secretary, accompanies Eliakim, the new master of the palace and head of the Judaean delegation sent to negotiate with the commander of the Assyrian armies, 2 K 18:18–19:7//Ls 36:3–37:7.

SHEBUEL

1. **Shebuel** (2), a Levite, son of Gershom, 1 Ch 23:16, a grandson of Moses, of the clan of Kohath; officer responsible for the treasuries, 1 Ch 26:24.

2. **Shebuel** (1), of the sons of Heman, 1 Ch 25:4.

= **Shubael** (1), head of the thirteenth class of cantors, 1 Ch 25:20.

SHECANIAH, "Yah has set up his dwelling."

1. **Shecaniah** (1), a priest, head of the tenth priestly class, 1 Ch 24:11.

2. **Shecaniah** (1), one of the ten Levites placed under the command of Kore, son of Imnah, for the distribution of foodstuffs in the time of King Hezekiah, 2 Ch 31:15.

3. **Shecaniah** (1), a descendant of King Jehoiachin via Zerubbabel and Hananiah, father of six sons, 1 Ch 3:21–22, one of whom is Hattush, 1 Ch 3:22 (acc. to Hb., Hattush is the grandson of Shecaniah); Ezr 8:2–3.

4. **Shecaniah son of Jahaziel** (1), an Israelite of the sons of Zattu (acc. to Gr.), returns from the exile with Ezra, Ezr 8:5.

5. **Shecaniah son of Jehiel, one of the sons of Elam** (1), suggests to Ezra the dismissal of foreign wives, Ezr 10:2–4.

6. **Shecaniah** (1), father of: SHEMAIAH 21.

7. **Shecaniah son of Arah** (1), father-in-law of Tobiah the Ammonite, governor of the Ammon region, Ne 6:18.

8. **Shecaniah** (1). See: SHEBANIAH 2.

SHECHEM (68), Hb. *Shekèm,* "Shoulder, Nape," see Gn 48:22 (cf. Migdal-shechem), Gr. *Sychem* or *Sikima.*

A town in the highlands of Ephraim, at the mouth of the gorge separating Mount Ebal and Mount: GERIZIM, Dt 11:30; Jos 8:33; cf. Jg 9:36, a junction for the roads between Jerusalem and Phoenicia, Jg 21:19; Ho 6:9, the Jordan and the Mediterranean ("the westward road"), Dt 11:30. A holy place for the patriarchs (Oak of: MOREH 2), Gn 12:6–7; 35:4. Jacob buys a field there from the sons of "Hamor, the father of Shechem," Gn 33:18–19 (Joseph will be buried there, Jos 24:32; cf. Ac 7:16, where Shechem is confused with Machpelah), and, like Abraham, builds an altar there, Gn 33:20. His sons pasture their flocks in the area, 37:12–14. The inhabitants of the town, who are linked to an eponymous Hivite ancestor, "Shechem, the son of Hamor the Hivite," 34:2–27; cf. Jg 9:28, are described as allied with the Israelites by a matrimonial pact because Shechem has offered to marry Dinah, the daughter of Jacob, whom he had raped, Gn 34:1–24. The rest of the story, 34:25–30, seems to say that the town of these "foreigners," cf. Jdt 9:2–4, was conquered by trickery and force, cf. Gn 48:22; 49:5; Ps 60:8// 108:8.

Shechem is assigned sometimes to Ephraim, 1 Ch 7:28; cf. Jos 8:33, sometimes (see below: **Shechem,** son of Manasseh) to Manasseh, these two tribes being lumped together as "the sons of Joseph," 1 Ch 7:28–29. It is a city of refuge, Jos 20:7, given to the Levites of the clan of Kohath, Jos 21: 21//1 Ch 6:52. Shechem—seat of the Ark, Jos 8:33, and place where the Canaanites worship Baal-berith, the god of the covenant, Jg 8:33; cf. 9:46—is the site of the great gathering of the tribes of Israel, at which "Joshua made a covenant for the people" and "laid down a statute and ordinance for them," Jos 24:1–28. It is at Shechem that Abimelech, son of Gideon/Jerubbaal and a Shechemite woman, Jg 8:31, has himself proclaimed king, 9:1–6. At the instigation of Jotham, brother of Abimelech, 9:7–21, the leaders of Shechem rebel against the king, who destroys the town, 9:22–49, 57. When Rehoboam comes to Shechem, the second capital of Solomon's kingdom, to have himself acknowledged as king of Israel, he provokes the political division between Judah and Israel, 1 K 12:1//2 Ch 10:1. The Israelites call Jeroboam to the assembly at Shechem and proclaim him king, 1 K 12:20; he makes the town the first capital of the northern kingdom, 1 K 12:25. After the exile the town becomes the metropolis of the: SAMARITANS, Si 50: 26, where the Jews take refuge who have been expelled from Jerusalem because of the law on mixed marriages, cf. Jr 41:5. Today *Tell Balata,* west of Nablus.

= **Shechem** (3), Hb. *Shekem,* son of Manasseh acc. to Jos 17:2, fourth of the six sons of Gilead, whose descendants form the **Shechemite** clan, Nb 26:31. In 1 Ch 7:19 Shechem is listed among the sons of Shemida (who is Shechem's "brother" in the other texts).

Opposite Shechem: MICHMETATH.
Its acropolis: MIGDAL-SHECHEM.
See: SYCHAR.

SHECHEMITE (1), Nb 26:31, belonging to the clan of: SHECHEM.

SHEDEUR (5), "Shaddai is Light"? (cf. Shaddai; Ur 2), father of: ELIZUR.

SHEEP GATE (3), Hb. *Zô'n,* Gr. *Probatikē* (cf. Rachel), in Jerusalem, N of the temple, rebuilt in the time of Nehemiah, Ne 3:1; 3:32; 12:39. The Pool of Bethzatha, or Sheep Pool, was near this gate, Jn 5:2.

SHEEP POOL (1). See: BETHZATHA.

SHEERAH (1), daughter of Ephraim, "who built both Lower and Upper Beth-horon and Uzzen-sheerah," 1 Ch 7:24.

SHEHARIAH (1), (cf. Shaharaim), a Benjaminite of the sons of Jeroham, head of a family in Jerusalem, 1 Ch 8:26.

SHELAH, Hb. 1: *Shélah,* "Request"? (cf. Saul); 2–4: *Shèlah* (cf. Methuselah; Shilhi; Shiloah).

1. **Shelah** (7), third son of Judah and Bath-shua, the Canaanite woman, Gn 38:5; 46:12//1 Ch 2:3. Following the premature death of his sons Er and Onan, married successively to Tamar, Judah refuses to give Shelah to his daughter-in-law, Gn 38:11, 14, 26. The descendants of Shelah, 1 Ch 4:21–23, form the **Shelanite** clan, Nb 26:20.

2. **Shelah** (10), "Javelin?," Gr. *Sala,* son of Arpachshad, son of Shem, and father of Eber, acc. to the Yahwist tradition, Gn 10:24//1 Ch 1:18, and the priestly tradition, Gn 11:12–15//1 Ch 1:24. Among the ancestors of Jesus acc. to Lk 3:35.

SHELANITE or **descendant of Shelah** (2), Nb 26:20; Ne 11:5, belonging to the clan of: SHELAH 1.

SHELEMIAH, "Yah has completed *or* preserved in peace" (cf. Salem).

1. **Shelemiah son of Cushi** (1). See: JEHUDI 2.

2. **Shelemiah son of Abdeel** (1). See: JERAHMEEL 3.

3. **Shelemiah** (2), father of: JUCAL.

4. **Shelemiah** (1), father of: IRIJAH.

5. **Shelemiah** (1). See: SHALLUM 11.

6. **Shelemiah** (1), an Israelite of the sons of Binnui, married to a foreign wife, whom he puts away, Ezr 10:39.

7. **Shelemiah** (1), an Israelite of the son of Zaccai, married to a foreign wife, whom he puts away, Ezr 10:41.

8. **Shelemiah** (1), father of: HANANIAH 10.

9. **Shelemiah** (1), a reliable priest, one of the supervisors of the temple storehouses in the time of Nehemiah, Ne 13:13.

SHELEPH (2), second of the thirteen sons of Joktan, a tribe or territory in southern Arabia, Gn 10:26//1 Ch 1:20.

SHELESH (1), (cf. Shilshah), an Asherite, one of the sons of Helem, 1 Ch 7:35.

SHELOMI (1), (cf. Salem), an Asherite, father of: AHIHUD.

SHELOMITH, fem. of *Shelomi* (cf. Salem).

1. **Shelomith daughter of Dibri, of the tribe of Dan** (1), wife of an Egyptian and mother of a blasphemer, Lv 24:11.

2. **Shelomith** (1), daughter of Zerubbabel, a descendant of King Jehoiachin, 1 Ch 3:19.

3. **Shelomith** (1), last of the four sons of Maacah and King Rehoboam, 2 Ch 11:20.

4. **Shelomith son of Josiphiah** (1), head of an Israelite family of the sons of Bani, who returns from the exile with Ezra, Ezr 8:10.

5. **Shelomith** (1), a Levite of the clan of Kohath, first of the sons of Izhar, 1 Ch 23:18.

= **Shelomoth** (2), 1 Ch 24:22.

SHELOMOTH (cf. Salem).

1. **Shelomoth** (1), a Levite of the clan of Gershon—son of Shimei?—one of the chiefs of Ladan, 1 Ch 23:9.

2. **Shelomoth** (2). See: SHELOMITH 5.

3. **Shelomoth** (3), a Levite of the clan of Kohath, a descendant of Moses through Eliezer, one of those responsible for the treasuries of votive offerings, 1 Ch 26:25, 26, 28.

SHELUMIEL (5), Gr. *Salamiel,* "God is my peace" (cf. Salem), **son of Zurishaddai** (5), leader of the tribe of Simeon, Nb 2:12; 7:36; 10:19, in charge of the census of his tribe, Nb 1:6, brings the offering for the dedication of the altar on the fifth day, Nb 7:36–41.

= **Salamiel son of Sarasadai** (1), an ancestor of Judith, Jdt 8:1.

SHEM (19), Gr. *Sem,* "Name, Renown" (cf. Samuel; Shemeber; Shemida), first of the three sons of Noah, Gn 5:32; 6:10; 10:1; 1 Ch 1:4. Saved from the flood, Gn 7:13; 9:18, he is one of the ancestors of the postdiluvian human race, cf. Gn 9:19, and the eponymous ancestor of the Semites.

Acc. to the Yahwist tradition, he is "the ancestor of all the sons of Eber," Gn 10:21, 24–29, 31//1 Ch 1:18–23. Canaan, son of Ham, will be subject to Shem and to Japhet, who will likewise increase at the expense of Shem, Gn 9:21–27. Acc. to the Elohist tradition, the sons of Shem are Elam, Asshur, Arpachshad, Lud, and Aram, Gn 10:22//1 Ch 1:17. It is through Arpachshad that Shem is the ancestor of Abraham, Gn 11:10–26//1 Ch 1:24–27. It is this genealogy that Luke incorporates into that of Jesus, Lk 3:34–36. Finally, Si 49:16 associates Shem and Seth.

SHEMA, Hb. 1: *Shema';* 2–5: *Shèma',* "Sound, Melodious sound" (cf. Shemaiah).

1. **Shema** (1), a town in the Negeb of Judah, Jos 15:26, formerly a town (Hb. *Sheba*) of Simeon, Jos 19:2. 25 km W of Beersheba.

2. **Shema** (2), a Calebite of the sons of Hebron, an ancestor of Jorkeam, 1 Ch 2:43–44.

3. **Shema** (1), a Reubenite, an ancestor of: BELA 3.

4. **Shema** (1), a Benjaminite, one of the family heads at Aijalon who defeat the people of Gath, 1 Ch 8:13.

Identical (?) with: SHIMEI 5.

5. **Shema** (1), an important layman who stands at Ezra's right during the solemn reading of the Law, Ne 8:4.

SHEMAIAH, Hb. *Shema'yah[u]*, "Yah has heard" (cf. Elishama; Eshtemoa; Hasshemar; Hoshama; Ishma; Ishmael; Ishmaiah; Mishma; Shama; Shammua; Shema 2–5; Shimea; Shimeath; Shimei; Simeon).

1. **Shemaiah** (5), "man of God," "prophet." Two interventions with King Rehoboam: after the breakaway of the northern tribes he advises the king not to have recourse to arms against Israel, 1 K 12:22–24//2 Ch 11:2–4; later, when Pharaoh Shishak (Sheshonk) threatens Jerusalem, he draws the attention of the king and the leaders to the religious causes of the political situation, 2 Ch 12:5–7. Acc. to 2 Ch 12:15 there exists an Annals of Shemaiah the prophet, in which the history of Rehoboam is recorded.

2. **Shemaiah** (1), father of the prophet: URIAH 3.

3. **Shemaiah** (4) **of Nehelam** (3), a deportee who is cursed owing to his fierce opposition to the letter of the prophet Jeremiah recommending that the exiles settle down in Babylonia because the exile will be a long one, Jr 29:24–32.

4. **Shemaiah** (1), father of: DELAIAH 1.

5. **Ben-shemaiah** (1), a Simeonite, head of a clan, 1 Ch 4:37.

6. **Shemaiah** (1), a Reubenite, son of Joel and ancestor of Beerah, 1 Ch 5:4.

7. **Shemaiah son of Hasshub, son of Azrikam, son of Hashabiah** (2), **son of Bunni** (1), acc. to Ne, **of the sons of Merari** (1), acc. to 1 Ch, a Levite living in Jerusalem, 1 Ch 9:14//Ne 11:15.

8. **Shemaiah** (1) = **Shammua** (1), father of the Levite: OBADIAH 11.

9. **Shemaiah** (2), a Levite official, of the sons of Elizaphan, takes part in the transferral of the Ark, 1 Ch 15:8, 11.

10. **Shemaiah son of Nethanel** (1), a Levite and scribe, 1 Ch 24:6.

11. **Shemaiah** (3), eldest son of Obed-edom, a gatekeeper; his sons are heads of families and valiant fighting men, 1 Ch 26:4, 6–7.

12. **Shemaiah** (1), one of the eight Levites sent by King Jehoshaphat, along with two priests and five officers, to instruct the towns of Judah in the Law, 2 Ch 17:7–9.

13. **Shemaiah** (1), a Levite, of the sons of Jeduthun, takes part in the purification of the temple during the reform of Hezekiah, 2 Ch 29:14.

14. **Shemaiah** (1), one of the six Levites in the service of Kore, son of Imnah, for the distributions of foodstuffs in the time of King Hezekiah, 2 Ch 31:15.

15. **Shemaiah** (1), one of the six heads of the Levites under King Josiah, 2 Ch 35:9.

16. **Shemaiah** (2), a descendant of King Jehoiachin, son of Shecaniah, 1 Ch 3:22.

17. **Shemaiah** (1), an Israelite of the sons of Adonikam, who returns from the exile with Ezra, Ezr 8:13.

18. **Shemaiah** (1), one of the messengers Ezra sends to Iddo, Ezr 8:16.

19. **Shemaiah** (1), a priest, of the sons of Harim, married to a foreign wife, whom he puts away, Ezr 10:21.

20. **Shemaiah** (1), an Israelite of the sons of Harim, married to a foreign wife, whom he puts away, Ezr 10:31.

21. **Shemaiah son of Shecaniah** (1), keeper of the East Gate, a volunteer in the rebuilding of the wall of Jerusalem, Ne 3:29.

22. **Shemaiah son of Delaiah, son of Mehetabel** (1), a prophet. He advises Nehemiah, when the latter is threatened with death, to use the right of sanctuary and take refuge in the temple; but in advising him to go into "the innermost part of the sanctuary," he is urging Nehemiah, a layman, to commit a serious sin, Ne 6:10–12.

23. **Shemaiah** (3), head of a priestly family who returns from the exile with Zerubbabel, Ne 12:6, a cosigner of the pledge to observe the Law, Ne 10:9. In the time of the high priest Joiakim, Jehonathan is the head of the family of Shemaiah, Ne 12:18.

24. **Shemaiah** (1), a descendant of Asaph and an ancestor of: ZECHARIAH 26.

25. **Shemaiah** (1), a priest, a trumpeter at the dedication of the wall of Jerusalem, Ne 12:34.

26. **Shemaiah** (1), a descendant of Asaph(?), an instrumentalist at the dedication of the wall, Ne 12:36.

27. **Shemaiah** (1), a priest accompanying Nehemiah at the dedication of the wall, Ne 12:42.

28. **Shemaiah the great** (1), Gr. *Semeias,* Tb 5:14, father of Jathan and: HANANIAH 15.

SHEMARIAH, "Yah has preserved" (cf. Ishmerai; Samaria; Shemer?; Shimrath; Shimri; Shimrith; Shimron; Shomer).

1. **Shemariah** (1), a Benjaminite who rallies to David before the latter becomes king, 1 Ch 12:6.

2. **Shemariah** (1), second of the three sons of Mahalath and King Rehoboam, 2 Ch 11:19.

3. **Shemariah** (2), two Israelites married to foreign wives, whom they put away: the first, of the sons of Harim, Ezr 10:32; the second, of the sons of Zaccai, 10:41.

SHEMEBER (1), Hb. *Shem'eber* (cf. Shem), **king of Zeboiim** (2), Gn 14:2, 8. Allied with: BERA.

SHEMED (1), a Benjaminite of the sons of Elpaal. "It was he who built Ono, and Lud with its outlying towns," 1 Ch 8:12.

SHEMER, "Sediment, Lees" (cf. Shemariah?).

1. **Shemer** (2), owner of the hill that King Omri of Israel buys and on which he builds "a town which he named Samaria after Shemer who had owned the hill," 1 K 16:24.

2. **Shemer** (1), a Levite of the clan of Merari, an ancestor of Ethan the cantor, 1 Ch 6:31.

SHEMIDA (3), Hb. *Shemida',* "The Name has known" (cf. Jada; Shem), last of the sons of Manasseh acc. to Jos 17:2, fifth of the sixth sons of Gilead, whose descendants form the **Shemidaite** clan, Nb 26:32. Among the sons of Shemida 1 Ch 7:19 lists Shechem and Likhi [= ? Helek], sons of Manasseh in Jos 17:2 and called sons of Gilead in Nb 26:30–32.

SHEMIDAITE (1), Nb 26:32, belonging to the clan of: SHEMIDA.

SHEMIRAMOTH, an Accad. fem. name, [Goddess?] *Sammuramat,* "Semiramis."

1. **Shemiramoth** (3), a Levite, a gatekeeper in the service of the Ark, 1 Ch 15:18, a player of the keyed harp, 15:20; 16:5.

2. **Shemiramoth** (1), one of the eight Levites sent by King Jehoshaphat, along with two priests and five officers, to instruct the towns of Judah in the Law, 2 Ch 17:7–9.

SHEMUEL. See: SAMUEL 1, 3.

SHENAZZAR (1), Hb. *Shena'zzar,* Accad. *Sin-uzur,* "Sin, protect!" (cf. Sharezer; Sin). See: SHESHBAZZAR.

SHEOL (65 in Hb.) or **Hades** (12 in Gr. NT) is translated in various ways: Sheol, Hades, dwelling of the dead, hell, underworld. *Hades* is derived from the name of the Gr. god of the dead, *Haidēs,* "The Invisible One," and usually designates the *dwelling place of the dead.* The Vulgate translates it as *Infernus* or *Inferus,* "Underworld."

Except in Lk 16:23, 28, where the rich man is tormented, Hades or Sheol is a "neutral" place, a pit, Si 21:10, in the depths of the earth, cf. Nb 16:30–33; Tb 4:19; 13:2; Si 51:5, to which the dead go down, Ba 3:19, be they good, Gn 37:35; Tb 3:10; 2 M 6:23; Jb 17:13, or wicked, Jb 21:13; Ps 9:18; 31:18, to live a gloomy afterlife, Jb 3:17–19; Ps 49:15; 88:4–13; Qo 9:5, 10. It is the land from which there is no returning, Ws 2:1; cf. Jb 7:9; 16:22.

Hades also stands for the inexorable power of death (cf. *the gates of the underworld,* Mt 16:18; cf. Jb 38:17), from which no human being can escape, 2 S 22:5–6//Ps 18:5–6; Ps 89:49; Pr 27:20; 30:15–16; Sg 8:6; Hab 2:5, which God alone can conquer, 1 S 2:6; Ps 49:16; Si 48:5; Dn 3:88; Rv 20:13–14, from which Christ will be rescued, Ac 2:24–31; Rv 1:18, as will the messianic community gathered by Jesus, Mt 16:18.

See: ABADDON; TARTARUS.

SHEPHAM

1. **Shepham** (2), a town on the theoretical NE boundary of the Promised Land, Nb 34:10–11.

2. **Shepham (of)** (1), native place of: ZABDI 3. Same as the preceding?

SHEPHAT (1), Tb 1:2. Precise location unknown.

SHEPHATIAH, "Yah has judged" (cf. Elishaphat; Jehoshaphat; Judgement; Shephat; Shiphtan).

1. **Shephatiah son of Abital** (2), fifth son of David born at Hebron, 2 S 3:4//1 Ch 3:3.

2. **Shephatiah from Hariph** (1), a Benjaminite, among the first to rally to David before the latter became king, 1 Ch 12:6.

3. **Shephatiah son of Maacah** (1), commissioner for the tribe of Simeon, 1 Ch 27:16.

4. **Shephatiah** (1), one of the six sons of King Jehoshaphat of Judah who are assassinated by their elder brother Jehoram after his accession to the throne, 2 Ch 21:2–4, 13.

5. **Shephatiah son of Mattan** (1), one of the four ministers of King Zedekiah who, during the Chaldaean siege of Jerusalem, have Jeremiah thrown into a cistern on the grounds that his words are demoralizing the remaining defenders of the city, Jr 38:1–6.

6. **Shephatiah** (1), a Benjaminite, father of: MESHULLAM 6.

7. **Shephatiah** (2), head of a family of Solomon's slaves who return from the exile, Ezr 2:57//Ne 7:59.

8. **Shephatiah** (3), an Israelite, head of a family whose sons return from the exile, some with Zerubbabel, Ezr 2:4//Ne 7:9, some with Ezra, Ezr 8:8.

9. **Shephatiah** (1), a Judaean, an ancestor of: ATHAIAH.

SHEPHER (2), a mountain, a stage of the Exodus between Sinai and Kadesh, Nb 33:23–24.

SHEPHI (1). See: SHEPHO.

SHEPHO (1), Gn 36:23, fourth of the five sons of Shobal, son of Seir.

= **Shephi** (1), 1 Ch 1:40.

SHEPHUPHAM (1), "Viper," one of the sons of Benjamin whose descendants form the **Shephuphamite** clan acc. to Nb 26:39.

= **Shephuphan** (1), a son of Bela, eldest son of Benjamin, acc. to 1 Ch 8:5.

SHEPHUPHAMITE (1), Nb 26:39, Hb. *Shuphami,* belonging to the clan of: SHEPHUPHAM.

SHEPHUPHAN (1). See: SHEPHUPHAM.

SHEREBIAH (8), **of the sons of Mahli son of Levi son of Israel** (1), "a capable man," a Levite leader who returns from Babylonia to Jerusalem with Ezra, Ezr 8:18, 24, a contemporary of the high priest Jeshua, Ne 12:8, 24, one of those in charge of the penitential ceremony in Ne 9:4–5, a cosigner of the pledge to observe the Law, Ne 10:13. Acc. to Ne 8:7 Sherebiah is one of the Levites who explain the Law to the people during its solemn reading by Ezra. One or several individuals.

SHERESH (1), "Root," a Manassite, a son of Machir and Maacah, 1 Ch 7:16.

SHESHAI (1), one of the three sons of: ANAK.

SHESHAK (2), Jr 25:26; 51:41, a cryptogram for *Babel,* "Babylon." See: LEB-KAMAI.

SHESHAN (5), of the clan of Jerahmeel. Acc. to 1 Ch 2:31, he is a son of Ishi and the father of Ahlai. Acc. to another tradition, 1 Ch 2:34–35, he has no sons but by one of his daughters, who marries his Egyptian servant, he is ancestor of Elishama.

SHESHBAZZAR (4), Neo-Babyl. *Sin-ab-uzur* (cf. Sin). This "prince of Judah" is the leader of the first convoy of repatriates, Ezr 1:8, 11, to whom is entrusted the official mission of restoring the temple in Jerusalem, Ezr 5:13–16; cf. 6:3–5. In fact, he will only lay the foundations of the temple.

= ? **Shenazzar** (1), one of the sons born to Jehoiachin, king of Judah, while a prisoner at Babylon, 1 Ch 3:18.

[SHESHONK]. See: SHISHAK.

SHETH (1). See: SETH 2.

SHETHAR (1), an official listed with: MEMUCAN.

SHETHAR-BOZENAI (4), associated with: TATTENAI.

SHEVA

1. **Sheva** (1), 2 S 20:25. See: SERAIAH 1.

2. **Sheva** (1), one of the sons of Maacah, concubine of Caleb, and "father of Machbenah and father of Gibea," 1 Ch 2:49.

SHIHOR, Hb. transcription of Egypt. *Shihor,* "Pool of Horus."

1. **Shihor** (2). See: WADI OF EGYPT.

2. **Nile** (2), Is 23:3 and Jr 2:18. See: NILE.

SHIKKERON (1), on the NW border of Judah, between Ekron and Jabneel, Jos 15:11. Not identified.

SHILHI (2), (cf. Shelah), father of: AZUBAH 2.

SHILHIM (1), a town in the Negeb of Judah, Jos 15:32.

= ? **Sharuhen** (1), a town formerly belonging to Simeon, Jos 19:6.

SHILLEM (2), "[Yah] has replaced [the dead child]" (cf. Salem. See Chalphi), the last of the four sons of Naphtali, Gn 46:24, whose descendants form the **Shillemite** clan, Nb 26:49.

= **Shallum** (1), 1 Ch 7:13.

SHILLEMITE (1), belonging to the clan of: SHILLEM.

SHILOAH, Gr. *Silōam,* "Sent" (Jn 9:7), "Conduit, Canal" (cf. Shelah).

1. **(Pool of) Shiloah** or **Siloam** (3), Is 8:6, SE of Jerusalem, a reservoir or terminus of the canal tunneled in the rock by King Hezekiah to bring the water of the Gihon spring into the city, cf. 2 K 20:20; 2 Ch 32:30; Si 48:17; Is 22:11. In Ne 3:15 the identification of the "conduit cistern" (Hb. *Shelah,* "canal") with Shiloah is disputed.

At the bidding of Jesus, the man born blind washes his eyes in the Pool of Siloam and recovers his sight, Jn 9:7, 11.

2. **Tower at Siloam** (1), not far from the Pool of Siloam. It falls and kills eighteen people, Lk 13:4.

SHILOH (32), Gr. *Sēlō* (cf. Tanaath-shiloh), **in the land of Canaan** (3), Jos 21:2; 22:9; Jg 21:12, a town "north of Bethel, east of the highway that runs from Bethel up to Shechem, and south of Lebonah," Jg 21:19. Site of an ancient sanctuary, 1 S 1:3, 9 (Hb.), 24; 2:14; cf. Jg 18:21, served by the family of Eli, 1 S 14:3; 1 K 2:27, where Samuel spends his childhood, 1 S 1:24; 2:11; 3:21, and where the Ark of the Covenant is kept, 1 S 4:3–4, 12; cf. Ps 78:60. There Joshua distributes their inheritance to the seven tribes still to be provided for after Judah, Ephraim, and Manasseh, Jos 18:1, 8–10; 19:51; cf. 22:9–12. A feast of Yahweh, which is an occasion for popular rejoicing, is celebrated each year at Shiloh, Jg 21:12, 19–21. The town is destroyed, doubtless by the Philistines, cf. Jr 7:12–14; 26:6–9, and the priests of Shiloh take refuge at Nob, 1 S 21:2; 22:19. But a brotherhood of prophets remains at Shiloh; see: AHIJAH 3. After the reform of Josiah and even after the destruction of the temple, the people of Shiloh come on pilgrimage to Jerusalem, cf. Jr 41:1. Today *Seilun*.

Priest: ELI 1.

SHILONITE or **of Shiloh** (6), Hb. *Shilôni*, 1 K 11:29; 12:15; 15:29; 2 Ch 9:29; 10:15 (for all these, see: AHIJAH 3); 1 Ch 9:5.

SHILSHAH (1), fem. of Hb. *Shelesh*, an Asherite, one of the eleven sons of Zophah, 1 Ch 7:37.

SHIMEA, Shimeah, Hb. 1–4: *Shim'ah* (1) or *Shim'a'* (2–4), (cf. Shemaiah); 5: *Shim'ah*.

1. **Shimeah** (4) or **Shimea** (1), a brother of David, 2 S 13:3, 32; 21:21; 1 Ch 2:13. See: SHAMMAH 2.

2. **Shimea** (1), a son of David. See: SHAMMUA 2.

3. **Shimea** (1), a Levite of the clan of Gershon, an ancestor of Asaph the cantor, 1 Ch 6:24.

4. **Shimeah** (1), 1 Ch 8:32, a Benjaminite, son of Mikloth, of the family of Saul, living in Jerusalem.

= **Shimeam** (1), 1 Ch 9:38.

SHIMEAH. See: SHIMEA 1, 4.

SHIMEAM (1), Hb. *Shim'am*. See: SHIMEA 4.

SHIMEATH (2), Hb. *Shim'at* (cf. Shemaiah), **the Ammonite woman** (1), mother of: JOZACAR.

SHIMEATHITES (1), Hb. *Shim'atim*, belonging to *Shimea?* to *Shimeath?*, a clan of Judah, descended from Salma, 1 Ch 2:55. Unknown.

SHIMEI, Hb. *Shim'i* (cf. Shemaiah).

1. **Shimei** (2), a Simeonite, a descendant of Shaul and father of sixteen sons and six daughters, 1 Ch 4:26–27.

2. **Shimei** (1), a Reubenite, a descendant of Joel and ancestor of Beerah, 1 Ch 5:4.

3. **Shimei** (8), brother of Libni/Ladan, son of Gershon, son of Levi, Ex 6:17// Nb 3:18//1 Ch 6:2. His descendants, 1 Ch 23:7–11, form the **Shimeite** clan, Nb 3:21; Zc 12:13. Shimei is an ancestor of Asaph the cantor acc. to 1 Ch 6:27.

4. **Shimei** (1), a Levite of the clan of Merari, an ancestor of Asaiah, 1 Ch 6:14.

5. **Shimei** (1), a Benjaminite, father of nine sons who are heads of families at Jerusalem, 1 Ch 8:21. The same (?) as: SHEMA 4.

6. **Shimei** (19) **son of Gera** (4), **a Benjaminite** (3) **from Bahurim** (2). When David is fleeing from his son Absalom, Shimei, "a man of the same clan as Saul's family," curses the king: "Yahweh has brought on you all the blood of the House of Saul whose sovereignty you have usurped," 2 S 16:5–13. When David returns from his exile, Shimei is the first to come out to meet him; the king pardons him, 2 S 19:17–24, but on his deathbed David bids Solomon turn aside the

curse by punishing Shimei, 1 K 2:8. Solomon then orders Shimei to remain strictly in Jerusalem and thus to have no contact with the members of his clan. Shimei breaks his promise (never to leave Jerusalem) when he hurries to Gath to bring back some runaway slaves. When he returns, Solomon has him put to death, 1 K 2:36–46. Shimei (Gr. *Semeias*) is an ancestor of: MORDECAI 2.

7. **Shimei** (1), in the matter of David's successor, rallies to Solomon against Adonijah, 1 K 1:8.

8. **Shimei son of Ela** (1), Solomon's administrator in Benjamin, 1 K 4:18.

9. **Shimei** (1), head of the tenth class of cantors, 1 Ch 25:17. His name must be supplied in 1 Ch 25:3, in order to fill out the list of the six sons of Jeduthun.

10. **Shimei of Ramah** (1), commissioner for the vineyards, 1 Ch 27:27.

11. **Shimei** (1), a Levite, of the sons of Heman, takes part in the purification of the temple during the reform of Hezekiah, 2 Ch 29:14.

12. **Shimei** (2), a Levite, brother of: CONANIAH 1.

13. **Shimei** (1), brother of Zerubbabel, a descendant of King Jehoiachin, 1 Ch 3:19.

14. **Shimei** (1), a Levite, married to a foreign wife, whom he puts away, Ezr 10:23.

15. **Shimei** (2), two Israelites married to foreign wives, whom they put away: the first, of the sons of Hashum, Ezr 10:33; the second, of the sons of Binnui, 10:38.

SHIMEITE (2), Nb 3:21; Zc 11:13, belonging to the clan of: SHIMEI 3.

SHIMEON (1). See: SIMEON 2.

SHIMON (1), Hb. *Shimôn,* a Judaean, father of four sons, 1 Ch 4:20.

SHIMRATH (1), (cf. Shemariah), a Benjaminite of the sons of Shimei, head of a family in Jerusalem, 1 Ch 8:21.

SHIMRI (cf. Shemariah).

1. **Ben-shimri** (1), a Simeonite, leader of a clan, 1 Ch 4:37.

2. **Shimri** (1), father of: JEDIAEL 2.

3. **Shimri** (1), a gatekeeper, the chief—though not the firstborn—of the sons of Hosah, a descendant of Merari, 1 Ch 26:10.

4. **Shimri** (1), a Levite, of the sons of Elizaphan (clan of Kohath), takes part in the purification of the temple during the reform of Hezekiah, 2 Ch 29:13.

SHIMRITH (1), (cf. Shemariah), **the Moabitess** (1). See: SHOMER 1.

SHIMRON (cf. Shemariah).

1. **Shimron** (3), last of the four sons of Issachar, Gn 46:13//1 Ch 7:1, whose descendants form the **Shimronite** clan, Nb 26:24.

2. **Shimron** (2), a former Canaanite town, whose king is among those conquered by Joshua, Jos 11:1; it becomes a town of Zebulun, Jos 19:15. About 10 km W of Nazareth.

SHIMRONITE (1), belonging to the clan of: SHIMRON 1.

SHIMSHAI (4), (cf. Samson; Shamsherai), secretary of Rehum, the governor of Samaria in the time of Artaxerxes I, Ezr 4:8–9, 17, 23.

SHINAB (1), Hb. *Shin'ab,* Accad. *Sin-abushu,* "[The god] Sin is his father" (cf. Sin), **king of Admah** (2), Gn 14:2, 8, allied with: BERA.

SHINAR (9), Hb. *Shin'ar.* Accad. *Sha-an-ha-ra.*

The **land of Shinar** (4) includes Babylonia with the cities of Babel, Erech, and Accad, Gn 10:10–11; the tower of Babel is built there, Gn 11:2; the people of God are exiled there, Is 11:11; cf. Dn 1:2. It is the symbolic center of Wickedness, Zc 5:11. Shinar is famous for its luxury, Jos 7:21. Outside the Bible, Shinar refers to an area of Upper Mesopotamia. Today *Jebel Sinjar.*

SHION (1), a town in Issachar, Jos 19:19.

SHIPHRAH (1), "Beauty" (cf. Shaphir), one of the Hebrew midwives in Egypt, Ex 1:15–21.

SHIPHTAN (1), (cf. Shephathiah), an Ephraimite, father of: KEMUEL 2.

SHISHA (1). See: SERAIAH 1.

SHISHAK (7), that is, *Sheshonk I,* **king of Egypt** (4), first Pharaoh of the twenty-second dynasty (950–929), with whom Jeroboam seeks refuge in his rebellion against Solomon, 1 K 11:40; cf. 12:2, and who ca. 926 marches on Jerusalem and takes the treasures of the temple and the royal palace, 1 K 14:25–26. The parallel but more detailed account in 2 Ch 12:2–12 speaks of a campaign in Judah and regards it as a punishment from Yahweh.

SHITRAI of Sharon (1), commissioner for the cattle in pasture in the plain of Sharon, 1 Ch 27:29.

SHITTIM, "Acacias" (cf. Beth-shittah).

1. **Shittim** (4), last encampment of Israel at the end of the Exodus, in Moab, Nb 25:1, before crossing the Jordan, Jos 3:1; cf. Mi 6:5; from here Joshua sends spies to explore the country at Jericho, Jos 2:1.

= **Abel-hash-shittim** (1), near the Jordan, in the plains of Moab, Nb 33:49. NE of the Dead Sea.

2. **The wadi of Acacias** (1), Jl 4:18. Location disputed: lower part of the wadi Kidron, *Wadi-en-Nar?* or NE of the Dead Sea, cf. 1, above?

SHIZA the Reubenite (1), father of: ADINA.

SHOA (1), Ezk 23:23, a Chaldaean tribe from eastern Babylonia, sometimes identified with the *Sutu* of the cuneiform inscriptions.

SHOBAB, "Return" (cf. Jashub).

1. **Shobab** (3), one of the sons of David born in Jerusalem, 2 S 5:14//1 Ch 3:5//14:4.

2. **Shobab** (1), son of Caleb and his wife Azubah, 1 Ch 2:18.

SHOBACH (2), 2 S 10:16, 18, commander of Hadadezer's army, conquered and executed by David.

= **Shophach** (2), 1 Ch 19:16, 18.

SHOBAI (2), head of a family of gatekeepers who return from the exile, Ezr 2:42//Ne 7:45.

SHOBAL

1. **Shobal** (5), second of the sons of Seir the Horite, Gn 36:20//1 Ch 1:38, and of the chiefs (or clans) of the Horites, Gn 36:29. He has five sons, Gn 36:23//1 Ch 1:40.

2. **Shobal** (4), a son of Judah acc. to 1 Ch 4:1; a son of Judah through Hur, and father of Kiriath-jearim, among others, acc. to 1 Ch 2:50; 52–53. Father of: REAIAH 1.

SHOBEK (1), (cf. Ishbak), a leader of the people and cosigner of the pledge to observe the Law, Ne 10:25.

SHOBI son of Nahash, from Rabbah of the Ammonites (1), a man greatly devoted to David during the latter's exile at Mahanaim, 2 S 17:27–29.

SHOHAM (1), "Cornelian," a Levite of the clan of Merari, one of the chiefs of the sons of Jaaziah, 1 Ch 24:27.

SHOMER (cf. Shemariah).

1. **Shomer** (1) = **Shimrith the Moabitess** (1), mother of: JOZABAD 10.

2. **Shomer** (1), an Asherite of the clan of Beriah, son of Heber and father of three sons, 1 Ch 7:32, 34.

SHOPHACH (2). See: SHOBACH.

SHUA, Hb. 1: *Shua'*, "Noble, magnanimous" (cf. Abishua; Bath-shua; Elishua; Joshua; Malchi-shua); 2: *Shu'a'*.

1. **Shua** (2), a Canaanite, father of: BATH-SHUA 1.

2. **Shua** (1), an Asherite, sister of the three sons of Heber, son of Beriah, 1 Ch 7:32.

SHUAH (2), Hb. *Shuah,* **of Shuah** (5), Hb. *Shuhi,* one of the six sons of Abraham and his concubine Keturah, a people or region of Arabia, Gn 25:2//1 Ch 1:32.
Native place of: BILDAD.

SHUAL, Hb. *Shu'al.* "Fox" (cf. Hazar-shual).
1. **Land of Shual** (1), 1 S 13:17, not far from Ophrah and Michmash. Location uncertain.
2. **Shual** (1), an Asherite, one of the eleven sons of Zophah, 1 Ch 7:36.

SHUBAEL
1. **Shubael** (2), a priest, a son of Amram, of the clan of Kohath, 1 Ch 24:20.
2. **Shubael** (1). See: SHEBUEL 2.

SHUHAH (1), "Pit," brother of Caleb, 1 Ch 4:11.

SHUHAM (1), son of Dan, whose descendants form the **Shuhamite** clan, the only clan of Dan that is named, Nb 26:42–43.
= **Hushim** (2), son of Dan, Gn 46:23; 1 Ch 7:12 (this v. 12 represents perhaps the remnant of a genealogy of Dan).

SHUHAMITE (2), Nb 26:42–43, belonging to the clan of: SHUHAM.

SHULAM (Maid of) (2), Hb. *Shulammit* (to be connected ? with: ABISHAG OF SHUNEM), a fem. form derived from "Solomon" and meaning *She who belongs to Solomon* or *The Pacified?* Name given to the spouse in Sg 7:1; cf. 8:10.

[SHULMAN]. See: SHALMANESER.

SHUMATHITES (1), a clan of Judah, descended from Shobal, 1 Ch 2:53.

SHUNAMMITESS or **of Shunem** (8), 1 K 1:3, 15; 2:17, 21–22; 2 K 4:12, 25, 36. See: SHUNEM.

SHUNEM (3), a town of Issachar, Jos 19:18, occupied by the Philistines in the time of Saul, 1 S 28:4. The prophet Elisha occasionally lodges there in the house of a woman of rank, 2 K 4:8–10. This Shunammitess, 4:12, 25, 26, gives birth to a child as Elisha had foretold. A few years later the little boy dies; the Shunammitess comes to complain to Elisha, who then brings the child back to life, 4:11–37. After a stay of seven years in Philistia, where she had taken refuge in a time of famine, the Shunammitess regains possession of "her house and lands" thanks to the intervention of Elisha, 8:1–6. A few km NE of Jezreel.
Native place of: ABISHAG.

SHUNI (2), third of the seven sons of Gad, Gn 46:16, whose descendants form the **Shunite** clan, Nb 26:15.

SHUNITE (1), belonging to the clan of: SHUNI.

SHUPPIM
1. **Shuppim** (2), associated with Huppim, is connected with Benjamin in 1 Ch 7:12 (but v. 12 may have been part of a genealogy of Dan, cf. Nb 26:42–43) and with Manasseh in 1 Ch 7:15.
2. **Shuppim** (1), a gatekeeper of the temple, 1 Ch 26:16.

SHUR (6), "Wall" (referring to the wall built by the Egyptians as a defense against invasion by Semites?), a wilderness, Ex 15:22, to the east of Egypt, Gn 25:18; 1 S 15:7; cf. 27:8, near Kadesh, Gn 20:1. Hagar sets out for it when she flees with Ishmael, Gn 16:7. Israel crosses it when leaving Egypt, Ex 15:22.

SHUTHELAH (5), a son of Ephraim, whose descendants form the **Shuthelahite** clan, Nb 26:35–36; cf. 1 Ch 7:20–21, 25 (corr. of Hb. *Resheph and Telah*).

SHUTHELAHITE (1), belonging to the clan of: SHUTHELAH.

SIA (1), Ne 7:47, = **Siaha** (1), Ezr 2:44, head of a family of "oblates" who return from the exile.

SIAHA (1). See: SIA.

SIBBECAI of Hushah (5), one of David's champions; in a battle with the Philistines he kills Saph, a descendant of Rapha, 2 S 21:18//1 Ch 20:4; 2 S 23:27 (corr. of Hb. *Mebunnai*)//1 Ch 11:29. Acc. to 1 Ch 27:11, where he is called a *Zerahite*, he is in charge of the (military) service for the eighth month.

SIBMAH (5), a town in Transjordania, linked with Heshbon, near which it lies, occupied by Reuben, Nb 32:38; Jos 13:19, then by Moab, and famous for its vineyards, Is 16:8–9; Jr 48:32.

= **Sebam** (1), Nb 32:3.

SIBRAIM (1), "lying between the territories of Damascus and Hamath," Ezk 47:16.

= ? **Ziphron** (1), Nb 34:9, a town on the northern border of the Promised Land. Location uncertain.

[SICILY]. See: SYRACUSE.

SICYON (1), Gr. *Sikyōn,* a town in the Peloponnesus, W of Corinth, to which the letter of the consul Lucius promulgating the alliance of Romans and Jews is addressed, 1 M 15:23.

SIDDIM (Valley of) (3), identified in Gn 14:3 with the "Salt Sea," the southern part of the Dead Sea, and containing "many bitumen wells," Gn 14:10; a place of battle between the kings of Sodom, Gormorrah, and the neighboring towns, on one side, and the four great kings, on the other, 14:8.

SIDE (1), (cf. Sidetes), a port of Pamphylia in Asia Minor, one of the places to which the letter of the consul Lucius promulgating the alliance of Romans and Jews is sent, 1 M 15:23.

[SIDETES], a surname of Antiochus VII, who is thus called because he had been brought up at Side in Pamphylia. See: ANTIOCHUS 6.

SIDON (34), Hb. *Zidôn,* "Fishing ground"? (cf. Bethsaida), **the Great** (2), Jos 11:8; 19:28.

a. **Sidon,** also called, "virgin daughter of Sidon," Is 23:12, first of the Canaanite cities acc. to the Yahwist, Gn 10:15//1 Ch 1:13; cf. Gn 10:19; Mt 15:21–22. An important Phoenician city, "the fortress of the sea" (later supplanted by Tyre), Is 23:4 (gloss), to the west of Mount Hermon, cf. Dt 3:9, famous for its oarsmen, Ezk 27:8, its woodsmen, 1 K 5:20; cf. 1 Ch 22:4; Ezr 3:7, its trade, Is 23:2, and its acumen, Zc 9:2, whose inhabitants live "in security, peaceful and trusting," Jg 18:7. It is listed as a city of Asher, Jos 19:28, in the opposite direction from Zebulun, a good distance from Laish/Dan, Jg 18:7, 28; but the Israelites, oppressed by the Sidonians, Jg 10:12; cf. 3:3, never possessed the city except in theory, Jos 13:4–6; cf. Jg 1:31. Israel—and especially King Solomon—allowed themselves to be led astray by the gods of Sidon, 1 K 11:5, 33; 2 K 23:13; cf. Jg 10:6; 1 K 11:1–2. The oracle in Ezk 28:21–23; cf. 32:30, is explained by the role Sidon played in the policy that led to Judah's downfall. The "strongly fortified city" threatened by the king of the North in Dn 11:15 is perhaps Sidon. Paul stops at Sidon on his journey to Rome, Ac 27:3–4. Today *Sa'ida.*

b. **Tyre and Sidon.** See: TYRE *b.*

King: ETHBAAL.

Local goddess: ASTARTE.

In the land of Sidon: ARAH 3; PHOENICIA; ZAREPHATH.

SIDONIAN (18), Dt 3:9; Jos 13:4, 6; Jg 3:3; 10:12; 18:7; 1 K 5:20; 11:1, 5, 33; 16:31; 2 K 23:13; 1 Ch 22:4; Ezr 3:7; Ez 32:30; Lk 4:26; Ac 12:20, from or of: SIDON.

SIHON (37), **the Amorite** (3), **the king of the Amorites** (13), **king of** (or who *rules* or *lives in*) **Heshbon** (17). Frequently named with Og, king of Bashan; cf. also **the two Amorite kings** (6), Dt 3:8; 4:47;

31:4; Jos 2:10; 9:10; 24:12; cf. Dt 3:21; Jos 13:12.

His kingdom, which has been increased at the cost of Moab, Nb 21:16–29; cf. Jr 48:45, extends beyond the Jordan, Dt 3:8; 4:47, from the Arnon, Dt 2:24, to the Jabbok, Jos 12:2, and from the wilderness to the Jordan, Jg 11:22. Sihon resists Israel with force when the latter seeks to cross his country, but the Israelites defeat him at Jahaz and conquer his territory, Nb 21:21–32; Dt 2:24–36; Jg 11:19–22, which is assigned to Reuben, Gad (cf. 1 K 4:19–20), and eastern Manasseh, Nb 32:33–41; Dt 29:6–7; Jos 13:8–11, 15–21, 24–27. The fate of Sihon will also be that of the legendary king Og, Nb 21:34; Dt 3:2, 6, and threatens the other enemies of Israel, Dt 3:21; 31:4; cf. Jos 2:10; 9:10. The victory over the two Amorite kings is recalled in Dt 1:4; 3:8; 4:46–47; Jos 13: 10–12, 21; 24:12 (which speaks of hornets being sent); Ne 9:22; Ps 135:11; 136:19–20.

Capital: HESHBON.

SILAS (13), Grecized form of *Saul,* with *Silvanus* as the Latin form. A Jewish Christian, a Roman citizen, Ac 16:37–38, a prophet, 15:32, Silas has an important place in the Christian community of Jerusalem, 15:22. With Judas, Barnabas, and Saul, he is a delegate from the Council of Jerusalem to the Church of Antioch, 15:22–34. He accompanies Paul on the latter's second missionary journey, 15:40 (at Lystra, Timothy joins them); at Philippi he is imprisoned with Paul, 16: 19, 25, 29, shares the latter's successes and trials at Thessalonika, 17:4, 10, remains at Beroea with Timothy while Paul goes to Athens, 17:14–15, then rejoins Paul at Corinth, 18:5.

= **Silvanus** (4), associated with Paul and Timothy in the preaching of the Gospel at Corinth, 2 Co 1:19, and in the sending of the two letters to the Thessalonians, 1 Th 1:1; 2 Th 1:1. Probably coauthor with Peter of the first letter of Peter, 1 P 5:12.

SILOAM. See: SHILOAH.

SILVANUS (4). See: SILAS.

SIMEON, Hb. *Shim'ôn,* "[Yah] has heard" (cf. Shemaiah), Gr. *Symeōn, Simōn.*

1. **Simeon** (46), a son of Jacob and a tribe of Israel.

Second son of Jacob and Leah, Gn 29:33; 35:23; Ex 1:2; 1 Ch 2:1; cf. Gn 48:5. As an individual person he appears only in the story of Joseph, who retains him as a hostage in Egypt in order to assure that Benjamin will be brought to him, Gn 42:24, 36; 43:23. The tribe of the **sons of Simeon** (16) or the **Simeonites** (4) plays a rather minor part in the history of Israel. The story told in Gn 34:25–31; cf. Gn 49:5, in which the two brothers Simeon and Levi use trickery in attacking Shechem the Hivite, is probably meant to show that the two sister tribes were initially settled near the Canaanite town of Shechem, before being "scattered among Israel," Gn 49: 7. Simeon—together with Judah, his "brother," Jg 1:3, 17—occupies the southern part of the Promised Land: these two tribes are cut off from the others by a kind of non-Israelite barrier, namely, Jerusalem, Gezer, and the Gibeonite federation. Simeon lives a nomadic existence in the Negeb, cf. 1 Ch 4:39–40. His clans are listed in Gn 46:10//Ex 6:15 and Nb 26:12//1 Ch 4:24, and their manpower is indicated in Nb 1:23//2:13 (59,300) and Nb 26:14 (22,200); cf. 1 Ch 4:38.

The territory of Simeon is described in Jos 19:1–9; 1 Ch 4:24–43. Simeon, weakened in the time of the judges, is rather quickly absorbed by Judah; this explains why twelve names of towns of Simeon are found in Judah, cf. Jos 15: 26–32, and why Simeon is not named in Dt 33.

Principal Simeonites: JUDITH 2; SHELUMIEL; UZZIAH 7; ZIMRI 1.

Simeon in the lists of the tribes: List, pages 410–11.

2. **Shimeon** (1), an Israelite of the sons of Harim, married to a foreign wife, whom he puts away, Ezr 10:31.

3. **Simeon** (1), an ancestor of: MATTITHIAH 6.

4. **Simon son of Onias** (1), a high priest (220–195), whose praises are sung in Si 50:1–21. Father of: ONIAS 3.

5. **Simon** (67) or **Simeon** (1), called **Thassi** (1), **son of Mattathias** (1), a descendant of Joarib, brother of Judas Maccabaeus, high priest and ethnarch of the Jews (143–134).

Second son of Mattathias, 1 M 2:3, he is commended to his brothers as "a man of sound judgement" who is to "take your father's place," 2:65; in fact, he will be only the third to lead the people. Simon is initially put in charge of several expeditions by his brother Judas: against Nicanor, 2 M 8:22, against the Idumaeans, 10:19–20, into Galilee to rescue Jews being oppressed by the pagans, 1 M 5:17–23, 55, and again against Nicanor, 2 M 14:17.

After the death of Judas, whom they bury at Modein, 1 M 9:19, Simon and Jonathan take refuge in the desert of Tekoa, 9:33–41. Simon forces the Syrian general Bacchides to lift the siege of Bethbasi, 9:62–68, and helps his brother Jonathan to defeat Apollonius at Joppa and Azotus, 10:74–82. Appointed "military commissioner of the region from the Ladder of Tyre to the frontiers of Egypt," that is, of the coastal region, 11:59, Simon recaptures Beth-zur, 11:64–65, occupies Joppa, 12:33, rebuilds Adida, 12:38, which he makes his base, 13:13. When Jonathan is imprisoned by Trypho, Simon takes his place, 13:1–10. He drives Trypho from Judaea, 13:12–24. He builds a tomb for his family at Modein, 13:25–30.

In 142, Simon takes the side of Demetrius II, who confirms the charter of 145, 1 M 11:30 ff., and thus acknowledges the religious and political independence of Judaea: "The rule of the pagans was lifted from Israel," and a new era begins with Simon, "great high priest, military commissioner, and leader of the Jews," 13:41–42. Rome and Sparta renew their alliance with Simon, 1 M 14:16–24; 15:15–24. Simon captures Gezer, 13:43–48, then, in June 141, the Citadel of Jerusalem, which had been a symbol of foreign domination, 13:49–52. Eulogy of Simon, 14:1–15. An inscription honoring Simon is set up on Mount Zion because he "secured the freedom" of Israel, 14:25–49. Simon receives a friendly letter from Antiochus VII, 15:1–9, but the latter suddenly becomes hostile, 15:27, and claims several towns from Simon, who refuses and sends his two sons against the governor Cendebaeus, 16:1–10. Simon dies tragically at Dok, being assassinated by his son-in-law Ptolemy; his son John succeeds him, 1 M 16:11–24; cf. 13:53.

6. **Simon** (7), **a priest of the tribe of Bilgah** (corr. of Gr. *Tribe of Benjamin*) (1), administrator of the temple, 2 M 3:4, a wild, double-dealing, and wicked man, 4:3–6, who, in his hatred for the high priest Onias, urges the expedition of Heliodorus for the purpose of confiscating the supposedly "untold wealth" that swells the treasury of the temple in Jerusalem, 3:4–11; 4:1–6.

Brother of: MENELAUS.

7. **Symeon** (1), an ancestor of Jesus, Lk 3:30.

8. **Simeon** (1), "an upright and devout man" who "looked forward to Israel's comforting" and who, along with the elderly prophetess Anna, welcomes the child Jesus to the temple; he foresees how difficult the mission of Jesus will be, Lk 2:25–35.

9. **Simon** (50) or **Simeon** (2), **son of John** (4) or **of Jonah** (1), Jewish name of: PETER.

10. **Simon** (4) **the Zealot** (4), Gr. *Kananaios,* "Canaanite; Zealous," or *Zelotēs,* "Zealot," Mt 10:3//Mk 3:18//Lk 6:15//Ac 1:13, one of the: TWELVE. See: ZEALOT; List, page 417.

11. **Simon** (1), a "brother" of Jesus, Mt 13:55//Mk 6:3.

12. **Simon Iscariot** (3), Jn 6:71; 13:2 (var.), 26; father of: JUDAH 12.

13. **Simon** (3) **the Pharisee** (4). He invites Jesus to his table, and Jesus, using the example of the sinful woman at the meal and the parable of the two debtors, reveals to him what it is to "love more," Lk 7:36–50. To be identified (?) with the following?

14. **Simon** (2), the leper of Bethany, welcomes Jesus to his table, Mt 26:6//Mk 14:3.

15. **Simon of Cyrene** (3), father of Alexander and Rufus, Mk 15:21, pressed into service to help Jesus carry his cross, Mt 27:32//Mk 15:21//Lk 23:26.

16. **Simon** (4), a magician of Samaria, tries to buy from the Apostles Peter and Paul the power to confer the Holy Spirit, Ac 8:9–24.

17. **Simon** (4), a leather tanner at Jaffa, in whose home Peter finds hospitality, Ac 9:43; 10:6, 17, 32.

18. **Simeon** called **Niger** (1), one of the five "prophets and teachers" of the Church at Antioch, Ac 13:1.

SIMEONITE or **of Simeon** (4), Hb. *Shim'ôni,* Nb 25:14; 26:14; Jos 21:4; 1 Ch 27:16, descendants of: SIMEON 1.

SIMON. See: SIMEON 4–6, 9–17.

SIN

1. **[Sin],** an Assyro-Babylonian lunar god whose daughter is Ishtar. He is not directly named in the Bible, but his name does enter as a component into several proper names (cf. Sanballat; Sennacherib; Shenazzar; Sheshbazzar; Shinab; Sinai?).

2. **Wilderness of Sin** (4), "between Elim and Sinai," Ex 16:1 (16:2–25, the manna and the quail); 17:1; Nb 33:11–12, a stage of the Israelites during the Exodus. Not to be confused with the wilderness of: ZIN.

3. **Sin** (2), "the stronghold of Egypt," Ez 30:15–16, a town in the eastern part of the Nile Delta. Perhaps the *Pelusium* of the Romans and Greeks.

SINAI (41), a word connected with the Hb. *Seneh,* "bush," see Ex 3:2–4, or with the god *Sin* (cf. Sin 1), a mountain and the wilderness around it in the Sinai peninsula.

Vocabulary: *Sinai* (7), Ex 16:1; Dt 33:2; Jg 5:5; Jdt 5:14; Ps 68:9 (Hb.), 18; Si 48:7. *Mount Sinai* (19), Ex (10×) 19:11, and so on; Lv 7:38; 25:1; 26:46; 27:34; Nb 3:1; 28:6; Ne 9:13; Ac 7:38; Ga 4:25. *Wilderness of Sinai* (13), Ex 19:1, 2; Lv 7:38; Nb (10×) 1:1, and so on. *The wilderness near Mount Sinai,* Ac 7:30. *Mountain of God,* Ex 4:27; 18:5; 24:13; cf. Ex 19:3. *Mountain of Yahweh,* Nb 10:33; cf. 1 K 19:11. *Mountain* (34), Ex (18×); Dt (15×) 4:11–10:10; 1 K 19:11. *Mountains,* Ex 32:12. *Wilderness* (± 120×). *Deserts,* Is 48:21.

Place of Moses' first encounter with God, who manifests himself in the burning bush, Ex 3:2–4; cf. Ac 7:30–35; Mk 12:26//Lk 20:37. God reveals himself to Moses and gives him his mission as liberator, Ex 3:1–4, 17. At the mountain of God, Moses is visited by his brother Aaron, Ex 4:27.

Sinai is one of the major stages of the Israelite Exodus between the departure from Egypt and the entry into the Promised Land, Ex 16:1; 19:1–2; 33:6; Nb 10:12, 33; 33:15–16; Dt 1:2, 6, 19; Jdt 5:14. It is there that the assembly in the wilderness takes place, Ex 19:7–15; Dt 4:10; 9:10; 10:4; 18:16; Ac 7:38, and that God speaks to his people, Dt 1:6; 4:15; 5:2; Ne 9:13. It is on Mount Sinai, amid "peals of thunder . . . and lightning flashes" and "a dense cloud," on the smoking mountain, Ex 19:16–25; Dt 5:2–5, 23–31, that God, Dt 33:2; Jg 5:5; Ps 68:9, 18, comes down in his glory, Ex 19:11, 20; 24:16; Ne 9:13, speaks to Moses, Ex 19:19; 31:18; 33:9–11; Lv 25:1; Nb 1:1; 3:1, 14; 9:1; Ac 7:38, allows him to see something of the divine glory, Ex 33:18–23; Si 45:3, gives him commandments for his people, Ex 20:1–21; Lv 26:46; 27:34; Si 45:3–5; Ml 3:22, and concludes the covenant, Dt 5:2–3; 28:69, with a sacrifice, Ex 24; cf. Nb 28:6. Moses spends forty days and forty nights on the mountain, Ex 24:18; 34:28; Dt 10:10, where, as the people below worship the golden calf, Ex 32:1–10; Dt 9:8; Ps 106:19, God gives him the tablets of the Law, Ex 24:12; 31:18; 32:15; 34:1–4, 28–29, which Moses places in the Ark of the Covenant, Ex 25:16, 21; 40:20; Dt 10:2–5; cf. 1 K 8:9//2 Ch 5:10.

The events and laws recorded in Ex 19–40; Lv 1–27; Nb 1–10, are presented in connection with Sinai, for example, the meeting of Moses and Jethro, Ex 18:5, the census of the people, Nb 1:19; 26:64, the death of Nadab and Abihu, Nb 3:4; cf. Lv 10:1–7, the celebration of the Passover, Nb 9:5, the presentation of the offerings, Lv 7:38, and holocausts, Nb 28:6; cf. Am 5:25; and so forth.

Once the people have settled in their own country, Mount Zion from which "the Law will go out," Is 2:3, becomes the new Sinai, cf. Ps 68:17–18. For Paul, Sinai represents the old covenant, which is now abrogated, Ga 4:24–26. Despite the important events and legislation connected with Sinai, the Israelites seem to have forgotten its exact location. Tradition identifies it with *Jebel Musa* (2245 m).

= **Horeb** (18).

Vocabulary: *Horeb* (15): Ex 17:6; Dt (10×) 1:1, 2, 6, 19; 4:10, 15; 5:2; 9:8; 19:16; 28:69; 1 K 8:9//2 Ch 5:10; Ps 106:19; Si 48:7; Ml 3:22. *Mount Horeb,* Ex 33:6. *Horeb, the mountain of God,* Ex 3:1; 1 K 19:8.

Horeb is the name given to Sinai in the deuteronomic history and in the deuteronomic redaction of the Book of Kings. The word *Horeb* is a gloss in Ex 3:1 and 17:6, just as *Sinai,* in Dt 33:2, comes from a different source from the rest of Dt. In Si 48:7 the two names are used as parallels. It is to Horeb that the prophet Elijah goes when fleeing the wrath of Jezebel, the journey taking him forty days and forty nights; there he meets God, 1 K 19:1–19; cf. Si 48:7, at the cave or "cleft of the rock" in which Moses had hidden himself during the divine manifestation, Ex 33:22.

SINIM (1). See: SYENE.

SINITES (2), a tribe on the Phoenician coast, connected with Canaan, Gn 10:17//1 Ch 1:15.

SIN-MAGIR (1), Jr 39:3, a town in the NE of Accad.

SIPHMOTH (1), a town in the south of Judah, 1 S 30:28.

SIPPAI (1). See: SAPH.

SIRA, Sirah

1. **Sira** (3), Gr. *Sirach,* father of Jesus. See: JOSHUA 10.

2. **Well of Sirah** (1), a well near Hebron, 2 S 3:26, where Joab meets Abner and assassinates him.

SIRAH. See: SIRA 2.

SIRION (3). See: HERMON.

SISERA, Hb. *Sisra',* Gr. *Sisara.*

1. **Sisera** (19), in the prose narrative in Jg 4, lives at Harosheth-ha-goiim and commands the army of Jabin, king of Hazor, 4:2. His army with its nine hundred iron-plated chariots is defeated at the wadi Kishon by the tribes of Naphtali and Zebulun under the command of Barak, 4:7–9, 12–16; cf. Ps 83:10. Sisera dies at the hand of a woman, Jael,

in whose tent he is hidden, Jg 4:17–22. In the poem in Jg 5, Sisera is portrayed as a king and as sole adversary of Israel, 5:20, 26, 28, 32. In 1 S 12:9 Sisera is called "general of the army of Hazor."

2. **Sisera** (2), head of a family of "oblates" who return from the exile, Ezr 2:53//Ne 7:55.

SISMAI (2), a descendant of the daughter of Sheshan, of the clan of Jerahmeel, 1 Ch 2:40.

SITHRI (1), (cf. Sethur), last of the three sons of Uzziel, a Levite of the clan of Kohath, Ex 6:22.

SITNAH (1), "Accusation" (cf. Satan), name of a well that is the subject of a dispute between the shepherds of Gerar and those of Isaac, Gn 26:21. Associated with the wells of Esek and Rehoboth. Between Gerar and Beersheba.

SKULL (4). See: GOLGOTHA.

SLOPE OF ZIZ (1). See: ZIZ.

SMYRNA (2), "Myrrh," the busiest port in Asia Minor and, with Pergamum, one of the centers of emperor worship. One of the seven letters to the churches of Asia is addressed to Smyrna and warns it of coming persecution, Rv 1:11; 2:8–11. Today *Izmir* in Turkey, about 60 km N of Ephesus.

SO, king of Egypt (1), 2 K 17:14, a name unknown for any king of Egypt. Probably to be identified with *Sibe,* commander-in-chief of the Egyptian army.

SOCO. See: SOCOH.

SOCOH

1. **Socoh** (3) or **Soco** (1) **of Judah** (1), a town in the lowlands of Judah, Jos 15:35. In the time of Saul there is a concentration of Philistines at Socoh, 1 S 17:1. Under Ahaz the town is captured by the Philistines, 2 Ch 28:18. 25 km SW of Jerusalem.

2. **Socoh** (1) or **Soco** (2), a town in the highlands of Judah, Jos 15:48; cf. 1 Ch 4:18, fortified by Rehoboam, 2 Ch 11:7. About 15 km SW of Hebron.

3. **Socoh** (1), a town in Solomon's third district, 1 K 4:10. 25 km NW of Shechem.

SODI (1), a Zebulunite, father of: GADDIEL.

SODOM (48), Hb. *Sedom,* and **Gomorrah,** the two best-known towns of the Pentapolis, that is, of the five "cities of the plain" to the south of the Dead Sea, Gn 13:12; 19:29; cf. 13:10; 19:28; Jr 50:40, and the expression "Sodom and her daughters," Ezk 16:46, 53.

A frontier town of the Canaanites, Gn 10:19, where Lot lives, Gn 13:12; 14:12; 19:12–15, 29; Si 16:8, and whose inhabitants are "vicious men, great sinners against Yahweh," Gn 13:13; 18:20; Is 3:9; Lm 4:6, because of their sexual perversion, Gn 19:4–11; Ws 19:17; 2 P 2:7–8; Jude 7, their pride, Si 16:8, their contempt for the laws of hospitality toward strangers, Gn 19:8, as represented by the two angels of Gn 19:1. The perversity of Sodom affects the entire population, young and old alike, Gn 19:4, to the point that it is impossible to find among them the "ten just men" who would win God's mercy on the town thanks to the intercession of Abraham, 18:32. God spares Lot, who is doubtless the only "virtuous man," Ws 10:6; 19:17; 2 P 2:7–8, and his family, Gn 19:12–16, 29, before he "rained on Sodom and Gomorrah brimstone and fire" and "overthrew these towns and the whole plain," Gn 19:24–29; Lk 17:19; 2 P 2:6, thus transforming this "garden of Yahweh," Gn 13:10, into "scorched earth, the whole land through," Dt 29:22; Ws 10:7, where stand "pillars of salt," one of which tradition has identified as the wife of Lot, Gn 19:26; Ws 10:7.

Sodom and Gomorrah stand as sad examples for two reasons:

—the catastrophe that destroyed them, Dt 29:12; Is 1:9//Rm 9:29; Is 13:19; Jr 49:18; 50:40; Am 4:11; Zp 2:9; cf. Ho 11:8;

—the sins that drew down such a punishment on these towns, and of which the chosen people in its turn becomes guilty, Dt 32:32; Is 1:10; 3:9; Jr 23:14; Mt 11:23–24; Lk 10:12, to such an extent that Jerusalem is called "Sodom" in Rv 11:8.

King of Sodom: BERA.

King of Gomorrah: BIRSHA.

SOLOMON, Hb. *Shelomoh,* "The Peaceful," see 1 Ch 22:9; cf. 1 K 5:4–5; Si 47:13, 16 (cf. Salem); Gr. *Salōmōn* (OT), *Solōmōn* (NT).

1. **Solomon** (303) **son of David** (6), king of Israel (970–931).

= **Jedidiah** (1), 2 S 12:24–25.

Solomon—perhaps a name given at his enthronement—occurs 162× in 1 and 2 K, 109× in 1 and 2 Ch, 12× in the NT.

Reign of Solomon

Born at Jerusalem, 2 S 5:14, of David and Bathsheba, who "had been Uriah's wife," Mt 1:6; cf. 2 S 11:26–27; 12:24–25, Solomon, despite the legitimate claims of his half-brother Adonijah, who is supported by Abiathar and Joab, and thanks to the intrigues of his mother and the prophet Nathan, succeeds his father David, who, "an old man now . . . made his son Solomon king over Israel," 1 Ch 23:1; cf. 29:22–23, 28; 2 Ch 1:1. He is anointed at the spring of Gihon, 1 K 1:28–40, and in order to strengthen his hold on the throne, 1 K 2:46; cf. 2:12; 2 Ch 1:1, rids himself of opposition by putting to death Adonijah, 1 K 1:52; 2:13–26, Joab his accomplice, 1 K 2:28–35, and Shimei, the only possible claimant to the dynasty of Saul, 1 K 2:36–46, and by excluding Abiathar from the priesthood, 1 K 2:26–27.

Solomon marries "Pharaoh's daughter" (daughter of Psusennis II?), 1 K 3:1; 7:8; 9:16, 24; 11:1. He offers extensive sacrifices at the old sanctuary of Gibeon and, during a prophetic dream, this beloved of Yahweh, 2 S 12:24–25; cf. 1 Ch 28:5; 29:1, receives magnificent promises, 1 K 3:4–15//2 Ch 1:3–12; cf. Ws 8:9–9:12. On the home scene Solomon reorganizes the administration of the kingdom, 1 K 4:1–6, establishes twelve districts or prefectures in Israel, 1 K 4:7–8, but gives Judah a special status, 1 K 4:19; he fortifies many towns, 1 K 9:15–19, builds up a force of chariots and horses, 1 K 10:26–29//2 Ch 1:14–17. In foreign affairs, he cultivates friendly relations with Phoenicia (Hiram of Tyre), 1 K 5:15, Arabia (the queen of Sheba), 1 K 10//2 Ch 9, Cilicia, 1 K 10:28, Ammon (marriage with Naamah, cf. 1 K 14:21). The fleet that he arms at Ezion-geber, 1 K 9:26–29// 2 Ch 8:17–18, assures him of profitable trade, cf. 1 K 10:11–12, 22. On the other hand, throughout his reign he must cope with enemies: Hadad the Edomite, 1 K 11:14–25, and Rezon the Aramaean, 1 K 11:23–24.

In the fourth year of his reign, 1 K 6:1, Solomon undertakes the building of the temple "on Mount Moriah," 2 Ch 3:1. He gets workmen and materials from the king of Tyre, 1 K 5:15–26, gains the assistance of Huram-abi, the Tyrian bronzeworker, 1 K 7:13–46, raises a levy throughout Israel for forced labor, 1 K 5:27–32; 9:15, 22 (the "sons of Solomon's slaves," Ezr 2:55–58//Ne 7:57–60; 11:3, are perhaps the descendants of the Canaanites assigned to work on the temple) with Adoram in charge of it, 1 K 4:6; 12:18, and increases taxes and duties, cf. 1 K 12:4, 9–10. The transfer of the Ark and the dedication of the temple are the occasion for a great celebration, which includes Solomon's all-embracing prayer, 1 K 8//2 Ch 5–6; cf. 2 M 2:8–11. According to the chronicler, the builder of the temple, 1 Ch 5:56; 6:17; 2 Ch 35:3; Ezr 5:11; cf. Ac 7:47, has only to carry out, 1 Ch 22:5–6; 29:1, what David had so carefully prepared, 1 Ch 22; 29:1–10. He establishes classes of priests and Levites, 2 Ch 8:14; cf. 35:4; Ne 12:45. Solomon's temple will be destroyed in 587. In addition to the temple, Solomon builds a palace for himself (thirteen years' work, 1 K 7:1; cf. 9:10), the Hall of the Forest of Lebanon, the Hall of the Throne, his private quarters, and a house for his Egyptian wife, 1 K 7:1–12. He builds the Millo or terreplein north of the City of David, 1 K 9:15, 24; 11:27.

Power, wealth, and renown cause the king's heart to change; under the influence of the women in his extensive harem, 1 K 11:1–3, he moves toward religious tolerance, cf. already 1 K 3:3, and idolatry, 1 K 11:4–8. Yahweh foretells punishment, 1 K 11:9–13; cf. Si 47:20–22. Political opposition takes shape in the person of the Ephraimite Jeroboam, son of Nebat, a man "in Solomon's service," 1 K 11:26–27; 2 Ch 13:6, and Ahijah of Shiloh expresses the hostility of prophetic circles to the king who has "forsaken" Yahweh, 1 K 11:29–39. At the death of Solomon, 1 K 11:43; Si 47:23, "the sovereignty was split in two, from Ephraim arose a rebel kingdom," Si 47:21.

Person of Solomon

Two traits mark the reign and person of Solomon in the eyes of history: glory and wisdom.

The "glory" of Solomon, which is a compound of ostentation, wealth, greatness, and fame, is summed up in these two texts: "Yahweh brought Solomon's greatness to its height in the sight of all Israel, and gave him a reign of such splendour as none that had reigned over Israel before him had ever known," 1 Ch 29:25; cf. 1 K 3:13; "In Jerusalem the king made silver common as pebbles, and cedars plentiful as the sycamores of the Lowlands," 1 K 10:27//2 Ch 1:16. When the queen of Sheba sees with her own eyes the luxury of the court at Jerusalem, it leaves her breathless, 1 K 10:1–13//2 Ch 9:1–12. On this fabulous wealth of Solomon cf. also 1 K 9:28//2 Ch 8:18; 1 K 10:24–29//2 Ch 9:13–25//2 Ch 1:14–17; 1 K 3:13; 5:14; Sg 3:7–11; Si 47:18. The stately and sumptuous character of the buildings, 1 K 6–7; cf. Qo 2, and the large harem of the king, 1 K 11:3, contribute to his prestige.

The wisdom of Solomon is proverbial: it is exemplified in the well-known "judgment of Solomon," 1 K 3:16–28; acc. to 1 K 5:10–11, "the wisdom of Solomon surpassed the wisdom of all the sons of the East, and all the wisdom of Egypt. He was wiser than any other." A number of passages recall this point: 1 K 3:6–12//2 Ch 1:8–12; cf. Ws 8:21–9:18; 1 K 5:21//2 Ch 2:11; 1 K 5:9–14, 26; 10:1–9, 23–24//2 Ch 9:1–8, 22–23; Si 47:12, 14–17. This reputation for wisdom caused the Bible to attribute to Solomon *two psalms,* Ps 72:1; 127:1, *Proverbs,* Pr 1:1; 10:1; 25:1, *Ecclesiastes,* Qo 1:1, 12, the *Son of Songs,* Sg 1:1, *Wisdom* (the Greek title of which is "Wisdom of Solomon"), cf. Ws 7–9, and, in addition, two apocryphal books, the *Odes of Solomon* and the *Psalms of Solomon.*

But Solomon's greatness should not make us overlook the forced contributions and forced labor that partially explain that greatness. Moreover, the wisdom of Solomon, much praised but largely secular in character, has another side to it; Solomon dies a man of divided spirit: "Solomon loved Yahweh," 1 K 3:3, but he also "loved many foreign women. . . . When Solomon grew old his wives swayed his heart to other gods, and his heart was not wholly with Yahweh his God as his father David's had been," 1 K 11:1, 4. Qoheleth regards all this happiness, wealth, and wisdom as so much "vanity" and "wind," Qo 1:12–2:12.

Jesus, a descendant of Solomon, Mt 1:6–7, likewise relativizes this glory of the king of Israel ("Solomon in all his regalia" was not clothed as splendidly as the lowliest flower of the field, Mt 6:29//Lk 12:27), and his wisdom as well (speaking of himself, Jesus says that "there is something greater than Solomon here," Mt 12:42//Lk 11:31).

His son and successor: REHOBOAM.

His daughters: BASEMATH 2; TAPHATH.

Solomon corrected to: SALMAH 3.

2. **Portico of Solomon** (3), a colonnade of the temple, alongside the esplanade. Jesus teaches there, Jn 10:23; the Christians of Jerusalem gather there, Ac 3:11; 5:12.

SON OF ABINADAB (1). See: ABINADAB 4.

SON OF DEKER (1). See: DEKER.

SON OF GEBER (1). See: GEBER 2.

SON OF HESED (1). See: HESED.

SON OF HUR (1). See: HUR 4.

SON OF TABEEL (1). See: TABEEL 1.

SONS OF HINNOM (Valley of the) (1). See: HINNOM.

SONS OF THE PEOPLE (Gate of the) (1), Hb. *Bene 'Am,* one of the gates of Jerusalem, probably the one most used, Jr 17:19.

SOPATER (1), Gr. *Sōpatros* (cf. Sosipater), **son of Pyrrhus, from Beroea** (1), one of Paul's companions on his return from his third missionary journey (from Greece to Syria), Ac 20:4.

Same (?) as: SOSIPATER 2.

SOPHERETH (1). See: HASSOPHERETH.

SOPHRITES (1), Hb. *Sopherim,* "Scribes" (cf. Hassophereth), Judaean clans descended from Salma and living at Jabez, 1 Ch 2:55. West of Jerusalem.

SOREK (Vale of) (1), "Rosy grape," native place of Delilah, with whom Samson falls in love, Jg 16:4. West of Jerusalem.

SORES (1), acc. to the Gr. text, a town in the highlands of Judah, Jos 15:59.

SOSIPATER, Lat. transcription of Gr. *Sōsipatros* (cf. Sopater).

1. **Sosipater** (2), a general in the army of Judas Maccabaeus, 2 M 12:19, captures Timotheus during a campaign in the country of the Tubians, 12:24.

2. **Sosipater** (1), a Jewish Christian of Corinth, a compatriot of Paul, Rm 16:21. Same (?) as: SOPATER.

SOSTHENES, Gr. *Sōsthenēs.*

1. **Sosthenes** (1), president of the synagogue at Corinth, beaten by the (Jewish? Pagan?) crowd after the proconsul Gallio's refusal to hear a case against Paul, Ac 18:17.

2. **Sosthenes** (1), a co-worker of Paul, 1 Co 1:1. Same as the preceding?

SOSTRATUS (2), Gr. *Sōstratos,* "Savior of the army," commandant of the Citadel at Jerusalem, is called, along with Menelaus, the high priest, to answer to Antiochus Epiphanes for the nonpayment of the taxes, 2 M 4:28–29.

SOTAI (2), head of a family of Solomon's slaves who return from the exile, Ezr 2:55//Ne 7:57.

SOUTH, Hb. *Negeb,* "Dry, *therefore* South."

1. **South** (10), used by Daniel to refer to *Egypt,* Dn 11:15, 29.

Kings: PTOLEMY 1–6.

2. **South** (2), Gr. *notos,* equivalent in Mt and Lk to: SHEBA 1.

3. See: NEGEB.

4. **Country of the South.** See: PATHROS.

SPAIN (3), conquered by the Romans, 1 M 8:3–4. During the winter of 57–58 Paul plans to go there, Rm 15:24, 28.

SPARTA (1), Gr. *Spartē,* 1 M 14:16, a city of Greece in the Peloponnesus. In 144, Jonathan Maccabaeus sends an embassy to the Spartans for the purpose of renewing the alliance between the two peoples, 1 M 12:2, 5–18; cf. 12:19–23. After the death of Jonathan, in 142, in a letter addressed to Simon Maccabaeus the Spartans renew the alliance with the Jews, 1 M 14:16–23. The letter of the consul Lucius, promulgating the alliance between the Romans and the Jews, is sent to Sparta, where there must have been a Jewish colony, 1 M 15:23. In 2 M 5:9 "to Sparta" represents the Gr. "to the **Lacedaemonians,"** Lacedaemon being another name for ancient Sparta. It was here that the high priest Jason went into exile and died in 168.

King: AREIOS.

SPARTANS (9), 1 M 12:2, 5–6, 20–21; 14:20, 23; 15:23, inhabitants of: SPARTA.

SPIES (Field of) (1), Hb. *Zophim* (cf. Mizpah), "toward the summit of Pisgah," Nb 23:14. In Transjordania, near Nebo.

SPRING OF JUDGEMENT (1), Hb. *En-mishpat* (cf. En-; Shephathiah). See: KADESH 1.

SPRING OF TAPPUAH (1). See: TAPPUAH 1.

STACHYS (1), "Ear of grain," a Christian of Rome, Rm 16:9.

STEPHEN (7), "Crown" (cf. Stephanas), one of the: SEVEN, a man "filled with the Spirit and with wisdom," Ac 6:3, "filled with grace and power," who "began to work miracles and great signs," 6:8, doubtless a Christian of Hellenistic origin, cf. 6:1, who wins the hatred of the Jews when they cannot match his wisdom, 6:10. Brought before the Sanhedrin, he makes an address that is a summary of sacred history, 7:1–53. His stoning under the approving gaze of the future Apostle Paul, 7:54–8:2; cf. 22:20, and his death, which resembles that of Jesus, 7:59–60, mark the beginning of a violent persecution against the Church, 8:1; 11:19.

STEPHANAS (3), (cf. Stephen), one of the earliest Christians of Corinth and Achaia, one of the rare individuals who, with his family, was baptized by Paul, 1 Co 1:16; 16:15. A very active Christian, he is probably the one who goes with Fortunatus and Achaicus to deliver the letter of the Corinthian Christians to Paul, 1 Co 16:16–18, and who brings back Paul's response, namely, the present "First Letter to the Corinthians."

STOICS (1), Gr. *Stoïkoi,* and Epicureans, whom Paul meets at Athens, are the two principal philosophical schools of this period, Ac 17:18.

STONE, Hb. *'eben,* Gr; *lithos* (cf. Ebenezer; Pavement).

1. **Stone of Bohan son of Reuben** (2), on the boundary between Judah and Benjamin, Jos 15:6; 18:17. NW of the Dead Sea.

2. **Sliding Stone** (1), Hb. *'Eben ha-Zohelet,* south of Jerusalem, near Fuller's Spring. Adonijah and his followers gather there when the question of David's successor arises, 1 K 1:9.

STRAIGHT, Gr. *eutheia,* a street in Damascus where a certain Judas lives. It is in his house that Saul meets Ananias, Ac 9:11.

SUAH (1), an Asherite, one of the eleven sons of Zophah, 1 Ch 7:36.

SUCATHITES (1), Hb. *Sukatim,* a Judaean clan descended from Salma, 1 Ch 2:55. Unidentified.

SUCCOTH, "Huts [of branches]" (cf. Secacah; Succoth-benoth).

1. **Succoth** (14), a stage in Jacob's return to Palestine, Gn 33:17 (etymology); cf. Ps 60:8. A town in Gad, Jos 13:27. Gideon punishes the people of Succoth for refusing him bread, Jg 8:5–6, 8, 14–16. Solomon has foundries between Succoth and Zarethan, 1 K 7:46//2 Ch 4:17. In the Jordan valley, probably at *Tell Akhsas.*

2. **Succoth** (1), first stage of the Exodus, between Rameses and Etham, Ex 12:37; 13:20; Nb 33:5–6. Perhaps the present-day *Tell el-Mashkhuta,* near Ismailia.

SUCCOTH-BENOTH (1), "Huts of the daughters [= sacral prostitutes?]" (cf. Succoth), an unidentified Babylonian divinity, whose worship is introduced into Samaria after the fall of the northern kingdom, 2 K 17:30. *Succoth* calls to mind the *Sakkuth* of Am 5:26.

SUD (1), an unidentified river in Babylonia, Ba 1:4.

SUKKIIM (1), Gr. *Trōglodytai,* an unidentified people who, with the Libyans and Ethiopians, serve in the army of Pharaoh Shishak, 2 Ch 12:3.

SUN, Hb. *Heres* or *Shemesh,* Gr. *Hēlios.* See: BETH-SHEMESH; HELIOPOLIS; HERES; IR HAHERES; RA.

SUPH, "Rushes, Reeds."

1. **Sea of Suph** or **of Reeds** (24). See: RED SEA.

2. **Suph** (1), in the southern part of Transjordania, Dt 1:1.

= **Suphah** (1), in Moab, Nb 21:14.

SUPHAH (1). See: SUPH 2.

SUR (1), Gr. *Sour,* possibly a dittography for Tyre (Hb. *Zor*), Jdt 2:28.

SUSA (24), Hb. **Shushan,** Gr. *Sousa.*

In addition to **Susa** (11), Est 1:1[b], 4, 8, 16, and so forth, there are references to the **citadel of Susa** (12), Ne 1:1; Est 1:2, 5; 2:3, 5, 8; 3:15; 8:14; 9:6, 11, 12; Dn 8:2, and the **people of Susa** (1), Ezr 4:9.

Capital of Elam and one of the capitals of the Persian empire, Susa is the winter residence of the Persian kings, cf. Ne 1:1 (Nehemiah, cupbearer of King Artaxerxes, lives there); Est 1:2; Dn 8:2. Susa is the scene of the events in the Book of Esther, Est 1:1[b], 5; 2:3, 5, 8; 3:15; 4:8, 16; 8:12[r], 14–15; 9:6, 11–15, 18. Today *Shush,* in Iran.

River: ULAI.

SUSANNA, Gr. *Sousanna,* Hb. *Shushân,* "Lily."

1. **Susansa** (11) **daughter of Hilkiah** (2), Dn 13:2, 29, wife of Joakim, "a woman of great beauty, and . . . God-fearing." Accused of adultery by two elders of the people who have not been able to seduce her, and sentenced to death, she is saved by young Daniel at the last moment, Dn 13.

2. **Susanna** (1), one of the women in the company of Jesus, Lk 8:3.

SUSI (1), a Manassite, father of: GADDI.

SYCHAR, a Samaritan town (1), where the well of Jacob is. There Jesus meets the Samaritan woman, Jn 4:5–6, 8, 28–30, 39–43. Perhaps on the site of the ancient *Shechem.*

SYENE (1), Hb. *Seveneh,* Gr. *Syēnē,* a town in the very south of Egypt, near the Ethiopian border, where there was an Israelite colony. The *Elephantine* of the Greeks; today *Aswan.*

The expression *from Migdol to Syene,* Ezk 29:10; 30:6, designates the northern and southern boundaries of Egypt.

= ? **Sinim** (1), a country whence Israelite exiles return, Is 49:12.

SYMEON. See: SIMEON 7.

SYMOON (1), Gr. for Hb. *Shimron Meron.* Its king is among those conquered by Joshua, Jos 12:20.

SYNTYCHE (1), a Greek name, "Chance, Encounter, Fortune" (cf. Eutychus), a Christian woman of Philippi whom Paul exhorts "to come to agreement" with Evodia. Both women "were a help to me when I was fighting to defend the Good News," Ph 4:2–3.

SYRACUSE (1), a port on the SE coast of Sicily. Coming from Malta en route to Rome, Paul stops there for three days, Ac 28:12–13.

SYRIA (15), Gr. *Syria,* probably an abbrev. of *Assyria,* translates the Hb.: ARAM 1.

SYRIAN (1), Gr. *Syros.* See: NAAMAN 3.

SYROPHOENICIAN (1), Gr. *Syrophoinikissa.* See: ARAM 1 *g.*

SYRTIS (1), very probably *Syrtis Maior,* the Gulf of Cyrene (modern Libya). The ship taking Paul to Rome tries to avoid it for fear of the shallows, Ac 27:17.

SYZYGUS (1), "Partner, Companion," an influential Christian of Philippi, Ph 4:3. Many translators take the Gr. *syzygos* as a common noun and translate it as "companion."

T

TAANACH (7), Hb. *Ta'nak* or *Ta'anak*, a former Canaanite town mentioned in Egyptian texts. Although its king is named in the list of kings conquered by Joshua, Jos 12:21, Taanach long remained independent, Jg 1:27; in the tribe of western Manasseh, Jos 17:11; 1 Ch 7:29. Barak defeats Sisera there, Jg 5:19. In Solomon's fifth district, 1 K 4:12. Assigned to Levites of the clan of Kohath, Jos 21:25 (//1 Ch 6:55, **Aner**). On the edge of the plain of Jezreel 8 km S of Megiddo.

TABBAOTH (2), "Rings, Seals," head of a family of "oblates" who return from the exile, Ezr 2:43//Ne 7:46.

TABBATH (1), a town on the left bank of the Jordan, near Abel-meholah. The Midianites flee there from Gideon, Jg 7:22.

TABEEL, Hb. *Tab'el,* "God is good" (cf. Tob).

1. **Son of Tabeel** (1), which the Masoretic text has vocalized as *Tabal,* "Good for nothing," probably an Aramaean of Damascus, a high official whom Razon, king of Damascus, and Pekah, king of Israel, propose to put on the throne of Jerusalem in place of Ahaz, who is a descendant of David, Is 7:6.

2. **Tabeel** (1), an official, probably Samaritan, of the king of Persia, a cosigner of the letter denouncing the Jews of Judah and Jerusalem to the king of Persia for undertaking to rebuild the wall, Ezr 4:7.

TABERAH (2), Hb. *Tab'erah,* "Pasture land *or* Burning," see Nb 11:1–3, a stage of the Exodus in the wilderness near Kibroth-hattaavah, one of the places where Israel indulged in lamentation, Nb 11:3; Dt 9:22.

TABITHA (2), an Aram. name, Gr. *Dorkas,* "Gazelle" (see Ophrah), a Christian woman of Jaffa "who never tired of doing good or giving in charity." She dies; Peter is called to her bedside and restores her to life, Ac 9:36–41.

= **Dorcas** (2), Ac 9:36–41.

TABOR, Gr. *Thabōr* (cf. Aznoth-tabor; Chisloth-tabor).

1. **Tabor** (7), a mountain on the border between the tribes of Issachar, Zebulun, and Naphtali (altitude 588 m). Barak assembles his troops there before attacking Sisera, Jg 4:6, 12, 14. Gideon's brothers die there in a battle against Midian, Jg 8:18. As an image of greatness and power, Tabor is compared with Carmel, Jr 46:18, and with Hermon, Ps 89:13. There was doubtless a sanctuary on the summit of Tabor, Ho 5:1; cf. Dt 33:19.

A tradition going back to the third century locates the transfiguration of Jesus on Tabor, cf. Mk 9:2–8 p.

2. **Tabor** (2), a town of Zebulun on the border with Issachar, Jos 19:22, assigned to the Levites of the clan of Merari, 1 Ch 6:62. At the foot of Mount Tabor.

3. **Oak of Tabor** (1), in the neighborhood of Bethel, 1 S 10:3.

TABRIMMON (1), "[The god] Rimmon is good" (cf. Tob; Rimmon), father of: BEN-HADAD 1.

TADMOR (2), a town in the Syrian wilderness, rebuilt by Solomon, 1 K 9:18 ([K]*Tamar;* [Q]*Tadmor*)//2 Ch 8:4. Tadmor is the *Palmyra* of the Greeks and Latins.

TAHAN (2), (cf. Hanan?), third son of Ephraim, whose descendants form the **Tahanite** clan, Nb 26:35; an ancestor of Joshua, 1 Ch 7:25.

= ? **Tahath** (2), 1 Ch 7:20.

TAHANITE (1), Nb 26:35, belonging to the clan of: TAHAN.

TAHASH (1), "Dolphin," one of the twelve sons of Nahor, brother of Abraham, born of his wife Reumah, Gn 22:24.

TAHATH, "In place of; Compensation."

1. **Tahath** (2), a stage of the Exodus between Sinai and Kadesh, Nb 33:26–27.

2. **Tahath** (2), a Levite of the clan of Kohath, an ancestor of Samuel and of Heman the cantor, acc. to 1 Ch 6:9, 22.

3. **Tahath** (2). See: TAHAN.

TAHPANHES (8), Hb. form of Egypt. "Fortress of the Black Man" (cf. Phinehas), Gr. *Taphnas,* the *Daphne* of the Greeks. A fortified town in the eastern part of the Nile Delta. Associated with Memphis, Jr 2:16; 44:1; 46:14; Ezk 30:13–18. After the destruction of Jerusalem in 587, a group of Judaeans takes up residence at Tahpanhes; among them is Jeremiah, who announces the invasion of Egypt by Nebuchadnezzar, king of Babylon, Jr 43:7–9; 44:1; 46:14; cf. Ezk 30:13.

TAHPENES (3), "She who protects the king *or* the palaces," an Egypt. title and not a proper name, explained by the Hb. title "Great Lady," which designates the queen mother; wife of Pharaoh and sister-in-law of Hadad, the Edomite prince, 1 K 11:19–20.

TAHREA (1). See: TAREA.

TALMAI (cf. Bartholomew).

1. **Talmai** (3), one of the three sons of: ANAK.

2. **Talmai** (3) **son of Ammihud** (1), **king of Geshur** (3), father-in-law of David, grandfather of Absalom, 2 S 3:3//1 Ch 3:2. After murdering his half-brother Amnon, Absalom finds refuge with Talmai, with whom he stays for three years, 2 S 13:37 (Hb. *Talmai son of* [K]*Ammihur*).

Father of: MAACAH 5.

TALMON (5), a gatekeeper, always associated with: AKKUB 2. To be identified (?) with: TELEM 2.

TAMAR, Gr. *Thamar,* "Palm tree" (cf. Baal-tamar; Palm; Palm trees).

1. **Tamar** (8), probably a Canaanite woman. Acc. to the Yahwist tradition, she is successively the wife of Er, eldest son of Judah, then, after the latter's death and in virtue of the levirate law, the wife of Onan, second son of Judah. But, upon the death of Onan, who never was willing to assure a posterity for his brother, Judah refuses to give his daughter-in-law his last son, Shelah. Tamar then disguises herself as a prostitute and is united to her father-in-law, Judah, by whom she has twins, Perez and Zerah, Gn 38:6–30; Rt 4:12; 1 Ch 2:4. She is listed among the ancestors of Jesus, Mt 1:3.

2. **Tamar** (14), full sister of Absalom, daughter of Maacah and David. Her half-brother Amnon, eldest son of David,

becomes obsessed with her and rapes her. Absalom avenges his sister by killing Amnon, 2 S 13:1–22, 32; 1 Ch 3:9.

3. **Tamar** (1), daughter of Absalom, 2 S 14:27.

4. **Tamar** (1), a town south of the Dead Sea, Ezk 47:18 (corr.), 19; 48:28, rebuilt by Solomon, 1 K 9:18 ([K]*Tamar;* [Q]*Tadmor*).

= **City of Palms** (1), where Hobab the Kenite, father-in-law of Moses, lives, Jg 1:16.

= **Hazazon-tamar** (2), occupied by the Amorites, who are conquered by Chedorlaomer, Gn 14:7. Identified with En-gedi in 2 Ch 20:2.

TAMMUZ (1), an Assyro-Babylonian divinity of the vegetation, venerated in Syria under the name of *Adoni* (Gr. *Adonis*), "the one whom women love," Dn 11:37, and referred to in Is 17:10–11 where "plants of delight" (literal translation) doubtless alludes to the *gardens of Adonis*. The worship of this god, whose death was solemnized in the fourth month (Tammuz = June–July) while the god was dwelling in the underworld, had made its way into Palestine, Ezk 8:14.

TANAATH-SHILOH (1), (cf. Shiloh), a town on the NE border of Ephraim, Jos 16:6. About 10 km SE of Shechem.

TANHUMETH (2), "Consolation" (cf. Nahum), father of: SERAIAH 6.

TANIS (2), Gr. form of: ZOAN.

TAPHATH (1), Gr. *Tabaat,* **daughter of Solomon** (1), wife of the prefect Son of Abinadab, 1 K 4:11.

TAPPUAH, "Apple tree" (cf. Beth-tappuah).

1. **Tappuah** (5), a Canaanite town in the list of kings conquered by Joshua, Jos 12:17, on the border between Ephraim and Manasseh, Jos 16:8; 17:7 **(Spring of Tappuah),** 8.

= **Tephon** (2), fortified by Bacchides, 1 M 9:50. 40 km N of Jerusalem.

2. **Tappuah** (1), a town in the lowlands of Judah, Jos 15:34. 20 km W of Bethlehem.

3. **Tappuah** (1), a Calebite of the sons of Hebron, 1 Ch 2:43. To be connected with the preceding or with: BETH-TAPPUAH.

TAPPUSH (1), a town cruelly punished by Menahem, king of Israel, for not opening its gates to him, 2 K 15:16. Text uncertain, site disputed.

TARALAH (1), a town in Benjamin, Jos 18:27.

TAREA (1), Hb. *Ta'rea',* 1 Ch 8:35, third son of Micah, a descendant of King Saul.

= **Tahrea** (1), Hb. *Tahrea',* 1 Ch 9:41.

TARSHISH, Gr. *Tarsis,* 1: "Foundry"; 2–3: "Precious Stone."

1. **Tarshish** (26), a city or land that Gn 10:4//1 Ch 1:7 connects with Javan (Ionia); some identify it with Tartessos on the SW coast of Spain, others with Sardinia; the LXX interprets it as Carthage in Is 23:1, 6, 10, 14; Ezk 27:12, 25; 38:13. However, on the basis of Gn 10:4 ("from these came the dispersal to the islands of the nations") it may be thought that Tarshish or the "daughter of Tarshish," Is 23:10, suggests "the ends of the world" (cf. Ps 19:5; 22:28; 61:3; 65:6; 67:8; Is 5:26; 24:16), a distant land, Is 23:6–7; 60:9; 66:19; Jon 1:3, famous for its wealth, 1 K 10:22//2 Ch 19:21; Ps 72:10; Is 2:16; Jr 10:9, and its merchants, Ezk 27:12; 38:13, and that it is reachable only in solidly built ships intended for long voyages, whence the proverbial expression "fleet *or* ships of Tarshish," 1 K 10:22//2 Ch 9:21; 1 K 22:49//2 Ch 20:36–37; Ps 48:8; Is 2:16; 23:1, 14; 60:9; Ezk 27:25; cf. Is 23:10. It is on one of these ships that Jonah tries to

"run away from Yahweh" instead of going to preach at Nineveh, Jon 1:3; 4:2.

2. **Tarshish** (1), a Benjaminite of the sons of Jediael, head of a family and a valiant fighting man, 1 Ch 7:10.

3. **Tarshish** (1), an officer listed with: MEMUCAN.

TARSUS (6) **in Cilicia** (2), Ac 21:39; 22:3, a "well-known city," Ac 21:39. Rebellion of the inhabitants of Tarsus under Antiochus Epiphanes, 2 M 4:30–31. Capital of the Roman province of: CILICIA; an intellectual center.

Native place of: APOLLONIUS 1; PAUL 1.

TARTAK (1), an unknown divinity introduced into Samaria by the Avvites, 2 K 17:31.

[TARTARUS], in. Gr. of 2 P 2:4, "the underworld." See: SHEOL.

TATAM (1), acc. to the Gr., a town in the highlands of Judah, Jos 15:59.

TATTENAI, satrap of Transeuphrates (4), **Shethar-bozenai,** and the authorities of the Transeuphrates region relate to King Darius of Persia the Jews who are rebuilding the temple, Ezr 5:3–17. Referring to the edict of Cyrus, who had given authorization "to rebuild the Temple of God," Darius authorizes the continuation of the work and orders Tattenai, Shethar-bozenai, and their colleagues to stop interfering, Ezr 6:6–13.

TEARS (Oak of) (1), Hb. *Bakût* (cf. Bochim), the place where Deborah, Rebekah's nurse, is buried, Gn 35:8. Perhaps identical with the *Palm of Deborah* the prophetess, Jg 4:5.

Perhaps to be connected with: BOCHIM.

TEBAH (1), "[Born at the time of a] massacre," one of the twelve sons of Nahor, brother of Abraham, born to him of his wife Reumah, Gn 22:14.

= **Tibhath** (1), 1 Ch 18:8. Location uncertain.

TEBALIAH (1), a gatekeeper, third of the sons of Hosah, a descendant of Merari, 1 Ch 26:11.

TEHINNAH (1), "Request for a favor, Supplication" (cf. Hanan), one of the sons of Eshton, a descendant of Chelub (= Caleb), 1 Ch 4:11.

TEKOA (9), Hb. *Teqoaʿ*, Gr. *Thekōe,* a town in the highlands of Judah, Jos 15:59 (acc. to Gr.); cf. Jr 6:1, Calebite in origin, 1 Ch 2:24; 4:5. Joab sends to Tekoa for "a quick-witted woman" who will induce David to call the exiled Absalom back to Jerusalem, 2 S 14:2, 4, 9. The town is restored by Jeroboam, 2 Ch 11:6. In the wilderness of Tekoa a holy war is waged by Jehoshaphat against a coalition of Ammon, Moab, and Edom, 2 Ch 20:20. After the return from the exile the people of Tekoa take part in rebuilding the wall of Jerusalem, Ne 3:5, 27. Jonathan and Simon Maccabaeus take refuge in the wilderness of Tekoa when Bacchides is searching for them, 1 M 9:33. 15 km S of Jerusalem.

Native place of: AMOS 2; IRA 2.

TEL ABIB (1), "Hill of the Ear [of Grain] *or* of the Springtime," substituted for the Accad. *Til-abubi,* "Hill of the Flood," a town in Babylonia on the river Chebar, where there is a colony of deported Jews, Ezekiel among them, Ezk 3:15. The name reoccurs in the modern *Tel Aviv,* in Israel.

TELAIM. See: TELEM 1.

TEL BASAR (2), Accad. *Tel-Baseri,* a town on the middle Euphrates, 2 K 19:12//Is 37:12 (corr. of Hb. *Telassar*).

TELEM

1. **Telem** (1), a town in the Negeb of Judah, Jos 15:24.

= **Telaim** (1), where Saul summons the people and reviews them before the campaign against Amalek, 1 S 15:4.

2. **Telem** (1), a gatekeeper, married to a foreign wife, whom he puts away, Ezr 10:24. To be connected (?) with: TALMON.

TEL-HARSHA (2), (cf. Harsha), a town in Babylonia, where a colony of deported Jews lives, Ezr 2:59//Ne 7:61.

TEL-MELAH (2), "Hill of Salt" (cf. Salt), a town in Babylonia, where a colony of deported Jews lives, Ezr 2:59// Ne 7:61.

TEMA (6), one of the twelve sons of Ishmael or Arab clans, Gn 25:15//1 Ch 1:30, associated with Dedan, Is 21:14; Jr 25:23, a people of caravaneers, Jb 6:19; Ba 3:23 (corr. of Gr. *Teman*). An oasis, cf. Is 21:14, in northern Arabia.

TEMAH (2), head of a family of "oblates" who return from the exile, Ezr 2:53//Ne 7:55.

TEMAN (13), Gr. *Thaïman,* "South" (cf. Jamin), first of the five sons of Eliphaz, called sons of Adah, the wife of Esau, Gn 36:11//1 Ch 1:36; one of the chiefs (or clans) of Edom, Gn 36:15, 42//1 Ch 1:53.

Between the wilderness of Sinai and the territory of Judah, Hab 3:3; cf. Zc 9:14. Famous for its wise men, Jr 49:7; Ba 3:22, 23 (in v. 23 some read *Tema*). A town included in the prophetic threats against Edom, Jr 49:20; Ezk 25:13; Am 1:12; Ob 9. Difficult to identify.

Native place of: ELIPHAZ 2; HUSHAM.

TEMANITE or **of Teman** (8), Gn 36: 34; 1 Ch 1:45; Jb 2:11; 4:1; 15:1; 22:1; 42:7, 9, from the land of: TEMAN.

TEPHON (2). See: TAPPUAH 1.

TERAH, Gr. *Thara.*

1. **Terah** (13), Gn 11:24; 1 Ch 1:26, a descendant of Shem and father of Abraham, Gn 11:10, 23–26//1 Ch 1:17, 26; Lk 3:34, living beyond the Euphrates and practicing a polytheistic religion, Jos 24:2. After the death of his youngest son, Haran, he leaves Ur of the Chaldaeans and sets out for Canaan, accompanied by his other two sons, Abram and Nahor and his nephew, Lot, "but on arrival in Haran they settled there," Gn 11:27–31. Terah dies at Haran, Gn 11: 32; cf. Ac 7:4. Terah is listed among the ancestors of Jesus, Lk 3:34.

2. **Terah** (2), Hb. *Tarah,* a stage of the Exodus, between Sinai and Kadesh, Nb 33:27–28.

TEREBINTH (Valley of the) (3), Hb. *'Emek ha-'Elah* (cf. Elah 1–5), place of confrontation between the Israelites and the Philistines, 1 S 17:2, 19; it is here that David kills Goliath, 21:10. Today *Wadi es-Sant,* about 20 km SW of Bethlehem.

TERESH (3), a eunuch associated with: BIGTHAN.

TERRORS (King of) (1), Hb. *Bahalôt,* Jb 18:14, a figure in Eastern (Moloch; Nergal) and Greek (Pluto) mythology, ruler of the kingdom of the dead.

TERTIUS (1), "Third," Paul's secretary, probably known to the Church at Rome, Rm 16:22.

TERTULLUS (2), an advocate who conducts the prosecution of Paul at Caesarea before Felix the governor and in the name of the Sanhedrin; he claims that the accused has disturbed the public peace and profaned the temple, Ac 24: 1–8.

THADDAEUS (2), derived from Aram. *Taddaï,* "The Courageous One"? or from

Theodotos or even from *Theudas?,* one of the Twelve. See: JUDAH 14.

THASSI (1), "The Zealous *or* The Guide." See: SIMEON 5.

[THEBES]. See: NO.

THEBEZ (4), a town about 15 km N of Shechem; the modern *Tubas.* Abimelech son of Jerubbaal besieges and captures it. But from a fortified tower in the center of the town a woman throws down a millstone that crushes the skull of Abimelech, Jg 9:50–53; cf. 2 S 11:21, 22 (acc. to Gr.).

THEODOTUS (1), Gr. *Theodotos,* "Given by God" (cf. Theophilus; Timothy; Dositheus), one of the three messengers from Nicanor to the Jews, 2 M 14:19.

THEOPHILUS (2), Gr. *Theophilos,* "Friend of God" (cf. Theodotus; Philetus), the addressee, probably Christian, of Luke's writings (third Gospel and Acts), Lk 1:3; Ac 1:1.

THESSALONIKA (5), Gr. *Thessalonikē,* "Victory of Thessaly" (cf. Andronicus), from the name of Alexander the Great's sister, the wife of King Cassander of Macedonia, who built the city. Capital of the Roman province of Macedonia from 146 B.C. A free city from the year 42 B.C. A flourishing commercial port at the inner end of the Thermaic Gulf. Many foreigners. A Jewish colony with a synagogue.

In 50, during his second missionary journey, Paul, accompanied by Silas and Timothy, preaches the Gospel there and meets with a more favorable response from the Greeks than from the Jews. The latter start a persecution of the new Christian community; Paul is obliged to leave the city for Beroea, where the Jews of Thessalonika pursue him, Ac 17:1–13; cf. Ph 4:16. After this sudden departure Paul, at Corinth, writes a *first,* then a *second letter to the Thessalonians;* Silas and Timothy join him in sending them, 1 Th 1:1; 2 Th 1:1. Acc. to some critics, 2 Th is the work of a forger. Paul doubtless passed through Thessalonika toward the end of his third missionary journey, cf. Ac 20:1, 3. At the end of Paul's life, one of his companions, Demas leaves him and goes to Thessalonika, 2 Tm 4:10. Today *Thessaloniki* or *Saloniki.*

Native place of: ARISTARCHUS; SECUNDUS.

THEUDAS (1), (cf. Thaddaeus), leader of a Jewish insurrection against the Roman conquerors, probably contemporary with the birth of Christ, Ac 5:36.

THISBE (1), a town in Upper Galilee, between Kadesh of Naphtali and Hazor, native place of Tobit, Tb 1:2.

THOMAS (11), Gr. *Thōmas,* from Aram. *Toma',* of which the Gr. translation is *Didymus,* "Twin." Called **the Twin** (3), ready to die with Jesus, Jn 11:16, whom he asks about the way to be followed, 14:5, Thomas is famous chiefly as the one who believes only what he sees, Jn 20:24–29. He is one of the group of Apostles to whom Jesus appears on the lake shore, 21:2–3. One of the: TWELVE; List, page 417.

THRACIAN (1), Gr. *Thrax* (cf. Samothrace), native of Thrace, a region between Macedonia and the Black Sea. In 2 M 12:35 Thracian cavalry in the Syrian army of Gorgias is mentioned.

THREE TAVERNS (1), Gr. *Treis Tabernai,* a way station on the Via Appia, 48 km S of Rome. Some Christians come there from Rome to meet Paul the prisoner, Ac 28:15.

THRESHING FLOOR OF THE BRAMBLE (2). See: GOREN-HA-ATAD.

THYATIRA (4), a town in Lydia in Asia Minor, native place of Lydia, a woman in the dye trade at Philippi, Ac 16:14. One of the seven letters to the churches of Asia, Rv 1:11, is addressed to the Church of Thyatira, 2:18–27, where a prophetess of the Nicolaitan sect is causing trouble, cf. Rv 2:6, 15.

[TIAMAT]. See: DEEP.

TIBERIAS (3), (cf. Tiberius), from the name of the reigning emperor, Tiberius, a city built by Herod Antipas between 17 and 22 on the SW shore of the Sea of Chinnereth. The Gospels do not say whether Jesus frequented the city. Only John mentions it, 6:23, and the Sea of Tiberias. See: CHINNERETH *b*.

TIBERIUS (1), (cf. Tiberias), *Tiberius Julius Caesar,* adopted son and successor of Augustus, a Roman emperor (14–37 A.D.). It is in the fifteenth year of his reign (27 or 28) that John the Baptist begins his preaching and Jesus his ministry, Lk 3:1.

TIBHATH (1). See: TEBAH.

TIBNI (3), **son of Ginath** (2). At the death of Zimri, he is proclaimed king by half the people of Israel, but the other party, with Omri at its head, wins the day. Tibni dies, and Omri exercises full kingship over Israel, 1 K 16:21–22.

TIDAL (2), Hb. *Tid'al,* equivalent to *Tudhalia* (a name of Hittite kings), **king of the Goiim** (2), allied with: AMRAPHEL.

TIGLATH-PILESER (6), Hb. *Tiglat-Pil'ésèr*, 2 K 15:29; 16:7, 10; *Tiglat-Pilnèsèr*, 1 Ch 5:6, 26; 2 Ch 28:20, Accad. *Tukulti-Apil-Esharra,* **king of Assyria** (12), **the great king** (1), Ho 5:13 (745–727).

Meant is Tiglath-pileser III, the real founder of the Assyrian Empire, who in his Annals lists "Menahem of Samaria" among those who pay tribute to him in 738, 2 K 15:19–20; cf. Ho 5:13. Under Pekah he invades Israel, and captures several towns, whose inhabitants he deports to Assyria, 2 K 15:29; cf. 1 Ch 5:6, 26. He agrees to protect Ahaz of Judah against the Syro-Ephraimite coalition; in return, Ahaz declares himself a vassal of Tiglath-pileser and pays him a substantial tribute. In 732 the king of Assyria captures Damascus and deports its inhabitants, 2 K 16:7–9//2 Ch 28:16, 20(?), 21. Tiglath-pileser and Ahaz meet at Damascus, 2 K 16:10–18.

= **Pul** (3), **king of Assyria** (4), an enthronement name taken by Tiglath-pileser III when he assumes power at Babylon in 729, 2 K 15:19; 1 Ch 5:26.

His son and successor: SHALMANESER.

TIGRIS (6), Hb. *Hiddeqel,* Aram. *Diqlat,* ancient Persian *Tigra,* Gr. *Tigris,* is one of the two largest rivers, Dn 10:4, of western Asia (1718 km), the other being the Euphrates to its west. With the Euphrates it provides the name of: MESOPOTAMIA. It is one of the four rivers of Paradise, Gn 2:14; cf. Si 24:25. Tobias and Raphael camp beside the Tigris, Tb 6:1–2. There Daniel has his vision of the man dressed in linen, Dn 10:4. See also Jdt 1:6.

Cities on the Tigris: ASSYRIA 1; NINEVEH.

TIKVAH, "Hope."

1. **Tikvah** (1) = **Tokhath** (1), father of: SHALLUM 7.

2. **Tikvah** (1), father of: JAHZEIAH.

TILON (1), Hb. [K]*Tolôn,* a Judaean, one of the sons of Shimon, 1 Ch 4:20.

TIMAEUS (1). See: BARTIMAEUS.

TIMNA, Timnah, Hb. 1–2: *Timna';* 3–4: *Tinnah* (cf. Timnath; Timnath-heres; Timnath-serah).

1. **Timna** (3), is, acc. to the Yahwist tradition, on the one hand the concubine of Eliphaz, son of Esau, and mother of Amalek, Gn 36:12, and on the other the sister of Lotan, son of Seir, Gn 36:22// 1 Ch 1:39.

2. **Timna** (3), sixth son of Eliphaz, son of Esau, acc. to 1 Ch 1:36, a leader (or clan) of Esau or Edom, Gn 36:40; 1 Ch 1:51.

3. **Timnah** (4), a town in the highlands of Judah, Jos 15:57. It is on the road to Timnah, where he is going for the sheepshearing, that Judah lies with his daughter-in-law Tamar, Gn 38:12–14. 15 km W of Bethlehem.

4. **Timnah** (8), a town in Dan, Jos 19:43 (corr. of Hb. *Timnata*), on the border of Judah, Jos 15:10. Samson marries a Philistine woman there, Jg 14:1–2, 5; 15:6. Under Ahaz, king of Judah, the Philistines capture the town, 2 Ch 28:18.

TIMNAH. See: TIMNA 3–4.

TIMNATH (1). See: TIMNATH-SERAH.

TIMNATH-HERES (1), (cf. Timnah 3–4; Heres). See: TIMNATH-SERAH.

TIMNATH-SERAH (2), (cf. Timnah 3–4), **in the highlands of Ephraim** (2), a town that is the inheritance assigned to Joshua; he is buried there, Jos 19:50; 24:30.

= **Timnath-heres, in the highlands of Ephraim** (1), Jg 2:9.

= **Timnath** (1), Gr. *Thamnatha,* fortified by Bacchides, 1 M 9:50.

TIMNITE

1. **Timnites** (1), Hb. *Temni,* a Judaean clan of the sons of Naarah, Calebite in origin, 1 Ch 4:6.

2. **Timnite** (1), Hb. *Timni,* Jg 15:6, an inhabitant of: TIMNA 4.

TIMON (1), Gr. *Timōn,* one of the: SEVEN.

TIMOTHEUS. See: TIMOTHY 1.

TIMOTHY, Gr. *Timotheos,* "Who honors God" (cf. Theodotus).

1. **Timotheus** (18), Syrian military commissioner in Transjordania, 1 M 5:6, 11; 2 M 12:2, more precisely in the territory of Gilead, cf. 1 M 5:9–10, defeated by Judas Maccabaeus, who has come to make war on the Ammonites; he is first put to flight by Judas, then overwhelmed by him in Gilead, 1 M 5:34, 37–43; cf. 2 M 12:10–25. The successes of Judas against Timotheus are mentioned again in 2 M 8:30–32; 9:3. The episode in 2 M 10:24–37 (invasion of Judaea by Timotheus, who there suffers a crushing defeat and is slain by Judas' men) has no parallel in 1 M. It must be placed after Judas' campaign against the Ammonites. Some critics think that the Timotheus of 2 M 10:24, 32, 37—or the Timotheus of 2 M 8:30–32; 9:3—is a different individual.

2. **Timothy** (24), disciple and companion of Paul.

A native of Lystra in Lycaonia, son of a pagan father and a Jewish-Christian mother, Ac 16:1–4, a "good servant," 1 Tm 4:6, of a faith passed on to him by his grandmother Lois, his mother Eunice, 2 Tm 1:5; 3:14, and above all by Paul, who calls him "true child of mine in the faith," 1 Tm 1:2, 18; 2 Tm 1:2; 2:1, his dear son, 1 Co 4:17; cf. Ph 2:22, educated while still very young in the knowledge of the Scriptures, 2 Tm 3:15. It is at Lystra, during the second missionary journey (49–52), that Paul makes him a fellow worker in the apostolate, after having circumcised him "on account of the Jews," Ac 16:1–4. He will become Paul's assistant, 19:22, companion, 20:4, co-worker, Rm 16:21; 1 Th 3:2, and brother, 2 Co 1:1; Col 1:1; 1 Th 3:2; Phm 1; Heb 13:23, who follows Paul in "my faith, my patience and my love; my constancy and the persecutions and hardships that came to me,"

2 Tm 3:10–11. Six letters of Paul are "signed" by Timothy as well: 2 Co 1:1; Ph 1:1; Col 1:1; 1 Th 1:1; 2 Th 1:1; Phm 1.

Timothy is young, 1 Tm 4:12; cf. 1 Co 16:10; 2 Tm 2:22, perhaps of weak health, 1 Tm 5:23. He accompanies Paul to Macedonia, cf. Ac 17:14, rejoins him at Athens, cf. Ac 17:15; 18:5, goes back to Thessalonika, 1 Th 3:2, 5, then returns to Corinth, 1 Th 3:6, where with Paul and Silas he preaches the Gospel, cf. 2 Co 1:19. During the third missionary journey Paul sends him from Ephesus to Macedonia, Ac 19:22; cf. Ph 2:19, then to Corinth, 1 Co 4:17; 16:10; at the end of the journey he again traverses Macedonia with Paul, Ac 20:4. He shares Paul's first imprisonment at Rome, cf. Col 1:1; Phm 1. When this imprisonment comes to an end, we find Timothy at Ephesus, 1 Tm 1:3, where Paul hopes to join him, 1 Tm 3:14; 4:13. When once again a prisoner at Rome, ca. 67, Paul asks Timothy to join him before the winter sets in, 2 Tm 4:9, 21, and bring the cloak Paul had left behind at Troas, 2 Tm 4:13. He tells Timothy that he always remembers him in prayer and longs to see him again, 2 Tm 1:3–4. We know nothing of the imprisonment of Timothy to which Heb 13:23 refers.

The two letters to Timothy remind him of his consecration as an Apostle, 1 Tm 1:18; 4:14, his mission as a man of God, 1 Tm 6:11, and faithful steward of the word of God, 2 Tm 2:15, that requires him to preserve the deposit of the faith, 1 Tm 6:20, show great care in the teaching of it, 1 Tm 4:16, and accept his share of suffering as a good soldier of Christ Jesus, 2 Tm 1:8; 2:3.

TIPHSAH (2), Gr. *Thapsakos,* "Ford," a town on the northern frontier of Solomon's kingdom, 1 K 5:4. In 2 K 15:16 *Tappuah* is probably to be read for Hb. *Tiphsah.* Today *Dibseh* on the Euphrates.

TIRAS (2), one of the seven sons of Japheth, Gn 10:2//1 Ch 1:5. Perhaps the ancestor of the Etruscans?

TIRATHITES (1), Hb. *Tir'atim,* a Judaean clan descended from Salma, 1 Ch 2:55. Unknown.

TIRHAKAH (2), Hb. *Tirhaqah,* Gr. *Tharaka,* **king of Cush** (2), a Pharaoh of the twenty-fifth dynasty, of Ethiopian origin (690–664). Acc. to 2 K 19:9//Is 37:9, a campaign of Tirhakah against Assyria forces Sennacherib to lift the siege of the Israelite city of Lachish.

TIRHANAH (1), a son of Maacah, the concubine of Caleb, 1 Ch 2:48.

TIRI-A (1), third of the sons of Jehallelel, a clan connected with Caleb, 1 Ch 4:16.

TIRZAH, Gr. *Thersa,* "Pleasure" (cf. Rizia?).

1. **Tirzah** (4), Nb 26:33; 27:1; 36:11; Jos 17:3, in Manasseh, one of the daughters of: ZELOPHEHAD.

To be compared with the following.

2. **Tirzah** (14), a former Canaanite town whose king is named among the kings conquered by Joshua, Jos 12:24. In Manasseh (see the preceding). After Shechem, Tirzah becomes the capital of the kingdom of Israel (cf. Sg 6:4: "beautiful as Tirzah"?): residence of Jeroboam I, 1 K 14:17, of Baasha, 15:21, 33—who is buried there, 1 K 16:6—of Elah, who is assassinated there, 16:8–9, of Zimri, who dies there in his burning palace after only a seven-day reign, 16:15, 17–18, of Omri, who reigns there for six years or until the foundation of Samaria, the new capital, 16:23. Tirzah is the place where Menahem begins the coup d'etat that brings him to the throne, 2 K 14:14, 16. Today *Tell Fari'a,* 10 km NE of Shechem.

TISHBE (1), acc. to the Gr. a town in Gilead, 1 K 17:1. Native place of: ELIJAH 1.

TISHBITE (6), 1 K 17:1; 21:17, 28; 2 K 1:3, 8; 9:36, a native of: TISHBE.

TITANS (1), Gr. *Titanes,* Jdt 16:8, where they are paralleled with "giants."

In the LXX *Titans* translates *Rephaim* in 2 S 5:18, 22. In Greek mythology the Titans are famous for their struggle against Zeus.

See: ANAK; GOLIATH; NEPHILIM; REPHAIM.

TITUS, Gr. *Titos.*

1. **Titus Manius** (1). See: MANIUS.

2. **Titus** (13), a Christian of pagan origin, Ga 2:3, whom Paul speaks of as "true child of mine in the faith that we share," Tt 1:4, who is his "colleague and fellow worker," 2 Co 8:23, and at the same time a beloved "brother," 2:13; 7:6, a generous Apostle, 7:13; 8:16, and a selfless one, 12:18. He accompanies Paul to the "Council" of Jerusalem, Ga 2:1. He is sent to Corinth and, on returning to Paul in Macedonia, gives an account of the welcome he received and of the success of his mission, 2 Co 7:6–15. Paul commissions him to conduct the collection at Corinth, 8:6, 16–23; 12:18. Later on, Paul sends him to Crete to complete the organization of the Church, Tt 1:5, then asks him in a letter (Tt) to join him at Nicopolis, where Paul intends to spend the winter, Tt 3:12. From Rome, where he is a prisoner, Paul sends Titus to Dalmatia, 2 Tm 4:10.

TIZITE (1), *from Tiz* or *Toz?* Place unidentified. Native place of: JOHA 2.

TOAH (1). See: TOHU.

TOB (4), "Good" (cf. Abitub; Ahitub; Tabeel; Tabrimmon; Tobijah; Tobias; Tobiel; Tobit). It is to the **land of Tob** that Jephthah flees, and it is there that the elders of Gilead seek him out when they are attacked by the Ammonites, Jg 11:3, 5. Some mercenaries from Tob are enlisted in the Ammonite army during the war against David, 2 S 10:6, 8. North of the Jabbok? In northern Transjordania, *et-Taiyibeh?*

[TOBIADS], a Jewish family that governs Ammanitis or the territory between Amman and the Jordan, known as the land of Tobiah. See: TOBIJAH 6.

Belonging to this family: HYRCANUS 1; JOHN 14; TOBIJAH 4–5.

TOBIAH. See: TOBIJAH.

TOBIAS. See: TOBIJAH.

TOBIEL (1), "God is good" (cf. Tob), a Naphtalite, father of Tobit and grandfather of Tobias, Tb 1:1; cf. 1:8.

TOBIJAH, Tobiah, Tobias, "Yah is good," Gr. *Tob(e)ia(s)* (cf. Tob. See Mehetabel).

1. **Tobijah** (1), one of the eight Levites sent by King Jehoshaphat with two priests and five officers to instruct the towns of Judah in the Law, 2 Ch 17:8.

2. **Tobijah** (2), one of the exiles who returns from Babylon to Jerusalem and proves especially generous, Zc 6:10, 14.

3. **Tobiah** (2), head of a family whose sons on returning from the exile cannot prove their authentic Israelite origin, Ezr 2:60//Ne 7:62.

4. **Tobiah** (13), called **the Ammonite** (3), Ne 2:10, 19; 3:35, because of his role as governor of the Ammonite territory, but in fact a Jew. With Sanballat, governor of Samaria, and Geshem, governor of the Arab federation of Kedar, he tries to obstruct the rebuilding of the wall of Jerusalem that Nehemiah has undertaken, Ne 2:10, 19–20; 3:33–35. The vigilance of Nehemiah frustrates their plans and threats: an attack on the

city, 4:1–3, attempts on Nehemiah, calumnies, 6:1–14. Tobiah has allies among the powerful of Judah—he is son-in-law of Shechaniah, son of Arah; his son Jehohanan is married to the daughter of Meshullam, son of Berechiah, 6:17–19—and even among the priests, 13:4–8.

5. **Tobias** (1), of the family of the preceding, father of: HYRCANUS 1.

6. **Tubians (among the)** (1), literally "in the [places] of Tobiah," that is, in Ammanitis or the territory between Amman and the Jordan, governed by the Jewish family of the Tobiads. Some Jews are massacred there, and their wives and children deported, 1 M 5:13. Judas launches a campaign against the Tubian Jews, 2 M 12:17. Dositheus, a Tubian cavalryman (corr. of Gr. *Bakēnor*), wins fame in Idumaea, 2 M 12:35.

7. **Tobias** (43) **son of Tobit** (2), Tb 3:17; 9:5, and Anna, 1:9, 20; 2:1. One Pentecost he tells his father that a murdered Jew is lying unburied in the marketplace, 2:1–3. Tobit, grown old, gives his son advice on how to live his life, 4:1–19, and sends him to Gabael in Media to recover a sizable amount of money left in Gabael's care, 4:20; cf. 1:14; 4:1. Tobias sets out with the angel Raphael; a long and eventful journey brings them, after an encampment on the banks of the Tigris (catch of a fish with miraculous powers), to Ecbatana and the home of Raguel, a cousin of Tobit, 5:1–7:9. Tobias marries Sarah, daughter of Raguel, 8:4–8. After the wedding Tobias and Sarah return to Nineveh, 9:1–10:13. Tobias again sees his father (whose blindness he cures) and mother, 11. After the death of his parents he returns to Ecbatana, where he dies at the age of 117, after having "had the opportunity of rejoicing over the fate of Nineveh," 14:14–15.

Son of: TOBIT.

TOBIT (27), Gr. *Tōbeit* or *Tōbit* (cf. Tob), a Naphtalite, Tb 1:1, father of Tobias.

Tobit is the principal hero of the "tale of Tobit," Tb 1:1; cf. 14:1, which opens with an autobiographical narrative, 1:3–3:6. Tobit describes himself as an Israelite from Naphtali in Galilee, a witness to the split of the ten tribes from the house of David, 1:4, a man faithful to the observances of the Law and especially to the practice of good works, 1:3, 5–8; cf. 14:1, married to Anna, by whom he has one son, 1:9; cf. 6:15, deported to Assyria with his tribe, 1:3, 10. His fidelity to God wins him the favor of "Shalmaneser," then persecution from "Sennacherib," 1:12–13, 15–20. Having become blind as a result of his zeal in burying the dead, 2:1–10; 7:7; 14:2, he endures the sarcasms of his wife, Anna, 2:14; 3:6.

Chapter 4 begins a narrative in the third person. Tobit, who has "come to the point of praying for death," 4:1–2, passes on to his son, Tobias, the principles of ancestral wisdom, 4:3–20; cf. 14:8, 11, recommends to him in particular that he marry someone who shares the blood of his fathers, 4:12–13; cf. 6:16–18, and decides to send him to Media to recover a sum of money left with Gabael, 4:1, 20; cf. 1:14. After approving of Azariah/Raphael as a guide for his son, Tobit sends them on their way, despite the objections of his wife, Anna, 5:1–22. Their journey takes them to Ecbatana and the home of Raguel, a cousin of Tobit, 9:6; cf. 6:11–12, 18; 7:2–5. Tobit counts the days, 10:1, finding that his son's absence is lasting too long. The latter finally reaches Nineveh and restores his father's sight, 11:1–15. Tobit gives his daughter-in-law, Sarah, a joyous welcome, 11:16–18, and Azariah reveals that he is in fact the angel Raphael, 12. Canticle of Tobit in praise of Zion, 13:1–14:1. Tobit "died in peace when he was a hundred and twelve years old," after having foretold the destruction of Nineveh and the exaltation of Jerusalem, and having given his son his final advice, 14:1–11.

TOCHEN (1), a town of Simeon, 1 Ch 4:32 (//Jos 19:7, *Ether*).

TOGARMAH (2), connected with Gomer (probably the Cimmerians) by the priestly tradition, Gn 10:3//1 Ch 1:16.

= **Beth-togarmah** (2), which sells "horses, chargers, mules" at Tyre, Ezk 27:14. With Gomer, an ally of Gog, Ezk 38:6. A region in northern Upper Mesopotamia, perhaps *Armenia.*

TOHU (1), an Ephraimite, an ancestor of Samuel, 1 S 1:1.

= **Toah** (1), an ancestor of Samuel, said to be a descendant of Levi, of the clan of Kohath, in 1 Ch 6:19 (//1 Ch 6:11, *Nahath*).

TOKHATH (1). See: TIKVAH 1.

TOLA, Hb. *Tola',* "Vermilion."

1. **Tola** (5), first of the four sons of Issachar, Gn 46:13//1 Ch 7:1, whose descendants form the **Tolaite** clan, Nb 26:24. Six sons of Tola are listed in 1 Ch 7:2.

2. **Tola son of Puah son of Dodo** (1), an Issacharite, from Shamir in the highlands of Ephraim, one of the "lesser" judges, Jg 10:1.

TOLAD (1). See: ELTOLAD.

TOLAITE (1), belonging to the clan of: TOLA 1.

TOPHEL (1), in the Arabah, Dt 1:1. Today probably *Tafileh,* SE of the Dead Sea.

TOPHETH (10), a word whose vocalization is borrowed from Hb. *boshet,* "shame" (see Astarte). The original word is perhaps *Tapheth,* "furnace," cf. Is 30:33. Topheth, in the Valley of Hinnom, at the gates of Jerusalem, is the place where children are sacrificed by fire in honor of Molech, 2 K 23:10; Jr 7:31–32; 19:6, 11–14. This type of sacrifice was practiced by Ahaz and Manasseh, kings of Judah, 2 K 16:3; 21:6.

TOU (4), Hb. *To'û,* 1 Ch 18:9–10, *To'i,* 2 S 8:9–10, **king of Hamath** (2), sends his son Hadoram to congratulate David on his victory over their common enemy, Hadadezer, king of Zobah, 2 S 8:9–10//1 Ch 18:9–10.

TOWER OF THE FLOCK (1). See: MIGDAL-EDER.

TRACHONITIS (1), from Gr. *trachōn,* "rocky soil." A region of volcanic rock located E of Galilee, NE of the Decapolis, and S of Damascus. At the time when John the Baptist begins his preaching, Philip is tetrarch of Trachonitis and Ituraea, Lk 3:1.

TRANSEUPHRATES, Hb. *'Ebèr (ha-) Nahar,* "Beyond the River [Euphrates]."

1. **Transeuphrates [Western]** (22), a satrapy of the Persian Empire, comprising the territory from the Euphrates to the Mediterranean and from the mountains of Cilicia to the wadi of Egypt, Ezr 4:10–20; 6–8; 7:25. The chronicler mentions its treasurers, Ezr 7:21, and governors, 8:36; Ne 2:7, 9; 3:7. A late addition to 1 K 5:4 uses "Transeuphrates" to signify the kingdom of Solomon. In 1 M 11:60 the Transeuphrates that Jonathan traverses is, in fact, Coele-Syria.

2. **[Transeuphrates, Eastern].** The phrase "beyond the River" (8) in Jos 24:2–3, 14–15; 2 S 10:16//1 Ch 19:16; 1 K 14:15, refers to: MESOPOTAMIA, and in Is 7:20 refers to: ASSHUR 1.

[TRANSJORDANIA]

1. **[Eastern Transjordania].** See: JORDAN 3.

2. **[Western Transjordania** or **Cisjordania].** See: JORDAN 4.

TRIPOLIS (1), "Three Cities": a conglomeration of Tyre, Sidon, and Aradus (cf. Pentapolis), a maritime city on the Phoenician coast between Byblos and Aradus. Demetrius, son of Seleucus, debarks there in the spring of 161 after his escape from Rome, 2 M 14:1//1 M 7:1.

TROAS (6), (*Alexandria of*) *Troas,* a harbor on the NE coast of the Aegean Sea, 15 km from ancient Troy. A Roman colony since the time of Augustus, in the province of Asia.

During his second missionary journey Paul has a vision there of a Macedonian who calls upon him to come over into Europe; he immediately takes ship for Macedonia with Silas and Timothy, Ac 16:8–11. During his third journey, after a stay at Ephesus, Paul stops there a first time in the hope of meeting Titus, 2 Co 2:12–13, then a second time at the end of this journey, when he stays for a week: on "the first day of the week," at a gathering of the community, Paul restores a young man, Eutychus, to life, Ac 20:5–12. Paul will return at least once more to Troas, 2 Tm 4:13.

TROGYLLIUM (1), a city in Asia Minor, S of Ephesus and opposite Samos. A port of call for Paul on his return from his third missionary journey, Ac 20:15.

TROPHIMUS (3), Gr. *Trophimos,* "Nourishing, Fruitful, Robust," **from Asia** (1), an **Ephesian** (1), a companion of Paul from Macedonia to Jerusalem (at the end of the third missionary journey), Ac 20:4; 21:29, and later at Miletus, where Paul leaves him ill, 2 Tm 4:20.

TRYPHAENA (1), Gr. *Tryphaina,* and **Tryphosa,** perhaps two sisters, Christian women of Rome, Rm 16:12.

TRYPHO (20), "Debauched," a surname of *Diodotus,* king of Syria (142–138).

A former supporter of Alexander Balas and tutor to the latter's son, Antiochus VI, 1 M 11:39–54, Trypho makes war on Demetrius II and captures Antioch, where he establishes Antiochus, 1 M 11:55–56. But "Trypho's ambition was to become king of Asia, assume the crown, and overpower King Antiochus," 1 M 12:39. Uneasy at the growing power of Jonathan Maccabaeus, Trypho sets a trap for him by enticing him to Ptolemais and taking him prisoner there, 12:41–49. Gathering a great army, 13:1, he prepares to invade Judaea, 13:12. Trypho proposes to Simon an exchange of Jonathan for two of the latter's sons as hostages and a sum of money, but he does not surrender the prisoner; after being repulsed from Judaea, he puts Jonathan to death at Baskama, 13:12–24, then treacherously kills Antiochus VI, "assuming the crown of Asia, and brought great havoc on the country," 13:13–34. Trypho is besieged in Dor by Antiochus VII, 15:10–14, 25, but manages to escape, 15:37–39.

TRYPHOSA (1), Gr. *Tryphōsa.* See: TRYPHAENA.

TUBAL (8), (cf. Tubal-cain), a people and country of Asia Minor (Cilicia?). Always associated with: MESHECH 1.

TUBAL-CAIN (2), (cf. Tubal; Cain), son of Lamech and Zillah, brother of Naamah, and "the ancestor of all metalworkers, in bronze or iron," Gn 4:22.

TUBIANS (2), 2 M 12:17, 35, from the land of: TOBIJAH 6.

TURTLEDOVE (1), Hb. *Yemimah,* the first of the three daughters who are born to Job after his trials and to whom he gives a share in the inheritance, Jb 42:14.

TWELVE (The) (26). This number, with its allusion to the twelve tribes of: ISRAEL *b,* cf. Mt 19:28, refers to the group of disciples chosen by Jesus and also called Apostles. They are the foundation of the new Jerusalem, Rv 21:12–14.

Used as a substantive: 26×, with 10× in Mk (3:16; 4:10; 6:7; 9:35; 10:32; 11:11; 14:10, 17, 20, 43), 6× in Lk (8:1; 9:1, 12; 18:31; 22:3, 47), 4× in Mt (20:17; 26:14, 20, 27), 4× in Jn (6:67, 70–71; 20:24); Ac 16:2, and 1 Co 15:5. Of these 26 occurrences, 8 mention Judas the betrayer as *one of the Twelve.*

Four lists of the Twelve: Mt 10:2–4; Mk 3:16–19; Lk 6:13–16; Ac 1:13, 25–26. Each list has three groups of four Apostles (always the same ones). The first man named in each group (Peter, Philip, and James, son of Alphaeus) does not vary from one list to another, but the order of the other members can change within each group (but in the first group, Mt = Lk; in the second, Mk = Lk; in the third, Mt = Mk). Judas is always at the end of the list; in Ac he is replaced by Matthias.

See: List, page 417.

TWIN (3), Gr. Didymos, Jn 11:16; 20:24; 21:2. See: THOMAS.

TWINS (1), Gr. *Dioskouroi,* "Sons of Zeus" (cf. Zeus), Castor and Pollux, protectors of sailors. Ac 28:11 speaks of an Alexandrian ship whose figurehead was the Twins.

TYCHICUS (5), Gr. *Tychikos,* "Fortuitous" (cf. Eutychus), a traveling companion of Paul (from Macedonia to Jerusalem), Ac 20:4, his "loyal helper," and delegate to the churches of Ephesus, Ep 6:21–22; 2 Tm 4:12, Colossae, Col 4:7–8, and perhaps Crete, Tt 3:12.

TYRANNUS (1), "Tyrant," perhaps a professor of rhetoric at Ephesus who lends or rents his lecture hall to Paul after the latter has broken with the Jewish community of the city, Ac 19:9–10.

TYRE (57), Hb. *Zor,* "Rock" (cf. Zur), Gr. *Tyros.*

a. **Tyre,** a famous Phoenician city that derives its name from the rocky island on which it is located, Ezk 26:4–5, 14; cf. 27:3–4, 32.

Because of its "mighty [position] on the sea," Ezk 26:17, "standing at the edge of the sea," Ezk 27:3, and its extensive trade, which is the source of great wealth, Is 23:3; Ezk 27:3, 9, 12–25; 28:4–5, 13, 16; Zc 9:3; cf. Ps 45:12 (*daughter of Tyre*); Ne 13:16; 2 M 4:32; Ac 12:20, Tyre is compared to "a ship perfect in beauty," Ezk 27:3–9. Good relations exist between Tyre and Israel from the time of David and Solomon, who are friends of Hiram of Tyre, 2 S 5:11//1 Ch 14:1; 1 K 5:15–16; 9:12–14; cf. Am 1:9. These relations are strengthened by the marriage of Ahab with a Tyrian princess, Jezebel, 1 K 16:31. Nonetheless, the impregnable city's sudden and spectacular fall is predicted by the prophets, Is 23; Ezk 26–28; cf. 29:18; Jr 47:4, because it sought to ensnarl Israel in alliances disapproved by Yahweh and because it rejoiced at the fall of Jerusalem, Ezk 26:2; cf. Ps 83:8; Am 1:9–10. But Tyre regains its prosperity, Is 23:17–18, and it is won over to hellenism in the time of the Maccabees, 2 M 4:18; cf. 4:44, 49.

Paul stops for seven days with the Christians of Tyre during his third missionary journey, Ac 21:3–7.

b. **Tyre and Sidon** (21). When named together, the two cities designate first of all a region, namely, the Phoenician coast, 2 S 24:6–7; 1 Ch 22:4; Ezr 3:7; Jdt 2:28; 1 M 5:15; Is 23:1–12; Jr 47:4; Ezk 27:8; Jl 4:4; Zc 9:2–3; Ac 12:20, whose kings are sometimes called kings of Tyre, 2 S 5:11, sometimes kings of the Sidonians, 1 K 16:31, sometimes kings of Tyre and Sidon, Jr 25:22; 27:3.

In the Gospels the expression "Tyre and Sidon," a pagan land to which Jesus journeys, Mk 7:31, has a theological significance: it underscores the opposition between Canaan—of which the Phoenicians are a part, Gn 10:15; cf. Mt 15: 21–22—and the house of Israel, Mt 15: 24, between the pagans and the chosen people. In responding to the request of a pagan woman, Jesus is saying that his message, though addressed first of all to the Jews, Mt 10:5–6; 15:24; looks also to the pagans, Mt 15:21–28//Mk 7:24–30, who are more receptive to the word, Mk 3:8//Lk 6:17, and the miracles of Jesus, Mt 11:21–22//Lk 10:13–14, than are the inhabitants of the Holy Land.

King of Tyre: HIRAM 1.
Local god: MELKART.
Tyrian: HIRAM 2.
See: LADDER OF TYRE.

TYRIAN (8), Hb. *Zori,* Gr. *Tyrios,* 1 K 7:14; 1 Ch 22:4; 2 Ch 2:13; Ezr 3:7; Ne 13:16; 2 M 4:49; Ac 12:20, an inhabitant of: TYRE.

U

UCAL (1), Hb. *'Ukal,* son or protégé of Agur?, Pr 30:1. Instead of *Ucal* it is possible to read "I am exhausted."

UEL (1), Hb. *'U'el,* an Israelite of the sons of Bani, married to a foreign wife, whom he puts away, Ezr 10:34.

ULAI (2), Hb. *'Ulai,* a river at Susa. In a vision of Daniel, Dn 8:2, 16. Compare with: HYDASPES.

ULAM, Hb. *'Ulam.*

1. **Ulam** (2), a Manassite, a descendant of Machir, 1 Ch 7:16, father of Bedan, 7:17.

2. **Ulam** (2), a Benjaminite, a descendant of King Saul, firstborn of Eshek. His sons are bowmen, 1 Ch 8:39–40.

ULLA (1), Hb. *'Ulla',* an Asherite, father of three sons, 1 Ch 7:39–40.

UNLOVED (2), Hb. *Lo-ruhamah* (cf. Jeroham), a symbolic name, which the prophet Hosea gives to his daughter born to Gomer, Ho 1:6, 8. This name will later be changed to "Beloved," *Ruhamah,* Ho 2:3.

UNNI (2), Hb. *'Unni,* a Levite gatekeeper in the service of the Ark, 1 Ch 15:18, a player of the keyed harp, 15:20.

UNNO (1), a Levite cantor who returns from the exile in the time of Jeshua, Ne 12:9.

UPPER (Gate), Hb. *ha-'Elyôn.*

1. **Upper Gate** (2), a gate of the Jerusalem temple, built by King Jotham, 2 K 15:35//2 Ch 27:3. Perhaps identical with "the Gate of Benjamin, the upper gate leading into the Temple of Yahweh," where Jeremiah is put into the stocks, Jr 20:2.

2. **Upper Gate** (1). See: GUARDS.

UPPER CILICIA, UPPER EGYPT, UPPER GALILEE, UPPER MESOPOTAMIA. See: CILICIA; EGYPT; GALILEE; MESOPOTAMIA.

UR. 1: Accad. *Uru;* 2: Hb. *'Ur,* "Light" (cf. Achior; Jair 1–3; Shedeur; Uri; Uriah; Uriel).

1. **Ur of the Chaldaeans** (4), native place of the family of Abraham, Gn 11:28, in Lower Mesopotamia. Abraham leaves Ur for the land of Canaan, Gn 11:31; 15:7; Ne 9:7.

= **Chaldaea** (1), lit. *Land of the Chaldaeans,* which Abraham leaves in order to settle at Haran, Ac 7:4.

2. **Ur** (1), 1 Ch 11:35, father of: ELIPHELET.

URBAN (1), Gr. *Ourbanos,* a Roman name, a Christian and active member of the Church of Rome, Rm 16:9.

URI, Hb. *'Uri,* "My Light" (cf. Ur 2).

1. **Uri** (6), a Judaean, a son of Hur, 1 Ch 2:20, and father of: BEZALEL.

2. **Uri** (1), father of: GEBER 1.

3. **Uri** (1), a gatekeeper, married to a foreign wife, whom he puts away, Ezr 10:24.

URIAH, Hb. *'Uriyyah, 'Uriyyahu,* "Yah is my light," Gr. *Ouria(s)* (cf. Ur 2).

1. **Uriah** (26) **the Hittite** (10), one of David's champions, 2 S 23:39//1 Ch 11:41. While Uriah is taking part in the siege of Rabbah of the Ammonites, King David seduces his wife Bathsheba, who becomes pregnant. When summoned back to Jerusalem by the king, Uriah refuses to go home to his wife while Joab and the bodyguard camp in the open fields. At David's orders, Uriah is placed in the front line at Rabbah and dies there, betrayed by his leaders, 2 S 11; 12:9; 1 K 15:5.

Husband of: BATHSHEBA.

2. **Uriah** (6), leader of the priests at Jerusalem, a contemporary of the prophet Isaiah, who chooses him as a witness to the writing down of Maher-shalal-hash-baz, Is 8:2. At the bidding of King Ahaz he builds at Jerusalem an altar modeled on that at Damascus and henceforth offers sacrifices on it, 2 K 16:10–11, 15–16.

3. **Uriah** (3) **son of Shemaiah, from Kiriath-jearim** (1), a prophet whose oracles against Jerusalem and Judah cause him to be pursued by King Jehoiakim to Egypt, where he had taken refuge. He is brought back to Jerusalem and executed, and his body is thrown into the common burying ground, Jr 26:20–23.

4. **Uriah** (3), father of the priest: MEREMOTH 1.

5. **Uriah** (1), a lay notable, stands on Ezra's right during the solemn reading of the Law, Ne 8:4.

URIEL, Hb. *'Uri'el,* "God is my light" (cf. Ur 2).

1. **Uriel** (1), a Levite of the clan of Kohath, an ancestor of Samuel acc. to 1 Ch 6:9.

2. **Uriel** (2), a Levite official of the clan of Kohath, takes part in the transferral of the Ark under David, acc. to 1 Ch 15:5, 11.

3. **Uriel from Gibeah** (1), 2 Ch 13:2, father of Micaiah. See: MAACAH 9.

URUK (1). See: ERECH.

UTHAI, Hb. *'Utai.*

1. **Uthai son of Ammihud son of Omri son of Imri son of Bani** (1), a Judaean of the clan of Perez, lives in Jerusalem after the exile, 1 Ch 9:4.

2. **Uthai son of Zabud** (1)—"son of" is added acc. to the Gr. of 3 Esdras 8:40; Hb. has *and Zabbud* ([K]*Zabud;* [Q]*Zaccur*)—an *Israelite of the sons of* Bigvai, returns from the exile with Ezra, Ezr 8:14.

UZ, Hb. *'Uz.*

1. **Uz** (2), first of the four sons of Aram, Gn 10:23//1 Ch 1:17.

2. **Uz** (1), firstborn of the twelve sons of Nahor, brother of Abraham, born to his wife Milcah, Gn 22:21.

3. **Uz** (2), first of the two sons of Dishan, the seventh son of Seir, Gn 36:28//1 Ch 1:42. See the following entry.

4. **Land of Uz** (3), in Edom, Lm 4:21; cf. Jr 25:21, native land of Job, Jb 1:1. To be connected with the preceding entries, especially no. 3.

UZAI (1), Hb. *'Uzai,* father of: PALAL.

UZAL (3), Hb. *'Uzal,* one of the thirteen sons of Joktan, Gn 10:27//1 Ch 1:21, a tribe or region of southern Arabia, Ezk 27:19 (Hb. *Meuzzal?*).

UZZA, Uzzah, Hb. *'Uzza* and *'Uzzah* (cf. Azaziah).

1. **Uzzah** (8), son of Abinadab, from Kiriath-jearim. With his brother Ahio he leads the cart in which the Ark of Yahweh is being carried from his father's house to Jerusalem. During the transferral he dies suddenly after touching the Ark. David supposedly gave the name *Perez-uzzah,* "Uzzah's Breach," to the

place where he fell, 2 S 6:3–8//1 Ch 13:7–11; cf. 15:13.

2. **Garden of Uzza** (2), at Jerusalem a garden of the royal palace where Kings Manasseh and Amon are buried, 2 K 21:18, 26.

3. **Uzza** (1), a Benjaminite, among the sons of Ehud, 1 Ch 8:7.

4. **Uzza** (2), head of a family of "oblates" who return from the exile, Ezr 2:49//Ne 7:51.

UZZAH. See: UZZA 1.

UZZEN-SHEERAH (1), 1 Ch 7:24, unknown. See: SHEERAH.

UZZI (cf. Azaziah).

1. **Uzzi** (4), a priest, a descendant of Aaron and ancestor of Zadok, 1 Ch 5:31–32; 6:36; Ezr 7:4.

2. **Uzzi** (2), first of the sons of Tola, son of Issachar. His family provides five military chiefs, 1 Ch 7:2–5.

3. **Uzzi** (1), a Benjaminite, second of the five sons of Bela, heads of families and valiant fighting men, 1 Ch 7:7.

4. **Uzzi** (1), a Benjaminite, father of: ELAH 5.

5. **Uzzi son of Bani son of Hashabiah son of Mattaniah son of Micah, of the sons of Asaph** (1), head of the Levites at Jerusalem, Ne 11:22.

6. **Uzzi** (1), a priest, head of the priestly family of Jedaiah in the time of the high priest Joiakim, Ne 12:19.

7. **Uzzi** (1), a priest, at Nehemiah's side during the dedication of the wall of Jerusalem, Ne 12:42.

UZZIA (1). See: UZZIAH 1.

UZZIAH, Uzzia, Hb. *'Uziyya'*, *'Uziyyah*, *'Uzziyyah(u)*, Gr. *Ozias*, "Yah is my strength" (cf. Azaziah).

1. **Uzzia from Ashtaroth** (1), one of David's champions, 1 Ch 11:44.

2. **Uzziah** (1), a Levite of the clan of Kohath, an ancestor of Samuel according to 1 Ch 6:9.

3. **Uzziah** (1), father of: JONATHAN 6.

4. **Uzziah** (25), tenth king of Judah (781–740). = **Azariah** (9), in Hb. text of 2 K 14:21; 15:1, 6–8, 17, 23, 27; 1 Ch 3:12, **son of Amaziah** (1)—whom he succeeds—and of Jecoliah, 2 K 15:1–2//2 Ch 26:3; cf. 1 Ch 3:12. The double name represents perhaps a name given at birth and a name given at enthronement (see: JEHOAHAZ 2; JEHOIAKIM 1; ZEDEKIAH 4). Uzziah is a contemporary of the kings of Israel Jeroboam II, Zechariah, Shallum, Menahem (Pekahiah and Pekah?), 2 K 15:1, 8, 13, 17, 23, 27, and of the prophets Amos, Am 1:1, Hosea, Hos 1:1, and Isaiah, Is 1:1; 6:1.

Regarding his reign, the Book of Kings says only that Uzziah reconquered Elath lost under Jehoram, 2 K 14:22, "did what is pleasing to Yahweh," and "became a leper till his dying day," so that he was forced to appoint his son as coregent, 2 K 15:3–7//2 Ch 26:4, 21–23; cf. 2 K 15:34//2 Ch 27:2. The chronicler, 2 Ch 26:6–15, offers further information: Uzziah does battle especially with the Philistines and Arabs, forces the Ammonites to pay a tribute, builds numerous fortifications at Jerusalem and in the wilderness, digs wells, develops agriculture, reorganizes the army. The same chronicler, 2 Ch 26:16–20, sees a usurpation of priestly functions by Uzziah (offering of incense) as the reason for his leprosy. In the reign of Uzziah there is an earthquake, Zc 14:5; cf. Am 1:1. Uzziah (Azariah) is an ancestor of Jesus according to Mt 1:8–9.

Father of: JOTHAM 2.

Grandfather of: AHAZ 1.

5. **Uzziah** (1), a priest of the sons of Harim, married to a foreign woman, whom he puts away, Ezr 10:21.

6. **Uzziah** (1), a Judaean, father of: ATHAIAH.

7. **Uzziah** (12) **son of Micah** (1), a Simeonite, one of the chief men of the town of Bethulia, along with the elders

Chabris and Charmis, places complete confidence in Judith's plan, Jdt 6:15–21; 7:23, 30; 8:9, 28–31, 35; 10:6; 13:18; 14:6; 15:4.

UZZIEL, Hb. *'Uzzi'ēl,* Gr. *Oziel,* "God is my strength" (cf. Azaziah).

1. **Uzziel** (11), last of the four sons of Kohath, son of Levi, Ex 6:18; Nb 3:19; 1 Ch 5:28; 6:3; 23:12. His sons, who are listed in Ex 6:22; 1 Ch 15:10; 23:20; 24:24, form the **Uzzielite** clan, Nb 3:27; 1 Ch 26:23 (Hb. *Ozzielite*). Initially associated with the transferral of the Ark, 1 Ch 15:10, they are subsequently assistants to the priests in the temple, cf. 1 Ch 23:25–32; 26:23.

Father of: ELZAPHAN.

2. **Uzziel** (1), a Levite, player of the lyre, 1 Ch 16:5 (Hb. *Jeiel*).

3. **Uzziel** (1), of the sons of Heman, 1 Ch 25:4.

= **Azarel** (1), head of the eleventh class of cantors, 1 Ch 25:18.

4. **Uzziel** (1), a Levite, of the sons of Jeduthun, takes part in the purification of the temple during the reform of Hezekiah, 2 Ch 29:14.

5. **Uzziel** (1), one of the Simeonite chiefs settled in the highland of Seir, 1 Ch 4:42.

6. **Oziel** (1), a Simeonite, an ancestor of Judith, Jdt 8:1.

7. **Uzziel** (1), a Benjaminite, third of the five sons of Bela, head of a family and a valiant fighting man, 1 Ch 7:7.

8. **Uzziel** (1), a member of the goldsmiths' guild (Hb. *son of Harhaiah*), a volunteer in the rebuilding of the Jerusalem wall, Ne 3:8.

UZZIELITE (2), Nb 3:27; 1 Ch 26:23, belonging to the clan of: UZZIEL 1.

V

VALE, VALLEY. See: BERACAH 2; CRAFTSMEN (Geharashim); ESHCOL; HAMON-GOG; HINNOM; HYENAS; IPHTAHEL; JOSHAPHAT 7; KING 2; REPHAIM 2; SALT 2; SIDDIM; SOREK; TEREBINTH; WEEPER; ZEPHATHAH.

VALE OF LEBANON, Hb. *Biqʻat ha-Lebanôn* (cf. Bikath-aven), Jos 11:17; 12:7, a high valley situated between the Lebanon and Anti-Lebanon ranges, 120 km long and 12 km wide. Today the *Bekaa.* See: BETH-REHOB; COELE-SYRIA.

VALLEY (Gate of the) (4), Hb. *Gayʼ*, at Jerusalem, on the SW side of the city, leading to the Valley of Hinnom. King Uzziah fortifies it, 2 Ch 26:9. It is at this gate that Nehemiah begins and ends his inspection of the walls, Ne 2:13, 15. It is restored together with the wall, Ne 3:13.

VANIAH (1), an Israelite of the sons of Bani, married to a foreign wife, whom he puts away, Ezr 10:36.

VASHTI (1), Persian *Vahista,* "The most beautiful *or* The desired," Gr. *Astin,* wife of the Persian king Ahasuerus (= Xerxes), repudiated for refusing to present herself to the king at a banquet, Est 1:9–19, and replaced by Esther, 2:1–4, 17.

[VENUS]. See: ISHTAR.

VOPHSI (1), Lat. *Vapsi,* a Naphtalite, father of: NAHBI.

W

WADI or **River** (10), Hb. *Nahal* (cf. Nahaliel), **of Egypt** (8), theoretical SW frontier of the Promised Land (with the Euphrates as the NW frontier), Gn 15: 18; Nb 34:5; 2 K 24:7//2 Ch 7:8; Is 27:12; Ezk 47:9 (Hb. *Nahalah*), and thus the SW border of Judah, Jos 15:4, 47. Cf. Jdt 1:9.

= **Shihor** (2) **of Egypt** (1), 1 Ch 13:5, or which is "east of Egypt," Jos 13:3. Today probably the *Wadi el-'Arish,* south of Gaza.

WAHEB (1), in Moab "by Suphah and the wadi Arnon," Nb 21:15. Unidentified.

WATCH GATE

1. **Watch Gate** (1), Hb. *Miphqad,* a gate of the temple, Ne 3:31.
2. **Watch Gate** (1), Hb. *Mattarah,* probably on the eastern side of Jerusalem, not far from the temple, Ne 12:39.

WATER GATE (5), Hb. *Mayim* (cf. Abel-maim; Me-zahab), at Jerusalem, a gate of the royal palace rather than of the eastern wall, Ne 3:26. Before this gate there is a large square where the Jews gather for the solemn reading of the Law by Ezra, Ne 8:1, 3, and where they set up shelters of branches, 8:16. At the dedication of the wall, the first choir advances as far as this gate, 12:37.

WEEPER (Valley of the), Hb. *Bakût,* that is, of the balsam tree, to the N of the Valley of Hinnom, W of Jerusalem, at the juncture of the roads from the north, west, and south, Ps 84:7.

WESTERN (Sea) (4). See: MEDITERRANEAN.

WILD GOATS (Rocks of the) (1), Hb. *Ye'elim* (cf. Jael). See: ROCK 7.

WILLOWS (Wadi of the) (1), Hb. *'Arabim,* Is 15:7, on the southern border of Moab? or in the north, the *Wadi Gharba,* a tributary of the Jordan along which willows abound?

X

XERXES (36), Gr. transcription of Hb. *'Ahashverosh,* whence the Lat. and Fr. transcriptions *Assuerus,* from the Pers. *Khshajarsha,* king of Persia, **the great king** (2), Est 3:13[a]; 8:12[b] (486–465). N.B. The LXX gives this name as *Asouēros* in Ezr 4:6, as *Xerxēs* in Dn 9:1 (where Theodotion has *Asouēros*). In the Book of Esther *Artaxerxes* appears everywhere because Xerxes is confused with his successors.

The person in question is Xerxes I the Great. Acc. to Ezr 4:6, "at the beginning of the reign of Xerxes" the enemies of Judah and Jerusalem "lodged a complaint against the inhabitants of Judah and Jerusalem." It is perhaps he who is meant by the *fourth king* of Persia who "will challenge all the kingdoms of Javan," Dn 11:2; in fact, he launched an expedition against Greece in 480.

Ahasuerus is chiefly known in the Bible from the Book of Esther, where he appears as a proud and pleasure-loving despot, cf. 1:4, 8–11, "whose empire stretched from India to Ethiopia and comprised one hundred and twenty-seven provinces," 1:1; 3:13[a]; 8:12[b]; cf. 10:1, in which numerous Jews live, 3:6; 4:3; 8:12; 9:2, 20, 30. After dismissing Vashti, he chooses another queen from among the women of his harem: Esther, who is a Jew, 2:1–18, and whose cousin and tutor Mordecai uncovers a plot of two eunuchs against Ahasuerus, 1:1[m]; 2:21–23; 6:2. Ahasuerus chooses as grand vizier Haman, an enemy of the Jews who is determined not only to get rid of Mordecai, of whom he is jealous, but to destroy all the Jews in the kingdom of Ahasuerus, 3. The intervention of Esther, supported by her cousin, prevents the extermination of the Jews and wins a decree of rehabilitation from Ahasuerus, 4–8.

See: CYAXARES; DARIUS 4.

His administrators: MEMUCAN.

His eunuchs: BIGTHA; HARBONA; MEHUMAN.

Y

YAH (54), abbrev. of: YAHWEH.

YAHU. See: YAHWEH *a*.

YAHWEH (± 6800×), Hb. *Yahveh,* Gr. *Kyrios,* "Lord," proper name of the God of Israel, abbreviated to *Yah.*

a. Statistics

Yahweh is the most frequently occurring word in the Bible. The variants in the manuscripts make it difficult to establish exact figures.

Pentateuch: 1818 (Gn, 166; Ex, 400; Lv, 310; Nb, 400; Dt, 542); Jos, 223; Jg, 175; Rt, 18; 1–2 S, 469; 1–2 K, 531; 1–2 Ch, 550; Ezr–Ne, 54; Jb, 32; Ps, 690; Pr, 84; Is, 438; Jr, 708; Lm, 35; Ezk, 422; Dn, 8 (ch. 9); Minor Prophets, 483 (Ho, 46; Jl, 31; Am, 79; Ob, 7; Jon, 24; Mi, 38; Na, 13; Hab, 12; Zp, 32; Hg, 35; Zc, 130; Ml, 46). Missing from Est and Qo. In a large number of instances *Yahweh* is connected with the verbs *speak/say. Yahweh* is used about 370× in the vocative: Ps, 205; 1–2 Ch, 25; Is, 19; Jr, 26.

Yah (55) occurs in the acclamation *Alleluia,* Hb. *hallelu-Yah,* "Praise Yah!" (28): at the beginning of Ps 106; 111; 112; 113; 135; 146; 147; 148; 149; 150; at the end of Ps 104; 105; 106; 113; 115; 116; 117; 135; 146; 147; 148; 149; 150; in Tb 13:17; Rv. 19:1, 3, 4, 6—and 27× in Ex 2:15//Ps 118:14//Is 12:2; Ex 17:16; Ps 68:5, 19; 77:12; 89:9; 94:7, 12; 102:19; 115:17; 118:5, 17–19; 122:4; 130:3; 135:3–4; 150:6; Sg 8:6; Is 26:4.

The name *Yahweh,* in the forms *Yah, Yahu, Jo, Jeho,* is a component part—prefix or suffix—of many proper names: *Abijah, Azaliah, Jehoiada, Jozabad,* and so on; cf. also *Jehu.*

b. Origin of the word

In the *Yahwist* document the name Yahweh appears as early as the story of creation, Gn 2:4; Enosh is "the first to invoke the name of Yahweh," 4:26; Noah blesses "Yahweh, God of Shem," 9:26; Yahweh is the name given to God throughout the story of the patriarchs, 12:1–39:23: Abram builds an altar to Yahweh and invokes his name, 12:8; 13:4, 18; 21:33; God says to Abraham, "I am Yahweh, who brought you out of Ur of the Chaldaeans," 15:7, and to Jacob, "I am Yahweh, the God of Abraham your father, and the God of Isaac," 28:13. But the *priestly* tradition maintains that the ancestors did not know God under the name Yahweh and knew him only as El Shaddai, Ex 6:3. And the *Elohist* account in Ex 3 makes the name Yahweh the object of a special revelation to Moses and the Israelites. Two points emerge from these divergences between the traditions: the name of God has a pre-Israelite origin and was known to some of the ancient tribes as early as their nomadic period; as a result of the revelation received at Sinai, Moses gave the name a religious meaning it had not previously had.

c. Meaning

The meaning is given in Ex 3:12–15. When Moses asks the "God of the fathers" what his name is, "God said to Moses, '*I Am who I Am.* This . . . is what you must say to the sons of Israel: "*I Am* has sent me to you." ' And God also said to Moses, 'You are to say to the sons of Israel: "*Yahweh,* the God of your fathers, the God of Abraham, the God of Isaac, and the God of Jacob, has sent me to you." This is my name for all time.' " In speaking of himself, God says: "I am" (*Ehyeh*); in speaking of God, men will follow Moses' lead and say: "He is" (*Yahweh*). This story links the name of God to an ancient form of the verb *hayah,* "to be."

In saying *Ehyeh asher ehyeh,* "I am he who I am *or* I am who I am *or* I am what I will be," God is underscoring several points:

—that he *is,* in an unqualified sense, always and for ever, the God of eternity, Gn 21:33; Is 40:28; 43:12; Si 36:17; cf. Lm 5:19, the eternal Rock, Is 26:4, the king of eternity, Jr 10:10, of the ages, 1 Tm 1:17; cf. "who is, who was, and who is to come," Rv 1:4, 8; 11:17; 16:5, whence the old translation of Yahweh as "the Eternal One";

—that he is *mysterious* and inaccessible, cf. Gn 32:30; Jg 13:18; 1 Tm 6:16;

—that he *is there,* cf. Ezk 48:35, *present and acting with* his people, Ex 8:18; 17:7; 29:46; Nb 11:20; 14:9, 14, 42–43; 16:3; Dt 2:7; 7:21; 20:1; 31:6, 8; Jos 22:31; Jg 1:22; 6:13; 1 K 8:57; 1 Ch 22:18; 2 Ch 13:12; 15:2; 20:17; 32:8; Ps 46:8, 12; Am 5:14; Mi 3:11; Zp 3:17; Hg 1:13; 2:4; Zc 10:5; cf. Is 7:14; 8:8, 10, *with* Moses and subsequently *with* the leaders of the people, Ex 3:12; 4:12, 15; Jos 1:5, 17; 3:7; 6:27; Jg 6:12; 1 S 3:19; 16:18; 17:37; 1 K 1:37; 2 K 18:7; 2 Ch 15:9; 17:3.

d. Yahweh and Adonai

(In this and the following sections the different formulas are found in the Hebrew text and not necessarily reflected in the English.)

It is generally thought that the holy name of God was pronounced *Yahweh.* But, beginning with the exile, a formalistic reverence pressures the Jews into a refusal to utter the real name of God, cf. Am 6:10; 1 M 2:21. It is usually replaced by another title, *Adon* (± 450×), "The Lord," Ps 114:7; Ml 3:1; the Lord of the whole earth, Jos 3:11, 13; Ps 97:5; Mi 4:13; Zc 4:14; 6:5, the Lord of lords, Dt 10:7; Ps 136:3. *Adon* with the possessive gives *Adoni,* "my Lord," or in a plural of intensity, *Adonai. Adonai,* "Lord," which is used alone about 130×, Gn 18:3, 27, 32; Ex 4:10, 13 . . . Jb 28:28; Ps (47×); Is (23×), Dn (9×), and so forth, is also used in combination with Yahweh: either *Yahweh Lord* (5×), Ps 68:21; 109:21; 140:8; 141:8; Hab 3:19; cf. Ne 10:30; Ps 8:2, 10; Is 51:22, or especially *Lord Yahweh* (282×), Gn 15:2, 8; Is (18×), Ezk (215×). . . .

To prevent the name Yahweh (or Iahweh or Jahweh) from being uttered in the reading of Scripture, the Massoretes intercalated between the four consonants ("Tetragram") of the sacred name YHWH the vowels a-o-a (written e-o-a) of the word Adonai, whence the artificial form *Jehovah* of old translations.

The Gr. *Kyrios* translated *Yahweh* ± 6350×, and *Adonai* ± 500× in the LXX. The "Lord" of modern translations corresponds at times to *Yahweh,* at times to *Adonai.*

e. Yahweh Sabaoth

("Yahweh of the armies." See: SABAOTH.)

Primitive formula: *Yahweh God Sabaoth* (19×), 2 S 5:10; 1 K 19:10, 14; Ps 59:6; 80:5, 20; 84:9; 89:9; Jr 5:14; 38:17; 44:7; Ho 12:6; Am 3:13; 4:13; 5:15–16, 27; 6:8, 14. Cf. God Sabaoth, Ps 80:7, 15. Note the more solemn formula in Am 5:16: "Yahweh . . . the God of Sabaoth, the Lord."

Usual formula: *Yahweh Sabaoth* (263×): 1 S 1:3, 11; 4:4; 15:2; 17:45; 2 S 6:2, 18; 7:8, 26–27; 1 K 18:15; 2 K 3:14; 19:31; 1 Ch 11:9; 17:7, 24; Ps 24:10; 46:8, 12; Is 1–55 (60×); Jr (77×); Mi 4:4; Na 2:14; 3:5; Hab 2:13; Zp 2:9–10; Hg (11×); Zc (55×); Ml (24×); cf. Rm 9:29; Jm 5:4, "the Lord of hosts."

Another formula: *the Lord Yahweh Sabaoth* (20×), Is 1:24; 3:1, 15 . . . 28:22; Jr 2:19; 46:10; 49:5; 50:25, 31; Am 9:5.

f. Yahweh God

(40×), Hb. *Yahweh 'Elohim* (34×), Gn (20×) 2:4–3:23; Ex 9:20; 2 S 7:25; 2 K 19:19; 1 Ch 17:16; 28:20; 29:1; 2 Ch 1:9; 6:41–42; 26:18; Ps 73:18; 84:12; Jr 10:10; Jon 4:6; or *Yahweh ha-'Elohim* (6×), 1 S 6:20; 1 Ch 22:1, 19; 2 Ch 32:16; Ne 6:8; 9:7; or *Yah 'Elohim,* Ps 68:19.

g. The Name Yahweh

Yahweh is the name God himself uses to designate himself, Ex 3:13–14; 6:3; Is 42:8; 51:15; Jr 12:16; 16:21, as he reveals that he is love, forgiveness, justice, Ex 33:19; 34:5–7. It is the name solemnly recalled in Ex 15:3; Dt 28:58; Ps 83:19; 135:13; Is 26:13; 47:4; 48:2; 54:5; Jr 16:21; 31:35; 32:18; 33:2; 46:18; 48:15; 51:19, 57; Ho 12:6; Am 4:13; 5:8, 27; 9:6. The name Yahweh—see also the possessives *my Name, your Name, his Name*—is the eternal name, Ex 3:15; Ps 135:13, the holy name, Lv 20:2; Ps 103:1; 11:9//Lk 1:49; Is 29:13 (cf. Mt 6:9); Ezk 20:39, the glorious name, great and awesome, Dt 28:58; 1 S 12:22; 1 Ch 16:29; Ps 148:13; Is 24:15; Jr 10:6; 44:26; Ml 1:11, to be feared, Ps 102:16; sought, Ps 83:17; cf. Is 26:8; Jr 3:17, known, Is 52:6, loved, 56:6, blessed and praised, Jb 1:21; Ps 113:1–3; 135:1; 148:5, 13; in which we must trust and from which we must seek help, Is 50:10; Ps 124:8, for it is a strong tower, Pr 18:10, which must therefore be invoked, Gn 4:26; 12:8; 13:4; Dt 32:3; 1 K 18:24; 2 K 5:11; Ps 20:8. It is "in the name of Yahweh *or* by the name of Yahweh" that men utter a blessing, Nb 6:27; 2 S 6:18//1 Ch 16:2; Ps 118:26; 129:8, or curse, 2 K 2:24, anoint kings, 1 Ch 29:22; 2 Ch 9:8, take oaths, Is 48:1; Jr 12:16, do battle, 1 S 17:45, prophesy, Jr 26:9, 16, 20; 29:9. . . . The Name of Yahweh is borne by the Ark, 2 S 6:2//1 Ch 13:6, the temple, 1 K 3:2; 5:17, 19; 8:16–20, the altar, 1 K 18:32, and the people, Jr 14:9.

The Name of Yahweh is, in the last analysis, Yahweh himself, Is 30:27. Cf. Dt 12:5; 1 K 8:29, etc., and especially the unqualified use of *the Name,* Hb. *Ha-Shem,* Lv 24:11, 16.

Jesus applies to himself the "I am" of Ex 3:14 in Jn 8:24, 28, 58; 13:14; cf. Ps 102:28//Heb 13:8, and the NT gives him the divine title of "Lord." See: JESUS *b.*

h. I Yahweh *or* I am Yahweh

Three kinds of formula in the mouth of God himself recall in a solemn and emphatic way the Name revealed to Moses:

I am Yahweh! or *It is I Yahweh!:* Ex 6:2, 6, 8, 29; 12:12; 20:5; Lv 18:2–6, 21, 30; 19 (16×); 20:7, 26; 21:12; 22: 2–3, 8–9, 30–31, 33; 23:42–43; 24:22; 25:17, 55; 26:1–2, 44–45; Nb 3:13; 10:10; 14:35; 35:34; Dt 5:9; Jg 6:10; Is 27:3; 41:4, 13; 42:6, 8; 43:3, 11, 15;

45:5–6, 18–19; 48:17; 60:22; 61:8; Jr 17:10; 32:27; Ezk 5:15, 17. Cf. the short profession of faith of the priest Eli: "*He is Yahweh;* let him do what he thinks good," 1 S 3:18.

I am (*or It is I*) *Yahweh who* . . . : Gn 15:7; Ex 4:17; 15:26; 20:2; Lv 11:44–45; 20:8, 24; 21:8, 16, 23; 22:16, 32; 25:38; 26:13; Nb 15:41; Dt 5:6; Ps 81:11; Is 44:24; 45:7–8; 51:15; Jr 9:23; Ezk 12:25; 14:4, 7, 9.

You (pl.) *will know* (or *you* [sing.] *will know* or *that they may know*) *that I am Yahweh* (or *that it is I Yahweh*) *who* . . . : Ex 6:7; 7:5, 17; 8:18; 10:2; 14:4, 18; 16:6, 12; 29:46; 31:13; Dt 29:5; 1 K 20:13, 28; 2 Ch 33:13; Is 45:3; 49:23, 26; 60:16; Ezk (60×); cf. Si 36:17.

i. Yahweh, the one God

This is the essential faith professed in Judaism and formulated in the *Shema:* "Yahweh our God is the one Yahweh" or "The Lord our God is the one Lord," Dt 6:4//Mk 12:29; cf. Zc 14:9; Ps 83:19. Yahweh, "the God of Israel," Jg 5:5; cf. Ezk 3:1–6; 19:18; Dt 33:16, is the God of gods, Dt 10:17; Jos 22:22; Ps 50:1; cf. Dn 2:47; 3:90; 11:36; greater than all the gods, Ex 18:11; Ps 95:3; 96:4; 97:9; 135:5, to whom no other is comparable, Ex 8:6; 15:11; Dt 4:34; 1 S 2:2–3; 1 K 8:23; 2 Ch 6:14; 32:19; Ps 89:7–9; 113:5; Is 44:7; 46:5; Jr 10:6, the living God, 1 S 19:6; 20:21; 26:10; 29:6; Ps 84:3; Jr 10:10; 16:14–15; 23:36, the only true God, Dt 4:35, 39; 7:9; Jos 2:11; 22:34; 2 S 7:22, 28; 22:32//Ps 18:32; 1 K 8:60; 2 K 19:15, 19//Is 37:16, 20; 1 Ch 16:26, 31; 17:20, 26; 2 Ch 13:9–10; 20:6–7; 33:13; Ps 100:3; 118:27; Is 37:20; 43:10–12; 44:6–8; 45:5–7, 14, 18; Jr 10:10, 16, the jealous God, Ex 20:5; 34:14; Dt 4:24; 5:9; 6:15, who does not permit men to serve other gods, Ex 20:4; Lv 19:4; Dt 7:4, 25; 32:12; Jos 24:14–24; Jg 6:10; 10:16; 1 S 7:3–4; 1 K 11:4.

j. Yahweh God of Israel

He is the God of the people's ancestors (see: ABRAHAM *c*), the *God of the Fathers,* Gn 32:10; Ex 3:15–16; 4:5; Dt 1:11, 21; 4:1; 6:3; 12:1; 26:7; 27:3; 29:24; Jos 18:3; Jg 2:12; 1 Ch 29:20; 2 Ch (20×); Ezr 7:27; 8:28; 10:11; cf. Ws 9:1; Ac 5:30.

He is the *God of the Hebrews,* Ex 3:18; 5:3; 7:16; 9:1, 13; 10:3; cf. Jon 1:9; "Yahweh brought you out of Egypt," Ex 13:9, 14, 16; 18:1; 29:46; Jos 24:17, and so on, in order to be their God, Lv 11:45; 22:33; 25:38; Nb 15:41, to make them his people, Ex 6:6–7, a free people, Lv 26:12–13.

He is the *God of Israel,* the *Holy One of Israel.* To these formulas (see: ISRAEL *g*) must be added the expressions *Yahweh your* (sing.) *God,* Dt (237×); Ps 81:11; Is 7:11, and so on; *Yahweh your* (pl.) *God,* Dt (46×); Ps 76:12; Jr 13:16, and so on; *Yahweh our God,* Dt (24×); Ps 20:8; 94:23; Is 26:13, and so on; *Yahweh their God,* Jr 3:21; 22:9; 30:9; 43:1; 50:4, and so on; so that Israel is called the *people of Yahweh,* Nb 11:29; 17:6; Dt 27:9; Jg 5:11; 1 S 2:24; 2 K 9:6; 11:17; Ezk 36:20, and so on, the *community of Yahweh,* Nb 16:3; 27:17; 31:16, the *assembly of Yahweh,* Nb 20:4; Dt 23:2–4, 9.

k. Other titles of the God of Israel

Baal, "Master, Owner, Lord, *and therefore* Spouse," Is 54:5 (husband); cf. Ho 2:18 (Baal). See the proper names with *Baal* as a component.

Melech, "King," Is 6:5; Jr 46:18; 48:15; 51:57; Ps 98:6; 145:1; Zc 14:16–17; King of eternity, Jr 10:10; King of glory, Ps 24:7–10; Jacob's king, Is 41:21; Israel's king, Is 44:6; Zp 3:15; King of the nations, Jr 10:7//Rv 15:4; King of all the earth, Ps 47:8; great King, Ps 47:3; 48:3; Ml 1:14; Mt 5:35. See the proper names with *Melech* as a component.

See also the names with *Ab,* "Father," *Ah,* "Brother" (see: AHI), and *Am,* "Uncle, Relative," as a component part.

l. Some veiled designations of God or Yahweh

The *angel of Yahweh* (50×). In some instances, the angel of Yahweh is distinguished from Yahweh, Nb 22:22–23; Gn 16:21, but most often he speaks and acts as God himself, cf. Gn 16:10 and 16:13; 22:15–16 and 12:1–2; Ex 14:19 and 20:2. Yahweh acts through him; his name is in him, Ex 23:21.

—*He who dwells in the Bush,* Dt 33:16.

—*Another place,* Est 4:14.

—*He who has his dwelling in heaven,* 2 M 3:39.

—*Heaven,* 1 M 3:18–19, 50, 60; 9:46; 12:15; 2 M 9:4; Mt 21:25 p; Lk 15:18, 21.

—*The heavens,* Dn 4:23 (pl. in Hb.).

See: ALMIGHTY; EL; MOST HIGH; SABAOTH; SHADDAI.

YAHWEH-IS-THERE, Hb. *Yahweh shammah,* the name of Jerusalem in the future, Ezk 48:35.

YAHWEH-NISSI (2), "Yahweh (is) my banner," name of an altar built by Moses, Ex 17:15.

YAHWEH-OUR-INTEGRITY (2), a symbolic name for the Messiah, Jr 23:6, and for Jerusalem, 33:16.

YAHWEH-PEACE (1), name of an altar Gideon builds for Yahweh, Jg 6:24.

YAHWEH PROVIDES (1), Hb. *Yahweh-yireh* (cf. Haroeh), Gn 22:14, the place where God provides the ram that Abraham is to sacrifice in place of Isaac.

YAHWEH SABAOTH. See: YAHWEH *e.*

YIRON (1), Hb. *Yir'ôn,* a fortified town in Naphtali, Jos 19:38. Today *Yarun* in Lebanon.

YOU ARE MY PEOPLE (1), Hb. *Ammi* (cf. Amad; Asaramel; Sons of the People. See Am-). See: NO-PEOPLE-OF-MINE.

Z

ZAANAN (1). See: ZENAN.

ZAANANNIM (1), Jg 4:11. See: ZANAANNIM.

ZAAVAN (2), Hb. *Za'avân,* second of the three sons of Ezer, himself the sixth of the sons of Seir, Gn 36:27//1 Ch 1:42.

ZABAD, "He has given a gift" (cf. Ammizabad; Elzabad; Jozabad; Zabdi; Zabdiel; Zabud; Zebadiah; Zebedee; Zebidah; Zebulun. See Nathan).

1. **Zabad** (2), a descendant of the daughter of Sheshan, of the clan of Jerahmeel, 1 Ch 2:36–37.

2. **Zabad** (1), an Ephraimite, 1 Ch 7:21.

3. **Zabad son of Ahlai** (1), one of David's champions, 1 Ch 11:41.

4. **Zabad son of Shimeath the Ammonite** (1). See: JOZACAR.

5. **Zabad** (3), three Israelites married to foreign wives, whom they put away: the first, of the sons of Zattu, Ezr 10:27; the second, of the sons of Hashum, 10:33; the third, of the sons of Nebo, 10:43.

ZABADAEANS (1), Gr. *Zabadaioi,* an Arabian tribe conquered by Jonathan Maccabaeus, 1 M 12:31. They must have lived between the Anti-Lebanon and Damascus; there the towns of *Zebdeni* and *Kefr Zebad* recall their name.

ZABBAI

1. **Zabbai** (1), an Israelite of the sons of Bebai, married to a foreign wife, whom he puts away, Ezr 10:28.

2. **Zabbai** (1), father of: BARUCH 2.

ZABDI, "My gift" (cf. Zabad).

1. **Zabdi** (3), Jos 7:1, 17–18, a Judaean, son of Zerah, ancestor of: ACHAN.

= ? **Zimri** (1), 1 Ch 2:6, one of the five sons of Zerah, son of Judah.

2. **Zabdi** (1), a Benjaminite of the sons of Shimei, head of a family in Jerusalem, 1 Ch 8:19.

3. **Zabdi of Shepham** (1), commissioner for those in the vineyards who look after the wine cellars, 1 Ch 27:27.

4. **Zabdi son of Asaph** (1). See: ZACCUR 4.

ZABDIEL, "Gift of God *or* My gift is God" (cf. Zabad).

1. **Zabdiel** (1), father of Jashobeam. See: ISHBAAL 2.

2. **Zabdiel son of Haggadol** (1), in charge of the priests living in Jerusalem, Ne 11:14.

3. **Zabdiel the Arab** (1), killer of Alexander Balas, 1 M 11:17. Diodorus speaks of Zabdiel under his Greek name, *Diocles.* It is to him that Alexander is said to have entrusted his son Antiochus. Zabdiel is perhaps the father of: IAMLEKU.

ZABUD (cf. Zabad).

1. **Zabud son of Nathan** (1), Friend of King Solomon; the Hb. text also calls him a priest, 1 K 4:5.

2. **Zabud** (1), father of: UTHAI 2.

ZACCAI, Zacchaeus, Gr. *Zakchaios,* perhaps a diminutive of *Zechariah* (cf. Zechariah)? or "The Pure"?

1. **Zaccai** (3), head of a family whose sons return from the exile with Zerubbabel, Ezr 2:9//Ne 7:14, and among whom are some individuals with foreign wives, whom they put away, Ezr 10:40.

2. **Zacchaeus** (1). See: ZECHARIAH 29.

3. **Zacchaeus** (3), a rich man, a senior tax collector at Jericho. Being small of stature, he climbs a sycamore in order better to see Jesus, welcomes the latter joyfully into his house, and announces that henceforth he will share his goods with the poor. Jesus acknowledges him as a worthy son of Abraham, Lk 19:1–10.

ZACCHAEUS. See: ZACCAI 2–3.

ZACCUR (cf. Zechariah).

1. **Zaccur** (1), a Reubenite, father of: SHAMMUA 1.

2. **Zaccur** (1), a Simeonite, a descendant of Shaul and the father of Shimei, 1 Ch 4:26.

3. **Zaccur** (1), a Levite of the clan of Merari, one of the heads of the sons of Jaaziah, 1 Ch 24:27.

4. **Zaccur** (3) **son of Asaph** (1), Ne 12:35; cf. 1 Ch 35:2, head of the third class of cantors, 1 Ch 25:10.

= **Zichri son of Asaph** (1), 1 Ch 9:15.

= **Zabdi son of Asaph** (1), Ne 11:17.

Ancestor of: MATTANIAH 5; ZECHARIAH 26.

5. **Zaccur son of Imri** (1), a volunteer in the rebuilding of the Jerusalem wall, Ne 3:2.

6. **Zaccur** (1), a Levite who cosigns the pledge to observe the Law, Ne 10:13.

7. **Zaccur son of Mattaniah** (1), father of: HANAN 6.

8. **Zaccur** (1), a cantor, married to a foreign wife, whom he puts away, Ezr 10:24.

ZADOK, Gr. *Sadōk,* from Hb. *zedek,* "Justice" (cf. Adoni-zedek; Jozadak; Melchizedek; Sadducees; Zedekiah. See Justus).

1. **Zadok** (47) **son of Ahitub** (2), a priest.

Zadok and Abiathar are always associated in 2 S and 1 K, and Zadok is always named first. Both are priests in the service of the Ark, 2 S 15:24–29; 1 Ch 15:11 (1 Ch 16:39 makes Zadok the priest of the high place at Gibeon) and are listed among the chief officials of David, 2 S 8:17; 20:25; (cf. 1 K 4:4, which is a gloss). During the revolt of Absalom, the two priests with the help of their two sons keep David informed about the developing situation in Jerusalem, 2 S 15:35–36; 17:15–16. At the death of this rebellious son, the two urge the elders of Judah to be the first to call David back to his throne, 2 S 19:12–15. But when the question of David's successor arises, Zadok sides with Solomon whereas Abiathar supports Adonijah, 1 K 1:7–45; cf. 2:22. After David's death Solomon exiles Abiathar to Anathoth and appoints "in place of Abiathar, Zadok the priest," 1 K 2:26–27, 35; cf. 1 Ch 29:32; 1 S 2:31–35. Subsequently the **sons of Zadok** are regarded as the only legitimate priests, Ezk 40:46; 43:19; 44:15; 48:11. But the chronicler seems to indicate a reconciliation of the two rival priestly families of Zadok and Abiathar by giving them both a common ancestor, Aaron, Zadok by way of Eleazar and Abiathar by way of Ithamar, 1 Ch 24:3, 6, 31; cf. 18:16.

Genealogy of Zadok (ancestry and posterity): List, page 415.

Father of: AHIMAAZ 2; AZARIAH 4.

2. **Zadok** (2), father of: JERUSHA.

3. **Zadok son of Immer** (1), another volunteer in the rebuilding of the wall, Ne 3:29.

4. **Zadok** (1), a leader of the people and a cosigner of the pledge to observe the Law, Ne 10:22.

5. **Zadok** (1), a reliable scribe, one of the supervisors of the temple storehouses in the time of Nehemiah, Ne 13:13.

6. **Zadok** (2), an ancestor of Jesus, Mt 1:14.

ZAHAM (1), "Disgust," last of the three sons of Mahalath and King Rehoboam, 2 Ch 11:19.

ZAHAR (1), linked with Helbon, probably a city or region N of Damascus, well-known for its wool, Ezk 27:18. Location unknown.

ZAIR (1), a town mentioned in connection with a war of King Jehoram of Judah against Edom, 2 K 8:21. Probably in Edom.

ZALAPH (1), "Caper-bush," father of: HANUN 3.

ZALMON, Hb. 1: "Statue, Image"?; 2–3: "Shadowy, Dark."

1. **Zalmon from Ahoh** (1), 2 S 23:28, one of David's champions.

= **Ilai from Ahoh** (1), 1 Ch 11:29.

2. **Zalmon** (1), an abutment of Mount Gerizim, Jg 9:48. Identical with the following?

3. **Dark Mountain** (1), Hb. *har-Zalmôn,* Ps 68:14. Identical with the preceding? Located in Bashan?

ZALMONAH (2), a stage of the Exodus, after Kadesh, Nb 33:41–42.

ZALMUNNA (12). See: ZEBAH.

ZAMZUMMIM (1), Dt 2:20. See: REPHAIM 1.

ZANAANNIM or **Zaanannim (Oak of)** (2), sacred tree on the boundary between Naphtali and Issachar, near Tabor, Jos 19:33; Jg 4:11.

ZANOAH

1. **Zanoah** (3), a town in the lowlands of Judah, Jos 15:34, occupied after the exile by Judaeans, Ne 11:30. The inhabitants of Zanoah take part in the rebuilding of the Jerusalem wall by restoring the Valley Gate, Ne 3:13.

2. **Zanoah** (2), a town in the highlands of Judah, Jos 15:56, probably Calebite in origin, 1 Ch 4:18.

ZAPHENATH-PANEAH (1), Egypt. "God says: he is living *or* God speaks and he [the new-born] lives," an Egyptian name, which Pharaoh gives to Joseph, son of Jacob, Gn 41:45.

ZAPHON (2), "North" (cf. Baal-zephon; Mizpah; North), a town in Transjordania, some km N of Succoth. Place of a confrontation between Ephraim and Gilead, Jg 12:1. A town in Gad, Jos 13:27.

ZAREPHATH (4), Hb. *Zarphat,* locative *Zarphatah,* Gr. *Sarepta,* a **Sidonian town** (2), 1 K 17:9; Lk 4:26, a town in Phoenicia between Tyre and Sidon. Today *Sarafand.*

The prophet Elijah stays there during the great drought, in the home of a widow, whose supplies he multiplies and whose son he raises from the dead, 1 K 17:9; cf. Lk 4:26. Acc. to Ob 20 Zarephath marks the northern boundary of the new Israel.

ZARETHAN (4), a town in the Jordan valley, near Adam, Jos 3:16; south of Beth-shan and Abel-meholah, 1 K 4:12. Gideon pursues the Midianites there, Jg 7:22 (corr. of Hb. *Zerera*). There are foundries nearby, 1 K 7:46.

= **Zeredah** (1), 2 Ch 4:17.

ZATTU (5), head of a family whose sons return from the exile with Zerubbabel, Ezr 2:8//Ne 7:13, and Ezra, Ezr 8:5 ("some sons of Zattu," acc. to Gr.). Some of the sons of Zattu who had married foreign wives put them away, Ezr 10:27. Zattu, a leader of the people, is among the signers of the pledge to observe the Law, Ne 10:15.

ZAZA (1), son of Jonathan, of the clan of Jerahmeel, 1 Ch 2:33.

ZEALOT (4), represents 2× the Aram. *Qanana,* Gr. *Kananaios,* "Canaanite," Mt

10:4//Mk 3:18, and 2× the Gr. *Zēlōtēs,* "Zealot," Lk 6:15//Ac 1:13. A member of a Jewish nationalist movement that is violently hostile to the occupying Roman forces? A violent integrist, pitiless toward Jews who are not faithful to the Law of Moses?

Surname of: SIMEON 10. To be compared (?) with: ISCARIOT.

ZEBADIAH, "Gift of Yah" (cf. Zabad).

1. **Zebadiah** (1), a Benjaminite of the sons of Beriah, head of a family at Jerusalem, 1 Ch 8:15.

2. **Zebadiah** (1), a Benjaminite of the sons of Elpaal, head of a family at Jerusalem, 1 Ch 8:17.

3. **Zebadiah** (1), a Benjaminite, brother of: JOELAH.

4. **Zebadiah** (1), son of David's champion, Asahel, and successor to his father as officer in charge of the (military) service for the fourth month, 1 Ch 27:7.

5. **Zebadiah** (1), a gatekeeper, a Korahite, third son of Meshelemiah, 1 Ch 26:2.

6. **Zebadiah** (1), one of the eight Levites sent by King Jehoshaphat, together with two priests and five officers, to explain the Law to the towns of Judah, 2 Ch 17:7–9.

7. **Zebadiah son of Ishmael** (1), controller of the House of Judah, judge in royal matters under Jehoshaphat, 2 Ch 19:11.

8. **Zebadiah son of Michael** (1), head of the family of the sons of Shephatiah, returns from the exile with Ezra, Ezr 8:8.

9. **Zebadiah** (1), a priest of the sons of Immer, married to a foreign wife, whom he puts away, Ezr 10:20.

ZEBAH (12), "[Born on the day of] sacrifice," and **Zalmunna,** the distorted or fictitious names of two **kings of Midian** (3). As a result of a military action against the region of Tabor, Gideon pursues, defeats, and executes them, Jg 8:5–28; cf. 9:17; Ps 83:10–12; Is 9:3.

ZEBEDEE (12), Gr. *Zebedaios,* "Gift of Yah" (cf. Zabad), a fisherman on the Sea of Chinnereth, Mt 4:21, probably somewhat well off because he employs workers, Mk 1:20.

Husband of: SALOME 1.

Father of the Apostles: JACOB 3; JOHN 23.

ZEBIDAH (1), (cf. Zabad), daughter of Pedaiah, from Rumah, mother of King Jehoiakim of Judah, 2 K 23:36.

ZEBINA (1), an Israelite of the sons of Nebo, married to a foreign wife, whom he puts away, Ezr 10:43.

ZEBOIIM (5), a derivative of *Zeboim,* "Hyenas" (cf. next entry)? A town in the Pentapolis, near Sodom and Gomorrah, Gn 10:9, and punished at the same time as these, Dt 29:22; Ho 11:8; cf. Ws 10:6.

King: SHEMEBER.

ZEBOIM (1), Hb. *Zeboʿim,* "Hyenas" (cf. Zibeon), a town inhabited by Benjaminites after the return from the exile, Ne 11:34.

ZEBUL (6), "Control, Domination" (cf. Jezebel; Zebulun), representative of Abimelech at Shechem. He sends a secret report to Abimelech about the uprising in the city that is being led by Gaal, an adventurer, and rids himself of the latter thanks to an armed intervention by Abimelech, Jg 9:28–41.

ZEBULUN (50), interpreted in Gn 30:20 as derived from *zebed,* "present," and therefore meaning "God has made me a present" (cf. Zabad), and then as derived from *zabal,* "to dwell *or* to treat as a prince, to honor" (cf. Zebul).

Zebulun is a son of Jacob and Leah, as is Issachar, with whom he is connected: they share the sacred mountain of Tabor and both live by trade, Dt 33:18–19; and the territory of Issachar was initially part of Zebulun, which may be suggested by Jg 1:22–36, which speaks of Zebulun, 1:30, but not of Issachar.

The territory of Zebulun, described in

Jos 19:10–16, is surrounded by those of Asher, Jos 19:27, Naphtali, 19:34, Issachar, and Manasseh. It never had a coastline, and the two oracles of Gn 49: 13: "Zebulun lives by the shore of the sea; he is a sailor," and Dt 33:19: "they taste the riches of the seas," means that "the people of Zebulun hired themselves out to the people on the coast" (de Vaux), cf. Mt 4:13.

Posterity and clans of Zebulun, Gn 46:14//Nb 26:26–27. Censuses, Nb 1: 30–31; 2:8; 26:27. Population mingled with the Canaanites, Jg 1:30. Levitical towns: Jos 21:7–34//1 Ch 6:48, 62.

The saying in Jg 5:18 perhaps alludes to the role that *Zebulun* and *Naphtali* played in the battle at the waters of Merom, Jos 11:5–8. These two tribes are also associated in the war against Sisera, Jg 4:6, 10; 5:14–15. Zebulun and Naphtali also join in taking part in Gideon's campaign against Midian, Jg 6:35. Although not named in 2 K 15:29, Zebulun, which had settled in Lower Galilee, must have experienced the campaigns of Tiglath-pileser and the deportation of 732. Isaiah predicts for this area of northern Palestine (see: GALILEE) a glorious future that will make up for these past humiliations, Is 8:23//Mt 4:15. Some people from Zebulun take part in the Passover of Hezekiah, 2 Ch 30:10–11, 18; cf. Ps 68:28.

Zebulun in the lists of the tribes: List, pages 410–11.

Native place of: ELON 2.

ZECHARIAH, "Yah remembers," Gr. *Zacharia(s)* (cf. Jozacar; Zaccai?; Zaccur; Zecher; Zichri).

1. **Zechariah** (1), a Reubenite of the sons of Joel, 1 Ch 5:7.

2. **Zechariah** (1), a Benjaminite. See: ZECHER.

3. **Zechariah** (1), a Manassite, father of: IDDO.

4. **Zechariah** (1), one of the five officers sent by King Jehoshaphat, along with two priests and eight Levites, to instruct the towns of Judah in the Law, 2 Ch 17:7–9.

5. **Zechariah** (1), one of the six sons of King Jehoshaphat of Judah who are assassinated by their elder brother Jehoram after his accession to the throne, 2 Ch 21:2–4, 13.

6. **Zechariah** (1) **son of Jehoiada the priest** (2), possessed by the prophetic spirit and stoned by order of his cousin, King Joash of Judah, in the court of the temple at Jerusalem, 2 Ch 24:20–22, 25.

= **Zechariah** (2) **son of Barachiah** (1), murdered "between the sanctuary and the altar," Mt 23:35 (where *son of Barachiah* is perhaps due to a confusion with Is 8:2; see: ZECHARIAH 8); Lk 11:51.

7. **Zechariah** (1), adviser to Uzziah of Judah, who "sought God devotedly" owing to Zechariah's influence, 2 Ch 26:5.

8. **Zechariah** (2), grandfather of King Hezekiah and father of: ABIJAH 4.

= **Zechariah son of Jeberechiah** (1), chosen by the prophet Isaiah as official witness to the inscription of Maher-shalal-hash-baz, Is 8:2.

9. **Zechariah** (3), **son of Jeroboam** (1) and his successor, fourteenth king of Israel (743), fifth and last of the dynasty of Jehu. After only six months on the throne he is assassinated by Shallum, son of Jabesh, who takes his place, 2 K 14: 29; 15:8–12.

10. **Zechariah** (1), a priest, one of these in charge of the temple under Josiah, 2 Ch 35:8.

11. **Zechariah** (3) **son of Meshelemiah** (1), 1 Ch 9:21, first of the seven sons of Meshelemiah, a Korahite gatekeeper (clan of Kohath), 26:2, a shrewd counselor, 26:14.

12. **Zechariah** (3), a Levite gatekeeper in the service of the Ark, 1 Ch 15:18, a player of the keyed harp, 15:20; 16:5.

13. **Zechariah** (1), a priest, a trumpeter before the Ark, 1 Ch 15:24.

14. **Zechariah** (1), a Levite of the sons of Uzziel (clan of Kohath), leader of the sons of Isshiah, 1 Ch 24:25.

15. **Zechariah** (1), a gatekeeper of the clan of Merari, the fourth of the sons of Hosah, 1 Ch 26:11.

16. **Zechariah** (1), of the sons of Asaph, father of: JAHAZIEL 4.

17. **Zechariah** (1), a Levite of the sons of Asaph, takes part in the purification of the temple during the reform of King Hezekiah, 2 Ch 29:13.

18. **Zechariah** (1), a Levite of the clan of Kohath, one of the masters of the works in the restoration of the temple under Josiah, 2 Ch 34:12.

19. **Zechariah** (1), Ne 11:12, an ancestor of the priest: ADAIAH 6.

20. **Zechariah** (1), a Judaean, an ancestor of: ATHAIAH.

21. **Zechariah** (1), a Judaean, an ancestor of: MAASEIAH 15.

22. **Zechariah** (7) **son of Iddo** (2), Ezr 5:1; 6:14, or **son of Berechiah son of Iddo** (2), Zc 1:1, 7, one of the twelve "minor prophets," whose activity is to be dated between October–November 520, Zc 1:1, 7, and November 518 at the earliest, Zc 7:1. A contemporary of the prophet Haggai, together with whom he exhorts the Jews to rebuild the temple in Jerusalem, Ezr 5:1; 6:14, Zechariah is a priest, head of the priestly family of Iddo in the time of the high priest Joiakim, Ne 12:16. In Zc 1–8, which is attributed to him, we can identify the *prophet* by his calls to conversion, 1:3–6; 7:4–14; 8:16–17, and his visions, 1:7–8; 2:1–2, 5–6, and so on, and the *priest* by his concern for the temple, cf. Ezr 5:1; 6:14; fasting, Zc 7:1–3; 8:18–19, and the "Holy Land," 2:16; cf. 5:1–11.

Some critics regard the mention of *son of Berechiah,* Zc 1:1, 7, as a gloss based on Is 8:2 (see: ZECHARIAH 8).

23. **Zechariah** (1), an Israelite, head of the family of the sons of Parosh who return from the exile with Ezra, Ezr 8:3.

24. **Zechariah son of Bebai** (1), an Israelite, head of the family of the sons of Bebai who return from the exile with Ezra, Ezr 8:11.

25. **Zechariah** (2), one of Ezra's messengers to Iddo, Ezr 8:16, and one his assistants at the solemn reading of the Law, Ne 8:4. One or two individuals.

26. **Zechariah son of Jonathan son of Shemaiah son of Mattaniah son of Micaiah son of Zaccur son of Asaph** (1), an instrumentalist at the dedication of the Jerusalem wall, Ne 12:35.

27. **Zechariah** (1), a priest, a trumpeter at the dedication of the wall, Ne 12:41.

28. **Zechariah** (1), an Israelite of the sons of Elam, married to a foreign wife, whom he puts away, Ezk 10:26.

29. **Zechariah** (2), father (?) of the army commander: JOSEPH 7.

= ? **Zacchaeus** (1), military commander who, with Joseph (his son) and Simon Maccabaeus, takes part in the siege of the Idumaean fortresses, 2 M 10:19.

30. **Zechariah** (9), a priest of the class of Abijah, husband of Elizabeth, a descendant of Aaron.

"Both were worthy in the sight of God," childless and on in years. During a service in the Temple at Jerusalem, Zechariah receives from the angel Gabriel the news that "Elizabeth is to bear you a son and you must name him John." But Zechariah doubts and asks for a sign. He is then struck deaf and dumb—this is the sign he asked for and a punishment for his disbelief—until the day of the child's circumcision, Lk 1:5–25, 59–64. On this latter occasion Luke puts a prophetic canticle or psalm, the *Benedictus,* on the lips of Zechariah, 1:67–79.

Father of: JOHN 22.

ZECHER (1), abbrev. of *Zechariah* (cf. Zechariah), a Benjaminite at Gibeon, 1 Ch 8:31.

= **Zechariah** (1), 1 Ch 9:37.

ZEDAD (2), on the (ideal) northern frontier of the Promised Land, Nb 34:8; Ezk 47:15.

ZEDEKIAH, Hb. *Zidqiyyah, Zidqiyyahu,* Lat. *Sedecias,* "Yah is my justice" (cf. Zadok).

1. **Zedekiah son of Chenaanah** (4), of the prophets at the court of King Ahab. By a symbolic gesture, that of the iron horns, he announces to Ahab his victory over the Aramaeans; he slaps the prophet Micaiah, son Imlah, who challenges the genuineness of his prophecy, 1 K 22:11, 24–25//2 Ch 18:10, 23–24.

2. **Zedekiah** (2) **son of Maaseiah** (1), a false prophet contemporary with Jeremiah, cursed and handed over, with Ahab, son of Kolaiah, to Nebuchadnezzar, who has them burned alive, Jr 29: 21–23.

3. **Zedekiah son of Hananiah** (1), one of the officials of King Jehoiakim who are overwhelmed as they hear the oracles of Jeremiah and unsuccessfully plead with the king not to burn the book, Jr 36:12–25.

4. **Zedekiah** (56) [third] **son of Josiah** (4), Jr 1:3; 27:1; 37:1; Ba 1:8, and of Hamital, 2 K 24:18//Jr 52:1, twentieth and last king of Judah (597–587).

= **Mattaniah** (1), 2 K 24:17, the name he has before his elevation to the throne (*Zedekiah* being an enthronement name).

Zedekiah is installed as king by Nebuchadnezzar after the latter has deposed Zedekiah's nephew Jehoiachin, 2 K 24: 17–18//2 Ch 36:10–11; Jr 37:1. His reign is notable chiefly for the fall of Jerusalem, which occurs in 587 and marks the end of the kingdom of Judah. Zedekiah having "rebelled against the king of Babylon" and looked for support from Egypt, Nebuchadnezzar begins the siege of Jerusalem at the end of December 589, 2 K 24:20–25:1//Jr 39:1. Eighteen months later (June–July 587), the wall is breached. Zedekiah flees. He is captured by the Chaldaeans in the plain of Jericho, taken to Nebuchadnezzar at Riblah; the latter has Zedekiah's sons slaughtered before his eyes, has the king himself blinded and then led in chains to Babylon, where he dies, 2 K 25:2–7// Jr 39:2, 4–7//52:3–11.

In the reign of Zedekiah, Jeremiah carries on his prophetic activity, Jr 1:3; 27:1; 28:1; 49:34. On several occasions Zedekiah consults Jeremiah, 21:1–7; 37: 3–7; 38:14–27. The prophet urges him to submit to the king of Babylon, 27:12, then warns him of the painful lot that awaits him if he does not submit, 24:8, and of his captivity, 32:4–5; 34:2–6, 21; 37:17; cf. 44:30; Lm 4:20 (*Yahweh's anointed*); Ezk 12:12–13; 17:15; 21:30 (*prince of Israel*). Zedekiah will have Jeremiah imprisoned, but then will relax the sentence, Jr 32:1–3; 37:18–31; 38:5–10. Acc. to Jr 29:3, Zedekiah sends an embassy to King Nebuchadnezzar at Babylon, cf. 51:59. And Jr 34:8 tells us that Zedekiah took steps to free the slaves in Jerusalem.

In 1 Ch 3:15–16 two Zedekiahs are distinguished: one an uncle, the other a brother of Jehoiachin.

5. **Zedekiah** (1), an ancestor of Baruch, Ba 1:1.

6. **Zedekiah** (1), a cosigner of the pledge to observe the Law, Ne 10:2.

ZEEB (6), Hb. *Ze'eb,* "Wolf." See: OREB.

ZEEB'S WINEPRESS (1), "Winepress of the Wolf." See: OREB.

ZELA (1), "Rib," in Benjamin, burial place of Saul and his family, 2 S 21:14.

= **Zela Haeleph** (1), in the list of towns of Benjamin, Jos 18:28 (acc. to Gr.; Hb., *Zela, Eleph*).

ZELA HAELEPH (1), "Rib of beef." See: ZELA.

ZELEK the Ammonite (2), one of David's champions, 2 S 23:37//1 Ch 11:39.

ZELOPHEHAD (11), "In the shadow of the Kinsman"? (cf. Kinsman of Isaac; Zillah), Gr. *Salpaad,* **son of Hepher** (3) **son of Gilead son of Machir son of Manasseh** (2). He dies during the Exodus "for his own sin," Nb 27:3, leaving no son but five daughters: **Mahlah, Noah, Hoglah, Milcah,** and **Tirzah,** Nb 26:33; 27:1–7; Jos 17:3 ff.; cf. 1 Ch 7:15. These daughters obtain from Moses the right to inherit from their father, Nb 27:1–8, but must marry within the tribe to prevent the breakup of the tribal territory, Nb 36:2–12. These five "daughters of Zelophehad" are the names of five clans that are perhaps to be located N and NE of Shechem.

ZEMARAIM (2), "The two summits," in the list of the towns of Benjamin, Jos 18:22. Perhaps near Mount Zemaraim "in the highlands of Ephraim," 2 Ch 13:4.

ZEMARITES (2), a Canaanite clan, Gn 10:18//1 Ch 1:16. On the Syrian coast (Tripolis?). Known to the Egyptians and Assyrians.

ZEMIRAH (1), "Song"?, a Benjaminite, one of the nine sons of Becher, a fighting man and head of a family, 1 Ch 7:8–9.

ZENAN (1), a town in the lowlands of Judah, Jos 15:37.

= ? **Zaanan** (1), threatened by an invasion, probably that of Sennacherib in 701, Mi 1:11.

ZENAS (1), abbrev. of *Zenodōros,* "Gift of Zeus" (cf. Dositheus; Zeus), a lawyer. Paul bids Titus "see to all the travelling arrangements" for Zenas and Apollos, Tt 3:13.

ZEPHANIAH, Gr. *Sophonias,* "Yahweh protects" (cf. Elzaphan).

1. **Zephaniah** (1), a descendant of Kohath, an ancestor of Heman the cantor, 1 Ch 6:21 (//1 Ch 6:9, *Uriel*).

2. **Zephaniah son of Cushi son of Gedaliah son of Amariah son of Hezekiah** (1), a prophet under Josiah, Zp 1:1. He may have experienced the destruction of Jerusalem (630–587?). A contemporary of Jeremiah. He announces "the day of Yahweh" that will bring the disintegration of the universe and the subsequent rebirth of God's people, "a humble and lowly people," Zp 3:12. One of the twelve "minor" prophets.

3. **Zephaniah** (6) **son of Maaseiah** (3), the priest second in rank, 2 K 25:18, listed twice among the messengers of King Zedekiah to Jeremiah, Jr 21:1 ff.; 37:3, in charge of the temple police; he refuses to put Jeremiah in the stocks as Shemaiah of Nehelam demands, Jr 29:25–29. He is a prisoner of the Babylonians at the fall of Jerusalem and is executed at Riblah, 2 K 25:18, 20–21//Jr 52:24, 26–27.

4. **Zephaniah** (2), perhaps identical with the preceding, father of: JOSIAH 2.

ZEPHATH (1). See: HORMAH.

ZEPHATHAH (Valley of) (1), near Mareshah; King Asa of Judah defeats Zerah the Cushite there, 2 Ch 14:9.

ZEPHI (1). See: ZEPHO.

ZEPHO (2), third of the sons of Eliphaz, who are called the sons of Adah, Esau's wife, Gn 36:11–12; one of the chiefs (or clans) of Edom, Gn 36:15.

= **Zephi** (1), 1 Ch 1:36.

ZEPHON (1), (cf. Zaphon), the first of the seven sons of Gad acc. to Nb 26:15; his descendants form the **Zephonite** clan.

= **Ziphion** (1), Gn 46:16.

ZEPHONITE (1), belonging to the clan of: ZEPHON.

ZER (1), a fortified town in Naphtali, Jos 19:35.

ZERAH, Gr. *Zara,* "Radiance, Brilliance" (cf. East 2).

1. **Zerah** (3), second of the four sons and chiefs of Reuel in Edom, called the sons of Basemath, wife of Esau, Gn 36:13, 17; 1 Ch 1:27.

2. **Zerah** (2), father of the king of Edom: JOBAB 2. To be connected with the preceding.

3. **Zerah** (12), born of the incestuous union of Judah with his—probably Canaanite—daughter-in-law Tamar, and twin brother of Perez, Gn 38:27–30; the

last of the five sons of Judah, Gn 46:12; 1 Ch 2:3–6. His descendants form the **Zerahite** clan, Nb 26:20; Jos 7:17, 1 Ch 27:11, 13. Zerah is listed among the ancestors of Jesus, Mt 1:3.

Of the clan of Zerah, or Zerahites: ACHAN; ETHAN 1; HEMAN; JEUEL; MAHARAI; SIBBECAI.

4. **Zerah** (2), son of Simeon. See: ZOHAR 2.

5. **Zerah** (2), a Levite of the clan of Gershon, 1 Ch 6:6, 26.

6. **Zerah the Cushite** (1) and the **Cushites** (4), Ethiopian mercenaries in the service of Egypt or nomads of the Negeb. They conduct a raid into the lowlands of Judah. King Asa stops them at Mareshah, routs them, and pursues them as far as Gerar, 2 Ch 14:8–14; cf. 16:8.

ZERAHIAH, "Yah has arisen *or* has shone" (cf. East 2).

1. **Zerahiah** (4), a priest, a descendant of Aaron and ancestor of Zadok, 1 Ch 5:32; 6:36; Ezr 7:4.

2. **Zerahiah** (1), father of: ELIEHOENAI 2.

ZERAHITE

1. **Zerahite** (4), belonging to the Judaean clan of: ZERAH 3.

2. **Zerahite** (1), Nb 26:13, belonging to the Simeonite clan of: ZERAH 4.

ZERED (Wadi) (4), in southern Moab, a stage of the Exodus, Nb 21:12; Dt 2:13–14.

ZEREDAH

1. **Zeredah** (1), native place of King Jeroboam I, 1 K 11:26. 45 km NW of Jerusalem.

2. **Zeredah** (1). See: ZARETHAN.

ZERESH (4), ancient Persian "Hairy head," Gr. *Zozara,* wife of Haman, the prime minister of Ahasuerus, Est 5:10, 14; 6:13.

ZERETH (1), a son of Helah and Ashhur, in Judah, 1 Ch 4:7.

ZERETH-SHAHAR (1), a town of Reuben, in the highlands of the Arabah, Jos 13:19.

ZERI (1), (cf. Zeruiah), of the sons of Jeduthun, 1 Ch 25:3.

= **Izri** (1), leader of the fourth class of cantors, 1 Ch 25:11.

ZEROR (1), "Little pouch; Pebble"?, ancestor of: KISH 1.

ZERUAH (1), "Leprosy," 1 K 11:26, mother of the king of Israel: JEROBOAM 1.

ZERUBBABEL (26), Accad. *Zer-Babili,* "Seed, Lineage of Babylon" (cf. Jezreel; Babylon), **son of Shealtiel** (1), Ezr 3:2, 8; 5:2; Ne 12:1; Hg 1:1, 12, 14; 2:2, 23; cf. Mt 1:12; Lk 3:27, but described as nephew of Shealtiel and son of Pedaiah in Ch 3:17, 19; grandson of King Jehoiachin and, therefore, a descendant of David, but does not "have the fortune to sit on the throne of David, or to rule in Judah," Jr 22:30. Born at Babylon—which explains his name—after the edict of Cyrus in 538, he becomes high commissioner for the repatriates.

Zerubbabel and Jeshua

Some time after the arrival in Jerusalem of a small group of exiles led by: SHESHBAZZAR, Zerubbabel and Jeshua head the list of twelve leaders, Ezr 2:2// Ne 7:7, who, between 538 and 522, accompany a second stream of repatriates, Ezr 2:1–70//Ne 7:6–72; cf. Si 49:11–12 (var.), among whom are doubtless the prophets Haggai and Zechariah. Zerubbabel takes the place of Sheshbazzar; he becomes **high commissioner** (Hb. *pehah*) **of Judah** or **of the Jews** (5), Ezr 6:7; Hg 1:1, 14; 2:2, 21; cf. Ne 12:47, and is entrusted by the Persians with the civil administration of the province, and his "second in command," Jeshua, son of Jozadak, becomes the first **high priest** of the Jews. The prophets Haggai (August–

December 520) and Zechariah (October/November 520–November 518) urge Zerubbabel and Jeshua, Ezr 5:1–2; 6:14; Hg 1:1, 12–14; 2:2–9; cf. Zc 4:6–10, to rouse the people from their "spiritual lethargy." The resumption of the work of rebuilding the temple, that had been begun under Sheshbazzar acc. to Ezr 3:1–9; 4:2–3; 6:7; Si 49:12, but had been quickly broken off, will be the proof of revitalized faith and zeal in the community and the pledge of restored divine blessings, cf. Hg 2:18–19. The two leaders of community after the exile concretize in their persons the "expectation of a government divided equally between priest and prince." They are the "two olive trees . . . the two anointed ones who stand before the Lord of the whole world," Zc 4:11–13. Jeshua, "a brand snatched from the fire," that is, saved amid his testing, receives investiture as high priest and, at the same time, an absolute control of the temple and cultic activities, Zc 3:1–9. Zerubbabel, for his part, has applied to him the language of royal messianism, Hg 2:23; cf. Si 49:11; Zc 6:12; cf. Jr 23:5. It is of Zerubbabel's crowning as Davidic ruler that Zc 6:11–13 is speaking, even though, after Zerubbabel's death, when the messianic expectation came to be concentrated in the person of the priest, an "inspired rereading" caused his name to be replaced by that of Jeshua.

Zerubbabel's descendants are listed in 1 Ch 3:19–24. He himself is counted among the ancestors of Jesus, Mt 1:12–13; Lk 3:27 (who connects Zerubbabel with David, not through Solomon and the royal line, but through Nathan, another son of David).

ZERUIAH (26), "Perfumed with the root of the mastic tree" (cf. Zeri), Lat. *Sarvia,* daughter of Jesse, sister of David and Abigail, 2 S 17:26; 1 Ch 2:16.

Mother of: ABISHAI; ASAHEL 1; JOAB 1.

ZETHAM (2), (cf. Olives?), a Levite of the clan of Gershon, one of the three family heads of Ladan, 1 Ch 23:8, in charge of the treasuries of the temple, 26:22.

ZETHAN (1), "He who takes care of the olive trees" (cf. Olives), a Benjaminite of the sons of Jediael, head of a family, a stout fighting man, 1 Ch 7:10.

ZETHAR (1), ancient Persian "Killer," a eunuch mentioned with: MEHUMAN.

ZEUS (5), a Gr. name, genitive *Dios* (cf. Dionysus; Diotrephes; Twins; Zenas), Lat. *Jupiter.*

The god of heaven (cf. Ac 19:35, Gr. *diopetēs,* lit. "fallen from Zeus = Fallen from heaven"), a personification of the divinized sky, the supreme god, father of gods and men; he dwells on Olympus, which is both a mountain and the heavenly dwelling place of the gods, whence the name *Olympian Zeus*—or *Zeus Hypsistos,* "Zeus Most High," to whom 2 M is perhaps referring.

Antiochus Epiphanes dedicates two sanctuaries to Zeus in Palestine: he profanes the temple in Jerusalem and rededicates it to *Olympian Zeus,* 2 M 6:2; the altar that he dedicates to Zeus is called "the abomination of desolation," 1 M 1:54; cf. Dn 9:27; 12:11; Mt 24:15. Then, at the request of the Samaritans, who wish to strengthen their sense of hospitality, in which they are unlike their brothers and enemies, the Jews, Antiochus dedicates the sanctuary on Mount Gerizim to *Zeus Xenios,* "Zeus, patron of strangers," 2 M 6:2, who is the equivalent of *Jupiter Hospitalis* of the Romans. In 2 M 11:21 the fact that no month of *Corinthian Zeus* is known leads some critics to correct *Dios Korinthiou* to *Dioscorou,* a month in the Cretan calendar.

At Lystra, in front of the temple of Zeus-outside-the-Gate (lit. "outside the city"), the crowd mistakes Barnabas for

Zeus and Paul for Hermes and seeks to offer a sacrifice to them, Ac 14:11–13.

ZIA (1), Hb. *Zi'a,* a Gadite, head of a family, 1 Ch 5:13.

ZIBA (16), former house servant of Saul, tells David of the existence of a survivor of the fallen royal family, namely, Meribbaal the cripple, 2 S 9:2–4. To Ziba, his fifteen sons and twenty slaves, 9:10; 19:18, David entrusts the working of Meribbaal's land, 9:9–12. During the rebellion of Absalom, Ziba brings the fugitive king many provisions and informs him that Meribbaal has remained in Jerusalem in hopes of regaining his ancestral throne. David then promises Ziba Meribbaal's possessions, 16:1–4. When David returns from exile, Meribbaal attempts to exonerate himself, claiming that Ziba has slandered him. Half-convinced, David gives Ziba only half of Meribbaal's estate, 19:16–19; 25–31.

ZIBEON (8), "Hyenas" (cf. Zeboim), third of the sons of Seir the Horite, Gn 36:20//1 Ch 1:38, and of the chiefs (or clans) of the Horites, Gn 36:29–30. He has two sons, Aiah and Anah, Gn 36:24//1 Ch 1:40. In Gn 36:2 and 14 the Hb. has: "Anah daughter of Zibeon." Zibeon raises donkeys, Gn 36:24.

See: OHOLIBAMAH.

ZIBIA, Zibiah, Hb. 1: *Zibia'*; 2: *Zibiah,* "Gazelle" (cf. Pochereth-haz-zebaim).

1. **Zibia** (1), a Benjaminite, head of a family, in Moab, 1 Ch 8:9.

2. **Zibiah of Beersheba** (2), mother of King Joash of Judah, 2 K 12:2//2 Ch 24:1.

ZIBIAH (2). See: ZIBIA 2.

ZICHRI, "My remembrance" (cf. Zechariah).

1. **Zichri** (1), a Levite of the clan of Kohath, the son of Izhar and the brother of Korah and Nepheg, Ex 6:21.

2. **Zichri** (1), a Benjaminite of the sons of Shimei, head of a family at Jerusalem, 1 Ch 8:19.

3. **Zichri** (1), a Benjaminite of the sons of Shashak, head of a family at Jerusalem, 1 Ch 8:23.

4. **Zichri** (1), a Benjaminite of the sons of Jeroham, head of a family at Jerusalem, 1 Ch 8:27.

5. **Zichri son of Asaph** (1). See: ZACCUR 4.

6. **Zichri** (1), a Levite of the clan of Kohath, a descendant of Amram through Moses and Eliezer, one of those responsible for the treasuries of votive offerings, 1 Ch 26:25.

7. **Zichri** (1), a Reubenite, father of: ELIEZER 4.

8. **Zichri** (1), a Judaean, father of: AMASIAH.

9. **Zichri** (1), father of: ELISHAPHAT.

10. **Zichri** (1), an "Ephraimite champion," who during the Syro-Ephraimite war against Ahaz, king of Judah "killed Maaseiah, son of the king, Azrikam the controller of the palace, and Elkanah the king's second-in-command," 2 Ch 28:7.

11. **Zichri** (1), a Benjaminite, father of: JOEL 12.

12. **Zichri** (1), head of the priestly family of Abijah in the time of the high priest Joiakim, Ne 12:17.

ZIDDIM, "Sides."

1. **Ziddim** (1), a fortified town in Naphtali, Jos 19:35.

2. **Field of Sides** (1), Hb. *Helqat ha-Ziddim* (corr. of Hb. *Helqat ha-Zurim,* "Field of Rocks"), at Gibeon, place of the bloody encounter between the twelve young soldiers of Benjamin and the twelve young soldiers from among David's followers, 2 S 2:16.

ZIHA (3), head of a family of "oblates" who return from the exile with Zerubbabel, Ezr 2:43//Ne 7:46. With Gishpa he is in charge of the "oblates" acc. to Ne 11:21.

ZIKLAG (15), Lat. *Siceleg,* a town in the Negeb that Achish, king of Gath, gives to David, whom Saul has forced into exile, 1 S 27:5–6; 30:1–14, 26; 2 S 1:1; 4:10. Acc. to 1 Ch 12:1–21 it is at Ziklag that men of Benjamin, Judah, Gad, and Manasseh rally to David before he becomes king.

Ziklag, a former town of Simeon, Jos 19:5//1 Ch 4:30, is listed among the towns in the Negeb of Judah, Jos 15:31. After the exile it is occupied by Judaeans, Ne 11:28. 18 km NNE of Beer-sheba.

ZILLAH (3), "Shadow, Protection" (cf. Bezalel; Hazzelelponi; Zelophehad), second wife of Lamech, mother of Tubal-cain and perhaps of Naamah, Gn 4:19–23.

ZILLE-THAI, Zillethai

1. **Zille-thai** (1), a Benjaminite of the sons of Shimei, head of a family in Jerusalem, 1 Ch 8:20.

2. **Zillethai** (1), a Manassite leader who rallies to David before the latter becomes king, 1 Ch 12:21.

ZILLETHAI (1). See: ZILLE-THAI.

ZILPAH (7), from Arabic "With a little nose." A slave-girl of Laban, then of his daughter Leah, and a concubine of Jacob, Gn 29:24; 30:9, to whom she bears two sons, Gad and Asher, 30:10–12; 35:26; 37:2; 46:18.

ZIMMAH (3), a Levite of the clan of Gershom, the son of Jahath, 1 Ch 6:5, or the grandson of this last and the ancestor of Asaph, 6:27.

Father of: JOAH 3.

ZIMRAM (2), one of the six sons of Abraham and his concubine Keturah, Gn 25:2//1 Ch 1:32. In Arabia.

ZIMRI, Gr. *Zambri.*

1. **Zimri son of Salu** (2), "leader of one of the patriarchal Houses of Simeon," put to death by Phinehas, at the same time as the Midianite woman Cozbi, daughter of Zur, with whom he had probably engaged in sacral prostitution, Nb 25:6–18; cf. 1 M 2:26 (Gr. *Zambri son of Salōm*).

2. **Zimri** (1), a Judaean. See: ZABDI 1.

3. **Zimri** (4), a Benjaminite, a descendant of King Saul and ancestor of the sons of Azel, 1 Ch 8:36//9:42.

4. **Zimri** (8), an officer in the Israelite army, "captain of half his [Elah's] chariotry," assassinates King Elah at the capital, Tirzah, in the house of Arza, master of the palace, and takes power. He speedily exterminates the house of Baasha, father of Elah. But Omri, the general, is proclaimed king; he besieges Tirzah. Zimri commits suicide by burning the royal palace over his head. His reign over Israel lasts only seven days (885), 1 K 16:9–12, 15–20; cf. 2 K 9:31.

5. **Zimri** (1), Jr 25:25, location unknown. Perhaps *Zimki* should be read, which would be a cryptogram for *Elam?* or perhaps *Gimri,* which can be connected with *Gomer,* son of Japheth, and would refer to the Cimmerians?

ZIN (10), a wilderness at the southern end of the Promised Land, Nb 13:21; 34:3–4//Jos 15:1–3. Kadesh is located there, Nb 20:1; 27:14; 33:36; Dt 32:51. Not to be confused with the wilderness of: SIN 2.

ZINA (1), Hb. *Zina'*. See: ZIZA 3.

ZION (176). See: JERUSALEM *b*.

ZIOR (1), a town in the highlands of Judah, Jos 15:54. 8 km NE of Hebron.

ZIPH

1. **Ziph** (1), a town in the Negeb of Judah, Jos 15:24. About 60 km S of Hebron.

2. **Ziph** (5), a town in the highlands of Judah, Jos 15:55, originally Calebite, 1 Ch 2:42; 4:16, fortified by Rehoboam, 2 Ch 11:8.

Around the town lies the **wilderness of Ziph** (4), where David hides to escape Saul's pursuit. His friend Jonathan comes there to encourage him, 1 S 23:14–18,

but some **men of Ziph** tell Saul that David is there, 23:19–24//26:1–2; cf. Ps 54:2.
See: HACHILAH; HORESH.

ZIPHAH (1), fem. form of *Ziph,* second of the four sons of Jehallelel, a clan connected with Caleb, 1 Ch 4:16.

ZIPHION (1). See: ZEPHON.

ZIPHITES or **men of Ziph** (3), 1 S 23:19; 26:1; Ps 54:1, the people of: ZIPH 2.

ZIPHRON (1). See: SIBRAIM.

ZIPPOR (7), "Bird" (cf. Zipporah; Zophar), Nb 22:2, 4, 10, 16; 23:18; Jos 24:9; Jg 11:25, father of: BALAK.

ZIPPORAH (3), fem. form of *Zippor,* Gr. *Sepphōra,* daughter of a priest of Midian—Reuel or Jethro—and **wife of Moses** (1), to whom she bears two sons, Ex 2:16–22. Acc. to the Yahwist tradition, Zipporah accompanies Moses when he returns to Egypt, and it is she who circumcises her son, 4:20, 25–26. In the Elohist account Moses returns alone to Egypt; during the Exodus, Jethro, with Zipporah and her two sons, comes looking for Moses in the desert, 18:2–6.

= ? **the Cushite woman** (2), Nb 12:1 (where *Cushite* would be a possible term for *Midianite*). Mother of Eliezer and: GERSHOM 1.

ZIZ (1), "Flower," an unidentified slope, 2 Ch 20:16. A deformation of the *Hazazon* in 20:2?

ZIZA, Zizah, Hb. 1–2: *Ziza'*; 3: *Zizah.*

1. **Ziza** (1), a Simeonite, head of a clan, 1 Ch 4:37.

2. **Ziza** (1), third of the four sons of Maacah and King Rehoboam, 2 Ch 11:20.

3. **Zizah** (1), 1 Ch 23:11.

= **Zina** (1), 1 Ch 23:10, a Levite of the clan of Gershon, second of the four sons of Shimei.

ZIZAH. See: ZIZA 3.

ZOAN (7), Gr. *Tanis,* a town in the NE of the Nile Delta, founded seven years after Hebron, Nb 13:22, a witness to the miracles that precede the Exodus, Ps 78:12, 43. King Hezekiah sends an embassy to Pharaoh at Zoan, Is 30:4 (*//Hanes*); but every alliance with Egypt is in vain, "the princes of Zoan are utter fools, and Pharaoh's wisest counsellors are stupid," Is 19:11, 13 (*//Memphis*). On the Day of Yahweh Zoan will be burned, Ezk 30:14 (*//Memphis; No; Pi-beseth; Tahpanhes*).

= **Tanis** (1), Jdt 1:10 (*//Memphis*).
To be identified (?) with: RAMESES 2.

ZOAR (10), Hb. *Zo'ar,* "Small, little," see Gn 19:20, a city of the Pentapolis, near Sodom and Gomorrah, Gn 13:14, SE of the Dead Sea, escapes destruction because Lot takes refuge there, Gn 19:20–23, 30. A town in Moab, Dt 34:3; Is 15:5; Jr 48:34.

= **Bela** (1), whose king is allied with: BERA.

ZOBA. See: ZOBAH.

ZOBAH or **Zoba** (13), an Aramaean state in the north of the Bekaa, the Anti-Lebanon, and the deserts NE of Damascus. War between Saul and the king of Zobah, 1 S 14:47. Aramaeans from Zobah are among the mercenaries in the first Ammonite campaign against David, 2 S 10:6, 8//1 Ch 19:6, 10.
King: HADADEZER.
Native place of: IGAL 2; JAASIEL 1.
See: HAMATH OF ZOBAH.

ZOHAR, "Ocher."

1. **Zohar** (2), a Hittite, father of: EPHRON 1.

2. **Zohar** (2), one of the (six) sons of Simeon, son of Jacob, Gn 46:10//Ex 6:15.

= **Zerah** (2), one of the (five) sons of Simeon, 1 Ch 4:24, whose descendants form the **Zerahite** clan, Nb 26:13.

3. **Zohar** (1), one of the sons of Helah and Ashhur, 1 Ch 4:7.

ZOHETH

1. **Zoheth** (1), first of the two sons of Ishi, connected with the clan of Caleb, 1 Ch 4:20.

2. **Ben-zoheth** (1), second of the two sons of Ishi, connected with the clan of Caleb, 1 Ch 4:20.

ZOPHAH (2), an Asherite, son of Helem and father of eleven sons, 1 Ch 7:35–37.

ZOPHAI (1). See: ZUPH *a.*

ZOPHAR (4), (cf. Zippor), **of Naamath** (4), Bildad of Shuah and Eliphaz of Teman, "three of his friends," who come to visit Job in his trials, to "offer him sympathy and consolation," Jb 2:11; 11:1; 20:1; (? 27:13–23); cf. 32:1–5. In the end, God blames them "for not speaking truthfully about me as my servant Job has done," 42:7–10.

ZORAH (10), a town about 25 km W of Jerusalem.

Zorah and **Eshtaol** (8) are initially Danite, Jos 19:41. The former is the native place of Samson, Jg 13:2, but it is between Zorah and Eshtaol, where the Camp of Dan is located, that he becomes aware of his call, 13:25, and will be buried, 16:31. It is from these two towns that the migration of the Danites to the north begins, 18:2–28. Zorah and Eshtaol figure later in the list of the towns in the lowlands of Judah, Jos 15:33; cf. 1 Ch 2:53.

Zorah is rebuilt by Rehoboam, 2 Ch 11:10, and after the exile it is once again inhabited by Judaeans, Ne 11:29. In 1 Ch 2:54 and 4:2 the **Zorathites** are once again linked to Judah.

ZORATHITES (3), 1 Ch 2:53, 54; 4:2, belonging to the town of: ZORAH.

ZUAR (5), an Issacharite, father of: NATHANAEL 1.

ZUPH (3)

a. **Zuph** (2), an ancestor of Elkanah and Samuel, an Ephraimite acc. to 1 S 1:1, a descendant of Levi acc. to 1 Ch 6:20.

= **Zophai** (1), 1 Ch 6:11, a descendant of Levi.

b. **Land of Zuph** (1), in Ephraim, native place of Samuel, where the latter and Saul meet, 1 S 9:5 ff. Elkanah, father of Samuel, is called a **Zuphite,** that is, from the land or clan of Zuph, 1 S 1:1 (corr. of Hb. *Zophim*).

ZUPHITE (1). See: ZUPH *b.*

ZUR, "Rock" (cf. Beth-zur; Elizur; Pedahzur; Tyre; Zuriel; Zurishaddai). To be compared with the Aram. *Kepha* (cf. Cephas).

1. **Zur** (3), chief of a Midianite clan, Nb 25:15, described as one of the five Midianite kings who are vassals of Sihon, Jos 13:21, and who are conquered and put to death by the Israelites during the Exodus, Nb 31:8.

Father of: COZBI.

2. **Zur** (2), a Benjaminite of Gibeon, 1 Ch 8:30//9:36.

3. See: ROCK 5–8.

ZURIEL (1), "God is my Rock" (cf. Zur), **son of Abihail** (1), head of a family in the clan of Merari, Nb 3:35.

ZURISHADDAI (5), Gr. *Sourisadai,* "Shaddai is my Rock" (cf. Shaddai; Zur).

= **Sarasadai** (1), a Simeonite.

Father of: SHELUMIEL.

ZUZIM (1), Gn 14:5. See: REPHAIM 1.

Lists

I. LISTS OF PROPER NAMES

1. Genealogical lists

a) *Descendants*

of Cain, Gn 4:17–22.
Seth, Gn 4:25–26.
Adam, Gn 5:1–32//1 Ch 1:1–4.
Shem to Abraham, Gn 11:10–32//1 Ch 1:24–27.
Nahor, Gn 22:20–24.
Keturah, Gn 25:1–4//1 Ch 1:32–33.
Ishmael, Gn 25:12–16//1 Ch 1:28–31.
Jacob. See: Lists of the Tribes of Israel, pp. 410–11.
Esau, Gn 36:1–5, 9–14//1 Ch 1:35–37.
Seir, Gn 36:20–28//1 Ch 1:38–42.
Sons of Jacob, Gn 46:8–27.
Moses and Aaron, Ex 6:16–25.
Judah, 1 Ch 2; 4:1–23.
Simeon, 1 Ch 4:24–27, 34–37.
Reuben, 1 Ch 5:1–8.
Gad, 1 Ch 5:11–15.
Manasseh, 1 Ch 5:24; 7:14–19.
Levi, 1 Ch 6:1–15.
Issachar, 1 Ch 7:1–3.
Benjamin, 1 Ch 7:6–12; 8:1–32.
Naphtali, 1 Ch 7:13.
Ephraim, 1 Ch 7:20–27.
Asher, 1 Ch 7:30–40.

b) *Ancestors and descendants*

of David, Rt 4:18–22//1 Ch 2:9–17; 3:1–24.
(Sons of David. See: Lists of the Sons of David, p. 414.)
Saul, 1 Ch 8:29–40//9:35–44.

c) *Genealogy*

of the high priests. See p. 415.
the great cantors, 1 Ch 6:18–29.
Judith, Jdt 8:1.
Jesus, Mt 1:1–17; Lk 3:23–38.

2. Other lists of persons

a) *Leaders, kings, authorities in Israel*

Leaders of the tribes, Nb 1:5–15; 2; 7:12–83; 10:13–27.
of the Levitical clans, Nb 3:17–35.
in charge of reconnoitering Canaan, Nb 13:3–16.
in charge of allocating Canaan, Nb 34:17–29.
High officials of David, 2 S 8:15–18//20:23–26.
High officials and prefects of Solomon, 1 K 4.
Kings of Judah, 1 Ch 3:10–16.
Civil and military authorities, 1 Ch 27.
Political and religious leaders, Lk 3:1–2.

b) *Leaders, kings, authorities outside of Israel*

Chiefs of Edom, Gn 36:15–19, 40–43//1 Ch 1:51–54.
Kings of Edom, Gn 36:31–39//1 Ch 1:43–50.
Chiefs of the Horites, Gn 36:29–30.
Kings of Midian, Nb 31:8.
High-ranking Persian and Median officials, Est 1:14.
Syrian military commissioners, 2 M 12:2.

c) *Priests, Levites, cantors, gatekeepers*

Priests and Levites at the transfer of the Ark, 1 Ch 15:4–24; 16:5–6.
Classes of Levites, 1 Ch 23:6–23; 24:20–30; 26:21–32.
of priests, 1 Ch 24:7–18.
of cantors, 1 Ch 25:1–31.
of gatekeepers, 1 Ch 26:1–19
Priests and Levites who return from the exile, Ne 12:1–9.
Levites at a penitential liturgy, Ne 9:4–5.
Priests and Levites in the time of the high priest Joiakim, Ne 12:12–26.

d) *Laymen, priests, Levites. . . .*

"Catechists" under Jehoshaphat, 2 Ch 17:7–8.
Returning from the exile, Ezr 2:1–61//Ne 7:6–63; Ezr 8:1–20.
Husbands of foreign wives, Ezr 10:18–44.
Volunteers in rebuilding the wall of Jerusalem, Ne 3:1–32.
Ezra's assistants at the solemn reading of the Law, Ne 8:4, 7.
Signers of the pledge to observe the Law, Ne 10:2–28.
Jewish population of Jerusalem, Ne 11:4–24//1 Ch 9:4–34.
Participants in the dedication of the Jerusalem wall, Ne 12:32–42.

e) *Various*

Champions of David. See pp. 412–13.
Eulogy of the ancestors, 1 M 2:51–60; Si 44:16–50:1; Heb 11:4–32.
The twelve Apostles. See p. 417.
The Seven, Ac 6:5.
The five prophets and teachers at Antioch, Ac 13:1.
Christians, Rm 16:1–15, 21–23; Col 4:7–17; 2 Tm 4:9–14, 19–20; Phm 1–2, 23–24.

3. Lists of tribes, peoples, countries

List of the peoples, Gn 10//1 Ch 1:5–23.
Peoples of: CANAAN *a*.
Tribes of Israel. See pp. 410–11.
Clans of Israel, Nb 26.
Conquests made by Israel, Ps 60:8–11.
Traditional enemies of Israel, Ps 83:7–12.
Neighbors of Israel, Ps 87:4.
Peoples allied with Nebuchadnezzar or threatened by him, Jdt 1:5–12.
Addressees of the letter of the consul Lucius, 1 M 15:22–23.
Jewish diaspora, Is 11:11.
Peoples represented at the first Christian Pentecost, Ac 2:9–11.
Christian diaspora, 1 P 1:1.
Various, Is 66:19; Jr 25:20–26; Ezk 27:10–25.

4. Lists of cities or towns and other places

a) *Cities or towns*

of Canaan, conquered by Joshua, Jos 12:7–24.
of Canaan, not occupied by Israel, Jg 1:27–35.
of Judah, Judaea, Jos 15:21–62; 1 S 30:27–31; 2 Ch 11:6–10; Ne 11:25–30; Mi 1:10–15; 1 M 9:50, 52.
of Simeon, Jos 19:2–8; 1 Ch 4:28–31.
of Benjamin, Jos 18:21–28; Ne 11:31–35.
of the other tribes of Israel, Jos 19:10–47 (passim).
of refuge, in Israel, Dt 4:41–43; Jos 20:7–8.
Levitical, Jos 21:9–42//1 Ch 6:39–66.
of Moab, Is 15//Jr 48.
of Egypt, Ezk 30:13–18.
of Asia (the seven churches), Rv 1:11; 2:1, 8, 12, 18; 3:1, 7, 14.
See: DECAPOLIS; PENTAPOLIS 1, 2.

b) *Boundaries*

Boundaries of Canaan, Nb 34:1–12; cf. Ezk 47:15–20.
Boundaries and towns of the tribes of Israel
  East of the Jordan, Jos 13:8–32; cf. Nb 32:3, 34–42.
  West of the Jordan, Jos 15:1–19:51.

c) *Routes*

of the Exodus, Nb 21:10–20; 33:1–49.
of the army of Holofernes, Jdt 2:21–28; 3:9–10.
of Judas Maccabaeus in Gilead, 1 M 5:24–54.
of the invader (of Jerusalem) coming from the north, Is 10:28–32.
of Paul's journeys:
  First journey, Ac 13:4–14:27.
  Second journey, Ac 15:40–18:22.
  Third journey, Ac 18:23–21:27.
  Journey to Rome, Ac 27:1–28:16.

d) *Topography of Jerusalem,* Ne 2:13–15; 3:1–32; 12:31–39.

II. TRIBES OF ISRAEL

Alphabetical order of the tribes, with names abbreviated:

A	Asher	L	Levi
B	Benjamin	M^e	Manasseh (east of the Jordan)
D	Dan	M^w	Manasseh (west of the Jordan)
E	Ephraim	N	Naphtali
G	Gad	R	Reuben
I	Issachar	S	Simeon
Jo	Joseph (= Ephraim and Manasseh)	Z	Zebulun
Ju	Judah		

According to Gn 29:32–30:25; 35:17–18, 22–26; 46:8–24:
sons of Leah: Simeon, Levi, Judah, Issachar, and Zebulun.
sons of Rachel: Joseph and Benjamin.
sons of Bilhah, Rachel's servant: Dan and Naphtali.
sons of Zilpah, Leah's servant: Gad and Asher.

For an understanding of the following table, see the article: ISRAEL *b*.

Lists of the Tribes

The twelve sons of Jacob

Gn 29:32–30:25; 35:17–18;	R	S	L	Ju	D	N	G	A	I	Z	Jo	B
35:22–26;	R	S	L	Ju	I	Z	Jo	B	D	N	G	A
46:8–24	R	S	L	Ju	I	Z	G	A	Jo	B	D	N
Ex 1:2–5	R	S	L	Ju	I	Z	B	D	N	G	A	Jo
1 Ch 2:1–2	R	S	L	Ju	I	Z	D	Jo	B	N	G	A
2–8	Ju	S	R	G	M^w	L	L	B	N	M	E	A

Blessings and curses

Gn 49:3–27	R	S	L	Ju	Z	I	D	G	A	N	Jo	B
Dt 33:6–24	R	Ju	L	B	Jo	Z	I	G	D	N	A	
27:12–13	S	L	Ju	I	Jo	B	R	G	A	Z	D	N
Jg 5:14–18	E	B	(M)	Z	I	(N)	R	(G)	D	A	Z	N

Leaders of the tribes

Nb 2:3–33	Ju	I	Z	R	S	G	E	M	B	D	A	N	
7:12–78	Ju	I	Z	R	S	G	E	M	B	D	A	N	
10:14–27	Ju	I	Z	R	S	G	E	M	B	D	A	N	
1:5–15	R	S	Ju	I	Z	E	M	B	D	A	G	N	
13:4–15	R	S	Ju	I	E	B	Z	M	D	A	N	G	
34:14, 19–28	R	G	M^e	Ju	S	B	D	M^w	E	Z	I	A	N
1 K 4:8–19	(E)							N	A	I	B	G	(Ju)
1 Ch 27:16–22	R	S	L	Ju	I	Z	N	E	M^w	M^e	B	D	

Allocation of the land

Jos 13–19	R	G	M^e	Ju	E	M^w	B	S	Z	U	A	N	D
Jg 1	Ju	S	B	Jo	M	E	Z	A	N	D			
Jos 21:4–7	Ju	S	B	E	D	M^w	M^e	I	A	N	Z	R	G
1 Ch 6:40–48	Ju	B				M^w	I	A	N	M^e	R	G	Z
Jos 21:9–38	Ju	S	B	E	D	M^w	M^e	I	A	N	Z	R	G
1 Ch 6:50–65	Ju	S	B	E		M^w	M^e	I	A	N	Z	R	G
Ezk 48:1–28	D	A	N	M	E	R	Ju	B	S	I	Z	N	
31–34	R	Ju	L	Jo	B	D	S	I	Z	G	A	G	

Censuses

Nb 1:20–43	R	S	G	Ju	I	Z	E	M	B	D	A	N		
26:5–50	R	S	G	Ju	I	Z	E	M	B	D	A	N		
1 Ch 12:25–38	Ju	S	L	B	E	M^w	I	Z	N	D	A	R	G	M^e
Rv 7:5–8	Ju	R	G	A	N	M	S	L	I	Z	Jo	B		

III. DAVID'S CHAMPIONS AND MILITARY LEADERS

CHAMPIONS		MILITARY LEADERS
2 S 23	**1 Ch 11**	**1 Ch 27**
8. These are the names of David's champions:	11. The principal champions of David:	2. The commissioner for the first order detailed for the first month was
Ishbaal the Hachmonite (Gr.)	Jashobeam the Hachmonite	Jashobeam son of Zabdiel.
9. Eleazar son of Dodo the Ahohite.	12. Eleazar son of Dodo the Ahohite	4. For the second month, Dodo the Ahohite.
11. Shamma son of Elah the Hararite.		
18. Abishai, the brother of Joab and son of Zeruiah.	20. Abishai, the brother of Joab.	
20. Benaiah son of Jehoiada.	22. Benaiah son of Jehoiada.	5. For the third month, Benaiah son of Jehoiada.
24. Asahel the brother of Joab;	26. The valiant champions: Asahel the brother of Joab.	7. For the fourth month, Asahel, brother of Joab.
Elhanan son of Dodo, from Bethlehem;	Elhanan son of Dodo, from Bethlehem.	
25. Shamma from Harod;	27. Shammoth from Harod.	8. For the fifth month, Shamhuth the Izrahite.
Elika from Harod;		
26. Helez from Beth-pelet;	Helez the Pelonite.	10. For the seventh month, Helez the Pelonite
Ira son of Ikkesh, from Tekoa;	28. Ira son of Ikkesh, from Tekoa.	9. For the sixth month, Ira son of Ikkesh of Takoa.
27. Abiezer from Anathoth;	Abiezer from Anathoth.	12. For the ninth month, Abiezer of Anathoth, a Benjaminite.
Sibbecai (Hb. *Mebunnai*) from Hushah;	29. Sibbecai from Hushah.	11. For the eighth month, Sibbecai of Hushah, a Zerahite.
28. Zalmon from Ahoh;	Ilai from Ahoh.	
Maharai from Netophah;	30. Maharai from Netophah.	13. For the tenth month, Maharai of Netophah, a Zerahite.
29. Heled (Hb. *Heleb*) son of Baanah, from Netophah;	Heled son of Baanah, from Netophah.	For the twelfth month, Heldai from Netophah, of Othniel.
Ittai son of Ribai, from Gibeah of Benjamin;	31. Ittai son of Ribai, from Gibeah of Benjamin.	
30. Benaiah from Pirathon;	Benaiah from Pirathon.	14. For the eleventh month, Benaiah of Pirathon, a son of Ephraim.
Hiddai from the wadis of Gaash;	32. Hurai from the wadis of Gaash	
31. Abialbon from Beth-arabah;	Abiel from Beth-ha-arabah.	
Azmaveth from Bahurim;	33. Azmaveth from Baharum.	

CHAMPIONS		MILITARY LEADERS
2 S 23	**1 Ch 11**	**1 Ch 27**
32. Eliahba from Shaalbon;	Eliahba from Shaalbon.	
(Hb. *The sons of*) Jashen from Gimzo;	34. Bene-hashem from Gizon.	
33. Jonathan son of Shammah, from Harar;	Jonathan son of Shagee, from Harar.	
Ahiam son of Sharar, from Harar;	35. Ahiam son of Sachar, from Harar.	
34. Eliphelet son of Ahasbai,	Eliphelet son of Ur.	
from Beth-maacah;	36. Hepher from Mecherah.	
Eliam son of Ahithophel, from Gilo;	Ahijah the Pelonite.	
35. Hezro from Carmel;	37. Hezro from Carmel.	
Paarai from Arab;	Naarai son of Ezbai.	
36. Igal son of Nathan, from Zobah;	38. Joel the brother of Nathan.	
Bani the Gadite;		
	Mibhar son of Hagri.	
37. Zelek the Ammonite.	39. Zelek the Ammonite.	
Naharai, from Beeroth, armour-bearer to Joab son of Zeruiah;	Naharai from Beeroth, armour-bearer to Joab son of Zeruiah.	
38. Ira from Jattit;	40. Ira from Jattir.	
Gareb from Jattir;	Gareb from Jattir.	
39. Uriah the Hittite— thirty-seven in all.	41. Uriah the Hittite.	
	Zabad son of Ahlai.	
	42. Adina son of Shiza the Reubenite.	
	43. Hanan son of Maacah.	
	Joshaphat the Mithnite.	
	44. Uzzia from Ashteroth.	
	Shama and Jeiel, sons of Hotham the Aroerite.	
	45. Jediael son of Shimri,	
	and Joha his brother, the Tizite.	
	46. Eliel the Mahavite.	
	Jeribai	
	and Joshaviah, sons of Elnaam.	
	Ithmah the Moabite.	
	47. Eliel, Obed, and Jaasiel from Zoba.	

IV. SONS OF DAVID

Born at Hebron

2 S 3	**1 Ch 3**
2. his firstborn Amnon,	1. the firstborn Amnon,
by Ahinoam of Jezreel;	by Ahinoam of Jezreel;
3. his second Chileab,	second, Daniel,
by Abigail, the wife	by Abigail of Carmel;
of Nabal from Carmel;	
the third Absalom,	2. third, Absalom,
the son of Maacah,	son of Maacah,
daughter of Talmai;	the daughter of Talmai;
4. the fourth Adonijah,	fourth, Adonijah,
the son of Haggith;	son of Haggith;
the fifth Shephatiah	3. fifth, Shephatiah,
the son of Abital;	by Abital;
5. the sixth Ithream,	sixth, Ithream
by Eglah, wife of David.	by his wife Eglah.

Born in Jerusalem

2 S 5	**1 Ch 3**	**1 Ch 14**
14. Shammua,	5. Shimea,	4. Shammua,
Shobab,	Shobab,	Shobab,
Nathan,	Nathan,	Nathan,
Solomon,	Solomon,	Solomon,
	the four of them	
	children of Bath-shua . . .	
15. Ibhar,	6. Ibhar,	5. Ibhar,
Elishua,	Elishama,	Elishua,
	Eliphelet,	Elpelet,
	7. Nogah,	6. Nogah,
Nepheg,	Nepheg,	Nepheg,
Japhia,	Japhia,	Japhia
16. Elishama,	8. Elishama,	7. Elishama,
Eliada,	Eliada,	Beeliada,
Eliphelet.	Eliphelet:	Eliphelet.
	nine.	

V. GENEALOGY OF THE HIGH PRIESTS OR ANCESTORS AND DESCENDANTS OF ZADOK

1Ch 5:29-40		1 Ch 6:35-38	Ezr 7:1-5	1 Ch 9:11	Ne 11:10-11
29. Aaron		35. Aaron	Aaron		
30. Eleazar		Eleazar	Eleazar		
Phinehas		Phinehas	Phinehas		
31. Abishua		Abishua	5. Abishua		
Bukki		36. Bukki	Bukki		
32. Uzzi		Uzzi	Uzzi		
Zerahiah		Zerahiah	4. Zerahiah		
33. Meraioth		37. Meraioth	Meraioth	Ahitub	Ahitub
	Azariah		Azariah		
Amariah	37. Amariah	Amariah	3. Amariah		
34. Ahitub	Ahitub	Ahitub	Ahitub	Meraioth	Meraioth
Zadok	**Zadok**	**Zadok**	**Zadok**	**Zadok**	**Zadok**
35. Ahimaaz		Ahimaaz			
Azariah					
36. Johanan					
		Ba 1:7			
	39. Shallum	Shallum	2. Shallum	Meshullam	Meshullam
	Hilkiah	Hilkiah	Hilkiah	Hilkiah	Hilkiah
	40. Azariah		Azariah	11. Azariah	
	Seraiah		Seraiah		11. Seraiah
	Jehozadak				
	Ne 12:10-11				
	Jeshua				
	Joiakim	Jehoiakım?			Joiakim (corr.)
					10. Jedaiah
	Eliashib				
	Joiada				
	Johanan				
	Jaddua				
			1. Ezra		

VI. DESCENDANTS OF LEVI, ACCORDING TO THE CHRONICLER

(1 Ch 5:27-29; 6; 23--26; cf. Ex 6:16-24; Nb 3:17-20)

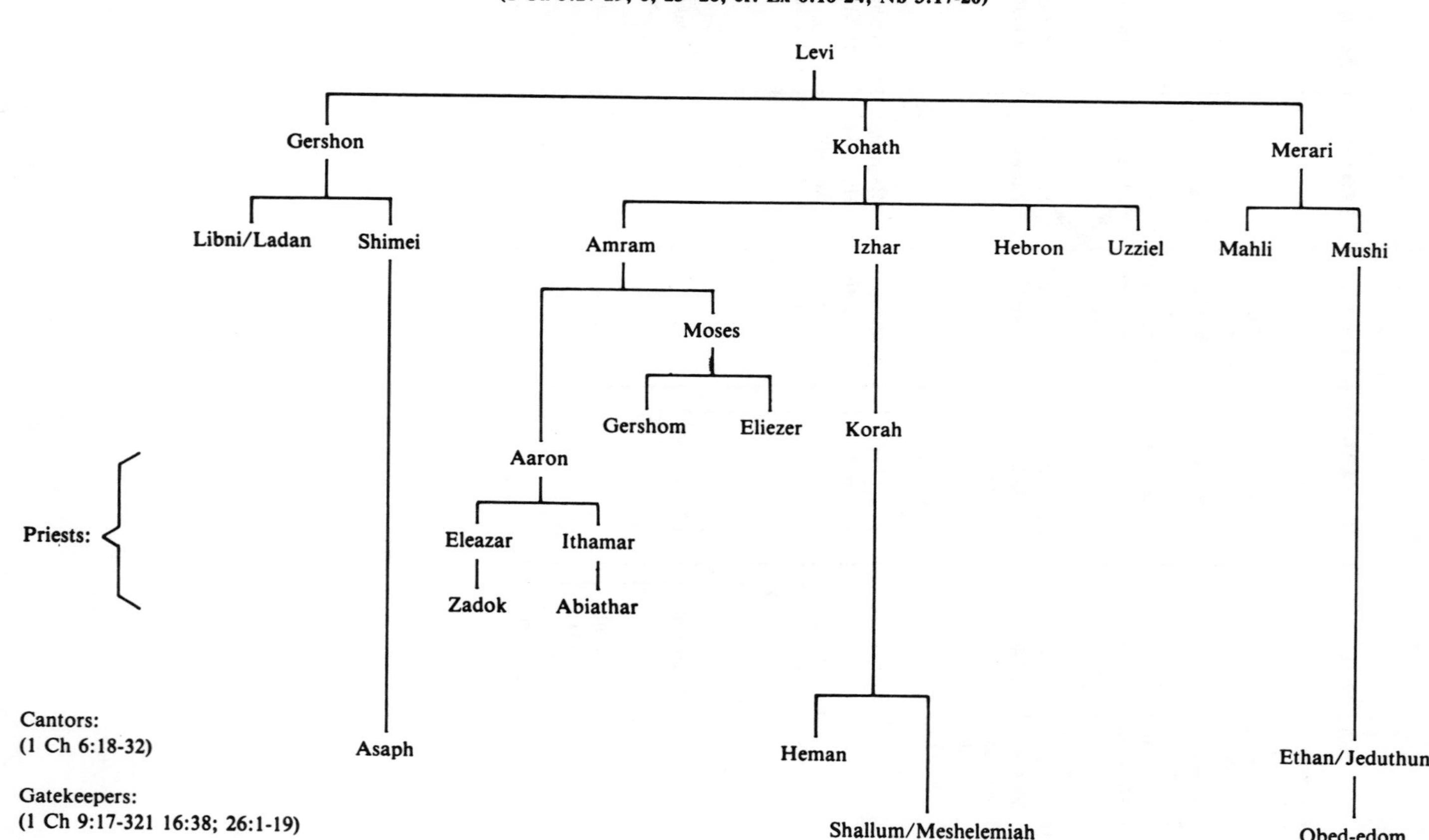

VII. LISTS OF THE TWELVE

(Three groups of four. The first man named in each group is always the same.
See: Twelve)

	Mt 10:2-4		Mk 3:16-19		Lk 6:13-16		Ac 1:13, 25-26
2.	Peter	16.	Peter	14.	Peter	13.	Peter
	his brother Andrew				Andrew		
							John
	James the son of Zebedee	17.	James		James		James
	his brother John		John		John		
		18.	Andrew				Andrew
3.	Philip		Philip		Philip		Philip
							Thomas
	Bartholomew		Bartholomew		Bartholomew		Bartholomew
	Thomas						
	Matthew		Matthew	15.	Matthew		Matthew
			Thomas		Thomas		
	James son of Alphaeus		James		James		James
	Thaddaeus		Thaddaeus				
4.	Simon the Zealot		Simon		Simon		Simon
				16.	Judas son of James		Jude son of James
	Judas Iscariot		Judas		Judas Iscariot	26.	Matthias

N.B. The boxes indicate groups that are identical at each level.

VIII. WOMEN

	WIVES AND CONCUBINES*		MOTHERS	DAUGHTERS	VARIOUS
1. Mothers of peoples and clans					
Adam	*Eve*				
Lamech	*Adah* 1			*Naamah* 1	
	Zillah				
Abraham	*Sarah*	*Hagar**			
		*Keturah**			
Isaac	*Rebekah*				nurse: *Deborah* 1.
Jacob	*Leah*	*Zilpah**		*Dinah*	
	Rachel	*Bilhah**			
Judah	*Bath-shua*	*Tamar** 1.			
Joseph	*Asenath*				
Asher				*Serah*	
Ephraim				*Sheerah*	
In Judah					
Caleb	*Azubah* 1	*Ephah**		*Achsah*	
	Ephrath	*Maacah** 2.			
Mered	*Bithiah*				
The sons of Hur					sister: *Hazzelelponi*
Ashhur	*Helah*				
	Naarah				
Jerahmeel	*Atarah*				
Abishur	*Abihail* 4.				
In Benjamin					
Shaharaim	*Baarah*				
(*or* Gera?)	*Hushim*				
	Hodesh				
Jeiel	*Maacah* 4.				
In Manasseh					
Machir	*Maacah* 3				
Zelophehad				*Hoglah*	
				Mahlah	
				Milcah 2.	
				Noah	
				Tirzah	
Gilead?					sister: *Malcath*
In Asher					
The sons of Heber					sister: *Shua* 2.
Related to the patriarchs:					
Haran				*Milcah* 1.	
				Iscah	
Nahor	*Milcah* 1	*Reumah**			
Esau	*Adah* 2.				
	Basemath 1.				
	Judith 1.				
	Mahalath 1.				
	Oholibamah				
Eliphaz		*Timnah**			

	WIVES AND CONCUBINES*		MOTHERS	DAUGHTERS	VARIOUS
	2. Women of the royal houses ("Mother" = Queen-mother)				
Saul	*Ahinoam* 1	*Rizpah**		*Merab*	
				Michal	
David	*Ahinoam* 2				*sisters:*
	Abigail 1				*Abigail* 2.
	Maacah 8.			*Tamar* 2	*Zeruiah*
	Haggith				niece
	Abital				*Abihail* 5
	Eglah				granddaughter:
	Michal				*Tamar* 3.
	Bathsheba				
	Abishag				
Solomon	*Naamah* 2		*Bathsheba*	*Basemath* 2.	
				Taphath	
Judah					
Rehoboam	*Maacah* 9.		*Naamah* 2.		
	Mahalath 2.				
Abijah			*Maacah* 9		
Asa			*Maacah* 9 (grand-mother)		
Jehoshaphat			*Azubah* 2		
Jehoram	*Athaliah*			*Jehosheba*	
Ahazaiah			*Athaliah*		
Jehoash			*Zibiah*		
Amaziah			*Jehoaddin*		
Uzziah			*Jecoliah*		
Jotham			*Jerusha*		
Hezekiah			*Abijah* 4.		
Manasseh			*Hephzibah*		
Amon			*Meshullemeth*		
Josiah			*Jedidah*		
Jehoahaz			*Hamital*		
Jehoiakim			*Zebidah*		
Jehoiachin			*Nehushta*		
Zedekiah			*Hamital*		
Israel					
Jeroboam I			*Zeruah*		
Ahab	*Jezebel* 1.			*Athaliah*	
Jehoram			*Jezebel* 1.		
Edom					
Hadad	*Mehetabel*				
Egypt					
Ptolemy V	[*Cleopatra 1.*]				
Ptolemy VIII (or XII)	*Cleopatra 3.*				
Syria					
Antiochus II	[*Laodice*]				
	[*Bernice 1*]				
Antiochus IV		*Antiochis**			
Alexander Balas	*Cleopatra* 2				
Demetrius II					
Persia					
Xerxes	*Vashti*				
	Esther				
Palestine					
[Herod] Philip					
	Herodias			[*Salome* 2]	
Herod [Antipas]					
Herod [Agrippa I]				*Bernice* 2	
				Drusilla	

3. Other women of the Old Testament

	WIVES AND CONCUBINES*	MOTHERS	DAUGHTERS	VARIOUS
Amram	*Jochebed*		*Miriam*	
Moses	*Zipporah*			
Aaron	*Elisheba*			
Zur			*Cozbi*	
Dibri			*Shelomith* 1	
Lappidoth	*Deborah* 2.			
Heber	*Jael*			
Samson	*Delilah**			
Elkanah	*Hannah* 1 *Peninnah*			
Elimelech	*Naomi*			daughters-in-law: *Ruth* *Orpah*
Boaz	*Ruth*			
Jozacar		*Shimeath*		
Jehozabad		*Shomer*		
Shallum	*Huldah*			
Hosea	*Gomer*		*Unloved*	
Zerubbabel			*Shelomith* 2.	
Job			*Cassia* *Mascara* *Turtledove*	
Tobit	*Anna*			grandmother: *Deborah* 3.
Raguel	*Edna*		*Sarah* 2	
Tobias	*Sarah* 2			
Manasseh	*Judith* 2.			
Haman	*Zeresh*			
Joakim	*Susanna* 1			
Phanuel			*Hannah* 3.	
Zechariah	*Elizabeth*			

Women mentioned without reference to a man: *Deborah* 1; *Puah; Shiphrah; Rahab* (but cf. Mt 1:5 which speaks of her as wife of Salmon); *Noadiah.*

4. Disciples of Jesus, Christian women
(see List IX)

IX. CHRISTIANS

THE TWELVE (see List VII)

Men		Women
PALESTINE–SYRIA		
Disciples not mentioned after Easter		
Joseph 10	Simeon 11	Mary 6
Joseph of Arimathaea	Zacchaeus	Martha
Lazarus		Mary 5
Nicodemus		Joanna
? Jairus		Salome 1
? Simon of Cyrene		Mary Magdalene
After Pentecost		
THE SEVEN		
Stephen	Timon	Mary, mother of Jesus
Philip	Parmenas	
Prochorus	Nicolaus	
Nicanor		
Agabus	Mnason	
Judas Barsabbas		
Jerusalem		
James the Younger		Mary 7
Joseph Barsabbas		Rhoda
Ananias		Sapphira
Lydda		
? Aeneas		
Jaffa		
Simon the leather tanner		Tabitha
Caesarea		
Cornelius		
Damascus		
Ananias	Judas	
Antioch		
THE FIVE		
Barnabas	Manaen	
Simeon	Saul/Paul	
Lucius		

CYPRUS

Sergius Paulus

ASIA MINOR

Lystra

Timothy

Lois
Eunice

Colossae

Epaphras
Philemon

Archippus
Onesimus

Apphia

Laodicea

Nymphas

Ephesus

Erastus 1
Trophimus

Onesiphorus
Nicolaitans

Pergamum

Antipas

Thyatira

Jezebel

Troas

Carpus

Eutychus

MACEDONIA–GREECE

Philippi

Clement
Epaphroditus
Syzygus

Lydia
Evodia
Syntyche

Doberus

Gaius 2

Thessalonika

Aristarchus
Secundus

? Jason 5

Beroea

Sopater

Athens

Dionysius

Damaris

Cenchreae

Phoebe

Corinth

Aquila
Achaicus
Crispus
Erastus 2
Fortunatus
Gaius 3
Jason 6

Lucius 3
Quartus
Sosipater 2
Sosthenes 2
Stephanas
Tertius
Justus 2

Priscilla
Chloe (*'s people*)

Rome

Ampliatus
Andronicus
Apelles
Asyncritus
Epaenetus
Eubulus
Hermas
Hermes
Herodion
Junias?
Linus
Aristobulus (*the household of*)
Narcissus (*the household of*)

Nereus
Olympas
Patrobas
Philologus
Phlegon
Pudens
Rufus
Stachys
Urban

Claudia
Julia
Mary 8
Persis
Tryphaena
Tryphosa

or Junia?

VARIOUS (men)

Fellow workers of Paul

Silas
Timothy
Mark
Luke
Apollos
Titus

Tychicus
Artemas
Jesus Justus
Crescens
Zenas

Men who break with Paul

Demas
Phygelus
Hermogenes

Alexander 6
Hymenaeus
Philetus

Others

Alexander 3
Demetrius
Diotrephes

Gaius 4
Jude
Theophilus

Indexes

I. WORDS IN THE ANCIENT LANGUAGES

1. Hebrew, Aramaic, or Syriac words

A

ʻAbed-Nabu	Abednego
ʻAbedyah	Bediah
ʼabib	Tel Abib
ʼAbikabod	Ichabod
ʼadamah	Holy Land
	Israel *c*
ʼAharôn	Aaron
ʼaharôn (heth)	Mediterranean
ʼAhashverosh	Xerxes
ʼAhiʼel	Hiel
ʼAhikabod	Ichabod
ʻam	Sons of the People
ʻAmorah	Gomorrah
ʻaphar	Beth-leaphrah
ʻaqab, *ʻaqeb*	Jacob
ʻarabim	Willows
ʻaralôt	Foreskins
ʼArbaʻ	Kiriath-arba
ʼArtahshast(a)	Artaxerxes
ʻash	Bear
ʼashpôt	Dung
ʻAshtart	Astarte
ʻAshtoret	Astarte
ʼAtad	Goren-ha-atad
ʻayish	Bear
ʻAzzah	Gaza

B

balahôt	Terrors
Barah	Beth-barah
bariah	Fleeing
Bassi	Bethbasi
baz	Maher-shalal-hash-baz
beli-yaʻal	Belial
Benayim	Jishi-be-nob
berit	Baal-berith
biqʻat	Vale (of Lebanon)
biqrah	Rebekah
Bireï	Beth-biri
boshet	Astarte
	Baal 1

D

Dagim	Fish
Dammeseq	Damascus
Dammim	Ephes-dammim
	Hakeldama
Daryavesh	Darius
Diqlat	Tigris

E

ʼebel	Abel-mizraim
ʻeber	Jordan 3.
	Transeuphrates
ʼehyeh	Yahweh *c*
ʼelah	Terebinth
ʼElishaʻ	Elisha
ʻEqed	Beth-eked
ʼerez	Israel *c*

G

Gaddi	En-gedi
gadol	Haggadol
galil	Galilee
gân	Beth-haggan
Gibʻon	Gibeon
Gidʻon	Gideon
Gilʻad	Gilead
Gilboaʻ	Gilboa

H

Haddata	Hazor-hadattah
hadre	Mansions of the South
halaq	Halak (Mount)
Ham	Ham
Hanân	Beth-hanan
har	Hor (Mount)
Harashim	Craftsmen
harsit	Potsherds
haruz	Decision
hash	Maher-shalal-hash-baz
(Ha)shmonaï	Hasmonaeans
hasidim	Hasidaeans

havvôt — Encampments of Jair
Hayil — Ben-hail
Hayyah — Eve
hebel — Abel 1
herem — Hormah
hevah — Beast
Hiddeqel — Tigris
hizzayôn — Vision
homotayim — Between the Two Walls
Huzôt — Kiriath-huzoth

I

'immanu'el — Immanuel
'ish — Ishbaal, and so forth
'Ishai — Jesse
'Iyyob — Job

K

kaphelta — Chaphenatha
Kar — Beth-car
Kasdim — Chaldaea
Kena'ân — Canaan
Kepha — Cephas
Kerem — Beth-hac-cherem
kikkar — Plain 1
kimah — Pleiades
kobes — Fuller 2
Kôresh — Cyrus

L

layelah — Lilith
Leaphra — Beth-leaphrah
Lebanôn — Lebanon
Lemek — Lamech
Lubim — Libyans

M

Mahleqôt — Divisions
maktesh — Mortar
maqqaba — Maccabaeus
mara' — Lord
Markabôt — Beth-marcaboth
mashah — Moses
mattarah — Watch (Gate)
mavet — Mot
mayim — Water (Gate)
melah — Salt
Menashshe — Manasseh
me'onenim — Diviners
meshiah — Jesus *b*
mesillôt — Mesaloth
Midyân — Midian
miqzoa' — Angle (Gate)
mishneh — Chaphenatha; New Town
mizrah — East 2
Mosheh — Moses

N

nahal — Nahaliel; Wadi (of Egypt)
nahar — Mesopotamia; Rehoboth-han-nahar; Transeuphrates
Na'omi — Naomi
Nebukadne'zzar — Nebuchadnezzar
Negeb — Adami-negeb
Nego — Abednego
nesheq — Armoury
Ninveh — Nineveh
nissi — Yahweh-nissi
Noah — Noah

O

'ozeb — Jabez
'Oni — Ben-oni
'ophim — Bakers

P

Pazzez — Beth-pazzez
pahad — Kinsman
paras, parsi — Persia, Persians
par'oh — Pharaoh
parush — Pharisee
pe'ah — Crop-heads
Peleshet — Philistia
perishayya — Pharisee
pesilim — Idols
pinnah — Corner (Gate)
puk — Mascara

Q

Qazin — Ittah-kazin
qanana — Zealot
qannah — El
qatân — Hakkatan

qezi'ah Cassia
qeziz Emek-keziz
qezuze Crop-heads
qeren Mascara
qetoret Keturah
Qidrôn Kidron
qodesh Holy Land

R

razim Guards (Gate)
Rahel Rachel
Rehab'am Rehoboam
Ribqah Rebekah
rish'atayim Cushan-rishathaim
rogel Fuller 1
roi Lahai roi
ro'im Beth-eked

S

Sanherib Sennacherib
Sannah Kiriath-sannah
sede Fields-of-the-Forest
Fuller 2
Sedom Sodom
seneh Sinai
sepher Kiriath-sepher
seqma Baskama
Seveneh Syene
Shahar Zereth-shahar
shai Abishai
shalal Mather-shalal-hash-baz
shalom Yahweh-Peace
shammah Yahweh-Is-There
Shamrai Shamsherai
shamrayin Samaria
shaqeh Rabshakeh
Shelishiyyah Eglath Shelishiyah
Shelomoh Solomon
shem Shem
shemesh Beth-shemesh
shiloah Shiloah
Shimshôn Samson
Shomrôn Samaria
Shophân Atroth-shophan
shophar Shaphir
Shulammit Shulam (of)
Shushân Susa
Susanna
susim Horses

T

ta'avah Kibroth-hattaavah
tabal Tabeel 1
tabbur Navel
tannurim Furnaces (Tower)
tavek Middle (Gate)
tehôm Deep

Y

Ya'aqob Jacob
Yarden Jordan
Yarob'am Jeroboam
yashar Jeshurun
ye'elim Wild Goats
Yehoshua' Joshua
yemimah Turtledove
ye'or Nile
Yephet Japheth
Yeriho Jericho
Yerushalayim Jerusalem
Yeshimot Beth-ha-jeshimoth
yesod Foundation (Gate)
Yizhaq Isaac
Yissa(s)kar Issachar
Yitrô Jethro
Yohu' Jehu

Z

zabal Zebulun
zebed Zebulun
Zebub Baalzebub
Zerubbabel Zerubbabel
zetim Olives

2. Greek words

A

Abdenagō Abednego
abyssos Deep
agros Hakeldama
akra Jerusalem *a*
anatolē Branch
ania Lysanias
Artemidōros Artemas

C

chōrion	Hakeldama

D

Damaskos	Damascus
diabolos	Satan
Dioclēs	Zabdiel 3
dios	Zeus
dynameis	Sabaoth

E

epaggelia	Promised Land
erythra	Red Sea
eutheia	Straight Street

G

gē	Holy Land
	Promised Land

H

hagios	Holy Land
haima	Hakeldama
hēlios	Sun
hērōs	Herod
hieros	Hierapolis
Hierosolyma	Jerusalem
hippos	Philip
hypsistos	Most High

K

Kaath	Kohath
Kaisar	Caesar
kaloi	Fair Havens
Kananaios	Zealot
Kariōth	Kerioth
klimax	Ladder of Tyre
Korinthios	Zeus
kyrios	Jesus *b*
	Lord

L

libertinoi	Freedmen
limenes	Fair Havens
lysis	Lysanias

M

machē	Lysimachus
Melitē	Malta
Minaioi	Meunites
Misach	Meshach
muia	Baalzebub

P

pagos	Areopagus
pantokratōr	Shaddai
	Almighty
paralia	Coastal Region
pedinē	Lowlands
pedion	Plain
peran	Jordan 3
Phagōr, Phogōr	Peor
Phoinikē	Phoenicia
polis	Amphipolis
potamos	Mesopotamia

S

sebastos	Augustus
sikarios	Iscariot
Spania	Spain
Stephanos	Stephen

T

tabernai	Three Taverns
thalassa	Red Sea
theos	Theodotus
thērion	Beast
Thersa	Tirzah
treis	Three Taverns
trōglodytai	Sukkiim

X

xenios	Zeus

3. Accadian, Arabic, Egyptian, Ugaritic, Persian, and so forth, words

A

abubi	Tel Abib
abushu	Shinab
Ahi-miti	Ahimoth
Allah	El
amur-pi-el	Amraphel
apal, apil, aplu	Abel 1
	Merodach-baladan
	Tiglath-pileser
avil	Evil-merodach

B

bab	Babylon
Basan	Bashan
be-el-shu-nu	Bilshan
belit	Belteshazzar
bibi	Bebai
bosphorus	Sepharad

D

dananu	Medan
dannatu	Dannah
Darayavahus	Darius
Dullupu	Dalphon

E

eriba	Sennacherib
esharra	Tiglath-pileser

H

Hapi	Apis
Harita	Aretas
Hatarikka	Hadrach
hi-ku-pta	Egypt
hurru	Horites

I

Iadason	Hydaspes
iddîn	Esarhaddon
	Baladan
	Nebuzaradan
ilu	El
infer(n)us	Sheol
izgad	Azgad

K

Khshajarsha	Xerxes
kudurri	Nebuchadnezzar
Kurush	Cyrus

L

Lotan	Leviathan

M

Maliku	Malchus
Mar·tu	Amorites

N

Ns-Nit	Asenath

P

per-âa	Pharaoh
Pitru	Pethor
Po-to-resi	Pathros

Q

Quds(el)	Jerusalem

R

ragimu	Regem

S

Sammuramat	Shemiramoth
Sarugi	Serug
Sha-an-ha-ra	Shinar
shadû	Shaddai
shar, sharru	Sharezer
	Sargon
stareh	Esther

T

til	Tel Abib
tukulti	Tiglath-pileser

U

uballit	Sanballat
uzur	Belshazzar
	Sharezer
	Shenazzar
Ufratu	Euphrates
ukîn	Sargon
Urushalimu	Jerusalem

V

Vahista	Vashti

W

(w)ardu	Jared

Z

zer	Nebuzaradan
	Zerubbabel

II. ENGLISH EQUIVALENTS OF BIBLICAL NAMES

A

abandoned	Azubah
abundance	Beth-ashbea
	Hothir
	Serah
acacias	Shittim
accord	Bishlam
account (take into)	Hashabiah
accuser/ accusation	Satan
acropolis	Citadel
	Ophir
act	Elpaal
add	Asaph
	Joseph
adorn	Eleadah
adversary	Antichrist
	Leb-kamai
	Satan
advocate	Meribbaal
alien	Gershom
almond	Luz
anathema, ban	Hormah
angry	Maaz
answer	Anaiah
antelope	Jael
apple tree	Tappuah
appointed	Maccabaeus
apportionment	Meni
arbitrate	Palal
arise	Azrikam
army	Sabaoth
	Sostratus
around	Amphipolis
ascend	Elealeh
aside	Azaliah
	Beth-ezel
ask for, request	Samuel
	Saul
	Tehinnah
ass	Hamor
assembly	Kehelathah
attractiveness	Jotbah
autumn	Hariph
awakened	Avaran

B

back (turn one's)	Orpah
bald, baldness	Halak
	Harbona
	Korah
bank, shore	Rakkath
banner	Yahweh-nissi
basil	Habakkuk
basket	Chelub
beast	Beast
	Behemoth
beautiful/beauty	Beautiful Gate
	Fair Havens
	Ishtar
	Joppa
	Shaphir
	Vashti
bee	Deborah
beef	Zela Haeleph
beetle	Gaal
beget	Molid
	Rameses
behind	Debir
being	Egypt
belong to	Lael
	Mishael
beloved	David
	Merari
benefactor	Euergetes
benevolent	Eumenes
bent, bowed	Ater
bestow	Jozabad
beyond	Hebrew
	Jordan 3–4
	Transeuphrates
bird	Zippor
	Etham 2–4
bitter/bitterness	Marah
black	Ethiopia
	Niger
	Phinehas
blessing/bless	Beracah
	Meremoth
blood	Hakeldama
bold	Chesil
bond	Moseroth
bone	Ezem

book	Kiriath-sepher
booty	Maher-shalal-hash-baz
born	Becorath
	Gahar
	Gazez
	Geshem
	Haggi
	Numenius
	Shabbethai
	Shaharaim
	Shamhuth
	Tebah
	Zebah
bottom, ground	Karka
bowl	Mortar
bramble, thorn-bush	Goren-ha-atad
	Koz
breach	Perez
bread	Bethlehem
break	Sheber
brilliance	Izhar
	Nogah
	Zerah
bring back, cause to return	Eliashib
bringer of ill-fortune	Achar
brother	Ahi
	Esarhaddon
	Hiram
	Joah
	Philadelphia
	Sennacherib
brute	Nabal
bronze (of)	Nehushtan
brook	Abel 2–3
bubbling	Giah
build	Benaiah
burning	Phlegon
	Rizpah
	Saraph
	Taberah
burning coal	Gomer 2
burnings	Misrephoth-maim
burnt (face)	Ethiopia
bull	Apis
bush	Sinai

C

cage	Chelub
cake (of figs)	Diblaim
calumniate	Satan
camel	Becher
camp	Mahanaim
can, be able	Jecoliah
canal	Pi-hahiroth
	Shiloah
canopy	Huppah
capable	Amok
caper-bush	Zalaph
carry	Amasa
	Amasiah
catastrophe	Shamhuth
cease (cause to)	Lysimachus
celebrate	Hodaviah
champion	Meribbaal
chance	Syntyche
chancellery	Hassophereth
chariot	Beth-marcaboth
charming/charm	Epaphroditus
	Jotbah
child	Bebai
	Hur
	Joseph
choice	Mibhar
circle (of stones)	Gilgal
cistern	Borashan
	Gebim
city	Amphipolis
	Ir 3
	Kiriath
	No
clamor	Rinnah
clarity	Izhar
	Nogah
cleft (nose)	Harumaph
cluster	Eshcol
combat	Lysimachus
commander	David
companion	Heber
	Ruth
	Syzygus
compassionate	Nahamani
compensation	Tahath
complete (to)	Shelemiah
conduit	Shiloah

conqueror	Andronicus
	Eliphaz
consecrated	Harim
consoled/ consolation	Nahum
constant	Eshtaol
contention	Meribah
converted (be)	Shear-jashub
copper	Irnahash
coquette	Delilah
cornelian	Shoham
counsel/ counselor	Adrammelech
	Eubulus
courageous	Ben-hail
	Thaddaeus
covenant	Baal-berith
	Hebron
cow	Leah
	Rebekah
crack	Sheber
craftsman	Geharashim
crafty	Apphus
create	Beraiah
	Elkanah
crooked	Ikkesh
cropped	Crop-heads
crown	Ataroth
	Stephen
cupbearer	Rabshakeh
cursed	Evil-merodach
cut	Gideon

D

dark	Kidron
	Zalmon 2–3
date-palm	Diklah
	Phoenicia
daughter	Bath-gallim
	Bath-rabbim
	Bath-shua
	Succoth-benoth
dawn	Shaharaim
death	Mot
debauched	Trypho
deceit/ deceive	Jacob
	Mirmah
decrepit	Jeshishai
dedication	Enoch
defend	Jerubbaal
delight	Baalis
	Hephzibah
delta	Naphtuh
demigod	Herod
depraved	Ikkesh
descendant/ lineage	Bacchides
	Eber
	Jerubbaal
descender	Jordan
desert/ desertlike	Eden 1
	Horeb
desire	Eldaah
	Vashti
destiny	Meni
destroyer	Apollyon
devastation	Beth-ha-jeshimoth
devil	Satan
dew	Abital
diadem	Atarah
difficulty	Amal
disgust	Zaham
dispel	Lysanias
distinguish	Eliphelehu
distress	Jabez 2
district	Galilee
ditch	Bethzatha
divide	Jahzeel
dog	Caleb
dolphin	Tahash
domination/ dominate	Raddai
	Zebul
donkey driver	Harbona
double	Chaphenatha
	Machpelah
dove	Jonah
drag	Joshaphat 7
draw out	Moses
droppings	Peresh
drunk	Ahithophel
dry	Horeb
	Jabesh
	Negeb
dung	Dung Gate
	Galal
	Madmenah
duration	Heled
dust	Beth-leaphrah

dwelling/dwell	Jishi-be-nob
	Maon
	Shecaniah
	Zebulun
	E
ear (of grain)	Stachys
	Tel Abib
earth	Adamah
	Navel of the Earth
eloquent	Omar
embankment	Millo
enclosure	Geder
	Gezer
	Hazar-
encounter	Noadiah
	Syntyche
encouragement/ encourage	Barnabas
enemy	Job
erect (to)	Jakim
establish	Jehoiachin
	Jekameam
	Jesimiel
eternity	El
evil (speak—of)	Satan
exalted	Athaliah
excrescence	Ophel
extend	Japheth
extricate	Delaiah
	Helez
eye	Eliehoenai
	Gehazi
	F
face	Ethiopia
	Penuel
faithful/fidelity	Amon 1–3
	Hesed
fallen (from heaven)	Nephilim
	Zeus
fat	Mishmannah
father	Ab-, -ab
	Antipater
	Barabbas
	Job
	Moab
father-in-law	Hamital
favorable, kind/ favor	Hanan
	Isaac
	Tehinnah
favored	Hanun
favorite	Apphus
felled	Felled Tree-trunk
fertile	Bashan
	Ephraim
festive/festival	Festus
	Haggi
fever	Harhur
field	Fuller 2
	Helkath
	Shaddai
fifth	Quintus
fig	Bethphage
	Diblaim
fight	Naphtali
fill up	Nedabiah
fire (red)	Pyrrhus
firm, steady	Chenaniah
	Jachin
firstborn	Becorath
fishing-ground, fishery	Bethsaida
	Sidon
five	Pentapolis
flame	Gaham
flat	Sharon
flea	Parosh
flood	Tel Abib
flower	Ziz
fly	Baalzebub
fool, madman	Evil-merodach
	Nabal
forbidden	Hermon
ford	Tiphsah
foresightful	Jakeh
forest	Horesh
	Jaar
forever	Amad
forget	Manasseh
fortress	Bezer
	Dannah
	Dura
	Maaziah
	Tahpanhes
fortuitous	Tychicus

fortune	Eutychus
	Gad
foundation	Jeruel
	Jerusalem
foundry	Tarshish 1
fountain	En-
four	Kiriath-arba
fourth	Quartus
fox	Shual
fragility	Chilion
free	Eleutherus
friend	Reuel
	Ruth
	Theophilus
frightening/fright	Emim
	Haradah
	Hatath
	Terrors
front	East 1
fruit	Carpus
fruitful	Ephrathah
	Trophimus
fulfillment	Gomer 2
fullness, plenitude	Salem
	Sheba
furnace	Topheth

G

garden	Beth-haggan
	Eden 1
gate	Babylon
	Beautiful Gate
	Jerusalem (references)
	Shaaraim
gathering/gather	Asaph
	Kabzeel
	Makheloth
gay	Festus
gazelle	Dishon
	Epher
	Jaalah
	Ophrah
	Tabitha
	Zibia 2
generous	Gennaeus
	Joshua
	Nadab
gift, donation/give	Baladan
	Dositheus
	Esarhaddon
	Ethnan
	Joash 1–6
	Kish
	Magdiel
	Nathan
	Nebuzaradan
	Potiphar
	Zabad
glory	Ichabod
glutton	Balaam
goat	En-gedi
god	Babylon
	God
	Gods
	El
	Herod
	Lael
	Theodotus
gold	Dizahab
	Eliphaz
good	Darius
	Eubulus
	Jamin
	Mehetabel
	Tob
good for nothing	Belial
governor	Hegemonides
	Pahath-moab
gracious	Naomi
grant	Seth
grape	Anab
	Sorek
grasp	Ahaz
grasshopper	Hagab
grassland	Beth-car
great	Haggadol
	Haman
	Pharaoh
	Rabbah
greed	Kibroth-hattaavah
ground	Karka
guide/to guide	Ahaz
	Jabal
	Thassi
gushing	Gihon

H

hairy	Esau
	Seir
	Zeresh
hammer	Maccabaeus
	Mark
hand	Bediah
happy/happiness	Asher
	Felix
hard	Gilead
haven	Fair Havens
head	Macron
	Rosh
healer/heal	Asa
	Raphael
hear	Azaniah
	Eshtemoa
	Jaazaniah
	Shemaiah
hearsay	Mishma
heart	Leb-kamai
hearth	Ariel
heaven	Baal-shamem
	Nephilim
	Zeus
heel	Jacob
heifer	Eglah
	En-eglaim
help	Elisha
	Ezer
	Joash 7–8
hiding place/hide	Amon 4
	Eliahba
	Hobaiah
	Maon
	Michmash
high/height	Alvah
	Bozkath
	Gabbatha
	Gibeon
	Ophel
	Ramah 1–6, 8–11
high place	Bamoth
hill	Areopagus
	Geba
	Gebal
	Ophel
	Tel Abib
	Tel-harsha
	Tel-melah
hillock	Gibbethon
hire out	Machir
hole	Horonaim
hollow	Coele-Syria
holy	Hierapolis
	Holy Land
	Jerusalem
	Kadesh
honey	Idbash
honor/to honor	Magdiel
	Timothy
	Zebulun
hope/to hope	Hacaliah
	Tikvah
hordes	Leummim
horn	Carnaim
	Jubal
	Shaphir
house	Beth-
	Egypt
	Pharaoh
	Pi-beseth
humpbacked/ hump	Ard
	Dabbesheth
husband	Baal
huts	Naioth
hyena	Zeboim
hypocritical	Iscariot
hyrax	Shaphan

I

ill-fortune	Achar
	Aven
image	Zalmon 1
immerse	Baptist
impetuous	Rahab 1
inauguration	Enoch
incense	Keturah
incomparable	Asyncritus
increase	Jeroboam
	Rehoboam
inheritance	Nahaliel
insolent	Chesil
integrity, wholeness	Jotham
	Salem
invisible	Hades

iron	Barzillai
issue	Moza

J

javelin	Nacon
	Shelah 2
jawbone	Lehi
jealous	El
jennet	Rithmah
joined to	Levi
journey	Evodia
judge	Dan
	Shephathiah
just/justice	Artaxerxes
	Jarib
	Justus
	Zadok

K

killer	Iscariot
	Zethar
king	Melech
	Sharezer
	Tahpenes
kinsman	Zelophehad
know	Eliada
	Jada

L

lady	Baalah
	Mary
lagoon	Merathaim
lamp	Ner
land, country	Holy Land
	Lowlands
	Pathros
	Promised Land
laugh	Isaac
laurel	Arnon
	Daphne
lawsuit	Dinah
lead/leader	Archelaus
	David
	Jabal
lees	Shemer
leprosy	Zeruah
liar	Iscariot
life/live	Belshazzar
	Jehiel
	Lahai Roi
	Zaphenath-paneah
light	Ur 2
lightning	Barak
	Lappidoth
	Regem
like Yah (who is)?	Micah
lily	Susanna
limped	Beth-nimrah
lion, lioness	Arieh
	Ariel
	Chephirah
	Laish
	Lebaoth
little	Hakkatan
	Zilpah
	Zoar
little town	Chephirah
loins	Chesulloth
long (head)	Macron
lookout, observation point	Dok
	Mizpah
lord	Bilshan
	Lord
lovable	Epaphroditus
	Erastus
love/loved	Abraham
	Eldad
	Meraiah
	Naamah
	Philetus
loving	Erastus
luck, opportunity	Eutychus
	Gad
	Jamin
luxuriant	Cozbi
lyre	Chinnereth

M

madder	Puah
magistrate	Ittah-kazin
magnanimous	Shua 1
magnify	Gedaliah
majesty	Geuel
	Hod
make	Asahel

man	Adam
	Alexander
	Enosh
	Eshbaal
	Evil-merodach
	Geber
	Ishbaal
	Ishhod
	Ishvi
	Jesse
	Methuselah
mangosteen	Nimshi
manifest, show	Apollophanes
	Hananiah
market (square)	Rehob
marriage	Hymenaeus
massacre	Tebah
master/to master, control	Almighty
	Aristarchus
	Baal
	Seraiah
	Zebul
mastic-tree	Zeruiah
meadow	Abel 2–3
mediation	Bediah
medlar	Azzur
mercenary	Machir
merciful/mercy	Bethesda (cf. Bethzatha)
	Harnepher
messenger	Azgad
	Malachi
metal	Aretas
mint	Habakkuk
misery	Reuben
mistress	Baalah
	Martha
month	Jerah
moon	Lebanah
	Numenius
moor-hen	Nekoda
morsel	Mishmannah
mother	Philometor
mountain	Armageddon
	Har-heres
	Mount Hor
mountain-dweller	Shaddai
mouse	Achbor
mouth	Amraphel
	Pi-hahiroth
multitude	Hamonah
murky	Kidron
myrrh	Smyrna
myrtle	Asa
	Hadassah

N

name	Hieronymus
	Jesus *b*
	Shem
	Yahweh *g*
nape	Shechem
narrative	Mispar
nations	Goiim
native	Ezrahite
necklace	Anak
new	Hadashah
	Hazor-hadattah
	Kir-heres
	Neapolis
night	Lilith
noble	Azel
	Eupator
	Gennaeus
	Herod
	Shua 1
north	Zephon
nose, nostrils	Harumaph
	Zilpah
nothing	Belial
	Cabul
	Lo-Debar
	Tabeel 1
nothingness	Beth-aven
nourishing	Trophimus
number	Mispar
nurseling	Diotrephes

O

oak	Elon 3–5
oath	Sheba
obstinate	Ezekiel
ocher	Zohar
offering	Abishai
oil	Gethsemane
old	New Town
	Jeshanah

open (to)	Jephthah
	Pekahiah
open (the womb)	Jeremiah
	Pethahiah
open (country)	Perizzites
oracle	Eshtaol
	Eshtemoa
	Massah 1
orchard	Carmel
order (of the world)	Artaxerxes
ornament	Adah
owner	Baal

P

palace	Tahpenes
parcel	Helkath
park	Hazar-
partner	Syzygus
partridge	Hoglah
	Kore
pasture land	Taberah
path	Mesaloth
peaceful/peace	Salem
	Shulam
	Yahweh-Peace
pearl	Peninnah
pebble	Zeror
perdition/destroy	Abaddon
	Asmodeus
perfect	Jotham
perfumed	Basemath
	Zeruiah
people	Nicodemus
	Nicolaus
permanent	Ethan
pierce	Avaran
pig	Hezir
pine	Arnon
pious	Hasidaeans
pistachio	Beten
pit	Shuhah
pitcher	Bakbuk
pity	Jeroham
place (in—of)	Antipater
	Tahath
plain	Bashan
	Beth-emek
	Lowlands
	Paddan
	Shaveh
plan	Heshbon
plantations	Netaim
plead against	Jerubbaal
pleader	En-hakkore
pleasure	Eden 1
	Tirzah
pock-marked	Gedor 3
pole (sacred)	Asherah
pomegranate	Rimmon 1–4
pool	King
	Shihor
poor	Bethany
populous	Bath-rabbim
portion, share/ apportion	Hilkiah
	Jahzeel
possession/ possess	Elkanah
posterity	Nebuzaradan
pouch	Zeror
powerful, mighty/power	Abihail
	Almighty
	Azgad
	Crates
	El
	On 2
praise/to praise	Hillel
	Judah
praiseworthy	Epaenetus
precious	Ahikar
	Tarshish 2–3
president	Qoheleth
press	Gath
pretty	Naamah
prey (bird of)	Etham 2–4
price	Mehir
prince	Zebulun
princess	Sarah
prisoner	Assir
profitable	Onesimus
promise	Promised Land
prostitute	Succoth-benoth
protection/ protect	Alexander
	Jacob
	Nebuchadnezzar

	Sharezer
	Tahpenes
	Ucal
	Zephaniah
	Zillah
provide	Yahweh Provides
pure	Zaccai
purple	Canaan
	Phoenicia
pursue	Matred

Q

quarrel	Esek
	Meribah
quarter	Reba
queen	Bithiah
quick	Maher-shalal-hash-baz

R

radiance	Zerah
rain	Gahar
	Geshem
ram	Beth-car
	Elon 1–2
ransom	Igal
	Pedaiah
raised up, noble	Barsabbas
	Eli
	Gabael
	Hadoram
	Jeremiah
	Seth
	Shahazimah
raven	Oreb
rebellion	Merathaim
red	Adamah
	Edom
	Pyrrhus
	Red (Sea)
	Rufus
reed	Cana
	Red (Sea)
reestablish	Eliashib
refuge	Mahseiah
	Maon
regard (to)	Nebat
reign	Iamleku
	Seraiah
rejoice	Jahdiel
relative	Am-, -am
	Kinsman
remember	Zechariah
remnant	Jether
	Shear-jashub
renown	Shem
replaced/replace	Chalphi
	Meshullam
	Sennacherib
rescue	Eliphelet
	Helez
	Jephthah
	Pedaiah
residence	Gur-baal
	Meconah
respected	Hasshub
rest (repose)	Beth-shan
	Nahath
	Noah
	Rephidim
retribution	Beth-gamul
return/to return	Belial
	Jashub
	Shobab
reward	Gamaliel
rib	Zela
right (hand)	Jamin
ring	Achsah
	Tabbaoth
rising/to rise	Branch
	East 2
	Izrahiah
river	Mesopotamia
	Rehoboth-han-nahar
	River
robust	Trophimus
rock	Cephas
	Peter
	Zur
rocky	Trachonitis
room	Rehabiah
root	Sheresh
rose	Rhoda
rosy (grape)	Sorek
ruin	Ai
	Iim
rumor	Mishma
rust	Helah

S

sabbath	Barsabbas
	Shabbethai
sacred	Hermon
	Hierapolis
sadness	Lysanias
safe and sound	Salem
salvation	Isaiah
sapphire	Sapphira
satiated	Gamul
savior/save	Hoshea
	Meshezabel
	Sostratus
scheme	Heshbon
scribes	Sophrites
sea	Chinnereth
	Dead (Sea)
	Mediterranean (Sea)
	Red (Sea)
seal	Hotham
	Tabbaoth
seas (high)	Pontus
second	Secundus
secret	Besodeiah
secretariat	Hassophereth
sediment	Shemer
seer, seeress	Haroeh
	Mary
sent	Siloam
separated	Pharisee
separation	Emek-keziz
serpent	Nahash
	Saraph
servant	Chedor-laomer
	Ebed
	Jered
seven	Seven
	Sheba
shades	Rephaim
shadowy/shadow	Zalmon 2–3
	Zillah
shame	Astarte
sharp	Hadad 5
shearing	Gazez
sheep	Immer
	Rachel
shepherd	Beth-eked
	Cyrus
shine	Izrahiah
	Phoebe
should	Cheteph
	Shechem
side	Cheteph
	Ziddim
silence	Dumah
sleep	Janum
	Jashen
sleepless	Dalphon
slide	Stone 2
sluice-gates	Arubboth
small	Hakkatan
	Zilpah
	Zoar
smash	Beth-pazzez
smile	Isaac
smith	Cain
smoke	Abel 1
	Ashan
smooth	Bashan
	Halak
snorer	Nahor
sold	Machir
solidarity	Hesed
son	Abel 1
	Bacchides
	Baladan
	Bar-
	Ben-, Bene-
	Moses
	Nebuchadnezzar
	Twins
	Ucal
song	Zemirah
soothsayer	Hallohesh
	Moreh
sorrow	Ben-oni
sound (melodious)	Shema 2–5
south	Jamin
	Negeb
	Pathros
sovereign	Sarah
sow/seed	Jezreel
	Zerubbabel
spared	Hamul
speak	Amariah
	Amraphel

	Kolaiah
	Philologus
	Zaphenath-paneah
speaker	Qoheleth
speedy	Maher-shalal-hash-baz
spitefulness	Bera
spoil	Maher-shalal-hash-baz
spring	Anath
	En-Hammath
	Moza 1–2
springtime	Tel Abib
square	Hazar-Rehob
stag	Aijalon
standing	Jachin
star	Esther
steppe	Arabah
	Eden 1
	Shaddai
stolen	Genubath
stone	Geder
	Gilgal
	Rizpah
	Stone
	Tarshish 2–3
stone pits, quarries	Shebarim
storm cloud	Anan
street	Haran 4
	Kiriath-huzoth
	Straight
strong/strength/strengthen, fortify	Amaziah
	Azaziah
	Boaz
	Gabriel
	Gaza
	Hezekiah
	Jehoiachin
	Medan
	Onan
	Seraiah
struggle	Seraiah
summit	Mareshah
	Zemaraim
sun	Heliodorus
	Heres
	Samson
superabundance	Jether
superior	Athaiah
	Shalmaneser
supplant	Jacob
supplication	Tehinnah
support, sustain	Ahimoth
	Josiah
	Semachiah
survivor	Pelet 1–2
	Sarid
swallowed up	Bela
swamp	Cabul
swarthy	Kedar
sweetness	Mithkah
	Naomi
swordfish	Gideon
sycamore	Baskama

T

tadpole	Hophni
tavern	Three Taverns
teacher	Moreh
tempestuous	Rahab 1
temptation	Massah 2
ten	Decapolis
tent	Ohel
terebinth	Elim
term (bring to)	Gemariah
terrace	Millo
thunder	Boanerges
third/three	Eglath Shelishiyah
	Tertius
	Three Taverns
	Tripolis
threshing	Joshaphat 7
threshing floor	Goren-ha-atad
	Nacon
thumb	Bohan
time	Ittah-kazin
tombs	Kibroth-hattaavah
torches	Lappidoth
tower	Migdol
	Samaria
trap	Pochereth-haz-zebaim
trembling	Harod

trial	Massah 2
tribe	Pamphylia
trough	Mortar
trumpet	Jubal
turn to	Hazzelelponi
	Job
turn (one's back)	Orpah
twin	Thomas
tyrant	Tyrannus
uncle	Am-, -am
uneven (ground)	Gilead
united to	Levi
useful/usefulness	Belial
	Onesimus

V

vagabond	Nod
valiant	Alcimus
vanity	Abel 1
vault	Gibbethon
vermilion	Tola
victory	Berenice
vigilant	Er
village	Hazar-
	Chephar-ammoni
vineyard	Beth-hac-cherem
viper	Shephupham
virile	Andrew
	Geber
vision/see	Hazael
	Irijah
	Reaiah
	Reuben
vulture	Aiah

W

wages	Issachar
	Mehir
	Sachar
wait	Jahleel
wall	Dura
	Between the Two Walls
	Kir 2
	Shur
wanderer	Nod
war	Eupolemus
watch/to watch	Guards
	Shecaniah
	Watch
watering place	Nahalal
waters	Moab
	Water (Gate)
weak/weakness	Chilion
	Rephaim 3
wealth	Baal-hamon
	Naphish
weapons	Armory
weepers	Bochim
well	Beer
	Hepher 1
wheat	Sheber
white/whiteness	Laban
Who belongs to God?	Mishael
Who is like God?	Michael
wicked	Nabal
wild ass	Aram
wild goats	Dishon
	Wild Goats
windows	Arubboth
with	Immanuel
	Ithiel
witness	Joed
wolf	Zeeb
womb (open the)	Jeremiah
	Pethahiah
wooded/wood	Harosheth-ha-goiim
work	Jezer
	Maaseiah
work (metal)	Aretas
would to God . . .	Ahlai

Y

young camel	Becher
young girl	Naarah 1
	Puah 3
young man	Jalam
youthfulness	Pethuel
zealous	Thassi
	Zealot

Chronological Tables

I. GENERAL CHRONOLOGY

The columns to the right of the date column deal with Palestinian and biblical history; those to the left deal with general history; but this distinction is less strict from the Christian era onwards. In the right-hand column, extra-biblical writings are in *italics*, and (before the Roman period) extra-biblical facts or those not taken from Josephus are also in *italics*.

The names of rulers, kings, governors and high priests are in SMALL CAPITALS or CAPITALS according to their importance. In the list of the kings of Judah the succession is from father to son unless anything different is indicated. The names of prophets, and of biblical books when mentioned at the time of their composition, are in **bold type**; and the most important of other items are also in **bold type.**

I. THE BEGINNINGS
Gn 1-11

	B.C.	
Prehistoric period: Stone Age		[Bible: popular account of creation]
Protohistoric period:	4000	[Popular account of man's inventions, Gn 4:16f]
Historical period: Writing, properly so called; more widespread use of bronze. Egypt: **Old Kingdom** (Great Pyramids). Capital: Memphis. Mesopotamia: Sumerians, followed by Akkadians	3000	*Palestine: Early Bronze Age*, 3100-2100. The **Canaanites.** Abraham's ancestors as nomads in Mesopotamia

II. THE PATRIARCHS
Gn 12-50

Egypt: **Middle Kingdom:** about 2030-1720. Mesopotamia: Sumerian revival (3rd dynasty of Ur) followed by the growing importance of the **Amorites**	2000	*Middle Bronze Age:* about 2100-1560. *In the 20c. and 21c. Egypt controls the Syro-Palestinian coast but not the interior (Memoirs of Sinuhe the Egyptian).* About 1850: **arrival of ABRAHAM in Canaan,** Gn 12
About this time, the *Akkadian poems of Creation* (Enuma elish) *and of the Flood* (Gilgamesh)		
18c. and 17c.: 1st Babylonian dynasty (Amorite): HAMMURABI about 1700 His code. Egypt: the **Hyksos,** about 1720-1560; capital: Tanis	1700	**The patriarchs in Egypt**

III. MOSES AND JOSHUA
Ex / Nb / Dt / Jos

Egypt: **New Kingdom:** 1560-715. Capital: Thebes. THUTMOSE III: 1502-1448 (campaigns in Palestine and Syria)	1500	*Late Bronze Age: about* 1550-1200
	1400	*The el-Amarna Letters; (the Habiru; Puti-hepa king of Jerusalem)*

	B.C.	
AKHNATON (= Amenophis IV): 1377-1358. His exclusive worship of the god Aton. The great hymn to Aton. Capital at Tell el-Amarna		
Tutankhamon: 1358-1349	1350	*Alphabetical tablets of Ugarit*
In Asia Minor and northern Syria, the **Hittites**: SHUPPILULIUMA about 1370		
Egypt: 19th dynasty, 1345-1200		
SETI I: 1317-1301		
RAMESES II: 1301-1234. Residence at Pi-Rameses. Struggle with the Hittites followed by an alliance	1300 1250	*Stelae of Seti I and Rameses II, his son, at Beth-shean.* Hebrews as forced labour for the building of Pi-Rameses, Ex 1:11. The **Exodus** between 1250 and 1230. MOSES, the **Law at Sinai**
MENEPTAH: 1234-1225. His fifth year: stele recording a victory over the 'people of Israel'		
Mesopotamia: 13c. and 12c., Assyrian preponderance		Between about 1220 and 1200, JOSHUA invades Palestine. *Excavations at the level of this period show ruins and impoverishment of dwellings and utensils*

IV. FROM THE JUDGES TO SOLOMON 1200-931

Jg / 1 S / 2 S / 1 K 1-11 / 1 Ch / 2 Ch 1-9

Egypt: 20th dynasty, 1200-1085. Rameses III: 1197-1165. Victory over the **'Peoples of the Sea'** who try to force an entry into Egypt	1200	*Iron Age I:* about 1200-900. The *Philistines, repulsed by Rameses III, occupy the Palestinian coast. Use of iron slowly spreads*
		The JUDGES: about 1200-1025
Mesopotamia: about 1100, Assyrian hegemony under Tiglath-Pileser I, followed by decline of Assyria and appearance of the **Aramaean kingdoms** (Damascus, Zobah, Hamath, temporarily Babylon, etc.)	1100	About 1125: Deborah and Barak triumph over the Canaanites at Taanach
Egypt: 21st dynasty, 1085-945. Capital: Tanis. Wenamon's journey to Byblos	1050	About 1050: Philistine victory at Aphek and death of Eli
		SAMUEL appears about 1040. The sanctuary at Shiloh
		SAUL: about 1030-1010. Resides at Gibeah. Victories over Ammonites and Philistines. Defeat at Gilboa and death of Saul
Siamon: 975-955	1000	DAVID: about 1010-970. **Capture of Jerusalem** about 1000. Victories over Philistines, Moabites, king of Zobah, Aramaeans of Damascus, Ammonites, Amalekites, Edomites. Alliance with Hamath, 2 S 8
Rezin, king of Damascus, 1 K 11:23f Psusennes II: 955-950	950	SOLOMON: about 970-931 Marries Pharaoh's daughter. In his 4th year: **the building of the Temple**, 1 K 6:1. *Excavations at Megiddo have uncovered Solomon's stables,* 1 K 5:6; 10:26. Commercial contacts with Phoenicia and Arabia. Literary activity: proverbs, historiography (2 S 9 - 1 K 2)

V. JUDAH AND ISRAEL 931-721
1 K 12-22 / 2 K 1-17 / 2 Ch 10-28 / Am / Ho / Is / Mi

	B.C.	*ISRAEL*	*JUDAH*
Egypt: 22nd dynasty: about 945-725 (Libyan). Capital: Bubastis		*Iron Age II: about* 900-600 Assembly at Shechem and **schism**, 1 K 12: about 931	
SHESHONK I: 945-925 Sheshonk's campaign in Palestine (the Karnak list)		Jeroboam I: 931-910. Residence at Tirzah. Worship at Dan and Bethel	Rehoboam: 931-913. In his 5th year, Temple pillaged by Sheshonk, 1 K 14:25f. *(Sheshonk's stele at Megiddo)*
Tabrimmon (son of Hezion) king of Damascus, 1 K 15:18		Nadab: 910-909	Abijah: 913-911
Ben-hadad I (his son), 1 K 15:18	900	Baasha: 909-886. Massacre of the House of Jeroboam	Asa: 911-870. Struggle against idolatry. Allies with Ben-hadad against Baasha
		Elah: 886-885	
		Zimri: 7 days	
Revival of **Assyria**: Assurnasirpal II: 883-859 Egypt's weakness in 9c. and first half of 8c.		OMRI: 885-874. Founds **Samaria.** Controls the territory of Moab	
Ben-hadad II, king of Damascus SHALMANESER III: 858-824. 853, victory at **Kharkar** on the Orontes over 12 kings, including Adadezer (= Ben-hadad) and Ahab		AHAB: 874-853. Marries Jezebel, daughter of Ittobaal, king of Tyre and Sidon. Temple of Baal. Enlarges his palace. *Samaritan ivories*, cf. 1 K 22:39. **Elijah** and the Yahwist reaction, 1 K 17-19; 21; 2 K 1. Wars against Ben-hadad II, 1 K 20; 22	JEHOSHAPHAT: 870-848. Struggle against idolatry. Allied to Ahab. Controls Edom
		Ahaziah: 853-852	
Mesha king of Moab. His stele about 840 (oppression of Omri and Ahab, then defeat of Israel) Hazael king of Damascus. 841, defeated by Shalmaneser III who reaches the sea and receives tribute from Jehu and the kings of Tyre and Sidon	850	Jehoram: 852-841, his brother. Campaigns with the king of Judah against Mesha. **Elisha,** 2 K 2-13. Jehoram defends Ramoth-gilead with Ahaziah of Judah against Hazael. Put to death, with his whole family, by Jehu	Jehoram: 848-841. Marries Athaliah daughter of Ahab. Baal-worship. Edom set free Ahaziah: 841. Killed on Jehu's orders
Ben-hadad III king of Damascus. Defeated by Shalmaneser III		Jehu: 841-814. Yahwist reaction. Hazael secures Gilead	Athaliah: 841-835. Massacre of the king's sons, except Joash. Jehoiada's plot and death of Athaliah
Adadnirari III: 810-783. 805, receives tribute from Ben-hadad III and the king of Israel	800	Jehoahaz: 841-798, son of Jehu. Harassed by Ben-hadad III, 2 K 13:3, cf. 2 K 6:24 +	Joash: 835-796, son of Ahaziah. Repairs the Temple. Hazael captures Gath
		Joash: 798-783. Death of Elisha. Joash regains lost cities from Ben-hadad, 2 K 13:25. Defeats Amaziah at Beth-shemesh	Amaziah: 796-781. Victory over Edom. Defeated by Joash of Israel. Killed at Lachish
783-745, Assyria weak Egypt: rivalry between 22nd dynasty (Bubastis) and 23rd (Thebes)	750	Jeroboam II: 783-743. Re-establishes Israel's boundaries. About 750, **Amos** and, a little later, **Hosea.** *Under Jeroboam or Joash: Samaritan ostraca*	Uzziah: 781-740 (= Azariah). Re-establishes his authority as far as Elath. Agriculture develops
TIGLATH-PILESER III: 745-727 (= Pulu in Babylon). **Conquered lands reduced to provinces: and populations exchanged**		Zechariah: 743 Shallum: 743	

		B.C.	
Rezin king of Damascus	Menahem: 743-738. Tribute to Pul, 2 K 15:19		740, call of **Isaiah**, Is 6:1
About 738, Tiglath-Pileser III receives tribute from Rezin, Menahem and the princes of the west	Pekahiah: 738-737. Killed by Pekah		Jotham: 740-736. First appearance of **Micah**
About 734, T.-Pileser III captures part of Galilee. Ahaz pays him tribute	Pekah: 737-732. Loses Galilee and Gilead, 2 K 15:29		Ahaz: 736-716 Rezin and Pekah besiege Jerusalem. **Oracle of Emmanuel.** Appeal to T.-Pileser III who takes Damascus and kills Rezin, 2 K 16:9
About 732, T.-Pileser's campaign against Rezin and end of Damascus' independence; he replaces Pekah by Hosea	Hoshea: 734-732. Makes alliance with Egypt		
Shalmaneser V: 726-722	Samaria besieged by Shalmaneser V		
SARGON II: 721-705. In 721, conquers Samaria, deports inhabitants and replaces them with foreign colonists	721, **conquest of Samaria**, deportation of inhabitants, installation of foreign colonists; religious syncretism; 2 K 17:5f		

VI. END OF THE KINGDOM OF JUDAH 721-587
2 K 18-25 / 2 Ch 29-36 / Zp / Na / Hab / Jr / Ezk

Sargon defeats Sibê the Egyptian at Raphia	Egypt: 24th dynasty. Capital: Sais		HEZEKIAH: 716-687. Sargon's army captures Ashdod, Is 20:1. Embassy of Merodach-baladan, 2 K 20:12f
His palace at Khorsabad near Nineveh			
711, Sargon captures Ashdod	Bocchoris: 715-709		
721-711 and 703, the Chaldaean Marduk-apal-iddinna II, king of Babylon	25th dynasty (Nubian)		
SENNACHERIB: 704-681	Shabaka: 710-696		
701, victory of Eltekeh over the Ekronites aided by Egyptians and Ethiopians (Nubians). He takes 46 towns from Hezekiah and imposes a tribute		700	Hezekiah's works at Jerusalem, and *inscription in the tunnel of Siloam*. Sennacherib invades Judaea. Hezekiah's tribute, 2 K 18:13-16 Literary activity. Pr 25:1
About 690, campaign in Arabia, as far as Dumah. On his return, capture of Lachish (relief of Nineveh, undated)	Shabatoka: 696-685 TIRHAKAH, his brother, born about 710 and co-regent about 690. King 685-664		Second (?) campaign of Sennacherib in Palestine, capture of Lachish, threat of Tirhakah, retreat of Sennacherib, 2 K 18: 17-19:37
ESARHADDON, 680-669			Manasseh, 687-642. Pagan cults in the Temple. Captivity in Babylon, 2 Ch 33:11
About 671, Esarhaddon takes Lower Egypt from Tirhakah. Tribute from the kings of the west, among whom, Manasseh			
ASHURBANIPAL: 668-621			
668, tribute from Manasseh. Tirhakah pushed back beyond Thebes			
About 663, his second Egyptian campaign, against Tirhakah; sack of Thebes	Tanutamon: 664-656 26th dynasty: 663/525. Capital, Sais		

		B.C.	
	PSAMMETICHUS I: 663-609		
The Library of Ashurbanipal at Nineveh	About 650, Assyrians driven from Egypt	650	
			Amon: 642-640
			JOSIAH: 640-609
			About 630, **Zephaniah**
			627, call of **Jeremiah, Jr 25:3**
Ashuretililani: 625-621	About 625, he checks the **Scythian invasion**		
Babylon: **neo-Babylonian dynasty,** 625-539			622, discovery of **'The Book of the Law'. Religious reform** which spreads to Samaria. Editing of historical documents in the spirit of Dt: 1st revision of the Books of **Joshua, Judges, Samuel** and **Kings**
NEBUPOLASSAR: 625-605			
Shinsharishkun: 620-612, king of Assyria			
612, CYAXARES, king of the Medes, and Nebupolassar take and destroy Nineveh			About 612, **Nahum**
Ashur-uballit II: 611-606; reigns in Haran			
609, Nebupolassar repulses the army of Neco coming to the aid of Assyria	Neco: 609-593		609, Josiah is killed while opposing Neco's armies
			609, Jehoahaz: replaced at the end of three months by his brother:
606, **Assyrian empire ended by Nebupolassar**			Jehoiakim: 609-598, at Neco's instigation
NEBUCHADNEZZAR: 604-562			In 605, Nebuchadnezzar, crown prince, defeats Neco at **Carchemish**. Jr 46:2, cf. 2 K 24:1,7; **prophecy of the 70 years of exile**, Jr 25:1,11; Jehoiakim a vassal for 3 years
His building at Babylon. Few texts concerning his campaigns			
		600	About 602, revolt of Jehoiakim and incursion of bands of Chaldaeans and Aramaeans, 2 K 24:2. The prophet **Habakkuk** (?)
			Jehoiachin: 598
Tablets naming Jehoiachin in the court records of Nebuchadnezzar			Siege of Jerusalem. After a reign of 3 months, Jehoiachin surrenders to Nebuchadnezzar. **Deportation to Babylon.** Jehoiachin replaced by his uncle:
			Zedekiah: 598-587 (son of Josiah)
	Psammetichus II: 593-588		Jeremiah and the false prophets. **Ezekiel** predicts the ruin of Jerusalem, Ezk 1-23
588-587, siege of Tyre; lasted 13 years	Hophra (Apries): 588-566		589, revolt of Zedekiah. In Dec. or Jan. beginning of the siege of Jerusalem
			Early 587, diversion by Hophra and lifting of siege, Ezk 29; Jr 37:5,11. *Letters of Lachish.* Jeremiah imprisoned
			Defeat of Hophra and renewal of siege

		B.C.	
			Siege of Tyre, Ezk 26f
			June-July 587, **capture of Jerusalem.** Capture of Zedekiah
Nebuzeriddinam heads a list of royal functionaries			One month later, Nebuzaradan destroys the Temple and the city. Fresh deportations
			Gedaliah as governor; assassinated Sept.-Oct. Jeremiah taken to Egypt, Jr 42f
			582/581, fresh deportations, Jr 52:30
568/567, campaign against Amasis	569: AMASIS co-regent. 566-526(?): king		
AVILMARDUK: 561-560			561, Evil-merodach pardons Jehoiachin
NERIGLISSAR: 559-556			
LABASHIMARDUK: 556			
NABONIDUS: 555-538. During his stay at Teima he is replaced by the crown prince BELSHAZZAR			
555, CYRUS king of the **Persians** revolts against his overlord Astyages king of the Medes			
549, Cyrus king of the Medes and Persians		550	**Is 40-55**
546, he captures Sardis (Croesus)			
	525, PSAMMETICHUS III		

VII. FROM THE RESTORATION TO THE PERSIAN PERIOD 538-333
Ezr / Ne / Hg / Zc / Ml

539, armies of Cyrus enter Babylon. He gives back to their original cities the idols carried off to Babylon		
		538, the **Edict of Cyrus.** Return from exile. SHESHBAZZAR high commissioner, Ezr 5:14
The palace of Pasargadae		Autumn of 538, restoration of the altar of holocausts, Ezr 3:3
		Spring 537, foundation of the **Second Temple,** Ezr 3:8; 5:16
CAMBYSES: 529-522. Son of Cyrus. Conquers Egypt which remains under Persian dominion till 400 (27th dynasty)		
DARIUS I: 522-486. Organises the Persian empire: Syria and Palestine form the 5th satrapy and Egypt the 6th		520-515, building of the **Second Temple,** Ezr 6:15; Hg 2:15. High Commissioner ZERUBBABEL; High Priest JOSHUA. The prophets **Haggai** and **Zechariah**
The palace of Persepolis	500	
490, battle of Marathon		498-399, *papyri from the Jewish colony of Elephantine*
XERXES I: 486-465. (Ahasuerus)		
480, he captures Athens but is defeated at Salamis		
ARTAXERXES I LONGIMANUS: 465-423. Revolts in Egypt and Syria		Opposition of the Samaritans to construction of the walls of Jerusalem, Ezr 4:6f
Athens: Pericles		458, Ezra's mission, if Ezr 7:7 refers to Artaxerxes I

	B.C.	
	450	445-443, the 1st mission of NEHEMIAH, Ne 2:1; 5:14, and the restoration of the walls. Hostility of Sanballat *(governor of Samaria, according to one of the Elephantine papyri)*, of Tobiah the Ammonite and Geshem the Arab
		Under Xerxes and Artaxerxes, **Malachi** and probably **Obadiah**, possibly also **Job**, **Proverbs**, **Song of Songs** and **Ruth** and many **Psalms** (428, Ezra's mission, if we read 37th in place of 7th year in Ezr 7:7f)
Xerxes II: 423		Before the death of Artaxerxes: 2nd mission of Nehemiah and the reforms inspired by Deuteronomy, Ne 13:6f
Darius II Nothus: 423-404		
Arsames satrap of Egypt		419, *Rescript of Darius on the Passover (Papyrus of Elephantine)*
		About 410, *the incident at the temple of Yaho at Elephantine*
		Prosperity of the Jews in Babylon (archives of the banking family of Murashu)
Artaxerxes II Mnemon: 404-358		
410, revolt of Cyrus the Younger and expedition of the Ten Thousand		
About 400, Egypt frees herself. (28th-30th dynasties: 400-342)	400	(398, EZRA'S mission, if Ezr 7:7 refers to Artaxerxes II. The legislation of the Pentateuch, unified by Ezra, is sanctioned by Artaxerxes, Ezr 7:26)
Plato		
Artaxerxes III Ochus: 358-338	350	Judaea is formed into a theocratic state with its own coinage *(drachmas inscribed YHD, Judah)*
In 342, reconquest of Egypt (31st dynasty: 342-332)		
Philip of Macedon. Aristotle		
Arsetis: 338-336		
Darius III Codomannus: 336-330		Before Alexander, the prophet **Joel** and doubtless the work of the Chronicler: the Books of **Chronicles** and **Ezra-Nehemiah.** At the time of Alexander, **Zc 9-14**
ALEXANDER THE GREAT: 336-323		
333, conquest of Syria		End of the Persian period, or beginning of the hellenistic period: **Jonah, Tobit**
332, capture of Tyre and Gaza; entry into Egypt		
331, foundation of **Alexandria**		
331, ends the Persian empire by his victory at **Arbela**		
330-326, conquest of the Eastern satrapies and India		
323, he dies in Babylon		

VIII. THE HELLENISTIC PERIOD 333-63
1 M / 2 M / Dn 11

Alexander's generals, the Diadochoi (or 'successors'), quarrel over his empire (319-287)		B.C.	
In Egypt: the LAGIDES	In Syria and Babylonia: the SELEUCIDS		**Judaea ruled by the Lagides** until 197
PTOLEMY I SOTER: 323-285			
Foundation of the 'Museum' at Alexandria. At Athens, a little before 300, foundation of the Epicurean and Stoic schools	SELEUCUS I NICATOR: 312-280. 300, foundation of **Antioch** on the Orontes	300	Ptolemy I establishes Jews in Egypt and Seleucus I in Antioch (Josephus)
PTOLEMY II PHILADELPHUS: 285-246	ANTIOCHUS I SOTER: 280-261. Defeats the Galatian invaders of Asia Minor		Ptolemy II orders Greek translation of the Law by the **Seventy** (the 'Septuagint', cf. *apocryphal letter of Aristeas)*
276-273, war with Syria; continues until arrival of the Romans	ANTIOCHUS II THEOS: 261-246		
252, gives his daughter Berenice to Antiochus II who repudiates Laodice, cf. Dn 11:6	About 250, displaced from Upper Asia by the Parthians (the Arsakidae, 250 B.C.-244 A.D.)	250	Active hellenisation in Palestine. Perhaps the Books of **Ecclesiastes** and **Esther**
PTOLEMY III EUERGETES: 246-221	SELEUCUS II CALLINICOS: 246-226		Tobiah the Ammonite *(his building at Araq el-Emir)*
Supremacy of Egypt	Laodice has Berenice and her son assassinated, cf. Dn 11:6		
PTOLEMY IV PHILOPATOR: 221-205	ANTIOCHUS III THE GREAT: 223-187		The victorious Ptolemy III and Ptolemy IV offer sacrifices at Jerusalem. (Josephus and 3 Maccabees)
217, victory over Antiochus at Raphia	Numerous campaigns, for the most part successful		
PTOLEMY V EPIPHANES: 205-180			
199-198, Scopas, Ptolemy's general, returns to the offensive	201, he reconquers Palestine; siege and capture of Gaza	200	
Besieged in Sidon, Scopas surrenders, cf. Dn 11:10-16	198, Antiochus defeats Scopas at Panias		

After the defeat at Panias, Egypt plays a minor role	**Judaea in subjection to the Seleucids**: 197-142. The charter of Antiochus sanctions the theocratic status of the Jewish nation (Josephus; cf. 2 M 4:11)
193, Antiochus III gives his daughter **Cleopatra (I)** to Ptolemy, cf. Dn 11:17	
189-188, Antiochus is defeated at **Magnesia** by the Scipios. Heavy indemnity to pay in annual instalments. His son Antiochus (IV) is a hostage in Rome	
187, Antiochus III killed during the pillage of the temple of Bel at Elymais, cf. Dn 11:19	
SELEUCUS IV PHILOPATOR: 187-175	SIMON II, son of Onias II, is high priest. Works undertaken at Jerusalem, Si 50. Ben Sira writes **Ecclesiasticus**
In Egypt: PTOLEMY VI PHILOMETOR: 180-145. His mother Cleopatra is regent	ONIAS III, son of Simon II, high priest. Seleucus IV sends Heliodorus to seize the Temple treasure, 2 M 3; Dn 11:20. Onias at Antioch, 2 M 4:5
Enthroned in 172	Hyrcanus the Tobiad is family governor of Amman, cf. 2 M 3:11
Seleucus IV killed by his minister HELIODORUS	

	B.C.
ANTIOCHUS IV EPIPHANES: 175-164/163. Dn 11:21. Brother of Seleucus IV. His son Demetrius (I) a hostage in Rome	Jason high priest, brother of Onias. With support of the king, introduces Greek customs in Jerusalem
	MENELAUS high priest: 172-162. Has Onias killed, 2 M 4:30f; Dn 9:25f; 11:22
170, 1st Egyptian campaign. Antiochus has himself crowned king of Egypt. On his return he pillages the Temple (Polybius)	170, 1st Egyptian campaign. On his return (169), Antiochus pillages the Temple, 1 M 1:16f; 2 M 5:15f; Dn 11:24-28
168, 2nd Egyptian campaign. Antiochus retires under orders from Popilius Laenas, cf. Dn 11:29f	168, 2nd Egyptian campaign, 2 M 5:1
	167-164, The Great Persecution
	167, massacres at Jerusalem, 1 M 1:29f; 2 M 5:24f; Dn 11:30. The Syrians build the **Citadel**
	Decree abolishing Jewish practices and establishing the cult of the Olympian Zeus in the Temple, 1 M 1:44f; 2 M 6:1f; Dn 11:31; cf. 8:12 etc.
	25th Chislev 167 (mid-Dec.), the first pagan sacrifice on the new altar, 2 M 10:5; cf. 1 M 1:59
	The priest MATTATHIAS (grandson of Simeon the Hasmonaean) takes refuge in Modin and, with his five sons, gives the signal of revolt. The Hasidaeans join with him. Martyrdom of Eleazar, cf. Dn 11:32f
	166, death of Mattathias. His son JUDAS MACCABAEUS succeeds him: 166-160
165, expedition of Antiochus in Upper Asia	Victories by Judas: at **Emmaus** over Nicanor and Gorgias, 165. Lysias' first campaign
	164, agreement with the king. 25th Chislev (mid-Dec.), purification of the Temple and resumption of the sacrifices *(Encaenia)* a little more than 3 years after the outbreak of the great persecution, cf. Dn 7:25; 12:7; 8:14; 9:27
	The Book of **Daniel** in its present form. The apocryphal Book of *Enoch* is in part anterior
	164-163, expeditions of Judas and his brothers throughout Judaea, 1 M 5; 2 M 10:15-23; 12:10-46 (sacrifice for the dead)

NOTE: If one takes into account the Babylonian tablet, B.M. 35.603, the table must be adjusted as from the autumn or winter of 164: the death of Antiochus IV occurs before the purification of the Temple (following the sequence of 2 M 9-10), and the campaign of Antiochus V and Lysias takes place in the autumn of 163. 1 and 2 M follow the autumnal Seleucid cursus (see Calendar), except for 1 M 1:54; 4:52; 9:3,54; 10:21; 16:14; 2 M 1:7,9; 13:1; 14:4 which seem to follow a religious calendar based on a vernal calculation agreeing with the Seleucid cursus of Babylon.

164/163, death of Antiochus IV at Tabae after the sack of the temple of Artemis at Elymais (Polybius)	164/163, death of Antiochus, 1 M 6:1f; 2 M 1:13f; 9:1f
ANTIOCHUS V EUPATOR: 163-162. Son of Antiochus IV, 12 years old. Philip is named regent, but the minister LYSIAS remains in power	
	162, Antiochus V and Lysias rout Judas at **Bethzechariah** and besiege Mount Zion. The arrival of Philip at Antioch forces them to negotiate, 1 M 6:28f; 2 M 13:1,2,9-26; 11:22-26

	B.C.	
DEMETRIUS I SOTER: 162-150. Cousin of Antiochus V, who along with Lysias is put to death by his orders		ALCIMUS high priest. BACCHIDES, governor of Syria, causes the death of sixty Hasidaeans
		160, Nicanor is defeated and killed at **Adasa**, the 'Day of Nicanor', 13th Adar (March)
		Jason of Cyrene writes the work subsequently adapted, about 124, by the author of the **Second Book of Maccabees**, cf. 2:19f and 1:9
		Alliance with Rome
		April 160, Judas defeated and killed at **Beerzeth**: tyranny of the Bacchides
		JONATHAN succeeds his brother: 160-142
		159-152, death of Alcimus and a period of peace
152, Alexander Balas lands at Ptolemais		152, JONATHAN named high priest by the pretender Alexander Balas. Demetrius I vainly tries to outbid him
ALEXANDER BALAS: 150-145	150	150/149, Jonathan named *strategos* and meridarch by Alexander
148, Macedonia becomes a Roman province		
147, Demetrius (II), son of Demetrius I, arrives in Cilicia		About this time, Onias, son of Onias III, founds the Jewish Temple at Leontopolis *(Tel el-Yehudiyeh, in the Delta)*; it survives until about 73 A.D. (Josephus)
146, destruction of Carthage and Corinth		About 146, Apollonius, named governor of Coele-Syria by Demetrius II, is defeated by Jonathan at Gaza
145, near Antioch, Ptolemy VI and Demetrius defeat Alexander Balas, who is killed soon after. Ptolemy dies of his wounds		The **Pharisees** and **Sadducees**. The **Essenes**: the monastery of Qumrân, *The Manual of Discipline*
PTOLEMY VII PHYSCON: 145-116		
		Apocryphal writings: *Jubilees*, and part of *Testament of the Twelve Patriarchs*
DEMETRIUS II: 145-138 and 129-125		Demetrius II confirms the conquests of Jonathan
ANTIOCHUS VI: 145-142. Son of Alexander Balas; put forward by Tryphon, one of Alexander's generals, against Demetrius who loses Syria		Antiochus VI names Jonathan governor of Syria and his brother Simon *strategos* of the coast. Jonathan holds the generals of Demetrius in check. Simon captures Bethzur
		143, Tryphon treacherously takes Jonathan prisoner
		SIMON high priest and ethnarch: 143-134. He occupies Jaffa to secure a port, 1 M 14:5
		Tryphon's campaign against Simon suffers a setback. 142, Tryphon has Jonathan killed
142, TRYPHON has Antiochus VI put to death and reigns until 138		142, Simon recognises Demetrius II, who confirms him as high priest and ethnarch. The Jews now autonomous, 1 M 13:41f
		June 141, the Citadel surrenders to Simon
140-138, campaign by Demetrius in Upper Asia; defeated by the Parthian king ARSACES VI and captive until 129		His son John Hyrcanus heads the army
		139, renewal of the Roman alliance

	B.C.	
ANTIOCHUS VII SIDETES: 138-129. Younger brother of Demetrius II. Tryphon is defeated and commits suicide (138)		The sons of Simon rout Cendebaeus, governor of the coast for Antiochus VII
		Feb. 134, Simon killed by his son-in-law Ptolemy. Hyrcanus escapes assassination
113, ATTALUS III, king of Pergamum, bequeathes his states to Rome, which organises province of Asia in 129		JOHN HYRCANUS (I): 134-104. High priest and ethnarch. Here **1 Maccabees** comes to an end (revision completed about 100)
129-64, the successors of Sidetes destroy themselves in family feuds; they have lost control of Palestine		John Hyrcanus conquers Moab and Samaria; destruction of the temple at Gerizim
		ARISTOBULUS I: 104-103. He assumes the title of king
About 84, ARETAS III, king of Nabataea, occupies Coele-Syria	100	ALEXANDER JANNAEUS: 103-76. New conquests. Struggle against the Pharisees
70, TIGRANES, king of Armenia, dominates the whole of Syria		ALEXANDRA: 76-67. Her son HYRCANUS II is high priest: 76-67, and again 63-40. In 67 he succeeds his mother but is soon supplanted by his younger brother
67, the Roman province of Crete-Cyrenaica		ARISTOBULUS II: 76-63. King and high priest
66-62, POMPEY in the East. Pontus and Bithynia become Roman provinces		Passover 65, Hyrcanus II and Aretas III besiege Jerusalem, but on instructions from Pompey they retire and are subsequently defeated by Aristobulus II
64, at Antioch, Pompey deposes Philip II, last of the Seleucids, and makes **Syria a Roman province**		Between 100 and 50, the Book of **Judith**

IX. ROMAN PALESTINE TO THE TIME OF HADRIAN 63 B.C.-135 A.D.

63, Pompey at Damascus. Arrogance of Aristobulus and incapacity of Hyrcanus		Summer or autumn 63, **Pompey takes Jerusalem,** names Hyrcanus high priest and sends Aristobulus and his son Antigonus to Rome
		The Idumaean ANTIPATER, minister of Hyrcanus, is the real ruler of Judaea. Rebellion of the last of the Hasmonaeans
CLEOPATRA VII, queen of Egypt: 51-30	50	About 50, in Alexandria, **Wisdom**
48, JULIUS CAESAR defeats Pompey at Pharsalia. Pompey killed in Egypt		*The Psalms of Solomon*
		47, Caesar names HYRCANUS ethnarch (47-41). Herod son of Antipater is named *strategos* of Galilee; the revolt of Hezekiah is suppressed
44, Caesar is assassinated		
41-30, ANTONY in the East		41, Antony names Herod and his brother Phasael as tetrarchs
40, **Parthians** in Syria and Palestine		
End of 40, the Senate declares Herod king		ANTIGONUS: king and high priest, 40-37. Herod flees to Rome. Hyrcanus is mutilated
38, Parthians driven from Syria and Palestine		39-37, struggle between Herod and Antigonus
		Early 37, Herod marries MARIAMNE I, granddaughter of Aristobulus II and Hyrcanus II

	B.C.
Sosius governor of Syria: 38-37	June(?) 37, **capture of Jerusalem by Sosius and Herod**
31, OCTAVIAN defeats Antony at naval battle of **Actium**	HEROD THE GREAT effectively king: 37-4 B.C.
30, suicide of Antony and Cleopatra. Egypt a Roman province	
29, Octavian, Imperator for life and, in 27, named AUGUSTUS	Herod builds the Antonia, and in 23 the Palace in the upper city. Founds or rebuilds Antipatris, Phaselis, Samaria (Sebaste), the Herodion and Caesarea
Syria an imperial province with a legate from Augustus	
Herod 'rex socius'	Numerous wives: in 23, Mariamne II, daughter of the High Priest Simon, son of Boethos. (Mariamne I was put to death in 29 and, some time after 30, her grandfather Hyrcanus)
25, Galatia a Roman province	
24, Herod is given Trachonitis, Batanaea and Auranitis and later Paneas	Winter of 20-19, start of the rebuilding of the Temple
13-11, M. Titius legate in Syria. His successor is not known	The Pharisees Hillel and Shammai and their rival schools
About 10(?), Sulpicius Quirinius (as legate of Syria?) subdues the Homonades of Taurus. Several indications of a census throughout the empire	The census of Lk 2:1f? Cf. the *lapis Venetus* inscription, undated, giving evidence of a census in Apamea (Syria) by order of Quirinius 'legate in Syria'. Cf. Lk 2:2
ARETAS IV succeeds his father Obodas II as king of Nabataea and reigns until 39	9-8, Herod violates the territory of the Nabataeans to capture the brigands of Trachonitis sheltered by the minister Syllaios, who complains to Augustus. Temporary disgrace of Herod
Sentius Saturninus, legate in Syria: 9-6	
	About the year 7, Herod has Alexander and Aristobulus, his two sons by Mariamne I, strangled
According to Tertullian, it is Saturninus who initiates the census of Judaea	More than 6000 Pharisees refuse to take the oath to Augustus on the occasion of a census (?) (which continues that of Quirinius?)
Quintilius Varus, legate in Syria: 6-4	Birth of JESUS, about 7-6(?)
	March of the year 4, the affair of the golden eagle in the Temple. Execution of Antipater, eldest son of Herod. Herod's will in favour of the sons of Malthake the Samaritan (Archelaus and Herod Antipas) and the son of Cleopatra (Philip)
	End of March, beginning of April, 4 B.C., **death of Herod** at Jericho. Archelaus takes his body to the Herodion
Sabinus, procurator for Augustus in Syria	4, at the Passover (11th April) Archelaus puts down a rebellion at Jerusalem, then goes to Rome to appeal to Augustus for the title of king
End of year 4, Augustus confirms Herod's last will, but omits the title of king for Archelaus	Sabinus comes to Jerusalem to make an inventory of the resources of the kingdom of Herod: sharp opposition and trouble throughout the country. At this time, possibly, the rebellion of Judas the Galilean, cf. Ac 5:37, and of the Pharisee Saddok who urged disobedience to Rome and refusal to pay taxes. (Origin of the Zealots, cf. Mt 22:17) Sabinus appeals to Varus who pursues the rebels; 2000 are crucified
Archelaus ethnarch of Judaea and Samaria: 4 B.C.-6 A.D.	
Herod Antipas tetrarch of Galilee and Peraea: 4 B.C.-39 A.D.	
Philip tetrarch of Gaulanitis, Batanaea, Trachonitis, Auranitis and the district of Paneas (Ituraea): 4 B.C.-34 A.D.	The *Assumption of Moses* (apoc.)

3-2 B.C., the successor to Varus is unknown. Some here place Quirinius as legate	B.C.	If Quirinus was in fact legate 3-2, he could have continued the census begun by Sabinus and ordered the census of Apamea (the undated *lapis Venetus*)
1/2 A.D. - 4, Quirinius is counsellor to young GAIUS CAESAR, grandson of Augustus, during his mission to the East	A.D. 1	Philip the tetrarch builds Julias (Bethsaida). He enriches the shrine of Pan (Paneas, the *Paneion*), which he names Caesarea in honour of Augustus
VOLUSIUS SATURNINUS, legate in Syria: 4-5 A.D.		
6, Augustus deposes Archelaus who is exiled to Vienne (Gaul)		
6-41, **Judaea a procuratorial province** (with Caesarea as the capital)		
6-8, COPONIUS procurator		
6, according to Josephus, QUIRINIUS legate in Syria(?)		6, according to Josephus, Quirinius comes to Judaea to make an inventory of possessions of Archelaus; this could have provoked the rebellion of Judas and Saddok. But for the year 6 Josephus repeats events he has described for the year 4
		ANNAS, son of Seth, high priest: 6(?)-15
		Between 5 and 10, birth of Paul at Tarsus; pupil of Gamaliel the Elder, Ac 22:3, cf. 5:34
14 (19th August), death of Augustus. TIBERIUS emperor: 14-37		
VALERIUS GRATUS procurator: 15-26		Valerius Gratus deposes Annas. Three other high priests follow, then JOSEPH CALLED CAIAPHAS: 18-36
17-19, GERMANICUS, adopted son of Tiberius, in the East		About 17, foundation of Tiberias by Antipas. Under Tiberius, LYSANIAS tetrarch of Abilene, Lk 3:1 *and inscriptions*
18, Cappadocia a Roman province		
26-36, PONTIUS PILATE procurator		About 27, Herod Antipas, married to the daughter of Aretas, marries Herodias, the wife of his brother Herod (son of Mariamne II)
The 15th year of Tiberius, Lk 3:1: 19th August 28 or 18th August 29, but according to the Syrian calculation: Sept.-Oct. 27 to Sept.-Oct. 28		Autumn of 27, the preaching of JOHN THE BAPTIST and the beginning of the ministry of Jesus. Cf. Lk 3:2 +
		28, Passover. Jesus in Jerusalem, Jn 2:13. The 46 years of Jn 2:20 begin from 20/19 B.C.
		Beginning of 29, John, imprisoned at Machaerus (Josephus), is beheaded, Mt 14:3
		29, shortly before the Passover, the multiplication of the loaves, Jn 6:1; Mt 14:13
		Feasts of Tabernacles and of the Dedication: Jesus in Jerusalem, Jn 7-10
'(The) Christ condemned to death by Pontius Pilate, under the Emperor Tiberius' (Tacitus, *Annals*)		30, on the eve of the Passover, i.e. 14th Nisan, a Friday, death of Jesus, Jn 19:31f. (The Passover fell on the Saturday, 8th April in 30 and 4th April in 33: the second date is too late, cf. Jn 2:20). Cf. Mt 26:17 +
		30, **Pentecost**, outpouring of the Spirit on the Church, Ac 2. The first community, Ac 2:42, etc.
33-34, Philip dies without an heir and Tiberius joins his tetrarchy with the province of Syria		Pontius Pilate has difficulties with the Jews: the incidents of the standards and shields (Philo). Pilate's aqueduct

	A.D.	
		Election of the seven hellenist deacons, Ac 6:1f
L. VITELLIUS, legate in Syria: 35-39. The father of the emperor Vitellius		About 35, Pontius Pilate orders the massacre of the Samaritans at Gerizim
He is given full powers in the East		36, Passover. Vitellius in Jerusalem. He replaces Caiaphas with JONATHAN, son of Annas
36, on the Euphrates, he concludes a pact with Artaban, king of the Parthians. Antipas is with him		36, the troops of Aretas defeat those of Antipas. Tiberius orders Vitellius to attack Aretas
		Autumn of 36, Pontius Pilate is sent to Rome by Vitellius to justify his conduct. He dies a violent death (execution or suicide)
36-37, winter. Vitellius concentrates the legions at Ptolemais		36-37, winter (?), **martyrdom of Stephen** and **dispersion** of part of the community. A little later, **conversion** of PAUL. Cf. Ac 9:1 +
37, March. Death of Tiberius. Vitellius breaks off his campaign against Aretas		37, Passover. Vitellius, on his way to Petra, stops at Jerusalem. He replaces Jonathan with his brother THEOPHILUS, high priest from 37-41
CALIGULA emperor: 37-41		
MARCELLUS procurator		Paul in 'Arabia', then in Damascus, Ac 9:19f; Ga 1:17f
37, Caligula gives AGRIPPA I, son of Aristobulus, the tetrarchies of Philip and Lysanias, with the title of king. (37-44)		
38, persecution of the Jews in Alexandria. 39, embassy of the Jewish philosopher Philo to Rome (he dies after 41)		
39-42, P. PETRONIUS legate in Syria		About 39, Paul escapes from Damascus, 2 Co 11:32f, and makes a first visit to the elders of the Church, Ga 1:18f (Cephas and James the brother of the Lord); Ac 9:25f
39, Caligula exiles Antipas to the Pyrenees and gives his tetrarchy to Agrippa I		39, Caligula orders the erection of his statue in the Temple. Thanks to Petronius and Agrippa I the affair drags on until the assassination of Caligula
41-54, CLAUDIUS emperor. Agrippa I, now in Rome, contributes to his success; Claudius concedes him Judaea and Samaria. His brother Herod becomes king of Chalcis (41-48) and marries Berenice (daughter of Agrippa)		The kingdom of Herod the Great is reconstituted. Agrippa builds the 3rd wall of Jerusalem, but at his death it is unfinished. Many buildings, in particular at Berytus (Beirut)
41, Claudius' edict and letter to the Alexandrians		
42-44, VIBIUS MARSIUS legate in Syria		About 43, Paul and Barnabas at **Antioch** which becomes the centre for the hellenistic Christians. PETER in Samaria (Simon the magician) and in the coastal plain (the centurion Cornelius)
44, spring. On the death of Herod Agrippa I, Judaea again becomes a procuratorial province, 44-66		43 or 44, before the Passover, Agrippa I orders the beheading of JAMES, BROTHER OF JOHN (James the Great); during the feast he imprisons Peter. Ac 12
CUSPIUS FADUS procurator 44-46		28th June 45, a rescript of Claudius gives the Jews the custody of the priestly vestments. Herod of Chalcis is named inspector of the Temple, with the right to nominate the high priest. In 47 he nominated Ananias, son of Nebadios (47-59), cf. Ac 23:2f
CASSIUS LONGINUS, the lawyer, legate in Syria: 45-50		

	A.D.	
		Fadus and the false prophet Theudas, cf. Ac 5:36
46-48, Tiberius Alexander procurator. Nephew of Philo, but an apostate. At this time, several famines throughout the empire		Between 45 and 49, **1st mission by Paul**: Antioch, Cyprus, Antioch in Pisidia, Lystra, ...Antioch, Ac 13:1f
48-52, Ventidius Cumanus procurator AGRIPPA II, son of Agrippa I, king of Chalcis 48-53. In 49 he is named inspector of the Temple, with the right to nominate the high priest		About 48, famine in Judaea, worsened by the sabbatical year 47/48. Visit to Jerusalem, by Helen, queen of Adiabene, a convert to Judaism; she brings relief to the population
49, Claudius 'drives from Rome the Jewish agitators stirred up by Chrestos' (Suetonius), cf. Ac 18:2		48-49, prophecy of Agabus and the aid given to the community at Jerusalem by that of Antioch. The **council of Jerusalem**: converts from paganism exempt from the Law, Ac 15:5f; Ga 2:1f
	50	About the year 50, the oral tradition of the gospel is put into written form: the **Aramaic Matthew,** and the complementary **collection.** The **Letter of James** (or about 58)
50-60, Ummidius Quadratus legate in Syria 52 (rather than 51), Gallio, brother of Seneca, proconsul of Achaia		50-52, 2nd mission by Paul: Lystra (Timothy), Phrygia, Galatia, Philippi, Thessalonika, Athens (sermon on the Areopagus)
		Winter of 50 to summer of 52, Paul in Corinth: the **Letters to the Thessalonians**; and, in the spring of 52, summoned to appear before Gallio. Summer 52, he goes to Jerusalem, Ac 18:22, and then to Antioch
Agrippa II in favour at Rome. Claudius exiles Cumanus		The Jews in their struggle against the Samaritans are supported by Cumanus. He is sent to Rome by Quadratus, who visits Jerusalem, Passover of 52
Antonius Felix procurator: 52-60. Brother of the freedman Pallas. Marries Drusilla, sister of Agrippa II, already married to Aziz, king of Emesa, cf. Ac 24:24		Felix checks brigandage
53, Claudius gives the tetrarchies of Philip and Lysanias to Agrippa II, in exchange for Chalcis, (53-93)		53-58, 3rd mission by Paul; Apollos at Ephesus and then at Corinth
54-68, NERO emperor 55, Nero adds a part of Galilee and Peraea to the kingdom of Agrippa		54-57, after passing through Galatia and Phrygia, Paul stays at Ephesus for 2¼ years. After 56(?), **Letter to the Philippians.** About Passover 57, **1 Corinthians.** Then a quick visit to Corinth, 2 Co 12:14. Return to Ephesus and **Letter to the Galatians**
		End of 57, passes through Macedonia. **2 Corinthians**
		Winter 57-58, at Corinth, Ac 20:3, cf. 1 Co 16:6; **Letter to the Romans**
		Passover 58, at Philippi, Ac 20:6, then, by sea, to Caesarea (Philip and Agabus)
		Summer 58, in Jerusalem. JAMES the Brother of the Lord heads the Judaeo-Christian community; his **Letter** to the Jews of the Dispersion (or possibly before 49)

	A.D.
	About 58, Felix disbands the followers of the Egyptian false prophet on the Mount of Olives, cf. Ac 21:38. He has the former High Priest Jonathan assassinated, in spite of the fact that he owed his position to Jonathan
	58, Pentecost. Paul arrested in the Temple and brought before Ananias and the Sanhedrin. Taken to Caesarea, he is brought before Felix
Between 59 and 67, Agrippa II nominates six high priests, among whom ANAN SON OF ANNAS (62)	58-60, Paul a captive at Caesarea, the scene of serious troubles between Jews and Syrians
60-63, CORBULO legate in Syria	60, Paul appears before Festus and appeals to Caesar. He pleads his cause before Agrippa and his sister Berenice
PORCIUS FESTUS, procurator : 60-62	
	Autumn of 60, Paul's voyage to Rome, the storm, he winters in Malta
	61-63, Paul in Rome under military guard. His apostolate, **Letters to Colossians, Ephesians, Philemon** (and **to Philippians?**)
LUCCEIUS ALBINUS procurator : 62-64	62, the High Priest Anan has **James** the brother of the Lord **stoned to death** (after the death of Festus and before the arrival of Albinus). SIMEON, son of Cleophas and of Mary (sister-in-law of the mother of Jesus), succeeded James as head of the church of Jerusalem (Eusebius)
	Anan deposed by Agrippa II
CESTIUS GALLUS legate in Syria: 63-66	63, Paul is set free, and possibly goes to Spain, Rm 15:24f
64, July, burning of Rome and persecution of the Christians	About **64, 1 Peter** and the **gospel of Mark**
	64 (or 67), **martyrdom of Peter** in Rome
64-66, GESSIUS FLORUS procurator. Nominated by influence of Poppaea, the Jewish wife of Nero	About 65, Paul at Ephesus, 1 Tm 1:3; in Crete, Tt 1:5; in Macedonia, whence he sends his **1st Letter to Timothy,** 1 Tm 1:3; and probably **Titus**
	The **Greek gospel of Matthew**; the **gospel of Luke** and the **Acts of the Apostles**: before 70? or about 80?
66, rising of the Alexandrian Jews. Tiberius Alexander, at that time prefect in Egypt, massacres several thousands	Summer 66, in Jerusalem, Florus crucifies some Jews, but a rising compels him to leave the city. Troubles in Caesarea and throughout the country
66-67, spectacular tour of Greece by Nero: he appoints VESPASIAN and his son TITUS to restore order in Palestine	Sept. 66, Jerusalem attacked by Cestius Gallus. He retires with heavy losses. Rebel government
	Exodus of people of importance and doubtless some Christians, cf. Lk 21:20f, who take refuge in Pella (Eusebius)
MUCIANUS legate in Syria: 67-69	67, Vespasian, with 60,000 men, reconquers Galilee (JOSEPHUS, its rebel governor, is taken prisoner)

	A.D.
	About 67, **Letter to the Hebrews**. Paul, a prisoner in Rome, writes **2 Timothy**. A little later he is beheaded
68, March, in Gaul the revolt of the legate Vindex	67-68, the Zealots of John of Gischala, escaped from Galilee, are masters of Jerusalem with the Idumaeans. Anan and the leading people are massacred
68, April, GALBA emperor 68, June, suicide of Nero	68, Vespasian occupies the maritime plain and the Valley of the Jordan (destruction of Qumrân). On Nero's death the siege of Jerusalem is broken off
69, January, OTHO proclaimed Emperor by the Praetorians and VITELLIUS by the legions in Germany	69, Simon Bargiora and the *sicarii* in Jerusalem. Vespasian subdues the rest of Judaea; the *sicarii* hold out in Jerusalem, and in the Herodion, Masada and Machaerus
69, July, Tiberius Alexander supports Vespasian. His lead is followed by all the East	
69-79, VESPASIAN emperor. He entrusts the siege of Jerusalem to Titus	70, Passover. Many pilgrims in Jerusalem. **Titus lays siege** to the city with four legions. Tiberius Alexander is second in command
End of 69, Vespasian in sole command of the empire	
	Capture of the 3rd wall, then of the 2nd. Circumvallation. Capture of the Antonia. Famine
	Beginning of August, sacrifices cease
	70, 29th August, capture of the Inner Court and **burning of the Temple** (the 10th of Loos, i.e. the 10th of the 5th month, the day when Nebuzaradan set fire to the first Temple, Jr 52:12 and Josephus)
	Sacrifice to the standards, in front of the Temple, cf. Mt 24:15. Titus hailed as Imperator
	70, Sept., capture of the Upper City and the palace of Herod. The inhabitants killed, sold into slavery or condemned to hard labour
70, end of the year, Judaea an imperial province; under the rule of the legate of the Xth Legion based in Jerusalem. Caesarea a Roman colony	Titus in Syria; many Jews killed in the gladiatorial games
	71, summer, triumph of Vespasian and Titus in Rome (with the Temple furnishings): execution of Simon Bargiora. The Arch of Titus
71-72, Lucilius Bassus legate in Judaea	The didrachma formerly subscribed to the Temple is now given to Jupiter Capitolinus
72, foundation of **Flavia Neapolis** (Naplus)	Capture of the Herodion and Machaerus, by L. Bassus
73, Flavius Silva legate in Judaea	Siege of **Masada** by F. Silva: Eleazar (descendant of Judas the Galilean) and his *sicarii* commit suicide rather than yield (Passover, 73)
A number of *sicarii* take refuge in Egypt, but are handed over to the Romans. Closing of the temple founded by Onias at Leontopolis	**Return** to Jerusalem of a group **of Judaeo-Christians** (Epiphanius). Rabbi Eleazar re-opens the synagogue of the Alexandrians
	Rabbi Johanan ben-Zakkai founds the **Academy of Yabneh** (Jamnia), successor to the Sanhedrin. Gamaliel II succeeds him; origins of the Mishna

	A.D.	
79-81, TITUS emperor		70-80, the **Letter of Jude**, then **2 Peter.** *2 Esdras* (apocryphal). About 78, the *Jewish War* (Josephus)
81-96, DOMITIAN emperor. Brother of Titus		About 93, *The Antiquities of the Jews* (Josephus)
95, has his cousin Flavius Clemens condemned to death as a Christian. Exiles his wife, Domitilla, to Pandataria		About 95, John exiled to Patmos. Final text of **Revelation.** *Letter of St Clement*, bishop of Rome, to the Corinthians
96-98, NERVA emperor 98-117, TRAJAN emperor		**Gospel of John**; then **1 John** (**3 John** and **2 John** are possibly earlier). He opposes Cerinthus and his Docetism
		The *Didache* (end of 1c.?)
CORNELIUS PALMA, legate in Syria, occupies the kingdom of Nabataea, which becomes the **province of Arabia,** capital Bostra (Bozra) (106)	100	At the beginning of Trajan's reign, **death of John at Ephesus**
Claudius Atticus Herodes governor of Judaea in 107		107, **martyrdom of Simeon,** 2nd bishop of Jerusalem. From now until the Second Revolt there are 13 other bishops, likewise Judaeo-Christians
111-113, PLINY THE YOUNGER legate in Bithynia. His letter on the persecution of the Christians and the **rescript of Trajan**		About 110, the seven *letters* of Ignatius, bishop of Antioch, and his martyrdom at Rome
114-116, annexation of Armenia, of Assyria and Mesopotamia. **The Roman empire at the height of its power**		A little later, the *Letter to the Philippians* of Polycarp, bishop of Smyrna and disciple of John († 156)
		The *Odes of Solomon* (apocryphal)
117, **rising of the Jews** throughout the East and revolt of the new provinces. These are recaptured by the Moor LUSIUS QUIETUS; he is named legate of Judaea		
117-138, HADRIAN emperor. Establishes the frontier of the empire on the Euphrates		Quietus erects the statue of Trajan in front of the altar of the Temple (Hippolytus). He is deposed and subsequently put to death by Hadrian
Hadrian's second tour of the empire, 128-134. At Athens the completion of the temple of the Olympian (or 'Capitoline') Zeus. Antiochus Epiphanes had contributed to its construction		About 130, the *Letter of Barnabas* (apocryphal). At Hierapolis in Phrygia, the bishop Papias. In Alexandria, the gnostic Basilides
Tineius Rufus legate in Judaea and Publicius Marcellus legate in Syria		130, Hadrian in Jerusalem. He decides to rebuild the city (Aelia Capitolina) and the Temple, now dedicated to Jupiter
		132-135, second Jewish rebellion
		Simeon Ben Koseba *(letters of Murabbaat)* seizes Jerusalem; Eleazar high priest. Ben Koseba acknowledged by Rabbi Akiba as Messiah and as the Star of Nb 24:17, whence his name of Bar Kokeba (Son of the Star). He persecutes the Christians because they refuse to join the revolt
		In spite of the reinforcements of Marcellus, Rufus is overrun by the rebels: Hadrian sends the legate in Britain, Julius Severus, and arrives in person
		Beginning of 134, **capture of Jerusalem**

A.D.

After the conquest of nearly 50 strongholds, Severus seizes **Bether,** where Bar Kokeba perishes (August, 135)

The captives are sold at Mamre and Gaza

The province of Judaea becomes the **province of Syria-Palestine.** Jerusalem a Roman colony, forbidden to the Jews

135, Rufus builds Aelia (the temple of Jupiter, Juno and Venus on the site of Calvary and the tomb of Christ). **The Temple is made into a sanctuary of Zeus and Hadrian**

The temple of Zeus Hypsistos at Gerizim and the sacred grove of Adonis around the Cave at Bethlehem

The bishop MARK (about 135-155) and the new Christian community. The Judaeo-Christians, dispersed in Transjordania and Syria, in time form the sect of the **Ebionites** (the 'Poor'), with the *Gospel of the Hebrews;* they do not accept the divinity of the Messiah and reject the Pauline Letters

II. SUCCESSORS OF ANTIOCHUS THE GREAT

The number preceding each name shows the order of succession among the Seleucid kings: thus, Antiochus the Great is the sixth in the dynasty. For the first five kings (see the General Chronology, VIII: Hellenistic Period), the succession is from father to son; the fifth king, Seleucus III, is brother to Antiochus the Great.

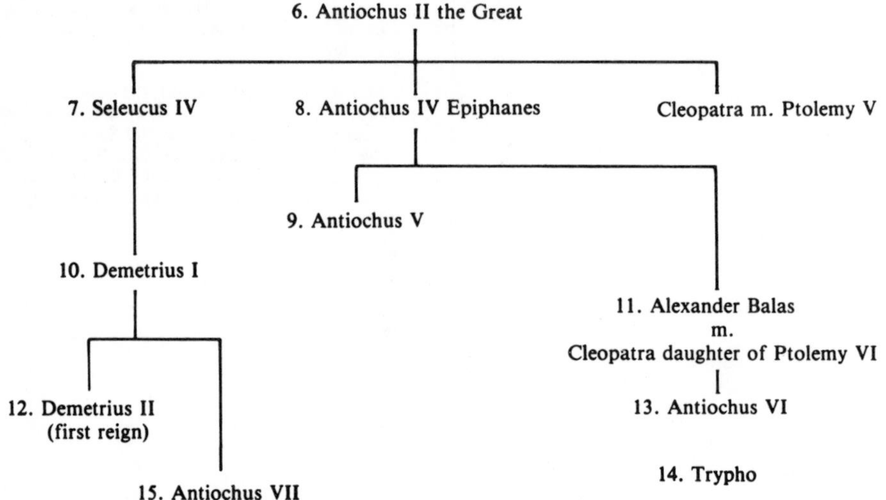

III. HASMONAEAN AND HERODIAN DYNASTIES

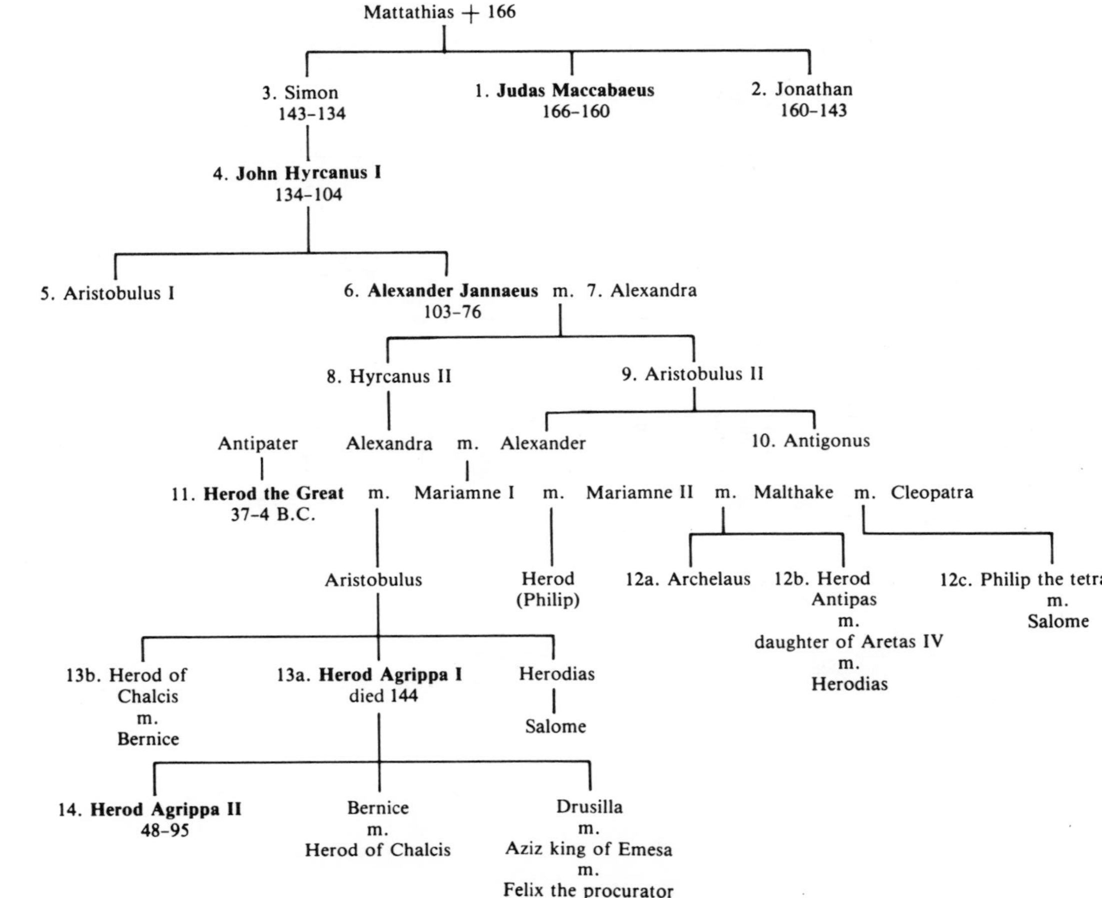

IV. OVERVIEW OF THE MAJOR PERSONALITIES OF THE BIBLE

1. FROM THE JUDGES TO SOLOMON

EGYPT				
Pharaohs				
	Cushan-rishathaim *(Edom? Aram Naharaiim?)*			1200
	Eglon *(Moab)*			
	Sisera *(Canaan)*			
	Oreb *and* Zeeb; Zebah *and* Zalmunna *(Midian)*			
				1050
	ARAM	AMMON	Others	
	Kings and others	Nahash	Agag *(Amalek)*	
	Geshur:			
	Talmai			1000
	Zobah:			
	Hadadezer			
	Shobach			
	Hamath:			
	Tou			
	Hadoram			
		Hanun	Hiram *(Tyre)*	
	DAMASCUS	Hadad *(Edom)*		
	Rezin			
[Psusennes II]				950

JUDAH and ISRAEL

Kings	*Ministers or military men*	*Prophets*	*Priests*
"Major" judges (in the order given in the Bible)			
	Othniel		
	Ehud		
	Barak	*and* Deborah	
	Gideon		
Abimelech *(Shechem)*			Eli *(at Shiloh)*
		Samuel	
Saul	Abner		Ahijah 1 Ahimelech 1 *(Nob)*
Ishbaal			
David	Joab	Gad	Abiathar
	Benaiah 1		Zadok
	Adoram	Nathan	Ira
	Joshaphat 3		
	Seraiah 1		
	Ahithophel		
Solomon	Elihoreph *and* Ahijah 2 Joshaphat 3 Azariah 3 Zabud Eliab 5 Adoram		Azariah 4

2. THE TWO PARALLEL KINGDOMS

EGYPT	DAMASCUS	ASSYRIA	Others		KINGDOM OF	
Pharaohs	*Kings and Officers*	*Kings*	*Kings*		*Kings*	*Ministers, Military Leaders*
Sheshonk					Rehoboam	
					Abijam	
	Tabrimmon				Asa	
	Ben-hadad I			900		
			Ethbaal *(Tyre)*			
					Jehoshaphat	Adnah *(military)*
	Ben-hadad II Naaman					
				850	Jehoram	
	Hazael		Mesha *(Moab)*			
					Ahaziah	
					Athaliah Jehoash	
	Ben-hadad III					
				800		
					Amaziah	
					Uzziah	Hananiah *(military)*
		Tiglath-pileser III	Shalman *(Moab)*	750		
					Jotham	
	Rezin *End of the kingdom of Damascus*	Shalmaneser V			Ahaz	Azrikam

JUDAH		KINGDOM OF ISRAEL			
Prophets	*Priests*	*Kings*	*Ministers*	*Prophets*	*Others*
Shemaiah 1		Jeroboam I		Ahijah 3	
Iddo 3		Nadab			
Oded 1		Baasha			
Azariah 10					
Hanani					
		Elah	Arza		
		Zimri			
		Omri			
		Ahab			Tibni
			Obadiah	Elijah	
Eliezer	Amariah 3			Elisha	
				Jehu 1	
				Micaiah son of Imlah	
				Zedekiah	
		Ahaziah			
		Jehoram			
		Jehu 2			Jonadab *(Rechabite)*
	Jehoiada 3				
Zechariah 6					
		Johoahaz			
		Joash			
	Azariah 7	Jeroboam II		Amos	Amaziah *(priest at Bethel)*
				Hosea	
				Jonah	
		Zechariah 9			
		Shallum			
		Menahem			
Micah of Moresheth					
		Pekahiah			
Isaiah	Uriah	Pekah		Oded 2	
		Hoshea			

End of the kingdom of Israel

EGYPT	BABYLON	ASSYRIA	Others
Pharaohs	*Kings and Officers*	*Kings*	*Kings*
		Sargon II	
[Shabaka]	Merodach-baladan		
		Sennacherib	
Tirhakah			
		Esarhaddon	
		Assurbanipal	
		MEDES	
		Cyaxares	
Neco			
	Nebuchadnezzar		
	Officers: Nebuzaradan Nergalsharezer Nebushazban		
Hophra			
			Baalis *(Ammon)*
	Evil-Merodach		
		Astyages	

KINGDOM OF JUDAH

	Kings	*Ministers, Military Leaders*	*Prophets*	*Priests*
	Hezekiah	Eliakim	Isaiah	Azariah 8
		Shebna		
700		Joah		
	Manasseh		Hozai	
650	Amon			
	Josiah			
		Ahikam	Zephaniah	Hilkiah 2
		Achbor		
		Asaiah		
		Shaphan		
		Joah	Jeremiah	
		Maaseiah	Huldah	
			Nahum	
	Jehoahaz			
	Jehoiakim		Uriah	
		Elishama		
		Delaiah		
		Elnathan		
		Gemariah		
		Zedekiah 3		
600				
			Habakkuk?	
	Jehoiachin			
	Zedekiah		Jeremiah	Seraiah 4
		Shephatiah	Hananiah 4	Jehoiada 4
		Gedaliah	*In exile:*	Zephaniah
		Jucal	Ezekiel	
		Pashhur 3	Ahab	
		Jonathan 9	Zedekiah 2	
		Seraiah3	Shemaiah 3	
	Governor:.	*Officers:*		
587	Gedaliah	Ishmael		
		Johanan 9		
		Jonathan 10		
		Seraiah		
		Jaazaniah		

3. PERSIAN PERIOD

PERSIA

Kings	High Officials	Governors of occupied territories	
Cyrus	Mithredath *(treasurer)*		550
		Tattenai *(Transeuphrates)*	
Darius I			
Xerxes (= Ahasuerus)		Rehum *(Samaria)*	500
Artaxerxes I			
	Nehemiah *(cupbearer)*		450
		Sanballat *(Samaria)*	
		Tobiah *(Ammonitis)*	
		Geshem (Kedar)	
Darius II			400
Darius III		MACEDONIA	350
		Kings	
		Philip II	
		Alexander the Great	

JUDAEA

Governors	*Officials*	*Prophets*	*High Priests*
Sheshbazzar			
Zerubbabel		Haggai Zechariah 22 ?Obadiah	Joshua 6
	District leaders Rephaiah Shallum 14 and 15 Malchijah Nehemiah Hashabiah		
Nehemiah		Noadiah	Eliashib
Secretary of State for Jewish Affairs Ezra			
		Joel	

4. HELLENISTIC PERIOD

EGYPT	SYRIA	Other Kingdoms	ROME	
Kings	*Kings and Authorities*	*Kings*	*Consuls and Legates*	
[Ptolemy I]	Seleucus I			300
[Ptolemy II]		Areius *(Sparta)*		
	Antiochus II			250
[Ptolemy III]	Seleucus II			
	Seleucus III			
[Ptolemy IV]	Antiochus III			
[Ptolemy V]	the Great			
				200
		Philip V *(Macedonia)*		
		Eumenes *(Pergamum)*	[Scipio]	
	Seleucus IV			
Ptolemy VI	Heliodorus			
	Apollonius 1			
	Antiochus IV Epiphanes			175
	Andronicus 1	Aretas I *(Nabataea)*		
	Apollonius 2	Perseus *(Macedonia)*		
	Seron			
	Lysias			
	Nicanor 1			
	Gorgias		Q. Memmius	
	Ptolemy 9		T. Manilius	
			M. Sergius	
	Antiochus V Eupator			
	Hegemonides			
	Gorgias			
	Demetrius I			
	Bacchides			
	Nicanor I			
	Alexander Balas			
Ptolemy VII	Demetrius II			150
	Apollonius 4			
	Lastnenes			
	Antiochus VI			
	Trypho	Arsaces VI *(Parthians)*	Lucius	
		Attalus II *(Pergamum)*		
		Ariarathes V		
		(Cappadocia)		
	Antiochus VII			
	Athenobius			
	Cendebaeus			
				134

JUDAEA

High Priests	*The Maccabees and Their Family*	*Military Leaders*	*Others*
Onias I			
Onias II			
Simon 4			
			John 20 *(Diplomat)*
Onias III			
			Simeon 6 *(Prefect of the Temple)*
Jason 3			Sostratus *(Prefect of the Citadel)*
Menelaus	Mattithiah 6		Philip 4 (*Commissioner*)
(Lysimachus)	Judah 7 (Macchabaeus)		
	Simeon 5		
		Zechariah 29	
Alicumus	Eleazar	Joseph 7	
		Azariah 23	
		Dositheus	
		Sosipater	Eupolemus *and* Jason 1 *(Ambassadors)*
	Jonathan 17		
	John 19		
Jonathan 17			
		Matthithiah 7	
		Judah 8	
			Numenius *and* Antipater
Simeon 5		Jonathan 18	*(Ambassadors)*
	John 21		
	Judah 9		
	Matthithiah 8		
		Judah 9	
John 21 [= Hyrcanus I]	Ptolemy 11		

5. ROMAN PERIOD

Roman Emperors	*Various Authorities*	*Procurators of Judaea*	
Augustus			
	Quirinius *(Syria)*		
			1
Tiberius			
	Lysanias *(Ituraea)*		
		Pontius Pilate	
			30
	Aretas IV *(king of Nabataea)*		
Claudius	Sergius Paulus *(Cyprus)*		
			50
	Gallio *(Achaia)*		
Nero		Felix	
	Publius *(Malta)*	Porcius Festus	60

Herodian Dynasty	*High Priests*	*"Christians"*	*Others*
Herod [the Great]			
		Jesus *(birth)*	?Judas the Galilean
Archelaus			?Theudas
Herod [Antipas]	Annas	John the Baptist	
[Herod] Philip 6	Caiphas		
[Herod] Philip 5			
		Jesus *(death)*	
		Peter	
		John 23	Gamaliel
		Stephen	
		Saul/Paul	
		Philip 8	Simon the Magician
		Barnabas	
Herod [Agrippa I]		James *(Brother of John)*	
		Silas	
		Timothy	
		Apollos	
	Hananiah 20	James *("Brother of the Lord")*	
		Paul *(prisoner)*	
Herod Agrippa II			

About the Authors

O. Odelain and R. Séguineau are connected with the famous Ecole Biblique de Jérusalem, the home of *The Jerusalem Bible,* and are two of the authors of the *Modern Concordance to the New Testament.*

Matthew J. O'Connell, the translator and adaptor, has translated several books, including *Catholic Pentecostalism* by René Laurentin, *God's Word and God's People* by Lucien Deiss, *The Humanity of God* and *The Humanity of Man,* the two-volume work by Edmond Barbotin, and, most recently, *A Materialist Reading of the Gospel of Mark* by Fernando Belo.

About the Authors

Maps

Lands of the Bible in Modern Times
International boundary
Armistice line, 1949
Israeli-occupied area
UN buffer zone
National capital
Ancient site
Port facility
Oil pipeline
Canal
0 20 40 60 80 100Mls
0 40 80 120 160Kms
Mediterranean Sea
ISRAEL
LEBANON
SYRIA
JORDAN
EGYPT
SAUDI ARABIA
Sinai Peninsula
Negeb
GAZA STRIP
West Bank
Golan Heights
Eastern Desert
Gulf of Suez
Gulf of Aqaba
Red Sea
Tripoli (Ţarābulus)
Cedars of Lebanon
Byblos
Baalbek
Beirut
Līţānī
Sidon
Damascus (Dimashq)
Az Zahrānī
Mt. Hermon
Tyre
Bāniyās
'Akko
Zefat
Tiberias
Lake Tiberias
Haifa
Nazareth
Irbid
Dar'ā
Caesarea
Janīn
Bet She'an
Netanya
Nābulus
'Ajlūn
Jordan
Tel Aviv-Yafo
Ramat Gan
Az Zarqā'
Holon
Jericho
Amman
Ashdod
Ramla
Jerusalem
Ashqelon
Bethlehem
Dead Sea
Gaza
Hebron
Dhībān
Masada
Beersheba
'Arad
Al Karak
Al 'Arīsh
Dimona
Sedom
Nizzana
'Oron
Tannur
Al Quşaymah
'En Yahav
Wādī al 'Arabah
Kadesh-barnea
Petra
Wādī Mūsá
Ma'ān
Ra's an Naqb
Al Kuntillah
Yotvata
Mikhrot Timna'
Elat
Al 'Aqabah
Al Mudawwārah
Ḩaql
Nuweiba
Dhahab
Jaba Mūsā (Mt. Sinai)
Maqna
Aţ Ţūr
Al Khuraybah
Str. of Tiran
Tīrān
Şanāfīr
Sharm ash Shaykh
Wādī al Arīsh
An Nakhl
Mitla Pass
Port Tawfīq
Suez
Ra's as Sidr
Ayn Sukhnah
Abū Zanīmah
Abū Rudays
Za'farānah
Ra's Ghārib
Baltīm
Damietta
Port Said
Tanis
Pelusium
Al Manşūrah
Suez Canal
Daphne
Tantā
Az Zaqāzīq
Ismailia
Succoth
Banhā
Bitter Lakes
Heliopolis (On)
Cairo (Al Qāhirah)
Ḩulwān
Nile
Banī Suwayf
Wādī aţ Ţarfā'
l el Amarna

Troy
ASSUWA
Sangarius
Halys
Alaca Huyuk
Hattusas
Ankuwa
HITTITE EMPIRE (HATTI)
L. Tuz
Kanish
Hermes
Karabel
Maeander
Beycesultan
ARZAWA
TAURUS MTS.
Kizzuwatna
LUKKA
Mersin
MINOAN-MYCENAEAN DOMAIN
Rhodes
Cnossus
CAPHTOR
(Crete)
Ugarit
Arvad
ALASHIYA, KITTIM
(Cyprus)
Mediterranean Sea
(Great or Upper Sea)
Gebal
(Byblos)
Sidon
Tyre
Hazor
Dor
Megiddo
Shechem
Joppa
Jericho
Jerusalem
Gaza
Hebron
Beer-sheba
Avaris
(Zoan)
Lower Egypt
On
Memphis
(Noph)
Kadesh-barnea
EGYPTIAN EMPIRE
Sinai
Heracleopolis
MIDIAN
Libyan Desert
Hermopolis
Akhetaton
(Tell el-Amarna)
Nile
Upper Egypt
Abydos
No
(Thebes)
Red Sea
NUBIA

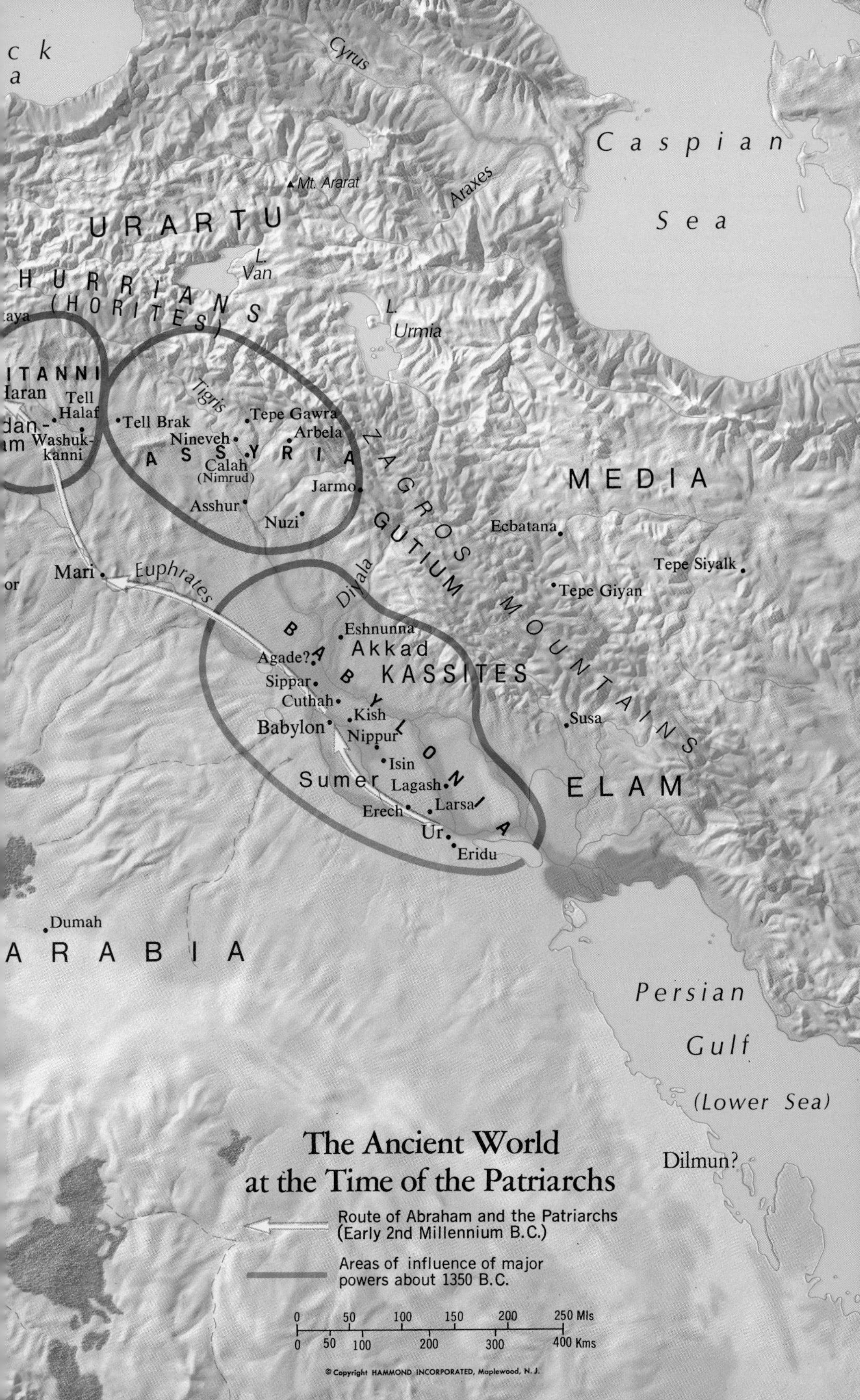

The Ancient World at the Time of the Patriarchs

The Exodus
Traditional route of the Exodus
Unsuccessful invasion of Canaan
Trade routes
0 20 40 60 80 100 Mls
0 40 80 120 160 Kms
© Copyright HAMMOND INCORPORATED, Maplewood, N. J.
The Great Sea
(Mediterranean Sea)
Gebal
Berytus
MT. LEBANON
Sidon
Damascus
Tyre
BASHA
Hazor
Acco
Ashtar
Mt. Carmel
Madon
Dor
Megiddo
Edrei
Taanach
Beth-shan
Shechem
Jabbok
Aphek
Jordan
Joppa
Shiloh
AMMO
Bethel
Ai
Jericho
Rabbah
Gezer
Heshbo
Ashdod
Mt. Nebo
Ashkelon
Jerusalem
CANAAN
Gaza
Eglon?
Lachish
Salt
Dibon
Hebron
Debir?
Sea
Arnon
Raphia
Arad
MOAB
Beer-sheba
Hormah
Kir-hareseth
Nile
Delta
Ramses
(Tanis)
Pelusium
(Sin)
The Way of the Sea
Brook of Egypt
Negeb
Zoar
Zered
Wilderness
Baal-zephon
Zilu
Ije-abarim
of Zin
Goshen
Wilderness of Shur
Bozrah
Kadesh-barnea
Pibeseth
(Bubastis)
Pithom
Jebel Helal
EDOM
Punon
Succoth
The Way to Shur
Arabah
EGYPT
Sela
Bitter
Lakes
Wilderness
Jebel Harun
Heliopolis
(On)
Wilderness
of
The King's Highway
of
Great
Pyramids
Memphis
(Noph)
Paran
Etham
Sinai
Ezion-geber
Marah?
Crocodilopolis
Peninsula
LAND
Elim?
(Gulf of Suez)
Wilderness
Heracleopolis
of
(Gulf of Aqaba)
Nile
Dophkah?
Sin
Hazeroth?
OF
Kibroth-hattaavah?
Alush?
Taberah?
Rephidim?
Mt. Sinai
MIDIAN
Akhetaton (Tell el-Amarna)
Red Sea

The Empire of David and Solomon
Boundary of the empire at its greatest extent
Territory conquered by David
Fortified places of Solomon
Copper mining centers
0 10 25 50 75 Mls
0 20 40 60 80 100 120 Kms
© Copyright HAMMOND INCORPORATED, Maplewood, N. J.
Hamath
Arvad
Kadesh
Zedad
Hazar-enan
ARAM– ZOBAH
Lebo-hamath
Gebal
Berothai
Berytus
BETH-REHOB
MT. LEBANON
PHOENICIA
Sidon
ARAM–DAMASCUS
Damascus
MT. HERMON
Tyre
Abel
Dan
Kedesh
Hazor
MAACAH
The Great Sea
(Mediterranean Sea)
Acco
ARGOB
Cabul
Mt. Carmel
GESHUR
Ashtaroth
Dor
TOB
Edrei
Megiddo
Jezreel
Taanach
Beth-shan
Ramoth-gilead
Salecah
Mt. Gilboa
Jordan
Hepher
Mahanaim
Shechem
Succoth
ISRAEL
Joppa
Gezer
Beth-horon
Rabbah
Bethel
AMMON
Gibeah
Jericho
Ashdod
Jerusalem
Heshbon
Beth-shemesh
Ashkelon
Gath?
Medeba
Hebron
Gaza
Lachish
Salt Sea
PHILISTIA
Aroer
Ziklag ?
Gerar
Raphia
Beer-sheba
Arad
MOAB
JUDAH
Kir-hareseth
Tamar
AMALEK
Bozrah
Kadesh-barnea
Punon
River of Egypt
EDOM
Arabah
Sela
Sinai
Ezion-geber

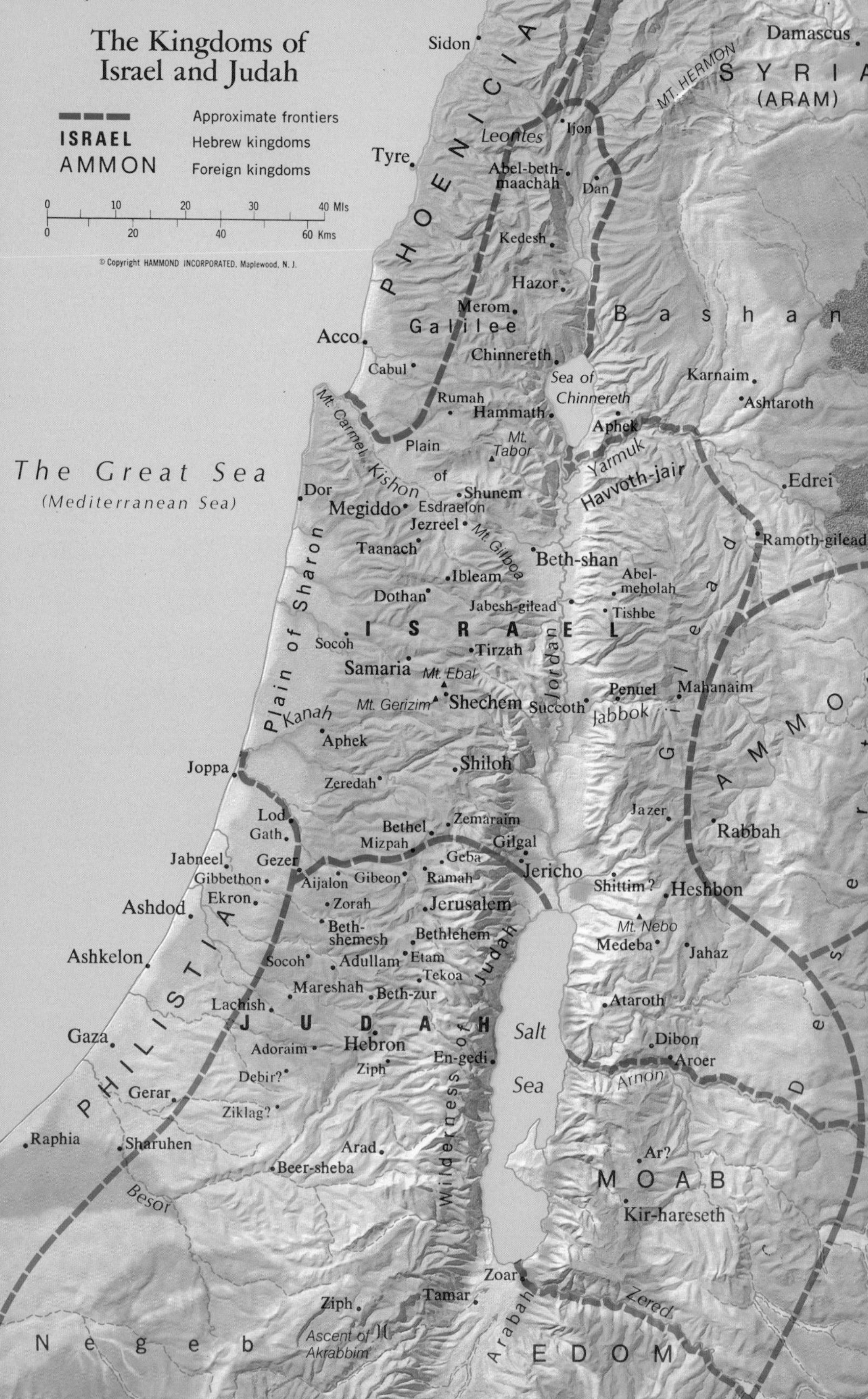

The Kingdoms of Israel and Judah
Approximate frontiers
ISRAEL Hebrew kingdoms
AMMON Foreign kingdoms
0 10 20 30 40 Mls
0 20 40 60 Kms
© Copyright HAMMOND INCORPORATED, Maplewood, N. J.
The Great Sea
(Mediterranean Sea)
Sidon
PHOENICIA
Damascus
MT. HERMON
SYRIA
(ARAM)
Ijon
Leontes
Tyre
Abel-beth-maachah
Dan
Kedesh
Hazor
Merom
Galilee
Bashan
Acco
Chinnereth
Cabul
Sea of Chinnereth
Karnaim
Ashtaroth
Mt. Carmel
Rumah
Hammath
Aphek
Plain of Esdraelon
Mt. Tabor
Yarmuk
Havvoth-jair
Edrei
Kishon
Dor
Shunem
Megiddo
Jezreel
Mt. Gilboa
Ramoth-gilead
Taanach
Beth-shan
Plain of Sharon
Ibleam
Abel-meholah
Dothan
Jabesh-gilead
Tishbe
ISRAEL
Socoh
Tirzah
Jordan
Gilead
Samaria
Mt. Ebal
Penuel
Mahanaim
Mt. Gerizim
Shechem
Succoth
Jabbok
Kanah
Aphek
AMMON
Joppa
Shiloh
Zeredah
Jazer
Rabbah
Lod
Bethel
Zemaraim
Gath
Mizpah
Gilgal
Jabneel
Gezer
Geba
Jericho
Gibbethon
Aijalon
Gibeon
Ramah
Shittim?
Heshbon
Ashdod
Ekron
Zorah
Jerusalem
Beth-shemesh
Bethlehem
Mt. Nebo
Medeba
Jahaz
Ashkelon
Socoh
Adullam
Etam
Tekoa
Mareshah
Beth-zur
PHILISTIA
Lachish
Ataroth
JUDAH
Salt Sea
Gaza
Hebron
Dibon
Adoraim
En-gedi
Aroer
Debir?
Ziph
Wilderness of Judah
Arnon
Gerar
Ziklag?
Raphia
Sharuhen
Arad
Ar?
Beer-sheba
MOAB
Besor
Kir-hareseth
Desert
Zoar
Tamar
Ziph
Zered
Negeb
Ascent of Akrabbim
Arabah
EDOM

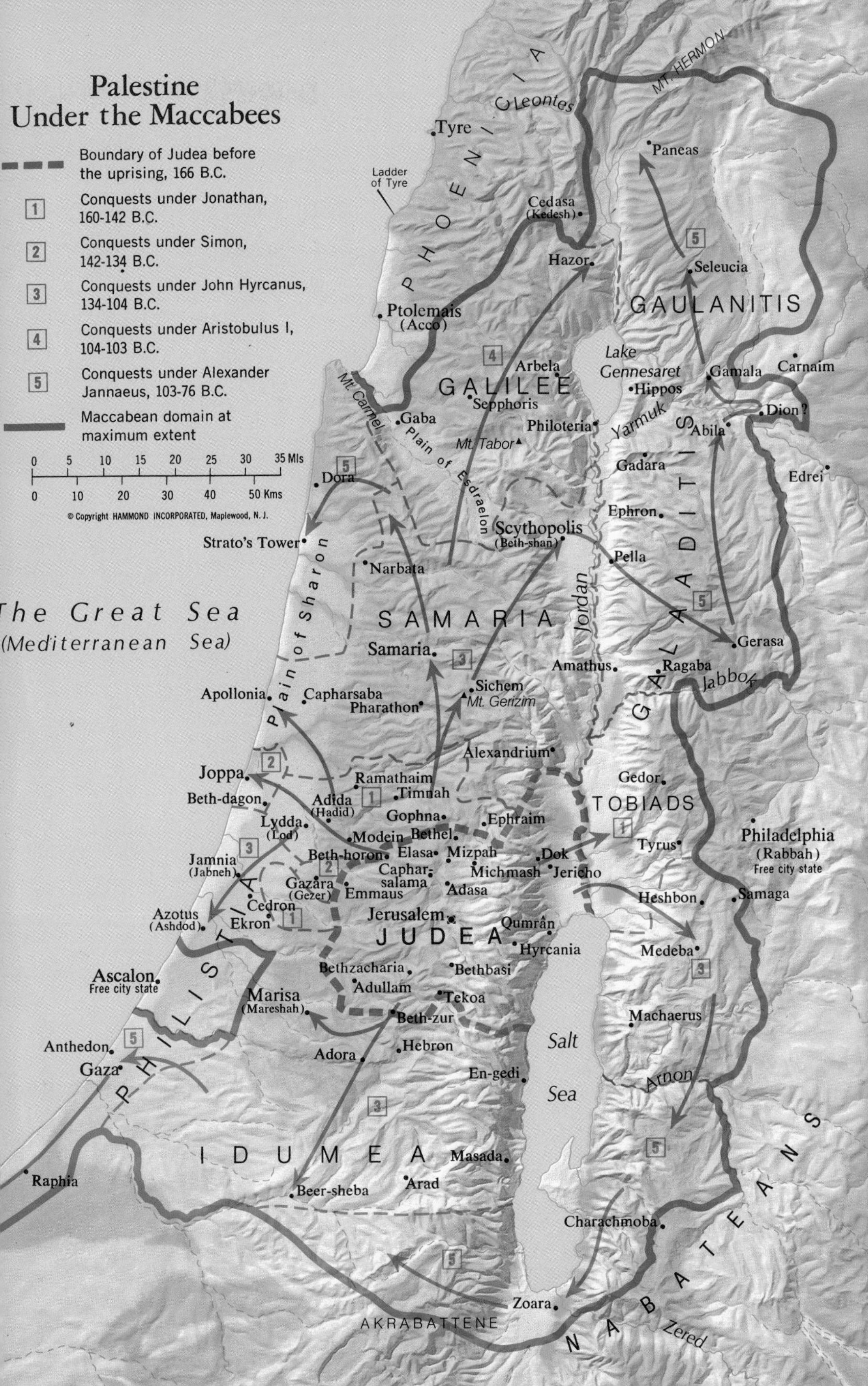

Palestine Under the Maccabees
Boundary of Judea before the uprising, 166 B.C.
1 Conquests under Jonathan, 160-142 B.C.
2 Conquests under Simon, 142-134 B.C.
3 Conquests under John Hyrcanus, 134-104 B.C.
4 Conquests under Aristobulus I, 104-103 B.C.
5 Conquests under Alexander Jannaeus, 103-76 B.C.
Maccabean domain at maximum extent
0 5 10 15 20 25 30 35 Mls
0 10 20 30 40 50 Kms
© Copyright HAMMOND INCORPORATED, Maplewood, N. J.
The Great Sea
(Mediterranean Sea)
PHOENICIA
Leontes
MT. HERMON
Tyre
Ladder of Tyre
Paneas
Cedasa (Kedesh)
Hazor
Seleucia
GAULANITIS
Ptolemais (Acco)
Lake Gennesaret
Arbela
GALILEE
Hippos
Gamala
Carnaim
Sepphoris
Mt. Carmel
Gaba
Plain of Esdraelon
Philoteria
Yarmuk
Abila
Dion?
Mt. Tabor
Gadara
Edrei
Dora
GALAADITIS
Ephron
Scythopolis (Beth-shan)
Strato's Tower
Plain of Sharon
Pella
Narbata
Jordan
SAMARIA
Samaria
Gerasa
Amathus
Ragaba
Jabbok
Sichem
Mt. Gerizim
Apollonia
Capharsaba
Pharathon
Alexandrium
Joppa
Ramathaim
Gedor
Beth-dagon
Adida (Hadid)
Timnah
TOBIADS
Lydda (Lod)
Gophna
Ephraim
Modein
Bethel
Tyrus
Philadelphia (Rabbah) Free city state
Jamnia (Jabneh)
Beth-horon
Elasa
Mizpah
Dok
Michmash
Jericho
Gazara (Gezer)
Caphar-salama
Emmaus
Adasa
Heshbon
Samaga
Cedron
Ekron
Azotus (Ashdod)
Jerusalem
JUDEA
Qumrân
Hyrcania
Medeba
PHILISTIA
Ascalon Free city state
Bethzacharia
Bethbasi
Adullam
Marisa (Mareshah)
Tekoa
Beth-zur
Machaerus
Anthedon
Gaza
Adora
Hebron
Salt Sea
En-gedi
Arnon
IDUMEA
Masada
Raphia
Beer-sheba
Arad
NABATEANS
Charachmoba
Zoara
AKRABATTENE
Zered

The Roman World
Limits of direct Roman rule or political influence at the birth of Christ
Provincial or state boundaries
SYRIA Roman provinces
LYCIA Client kingdoms or states
0 100 200 300 400 500 Mls
0 200 400 600 800 Kms
Britannia
Atlantic
Ocean
Lost to Rome in A.D. 9
Albis
(Elbe)
Rhine
Germania
Augusta Treverorum
Lutetia
BELGICA
LUGDUNENSIS
Gaul
AQUITANIA
Burdigala
Lugdunum
Danube
RAETIA
NORICUM
ALPS
ALPES
NARBONENSIS
Narbo
Aquileia
PANNONIA
Sarmatia
CARPATHIANS
Dacia
Ister (Danube)
Rha (Volga)
Caspian Sea
BOSPORUS KDM.
CAUCASUS
Colchis
Iberia
Albania
Black Sea
TARRACONENSIS
LUSITANIA
Caesarea Augusta
Hispania
Emerita Augusta
Tarraco
BAETICA
Corduba
Tingis
CORSICA
AND
SARDINIA
Caralis
Rubicon
ITALY
Rome
Tarentum
ILLYRICUM
Salonae
MOESIA
THRACE
MACEDONIA
Byzantium
Thessalonica
Sea of Adria
Sinope
Trapezus
Artaxata
ARMENIA
BITHYNIA & PONTUS
CAPPADOCIA
Ancyra
COMMAGENE
GALATIA
Pergamum
ASIA
Ephesus
Aegean Sea
ACHAIA
Athens
Corinth
CILICIA
Tarsus
LYCIA
PAMPHYLIA
Antioch
SYRIA
PARTHIAN EMPIRE
Tigris
Euphrates
Ctesiphon
Mare
Caesarea
MAURETANIA
Cirta
Carthage
SICILIA
Syracuse
(Mediterranean Sea)
Internum
CRETA
CYPRUS
KDM. OF HEROD
Jerusalem
NABATEA
AFRICA
Leptis Magna
Cyrene
CYRENAICA
Alexandria
Memphis
EGYPT
Nile
Thebes
Arabia
Red S

Palestine in New Testament Times
Political boundaries A.D. 6-44
Cities of the Decapolis
Fortresses
0 10 20 30 40 Mls
0 20 40 60 Kms
© Copyright HAMMOND INCORPORATED, Maplewood, N. J.
Mediterranean Sea
Phoenicia
SYRIA
ABILENE
Abila
Iturea
Damascus
MT. LEBANON
MT. HERMON
Sidon
Sarepta
Leontes
Tyre
Paneas
Caesarea Philippi (Paneas)
Ulatha
Gaulanitis
Trachonitis
Batanea
Raphana
Cadasa
Gischala
Ladder of Tyre
Ecdippa
Ptolemais
Chorazin
Bethsaida-Julias
GALILEE
Capernaum
Cana
Magadan
Asochis
Tiberias
Sea of Galilee
Hippos
Dion?
Sepphoris
Yarmuk
Mt. Carmel
Nazareth
Mt. Tabor
Abila
Plain of Esdraelon
Gadara
Nain
Capitolias
Dora
Agrippina
Crocodilion
Arbela
Caesarea
Scythopolis
DECAPOLIS
Pella
Narbata
Ginae
Salim
Aenon
Jordan
SAMARIA
Plain of Sharon
Gerasa
Sebaste (Samaria)
Amathus
Neapolis
Mt. Ebal
Apollonia
Mt. Gerizim
Sychar
Jabbok
Antipatris
Alexandrium
Joppa
Arimathea?
Phasaelis
Gadara
PEREA
Ephraim
Philadelphia
Lydda
Gophna
Archelais
Jamnia
Jericho
Betharamphtha (Livias, Julias)
Emmaus (Nicopolis)
Cyprus
Emmaus?
Esbus
Jerusalem
Bethany
Azotus
Qumran
Medeba
Bethlehem
Hyrcania
Ascalon
JUDEA
Herodium
Callirrhoe
Marisa
Bethsura
Machaerus
Agrippias
Hebron
Gaza
Engaddi
Arnon
Lake Asphaltitis (Dead Sea)
NABATEA
Masada
IDUMEA
Areopolis
Bersabe
Malatha
Charachmoba

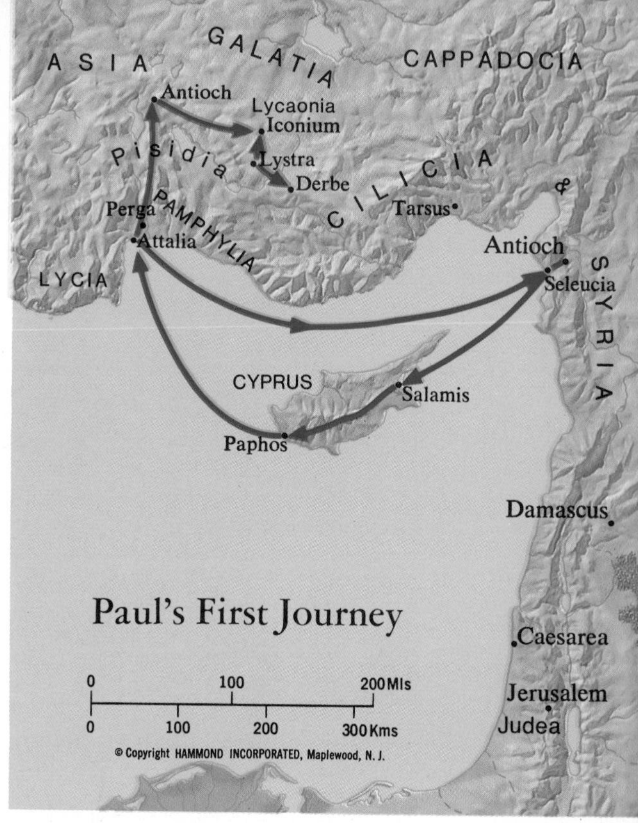

Paul's First Journey

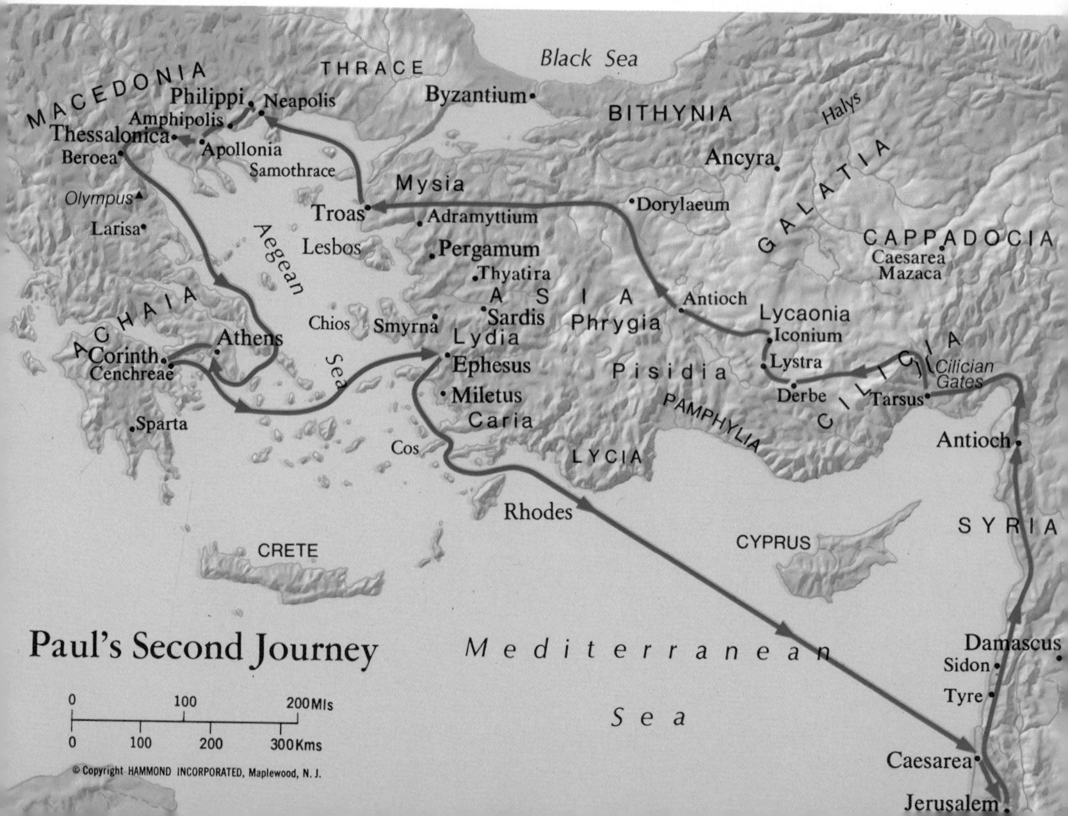

Paul's Second Journey

Black Sea
THRACE
MACEDONIA
Philippi
Neapolis
Byzantium
BITHYNIA
Halys
Amphipolis
Thessalonica
Apollonia
Beroea
Samothrace
Ancyra
GALATIA
Mysia
Olympus
Troas
Adramyttium
Dorylaeum
Larisa
Aegean
Lesbos
Pergamum
CAPPADOCIA
Caesarea Mazaca
Thyatira
ACHAIA
ASIA
Antioch
Lycaonia
Iconium
Chios
Smyrna
Sardis
Phrygia
Athens
Lydia
Corinth
Cenchreae
Sea
Ephesus
Pisidia
Lystra
CILICIA
Cilician Gates
Derbe
Tarsus
Miletus
PAMPHYLIA
Caria
Sparta
Cos
LYCIA
Antioch
Rhodes
SYRIA
CRETE
CYPRUS
Mediterranean Sea
Damascus
Sidon
Tyre
Caesarea
Jerusalem
0 100 200 Mls
0 100 200 300 Kms

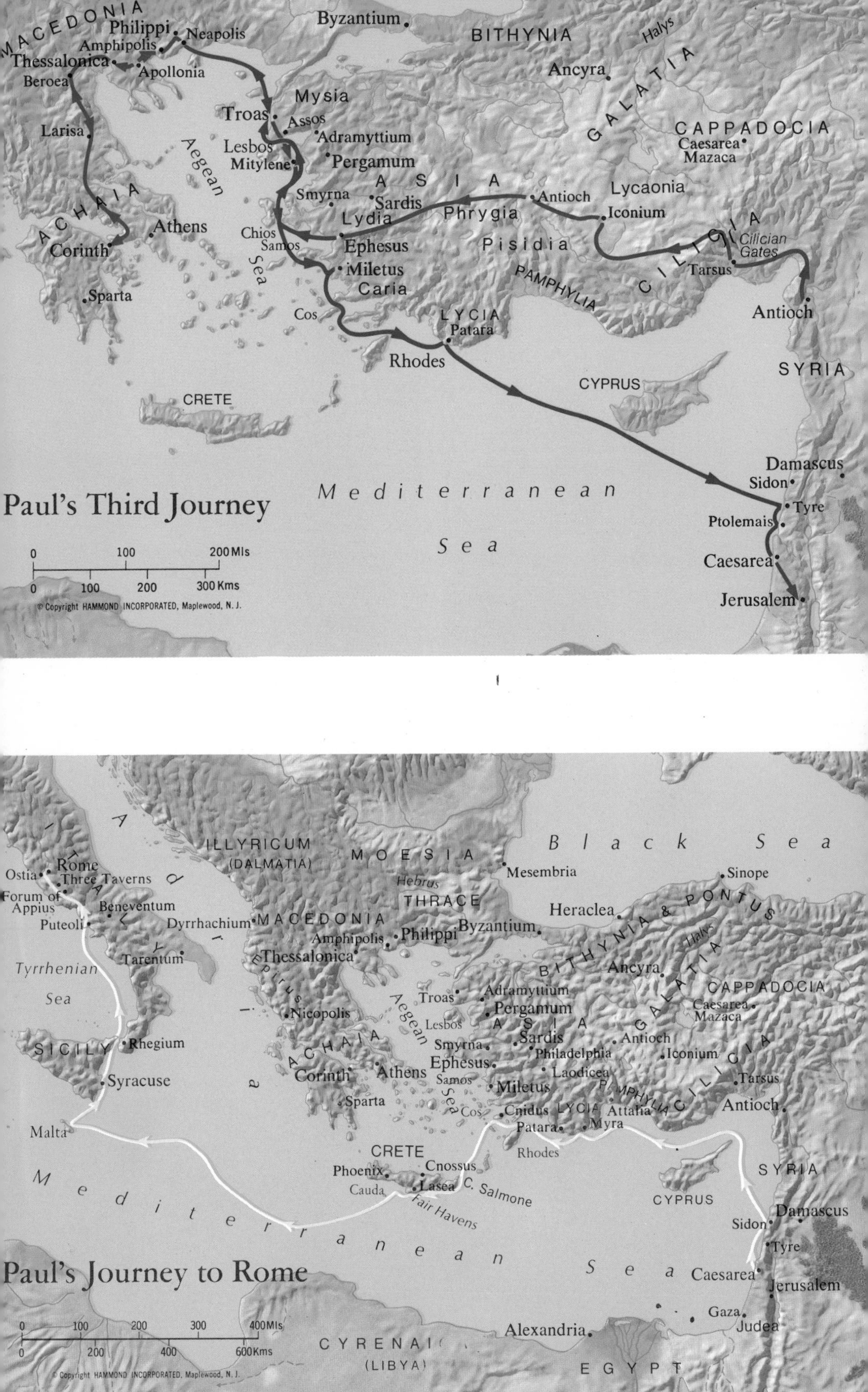
Paul's Third Journey
MACEDONIA
Philippi
Neapolis
Amphipolis
Thessalonica
Apollonia
Beroea
Larisa
ACHAIA
Corinth
Athens
Sparta
Byzantium
BITHYNIA
Halys
GALATIA
Ancyra
CAPPADOCIA
Caesarea Mazaca
Mysia
Troas
Assos
Adramyttium
Lesbos
Mitylene
Pergamum
Aegean Sea
ASIA
Smyrna
Sardis
Lydia
Chios
Samos
Ephesus
Miletus
Caria
Phrygia
Antioch
Lycaonia
Iconium
Pisidia
PAMPHYLIA
CILICIA
Cilician Gates
Tarsus
Antioch
Cos
LYCIA
Patara
Rhodes
CRETE
CYPRUS
SYRIA
Mediterranean Sea
Damascus
Sidon
Tyre
Ptolemais
Caesarea
Jerusalem
0 100 200 Mls
0 100 200 300 Kms
© Copyright HAMMOND INCORPORATED, Maplewood, N. J.
Paul's Journey to Rome
ITALY
Adriatic Sea
ILLYRICUM (DALMATIA)
MOESIA
Black Sea
Ostia
Rome
Three Taverns
Forum of Appius
Beneventum
Puteoli
Dyrrhachium
MACEDONIA
Amphipolis
Philippi
Thessalonica
THRACE
Hebrus
Mesembria
Byzantium
Heraclea
Sinope
BITHYNIA & PONTUS
Halys
Ancyra
GALATIA
CAPPADOCIA
Caesarea Mazaca
Tarentum
Tyrrhenian Sea
Epirus
Nicopolis
Troas
Adramyttium
Pergamum
Lesbos
Aegean Sea
ASIA
Sardis
Philadelphia
Antioch
Iconium
Smyrna
Ephesus
Laodicea
ACHAIA
Corinth
Athens
Samos
Miletus
PAMPHYLIA
CILICIA
Tarsus
Sparta
Cos
Cnidus
LYCIA
Attalia
Antioch
Patara
Myra
Rhodes
SICILY
Rhegium
Syracuse
Malta
CRETE
Phoenix
Cnossus
Cauda
Lasea
C. Salmone
Fair Havens
SYRIA
CYPRUS
Damascus
Sidon
Tyre
Mediterranean Sea
Caesarea
Jerusalem
Gaza
Judea
Alexandria
CYRENAICA (LIBYA)
EGYPT
0 100 200 300 400 Mls
0 200 400 600 Kms
© Copyright HAMMOND INCORPORATED, Maplewood, N. J.

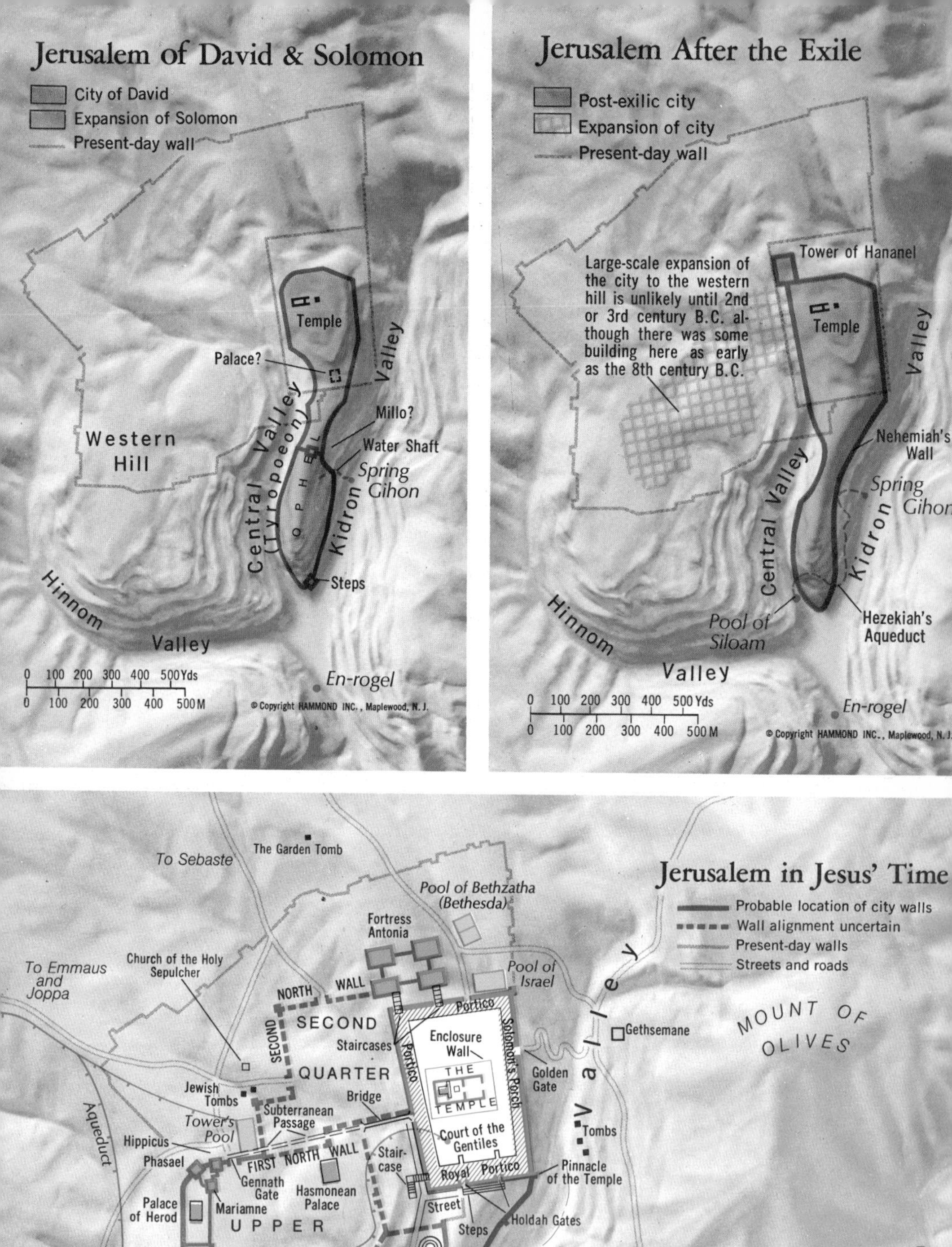

Jerusalem of David & Solomon
City of David
Expansion of Solomon
Present-day wall
Temple
Palace?
Valley
Central Valley (Tyropoeon)
OPHEL
Millo?
Water Shaft
Spring Gihon
Western Hill
Kidron
Steps
Hinnom
Valley
En-rogel
0 100 200 300 400 500 Yds
0 100 200 300 400 500 M
© Copyright HAMMOND INC., Maplewood, N. J.
Jerusalem After the Exile
Post-exilic city
Expansion of city
Present-day wall
Tower of Hananel
Large-scale expansion of the city to the western hill is unlikely until 2nd or 3rd century B.C. although there was some building here as early as the 8th century B.C.
Temple
Valley
Nehemiah's Wall
Spring Gihon
Central Valley
Kidron
Pool of Siloam
Hezekiah's Aqueduct
Hinnom
Valley
En-rogel
0 100 200 300 400 500 Yds
0 100 200 300 400 500 M
© Copyright HAMMOND INC., Maplewood, N. J.
Jerusalem in Jesus' Time
Probable location of city walls
Wall alignment uncertain
Present-day walls
Streets and roads
The Garden Tomb
To Sebaste
Pool of Bethzatha (Bethesda)
Fortress Antonia
To Emmaus and Joppa
Church of the Holy Sepulcher
Pool of Israel
NORTH WALL
SECOND
SECOND QUARTER
Portico
Staircases
Enclosure Wall
Solomon's Porch
THE TEMPLE
Golden Gate
Gethsemane
MOUNT OF OLIVES
Jewish Tombs
Bridge
Subterranean Passage
Tower's Pool
Hippicus
Phasael
FIRST NORTH WALL
Court of the Gentiles
Stair-case
Royal Portico
Pinnacle of the Temple
Tombs
Valley
Gennath Gate
Mariamne
Hasmonean Palace
Palace of Herod
Street
Steps
Holdah Gates
UPPER CITY
Aqueduct
Herod's Family Tomb
Theater?
Hippo-drome
To Bethany
LOWER CITY
Tyropoeon Valley
Spring Gihon
House of Caiaphas?
Upper Room?
Hezekiah's Tunnel
Serpent's Pool
Pool of Siloam
Kidron
Hinnom Valley
Aqueduct
Water Gate
To Bethlehem and Hebron
To the Dead Sea
0 200 400 600 Yards
0 200 400 600 Meters
© Copyright HAMMOND INCORPORATED, Maplewood, N. J.